Advance Praise for *African American Literature*

"This anthology succeeds in engaging young undergraduate scholars not only in a reading of key texts but in a critical/intellectual interaction with those texts as well."

Maxine Montgomery
Florida State University

"The text is highly readable, engaging and thought-provoking for my African American literature students."

Barbara J. Hunt
Washtenaw Community College

"I do think the introductions would be particularly helpful for my students—and in this respect much more than in anthologies currently available—because of the regular comparisons and connections made between and among the texts in that chapter . . . these links are refreshing and illuminating."

Kristine Yohe
Northern Kentucky University

"I believe the introductions and the anthology are very teachable. Both instructors and students should find it enjoyable to use. . . . All in all, this anthology has great potential."

Sandra Carleton Alexander
North Carolina A&T State University

About the Authors

Keith Gilyard is Professor of English at The Pennsylvania State University. He has written and lectured widely about language, literature, and education. A writing teacher (and teaching writer) for more than a quarter century, his books include *Voices of the Self: A Study of Language Competence*, for which he received an American Book Award in 1992; *Let's Flip the Script: An African American Discourse on Language, Literature, and Learning; Liberation Memories: The Rhetoric and Poetics of John Oliver Killens;* and the edited collection *Race, Rhetoric, and Composition*. Gilyard has also published the poetry volumes *American 40, Poemographies,* and *How I Figure,* and edited *Spirit & Flame: An Anthology of Contemporary African American Poetry*. Long active in professional organizations, he has served on the executive committees of the National Council of Teachers of English (NCTE), the Conference on English Education (CEE), and the Conference on College Composition and Communication (CCCC). Gilyard served as Chair of CCCC in 2000. He resides with his family in State College, Pennsylvania.

Anissa Janine Wardi is Assistant Professor of English and Director of Cultural Studies and African American Studies at Chatham College in Pittsburgh, Pennsylvania. She has lectured and published in the area of twentieth-century African American literature, focusing on literary constructions of the American South. She is the author of *Death and the Arc of Mourning in African American Literature*, which examines of gravesites and death as modes of memory in the work of Jean Toomer, Gloria Naylor, Toni Morrison, and Ernest Gaines. She is a past contributor to *African American Review, Griot, College Language Association Journal,* and *Melus,* and has published in anthologies including *Gloria Naylor: Strategy and Technique, Magic and Myth,* and *Race, Rhetoric, and Composition*. She lives in Pittsburgh with her husband, Casey Kurtz.

African American Literature

Keith Gilyard
The Pennsylvania State University,
Department of English

Anissa Janine Wardi
Chatham College,
Department of English

PENGUIN ACADEMICS

New York   San Francisco   Boston
London   Toronto   Sydney   Tokyo   Singapore   Madrid
Mexico City   Munich   Paris   Cape Town   Hong Kong   Montreal

Vice President and Editor-in-Chief: Joseph Terry
Senior Marketing Manager: Melanie Craig
Production Manager: Denise Phillip
Project Coordination, Text Design, and Electronic Page Makeup:
    Electronic Publishing Services Inc., NYC
Cover Designer/Manager: John Callahan
Cover Image: Courtesy of Photodisc
Senior Manufacturing Buyer: Alfred C. Dorsey
Printer and Binder: Courier Corporation
Cover Printer: Phoenix Color Corporation

For permission to use copyrighted material, grateful acknowledgment is made
to the copyright holders on pp. 1337–1346, which are hereby made part of
this copyright page.

Library of Congress Cataloging-in-Publication Data

African American literature / Keith Gilyard, Anissa
Janine Wardi.— 1st ed.
    p. cm.

Includes bibliographical references and index.

  ISBN 0-321-11341-1

  1. American literature—African American authors. 2. African
Americans—Literary collections. I. Gilyard, Keith, 1952– II. Wardi,
Anissa Janine, 1969–

PS508.N3A58 2004
810.8′0896073—dc22

                              2003020621

Please visit us at http://www.ablongman.com

ISBN 0–321–11341–1

  2 3 4 5 6 7 8 9 10—CRW—09 08 07

Contents

CHAPTER 2   The Influence of the Spirituals   117

CHAPTER 3   The South as Literary Landscape   237

CHAPTER 6   Stories of Migration   561

CHAPTER 7   Urban Landscapes 695

CHAPTER 8   A Strand of Social Protest   795

CHAPTER 11 Statements of Feminism 1141

Preface

"Communication is only important because it is the broadest root of education. And all cultures communicate exactly what they have, a powerful motley of experience." Amiri Baraka, writing as LeRoi Jones, stated this realization in 1963. Baraka understood that literature, as well as other aspects of expressive culture like visual design, culinary arts, and celebratory traditions, has been a central element of the collective African American cultural and political statement. The folklore, stories, songs, poems, speeches, essays, and plays created by African Americans represent a brilliant and forceful assertion of African American humanity in the face of enduring hardship. This written and verbal output speaks poignantly of the complex sociohistorical circumstances of being Black in America, but its intense, powerful, and insightful testimony also enriches our understanding of human drama in general.

African American Literature is a fairly comprehensive, thematic treatment of the African American literary tradition, and it is intended primarily for use in one-semester, introductory college courses. We feel this text offers two distinct advantages. First, because this book is organized primarily around theme rather than by chronology, we feel it affords a more coherent examination of the literature than chronologically driven collections. We focus on the connective tissue, or intertextuality, that helps to bind a wide array of texts. Intertextuality is one of the primary characteristics of the tradition, because texts speak to one another in multiple ways, whether it is by authors recycling themes, repeating images, or even revising characters created by other authors. African American writers, in short, habitually participate in literary conversations that transpire over lengthy stretches of time, even centuries. We remained acutely aware of this reality as we compiled this book. One result, to give an example of how our thematic approach shapes this collection, is that Ishmael Reed's poetry is included in the same chapter as some of the much older folklore that directly informs it. In a lengthy book organized strictly by historical period or authors' birth dates, these works might be separated by hundreds of pages, without commentary that reveals and stresses the links that exist between and among them. So, while some sequential principle is at work in this anthology—it makes historical sense to have a chapter on the Middle Passage precede one on migration, feminism, or the Black Aesthetic—the reader will find that each chapter is a blend of traditional and contemporary selections that are united around their distinguishing characteristics. The reader will find the writing of Olaudah Equiano in relatively close proximity to the words of Julie Dash; Paul Laurence Dunbar's work near Ralph Ellison's and Toni Morrison's; and that Langston Hughes shows up in the vicinity of Nikki Giovanni and Kenneth Carroll.

Second, we feel that a thematic approach, calibrated to the rhythm of a semester, provides a more concise, yet balanced, overview of African American literature than the approach of anthologies whose major aim is to establish a canon. Such works typically run several thousand pages and prove physically and intellectually unwieldy for a single course. Of course, all anthologies participate in canon formation, but we do not claim that we have featured all of the noteworthy writers or texts in the African American literary tradition. We have tried, instead, to develop a book that is more manageable for students and their instructors while still providing enough choices to allow teachers some flexibility when structuring their syllabi.

We believe that, ideally, the best use of this volume is during the first half of a two-semester survey course, which is available on some campuses and allows for wider or deeper examination of African American literary texts. We feel that this book would comprise a strong core for the first semester of study, while the second semester could build upon the knowledge developed during the first semester and be devoted to the study of full-length texts.

We have identified 12 themes around which African American literature coheres, namely, 1) the Middle Passage/mourning rituals, 2) the infusion of the Spirituals, 3) representations of the South, 4) folklore traditions, 5) the incorporation of blues and jazz, 6) migration, 7) urban landscapes, 8) social protest, 9) jeremiadic discourse, 10) Black nationalist discourse, 11) feminist discourse, and 12) the Black Aesthetic. Of course, this arrangement is only one of many possible arrangements, but we feel these topics and this ordering of them allow us to include a sufficiently impressive range of texts while maintaining the cohesiveness necessary for fruitful inspection. Recurring elements resonate through the selections in this volume, transcending not only chronological divisions, but chapter demarcations as well, allowing both instructors and students to map alternative reading paths through the anthology. The book fosters close reading practices by enabling students to locate similarities among chronologically disparate texts and recognize the myriad ways in which recurring tropes or patterns accumulate textual meaning over time. Moreover, the very construction of the anthology, with its particular literary selections, encourages intertextual analysis and, therefore, introduces students to a fundamental approach to the study of African American literature.

Not lost in this thematic approach, however, is the historical undergirding of the literature. The editors' chapter introductions, which precede each grouping of literary selections, disclose significant historical and cultural contexts, including, for example, conditions aboard slave ships, religious practices, lynching rituals, the Harlem Renaissance, and folk customs. To promote further study, biographical and framing headnotes accompany each selection, and each chapter includes suggestions for further reading, for research, and for writing.

Because we have organized this anthology through the prism of intertextuality, that is, tracing the manifold ways texts call and respond to one another, it is apt that we incorporate a wide range of oral texts. Indeed, one of the most notable features of the book is its inclusion of oral performances, which contextualize African American literary arts within a larger expressive tradition. Threaded throughout the volume are numerous examples of verbal arts, ranging from formal speeches and oratorical performances, such as the dozens, signifying, and toasts, to blues songs and hip-hop lyrics. The infusion of oral texts into the thematically based chapters highlights a more comprehensive trajectory of African American artistry and foregrounds the import of the spoken word throughout the tradition. The imprint of oral practices is indelible in African American literature; therefore, introducing students to the vitality of oral literature will enhance their examination of the selected texts in this volume and broaden their understanding of the larger African American literary tradition.

In addition, students can strengthen their grasp of the tradition by reading several books that could not be included—or included in full—in *African American Literature* but are being made available at reduced rates to users of the book. These works include *Narrative of the Life of Frederick Douglass, an American Slave, Written by Himself, Incidents in the Life of a Slave Girl* by Harriet Jacobs, and Nella Larsen's novel *Passing*. Moreover, print supplements, like *Analyzing Literature* by Sharon James McGee and *Glossary of Literary Terms* by Heidi Jacobs, also are available to students and can serve as important study aids.

Finally, we wish to thank several people whose insights and energy made this book possible. Joe Terry and Lynn Huddon (even when she was supposed to be working on something else!) helped us to see important possibilities in the early stages of this project. We remain in their debt. Michele Cronin admirably managed the growing manuscript, getting the right things sent to the right places—no easy task. We wish to thank our production manager, Denise Phillip, and production editor, Jim Hill, for as smooth a passage through the production process as one can imagine. Big thanks also to copy editor Kay Mallett and permissions editor Doug Hernandez for performing gargantuan tasks with efficiency and grace. Several reviewers provided indispensable feedback, including Sandra Carlton Alexander, North Carolina A&T; Barbara J. Hunt, Washtenaw Community College; Maxine L. Montgomery, Florida State University; Jennifer Palmgren, Saint Paul's College; and Kristine Yohe, Northern Kentucky University. Our spouses—Sharyn Gilyard and Casey Kurtz—sacrificed much to allow this project to happen. We are especially grateful for their cheerleading and for the additional support given by our entire families.

Keith Gilyard

Anissa Janine Wardi

CHAPTER ONE

THE MIDDLE PASSAGE, MOURNING, AND SURVIVAL

The term "Middle Passage" derives from the triangular trade route by which ships from England, loaded with manufactured goods such as guns and textiles, sailed to West Africa, then to the Americas, and then back to England. The goods from England were traded for African captives, who were forcibly placed on sailing vessels bound for ports in North America, South America, and the Caribbean. There, the African captives were traded for raw materials such as sugarcane, wine, tobacco, and rum, which were to be sold back in England. The Middle Passage specifically designates the second leg, that is, the transatlantic voyage from Africa to the Americas, which, depending upon the port of destination and weather conditions, ranged from five to twelve weeks in duration.

The Atlantic slave trade began in the fifteenth century and continued to the nineteenth century. Earlier in the slave trade, Africans primarily were sold to Spanish colonies in South and Central America to work on sugarcane plantations, but by the mid-1700s the majority of the slave ships were bound for territories that now make up the United States.

The horror of this journey, however, did not begin on the slave ships; the captives were forced to endure weeks and sometimes months of imprisonment in forts and castles that lined the coasts, where they waited to be loaded onto slaving vessels. Some estimates suggest that less than half of those Africans captured inland even made it to these slaving centers. One of the earliest European-constructed forts, El Mina, was built in the late fifteenth century in modern-day Ghana. Subsequently, many slaving centers were built along the Gold Coast. These dungeons housed between 300 to 500 Africans, so the prisoners' movement was severely limited. These shoreline structures foretold the circumstances that the captives were to endure on the ships.

Conditions on the slave ships can be described only as hellish. Motivated by greater profits, many slavers packed their human cargo as tightly as possible into the ships. Although some slave captains believed in loosely packing their ships in the hopes of capitalizing on profits by delivering a larger percentage of healthy Africans to shore, most slavers fell into the former category. The average vessel carried between 250 and 300 passengers. Captives, who were chained to one another by handcuffs and leg shackles, were herded below deck into dark and suffocating spaces that measured no more than four feet in height. These cramped quarters often prohibited the captives from sitting upright; thus, they were forced to assume a perpetually prone posture, which caused severe muscular and limb numbness. The unsanitary conditions of this voyage are perhaps difficult to comprehend. In this space of utter dehumanization, diseases such as scurvy, smallpox, measles, and dysentery ran rampant as people lay in their own filth for days at a time and were permitted very little food or water. As a result, death was not uncommon below deck, which compounded the horror for the living who found themselves chained to the dead.

Often, slavers threw ill captives overboard out of fear of infecting a ship's entire population. On the other hand, many of the enslaved chose death over enslavement and the nightmare of the slave ship. Many who attempted to starve themselves were force-fed by their captors and severely beaten. Indeed, schools of sharks often trailed the slave vessels, following the scent of the captives' blood and bodies. Other slaves, when given the opportunity, jumped overboard to their deaths.

Brutal violation extended to all areas of the captives' lives. While men and women suffered similar horrors, each group bore its own heinous ordeals on the vessels. Because of the fear of insurrection, especially in later years, men were often subject to violent treatment and threatening behavior from the crew. Women, on the other hand, were not only physically assaulted, but were sexually violated at will by crew members and captains.

Because the crews recognized that more of the captives would die if not given periodic exercise and fresh air, they allowed the enslaved reprieves from the ships' subterranean coffins. However, the captives could not exercise their agency on the upper decks, but were subject to further humiliations as they were forced to jump and dance for the pleasure of the crew. Records suggest that these spectacles had a very long history and were often cited by slavers as evidence of their humane treatment of their live cargoes. Because of the slavers' fear of mutiny, male captives generally were chained throughout this ordeal; thus, these brief periods of seeming freedom from the ships' holds cannot be interpreted as moments of liberation.

Madness certainly took hold of some captives in this tomb-like environment. Accounts of wails and screams punctuating the ships' eternal rockings are recorded not only in African American writing, but are inscribed in slavers' logs and journals as well. Although numbers range significantly, most estimates suggest that between 30 and 60 million Africans were subject to the horror of the Middle Passage, and that nearly one-third survived, only to later be sold in slave markets of the so-called New World.

In African American literature, the Middle Passage often is employed as a metaphor for the slave experience. The unspeakable horror of the Middle Passage and the suffering of the "60 million and more," Toni Morrison's reference to the unnamed captives who died during the sea voyages, are woven into the texture of many expressive works. Novelistic attempts to render the Middle Passage range from the most abstract, enigmatic, and obscure to precise, detailed accounts as writers attempt to capture the horror, the suffering, and the mourning of millions. Olaudah Equiano's *The Interesting Life of Olaudah Equiano* (1789) is a particularly important treatment of the Middle Passage because it provides a firsthand account of Equiano's capture at age 11, his journey to the coast, and his terrifying transatlantic voyage. By contrast, both Robert Hayden's and Toni Morrison's narratives about the voyage are fragmented and disrupted. Hayden's modernist history poem, "Middle Passage" (1945), which makes use of multiple points of view, is based on the famous uprising aboard the slave ship *Amistad*. The Middle Passage section of Morrison's *Beloved* (1987) exemplifies the utter failure of language to encapsulate the horrors of the Middle Passage, an experience that "breaks the back of words."

The return to the Middle Passage is, as exemplified in the work of Henry Dumas, August Wilson, and Everett Hoagland, a confrontation with the dead. In Dumas' masterful short story "Ark of Bones" (1974), he provides a symbolic treatment of the Middle Passage. The ark that lands in an Arkansas river is a symbolic slave vessel that contains the bones of all of those who lost their lives during the Middle Passage, yet it is only a young boy who can hear the wails of the dispossessed. Playwright August Wilson's *Joe Turner's Come and Gone* (1988) contains a powerful, albeit brief, section on the Middle Passage that also employs the symbol of bones to suggest death on the Atlantic.

Hoagland's three poems, "Homecoming," "Goree," and "Dust" (2000), map the trajectory of the Middle Passage, speaking of and to the "many thousand" who "did not make it," the drowned, "lost forgotten family." The Middle Passage is an important site in African American history as it reflects the origins of African Americans' hybrid identity. The Middle Passage did not mark a clean break from Africa; Africans on the ships carried with them their rich culture, including language, spirituality, history, and death customs. However, since the captives were dispossessed from their homelands, they developed new strategies for keeping those traditions alive while integrating them with their new cultural and physical surroundings. The transatlantic voyage did not represent a division, as much as it did a porous site in which African and American cultures were bridged and inextricably linked. The Middle Passage was both symbolically and literally a voyage of death, and rituals concerning the dead survived the ordeal. Certainly, African American burial grounds and the accompanying mortuary customs are material signs of the vitality and continuation of African cultures in America. In the selections by Ernest Gaines, Alice Walker, and Julie Dash included in this chapter, burial grounds are cast as sacred ancestral landscapes that mark a connection between the living community and the dead.

Despite the importance of African burial traditions during slavery, records indicate that the ability to practice these customs ranged considerably depending on a slave master's will. Some accounts indicate that the enslaved were given full control over burial rites and were granted passes to attend funerals on nearby plantations to pay their respects. The vast majority of slave funerals were attended by whites, who sometimes even delivered eulogies. However, other slave owners refused even to acknowledge that a death had occurred and prevented any overt display of mourning among their slaves. Some masters prohibited funerals and other public gatherings because they feared that slaves would plan insurrections. In 1687, Virginia banned public funerals for slaves, and in 1772, New York began requiring that slave funerals be held in the daylight and be attended by no more than 12 mourners. Regardless of the latitude granted by whites, Africans in America managed to maintain their honored rituals.

Grave decorating is perhaps the most notable African tradition that still is practiced in areas of the Deep South and Low Country today. In this tradition, many objects that belonged to the deceased or that represent water (such as broken bottles, pitchers, shells, and mirrors) are placed on the gravesite. According to the Bakongo people from West Africa, the spirit world is located on the watery floors of oceans and rivers; thus, these water images indicate the territory of the dead and may aid in the departed's transition to the spirit world. Drums also figured prominently in funerals both during and after slavery to announce that a person had passed. Mourners often beat drums on their way to funerals and performed what was known as the "death march" as the bereaved formed a ringed procession around the grave. Paul Laurence Dunbar's "A Death Song" (1913), Zora Neale Hurston's autobiography *Dust Tracks on a Road* (1942), and Arna Bontemps's *Black Thunder* (1936) reveal the importance of administering funerary rites. In fact, there are numerous traditions represented in these works, such as covering mirrors after a death, burying the dead at night, and providing grave offerings, all of which evidence the living community's intimate relationship with the dead. In this way, all of the writers represented in this chapter give voice to an important aspect of African American history and culture and in so doing pay tribute to the lives of their ancestors.

Further Reading

Burnside, Madeleine, and Rosemarie Robotham. *Spirits of the Passage: The Transatlantic Slave Trade in the Seventeenth Century.* New York: Simon and Schuster, 1997.

Diedrich, Maria, Henry Louis Gates, Jr., and Carl Pedersen. *Black Imagination and the Middle Passage.* New York: Oxford University Press, 1999.

Genovese, Eugene D. *Roll, Jordan, Roll: The World the Slaves Made.* New York: Vintage Books, 1974.

Georgia Writer's Project Work Project Administration. *Drums and Shadows: Survival Studies Among the Georgia Coastal Negroes.* Athens: University of Georgia Press, 1940.

Holloway, Karla. *Passed On: African American Mourning Stories.* Durham: Duke UP, 2002.

Jamieson, Ross W. "Material Culture and Social Death: African American Burial Practices." *Historical Archaeology* 29.4 (1995): 39–58.

Johnson, Charles, Patricia Smith, and the WGBH Series Research Team. *Africans in America: America's Journey through Slavery.* New York: Harcourt Brace, 1998.

Kruger-Kahloula, Angelika. "Homage and Hegemony: African American Grave Inscription and Decoration." *Slavery in the Americas.* Ed. Wolfgang Binder. Wurzburg: Konigshausen & Neumann, 1993. 317–35.

Olauдah Equiano

(1745–1797)

Olaudah Equiano's narrative, which chronicles his capture from his Nigerian village when he was 11*, his experiences during the Middle Passage, his work as a sailor, and his eventual purchase of his own freedom in 1766, is hailed as a powerful account of life under slavery. Moreover, as the author of one of the first slave narratives, The Interesting Narrative of the Life of Olaudah Equiano, or Gustavus Vassa, the African, *Equiano gave shape to this autobiographic genre, which chronicled the atrocities of slavery, Christianity's influence on the slave trade, and the immorality of human bondage. Indeed, subsequent slave narratives, like those written by Frederick Douglass and Harriet Jacobs, were written in this literary tradition and bear the mark of Equiano's early account. Between 1780 and 1857, Equiano's narrative went through 36 editions and was translated into Dutch, Russian, and German. Equiano, a powerful voice in the abolitionist movement, eventually settled in England, married an Englishwoman, and had two daughters. The following reading is an excerpt from* The Interesting Narrative of the Life of Olaudah Equiano.

The Interesting Narrative of the Life of Olaudah Equiano

1   *The Author's birth and parentage—His being kidnapped with his sister—Their separation—Surprise at meeting again—Are finally separated—Account of the different places and incidents the Author met with till his arrival on the coast—The effect the sight of a slave-ship had on him—He sails for the West-Indies—Horrors of a slave-ship—Arrives at Barbadoes, where the cargo is sold and dispersed.*

2   I hope the reader will not think I have trespassed on his patience in introducing myself to him with some account of the manners and customs of my country. They had been implanted in me with great care, and made an impression on my mind, which time could not erase, and which all the adversity and variety of fortune I have since expe-

---

*Recent scholarship suggests that Equiano could have been born in South Carolina, but the prevailing opinion is that he was indeed born in Africa.

rienced served only to rivet and record: for, whether the love of one's country be real or imaginary, or a lesson of reason, or an instinct of nature, I still look back with pleasure on the first scenes of my life, though that pleasure has been for the most part mingled with sorrow.

3 I have already acquainted the reader with the time and place of my birth. My father, besides many slaves, had a numerous family, of which seven lived to grow up, including myself and a sister, who was the only daughter. As I was the youngest of the sons, I became, of course, the greatest favourite with my mother, and was always with her; and she used to take particular pains to form my mind. I was trained up from my earliest years in the arts of agriculture and war: my daily exercise was shooting and throwing javelins; and my mother adorned me with emblems, after the manner of our greatest warriors. In this way I grew up till I was turned the age of eleven, when an end was put to my happiness in the following manner:—Generally, when the grown people in the neighbourhood were gone far in the fields to labour, the children assembled together in some of the neighbours' premises to play; and commonly some of us used to get up a tree to look out for any assailant, or kidnapper, that might come upon us; for they sometimes took those opportunities of our parents' absence, to attack and carry off as many as they could seize. One day, as I was watching at the top of a tree in our yard, I saw one of those people come into the yard of our next neighbour but one, to kidnap, there being many stout young people in it. Immediately, on this, I gave the alarm of the rogue, and he was surrounded by the stoutest of them, who entangled him with cords, so that he could not escape till some of the grown people came and secured him. But, alas! ere long it was my fate to be thus attacked, and to be carried off, when none of the grown people were nigh. One day, when all our people were gone out to their works as usual, and only I and my dear sister were left to mind the house, two men and a woman got over our walls, and in a moment seized us both; and, without giving us time to cry out, or make resistance, they stopped our mouths, tied our hands, and ran off with us into the nearest wood; and continued to carry us as far as they could, till night came on, when we reached a small house, where the robbers halted for refreshment, and spent the night. We were then unbound, but were unable to take any food; and, being quite overpowered by fatigue and grief, our only relief was some sleep, which allayed our misfortune for a short time. The next morning we left the house, and continued travelling all the day. For a long time we had kept the woods, but at last we came into a road which I

believed I knew. I had now some hopes of being delivered for we had advanced but a little way before I discovered some people at a distance, on which I began to cry out for their assistance; but my cries had no other effect than to make them tie me faster, and stop my mouth, and then they put me into a large sack. They also stopped my sister's mouth, and tied her hands; and in this manner we proceeded till we were out of the sight of these people.—When we went to rest the following night they offered us some victuals; but we refused them; and the only comfort we had was in being in one another's arms all that night, and bathing each other with our tears. But, alas! we were soon deprived of even the smallest comfort of weeping together. The next day proved a day of greater sorrow than I had yet experienced; for my sister and I were then separated, while we lay clasped in each other's arms. It was in vain that we besought them not to part us: she was torn from me, and immediately carried away, while I was left in a state of distraction not to be described. I cried and grieved continually; and for several days I did not eat any thing but what they forced into my mouth. At length, after many days travelling, during which I had often changed masters, I got into the hands of a chieftain, in a very pleasant country. This man had two wives and some children, and they all used me extremely well, and did all they could to comfort me; particularly the first wife, who was something like my mother. Although I was a great many days journey from my father's house, yet these people spoke exactly the same language with us. This first master of mine, as I may call him, was a smith and my principal employment was working his bellows, which were the same kind as I had seen in my vicinity. They were in some respects not unlike the stoves here in gentlemen's kitchens; and were covered over with leather; and in the middle of that leather a stick was fixed, and a person stood up, and worked it, in the same manner as is done to pump water out of a cask with a hand-pump. I believe it was gold he worked, for it was of a lovely bright yellow colour, and was worn by the women on their wrists and ancles. I was there I suppose about a month, and they at last used to trust me some little distance from the house. This liberty I used in embracing every opportunity to inquire the way to my own home; and I also sometimes, for the same purpose, went with the maidens, in the cool of the evenings, to bring pitchers of water from the springs for the use of the house. I had also remarked where the sun rose in the morning, and set in the evening, as I had travelled along; and I had observed that my father's house was towards the rising of the sun. I therefore determined to seize the first opportunity of making my escape, and to shape my course for that quarter; for I was quite oppressed and weighed down by grief after my mother and friends; and my love of liberty, ever great, was strengthened by the mortifying circumstance of not daring to eat with the free-born children, although I was mostly their companion.—While I was projecting my escape one day, an unlucky event happened, which quite disconcerted my plan, and put an end to my hopes. I used to be sometimes employed in assisting an elderly woman slave to cook and take care of the poultry; and one morning, while I was feeding some chickens, I happened to toss a small pebble at one of them, which hit it on the middle, and directly killed it. The old slave, having soon after missed the chicken, inquired after it; and on my relating the accident (for I told her the truth, because my mother would never suffer me to tell a lie) she flew into a violent passion, threatened that I should suffer for it; and, my master being out, she immediately went and told her mistress what I had done. This alarmed me very much, and I expected an instant correction, which to me was uncommonly dreadful; for I had seldom been beaten at home. I therefore resolved to fly; and accordingly I ran into a thicket that was hard by, and hid myself in the bushes. Soon afterwards my mistress and the slave returned, and, not seeing me, they searched all the house, but, not finding me, and I not making answer when they called to me, they thought I had run away, and the whole neighbourhood was raised in the pursuit of me. In that part of the country (as well as ours) the houses and villages were skirted with woods, or shrubberies, and the bushes were so thick, that a man could readily conceal himself in them, so as to elude the strictest search. The neighbours continued the whole day looking for me, and several times many of them came within a few yards of the place where I lay hid. I expected every moment, when I heard a rustling among the trees, to be found out, and punished by my master; but they never discovered me, though they were often so near that I even heard their conjectures as they were looking about for me; and I now learned from them, that any attempt to return home would be hopeless. Most of them supposed I had fled towards home; but the distance was so great, and the way so intricate, that they thought I could never reach it, and that I should be lost in the woods. When I heard this I was seized with a violent panic, and abandoned myself to despair. Night too began to approach, and aggravated all my fears. I had before entertained hopes of getting home, and I had determined when it should be dark to make the attempt; but I was now convinced it was fruitless, and I began to consider that, if possibly I could escape all other animals, I could not those of the human kind; and that, not knowing the way, I must perish in the woods.—Thus was I like the hunted deer:

> *Ev'ry leaf and ev'ry whisp'ring breath*
> *Convey'd a foe, and ev'ry foe a death.*

4   I heard frequent rustlings among the leaves; and, being pretty sure they were snakes, I expected every instant to be stung by them.—This increased my anguish, and the horror of my situation became now quite insupportable. I at length quitted the thicket, very faint and hungry, for I had not eaten or drank any thing all the day, and crept to my master's kitchen, from whence I set out at first, and which was an open shed, and laid myself down in the ashes, with an anxious wish for death to relieve me from all my pains. I was scarcely awake in the morning when the old woman slave, who was the first up, came to light the fire, and saw me in the fire-place. She was very much surprised to see me, and could scarcely believe her own eyes. She now promised to intercede for me, and went for her master, who soon after came, and, having slightly reprimanded me, ordered me to be taken care of, and not ill-treated.

5   Soon after this my master's only daughter and child by his first wife sickened and died, which affected him so much that for some time he was almost frantic, and really would have killed himself had he not been watched and prevented. However, in a small time afterwards he recovered, and I was again sold. I was now carried to the left of the sun's rising, through many dreary wastes and dismal woods, amidst the hideous roarings of wild beasts.—The people I was sold to used to carry me very often, when I was tired, either on their shoulders or on their backs. I saw many convenient well-built sheds along the roads, at proper distances, to accommodate the merchants and travellers, who lay in those buildings along with their wives, who often accompany them; and they always go well armed.

6   From the time I left my own nation I always found somebody that understood me till I came to the sea coast. The languages of different nations did not totally differ, nor were they so copious as those of the Europeans, particularly the English. They were therefore easily learned; and, while I was journeying thus through Africa, I acquired two or three different tongues. In this manner I had been travelling for a considerable time, when one evening, to my great surprise, whom

should I see brought to the house where I was but my dear sister. As soon as she saw me she gave a loud shriek, and ran into my arms.— I was quite overpowered; neither of us could speak, but, for a considerable time, clung to each other in mutual embraces, unable to do any thing but weep. Our meeting affected all who saw us; and indeed I must acknowledge, in honour of those sable destroyers of human rights, that I never met with any ill treatment, or saw any offered to their slaves, except tying them, when necessary, to keep them from running away. When these people knew we were brother and sister they indulged us to be together; and the man, to whom I supposed we belonged, lay with us, he in the middle, while she and I held one another by the hands across his breast all night; and thus for a while we forgot our misfortunes in the joy of being together: but even this small comfort was soon to have an end; for scarcely had the fatal morning appeared, when she was again torn from me for ever! I was now more miserable, if possible, than before. The small relief which her presence gave me from pain was gone, and the wretchedness of my situation was redoubled by my anxiety after her fate, and my apprehensions lest her sufferings should be greater than mine, when I could not be with her to alleviate them. Yes, thou dear partner of all my childish sports! thou sharer of my joys and sorrows! happy should I have ever esteemed myself to encounter every misery for you, and to procure your freedom by the sacrifice of my own. Though you were early forced from my arms, your image has been always rivetted in my heart, from which neither *time nor fortune* have been able to remove it: so that, while the thoughts of your sufferings have damped my prosperity, they have mingled with adversity, and increased its bitterness.— To that heaven which protects the weak from the strong, I commit the care of your innocence and virtues, if they have not already received their full reward; and if your youth and delicacy have not long since fallen victims to the violence of the African trader, the pestilential stench of a Guinea ship, the seasoning in the European colonies, or the lash and lust of a brutal and unrelenting overseer.

7   I did not long remain after my sister. I was again sold, and carried through a number of places, till, after travelling a considerable time, I came to a town called Tinmah, in the most beautiful country I had yet seen in Africa. It was extremely rich, and there were many rivulets which flowed through it; and supplied a large pond in the center of the town, where the people washed. Here I first saw and tasted cocoa nuts, which I thought superior to any nuts I had ever tasted before; and the trees, which were loaded, were also interspersed

amongst the houses, which had commodious shades adjoining, and were in the same manner as ours, the insides being neatly plastered and whitewashed. Here I also saw and tasted for the first time sugarcane. Their money consisted of little white shells, the size of the finger nail: they are known in this country by the name of *cores*. I was sold here for one hundred and seventy-two of them by a merchant who lived and brought me there. I had been about two or three days at his house, when a wealthy widow, a neighbour of his, came there one evening, and brought with her an only son, a young gentleman about my own age and size. Here they saw me; and, having taken a fancy to me, I was bought of the merchant, and went home with them. Her house and premises were situated close to one of those rivulets I have mentioned, and were the finest I ever saw in Africa: they were very extensive, and she had a number of slaves to attend her. The next day I was washed and perfumed, and when meal-time came, I was led into the presence of my mistress, and ate and drank before her with her son. This filled me with astonishment: and I could scarce help expressing my surprise that the young gentleman should suffer me, who was bound to eat with him who was free; and not only so, but that he would not at any time either eat or drink till I had taken first, because I was the eldest, which was agreeable to our custom. Indeed every thing here, and all their treatment of me, made me forget that I was a slave. The language of these people resembled ours so nearly, that we understood each other perfectly. They had also the very same customs as we. There were likewise slaves daily to attend us, while my young master and I, with other boys, sported with our darts and bows and arrows, as I had been used to do at home. In this resemblance to my former happy state I passed about two months, and I now began to think I was to be adopted into the family, and was beginning to be reconciled to my situation, and to forget by degrees my misfortunes, when all at once the delusion vanished; for without the least previous knowledge, one morning early, while my dear master and companion was still asleep, I was awakened out of my reverie to fresh sorrow, and hurried away even amongst the uncircumcised.

8   Thus, at the very moment I dreamed of the greatest happiness, I found myself most miserable: and it seemed as if fortune wished to give me this taste of joy only to render the reverse more poignant. The change I now experienced was as painful as it was sudden and unexpected. It was a change indeed from a state of bliss to a scene which is inexpressible by me, as it discovere to me an element I had never

before beheld, and till then had no idea of, and wherein such instances of hardship and cruelty continually occurred as I can never reflect on but with horror.

9   All the nations and people I had hitherto passed through resembled our own in their manners, customs and language: but I came at length to a country, the inhabitants of which differed from us in all those particulars. I was very much struck with this difference, especially when I came among a people who did not circumcise, and eat without washing their hands. They cooked also in iron pots, and had European cutlasses and cross bows, which were unknown to us, and fought with their fists amongst themselves. Their women were not so modest as ours, for they eat, and drank, and slept with their men. But, above all, I was amazed to see no sacrifices or offerings among them. In some of those places the people ornamented themselves with scars, and likewise filed their teeth very sharp. They wanted sometimes to ornament me in the same manner, but I would not suffer them; hoping that I might some time be among a people who did not thus disfigure themselves, as I thought they did. At last, I came to the banks of a large river, which was covered with canoes, in which the people appeared to live with their household utensils and provisions of all kinds. I was beyond measure astonished at this, as I had never before seen any water larger than a pond or a rivulet; and my surprise was mingled with no small fear when I was put into one of these canoes, and we began to paddle and move along the river. We continued going on thus till night; and when we came to land, and made fires on the banks, each family by themselves, some dragged their canoes on shore, others staid and cooked in theirs, and laid in them all night. Those on the land had mats, of which they made tents, some in the shape of little houses: In these we slept; and after the morning meal we embarked again, and proceeded as before. I was often very much astonished to see some of the women, as well as the men, jump into the water, dive to the bottom, come up again, and swim about. Thus I continued to travel, sometimes by land, sometimes by water, through different countries, and various nations, till, at the end of six or seven months after I had been kidnapped, I arrived at the sea coast. It would be tedious and uninteresting to relate all the incidents which befel me during this journey, and which I have not yet forgotten; of the various hands I passed through, and the manners and customs of all the different people among whom I lived: I shall therefore only observe, that, in all the places where I was, the soil was exceedingly rich; the pomkins, cadas, plantains, yams, &c. &c. were

in great abundance, and of incredible size. There were also vast quantities of different gums, though not used for any purpose; and every where a great deal of tobacco. The cotton even grew quite wild; and there was plenty of red wood. I saw no mechanic whatever in all the way, except such as I have mentioned. The chief employment in all these countries was agriculture, and both the males and females, as with us, were brought up to it, and trained in the arts of war.

The first object which saluted my eyes when I arrived on the coast was the sea, and a slave-ship, which was then riding at anchor, and waiting for its cargo. These filled me with astonishment, which was soon converted into terror, which I am yet at a loss to describe, nor the then feelings of my mind. When I was carried on board I was immediately handled, and tossed up, to see if I were sound, by some of the crew; and I was now persuaded that I had gotten into a world of bad spirits, and that they were going to kill me Their complexions too differing so much from ours, their long hair, and the language they spoke, which was very different from any I had ever heard, united to confirm me in this belief. Indeed, such were the horrors of my views and fears at the moment, that, if ten thousand worlds had been my own, I would have freely parted with them all to have exchanged my condition with that of the meanest slave in my own country. When I looked round the ship too, and saw a large furnace of copper boiling, and a multitude of black people of every description chained together, every one of their countenances expressing dejection and sorrow, I no longer doubted of my fate, and, quite overpowered with horror and anguish, I fell motionless on the deck and fainted. When I recovered a little, I found some black people about me, who I believed were some of those who brought me on board, and had been receiving their pay: they talked to me in order to cheer me, but all in vain, I asked them if we were not to be eaten by those white men with horrible looks, red faces, and long hair? They told me I was not; and one of the crew brought me a small portion of spirituous liquor in a wine glass; but, being afraid of him, I would not take it out of his hand. One of the blacks therefore took it from him and gave it to me, and I took a little down my palate, which, instead of reviving me, as they thought it would, threw me into the greatest consternation at the strange feeling it produced, having never tasted any such liquor before. Soon after this, the blacks who brought me on board went off, and left me abandoned to despair. I now saw myself deprived of all chance of returning to my native country, or even the least glimpse of hope of gaining the shore, which I now considered as friendly: and I even wished for my former slavery in preference to my present situation, which was filled with horrors of every kind, still heightened by my ignorance of what I was to undergo. I was not long suffered to indulge my grief; I was soon put down under the decks, and there I received such a salutation in my nostrils as I had never experienced in my life; so that with the loathsomeness of the stench, and crying together, I became so sick and low that I was not able to eat, nor had I the least desire to taste any thing. I now wished for the last friend, Death, to relieve me; but soon, to my grief, two of the white men offered me eatables; and, on my refusing to eat, one of them held me fast by the hands, and laid me across, I think, the windlass, and tied my feet, while the other flogged me severely. I had never experienced any thing of this kind before; and although, not being used to the water, I naturally feared that element the first time I saw it; yet, nevertheless, could I have got over the nettings, I would have jumped over the side, but I could not; and, besides, the crew used to watch us very closely who were not chained down to the decks, lest we should leap into the water; and I have seen some of these poor African prisoners most severely cut for attempting to do so, and hourly whipped for not eating. This indeed was often the case with myself. In a little time after, amongst the poor chained men, I found some of my own nation, which in a small degree gave ease to my mind. I inquired of these what was to be done with us? they gave me to understand we were to be carried to these white people's country to work for them. I then was a little revived, and thought, if it were no worse than working, my situation was not so desperate: but still I feared I should be put to death, the white people looked and acted, as I thought, in so savage a manner; for I had never seen among any people such instances of brutal cruelty; and this not only shewn towards us blacks, but also to some of the whites themselves. One white man in particular I saw, when we were permitted to be on deck, flogged so unmercifully with a large rope near the foremast, that he died in consequence of it; and they tossed him over the side as they would have done a brute. This made me fear these people the more; and I expected nothing less than to be treated in the same manner. I could not help expressing my fears and apprehensions to some of my countrymen. I asked them if these people had no country, but lived in this hollow place the ship? they told me they did not, but came from a distant one. "Then," said I, "how comes it in all our country we never heard of them?" They told me, because they lived so very far off. I then asked where were their women? had they any like themselves? I was told they had: "And why," said I, "do we not see them?" they answered, because they were left behind. I asked how the vessel could go? they told me they could not tell; but that there were cloths put upon the masts by the help of the ropes I saw, and then the vessel went on; and the white men had some spell or magic they put in the water when they liked in order to stop the vessel. I was exceedingly amazed at this account, and really thought they were spirits. I therefore wished much to be from amongst them, for I expected they would sacrifice me: but my wishes were vain; for we were so quartered that it was impossible for any of us to make our escape. While we staid on the coast I was mostly on deck; and one day, to my great astonishment, I saw one of these vessels coming in with the sails up. As soon as the whites saw it, they gave a great shout, at which we were amazed; and the more so as the vessel appeared larger by approaching nearer. At last she came to an anchor in my sight, and when the anchor was let go, I and my countrymen who saw it were lost in astonishment to observe the vessel stop; and were now convinced it was done by magic. Soon after this the other ship got her boats out, and they came on board of us, and the people of both ships seemed very glad to see each other. Several of the strangers also shook hands with us black people, and made motions with their hands, signifying, I suppose, we were to go to their country; but we did not understand them. At last, when the ship we were in had got in all her cargo, they made ready with many fearful noises, and we were all put under deck, so that we could not see how they managed the vessel. But this disappointment was the least of my sorrow. The stench of the hold while we were on the coast was so intolerably loathsome, that it was dangerous to remain there for any time, and some of us had been permitted to stay on the deck for the fresh air; but now that the whole ship's cargo were confined together, it became absolutely pestilential. The closeness of the place, and the heat of the climate, added to the number in the ship, which was so crowded that each had scarcely room to turn himself, almost suffocated us. This produced copious perspirations, so that the air soon became unfit for respiration, from a variety of loathsome smells, and brought on a sickness among the slaves, of which many died, thus falling victims to the improvident avarice, as I may call it, of their purchasers. This wretched situation was again aggravated by the galling of the chains, now become insupportable; and the filth of the necessary tubs, into which the children often fell, and were almost suffocated. The shrieks of the women, and the groans of the dying, rendered the whole a scene of horror almost inconceiveable. Happily perhaps for myself I was soon reduced so low here that it was thought necessary to keep me almost always on deck; and from my extreme youth I was not put in fetters. In this situation I expected every hour to share the fate of my companions, some of whom were almost daily brought upon deck at the point of death, which I began to hope would soon put an end to my miseries. Often did I think many of the inhabitants of the deep much more happy than myself; I envied them the freedom they enjoyed, and as often wished I could change my condition for theirs. Every circumstance I met with served only to render my state more painful, and heighten my apprehensions, and my opinion of the cruelty of the whites. One day they had taken a number of fishes; and when they had killed and satisfied themselves with as many as they thought fit, to our astonishment who were on the deck, rather than give any of them to us to eat, as we expected they tossed the remaining fish into the sea again, although we begged and prayed for some as well as we could, but in vain; and some of my countrymen, being pressed by hunger, took an opportunity, when they thought no one saw them, of trying to get a little privately; but they were discovered, and the attempt procured them some very severe floggings.

11   One day, when we had a smooth sea, and moderate wind, two of my wearied countrymen, who were chained together (I was near them at the time), preferring death to such a life of misery, somehow made through the nettings, and jumped into the sea: immediately another quite dejected fellow, who, on account of his illness, was suffered to be out of irons, also followed their example; and I believe many more would very soon have done the same, if they had not been prevented by the ship's crew, who were instantly alarmed. Those of us that were the most active were, in a moment, put down under the deck; and there was such a noise and confusion amongst the people of the ship as I never heard before, to stop her, and get the boat out to go after the slaves. However, two of the wretches were drowned, but they got the other, and afterwards flogged him unmercifully, for thus attempting to prefer death to slavery. In this manner we continued to undergo more hardships than I can now relate; hardships which are inseparable from this accursed trade—Many a time we were near suffocation, from the want of fresh air, which we were often without for whole days together. This, and the stench of the necessary tubs, carried off many. During our passage I first saw flying fishes, which surprised me very much: they used frequently to fly across the ship, and many of them fell on the deck. I also now first saw the use of the quadrant. I had often with astonishment seen the mariners make observations with it, and I could not think what it meant. They at last took notice of my surprise; and one of them, willing to increase it, as well as to gratify my curiosity, made me one day

look through it. The clouds appeared to me to be land, which disappeared as they passed along. This heightened my wonder; and I was now more persuaded than ever that I was in another world, and that every thing about me was magic. At last we came in sight of the island of Barbadoes, at which the whites on board gave a great shout, and made many signs of joy to us. We did not know what to think of this; but as the vessel drew neater we plainly saw the harbour, and other ships of different kinds and sizes: and we soon anchored amongst them off Bridge Town. Many merchants and planters now came on board, though it was in the evening. They put us in separate parcels, and examined us attentively. They also made us jump, and pointed to the land, signifying we were to go there. We thought by this we should be eaten by these ugly men, as they appeared to us; and, when soon after we were all put down under the deck again, there was much dread and trembling among us, and nothing but bitter cries to be heard all the night from these apprehensions, insomuch that at last the white people got some old slaves from the land to pacify us. They told us we were not to be eaten, but to work, and were soon to go on land, where we should see many of our country people. This report eased us much; and sure enough, soon after we were landed, there came to us Africans of all languages. We were conducted immediately to the merchant's yard, where we were all pent up together like so many sheep in a fold, without regard to sex or age. As every object was new to me, every thing I saw filled me with surprise. What struck me first was, that the houses were built with bricks, in stories, and in every other respect different from those in I have seen in Africa but I was still more astonished on seeing people on horseback. I did not know what this could mean; and indeed I thought these people were full of nothing but magical arts. While I was in this astonishment, one of my fellow prisoners spoke to a countryman of his about the horses, who said they were the same kind they had in their country. I understood them, though they were from a distant part of Africa, and I thought it odd I had not seen any horses there; but afterwards, when I came to converse with different Africans, I found they had many horses amongst them, and much larger than those I then saw. We were not many days in the merchant's custody before we were sold after their usual manner, which is this:—On a signal given, (as the beat of a drum), the buyers rush at once into the yard where the slaves are confined, and make choice of that parcel they like best. The noise and clamour with which this is attended, and the eagerness visible in the countenances of the buyers, serve not a little to increase the apprehensions of the terrified Africans, who may well be supposed to consider them as the ministers of that destruction to which they think themselves devoted. In this manner, without scruple, are relations and friends separated, most of them never to see each other again. I remember in the vessel in which I was brought over, in the men's apartment, there were several brothers, who, in the sale, were sold in different lots; and it was very moving on this occasion to see and hear their cries at parting. O, ye nominal Christians! might not an African ask you, learned you this from your God? who says unto you, Do unto all men as you would men should do unto you? Is it not enough that we are torn from our country and friends to toil for your luxury and lust of gain? Must every tender feeling be likewise sacrificed to your avarice? Are the dearest friends and relations, now rendered more dear by their separation from their kindred, still to be parted from each other, and thus prevented from cheering the gloom of slavery with the small comfort of being together and mingling their sufferings and sorrows? Why are parents to lose their children, brothers their sisters, or husbands their wives? Surely this is a new refinement in cruelty, which, while it has no advantage to atone for it, thus aggravates distress, and adds fresh horrors even to the wretchedness of slavery.

Robert Hayden

(1913–1980)

Born in Detroit on August 4, 1913, Robert Hayden was named Asa Bundy Sheffey at birth. He took the name Hayden from his foster parents, who raised him. Hayden graduated from Detroit City College (later renamed Wayne State University) and earned a master's degree from the University of Michigan, where he studied with W. H. Auden. Hayden evolved into a modernist poet, becoming very adept at the latest poetic techniques. He was often subjected to criticism, particularly during the 1960s, because he would not embrace the idea that art is racial. Notwithstanding, he wrote some of the most memorable verses about African American experience. His volumes include Heart-Shape in the Dust: Poems *(1940),* The Lion and the Archer *(1948),* The Ballad of Birmingham *(1962),* Words in the Mourning Time: Poems *(1970), and* American Journal *(1978). Hayden won the grand prize for poetry at the First World Festival of Negro Arts at Dakar, Senegal, in 1966, and was appointed consultant in poetry at the Library of Congress in 1976. He also edited* Kaleidoscope: Poems by American Negro Poets *(1967). One of his most celebrated works, "Middle Passage," first published in the journal* Phylon *in 1945, is reprinted below.*

Middle Passage

I.

1   *Jesús Estrella, Esperanza, Mercy:*
    Sails flashing to the wind like weapons,
    sharks following the moans the fever and the dying;
    horror the corposant and compass rose.

5   Middle Passage:
    voyage through death
       to life upon these shores.

    "10 April 1800—
    Blacks rebellious. Crew uneasy. Our linguist says
10   their moaning is a prayer for death,
    ours and their own. Some try to starve themselves.
    Lost three this morning leaped with crazy laughter
    to the waiting sharks, sang as they went under."

    Desire, Adventure, Tartar, Ann:

15   Standing to America, bringing home
    black gold, black ivory, black seed.

       Deep in the festering hold thy father lies,
       of his bones New England pews are made,
       those are altar lights that were his eyes.

    Jesus Saviour Pilot Me
    Over Life's Tempestuous Sea.

    We pray that Thou wilt grant, O Lord,
20 safe passage to our vessels bringing
    heathen souls unto Thy chastening.
    Jesus Saviour

       "8 bells, I cannot sleep, for I am sick
       with fear, but writing eases fear a little
25   since still my eyes can see these words take shape
       upon the page & so I write, as one
       would turn to exorcism, 4 days scudding,
       but now the sea is calm again. Misfortune
       follows in our wake like sharks (our grinning

30   tutelary gods). Which one of us
has killed an albatross? A plague among
our blacks—Ophthalmia: blindness—& we
have jettisoned the blind to no avail.
It spreads, the terrifying sickness spreads.
35   Its claws have scratched sight from the Capt.'s eyes
& there is blindness in the fo'c'sle
& we must sail 3 weeks before we come
to port."

> *What port awaits us, Davy Jones'*
> *or home? I've heard of slavers drifting, drifting,*
> *playthings of wind and storm and chance, their crews*
> *gone blind, the jungle hatred*
> *crawling up on deck.*

Thou Who Walked On Galilee

40   "Deponent further sayeth *The Bella J*
left the Guinea Coast
with cargo of five hundred blacks and odd
for the barracoons of Florida:

"That there was hardly room 'tween-decks for half
45   the sweltering cattle stowed spoon-fashion there;
that some went mad of thirst and tore their flesh
and sucked the blood:

"That Crew and Captain lusted with the comeliest
of the savage girls kept naked in the cabins;
50   that there was one they called The Guinea Rose
and they cast lots and fought to lie with her:

"That when the Bo's'n piped all hands, the flames
spreading from starboard already were beyond
control, the negroes howling and their chains
55   entangled with the flames:

"That the burning blacks could not be reached,
that the Crew abandoned ship,
leaving their shrieking negresses behind,
that the Captain perished drunken with the wenches:

60   "Further Deponent sayeth not."

Pilot Oh Pilot Me

II.

Aye, lad, and I have seen those factories,
Gambia, Rio Pongo, Calabar;
have watched the artful mongos baiting traps
65 of war wherein the victor and the vanquished

Were caught as prizes for our barracoons.
Have seen the nigger kings whose vanity
and greed turned wild black hides of Fellatah,
Mandingo, Ibo, Kru to gold for us.

70 And there was one—King Anthracite we named him—
fatish face beneath French parasols
of brass and orange velvet, impudent mouth
whose cups were carven skulls of enemies:

He'd honor us with drum and feast and conjo
75 and palm-oil-glistening wenches deft in love,
and for tin crowns that shone with paste,
red calico and German-silver trinkets

Would have the drums talk war and send
his warriors to burn the sleeping villages
80 and kill the sick and old and lead the young
in coffles to our factories.

Twenty years a trader, twenty years,
for there was wealth aplenty to be harvested
from those black fields, and I'd be trading still
85 but for the fevers melting down my bones.

III.

Shuttles in the rocking loom of history,
the dark ships move, the dark ships move,
their bright ironical names
like jests of kindness on a murderer's mouth;
90 plough through thrashing glister toward
fata morgana's lucent melting shore,
weave toward New World littorals that are
mirage and myth and actual shore.

Voyage through death,
95   voyage whose chartings are unlove.

A charnel stench, effluvium of living death
spreads outward from the hold,
where the living and the dead, the horribly dying,
lie interlocked, lie foul with blood and excrement.

Deep in the festering hold thy father lies,
the corpse of mercy rots with him,
rats eat love's rotten gelid eyes.

But, oh, the living look at you
with human eyes whose suffering accuses you,
whose hatred reaches through the swill of dark
to strike you like a leper's claw.

You cannot stare that hatred down
or chain the fear that stalks the watches
and breathes on you its fetid scorching breath;
cannot kill the deep immortal human wish,
the timeless will.

100 "But for the storm that flung up barriers
of wind and wave, *The Amistad,* señores,
would have reached the port of Principe in two,
three days at most; but for the storm we should
have been prepared for what befell.
105 Swift as the puma's leap it came. There was
that interval of moonless calm filled only
with the water's and the rigging's usual sounds,
then sudden movement, blows and snarling cries
and they had fallen on us with machete
110 and marlinspike. It was as though the very
air, the night itself were striking us.
Exhausted by the rigors of the storm,
we were no match for them. Our men went down
before the murderous Africans. Our loyal
115 Celestino ran from below with gun
and lantern and I saw, before the cane-knife's
knife's wounding flash, Cinquez,
that surly brute who calls himself a prince,
directing, urging on the ghastly work.

120 He hacked the poor mulatto down, and then
he turned on me. The decks were slippery
when daylight finally came. It sickens me
to think of what I saw, of how these apes
threw overboard the butchered bodies of
125 our men, true Christians all, like so much jetsam.
Enough, enough. The rest is quickly told:
Cinquez was forced to spare the two of us
you see to steer the ship to Africa,
and we like phantoms doomed to rove the sea
130 voyaged east by day and west by night,
deceiving them, hoping for rescue,
prisoners on our own vessel, till
at length we drifted to the shores of this
your land, America, where we were freed
135 from our unspeakable misery. Now we
demand, good sirs, the extradition of
Cinquez and his accomplices to La
Havana. And it distresses us to know
there are so many here who seem inclined
140 to justify the mutiny of these blacks.
We find it paradoxical indeed
that you whose wealth, whose tree of liberty
are rooted in the labor of your slaves
should suffer the august John Quincy Adams
145 to speak with so much passion of the right
of chattel slaves to kill their lawful masters
and with his Roman rhetoric weave a hero's
garland for Cinquez. I tell you that
we are determined to return to Cuba
150 with our slaves and there see justice done, Cinquez—
or let us say 'the Prince'—Cinquez shall die."

The deep immortal human wish,
the timeless will:

Cinquez its deathless primaveral image,
155 life that transfigures many lives.

Voyage through death
            to life upon these shores.

Henry Dumas

(1934–1968)

Henry Dumas, short story writer, poet, and Civil Rights worker, was born on July 20, 1934, in Sweet Home, Arkansas, where he spent the first 10 years of his life before moving to Harlem. After graduating from Commerce High School, Dumas enrolled in City College, but soon left to join the U.S. Air Force. He attended Rutgers University, but did not complete his degree. In 1967, Dumas accepted a teaching position at Southern Illinois University, where he became friends with fellow writer and teacher Eugene Redmond. Redmond has been essential to the literary legacy of Dumas: He edited and published Dumas's work, including "Ark of Bones" and Other Stories *(1974),* Play Ebony: Play Ivory *(1974),* Goodbye, Sweetwater *(1988), and* Knees of a Natural Man: The Selected Poetry of Henry Dumas *(1989). Dumas was shot and killed at the age of 33 by a New York City Transit policeman.*

Ark of Bones

1   Headeye, he was followin me. I knowed he was followin me. But I just kept goin, like I wasn't payin him no mind. Headeye, he never fish much, but I guess he knowed the river good as anybody. But he ain't know where the fishin was good. Thas why I knowed he was followin me. So I figured I better fake him out. I ain't want nobody with a mojo bone followin me. Thas why I was goin along downriver stead of up, where I knowed fishin was good. Headeye, he hard to fool. Like I said, he knowed the river good. One time I rode across to New Providence with him and his old man. His old man was drunk. Headeye, he took the raft on across, Me and him. His old man stayed in New Providence, but me and Headeye come back. Thas when I knowed how good of a river-rat he was.

2   Headeye, he o.k., cept when he get some kinda notion in that big head of his. Then he act crazy. Tryin to show off his age. He older'n me, but he little for his age. Some people say readin too many books will stunt your growth. Well, on Headeye, everything is stunted cept his eyes and his head. When he get some crazy notion runnin through his head, then you can't get rid of him till you know what's on his mind. I knowed somethin was eatin on him, just like I knowed it was *him* followin *me*.

3 I kept close to the path less he think I was tryin to lose him. About a mile from my house I stopped and peed in the bushes, and then I got a chance to see how Headeye was movin along.

4 Headeye, he droop when he walk. They called him Headeye cause his eyes looked bigger'n his head when you looked at him sideways. Headeye bout the ugliest guy I ever run upon. But he was good-natured. Some people called him Eagle-Eye. He bout the smartest nigger in that raggedy school, too. But most time we called him Head-eye. He was always findin things and bringin 'em to school, or to the cotton patch. One time he found a mojo bone and all the kids cept me went round talkin bout him puttin a curse on his old man. I ain't say nothin. It wont none of my business. But Headeye, he ain't got no devil in him. I found that out.

5 So, I'm kickin off the clay from my toes, but mostly I'm thinkin about how to find out what's on his mind. He's got this notion in his head about me hoggin the luck. So I'm fakin him out, lettin him droop behind me.

6 Pretty soon I break off the path and head for the river. I could tell I was far enough. The river was gettin ready to bend.

7 I come up on a snake twistin toward the water. I was gettin ready to bust that snake's head when a fox run across my path. Before I could turn my head back, a flock of birds hit the air pretty near scarin me half to death. When I got on down to the bank, I see somebody's cow lopin on the levee way down the river. Then to really upshell me, here come Headeye droopin long like he had ten tons of cotton on his back.

8 "Headeye, what you followin me for?" I was mad.

9 "Ain't nobody thinkin bout you," he said, still comin.

10 "What you followin long behind me for?"

11 "Ain't nobody followin you."

12 "The hell you ain't."

13 "I ain't followin you."

14 "Somebody's followin me, and I like to know who he is."

15 "Maybe somebody's followin me."

16 "What you mean?"

17 "Just what you think."

18 Headeye, he was gettin smart on me. I give him one of my looks, meanin that he'd better watch his smartness round me, cause I'd have him down eatin dirt in a minute. But he act like he got a crazy notion.

19 "You come this far ahead me, you must be got a call from the spirit."

20 "What spirit?" I come to wonder if Headeye ain't got to workin his mojo too much.

21   "Come on."

22   "Wait." I grabbed his sleeve.

23   He took out a little sack and started pullin out something.

24   "You fishin or not?" I ask him.

25   "Yeah, but not for the same thing. You see this bone?" Headeye, he took out that mojo. I stepped back. I wasn't scared of no ole bone, but everybody'd been talkin bout Headeye and him gettin sanctified. But he never went to church. Only his mama went. His old man only went when he sober, and that be about once or twice a year.

26   So I look at that bone. "What kinda voodoo you work with that mojo?"

27   "This is a keybone to the culud man. Ain't but one in the whole world."

28   "And *you* got it?" I act like I ain't believe him. But I was testin him. I never rush upon a thing I don't know.

29   "We got it."

30   "We got?"

31   "It belongs to the people of God."

32   I ain't feel like the people of God, but I just let him talk on.

33   "Remember when Ezekiel was in the valley of dry bones?"

34   I reckoned I did.

35   ". . . And the hand of the Lord was upon me, and carried me out in the spirit to the valley of dry bones.

36   "And he said unto me, 'Son of man, can these bones live?' and I said unto him, 'Lord, thou knowest.'

37   "And he said unto me, 'Go and bind them together. Prophesy that I shall come and put flesh upon them from generations and from generations.'

38   "And the Lord said unto me, 'Son of man, these bones are the whole house of thy brothers, scattered to the islands. Behold, I shall bind up the bones and you shall prophesy the name.'"

39   Headeye, he stopped. I ain't say nothin. I never seen him so full of the spirit before. I held my tongue. I ain't know what to make of his notion.

40   He walked on pass me and loped on down to the river bank. This here old place was called Deadman's Landin because they found a dead man there one time. His body was so rotted and ate up by fish and craw dads that they couldn't tell whether he was white or black. Just a dead man.

41   Headeye went over to them long planks and logs leanin off in the water and begin to push them around like he was makin somethin.

42   "You was followin me." I was mad again.

43   Headeye acted like he was iggin me. He put his hands up to his eyes and looked far out over the water. I could barely make out the other side of the river. It was real wide right along there and take coupla hours by boat to cross it. Most I ever did was fish and swim. Headeye, he act like he iggin me. I began to bait my hook and go down the bank to where he was, I was mad enough to pop him side the head, but I shoulda been glad. I just wanted him to own up to the truth. I walked along the bank. That damn river was risin. It was lappin up over the planks of the landin and climbin up the bank.

44   Then the funniest thing happened. Headeye, he stopped movin and shovin on those planks and looks up at me. His pole is layin back under a willow tree like he wan't goin to fish none. A lot of birds were still flyin over and I saw a bunch of wild hogs rovin along the levee. All of a sudden Headeye, he say:

45   "I ain't mean no harm what I said about you workin with the devil. I take it back."

46   It almost knocked me over. Me and Headeye was arguin a while back bour how many niggers there is in the Bible. Headeye, he know all about it, but I ain't give on to what I know. I looked sideways at him. I figured he was tryin to make up for followin me. But there was somethin funny goin on so I held my peace. I said 'huh-huh,' and I just kept on lookin at him.

47   Then he points out over the water and up in the sky wavin his hand all round like he was twirlin a lasso.

48   "You see them signs?"

49   I couldn't help but say 'yeah.'

50   "The Ark is comin."

51   "What Ark?"

52   "You'll see."

53   "Noah's Ark?"

54   "Just wait. You'll see."

55   And he went back to fixin up that landin. I come to see what he was doin pretty soon. And I had a notion to go down and pitch in. But I knowed Headeye. Sometimes he gets a notion in his big head and he act crazy behind it. Like the time in church when he told Rev. Jenkins that he heard people moanin out on the river. I remember that. Cause papa went with the men. Headeye, his old man was with them out in that boat. They thought it was somebody took sick and couldn't row ashore. But Headeye, he kept tellin them it was a lot of people, like a multitude.

56   Anyway, they ain't find nothin and Headeye, his daddy hauled off and smacked him side the head. I felt sorry for him and didn't laugh as much as the other kids did, though sometimes Headeye's notions get me mad too.

57   Then I come to see that maybe he wasn't followin me. The way he was actin I knowed he wasn't scared to be there at Deadman's Landin. I threw my line out and made like I was fishin, but I wasn't, cause I was steady watchin Headeye.

58   By and by the clouds started to get thick as clabber milk. A wind come up. And even though the little waves slappin the sides of the bank made the water jump around and dance, I could still tell that the river was risin. I looked at Headeye. He was wanderin off along the bank, wadin out in the shallows and leanin over like he was lookin for somethin.

59   I comest to think about what he said, that valley of bones. I comest to get some kinda crazy notion myself. There was a lot of signs, but they weren't nothin too special. If you're sharp-eyed you always seein somethin along the Mississippi.

60   I messed around and caught a couple of fish. Headeye, he was wadin out deeper in the Sippi, bout hip-deep now, standin still like he was listenin for somethin. I left my pole under a big rock to hold it down and went over to where he was.

61   "This ain't the place," I say to him.

62   Headeye, he ain't say nothin. I could hear the water come to talk a little. Only river people know how to talk to the river when it's mad. I watched the light on the waves way upstream where the ole Sippi bend, and I could tell that she was movin faster. Risin. The shakin was fast and the wind had picked up. It was whippin up the canebrake and twirlin the willows and the swamp oak that drink themselves full along the bank.

63   I said it again, thinkin maybe Headeye would ask me where was the real place. But he ain't even listen.

64   "You come out here to fish or fool?" I asked him. But he waved his hand back at me to be quiet. I knew then that Headeye had some crazy notion in his big head and that was it. He'd be talkin about it for the next two weeks.

65   "Hey!" I hollered at him. "Eyehead, can't you see the river's on the rise? Let's shag outa here."

66   He ain't pay me no mind. I picked up a coupla sticks and chunked them out near the place where he was standin just to make sure he ain't fall asleep right out there in the water. I ain't never knowed

Headeye to fall asleep at a place, but bein as he is so damn crazy, I couldn't take the chance.

67   Just about that time I hear a funny noise. Headeye, he hear it too, cause he motioned to me to be still. He waded back to the bank and ran down to the broken down planks at Deadman's Landin. I followed him. A couple drops of rain smacked me in the face, and the wind, she was whippin up a sermon.

68   I heard a kind of moanin, like a lot of people. I figured it must be in the wind. Headeye, he is jumpin around like a perch with a hook in the gill. Then he find himself. He come to just stand alongside the planks. He is in the water about knee deep. The sound is steady not gettin any louder now, and not gettin any lower. The wind, she steady whippin up a sermon. By this time, it done got kinda dark, and me, well, I done got kinda scared.

69   Headeye, he's all right though. Pretty soon he call me.

70   "Fish-hound?"

71   "Yeah?"

72   "You better come on down here."

73   "What for? Man, can't you see it gettin ready to rise?"

74   He ain't say nothin. I can't see too much now cause the clouds done swole up so big and mighty that everything's gettin dark.

75   Then I sees it. I'm gettin ready to chunk another stick out at him, when I see this big thing movin in the far off, movin slow, down river, naw, it was up river. Naw, it was just movin and standin still at the same time. The damnest thing I ever seed. It just about a damn boat, the biggest boat in the whole world. I looked up and what I took for clouds was sails. The wind was whippin up a sermon on them.

76   It was way out in the river, almost not touchin the water, just rockin there, rockin and waitin.

77   Headeye, I don't see him.

78   Then I look and I see a rowboat comin. Headeye, he done waded out about shoulder deep and he is wavin to me. I ain't know what to do. I guess he bout know that I was gettin ready to run, because he holler out. "Come on, Fish! Hurry! I wait for you."

79   I figured maybe we was dead or somethin and was gonna get the Glory Boat over the river and make it on into heaven. But I ain't say it out aloud. I was so scared I didn't know what I was doin. First thing I know I was side by side with Headeye, and a funny-lookin rowboat was drawin alongside of us. Two men, about as black as anybody black wants to be, was steady strokin with paddles. The rain

had reached us and I could hear that moanin like a church full of people pourin out their hearts to Jesus in heaven.

80   All the time I was tryin not to let on how scared I was. Headeye, he ain't payin no mind to nothin cept that boat. Pretty soon it comest to rain hard. The two big black jokers rowin the boat ain't say nothin to us, and everytime I look at Headeye, he poppin his eyes out tryin to get a look at some-thin far off. I couldn't see that far, so I had to look at what was close up. The muscles in those jokers' arms was movin back an forth every time they swung them oars around. It was a funny ride in that rowboat, because it didn't seem like we was in the water much. I took a chance and stuck my hand over to see, and when I did that they stopped rowin the boat and when I looked up we was drawin longside this here ark, and I tell you it was the biggest ark in the world.

81   I asked Headeye if it was Noah's Ark, and he tell me he didn't know either. Then I was scared.

82   They was tyin that rowboat to the side where some heavy ropes hung over. A long row of steps were cut in the side near where we got out, and the moanin sound was real loud now, and if it wasn't for the wind and rain beatin and whippin us up the steps, I'd swear the sound was comin from someplace inside the ark.

83   When Headeye got to the top of the steps I was still makin my way up. The two jokers were gone. On each step was a number, and I couldn't help lookin at them numbers. I don't know what number was on the first step, but by the time I took notice I was on 1608, and they went on like that right on up to a number that made me pay attention: 1944. That was when I was born. When I got up to Headeye, he was standin on a number, 1977, and so I ain't pay the number any more mind.

84   If that ark was Noah's, then he left all the animals on shore because I ain't see none. I kept lookin around. All I could see was doors and cabins. While we was standin there takin in things, half scared to death, an old man come walkin toward us. He's dressed in skins and his hair is grey and very woolly. I figured he ain't never had a haircut all his life. But I didn't say nothin. He walks over to Headeye and that poor boy's eyes bout to pop out.

85   Well, I'm standin there and this old man is talkin to Headeye. With the wind blowin and the moanin, I couldn't make out what they was sayin. I got the feelin he didn't want me to hear either, because he was leanin in on Headeye. If that old fellow was Noah, then he wasn't like the Noah I'd seen in my Sunday School picture cards. Naw, sir. This old guy was wearin skins and sandals and he was black as Headeye and

me, and he had thick features like us, too. On them pictures Noah was always white with a long beard hangin off his belly.

86   I looked around to see some more people, maybe Shem, Ham and Japheh, or wives and the rest who was suppose to be on the ark, but I ain't see nobody. Nothin but all them doors and cabins. The ark is steady rockin like it is floatin on air. Pretty soon Headeye come over to me. The old man was goin through one of the cabin doors. Before he closed the door he turns around and points at me and Headeye. Headeye, he don't see this, but I did. Talkin about scared. I almost ran and jumped off that boat. If it had been a regular boat, like somethin I could stomp my feet on, then I guess I just woulda done it. But I held still.

87   "Fish-hound, you ready?" Headeye say to me.

88   "Yeah, I'm ready to get ashore." I meant it, too.

89   "Come on. You got this far. You scared?"

90   "Yeah, I'm scared. What kinda boat is this?"

91   "The Ark. I told you once."

92   I could tell now that the roarin was not all the wind and voices. Some of it was engines. I could hear that chug-chug like a paddle wheel whippin up the stern.

93   "When we gettin off here? You think I'm crazy like you?" I asked him. I was mad. "You know what that old man did behind your back?"

94   "Fish-hound, this is a soulboat."

95   I figured by now I best play long with Headeye. He got a notion goin and there ain't nothin mess his head up more than a notion. I stopped tryin to fake him out. I figured then maybe we both was crazy. I ain't feel crazy, but I damn sure couldn't make heads or tails of the situation. So I let it ride. When you hook a fish, the best thing to do is just let him get a good hold, let him swallow it. Specially a catfish. You don't go jerkin him up as soon as you get a nibble. With a catfish you let him go. I figured I'd better let things go. Pretty soon, I figured I'd catch up with somethin. And I did.

96   Well, me and Headeye were kinda arguin, not loud, since you had to keep your voice down on a place like that ark out of respect. It was like that. Headeye, he tells me that when the cabin doors open we were suppose to go down the stairs. He said anybody on this boat could consider hisself *called.*

97   "Called to do what?" I asked him. I had to ask him, cause the only kinda callin I knew about was when somebody *hollered* at you or when the Lord *called* somebody to preach. I figured it out. Maybe the Lord had called him, but I knew dog well He wasn't *callin* me. I hardly ever went to church and when I did go it was only to play with

the gals. I knowed I wasn't fit to whip up no flock of people with holiness. So when I asked him, called for what, I ain't have in my mind nothin I could be called for.

98   "You'll see," he said, and the next thing I know we was goin down steps into the belly of that ark. The moanin jumped up into my ears loud and I could smell somethin funny, like the burnin of sweet wood. The churnin of a paddle wheel filled up my ears and when Headeye stopped at the foot of the steps, I stopped too. What I saw I'll never forget as long as I live.

99   Bones. I saw bones. They were stacked all the way to the top of the ship. I looked around. The under side of the whole ark was nothin but a great bonehouse. I looked and saw crews of black men handlin in them bones. There was crew of two or three under every cabin around that ark. Why, there must have been a million cabins. They were doin it very carefully, like they were holdin onto babies or somethin precious. Standin like a captain was the old man we had seen top deck. He was holdin a long piece of leather up to a fire that was burnin near the edge of an opening which showed outward to the water. He was readin that piece of leather.

100   On the other side of the fire, just at the edge of the ark, a crew of men was windin up a rope. They were chantin every time they pulled. I couldn't understand what they was sayin. It was a foreign talk, and I never learned any kind of foreign talk. In front of us was a fence so as to keep anybody comin down the steps from bargin right in. We just stood there. The old man knew we was there, but he was busy readin. Then he rolls up this long scroll and starts to walk in a crooked path through the bones laid out on the floor. It was like he was walkin frontwards, backwards, sidewards and every which a way. He was bein careful not to step on them bones. Headeye, he looked like he knew what was goin on, but when I see all this I just about popped my eyes out.

101   Just about the time I figure I done put things together, somethin happens. I bout come to figure them bones were the bones of dead animals and all the men wearin skin clothes, well, they was the skins of them animals, but just about time I think I got it figured out, one of the men haulin that rope up from the water starts to holler. They all stop and let him moan on and on.

102   I could make out a bit of what he was sayin, but like I said, I never was good at foreign talk.

> *Aba aba, al ham dilaba*
> *aba aba, mtu brotha*
> *aba aba, al ham dilaba*
> *aba aba, bretha brotha*
> *aba aba, djuka brotha*
> *aba, aba, al ham dilaba*

103   Then he stopped. The others begin to chant in the back of him, real low, and the old man, he stop where he was, unroll that scroll and read it, and then he holler out: "Nineteen hundred and twenty-three!" Then he close up the scroll and continue his comin towards me and Headeye. On his way he had to stop and do the same thing about four times. All along the side of the ark them great black men were haulin up bones from that river. It was the craziest thing I ever saw. I knowed then it wasn't no animal bones. I took a look at them and they was all laid out in different ways, all making some kind of body and there was big bones and little bones, parts of bones, chips, rid-bits, skulls, fingers and everything. I shut my mouth then. I knowed I was onto somethin. I had fished out somethin.

104   I comest to think about a sermon I heard about Ezekiel in the valley of dry bones. The old man was lookin at me now. He look like he was sizin me up.

105   Then he reach out and open the fence. Headeye, he walks through and the old man closes it. I keeps still. You best to let things run their course in a situation like this.

106   "Son, you are in the house of generations. Every African who lives in America has a part of his soul in this ark. God has called you, and I shall anoint you."

107   He raised the scroll over Headeye's head and began to squeeze like he was tryin to draw the wetness out. He closed his eyes and talked very low.

108   "Do you have your shield?"

109   Headeye, he then brings out this funny cloth I see him with, and puts it over his head and it flops all the way over his shoulder like a hood.

110   "Repeat after me," he said. I figured that old man must be some kind of minister because he was ordaining Headeye right there before my eyes. Everythin he say, Headeye, he sayin behind him.

> *Aba, I consecrate my bones.*
> *Take my soul up and plant it again.*
> *Your will shall be my hand.*

When I strike you strike.
My eyes shall see only thee.
I shall set my brother free.
Aba, this bone is thy seal.

111   I'm steady watchin. The priest is holdin a scroll over his head and I see some oil fallin from it. It's black oil and it soaks into Headeye's shield and the shield turns dark green. Headeye ain't movin. Then the priest pulls it off.

112   "Do you have your witness?"

113   Headeye, he is tremblin. "Yes, my brother, Fish-hound."

114   The priest points at me then like he did before.

115   "With the eyes of your brother Fish-hound, so be it?" He was askin me. I nodded my head. Then he turns and walks away just like he come.

116   Headeye, he goes over to one of the fires, walkin through the bones like he been doin it all his life, and he holds the shield in till it catch fire. It don't burn with a flame, but with a smoke. He puts it down on a place which looks like an altar or somethin, and he sits in front of the smoke cross-legged, and I can hear him moanin. When the shield it all burnt up, Headeye takes out that little piece of mojo bone and rakes the ashes inside. Then he zig-walks over to me, opens up that fence and goes up the steps. I have to follow, and he ain't say nothin to me. He ain't have to then.

117   It was several days later that I see him again. We got back that night late, and everybody wanted to know where we was. People from town said the white folks had lynched a nigger and threw him in the river. I wasn't doin no talkin till I see Headeye. Thas why he picked me for his witness. I keep my word.

118   Then that evenin, whilst I'm in the house with my ragged sisters and brothers and my old papa, here come Headeye. He had a funny look in his eye. I knowed some notion was whippin his head. He must've been runnin. He was out of breath.

119   "Fish-hound, broh, you know what?"

120   "Yeah," I said. Headeye, he know he could count on me to do my part, so I ain't mind showin him that I like to keep my feet on the ground. You can't never tell what you get yourself into by messin with mojo bones.

121   "I'm leavin." Headeye, he come up and stand on the porch. We got a no-count rabbit dog, named Heyboy, and when Headeye come up on the porch Heyboy, he jump up and come sniffin at him.

122   "Git," I say to Heyboy, and he jump away like somebody kick him. We hadn't seen that dog in about a week. No tellin what kind of devilment he been into.

123   Headeye, he ain't say nothin. The dog, he stand up on the edge of the porch with his two front feet lookin at Headeye like he was goin to get piece bread chunked out at him. I watch all this and I see who been takin care that no-count dog.

124   "A dog ain't worth a mouth of bad wine if he can't hunt," I tell Headeye, but he is steppin off the porch.

125   "Broh, I come to tell you I'm leavin."

126   "We all be leavin if the Sippi keep risin," I say.

127   "Naw," he say.

128   Then he walk off. I come down off that porch.

129   "Man, you need another witness?" I had to say somethin.

130   Headeye, he droop when he walk. He turned around, but he ain't droopin.

131   "I'm goin, but someday I be back. You is my witness."

132   We shook hands and Headeye, he was gone, movin fast with that no-count dog runnin long side him.

133   He stopped once and waved. I got a notion when he did that. But I been keepin it to myself.

134   People been askin me where'd he go. But I only tell em a little somethin I learned in church. And I tell em bout Ezekiel in the valley of dry bones.

135   Sometimes they say, "Boy, you gone crazy?" and then sometimes they'd say, "Boy, you gonna be a preacher yet," or then they'd look at me and nod their heads as if they knew what I was talkin bout.

136   I never told em about the Ark and them bones. It would make no sense. They think me crazy then for sure. Probably say I was gettin to be as crazy as Headeye, and then they'd turn around and ask me again:

137   "Boy, where you say Headeye went?"

Toni Morrison

(1931–)

Born Chloe Anthony Wofford in Lorain, Ohio, on February 18, 1931, Toni Morrison is unquestionably one of the most important writers of the twentieth century. Her parents, Ramah Willis and George Wofford, were recent Southern migrants, and the South and its accompanying issues of migration and displacement are recurring themes in Morrison's oeuvre, along with topics ranging from African American history and folk traditions to gender relationships and language practices. Morrison received her undergraduate degree from Howard University and her master's degree from Cornell University. She has published eight novels, including The Bluest Eye *(1970);* Sula *(1973);* Song of Solomon *(1977), which won the National Book Critics Circle award and earned Morrison national repute; and* Tar Baby *(1981). Morrison characterizes her next three novels as a trilogy about love.* Beloved *(1987), a powerful account of the institution of slavery as understood through mother love, won the novelist the Pulitzer Prize. The passage from the novel that voices the trauma of the Middle Passage is reprinted below.* Jazz *(1991), set in 1920s Harlem, takes up the issue of romantic love.* Paradise *(1998) examines the love of God through a story that moves from Reconstruction to 1970s Oklahoma. Morrison's most recent novel is titled, perhaps not surprisingly,* Love *(2003). Morrison received the Nobel Prize for literature in 1993, making her the first African American writer to be so honored. In addition to her fiction, Morrison has become an important cultural and literary critic. She currently is the Robert F. Goheen Professor of Humanities at Princeton University.*

Beloved

1   I am beloved and she is mine. I see her take flowers away from leaves she puts them in a round basket the leaves are not for her she   fills the basket   she opens the grass   I would help her but the clouds are in the way   how can I say things that are pictures   I am not separate from her   there is no place where I stop   her face is my own and I want to be there in the place where her face is and to be looking at it too   a hot thing

2   All of it is now   it is always now   there will never be a time when I am not crouching and watching others who are crouching too   I am always crouching   the man on my face is dead   his face is not mine   his mouth smells sweet but his eyes are locked

3   some who eat nasty themselves   I do not eat   the men without skin bring us their morning water to drink   we have none   at night I cannot see the dead man on my face   daylight comes through the cracks and I can see his locked eyes   I am not big   small rats do not wait for us to sleep   someone is thrashing but there is no room

to do it in   if we had more to drink we could make tears   we cannot make sweat or morning water so the men without skin bring us theirs   one time they bring us sweet rocks to suck   we are all trying to leave our bodies behind   the man on my face has done it   it is hard to make yourself die forever   you sleep short and then return   in the beginning we could vomit   now we do not

4   now we cannot   his teeth are pretty white points   someone is trembling   I can feel it over here   he is fighting hard to leave his body which is a small bird trembling   there is no room to tremble so he is not able to die   my own dead man is pulled away from my face I miss his pretty white points

5   We are not crouching now   we are standing but my legs are like my dead man's eyes   I cannot fall because there is no room to   the men without skin are making loud noises   I am not dead the bread is sea-colored   I am too hungry to eat it   the sun closes my eyes   those able to die are in a pile   I cannot find my man the one whose teeth I have loved   a hot thing   the little hill of dead people   a hot thing   the men without skin push them through with poles   the woman is there with the face I want   the face that is mine   they fall into the sea which is the color of the bread   she has nothing in her ears   if I had the teeth of the man who died on my face I would bite the circle around her neck   bite it away I know she does not like it   now there is room to crouch and to watch the crouching others   it is the crouching that is now always now   inside   the woman with my face is in the sea   a hot thing

6   In the beginning I could see her   I could not help her because the clouds were in the way   in the beginning I could see her   the shining in her ears   she does not like the circle around her neck I know this   I look hard at her so she will know that the clouds are in the way I am sure she saw me   I am looking at her see me   she empties out her eyes   I am there in the place where her face is and telling her the noisy clouds were in my way   she wants her earrings   she wants her round basket   I want her face   a hot thing

7   in the beginning the women are away from the men and the men are away from the women   storms rock us and mix the men into the women and the women into the men   that is when I begin to be on the back of the man   for a long time I see only his neck and his wide shoulders above me   I am small   I love him because he has a song   when he turned around to die I see the teeth he sang through

his singing was soft   his singing is of the place where a woman takes
flowers away from their leaves and puts them in a round basket
before the clouds   she is crouching near us   but I do not see her
until he locks his eyes and dies on my face   we are that way   there
is no breath coming from his mouth and the place where breath
should be is sweet-smelling   the others do not know he is dead   I
know   his song is gone   now I love his pretty little teeth instead

8   I cannot lose her again   my dead man was in the way like the
noisy clouds   when he dies on my face I can see hers   she is going
to smile at me   she is going to   her sharp earrings are gone   the
men without skin are making loud noises   they push my own man
through   they do not push the woman with my face through   she goes
in   they do not push her   she goes in   the little hill is gone   she
was going to smile at me   she was going to   a hot thing

9   They are not crouching now   we are   they are floating on the
water   they break up the little hill and push it through   I cannot
find my pretty teeth   I see the dark face that is going to smile at me
it is my dark face that is going to smile at me   the iron circle is around
our neck   she does not have sharp earrings in her ears or a round basket   she goes in the water   with my face

10   I am standing in the rain falling   the others are taken   I am not
taken   I am falling like the rain is   I watch him eat   inside I am
crouching to keep from falling with the rain   I am going to be in
pieces   he hurts where I sleep   he puts his finger there   I drop the
food and break into pieces   she took my face away.

11   there is no one to want me   to say me my name   I wait on the
bridge because she is under it   there is night and there is day

12   again   again   night day   night day   I am waiting   no iron circle is around my neck   no boats go on this water   no men without
skin   my dead man is not floating here   his teeth are down there
where the blue is and the grass   so is the face I want   the face that
is going to smile at me   it is going to   in the day diamonds are in
the water where she is and turtles   in the night I hear chewing and
swallowing and laughter   it belongs to me   she is the laugh   I am
the laugher   I see her face which is mine   it is the face that was
going to smile at me in the place where we crouched   now she is going
to   her face comes through the water   a hot thing   her face is mine
she is not smiling   she is chewing and swallowing   I have to have

my face   I go in   the grass opens   she opens it   I am in the water
and she is coming   there is no round basket   no iron circle around
her neck   she goes up where the diamonds are   I follow her   we
are in the diamonds which are her earrings now   my face is coming
I have to have it   I am looking for the join   I am loving my face so
much   my dark face is close to me   I want to join   she whispers to
me   she whispers   I reach for her   chewing and swallowing she
touches me   she knows I want to join   she chews and swallows me
I am gone   now I am her face   my own face has left me   I see me
swim away   a hot thing   I see the bottoms of my feet   I am alone
I want to be the two of us   I want the join

13   I come out of blue water   after the bottoms of my feet swim away
from me I come up   I need to find a place to be   the air is heavy
I am not dead   I am not   there is a house   there is what she whispered to me   I am where she told me   I am not dead   I sit   the sun
closes my eyes   when I open them I see the face I lost   Sethe's is
the face that left me   Sethe sees me see her and I see the smile   her
smiling face is the place for me   it is the face I lost   she is my face
smiling at me   doing it at last   a hot thing   now we can join   a
hot thing

Charles Johnson

(1948–)

*Charles Johnson, born in Evanston, Illinois, in 1948, is a celebrated
contemporary novelist who won the 1990 National Book Award for his
best-selling novel,* Middle Passage, *excerpted below. Johnson is only
the second African American man (after Ralph Ellison) to be so honored. His other publications include the novels* Faith and the Good
Thing *(1974),* Oxherding Tale *(1982), and* Dreamer *(1998), as well as
a collection of stories,* The Sorcerer's Apprentice *(1986). In addition to
his creative writing, Johnson is an illustrator, a philosopher, and a
critic. His political cartoons have been published in two separate collections,* Black Humor *(1970) and* Half-Past Nation Time *(1972).
Johnson's aesthetic largely is informed by his philosophical training;
he received an undergraduate degree from Southern Illinois University
and did graduate work in philosophy at that University and SUNY-
Stony Brook. He is also the author of* Being and Race: Black Writing
Since 1970 *(1988). Johnson is currently a professor of English at the
University of Washington in Seattle.*

Middle Passage
Entry, the sixth
July 3, 1830

1   Twenty blacks were brought from below to dance them a bit to music
from Tommy's flute and let them breathe. They climbed topside and
stood crushed together, blinded by the sun, for that morning the
weather was fair, yet hushed. Meadows and Ngonyama searched the
fusty spaces between decks for Africans unable to come up on their
own. There were always a few of these since Ebenezer Falcon
rearranged their position after the storm. He was, as they say, a
"tight-packer," having learned ten years ago from a one-handed
French slaver named Captain Ledoux that if you arranged the
Africans in two parallel rows, their backs against the lining of the
ship's belly, this left a free space at their rusty feet, and *that*, given
the flexibility of bone and skin, could be squeezed with even more
slaves if you made them squat at ninety-degree angles to one another.
Flesh could conform to anything. So when they came half-dead from
the depths, these eyeless contortionists emerging from a shadowy Pla-
tonic cave, they were stiff and sore and stank of their own vomit and
feces. Right then I decided our captain was more than just evil. He
was the Devil. Who else could twist the body so terribly? Who else
could enslave gods and men alike? All, like livestock, bore the initials
of the *Republic's* financiers burned into their right buttock by a
twisted wire—*ZS*, *PZ*, *EG*, a cabal of Louisiana speculators whose
names I would learn soon enough.

2   Meadows snapped his head away, his nose wrinkled, and he
splashed buckets of salt water on them, then told Tommy to play. The
cabin boy, taking his place on the capstan head, had not stopped smiling since seeing the Allmuseri god. Snapping together his three-piece
flute and touching it to lips shaped in that strangely mad, distant
smile unreadable as a mask, he let his chest fall, forcing wind into
wood that transformed his exhalations into a rill of sound-colors all
on board found chilling—less music, if you ask me, than the boy's
air alchemized into emotion, or the song of hundred-year-old trees
from which the narrow flute was torn.

3   One side of Falcon's face tightened. "Methinks that's too damned
melancholy. Even niggers can't dance to that. A lighter tune, if you

will, Tommy." The cabin boy obeyed, striking up a tune of lighter tempo. Falcon, pleased, tapped his foot, stopping only to stare as Ngonyama and Meadows carried an African's corpse from below. As with previous cases like these, Falcon ordered his ears sliced off and preserved below in oil to prove to the ship's investors that he had in fact purchased in Bangalang as many slaves as promised. This amputation proved tough going for Meadows, for the last stages of rigor mortis froze the body hunched forward in a grotesque hunker, like Lot's wife. Hence, after shearing off his ears, they toted him to the rail as you might a chair or the ship's figurehead, then found him too heavy to heave over.

4   "Lend us a hand here, Mr. Calhoun." Meadows wiped sweat off his upper lip.

5   I stayed where I was. Beside me, a moan burst from a carpenter standing too close to the slaves. They danced in place like men in a work-gang, but one had slipped when the ship rolled, falling on his back and accidentally, it seemed, kicking the sailor in his stomach. And a good kick it was, knocking the wind out of him. The mate looked puzzled; he ran two fingers over his forehead.

6   "You should earn your keep, my boy." Falcon nudged me toward them, then brought a handkerchief to his brow. "One hundred bars overboard. Gawd, I hate waste."

7   Ngonyama was holding the boy—for so he proved to be when I stepped closer—under his arms. Meadows had him by legs cooled to the lower temperatures of the hold. Though he was semistiff, blood giving way to the pull of gravity, motionless in his veins, was settling into his lower limbs, purplish in color as he entered the first stages of stench and putrefaction. The young rot quickest, you know. The underside of his body had the squishy, fluid-squirting feel of soft, overripe fruit. If you squeezed his calves, a cheeselike crasis oozed through the cracks and cuts made in his legs by the chains. It was this side of him Meadows wanted me to grab, providing him and Ngonyama the leverage they needed to swing him past the rail. I cannot say how sickened I felt. The sight and smell of him was a wild thing turned loose in my mind. Never in my life had I handled the dead. It did not matter that I knew nothing of this boy. Except for Ngonyama, the males had generally been kept below, but I'd seen him among the others when Falcon made the Africans dance. Judging by what little was left of his face, hard as wood on one side and melting into worm-eaten pulp on the other as rigor mortis began to reverse, he was close to my own age, perhaps had been torn from a

lass as lovely as, lately, I now saw Isadora to be, and from a brother as troublesome as my own. His open eyes were unalive, mere kernels of muscle, though I still found myself poised vertiginously on their edge, falling through these dead holes deeper into the empty hulk he had become, as if his spirit had flown and mine was being sucked there in its place.

8   "'Ere now," said Meadows, "come about, Calhoun. I'm gettin' tired of holdin' him." I gripped the boy from below, slipping my right hand behind his back, my other under his thigh, so cool and soft, like the purple casing of a plum, that my ragged, unmanicured nails punctured the meat with a hiss as if I'd freed a pocket of air. A handful of rotting leg dropped into my hand before I was able to push hard enough for the others to swing him, just before his limbs disconnected like a doll's, to sharks circling the hull. That bloody piece of him I held, dark and porous, with the first layers of liquefying tissue peeling back to reveal an orange underlayer, fell from my fingers onto the deck: a clump from the butcher's block, it seemed, and the ship's dogs strained their collars trying to get it.

9   Ngonyama wrapped it in a scrap of canvas and pitched it as hard as he could into a wave. My stained hand still tingled. Of a sudden, it no longer felt like my own. Something in me said it would never be clean again, no matter how often I scrubbed it or with what stinging chemicals, and without thinking I found my left hand lifting the knife from my waist, then using its blade to scrape the boy's moist, black flesh off my palm, and at last I swung it up to slice it across my wrist and toss that into the ocean too. "No." Ngonyama placed his fingers on my forearm. He must have felt me wobble. His hands steadied and guided me to the rail, where I gasped for wind, wanting to retch but unable to. Saying nothing, he waited, and as always his expression was difficult to decipher. Weeks before I'd felt that no matter how I tried to see past his face to his feelings, the signs he threw off were so different at times from those I knew they could not be uncoded. It was said, for example, that the Allmuseri spat at the feet of visitors to their village and, as you might expect, this sometimes made travelers draw their swords in rage, though the Allmuseri meant only that the stranger's feet must be hot and tired after so long a journey and might welcome a little water on his boots to cool them. Nay, you could assume nothing with them. But of one thing I was sure: There was a difference in them. They were leagues from home—indeed, without a home—and in Ngonyama's eyes I saw a displacement, an emptiness like maybe all of his brethren as he once knew them were dead. To wit, I saw myself. A man remade by virtue of his

contact with the crew. My reflection in his eyes, when I looked up, gave back my flat image as phantasmic, the flapping sails and sea behind me drained of their density like figures in a dream. Stupidly, I had seen their lives and culture as timeless product, as a finished thing, pure essence or Parmenidean meaning I envied and wanted to embrace, when the truth was that they were process and Heraclitean change, like any men, not fixed but evolving and as vulnerable to metamorphosis as the body of the boy we'd thrown overboard. Ngonyama and maybe all the Africans, I realized, were not wholly Allmuseri anymore. We had changed them. I suspected even he did not recognize the quiet revisions in his voice after he learned English as it was spoken by the crew, or how the vision hidden in their speech was deflecting or redirecting his own way of seeing. Just as Tommy's exposure to Africa had altered him, the slaves' life among the lowest strata of Yankee society—and the horrors they experienced—were subtly reshaping their souls as thoroughly as Falcon's tight-packing had contorted their flesh during these past few weeks, but into what sort of men I could not imagine. No longer Africans, yet not Americans either. Then what? And of what were they now capable?

August Wilson

(1945–)

One of the leading dramatists of our time, Pittsburgh playwright August Wilson was born on April 27, 1945, in the Hill District, a working-class neighborhood in the city, which figures largely in the landscape of his work. It is the people, culture, language, and music of his upbringing to which Wilson has turned in creating his 10-cycle play sequence designed to represent each decade of the twentieth century. At this point, Wilson has published seven plays toward this effort, including Jitney, Ma Rainey's Black Bottom, Fences, Joe Turner's Come and Gone, The Piano Lesson, Two Trains Running, *and* Seven Guitars, *and he has staged two others,* King Hedley II *and* Gem of the Ocean. *Both* Fences *and* The Piano Lesson *earned the playwright Pulitzer Prizes. Wilson has been both critically recognized, winning numerous awards, including Bush, McKnight, Rockefeller, and Guggenheim Foundation fellowships, as well as commercially successful. He is the first African American to have two plays—*Fences *and* Joe Turner's Come and Gone—*running simultaneously on Broadway, and he has won New York Drama Critics Circle and Tony awards. Wilson began his writing career as a poet, and the lyricism of the dialogue in his plays bears the imprint of that experience. The following scene from*

Joe Turner's Come and Gone *portrays an evening in a rooming house where the boarders are enjoying themselves with dance and song. However, Loomis, one of the inhabitants, disrupts this levity with a powerful vision of the Middle Passage.*

Joe Turner's Come and Gone

ACT ONE

Scene Four

The lights come up on the kitchen. It is later the same evening. MATTIE *and all the residents of the house, except* LOOMIS, *sit around the table. They have finished eating and most of the dishes have been cleared.*

1 **MOLLY:** That sure was some good chicken.

JEREMY: That's what I'm talking about. Miss Bertha, you sure can fry some chicken. I thought my mama could fry some chicken. But she can't do half as good as you.

SETH: I know it. That's why I married her. She don't know that, though. She think I married her for something else.

BERTHA: I ain't studying you, Seth. Did you get your things moved in alright, Mattie?

5 **MATTIE:** I ain't had that much. Jeremy helped me with what I did have.

BERTHA: You'll get to know your way around here. If you have any questions about anything just ask me. You and Molly both. I get along with everybody. You'll find I ain't no trouble to get along with.

MATTIE: You need some help with the dishes?

BERTHA: I got me a helper. Ain't I, Zonia? Got me a good helper.

ZONIA: Yes, ma'am.

10 **SETH:** Look at Bynum sitting over there with his belly all poked out. Ain't saying nothing. Sitting over there half asleep. Ho, Bynum!

BERTHA: If Bynum ain't saying nothing what you wanna start him up for?

SETH: Ho, Bynum!

BYNUM: What you hollering at me for? I ain't doing nothing.

SETH: Come on, we gonna Juba.

15 **BYNUM:** You know me, I'm always ready to Juba.

    SETH: Well, come on, then.

> (*SETH pulls out a haromnica and blows a few notes.*)

Come on there, Jeremy. Where's your guitar? Go get your guitar. Bynum say he's ready to Juba.

JEREMY: Don't need no guitar to Juba. Ain't you never Juba without a guitar?

> (*JEREMY begins to drum on the table.*)

SETH: It ain't that. I ain't never Juba with one! Figured to try it and see how it worked.

BYNUM: (*Drumming on the table.*) You don't need no guitar. Look at Molly sitting over there. She don't know we Juba on Sunday. We gonna show you something tonight. You and Mattie Campbell both. Ain't that right, Seth?

20 **SETH:** You said it! Come on, Bertha, leave them dishes be for a while. We gonna Juba.

    BYNUM: Alright. Let's Juba down!

> (*The Juba is reminiscent of the Ring Shouts of the African slaves. It is a call and response dance. BYNUM sits at the table and drums. He calls the dance as others clap hands, shuffle and stomp around the table. It should be as African as possible, with the performers working themselves up into a near frenzy. The words can be improvised, but should include some mention of the Holy Ghost. In the middle of the dance HERALD LOOMIS enters.*)

LOOMIS: (*In a rage.*) Stop it! Stop!

> (*They stop and turn to look at him.*)

You all sitting up here singing about the Holy Ghost. What's so holy about the Holy Ghost? You singing and singing. You think the Holy Ghost coming? You singing for the Holy Ghost to come? What he gonna do, huh? He gonna come with tongues of fire to burn up your woolly heads? You gonna tie onto the Holy Ghost and get burned up? What you got then? Why God got to be so big? Why he got to be bigger than me? How much big is there? How much big do you want?

> (*LOOMIS starts to unzip his pants.*)

SETH: Nigger, you crazy!

LOOMIS: How much big you want?

25 **SETH:** You done plumb lost your mind!

(LOOMIS begins to speak in tongues and dance around the kitchen. SETH starts after him.)

BERTHA: Leave him alone, Seth. He ain't in his right mind.

LOOMIS: (*Stops suddenly.*) You all don't know nothing about me. You don't know what I done seen. Herald Loomis done seen some things he ain't got words to tell you.

(LOOMIS starts to walk out the front door and is thrown back and collapses, terror-stricken by his vision. BYNUM crawls to him.)

BYNUM: What you done seen, Herald Loomis?

LOOMIS: I done seen bones rise up out the water. Rise up and walk across the water. Bones walking on top of the water.

30 **BYNUM:** Tell me about them bones, Herald Loomis. Tell me what you seen.

LOOMIS: I come to this place . . . to this water that was bigger than the whole world. And I looked out . . . and I seen these bones rise up out the water. Rise up and begin to walk on top of it.

BYNUM: Wasn't nothing but bones and they walking on top of the water.

LOOMIS: Walking without sinking down. Walking on top of the water.

BYNUM: Just marching in a line.

35 **LOOMIS:** A whole heap of them. They come up out the water and started marching.

BYNUM: Wasn't nothing but bones and they walking on top of the water.

LOOMIS: One after the other. They just come up out the water and start to walking.

BYNUM: They walking on the water without sinking down. They just walking and walking. And then . . . what happened, Herald Loomis?

LOOMIS: They just walking across the water.

40 **BYNUM:** What happened, Herald Loomis? What happened to the bones?

LOOMIS: They just walking across the water . . . and then . . . they sunk down.

BYNUM: The bones sunk into the water. They all sunk down.

LOOMIS: All at one time! They just all fell in the water at one time.

BYNUM: Sunk down like anybody else.

45   **LOOMIS:**   When they sink down they made a big splash and this here wave come up . . .

BYNUM: A big wave, Herald Loomis. A big wave washed over the land.

LOOMIS: It washed them out of the water and up on the land. Only . . . only . . .

BYNUM: Only they ain't bones no more.

LOOMIS: They got flesh on them! Just like you and me!

50   **BYNUM:**   Everywhere you look the waves is washing them up on the land right on top of one another.

LOOMIS: They black. Just like you and me. Ain't no difference.

BYNUM: Then what happened, Herald Loomis?

LOOMIS: They ain't moved or nothing. They just laying there.

BYNUM: You just laying there. What you waiting on, Herald Loomis?

55   **LOOMIS:**   I'm laying there . . . waiting.

BYNUM: What you waiting on, Herald Loomis?

LOOMIS: I'm waiting on the breath to get into my body.

BYNUM: The breath coming into you, Herald Loomis. What you gonna do now?

LOOMIS: The wind's blowing the breath into my body. I can feel it. I'm starting to breathe again.

60   **BYNUM:**   What you gonna do, Herald Loomis?

LOOMIS: I'm gonna stand up. I got to stand up. I can't lay here no more. All the breath coming into my body and I got to stand up.

BYNUM: Everybody's standing up at the same time.

LOOMIS: The ground's starting to shake. There's a great shaking. The world's busting half in two. The sky's splitting open. I got to stand up.

(LOOMIS attempts to stand up.)

My legs . . . my legs won't stand up!

BYNUM: Everybody's standing and walking toward the road. What you gonna do, Herald Loomis?

65   **LOOMIS:**   My legs won't stand up.

BYNUM: They shaking hands and saying goodbye to each other and walking every whichaway down the road.

LOOMIS: I got to stand up!

BYNUM: They walking around here now. Mens. Just like you and me. Come right up out the water.

LOOMIS: Got to stand up.

70 **BYNUM:** They walking, Herald Loomis. They walking around here now.

LOOMIS: I got to stand up. Get up on the road.

BYNUM: Come on, Herald Loomis.

(LOOMIS tries to stand up.)

LOOMIS: My legs won't stand up! My legs won't stand up!

(LOOMIS collapses on the floor as the lights go down to black.)

Everett Hoagland

(1942–)

Born on December 18, 1942, and raised in Philadelphia, Pennsylvania, Everett Hoagland received his undergraduate degree from Lincoln University in Pennsylvania and a master's degree in creative writing from Brown University in 1973. Hoagland's work has been widely anthologized, appearing in Clarence Major's 1968 collection, The New Black Poetry, *Dudley Randall's 1970 anthology,* The Black Poets, *and numerous literary journals, including* The American Poetry Review, The Massachusetts Review, The Iowa Review, *and* The Crisis. *His first full-length volume of poetry,* This City and Other Poems, *was published in 1997. Hoagland, who has been the recipient of the Gwendolyn Brooks Award, has twice received the Massachusetts Artist Foundation Fellowship, and in 1994 he was designated the Poet Laureate of New Bedford, Massachusetts. He has been an English professor at the University of Massachusetts for more than 20 years.*

Homecoming

1 *"Do ba-na co-ba, gene me, ge-ne me!*
Do ba-na co-ba, gene me, ge-ne me!"

"Do ba-na co-ba, gene me, ge-ne me!
Do ba-na co-ba, gene me, ge-ne me!"*

5 we who are
american made who
feel and act like we are
        making it in america

ensconced in mansions
10 with yachts
and other leisure craft
sometimes forget last

time we crossed

over the atlantic we
15 had to
we had

. . . we . . .

were so many too
few to . . . by twos
20 by the score in lots sold
singly or by the dirty dozens

baptized by inhumanity
in the name of the slaveship
in the name of our "owners"
25 and the power and the glory
of their successive sons many thousand-
thousands did not make it

. . . gone . . .

we who are american made
30 who act and feel like we
have it made in america some-

times forget

his craft and power are great
and still armed with steel gray greed
35 and hate that enforce foreign policy
begun with middle

passage forgive

the heavy air this plaint
brings to our affair
40 here you see
my great-grandparents' grandparents
came from somewhere in the old gold coast

indulge me you see the last time
the we in me crossed the sea
45 sickened naked branded we barely
made it we

traveled so lightly forgive
this funk those of us who
were not sick and jettisoned
50 like junk survived to make

possible succeeding amber waves of we
who currently seem to have it made
in america had seaborne ancestors
who in me are just recently airborne

55 here who

endured floggings and rapes in the name
of moral and cultural superiority who
bore up under ten stone bales of cotton
who rose in negro spirituals from christenings

60 in their own blood from baptismals awash
with their urine vomit liquid feces and pus
and walked free of the heavy air of the hold
into the sea-deep blues of american slavery

and its legacies pardon them
65 for returning in mixed company in me
for returning so ponderously my air
is heavy because I am here for them

fresh out of the funky hold of america
in the name of their lost forgotten family
70 chained names thrown overboard or otherwise drowned in troubled water named nameless
middle passage cape fear river "negroes"
gone
down in holy water drowned to be reborn
75 from kofi to cuffee to cousins
flourishing somewhere among the humanity

here i am
distant family extended nearly to the point
of no return but not as had been hoped for
80 by the slave breakers not beyond endurance
beyond belief for by-and-by by real miracles

of rebellion escape cross-
overcoming by bullets ballots births
beliefs blessings
85 they are here in me
by invitation
by way of high john
hambone ring shouts jazz and pan
african airways

90 *"Do ba-na co-ba, gene me, ge-ne me!*
*Ben-de nu-li, nuli, nuli, ben-de le"**

Gorée

". . . necessary and inevitable
like the 'inevitable' slave past
through consciousness like the present. . . ."
FROM "THE PATH OF THE STARS" BY AUGUSTINO NETO

Gorée ten miles off shore beckons
from the western horizon like the landscape
of the troubled dream and we sleepwalk to the ferry.

Twenty thousand-thousand gone through the Gorée trade alone
5 we are told.

This is a Catholic isle off a Moslem land.
This the church where truth was chained.
Here Jesus died and rose again.
The beads we say are knots of blood.
10 *Here they force-fed us after the trek in chains.*
Here men were sold by size, nubile women penned
and prized for comeliness. Mulattoes conceived here,
and their mothers, were boated back to the main-

*From Chapter 14, "The Souls of Black Folk" by W. E. B. Du Bois.

land to buffer tides of rage. Here children's
15 *chains are sold as souvenirs; they anchor history*
and the mind. Here they took, selected the best;
the rest: lame, old, small and sick were helped
to die.

The writing is on the stockade walls: poster sized
20 revolutionary rhetoric, Pan-African credos, race
pride logos, reminders, challenges and warnings
written in black by the descendants
of the survivors of the dried blood red walls
of the pastel colonial buildings'
25 shuttered silence.

We've had to come all the way
back to see, clearly poetry kill people, blind them,
cause them to cough blood and be crippled
in a French provincial palace of mind,
30 with a court, an overmonied ten percent
of the population, prospering lords and ladies,
fronting masks. Eighty percent of each dollar spent
on the slave factory island, on a ROOTS tee shirt
goes to France. *"See Your Roots"* cotton
35 shirts off bony backs are hawked by hungry hustlers
inside the barracoon's walls. Bloods at its
doors trade cowry shells for your money or
urge on you a brand new djuju bag—

for fifty Central African francs.

40 At sunset on Gorée Island, where scavenging
brown hawks wheel above the huge metal cross
stop the island's highest point, the volcano
sleeps silent as the broken cannon pointed there
over the Middle Passage. . . .
45 down a long dark corridor a doorless doorway
to the past and future opens
to the surf's wash and soft thud on the black
boulders. The blue-eyed horizon of this eastern shore . . . gone.
You are your shadow silhouetted in the rectangular
50 frame that is the grave of time, where so much went
underground. You had to, had to, you
had to come all the way back

to the rock fortress, to the slave pens,
get down
50 on your hands and knees and crawl into
the stone oven of a cell
where the African rebels' yell and defiance were kept
in solitary. Compressed by silence and circumstance
to diamond-hard blues. Completely black
60 inside the cell alone, one sees and hears things
clearly in the deep darkness. Overhead are heard
the voices of African-American tourists
calling their mates to, "Come look at this
Tyree. Come see this Dee. . . ." One hears a sea
65 of twenty thousand thousand voices at once

but also this from the shadows that always crowd
your view-finder, even in the dark:
"Do you tan? The native women are
charming. Does he take Master Charge? How
70 can they be so resigned? Gee, Gorée is neat fun!"
inside the cowry shell you hold to your ear
you hear your name and heartbeat;
you finger the humming walls of the
cubicle and chip the tactile darkness
75 for a keepsake to put in your
djuju bag: ancient black lava rock.

You crawl out into the light
of the setting sun, face the western horizon
and, stripping as you go, hanging your watch
80 and jeans, western shirt and shoes on your white
shadow, you wade into
the east shore of the Middle Passage—
the hyphen between African
and American—
85 the surf hisses and steams off you
like water around white hot iron.
You walk out farther, level with your
heart. Farther, until the edge of life
is just over your head. You hold your
90 breath under water, open your eyes, clench
your fists and let the bellow bubble out

of you.
But you bound off the sand and obsidian
bottom and beat your breath back to the surface. . . .

95 As we board the ferry back to Dakar
the ghosts of twenty million swarm the wharf;
waifs with open palms and eyes closed by
disease and blindness, with ringworm in their
rusty dreadlocks, beg
100 for fifty Central African francs.

The Paris of Africa.

At sunset, the sea around Gorée is red;
it recedes revealing twenty thousand-
thousand gone and western rigs drilling
105 offshore for new black gold.

Later, alone in the bush, squatting
at the base of an ashy baobab, you contemplate
it all: your blue jeans,
the same old cotton, under
110 the same old sun,
the same old so-called "communes,"
the same old mules,
the same gaunt shadows lengthening
in the light. And how
115 oppression always
smells the same, looks the same, how
poverty personified is always full
of the same self
hate and hospitality.

120 You look at, listen to
the little whirlwinds, dust devils
swirling on the dry red road
and think of goopher,
think of vévé.
125 You take a twig and score
your name under a poem
you are able to read in the deep
red dust:

Dust

We are dust.

Rock is the placenta of time.
But rock can be shattered.

You cannot break dust;
5 it defies the hammer.
Chisels cannot carve up-

on it. Its stuff will not
make good statues of your heroes.
Heroes are made of it. Blown up?
10 Explosives never destroy it.
It cannot be slung or thrown.
Primitive

but it can kill you.

W. E. B. Du Bois

(1868–1963)

*Generally regarded as the most accomplished intellectual in the
African American tradition, William Edward Burghardt Du Bois was
born in Great Barrington, Massachusetts, on February 23, 1868.
Rising from humble beginnings, he earned baccalaureate degrees at
both Fisk University (1888) and Harvard University (1890). He pursued graduate study at Harvard, receiving an M.A. in 1891. Du Bois
did further work at Harvard but also traveled to Germany to study
history and sociology for two years at the University of Berlin. He
returned to become, in 1896, the first African American to receive a
doctorate from Harvard. Du Bois taught at Wilberforce and Atlanta
universities, was the only African American founding member of the
National Association for the Advancement of Colored People
(NAACP), and was the founder and editor of the* Crisis, *the magazine sponsored by the NAACP. However, he rose to national prominence because of his writing—more specifically, with the publication
of* The Souls of Black Folk *(1903), a chapter of which is reprinted
below. In this piece, Du Bois contextualizes the subject of his infant
son's death with the pain of racism and oppression. Other significant works include the academic treatises* The Suppression of the

Africa Slave-Trade to the Unites States of America 1638–1870 *(1896), and* The Philadelphia Negro *(1898); the novels* The Quest of the Silver Fleece *(1911) and* Dark Princess *(1928); and the autobiographies* Dusk of Dawn: An Essay Toward an Autobiography of a Race Concept *(1940) and the posthumously published* The Autobiography of W.E.B. Du Bois: A Soliloquy on Viewing My Life from the Last Decade of Its First Century *(1968). Du Bois was a consistent fighter for justice and equality both in the United States and abroad. For his activism in the peace movement, he was arrested and indicted in 1951, when he was 83 years old. Having become increasingly disillusioned in America, Du Bois relocated to Ghana in 1959 and later renounced his U.S. citizenship. On August 27, 1963, as thousands were gathering in Washington, D.C., for the next day's March on Washington, Du Bois, one of the guiding spirits behind that event, died in Accra, Ghana, at the age of 95.*

The Souls of Black Folk

OF THE PASSING OF THE FIRST-BORN

O sister, sister, thy first-begotten,
The hands that cling and the feet that follow,
The voice of the child's blood crying yet,
Who hath remembered me? who hath forgotten?
Thou has forgotten, O summer swallow,
But the world shall end when I forget.

Swinburne

1   "Unto you a child is born," sang the bit of yellow paper that fluttered into my room one brown October morning. Then the fear of fatherhood mingled wildly with the job of creation; I wondered how it

looked and how it felt,—what were its eyes, and how its hair curled and crumpled itself. And I thought in awe of her,—she who had slept with Death to tear a man-child from underneath her heart, while I was unconsciously wandering. I fled to my wife and child, repeating the while to myself half wonderingly, "Wife and child? Wife and child?"—fled fast and faster than boat and steam-car, and yet must ever impatiently await them; away from the hard-voiced city, away from the flickering sea into my own Berkshire Hills that sit all sadly guarding the gates of Massachusetts.

2   Up the stairs I ran to the wan mother and whimpering babe, to the sanctuary on whose altar a life at my bidding had offered itself to win a life, and won. What is this tiny formless thing, this new-born wail from an unknown world,—all head and voice? I handle it curiously, and watch perplexed its winking, breathing, and sneezing. I did not love it then; it seemed a ludicrous thing to love; but her I loved, my girl-mother, she whom now I saw unfolding like the glory of the morning—the transfigured woman.

3   Through her I came to love the wee thing, as it grew and waxed strong; as its little soul unfolded itself in twitter and cry and half-formed word, and as its eyes caught the gleam and flash of life. How beautiful he was, with his olive-tinted flesh and dark gold ringlets, his eyes of mingled blue and brown, his perfect little limbs, and the soft voluptuous roll which the blood of Africa had moulded into his features! I held him in my arms, after we had sped far away to our Southern home,—held him, and glanced at the hot red soil of Georgia and the breathless city of a hundred hills, and felt a vague unrest. Why was his hair tinted with gold? An evil omen was golden hair in my life. Why had not the brown of his eyes crushed out and killed the blue?—for brown were his father's eyes, and his father's father's. And thus in the Land of the Color-line I saw, as it fell across my baby, the shadow of the Veil.

4   Within the Veil was he born, said I; and there within shall he live,— a Negro and a Negro's son. Holding in that little head—ah, bitterly!— the unbowed pride of a hunted race, clinging with that tiny dimpled hand—ah, wearily!—to a hope not hopeless but unhopeful, and seeing with those bright wondering eyes that peer into my soul a land whose freedom is to us a mockery and whose liberty a lie. I saw the shadow of the Veil as it passed over my baby, I saw the cold city towering above the blood-red land. I held my face beside his little cheek, showed him the star-children and the twinkling lights as they began to flash, and stilled with an even-song the unvoiced terror of my life.

5   So sturdy and masterful he grew, so filled with bubbling life, so tremulous with the unspoken wisdom of a life but eighteen months distant from the All-life,—we were not far from worshipping this revelation of the divine, my wife and I. Her own life builded and moulded itself upon the child; he tinged her every dream and idealized her every effort. No hands but hers must touch and garnish those little limbs; no dress or frill must touch them that had not wearied her fingers; no voice but hers could coax him off to Dreamland, and she and he together spoke some soft and unknown tongue and in it held communion. I too mused above his little white bed; saw the strength of my own arm stretched onward through the ages through the newer strength of his; saw the dream of my black fathers stagger a step onward in the wild phantasm of the world; heard in his baby voice the voice of the Prophet that was to rise within the Veil.

6   And so we dreamed and loved and planned by fall and winter, and the full flush of the long Southern spring, till the hot winds rolled from the fetid Gulf, till the roses shivered and the still stern sun quivered its awful light over the hills of Atlanta. And then one night the little feet pattered wearily to the wee white bed, and the tiny hands trembled; and a warm flushed face tossed on the pillow, and we knew baby was sick. Ten days he lay there,—a swift week and three endless days, wasting, wasting away. Cheerily the mother nursed him the first days, and laughed into the little eyes that smiled again. Tenderly then she hovered round him, till the smile fled away and Fear crouched beside the little bed.

7   Then the day ended not, and night was a dreamless terror, and joy and sleep slipped away. I hear now that Voice at midnight calling me from dull and dreamless trance,—crying, "The Shadow of Death! The Shadow of Death!" Out into the starlight I crept, to rouse the gray physician,—the Shadow of Death, the Shadow of Death. The hours trembled on; the night listened; the ghastly dawn glided like a tired thing across the lamplight. Then we two alone looked upon the child as he turned toward us with great eyes, and stretched his string-like hands,—the Shadow of Death! And we spoke no word, and turned away.

8   He died at eventide, when the sun lay like a brooding sorrow above the western hills, veiling its face; when the winds spoke not, and the trees, the great green trees he loved, stood motionless. I saw his breath beat quicker and quicker, pause, and then his little soul leapt like a star that travels in the night and left a world of darkness in its train. The day changed not; the same tall trees peeped

in at the windows, the same green grass glinted in the setting sun. Only in the chamber of death writhed the world's most piteous thing—a childless mother.

9   I shirk not. I long for work. I pant for a life full of striving. I am no coward, to shrink before the rugged rush of the storm, nor even quail before the awful shadow of the Veil. But hearken, O Death! Is not this my life hard enough,—is not that dull land that stretches its sneering web about me cold enough,—is not all the world beyond these four little walls pitiless enough, but that thou must needs enter here,—thou, O Death? About my head the thundering storm beat like a heartless voice, and the crazy forest pulsed with the curses of the weak; but what cared I, within my home beside my wife and baby boy? Was thou so jealous of one little coign of happiness that thou must needs enter there,—thou, O Death?

10   A perfect life was his, all joy and love, with tears to make it brighter,—sweet as a summer's day beside the Housatonic. The world loved him; the women kissed his curls, the men looked gravely into his wonderful eyes, and the children hovered and fluttered about him. I can see him now, changing like the sky from sparkling laughter to darkening frowns, and then to wondering thoughtfulness as he watched the world. He knew no color-line, poor dear,—and the Veil, though it shadowed him, had not yet darkened half his sun. He loved the white matron, he loved his black nurse; and in his little world walked souls alone, uncolored and unclothed. I—yea, all men—are larger and purer by the infinite breath of that one little life. She who in simple clearness of vision sees beyond the stars said when he had flown, "He will be happy There; he ever loved beautiful things." And I, far more ignorant, and blind by the web of mine own weaving, sit alone winding words and muttering, "If still he be, and he be There, and there be a There, let him be happy, O Fate!"

11   Blithe was the morning of his burial, with bird and song and sweet-smelling flowers. The trees whispered to the grass, but the children sat with hushed faces. And yet it seemed a ghostly unreal day,— the wraith of Life. We seemed to rumble down an unknown street behind a little white bundle of posies, with the shadow of a song in our ears. The busy city dinned about us; they did not say much, those pale-faced hurrying men and women; they did not say much,—they only glanced and said, "Niggers!"

12   We could not lay him in the ground there in Georgia, for the earth there is strangely red; so we bore him away to the northward, with his

flowers and his little folded hands. In vain, in vain!—for where, O God! beneath thy broad blue sky shall my dark baby rest in peace,—where Reverence dwells, and Goodness, and a Freedom that is free?

13   All that day and all that night there sat an awful gladness in my heart,—nay, blame me not if I see the world thus darkly through the Veil,—and my soul whispers ever to me, saying, "Not dead, not dead, but escaped; not bond, but free." No bitter meanness now shall sicken his baby heart till it die a living death, no taunt shall madden his happy boyhood. Fool that I was to think or wish that this little soul should grow choked and deformed within the Veil! I might have known that yonder deep unworldly look that ever and anon floated past his eyes was peering far beyond this narrow Now. In the poise of his little curl-crowned head did there not sit all that wild pride of being which his father had hardly crushed in his own heart? For what, forsooth, shall a Negro want with pride amid the studied humiliations of fifty million fellows? Well sped, my boy, before the world had dubbed your ambition insolence, had held your ideals unattainable, and taught you to cringe and bow. Better far this nameless void that stops my life than a sea of sorrow for you.

14   Idle words; he might have borne his burden more bravely than we,—aye, and found it lighter too, some day; for surely, surely this is not the end. Surely there shall yet dawn some mighty morning to lift the Veil and set the prisoned free. Not for me,—I shall die in my bonds,—but for fresh young souls who have not known the night and waken to the morning; a morning when men ask of the workman, not "Is he white?" but "Can he work?" When men ask artists, not "Are they black?" but "Do they know?" Some morning this may be, long, long years to come. But now there wails, on that dark shore within the Veil, the same deep voice, *Thou shalt forego!* And all have I foregone at that command, and with small complaint,—all save that fair young form that lies so coldly wed with death in the nest I had builded.

15   If one must have gone, why not I? Why may I not rest me from this restlessness and sleep from this wide waking? Was not the world's alembic, Time, in his young hands, and is not my time waning? Are there so many workers in the vineyard that the fair promise of this little body could lightly be tossed away? The wretched of my race that line the alleys of the nation sit fatherless and unmothered; but Love sat beside his cradle, and in his ear Wisdom waited to speak. Perhaps now he knows the All-love, and needs not to be wise. Sleep, then, child,—sleep till I sleep and waken to a baby voice and the ceaseless patter of little feet—above the Veil.

Paul Laurence Dunbar

(1872–1906)

The son of former slaves, Joshua and Matilda Dunbar, Paul Laurence Dunbar was born in Dayton, Ohio, on June 27, 1872. Dunbar was educated in Ohio public schools and was the only African American to attend Dayton's Central High School. After graduating in 1891, he assumed employment as an elevator operator. Dunbar made use of folk culture, most especially folk idiom, in some of his verse, an artistic choice that has generated a great deal of controversy. He published 11 volumes of poetry, including Oak and Ivy *(1893),* Majors and Minors *(1895),* Lyrics of Lowly Life *(1896),* Lyrics of the Hearthside *(1899), and* Lyrics of Sunshine and Shadow *(1905). Although best known for his poetry, Dunbar also published fiction, including* The Uncalled *(1898),* Folks from Dixie *(1898),* The Fanatics *(1901), and his most notable novel,* Sport of the Gods *(1901), which captures the psychological costs of Urban Migration. "A Death Song" can be found in the* Complete Poems of Paul Laurence Dunbar *(1913).*

A Death Song

LAY me down beneaf de willers in
    de grass,
Whah de branch 'll go a-singin' as
    it pass.
5   An' w'en I's a-layin' low,
    I kin hyeah it as it go
Singin', "Sleep, my honey, tek yo'
    res' at las'."

Lay me nigh to whah hit meks a
10   little pool,
An' de watah stan's so quiet lak
    an' cool,
    Whah de little birds in spring,
    Ust to come an' drink an' sing,
15 An' de chillen waded on dey way
    to school.

Let me settle w'en my shouldahs
    draps dey load

Nigh enough to hyeah de noises in
20   de road;
     Fu' I t'ink de las' long res'
     Gwine to soothe my sperrit bes'
Ef I's layin' 'mong de t'ings I's
     allus knowed.

Countee Cullen

(1903–1946)

Born in Louisville, Kentucky, on March 30, 1903, Countee Cullen was raised in New York City after being adopted by Reverend Frederick Cullen, a Harlem minister, and his wife Carolyn Belle Cullen. Cullen received his bachelor's degree from New York University and his master's degree from Harvard University in 1926. His first three volumes of poems, Color *(1925),* Copper Sun *(1927), and* The Ballad of the Brown Girl *(1927), in addition to his column, "The Dark Tower," in* Opportunity *magazine established Cullen as a major literary and cultural figure of the New Negro Movement, also known as the Harlem Renaissance. Cullen married W.E.B. Du Bois's daughter, Yolande Du Bois, in his father's Harlem church in one of the most extravagant weddings of the time; however, the marriage was short-lived. Cullen received many literary accolades throughout his life, winning more major literary prizes than any other African American writer of the 1920s. Cullen wrote a novel,* One Way to Heaven *(1934), a satire of the Harlem Renaissance, and at the time of his death was at work on a musical with Arna Bontemps.*

A Brown Girl Dead

With two white roses on her breasts,
    White candles at head and feet,
Dark Madonna of the grave she reats;
    Lord Death has found her sweet.

5 Her mother pawned her wedding ring
    To lay her out in white;
She'd be so proud she'd dance and sing
    To see herself tonight.

Arna Bontempó

(1902–1973)

*While Arna Bontemps was born in Alexandria, Louisiana, on October
13, 1902, his family moved to Los Angeles, California, when he was
only 3 years old, to avoid the dangerous racial climate of the South.
Bontemps received his undergraduate degree in 1923 from Pacific
Union College and then accepted a teaching position in Harlem, at the
height of the Harlem Renaissance. Bontemps's work ranged considerably, including fiction, poetry, history, and criticism. The excerpt
reprinted below, from* Black Thunder, *features the death and mourning rituals performed for one of the community elders, Bundy, who is
killed by his master. This is an important scene because the funeral is
the final impetus for Gabriel's rebellion. Along with Langston Hughes,
Bontemps edited* Poetry of the Negro *(1949) and* The Book of Negro
Folklore *(1959). Also in collaboration with Hughes, Bontemps published the children's books* Popo and Fifina: Children of Haiti *(1932),*
Sad-faced Boy *(1937), and* The Fast Sooner Hound *(1942). After
receiving his master's degree in Library Science from the University of
Chicago in 1945, he worked at the Fisk University Library in
Nashville, Tennessee, for more than 20 years.*

Black Thunder

1   Old Bundy was dying when Ben got the word. It was night again, and
the old great house was still and dark, but Ben was not alone. While
Mr. Moseley Sheppard and his son slept in the large bedrooms at the
top of the stairs, the frizzly whiskered major-domo and the female
house servants buzzed quietly in the kitchen.

2   Drucilla was preparing her next day's vegetables by the flicker
of a candle, and Mousie, the grown daughter that did the scrubbing,
had stayed to help her. Mousie was picking and cleaning greens while
her old black mother shelled peas. Ben stood at the lamp table blowing his breath on a smoked chimney and polishing it with a soft cloth.
There was an octagonal ring on his finger. It was about the thickness of a woman's wedding band, and it kept clicking against the glass
as Ben turned his hand inside the chimney.

3   Presently there was a little scraping noise at the back door, a sound
like the pawing of a dog. Ben opened it and looked out. Criddle was

there, terrified and panting, the two little domino spots showing plain on his bullet head.

4   "Bundy—"

5   "Hush that loud talk, boy. The white folks is sleep," Ben said.

6   "Well, I help you to say hush," Drucilla whispered.

7   "What about Bundy?"

8   "He's dying, I reckon."

9   "Dying!"

10   "H'm."

11   "Dying from what?"

12   "From day before yestiddy; from what happened in the field."

13   They all became silent and looked one at the other. The candle on the table gasped as if catching its breath. Ben put the lamp chimney down, knotted his brow and looked at the boy.

14   "I ain't heard nothing about day before yestiddy."

15   "Marse Prosser whupped Bundy about coming here," Criddle said. "He whupped him all up about the head and stepped on him with his horse."

16   Mousie turned her head petulantly.

17   "That's one mo' mean white man, that Marse Prosser."

18   "H'm," Criddle murmured, "That's what Gabriel and the rest of them is saying now. They say it ain't no cause to beat a nigger up about the head and step on him in the bushes with a horse."

19   "Po' old Bundy," Ben said, "He was worried about making me a mason."

20   "That's howcome he sent me," Criddle said. "He say don't you stay away on account of him. He want you to talk to Gabriel about j'ining up."

21   "I wasn't aiming to go," Ben said. "I ain't strong on that chillun's foolishness, but you needn't mention it to Bundy if he's all that bad off."

22   "I reckon he dying all right."

23   "Bundy used to talk a heap about freedom," Drucilla said. "Used to swear he's going to die free."

24   "He ain't apt to do that now."

25   "Nah," Criddle said; "leastwise, not less'n the good Lord sets him free."

26   "Po' old Bundy," Ben said. "He kept drinking up all that rum because he couldn't get up enough nerve to make his getaway."

27   "Must I tell him you said yes, Uncle Ben?"

28   "Tell him I said I reckon. That mason business is chillun's foolishness."

29   Criddle slipped away, dissolved in the shadows. Ben took a candle and went through the dark house trying the doors, adjusting the windows and hangings. His hand trembled on the brass knobs. Old Bundy was dying. A squirrel sprang from a bough, ran across the roof. Poor old Bundy. It seemed like just the other day since he was a young buck standing cross-legged against a tree and telling the world he was going to die free. He had grown old and given up the notion, it seemed, but Ben could well imagine his feelings. A slave's life was bad enough when he belonged to quality white folks; it must have been torment on that Prosser plantation.

30   They were praying for old Bundy's life when Criddle returned. Moonlight made shadows of uplifted arms on the wall above his heap of rags. There was a chorus of moaning voices. There were faces bowing to the earth and bodies swaying like barley.

31   Oh, Lord, Lord-Lord . . . Knee-bent and body-bound, thy unworthy chilluns is crying in Egypt land . . . La-aawd, Lord . . . Wilt thou please, Oh, Massa Jesus, to look upon him what's lowly bowed and raise him up if it is thy holy and righteous will. Oh, La-aawd. La-aaaawd-Lord! . . .

32   "Amen," old Bundy said feebly. "*Amen!*"

33   They were praying for old Bundy's life, but there was one who didn't pray. He stood naked to the waist in the hot cabin, stood above the others with hands on his hips and head bowed sorrowfully. His shadow, among the waving hands on the wall, was like a giant in a field of grain.

34   Old Bundy's eyes opened; he looked at the big fellow.

35   "That there head of yo's is mighty low, long boy, mighty low."

36   "Yeah, old Bundy, I reckon it is," Gabriel said.

37   "And it don't pleasure me a bit to see it like that neither."

38   "I'm sorry, old man; I'm sorry as all-out-doors. I'd lift it up for a penny, and I'd pleasure you if I could."

39   "It's that yellow woman, I 'spect, that white men's Melody waving her hand out the window."

40   "No woman, old Bundy, no woman."

41   "That brown gal Juba then—her with her petticoats on fire?"

42   "She belongs to me, that Juba, but she ain't got my head hung down."

43   "Not her? Well, you's thinking again, boy."

44   "Thinking again. It's all like we been talking. You know."

45   "H'm. I was aiming to die free, me. I heard tell how in San Domingo—"

46   "Listen, old man. You ain't gone yet."

47   "I don't mind dying, but I hates to die not free. I wanted to see y'-all do something like Toussaint done. I always wanted to be free powerful bad."

48   "That you did, and we going to do something too. You know how we talked it, you and me. And you know right well how I feel when my head's bowed low."

49   "Feel bad—I know. I feel bad too, plenty times."

50   One of the moaners on the ground raised a fervent voice, cried in a wretched sing-song.

51   "When Marae Prosser beat you with a stick, how you feel, old man?"

52   "Feel like I wants to be free, chile."

53   Gabriel gave the others his back, strolled to the door, reated one hand on the sill overhead. The chant went on.

54   "When the jug get low and you can't go to town, how you feel?"

55   "Bound to be free, chillun, bound to be free."

56   Gabriel left the others, walked outdoors.

57   "When the preacher preach about Moses and the chillun, about David and the Philistines, how you feel, old man?"

58   "Amen, boy. Bound to be free. You hear me? Bound to be free."

59   Gabriel did not turn. Even when the moaning and chanting stopped, he continued to walk.

60   They were burying old Bundy in the low field by the swamp. They were throwing themselves on the ground and wailing savagely. (The Negroes remembered Africa in 1800.) But there was one that did not wail, and there were some that did not wail for grief. Some were too mean to cry; some were too angry. They had made a box for him, and black men stood with ropes on either side the hole.

61   Down, down, down: old Bundy's long gone now. Put a jug of rum at his feet. Old Bundy with his legs like knotty canes. Roast a hog and put it on his grave. Down, down. How them victuals suit you, Bundy? How you like what we brung you? Anybody knows that dying ain't nothing. You got one eye shut and one eye open, old man. We going to miss you just the same, though, we going to miss you bad, but we'll meet you on t'other side, Bundy. We'll do that sure's you born. One eye shut and one eye open: down, down, down. Lord, Lord. Mm-mm-mm-mm. Don't let them black boys cover you up in that hole, brother.

62 They had raised a song without words. They were kneeling with their faces to the sun. Their hands were in the air, the fingers apart, and they bowed and rose together as they sang. Up came the song like a wave, and down went their faces in the dirt.

63 Easy down, black boys, easy down. I heard tell of niggers dropping a coffin one time. They didn't have no more rest the balance of their borned days. The dead man's spirit never would excuse a careleasness like that. Easy down, black boys. Keep one eye open, Bundy. Don't let them sprinkle none of that dirt on you. Dying ain't nothing. You know how wood burns up to ashes and smoke? Well, it's just the same way when you's dying. The spirit and the skin been together like the smoke and the ashes in the wood; when you dies, they separates. Dying ain't nothing. The smoke goes free. Can't nobody hurt smoke. A smoke man—that's you now, brother. A *real* smoke man. Smoke what gets in yo' eyes and makes you blink. Smoke what gets in yo' throat and chokes you. Don't let them cover you up in that hole, Bundy. Mm-mm-mm-mm.

64 Ben crossed a field and came to the place. The sun was far in the west; it was slipping behind the hills fast. But there were small suns now in every window on the countryside, numberless small suns. A blue and gold twilight sifted into the low field. The black folks, some of them naked to the waist, kept bowing to the sun, bowing and rising as they sang. Their arms quivered above their heads.

65 That's all right about you, Bundy, and it's all right about us. Marse Prosser thunk it was cheaper to kill a old wo'-out mule than to feed him. But they's plenty things Marse Prosser don't know. He don't even know a tree got a soul same as a man, and he don't know you ain't in that there hole, Bundy. We know, though. We can see you squatting there beside that pile of dirt, squatting like a old grinning bullfrog on a bank. Marse Prosser act like he done forgot smoke get in his eyes and make him blink. You'll be in his eyes and in his throat too, won't you, Bundy?

66 Ben knelt down and joined the song, moaning with the others at the place where the two worlds meet. He watched the young black fellows cover the hole, and he kept thinking about the old crochety slave who loved a jug of rum. Bundy wanted Ben to talk with Gabriel, and Ben knew now he would have to do it. There was something about a dead man's wish that commanded respect. The

twilight thickened in the low field. Two or three stray whites who had been standing near by walked away.

67   Dead and gone, old Bundy. Something—something no denser than smoke—squatting by the hole, grinning pleasantly with one eye on the jug of rum.

68   The Negroes became still; and Martin, the smaller of Gabriel's two brothers, stood up to speak.

69   "Is there anybody what ain't swore?"

70   Ben wrinkled his forehead, scratched his frizzly salt-and-pepper whiskers.

71   "Swore about what?" he murmured.

72   "I reckon you don't know." Martin said. "Here's the Book, and here's the pot of blood, and here's the black-cat bone. Swear."

73   "Swear what?"

74   "You won't tell none of what you's apt to hear in this meeting. You'll take a curse and die slow death if you tells. On'erstand?"

75   Ben felt terrified. All eyes were on him. All the others seemed to know. Something like a swarm of butterflies was suddenly let loose in his mind. After a dreadful pause his thought became clear again. Well, he wouldn't be swearing to do anything he didn't want to do; he would just be swearing that he'd keep his mouth closed. It was no more than he'd have done had he not come to the burying. And by now, anyhow, so great was his curiosity, he couldn't possibly resist the desire to hear. Gossip was sweet at his age.

76   "I won't tell nobody. Martin," he said. "I swears."

77   There were a few others to be sworn. This done, Martin knelt quietly, and Gabriel took his place in the center of the circle. Near him on the ground was Ditcher, powerful and beast-like. General John Scott knelt in his rags. Criddle looked up, his mouth hanging open, the domino spots bright in his bullet head. Juba, the thin-waisted brown girl with hair bushed on her head, curled both feet under her body and leaned back insolently, her hands behind her on the ground. Solomon, Gabriel's oldest brother, sat with his chin in his palm like a thinker. His head was bald in front, and his forehead glistened. Something imaginary, perhaps the smoke of old Bundy, squatted beside the hole that the black boys had covered, squatted and grinned humorously, one eye on the jug of rum. Gabriel called for a prayer.

78   Oh, battle-fighting God, listen to yo' little chilluns; listen to yo' lambs. Remember how you brung deliverance to the Israelites

in Egypt land; remember how you fit for Joshua. Remember Jericho. Remember Goliath, Lord. Listen to yo' lambs. Oh, battle-fighting God . . .

79 "That's enough," Gabriel said. "Hush moaning and listen to me now. God don't like ugly. Some of y'-all heard Mingo read it."

80 He gave a quick summary of the Scriptures Mingo had read. Then he paused a long time. His eye flashed in the growing dusk. He looked at those near him in the circle, one by one, and one by one they broke their gaze and dropped their heads.

81 Another sweeping gaze.

82 Then he spoke abruptly.

83 "We's got enough to take the town already. This going to be the sign: When you see somebody riding that black colt Araby, galloping him for all he's worth in the big road, wearing a pair of Marse Prosser's shiny riding boots, you can know that the time's come. You going to know yo' captains, and that's going to be the sign to report. You on'erstand me?"

84 Ben caught his breath with difficulty. Lordy. The young speaker was deeply in earnest, but Ben couldn't make himself believe that Gabriel meant what his words seemed to mean. It sounded like a dream. Two or three phrases, a few words, fluttered in his mind like rags on a clothes wire. Take the town. Captains . . . Ben shuddered violently. Somebody wearing Marse Prosser's riding boots, galloping Araby in the big road. Where would Marse Prosser be when they took his shiny boots off him? Did they mean that they were going to murder?

85 And so this was what old Bundy wanted him to hear from Gabriel, was it? Did he think Ben would get mixed up in any such crazy doings? Ben's lips twitched. His thought broke off abruptly. Something squatting beside the covered hole turned a quizzical eye toward the frizzly whiskered house servant. Ben wrung his hands; he bowed his head, and heavy jolting sobs wrenched his body. He wasn't in for no such cutting up as all that. The devil must of got in Bundy before he died. What could he do now with that eye on him? Ben bowed lower."

86 "Oh, Lord Jesus," he said, crying.

87 A powerful elbow punched his ribs, and Ben raised his head without opening his eyes.

88 "What's the matter, nigger, don't you want to be free?"

89 Ben stopped sobbing, thought a long moment.

90 "I don't know," he said.

91 Gabriel was talking again by now.

92 "This the way how you line up: Ditcher's the head man of all y'-all from across the branch. Gen'l John is going to—"

93 He stopped talking for a moment. A little later he whispered, "Who that coming across that field?"

94 "Marse Prosser."

95 "It is, hunh? Well, strike up a song, Martin."

96 They began moaning softly. The voices rose bit by bit, a full wave. Again there was the same swaying of bodies, the same shouts punctuating the song. Gabriel faced the west, his hands locked behind him, his varnished coachman's hat tilted forward. Ben fell on his face crying. It became quite dark.

Zora Neale Hurston

(1891–1960)

Folklorist, playwright, anthropologist, and novelist Zora Neale Hurston was born on January 7, 1891, in Notasulga, Alabama, but was raised in the all-Black town of Eatonville, Florida. Her hometown figures largely in the landscape of her fictional and autobiographical writings. Hurston was a teenager when her mother died, and after her father remarried she was in and out of schools and held a number of odd jobs. She attended Howard University and Barnard College, and studied anthropology with Franz Boas, a pioneer in the field. This daughter of the South formally studied and documented the vibrant culture of the rural, Black, Southern community in two collections of folklore, Mules and Men *(1935) and* Tell My Horse *(1938). While Hurston was a notable figure in the Harlem Renaissance and afterward, her immense fame came posthumously. More than a decade after she died in poverty in Florida, she was claimed as an early feminist and literary foremother by numerous African American writers, most notably Alice Walker. Hurston's novels include* Jonah's Gourd Vine *(1934),* Moses, Man of the Mountain *(1939), and* Seraph on the Suwanee *(1948). Reprinted below is a chapter from Hurston's memoir,* Dust Tracks on a Road, *which recounts the rituals accompanying her mother's passing and some of the impact on Hurston's life as a result of her being left motherless.*

Dust Tracks on a Road

WANDERING

1   I knew that Mama was sick. She kept getting thinner and thinner and her chest cold never got any better. Finally, she took to bed.

2   She had come home from Alabama that way. She had gone back to her old home to be with her sister during her sister's last illness. Aunt Dinky had lasted on for two months after Mama got there, and so Mama had stayed on till the last.

3   It seems that there had been other things there that worried her. Down underneath, it appeared that Grandma had never quite forgiven her for the move she had made twenty-one years before in marrying Papa. So that when Mama suggested that the old Potts place be sold so that she could bring her share back with her to Florida, her mother urged on by Uncle Bud, Mama's oldest brother, refused. Not until Grandma's head was cold, was an acre of the place to be sold. She had long since quit living on it, and it was pretty well run down, but she wouldn't, that was all. Mama could just go on back to that yaller rascal she had married like she came. I do not think that the money part worried Mama as much as the injustice and spitefulness of the thing.

4   Then Cousin Jimmie's death seemed to come back on Mama during her visit. How he came to his death is an unsolved mystery. He went to a party and started home. The next morning his headless body was found beside the railroad track. There was no blood, so the train couldn't have killed him. This had happened before I was born. He was said to have been a very handsome young man, and very popular with the girls. He was my mother's favorite nephew and she took it hard. She had probably numbed over her misery, but going back there seemed to freshen up her grief. Some said that he had been waylaid by three other young fellows and killed in a jealous rage. But nothing could be proved. It was whispered that he had been shot in the head by a white man unintentionally, and then beheaded to hide the wound. He had been shot from ambush, because his assailant mistook him for a certain white man. It was night. The attacker expected the white man to pass that way, but not Jimmie. When he found out his mistake, he had forced a certain Negro to help him move the body to the railroad track without the head, so that it would look as if he had been run over by the train. Anyway, that is what the Negro wrote back after he had moved

to Texas years later. There was never any move to prove the charge, for obvious reasons. Mama took the whole thing very hard.

5   It was not long after Mama came home that she began to be less active. Then she took to bed. I knew she was ailing, but she was always frail, so I did not take it too much to heart. I was nine years old, and even though she had talked to me very earnestly one night, I could not conceive of Mama actually dying. She had talked of it many times.

6   That day, September eighteenth, she had called me and given me certain instructions. I was not to let them take the pillow from under her head until she was dead. The clock was not to be covered, nor the looking-glass. She trusted me to see to it that these things were not done. I promised her as solemnly as nine years could do, that I would see to it.

7   What years of agony that promise gave me! In the first place, I had no idea that it would be soon. But that same day near sun-down, I was called upon to set my will against my father, the village dames and village custom. I know now that I could not have succeeded.

8   I had left Mama and was playing outside for a little while when I noted a number of women going inside Mama's room and staying. It looked strange. So I went on in. Papa was standing at the foot of the bed looking down on my mother, who was breathing hard. As I crowded in, they lifted up the bed and turned it around so that Mama's eyes would face the east. I thought that she looked to me as the head of the bed was reversed. Her mouth was slightly open, but her breathing took up so much of her strength that she could not talk. But she looked at me, or so I felt, to speak for her. She depended on me for a voice.

9   The Master-Maker in His making had made Old Death. Made him with big, soft feet and square toes. Made him with a face that reflects the face of all things, but neither changes itself, nor is mirrored anywhere. Made the body of Death out of infinite hunger. Made a weapon for his hand to satisfy his needs. This was the morning of the day of the beginning of things.

10   But Death had no home and he knew it at once.

11   "And where shall I dwell in my dwelling?" Old Death asked, for he was already old when he was made.

12   "You shall build you a place close to the living, yet far out of the sight of eyes. Wherever there is a building, there you have your platform that comprehends the four roads of the winds. For your hunger, I give you the first and last taste of all things."

13   We had been born, so Death had had his first taste of us. We had built things, so he had his platform in our yard.

14   And now, Death stirred from his platform in his secret place in our yard, and came inside the house.

15   Somebody reached for the clock, while Mrs. Mattie Clarke put her hand to the pillow to take it away.

16   "Don't!" I cried out. "Don't take the pillow from under Mama's head! She said she didn't want it moved!"

17   I made to stop Mrs. Mattie, but Papa pulled me away. Others were trying to silence me. I could see the huge drop of sweat collected in the hollow at Mama's elbow and it hurt me so. They were covering the clock and the mirror.

18   "Don't cover up that clock! Leave that looking-glass like it is! Lemme put Mama's pillow back where it was!"

19   But Papa held me tight and the others frowned me down. Mama was still rasping out the last morsel of her life. I think she was trying to say something, and I think she was trying to speak to me. What was she trying to tell me? What wouldn't I give to know! Perhaps she was telling me that it was better for the pillow to be moved so that she could die easy, as they said. Perhaps she was accusing me of weakness and failure in carrying out her last wish. I do not know. I shall never know.

20   Just then, Death finished his prowling through the house on his padded feet and entered the room. He bowed to Mama in his way, and she made her manners and left us to act out our ceremonies over unimportant things.

21   I was to agonize over that moment for years to come. In the midst of play, in wakeful moments after midnight, on the way home from parties, and even in the classroom during lectures. My thoughts would escape occasionally from their confines and stare me down.

22   Now, I know that I could not have had my way against the world. The world we lived in required those acts. Anything else would have been sacrilege, and no nine-year-old voice was going to thwart them. My father was with the mores. He had restrained me physically from outraging the ceremonies established for the dying. If there is any consciousness after death, I hope that Mama knows that I did my best. She must know how I have suffered for my failure.

23   But life picked me up from the foot of Mama's bed, grief, self-despisement and all, and set my feet in strange ways. That moment was the end of a phase in my life. I was old before my time with grief of loss, of failure, of remorse of failure. No matter what the

others did, my mother had put her trust in me. She had felt that I could and would carry out her wishes, and I had not. And then in that sunset time, I failed her. It seemed as she died that the sun went down on purpose to flee away from me.

24   That hour began my wanderings. Not so much in geography, but in time. Then not so much in time as in spirit.

25   Mama died at sundown and changed a world. That is, the world which had been built out of her body and her heart. Even the physical aspects fell apart with a suddenness that was startling.

26   My oldest brother was up in Jacksonville in school, and he arrived home after Mama had passed. By then, she had been washed and dressed and laid out on the ironing board in the parlor.

27   Practically all of the village was in the front yard and on the porch, talking in low tones and waiting. They were not especially waiting for my brother Bob. They were doing that kind of waiting that people do around death. It is a kind of sipping up the drama of the thing. However, if they were asked, they would say it was the sadness of the occasion which drew them. In reality it is a kind of feast of the Passover.

28   Bob's grief was awful when he realized that he was too late. He could not conceive at first that nothing could be done to straighten things out. There was no ear for his excuse nor explanation—no way to ease what was in him. Finally it must have come to him that what he had inside, he must take with him wherever he went. Mama was there on the cooling board with the sheet draped over her blowing gently in the wind. Nothing there seemed to hear him at all.

29   There was my sister Sarah in the kitchen crying and trying to quiet Everett, who was just past two years old. She was crying and trying to make him hush at the same time. He was crying because he sensed the grief around him. And then, Sarah, who was fifteen had been his nurse and he would respond to her mood, whatever it was. We were all grubby bales of misery, huddled about lamps.

30   I have often wished I had been old enough at the time to look into Papa's heart that night. If I could know what that moment meant to him, I could have set my compass towards him and been sure. I know that I did love him in a way, and that I admired many things about him. He had a poetry about him that I loved. That had made him a successful preacher. He could hit ninety-seven out of a hundred with a gun. He could swim Lake Maitland from Maitland to Winter Park, and no man in the village could put my father's shoulders to the ground. We were so certain of Papa's invincibility in combat that when a village woman scolded Everett for some misdemeanor, and told him that God would

punish him, Everett, just two years old, reared back and told her, "He better not bother me. Papa will shoot Him down." He found out better later on, but that goes to show you how big our Papa looked to us. We had seen him bring down bears and panthers with his gun, and chin the bar more times than any man in competing distance. He had to our knowledge licked two men who Mama told him had to be licked. All that part was just fine with me. But I was Mama's child. I knew that she had not always been happy, and I wanted to know just how sad he was that night.

31   I have repeatedly called up that picture and questioned it. Papa cried some too, as he moved in his awkward way about the place. From the kitchen to the front porch and back again. He kept saying, "Poor thing! She suffered so much." I do not know what he meant by that. It could have been love and pity for her suffering ending at last. It could have been remorse mixed with relief. The hard-driving force was no longer opposed to his easy-going pace. He could put his potentialities to sleep and be happy in the laugh of the day. He could do next year or never, what Mama would have insisted must be done today. Rome, the eternal city, meant two different things to my parents. To Mama, it meant, you must build it today so it could last through eternity. To Papa, it meant that you could plan to lay some bricks today and you have the rest of eternity to finish it. With all that time, why hurry? God had made more time than anything else, anyway. Why act so stingy about it?

32   Then too, I used to notice how Mama used to snatch Papa. That is, he would start to put up an argument that would have been terrific on the store porch, but Mama would pitch in with a single word or a sentence and mess it all up. You could tell he was mad as fire with no words to blow it out with. He would sit over in the corner and cut his eyes at her real hard. He was used to being a hero on the store porch and in church affairs, and I can see how he must have felt to be always outdone around home. I know now that that is a griping thing to a man—not to be able to whip his woman mentally. Some women know how to give their man that conquesting feeling. My mother took her over-the-creek man and bare-knuckled him from brogans to broadcloth, and I am certain that he was proud of the change, in public. But in the house, he might have always felt over-the-creek, and because that was not the statue he had made for himself to look at, he resented it. But then, you cannot blame my mother too much if she did not see him as his entranced congregations did. The one who

makes the idols never worships them, however tenderly he might have molded the clay. You cannot have knowledge and worship at the same time, Mystery is the essence of divinity. Gods must keep their distances from men.

33   Anyway, the next day, Sam Moseley's span of fine horses, hitched to our wagon, carried my mother to Macedonia Baptist Church for the last time. The finality of the thing came to me fully when the earth began to thud on the coffin.

34   That night, all of Mama's children were assembled together for the last time on earth. The next day, Bob and Sarah went back to Jacksonville to school. Papa was away from home a great deal, so two weeks later, I was on my way to Jacksonville, too. I was under age, but the school had agreed to take me in under the circumstances. My sister was to look after me, in a way.

35   The midnight train had to be waved down at Maitland for me. That would put me into Jacksonville in the daytime.

36   As my brother Dick drove the mile with me that night, we approached the curve in the road that skirts Lake Catherine, and suddenly I saw the first picture of my visions. I had seen myself upon that curve at night leaving the village home, bowed down with grief that was more than common. As it all flashed back to me, I started violently for a minute, then I moved closer beside Dick as if he could shield me from those others that were to come. He asked me what was the matter, and I said I thought I heard something moving down by the lake. He laughed at that, and we rode on, the lantern showing the roadway, and me keeping as close to Dick as I could. A little, humped-up, shabby-backed trunk was behind us in the buckboard. I was on my way from the village, never to return to it as a real part of the town.

37   Jacksonville made me know that I was a little colored girl. Things were all about the town to point this out to me. Street cars and stores and then talk I heard around the school. I was no longer among the white people whose homes I could barge into with a sure sense of welcome. These white people had funny ways. I could tell that even from a distance. I didn't get a piece of candy or a bag of crackers just for going into a store in Jacksonville as I did when I went into Galloway's or Hill's at Maitland, or Joe Clarke's in Eatonville.

38   Around the school I was an awful bother. The girls complained that they couldn't get a chance to talk without me turning up somewhere to be in the way. I broke up many good "He said" conferences just by showing up. It was not my intention to do so. What I wanted was for

it to go full stream ahead and let me listen. But that didn't seem to please. I was not in the "he said" class, and they wished I would kindly please stay out of the way. My underskirt was hanging, for instance. Why didn't I go some place and fix it? My head looked like a hoo-raw's nest. Why didn't I go comb it? If I took time enough to match my stockings, I wouldn't have time to be trying to listen in on grown folk's business. These venerable old ladies were anywhere from fifteen to eighteen.

39   In the classroom I got along splendidly. The only difficulty was that I was rated as sassy. I just had to talk back at established authority and that established authority hated back talk worse than barbed-wire pie. My brother was asked to speak to me in addition to a licking or two. But on the whole, things went along all right. My immediate teachers were enthusiastic about me. It was the guardians of study-hour and prayer meetings who felt that their burden was extra hard to bear.

40   School in Jacksonville was one of those twilight things. It was not dark, but it lacked the bold sunlight that I craved. I worshipped two of my teachers and loved gingersnaps with cheese, and sour pickles. But I was deprived of the loving pine, the lakes, the wild violets in the woods and the animals I used to know. No more holding down first base on the team with my brothers and their friends. Just a lagged hole where my home used to be.

41   At times, the girls of the school were lined up two and two and taken for a walk. On one of these occasions, I had an experience that set my heart to fluttering. I saw a woman sitting on a porch who looked at a distance like Mama. Maybe it *was* Mama! Maybe she was not dead at all. They had made some mistake. Mama had gone off to Jacksonville and they thought that she was dead. The woman was sitting in a rocking chair just like Mama always did. It must be Mama! But before I came abreast of the porch in my rigid place in line, the woman got up and went inside. I wanted to stop and go in. But I didn't even breathe my hope to anyone. I made up my mind to run away someday and find the house and let Mama know where I was. But before I did, the hope that the woman really was my mother passed. I accepted my bereavement.

Alice Walker

(1944–)

Born in Eatonville, Georgia, on February 9, 1944, to sharecropping parents, Alice Walker is an acclaimed novelist, short-story writer, poet, essayist, and activist. Walker attended Spelman College for two years and graduated from Sarah Lawrence College during the Civil Rights era. Walker's most acclaimed novel, The Color Purple *(1982), was awarded the Pulitzer Prize, the National Book Award, and the American Book Award, and was made into a major motion pictured directed by Steven Spielberg. However, Walker began publishing more than a decade before writing* The Color Purple, *starting with her first collection of poetry,* Once *(1968). Walker's other books include the novels* The Third Life of Grange Copeland *(1970),* Meridian *(1976),* The Temple of My Familiar *(1989),* Possessing the Secret of Joy *(1992), and* By the Light of My Father's Smile *(1998). A consistent theme running through her creative and critical work is Black feminism, which she labels "womanism," a concept that she puts forth in her famous essay collection* In Search of Our Mothers' Gardens *(1983). "Looking for Zora," reprinted below, is from this collection, and the poems are taken from her third collection of poetry,* Revolutionary Petunias and Other Poems, *published in 1972. Walker also has published additional essay collections, including* Living By the Word *(1988) and* The Same River Twice *(1996).*

Looking for Zora

On January 16, 1959, Zora Neale Hurston, suffering from the effects of a stroke and writing painfully in longhand, composed a letter to the "editorial department" of Harper & Brothers inquiring if they would be interested in seeing "the book I am laboring upon at present—a life of Herod the Great." One year and twelve days later, Zora Neale Hurston died without funds to provide for her burial, a resident of the St. Lucie County, Florida, Welfare Home. She lies today in an unmarked grave in a segregated cemetery in Fort Pierce, Florida, a resting place generally symbolic of the black writer's fate in America.

Zora Neale Hurston is one of the most significant unread authors in America, the author of two minor classics and four other major books.

—ROBERT HEMENWAY,
"ZORA HURSTON AND THE EATONVILLE ANTHROPOLOGY,"
IN THE HARLEM RENAISSANCE REMEMBERED

1   On August 15, 1973, I wake up just as the plane is lowering over San-
ford, Florida, which means I am also looking down on Eatonville, Zora
Neale Hurston's birthplace. I recognize it from Zora's description in
Mules and Men, "the city of five "lakes, three croquat courts, three hundred brown skins, three hundred good swimmers, plenty guavas, two
schools, and no jailhouse." Of course I cannot see the guavas, but the
five lakes are still there, and it is the lakes I count as the plane prepares to land in Orlando.

2   From the air, Florida looks completely flat, and as we near the
ground this impression does not change. This is the first time I have
seen the interior of the state, which Zora wrote about so well, but
there are the acres of orange groves, the sand, mangrove trees, and
scrub pine that I know from her books. Getting off the plane I walk
through the humid air of midday into the tacky but air-conditioned
airport. I search for Charlotte Hunt, my companion on the Zora
Hurston expedition. She lives in Winter Park, Florida, very near
Eatonville, and is writing her graduate dissertation on Zora. I see her
waving—a large, pleasant-faced white woman in dark glasses. We
have written to each other for several weeks, swapping our latest
finds (mostly hers) on Zora, and trying to make sense out of the mass
of information obtained (often erroneous or simply confusing) from
Zora herself—through her stories and autobiography—and from
people who wrote about her.

3   Eatonville has lived for such a long time in my imagination that
I can hardly believe it will be found existing in its own right. But after
twenty minutes on the expressway, Charlotte turns off and I see a
small settlement of houses and stores set with no particular pattern
in the sandy soil off the road. We stop in front of a neat gray building that has two fascinating signs: EATONVILLE POST OFFICE and
EATONVILLE CITY HALL.

4   Inside the Eatonville City Hall half of the building, a slender, dark-
brown-skin woman sits looking through letters on a desk. When she
hears we are searching for anyone who might have known Zora Neale
Hurston, she leans back in thought. Because I don't wish to inspire
foot-dragging in people who might know something about Zora
they're not sure they should tell, I have decided on a simple, but I feel
profoundly *useful*, lie.

5   "I am Miss Hurston's niece," I prompt the young woman, who
brings her head down with a smile.

6   "I think Mrs. Moseley is about the only one still living who might
remember her," she says.

7   "Do you mean *Mathilda* Moseley, the woman who tells those 'woman-is-smarter-than-man' lies in Zora's book?"

8   "Yes," says the young woman. "Mrs. Moseley is real old now, of course. But this time of day, she should be at home."

9   I stand at the counter looking down on her, the first Eatonville resident I have spoken to. Because of Zora's books, I feel I know something about her; at least I know what the town she grew up in was like years before she was born.

10 "Tell me something," I say, "Do the schools teach Zora's books here?"

11 "No," she says, "they don't. I don't think most people know anything about Zora Neale Hurston, or know about any of the great things she did. She was a fine lady. I've read all of her books myself, but I don't think many other folks in Eatonville have."

12 "Many of the church people around here, as I understand it," says Charlotte in a murmured aside, "thought Zora was pretty loose. I don't think they appreciated her writing about them."

13 "Well," I say to the young woman, "thank you for your help." She clarifies her directions to Mrs. Moseley's house and smiles as Charlotte and I turn to go.

The letter to Harper's does not expose a publisher's rejection of an unknown masterpiece, but it does reveal how the bright promise of the Harlem Renaissance deteriorated for many of the writers who shared in its exuberance. It also indicates the personal tragedy of Zora Neale Hurston: Barnard graduate, author of four novels, two books of folklore, one volume of autobiography, the most important collector of Afro-American folklore in America, reduced by poverty and circumstance to seek a publisher by unsolicited mail.

—ROBERT HEMENWAY

Zora Hurston was born in 1901, 1902, or 1903—depending on how old she felt herself to be at the time someone asked.

—LIBRARIAN, BEINECKE LIBRARY, YALE UNIVERSITY

14 The Moseley house is small and white and snug, its tiny yard nearly swallowed up by oleanders and hibiscus bushes. Charlotte

and I knock on the door. I call out. But there is no answer. This strikes us as peculiar. We have had time to figure out an age for Mrs. Moseley—not dates or a number, just old. I am thinking of a quivery, bedridden invalid when we hear the car. We look behind us to see an old black-and-white Buick—paint peeling and grillwork rusty—pulling into the drive. A neat old lady in a purple dress and with white hair is straining at the wheel. She is frowning because Charlotte's car is in the way.

15   Mrs. Moseley looks at us suspiciously. "Yes, I knew Zora Neale," she says, unsmilingly and with a rather cold stare at Charlotte (who, I imagine, feels very *white* at that moment), "but that was a long time ago, and I don't want to talk about it."

16   "Yes, ma'am," I murmur, bringing all my sympathy to bear on the situation.

17   "Not only that," Mrs. Moseley continues, "I've been sick. Been in the hospital for an operation. Ruptured artery. The doctors didn't believe I was going to live, but you see me alive, don't you?"

18   "Looking well, too," I comment.

19   Mrs. Moseley is out of her car. A thin, sprightly woman with nice gold-studded false teeth, uppers and lowers. I like her because she stands there *straight* beside her car, with a hand on her hip and her straw pocketbook on her arm. She wears white T-strap shoes with heels that show off her well-shaped legs.

20   "I'm eighty-two years old, you know," she says. "And I just can't remember things the way I used to. Anyhow, Zora Neale left here to go to school and she never really came back to live. She'd come here for material for her books, but that was all. She spent most of her time down in South Florida."

21   "You know, Mrs. Moseley, I saw your name in one of Zora's books."

22   "You did?" She looks at me with only slightly more interest. "I read some of her books a long time ago, but then people got to borrowing and borrowing and they borrowed them all away."

23   "I could send you a copy of everything that's been reprinted," I offer. "Would you like me to do that?"

24   "No," says Mrs. Moseley promptly. "I don't read much any more. Besides, all of that was *so* long ago. . . ."

25   Charlotte and I settle back against the car in the sun. Mrs. Moseley tells us at length and with exact recall every step in her recent operation, ending with: "What those doctors didn't know—when they were expecting me to die (and they didn't even think I'd live long enough for them to have to take out my stitches!)—is that

Jesus is the best doctor, and if *He* says for you to get well, that's all that counts."

26 With this philosophy, Charlotte and I murmur quick assent: being Southerners and church bred, we have heard that belief before. But what we learn from Mrs. Moseley is that she does not remember much beyond the year 1938. She shows us a picture of her father and mother and says that her father was Joe Clarke's brother. Joe Clarke, as every Zora Hurston reader knows, was the first mayor of Eatonville, his fictional counterpart is Jody Starks of *Their Eyes Were Watching God.* We also get directions to where Joe Clarke's store *was*—where Club Eaton is now. Club Eaton, a long orange-beige nightspot we had seen on the main road, is apparently famous for the good times in it regularly had by all. It is, perhaps, the modern equivalent of the store porch, where all the men of Zora's childhood came to tell "lies," that is, black folk tales, that were "made and used on the spot," to take a line from Zora. As for Zora's exact birthplace, Mrs. Moseley has no idea.

27 After I have commented on the healthy growth of her hibiscus bushes, she becomes more talkative. She mentions how much she *loved* to dance, when she was a young woman, and talks about how good her husband was. When he was alive, she says, she was completely happy because he allowed her to be completely free. "I was so free I had to pinch myself sometimes to tell if I was a married woman."

28 Relaxed now, she tells us about going to school with Zora. "Zora and I went to the same school. It's called Hungerford High now. It *was* only to the eighth grade. But our teachers were so good that by the time you left you knew college subjects. When I went to Morris Brown in Atlanta, the teachers there were just teaching me the same things I had already learned right in Eatonville. I wrote Mama and told her I was going to come home and help her with her babies. I wasn't learning anything new."

29 "Tell me something, Mrs. Moseley," I ask. "Why do you suppose Zora was against integration? I read somewhere that she was against school desegregation because she felt it was an insult to black teachers."

30 "Oh, one of them [white people] came around asking me about integration. One day I was doing my shopping. I heard 'em over there talking about it in the store, about the schools. And I got on out of the way because I knew if they asked me, they wouldn't like what I was going to tell 'em. But they came up and asked me anyhow. 'What do you think about this integration?' one of them said. I acted like I thought I had heard wrong. 'You're asking *me* what

I think about integration?' I said. 'Well, as you can see, I'm just an old colored woman'—I was seventy-five or seventy-six then— 'and this is the first time anybody ever asked me about integration. And nobody asked my grandmother what she thought, either, but her daddy was one of you all' " Mrs. Moseley seems satisfied with this memory of her rejoinder. She looks at Charlotte. "I have the blood of three races in my veins," she says belligerently, "white, black, and Indian, and nobody asked me *anything* before."

31   "Do you think living in Eatonville made integration less appealing to you?"

32   "Well, I can tell you this: I have lived in Eatonville all my life, and I've been in the governing of this town. I've been everything but mayor and I've been *assistant* mayor. Eatonville was and is an all-black town. We have our own police department, post office, and town hall. Our own school and good teachers. Do I need integration?

33   "They took over Goldsboro, because the black people who lived there never incorporated, like we did. And now I don't even know if any black folks live there. They built big houses up there around the lakes. But we didn't let that happen in Eatonville, and we don't sell land to just anybody. And you see, we're still here."

34   When we leave, Mrs. Moseley is standing by her car, waving. I think of the letter Roy Wilkins wrote to a black newspaper blasting Zora Neale for her lack of enthusiasm about the integration of schools. I wonder if he knew the experience of Eatonville she was coming from. Not many black people in America have come from a self-contained, all-black community where loyalty and unity are taken for granted. A place where black pride is nothing new.

35   There is, however, one thing Mrs. Moseley said that bothered me.

36   "Tell me, Mrs. Moseley," I had asked, "why is it that thirteen years after Zora's death, no marker has been put on her grave?"

37   And Mrs. Moseley answered: "The reason she doesn't have a stone is because she wasn't buried here. She was buried down in South Florida somewhere. I don't think anybody really knew where she was."

Only to reach a wider audience, need she ever write books— because she is a perfect book of entertainment in herself. In her youth she was always getting scholarships and things from wealthy white people, some of whom simply paid her just to sit around and represent the Negro race for them, she did it in such a racy fashion. She was full of sidesplitting anecdotes, humorous tales, and tragicomic stories, remembered out of her life in the South as a daughter of a traveling minister of God. She could make you laugh one minute and cry the next. To many of her white friends, no doubt, she was a perfect "darkie," in the nice meaning they give the term—that is, a naïve, childlike, sweet, humorous, and highly colored Negro.

But Miss Hurston was clever, too—a student who didn't let college give her a broad "a" and who had great scorn for all pretensions, academic or otherwise. That is why she was such a fine folklore collector, able to go among the people and never act as if she had been to school at all. Almost nobody else could stop the average Harlemite on Lenox Avenue and measure his head with a strange-looking, anthropological device and not get bawled out for the attempt, except Zora, who used to stop anyone whose head looked interesting, and measure it.

—LANGSTON HUGHES,
THE BIG SEA

What does it matter what white folks must have thought about her?

—STUDENT, BLACK WOMEN WRITERS CLASS
WELLESLEY COLLEGE

38   Mrs. Sarah Peek Patterson is a handsome, red-haired woman in her late forties, wearing orange slacks and gold earrings. She is the director of Lee-Peek Mortuary in Fort Pierce, the establishment that handled Zora's burial. Unlike most black funeral homes in Southern towns that sit like palaces among the general poverty, Lee-Peek has a run-down, *small* look. Perhaps this is because it is painted purple and white, as are its Cadillac chariots. These colors do not age well. The rooms are cluttered and grimy, and the bathroom is a tiny, stale-smelling prison, with a bottle of black hair dye (apparently used to touch up the hair of the corpses) dripping into the face bowl. Two pine burial boxes are resting in the bathtub.

39   Mrs. Patterson herself is pleasant and helpful.

40   "As I told you over the phone, Mrs. Patterson," I begin, shaking her hand and looking into her penny-brown eyes, "I am Zora Neale Hurston's niece, and I would like to have a marker put on her grave. You said, when I called you last week that you could tell me where the grave is."

41   By this time I am, of course, completely into being Zora's niece, and the lie comes with perfect naturalness to my lips. Besides, as far as I'm concerned, she *is* my aunt—and that of all black people as well.

42   "She was buried in 1960," exclaims Mrs. Patterson. "That was when my father was running this funeral home. He's sick now or I'd let you talk to him. But I know where she's buried. She's in the old cemetery, the Garden of the Heavenly Rest, on Seventeenth Street. Just when you go in the gate there's a circle, and she's buried right in the middle of it. Hers is the only grave in that circle—because people don't bury in that cemetery any more."

43   She turns to a stocky, black-skinned woman in her thirties, wearing a green polo shirt and white jeans cut off at the knee. "This lady will show you where it is," she says.

44   "I can't tell you how much I appreciate this," I say to Mrs. Patterson, as I rise to go. "And could you tell me something else? You see, I never met my aunt. When she died, I was still a junior in high school. But could you tell me what she died of, and what kind of funeral she had?"

45   "I don't know exactly what she died of," Mrs. Patterson says. "I know she didn't have any money. Folks took up a collection to bury her. . . . I believe she died of malnutrition."

46   "*Malnutrition?*"

47   Outside, in the blistering sun, I lean my head against Charlotte's even more blistering car top. The sting of the hot metal only intensifies my anger. "*Malnutrition,*" I manage to mutter. "Hell, our condition hasn't changed *any* since Phillis Wheatley's time. *She* died of malnutrition!"

48   "Really?" says Charlotte. "I didn't know that."

> One cannot overemphasize the extent of her commitment. It was so great that her marriage in the spring of 1927 to Herbert Sheen was short-lived. Although divorce did not come officially until 1931, the two separated amicably after only a few months, Hurston to continue her collecting, Sheen to attend Medical School. Hurston never married again.
>
> —Robert Hemenway

49   "What is your name?" I ask the woman who has climbed into the back seat.

50   "Rosalee," she says. She has a rough, pleasant voice, as if she is a singer who also smokes a lot. She is homely, and has an air of ready indifference.

51 "Another woman came by here wanting to see the grave," she says, lighting up a cigarette. "She was a little short, dumpty white lady from one of these Florida schools. Orlando or Daytona. But let me tell you something before we gets started. All I know is where the cemetery is. I don't know one thing about that grave. You better go back in and ask her to draw you a map."

52 A few moments later, with Mrs. Patterson's diagram of where the grave is, we head for the cemetery.

53 We drive past blocks of small, pastel-colored houses and turn right onto Seventeenth Street. At the very end, we reach a tall curving gate, with the words "Garden of the Heavenly Rest" fading into the stone. I expected, from Mrs. Patterson's small drawing, to find a small circle—which would have placed Zora's grave five or ten paces from the road. But the "circle" is over an acre large and looks more like an abandoned field. Tall weeds choke the dirt road and scrape against the sides of the car. It doesn't help either that I step out into an active ant hill.

54 "I don't know about y'all," I say, "but I don't even believe this." I am used to the haphazard cemetery-keeping that is traditional in most Southern black communities, but this neglect is staggering. As far as I can see there is nothing but bushes and weeds, some as tall as my waist. One grave is near the road, and Charlotte elects to investigate it. It is fairly clean, and belongs to someone who died in 1963.

55 Rosalee and I plunge into the weeds; I pull my long dress up to my hips. The weeds scratch my knees, and the insects have a feast. Looking back, I see Charlotte standing resolutely near the road.

56 "Aren't you coming?" I call.

57 "No," she calls back. "I'm from these parts and I know what's out there." She means makes.

58 "Shit," I say, my whole life and the people I love flashing melodramatically before my eyes. Rosalee is a few yards to my right.

59 "How're you going to find anything out here?" she asks, And I stand still a few seconds, looking at the weeds. Some of them are quite pretty, with tiny yellow flowers. They are thick and healthy, but dead weeds under them have formed a thick gray carpet on the ground. A snake could be lying six inches from my big toe and I wouldn't see it. We move slowly, very slowly, our eyes alert, our legs trembly. It is hard to tell where the center of the circle is since the circle is not really round, but more like half of something round. There are things crackling and hissing in the grass. Sandspurs are sticking to the inside of my skirt. Sand and ants cover my feet. I look toward

the road and notice that there are, indeed, *two* large curving stones, making an entrance and exit to the cemetery. I take my bearings from them and try to navigate to exact center. But the center of anything can be very large, and a grave is not a pinpoint. Finding the grave seems positively hopeless. There is only one thing to do:

60   "Zora!" I yell, as loud as I can (causing Rosalee to jump). "Are you out here?"

61   "If she is, I sho hope she don't answer you. If she do, I'm gone."

62   "Zora!" I call again. "I'm here, Are you?"

63   "If she is," grumbles Rosalee, "I hope she'll keep it to herself."

64   "Zora!" Then I start fussing with her. "I hope you don't think I'm going to stand out here all day, with these snakes watching me and these ants having a field day. In fact, I'm going to call you just one or two more times." On a clump of dried grass, near a small bushy tree, my eye falls on one of the largest bugs I have ever seen. It is on its back, and is as large as three of my fingers. I walk toward it, and yell "Zo-ra!" and my foot sinks into a hole. I look down. I am standing in a sunken rectangle that is about six feet long and about three or four feet wide. I look up to see where the two gates are.

65   "Well," I say, "this is the center, or approximately anyhow. It's also the only sunken spot we've found. Doesn't this look like a grave to you?"

66   "For the sake of not going no farther through these bushes," Rosalee growls, "yes, it do."

67   "Wait a minute," I say, "I have to look around some more to be sure this is the only spot that resembles a grave. But you don't have to come."

68   Rosalee smiles—a grin, really—beautiful and tough.

69   "Naw," she says, "I feels sorry for you. If one of these snakes got ahold of you out here by yourself I'd feel *real* bad." She laughs. "I done come this far, I'll go on with you."

70   "Thank you, Rosalee," I say, "Zora thanks you too."

71   "Just as long as she don't try to tell me in person," she says, and together we walk down the field.

The gusto and flavor of Zora Neal[e] Hurston's storytelling, for example, long before the yarns were published in "Mules and Men" and other books, became a local legend which might have spread further under different conditions. A tiny shift in the center of gravity could have made them best-sellers.

    —ARNA BONTEMPS,
    PERSONALS

> Bitter over the rejection of her folklore's value, especially in the black community, frustrated by what she felt was her failure to convert the Afro-American world view into the forms of prose fiction, Hurston finally gave up.
>
> —ROBERT HEMENWAY

72   When Charlotte and I drive up to the Merritt Monument Company, I immediately see the headstone I want.

73   "How much is this one?" I ask the young woman in charge, pointing to a tall black stone. It looks as majestic as Zora herself must have been when she was learning voodoo from those root doctors down in New Orleans.

74   "Oh, *that* one," she says, "that's our finest, That's Ebony Mist."

75   "Well, how much is it?"

76   "I don't know. But wait," she says, looking around in relief, "here comes somebody who'll know."

77   A small, sunburried man with squinty green eyes comes up. He must be the engraver, I think, because his eyes are contracted into slits, as if he has been keeping stone dust out of them for years.

78   "That's Ebony Mist," he says. "That's our best."

79   "How much is it?" I ask, beginning to realize I probably *can't* afford it.

80   He gives me a price that would feed a dozen Sahelian drought victims for three years. I realize I must honor the dead, but between the dead great and the living starving, there is no choice.

81   "I have a lot of letters to be engraved," I say, standing by the plain gray marker I have chosen. It is pale and ordinary, not at all like Zora, and makes me momentarily angry that I am not rich.

82   We go into his office and I hand him a sheet of paper that has:

ZORA NEALE HURSTON
"A GENIUS OF THE SOUTH"
NOVELIST FOLKLORIST
ANTHROPOLOGIST
1901   1960

83   "A genius of the South" is from one of Jean Toomer's poems.

84   "Where is this grave?" the monument man asks. "If it's in a new cemetery, the stone has to be flat."

85   "Well, it's not a new cemetery and Zora—my aunt—doesn't need anything flat, because with the weeds out there, you'd never be able to see it. You'll have to go out there with me."

86   He grunts.

87   "And take a long pole and 'sound' the spot," I add. "Because there's no way of telling it's a grave, except that it's sunken."

88   "Well," he says, after taking my money and writing up a receipt, in the full awareness that he's the only monument dealer for miles, "you take this flag" (he hands me a four-foot-long pole with a red-metal marker on top) "and take it out to the cemetery and put it where you think the grave is. It'll take us about three weeks to get the stone out there."

89   I wonder if he knows he is sending me to another confrontation with the snakes. He probably does. Charlotte has told me she will cut my leg and suck out the blood if I am bit.

90   "At least send me a photograph when it's done, won't you?"

91   He says he will.

Hurston's return to her folklore-collecting in December of 1927 was made possible by Mrs. R. Osgood Mason, an elderly white patron of the arts, who at various times also helped Langston Hughes, Alain Locke, Richmond Barthe, and Miguel Covarrubias. Hurston apparently came to her attention through the intercession of Locke, who frequently served as a kind of liaison between the young black talent and Mrs. Mason. The entire relationship between this woman and the Harlem Renaissance deserves extended study, for it represents much of the ambiguity involved in white patrorage of black artists. All her artists were instructed to call her "Godmother"; there was a decided emphasis on the "primitive" aspects of black culture, apparently a holdover from Mrs. Mason's interest in the Plains Indians. In Hurston's case there were special restrictions imposed by her patron: although she was to be paid a handsome salary for her folklore collecting, she was to limit her correspondence and publish nothing of her research without prior approval.

—Robert Hemenway

You have to read the chapters Zora *left out* of her autobiography.

—Student, Special Collections Room
Beinecke Library, Yale University

92   Dr. Benton, a friend of Zora's and a practicing M.D. in Fort Pierce, is one of those old, good-looking men whom I always have trouble not

liking. (It no longer bothers me that I may be constantly searching for father figures; by this time, I have found several and dearly enjoyed knowing them all.) He is shrewd, with steady brown eyes under hair that is almost white. He is probably in his seventies, but doesn't look it. He carries himself with dignity, and has cause to be proud of the new clinic where he now practices medicine. His nurse looks at us with suspicion, but Dr. Benton's eyes have the penetration of a scalpel cutting through skin. I guess right away that if he knows anything at all about Zora Hurston, he will not believe I am her niece. "Eatonville?" Dr. Benton says, leaning forward in his chair, looking first at me, then at Charlotte. "Yes, I know Eatonville, I grew up not far from there. I knew the whole bunch of Zora's family." (He looks at the shape of my cheekbones, the size of my eyes, and the nappiness of my hair.) "I knew her daddy. The old man. He was a hardworking, Christian man. Did the best he could for his family. He was the mayor of Eatonville for a while, you know.

93   "My father was the mayor of Goldsboro. You probably never heard of it. It never incorporated like Eatonville did, and has just about disappeared. But Eatonville is still all black."

94   He pauses and looks at me. "And you're Zora's niece," he says wonderingly.

95   "Well," I say with shy dignity, yet with some tinge, I hope, of a nineteenth-century blush, "I'm illegitimate. That's why I never knew Aunt Zora."

96   I love him for the way he comes to my rescue. "You're not illegitimate!" he cries, his eyes resting on me fondly. "All of us are God's children! Don't you even *think* such a thing!"

97   And I hate myself for lying to him. Still, I ask myself, would I have gotten this far toward getting the headstone and finding out about Zora Hurston's last days without telling my lie? Actually, I probably would have. But I don't like taking chances that could get me stranded in central Florida.

98   "Zora didn't get along with her family. I don't know why. Did you read her autobiography, *Dust Tracks on a Road?*"

99   "Yes, I did," I say. "It pained me to see Zora pretending to be naïve and grateful about the old white 'Godmother' who helped finance her research, but I loved the part where she ran off from home after falling out with her brother's wife."

100   Dr. Benton nods. "When she got sick, I tried to get her to go back to her family, but she refused. There wasn't any real hatred; they just never had gotten along and Zora wouldn't go to them. She didn't want

to go to the county home, either, but she had to, because she couldn't do a thing for herself."

101   "I was surprised to learn she died of malnutrition."

102   Dr. Benton seems startled. "Zora *didn't* die of malnutrition," he says indignantly. "Where did you get that story from? She had a stroke and she died in the welfare home." He seems peculiarly upset, distressed, but sits back reflectively in his chair. "She was an incredible woman," he muses. "Sometimes when I closed my office, I'd go by her house and just talk to her for an hour or two. She was a well-read, well-traveled woman and always had her own ideas about what was going on. . . ."

103   "I never knew her, you know. Only some of Carl Van Vechten's photographs and some newspaper photographs . . . What did she look like?"

104   "When I knew her, in the fifties, she was a big woman, *erect*. Not quite as light as I am [Dr. Benton is dark beige], and about five foot, seven inches, and she weighed about two hundred pounds. Probably more. She . . ."

105   "What! Zora was *fat!* She wasn't, in Van Vechten's pictures!"

106   "Zora loved to eat," Dr. Benton says complacently. "She could sit down with a mound of ice cream and just eat and talk till it was all gone."

107   While Dr. Benton is talking, I recall that the Van Vechten pictures were taken when Zora was still a young woman. In them she appears tall, tan, and healthy. In later newspaper photographs—when she was in her forties—I remembered that she seemed heavier and several shades lighter. I reasoned that the earlier photographs were taken while she was busy collecting folklore materials in the hot Florida sun.

108   "She had high blood pressure. Her health wasn't good. . . . She used to live in one of my houses—on School Court Street. It's a block house. . . . I don't recall the number. But my wife and I used to invite her over to the house for dinner. *She always ate well,*" he says emphatically.

109   "That's comforting to know," I say, wondering where Zora ate when she wasn't with the Bentons.

110   "Sometimes she would run out of groceries—after she got sick—and she'd call me. 'Come over here and see 'bout me,' she'd say. And I'd take her shopping and buy her groceries.

111   "She was always studying. Her mind—before the stroke—just worked all the time. She was always going somewhere, too. She once went to Honduras to study something. And when she died, she was working on that book about Herod the Great. She was so intelligent! And really had perfect expressions. Her English was beautiful." (I sus-

pect this is a clever way to let me know Zora herself didn't speak in the "black English" her characters used.)

112   "I used to read all of her books," Dr. Benton continues, "but it was a long time ago. I remember one about. . . it was called, I think, 'The Children of God' [*Their Eyes Were Watching God*], and I remember Janie and Teapot [Teacake] and the mad dog riding on the cow in that hurricane and bit old Teapot on the cheek. . . ."

113   I am delighted that he remembers even this much of the story, even if the names are wrong, but seeing his affection for Zora I feel I must ask him about her burial. "Did she *really* have a pauper's funeral?"

114   "She *didn't* have a pauper's funerall" he says with great heat. "Everybody around here *loved* Zora."

115   "We just came back from ordering a headstone," I say quietly, because he *is* an old man and the color is coming and going on his face, "but to tell the truth, I can't be positive what I found is the grave. All I know is the spot I found was the only grave-size hole in the area."

116   "I remember it wasn't near the road," says Dr. Benton, more calmly. "Some other lady came by here and we went out looking for the grave and I took a long iron stick and poked all over that part of the cemetery but we didn't find anything. She took some pictures of the general area. Do the weeds still come up to your knees?"

117   "And beyond," I murmur. This time there isn't any doubt. Dr. Benton feels ashamed.

118   As he walks us to our car, he continues to talk about Zora. "She couldn't really write much near the end. She had the stroke and it left her weak; her mind was affected. She couldn't think about anything for long.

119   "She came here from Daytona, I think. She owned a houseboat over there. When she came here, she sold it. She lived on that money, then she worked as a maid—for an article on maids she was writing—and she worked for the *Chronicle* writing the horoscope column.

120   "I think black people here in Florida got mad at her because she was for some politician they were against. She said this politician *built* schools for blacks while the one they wanted just talked about it. And although Zora wasn't egotistical, what she thought, she thought; and generally what she thought, she said."

121   When we leave Dr. Benton's office, I realize I have missed my plane back home to Jackson, Mississippi. That being so, Charlotte and I decide to find the house Zora lived in before she was taken to the county welfare home to die. From among her many notes,

Charlotte locates a letter of Zora's she has copied that carries the address: 1734 School Court Street. We ask several people for directions. Finally, two old gentlemen in a dusty gray Plymouth offer to lead us there. School Court Street is not paved, and the road is full of mud puddles. It is dismal and squalid, redeemed only by the brightness of the late afternoon sun. Now I can understand what a "block" house is. It is a house shaped like a block, for one thing, surrounded by others just like it. Some houses are blue and some are green or yellow. Zora's is light green. They are tiny—about fifty by fifty feet, squatty with flat roofs. The house Zora lived in looks worse than the others, but that is its only distinction. It also has three ragged and dirty children sitting on the steps.

122 "Is this where y'all live?" I ask, aiming my camera.

123 "No, ma'am" they say in unison, looking at me earnestly. "We live over yonder. This Miss So-and-So's house; but she in the hospital."

124 We chatter inconsequentially while I take more pictures. A car drives up with a young black couple in it. They scowl fiercely at Charlotte and don't look at me with friendliness, either. They get out and stand in their doorway across the street. I go up to them to explain. "Did you know Zora Hurston used to live right across from you?" I ask.

125 "Who?" They stare at me blankly, then become curiously attentive, as if they think I made the name up. They are both Afroed and he is somberly dashikied.

126 I suddenly feel frail and exhausted. "It's too long a story," I say, "but tell me something: is there anybody on this street who's lived here for more than thirteen years?"

127 "That old man down there," the young man says, pointing. Sure enough, there is a man sitting on his steps three houses down. He has graying hair and is very neat, but there is a weakness about him. He reminds me of Mrs. Turner's husband in *Their Eyes Were Watching God*. He's rather "vanishing"-looking, as if his features have been sanded down. In the old days, before black was beautiful, he was probably considered attractive, because he has wavy hair and light-brown skin; but now, well, light skin has ceased to be its own reward.

128 After the preliminaries, there is only one thing I want to know: "Tell me something," I begin, looking down at Zora's house. "Did Zora like flowers?"

129 He looks at me queerly. "As a matter of fact," he says, looking regretfully at the bare, rough yard that surrounds her former house, "she was crazy about them. And she was a great gardener. She loved azaleas, and that running and blooming vine [morning-glories], and

she really loved that night-smelling flower [gardenia]. She kept a vegetable garden year-round, too. She raised collards and tomatoes and things like that.

130 "Everyone in this community thought well of Miss Hurston. When she died, people all up and down this street took up a collection for her burial. We put her away nice."

131 "Why didn't somebody put up a headstone?"

132 "Well, you know, one was never requested. Her and her family didn't get along. They didn't even come to the funeral."

133 "And did she live down there by herself?"

134 "Yes, until they took her away. She lived with—just her and her companion, Sport."

135 My ears perk up. "Who?"

136 "Sport, you know, her dog. He was her only companion. He was a big brown-and-white dog."

137 When I walk back to the car, Charlotte is talking to the young couple on their porch. They are relaxed and smiling.

138 "I told them about the famous lady who used to live across the street from them," says Charlotte as we drive off. "Of course they had no idea Zora ever lived, let alone that she lived across the street. I think I'll send some of her books to them."

139 "That's real kind of you," I say.

> I am not tragically colored. There is no great sorrow dammed up in my soul, nor lurking behind my eyes. I do not mind at all. I do not belong to the sobbing school of Negrohood who hold that nature somehow has given them a lowdown dirty deal and whose feelings are all hurt about it. . . . No, I do not weep at the world—I am too busy sharpening my oyster knife.
> —ZORA NEALE HURSTON,
> *"HOW IT FEELS TO BE COLORED ME,"*
> WORLD TOMORROW, 1928

140 There are times—and finding Zora Hurston's grave was one of them—when normal responses of grief, horror, and so on do not make sense because they bear no real relation to the depth of the emotion one feels. It was impossible for me to cry when I saw the field full of weeds where Zora is. Partly this is because I have come to know Zora through her books and she was not a teary sort of person herself, but partly, too, it is because there is a point at which even grief feels absurd. And at this point, laughter gushes up to retrieve sanity.

141   It is only later, when the pain is not so direct a threat to one's own existence, that what was learned in that moment of comical lunacy is understood. Such moments rob us of both youth and vanity. But perhaps they are also times when greater disciplines are born.

1975

Burial

I

They have fenced in the dirt road
that once led to Wards Chapel
A.M.E. church,
and cows graze
5   among the stones that
mark my family's graves.
The massive oak is gone
from out the church yard,
but the giant space is left
10   unfilled;
despite the two-lane blacktop
that slides across
the old, unalterable
roots.

II

15   Today I bring my own child here;
to this place where my father's
grandmother rests undisturbed
beneath the Georgia sun,
above her the neatstepping hooves
20   of cattle.
Here the graves soon grow back into the land.
Have been known to sink. To drop open without
warning. To cover themselves with wild ivy,
blackberries. Bittersweet and sage.
25   No one knows why. No one asks.
When Burning Off Day comes, as it does

some years,
the graves are haphazardly cleared and snakes
hacked to death and burned sizzling
30 in the brush. . . . The odor of smoke, oak
leaves, honeysuckle.
Forgetful of geographic resolutions as birds,
the farflung young fly South to bury
the old dead.

III

35 The old women move quietly up
and touch Sis Rachel's face.
"Tell Jesus I'm coming," they say.
"Tell Him I ain't goin' to *be*
long."

My grandfather turns his creaking head
40 away from the lavender box.
He does not cry. But looks afraid.
For years he called her "Woman";
shortened over the decades to
" 'Oman."
45 On the cut stone for " 'Oman's" grave
he did not notice
they had misspelled her name.
(The stone reads *Racher Walker*—not "Rachel"—
Loving Wife, Devoted Mother.)

IV

50 As a young woman, who had known her? Tripping
eagerly, "loving wife," to my grandfather's
bed. Not pretty, but serviceable. A hard
worker, with rough, moist hands. Her own two
babies dead before she came.
55 *Came to seven children.*
To aprons and sweat.
Came to quiltmaking.
Came to canning and vegetable gardens
big as fields.

60 *Came to fields to plow.*
Cotton to chop.
Potatoes to dig.
Came to multiple measles, chickenpox,
and croup.
65 *Came to water from springs.*
Came to leaning houses one story high.
Came to rivalries. Saturday night battles.
Came to straightened hair, Noxzema, and
feet washing at the Hardshell Baptist church.
70 *Came to zinnias around the woodpile.*
Came to grandchildren not of her blood
whom she taught to dip snuff without
sneezing.
Came to death blank, forgetful of it all.

75 *When he called her "'Oman" she no longer*
listened. Or heard, or knew, or felt.

V

It is not until I see my first grade teacher
review her body that I cry.
Not for the dead, but for the gray in my
80 first grade teacher's hair. For memories
of before I was born, when teacher and
grandmother loved each other; and later
above the ducks made of soap and the orange-
legged chicks Miss Reynolds drew over
85 my own small hand
on paper with wide blue lines.

VI

Not for the dead, but for memories. None of
them sad. But seen from the angle of her
death.

View from Rosehill Cemetery: Vicksburg
for Aaron Henry

Here we have watched ten thousand
seasons
come and go.
And unmarked graves atttangled
5 in the brush
turn our own legs to trees
vertical forever between earth
and sun.
Here we are not quick to disavow
10 the pull of field and wood
and stream;
we are not quick to turn
upon our dreams.

Ernest Gaines

(1933–)

*One of the most powerful contemporary Southern voices, Ernest Gaines
was born on January 15, 1933, in Pointe Coupee, a Louisiana plantation. Louisiana, with its rich and varied cultural traditions—Creole,
Cajun, and African American—and its attendant racial codes of conduct, is the landscape of Gaines's fiction. While Gaines's work gives voice
to the complexity of the state, he is most interested in capturing the oral
traditions of the African American elders of his childhood, which is
clearly evident in the* Autobiography of Miss Jane Pittman *(1971), one of
his most popular and acclaimed novels. Gaines moved to California at
the age of 15 to join his mother and stepfather because his family wanted him to continue his education, an impossibility in his Louisiana
town. Once in California, Gaines enrolled in a junior college and later
finished his education at San Francisco State College, graduating in
1957. He has published a short story collection,* Bloodline *(1968), but is
primarily recognized as a novelist. His critically celebrated body of work*

includes Catherine Carmier *(1964)*, Of Love and Dust *(1967)*, In My Father's House *(1978)*, A Gathering of Old Men *(1983)*, *and* A Lesson Before Dying *(1993)*. *The excerpt below is a scene from* A Gathering of Old Men, *in which the men underscore their connection to their ancestors by visiting their people's graves. This is a particularly important moment for the elderly men as they are on a journey to claim their manhood by taking responsibility for the murder of a Cajun overseer, a symbolic representation of institutional injustices.*

A Gathering of Old Men
Grant Bello
aka
Cherry

1   Yank was waiting for us behind a bush on the riverbank side of the road. Clatoo didn't have to stop, just slow down, and old Yank hopped in the back of the truck. Yank was in his early seventies, but he still thought he was a cowboy. He used to break horses and mules thirty, forty years ago, and he still wore the same kinda clothes he wore back then. His straw hat was draped like a cowboy hat. Wore a faded red polka-dotted handkerchief, tied in a loose knot round his neck. His pants legs was stucked down in his rubber boots—not cowboy boots. Back, shoulders had been broke I don't know how many times; made him walk leaning forward. Hands had been broke and rebroke; now he couldn't shut them too tight, or open them too wide. But he still thought he was a cowboy. He spoke when he first got in the truck, but after that we didn't do much talking. We was just feeling proud. I could see it on Yank's face; I could feel it sitting next to Chimley and Mat. Proud as we could be.

2   A mile or so after we picked up Yank, we picked up Dirty Red at Talbot. Clatoo had to blow the horn twice before we saw Dirty Red shuffling from behind the house. He carried the old shotgun by the barrel, the stock almost touching the ground. He had a self-rolled cigarette hanging from the corner of his mouth. He had as much ashes hanging on the cigarette as the cigarette was long. Dirty Red wouldn't take time to knock the ashes off a cigarette. Ashes fell off when it couldn't hang on any longer. Dirty Red got in the truck and spoke to everybody.

3   "Hoa," he said. We greeted him back. He looked at Chimley. "What's happening there, Chimley?"

4   Chimley nodded. Dirty Red grinned at him.

5   Three or four miles after we picked up Dirty Red. Clatoo turned off the main highway, down a dirt road that separated Morgan and the Marshall plantations. There was a cane on both sides, Morgan on on one side, Marshall on the other. The cane was so tall the blades hung over the ditches and over the road. After going a little ways so the people on the highway couldn't see us. Clatoo stopped the truck and told us to get out. He had to go farther up the highway for another load. He told us to wait for them at the graveyard, and we would all walk up to Mathu's house together. He thought that would look better than if we straggled in one or two at a time. He turned the truck around and headed back to the highway, and we started walking.

6   Jacob and Mat was in front, Chimley right behind them. Jacob had his gun over his shoulder, carrying it like a soldier. Mat had his tucked under his arm, barrel pointed toward the ground, like a hunter. Chimley had his under his arm, too, but he didn't walk nearly as straight as Mat or Jacob. Just shuffling along, head down, like he was following their tracks in the dust. If they had made a quick stop, Chimley woulda butt into them, I'm sure. Me and Yank followed Chimley, with Dirty Red and Billy Washington behind us. Billy carried his gun over his shoulder, but carried it too loosely. More like he was carrying a stick of wood than a gun. Billy couldn't hit the broad side of a barn if he stood two feet in front of it. Next to him. Dirty Red was nearly dragging his gun in the dust. I don't know who looked worse, Dirty Red, Billy Washington, or Chimley. Neither one of them looked like he was ready for battle, that's for sure.

7   We still had cane, tall and blue-green, on both sides of the road Morgan on the left, Marshall on the right. But it wasn't Marshall cane anymore. Beau Boutan was leasing the plantation from the Marshall family. Beau and his family had been leasing all the land the past twenty-five, thirty years. The very same land we had worked, our people had worked, our people's people had worked since the time of slavery. Now Mr. Beau had it all. Or, I should say, he had it all up to about twelve o'clock that day.

8   After about half a mile, we turned right on another headland. You had cane here, too, but just on one side. On the left the cane had been cut and hauled away, and you could see all the way back to the

swamps. It made me feel lonely. In my old age, specially in grinding, when I saw an empty cane field, it always made me feel lonely. The rows looked so naked and gray and lonely—like an old house where the people have moved from. Where good friends have moved from, leaving the house empty and bare, with nothing but ghosts now to keep it company.

9   I was still looking across the field when I heard the shot. I turned just in time to see a little rabbit bobbing across the empty rows. By the time I took aim, he was already down one of the middles, and all I could see was his little ears bobbing every now and then. I looked back at Billy and Dirty Red. Billy was just bringing the gun down from his shoulder. Me and Yank waited for him and Dirty Red to catch up.

10   "Missed him, huh, Billy?" I asked.

11   Billy didn't answer. He wouldn't even look at me or Yank. He was too 'shamed.

12   "I hope he don't miss Fix like that," Dirty Red teased Billy. Dirty Red had a cigarette hanging from the corner of his mouth, and he helt his head a little to the side to keep the smoke out his eyes. "Rabbit was so close I started to hit him in the head with the butt of my gun, but I wanted Billy to have him."

13   "He was moving," Billy said. He said it quietly. He wouldn't look at us.

14   "After you stumbled over him, he started moving," Dirty Red teased Billy.

15   Billy kept his head down.

16   "You'll get another chance, Billy, you just wait," I told him.

17   We started walking again. Me and Yank in front, and Billy and Dirty Red following us. Mat, Jacob, and Chimley had stopped for a second, and started walking again. Behind us, I could hear Dirty Red laughing. He would be quiet a second, then laugh again. I knowed he was still laughing at Billy. I hoped Billy missing that rabbit wasn't a bad sign for the rest of that day.

18   Now, up ahead, I could see the pecan and oak trees in the graveyard at Marshall. You had a dozen trees spread out over the graveyard, and about that same number of headstones, maybe two or three more. But twenty-five, thirty years ago you didn't have more than two or three headstones in there all total. Back there when I was growing up, people didn't even mark the graves. Each family had a little plot, and everybody knowed where that little plot was. If it was a big family, then they had to have a little bit more, sometimes from the plot of a smaller family. But who cared? They had all come from the

same place, they had mixed together when they was alive, so what's the difference if they mixed together now? That old graveyard had been the burial ground for black folks ever since the time of slavery. I was seventy-four, and I had grandparents in there.

19   We squatted under a pecan tree just outside the graveyard fence. You had pecans on the ground all around you, and if you looked up you could see them hanging loose in the shells. The next good wind or rain was go'n bring them all down. It was a good year for pecans.

20   We hadn't been there more than ten, maybe fifteen minutes when Jacob stood up and went inside the graveyard. I looked back over my shoulder, and I seen him pulling up weeds from Tessie's grave. Tessie was his sister. She was one of them great big pretty mulatto gals who messed around with the white man and the black man. The white men wanted her all for themself, and they told her to stay away from the niggers. But she didn't listen, and they killed her. Ran her through the quarters out into that St. Charles River—Mardi Gras Day, 1947.

21   But listen to this now. Her own people at the old Mulatto Place wouldn't even take her body home. They was against her living here in the first place round the darker people. I'm not dark myself, I'm light as them, but I'm not French, not quality. Them, they're quality, them; but they wouldn't even take her body home. Buried her with the kind she had lived with. Maybe that's why Jacob was here today, to make up for what he had done his sister over thirty years ago. After pulling up the weeds, he knelt down at the head of the grave and made the sign of the cross. Next thing you knowed, every last one of us was in there visiting our people's graves.

22   You had to walk in grass knee-high to reach some of the graves. The people usually cleaned up the graveyard if they had to bury somebody, or for La Toussaint. But nobody had been buried there in a good while, and La Toussaint wasn't for another month, so you had grass, weeds everywhere. Pecans and acorns—you could feel them under your feet, you could hear them crack when you stepped on them.

23   We went to our different little family plots. But we wasn't too sure about all the graves. If they had been put there the last twenty, twenty-five years, yes, then we could tell for sure. But, say, if they had been put there forty, fifty years ago, it was no way we could tell if we was looking at the right grave for the right person. Most of the graves after a while had just shifted and mixed with all the others.

24   Dirty Red was a little bit farther away from the rest of us, more over into the corner. We had never mixed too well with his people. We

thought they was too trifling, never doing anything for themself. Dirty Red was the last one. Maybe that's why he was here today, to do something for all the others. But maybe that's why we was all there, to do something for the others.

25 After I had knelt down and prayed over my own family plot, I wandered over to where Dirty Red was standing all by himself. He was eating a pecan and looking down at the weeds that covered the graves. Dirty Red hadn't knelt down or pulled one weed from one grave. Some of the graves was all sunked in.

26 "My brother Gabe there," Dirty Red said. I didn't know for sure what spot he was looking at, because soon as he said it he cracked another pecan with his teeth. Not cracking couple of them together in his hand, but cracking them one at a time with his teeth. "My mon, Jude; my pa, François, right there," he said. I still didn't know for sure where he was looking. "Uncle Ned right in there—somewhere," he said.

27 The whole place was all sunked in, and you had weeds everywhere, so I couldn't tell for sure where Dirty Red was looking. I never looked at his eyes to see if they shifted from one spot to another. But, knowing Dirty Red, I figured they probably didn't. That woulda been too much like work. Even to bat his eyes was too much work for Dirty Red.

28 "You got plenty of us in here," I said, looking around the graveyard. I could see Mat, Chimley, Yank—all of them standing near their people's graves. "This where you want them to bring you?" I asked Dirty Red.

29 "Might as well, if it's still here," he said.

30 "They getting rid of these old graveyards more and more," I said. "These white folks coming up today don't have no respect for the dead."

31 Dirty Red cracked another pecan with his teeth.

32 "Graveyard pecan always taste good," he said. "You tried any of them?"

33 "I'll gather me up a few before we leave," I said.

34 I looked out on the empty field on the other side of the fence. The cane rows came up to twenty or thirty feet of the graveyard. Beau had cut and hauled the cane away, and I could see all the way back to the swamps. Them long old lonely cane rows took me back back, I can tell you that.

35 "Him and Charlie had a chance to get some of it done," I said to Dirty Red.

36 "He sure won't be getting no more done," Dirty Red said.

37 "What you think of all this, Dirty Red?" I asked him.

38   "Well, I look at it this way," he said. "How many more years I got here on this old earth?"

39   That was all he had to say. He stopped right there. Just like Dirty Red not to finish something. That woulda taken too much of his strength, and him and his people believed in saving as much strength as they could.

40   "With that little time left, you thought you ought to do something worthwhile with your life?" I asked, trying to coax him on.

41   "Something like that," he said. He ate another pecan.

42   "Your people will be proud of you, Dirty Red."

43   "I reckon lot of them in here go'n be proud after this day is over," he said. "Might have some of us joining them, too."

44   "You think it might come to that?"

45   "That's up to Fix," he said. He looked at me and grinned. Then he looked past me and nodded. "Here come Clatoo and them."

46   They came down the road, where the old railroad tracks used to be. Clatoo was in front, with his gun in one hand and a shoe box under his left arm. Bing and Ding Lejeune from the Two Indian Bayou was a step behind him. Both had on khakis and both had on straw hats, and you had to get right on them to tell who was who, and if you didn't know Ding had the scar 'cross the left side of his face, you still couldn't tell which one you was talking to. Clabber Hornsby, the albino from Jarreau, came behind Bing and Ding Lejeune, walking by himself. Clabber's head and face from this distance was all one color—white white. What he had a gun for, only God knows. He couldn't stop blinking long enough to sight, let alone kill somebody. Behind Clabber came Jean Pierre Ricord and Gable Rauand. Now, that was somebody, Gable, I never woulda expected to see. He very seldomed ever left home. To church, maybe, but that was about all. Behind him and Jean Pierre came Cedrick Tucker and Sidney Brooks, Cedrick's brother Silas was the last black sharecropper on the place. He was buried here. Walking next to Cedrick was Sidney Brooks—we all called him Coot. Old Coot was in his World War I uniform. Even had on the cap, and the belt 'cross his shoulder. He carried his gun 'cross the other shoulder in a soldier's manner. We left the graveyard to meet them. We met under the pecan tree, and couple of the fellows squatted down against the wire fence.

47   "Everybody shot?" Clatoo asked soon as he walked up.

48   "Billy shot at a rabbit on his foot and missed him," Dirty Red said. Ditty Red was squatting by the fence.

49   Couple of the fellows laughed at Dirty Red.

50   "That rabbit was moving, Dirty Red," Billy told him. "But you ain't, and don't forget it."

51   The men laughed again. Not loud. Quiet. Thoughtful. More from nervousness than anything else.

52   "Save your fighting for later," Clatoo told Billy Washington. "Them ain't shot, shoot," he said. "She told us to bring empty shells."

53   "What we suppose to do with them empties, throw them at Fix?" I asked Clatoo.

54   "You can ask her that when you get there," Clatoo said. "Them ain't shot yet, shoot up in them trees. Let them down there hear you."

55   Five or six of us raised our guns and shot. A few pecans, a few acorns, some moss and leaves fell down on the sunked-in graves under the trees.

56   "Anybody got anything to say 'fore we get started?" Clatoo asked. "Anybody feel like turning around? It can get a little hot out there today. Anybody?"

57   Nobody said they wanted to turn around.

58   "All right," Clatoo said. "Let's get moving. Heads up and backs straight. We going in like soldiers, not like tramps. All right?"

59   He started out first, gun in one hand, shoe box under his arm. Mat and Jacob followed, then the rest of us. Jean Pierre, Billy Washington, and Chimley was doing all they could to walk with their heads up and backs straight.

Julie Dash

(1952–)

Born and raised in New York City, Julie Dash is an accomplished film-maker, receiving her BA in film production from City College in 1974. She earned her MFA in Film and Television Production from UCLA in 1986. Illusions, *a short film, won her critical acclaim, and she followed up this success with the hugely popular 1992 film,* Daughters of the Dust. *Set in the Sea Islands at the turn of the twentieth century, this film traces the migration of one Gullah family as they migrate from the South to the North. In so doing, the film pays homage to the Gullah cul-ture and highlights women as the bearers of this cultural tradition.* Daughters of the Dust *marked the first full-length film debut by an African American woman to have a general theatric release. This film has received numerous honors: It was cited by* Filmmaker's *Magazine as*

*one of the 50 most important independent films ever made, and, in
1999, the 25th Annual Newark Black Film Festival honored it as one of
the most important cinematic achievements in Black Cinema in the
twentieth century. Dash also has written a novel with the same title,
which continues the story of the Sea Islands community. The passage
reprinted below illustrates an ancestral burial ritual. This important
public ceremony follows the discovery by one of the community members, Lucy, of shackled human bones buried in the fields.*

Daughters of the Dust

1   Elizabeth stood at the edge of the yard and felt the wind rise and
sweep across the sand. The hair on her arms and neck prickled as she
contemplated the long night ahead. She looked up at the sky; it was
clearing after having been overcast all day. The last streaks of light
faded quickly as the dark approached across the water. She heard
Amelia come up behind her and saw the light from the kerosene lamp
she carried. "You got de charm I made for you?" she asked when
Amelia handed her a jacket. Amelia touched the charm that lay under
her blouse.

2   Elizabeth, Amelia, Eula, and several other women had both
worked hard these last two days to get the ancestor ground ready
for the ceremony. Iona and Clemmie arrived the second day to help
with the preparations, word having reached them back in the
swamp. The women worked together easily, clearing the weeds from
the place by the old burial ground, sweeping the dirt to level the
ground, and constructing the altar according to Miz Emma Julia's
instructions. As they went about their work, each woman felt what
they had missed when Nana and the others had passed on and this
ritual had disappeared from their lives. Clemmie was charged with
gathering the items that would dress the altar. Elizabeth tried to
get Lucy to join in collecting the waters, the shells, the earth, and
other things that were required, but Lucy refused to move from her
bed. Amelia had found a large blue cloth with a crackled design
among some old burlap sacks that had been sewn together to make
sheets, perfect for draping the altar. Eli and Ben built the solid pine
coffin that would hold the bones after the ceremony. Ben had
inscribed it with the markings as scratched in the sand by Miz

Emma Julia. Together they carried it to the old burial ground, setting it behind the altar.

3   With the help of the other women, Iona and Carrie Mae had set up the cooking place and brought the huge pots for the feast that would follow. Willis George and the men had been up since early morning, casting their nets, pulling in the shrimp, croaker, flounder, and crab that would be prepared. Today returned from her hunt with two large wild turkeys, a couple of wood hens, and several rabbits. People had begun arriving in the late morning, hauling wagons filled with vegetables taken from their winter storage.

4   It had been two days of continuous activity since Miz Emma Julia had made the pronouncement. It seemed that almost everyone had put aside their chores to make sure everything was ready for the journey. Everything would be ready when Miz Emma Julia returned.

5   Ol Trent hung at the edges of the activity, watching every preparation suspiciously, haranguing people about devil worshipping and false gods. It was only when Carrie Mae threatened him with Miz Emma Julia that he backed off, muttering angrily, but no longer interfering. Elizabeth gazed at Ol Trent, trying to summon the confident image of the young man in the photograph.

6   Sallie Lee had shown up when Willis George had not come back directly that day. She collected her children with barely a "thank you" to Eula. Amelia had felt pity for the little boy who stood by Lucy's bed and patted her on the back to tell her "good-bye." In her one display of emotion, Lucy had turned and hugged him until he squealed and then let him go. He continued to wave to them on the front porch as he followed his mother and big brother down the road.

7   They arrived at the ancestor ground and found Eula, Iona, and Clemmie checking to make sure everything was in order. Lucy stared at the wooden tablets that marked the graves of the ancients. Amelia immediately crossed to her. "I'm glad you've come, Lucy."

8   Lucy looked at her with hollow eyes, "Mama an Daddy wouldnt have it no other way."

9   Rebecca ran up, brimming with excitement. "I been in de cleanin house! Dey dont let no boys in de cleanin house!"

10   Folks arrived quickly as darkness settled around them. Sitting on the ground around the altar, they remained quiet, awaiting Miz Emma Julia's arrival. A gust of wind blew through the treetops, sending leaves tumbling down on the ceremonial ground. They heard the creak of a cart wheel, and Miz Emma Julia rode into view. Eli and J.C. stepped forward to carry her from the cart. A gasp went through the

crowd as she waved them aside and pulled herself up. She stood at the edge of the cart and took in everyone. Nodding with satisfaction, she said, "It good. All de chilren come home!" She gestured for Eli and J.C. to help her down. When her feet reached the ground, she leaned on them to steady herself, then stepped forward tentatively. With each tread, her step became more sure until she was moving slowly but with confidence. She moved through the crowd followed by Aubrey and Ell.

11   "How many chilren dis make, Mary?" she asked one women as she passed her.

12   "Leven," came the reply.

13   She looked at a young man. "You still creepin where you dont belong?"

14   The man stepped back. "Aw, Miz Emma Julia, why you got to say dat?"

15   "Cause you dont deserve dat good woman!" she snapped. She stopped in front of Carrie Mae and grinned, showing the one tooth in her mouth. "I caint do nuttin for you! All dat devilment you into!" Miz Emma Julia declared. Despite herself, Carrie Mae blushed. "I just here for de journey!" Miz Emma Julia cackled. "Dem ol ones take anybody wit dem! Dey aint too particular!" She moved on, but then turned back, "You still got dat barley water?"

16   "Yes, ma'am."

17   "Send me a lil taste. I aint had none in a long time!"

18   She peered through the crowd and spotted a middle-aged man with thick salt-and-pepper hair. "Lorda mercy! Leroy, you still de best-lookin coal-black man I ever set dese eyes on!"

19   The man grinned at her. "How you, Miz Emma Julia?"

20   "I fine now!"

21   She reached the altar and inspected the items that had been laid out. She lifted the top from the stew pot and dipped her fingers in the dirt. She pointed to the bottles filled with different types of water. "You get dis water from de river, de swamp, de pond, de creek, de big water like I say?"

22   Clemmie stepped forward. "Yes, maam."

23   Recognizing the girl she asked, "Where you mama?"

24   "She at de cooking place."

25   "Dat right where her need to be. Tell her no salt. Salt scare de ol spirits, an us need dem tonight!" Clemmie left to give her mother the warning. Miz Emma Julia turned the seashells in the direction of the sea, then moved the herb pot to the middle of the table. She

reached into her apron pockets and brought out a box of matches and lit the herb pot. "Lil Bet!" she called. Elizabeth moved quickly to her side. "Start de fires!" Elizabeth drew a twig from the pile that lay on the altar and lit it from the herb pot. She then lit the fires under the water-filled iron pots that sat in front of the altar. Miz Emma Julia reached into her blouse and pulled out a sack. She stood before each hot pot and muttered silently before she dropped a handful of herbs from the sack into the kettles.

26   Abruptly, she ordered, "Bring me de quilts, bring me de bones of dose dat come afore we!" Eula and Eli brought one quilt forward and laid it at her feet, then brought the other. They stepped back into the group as Miz Emma Julia lifted her arms and began her incantation, throwing her voice to the sky.

> *Chango! Agwe! Mami Wata! Yemaya! Allah!*
> *Gods of de many peoples of Africa, hear my call!*
> *Ogun! Igwe! Dan Bada! Asaso-Yaa! Kamalu!*
> *You chilren callin you from all de places of dis earth!*
> *De chilren stolen from de lands of Ibo, Yoruba, Kissee,*
> *Dahomey, Angola, Gambia, Whydah!*
> *Come! Come! Hear de chilren calling you!*

27   The night was complete silence, with not even a sound from the woods. Suddenly a large gust of wind swirled through the group, lifting skirts, tugging at jackets, snatching the breath from the babies. The flames from the torches shot up in the air. While some fell to their knees, Eula, Eli, and others looked to the skies as the clouds parted to show the moon. Lucy shrank as the wind seemed to circle her, moving along the edge of the group. Amelia felt the soft caress of the breeze on the back of her neck, her body relaxing. Elizabeth held her arms out and let the wind pass through her body. Miz Emma Julia stood resolutely against the wind as it threatened to bowl her over. Then it stopped as suddenly as it had come up.

28   Miz Emma Julia looked to Lucy, holding her hand out. "Come, chile, you brought dem to us. You gotta help dem go home," Lucy shook her head, but Miz Emma Julia continued to hold out her hand. Lucy slowly moved toward her as if pulled by a force. "You a lil gal. You gonna need a helper to send dem home." When Lucy turned to her with pleading eyes, Amelia got to her feet to stand beside her.

29   "Take de quilts an open dem up." Lucy took one end and Amelia the other and gently spread the quilt. They moved to the second

quilt and opened it, Lucy turning her head from the bones that lay in the quilt. Miz Emma Julia held out her hand. "Spread out de shackles an de chain as dey lay in de ground." Amelia and Lucy picked up the pieces and strung them out as best they could. Mis Emma Julia spoke, "Now, spread out de bones so we can see de old ones." Lucy looked as if she was about to flee. Caught by Miz Emma Julia's gaze, she began to sob. Eula pressed her hands to her mouth to keep from crying out to her daughter. Eli put his arm around Eula, holding her close.

30   "Go on, gal. Let dem saltwater tears wash down an cleanse dem. Aint nobody cry for dem for years. Dey lay out in dat field for nobody know how long. Dat why dat field so rich wit de earth. Our elders give it dey life blood. Dey give to we what was took from dem." She gestured for Amelia to spread the bones. Amelia leaned down, hands trembling, and reached for a long piece of bone. When her shaking fingers touched it, she felt a joit and pulled back. Miz Emma Julia nodded encouragingly. "Dey reachin out to you. Take what dey got to offer." Amelia wanted to refuse, then saw the fear in Lucy's eyes. Heart pounding and breathing heavily, she picked up the bone. She thought it was her imagination, the tingling that started in her fingers and began to spread up her arm. But as it spread over her body, she felt it in every pore as sweat broke out and her skin seemed to flush with blood. She held the bone above her head with both hands and cried out when she felt the waves of fear, pain, and despair wash over her. The others flinched and moaned with her, while Lucy hid her face. Amelia slowly lowered the bone, her arms trembling, her clothes soaking. Miz Emma Julia placed Amelia's coat on her shoulders and stroked her head.

31   The old woman then reached down and picked up a skull, crossing to Lucy, who cried out and shrank from her. Relentlessly, she grabbed Lucy's hand, struggling with her, and thrust the skull into it. She hissed at her, "Feel deir pain, gal! Feel deir hurt! Only when you feel de pain do de healin begin!"

32   Lucy shook as she stared at the skull. Just as she was about to let it roll off her palm, her head snapped back as the force hit her. She jerked as if her body were receiving invisible blows, her head lolling and her arms flinging in every direction. Painfully she closed her fingers around the skull and struggled to bring it closer to her. Only when she clasped it to her chest did the force seem to take pity on her. Her head hung low; her body was limp.

33   Miz Emma Julia stepped in front of the altar, waving the herb pot, the smoke swirling up and disappearing into the night air. "It take

a strong people, snatch from de cradle, de wood, de village, put on de boat, an took cross de big water to land dey never know." Miz Emma Julia moved back and forth in front of the altar, acting out the story. Her age fell away as her words rose. "It take a strong people to keep dey all about dem, to hold on de ol ways, to keep de lies true, to know who dey be! It take a strong people to work from day clean to day over to clear de lan, build de house, plow de field, make de indigo, sow de rice, pick de cotton, all to de good of de buckra. Some of we forget how strong dem people was, us look past de old ways, put aside what dey was tellin we bout de right way to live. An now dey come back to we, de ancients who seed dis earth wit deir tears, sweat, an blood!" She leaned over and picked up a skull and a large piece of bone, holding them up for all to see. She began to shake as the forces moved through her, the people in front of her ducking when spikes of electricity flew from her body.

> *Ogun Iree Ni Tala Conje!*
> *Ogun, God of Iron!*
> *Opah Ne Sole Tu Bayai Se Fue!*
> *Give We You Strength to Carry On!*
>
> *Yemoja, Ose Bo Kinya To Le!*
> *Yemoja, Mother of Our World!*
> *Bon Me No Candona Kikwala!*
> *Mbata Ke Bil*
> *Let You Waters Wash We With*
> *De Wisdom of Life!*
>
> *Elegba, Obebe Ko Nande Be Soma!*
> *Elegba, de Trickster of Man an Woman!*
> *Aru Be Ne Royo Te Ndebe! Pa Li Be Onota!*
> *When de Roads Coms Together!*
> *Show We de Right Way!*
>
> *Oshun, On Ye Ye O Talalu Be Me!*
> *Oshun, She Who Brings Love an Beauty!*
> *Ode Asasu Mbotele So Indo!*
> *Teach We to Treasure Who Us Come From!*
> *Me Ti Lo!*
> *Who Us Are!*

34   The trees behind the altar began to shake with her force. People grabbed onto each other and wailed as the earth began to move. Miz

Emma Julia threw her head back and laughed. "Come, chilren, dey telling you to rise up! Free de souls!" she commanded as they slowly got to their feet, holding on to each other as the earth rolled. "We done took de pain an de sadness! All dat lef is de healin!" At her words, there was the sound of drums. Aubrey and two other men took their places behind the altar, alternating the rhythms between them.

35   Moving to the beat of the drums, Miz Emma Julia picked up the stew pot and began to sprinkle the dirt across the bones, making a full circle around the quilts. She waved for Amelia and Lucy to follow her.

> *Dis de earth dat mark de spot where*
> *de ancients lay for no telling how long!*

She poured water from each bottle onto the bones, changing the direction of the circle. Carrie Mae, Clemmie, and Elizabeth joined the line following her, the tempo of the drums picking up.

> *De water give dem safe passage back to*
> *de old world!*

Rice sprayed from her hands as she flung it to the sky. Eli and Eula moved into the line. Rebecca and several other children ran forward, trying to catch the rice as it rained down upon them. They began to imitate the adults, dancing around the quilt.

> *Dis will provide de sustenance to see you*
> *through de rough journey!*

She laid her hands on the found objects, the oddly shaped piece of wood, the bright tallfeather of the parrot, the stone worn smooth by the waters, and the spiral-shaped seashell.

> *Dis wood will pay de passage to Ogun!*
> *Oshun, her love de colors of de bird!*
> *Elegba use dis stone to mark de place in de road!*
> *Yemaja blow in de shell to let dem know you coming!*

Toady and Ben stepped forward as she raised her hands, exhorting the others to join her in this dance of celebration.

Ash the Watchman how long—
How long, Watchman, how long?
Oh, we dont know how long—
Oh, how long, Watchman, how long?

36   The wind blew strongly, threatening to extinguish the flames
from the torches that surrounded the old burial ground. Amelia
looked at the faces of the men, women, and children who solemnly
watched Eli and the other men dig the common grave for the bones.
Deep sadness had replaced the fear and anxiety that had earlier
marked their faces, each one remembering a loved one who lay just
beyond the light.

Oh, ask my brother how long—
How long, Watchman, how long?

37   Slipping her hand into her pocket, Amelia grasped the piece of
iron from the shackles. Miz Emma Julia had insisted that everyone take
a piece so they would always remember the price the old ones paid
for their freedom. Listening to the melancholy dirge that set the rhythm
for the shovels as they dug into the soft dirt, Amelia wondered how
many more captives lay in secret places, waiting to be uncovered and
brought home. She had discovered that folks did not find it easy to talk
about slavery. It had not been long ago, and the stories and experiences
as drawn from the collective memory and shared from one generation
to the next remained fresh. There was still much pain among the elders,
and she would never forget how one woman had thrown her apron over
her head, crying bitter tears when asked about her family. The young
ones knew these stories, having heard them all their lives, and burned
with fresh anger at their retelling.

38   The men stopped digging, and Miz Emma Julia, who lay in the back
of her cart, signaled for them to bring the coffin forward. Amelia could
see the groundwater that was already seeping through into the grave.
Eli and Ben lifted the lid from the coffin. Amelia and Lucy stepped forward with one quilt of bones, Clemmie and Elizabeth with the other.
Amelia heard the murmur of many prayers as they gently lowered the
quilts into the coffin. All quieted as Miz Emma Julia sat up.

Olodumare, God of All Worlds!
It time for de ancient ones to start de

journey back across de big water!
Back to where de spirits of deir modders
an fadders wait for dem so dey can start de
journey to de land where de moon an de sun play together!
Olodumare, God of All Worlds!
Help dem cross de way an send down you
blessin on we, you poor chilren who dey leave
behind!

39   At Miz Emma Julia's nod, the lid was hammered into the coffin. The men stepped forward and lifted the ropes holding the coffin and swung it over the open grave.

Oh, ask my mother, how long!
How long, Watchman, how long?

They sang louder as the coffin was lowered into the grave, swaying to the beat and clapping their hands. Amelia shivered when the first shovel of dirt fell on the coffin. Now, at the end, she was weak with tiredness and could see the exhaustion from the long night in the others' faces. She swayed on her feet and felt Elizabeth's arm go around her and squeeze her encouragingly.

40   "That was a good thing you did! Standing with Lucy!" Elizabeth whispered in her ear. They both glanced over at Lucy, who stood within the protective shelter of Eli's arms, singing solemnly while the coffin disappeared under the dirt.

Ask the Watchman how long—
How long, Watchman, how long?
Oh, we don't know how long—
Oh, how long, Watchman, how long?

When the coffin was completely covered, folks stepped forward to lay their offerings on the grave; pots of food, a handkerchief, a single earring, a jar of liquor, a wooden carving, a clump of hair, whatever they wanted to leave of themselves. After each person made their offering, they fell in line behind Miz Emma Julia's cart, which led them to the morning feast that awaited them.

Writing Assignments

1. Using the historical information presented in this chapter's introduction, as well as the literary selections, write a narrative or poetic description of the Middle Passage. Think about what language you will use to capture the conditions aboard the slaving vessels. How does your text compare with the approaches taken by the authors presented in this chapter?

2. In Toni Morrison's rendering of the Middle Passage in *Beloved* and in W. E. B. Du Bois' presentation of his son's death in *Souls of Black Folk*, these specific events take on larger significance. How do these representations of suffering serve as symbols of broader themes in African American history?

3. Many cultures perform rituals to honor the dead. Compile a list of African American death and funerary customs that are referenced in the following works: "A Death Song," "A Brown Girl Dead," *Black Thunder*, and *Dust Tracks on a Road*. What narrative function do these rituals serve in the context of the literary selections?

4. Alice Walker's "Looking for Zora" and Julie Dash's *Daughters of the Dust* feature unmarked burial grounds. What is the metaphoric significance of these erased cemeteries? What might the acts of burying the dead and marking their graves signify in the texts?

CHAPTER TWO

THE INFLUENCE OF THE SPIRITUALS

The spirituals sung originally by Blacks, also known as the Negro spirituals, are among the oldest and most pervasive influences reflected in African American literature. The songs—there are more than six thousand—evolved as powerful statements about pain, hope, faith, and the Black struggle for freedom. They largely represent a brilliant assertion of humanity and perseverance by an enslaved community that ingeniously blended its experience in the American slavocracy, particularly the exposure to Protestant Christianity and the King James Bible, with patterns and themes of African creative discourse. It is a remarkable achievement, one that has inspired generations of African American creative writers like Frances E. W. Harper, Paul Laurence Dunbar, James Weldon Johnson, John Oliver Killens, and William Melvin Kelley—and also major white authors like Eugene O'Neill (*All God's Chillun Got Wings*, 1924) and William Faulkner (*Go Down, Moses*, 1942). Numerous poems, plays, and fictional works rely upon the spirituals and the related biblical stories for content, plot, and style. No definitive assessment of the spirituals exists. Scholars and laypersons still debate the exact nature of their structure and their religious and political intent. However, the spirituals remain, above all things, irresistible.

Although the precise advent of the spirituals is in dispute, it can reasonably be argued that captured Africans were analyzing and commenting upon their social plight, as well as melding expressive forms, from the beginnings of the Middle Passage. What is certain is that they did not leave their African culture entirely behind. African epics and praise poems inform spirituals like "Go Down, Moses" (an epic) and

"Joshua Fit de Battle of Jericho" (a praise poem). Therefore, the spirituals can be labeled a poetic creole, that is, they largely consist of a New World vocabulary (the Bible) mixed with African poetic patterns or syntax. "Go Down, Moses," the most popular spiritual and the first to be written down (sometime in the nineteenth century) according to Richard Newman, serves as an example. It draws upon the story of Exodus, resembles typical African epics in that the hero's triumph is made possible through sorcery, not simply brute strength, and exemplifies the call-and-response element that is fundamental to African group singing. Despite the fact that the Bible represented the religion of the enslavers, the enslaved were artistically and politically seduced by visions of an ultimately just God, prospects of divine deliverance, and heroes both mystical and powerful, especially Old Testament icons like Moses and Joshua. In addition, the enslaved imbued the Scriptures with additional layers of meaning. The spirituals popularized the metaphor of the antebellum South as the American Egypt— with Blacks the chosen and enslaved people laboring under an evil Pharoah, seeking the Promised Land (the North) and, most important, capable of producing a Moses.

Indeed, the Egypt or Moses motif has been one of the most captivating and enduring in African American literature. Harper, a major nineteenth-century author who often employed religious themes in her verse, published a lengthy poem in 1869 titled "Moses: A Story of the Nile." Dunbar incorporated the story of Moses into his poem "Ante-Bellum Sermon" (1895). In 1908, James Weldon Johnson continued the tribute in formal poetry to the folk poetry of the spirituals in general, and to "Go Down, Moses" in particular, in his famous "O Black and Unknown Bards." Kelley's 1962 novel, *A Different Drummer*, is emblematic of the Moses trope, and the theme has been explored in more recent times by the likes of Lauryn Hill, whose work, including the 1998 "The Final Hour," is steeped in biblical imagery.

Although not all spirituals are overtly political, it is precisely the arguably political ones that have been of most interest to African American writers. As Killens portrays in his 1954 novel *Youngblood*, many listeners and readers insist that the spirituals reflect more than religious servility. Listeners reason that the songs contain numerous coded messages about rebellion and escape. "Swing Low, Sweet Chariot," they argue, may have signaled the arrival of the Underground Railroad. "Steal Away to Jesus," it is speculated, may have similarly announced an escape attempt. It has been surmised that "God's Going to Trouble the Water" was employed by Harriet Tubman to caution runaways to travel by water as much as possible in order to confuse bloodhounds. Certainly, there are all kinds of movement in the songs—by way of chariots, trains, the Gospel ship, even foot—to suggest meaning beyond the concern of a soul's passage to heaven. Not all messages, however, were coded enough to fool slave masters. The singing of "Go Down, Moses," for example, was banned on many plantations.

Although literature by African Americans eventually matched, even surpassed, the boldness of "Go Down, Moses" or the even more radical "Didn't My Lord Deliver Daniel?," the first formal poetry by Africans—namely that of eighteenth-century poets Jupiter Hammon and Phillis Wheatley—lacked the Old Testament fervor that characterized many of the spirituals. We make this point not to follow the rather conventional assumption that Hammon and Wheatley were apolitical; they were not. We make it simply to acknowledge that the constraints surrounding a Black poet being published at that time were such that a certain subtlety, what may even be termed a softer, New Testament sensibility, was required in order for Black poets to be sponsored.

Hammon wrote the first poem published by a Black writer in America, "An Evening Thought: Salvation by Christ, with Penetential Cries" (1760). Although contemporary readers may balk at Hammon's preoccupation with Christian doctrine at the expense of social protest—his poetry contains numerous biblical citations but no blunt indictment of slavery—"Salvation by Christ" does represent the rejection of a racial hierarchy, arguing that redemption is both possible to all, regardless of race and condition of servitude, and possible only through Christ. While certainly not a forceful decree, it was perhaps the strongest entry into public discourse that an enslaved poet, who needed the permission of his master to publish, could make. Thus Hammon, like the creators of the spirituals, can also be said to have worked in code, though within a more restricted and moderate range. He made seemingly benign statements to whites while aiming a subversive message to any potential Black audience.

Phillis Wheatley, the first Black to publish a volume of poetry, constructed similar, veiled verses. Of her poems, "On Being Brought from Africa to America," which is included in the historic *Poems on Various Subjects, Religious and Moral* (1773), is the most anthologized and perhaps the most representative. Wheatley's opening lines jar some contemporary readers, given the lines' suggestion that Africans were morally ignorant pagans who were mercifully enslaved in order to be exposed to Christianity. However, Wheatley does argue for racial equality—anyone, meaning all Blacks, can qualify for redemption—and highlights the hypocrisy of white Christians who supported slavery. Thus Wheatley's poems, and Wheatley's very presence itself as the author of those poems, were important developments. The bolder tone of her "Letter to Samson Occum" (1774) ought to be noted as well.

Among nineteenth-century African American writers, Harper made the most extensive and perhaps most creative use of biblical sources. Her previously mentioned "Moses" stands as a landmark not only because of its in-depth portrayal of the archetypal hero, but because, as Melba Joyce Boyd points out, it represents a blending of New Testament material with the basic story provided by Exodus. One effect of this is the formal aligning of Jesus with active social protest. In addition, Harper's "Moses" highlights the voices of Moses's Egyptian and Hebrew mothers, which makes her work, as Boyd informs us, significant in terms of the development of a feminist voice in African American poetry. Harper never specifically mentions race in her poem, but her Moses is clearly a self-sacrificing liberator on behalf of Blacks as well as women.

In the early decades of the twentieth century, James Weldon Johnson was the writer who perhaps made the most noteworthy use of the Scriptures. As mentioned previously, Johnson paid tribute to the creators of the spirituals in "O Black and Unknown Bards." He also authored *God's Trombones*, (1927), a volume of verse that stands as his major poetic achievement. Although an agnostic, Johnson greatly valued the intellect and artistry of the "old-time Negro preacher." He thought that Christianity, which he referred to as a "narcotic doctrine," could promote passivity; nonetheless, he recognized the crucial role that Black folk preachers played in giving inspiration, strength, and hope to an oppressed people. Johnson specifically sought to render poetically the "stereotyped sermon," as he termed it, "which had no definite subject, and which was quite generally preached; it began with the Creation, went on to the fall of man, rambled through the trials and tribulations of the Hebrew Children, came down to the redemption by Christ, and ended with the Judgment Day and a warning and an exhortation to sinners." Johnson adds that "this was the framework of a sermon that allowed the individual preacher the widest latitude that could be desired for all his arts and powers." Accordingly, *God's Trombones* opens with a preliminary prayer in verse followed by seven sermons, "The Creation," "The Prodigal Son," "Go Down Death," "Noah Built the Ark," "The Crucifixion," "Let My People Go," and "The Judgment Day." *God's Trombones* remains among the most anthologized and performed African American poetry.

Since the late 1960s (although not a phenomenon exclusive to this era), the spirituals and accompanying biblical stories have received alternately hostile and sympathetic treatment by African American writers. No example of the former sentiment stands out more than Amiri Baraka's "When We'll Worship Jesus" (1972). Carolyn Rodgers, on the other hand, is dubious but not as uncompromising as Baraka in her 1969 "Jesus Was Crucified, or It Must Be Deep" and "It Is Deep" (1969). Rodgers, like Johnson before her, recognizes and celebrates the source of strength the Bible has represented for many African Americans. She realizes that a modern, revolutionary vision, whatever shape it ultimately may take, is possible only because of the contributions of everyday Christians like the mother in her poems.

Charlie Braxton goes further. Rather than dismissing Jesus as a pacifist, he creates an Old Testament-style figure in his poem, "Apocalypse" (1990), to whom perhaps even Baraka could pay homage. And the "wading in the water" that Nicole Breedlove espouses in her poem, "The New Miz Praise De Lawd" (1990), is a direct and explicit expression of activism linked to the spirituals.

Popular culture, of course, has also reflected the spirituals; the spirituals are indeed popular culture. We include lyrics by the likes of Lauryn Hill, Curtis Mayfield, and James Brown to illustrate the connection between these verbal forms and the spirituals, a link that may not always be acknowledged.

Further Reading

Boyd, Melba Joyce. *Discarded Legacy: Politics and Poetics in the Life of Francis E. W. Harper, 1825–1911.* Detroit: Wayne State UP, 1994.

Cone, James H. *The Spirituals and the Blues: An Interpretation.* New York: Seabury Press, 1972.

Dixon, Christa K. *Negro Spirituals: From Bible to Folksong.* Philadelphia: Fortress Press, 1976.

Du Bois, W. E. B. *The Souls of Black Folk: Essays and Sketches.* Chicago: A. C. McClurg & Co., 1903.

Epstein, Dena J. Polachek. *Sinful Tunes and Spirituals: Black Folk Music to the Civil War.* Urbana: University of Illinois Press, 1977.

Jones, Arthur C. *Wade in the Water: The Wisdom of the Spirituals.* Maryknoll, N.Y.: Orbis Books, 1993.

Levine, Lawrence W. *Black Culture and Black Consciousness: Afro-American Folk Thought from Slavery to Freedom.* Oxford: Oxford UP, 1978.

Lovell, John, Jr. *Black Song: The Forge and the Flame.* New York: Macmillan, 1972.

Newman, Richard. *Go Down Moses: A Celebration of the African-American Spiritual.* New York: Clarkson Potter, 1998.

Roberts, John W. *From Trickster to Badman: The Black Folk Hero in Slavery and Freedom.* Philadelphia: University of Pennsylvania Press, 1989.

Anonymous

God's Going to Trouble the Water

Wade in the water, children,
Wade in the water, children,
Wade in the water, children,
God's going to trouble the water.
5 See that host all dressed in white,
The leader looks like the Israelite;
See that band all dressed in red,
Looks like the band that Moses led.
Wade in the water, children,
10 Wade in the water, children,
Wade in the water, children,
God's going to trouble the water.

Didn't My Lord Deliver Daniel

Sung in Unison.

Did-n't   my Lord   de‑liv‑er   Dan‑iel,   D'liver

Dan - iel, d'liver Dan - iel, Did-n't my Lord de - liv - er

1ST VERSE.

Dan - iel, And why not a ev - e - ry man? He de -

liv - er'd Dan-iel, from the li - on's den, Jo-nah from the

bel- ly of the whale, And the He-brew children from the

fie - ry fur-nace, And why not ev - e - ry man?

Did - n't my Lord de - liv - er Dan - iel. D'liver

Dan - iel, d'liver Dan-iel, Did- n't my Lord de - liv - er

Dan - iel, And why not a ev - e - ry man?

2D Verse.

The moon run down in a purple-stream, The sun for-bear to

D.C. "Didn't my Lord."

shine, And ev-e-ry star dis-ap-pear, King Jesus shall be mine.

3D Verse.

The wind blows East, and the wind blows West, It

blows like the judg-ment day, And ev-ery poor soul that

D.C. "Didn't my Lord."

nev-er did pray, 'll be glad to pray that day.

4TH Verse.

I set my foot on the Gos-pel ship, And the

ship it be-gin to sail, It land-ed me o-ver on

D.C. "Didn't my Lord."

Ca-naan's shore, And I'll nev-er come back a-ny more.

Swing Low, Sweet Chariot

Swing low, sweet char-i-ot, Com-ing for to car-ry me home,

Swing low, sweet char-i-ot, Com-ing for to car-ry me home.

FINE.

1. I looked o - ver Jor - dan, and what did I see,
2. If you get there be - fore I do,
3. The bright - est day that ev - er I saw,
4. I'm some - times up and some - times down,

Com-ing for to car - ry me home? A band of an - gels
Com-ing for to car - ry me home, Tell all my friends I'm
Com-ing for to car - ry me home, When Je - sus wash'd my
Com-ing for to car - ry me home, But still my soul feels

D.C.

com-ing af - ter me, Com-ing for to car - ry me home.
com - ing too, Com-ing for to car - ry me home.
sins a - way, Com-ing for to car - ry me home.
heaven - ly bound, Com-ing for to car - ry me home.

Steal Away

Steal a-way, steal a-way, steal a-way to Je-sus!

Steal a-way, steal a-way, home, I hain't got long to stay here.

1. My Lord calls me, He calls me by the thunder; The
2. Green trees are bending, Poor sin-ners stand trembling; The,&c

trumpet sounds it in my soul: I hain't got long to stay here.

My Lord calls me,
Tombstones are bursting,
He calls me by the lightning;
Poor sinners are trembling;
The trumpet sounds it in my soul:
The trumpet sounds it in my soul:
I hain't got long to stay here.
I hain't got long to stay here.

Chorus: Steal away . . .

Chorus: Steal away . . .

Jupiter Hammon

(1711–1806)

Jupiter Hammon published the first poem in the African American literary tradition. His "An Evening Thought: Salvation by Christ, with Penetential Cries," a poem commemorating the birth of Jesus Christ, appeared on December 25, 1760. Born on October 17, 1711, on the Lloyd plantation in Oyster Bay, Long Island, Hammon worked as a clerk for his owners. Also a preacher, he authored a series of religious poems and essays. Hammon's work may seem too passive for some contemporary readers, but it should be remembered that, as a slave, he wrote under constraints that amounted to censorship. Nonetheless, there is an undertone in his work that reflects criticism of the institution of slavery and expresses a desire for freedom.

An Evening Thought: Salvation by Christ, with Penetential Cries

Salvation comes by Jesus Christ alone,
    The only Son of God;
Redemption now to every one,
    That love his holy Word.
5 Dear Jesus we would fly to Thee,
    And leave off every Sin.

Thy tender Mercy well agree;
    Salvation from our King.
Salvation comes now from the Lord,
10   Our victorious King;
His holy Name be well ador'd,
    Salvation surely bring.
Dear Jesus give thy Spirit now,
    Thy Grace to every Nation,
15 That han't the Lord to whom we bow,
    The Author of Salvation.
Dear Jesus unto Thee we cry,
    Give us the Preparation;
Turn not away thy tender Eye;
20   We seek thy true Salvation.
Salvation comes from God we know,
    The true and only one;
It's well agreed and certain true,
    He gave his only Son.
25 Lord hear our penetential Cry:
    Salvation from above;
It is the Lord that doth supply,
    With his Redeeming Love.
Dear Jesus by thy precious Blood,
30   The World Redemption have:
Salvation now comes from the Lord,
    He being thy captive slave.
Dear Jesus let the Nations cry,
    And all the People say,
35 Salvation comes from Christ on high,
    Haste on Tribunal Day.
We cry as Sinners to the Lord,
    Salvation to obtain;
It is firmly fixt his holy Word,
40   *Ye shall not cry in vain.*
Dear Jesus unto thee we cry,
    And make our Lamentation:
O let our Prayers ascend on high;
    We felt thy Salvation.
45 Lord turn our dark benighted Souls;
    Give us a true Motion,
And let the Hearts of all the World,

Make Christ their Salvation.
Ten Thousand Angels cry to Thee,
50   Yea louder than the Ocean.
Thou art the Lord, we plainly see;
Thou art the true Salvation.
Now is the Day, excepted Time;
The Day of Salvation;
55   Increase your Faith, do not repine:
Awake ye every Nation.
Lord unto whom now shall we go,
Or seek a safe Abode;
Thou hast the Word Salvation too
60   The only son of God.
Ho! every one that hunger hath,
Or pineth after me,
Salvation be thy leading Staff,
To set the Sinner free.
65   Dear Jesus unto Thee we fly;
Depart, depart from Sin,
Salvation doth at length supply,
The Glory of our King.

Phillis Wheatley

(1753?–1784)

Because she was the first African in America to publish a book of poetry, receive critical acclaim, and dramatically link literary prowess to the African, Phillis Wheatley is often regarded as the mother of African American literature. Abducted from West Africa as a small child, Wheatley was sold on the auction block in Boston to John and Susannah Wheatley in 1761. Although trained primarily to perform domestic labor, she also became literate and fairly well educated, largely through the efforts of Mary Wheatley, her owners' daughter. Taking a particular interest in the poetry of John Milton and Alexander Pope, Wheatley began publishing single poems in 1767, while still an adolescent. Her collection of verse, Poems on Various Subjects, Religious and Moral, *was first published in England in 1773. Although the book was a success, the American edition did not appear until 1787, three years after her death, because of the refusal by many to accept and promote the idea that an African could be an accomplished poet in the English*

*language, despite the fact that a group of prominent Bostonians pro-
vided written affirmation, included in the book, that Wheatley was the
author. Emanicipated in early adulthood, Wheatley married John
Peters and bore three children, all of whom died as youth. Wheatley's
marriage eventually disintegrated, and she died in poverty in 1784. As
is the case with the work of Hammon, her poetry is sometimes viewed
as being too submissive, although her voice is pretty clear on behalf of
freedom and social equality. Her "Letter to Samson Occum," condemning slavery, was published in a dozen New England newspapers.*

On Being Brought from Africa to America

'TWAS mercy brought me from my *Pagan* land,
Taught my benighted foul to understand
That there's a God, that there's a *Saviour* too;
Once I redemption neither fought nor knew.
5 Some view our fable race with scornful eye,
"Their colour is a diabolic die."
Remember, *Christians*, *Negros*, black as *Cain*,
May be refin'd, and join th' angelic train.

Letter to Samson Occom

Reverend and Honoured Sir [Samson Occom],
I have this Day received your obliging kind Epistle, and am greatly
satisfied with your Reasons respecting the Negroes, and think highly reasonable what you offer in Vindication of their natural Rights: Those that
invade them cannot be insensible that the divine Light is chasing away
the thick Darkness which broods over the Land of Africa; and the Chaos
which has reigned so long, is converting into beautiful Order, and reveals
more and more clearly, the glorious Dispensation of civil and religious
Liberty, which are so inseparably united, that there is little or no Enjoyment of one without the other: Otherwise, perhaps, the Israelites had

been less solicitous for their Freedom from Egyptian Slavery; do not say they would have been contented without it, by no Means, for in every human Breast, God has implanted a Principle, which we call Love of Freedom; it is impatient of Oppression, and pants for Deliverance; and by the Leave of our Modern Egyptians I will assert, that the same Principle lives in us. God grant Deliverance in his own way and Time, and get him honor upon all those whose Avarice impels them to countenance and help forward the Calamities of their Fellow Creatures. This I desire not for their Hurt, but to convince them of the strange Absurdity of their Conduct whose Words and Actions are so diametrically opposite. How well the Cry for Liberty, and the reverse Disposition for the Exercise of oppressive Power over others agree,—I humbly think it does not require the Penetration of a Philosopher to determine.

[February 11, 1774]

Anonymous

Go Down, Moses

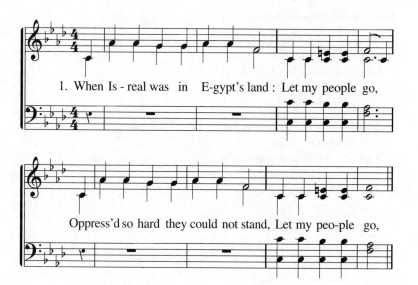

1. When Is - real was in E-gypt's land : Let my people go,

Oppress'd so hard they could not stand, Let my peo-ple go,

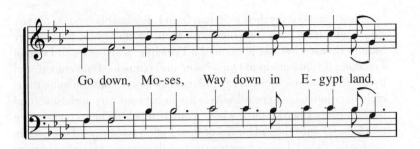

Go down, Mo-ses, Way down in E - gypt land,

Tell ole Pha - roh, Let my peo - ple go.

Thus saith the Lord, bold Moses said,
   Let my people go;
If not I'll smite your first-born dead,
   Let my people go.
5   Go down, Moses . . .

No more shall they in bondage toil,
   Let my people go;
Let them come out with Egypt's spoil,
   Let my people go.
10   Go down, Moses . . .

When Israel out of Egypt came,
   Let my people go;
And left the proud oppressive land,
   Let my people go.
15   Go down, Moses . . .

O, 'twas a dark and dismal night,
   Let my people go;
When Moses led the Israelites,
   Let my people go.
20   Go down, Moses . . .

'Twas good old Moses and Aaron, too,
   Let my people go;
'Twas they that led the armies through,
   Let my people go.
25   Go down, Moses . . .

The Lord told Moses what to do,
   Let my people go;
To lead the children of Israel through,
   Let my people go.
30   Go down, Moses . . .

O come along, Moses, you'll not get lost,
   Let my people go;
Stretch out your rod and come across,
   Let my people go.
35   Go down, Moses . . .

As Israel stood by the waterside,
   Let my people go;
At the command of God it did divide,
   Let my people go.
40   Go down, Moses . . .

When they had reached the other shore,
   Let my people go;
They sang a song of triumph o'er,
   Let my people go.
45   Go down, Moses . . .

Pharaoh said he would go across,
   Let my people go;
But Pharaoh and his host were lost,
   Let my people go.
50   Go down, Moses . . .

O, Moses, the cloud shall cleave the way,
   Let my people go;
A fire by night, a shade by day,
   Let my people go.
55   Go down, Moses . . .

You'll not get lost in the wilderness,
   Let my people go;
With a lighted candle in your breast,

Let my people go.
60   Go down, Moses . . .

Jordan shall stand up, like a wall,
    Let my people go;
And the walls of Jericho shall fall,
    Let my people go.
65   Go down, Moses . . .

Your foes shall not before you stand,
    Let my people go;
And you'll possess fair Canaan's land,
    Let my people go.
70   Go down, Moses . . .

'Twas just about in harvest time,
    Let my people go;
When Joshua led his host divine,
    Let my people go.
75   Go down, Moses . . .

O let us all from bondage flee,
    Let my people go;
And let us all in Christ be free,
    Let my people go.
80   Go down, Moses . . .

We need not always weep and moan,
    Let my people go;
And wear these slavery chains forlorn,
    Let my people go.
85   Go down, Moses . . .

This world's a wilderness of woe,
    Let my people go;
O, let us on to Canaan go,
    Let my people go.
90   Go down, Moses . . .

What a beautiful morning that will be,
    Let my people go;
When time breaks up in eternity,
    Let my people go.
95   Go down, Moses . . .

O brethren, brethren, you'd better be engaged,
   Let my people go;
For the Devil he's out on a big rampage,
   Let my people go.
100   Go down, Moses . . .

The Devil he thought he had me fast,
   Let my people go;
But I thought I'd break his chains at last,
   Let my people go.
105   Go down, Moses . . .

O take your shoes from off your feet,
   Let my people go;
And walk into the golden street,
   Let my people go.
110   Go down, Moses . . .

I'll tell you what I like the best,
   Let my people go;
It is the shouting Methodist,
   Let my people go.
115   Go down, Moses . . .

I do believe without a doubt,
   Let my people go;
That a Christian has the right to shout,
   Let my people go.
120   Go down, Moses . . .

Frances E. W. Harper
(1825–1911)

*Although Maryland was a slave state during the antebellum period,
Frances Ellen Watkins Harper, who emerged as one of the most distinguished African Africans of the nineteenth century, was born to free parents in Baltimore on September 24, 1825. As a young woman, she
relocated to Columbus, Ohio, where she taught school until further travels and observations led her to embark upon a career as a social
activist. Her career gained great momentum between 1854 and 1865,
the period during which she worked for the Maine Antislavery Society.
She frequently received accolades from Frederick Douglass and William*

Lloyd Garrison. *A compelling orator, Harper became one of the most visible spokespersons in the country on behalf of the abolitionist, women's suffrage, and temperance movements. A prolific author, perhaps the best-known African American creative writer of the nineteenth century, her works include the poetry volumes* Poems on Miscellaneous Subjects *(1854),* Moses: A Story of the Nile *(1869),* Poems *(1871),* Sketches of Southern Life *(1872), and* Atlanta Offering: Poems *(1895). Her novels include* Trial and Triumph *(1888–89) and her most well-known work of fiction,* Iola LeRoy; or, Shadows Uplifted *(1892).*

Moses: A Story of the Nile

THE PARTING
CHAPTER I

Moses

Kind and gracious princess, more than friend,
I've come to thank thee for thy goodness,
And to breathe into thy generous ears
My last and sad farewell. I go to join
5 The fortunes of my race, and to put aside
All other bright advantages, save
The approval of my conscience and the meed
Of rightly doing.

Princess

What means, my son, this strange election?
10 What wild chimera floats across thy mind?
What sudden impulse moves thy soul? Thou who
Hast only trod the court of kings, why seek
Instead the paths of labor? Thou, whose limbs
Have known no other grab than that which well
15 Befits our kingly state, why rather choose
The badge of servitude and toil?

Moses

Let me tell thee, gracious princess; 'tis no
Sudden freak nor impulse wild that moves my mind.

I feel an earnest purpose binding all
20 My soul until a strong resolve, which bids
Me put aside all other ends and aims,
Until the hour shall come when God—the God
Our fathers loved and worshipped—shall break our chains,
And lead our willing feet to freedom.

Princess

25 Listen to me, Moses: thou art young,
And the warm blood of youth flushes thy veins
Like generous wine; thou wearest thy manhood
Like a crown; but what king e'er cast
His diadem in the dust, to be trampled
30 Down by every careless foot? Thou hast
Bright dreams and glowing hopes; could'st thou not live
Them out as well beneath the radiance
Of our throne as in the shadow of those
Bondage-darkened huts?

Moses

35 Within those darkened huts my mother plies her tasks,
My father bends to unrequited toil;
And bitter tears moisten the bread my brethren eat.
And when I gaze upon their cruel wrongs
The very purple on my limbs seems drenched
40 With blood, the warm blood of my own kindred race;
And then thy richest viands pall upon my taste,
And discord jars in every tone of song.
I cannot live in pleasure while they faint
In pain.

Princess

45 How like a dream the past floats back: it seems
But yesterday when I lay tossing upon
My couch of pain, a torpor creeping through
Each nerve, a fever coursing through my veins.
And there I lay, dreaming of lilies fair,
50 Of lotus flowers and past delights, and all
The bright, glad hopes, that give to early life

Its glow and flush; and thus day after day
Dragged its slow length along, until, one morn,
The breath of lilies, fainting on the air,
55 Floated into my room, and then I longed once more
To gaze upon the Nile, as on the face
Of a familiar friend, whose absence long
Had made a mournful void within the heart.
I summoned to my side my maids, and bade
60 Them place my sandals on my feet, and lead
Me to the Nile, where I might bathe my weary
Limbs within the cooling flood, and gather
Healing from the sacred stream.
I sought my favorite haunt, and, bathing, found
65 New tides of vigor coursing through my veins.
Refreshed, I sat me down to weave a crown of lotus leaves
And lilies fair, and while I sat in a sweet
Revery, dreaming of life and hope, I saw
A little wicker-basket hidden among
70 The flags and lilies of the Nile, and I called
My maidens and said, "Nillias and Osiris,
Bring me that little ark which floats beside
The stream." They ran and brought me a precious burden.
'Twas an ark with rushes and daubed
75 With slime, and in it lay a sleeping child;
His little hand amid his clustering curls,
And a bright flush upon his glowing cheek.
He wakened with a smile, and reached out his hand
To meet the welcome of the mother's kiss,
80 When strange faces met his gaze, and he drew back
With a grieved, wondering look, while disappointment
Shook the quivering lip that missed the mother's
Wonted kiss, and the babe lifted his voice and wept.
Then my heart yearned towards him, and I resolved
85 That I would brave my father's wrath and save
The child; but while I stood gazing upon
His wondrous beauty, I saw beside me
A Hebrew girl, her eyes bent on me
With an eager, questioning look, and drawing
90 Near, she timidly said, "Shall I call a nurse?"
I bade her go; she soon returned, and with her
Came a woman of the Hebrew race, whose

Sad, sweet, serious eyes seemed overflowing
With a strange and sudden joy. I placed the babe
95 Within her arms and said, "Nurse this child for me;"
And the babe nestled there like one at home,
While o'er the dimples of his face rippled
The brightest, sweetest smiles, and I was well
Content to leave him in her care; and well
100 Did she perform her part. When many days had
Passed she brought the child unto the palace;
And one morning, while I sat toying with
His curls and listening to the prattle of his
Untrained lips, my father, proud and stately,
105 Saw me bending o'er the child and said,
"Charmian, whose child is this? who of my lords
Calls himself father to this goodly child?
He surely must be a happy man."
                    Then I said, "Father, he is mine. He is a
110 Hebrew child that I have saved from death." He
Suddenly recoiled, as if an adder
Had stung him, and said, "Charmian, take that
Child hence. How darest thou bring a member
Of that mean and servile race within my doors?
115 Nay, rather let me send for Nechos, whose
Ready sword shall rid me of his hateful presence."
Then kneeling at his feet, and catching
Hold of his royal robes, I said, "Not so,
Oh! honored father, he is mine; I snatched
120 Him from the hungry jaws of death, and foiled
The greedy crocodile of his prey; he has
Eaten bread within thy palace walls, and thy
Salt lies upon his fresh young lips; he has
A claim upon thy mercy."
125   "Charmian," he said
"I have decreed that every man child of that
Hated race shall die. The oracles have said
The pyramids shall wane before their shadow.
And from them a star shall rise whose light shall
130 Spread over earth a baleful glow; and this is why
I root them from the land; their strength is weakness
To my throne. I shut them from the light lest they
Bring darkness to my kingdom. Now, Charmian,

Give me up the child, and let him die."
135 Then clasping the child closer to my heart,
I said, "The pathway to his life is through my own;
Around that life I throw my heart, a wall
Of living, loving clay." Dark as the thunder
Clouds of distant lands became my father's brow,
140 And his eyes flashed with the fierce lightnings
Of his wrath; but while I plead, with eager
Eyes upturned, I saw a sudden change come
Over him; his eyes beamed with unwanted
Tenderness, and he said, "Charmian, arise,
145 Thy prayer is granted; just then thy dead mother
Came to thine eyes, and the light of Asenath
Broke over thy face. Asenath was the light
Of my home; the star that faded out too
Suddenly from my dwelling, and left my life
150 To darkness, grief and pain, and for her sake,
Not thine, I'll spare the child." And thus I saved
Thee twice—once from the angry sword and once
From the devouring flood. Moses, thou art
Doubly mine; as such I claimed thee then, as such
155 I claim thee now. I've nursed no other child
Upon my knee, and pressed upon no other
Lips the sweetest kisses of my love, and now,
With rash and careless hand, thou dost thrust aside that love.
There was a painful silence, a silence
160 So hushed and still that you might have almost
Heard the hurried breathing of one and the quick
Throbbing of the other's heart: for Moses,
He was slow of speech, but she was eloquent
165 With words of tenderness and love, and had breathed
Her full heart into her lips; but there was
Firmness in the young man's choice, and he beat back
The opposition of her lips with the calm
Grandeur of his will, and again he essayed to speak.

Moses

170 Gracious lady, thou remembrest well
The Hebrew nurse to whom thou gavest thy foundling.
That woman was my mother; from her lips I

Learned the grand traditions of our race that float
With all their weird and solemn beauty, around
175 Our wrecked and blighted fortunes. How oft!
With kindling eye and glowing cheek, forgetful
Of the present pain, she would lead us through
The distant past: the past, hallowed by deeds
Of holy faith and lofty sacrifice.
180 How she would tell us of Abraham,
The father of our race, that he dwelt in Ur;
Of the Chaldees, and when the Chaldean king
Had called him to his sacrifice, that he
Had turned from his dumb idols to the living
185 God, and wandered out from kindred, home and race,
Led by his faith in God alone; and she would
Tell us,—(we were three,) my brother Aaron,
The Hebrew girl thou sentest to call a nurse,
And I, her last, her loved and precious child;
190 She would tell us that one day our father
Abraham heard a voice, bidding him offer
Up in sacrifice the only son of his
Beautiful and beloved Sarah; that the father's
Heart shrank not before the bitter test of faith,
195 But he resolved to give his son to God
As a burnt offering upon Moriah's mount;
That the uplifted knife glittered in the morning
Sun, when, sweeter than the music of a thousand
Harps, he heard a voice bidding him to stay his hand,
200 And spare the child; and how his faith, like gold
Tried in the fiercest fire, shone brighter through
Its fearful test. And then she would tell us
Of a promise, handed down from sire to son,
That God, the God our fathers loved and worshiped,
205 Would break our chains, and bring to us a great
Deliverance; that we should dwell in peace
Beneath our vines and palms, our flocks and herds
Increase, and joyful children crowd our streets;
And then she would lift her eyes unto the far
210 Off hills and tell us of the patriarchs
Of our line, who sleep in distant graves within
That promised land; and now I feel the hour
Draws near which brings deliverance to our race.

Princess

These are but the dreams of thy young fancy;
215 I cannot comprehend thy choice. I have heard
Of men who have waded through slaughter
To a throne; of proud ambitions, struggles
Fierce and wild for some imagined good; of men
Who have even cut in twain the crimson threads
220 That lay between them and a throne; but I
Never heard of men resigning ease for toil,
The splendor of a palace for the squalor
Of a hut, and casting down a diadem
To wear a servile badge.
225   Sadly she gazed
Upon the fair young face lit with its lofty
Faith and high resolves—the dark prophetic eyes
Which seemed to look beyond the present pain
Unto the future greatness of his race.
230 As she stood before him in the warm
Loveliness of her ripened womanhood,
Her languid eyes glowed with unwonted fire,
And the bright tropical blood sent its quick
Flushes o'er the olive of her cheek, on which
235 Still lay the lingering roses of her girlhood.
Grief, wonder, and surprise flickered like shadows
O'er her face as she stood slowly crushing
With unconscious hand the golden tassels
Of her crimson robe. She had known life only
240 By its brightness, and could not comprehend
The grandeur of the young man's choice; but she
Felt her admiration glow before the earnest
Faith that tore their lives apart and led him
To another destiny. She had hoped to see
245 The crown of Egypt on his brow, the sacred
Leopard skin adorn his shoulders, and his seat
The throne of the proud Pharaoh's; but now her
Dream had faded out and left a bitter pang
Of anguish in its stead. And thus they parted,
250 She to brood in silence o'er her pain, and he
To take his mission from the hands of God
And lead his captive race to freedom.

With silent lips but aching heart she bowed
Her queenly head and let him pass, and he
255 Went forth to share the fortune of his race,
Esteeming that as better far than pleasures
Bought by sin and gilded o'er with vice.
And he had chosen well, for on his brow,
God poured the chrism of a holy work.
260 And thus anointed he has stood a bright
Ensample through the changing centuries of time.

CHAPTER II

It was a great change from the splendor, light
And pleasure of a palace to the lowly huts
Of those who sighed because of cruel bondage.
265   As he passed
Into the outer courts of that proud palace,
He paused a moment just to gaze upon
The scenes 'mid which his early life had passed—
The pleasant haunts amid the fairest flowers,—
270 The fountains tossing on the air their silver spray—
The statues breathing music soft and low
To greet the first faint flushes of the morn,—
The obelisks that rose in lofty grandeur
From their stony beds—the sphynxes gaunt and grim,
275 With unsolved riddles on their lips—and all
The bright creation's painters art and sculptors
Skill had gathered in those regal halls, where mirth
And dance, and revelry, and song had chased
With careless feet the bright and fleeting hours.
280 He was leaving all; but no regrets came
Like a shadow o'er his mind, for he had felt
The quickening of a higher life, as if his
Soul had wings and he were conscious of their growth;
And yet there was a tender light in those
285 Dark eyes which looked their parting on the scenes
Of beauty, where his life had been a joyous
Dream enchanted with delight; but he trampled
On each vain regret as on a vanquished foe,
And went forth a strong man, girded with lofty

290 Purposes and earnest faith. He journeyed on
     Till palaces and domes and lofty fanes,
     And gorgeous temples faded from his sight,
     And the lowly homes of Goshen came in view.
     There he saw the women of his race kneading
295 Their tale of bricks; the sons of Abraham
     Crouching beneath their heavy burdens. He saw
     The increasing pallor on his sister's cheek,
     The deepening shadows on his mother's brow,
     The restless light that glowed in Aaron's eye,
300 As if a hidden fire were smouldering
     In his brain; and bending o'er his mother
     In a tender, loving way, he said, "Mother,
     I've come to share the fortunes of my race,—
     To dwell within these lowly huts,—to wear
305 The badge of servitude and toil, and eat
     The bitter bread of penury and pain."
     A sudden light beamed from his mother's eye,
     And she said, "How's this, my son? but yesterday
     Two Hebrews, journeying from On to Goshen,
310 Told us they had passed the temple of the Sun
     But dared not enter, only they had heard
     That it was a great day in On; that thou hadst
     Forsworn thy kindred, tribe and race; hadst bowed
     Thy knee to Egypt's vain and heathen worship:
315 Hadst denied the God of Abraham, of Isaac,
     And of Jacob, and from henceforth wouldst
     Be engrafted in Pharaoh's regal line,
     And be called the son of Pharaoh's daughter.
     When thy father Amram heard the cruel news
320 He bowed his head upon his staff and wept.
     But I had stronger faith than that. By faith
     I hid thee when the bloody hands of Pharaoh
     Were searching 'mid our quivering heart strings,
     Dooming our sons to death; by faith I wove
325 The rushes of thine ark and laid thee 'mid
     The flags and lilies of the Nile, and saw
     The answer to that faith when Pharaoh's daughter
     Placed thee in my arms, and bade me nurse the child
     For her: and by that faith sustained, I heard
330 As idle words the cruel news that stabbed

Thy father like a sword."
"The Hebrews did not hear aright; last week
There was a great day in On, from Esoan's gate
Unto the mighty sea; the princes, lords
335 And chamberlains of Egypt were assembled;
The temple of the sun was opened. Isis
And Osiris were unveiled before the people.
Apis and Orus were crowned with flowers;
Golden censers breathed their fragrance on the air;
340 The sacrifice was smoking on the altar;
The first fruits of the Nile lay on the tables
Of the sun; the music rose in lofty swells,
Then sank in cadences so soft and low
Till all the air grew tremulous with rapture.
345 The priests of On were there, with sacred palms
Within their hands and lotus leaves upon their
Brows; Pharaoh and his daughter sat waiting
In their regal chairs; all were ready to hear
Me bind my soul to Egypt, and to swear
350 Allegiance to her gods. The priests of On
Drew near to lay their hands upon my head
And bid me swear, "Now, by Osiris, judge
Of all the dead, and Isis, mother of us
All," that henceforth I'd forswear my kindred,
355 Tribe and race; would have no other gods
Than those of Egypt; would be engrafted
Into Pharaoh's royal line, and be called
The son of Pharaoh's daughter. Then, mother
Dear, I lived the past again. Again I sat
360 Beside thee, my lips apart with childish
Wonder, my eyes uplifted to thy
Glowing face, and my young soul gathering
Inspiration from thy words. Again I heard
Thee tell the grand traditions of our race,
365 The blessed hopes and glorious promises
That weave their golden threads among the sombre
Tissues of our lives, and shimmer still amid
The gloom and shadows of our lot. Again
I heard thee tell of Abraham, with his constant
370 Faith and earnest trust in God, unto whom
The promise came that in his seed should all

The nations of the earth be blessed. Of Isaac
Blessing with disappointed lips his first born son,
From whom the birthright had departed. Of Jacob,
375 With his warm affections and his devious ways,
Flying before the wrath of Esau; how he
Slumbered in the wild, and saw amid his dreams
A ladder reaching to the sky, on which God's
Angels did descend, and waking with a solemn
380 Awe o'ershadowing all, his soul exclaimed, "How
Dreadful is this place. Lo! God is here, and I
Knew it not." Of Joseph, once a mighty prince
Within this land, who shrank in holy horror
From the soft white hand that beckoned him to sin;
385 Whose heart, amid the pleasures, pomp and pride
Of Egypt, was ever faithful to his race,
And when his life was trembling on its frailest chord
He turned his dying eyes to Canaan, and made
His brethren swear that they would make his grave
390 Among the patriarchs of his line, because
Machpelah's cave, where Abraham bowed before
The sons of Heth, and bought a place to lay
His loved and cherished dead, was dearer to his
Dying heart than the proudest tomb amid
395 The princely dead of Egypt.
              Then, like the angels, mother dear, who met
Our father Jacob on his way, thy words
Came back as messengers of light to guide
My steps, and I refused to be called the son
400 Of Pharaoh's daughter. I saw the priests of On
Grow pale with fear, an ashen terror creeping
O'er the Princess' face, while Pharaoh's brow grew
Darker than the purple of his cloak. But I
Endured, as seeing him who hides his face
405 Behind the brightness of his glory.
And thus I left the pomp and pride of Egypt
To cast my lot upon the people of my race."

FLIGHT INTO MIDIAN
CHAPTER III

The love of Moses for his race soon found
A stern expression. Pharaoh was building

410 A pyramid; ambitious, cold and proud,
He scrupled not at means to gain his ends.
When he feared the growing power of Israel
He stained his hands in children's blood, and held
A carnival of death in Goshen; but now
415 He wished to hand his name and memory
Down unto the distant ages, and instead
Of lading that memory with the precious
Fragrance of the kindest deeds and words, he
Essayed to write it out in stone, as cold
420 And hard, and heartless as himself.
                                    And Israel was
The fated race to whom the cruel tasks
Were given. Day after day a cry of wrong
And anguish, some dark deed of woe and crime,
425 Came to the ear of Moses, and he said,
"These reports are ever harrowing my soul;
I will go unto the fields where Pharaoh's
Officers exact their labors, and see
If these things be so—if they smite the feeble
430 At their tasks, and goad the aged on to toils
Beyond their strength—if neither age nor sex
Is spared the cruel smiting of their rods."
And Moses went to see his brethren.
                                    'Twas eventide,
435 And the laborers were wending their way
Unto their lowly huts. 'Twas a sad sight,—
The young girls walked without the bounding steps
Of youth, with faces prematurely old,
As if the rosy hopes and sunny promises
440 Of life had never flushed their cheeks with girlish
Joy; and there were men whose faces seemed to say
We bear our lot in hopeless pain, we've bent unto
Our burdens until our shoulders fit them,
And as slaves we crouch beneath our servitude
445 And toil. But there were men whose souls were cast
In firmer moulds, men with dark secretive eyes,
Which seemed to say, to-day we bide our time,
And hide our wrath in every nerve, and only
Wait a fitting hour to strike the hands that press
450 Us down. Then came the officers of Pharaoh;
They trod as lords, their faces flushed with pride

And insolence, watching the laborers
Sadly wending their way from toil to rest.
And Moses' heart swelled with a mighty pain; sadly
455 Musing, he sought a path that led him
From the busy haunts of men. But even there
The cruel wrong trod in his footsteps; he heard
A heavy groan, then harsh and bitter words,
And, looking back, he saw an officer
460 Of Pharaoh smiting with rough and cruel hand
An aged man. Then Moses' wrath o'erflowed
His lips, and every nerve did tremble
With a sense of wrong, and bounding forth he
Cried unto the smiter, "Stay thy hand; seest thou
465 That aged man? His head is whiter than our
Desert sands; his limbs refuse to do thy
Bidding because the cruel tasks have drained
Away their strength." The Egyptian raised his eyes
With sudden wonder; who was this that dared dispute
470 His power? Only a Hebrew youth. His
Proud lip curved in scornful anger, and he
Waved a menace with his hand, saying, "Back
To the task base slave, nor dare resist the will
Of Pharaoh." Then Moses' wrath o'erleaped the bounds
475 Of prudence, and with a heavy blow he felled
The smiter to the earth, and Israel had
One tyrant less. Moses saw the mortal paleness
Chase the flushes from the Egyptian's face,
The whitening lips that breathed no more defiance
480 And the relaxing tension of the well knit limbs.
And when he knew that he was dead, he hid
Him in the sand and left him to his rest.
                              Another day Moses walked
Abroad, and saw two brethren striving
485 For mastery; and then his heart grew full
Of tender pity. They were brethren, sharers
Of a common wrong; should not their wrongs more
Closely bind their hearts, and union, not division,
Be their strength? And feeling thus, he said, "Ye
490 Are brethren, wherefore do ye strive together?"
But they threw back his words in angry tones
And asked if he had come to judge them, and would

Mete to them the fate of the Egyptians?
Then Moses knew the sand had failed to keep
495 His secret, that his life no more was safe
In Goshen, and he fled unto the deserts
Of Arabia and became a shepherd
For the priest of Midian.

Chapter IV

Men grow strong in action, but in solitude
500 Their thoughts are ripened. Like one who cuts away
The bridge on which he has walked in safety
To the other side, so Moses cut off all retreat
To Pharaoh's throne, and did choose the calling
Most hateful to an Egyptian; he became
505 A shepherd, and led his flocks and herds amid
The solitude and wilds of Midian, where he
Nursed in silent loneliness his earnest faith
In God and a constant love for kindred, tribe
And race. Years stole o'er him, but they took
510 No atom from his strength, nor laid one heavy weight
Upon his shoulders. The down upon his face
Had ripened to a heavy beard; the fire
That glowed within his youthful eye had deepened
To a calm and steady light, and yet his heart
515 Was just as faithful to his race as when he had
Stood in Pharaoh's courts and bade farewell
Unto his daughter.
There was a look of patient waiting on his face,
A calm, grand patience, like one who had lifted
520 Up his eyes to God and seen, with meekened face,
The wings of some great destiny o'ershadowing
All his life with strange and solemn glory.
But the hour came when he must pass from thought
To action.—when the hope of many years
525 Must reach its grand fruition, and Israel's
Great deliverance dawn. It happened thus:
One day, as Moses led his flocks, he saw
A fertile spot skirted by desert sands,—
A pleasant place for flocks and herds to nip
530 The tender grass and rest within its shady nooks;

And as he paused and turned, he saw a bush with fire
Aglow; from root to stem a lambent flame
Sent up its jest and sprays of purest light,
And yet the bush, with leaves uncrisped, uncurled,
535 Was just as green and fresh as if the breath
Of early spring were kissing every leaf.
Then Moses said, "I'll turn aside to see
This sight," and as he turned he heard a voice
Bidding him lay his sandals by, for Lo! he
540 Stood on holy ground. Then Moses bowed his head
Upon his staff and spread his mantle o'er
His face, lest he should see the dreadful majesty
Of God; and there, upon that lonely spot,
By Horeb's mount, his shrinking hands received
545 The burden of his God, which bade him go
To Egypt's guilty king, and bid him let
The oppressed go free.
                                 Commissioned thus
He gathered up his flocks and herds and sought
550 The tents of Jethro, and said "I pray thee
Let me go and see if yet my kindred live;"
And Jethro bade him go in peace, nor sought
To throw himself across the purpose of his soul.
Yet there was tender parting in that home;
555 There were moistened eyes, and quivering lips,
And lingering claspings of the parting hand, as Jethro
And his daughters stood within the light of that
Clear morn, and gave to Moses and his wife
And sons their holy wishes and their sad farewells.
560 For he had been a son and brother in that home
Since first with manly courtesy he had filled
The empty pails of Reuel's daughters, and found
A shelter 'neath his tent when flying from
The wrath of Pharaoh.
565   They journeyed on,
Moses, Zipporah and sons, she looking back
With tender love upon the home she had left,
With all its precious memories crowding round
Her heart, and he with eager eyes tracking
570 His path across the desert, longing once more
To see the long-lost faces of his distant home,

The loving eyes so wont to sun him with their
Welcome, and the aged hands that laid upon
His youthful head their parting blessing. They
575 Journeyed on till morning's flush and noonday
Splendor gilded into the softened, mellowed
Light of eve, and the purple mists were deep'ning
On the cliffs and hills, when Horeb, dual
Crowned, arose before him; and there he met
580 His brother Aaron, sent by God to be
His spokesman and to bear him company
To Pharaoh. Tender and joyous was their greeting.
They talked of home and friends until the lighter
Rapple of their thoughts in deeper channels flowed;
585 And then they talked of Israel's bondage,
And the great deliverance about to dawn
Upon the fortunes of their race; and Moses
Told him of the burning bush, and how the message
Of his God was trembling on his lips. And thus
590 They talked until the risen moon had veiled
The mount in soft and silvery light; and then
They rested until morn, and rising up, refreshed
From sleep, pursued their way until they reached
The land of Goshen, and gathered up the elders
595 Of their race, and told them of the message
Of their Father's God. Then eager lips caught up
The words of hope and passed the joyful news
Around, and all the people bowed their heads
And lifted up their hearts in thankfulness
600 To God.
                        That same day
Moses sought an audience with the king. He found
Him on his throne surrounded by the princes
Of his court, who bowed in lowly homage
605 At his feet. And Pharaoh heard with curving lip
And flushing cheek the message of the Hebrew's God
Then asked in cold and scornful tones, "Has
Israel a God, and if so where has he dwelt
For ages? As the highest priest of Egypt
610 I have prayed to Isis, and the Nile has
Overflowed her banks and filled the land
With plenty, but these poor slaves have cried unto

Their God, they crept in want and sorrow
To their graves. Surely, Mizraim's God is strong
615 And Israel's is weak; then wherefore should
I heed his voice, or at this bidding break
A single yoke?" Thus reasoned that proud king,
And turned a deafened ear unto the words
Of Moses and his brother, and yet he felt
620 Strangely awed before their presence, because
They stood as men who felt the grandeur
Of their mission, and thought not of themselves
But of their message.

CHAPTER V

On the next day Pharaoh called a council
625 Of his mighty men, and before them laid
The message of the brethren: then Amorphel,
Keeper of the palace and nearest lord
Unto the king, arose, and bending low
Before the throne, prayed leave to speak a word.
630 Amorphel was a crafty, treacherous man,
With oily lips well versed in flattery
And curtly speech, a supple reed ready
To bend before his royal master's lightest
Breath—Pharaoh's willing tool. He said
635 "Gracious king, thou has been too lenient
With these slaves; light as their burdens are, they
Fret and chafe beneath them. They are idle
And the blood runs riot in their veins. Now
If thou would'st have those people dwell in peace,
640 Increase, I pray thee, their tasks and add unto
Their burdens; if they faint beneath their added
Tasks, they will have less time to plot sedition
And revolt."

Then Rhadma, oldest lord in Pharaoh's court,
645 Arose. He was an aged man, whose white
And heavy beard hung low upon his breast,
Yet there was a hard cold glitter in his eye,
And on his face a proud and evil look.

He had been a servant to the former king,
650 And wore his signet ring upon his hand.
He said, "I know this Moses well. Fourscore
Years ago Princess Charmian found him
By the Nile and rescued him from death, and did
Choose him as her son, and had him versed in all
655 The mysteries and lore of Egypt. But blood
Will tell, and this base slave, with servile blood
Within his veins, would rather be a servant
Than a prince, and so, with rude and reckless hand,
He thrust aside the honors of our dear
660 Departed king. Pharaoh was justly wroth,
But for his daughter's sake he let the trespass
Pass. But one day this Moses slew an Egyptian
In his wrath, and then the king did seek his life;
But he fled, it is said, unto the deserts
665 Of Arabia, and became a shepherd for the priest
Of Midian. But now, instead of leading flocks
And herds, he aspires to lead his captive race
To freedom. These men mean mischief; sedition
And revolt are in their plans. Decree, I pray thee,
670 That these men shall gather their own straw
And yet their tale of bricks shall be the same."
And these words pleased Pharaoh well, and all his
Lords chimed in with one accord. And Pharaoh
Wrote the stern decree and sent it unto Goshen—
675 That the laborers should gather their own straw,
And yet they should not 'minish of their tale of bricks.
                    'Twas a sad day in Goshen;
The king's decree hung like a gloomy pall
Around their homes. The people fainted 'neath
680 Their added tasks, then cried unto the king,
That he would ease their burdens; but he hissed
A taunt into their ears and said, "Ye are
Idle, and your minds are filled with vain
And foolish thoughts; get you unto your tasks,
685 And ye shall not 'minish of your tale of bricks."
                    And they turned their eyes
Reproachfully to Moses and his brother,
And laid the cruel blame upon their shoulders.

'Tis an old story now, but then 'twas new
690 Unto the brethren,—how God's anointed ones
Must walk with bleeding feet the paths that turn
To lines of living light; how hands that bring
Salvation in their palms are pierced with cruel
Nails, and lips that quiver first with some great truth
695 Are steeped in bitterness and tears, and brows
Now bright beneath the aureola of God,
Have bent beneath the thorny crowns of earth.
                              There was no hope for Israel,
But they did not see the golden fringes
700 Of their coming morn; they only saw the cold,
Grey sky, and fainted 'neath the cheerless gloom.

Moses sought again the presence of the king:
And Pharaoh's brow grew dark with wrath,
And rising up in angry haste, he said
705 Defiantly, "If thy God be great, show
Us some sign or token of his power."
Then Moses threw his rod upon the floor,
And it trembled with a sign of life;
The dark wood glowed, then changed into a thing
710 Of glistening scales and golden rings, and green
And brown and purple stripes; a hissing, hateful
Thing, that glared its fiery eye, and darting forth
From Moses' side, lay coiled and panting
At the monarch's feet. With wonder open-eyed
715 The king gazed on the changed rod, then called
For his magicians—wily men, well versed
In sinful lore—and bade them do the same.
And they, leagued with the powers of night, did
Also change their rods to serpents; then Moses'
720 Serpent darted forth, and with a startling hiss
And angry gulp, he swallowed the living things
That coiled along his path. And thus did Moses
Show that Israel's God had greater power
Than those dark sons of night.
725   But not by this alone
Did God his mighty power reveal: He changed
Their waters; every fountain, well and pool
Was red with blood, and lips, all parched with thirst,

Shrank back in horror from the crimson draughts.
730 And then the worshiped Nile grew full of life:
Millions of frogs swarmed from the stream—they clogged
The pathway of the priests and filled the sacred
Fanes, and crowded into Pharaoh's bed, and hopped
Into his trays of bread, and slumbered in his
735 Ovens and his pans.

There came another plague, of loathsome vermin;
They were gray and creeping things, that made
Their very clothes alive with dark and sombre
Spots—things of loathsome in the land, they did
740 Suspend the service of the temple; for no priest
Dared to lift his hand to any god with one
Of those upon him. And then the sky grew
Dark, as if a cloud were passing o'er its
Changeless blue; a buzzing sound broke o'er
745 The city, and the land was swarmed with flies.
The Murrain laid their cattle low; the hail
Cut off the first fruits of the Nile; the locusts
With their hungry jaws, destroyed the later crops,
And left the ground as brown and bare as if a fire
750 Had scorched it through.
                         Then angry blains
And fiery boils did blur the flesh of man
And beast; and then for three long days, nor saffron
Tint, nor crimson flush, nor soft and silvery light
755 Divided day from morn, nor told the passage
Of the hours; men rose not from their seats, but sat
In silent awe. That lengthened night lay like a burden
On the air,—a darkness one might almost gather
In his hand, it was so gross and thick. Then came
760 The last dread plague—the death of the first born
                         'Twas midnight,
And a startling shriek rose from each palace,
Home and hut of Egypt, save the blood-besprinkled homes
Of Goshen; the midnight seemed to shiver with a sense
765 Of dread, as if the mystic angel's wing
Had chilled the very air with horror.
Death! Death! was everywhere—in every home
A corpse—in every heart a bitter woe.

There were anxious fingerings for the pulse
770 That ne'er would throb again, and eager listenings
For some sound of life—a hurrying to and fro—
Then burning kisses on the cold lips
Of the dead, bitter partings, sad farewells,
And mournful sobs and piercing shrieks,
775 And deep and heavy groans throughout the length
And breadth of Egypt. 'Twas the last dread plague,
But it had snapped in twain the chains on which
The rust of ages lay, and Israel was freed;
Not only freed, but thrust in eager haste
780 From the land. Trembling men stood by, and longed
To see them gather up their flocks and herds,
And household goods, and leave the land; because they felt
That death stood at their doors as long as Israel
Lingered there; and they went forth in haste,
785 To tread the paths of freedom.

CHAPTER VI

But Pharaoh was strangely blind, and turning
From his first-born and his dead, with Egypt's wail
Scarce still upon his ear, he asked which way had
Israel gone? They told him that they journeyed
790 Towards the mighty sea, and were encamped
Near Baalzephen.
Then Pharaoh said, "the wilderness will hem them in,
The mighty sea will roll its barriers in front,
And with my chariots and my warlike men
795 I'll bring them back, or mete them out their graves."
                    Then Pharaoh's officers arose
And gathered up the armies of the king
And made his chariots ready for pursuit
With proud escutcheons blazoned to the sun,
800 In his chariot of ivory, pearl and gold,
Pharaoh rolled out of Egypt; and with him
Rode his mighty men, their banners floating
On the breeze, their spears and armor glittering
In the morning light; and Israel saw,
805 With fainting hearts, their old oppressors on their
Track: then women wept in hopeless terror;

Children hid their faces in their mothers' robes,
And strong men bowed their head in agony and dread;
And then a bitter, angry murmur rose,—
810 "Were there no graves in Egypt, that thou hast
Brought us here to die?"
Then Moses lifted up his face, aglow
With earnest faith in God, and bade their fainting hearts
Be strong and they should his salvation see.
815 "Stand still," said Moses to the fearful throng
Whose hearts were fainting in the wild, "Stand still."
Ah, that was Moses' word, but higher and greater
Came God's watchword for the hour, and not for that
Alone, but all the coming hours of time
820 "Speak ye unto the people and bid them
Forward go; stretch thy hand across the waters
And smite them with thy rod." And Moses smote
The restless sea; the waves stood up in heaps,
Then lay as calm and still as lips that
825 Had tasted death. The secret-loving sea
Laid bare her coral caves and iris-tinted
Floor; that wall of flood which lined the people's
Way was God's own wondrous masonry;
The signal pillar sent to guide them through the wild
830 Moved its dark shadow till it fronted Egypt's
Camp, but hung in fiery splendor, a light
To Israel's path. Madly rushed the hosts
Of Pharaoh upon the people's track, when
The solemn truth broke on them—that God
835 For Israel fought. With cheeks in terror
Blenching, and eyes astart with fear, "Let
Us flee," they cried, "from Israel, for their God
Doth fight against us; he is battling on their side."
They had trusted in their chariots, but now
840 That hope was vain; God had loosened every
Axle and unfastened every wheel, and each
Face did gather blackness and each heart stood still
With fear, as the livid lightnings glittered
And the thunder roared and muttered on the air,
845 And they saw the dreadful ruin that shuddered
O'er their heads, for the waves began to tremble
And the wall of flood to bend. Then arose

A cry of terror, baffled hate and hopeless dread,
A gurgling sound of horror, as "the waves
850 Came madly dashing, wildly crashing, seeking
Out their place again," and the flower and pride
Of Egypt sank as lead within the sea
Till the waves threw back their corpses cold and stark
Upon the shore, and the song of Israel's
855 Triumph was the requiem of their foes.
Oh the grandeur of that triumph; up the cliffs
And down the valleys, o'er the dark and restless
Sea, rose the people's shout of triumph, going
Up in praise to God, and the very air
860 Seemed joyous for the choral song of millions
Throbbed upon its viewless wings.
Then another song of triumph rose in accents
Soft and clear; 'twas the voice of Moses' sister
Rising in the tide of song. The warm blood
865 Of her childhood seemed dancing in her veins;
The roses of her girlhood were flushing
On her cheek, and her eyes flashed out the splendor
Of long departed days, for time itself seemed
Pausing, and she lived the past again; again
870 The Nile flowed by her; she was watching by the stream,
A little ark of rushes where her baby brother lay;
The tender tide of rapture swept o'er her soul again
She had felt when Pharaoh's daughter had claimed
Him as her own, and her mother wept for joy
875 Above her rescued son. Then again she saw
His choosing "twixt Israel's pain and sorrow
And Egypt's pomp and pride." But now he stood
Their leader triumphant on that shore, and loud
She struck the cymbals as she led the Hebrew women
880 In music, dance and song, as they shouted out
Triumphs in sweet and glad refrains.

Paul Laurence Dunbar

(1872–1906)

*For biographical information about Dunbar, see page 62. "An Ante-Bellum
Sermon" was first published in 1895 and was included in the poet's first
professionally produced book,* Lyrics of Lowly Life *(1896).*

An Ante-Bellum Sermon

We is gathahed hyeah, my brothahs,
    In dis howlin' wildaness,
Fu' to speak some words of comfo't
    To each othah in distress.
5 An' we chooses fu' ouah subjic'
    Dis—we'll' splain it by an' by;
"An' de Lawd said, 'Moses, Moses,'
    An' de man said, 'Hyeah am I.'"

Now ole Pher'oh, down in Egypt,
10   Was de wuss man evah bo'n,
And he had de Hebrew chillun
    Down dah wukin' in his co'n;
'T well de Lawd got tiahed o' his foolin',
    An' sez he: "I'll let him know—
15 Look hyeah, Moses, go tell Pher'oh
    Fu' to let dem chillun go."

"An' ef he refuse to do it,
    I will make him rue de houah,
Fu' I'll empty down on Egypt
20   All de vials of my powah."
Yes, he did—an' Pher'oh's ahmy
    Was n't wuth a ha'f a dime;
Fu' de Lawd will he'p his chillun,
    You kin trust him evah time.

An' yo' enemies may 'sail you
    In de back an' in de front;
But de Lawd is all aroun' you,
    Fu' to ba' de battle's brunt.
Dey kin fo'ge yo' chains an' shackles
30   F'om de mountains to de sea;
But de Lawd will sen' some Moses
    Fu' to set his chillun free.

An' de lan' shall hyeah his thundah,
    Lak a blas' f'om Gab'el's ho'n,
35 Fu' de Lawd of hosts is mighty
    When he girds his ahmor on.

Bu fu' feah some one mistakes me,
    I will pause right hyeah to say,
Dat I'm still a-preachin' ancient,
40   I ain't talkin' 'bout to-day.

But I tell you, fellah christuns,
    Things'll happen mighty strange;
Now, de Lawd done dis fu' Isrul,
    An' his ways don't nevah change,
45 An' de love he showed to Isrul
    Was n't all on Isrul spent;
Now don't run an' tell yo' mastahs
    Dat I's preachin' discontent.

'Cause I is n't; I'se a-judgin'
50   Bible people by deir ac's;
I'se a-givin' you de Scriptuah,
    I'se a-handin' you de fac's.
Cose ole Pher'oh b'lieved in slav'ry,
    But de Lawd he let him see,
55 Dat de people he put bref in,—
    Evah mothah's son was free.

An' dahs othahs thinks lak Pher'oh,
    But dey calls de Scriptuah liar,
Fu' de Bible says "a servant
60   Is a-worthy of his hire."
An' you cain't git roun' nor thoo dat,
    An' you cain't git ovah it,
Fu' whatevah place you git in,
    Dis hyeah Bible too'll fit.
65 So you see de Lawd's intention,
    Evah sence de worl' began,
Was dat His almighty freedom
    Should belong to evah man,
But I think it would be bettah,
70   Ef I'd pause agin to say,
Dat I'm talkin' 'bout ouah freedom
    In a Bibleistic way.

But de Moses is a-comin',
    An' he's comin', suah and fas'

75 We kin hyeah his feet a-trompin',
    We kin hyeah his trumpit blas'.
But I want to wa'n you people,
    Don't you git too brigity;
An' don't you git to braggin'
80   'Bout dese things, you wait an' see.

But when Moses wif his powah
    Comes an' sets us chillun free,
We will praise de gracious Mastah
    Dat has gin us liberty;
85 An' we'll shout ouah halleluyahs,
    On dat mighty reck'nin' day,
When we'se reco'nised ez citiz'—
    Huh uh! Chillun, let us pray!

Anonymous

God's Gonna Set This World on Fire

God's gonna set this world on fire,
One of these days;
God's gonna set this world on fire,
One of these days,
5 O, God's gonna set this world on fire,
One of these days.

I'm gonna drink from the healing cup,
One of these days;
I'm gonna drink from the healing cup,
10 I'm gonna drink from the healing cup,
I'm gonna drink from the healing cup,
One of these days.

Dry Bones

God called Ezekiel by His word,
"Go down and prophesy!"
"Yes, Lord!"
Ezekiel prophesied by the power of God,
5 Commanded the bones to rise.

They gonna walk around, dry bones,
They gonna walk around, with the dry bones,
They gonna walk around, dry bones,
Why don't you rise and hear the word of the Lord?
10 "Tell me, how did the bones get together with the long bones?
Prophesy?"

Ah, well, the toe bone connected with the foot bone,
The foot bone connected with the ankle bone,
The ankle bone connected with the leg bone,
The leg bone connected with the knee bone,
15 The knee bone connected with the thigh bone,
Rise and hear the word of the Lord!

James Weldon Johnson

(1871–1938)

Born in Jacksonville, Florida, on June 17, 1871, James Weldon Johnson, poet, novelist, critic, composer, diplomat, educator, and activist, is one of the foremost figures in the African American artistic and activist traditions. After graduating from Atlanta University in 1894, he assumed the post of principal at Stanton School, which he himself had attended as a boy in Jacksonville. He moved to New York City in 1902 to pursue a songwriting career with his younger brother Rosamond, with whom he had written, in 1900, "Lift Ev'ry Voice and Sing," a song also known as the Negro National Anthem. Johnson subsequently became a key force in the Harlem Renaissance and in the National Association for the Advancement of Colored People (NAACP), serving as the organization's first African American executive secretary. His books include the acclaimed novel Autobiography of an Ex-Coloured Man *(1912); the poetry collections* Fifty Years and Other Poems *(1917) and* God's Trombones:

Seven Negro Sermons in Verse *(1927); and the memoir* Along This Way *(1933). Johnson edited* The Book of Negro American Poetry *(1922),* The Book of Negro American Spirituals *(1925), and* The Second Book of Negro American Spirituals *(1926). In 1931, he became the Adam K. Spence Chair of Creative Literature at Fisk University. He died when a train struck his car while he was vacationing in Maine on June 26, 1938.*

O Black and Unknown Bards

O black and unknown bards of long ago,
How came your lips to touch the sacred fire?
How, in your darkness, did you come to know
The power and beauty of the minstrel's lyre?
5 Who first from midst his bonds lifted his eyes?
Who first from out the still watch, lone and long,
Feeling the ancient faith of prophets rise
Within his dark-kept soul, burst into song?

Heart of what slave poured out such melody
10 As "Steal away to Jesus"? On its strains
His spirit must have nightly floated free,
Though still about his hands he felt his chains.
Who heard great "Jordan roll"? Whose starward eye
Saw chariot "swing low"? And who was he
15 That breathed that comforting, melodic sigh,
"Nobody knows de trouble I see"?

What merely living clod, what captive thing,
Could up toward God through all its darkness grope,
And find within its deadened heart to sing
20 These songs of sorrow, love and faith, and hope?
How did it catch that subtle undertone,
That note in music heard not with the ears?
How sound the elusive reed so seldom blown,
Which stirs the soul or melts the heart to tears.
25 Not that great German master in his dream
Of harmonies that thundered amongst the stars
At the creation, ever heard a theme

Nobler than "Go down, Moses." Mark its bars
How like a mighty trumpet-call they stir
30 The blood. Such are the notes that men have sung
Going to valorous deeds; such tones there were
That helped make history when Time was young.

There is a wide, wide wonder in it all,
That from degraded rest and servile toil
35 The fiery spirit of the seer should call
These simple children of the sun and soil.
O black slave singers, gone, forgot, unfamed,
You—you alone, of all the long, long line
Of those who've sung untaught, unknown, unnamed,
40 Have stretched out upward, seeking the divine.

You sang not deeds of heroes or of kings;
No chant of bloody war, no exulting paean
Of arms-won triumphs; but your humble strings
You touched in chord with music empyrean.
45 You sang far better than you knew; the songs
That for your listeners' hungry hearts sufficed
Still live,—but more than this to you belongs:
You sang a race from wood and stone to Christ.

The Judgment Day

In that great day,
People, in that great day,
God's a-going to rain down fire.
God's a-going to sit in the middle of the air
5 To judge the quick and the dead.

Early one of these mornings,
God's a-going to call for Gabriel,
That tall, bright angel, Gabriel;
And God's a-going to say to him: Gabriel,
10 Blow your silver trumpet,
And wake the living nations.

And Gabriel's going to ask him: Lord,
How loud must I blow it?
And God's a-going to tell him: Gabriel,
15 Blow it calm and easy.
Then putting one foot on the mountain top,
And the other in the middle of the sea,
Gabriel's going to stand and blow his horn,
To wake the living nations.

20 Then God's a-going to say to him: Gabriel,
Once more blow your silver trumpet,
And wake the nations underground.

And Gabriel's going to ask him: Lord
How loud must I blow it?
25 And God's a-going to tell him: Gabriel,
Like seven peals of thunder.
Then the tall, bright angel, Gabriel,
Will put one foot on the battlements of heaven
And the other on the steps of hell,
30 And blow that silver trumpet
Till he shakes old hell's foundations.

And I feel Old Earth a-shuddering—
And I see the graves a-bursting—
And I hear a sound,
35 A blood-chilling sound.
What sound is that I hear?
It's the clicking together of the dry bones,
Bone to bone—the dry bones.
And I see coming out of the bursting graves,
40 And marching up from the valley of death,
The army of the dead.
And the living and the dead in the twinkling of an eye
Are caught up in the middle of the air,
Before God's judgment bar.

45 Oh-o-oh, sinner,
Where will you stand,
In that great day when God's a-going to rain down fire?
Oh, you gambling man—where will you stand?
You whore-mongering man—where will you stand?

50 Liars and backsliders—where will you stand,
In that great day when God's a-going to rain down fire?

And God will divide the sheep from the goats,
The one on the right, the other on the left.
And to them on the right God's a-going to say:
55 Enter into my kingdom.
And those who've come through great tribulations,
And washed their robes in the blood of the Lamb,
They will enter in—
Clothed in spotless white,
60 With starry crowns upon their heads,
And silver slippers on their feet,
And harps within their hands;—

And two by two they'll walk
Up and down the golden street,
65 Feasting on the milk and honey
Singing new songs of Zion,
Chattering with the angels
All around the Great White Throne.
And to them on the left God's a-going to say:
70 Depart from me into everlasting darkness,
Down into the bottomless pit.
And the wicked like lumps of lead will start to fall,
Headlong for seven days and nights they'll fall,
Plumb into the big, black, red-hot mouth of hell,
75 Belching out fire and brimstone.
And their cries like howling, yelping dogs,
Will go up with the fire and smoke from hell,
But God will stop his ears.

Too late, sinner! Too late!
80 Good-bye, sinner! Good-bye!
In hell, sinner! In hell!
Beyond the reach of the love of God.

And I hear a voice, crying, crying:
Time shall be no more!
85 Time shall be no more!
Time shall be no more!
And the sun will go out like a candle in the wind,

The moon will turn to dripping blood,
The stars will fall like cinders,
90 And the sea will burn like tar;
And the earth shall melt away and be dissolved,
And the sky will roll up like a scroll.
With a wave of his hand God will blot out time,
And start the wheel of eternity.

95 Sinner, oh, sinner,
Where will you stand
In that great day when God's a-going to rain down fire?

Robert Hayden

(1913–1980)

For biographical information about Hayden, see page 19. "Runagate Runagate" is part of a series of poems that Hayden wrote about African American history.

Runagate Runagate

I.

Runs falls rises stumbles on from darkness into darkness
and the darkness thicketed with shapes of terror
and the hunters pursuing and the hounds pursuing
and the night cold and the night long and the river
5 to cross and the jack-muh-lanterns beckoning beckoning
and blackness ahead and when shall I reach that somewhere
morning and keep on going and never turn back and keep on
going
        Runagate
            Runagate
10   Runagate
Many thousands rise and go
many thousands crossing over
                  O mythic North

O star-shaped yonder Bible city

15   Some go weeping and some rejoicing
      some in coffins and some in carriages
      some in silks and some in shackles
                Rise and go or fare you well
      No more auction block for me
20   no more driver's lash for me
      If you see my Pompey, 30 yrs of age,
      new breeches, plain stockings, negro shoes;
      if you see my Anna, likely young mulatto
      branded E on the right cheek, R on the left,
25   catch them if you can and notify subscriber.
      Catch them if you can, but it won't be easy.
      They'll dart underground when you try to catch them,
      plunge into quicksand, whirlpools, mazes,
      turn into scorpions when you try to catch them.

30   And before I'll be a slave
      I'll be buried in my grave
      North star and bonanza gold
      I'm bound for the freedom, freedom-bound
      and oh Susyanna don't you cry for me
35   Runagate
                      Runagate

II.

      Rises from their anguish and their power,
                      Harriet Tubman,
                      woman of earth, whipscarred,
40   a summoning, a shining
                      Mean to be free
      And this was the way of it, brethren, brethren,
      way we journeyed from Can't to Can.
      Moon so bright and no place to hide,
45   the cry up and the patterollers riding,
      hound dogs belling in bladed air.
      And fear starts a-murbling. Never make it,
      we'll never make it. *Hush that now,*
      and she's turned upon us, levelled pistol

50 glinting in the moonlight:
    Dead folks can't jaybird-talk, she says;
    you keep on going now or die, she says.
    Wanted Harriet Tubman alias The General
    alias Moses   Stealer of Slaves
55 In league with Garrison   Alcott   Emerson
    Garrett   Douglass   Thoreau   John Brown
    Armed and known to be Dangerous
    Wanted   Reward   Dead or Alive
        Tell me, Ezekiel, oh tell me do you see
60   mailed Jehovah coming to deliver me?
    Hoot-owl calling in the ghosted air,
    five times calling to the hants in the air,
    Shadow of a face in the scary leaves,
    shadow of a voice in the talking leaves.
65 Come ride-a my train

        Oh that train, ghost-story train
        through swamp and savanna movering movering,
        over trestles of dew, through caves of the wish,
        Midnight Special on a sabre track movering movering,
        first stop Mercy and the last Hallelujah.

    Come ride-a my train
    Mean mean mean to be free.

Lauryn Hill

(1975–)

*A singer, an MC, a songwriter, a producer, an actress, and the daugh-
ter of a high school English teacher (her mother), Lauryn Hill was
born on May 26, 1975, in New Jersey. She was a pivotal member of
the Fugees (originally known as Tranzlator Crew), and recorded with
them the albums* Blunted on Reality *(1993) and the highly successful*
The Score *(1996). She made her solo debut with* The Miseducation of
Lauryn Hill *(1998), a Grammy-winning album from which the following selection is drawn.*

Final Hour

I treat this like my thesis
Well-written topic, broken down into pieces
I introduce then produce
Words so profuse it's abuse how I juice up this beat
5 Like I'm deuce, two people both equal
Like I'm Gemini, rather Simeon
If I Jimmy on this lock I could pop it
You can't stop it, drop it
Your whole crew's microscopic
10 Like particles while I make international articles
And on the cover
Don't discuss the baby mother business
I been in this third LP you can't tell me, I witness
First handed I'm candid
15 You can't stand it, respect demanded
And get flown around the planet
Rock Hard like granite or steel
People feel Lauryn Hill from New-Ark to Israel
And this is real, so I keep makin' the street's ballads
20 While you lookin' for dressin' to go with your tossed salad
You can get the money!
You can get the power!
But keep your eyes on the Final Hour!
I'm about to change the focus from the richest to the brokest
25 I wrote this opus, to reverse the hypnosis
Whoever's closest to the line's gonna win it
You gonna fall trying to ball
While my team win the pennant
I'm about to begin it
30 For a minute, then run for senate
Make a slum lord be the tenant give his money to kids to spend it

And then amend it, every law that ever prevented
Our survival since our arrival

Documented in The Bible, like Moses and Aaron
35 Things gon' change, it's apparent
And all the transparent gonna

Be seen through, let God redeem you
Keep your deen true
You can get the green too
40 Watch out what you cling to
Observe how a queen do
And I remain calm reading the 73 Psalm
'Cause with all this going on I got the world in my palm
You can get the money!
45 You can get the power!
But keep your eyes on the Final Hour!
Now I be breaking bread sipping
Manichevitz wine
Pay no mind party like it's 1999
50 But when it comes down to ground beef like Palestine
Say your rhymes, let's see if that get you out your bind
Now I'm a get the mozzarella like a Rockerfeller
Still be in the church of Lalibela, singing hymns a cappella
Whether posed in Maribella in Couture
55 Or collecting residuals from off The Score
I'm making sure I'm with the 144
I've been here before this ain't a battle, this is war
Word to Boonie
I makes a lot like a Sunni
60 Get diplomatic immunity in every ghetto community
Had opportunity went from Hoodshock to Hood-chic
But it ain't what you cop, it's about what you keep
And even if there are leaks, you can't capsize this ship
Cause I baptize my lips every time I take a sip (Every time I take
    sips!)

Anonymous

Walk Together, Children

Walk together, children,
Don't you get weary,
Walk together, children,
Don't you get weary,

5 O, walk together children,
  Don't you get weary,
  There's a great camp meeting
  In the promised land.

  Going to mourn and never tire,
10 Mourn and never tire,
  Mourn and never tire.
  There's a great camp meeting
  In the Promised Land.

  O, sing together, children, children,
15 Don't you get weary,
  Sing together, children,
  Don't you get weary, children.

  Stand together, children, children,
  Don't you get weary,
20 There's a great camp meeting
  In that Promised Land;
  O, walk together,
  Keep on a-walking,
  There's a great camp meeting
  In that Promised Land.

John Oliver Killens

(1916–1987)

John Oliver Killens was born in Macon, Georgia, on January 14, 1916. He resided in Macon until he left to attend college, first at Edward Waters in Jacksonville and then at Morris Brown in Atlanta. He left school in 1936 to take a job as a messenger at the newly formed National Labor Relations Board in Washington, D.C., where he became the first African American employee. While on a military tour of duty in the South Pacific during World War II, Killens began writing obsessively. He moved from Washington to New York in 1948 and became the founding chairman of the Harlem Writers Guild in 1950. Known for writing that is expressly political and celebratory of African American culture, his books include the novels Youngblood *(1954),* And Then We Heard the Thunder *(1962),* 'Sippi *(1967),* The Cotillion *(1971), and the posthumously published* Great Black Russian: A Novel on the Life and Times of Alexander Pushkin *(1989). He also wrote the essay collection* Black Man's Burden

(1965). Among his professional appointments, Killens served on the faculties of Columbia, Fisk, and Howard universities; he last taught at Medgar Evers College of the City University of New York. The following selection consists of chapters 2–4 from Part Three of Youngblood, *which is titled "Jubilee," which is a word that connotes freedom or a free space. The novel is largely Rob Youngblood's coming-of-age story set against the backdrop of the segregated South during the first third of the twentieth century. The selection below details the reactions of Rob and his classmates to the fact they are being required to give a performance of the spirituals before whites on Jubilee Day.*

Youngblood

Chapter 2

1   Rob would stay after school and ask Mr. Myles about it. That's all there was to it. A long time had passed since Mama had beaten him down at the courthouse, and he was getting older and growing up and he understood what made Mama do it, and he pretended that everything was just as it used to be between him and his mother. He wanted to forget that day in Mr. Cross's courthouse forever and ever but he just couldn't do it.

2   A few days ago at recess time he had been standing on the school grounds daydreaming about Mama, when Biff Roberts and Skinny Johnson had come up to him.

3   "You and your Mr. Myles this and Mr. Myles that. He ain't any better than anybody else. Just as big a *sambo* as old man Mulberry used to be." Skinny Johnson leered at Rob, his eyes almost closed.

4   "You bet not be talking like that in front of the teacher's pet. He doesn't allow anybody to talk about Professor Myles from New York City," Biff said to Skinny.

5   Rob stood there looking from one of them to the other. It was a Monday in January and a chill in the air and the children chased each other all over the grounds to keep their bodies warm. Crying, yelling, laughing, fighting—

6   Biff said, "Your Professor so tough with the crackers, how come he gon be in charge of Jubilee Day?"

7   Rob felt an uneasiness all through his body. "You all bet not go around putting that lie out on Mr. Myles."

8   "If it's a lie how come Mr. Blake told my father when he was at the house for dinner yesterday?"

9   Rob's hands clenched unconsciously. "You all aren't telling nothing but a pop-eyed lie. They haven't had Jubilee since Mr. Myles been here."

10   "They sure gon have it this year. You don't have to take my word for it. You can read it yourself on next Sunday's Colored Page. It'll be right in there for everybody to see."

11   "Your *Pa* is a damn Uncle Tom. Mr. Myles isn't," Rob shouted at them and walked away from them. But they followed him all over the school grounds till he turned upon Biff in particular. "What you following me all over everywhere for? You want to start something? If you do, I'm ready for you." He balled up his fist and Biff and Skinny decided suddenly to leave him alone.

12   But he had carried it around with him all week since Monday, and he had taken it home with him and had dreamed about it, and it couldn't be true, but it *was* true, because he heard it everywhere. And now it was Thursday and he wasn't going to walk around in doubt any longer. He was going to stay after school and ask Mr. Myles.

13   The letting-out bell startled him, bringing him sharply back from his daydream world. He sat at his desk, watching absently, the children gathering up their books and filing out of the classroom. His eyes dwelled particularly on Ida Mae Raglin as she walked toward the door with the rest of the children.

14   After they had gone Mr. Myles came over to Robby and he sat on top of one of the desks. He smiled at Robby. "Well, Mr. Youngblood, what's on your mind?"

15   Robby looked up into the teacher's friendly face and away again. He cleared his throat in a nervous agitation.

16   "How's your family?" Mr. Myles asked him.

17   "Just fine, thank you." He wouldn't beat around the bush, he would just out-with-it and let it be done with, and besides he and Mr. Myles were friends, so he didn't have to hem and haw with the teacher.

18   "What's on your mind? Anything in particular?"

19   "Yes, sir." He was aware of the boy and girl on the other side of the room cleaning the blackboards. He lowered his voice. "I-I-I hear them say—They—They say they going to have that spiritual singing to-do for white folks again this year."

20   "Nothing's wrong with spirituals."

21   "I know ain't nothing—isn't anything wrong with them," Robby said heatedly. Mr. Myles had a way of looking at you as if what you

were saying were the most important thing in the world. He watched the words as they started out of your mouth.

22   "Well, what's the problem?" he said to Rob.

23   "It's alright to sing them," Rob argued, "but not for them white folks that turn out every year to poke fun at us. That's what I'm talking about. Spend all that time practicing and singing just for a bunch of rich white folks."

24   Mr. Myles still smiled but his voice had a little bit of irritation in it, unusual to Rob. "Well, there's nothing I can do about it. I wouldn't worry about it anyhow if I were you."

25   "You think it's alright?" Rob asked in bitter disappointment. "You think it's alright Uncle-Tomming for white folks?"

26   "I didn't say it was alright. I simply said there was nothing I could do about it. What do you want me to do?" He loved this boy like a son, more like a younger brother.

27   "I hear them say you going to be the one in charge." It was the first time he had ever had a real disagreement with Mr. Myles, and it put a funny feeling in his stomach and his body grew warm and outside Ida Mae was waiting for him and the great big boys probably picking at her—Maybe she was waiting.

28   "Well, what about it, if I am? If I didn't do it, another teacher would. What do you want me to do?" It seemed to Rob that even Mr. Myles's voice had changed and now it had a strange harshness in it.

29   "Anyhow," Rob argued, "let somebody else do it. Don't let it be you. Everybody around town'll sure be disappointed in you. They think that you one colored man in Cross County that wouldn't Uncle Tom for white folks don't care what."

30   "Negroes in town don't like Jubilee Day?" Mr. Myles asked Rob. Mr. Blake had told him that Negroes liked singing the spirituals for the white folks. "The trouble with you, Myles, you don't understand the psychology of the lower class southern Negro," Mr. Blake had told him.

31   "Shoot naw, Mr. Myles. And especially the students. That's the one thing we hated about Mr. Mulberry. You ought to see how them crackers look—grinning like they looking at monkeys in a circus."

32   He looked at Rob and he thought about Brooklyn, hundreds of miles away, and Hank Saunders dead, and he thought about Laurie Youngblood and Joe Youngblood and he looked again at the boy in front of him—a boy that was growing into the handsomest youngster in Cross County and big and serious-minded like an adult and still growing in all kinds of directions. Growing gradually and quickly away from his shyness.

33   "As long as we help the white make monkeys out of us, they gonna always do it. I don't understand you at all, Mr. Myles. You'd be the last person I would've thought—Look, it ain't nothing against the spirituals, it's the way the crackers make us use them—Don't you see what I mean?"

34   "Of course I do."

35   "Don't you be in charge of it anyhow, Mr. Myles. Too many people taking pattern after you."

36   "I'll see what I can do," he said vaguely, knowing fully well there was nothing he could do. He could refuse to have anything to do with it like Robby suggested and not come back next year. He could resign his teaching job and go back to Brooklyn where he came from—If he didn't do it, somebody else would—

37   The boy didn't wait another second. It was as if Mr. Myles had said—Take my word for it. There will be no Jubilee Day. Rob said, "Yes, sir. I'll be seeing you."

38   Richard Myles wanted to call him back and say that he wasn't sure what could be done, but he didn't say a word. He sat for awhile where Rob had left him, until the two children had finished cleaning up the room. When he left the schoolhouse he caught the bus into town. He walked across the wide square toward the post office. He still hadn't gotten used to Crossroads, Georgia, and he thought he never would. Everybody walked as if they were already beyond the Pearly Gates where the streets were paved with gold and flowing with honey and life was peaceful and wonderful and pretty, so what was the use of getting excited or being in a hurry, the colored and the white. The accent of the so-called educated South was soft and slow and easy and sweet and dripping with honey. "Colored and white get along just *fine*." The last word lingering soft and sweet like an unanswered question. And sometimes it seemed even to Richard that the relationship was smooth and peaceful and totally without friction or resentment from either side.

39   He came out of the post office and started back across the Square. He saw two crackers standing near the corner. He felt their hostile eyes heavily upon him. "New York City—" he heard one of them say contemptuously. Over in Pleasant Grove he always knew a secure kind of feeling of being at home and among his people. But the moment he came downtown to attend to any kind of business, he was back in that foreign country again. Because he sensed that beneath the surface of the complacency and the politeness and the peaceful relationship, there was a great big rattlesnake poised for the strike,

like a streak of lightning chained and ready. Beneath the surface of the How you Mr. Jamison and the Howdy Josephus, his sensitive ears could hear an almighty rumble like a storm making up in the midst of the quiet.

40   He caught the bus heading back to the colored section. It went up Jeff Davis Boulevard past the beautiful mansions where the rich white folks lived. It was a beautiful town if you just looked upon the outside beauty in the white folks section. He rode through the whiteness of Peckerwood Town. Crossroads, Georgia was the most tranquil city in all the world. On the outskirts of Pleasant Grove was where the colored folks lived that were a little better off than the other colored folks. Since he had been in Crossroads, they had even put pavement on Monroe Terrace. All the homes on the Terrace had electric lights and telephones and bathrooms with real bathtubs. The three colored doctors lived on this street and the two dentists and a couple of mail carriers and school teachers and a pullman porter and William Roberts lived in the middle of the block in a big brick two-story house with a built-in garage. William Roberts Sr. was Biff Roberts' father and the editor of the colored page of the *Daily Telegram.* When Richard Myles first came to town most of the colored people on this street told him all about how much progress was being made in the south and especially Crossroads. And all the intelligent Negro had to do was to prepare himself and make the best of it.

41   He got off the bus and walked to the end of the street where Reverend Ledbetter lived. He liked Reverend Ledbetter. He liked almost everybody who lived on the Terrace, but they made him nervous sometimes, the way they always made a point of exaggerating to him the progress that the Negroes were making in the south especially in Crossroads and the liberalism of the educated and well-to-do white folks. Every time he talked with any of them, they would pour it on thicker than ever, as if they had to justify to him their being born in the Southland and staying in the Southland. They embarrassed him. It was as if he brought their insecurity to the surface, aroused them from their tissue-paper smugness against their will. They made him feel like an outsider trying to get the inside dope and they trying to show him the bright side only.

42   He was seated in the Ledbetter living room now, and the personality of the pastor was everywhere in the modest room that was comfortable and livable with a serenity all its own. And books all over the place. The pastor came in.

43   "Well—well—well—My learned friend from the big city."

44   He reminded Richard somehow of his father. He was a small black man with tiny eyes, but they didn't have the nervousness that his father's possessed. They were always calm and self-assuring.

45   "How are you, Reverend Ledbetter?" Richard never understood why a man of the pastor's intelligence and drive was content to stay in a small town like Crossroads. He could have a big church in any big city.

46   They sat facing each other, looking each other over. Reverend Ledbetter smiled. "Well, what is it today? Getting more material for your book?"

47   "What book, Reverend Ledbetter?"

48   "I have tried to figure out why a brilliant young man like you would waste your time in a place like this, and I came to the conclusion that you must be collecting material for a book about *us*. If you are, you just wasting your time on Monroe Terrace. You need to spend some time over in The Quarters, and with the working people in Pleasant Grove, and also the young people you in touch with every day at school. They're the ones gon really change things with the help of the Good Lord. We folks up here on the Terrace, we're scared of our shadow." He looked at Richard's questioning face and laughed as if he were enjoying a private joke. "Yes—sir—ree"—

49   "But why—why? You would think—I mean the people on the Terrace have more education—"

50   "Why? Why? We're just scared—that's why. Scared we'll lose this little bit of security the white man handed down to us. We teach school in the white man's school system. We carry mail for the white man's post office. We take care of the colored folks in the white man's newspaper. We got a paved street. We got a nice home with right pretty furniture. We're business men. We're doctors. Sometimes I think we more scared of the Negroes over in the Quarters than we are of the white folks." He stood up nervously and at that moment painfully reminded Richard of his father, but he sat back down and a calm moved over him.

51   "Look—You know where Monroe Terrace is located? Our Street is two blocks long. It runs to the west smack into Peckerwood Town, but north of us is the rich white folks and south of us is the black folks. And here we are in the middle. And you know what it is to be in the middle." He laughed and he slapped his knee with his hands. "Yes—sir—ree—You don't know—"

52   "Yes," Richard said. "Yes—But you—"

53   "I'm the only feller on the street with any kind of independence. My support comes from the people south of the border. A Negro

preacher is in a better, more independent position to serve his people than any other colored professional man in the United States. Two powers we have to answer to, and that's our congregation and God Almighty, and ain't neither one of them white. I tell all the other preachers—I tell them all—they don't have to be scared of the white man—They don't owe him nothing—Not a thing—Everything they owe is to God and the black folks." He was getting excited and he realized he was getting excited. He smiled at Richard and lowered his voice again. "Well, you didn't come here to hear me preach a sermon. If you liked my preaching you would come to church more regular."

54   There was a brief silence before the young man cleared his throat. "I wanted to talk to you about the Negro spirituals and Jubilee Day."

55   "What about them?"

56   "The children don't like it. They don't like all that spiritual singing for the white man."

57   "There is nothing wrong with the Negro spirituals, son. They're some of the most beautiful songs ever conceived by man, and they weren't conceived for the pleasure of white folks, I can state you that."

58   "That's just the point," Richard said.

59   "Now I can understand the stylish people on this street being ashamed of the spirituals," the Reverend said. "Some of them shame of everything colored. Think everything we invent or anything we do is no-count. To let them tell it they don't like jazz—too high class for the blues, and ain't got nothing for the spirituals to do. But the young folks in the school they should be taught to be proud of the spirituals. And you—"

60   "We don't mind the spirituals, Reverend Ledbetter. We just don't like the use that is made of them on Jubilee Day. We want to sing spirituals when we want to sing them. Not for the pleasure of a bunch of white folks that think they're dealing with a bunch of monkeys." He could see the worried face of Rob Youngblood, hear his angry voice.

61   "Never mind what the white folks think, as long as we know what the spirituals mean, why should we always be worried about what the white man thinks?"

62   Richard looked down at the carpeted floor. Maybe he was whipping a dead horse. Maybe he and Rob Youngblood were wrong. "But—but—the colored folks would prefer that we forget all about Jubilee Night. It's the white folks—the Board of Education's demanding it. I've been to Mr. Blake, and he says it's something that was done every year before I came and the Board of Education say they're going

to start doing it again. No ifs, ands or buts. He says it's out of his hands and he can't see where it does any harm anyhow."

63   The little preacher went to his desk and he came back with a big book in his hand. "Here is a book, son. Here is a book. Next to the Bible it's my favorite book. Next to the Holy Bible." It was the *Life and Times of Frederick Douglass.*

64   "I have read this book," Reverend Ledbetter said. "Exactly nine times, through and through, from cover to cover. Exactly nine times, and I'll probably read it nine more times, the Good Lord willing that I live long enough. This is one of the greatest testimonies to the equality of man and the human spirit." He waved the big book in his right hand. "This is a monument to the God-given right of every man to be free." He stopped and laughed, "Reverend Ledbetter, what the devil has all this got to do with Jubilee Day?" he said to himself.

65   "I have read that book, sir," Richard Myles said. They sat for awhile, saying nothing. The preacher appeared to be lost in his thoughts, listening to something from another world.

66   "Frederick Douglass wasn't ashamed of the Negro spirituals," he finally said, "and he wasn't ashamed of the colored folks' religion, but he didn't give a hoot for the hypocrisy of the white man's religion."

67   "Nobody's ashamed of the spirituals, Reverend Ledbetter. The children don't object to the spirituals as such. They just want to sing them on their own terms."

68   Reverend Ledbetter sat there with the great book on his knees, rubbing it nervously with the palm of his hand. Suddenly he slapped his other hand on his other knee. "The children are right," he said aloud to himself. "The children are right."

69   Of course the children are right, Richard thought to himself.

70   The preacher jumped up as if something had bitten him, and again he reminded Richard sharply and painfully of his father in far-away Brooklyn. He sat back down. "We'll do what the children want us to do," Reverend Ledbetter said. "We'll have a Jubilee on our own terms. A real Jubilee. We can have a Jubilee Day these crackers round here will never forget. Make them wish they had never thought it up. Get the point? Ain't nothing Uncle-Tom about the Negro spirituals. They the fightinest songs ever known to man. We'll tell the people how they came into being. Fix a program around the history of the spirituals."

71   Richard stared at the preacher. The impact of the preacher's suggestion had him speechless for a moment.

72   Reverend Ledbetter continued. "You know how to do it, son. Tell them what 'Swing Low Street Chariot' really means. Tell them all about

that underground railroad, son. I'm glad they put you in charge. You're really the right man for the job." Reverend Ledbetter looked at his big pocket watch. "Excuse my manners, son. I just got to run down to the church for awhile. Got a real important engagement."

73 "A very good idea," Richard Myles said with a tremble in his voice. "An excellent idea."

74 He was roused by the preacher's melodious pulpit voice, which was a little different from his regular voice—richer, fuller, deeper. "Can't you hear them singing, son? Way back yonder—Can't you just hear them? My father and your grandfather?—Make you proud to be a black man. Great God Almighty! Just one verse:—

> *Green trees A-bending*
> *Poor sinner stands a-trembling*
> *The trumpet sounds within-a my soul*
> *I ain't got long to stay here*
> *Steal away*
> *Steal away*
> *Steal away to Je—sus*
> *Steal away*
> *Steal away home*
> *I ain't got long to stay here—*

75 "Steal Away To Jesus," he repeated. "Son, as far as the black man in slavery was concerned, wasn't no Jesus in Georgia, Jesus was in Heaven and Jesus was up above that Mason and Dixon line. Great-GodAlmighty. Jesus was freedom." He laughed at himself. "When is this here Jubilee business?"

76 "It's the last Friday night in February."

77 "Got plenty of time. Sorry I got to rush you. Come back to see me next week after you talk to yourself and get it clearer in your own mind."

78 "Yes, sir."

79 They shook hands and said good-night and started toward the door. Richard walked out into the early evening. The pastor called after him, "Don't talk to too many people about it outside of your own self. If you do, Marser Charlie get the news before daybreak."

80 He heard the preacher laughing as he walked down the steps, and at that moment he had a wonderful full-blown feeling about Negro preachers and Negro churches and black folks' religion and black folks everywhere no matter their color, and his people marching through the pages of history down through the years with Frederick Douglass

and Harriet Tubman and his people over in Pleasant Grove and out in the Quarters in their ugly shacks and in Joe Jesup's Barber Shop, his people in far away places like New York City where his father lived and where he came from, and even those on Monroe Terrace and and and he loved his people—and proud proud proud—

CHAPTER THREE

81   After he left Reverend Ledbetter's house, he didn't catch the bus home. He walked all the way through the early evening and the darkness falling fast, and a sharp chilly breeze blowing through the town. The boldness of the preacher's suggestion gradually sinking into his whole being, and the possibilities—the possibilities— But why hadn't he thought of it? He had thought only in terms of going through with the white folks' version of Jubilee Day; either that, or giving up his job. The answer had been there all of the time just out of reach. With all he had learned about religion keeping the people from thinking, Reverend Ledbetter was one of the boldest thinkers he had ever met.

82   The next evening, as he sat in his room, mulling it over in his mind, he wished for somebody to discuss it with. There were so many ifs, ands and buts about it. Maybe he would be just stirring up trouble between colored and white. He couldn't just sit alone and plan, because maybe the idea wasn't as good as it sounded, and other people might not think like the preacher.

83   He put on his topcoat. He would go to the Youngbloods, place the whole thing before them, and see what they thought. He gathered up the notes he had made. Marser Charlie wouldn't get any news from the Youngbloods—he hoped.

84   It was a dark cold night and they were seated by the fireplace when he got there, and he could tell they were surprised, but very glad to see him.

85   "Thought you weren't gon never get back to see us." Joe smiled at the teacher. "I declare I thought you had put us colored folks down."

86   "I keep so busy," Richard Myles said self-consciously. "I meant to come long before now, but I just kept putting it off. You know how it is." He could feel Robby's eyes heavily upon him.

87   "You know you always welcome," Mrs. Youngblood said.

88   Joe gave him a chair and Richard Myles sat with them, and he glanced at the boy and then at the girl, and Jenny Lee's face flushed

painfully for everyone to notice, and she tried to pull her dress further below her knees than it already was, and the young teacher smiled his own embarrassment.

89   Joe Youngblood took the poker and poked at the fire in the fireplace. "Kinda chilly out there tonight, ain't it?"

90   "Yes, indeed," Richard Myles answered. "It's colder than chilly."

91   "What you need this kind of weather is little old tarty every now and then to keep that old blood warm and carrying on." Joe smiled slyly. "Ain't got nothing like that in the house is we, Mrs. Youngblood? Got anything for snake bites around here?"

92   Rob laughed out loud, and the rest of them laughed.

93   "I don't believe we got that kind of medicine on the shelf this time," Laurie Lee said. "I reckon I can stir up a few cups of coffee though. That ought to help a little." She got up from her rocker.

94   "Don't bother, Mrs. Youngblood. Really, don't go to any trouble."

95   "Isn't any trouble, Mr. Myles. No trouble at all."

96   "Set still, Laurie Lee. I'll take care the coffee. You talk to the teacher. He didn't come here to keep company with a great big old hard head like me." Without another word, he went in the kitchen. Laurie Lee watched him with her narrow eyes widened in genuine surprise. She thought about the night the teacher had brought Rob back home and the talk they had had far into the night and she shook her head unconsciously, and she smiled at the teacher.

97   Richard Myles sat there staring into the sleepy-looking fire. He glanced at Rob. "Are you ready for that history test tomorrow?"

98   "Yes, sir."

99   Big Sister looked boldly up into Richard Myles's face for one brief second. "To let him tell it, he got everybody's waters on in your class, Mr. Myles. That's all he talk about—Negro history." Her face flushed warm again, and she got up quickly and went into the kitchen where her father was.

100   Mr. Myles and Mama laughed.

101   "You just telling a great big something-ain't-so," Rob said.

102   And the grown folks had coffee and bread and home-made jam and the children had hot water tea and bread and jam, and they all sat relaxing before the fire and talking about first one thing and then another, and Big Sister glancing self-consciously at the nice looking, pretty-talking young teacher, but most of the time her eyes looking holes in the floor near the hearth, and Rob fidgeting like ants were in his britches, and the quiet noises of the fire in the fireplace and the shadows on the hearth.

103   Joe cleared his throat and told Richard Myles, with everynow-and-then a tremble in his soft booming voice, about the argument he had with the paymaster and the way the Negroes gathered around him and the cracker saying "Howdy," and the cracker since then walking out of the gate with him and talking to him friendly-like. "Yes, sir," Joe said, smiling and slapping his big thighs, "I got to thinking and studying about what you said when you was here that night, and I said to myself, that Professor Myles must be one of the Major Prophets sent down here on earth by Great God Almighty." Joe laughed out loud and all of them laughed including Richard. Then everything got quiet again.

104   And Rob just couldn't hold it any longer. "What you going to do about Jubilee Day?" he asked Mr. Myles. The Youngbloods looked at Rob in surprise.

105   "What would you say, if I told you we *were* going through with it?"

106   "You mean you going to have it?"

107   "That's exactly what I mean."

108   "And you going to be in charge?"

109   "What would you say, if I asked you to take part in it?" Mr. Myles smiled at the angry disappointment on Rob's face, and it made the boy angrier.

110   "Me?" he shouted. "I wouldn't be in it for a million dollars. I can't sing nohow."

111   "I think everybody is going to enjoy this Jubilee Day—All the colored folks I mean. After you spoke to me, I went to see Reverend Ledbetter and discussed it with him, and he said we ought to have a Jubilee Day, but we ought to have the kind colored folks will be proud of. Teach the white folks a lesson."

112   "You mean there won't be any spirituals?"

113   "There'll be plenty of spirituals, but we're going to build a program around the spirituals."

114   "And you talked Reverend Ledbetter into it too?" Rob said angrily.

115   "I didn't talk him into anything. It's his own idea. Wait a minute. Listen—We're going to give the meaning and the history of the spirituals. We're going to tell them, the white and the colored, how the Negro spirituals came into being." He looked around into all of their faces that were fixed upon him now. And he told them how the Negro spirituals were born in the fields on the great slave plantations and in the slave cabins, and wherever else slaves could get together to pass the word along, sometimes right under the nose of the master. He hazily outlined the program to them, which had been forming in his

head the last couple of days, becoming clearer to him as he talked
to them, trying to read the meanings of the expressions in their faces
as he went along, and when he finished there was a silence in the room
that was painful to him, and the crackling of the burning wood in the
fireplace sounded like angry shots from a pistol.

116   Joe looked at Laurie and cleared his throat. "Never knowed spirituals meant all them things you say they mean."

117   Laurie Lee's rocker went back and forth, her narrow eyes nar-
rowed in a deep meditation. "This is the kind of Jubilee Day we've
been needing for the longest kind of time. This the kind of religion
the colored man needs everywhere."

118   Joe said to the teacher, "Don't get me wrong, Professor Myles.
I'm behind the proposition every step of the way, but how you know
the spirituals mean the kind of things you say they mean?"

119   "Learned it from Negro history—from Frederick Douglass—from
Paul Lawrence Dunbar—Carter G. Woodson—from Reverend Ledbetter right here in Crossroads—and from the Negro spirituals themselves—Just about all of the spirituals back there in slavery had
double meanings. The slaves weren't fools. They knew what would
happen if they came right out and said what they wanted to say."

120   "If they didn't have double meaning," Laurie Lee said, "they just
ought to have."

121   "Listen," Richard Myles said. "Listen to the words." He began
to sing in his rich baritone, self-conscious at first.

> *Swing Low Sweet Chariot*
> *Coming for to carry me home,*
> *Swing Low Sweet Chariot*
> *Coming for to carry me home.*

122   He heard Joe's thundering bass join in. *If you git there before I
do, tell all of my friends I'm coming too,* and Laurie Lee's soprano,
and before the first verse was finished the children were singing.

123   "You know where home was," Richard Myles said after the song
had ended. "It wasn't only in Heaven. It was up north to freedom."

124   "Great Day in the morning," Joe said. "Many times as I done sung
that song, it ain't never sounded that good before."

125   "It hasn't felt that good either," Laurie Lee said, thinking about
Big Mama.

126   They sang a couple of more spirituals including Joe's favorite,
"Walk Together Children," and the room was filled with a Jubilee

spirit. Joe got up and turned his back and wiped his eyes on the sly, and he blew his nose. "I declare I believe I'm catching a fresh cold. That tarty sure would come in handy."

127 Laurie Lee nodded her head and smiled at the teacher. "You say Reverend Ledbetter going to take part in it?"

128 "He certainly is. It's his idea to begin with." Thinking to himself it would be a good idea to get the minister to participate in the program itself, and not just the planning. . . .

129 "That'll be good—mighty mighty good."

130 Rob was so filled up he could hardly speak. "Wh-wh-what you want me do do? I got a pretty nice voice for calling hogs, but it isn't good enough to sing in any chorus."

131 "We have something special for you to do," Richard Myles answered. "You're going to have something to say before each number. You're going to be the narrator. You're going to give the history and the background. You and Reverend Ledbetter and I will work out the content."

132 "Me!" Rob sat there with his mouth open.

133 "You don't reckin we'll have any trouble with the crackers," Laurie Lee said anxiously.

134 "Can I be in the chorus?" Jenny Lee asked. "I can sing pretty good. Can't I, Mama? I coulda been in it last year. I just didn't want to."

135 "You don't reckin there'll be any trouble. Do you, Mr. Myles?" Laurie Lee repeated.

136 "I sure do want to be in this Jubiles Day," Jenny Lee insisted.

137 "Quiet girl," Mama said. "Haven't you got any manners?" She looked at Mr. Myles.

138 He looked briefly into the depths of her anxious eyes. "I hope there won't be any trouble, Mrs. Youngblood. But you folks would know the answer to that question better than I would."

139 "If the crackers don't like it, shame on them," Jenny Lee said, batting her big eyes. "Can I be in the chorus? I got a good voice."

140 "There'll be so many Negroes there, won't make no difference what the crackers like," Joe said.

141 Laurie Lee looked anxiously at Rob and then at the teacher. "But what about afterwards? What about you, Mr. Myles and what about Rob?"

142 "Don't worry about the narrator," Rob said.

143 "I'm thinking about what will come after. These crackers won't take nothing like this lying down. They might make trouble for Rob,

and they'll sure be giving you your walking papers, even if they don't do you no bodily harm."

144   "I've thought about that, but as far as I am concerned, if they do send me away, it will be well worth it." He didn't want to leave Crossroads.

145   "We won't let them!" Jenny Lee said.

146   Joe Youngblood stood up and he poked at the fire again. He stared up at the ceiling. He remembered the last time the teacher was there in the same room, and the fire in the fireplace seemed to be the same, and the smell of firewood burning, and the feeling everywhere. He remembered the words spoken about standing together and what Laurie Lee had said. He had thought about them enough since then. He cleared his throat and looked down into their faces. "Look like to me if the colored stick together, ain't gon be no need to worry about what the crackers gon do."

147   Laurie Lee looked at Joe. "You right about that Joe—Yet and still—You right about that Joe," she repeated. "And especially if Reverend Ledbetter is going to be in it. Get all the church folks and the lodge folks behind you, crackers can't do nothing. Crackers don't ever start anything unless they outnumber you a hundred to one. Whatever they start we'll sure God finish."

148   "And one thing we aren't going to stand for," Jenny Lee said. "We're not going to let them send Mr. Myles away."

149   "You'll be in the chorus," Mr. Myles told her. "No doubt about it."

150   The Youngbloods laughed.

151   Rob had a feeling that he would burst wide open any minute, he was so filled up. He got up and walked over to Mr. Myles and he held out his hand. "I knew you would find some kind of a way Mr. Myles, and I want you to know us Youngbloods are with you one hundred percent."

152   Richard grabbed the boy's hand, and he squeezed it so hard he himself was embarrassed. He stood up to go, and he wanted to say to them not to tell anybody about the plan right away, but he didn't know how to say it, because he didn't want them to think he didn't have confidence in the Negro people of Crossroads, Georgia. He shook all of their hands, and when he was about to leave, he said, "Up to now you're the only folks that know about the plan besides Reverend Ledbetter and me."

153   Laurie Lee smiled. "And nobody else going to know about it from us. You tell too many Mr. Charlie'll know it."

154   All of them laughed including Richard Myles.

155   He felt good when he left them, and, as late as it was, he walked through the brisk night to the Terrace where Josephine Rollins lived carrying with him an unexplored feeling of being a part of the Youngblood family. He missed his family in far away Brooklyn, and he needed the Youngbloods.

156   He liked Josephine Rollins more than a little. They liked each other. And he told her about the Jubilee plan as they sat in her prim little living room facing each other, she in her light blue bathrobe with the bottom edge of her nightgown showing, her soft friendly eyes heavy with sleep. When he finished talking she said he was just going to stir up a whole lot of trouble. White folks and colored got along fairly well in Crossroads—better than most places down here. And they talked about it till it got quite late, early in the morning. He tried awfully hard to keep the anger out of his voice, and he was twice as angry with her as he would have been with anybody else because he liked her so much. She told him Mr. Blake wouldn't allow it anyhow, and he said Mr. Blake wouldn't have to know about it ahead of time. Nobody had to know about it, not even the children in the chorus. They became angrier and angrier with each other, polite and angry. And when she said people from up north do more harm than good, he asked her was it true what they said about the Southern Negro being happy and contented. At that point she got to her feet and said it was getting quite late and thanks for taking her into his confidence, but she was not going to be in this colored folks' mess. "I'll just play the piano like I always did, during the practice and Jubilee Night. I'm not going to run and carry tales to the *man*, so don't worry about that. I'm just going to forget you paid me a visit." She wouldn't look into his eyes now. Her usually sweet voice was husky and strange. She walked toward the front door and she stood there as they said good-night, the ceiling lamp casting soft reflections on her dark sweet face.

157   It was two or three days later before the practice for Jubilee Day really got under way. From then on every afternoon at two o'clock, the children in the chorus would happily leave their classes and go to the auditorium for Jubilee practice. He told them the first day this was going to be the best Jubilee Day in the history of Crossroads and Pleasant Grove School, and he wanted them to practice hard and this was one Jubilee the Negro people of Crossroads would be proud of. Josephine Rollins played the piano and helped him with the children in the chorus as if nothing had happened. Maybe his going to see her that night had not happened at all. Maybe he'd dreamed it.

158   The day before the Jubilee the children in the chorus marched all the way downtown to the city hall auditorium where the Jubilee was to be held. They marched two abreast and full of pride and happiness and devilment through Peckerwood Town and down Jeff Davis Boulevard past the great big mansions where the rich white folks lived, and they practiced in the great big auditorium. Richard Myles had convinced most of them that this was one Jubilee they would be proud to be a part of. Reverend Led-better announced it from his pulpit every Sunday morning and all through the week, and he sent the announcement out in his weekly bulletin. "Your children will not be singing for the benefit of our white friends, welcome as they are. They will be singing for us. The Great Lord be praised. They will be singing for our fathers and our fathers' fathers back through the ages and for generations to come. So come on out on Friday night, Brothers and Sisters. Come on out and bring *everybody* and join in the great Jubilee—"

159   Richard Myles found himself leaving the auditorium the evening before Jubilee Day, with Josephine Rollins. The final practice had just ended and the children had left, and they had stayed behind looking after first one thing and then another. She was tense and all tuned up to a very high pitch, which she tried to disguise. They walked down the long white marble steps and she looked sideways at him and away again.

160   "Well, professor, I reckin you got everything in order. You ready to take your flock right smack up to the Pearly Gates?" She gave a quick laugh.

161   He felt a sudden flash of anger toward her. After all those weeks of practice, she had not once mentioned the new kind of program she knew he and Reverend Ledbetter and Robby were feverishly planning. She had never even alluded to it by a word or a look or the bat of an eyelash. She had just been her same soft sweet-faced cooperative self throughout the entire practice period. And now he wasn't in the mood for flippancy on anybody's part, but especially hers. He wondered how the children would take it when he told them about the special part of the program tomorrow evening before it began. He was really worried about how the audience would take it, especially the crackers. "I think everything is ready," he told Josephine. He said goodnight and turned quickly away.

162   Before he got home it started to rain and it rained all night long till about seven in the morning. The sky was dark and gray with

clouds everywhere. Before he left for school Reverend Ledbetter phoned him.

163   "Well, my learned intellectual fighter, have you been on your knees this morning?" The Reverend was mimicking his own pulpit voice.

164   "No, sir, I haven't as yet. I thought that was your department," Richard said in the same joking spirit, edged with a little nervous anxiety. "You've had a whole lot more experience along those lines."

165   "Bad as some of these crackers are and bad as that weather outside looks, it's going to take a whole heap of knee-bending."

166   Even after the preacher hung up Richard seemed to hear the rich peals of laughter reaching toward him through the telephone and washing away his early-morning nervousness.

167   The sun came out about two thirty in the afternoon and it stayed out. The program was supposed to begin at eight thirty sharp. The children were to get to the auditorium at seven. When Richard Myles arrived people were already there standing on the outside, colored and white, mostly colored and mostly country people. It looked like in-town-Saturday-afternoon. Wagons and trucks parked nearby, and talking and laughing like being on a picnic. He walked through a crowd of people and he heard somebody say—

168   "There go the professor. He the one in charge."

169   And hostile glances from the red-faced peckerwoods.

170   "Is that Professor Myles?"

171   "From New York City—"

172   "Where Rev. Ledbetter?"

173   When he went backstage some of the children had already arrived. Rob Youngblood was there. "How do you feel, Robert?"

174   He looked Richard Myles full in the face. "I'm ready," he said.

175   The children drifted in from seven to seven thirty. By a quarter to eight most of them had arrived. Richard Myles called them together, and they lined up just as they would when the program began. When he began to speak to them the air was so tense, you could actually feel it moving around. He hoped that the children were not as nervous as he was.

176   He thanked them for their cooperation and for the confidence they had shown in Miss Rollins and him. "I know what most of us think about previous Jubilee Days and about singing Negro spirituals for rich white folks who come along for the laughs. And we promised that this one would be different, but you had to take our word for it, because we couldn't say anymore than that then. Now we can tell you." He could see their beautiful children faces, dark-eyed and

bright-eyed and confident and nervous, and black and brown and light brown faces, all turned toward him in anxious expectancy.

177   "This Jubilee Day, along with the glorious spirituals and throughout the program, we are going to give the history and meaning of the spirituals, most of which were born in the struggle of our forefathers against the inhumanity of slavery. There was never anything Uncle-Tom about Negro spirituals and we're going to prove it tonight. We're going to give the white folks a real education. All of us are going to be teachers tonight. We're going to teach history and we're going to make history. Robert Youngblood will be the narrator."

178   A murmur went through the chorus, and he wondered nervously had he put the thing over.

179   "You have done wonderfully in practice, and now with a noble purpose in mind, the purpose of Freedom which we haven't won yet, you will do even better than ever before. Any questions?"

180   He looked into their anxious faces. His stomach flip-flopped as he heard Biff Robert's voice coming from the back line of the chorus. "I don't know about all that history and meaning stuff, Mr. Myles. I believe it's just going to stir up a whole heap of trouble with the white folks."

181   "We'll just speak the truth," Mr. Myles said. "The truth never hurt anybody, unless he is guilty of something."

182   "I don't know about that, Mr. Myles. All I know is, ain't no use of stirring up trouble between colored and white."

183   He should have been prepared for this, Richard Myles thought. This boy could disrupt the entire business if he tried hard enough. He had focused all of his anxieties and anticipation on the crackers and Uncle Tom Negro adults, had taken the children for granted.

184   "I don't know about the rest of them," Biff Roberts said. "But I don't want to get in no mess—get put out of school—sent to the reformatory—We ain't nothing but innocent children. You shouldn't be putting us in the middle of everything. I don't know about the rest, but you can count me out."

185   There were wide-eyed looks of fear and confusion on the children's faces. All of the planning and work, the weeks and weeks of practicing and planning and worrying and the work.. . .

186   He saw Jenny Lee Youngblood step out of the front line and look toward the back of the chorus. "Get on out of line then," she shouted. "Ain't nobody scared of these crackers but you. Everybody in town knows your whole family ain't nothing but a bunch of Uncle Toms from your daddy on down. Mr. Myles spend all his time studying how

to bring the race up, and you trying to tear it down. Get on out if you so scared of crackers. Anybody else scared get out too. I'm standing by my own."

187   There was a frightening moment of painful silence and then Richard Myles heard the "Me too's" coming from all over the chorus and he wanted to go to big-eyed Jenny Lee Youngblood and pick her up and give her the biggest hug anybody ever gave her, as she stood there with the other children, an angry pout on her upturned mouth.

188   "Ain't nobody scared," Biff Roberts said.

189   Richard Myles asked were there any more questions. There was nothing but mumbles. "Anybody want to drop out?"

190   "I'm with you, Mr. Myles," Rob Youngblood said. "Crackers don't scare me."

191   "Me too," Bruh Robinson said.

192   "Me too."

193   "Count me in."

194   "How about you, William?"

195   "Ain't nobody scared," Biff Roberts answered.

196   Myles could feel the perspiration pouring from him all over his body. "Thank you," he said. "I guess that's all. Relax until the bell rings at eight fifteen. Then assemble in your places. Good luck, God bless you," he added with the greatest sincerity.

197   Every now and then he would look out from behind the great curtain at the audience assembling. They came in dribbles at first, then at about ten minutes after eight, they began to flow in. By eight-twenty-five every seat was taken, except a few vacants in the section roped off for white folks up front on the right. Even so there were almost a hundred white people present, most of them dressed like important looking people. He saw the Mayor come in with the Superintendent of the Board of Education. All the children in the chorus had arrived but five or six, and they could start without them, except that Willabelle Braxton had not come yet and she was the best alto in the entire chorus. As he stood there thinking about how the Mayor and the Superintendent would react to his program, he felt somebody poke him in the ribs and he jumped nervously. He turned and looked into the smiling face of Josephine Rollins.

198   "Don't worry about a thing," she said. "The folks are here tonight. They are standing along the sides. Fred and Harriet's folks I mean."

199   He laughed nervously.

200   "What time are you going to start the program by?" she asked him. "Eastern Standard or Colored People's Time?"

201   He looked at her sweet face and he laughed a good laugh this time, suddenly feeling a great relief flow through his body. "We're going to throw *C P T* out the window this night of our Lord," he burlesqued. Both of them laughed.

202   Willabelle Braxton came in out of breath and she was very very sorry, and he said it was all right and he briefed her quickly about the meaning of the program.

203   Mr. Blake came over to them from the other side of the stage. "Everything in readiness?" he asked, a nervous look beneath the customary beam of his countenance.

204   "Everything ready to roll, Mr. Blake," Richard said. He glanced at Josephine Rollins. "Almost everybody is on time, including the audience, and we're going to start as close to eight thirty as possible."

205   "Well," Mr. Blake said, "I'm sure it will come off all right with you and Miss Rollins taking care of things." He smiled at Miss Rollins and he cleared his throat.

206   He might as well tell Mr. Blake now, this minute. "I think you're going to find it rather interesting," Richard Myles said. "We're doing it just a little bit differently this time. We're going to give a bit of historical background."

207   "Historical background?" the principal said with a worried look. "Historical background—Well I guess it can't hurt any," he said to himself. "Good—Good—You should have told me about it before now. I guess it's all right though."

CHAPTER FOUR

208   At eight-thirty-eight the curtains parted and the children stood up, and Richard Myles came on the stage with Josephine Rollins and a silence fell gradually upon the audience. Miss Rollins sat down at the piano and began to play the National Anthem, and everybody stood up and sang the first verse—

> *Oh say can you see by the dawn's early light—*
> *What so proudly we hailed—*

209   Reverend Ledbetter walked out from the wing, the people still standing, and he raised his arms and he asked the blessings of the Lord on the gathering, "We are come, oh Lord, to pay tribute to black men and black women and to sing Negro spirituals which

our fore-fathers gave to this great country in the days of slavery a-way down in Egypt Land—"

210   And when the Amens died softly away, and some of the lights went off all over the great big beautiful auditorium, Robert Youngblood, seated at the left of the chorus, stood up and walked with proud nervous dignity towards the center of the stage. He was all dressed up in his Sunday-go-to-meeting dark blue suit. He looked out beyond the footlights at the upturned faces, and, in a brief second, he glimpsed his mother and his father and Ida Mae Raglin and Fat Gus and a thousand other faces, and black and white faces—brown and light brown. He cleared his throat and he looked bleary-eyed at the paper in his hand and he opened his mouth and worked his jaws but nothing came out. But sweat broke out all over his face. He licked his lips and tried again, and the sound of his voice shocked the fear out of him, for the moment at least.

211   "In the words of Frederick Douglass, the greatest of all Americans, past or present, the Negro spirituals were tones, loud, long and deep, breathing the prayer and complaint of souls boiling over with the bitterest anguish. Every tone was a testimony against slavery, and a prayer to God for deliverance from chains. Thus were the Negro spirituals born." His young voice trembled. He cleared his throat. "The first of these spirituals to be sung by the chorus is 'Nobody knows the trouble I see.'" He turned and walked shakily back to his seat, his heart pounding heavily, and he heard Miss Josephine start the introduction and the chorus standing and the children's voices and the soprano voices and Willabelle Braxton and her alto voice and the tenor voices and Jenny Lee's voice and the voices that tried to be baritone and bass, and soft and clear and pretty and sometimes too loud, and the girls in white dresses and the boys in white shirts and dark trousers and the whole thing wonderful. . . .

> *Nobody knows the trouble I see*
> *Nobody knows but Jesus*
> *Nobody knows the trouble I see Glory Hallelu—yah*
> *Sometimes I'm up—sometimes I'm down Yes my Lord*
> *Sometimes I'm almost to the ground Yes my Lord.*

212   After it ended he heard the chorus sit down and Mr. Myles took his place and Rob walked back to the center of the stage. He could hear the Amens clearly now and the Yes My Lords coming from all over

the auditorium, and he felt the spirit, and all eyes were on him. He lifted his voice.

213   "In the evil days when slavery was in the land, the Negro people were oppressed so hard they could not stand. They wanted to be free, and they took every chance they got to run away from their shackles and their chains. With their white and black friends up north they organized an underground railroad that reached from deep in Dixie all the way to Canada and they made up religious songs about it, as they joined together their faith in God with their uncompromising determination to be free, and they sang those songs right under the noses of the slaveholders, and one of those beautiful songs is 'Swing Low Sweet Chariot.' "

> *Swing low sweet chariot—Coming for to carry me home*
> *Swing low sweet chariot—Coming for to carry me home*
> *I looked over Jordan and what did I see*
> *Coming for to carry me home*
> *A band of angels coming after me*
> *Coming for to carry me home*

214   The chorus had lost the shakiness in its voice. It was clear and as pretty as a Sunday church bell. And Rob was caught up by the songs and the meanings and the spirit of the people and the Amens and the sobs that he heard in the audience, and he completely forgot about his nervousness. He walked pigeon-toed to the center of the stage.

215   "Coming for to carry me home," he repeated. "Home was in Heaven, but Home wasn't only in Heaven. Home was up north in the Promised Land. Away from the chains of slavery—Away from the lash of the whip—Away from man's inhumanity—" Rob heard his people's voices all over the auditorium—"The Lord be praised" and "Merciful Father" and "Yes—Yes—Yes."

216   "And every chance a slave could get he would get on board that Glory train and—'Steal away to Jesus.' " He heard Jenny Lee's voice and heard Willabelle's, and the other children coming and going like the rolling billows of an imagined ocean, and the sweet mournful harmony made his stomach turn, head over heels, and he felt the fiercest kind of love for his people—

> *My Lord he calls me*
> *He calls me by the thunder*

> *The trumpet sounds within-a my soul*
> *I ain't got long to stay here*
> *Steal away—steal away*
> *Steal away to Jesus*
> *Steal away—steal away home*
> *I ain't got long to stay here.*

217   After he introduced the next number and went back to his place, he fought himself hard to keep from crying, when he heard Bruh Robinson leading the chorus. *Didn't my Lord deliver Daniel? Why not every man?*

218   Chills went up and down Rob's back, as he walked to the center of the stage again, and heard people crying in the audience, and over on the left he saw two men holding a shouting woman.

219   "In the evil days of slavery men and women were sold like cattle. From an auction block. But when Abraham Lincoln signed the Proclamation of Emancipation a new song was born."

> *No more auction block for me*
>   *No more—no more*
> *No more auction block for me*
>   *Many thousands gone . . .*
> *No more peck of corn for me. . . .*
>   *. . . . .*
> *No more drivers lash for me . . .*
>   *Many thousands gone*

220   And then the intermission.

221   Mama told Robby, "Boy, you really put it on!"

222   He wanted to put his arms around her and kiss her, but he wouldn't because sometimes he still wanted to be mean to her and angry with her.

223   Sarah Raglin said, "Willabelle Braxton, honey, you got a voice like an angel."

224   Richard Myles had very little to say. The children and the response of his own people to the children singing had filled him up with a spirit and strength he had never possessed before, but nevertheless he had been aware of the angry expressions in the white folks' faces, and some of them leaving all during the first half of the program, and at the intermission the way they left in groups was an ominous threat. And the Superintendent of the Board of Education seated with Mayor Livingston. He had seen these two high-ranking white gentlemen

talking to Ben Blake in the back of the auditorium, and he could just imagine what they were talking about.

225   Mr. Blake was fuming when he came backstage. "Why wasn't I told about this in the first place?" he yelled.

226   "Didn't want to bother you with details," Richard Myles said calmly. "I was sure you would like it."

227   "Like it?" he said. "Like it! It—it—it's an insult to the citizenry of Crossroads. That's what it is!" he shouted. He lowered his voice so others wouldn't hear. "I came around often. I watched the practice regularly. I didn't see—"

228   Laurie Lee Youngblood came over to them. "I must give my congratulations to all three of you. Mr. Blake, this is the best Jubilee ever been anywhere. And I'm not just saying so cause Rob and Jenny Lee are in it. I know you just as proud as you can be. Everybody say it's just the best ever." She didn't wait for an answer from him.

229   He turned back to Richard and Josephine. "Well, anyhow," he said softly but doggedly, "just leave out the background during the next half, and let them just sing the spirituals."

230   "But the audience likes it the way we're doing it. They wouldn't understand," Richard said with a make-believe calm.

231   "Man, do you think we're playing ring games?" Ben Blake exploded, "Do you know that Mr. Johnson is out there and the Mayor of Crossroads is out there with him? I'm not playing, man. Leave it out! Leave it out!" His desperate eyes begged Richard Myles to be reasonable. "You standing there looking so smug and righteous!"

232   Richard Myles didn't feel any smugness or righteousness, and he wished Josephine would have something to say, at the same time afraid of what she might say. "At the beginning of the second half, I'll have to explain to the audience that you thought it wasn't proper," he said to Mr. Blake.

233   "Don't you dare! What are you trying to do to me, Myles?" He turned to Josephine. "You take over, Miss Rollins. You know how it's done. Just let them sing the good old spirituals."

234   Richard Myles felt his belly contracting and fresh perspiration all over his body. He didn't dare to look in her direction. He didn't want to hear her but he heard her say with a calm in her voice—"I like it the way it's going now, Mr. Blake. I helped to plan it this way. It's honest and it's Christian and truthful. It's just about the best thing ever happened in Crossroads."

235   Two Negro women walked across the stage towards them, beaming with smiles, as the bell rang for the end of the intermission,

and Mr. Blake walked off mumbling to himself that he was going to have both of their jobs, and they would be sorry they ever messed with Ben Blake.

236   "You shouldn't have done that," he said to Josephine. "You shouldn't have implicated yourself like that."

237   "What do you take me for, Richard Myles?" she asked him angrily.

238   "You heard what he said. You may lose your job."

239   "So what? *You* may lose *your* job."

240   He looked at her sweet face which seemed to have acquired a new defiant kind of beauty, and an unreasoning happiness drowned out the doubts and fears ringing in the ears of his mind. He started to say something like I love you, Josephine. But he just said thanks.

241   She said, "Don't thank me."

242   The bell rang again to begin the second half, sharp and impatient.

243   The children were in their seats, the curtains parted and a quiet came gradually over the audience. Robert Youngblood recited "O Black and Unknown Bards" by James Weldon Johnson, and Carrie Lou Jackson led the chorus in—

> *Sometimes I feel like a motherless child . . .*
> *. . . A long ways from home. . . .*

244   There was unashamed weeping now throughout the audience and a few people shouting here and there, as the chorus sang like angels in a beautiful black Heaven. It was wonderful. It was glorious.

> *I got shoes—you got shoes*
> *All of God's chillun got shoes*
> *When you git to Heaven gonna put on your shoes*
> *Gonna walk all over God's Heaven.*

and

> *Bye and bye I'm gonna lay down this heavy load. . . .*

245   It was getting closer and closer to the end of the program, and each time Rob would get up to introduce a number, he was lifted higher and higher and filling up to the overflowing. He tried to keep from looking out at the people in the audience. He had seen all of his friends and acquaintances out there at one time or another. He had even looked in the white section and had seen some real big people

who were getting the surprise of their lives. Some of them left at the intermission. But many had remained. Even a few red-faced crackers were still in their seats. His knees weren't shaking any more and his voice had stopped going froggy on him. He became aroused by the sound of his own voice and the words that he spoke.

246 "And there was a great white man by the name of John Brown, an angry God-fearing man, who hated slavery and gave his life at Harpers Ferry so that black men and women might be free. White and black stood together, died side by side. And there was a little black woman named Harriet Tubman, a friend of John Brown, a woman of greatness. Harriet Tubman overpowered her whipping boss and escaped from slavery. But she wasn't satisfied with just her own freedom when she crossed over Jordan. She couldn't sit still till the South was free. She went back south, she went down in Egypt Land, time and again, and she led the Hebrew children to freedom. And they called her Harriet and they called her Moses. The next selection by the Pleasant Grove School Chorus will be 'Go Down Moses.' "

247 He almost burst out laughing, and at the same time crying, when he heard Fat Gus's mother, Miss Lulabelle, who was seated in the front row, say—"Moses been going down too damn long now—He need to git up off his devilish knees and stand up and fight!"

> *When Israel was in Egypt Land*
> *Let my people go*
> *Oppressed so hard they could not stand*
> *Let my people go*
> *Go down Moses—way down in Egypt Land*
> *And tell old Pharaoh*
> *To let my people go.*

248 The last spiritual they sang turned the auditorium inside out. There was humming by the people in the audience and weeping and patting of feet and Amen-ning and a spirit so strong that it reached out toward the children in the chorus and lifted them up and carried them away toward the Evening star and the River of Jordan, and they sang as they never sang before, and it embarrassed Rob to see the tears spill down the young teacher's face.

> *O freedom*
> *O freedom*
> *O freedom over me*

And before I be a slave
I'd be buried in my grave
And go home to my Lord
And be free.

249 As Richard Myles turned toward the audience and motioned for everybody to stand, he was still worried and anxious about the crackers who left in droves and groups during the intermission and some of the evil white expressions on the faces of some who still remained, and they might start trouble any minute and they might have guns, and it would be all his fault, and he looked out towards his own people and he saw Laurie Lee Youngblood's face and Joe Youngblood's and hundreds of black and brown faces, and he remembered what Laurie Lee Youngblood had said the night he had talked with them about Jubilee Day—Crackers don't ever start anything unless they outnumber you. Whatever they start we'll sure God finish. He felt growth and understanding and an overpowering strength, as he raised his arms to his people, and Josephine Rollins played the introduction to the National Negro Anthem, and everybody sang, except some of the white folks.

Lift every voice and sing
Till earth and Heaven ring,
Ring with the harmonies of liberty:
Let our rejoicing rise
High as the listening skies,
Let it resound loud as the rolling sea.
Sing a song full of the faith that the dark past has taught us,
Sing a song full of the hope that the present has brought us,
Facing the rising sun of our new day begun
Let us march on till victory is won.

250 Reverend Ledbetter came forward and raised his arms and every head bowed, including most of the white folks.

251 "We thank you, O Heavenly Father, for this great gathering here tonight of black and white citizens, children of the Heavenly King. We hope that all of them have been caught up by the spirit of the Negro spirituals, the spirit of peace on earth, good will to all men no matter their nationality or religion. We are humbly proud, Dear Father, of our spirituals, for they are some of the most glorious songs ever sung in the name of your Son, Jesus. But we want the world to know, O Merciful Father, that we, your black sons and daughters, haven't sung any

songs like we're going to sing them one of these days—In that Great-Getting-Up-Morning, when we all cross over the River of Jordan, when all men on earth will be truly brothers in the sight of God and man, O Lord. We're going to sing a song we never sang before—We're going to sing like nobody ever sang before—"

252   After it was over and the lights on bright all over the big auditorium, many of the people came backstage, and the congratulations, and the handshakes and the hugging and the kissing. And Mr. Blake standing there with the rest of them, not knowing what to do because it was plain to see that all the people were just crazy about the Jubilee Program.

253   Big Sister ran up to Mr. Myles in front of everybody and put her arms around him and kissed him on the mouth. "Mr. Myles! Mr. Myles! It was really wonderfull" And many of the grown folks laughed at her.

254   Everything became suddenly quiet, as two white people walked across the stage toward Richard Myles. Mrs. Cross and her daughter walked right up to the young teacher and the tall handsome yellow-haired woman held out her hand in the sight of everybody. "Magnificent, Mr. Myles. It was simply magnificent. The most moving thing I have ever experienced." Everybody heard. And the big rich white girl standing beside her mother with her pinkish face red and glowing like the first rose of summer. Mrs. Cross Junior asked for Rob Youngblood, but he was nowhere to be seen at the moment. After the white folks left, the stage became noisy with the jubilee spirit all over again, until another white person came, a long skinny ugly man with a broad pink forehead and a friendly smile and along with him a broad-shouldered blond-haired man that dragged behind the skinny one and seemed embarrassed.

255   "Good evening, Professor," the long skinny one said to Richard in a southern drawl that was somehow cultured and different from the average cracker. "I'm Doctor Riley and this is Dr. Crump. We're from the University. We sure did enjoy your program immensely. It was a real revelation."

256   "Well, thank you a lot," Richard Myles said. He couldn't think of anything else to say, he was so surprised. The skinny man shook hands warmly with Richard. The stocky one's hand was limp. They both stood there for a moment amongst all those colored folks and their faces flushed and they both looked embarrassed. Richard Myles finally said, "Well we're certainly glad you liked the program."

257   "Yes, indeed," Dr. Riley said, and both of them smiled and said goodnight.

258   Rob and Mr. Myles and Josephine Rollins left the stage together. People still stood around in the auditorium laughing and talking, a few of them white. Joe Youngblood came over and shook the teacher's hand and he and two other men stayed close to Richard as they went down the aisle toward the door. They approached a group of red-faced pecks. Let them scowl their ugly heads off, Richard thought to himself. One of them, a square-shouldered, heavy-set cracker, left the group and walked toward Richard and Rob and Joe and the rest. Richard Myles felt his own body stiffen, but he kept walking in the middle of the others, as if nothing at all was about to happen. The auditorium got suddenly quiet again.

259   The chunky-shouldered cracker stopped walking toward them about five feet away and stood blank-faced and waiting with his hands in his pockets, and Richard Myles and Josephine Rollins and Robby and Joe and Laurie Lee and Jenny Lee and Lee Patterson and Clyde Waters kept coming. When they came up to the cracker they stopped.

260   The cracker's face turned redder than it already was. He looked into Richard Myles' face. "That was a mighty nice program," he said in a husky crackerish drawl. "And I sure did enjoy it mighty mighty much."

261   Richard Myles said, "Thanks" when his voice came to him. The cracker turned to Joe and said How you Joe and Joe said Howdy and the cracker said—"A mighty nice program, yes indeed." And he turned and walked back to the other crackers who scowled more than ever, and one of them spat on the pretty marble floor and said "the goddamn sassy ass niggers. . . ."

262   Richard and the rest continued toward the door. When they got outside Joe said, "That was Oscar Jefferson. That's the one I was talking to you about. Real funny old cracker."

263   Before he could say anything in reply, he looked down the long wide white marble steps and he saw a gathering of mean-looking white men at the foot of the steps. They were waiting for him and he knew it. He felt his whole body suck in the cold night air and his body growing quickly from warm to hot. But the group he was with didn't hesitate a moment. Then he felt an excitement seize hold of him and relief ran through him as he saw a large group of men move

past the crackers and come up to meet them—black and brown men. Just before the men reached them, Joe Youngblood stepped forward to meet them and he said a few mumbled words to a couple of them, one was Ray Morrison, and they moved in quietly and surrounded the group and went down the steps and past the crackers. Joe Youngblood whispered softly to Richard Myles, "Ain't gon be no whole lot of who-shot-John-tonight, cause we got the business. If they start anything, we'll sure God finish it."

264   They took them to where Reverend Ledbetter's car was waiting, and Jenny Lee and Laurie Lee and Rob and Josephine and Richard and Joe piled in, Reverend Ledbetter driving. As they pulled away from the curb, Richard Myles heard another car motor warming up and he sensed the other car pulling out behind them.

265   Joe's deep booming voice broke into his thoughts, "Don't worry about nothing. Them the members of Frederick Douglass Lodge—five-hundred-and-six. We got the cat by his natural tail."

266   Richard Myles laughed as they rode through the night toward the Youngbloods' house, where that afternoon Laurie Lee had prepared sandwiches and lemonade.

William Melvin Kelley

(1937–)

Born in the Bronx on November 1, 1937, William Melvin Kelley attended the exclusive Fieldston School in New York City and then enrolled at Harvard University. In 1960, he won the Dana Reed Prize for best writing by a Harvard undergraduate. Consumed by the desire to write, he left Harvard and began working on his first novel, A Different Drummer *(1962), which is a parody of the story of Exodus, as African Americans depart from a mythical Southern state. For this novel he won the Rosenthal Award of the National Institute of Arts and Letters in 1963. His subsequent novels include* A Drop of Patience *(1965),* dem *(1967), and* Dunfords Travels Everywhere *(1970). He also published a collection of short stories,* Dancers on the Shore *(1964). Kelley has taught at the State University of New York at Geneseo, the New School for Social Research, the University of Paris, Nanterre, and Sarah Lawrence College. The following selection is the opening of* A Different Drummer.

A Different Drummer

THE STATE

An excerpt from THE THUMB-NAIL ALMANAC, 1961 . . . page 643:
*An East South Central state in the Deep South, it is
bounded on the north by Tennesses; east by Alabama; south
by the Gulf of Mexico; west by Mississippi.*
CAPITAL: *Willson City.* AREA: *50,163 square miles.*
POPULATION: *(1960 Census, preliminary) 1,802,268.* MOTTO:
With Honor and Arms We Dare Defend Our Rights. ADMITTED
TO UNION: *1818*

Early History — Dewey Wilson:

*Although the state's history is a rich and varied one, it is known
predominately as the home of Confederate General Dewey Willson, who, in 1825, was born in Sutton, a small town 27 miles
north of the Gulfport city of New Marsails. Willson matricu-
lated at the United States Military Academy at West Point (class
of 1842), rose to the rank of colonel in the Federal Army before
the outbreak of the Civil War. Upon the state's secession in 1861,
he resigned his commission and was given the rank of General of
the Confederate Army. He was the chief architect of the two well-
known southern victories at Bull's Horn Creek and at Harmon's
Draw, the latter fought less than 3 miles from his birthplace. His
victory at Harmon's Draw permanently frustrated northern
attempts to reach and capture New Marsails.*

*In 1870, with the state's re-admittance to the Union, Will-
son became its governor. Shortly thereafter, be chose the site,
initiated construction, and, in large part, designed the new
state capital which now bears his name. Upon his retirement
from public life in 1878, be returned to Sutton. On April 5,
1889, having just returned from the dedication of a ten-foot
bronze likeness of himself which the townspeople of Sutton had
erected in their Square, he was stricken and died. He is considered by most historians to have been, after Lee, the Confederacy's greatest general.*

Recent History:

In June 1957, for reasons yet to be determined, all the state's Negro inhabitants departed. Today, it is unique in being the only state in the Union that cannot count even one member of the Negro race among its citizens.

THE AFRICAN

1   It was over now. Most of the men standing, slouching, or sitting on the porch of the Thomason Grocery Company had been at Tucker Caliban's farm on Thursday when it all started, though, with the possible exception of Mister Harper, none of them had known it was the start of anything. All during Friday and most of Saturday they had watched the Negroes of Sutton, with suitcases or empty-handed, waiting at the end of the porch for the hourly bus which would carry them up Eastern Ridge, through Harmon's Draw, to New Marsails and the Municipal Railroad Depot. From the radio and the newspapers they knew Sutton was not the only town, knew that all the Negroes in all the cities, towns, and crossroads in the state had been using any means of transportation available, including their own two legs to journey toward the state's borders, to cross over into Mississippi or Alabama or Tennessee, even if some (most did not) stopped right there and began looking for shelter and work. They knew most would not stop just over the borders, would go on until they came to a place where they had merely the smallest opportunity to live, or die decently, for the men had seen pictures of the depot jammed with black people, and being on the Highway between New Marsails and Willson City, had watched the line of cars crammed with Negroes and enough belongings to convince the men that the Negroes had not gone to all this trouble to move a mere hundred miles or so. And they all read the governor's statement: "There ain't nothing to worry about. We never needed them, never wanted them, and we'll get along fine without them; the South'll get along fine without them. Even though our population's been cut by a third, we'll fare all right. There's still lots of good men left."

2   They all wanted to believe this. They had not lived long enough in a world without black faces to know anything for certain, but hoped everything would be all right, tried to convince themselves it was really over, but sensed, that for them, it was just beginning.

3   Though they had been present at the very start, they had fallen behind the rest of the state, for they had not yet experienced the anger and bitter resentment which they read about in the papers, had not tried to stop the Negroes from leaving, as had other white men in other towns, feeling it was their right and duty to tear suitcases from any black hands which held them; or thrown any punches. They had been spared the disheartening discovery that such gestures were futile or had been barred from such demonstrations of righteous anger— Mister Harper had made them see that the Negroes could not be stopped; Harry Leland had gone so far as to express the idea that the Negroes had the right to leave—and so, now, late Saturday afternoon, as the sun swooped behind the flat-faced, unpainted buildings across the Highway, they turned back to Mister Harper and tried for the thousandth time in three days to discover how it ever began in the first place. They could not know it all, but what they did know might give them some part of an answer and they wondered if what Mister Harper said about "blood" could possibly be true.

4   Mister Harper usually appeared on the porch at eight in the morning, where for twenty years he had held court in a wheel chair as old and awkward as a throne. He was a retired army man, who had gone North to West Point, having been nominated to the Academy by the General himself, Dewey Willson. At West Point, Mister Harper had learned to wage the wars he would never have the opportunity to fight: he was too young for the War Between the States, did not arrive in Cuba until long after the Spanish-American War had ended, and was too old for World War I, which had taken his son from him. War had given him nothing, but had deprived him of everything, and so, thirty years before, he decided life was not worth meeting on foot, since it always knocked you down, and seated himself in a wheel chair to view the world from the porch, explaining its chaotic pattern to the men who clustered around him each day.

5   In all those thirty years, when the world could see it, he had climbed from the wheel chair only once—on Thursday, to go to Tucker Caliban's farm. Now he was again rooted as firmly as though he had never left it, his limp white hair, parted in the middle and long, falling almost like a woman's on either side of his face. His hands were folded over a small but protruding stomach.

6   Thomason, who, because he did so little business, was hardly ever in his store, stood just behind Mister Harper, his back pressed against the dirty plate glass of his show window. Bobby-Joe McCollum, the youngest member of the group, barely twenty, sat on the porch steps

with his feet in the gutter, smoking a cigar. Loomis, a habitual member of the group, was in a chair, reared back on its two hind legs. He had been upstate to the university at Willson, though he had lasted only three weeks, and thought Mister Harper's explanation of the happenings too fantastic, too simple. "Now, I just can't believe this here blood business."

7 "What else can it be?" Mister Harper turned to Loomis and squinted through his hair. He spoke differently from the rest of the men; his voice, high, breathy, dry, distinct, like a New Englander's. "Mind you, I'm not one of these superstitious folks; I don't take account of ghosts and such. But the way I see it, it's pure genetics: something special in the blood. And if anybody in this world got something special in his blood, his name is Tucker Caliban." He lowered his voice, spoke almost in a whisper. "I can see whatever was in his blood just a-laying there sleeping, waiting, and then one day waking up, making Tucker do what he did. Can't be no other reason. We never had no trouble with him, nor him with us. But all at once his blood started to itch in his veins, and he started this here . . . this here revolution. And I know all about revolution; that's one of the things we studied at the Point. Why d'you reckon I thought it was important enough to get up out of my chair?" He stared across the street. "It's got to be the African's blood! That's simple!"

8 Bobby-Joe's chin was cupped in his hands. He did not turn around to look at the old man, and so Mister Harper did not realize immediately the boy was making fun of him. "I hear tell about this African, and can even remember somebody telling the story to me a long time ago, but I JUST CAN'T seem to remember how it went." Mister Harper had told the story the day before, and many times before that. "Why don't you tell it, Mister Harper, and let us see how it got something to do with all this. How about that?"

9 By now Mister Harper realized what was going on, but it did not matter. He knew too some of the men thought he was too old and ought to be dead instead of coming to the porch each morning. But he liked to tell the story. Even so, they would have to coax him. "You all know that story as well as me."

10 "Awh now, Mister Harper, we just want to hear you tell it again." Bobby-Joe tried to make the man a child by the coddling tone in his voice. Someone behind Mister Harper laughed.

11 "Hell! I don't care. I'll tell it even if you don't want to hear it—just for spite!" He leaned back and took a deep breath. "Now, ain't nobody claiming this here story is ALL true."

12 "That's true if nothing else is." Bobby-Joe drew on his cigar and spat.

13   "All right, suppose you just let me tell this story."

14   "Yes, SIR." Bobby-Joe exaggerated his apology, but turning, found no approval on the other men's shadowed faces; Mister Harper had captured them already. "Yes, sir." This time Bobby-Joe meant it.

15   Like I said, nobody's claiming this story is all truth. It must-a started out that way, but somebody along the way or a whole parcel of somebodies must-a figured they could improve on the truth. And they did. It's a damn sight better story for being half lies. Can't a story be good without some lies. You take the story of Samson. Might not all be true as you read it in the Bible; folks must-a figured if you got a man just a little bit stronger than most, it couldn't do no real harm if you make him a whole lot stronger. So that's probably what folks hereabouts did; take the African, who must-a been pretty big and strong to start and make him even bigger and stronger.

16   I reckon they wanted to make certain we'd remember him. But when you think on it, there's no reason why we'd ever forget the African, even though this all happened a long time ago, because just like Tucker Caliban, the African was working for the Willsons, who was the most important folks around these parts. Only folks liked those Willsons a hell of a lot more in them days than we do now. They weren't so uppity as our Willsons.

17   But we're not talking about the Willsons of nowadays; we're talking about the African, who was owned by the General's father, Dewitt Willson, even though Dewitt never got no work out of him. But he owned him all the same.

18   Now the first time New Marsails (it was still New Marseilles then, after the French city) ever saw the African was in the morning, just after the slave ship he was riding pulled into the harbor. In them days, a boat coming was always a big occasion and folks used to walk down to the dock to greet it; it wasn't a far piece since the town wasn't no bigger than Sutton is today.

19   The slaver came up, her sails all plump, and tied up, and let fall her gangplank. And the ship's owner, who was also the leading slave auctioneer in New Marsails—he talked so good and so fast he could sell a one-armed, one-legged, half-witted Negro for a premium price— he ambled up the gangplank. I'm told he was a spindly fellow, with no muscles whatever. He had hard-bargain-driving eyes and a nose all round and puffy and pocked like a rotten orange, and he always wore a blue old-time suit with lace at the collar, and a sort of derby of green felt. And following him, exactly three paces behind, was a Negro. Some

folks said this was the auctioneer's son by a colored woman. I don't know that for certain, but I DO know this here Negro looked, walked, and talked just like his master. He had that same build, and the same crafty eyes, and dressed just like him too—green derby and all—so that the two of them looked like a print and a negative of the same photograph, since the Negro was brown and had kinky hair. This Negro was the auctioneer's bookkeeper and overseer and anything else you can think of. So then these two went up on deck, and while the Negro stood by, the auctioneer shook hands with the captain, who was standing on deck watching his men do their chores. You understand, they spoke different in them days, so I can't be certain exactly what they said, but I reckon it was something like: "How do, How was the trip?"

20   Already some folks standing on the dock could see the captain looked kind of sick. "Fine, excepting we had one real ornery son of a bitch. Had to chain him up, alone, away by himself."

21   "Let's have a look at him," said the auctioneer. The Negro behind him nodded, which he did every time the auctioneer spoke, so that he looked like he was a ventriloquist, and the auctioneer was his dummy, either that way or the other way around.

22   "Not yet. God damn! I'll bring him up after the rest of them niggers is OFF the boat. Then we can ALL hold him down. Damn!" He put his hand up to his brow, and that's when folks with good eyes could see the oily blue mark on his head like somebody spat axle grease on him and he hadn't had time yet to wipe it off. "God damn!" he said again.

23   Well, of course folks was getting real anxious, not just out of common interest like usual, but to see this son of a bitch that was causing all the trouble.

24   Dewitt Willson was there too. He hadn't come to see the boat, or even to buy slaves. He was there to pick up a grandfather clock. He was building himself a new house outside of Sutton and he'd ordered this clock from Europe and he wanted, it to come as fast as possible, and the fastest way was for it to come by slaver. He'd heard how carrying things on a slaver was seven kinds of bad luck, but still, because he was so anxious to get the clock, he let them send it that way. The clock rode in the captain's cabin and was all padded up with cotton, and boxed in, and crated around, and wadded secure. And he'd come to get it, bringing in a wagon to carry it out to his house and surprise his wife with it.

25   Dewitt and everybody was waiting, but first the crew went down and cracked their whips and herded this long line of Negroes out of

the hold. The women had breasts hanging most down to their waists, and some carried black babies. The men, their faces was all twisted up sullen as the inside of lemons. Most all the slaves was bone-naked and they stood on the deck, blinking; none of them had seen the sun in a long time. The auctioneer and his Negro walked up and down the row, as always, inspecting teeth, feeling muscles, looking over the goods, you might say. Then the auctioneer said, "Well, let's bring up this troublemaker, what say."

26   "No, sir!" yelled the captain.

27   "Why not?"

28   "I told you. I don't want him brung up until the rest of these niggers is off the boat."

29   "Yes, surely," said the auctioneer, but looked sort of blank. And so did his Negro.

30   The captain rubbed that shining grease-spot wound. "Don't you understand? He's their chief. If he says the word we'll have more trouble here than God has followers. I had enough already!" And he rubbed that spot again.

31   The crewmen pushed them Negroes down the gangplank and the folks on the dock stepped out of the way and watched them go by. Them Negroes even SMELLED angry, having been crammed together, each of them with no more room to himself than a baby in a crib. They was dirty, and mad, and ready for a fight. So the captain sent down some crewmen with rifles to keep them company. And the other crewmen, twenty or thirty there was, they just stood on deck fidgeting and shuffling. Folks on the dock knew right off what was the matter: them crewmen was afraid. You could see it in their eyes. All them grown men scared of whatever was down in the hold of that boat chained to the wall.

32   The captain looked sort of scared himself and fingered his wound and sighed and said to his mate: "I reckon you might as well go down there and get him." And to the twenty or thirty men standing around: "You go down there with him—all of you. Maybe you can manage."

33   Folks held their breath like youngsters at a circus waiting for a high-wire fellow to make it to his nest, because even if an old deaf-blind lady had-a been standing on that dock, she would-a known there was something down in the hold that was getting ready to make an appearance. Everybody got quiet and over the waves slapping against the hull they could hear all them crewmen tramping downstairs, the whole swarm of them in heavy bro-GANS, taking their time about informing that thing in the hold it was wanted on deck.

34   Then, out of the bottom of the ship, way off in some dark place, came this roar, louder'n a cornered bear or maybe two bears mating. It was so loud the sides of the boat bulged out. They all knew it was from one throat since there wasn't no blending, just one loud sound. And then, right in front of their eyes, in the side of the boat, way down near the water line, they saw a hole tear open, and splinters fly, splashing like when you toss a handful of pebbles into a pond. There was a lot of muffled fighting, pushing, and hollering going on, and after a while this fellow staggered on deck with blood dripping from his head. "God damn—if he ain't pulled his chain outen the wall of the boat," he says. And everybody stared at that hole again, and didn't take note that the crewman had just passed on from a cracked skull.

35   Well sir, you can believe that folks got into close knots for protection in case that thing in the bottom of the ship should somehow get loose and start a-raging through the peaceful town of New Marsails. Then it got sort of quiet again, even on the inside of the ship, and folks leaned forward, listening. They heard chains dragging and then they saw the African for the first time.

36   To begin with, they seen his head coming up out of the gangway, and then his shoulders, so broad he had to climb those stairs sideways; then his body began, and long after it should-a stopped it was still coming. Then he was full out, skin-naked except for a rag around his parts, standing at least two heads taller than any man on the deck. He was black and glistened like the captain's grease-spot wound. His head was as large as one of them kettles you see in a cannibal movie and looked as heavy. There was so many chains hung on him he looked like a fully trimmed Christmas tree. But it was his eyes they kept looking at; sunk deep in his head they was, making it look like a gigantic black skull.

37   There was something under his arm. At first they thought it was a tumor or growth and didn't pay it no mind, and it wasn't until it moved all by itself and they noticed it had eyes that they saw it was a baby. Yes sir, a baby tucked under his arm like a black lunch box, just peeping out at everybody.

38   So now they'd seen the African, and they stepped back a little as if the distance between him and them wasn't at all far enough, as if he could reach out over the railing of the ship, and down at them and pop off their heads with a flick of his fingers. But he was quiet now, not blinking in the sun like them others, just basking like it was his very own and he'd ordered it to come out and shine on him.

39   Dewitt Willson just stared. It was hard to tell what he was thinking but some folks said they heard him saying slowly to himself over

and over again: "I'll own him. He'll work for me. I'll break him. I have
to break him." They said he just stared and talked to himself.

40   And the auctioneer's Negro, he just stared too. But he wasn't
mumbling or talking. Folks said he just looked like he was pricing
something—looking at the African from head to toe and adding
totals: so much for the head and the brain; so much for the build
and the muscles; so much for the eyes—making notes on a piece
of paper with a crayon.

41   The captain had yelled down to his men to get them Negroes over
to the auction place, a mound of dirt in the center of New Marsails in
what is now Auction Square. Some men cleared a way and some others came down off the boat and started pushing the line of chained
Negroes. Then came all the people on the dock who was going over
to the Square to see what the going price for a good slave was on that
day, like folks read the stock market reports nowadays, and more
important, to see how much the African would sell for. And after they'd
gone away some, came the African and his escort, twenty men at least,
each holding a chain so he looked like a Maypole with all the men
around him in a circle staying a good healthy distance out of his reach.

42   When they got to the Square they pulled them other Negroes way
off to one side and the African and his attendants went right up on
the hill. Then the auctioneer, with his Negro behind him those same
three steps, started his selling:

43   "Now folks, you see here before you about the most magnificent
piece of property any man'd ever want to own. Note the height, the
breadth, the weight; note the extraordinary muscular development,
the regal bearing. This is a chief so he's got to have great leadership ability. He's gentle with children as you may be able to see
there under his arm. True, he's capable of destruction, but I maintain this is merely a sign of his ability to get a job done. I don't
think you need any proof of all I say; just to look at him is proof
enough. Why, if I didn't own him already, and if I had a farm or
a plantation, I'd sell half my land and all my slaves just to scrape
up enough money to buy him to work the other half. But I DO own
him, and I don't have any land. That's my problem. I can't use him;
I don't need him; I got to get rid of him. And that's where you come
in, friends. One of you has to take him off my hands. I'll pay you
for that kindness. Yes, sir! Don't let anybody tell you I'm not grateful for the good turns my friends do for me. What I'll do is this:
I'll toss right in this deal, at two for the price of one, that little baby
he's got under his arm."

44 (Now some folks said they found out later the auctioneer HAD to make that deal, since it was the captain who'd tried in the first place to get that baby from the African, and that's how come he'd got his head smashed. So I reckon the auctioneer couldn't very well sell them two as separate items without having to kill one to get the other.)

45 "Now, you know that's a bargain," he was going on to say, "because that baby will grow up to be just like his daddy. So now just picture it: when this here man gets too old to work, you'll have his spitting image all set to take over for him.

46 "I reckon you must know I'm not very sharp when it comes to prices and costs, but I'd say right off this here worker shouldn't go for less than five hundred dollars. What say, Mister Willson, you figure he's worth that much?"

47 Dewitt Willson didn't answer, didn't say nothing, just reached into his pocket and pulled out one thousand cash, as calm as you'd pick lint off a suit, walked halfway up the hill and handed that money to the auctioneer.

48 The auctioneer rapped his green derby against his knee. "Sold!"

49 Nobody, not even folks what claims to-a seen it, is really certain about what happened next. It must-a been them crewmen, who was still holding all them chains, relaxed when they saw all that money, because the African spun around once and nobody was holding nothing except maybe a fist full of blood and skin where them chains had rushed through like a buzz saw. And now the African was holding ALL them chains, had gathered them up like a woman grabs up her skirts climbing into an auto, and right off he started for the auctioneer like he understood what that man was saying and doing, which could not-a been since he was African and likely spoke that gibberish them Africans use. But leastways, he DID go after the auctioneer and some folks swears, though not all, that, using his chains, he sliced his head off—derby and all—and that the head sailed like a cannon ball through the air a quarter mile, bounced another quarter mile and still had up enough steam to cripple a horse some fellow was riding into New Marsails. Fellow came into town babbling about having to shoot his horse after its leg got splintered by a flying head wearing a green derby.

50 Some strange things happened just then. The auctioneer's Negro, who'd taken a step or two back when the African got loose and didn't seem to take notice of the headless auctioneer except to make certain he didn't have no blood splattered on him to ruin his clothes, he ran up to the African, who was just standing near the body which hadn't

even had time to fall yet, and grabbed his arm and pointed and started yelling: "This way! This way!"

51   I reckon the African didn't really understand but he knew the Negro was trying to help him and started out in the direction the Negro was pointing, and the Negro followed him just like he'd followed the auctioneer, a distance of three steps back, and the African ran down off the hill though he must-a been carrying close to three hundred pounds of chains on him, swinging them, breaking seven or eight arms and a leg, carving himself and the Negro a path through the townspeople of New Marsails. Some men raised rifles and took aim, and maybe could-a hit them (not saying, mind you, they could-a stopped the African), but Dewitt Willson ran up on the hill like a crazy man, and got between the men and the African and Negro, screaming all the while: "Don't shoot my property! I'll sue! That's my property!" And by that time the African was out of range and heading south into the swamps at the end of town. So the men and Dewitt got horses and more rifles and after a while set out after him.

52   The African was traveling pretty fast (he must-a been carrying not only his baby and the chains but the Negro too because I don't see how that small Negro could-a kept up), and Dewitt and the men might-a never trailed him except that he went straight through the woods and swamps and left this trail of torn-up bushes, grass, and small trees where them chains had caught on things and he'd pulled them right out of the ground, heading straight for the sea. They just set out on this trail, wide enough for two horses to go abreast, as straight as a plumb line, and followed it through the swamp, right down to the sand and into the water. That's where it stopped.

53   The men figured the African must-a just tried to swim back home (some said he could-a made it—chains, baby and all) and that auctioneer's Negro must-a lit out on his own, and now they was sort of tired and wanted to go home and forget about it, but Dewitt was sure the African wasn't gone, not swimming, and was coming back, and got the men to look up and down the beach for some sign. They did, and half mile down the beach they found two sets of tracks going into the woods.

54   Right about now it got hard for Dewitt Willson to get men to help him chase his property. First of all, it was getting dark. Second of all, there wasn't no wide trail like before because the African must-a been holding them chains off the ground so they wouldn't catch on anything, like a little girl holds up her skirts around her waist when she goes wading. So the men just naturally cooled down when it came to tracking a wild man through the woods at night when, at beat, it

would be hard to see him and when you couldn't be sure where he was, and he could pay you a visit and slice off your head even before you knew he was calling. So they camped on the beach, and some men went for supplies and at daybreak they took out after him again.

55 But that one night was all the time the African and the auctioneer's Negro needed and it was going to be harder than ever to catch him now because when they came into a clearing about a mile into the woods, shining in the sun was a pile of broken stones, and links, and bracelets where the African had spent the night cleaning them off himself. So now he was loose, free of his chains, and was somewhere in the area. He was so big and so fast you didn't dare make a guess at WHERE he might be, since folks began to realize he could-a been anywhere within a distance of a hundred miles. But Dewitt, with fewer men now, kept going and tracked his property for two weeks, halfway to where Willson City is now, and back, which is a total of two hundred miles, and all along the Gulf Coast almost to Mississippi and the other way into Alabama, and finally, those men still with Dewitt noticed he was looking sort of funny. He didn't sleep at all, or eat, spent twenty-four hours a day on his horse and was talking to himself, saying: "I'll catch you . . . I'll catch you . . . I'll catch you." And then, nearly a month after the African got away, in which time Dewitt hadn't been home at all, while the men watched, he keeled off his horse and didn't wake up until they'd taken him home in a litter to his plantation and he'd slept in a featherbed for another week. His wife told folks he kept right on talking to himself and when he did wake up, he came up screaming: "But I am. I'm worth a thousand too! I am!"

56 Now the African changed his tactics.

57 One afternoon Dewitt and his wife was sitting on their front porch. Dewitt was trying to get back his strength by sipping something cool and taking in the sun. And up the front lawn, dressed in African clothes of bright colors, with a spear and a shield, comes the African, bearing down on the house like he was a train and it was a tunnel and he was going right through—which he did, on out the back door, across the back lawn to the slave quarters, where he freed every last one of Dewitt's Negroes and led them off into the dark of the woods before Dewitt could even set down his glass and get up out of his chair.

58 Well, if that wasn't enough, the next night almost the same thing happened to a fellow east of New Marsails. He came into town and told everybody about it: "I was sleeping peaceful when I heared this noise outside down by the slave cabins. God damn, when I rushed to the window if I didn't see all my niggers heading into the woods

behind a man who was as big anyways as a black horse on its hind legs. And there was another one too," the fellow went on, "never more than a few steps behind the big one, waving his arms and telling MY niggers what to do and where to go."

59   Even though he was still ailing, Dewitt Willson came into town and stood up in front of a big meeting they was holding to try and solve the problem and said: "Now I swear to you, I'm not going home until I can take the African or what's left of him with me. And let everybody know this: white or black, anybody who can give me news that'll help me catch the African will be walking around the next day with a thousand of my dollars in his pocket." And that news spread like the smell of cooking cabbage, spread all up and down the region so that years after, if you'd gone into Tennessee and mentioned you was from down this way, somebody'd ask: "Say, who DID get Dewitt Willson's thousand?"

60   Dewitt Willson kept his word; he set out after the African again. He tracked and trailed him for another month all over the state. Sometimes they'd come pretty close to getting him too, but not quite close enough. They'd come on him and his band, which they managed to thin out and keep down to twelve or so what with killing and capturings, and have a battle, but the African'd always wriggle out some way. One time they thought they had him trapped with his back to the river and he just turned around, dove in and swam it underwater. And you know some fellows can't even throw a stone that far. They could never get their hands on that auctioneer's Negro neither. He was always around, holding the baby while the African fought, looking at what went on out of them money-filled eyes which gleamed under that green derby. Yes sir, he still had the derby, though nothing else, was dressed now like the African in one of them long, multi-colored sheets.

61   Dewitt was changing again, doing the same things he'd done before he collapsed, not talking to anybody, not even to himself now, moody and silent all the time. And so it went on, the African raiding and freeing slaves, Dewitt Willson catching up with the band and taking most of the slaves back and killing more, keeping the African's men down to twelve or thirteen, and the African and the auctioneer's Negro never getting caught.

62   Then one night they was camped a little north of New Marsails. Everybody was asleep except Dewitt, who was sitting on his horse looking into the fire. He heard a voice behind him, what seemed like it could-a been the voice of the auctioneer's ghost, but wasn't. "You want the African? I'll take you to him."

63 Dewitt turned around and saw the auctioneer's Negro standing there, wearing his sheet and his derby; he'd got into camp without being heard or seen.

64 "Where is he?" Dewitt asked.

65 "I'll take you to him. I'll go up to him and slap him on the cheek if you want it that way," said the Negro.

66 So Dewitt went. He said later he wasn't sure he'd done the right thing following that Negro because it could-a been an ambush or a trap. But he said, too, he didn't think the African'd do something like that. Some of the men with him said Dewitt was crazy enough by that time to do anything to catch the African, would-a gone anywhere with anyone to get him.

67 So Dewitt roused his men, and they rode out after the Negro. They didn't have to go more than a mile before they came into the African's camp. There was no fire and the Negroes, maybe twelve, was lying on the bare ground with no cover, sleeping. Right in the middle of the clearing, his back against a huge rock, the black baby across his knees, sat the African. He had a cloth over his head and set up in front of him was a pile of stones, which he seemed to be a-mumbling at.

68 Dewitt Willson couldn't figure out why no one'd warned the African, how come he'd been able to sneak up on him, and leaned down to the Negro and said: "Why aren't there no guards? He knew I was right close by. Why aren't there no guards?"

69 The Negro smiled up at him. "There WAS one guard. Me."

70 "Why'd you do this? Why'd you turn on him?"

71 The Negro smiled again. "I'm an American; I'm no savage. And besides, a man's got to follow where his pocket takes him, doesn't he?"

72 Dewitt Willson nodded. Some folks said he almost turned around and went back to his own camp and wanted to forget all about catching his property this way and then come back in the morning when the African would be gone and chase him until he caught him fair and square, because it seems like after all those weeks of chasing the African through the woods, after all that time of following his trail and thinking maybe he'd get him this time and finding he didn't any more have him than a dwarf has a chance of being a professional basketball player, after all the sweating and riding and bad food and hard sleeping, he'd come to respect this man, and I reckon he must-a been a little sad that when he finally caught up with his property it was because some fellow the African'd trusted would turncost and lead the white men into camp. But the other men didn't feel that way. They wanted the African any way they

could get him because he'd been making fools of them and they knew it and they wanted an end to that.

73   So the white men circled the camp and when they had it surrounded, Dewitt Willson called out for the Negroes to give up. The white men lit torches so the African could see he was ringed by fire, horses, and men with rifles. The Negroes jumped to their feet and right away saw it wasn't no use, since all they had was African weapons, and they threw them down on the ground. But the African bolted up on top of the rock straddling the baby and made a full circle taking stock of what he was up against because he was alone and he knew it, since by then all the Negroes had scattered into the bushes or were standing around like they'd never seen him before and didn't know him from a third-century Roman Catholic Pope.

74   There he stood on the rock, alone, glistening in the fire, almost naked, his eyes just hollows of black. Then he stepped down. Someone raised a rifle.

75   "Wait!" Dewitt shouted. "See if we can take him alive. Don't you understand? That's the point. Take him alive!" He was standing up in his stirrups waving his arms for attention in the firelight.

76   Some fellow took this to mean that he should be a hero, and thinking he could run down the African, raced his horse straight at him, but the African just grabbed the fellow off the horse's back like you might catch a ring on a carousel and popped his back over his knee like a dry wishbone and tossed him aside.

77   "If you shoot, aim for his limbs," Dewitt was yelling.

78   Someone from the other side of the circle fired, and they could see the bullet go right through the African's hand and dig into the ground near Dewitt's horse, but the African didn't seem to connect the report with any pain he might-a felt in his hand, didn't even wince or move. Someone else shot him just above the knee and blood ran down his leg like a ribbon.

79   Keeping his back to the rock, where the baby was sleeping, he made a full, slow circle, eying them all, eying the auctioneer's Negro too, who was standing next to Dewitt, but not stopping at him, or showing any anger or bitterness, stopping only when he came to Dewitt Willson and staring at him. They stared at each other, not like they was trying to stare each other down, more like they was discussing something without using words. And finally it seemed like they came to an agreement because the African bowed slightly like a fighter bows at the beginning of a match, and Dewitt Willson raised his rifle, sighted the African's upturned face, and shot him cleanly just above the bridge of his wide nose.

80   It hit him all right, but the African just stood there, and then finally sunk to his knees, and then forward on his hands. He seemed to be melting away, and then suddenly, he looked up with shock on his face, like he'd just remembered something and had to do it before he passed on, and gave a loud wail, and started crawling toward the sleeping baby, his eyes filled with blood, and a good-sized rock in his fist. He raised the rock above the baby, but Dewitt Willson shattered the back of his head before he could smash it down. And so the African died.

81   None of the men moved. They sat, disappointed, on their horses because they, each of them, had wanted to go back and say they'd gotten the bullet into the African what had killed him.

82   Dewitt Willson climbed down off his horse, walked to the baby, which was still sleeping, not knowing his daddy was dead, not knowing, I reckon, his daddy'd ever been alive. Coming back to his horse, Dewitt tripped over that pile of stones the African'd been talking to. They was all very flat stones, and Dewitt Willson stared down at them for a long time, and after a while he bent over, picked up the smallest one, a white one, and put it in his pocket.

83   Mister Harper was getting hoarse. He paused for a moment, cleared his throat, went on. "Dewitt Willson went back to New Marsails, got his clock, which he hadn't called for yet, and rode on home, with the African's baby beside him on the wagon seat, the auctioneer's Negro and the clock ticking in the wagon bed, that same clock you saw out at Tucker's farm on Thursday." He stopped and turned to face those behind him. "Well, that's the story and you all know as well as me how that baby got named Caliban by the General, when the General was twelve years old."

84   That's right. After the General read that there book by Shakespeare," Loomis added, sighing.

85   "Not a book, a play, *The Tempest.* Shakespeare didn't write no books; nobody wrote books then, just poems and plays. No books. You must not-a learned NOTHING your three weeks up at the university." Mister Harper stared Loomis down.

86   "All right then, a play," Loomis agreed, sheepishly.

87   It was near dinner time now. Several men left the porch. A warm wind blew down off Eastern Ridge. A car, filled with solemn-faced Negroes, sputtered through, going north.

88   "And Caliban, whose Christian name got to be First after he got a family and there was more than just one Caliban, was John Caliban's father, and John Caliban's grandson is Tucker Caliban and

the African's blood is running in Tucker Caliban's veins." Mister Harper sat back, satisfied.

89 "That's what you say." Bobby-Joe tossed his cigar into the street.

90 "Boy, I'll forgive you for being so damned stupid. You'll find out one of these days that I'm no fool. You can believe me now or not— it makes no difference to me—but sooner or later you WILL agree and you'll have to apologize."

91 The men grumbled. "That's right."

92 "Now look here, Mister Harper," Bobby-Joe started very softly, not even turning to face the old man, rather looking up and down the street before him, "Tucker Caliban worked for the Willsons every day of his life. How come he picked Thursday to up and feel his African's blood." He turned now. "Tell me that?"

93 "Well, boy, a good man won't lie to you; he won't tell you something is true if he's not sure. And I'll tell you right out I can't answer your question. I just say Tucker Caliban felt the blood and had to move and even though it was different from what the African would-a done, it amounts to the same thing. But why on Thursday? I can't tell you." The old man nodded his head as he talked, looking over the roof tops at the sky.

94 They all heard the clomping of old woman's shoes, then saw Mister Harper's daughter. She was fifty-five, a spinster, with limp yellow hair. "You ready to come home and eat, Papa?"

95 "Yes, honey. Yes, I am."

96 "Will some of you men help him down?" She asked that same question each night.

97 "Well now, I don't reckon I'll be coming back tonight, so I'll see you all tomorrow after church." Mister Harper was in the street now, his daughter behind him, her hands on the high thronelike back, waiting.

98 "Yes, sir." They answered together.

99 "Good night then. Don't get into no trouble." The wheels creaked the old man away.

100 Once Mister Harper was out of earshot, Bobby-Joe turned to the other men. "You really believe that blood business? You think that explains all this?" He thought that once the old man was gone they would not be so kind to his opinions.

101 "If that's what Mister Harper says, it's got to be part of the answer anyways." Thomason pushed himself off the wall and started toward the door.

102 "Yes, that's so." Loomis rocked forward and placed his hands on his knees, preparing to get up.

103   "You REALLY think it's simple as that?"

104   "Well, put it this way." Thomason opened the door, went inside and pressed his nose against the screening. "Can you give a better reason?"

105   "No." Bobby-Joe looked at Thomason's stomach pressed flat against the screen door. "No, I can't right now. But I'm thinking on it."

Amiri Baraka

(1934–)

One of the foremost innovators in African American literature, Amiri Baraka was named Everett Leroy Jones upon his birth on October 7, 1934, in Newark, New Jersey. He attended Rutgers and Howard universities before serving in the Air Force, though he never felt at ease in any of those institutions. Following his dishonorable discharge (for disciplinary violations) from the military in 1957, he relocated to New York City and became a notable member of the avant-garde in Greenwich Village. He achieved national prominence with his play Dutchman *(1964), for which he received an Obie award. Following the assassination of Malcolm X in 1965, Baraka embraced Black nationalism and left the bohemian scene in Greenwich Village for Harlem, where he became known as the leading proponent of the Black Arts Movement and founded the Black Arts Repertory Theatre. Baraka was back in Newark by 1968. That year, he changed his name to Imamu Amiri Baraka, meaning "blessed spiritual leader." In 1974, he adopted the ideology of Marxism-Leninism. Baraka has long been involved in political organizing, both locally and nationally, and he served on the faculty of the State University of New York at Stony Brook. His dozens of literary works span the genres of poetry, drama, fiction, and criticism. These works include the poetry volumes* Preface to a Twenty Volume Suicide Note *(1961),* The Dead Lecturer *(1964),* Black Art *(1966),* It's Nation Time *(1970),* Reggae or Not! *(1982), and* Transbluescency; *the novel* The System of Dante's Hell *(1965); the plays* Slave *and* The Baptism; *the critical works* Blues People *(1963) and* What the Music Said; *the essay collections* Home: Social Essays *(1966), and* Raise Race Rays Raze *(1972); and the memoir* The Autobiography of LeRoi Jones/Amiri Baraka. *With Larry Neal, he edited* Black Fire: An Anthology of Afro-American Writing *(1968). "When We'll Worship Jesus" appeared in his 1972 volume of poetry* Hard Facts.

When We'll Worship Jesus

We'll worship Jesus
When jesus do
Somethin
When jesus blow up
5   the white house
or blast nixon down
when jesus turn out congress
or bust general motors to
yard bird motors
10 jesus we'll worship jesus
when jesus get down
when jesus get out his yellow lincoln
w/the built in cross stain glass
window&box w/black peoples
15 enemies we'll worship jesus when
he get bad enough to at least scare
somebody—cops not afraid
of jesus
pushers not afraid
20 of jesus, capitalists racists
imperialists not afraid
of jesus shit they makin money
off jesus
we'll worship jesus when mao
25 do, when toure does
when the cross replaces Nkrumah's
star
Jesus need to hurt some a our
enemies, then we'll check him
30 out, all that screaming and hollering
&wallering and moaning talkin bout
jesus, jesus, in a red
check velvet vine + 8 in. heels
jesus pinky finger
35 got a goose egg ruby
which actual bleeds
jesus at the apollo
doin splits and helpin

         nixon trick niggers
40   jesus w/his one eyed self
         tongue kissing johnny carson
         up the behind
         jesus need to be busted
         jesus need to be thrown down and whipped
45   till something better happen
         jesus aint did nothin for us
         but kept us turned toward the
         sky (him and his boy allah
         too, need to be checked
50   out!)
         we'll worship jesus
         when he get a boat load of ak-47s
         and some dynamite
         and blow up abernathy robotin
55   for gulf
         jesus need to be busted
         we ain't gonna worship nobody
         but niggers gettin up off
         the ground
60   not gon worship jesus
         unless he just a tricked up
         nigger somebody named
         outside his race
         need to worship yo self fo
65   you worship jesus
         need to bust jesus (+ check
         out his spooky brother
         allah while you heavy
         on the case
70   cause we ain gon worship jesus
         we aint gon worship
         jesus
         we aint gon worship
         jesus
75   not till he do somethin
         not till he help us
         not till the world get changed
         and he ain, jesus ain, he cant change the world
         we can change the world

80   we can struggle against the forces of backwardness, we can
      change the world
  we can struggle against our selves, our slowness, our connection
      with
  the oppressor, the very cultural aggression which binds us to
85   our enemies
      as their slaves.
  we can change the world
  we aint gonna worship jesus cause jesus dont exist
  except in song and story except in ritual and dance, except in
90   slum stained
  tears or trillion dollar opulence stretching back in history, the
      history
  of the oppression of the human mind
  we worship the strength in us
95   we worship our selves
  we worship the light in us
  we worship the warmth in us
  we worship the world
  we worship the love in us
100   we worship our selves
  we worship nature
  we worship ourselves
  we worship the life in us, and science, and knowledge, and
      transformation
105 of the visible world
  but we aint gonna worship no jesus
  we aint gonna legitimize the witches and devils and spooks and
      hobgoblins
  the sensuous lies of the rulers to keep us chained to fantasy and
110   illusion
  sing about life, not jesus
  sing about revolution, not no jesus
  stop singing about jesus,
  sing about, creation, our creation, the life of the world and
115   fantastic
  nature how we struggle to transform it, but dont victimize our
      selves by
  distorting the world
  stop moanin about jesus, stop sweatin and crying and stompin
120   and dyin for jesus

unless thats the name of the army we building to force the land
    finally to
change hands. And lets not call that jesus, get a quick
    consensus, on that,
125 lets damn sure not call that black fire muscle
    no invisible psychic dungeon
no gentle vision strait jacket, lets call that peoples army, or
    wapenduzi or
    simba
130 wachanga, but we not gon call it jesus, and not gon worship
    jesus, throw
jesus out yr mind. Build the new world out of reality, and new
    vision
we come to find out what there is of the world
135 to understand what there is here in the world!
to visualize change, and force it.
we worship revolution

Carolyn Rodgers
(1945–)

*Born December 14, 1945, in Chicago, Carolyn Rodgers became, in the
1960s, an important member of the Chicago-based Organization of
Black American Culture (OBAC). She emerged as a leading voice among
African American poets both locally and nationally. Her work has been
visionary yet grounded in everyday African American experience, and, as
indicated by the following selections, her work exemplifies a complexity
of engagement. Her poetry volumes include* Paper Soul *(1969),* 2 Love
Raps *(1969),* Now Ain't That Love *(1969),* Songs of a Black Bird *(1969),*
how i got ovah: New and Selected Poems *(1975),* The Heart As Ever
Green *(1978), and* Morning Glory *(1989).*

Jesus Was Crucified or: It Must Be Deep

(*an epic pome*)

i was sick
and my motha called me
tonight yeah, she did she

sd she was sorri
5 i was sick, but what
     she wanted tuh tell
me was that i shud pray or
have her (hunky) preacher
pray fuh me, she sd. i
10 had too much hate in me
she sd u know the way yuh think is
got a lots to do
wid the way u feel, and i
agreed, told her i WAS angry a lot THESE days
15 and maybe my insides was too and she sd
     why it's somethin wrong wid yo mind girl
that's what it is
          and i sd yes, i was aware a lot
lately and she sd if she had evah known educashun
20 wouda mad me crazi, she woulda neva sent me to
school (college that is)
she sd the way i worked my fingers to the bone in
this white mans factori to make u a de-cent somebodi
and here u are actin not like decent folks
25   talkin bout hatin white folks&revolution
 &such and runnin round wid Negroes
     WHO CURSE IN PUBLIC!!! (she sd)
THEY COMMUNIST GIRL!!! DON'T YUH KNOW
THAT???
30   **DON'T YUH READ***THE NEWSPAPERS??????
                (and i sd)
i don't believe—(and she sd) U DON'T BELIEVE IN
           GOD NO MO DO U?????
u wudn't raised that way! U gon die and go tuh HELL
35 and i sd i hoped it wudn't be NO HUNKIES there
and she sd
what do u mean, there is some good white people and
some bad ones, just like there is negroes
and i says a had neva seen ONE (wite good that is) but
40 she sd negroes ain't redi, i knows this and
deep in yo heart you do too and i sd yes u right
negroes ain't readi and she sd
why just the utha day i was in the store and there was
uh negro packin clerk put uh colored woman's ice cream

45   in her grocery bag widout wun of them "don't melt" bags
      and the colored ladi sd to the colored clerk
      "how do u know mah ice cream ain't gon tuh melt befo I
      git home."
         clerk sd. "i don't" and took the ice cream
50   back out and put it in wun of them "stay hard"
      bags
      and me and that ladi sd see, ne-groes don't treat
      nobody right why that clerk packin groceries was un
      grown main, acted mad. White folks wudn't treat yuh that
55   way, why when i went tuh the BANK the otha day to deposit
      some MONEY
        this white man helped me fast and nice. u gon die girl
      and go tuh hell if yuh hate white folks. i sd, me and
      my friends could dig it . . . hell, that is
60   she sd du u pray? i sd sorta when i hear Coltrane and
      she sd if yuh read yuh bible it'll show u read genesis
      revelation and she couldn't remember the otha chapter
      i should read but she sd what was in the bible was
      happnin now, fire&all and she sd just cause i didn't
65   believe the bible don't make it not true
                       (and i sd)
      just cause she believed the bible didn't make it true
      and she sd it is it is and deep deep down
      in yo heart u know it's true
70   (and i sd)
      it must be deeep
      she sd i gon pray fuh u tuh be saved. i sd thank yuh
        but befo she hung up my motha sd
        well girl, if yuh need me call me
75   i hope we don't have to straighten the truth out no mo.
      i sd i hoped we didn't too
           (it was 10 P.M. when she called)
      she sd, i got tuh go so i can git up early tomorrow
      and go tuh the social security board to clarify my
80   record cause i need my money.
      work hard for 30 yrs. and they don't want tuh give me
      $28.00 once every two weeks.
           i sd yeah . . .
      don't let em nail u wid no technicalities
85   git yo checks . . . (then i sd)

catch yuh later on Jesus, i mean motha I
it must be
deeeeep. . . .

It is Deep

(don't never forget the bridge that you crossed over on)

Having tried to use the
witch cord
that erases the stretch of
thirty-three blocks
5 and tuning in the voice which
woodenly stated that the
talk box was "disconnected"

My mother, religiously girdled in
her god, slipped on some love, and
10 laid on my bell like a truck,
blew through my door warm wind from the south
concern making her gruff and tight-lipped
and scared
that her "baby" was starving.
15 she, having learned, that disconnection results from,
non-payment of bill (s).

She did not
recognize the poster of the
grand le-roi*
20 had never even seen the book of

Black poems that I have written
thinks that I am under the influence of
communists
when I talk about Black as anything
25 other than something ugly to kill it befo it grows
in any impression she would not be
considered "relevant" or "Black"
but

---

* LeRoi Jones, who changed his name to Amiri Baraka.

there she was, standing in my room
30 not loudly condemning that day and
not remembering that I grew hearing her
curse the factory where she "cut uh slave"
and the cheep j-boss wouldn't allow a union,
not remembering that I heard the tears when
35 they told her a high school diploma was not enough
and here now, not able to understand, what she had
been forced to deny, still—

she pushed into my kitchen so
she could open my refrigerator to see
40 what I had to eat, and pressed fifty
bills in my hand saying "pay the talk bill and buy
some food; you got folks who care about you . . ."

My mother, religious-negro, proud of
having waded through a storm, is very obviously,
45 a sturdy Black bridge that I
crossed over, on.

Anonymous

There's No Hiding Place Down There

There's no hiding place down there,
There's no hiding place down there.

O, I went to the rock to hide my face,
The rock cried out, "No hiding place."
5 There's no hiding place down there.

O, the rock cried, "I'm burning, too,"
O, the rock cried, "I'm burning, too,"
O, the rock cried, "I'm burning, too,"

I want to go to Heaven as well as you,
10 There's no hiding place down there.

O, the sinner man, he gambled and fell,
O, the sinner man, he gambled and fell,
O, the sinner man, he gambled and fell;
He wanted to go to Heaven,
15 But he had to go to Hell.
There's no hiding place down there.

Curtis Mayfield

(1942–1997)

Born in Chicago on June 3, 1942, Curtis Mayfield was a member of
The Impressions, a singing group whose popular music, heavily
influenced by gospels and spirituals, is closely identified with the
modern Civil Rights Movement. Mayfield was singing by the age of
seven and taught himself how to play the guitar. He paid particular
attention to the Northern Jubilee Gospel Singers, whose members
included three of his cousins as well as childhood friend Jerry But-
ler. In 1957, Butler invited Mayfield to join The Roosters, a group
whose name was subsequently changed to The Impressions. The
group achieved success throughout the 1960s with socially conscious
hits like "People Get Ready" (1965) and "We're a Winner" (1968).
Mayfield embarked upon an enormously successful solo career in
1970. In 1990, he was paralyzed by an accident prior to an outdoor
concert at Wingate High School in Brooklyn, where he was felled by
a lighting rig that had been dislodged by winds. Mayfield died in
Roswell, Georgia, on December 26, 1997.

"People Get Ready"

People get ready
There's a train comin'

Don't need no baggage
You just get on board
5 All we need is faith

To hear the diesel's humming
Don't need no ticket
We'll just thank the Lord.

People get ready
10 for the train to Jordan
It's pickin' up passengers
from coast to coast.
Faith is the key,
open the doors and borders
15 That's all . . . among his love and though
I believe, I believe
I believe, I do believe.

There ain't no room for the hopeless sinner
Have pity on those
20 whose chances grow thinner.
There's no hidin' place
against the kingdom's throne.

Anonymous

I've Been 'Buked

I've been 'buked and I've been scorned,
O, Lord—
I've been 'buked and I've been scorned,
Children—
5 I've been 'buked and I've been scorned,
I've been talked about sure's you're born.
But, ain't goin' to lay my religion down,
No, Lord—
Ain't goin' to lay my religion down,
10 Children—
No, ain't goin' to lay my religion down,
Ain't goin' to lay my religion down.

James Brown

(1933–)

Known widely and fondly by several nicknames, including "The Godfather of Soul" and "Soul Brother Number One," James Brown was born in rural Georgia on May 3, 1933. He grew up economically impoverished in Augusta, Georgia. Brown hustled on the streets, served a sentence for armed robbery, and tried his hand at sports before launching a music career that became characterized by pulsating beats and live dance performances that were so energetic that Brown routinely lost seven pounds or so each night. Over the course of his career, he has placed ninety-eight singles on Billboard's rhythm and blues Top 40, including number one hits like "Papa's Got a Brand New Bag" (1965), "Cold Sweat" (1967), "I Got the Feelin" (1968), and "Say It Loud—I'm Black and I'm Proud" (1968). Although an innovator of funk and a precursor to disco and hip hop, Brown's musical roots are the gospels and spirituals of his youth, as one can see in "I'm Black and I'm Proud."

Say It Loud, I'm Black and I'm Proud

Say it loud, I'm black and I'm proud
Whee it's hurting me, if it's alright, it's alright,
You're too tough, you're tough enough,
You're alright and you're out of sight,
5   Say it loud, I'm black and I'm proud.

I say we won't quit moving until we get what we deserve,
We've been 'buked and we've been scorned,
We've been treated bad, as sure as you've been borned,
But just as it takes two eyes to make a pair,
We're not gonna quit until we get our share.

Charlie Braxton

(1961–)

A Mississippi-born poet, playwright, and journalist, Charlie Braxton was born on June 19, 1961. Raised in McComb, Mississippi, he majored in Mass Communication with a minor in English at Jackson

State University. At the university, he cofounded Black Poets for a New Day, a workshop for student and community writers. Braxton has worked primarily as a journalist, although his poetry has been published in journals such as African American Review *and* Minnesota Review. *The following poem is taken from his volume* Ascension from the Ashes *(1990).*

Apocalypse

across the sandy dry plains

of the good old wild wild west

the thunderous din of dead buffalo

hoof beat out a desperate warning

5   to one and all

beware

beware

beware

jesus is a big mean assed black man

10   painted smokey grey

and boy is he mad upset pissed off

dressed in a camouflage shroud

a three day beard and packing

a steel blue jammie

15   last seen kicking asses

and calling names

headed straight for the second

coming

Nicole Breedlove

(1970–)

Born and raised in the Bedford-Stuyvesant section of Brooklyn, New York, Nicole Breedlove joined a writing group as a teenager but decided that the group had fallen into the "art-for-art's-sake-only" trap. She wanted her writing to be geared toward the liberation of oppressed people. Breedlove appeared on the PBS series Words in Your Face, *in 1991. The following poem was published in Ras Baraka and Kevin Powell's* In the Tradition *(1992).*

The New Miz Praise De Lawd

wade in the water
wade in the water children
wade in the water
God's gonna trouble the water
5   Hey y'all I'm Miz Mary but peoples call me Missy
cause they say I never miss the point
I'm also a God-fearing woman I mean I pray and things
are alright by me . . . Now don't get me wrong I ain't blind
I know God only helps those who helps themselves.
10 I also know that Jesus was a black prophet who was lynched
by Roman soldiers 2,000 years ago! (Now even I knew since I
was wee old that ain't no way a man could live during that
time in that heat and have white skin, blond hair and blue eyes).
I don't want nothin from nobody and I don't owe nothin
15 to anybody but the good Lord above. The bible say, "Whatsoever
thy hand findeth to do, do it with thy, might;"

Ecclesiastes Chapter 9 Verse 10! Thats why I give praise
everyday God gave us Larry Davis, Malcolm X and Steven Biko.
I don't believe in the Dream Martin had that Blacks are suppose
20 to be meek and abide by the Bible. I agree that his bringing
together blacks for freedom by way of religion was a good idea
but I think we've been obedient for too long. Now I know I
just said I was a God-fearing woman and I know that the Bible
says to turn the other cheek but Lord. . .that one has been
25 slapped too! I don't never propose violence but seeing what's
happenin' to young black people and older black people and
poor black people everywhere, an eye for an eye and a tooth
for a tooth is becoming more appealing as I grow older!!
wade in the water wade in the water children
wade in the water Missy's gonna trouble the water . . .

Writing Assignments

1. Develop your viewpoint on the central meaning of the spirituals.
   Do you see them as overtly political in the ways that some argue?
   Or does your opinion differ? Make reference to specific lines or passages to construct your argument. You may want to consult material on the suggested reading list.

2. Compare and contrast the work of two poets from among a group
   that includes Jupiter Hammon, Phillis Wheatley, Frances E. W.
   Harper, Paul Laurence Dunbar, James Weldon Johnson, and Robert
   Hayden. Feel free to include discussion of poems by these poets that
   are not included in this chapter. Analyze both form and the use of
   biblical themes in the poetry you consider.

3. What is your assessment of the dynamics expressed in the poems
   by Carolyn Rodgers, Amiri Baraka, Charlie Braxton, and Nicole
   Breedlove? Which poet expresses sentiments most similar to your
   own? How does this poet's work compare, in your view, with poetry
   by the likes of Harper and Johnson?

4. In your estimation, which work of fiction in this chapter is most
   successful in terms of incorporating biblical themes into the story?
   Explain your choice with respect to such elements as character, plot,
   and tone.

5. After tracing the specific textual connections between some of the spirituals in this chapter and the lyrics by Sam Cooke, Lauryn Hill, Curtis Mayfield, and James Brown, compile a list of additional songs that you think are directly traceable to spirituals. Compare and contrast the messages of the songs with those of the spirituals.

CHAPTER THREE

THE SOUTH AS LITERARY LANDSCAPE

The American South materializes as a complicated landscape in African American literature. While the South is located below the Mason-Dixon line, the precise contours by which it is defined are ambiguous, and thus it is more a symbolic geography than a specifically definable region. Despite the fact that chattel slavery existed throughout the nation, the South relied on this "peculiar institution" as the foundation for its economic, social, and cultural landscape. Further, the South was a primary port of entry for slaving vessels. More than half of the African captives headed for America landed in South Carolina, which contained the largest seaport in all of North America.

It is, therefore, reasonable to conclude that the South, in the words of Amiri Baraka, is the "scene of the crime," a sentiment echoed strongly in American slave narratives. This chapter begins with an excerpt from the most famous slave autobiography, *Narrative of the Life of Frederick Douglass, An American Slave, Written by Himself* (1845). The memoir chronicles the horrors of chattel slavery, focusing on familial separation, the slaveholder's penchant for corporal punishment, and the spectrum of physical and psychological abuse that dehumanizes the captives. The author's journey from enslavement to freedom is coterminous with his move from the rural to the urban, and eventually the South to the North. Thus Douglass' initial move from his birthplace in rural Maryland to the city of Baltimore, where he acquires literacy, the necessary tool of freedom, concludes the section collected in this chapter. Not only was the South a notorious site of slavery Reconstruction it was a landscape of racial terror and widespread violence. A culture of lynching, sharecropping, and tenant farming characterized life for many even decades after the Emancipation

Proclamation. In this chapter, Richard Wright's "Big Boy Leaves Home," from his short-story collection *Uncle Tom's Children* (1938), clearly articulates the brutal social conditions of the South in the early part of the twentieth century. Wright's story poignantly exposes the oppressive laws, known as Jim Crow, that circumscribed African American lives. This series of laws and customs mandated segregation in nearly all aspects of Black and white life in the South, from schools to public transportation to workplaces. In fact, some codes even prevented Black and white laborers from working in the same room together or from using the same entrances and doorways. Wright's story dramatizes the heinous violence, including the all-too-familiar spectacle of lynching, triggered by the young protagonists' transgression of Southern racial conventions. Lynching, the emblematic act of Southern violence, is a chord that is sounded through many pieces in this chapter, from Billie Holiday's signature song, "Strange Fruit" (1938), to excerpts from Jean Toomer's *Cane* (1923) to Maya Angelou's *Gather Together in My Name* (1974).

Despite the region's conflation with these horrors, it also emerges in African American literature as a landscape of family networks, close community, and agrarian-based kinship. In short, it often is the site of the ancestor, an African American homeland of construction, nurturing, continuance of African cultural practices, and spiritual renewal.

Considering that as late as 1900, 90 percent of African Americans lived in the South, it is no wonder that this landscape has taken on a great deal of cultural and historical significance. Literary musings on the South are complex and often paradoxical, as the region emerges repeatedly as a site of home—James Baldwin called the South the "Old Country," and Addison Gayle characterized the South as the "first home away from home" for African Americans—that is nevertheless paired with feelings of alienation and antipathy.

Jean Toomer's masterpiece, *Cane*, captures the complexity of the South. Indeed, the "pain and beauty" of the South are at once palpable on nearly every page. The personified Georgia landscape is perhaps the most significant character in the selections from *Cane* reprinted in this chapter, for much of the action plays out against its geography. In "Karintha," "Georgia Dusk," and "Blood Burning Moon," the landscape that bears witness to the many tragedies gives voice to the residents' lives: The moon casts spells, cane fields whisper, and the night winds sing." Despite the lyricism of the text, Toomer never lets the reader forget about the horrors that were performed on that very landscape. As a result, the eeriness of the text is due in no small measure to Toomer's constant pairing of oppression with beauty, an incongruity that numerous writers have captured.

Many of the texts in this chapter are not set directly in the South; however, that location recurs as a memory of home and can be conjured through fond remembrances of family and community or through terrifying recollections of violence and subjugation. This psychological distance is further indicated by the fact that not all of the writers in this section are Southern by birth. However, many writers visit or return to this region in their fiction, indicating that "down home" is a highly symbolic location.

African American writers' association of home and culture with the South and the implications of leaving and returning to the South are theorized by Robert Stepto in *Behind the Veil: A Study of Afro-American Narrative*. He proposes a template for reading these literary journeys away from and toward the South through what he labels "rituals of ascension" and "rituals of immersion." The ritual of ascension is a movement away from a stultifying South to a relatively freer North, while the ritual of immersion is essentially the reverse, as the protagonist leaves a relatively free environment (the North) and travels to a seemingly more oppressive environment (the South). Through this odyssey, "tribal literacy"—an awareness of history and ancestry—is achieved. What is interesting about Stepto's conceptualization of the immersion ritual is that it typically concludes with the character enjoying a sense of community despite being located in perhaps more repressive social climes. In this chapter, the immersion ritual is illustrated in Arrested Development's "Tennessee," as the speaker who is "stressed out and down" is guided back "home" to Tennessee. By walking on the "roads [his] forefathers walked," and climbing "the trees [his] forefathers hung from," he has gained "all of their wisdom." It is only in the South that he is able to lay claim to his "family tree" and his "family name."

No discussion of the South in African American literature is complete without reference to Zora Neale Hurston's body of work. Hurston was a novelist, a folklorist, and an anthropologist who was raised in Eatonville, Florida, the first incorporated all-Black town in America. This unique experience is evident throughout Hurston's literary texts, which integrate the mores, social customs, and language of African American Southern culture. Indeed, she creates an aesthetic that is beautifully informed by the rich oral traditions of the South.

As an anthropologist, Hurston formalized her passion for African American folk culture by traveling to the rural South to gather stories, music, poetry, and folkloric traditions, including New Orleans practices of hoodoo. This folk culture is presented in her important collection, *Mules and Men* (1935), an early study that validates the worth of such traditions. Hurston's anthropological work was not solely an academic exercise; her collection of folk culture further reinforced Hurston's sense of her Southern identity. Indeed, in her memoir *Dust Tracks on a Road* (1942), she unabashedly asserts her Southernness, claiming she has a "map of Dixie on [her] tongue."

The selections in this chapter are designed to map out the complexities of the region and the varied and often contradictory responses to Southern conditions. However, common themes are echoed and provide a glimpse into the magnitude of the South in African American letters. While these texts span the twentieth century, the South as subject and theme has had a much longer trajectory in the tradition. In fact, throughout this volume there are several works, from folktales to spirituals to slave narratives, that also manifest Southern concerns.

It is perhaps Margaret Walker's poem, "Southern Song" that best characterizes the complex literary representations of the South in a great deal of African American literature, for the speaker at once basks in the beauty of her homeland ("I want my body bathed again by southern suns"), yet at the same time experiences a homecoming complicated by the threat of Southern violence ("I want no mobs to wrench me from my southern rest"). Regardless of its manifestation, the theme of the Southern home and its layered history is a prevalent one throughout the tradition of African American literature.

Further Reading

Baker, Houston A. and Dana D. Nelson, eds. "Violence, the Body and 'The South.'" *American Literature* 73.2 (2001).

Campbell, Edward D.C., ed. *Before Freedom Came: African-American Life in the Antebellum South.* Charlottesville: University Press of Virginia, 1991.

Harris, Trudier. *The Power of the Porch: The Storyteller's Craft in Zora Neale Hurston, Gloria Naylor, and Randall Kenan.* Athens: University of Georgia Press, 1996.

Jones, Carolyn. "Southern Landscape as Psychic Landscape in Morrison's Fiction. *Studies in the Literary Imagination* 31.2 (1998): 37–48.

Killens, John Oliver and Jerry W. Ward, Jr., eds. *Black Southern Voices: An Anthology of Fiction, Poetry, Drama Nonfiction and Critical Essays.* New York: Meridian, 1992.

Murray, Albert. *South to a Very Old Place.* New York: Vintage Books, 1991.

Stepto, Robert. *From Behind the Veil: A Study of Afro-American Narrative.* 2nd ed. Chicago: University of Illinois Press, 1991.

Walker, Alice. "The Black Writer and the Southern Experience." *In Search of Our Mothers' Gardens: Womanist Prose.* New York: Harcourt, 15–21.

Frederick Douglass

(1818–1895)

Perhaps the most important African American writer of the nineteenth century, Frederick Douglass was born into slavery in 1818 on Maryland's Eastern Shore. Named Frederick Augustus Bailey at birth, he took the name "Douglass" after he escaped from slavery, with the help of his future wife Anna Murray, in 1838. Douglass settled in New Bedford, Massachusetts, and became active in the abolition movement, lecturing often under the sponsorship of William Lloyd Garrison. An orator with few peers, he made brilliantly eloquent appeals for freedom, justice, and a racially integrated United States. Also an outstanding writer, he penned the classic Narrative of the Life of Frederick Douglass, an American Slave, Written by Himself *(1845);* The Heroic Slave *(1853), considered the first novella in African American literature;* My Bondage and My Freedom *(1855); and* Life and Times of Frederick Douglass *(1881/1992). He spent his latter years in Washington, D.C., serving part of the time as federal marshal of the District of Columbia.*

Narrative of the Life of Frederick Douglass, an American Slave, Written by Himself.

CHAPTER 1.

1   I was born in Tuckahoe, near Hillsborough, and about twelve miles from Easton, in Talbot county, Maryland. I have no accurate knowledge of my age, never having seen any authentic record containing it. By far the larger part of the slaves know as little of their ages as horses know of theirs, and it is the wish of most masters within my knowledge to keep their slaves thus ignorant. I do not remember to have ever met a slave who could tell of his birthday. They seldom come nearer to it than planting-time, harvest-time, cherry-time, spring-time, or fall-time. A want of information concerning my own

was a source of unhappiness to me even during childhood. The white children could tell their ages. I could not tell why I ought to be deprived of the same privilege. I was not allowed to make any inquiries of my master concerning it. He deemed all such inquiries on the part of a slave improper and impertinent, and evidence of a restless spirit. The nearest estimate I can give makes me now between twenty-seven and twenty-eight years of age. I come to this, from hearing my master say, some time during 1835, I was about seventeen years old.

2   My mother was named Harriet Bailey. She was the daughter of Isaac and Betsey Bailey, both colored, and quite dark. My mother was of a darker complexion than either my grandmother or grandfather.

3   My father was a white man. He was admitted to be such by all I ever heard speak of my parentage. The opinion was also whispered that my master was my father; but of the correctness of this opinion, I know nothing; the means of knowing was withheld from me. My mother and I were separated when I was but an infant—before I knew her as my mother. It is a common custom, in the part of Maryland from which I ran away, to part children from their mothers at a very early age. Frequently, before the child has reached its twelfth month, its mother is taken from it, and hired out on some farm a considerable distance off, and the child is placed under the care of an old woman, too old for field labor. For what this separation is done, I do not know, unless it be to hinder the development of the child's affection toward its mother, and to blunt and destroy the natural affection of the mother for the child. This is the inevitable result.

4   I never saw my mother, to know her as such, more than four or five times in my life; and each of these times was very short in duration, and at night. She was hired by a Mr. Stewart, who lived about twelve miles from my home. She made her journeys to see me in the night, travelling the whole distance on foot, after the performance of her day's work. She was a field hand and a whipping is the penalty of not being in the field at sunrise, unless a slave has special permission from his or her master to the contrary—a permission which they seldom get, and one that gives to him that gives it the proud name of being a kind master. I do not recollect of ever seeing my mother by the light of day. She was with me in the night. She would lie down with me, and get me to sleep, but long before I waked she was gone. Very little communication ever took place between us. Death soon ended what little we could have while she lived, and with it her hardships and suffering. She died when I was about seven years

old, on one of my master's farms, near Lee's Mill. I was not allowed to be present during her illness, at her death, or burial. She was gone long before I knew any thing about it. Never having enjoyed, to any considerable extent, her soothing presence, her tender and watchful care, I received the tidings of her death with much the same emotions I should have probably felt at the death of a stranger.

5   Called thus suddenly away, she left me without the slightest intimation of who my father was. The whisper that my master was my father, may or may not be true; and, true or false, it is of but little consequence to my purpose whilst the fact remains, in all its glaring odiousness, that slaveholders have ordained, and by law established, that the children of slave women shall in all cases follow the condition of their mothers, and this is done too obviously to administer to their own lusts, and make a gratification of their wicked desires profitable as well as pleasurable; for by this cunning arrangement, the slaveholder, in cases not a few, sustains to his slaves the double relation of master and father.

6   I know of such cases; and it is worthy of remark that such slaves invariably suffer greater hardships, and have more to contend with, than others. They are, in the first place, a constant offence to their mistress. She is ever disposed to find fault with them; they can seldom do any thing to please her; she is never better pleased than when she sees them under the lash, especially when she suspects her husband of showing to his mulatto children favors which he withholds from his black slaves. The master is frequently compelled to sell this class of his slaves, out of deference to the feelings of his white wife; and, cruel as the deed may strike any one to be, for a man to sell his own children to human flesh-mongers, it is often the dictate of humanity for him to do so; for, unless he does this, he must not only whip them himself, but must stand by and see one white son tie up his brother, of but few shades darker complexion than himself, and ply the gory lash to his naked back; and if he lisp one word of disapproval, it is set down to his parental partiality, and only makes a bad matter worse, both for himself and the slave whom he would protect and defend.

7   Every year brings with it multitudes of this class of slaves. It was doubtless in consequence of a knowledge of this fact, that one great statesman of the south predicted the downfall of slavery by the inevitable laws of population. Whether this prophecy is ever fulfilled or not, it is nevertheless plain that a very different-looking class of people are springing up at the south, and are now held in slavery,

from those originally brought to this country from Africa; and if their increase will do no other good, it will do away the force of the argument, that God cursed Ham, and therefore American slavery is right. If the lineal descendants of Ham are alone to be scripturally enslaved, it is certain that slavery at the south must soon become unscriptural; for thousands are ushered into the world, manually, who, like myself, owe their existence to white fathers, and those fathers most frequently their own masters.

8   I have had two masters. My first master's name was Anthony. I do not remember his first name. He was generally called Captain Anthony—a title which, I presume, he acquired by sailing a craft on the Chesapeake Bay. He was not considered a rich slaveholder. He owned two or three farms, and about thirty slaves. His farms and slaves were under the case of an overseer. The overseer's name was Plummer. Mr. Plummer was a miserable drunkard, a profane swearer, and a savage monster. He always went armed with a cowskin and a heavy cudgel. I have known him to cut and slash the women's heads so horribly, that even master would be enraged at his cruelty, and would threaten to whip him if he did not mind himself. It required extraordinary barbarity on the part of an overseer to affect him. He was a cruel man, hardened by a long life of slaveholding. He would at times seem to take great pleasure in whipping a slave. I have often been awakened at the dawn of day by the most heart-reading shrieks of an own aunt of mine, whom he used to tie up to a joint, and whip upon her naked back till she was literally covered with blood. No words, no tears, no prayers, from his gory victim, seemed to move his iron heart from its bloody purpose. The louder she screamed, the harder he whipped; and where the blood ran fastest, there he whipped longest. He would whip her to make her scream, and whip her to make her hush; and not until overcome by fatigue, would he cease to swing the blood-clotted cowskin. I remember the first time I ever witnessed this horrible exhibition. I was quite a child, but I well remember it. I never shall forget it whilst I remember any thing. It was the first of a long series of such outrages, of which I was doomed to be a witness and a participant. It struck me with awful force. It was the blood-stained gate, the entrance to the hell of slavery, through which I was about to pass. It was a most terrible spectacle. I wish I could commit to paper the feelings with which I beheld it.

9   This occurrence took place very soon after I went to live with my old master, and under the following circumstances. Aunt Hester went out one night,—where or for what I do not know,—and happened

to be absent when my master desired her presence. He had ordered her not to go out evenings, and warned her that she must never let him catch her in company with a young man, who was paying attention to her, belonging to Colonel Lloyd. The young man's name was Ned Roberts, generally called Lloyd's Ned. Why master was so careful of her, may be safely left to conjecture. She was a woman of noble form, and of graceful proportions, having very few equals, and fewer superiors, in personal appearance, among the colored or white women of our neighborhood.

10   Aunt Hester had not only disobeyed his orders in going out, but had been found in company with Lloyd's Ned; which circumstance, I found, from what he said while whipping her, was the chief offence. Had he been a man of pure morals himself, he might have been thought interested in protecting the innocence of my aunt; but those who knew him will not suspect him of any such virtue. Before he commenced whipping Aunt Hester, he took her into the kitchen, and stripped her from neck to waist, leaving her neck, shoulders, and back, entirely naked. He then told her to cross her hands, calling her at the same time a d——d b——h. After crossing her hands, he tied them with a strong rope, and led her to a stool under a large hook in the joist, put in for the purpose. He made her get upon the stool, and tied her hands to the hook. She now stood fair for his infernal purpose. Her arms were stretched up at their full length, so that she stood upon the ends of her toes. He then said to her, "Now, you d——d b——h, I'll learn you how to disobey my orders!" and after rolling up his sleeves, he commenced to lay on the heavy cowskin, and soon the warm, red blood (amid heart-rending shrieks from her, and horrid oaths from him) came dripping to the floor. I was so terrified and horror-stricken at the sight, that I hid myself in a closet, and dared not venture out till long after the bloody transaction was over. I expected it would be my turn next. It was all new to me. I had never seen anything like it before. I had always lived with my grandmother on the outskirts of the plantation, where she was put to raise the children of the younger women. I had therefore been, until now, out of the way of the bloody scenes that often occurred on the plantation.

CHAPTER II.

11   My master's family consisted of two sons, Andrew and Richard, one daughter, Lucretia, and her husband, Captain Thomas Auld. They lived in one house, upon the home plantation of Colonel Edward

Lloyd. My master was Colonel Lloyd's clerk and superintendent. He was what might be called the overseer of the overseers. I spent two years of childhood on this plantation in my old master's family. It was here that I witnessed the bloody transaction recorded in the first chapter; and as I received my first impressions of slavery on this plantation, I will give some description of it, and of slavery as it there existed. The plantation is about twelve miles north of Easton, in Talbot county, and is situated on the border of Miles River. The principal products raised upon it were tobacco, corn, and wheat. These were raised in great abundance; so that, with the products of this and the other farms belonging to him, he was able to keep in almost constant employment a large sloop, in carrying them to market at Baltimore. This sloop was named Sally Lloyd, in honor of one of the colonel's daughters. My master's son-in-law, Captain Auld, was master of the vessel; she was otherwise manned by the colonel's own slaves. Their names were Peter, Isaac, Rich, and Jake. These were esteemed very highly by the other slaves, and looked upon as the privileged ones of the plantation; for it was no small affair, in the eyes of the slaves, to be allowed to see Baltimore.

12　　Colonel Lloyd kept from three to four hundred slaves on his home plantation, and owned a large number more on the neighboring farms belonging to him. The names of the farms nearest to the home plantation were Wye Town and New Design. "Wye Town" was under the overseership of a man named Noah Willis. New Design was under the overseership of a Mr. Townsend. The overseers of these, and all the rest of the farms, numbering over twenty, received advice and direction from the managers of the home plantation. This was the great business place. It was the seat of government for the whole twenty farms. All disputes among the overseers were settled here. If a slave was convicted of any high misdemeanor, became unmanageable, or evinced a determination to run away, he was brought immediately here, severely whipped, put on board the sloop, carried to Baltimore, and sold to Austin Woolfolk, or some other slave-trader, as a warning to the slaves remaining.

13　　Here, too, the slaves of all the other farms received their monthly allowance of food, and their yearly clothing. The men and women slaves received, as their monthly allowance of food, eight pounds of pork, or its equivalent in fish, and one bushel of corn meal. Their yearly clothing consisted of two coarse linen shirts, one pair of linen trousers, like the shirts, one jacket, one pair of trousers for winter, made of course negro cloth, one pair of stockings, and one pair of shoes; the whole of which could not have cost more than seven dollars. The allowance of the slave children was given to their mothers, or the old women having the care of them. The children unable to work in the field had neither shoes, stockings, jackets, nor trousers, given to them; their clothing consisted of two coarse linen shirts per year. When these failed them, they went naked until the next allowance-day. Children from seven to ten years old, of both sexes, almost naked, might be seen at all seasons of the year.

14   There were no beds given the slaves, unless one coarse blanket be considered such, and none but the men and women had these. This, however, is not considered a very great privation. They find less difficulty from the want of beds, than from the want of time to sleep; for when their day's work in the field is done, the most of them having their washing, mending, and cooking to do, and having few or none of the ordinary facilities for doing either of these, very many of their sleeping hours are consumed in preparing for the field the coming day; and when this is done, old and young, male and female, married and single, drop down side by side, on one common bed,— the cold, damp floor,—each covering himself or herself with their miserable blankets; and here they sleep till they are summoned to the field by the driver's horn. At the sound of this, all must rise, and be off to the field. There must be no halting; every one must be at his or her post; and woe betides them who hear not this morning summons to the field; for if they are not awakened by the sense of hearing, they are by the sense of feeling: no age nor sex finds any favor. Mr. Severe, the overseer, used to stand by the door of the quarter, armed with a large hickory stick and heavy cowskin, ready to whip any one who was so unfortunate as not to hear, or, from any other cause, was prevented from being ready to start for the field at the sound of the horn.

15   Mr. Severe was rightly named; he was a cruel man. I have seen him whip a woman, causing the blood to run half an hour at the time; and this, too, in the midst of her crying children, pleading for their mother's release. He seemed to take pleasure in manifesting his fiendish barbarity. Added to his cruelty, he was a profane sweater. It was enough to chill the blood and stiffen the hair of an ordinary man to hear him talk. Scarce a sentence escaped him but that was commenced or concluded by some horrid oath. The field was the place to witness his cruelty and profanity. His presence made it both the field of blood and blasphemy. From the rising till the going down of the sun, he was cursing, raving, cutting, and slashing among the

slaves of the field, in the most frightful manner. His career was short. He died very soon after I went to Colonel Lloyd's; and he died as he lived, uttering, with his dying groans, bitter curses and horrid oaths. His death was regarded by the slaves as the result of a merciful providence.

16 Mr. Severe's place was filled by a Mr. Hopkins. He was a very different man. He was less cruel, less profane, and made less noise, then Mr. Severe. His course was characterized by no extraordinary demonstrations of cruelty. He whipped, but seemed to take no pleasure in it. He was called by the slaves a good overseer.

17 The home plantation of Colonel Lloyd wore the appearance of a country village. All the mechanical operations for all the farms were performed here. The shoemaking and mending, the black-smithing, cartwrighting, coopering, weaving, and grain-grinding, were all performed by the slaves on the home plantation. The whole place wore a business-like aspect very unlike the neighboring farms. The number of houses, too, conspired to give it advantage over the neighboring farms. It was called by the slaves the *Great House Farm*. Few privileges were esteemed higher, by the slaves of the out-farms, than that of being selected to do errands at the Great House Farm. It was associated in their minds with greatness. A representative could not be prouder of his election to a seat in the American Congress, than a slave on one of the out-farms would be of his election to do errands at the Great House Farm. They regarded it as evidence of great confidence reported in them by their overseers; and it was on this account, as well as a constant desire to be out of the field from under the driver's lash, that they esteemed it a high privilege, one worth careful living for. He was called the smartest and most trusty fellow, who had this honor conferred upon him the most frequently. The competitors for this office sought as diligently to please their overseers, as the office-seekers in the political parties seek to please and deceive the people. The same traits of character might be seen in Colonel Lloyd's slaves, as are seen in the slaves of the political parties.

18 The slaves selected to go to the Great House Farm, for the monthly allowance for themselves and their fellow-slaves, were peculiarly enthusiastic. While on their way, they would make the dense old woods, for miles around, reverberate with their wildsongs, revealing at once the highest joy and the deepest sadness. They would compose and sing as they went along, consulting neither time nor tune. The thought that came up, came out—if not in the word, in the sound;—and as frequently in the one as in the other. They would

sometimes sing the most pathetic sentiment in the most rapturous tone, and the most rapturous sentiment in the most pathetic tones. Into all of their songs they would manage to weave something of the Great House Farm. Especially would they do this, when leaving home. They would then sing most exhultingly the following words:—

I am going away to the Great House Farm!
O, yea! O, yea! O!

This they would sing, as a chorus, to words which to many would seem unmeaning jargon, but which, nevertheless, were full of meaning to themselves. I have sometimes thought that the mere hearing of those songs would do more to impress some minds with the horrible character of slavery, than the reading of whole volumes of philosophy on the subject could do.

19 I did not, when a slave, understand the deep meaning of those rude and apparently incoherent songs. I was myself within the circle; so that I neither saw nor heard as those without might see and hear. They told a tale of woe which was then altogether beyond my feeble comprehension; they were tones loud, long, and deep; they breathed the prayer and complaint of souls boiling over with the bitterest anguish. Every tone was a testimony against slavery, and a prayer to God for deliverance from chains. The hearing of those wild notes always depressed my spirit, and filled me with ineffable sadness. I have frequently found myself in tears while hearing them. The mere recurrence to those songs, even now, afflicts me; and while I am writing these lines, an expression of feeling has already found its way down my cheek. To those songs I trace my first glimmering conception of the dehumanizing character of slavery. I can never get rid of that conception. Those songs still follow me, to deepen my hatred of slavery, and quicken my sympathies for my brethren in bonds. If any one wishes to be impressed with the soul-killing effects of slavery, let him go to Colonel Lloyd's plantation, and, on allowance-day, place himself in the deep pine woods, and there let him, in silence, analyze the sounds that shall pass through the chambers of his soul,—and if he in not thus impressed, it will only be because "there is no flesh in his obdurate heart."

20 I have often been utterly astonished, since I came to the north, to find persons who could speak of the singing, among slaves, as evidence of their contentment and happiness. It is impossible to conceive of a greater mistake. Slaves sing most when they are most unhappy.

The songs of the slave represent the sorrows of his heart; and he is relieved by them, only as an aching heart is relieved by its tears. At least, such is my experience. I have often sung to drown my sorrow, but seldom to express my happiness. Crying for joy, and singing for joy, were alike uncommon to me while in the jaws of slavery. The singing of a man cast away upon a desolate island might be as appropriately considered as evidence of contentment and happiness, as the singing of a slave; the songs of the one and of the other are prompted by the same emotion.

CHAPTER III.

21 Colonel Lloyd kept a large and finely cultivated garden, which afforded almost constant employment for four men, besides the chief gardener, (Mr. M'Durmond.) This garden was probably the greatest attraction of the place. During the summer months, people came from far and near—from Baltimore, Easton, and Annapolis—to see it. It abounded in fruits of almost every description, from the hardy apple of the north to the delicate orange of the south. This garden was not the least source of trouble on the plantation. Its excellent fruit was quite a temptation to the hungry swarms of boys, as well as the older slaves, belonging to the colonel, few of whom had the virtue or the vice to resist it. Scarcely a day passed, during the summer, but that some slave had to take the lash for stealing fruit. The colonel had to resort to all kinds of stratagems to keep his slaves out of the garden. The last and most successful one was that of tarring his fence all around; after which, if a slave was caught with any tar upon his person, it was deemed sufficient proof that he had either been into the garden, or had tried to get in. In either case, he was severely whipped by the chief gardener. This plan worked well; the slaves became as fearful of tar as of the lash. They seemed to realize the impossibility of TAR without being defiled.

22 The colonel also kept a splendid riding equipage. His stable and carriage-house presented the appearance of some of our large city livery establishments. His horses were of the finest form and noblest blood. His carriage-house contained three splendid coaches, three or four gigs, besides dearborns and barouches of the most fashionable style.

23 This establishment was under the care of two slaves—old Barney and young Barney—father and son. To attend to this establishment was their sole work. But it was by no means an easy employment; for in nothing was Colonel Lloyd more particular than

in the management of his horses. The slightest inattention to these was unpardonable, and was visited upon those, under whose care they were placed, with the severest punishment; no excuse could shield there, if the colonel only suspected any want of attention to his horses—a supposition which he frequently indulged, and one which, of course, made the office of old and young Barney a very trying one. They never knew when they were safe from punishment. They were frequently whipped when least deserving, and escaped whipping when most deserving it. Every thing depended upon the looks of the horses, and the state of Colonel Lloyd's own mind when his horses were brought to him for use. If a horse did not move fast enough, or hold his head high enough, it was owing to some fault of his keepers. It was painful to stand near the stable-door, and hear the various complaints against the keepers when a horse was taken out for use. "This horse has not had proper attention. He has not been sufficiently rubbed and curried, or he has not been properly fed; his food was too wet or too dry; he got it too soon or too late; he was too hot or too cold; he had too much hay, and not enough of grain; or he had too much grain, and not enough of hay; instead of old Barney's attending to the horse, he had very improperly left it to his son." To all these complaints, no matter how unjust, the slave must answer never a word. Colonel Lloyd could not brook any contradiction from a slave. When he spoke, a slave must stand, listen, and tremble; and such was literally the case. I have seen Colonel Lloyd make old Barney, a man between fifty and sixty years of age, uncover his bold head, kneel down upon the cold, damp ground, and receive upon his naked and toil-worn shoulders more than thirty lashes at the time. Colonel Lloyd had three sons—Edward, Murray, and Daniel,—and three sons-in-law, Mr. Winder, Mr. Nicholson, and Mr. Lowndes. All of these lived at the Great House Farm, and enjoyed the luxury of whipping the servants when they pleased, from old Barney down to William Wilkes, the coach-driver. I have seen Winder make one of the house-servants stand off from him a suitable distance to be touched with the end of his whip, and at every stroke raise great ridges upon his back.

24   To describe the wealth of Colonel Lloyd would be almost equal to describing the riches of Job. He kept from ten to fifteen house-servants. He was said to own a thousand slaves, and I think this estimate quite within the truth. Colonel Lloyd owned so many that he did not know them when he saw them; nor did all the slaves of the out-farms know him. It is reported of him, that, while riding along the road one day, he met a colored man, and addressed him in the

usual manner of speaking to colored people on the public highways of the south: "Well, boy, whom do you belong to?" "To Colonel Lloyd," replied the slave. "Well, does the colonel treat you well?" "No, sir," was the ready reply. "What, does he work you too hard?" "Yes, sir." "Well, don't he give you enough to eat?" "Yes, sir, he gives me enough, such as it is."

25 The colonel, after ascertaining where the slave belonged, rode on; the man also went on about his business, not dreaming that he had been conversing with his master. He thought, said, and heard nothing more of the matter, until two or three weeks afterwards. The poor man was then informed by his overseer that, for having found fault with his master, he was now to be sold to a Georgia trader. He was immediately chained and handcuffed; and thus, without a moment's warning, he was snatched away, and forever sundered, from his family and friends, by a hand more unrelenting than death. This is the penalty of telling the truth, of telling the simple truth, in answer to a series of plain questions.

26 It is partly in consequence of such facts, that slaves, when inquired of as to their condition and the character of their masters, almost universally say they are contented, and that their masters are kind. The slaveholders have been known to send in spies among their slaves, to ascertain their views and feelings in regard to their condition. The frequency of this has had the effect to establish among the slaves the maxim, that a still tongue makes a wise head. They suppress the truth rather than take the consequences of telling it, and in so doing prove themselves a part of the human family. If they have any thing to say of their masters, it is generally in their masters' favor, especially when speaking to an untried man. I have been frequently asked, when a slave, if I had a kind master, and do not remember ever to have given a negative answer; nor did I, in pursuing this course, consider myself as uttering what was absolutely false; for I always measured the kindness of my master by the standard of kindness set up among slaveholders around us. Moreover, slaves are like other people, and imbibe prejudices quite common to others. They think their own better than that of others. Many, under the influence of this prejudice, think their own masters are better than the masters of other slaves; and this, too, in some cases, when the very reverse is true. Indeed, it is not uncommon for slaves even to fall out and quarrel among themselves about the relative goodness of their masters, each contending for the superior goodness of his own over that of the others. At the very same time, they mutually execrate their masters when

viewed separately. It was so on our plantation. When Colonel Lloyd's slaves met the slaves of Jacob Jepson, they seldom parted without a quarrel about their masters; Colonel Lloyd's slaves contending that he was the richest, and Mr. Jepson's slaves that he was the smartest, and most of a man. Colonel Lloyd's slaves would boast his ability to buy and sell Jacob Jepson, Mr. Jepson's slaves would boast his ability to whip Colonel Lloyd. These quarrels would almost always end in a fight between the parties, and those that whipped were supposed to have gained the point at issue. They seemed to think that the greatness of their masters was transferable to themselves. It was considered as being bad enough to be a slave; but to be a poor man's slave was deemed a disgrace indeed!

CHAPTER IV.

27   Mr. Hopkins remained but a short time in the office of overseer. Why his career was so short, I do not know, but suppose he lacked the necessary severity to suit Colonel Lloyd. Mr. Hopkins was succeeded by Mr. Austin Gore, a man possessing, in an eminent degree, all those traits of character indispensable to what is called a first-rate overseer. Mr. Gore had served Colonel Lloyd, in the capacity of overseer, upon one of the out-forms, and had shown himself worthy of the high station of overseer upon the home or Great House Farm.

28   Mr. Gore was proud, ambitions, and persevering. He was artful, cruel, and obdurate. He was just the man for such a place, and it was just the place for such a man. It afforded scope for the full exercise of all his powers, and he seemed to be perfectly at home in it. He was one of those who could torture the slightest look, word, or gesture, on the part of the slave, into impudence, and would treat it accordingly. There must be no answering back to him; no explanation was allowed a slave, showing himself to have been wrongfully accused. Mr. Gore acted fully up to the maxim laid down by slaveholders,—"It is better that a dozen slaves suffer under the lash, than that the overseer should be convicted, in the presence of the slaves, of having been at fault." No matter how innocent a slave might be—it availed him nothing, when accused by Mr. Gore of any misdemeanor. To be accused was to be convicted, and to be convicted was to be punished; the one always following the other with immutable certainty. To escape punishment was to escape accusation; and few slaves had the fortune to do either, under the overseership of Mr. Gore. He was just proud enough to demand the most debasing homage of the slave,

and quite servile enough to crouch, himself, at the feet of the master. He was ambitious enough to be contented with nothing short of the highest rank of overseers, and persevering enough to reach the height of his ambition. He was cruel enough to inflict the severest punishment, artful enough to descend to the lowest trickery, and obdurate enough to be insensible to the voice of a reproving conscience. He was, of all the overseers, the most dreaded by the slaves. His presence was painful; his eye flashed confusion; and seldom was his sharp, shrill voice heard, without producing horror and trembling in their ranks.

29   Mr. Gore was a grave man, and, though a young man, he indulged in no jokes, said no funny words, seldom smiled. His words were in perfect keeping with his looks, and his looks were in perfect keeping with his words. Overseers will sometimes indulge in a witty word, even with the slaves; not so with Mr. Gore. He spoke but to command, and commanded but to be obeyed; he dealt sparingly with his words, and bountifully with his whip, never bring the former where the latter would answer as well. When he whipped, he seemed to do so from a sense of duty, and feared no consequences. He did nothing reluctantly, no matter how disagreeable; always at his post, never inconsistent. He never promised but to fulfill. He was, in a word, a man of the most inflexible firmness and stone-like coolness.

30   His savage barbarity was equalled only by the consummate coolness with which he committed the grossest and most savage deeds upon the slaves under his charge. Mr. Gore once undertook to whip one of Colonel Lloyd's slaves, by the name of Demby. He had given Demby but few stripes, when, to get rid of the scourging, he ran and plunged himself into a creek, and stood there at the depth of his shoulders, refusing to come out. Mr. Gore told him that he would give him three calls, and that, if he did not come out at the third call, he would shoot him. The first call was given. Demby made no response, but stood his ground. The second and third calls were given with the same result. Mr. Gore then, without consultation or deliberation with any one, not even giving Demby an additional call, raised his musket to his face, taking deadly aim at his standing victim, and in an instant poor Demby was no more. His mangled body rank out of sight, and blood and brains marked the water where he had stood.

31   A thrill of horror flashed through every soul upon the plantation, excepting Mr. Gore. He alone seemed cool and collected. He was asked by Colonel Lloyd and my old master, why he resorted to this extraordinary expedient. His reply was, (as well as I can remember,) that

Demby had become unmanageable. He was setting a dangerous example to the other slaves,—one which, if suffered to pass without some such demonstration on his part, would finally lead to the total subversion of all rule and order upon the plantation. He argued that if one slave refused to be corrected, and escaped with his life, the other slaves would soon copy the example; the result of which would be, the freedom of the slaves, and the enslavement of the whites. Mr. Gore's defence was satisfactory. He was continued in his station as overseer upon the home plantations. His fame as an overseer went abroad. His horrid crime was not even submitted to judicial investigation. It was committed in the presence of slaves, and they of course could neither institute a suit, nor testify against him; and thus the guilty perpetrator of one of the bloodiest and most foul murders goes unwhipped of justice, and uncensored by the community in which he lives. Mr. Gore lived in St. Michael's, Talbot county, Maryland, when I left there; and if he is still alive, he very probably lives there now; and if so, he is now, as he was then, as highly esteemed and as much respected as though his guilty soul had not been stained with his brother's blood.

32   I speak advisedly when I say this,—that killing a slave, or any colored person, in Talbot county, Maryland, is not treated as a crime, either by the courts or the community. Mr. Thomas Lanman, of St. Michael's, killed two slaves, one of whom he killed with a hatchet, by knocking his brains out. He used to boast of the commission of the awful and bloody deed. I have heard him do so laughingly, saying, among other things, that he was the only benefactor of his country in the company, and that when others would do as much as he had done, we should be relieved of "the d——d niggers."

33   The wife of Mr. Giles Hick, living but a short distance from where I used to live, murdered my wife's cousin, a young girl between fifteen and sixteen years of age, mangling her person in the most horrible manner, breaking her nose and breastbone with a stick, so that the poor girl expired in a few hours afterward. She was immediately buried, but had not been in her untimely grave but a few hours before she was taken up and examined by the coroner, who decided that she had come to her death by severe beating. The offence for which this girl was thus murdered was this:—She had been set that night to mind Mrs. Hick's baby, and during the night she fell asleep, and the baby cried. She, having lost her rest for several nights previous, did not hear the crying. They were both in the room with Mrs. Hicks. Mrs. Hicks, finding the girl slow to move, jumped from her bed, seized

an oak stick of wood by the fireplace, and with it broke the girl's nose and breastbone, and thus ended her life. I will not say that this most horrid murder produced no sensation in the community. It did produce sensation, but not enough to bring the murderess to punishment. There was a warrant issued for her arrest, but it was never served. Thus she escaped not only punishment, but even the pain of being arraigned before a court for her horrid crime.

34   Whilst I am detailing bloody deeds which took place during my stay on Colonel Lloyd's plantation, I will briefly narrate another, which occurred about the same time as the murder of Demby by Mr. Gore.

35   Colonel Lloyd's slaves were in the habit of spending a part of their nights and Sundays in fishing for oysters, and in this way made up the deficiency of their scanty allowance. An old man belonging to Colonel Lloyd, while thus engaged, happened to get beyond the limits of Colonel Lloyd's, and on the premises of Mr. Beal Bondly. At this trespass, Mr. Bondly took offence, and with his musket came down to the shore, and blew its deadly contents into the poor old man.

36   Mr. Bondly came over to see Colonel Lloyd the next day, whether to pay him for his property, or to justify himself in what he had done, I know not. At any rate, this whole fiendish transaction was soon bushed up. There was very little said about it at all, and nothing done. It was a common saying, even among little white boys, that it was worth a half-cent to kill a "nigger," and a half-cent to bury one.

CHAPTER V.

37   As to my own treatment while I lived on Colonel Lloyd's plantation, it was very similar to that of the other slave children. I was not old enough to work in the field, and there being little else than field work to do, I had a great deal of leisure time. The most I had to do was to drive up the cows at evening, keep the fowls out of the garden, keep the front yard clean, and run of errands for my old master's daughter, Mrs. Lueretia Auld. The most of my leisure time I spent in helping Master Daniel Lloyd in finding his birds, after he had shot them. My connection with Master Daniel was of some advantage to me. He became quite attached to me, and was a sort of protector of me. He would not allow the older boys to impose upon me, and would divide his cakes with me.

38   I was seldom whipped by my old master, and suffered little from any thing else than hunger and cold. I suffered much from hunger, but much more from cold. In hottest summer and coldest winter, I was

kept almost naked—no shoes, no stockings, no jacket, no trousers, nothing on but a course tow linen shirt, reaching only to my knees. I had no bed. I must have perished with cold, but that, the coldest nights, I used to steal a bag which was used for carrying corn to the mill. I would crawl into this bag, and there sleep on the cold, damp, clay floor, with my head in and feet out. My feet have been so cracked with the frost, that the pen with which I am writing might be laid in the gashes.

39   We were not regularly allowanced. Our food was coarse corn meal boiled. This was called *mush*. It was put into a large wooden tray or trough, and set down upon the ground. The children were then called, like so many pigs, and like so many pigs they would come and devour the mush; some with oystershells, others with pieces of shingle, some with naked hands, and none with spoons. He that ate fastest got most; he that was strongest secured the best place; and few left the trough satisfied.

40   I was probably between seven and eight years old when I left Colonel Lloyd's plantation. I left it with joy. I shall never forget the ecstasy with which I received the intelligence that my old master (Anthony) had determined to let me go to Baltimore, to live with Mr. Hugh Auld, brother to my old master's son-is-law, Captain Thomas Auld. I received this information about three days before my departure. They were three of the happiest days I ever enjoyed. I spent the most part of all these three days in the crock, washing off the plantation scurf, and preparing myself for my departure.

41   The pride of appearance which this would indicate was not my own. I spent the time in washing, not so much because I wished to, but because Mrs. Lucretia had told me I must get all the dead skin off my feet and knees before I could go to Baltimore; for the people in Baltimore were very cleanly, and would laugh at me if I looked dirty. Besides, she was going to give me a pair of trousers, which I should not put on unless I got all the dirt off me. The thought of owning a pair of trousers was great indeed! It was almost a sufficient motive, not only to make me take off what would be called by pig-drovers the mange, but the skin itself. I went at it in good earnest, working for the first time with the hope of reward.

42   The ties that ordinarily bind children to their homes were all suspended in my case. I found no severe trial in my departure. My home was charmless; it was not home to me; on parting from it, I could not feel that I was leaving any thing which I could have enjoyed by staying. My mother was dead, my grandmother lived far off, so that

I seldom saw her. I had two sisters and one brother, that lived in the same house with me; but the early separation of us from our mother had well nigh blotted the fact of our relationship from our memories. I looked for home elsewhere, and was confident of finding none which I should relish less than the one which I was leaving. If, however, I found in my new home hardship, hunger, whipping, and nakedness, I had the consolation that I should not have escaped any one of them by staying. Having already had more than a taste of them in the house of my old master, and having endured them there, I very naturally inferred my ability to endure them elsewhere, and especially at Baltimore; for I had something of the feeling about Baltimore that is expressed in the proverb, that "being hanged in England is preferable to dying a natural death in Ireland." I had the strongest desire to see Baltimore. Cousin Tom, though not fluent in speech, had inspired me with that desire by his eloquent description of the place. I could never point out any thing at the Great House, no matter how beautiful or powerful, but that he had seen something at Baltimore for exceeding, both in beauty and strength, the object which I pointed out to him. Even the Great House itself, with all its pictures, was far inferior to many buildings in Baltimore. So strong was my desire, that I thought a gratification of it would fully compensate for whatever loss of comforts I should sustain by the exchange. I left without a regret, and with the highest hopes of future happiness.

43   We sailed out of Miles River for Baltimore on a Saturday morning. I remember only the day of the week, for at that time I had no knowledge of the days of the month, nor the months of the year. On setting sail, I walked aft, and gave to Colonel Lloyd's plantation what I hoped would be the last look. I then placed myself in the bows of the sloop, and there spent the remainder of the day in looking ahead, interesting myself in what was in the distance rather than in things near by or behind.

44   In the afternoon of that day, we reached Annapolis, the capital of the State. We stopped but a few moments, so that I had no time to go on shore. It was the first large town that I had ever seen, and though it would look small compared with some of our New England factory villages, I thought it a wonderful place for its size—more imposing even than the Great House Farm!

45   We arrived at Baltimore early on Sunday morning, landing at Smith's Wharf, not far from Bowley's Wharf. We had on board the sloop a large flock of sheep; and after aiding in driving them to the

slaughterhouse of Mr. Curtis on Louden Slater's Hill, I was conducted by Rich, one of the hands belonging on board of the sloop, to my new home in Alliciana Street, near Mr. Gardner's ship-yard, on Fells Point.

46 Mr. and Mrs. Auld were both at home, and met me at the door with their little son Thomas, to take care of whom I had been given. And here I saw what I had never seen before; it was a white face beaming with the most kindly emotions; it was the face of my new mistress, Sophia Auld. I wish I could describe the rapture that flashed through my soul as I beheld it. It was a new and strange sight to me, brightening up my pathway with the light of happiness. Little Thomas was told, there was his Freddy,—and I was told to take care of little Thomas; and thus I entered upon the duties of my new home with the most cheering prospect ahead.

47 I look upon my departure from Colonel Lloyd's plantation as one of the most interesting events of my life. It is possible, and even quite probable, that but for the mere circumstance of being removed from that plantation to Baltimore, I should have to-day, instead of being here seated by my own table, in the enjoyment of freedom and the happiness of home, writing this Narrative, been confined in the galling chains of slavery. Going to live at Baltimore laid the foundation, and opened the gateway, to all my subsequent prosperity. I have ever regarded it as the first plain manifestation of that kind providence which has ever since attended me, and marked my life with so many favors. I regarded the selection of myself as being somewhat remarkable. There were a number of slave children that might have been sent from the plantation to Baltimore. There were those younger, those older, and those of the same age. I was chosen from among them all, and was the first, last, and only choice.

48 I may be deemed superstitions, and even egotistical, in regarding this event as a special interposition of divine Providence in my favor. But I should be false to the earliest sentiments of my soul, if I suppressed the opinion. I prefer to be true to myself, even at the hazard of incurring the ridicule of others, rather than to be false, and incur my own abhorrence. From my earliest recollection, I date the entertainment of a deep conviction that slavery would not always be able to hold me within its foul embrace; and in the darkest hours of my career in slavery, this living word of faith and spirit of hope departed not from me, but remained like ministering angels to cheer me through the gloom. This good spirit was from God, and to him I offer thanksgiving and praise.

Margaret Walker

(1915–1998)

A prominent poet, author, and scholar, Margaret Abigail Walker Alexander was born in Birmingham, Alabama, on July 7, 1915, to an educated, middle-class family that later relocated to New Orleans, Louisiana. Walker was herself highly educated; in 1935 she received a bachelor's degree from Northwestern University, in 1940 a master's degree from the same school, and in 1965 a doctorate from the University of Iowa. Still considered one of her finest works, her first volume of poetry, For My People, *was published in 1942 and won the Yale University Younger Poets Award. Walker was professor at Jackson State University in Jackson, Mississippi, for 30 years, where she was instrumental in founding the Institute for the Study of the History, Life and Culture of Black People. Walker won a number of awards, including a Fulbright Scholarship in 1971. Her books include the poetry volumes* Prophets for a New Day *(1970),* October Journey *(1973), and* This Is My Century: New and Selected Poems *(1989); the novel* Jubilee *(1966); and a critical study,* Richard Wright: Daemonic Genius *(1988). "Southern Song" First appeared in* For My People *(1942).*

Southern Song

I want my body bathed again by southern suns, my soul
    reclaimed again from southern land. I want to rest
    again in southern fields, in grass and hay and clover
    bloom; to lay my hand again upon the clay baked by
5   a southern sun, to touch the rain-soaked earth and
    smell the smell of soil.

I want my rest unbroken in the fields of southern earth;
    freedom to watch the corn wave silver in the sun and
    mark the splashing of a brook, a pond with ducks
10   and frogs and count the clouds.

I want no mobs to wrench me from my southern rest; no
    forms to take me in the night and burn my shack and
    make for me a nightmare full of oil and flame.

I want my careless song to strike no minor key; no fiend to
15   stand between my body's southern song—the fusion
    of the South, my body's song and me.

Jean Toomer

(1894–1967)

Celebrated Harlem Renaissance writer Jean Toomer, born Nathan Pinchback Toomer in Washington, D.C., on March 29, 1894, was the only child of Nina Pinchback and Nathan Toomer. Within a year of Toomer's birth, his father abandoned the family, and Toomer and his mother moved in with his maternal grandparents. Toomer's grandfather, P. B. S. Pinchback, was a notable Louisiana politician and played a major role in Toomer's life. Toomer attended several colleges, and in 1921 accepted a position as the acting principal of Sparta Agricultural and Industrial Institute in Sparta, Georgia. His brief experience in the rural South was the catalyst for Cane, *a modernist collection of short stories, character vignettes, poetry, and drama. Soon after the release of* Cane *(1923), Toomer, who was of mixed racial heritage, argued that he was "of no particular race" and adopted the philosophy of Armenian mystic George Gurdfieff. Later in life he rejected this philosophy for the Quaker religion. Toomer continued to write after the publication of* Cane, *but none of his subsequent work came close to matching that literary masterpiece.*

Cane*

KARINTHA

> Her skin is like dusk on the eastern horizon,
> O cant you see it, O cant you see it,
> Her skin is like dusk on the eastern horizon
> . . . When the sun goes down.

1 Men had always wanted her, this Karintha, even as a child, Karintha carrying beauty, perfect as dusk when the sun goes down. Old men

---

*Cane comprises three general sections. The first section is set in the rural South, with an emphasis on stories of individual women. The second section takes place, for the most part, in urban settings, such as Washington, D.C., and Chicago. The third section, Kabnis, is a drama set in a single locality in the South.

rode her hobby-horse upon their knees. Young men danced with her at frolics when they should have been dancing with their grown-up girls. God grant us youth, secretly prayed the old men. The young fellows counted the time to pass before she would be old enough to mate with them. This interest of the male, who wishes to ripen a growing thing too soon, could mean no good to her.

2   Karintha, at twelve, was a wild flash that told the other folks just what it was to live. At sunset, when there was no wind, and the pine-smoke from over by the sawmill hugged the earth, and you couldn't see more than a few feet in front, her sudden darting past you was a bit of vivid color, like a black bird that flashes in light, With the other children one could hear, some distance off, their feet flopping in the two-inch dust. Karintha's running was a whir. It had the sound of the red dust that sometimes makes a spiral in the road. At dusk, during the hush just after the sawmill had closed down, and before any of the women had started their supper-getting-ready songs, her voice, high-pitched, shrill, would put one's ears to itching. But no one ever thought to make her stop because of it. She stoned the cows, and beat her dog, and fought the other children . . . Even the preacher, who caught her at mischief, told himself that she was as innocently lovely as a November cotton flower. Already, rumors were out about her. Homes in Georgia are most often built on the two-room plan. In one, you cook and eat, in the other you sleep, and there love goes on. Karintha had seen or heard, perhaps she had felt her parents loving. One could but imitate one's parents, for to follow them was the way of God. She played "home" with a small boy who was not afraid to do her bidding. That started the whole thing. Old men could no longer ride her hobby-horse upon their knees. But young men counted faster.

> *Her skin is like dusk,*
> *O cant you see it,*
> *Her skin is like dusk,*
> *When the sun goes down.*

3   Karintha is a woman. She who carries beauty, perfect as dusk when the sun goes down. She has been married many times. Old men remind her that a few years back they rode her hobby-horse upon their knees. Karintha smiles, and indulges them when she is in the

mood for it. She has contempt for them. Karintha is a woman. Young men run stills to make her money. Young men go to the big cities and run on the road. Young men go away to college. They all want to bring her money. These are the young men who thought that all they had to do was to count time. But Karintha is a woman, and she has had a child. A child fell out of her womb onto a bed of pine-needles in the forest. Pine-needles are smooth and sweet. They are elastic to the feet of rabbits . . . A sawmill was nearby. Its pyramidal sawdust pile smouldered. It is a year before one completely burns. Meanwhile, the smoke curls up and hangs in odd wraiths about the trees, curls up, and spreads itself out over the valley . . . Weeks after Karintha returned home the smoke was so heavy you tasted it in water. Some one made a song:

> *Smoke is on the hills. Rise up.*
> *Smoke is on the hills. O rise*
> *And take my soul to Jesus.*

4   Karintha is a woman. Men do not know that the soul of her was a growing thing ripened too soon. They will bring their money; they will die not having found it out . . . Karintha at twenty, carrying beauty, perfect as dusk when the sun goes down. Karintha . . .

> *Her skin is like dusk on the eastern horizon,*
> *O cant you see it, O cant you see it,*
> *Her skin is like dusk on the eastern horizon*
> *. . . When the sun goes down.*

> *Goes down . . .*

GEORGIA DUSK

The sky, lazily disdaining to pursue
    The setting sun, too indolent to hold
    A lengthened tournament for flashing gold,
Passively darkens for night's barbecue,

5 A feast of moon and men and barking hounds,
    An orgy for some genius of the South
    With blood-hot eyes and cane-lipped scented mouth,
Surprised in making folk-songs from soul sounds.

The sawmill blows its whistle, buzz-saws stop,
10   And silence breaks the bud of knoll and hill,
    Soft settling pollen where plowed lands fulfill
Their early promise of a bumper crop.

Smoke from the pyramidal sawdust pile
    Curls up, blue ghosts of trees, tarrying low
15   Where only chips and stumps are left to show
The solid proof of former domicile.

Meanwhile, the men, with vestiges of pomp,
    Race memories of king and caravan,
    High-priests, an ostrich, and a juju-man,
20 Go singing through the footpaths of the swamp.

Their voices rise .. the pine trees are guitars,
    Strumming, pine-needles fall like sheets of rain ..
    Their voices rise .. the chorus of the cane
Is caroling a vesper to the stars..

25 O singers, resinous and soft your songs
    Above the sacred whisper of the pines,
    Give virgin lips to cornfield concubines,
Bring dreams of Christ to dusky cane-lipped throngs.

BLOOD-BURNING MOON

1

1 Up from the skeleton stone walls, up from the rotting floor boards and
the solid hand-hewn beams of oak of the pre-war cotton factory, dusk
came. Up from the dusk the full moon came. Glowing like a fired
pine-knot, it illumined the great door and soft showered the Negro
shanties aligned along the single street of factory town. The full moon
in the great door was an omen. Negro women improvised songs
against its spell.

2   Louisa sang as she came over the crest of the hill from the white
folks' kitchen. Her skin was the color of oak leaves on young trees
in fall. Her breasts, firm and up-pointed like ripe acorns. And her
singing had the low murmur of winds in fig trees. Bob Stone, younger
son of the people she worked for, loved her. By the way the world
reckons things, he had won her. By measure of that warm glow which
came into her mind at thought of him, he had won her. Tom Bur-

well, whom the whole town called Big Boy, also loved her. But working in the fields all day, and far away from her, gave him no chance to show it. Though often enough of evenings he had tried to. Somehow, he never got along. Strong as he was with hands upon the ax or plow, he found it difficult to hold her. Or so he thought. But the fact was that he held her to factory town more firmly than he thought for. His black balanced, and pulled against, the white of Stone, when she thought of them. And her mind was vaguely upon them as she came over the crest of the hill, coming from the white folks' kitchen. As she sang softly at the evil face of the full moon.

3   A strange stir was in her. Indolently, she tried to fix upon Bob or Tom as the cause of it. To meet Bob in the canebrake, as she was going to do an hour or so later, was nothing new. And Tom's proposal which she felt on its way to her could be indefinitely put off. Separately, there was no unusual significance to either one. But for some reason, they jumbled when her eyes gazed vacantly at the rising moon. And from the jumble came the stir that was strangely within her. Her lips trembled. The slow rhythm of her song grew agitant and restless. Rusty black and tan spotted hounds, lying in the dark corners of porches or prowling around back yards, put their noses in the air and caught its tremor. They began plaintively to yelp and howl. Chickens woke up and cackled. Intermittently, all over the countryside dogs barked and roosters crowed as if heralding a weird dawn or some ungodly awakening. The women sang lustily. Their songs were cotton-wads to stop their ears. Louisa came down into factory town and sank wearily upon the step before her home. The moon was rising towards a thick cloud-bank which soon would hide it.

> *Red nigger moon. Sinner!*
> *Blood-burning moon. Sinner!*
> *Come out that fact'ry door.*

2

4   Up from the deep dusk of a cleared spot on the edge of the forest a mellow glow arose and spread fan-wise into the low-hanging heavens. And all around the air was heavy with the scent of boiling cane. A large pile of cane-stalks lay like ribboned shadows upon the ground. A mule, harnessed to a pole, trudged lazily round and round the pivot of the grinder. Beneath a swaying oil lamp, a Negro alternately whipped out at the mule, and fed cane-stalks to the grinder. A fat boy

waddled pails of fresh ground juice between the grinder and the boiling stove. Steam came from the copper boiling pan. The scent of cane came from the copper pan and drenched the forest and the hill that sloped to factory town, beneath its fragrance. It drenched the men in circle seated around the stove. Some of them chewed at the white pulp of stalks, but there was no need for them to, if all they wanted was to taste the cane. One tasted it in factory town. And from factory town one could see the soft haze thrown by the glowing stove upon the low-hanging heavens.

5   Old David Georgia stirred the thickening syrup with a long ladle, and ever so often drew it off. Old David Georgia tended his stove and told tales about the white folks, about moonshining and cotton picking, and about sweet nigger gals, to the men who sat there about his stove to listen to him. Tom Burwell chewed cane-stalk and laughed with the others till some one mentioned Louisa. Till some one said something about Louisa and Bob Stone, about the silk stockings she must have gotten from him. Blood ran up Tom's neck hotter than the glow that flooded from the stove. He sprang up. Glared at the men and said, "She's my gal." Will Manning laughed. Tom strode over to him. Yanked him up and knocked him to the ground. Several of Manning's friends got up to fight for him. Tom whipped out a long knife and would have cut them to shreds if they hadnt ducked into the woods. Tom had had enough. He nodded to Old David Georgia and swung down the path to factory town. Just then, the dogs started barking and the roosters began to crow. Tom felt funny. Away from the fight, away from the stove, chill got to him. He shivered. He shuddered when he saw the full moon rising towards the cloud-bank. He who didnt give a godam for the fears of old women. He forced his mind to fasten on Louisa. Bob Stone. Better not be. He turned into the street and saw Louisa sitting before her home. He went towards her, ambling, touched the brim of a marvelously shaped, spotted, felt hat, said he wanted to say something to her, and then found that he didnt know what he had to say, or if he did, that he couldnt say it. He shoved his big fists in his overalls, grinned and started to move off.

6   "Youall want me, Tom?"

7   "Thats what us wants, sho, Louisa."

8   "Well, here I am—"

9   "An here I is, but that aint ahelpin none, all th same."

10   "You wanted to say something?.."

11   "I did that, sho. But words is like th spots on dice: no matter how y fumbles em, there's times when they jes wont come. I dunno why.

Seems like th love I feels fo yo done stole m tongue. I got it now. Wheel Louisa, honey, I oughtnt tell y, I feel I oughtnt cause yo is young an goes t church an I has had other gals, but Louisa I sho do love y. Lil gal, Ise watched y from them first days when youall sat right here befo yo door befo th well an sang sometimes in a way that like t broke m heart. Ise carried y with me into th fields, day after day, an after that, an I sho can plow when yo is there, an I can pick cotton. Yassur! Come near beatin Barlo yesterday. I sho did. Yassur! An next year if ole Stone'll trust me, I'll have a farm. My own. My bales will buy yo what y gets from white folks now. Silk stockings an purple dresses—course I dont believe what some folks been whisperin as t how y gets them things now. White folks always did do for niggers what they likes. An they jes cant help alikin yo, Louisa, Bob Stone likes y. Course he does. But not th way folks is awhisperin. Does he, hon?"

12   "I dont know what you mean, Tom."

13   "Course y dont. Ise already cut two niggers. Had t hon, t tell em so. Niggers always tryin t make somethin out a nothin. An then besides, white folks aint up t them tricks so much nowadays. Godam better not be. Leastawise not with yo. Cause I wouldnt stand f it. Nassur."

14   "What would you do, Tom?"

15   "Cut him jes like I cut a nigger."

16   "No, Tom—"

17   "I said I would an there aint no mo to it. But that aint th talk f now. Sing, honey Louisa, an while I'm listenin t y I'll be makin love."

18   Tom took her hand in his. Against the tough thickness of his own, hers felt soft and small. His huge body slipped down to the step beside her. The full moon sank upward into the deep purple of the cloud-bank. An old woman brought a lighted lamp and hung it on the common well whose bulky shadow squatted in the middle of the road, opposite Tom and Louisa. The old woman lifted the well-lid, took hold the chain, and began drawing up the heavy bucket. As she did so, she sang. Figures shifted, restlesslike, between lamp and window in the front rooms of the shanties. Shadows of the figures fought each other on the gray dust of the road. Figures raised the windows and joined the old woman in song. Louisa and Tom, the whole street, singing:

> *Red nigger moon. Sinner!*
> *Blood-burning moon. Sinner!*
> *Come out that fact'ry door.*

3

19 Bob Stone sauntered from his veranda out into the gloom of fir trees and magnolias. The clear white of his skin paled, and the flush of his cheeks turned purple. As if to balance this outer change, his mind became consciously a white man's. He passed the house with its huge open hearth which, in the days of slavery, was the plantation cookery. He saw Louisa bent over that hearth. He went in as a master should and took her. Direct, honest, bold. None of this sneaking that he had to go through now. The contrast was repulsive to him. His family had lost ground. Hell no, his family still owned the niggers, practically. Damned if they did, or he wouldnt have to duck around so. What would they think if they knew? His mother? His sister? He shouldnt mention them, shouldnt think of them in this connection. There in the dusk he blushed at doing so. Fellows about town were all right, but how about his friends up North? He could see them incredible, repulsed. They didnt know. The thought first made him laugh. Then, with their eyes still upon him, he began to feel embarrassed. He felt the need of explaining things to them. Explain hell. They wouldnt understand, and moreover, who over heard of a Southerner getting on his knees to any Yankee, or anyone. No sir. He was going to see Louisa to-night, and love her. She was lovely—in her way. Nigger way. What way was that? Damned if he knew. Must know. He'd known her long enough to know. Was there something about niggers that you couldnt know? Listening to them at church didnt tell you anything. Looking at them didnt tell you anything. Talking to them didnt tell you anything—unless it was gossip, unless they wanted to talk. Of course, about farming, and licker, and craps— but those werent nigger. Nigger was something more. How much more? Something to be afraid of, more? Hell no. Who ever heard of being afraid of a nigger? Tom Burwell. Cartwell had told him that Tom went with Louisa after she reached home. No sir. No nigger had ever been with his girl. He'd like to see one try. Some position for him to be in. Him, Bob Stone, of the old Stone family, in a scrap with a nigger over a nigger girl. In the good old days . . . Ha! Those were the days. His family had lost ground. Not so much, though. Enough for him to have to cut through old Lemon's canefield by way of the woods, that he might meet her. She was worth it. Beautiful nigger gal. Why nigger? Why not, just gal? No, it was because she was nigger that he went to her. Sweet . . . The scent of boiling cane came to him. Then he saw the rich glow of the stove. He heard the

voices of the men circled around it. He was about to skirt the clearing when he heard his own name mentioned. He stopped. Quivering. Leaning against a tree, he listened.

20 "Bad nigger. Yassur, he sho is one bad nigger when he gets started."

21 "Tom Burwell's been on th gang three times of cuttin men."

22 "What y think he's agwine t do t Bob Stone?"

23 "Dunno yet. He aint found out. When he does—Baby!"

24 "Aint no tellin."

25 "Young Stone aint no quitter an I ken tell y that. Blood of th old uns in his veins."

26 "Thats right. He'll scrap, sho."

27 "Be gettin too hot f niggers round this away."

28 "Shut up, nigger. Y dont know what y talkin bout."

29 Bob Stone's ears burned as though he had been holding them over the stove. Sizzling heat welled up within him. His feet felt as if they rested on red-hot coals. They stung him to quick movement. He circled the fringe of the glowing. Not a twig cracked beneath his feet. He reached the path that led to factory town. Plunged furiously down it. Halfway along, a blindness within him veered him aside. He crashed into the bordering canebrake. Cane leaves cut his face and lips. He tasted blood. He threw himself down and dug his fingers in the ground. The earth was cool. Cane-roots took the fever from his hands. After a long while, or so it seemed to him, the thought came to him that it must be time to see Louisa. He got to his feet and walked calmly to their meeting place. No Louisa. Tom Burwell had her. Veins in his forehead bulged and distended. Saliva moistened the dried blood on his lips. He bit down on his lips. He tasted blood. Not his own blood; Tom Burwell's blood. Bob drove through the cane and out again upon the road. A hound swung down the path before him towards factory town. Bob couldnt see it. The dog loped aside to let him pass. Bob's blind rushing made him stumble over it. He fell with a thud that dazed him. The hound yelped. Answering yelps came from all over the countryside. Chickens cackled. Roosters crowed, heralding the bloodshot eyes of southern awakening. Singers in the town were silenced. They shut their windows down. Palpitant between the rooster crows, a chill hush settled upon the huddled forms of Tom and Louisa. A figure rushed from the shadow and stood before them. Tom popped to his feet.

30 "Whats y want?"

31 "I'm Bob Stone."

32   "Yassur—an I'm Tom Burwell. Whats y want?"

33   Bob lunged at him. Tom side-stepped, caught him by the shoulder, and flung him to the ground. Straddled him.

34   "Let me up."

35   "Yassur—but watch yo doins, Bob Stone."

36   A few dark figures, drawn by the sound of scuffle, stood about them. Bob sprang to his feet.

37   "Fight like a man, Tom Burwell, an I'll lick y."

38   Again he lunged. Tom side-stepped and flung him to the ground. Straddled him.

39   "Get off me, you godam nigger you."

40   "Yo sho has started somethin now. Get up."

41   Tom yanked him up and began hammering at him. Each blow sounded as if it smashed into a precious, irreplaceable soft something. Beneath them, Bob staggered back. He reached in his pocket and whipped out a knife.

42   "Thats my game, sho."

43   Blue flash, a steel blade slashed across Bob Stone's throat. He had a sweetish sick feeling. Blood began to flow. Then he felt a sharp twitch of pain. He let his knife drop. He slapped one hand against his neck. He pressed the other on top of his head as if to hold it down. He groaned. He turned, and staggered towards the crest of the hill in the direction of white town. Negroes who had seen the fight slunk into their homes and blow the lamps out. Louisa, dazed, hysterical, refused to go indoors. She slipped, crumbled, her body loosely propped against the woodwork of the well. Tom Burwell leaned against it. He seemed rooted there.

44   Bob reached Broad Street. White men rushed up to him. He collapsed in their arms.

45   "Tom Burwell. . . ."

46   White men like ants upon a forage rushed about. Except for the taut hum of their moving, all was silent. Shotguns, revolvers, rope, kerosene, torches. Two high-powered cars with glaring search-lights. They came together. The taut hum rose to a low roar. Then nothing could be heard but the flop of their feet in the thick dust of the road. The moving body of their silence preceded them over the crest of the hill into factory town. It flattened the Negroes beneath it. It rolled to the wall of the factory, where it stopped. Tom knew that they were coming. He couldnt move. And then he saw the search-lights of the two cars glaring down on him. A quick shock went through him. He stiffened. He started to run. A yell went up from the mob. Tom

wheeled about and faced them. They poured down on him. They swarmed. A large man with dead-white face and flabby cheeks came to him and almost jabbed a gun-barrel through his guts.

47 "Hands behind y, nigger."

48 Tom's wrists were bound. The big man shoved him to the well. Burn him over it, and when the woodwork caved in, his body would drop to the bottom. Two deaths for a godam nigger. Louisa was driven back. The mob pushed in. Its pressure, its momentum was too great. Drag him to the factory. Wood and stakes already there. Tom moved in the direction indicated. But they had to drag him. They reached the great door. Too many to get in there. The mob divided and flowed around the walls to either side. The big man shoved him through the door. The mob pressed in from the sides. Taut humming. No words. A stake was sunk into the ground. Rotting floor boards piled around it. Kerosene poured on the rotting floor boards. Tom bound to the stake. His breast was bare. Nail's scratches let little lines of blood trickle down and mat into the hair. His face, his eyes were set and stony. Except for irregular breathing, one would have thought him already dead. Torches were flung onto the pile. A great flare muffled in black smoke shot upward. The mob yelled. The mob was silent. Now Tom could be seen within the flames. Only his head, erect, lean, like a blackened stone. Stench of burning flesh soaked the air. Tom's eyes popped. His head settled downward. The mob yelled. Its yell echoed against the skeleton stone walls and sounded like a hundred yells. Like a hundred mobs yelling. Its yell thudded against the thick front wall and fell back. Ghost of a yell slipped through the flames and out the great door of the factory. It fluttered like a dying thing down the single street of factory town. Louisa, upon the step before her home, did not hear it, but her eyes opened slowly. They saw the full moon glowing in the great door. The full moon, an evil thing, an omen, soft showering the homes of folks she knew. Where were they, these people? She'd sing, and perhaps they'd come out and join her. Perhaps Tom Burwell would come. At any rate, the full moon in the great door was an omen which she must sing to:

> Red nigger moon. Sinner!
> Blood-burning moon. Sinner!
> Come out that fact'ry door.

Richard Wright

(1908–1960)

Richard Wright, one of the premier writers of the twentieth century, was born on a farm near Natchez, Mississippi, on September 4, 1908. Wright had a difficult childhood, enduring paternal abandonment, poverty, hunger, and racial segregation, which he recounts in his mem-oir Black Boy *(1945). Attempting to escape the pathology of his South-ern experiences, Wright relocated to Chicago among a wave of urban migration in 1927, which he details in* American Hunger, *posthu-mously published in 1977. During this period, Wright joined the Amer-ican Communist party and contributed to magazines such as* Daily Worker *and* New Masses. *In 1938, he published a collection of short stories,* Uncle Tom's Children, *for which he won a Guggenheim Fellow-ship. Wright became a literary giant and a commercial success in 1940 with the publication of his masterpiece,* Native Son. *This water-shed in American literature was the first African American Book-of-the-Month Club selection, selling two hundred thousand copies in less than one month. At this time Wright's place in the annals of American literature was firmly established. After the publication of* Native Son, *Wright continued to publish works of fiction, including* The Outsider *(1953),* Savage Holiday *(1954), and* The Long Dream *(1958), as well as nonfiction, including a photographic essay,* 12 Million Black Voices: A Folk History of the American Negro *(1941), and* Black Power *(1954), a diary written during his visits to the Gold Coast. In 1947, Wright became an expatriate, living the rest of his life in France. This reading is from* Uncle Tom's Children.

Uncle Tom's Children

ONE: BIG BOY LEAVES HOME

I

1   *Yo mama don wear no drawers* . . .

2   Clearly, the voice rose out of the woods, and died away. Like an echo another voice caught it up:

3   *Ah seena when she pulled em off* . . .

4   Another, shrill, cracking, adolescent:

5   *N she washed'em in alcohol* . . .

6   Then a quarter of voices, blending in harmony, floated high above the tree tops:

7   *N she hung 'em out in the hall . . .*

8   Laughing easily, four black boys came out of the woods into cleared pasture. They walked lollingly in bare feet, beating tangled vines and bushes with long sticks.

9   "Ah wished Ah knowed some mo lines t tha song."

10   "Me too."

11   "Yeah, when yuh gits t where she hangs em out in the hall yuh has t stop."

12   "Shucks, whut goes wid *hall?*"

13   "*Call.*"

14   "*Fall.*"

15   "*Wall.*"

16   "*Quall.*"

17   They threw themselves on the grass, laughing.

18   "Big Boy?"

19   "Huh?"

20   "Yuh know one thing?"

21   "Whut?"

22   "Yuh sho is crazy!"

23   "Crazy?"

24   "Yeah, yuh crazys a bed-bug!"

25   "Crazy bout whut?"

26   "Man, whoever hearda *quall?*"

27   "Yuh said yuh wanted something to go wid *hall*, didn't yuh?"

28   "Yeah, but whuts a *quall?*"

29   "Nigger, a *qualls* a *quall.*"

30   They laughed easily, catching and pulling long green blades of grass with their toes.

31   "Waal, ef a *qualls* a *quall*, whut IS a *quall?*"

32   "Oh, Ah know."

33   "Whut?"

34   "Tha ol song goes something like this:

> *Yo mama don wear no drawers.*
> *Ah seena when she pulled em off,*
> *N she washed em in alcohol,*
> *N she hung em out in the hall,*
> *N then she put em back on her QUALL!*"

35   They laughed again. Their shoulders were flat to the earth, their knees propped up, and their faces square to the sun.

36   "Big Boy, yuhs CRAZY!"

37   "Don ax me nothin else."

38   "Nigger, yuhs CRAZY!"

39   They fell silent, smiling, dropping the lids of their eyes softly against the sunlight.

40   "Man, don the groun feel warm?"

41   "Jus lika bed."

42   "Jeeesus, Ah could stay here ferever."

43   "Me too."

44   "Ah kin feel tha ol sun goin all thu me."

45   "Feels like mah bones is warm."

46   In the distance a train whistled mournfully.

47   "There goes number fo!"

48   "Hittin on all six!"

49   "Highballin it down the line!"

50   "Boun for up Noth, Lawd, bound for up Noth!"

51   They began to chant, pounding bare heels in the grass.

> *Dis train bound fo Glory*
> *Dis train, Oh Hallelujah*
> *Dis train bound fo Glory*
> *Dis train, Oh Hallelujah*
> *Dis train bound to Glory*
> *Ef yuh ride no need fer fret er worry*
> *Dis train, Oh Hallelujah*
> *Dis train . . .*
> *Dis train don carry no gambler*
> *Dis train, Oh Hallelujah*
> *Dis train don carry no gambler*
> *Dis train, Oh Hallelujah*
> *Dis train don carry no gambler*
> *No to day creeper er midnight rambler*
> *Dis train, Oh Hallelujah*
> *Dis train . . .*

52   When the song ended they burst out laughing, thinking of a train bound for Glory.

53   "Gee, thas a good ol song!"

54   "Huuuuummmmmmmmman . . ."

55   "Whut?"

56   "Goeee whiiiiiiz . . ."

57   "Whut?"

58 "Somebody done let win! Das whut!"

59 Buck, Bobo and Lester jumped up. Big Boy stayed on the ground, feigning sleep.

60 "Jeeesus, tha sho stinks!"

61 "Big Boy!"

62 Big Boy feigned to snore.

63 "Big Boy!"

64 Big Boy stirred as though in sleep.

65 "Big Boy!"

66 "Hunh?"

67 "Yuh rotten inside!"

68 "Rotten?"

69 "Lawd, cant yuh smell it?"

70 "Smell whut?"

71 "Nigger, yuh mus gotta bad coll"

72 "*Smell whut?*"

73 "NIGGER, YUH BROKE WIN!"

74 Big Boy laughed and fall back on the grass, closing his eyes.

75 "The hen whut cackles is the hen whut laid the egg."

76 "We ain no hens."

77 "Yuh cackled, didnt yuh?"

78 The three moved off with noses turned up.

79 "C mon!"

80 "Where yuh-all goin?"

81 "T the creek fer a swim."

82 "Yeah, les swim."

83 "Naw buddy naw!" said Big Boy, slapping the air with a scornful palm.

84 "Aa, c mon! Don be a heel!"

85 "N git *lynched?* Hell naw!"

86 "He ain gonna see us."

87 "How yuh know?"

88 "Cause he ain."

89 "Yuh-all go on. Ahma stay right here," said Big Boy.

90 "Hell, let im stay! C mon, les go," said Buck.

91 The three walked off, swishing at grass and bushes with sticks. Big Boy looked lazily at their backs.

92 "Hey!"

93 Walking on, they glanced over their shoulders.

94 "Hey, niggers!"

95 "C mon!"

96 Big Boy grunted, picked up his stick, pulled to his feet, and stumbled off.

97 "Wait!"

98 "C mon!"

99 He ran, caught up with them, leaped upon their backs, bearing them to the ground.

100 "Quit, Big Boy!"

101 "Gawddam, nigger!"

102 "Git t hell offa me!"

103 Big Boy sprawled in the grass beside them, laughing and pounding his heels in the ground.

104 "Nigger, whut yuh think we is, hosses?"

105 "How come yuh awways hoppin on us?"

106 "Lissen, wes gonna doubt-team on yuh one of these days n beat yo ol ass good."

107 Big Boy smiled.

108 "Sho nough?"

109 "Yeah, don yuh like it?"

110 "We gonna beat yuh sos yuh cant walk!"

111 "N dare yuh t do nothin erbout it!"

112 Big Boy bared his teeth.

113 "C mon! Try it now!"

114 The three circled around him.

115 "Say, Buck, yuh grab his feets!"

116 "N yuh git his head, Lester!"

117 "N Bobo, yuh get berhin n grab his arms!"

118 Keeping more than arm's length, they circled round and round Big Boy.

119 "C mon!" said Big Boy, feinting at one and then the other.

120 Round and round they circled, but could not seem to get any closer. Big Boy stopped and braced his hands on his hips.

121 "Is all three of yuh-all scareda me?"

122 "Les git im some other time," said Bobo, grinning.

123 "Yeah, we kin ketch yuh when yuh ain thinkin," said Lester.

124 "We kin trick yuh," said Buck.

125 They laughed and walked together.

126 Big Boy belched.

127 "Ahm hongry," he said.

128 "Me too."

129 "Ah wished Ah hada big hot pota belly-busters!"

130 "Cooked wid some good ol saltry ribs . . ."

131 "N some good ol egg cornbread . . ."

132 "N some buttermilk . . ."

133 "N some hot peach cobbler swimmin in juice . . ."

134 "Nigger, hush!"

135 They began to chant, emphasizing the rhythm by cutting at grass with sticks.

> *Bye n bye*
> *Ah wanna piece of pie*
> *Pies too sweet*
> *Ah wanna piece of meat*
> *Meats too red*
> *Ah wanna piece of bread*
> *Breads too brown*
> *Ah wanna go t town*
> *Towns too far*
> *Ah wanna ketch a car*
> *Cars too fas*
> *Ah fall n break mah ass*
> *Ahll understan it better bye n bye . . .*

136 They climbed over a barbed-wire fence and entered a stretch of thick woods. Big Boy was whistling softly, his eyes half-closed.

137 "LES GIT IM!"

138 Buck, Lester, and Bobo whirled, grabbed Big Boy about the neck, arms, and legs, bearing him to the ground. He grunted and kicked wildly as he went back into weeds.

139 "Hol im tight!"

140 "Git his arms! Git his arms!"

141 "Set on his legs so he cant kick!"

142 Big Boy puffed heavily, trying to get loose.

143 "WE GOT YUH NOW GAWDDAMMIT, WE GOT YUH NOW!"

144 "Thas a Gawddam lie!" said Big Boy. He kicked, twisted, and clutched for a hold on one and then the other.

145 "Say, yuh-all hep me hol his arms!" said Bobo.

146 "Aw, we got this bastard now!" said Lester.

147 "Thas a Gawddam lie!" said Big Boy again.

148 "Say, yuh-all hep me hol his arms!" called Bobo.

149 Big Boy managed to encircle the neck of Bobo with his left arm. He tightened his elbow scissors-like and hissed through his teeth:

150 "Yuh got me, ain yuh?"

151 "Hol im!"

152 "Les beat this bastard's ass!"

153 "Say, hep me hol his *arms!* Hes got aholda mah *neck!*" cried Bobo.

154 Big Boy squeezed Bobo's neck and twisted his head to the ground.

155 "Yuh got me, ain yuh?"

156 "Quit, Big Boy, yuh chokin me! Yuh hurtin mah neck!" cried Bobo.

157 "Turn me loose!" said Big Boy.

158 "Ah ain got yuh! Its the others whut got yuh!" pleaded Bobo.

159 "Tell them others t git t hell offa me or Ahma break yo neck," said Big Boy.

160 "Ssssay, yyyuh-al gggit ooooffa-Bbig Boy. Hhhes got me," gurgled Bobo.

161 "Cant yuh hol im?"

162 "Nnaw, hhes ggot mmah nneck . . ."

163 Big Boy squeezed tighter.

164 "N Ahma break it too les yuh tell em t git t hell offa me!"

165 "Ttturn mmmeee. llloose," panted Bobo, tears-gushing.

166 "Cant yuh hol im, Bobo?" asked Buck.

167 "Nnaw, yuh-all tturn im lloose; hhhes got mah nnneck . . ."

168 "Grab his neck, Bobo . . ."

169 "Ah cant; yugurgur . . ."

170 To save Bobo, Lester and Buck got up and ran to a safe distance. Big Boy released Bobo, who staggered to his feet, slobbering and trying to stretch a crick out of his neck.

171 "Shucks, nigger, yuh almos broke mah neck," whimpered Bobo.

172 "Ahm gonna break yo ass nex time," said Big Boy."

173 "Ef Bobo coulda hel yuh we woulda had yuh," yelled Lester.

174 "Ah waznt gonna let im do that," said Big Boy.

175 They walked together again, swishing sticks.

176 "Yuh ses," began Big Boy, "when a ganga guys jump on yuh, all yuh gotta do is put the heat on one of them n make im tell the others t let up, see?"

177 "Gee, thas a good ideel!"

178 "Yeah, thas a good ideel"

179 "But yuh almos broke mah neck, man," said Bobo.

180 "Ahma smart nigger," said Big Boy, thrusting out his chest.

II

181 They came to the swimming hole.

182 "Ah ain goin in," said Bobo.

183 "Done got scared?" asked Big Boy.

184 "Naw, Ah ain scared . . ."

185 "How come yuh ain goin in?"

186 "Yuh know ol man Harvey don erllow no niggers t swim in this hole."

187 "N jus las year he took a shot at Bob fer swimming in here," said Lester.

188 "Shucks, ol man Harvey ain studyin bout us niggers," said Big Boy.

189 "Hes at home thinking about his jelly-roll," said Buck.

190 They laughed.

191 "Buck, yo mins lowern a snakes belly," said Lester.

192 "Ol man Harveys too doggone ol t think erbout jelly-roll," said Big Boy.

193 "Hes dried up; all the saps done lef im," said Bobo.

194 "C mon, les go!" said Big Boy.

195 Bobo pointed.

196 "See tha sign over yonder?"

197 "Yeah."

198 "Whut it say?"

199 "NO TRESPASSIN," read Lester.

200 "Know whut tha mean?"

201 "Mean ain no dogs n niggers erllowed," said Buck.

202 "Waal, wes here now," said Big Boy. "Ef he ketched us even like this thered be trouble, so we just as waal go on in . . ."

203 "Ahm wid the nex one!"

204 "Ahll go ef anybody else goes!"

205 Big Boy looked carefully in all directions. Seeing nobody, he began jerking off his overalls.

206 "LAS ONE INS A OL DEAD DOG!"

207 "THAS YO MA!"

208 "THAS YO PA!"

209 "THAS BOTH YO MA N YO PA!"

210 They jerked off their clothes and threw them in a pile under a tree. Thirty seconds later they stood, black and naked, on the edge of the hole under a sloping embankment. Gingerly Big Boy touched the water with his foot.

211 "Man, this waters col," he said.

212 "Ahm gonna put mah cloes back on," said Bobo, with-drawing his foot.

213 Big Boy grabbed him about the waist.

214 "Like hell yuh is!"

215   "Git outta the way, nigger!" Bobo yelled.

216   "Thow im in!" said Lester.

217   "Duck im!"

218   Bobo crouched, spread his legs, and braced himself against Big Boy's body. Locked in each other's arms, they tussled on the edge of the hole, neither able to throw the other.

219   "C mon, les me n yuh push em in."

220   "O.K."

221   Laughing, Lester and Buck gave the two locked bodies a running push. Big Boy and Bobo splashed, sending up silver spray in the sunlight. When Big Boy's head came up he yelled:

222   "Yuh bastard!"

223   "Tha wuz yo ma yuh pushed!" said Bobo, shaking his head to clear the water from his eyes.

224   They did a surface dive, came up and struck out across the creek. The muddy water foamed. They swam back, waded into shallow water, breathing heavily and blinking eyes.

225   "C mon in!"

226   "Man, the water's fine!"

227   Lester and Buck hesitated.

228   "Les wet em," Big Boy whispered to Bobo.

229   Before Lester and Buck could back away, they were dripping wet from handfuls of scooped water.

230   "Hey, quit!"

231   "Gawddam, nigger; tha waters col!"

232   "C mon in!" called Big Boy.

233   "We just as waal go on in now," said Buck.

234   "Look n see ef anybody's comin."

235   Kneeling, they squinted among the trees.

236   "Ain nobody."

237   "C mon, les go."

238   They waded in slowly, pausing each few steps to catch their breath. A desperate water battle began. Closing eyes and backing away, they shunted water into one another's faces with the flat palms of hands.

239   "Hey, cut it out!"

240   "Yeah, Ahm bout drownin!"

241   They came together in water up to their navels, blowing and blinking. Big Boy ducked, upsetting Bobo.

242   "Look out, nigger!"

243   "Don holler so loud!"

244 "Yeah, they kin hear yo ol big mouth a mile erway."

245 "This waters too col fer me."

246 "Thas cause it rained yistiddy."

247 They swam across and back again.

248 "Ah wish we hada bigger place t swim in."

249 "The white folks got plenty swimming pools n we ain got none."

250 "Ah useta swim in the ol Missippi when we lived in Vicksburg."

251 Big Boy put his head under the water and blew his breath. A sound came like that of a hippopotamus.

252 "C mon, les be hippos."

253 Each went to a corner of the creek and put his mouth just below the surface and blew like a hippopotamus. Tiring, they came and sat under the embankment.

254 "Look like Ah gotta chill."

255 "Me too."

256 "Les stay here n dry off."

257 "Jeeesus Ahm col!"

258 They kept still in the sun, suppressing shivers. After some of the water had dried off their bodies they began to talk through clattering teeth.

259 "Whut would yuh do ef ol man Harveyd come erlong right now?"

260 "Run like hell!"

261 "Man, Ahd run so fas hed thinka black streaka lightnin shot pass im."

262 "But spose he hada gun?"

263 "Aw, nigger, shut up!"

264 They were silent. They ran their hands over wet, trembling legs, brushing water away. Then their eyes watched the sun sparkling on the restless creek.

265 Far away a train whistled.

266 "There goes number seven!"

267 "Headin fer up Noth!"

268 "Blazin it down the line!"

269 "Lawd, Ahm goin Noth some day."

270 "Me too, man."

271 "They say colored folks up Noth is got ekual rights."

272 They grew pensive. A black winged butterfly hovered at the water's edge. A bee droned. From somewhere came the sweet scent of honeysuckles. Dimly they could hear sparrows twittering in the woods. They rolled from side to side, letting sunshine dry their skins and warm their blood. They plucked blades of grass and chewed them.

273   "Oh!"

274   They looked up, their lips parting.

275   "Oh!"

276   A white woman, poised on the edge of the opposite embankment, stood directly in front of them, her hat in her hand and her hair lit by the sun.

277   "Its a woman!" whispered Big Boy in an underbreath. "A *white* woman!"

278   They stared, their hands instinctively covering their groins. Then they scrambled to their feet. The white woman backed slowly out of sight. They stood for a moment, looking at one another.

279   "Les git outta here!" Big Boy whispered.

280   "Wait till she goes erway."

281   "Les run, theyll ketch us here naked like this!"

282   "Mabbe theres a man wid her."

283   "C mon, les git our cloes," said Big Boy.

284   They waited a moment longer, listening.

285   "What t hell! Ahma git mah cloes," said Big Boy.

286   Grabbing at short tufts of grass, he climbed the embankment.

287   "Don run out there now!"

288   "C mon back, fool!"

289   Bobo hesitated. He looked at Big Boy, and then at Buck and Lester.

290   "Ahm goin wid Big Boy n git mah cloes," he said.

291   "Don run out there naked like tha, fool!" said Buck. "Yuh don know whos out there!"

292   Big Boy was climbing over the edge of the embankment.

293   "C mon," he whispered.

294   Bobo climbed after. Twenty-five feet away the woman stood. She had one hand over her mouth. Hanging by fingers, Buck and Lester peeped over the edge.

295   "C mon back; that womans scared," said Lester.

296   Big Boy stopped, puzzled. He looked at the woman. He looked at the bundle of clothes. Then he looked at Buck and Lester.

297   "C mon, les git our cloes!"

298   He made a step.

299   "Jim!" the woman screamed.

300   Big Boy stopped and looked around. His hands hung loosely at his side. The woman, her eyes wide, her hand over her mouth, backed away to the tree where their clothes lay in a heap.

301   "Big Boy, come back here n wait till shes gone!"

302   Bobo ran to Big Boy's side.

303 "Les go home! Theyll ketch us here," he urged.

304 Big Boy's throat felt tight.

305 "Lady, we wanna git our cloes," he said.

306 Buck and Lester climbed the embankment and stood indecisively. Big Boy ran toward the tree.

307 "Jim!" the woman screamed. "Jim! Jim!"

308 Black and naked, Big Boy stopped three feet from her.

309 "We wanna git our cloes," he said again, his words coming mechanically.

310 He made a motion.

311 "You go away! You go away! I tell you, you go away!"

312 Big Boy stopped again, afraid. Bobo ran and snatched the clothes. Buck and Lester tried to grab theirs out of his hands.

313 "You go away! You go away! You go away!" the woman screamed.

314 "Les go!" said Bobo, running toward the woods.

315 CRACK!

316 Lester grunted, stiffened, and pitched forward. His forehead struck a toe of the woman's shoes.

317 Bobo stopped, clutching the clothes. Buck whirled. Big Boy stared at Lester, his lips moving.

318 "Hes gotta gun; hes gotta gun!" yelled Buck, running wildly.

319 CRACK!

320 Buck stopped at the edge of the embankment, his head jerked backward, his body arched stiffly to one side; he toppled headlong, sending up a shower of bright spray to the sunlight. The creek bubbled.

321 Big Boy and Bobo backed away, their eyes fastened fearfully on a white man who was running toward them. He had a rifle and wore an army officer's uniform. He ran to the woman's side and grabbed her hand.

322 "You hurt, Bertha, you hurt?"

323 She stared at him and did not answer.

324 The man turned quickly. His face was red. He raised the rifle and pointed it at Bobo. Bobo ran back, holding the clothes in front of his chest.

325 "Don shoot me, Mistah, don shoot me . . ."

326 Big Boy lunged for the rifle, grabbing the barrel.

327 "You black sonofabitch!"

328 Big Boy clung desperately.

329 "Let go, you black bastard!"

330 The barrel pointed skyward.

331 CRACK!

332   The white man, taller and heavier, flung Big Boy to the ground. Bobo dropped the clothes, ran up, and jumped onto the white man's back.

333   "You black sonsofbitches!"

334   The white man released the rifle, jerked Bobo to the ground, and began to batter the naked boy with his fists. Then Big Boy swung, striking the man in the mouth with the barrel. His teeth caved in, and he fell, dazed. Bobo was on his feet.

335   "C mon, Big Boy, les go!"

336   Breathing hard, the white man got up and faced Big Boy. His lips were trembling, his neck and chin wet with blood. He spoke quietly.

337   "Give me that gun, boy!"

338   Big Boy leveled the rifle and backed away.

339   The white man advanced.

340   "Boy, I say give me that gun!"

341   Bobo had the clothes in his arms.

342   "Run, Big Boy, run!"

343   The man came at Big Boy.

344   "Ahll kill yuh; Ahll kill yuh!" said Big Boy.

345   His fingers fumbled for the trigger.

346   The man stopped, blinked, spat blood. His eyes were bewildered. His face whitened. Suddenly, he lunged for the rifle, his hands outstretched.

347   CRACK!

348   He fell forward on his face.

349   "Jim!"

350   Big Boy and Bobo turned in surprise to look at the woman.

351   "Jim!" she screamed again, and fell weakly at the foot of the tree.

352   Big Boy dropped the rifle, his eyes wide. He looked around. Bobo was crying and clutching the clothes.

353   "Big Boy, Big Boy . . ."

354   Big Boy looked at the rifle, started to pick it up, but didn't. He seemed at a loss. He looked at Lester, then at the white man; his eyes followed a thin stream of blood that seeped to the ground.

355   "Yuh done killed im," mumbled Bobo.

356   "Les go home!"

357   Naked, they turned and ran toward the wood. When they reached the barbed-wire fence they stopped.

358   "Les git our cloes on," said Big Boy.

359   They slipped quickly into overalls. Bobo held Lester's and Buck's clothes.

360   "Whut we gonna do wid these?"

361 Big Boy stared. His hands twitched.

362 "Leave em."

363 They climbed the fence and ran through the woods. Vines and leaves switched their faces. Once Bobo tripped and fell.

364 "C mon!" said Big Boy.

365 Bobo started crying, blood streaming from his scratches.

366 "Ahm scared!"

367 "C mon! Don cry! We wanna git home fo they ketches us!"

368 "Ahm scared!" said Bobo again, his eyes full of tears.

369 Big Boy grabbed his hand and dragged him along.

370 "C mon!"

III

371 They stopped when they got to the end of the woods. They could see the open road leading home, to ma and pa. But they hung back, afraid. The thick shadows cast from the trees were friendly and sheltering. But the wide glare of sun stretching out over the fields was pitiless. They crouched behind an old log.

372 "We gotta git home," said Big Boy.

373 "Theys gonna lynch us," said Bobo, half-questioningly.

374 Big Boy did not answer.

375 "Theys gonna lynch us," said Bobo again.

376 Big Boy shuddered.

377 "Hush!" he said. He did not want to think of it. He could not think of it; there was but one thought, and he clung to that one blindly. He had to get home, home to ma and pa.

378 Their heads jerked up. Their ears had caught the rhythmic jingle of a wagon. They fell to the ground and clung flat to the side of a log. Over the crest of the hill came the top of a hat. A white face. Then shoulders in a blue shirt. A wagon drawn by two horses pulled into full view.

379 Big Boy and Bobo held their breath, waiting. Their eyes followed the wagon till it was lost in dust around a bend of the road.

380 "We gotta git home," said Big Boy.

381 "Ahm scared," said Bobo.

382 "C mon! Les keep t the fields."

383 They ran till they came to the cornfields. Then they went slower, for last year's corn stubbles bruised their feet.

384 They came in sight of a brickyard.

385 "Wait a minute," gasped Big Boy.

386 They stopped.

387 "Ahm goin on t mah home n yuh better go on t yos."

388 Bobo's eyes grew round.

389 "Ahm scared!"

390 "Yuh better go on!"

391 "Lemme go wid yuh; theyll ketch me . . ."

392 "Ef yuh kin git home mabbe yo folks kin hep yuh t git erway."

393 Big Boy started off. Bobo grabbed him.

394 "Lemme go wid yuh!"

395 Big Boy shook free.

396 "Ef yuh stay here theys gonna lynch yuh!" he yelled, running.

397 After he had gone about twenty-five yards he turned and looked; Bobo was flying through the woods like the wind.

398 Big Boy slowed when he came to the railroad. He wondered if he ought to go through the streets or down the track. He decided on the tracks. He could dodge a train better than a mob.

399 He trotted along the ties, looking ahead and back. His cheek itched, and he felt it. His hand came away smeared with blood. He wiped it nervously on his overalls.

400 When he came to his back fence he heaved himself over. He landed among a flock of startled chickens. A bantam rooster tried to spur him. He slipped and fell in front of the kitchen steps, grunting heavily. The ground was slick with greasy dishwater.

401 Panting, he stumbled through the doorway.

402 "Lawd, Big Boy, whuts wrong wid yuh?"

403 His mother stood gaping in the middle of the floor. Big Boy flopped wordlessly onto a stool, almost toppling over. Pots simmered on the stove. The kitchen smelled of food cooking.

404 "Whuts the matter, Big Boy?"

405 Mutely, he looked at her. Then he burst into tears. She came and felt the scratches on his face.

406 "Whut happened t yuh, Big Boy? Somebody been botherin yuh?"

407 "They after me, Ma! They after me . . ."

408 "Who!"

409 "Ah . . . Ah . . . We . . ."

410 "Big Boy, whuts wrong wid yuh?"

411 "He killed Lester n Buck," he muttered simply.

412 "Killed!"

413 "Yessum."

414 "Lester n Buck!"

415 "Yessum, Ma!"

416 "How killed?"

417 "He shot em, Ma!"

418 "Lawd Gawd in Heaven, have mercy on us all! This is mo trouble, mo trouble," she moaned, wringing her hands.

419 "N Ah killed im, Ma . . ."

420 She stared, trying to understand.

421 "Whut happened, Big Boy?"

422 "We tried t git our cloes from the tree . . ."

423 "Whut tree?"

424 "We wuz swimmin, Ma. N the white woman . . ."

425 "*White* woman? . . ."

426 "Yessum. She wuz at the swimmin hole . . .

427 "Lawd have mercy! Ah knowed yuh boys wuz gonna keep on till yuh got into somethin like this!"

428 She ran into the hall.

429 "Lucy!"

430 "Mam?"

431 "C mere!"

432 "Mam?"

433 "C mere, Ah say!"

434 "Whutcha wan, Ma? Ahm sewin."

435 "Chile, will yuh c mere like Ah ast yuh?"

436 Lucy came to the door holding an unfinished apron in her hands. When she saw Big Boy's face she looked wildly at her mother.

437 "Whuts the matter?"

438 "Wheres Pa?"

439 "He's out front, Ah reckon."

440 "Git im, quick!"

441 "Whuts the matter, Ma?"

442 "Go git yo Pa, Ah say!"

443 Lucy ran out. The mother sank into a chair, holding a dish rag. Suddenly, she sat up.

444 "Big Boy, Ah thought yuh wuz at school?"

445 Big Boy looked at the floor.

446 "How come yuh didn't go t school?"

447 "We went t the woods."

448 She sighed.

449 "Ah done done all Ah kin fer yuh, Big Boy. Only Gawd kin help yuh now."

450   "Ma, don let em git me; don let em git me . . ."

451   His father came into the doorway. He stared at Big Boy, then at his wife.

452   "Whuts Big Boys inter now?" he asked sternly.

453   "Saul, Big Boys done gone n got inter trouble wid the white folks."

454   The old man's mouth dropped, and he looked from one to the other.

455   "Saul, we gotta git im erway from here."

456   "Open yo mouth n talk! Whut yuh been doin?" The old man gripped Big Boy's shoulders and peered at the scratches on his face.

457   "Me n Lester n Buck n Bobo wuz out on ol man Harveys place swimmin . . ."

458   "Saul, its a *white* woman!"

459   Big Boy winced. The old man compressed his lips and stared at his wife. Lucy gaped at her brother as though she had never seen him before.

460   "Whut happened? Cant yuh all talk?" the old man thundered, with a certain helplessness in his voice.

461   "We wuz swimmin," Big Boy began, "n then a white woman comes up t the hole. We got up right erway to git our cloes sos we could git erway, n she started screamin. Our cloes wuz right by the tree where she wuz standin, n when we started t git em she jus screamed. We told her we wanted our cloes . . . Yuh see, Pa, she was standin' right *by* our cloes; n when we went t git em she jus screamed . . . Bobo got the cloes, n then he shot Lester . . ."

462   "*Who* shot Lester?"

463   "The white man."

464   "Whut white man?"

465   "Ah dunno, Pa. He wuz a soljer, n he had a rifle."

466   "A soljer?"

467   "Yessuh."

468   "A *Soljer?*"

469   "Yessuh, Pa. A soljer."

470   The old man frowned.

471   "N then what yuh-all do?"

472   "Waal, Buck said, 'Hes gotta gun!' N we started runnin. N then he shot Buck, n he fell in the swimmin hole. We didn't see im no mo . . . He wuz close on us then. He looked at the white woman n then he started t shoot Bobo. Ah grabbed the gun, n we started fightin. Bobo jumped on his back. He started beatin Bobo. Then Ah hit im wid the gun. Then he started at me n Ah shot im. Then we run . . ."

473   "Who seen?"

474 "Nobody."

475 "Wheres Bobo?"

476 "He went home."

477 "Anybody run after yuh-all?"

478 "Nawsuh."

479 "Yuh see anybody?"

480 "Nawsuh. Nobody but a white man. But he didnt see us."

481 "How long fo yuh-all lef the swimmin hole?"

482 "Little while ergo."

483 The old man nervously brushed his hand across his eyes and walked to the door. His lips moved, but no words came.

484 "Saul, whut we gonna do?"

485 "Lucy," began the old man, "go t Brother Sanders n tell im Ah said c mere; n go t Brother Jenkins n tell im Ah said c mere; n go t Elder Peters n tell im Ah said c mere. N don say nothin t nobody but whut Ah tol yuh. N when yuh git thu come straight back. Now go!"

486 Lucy dropped her apron across the back of a chair and ran down the steps. The mother bent over, crying and praying. The old man walked slowly over to Big Boy.

487 "Big Boy?"

488 Big Boy swallowed.

489 "Ahm talkin t yuh!"

490 "Yessuh."

491 "How come yuh didnt go t school this mawnin?"

492 "We went t the woods."

493 "Didnt yo ma send yuh t school?"

494 "Yessuh."

495 "How come yuh didnt go?"

496 "We went t the woods."

497 "Don yuh know thas wrong?"

498 "Yessuh."

499 "How come yuh go?"

500 Big Boy looked at his fingers, knotted them, and squirmed in his seat.

501 "AHM TALKIN T YUH!"

502 His wife straightened up and said reprovingly:

503 "Saul!"

504 The old man desisted, yanking nervously at the shoulder straps of his overalls.

505 "How long wuz the woman there?"

506 "Not long."

507   "Wuz she young?"

508   "Yessuh. Lika gal."

509   "Did yuh-all say anythin t her?"

510   "Nawsuh. We jes said we wanted our cloes."

511   "N what she say?"

512   "Nothin, Pa. She jus backed erway t the tree n screamed."

513   The old man stared, his lips trying to form a question.

514   "Big Boy, did yuh-all bother her?"

515   "Nawsuh, Pa. We didnt *touch* her."

516   "How long fo the white man come up?"

517   "Right erway."

518   "Whut he say?"

519   "Nothin. He jus cussed us."

520   Abruptly the old man left the kitchen.

521   "Ma, cant Ah go fo they ketches me?"

522   "Sauls doin whut he kin."

523   "Ma, Ma, Ah don want em t ketch me . . ."

524   "Sauls doin what he kin. Nobody but the good Lawd kin hep us now."

525   The old man came back with a shotgun and leaned it in a corner. Fascinatedly, Big Boy looked at it.

526   There was a knock at the front door.

527   "Liza, see whos there."

528   She went. They were silent, listening. They could hear her talking.

529   "Whos there?"

530   "Me."

531   "Who?"

532   "Me, Brother Sanders."

533   "C mon in. Sauls waitin fer yuh."

534   Sanders paused in the doorway, smiling.

535   "Yuh sent fer me, Brother Morrison?"

536   "Brother Sanders, wes in deep trouble here."

537   Sanders came all the way into the kitchen.

538   "Yeah?"

539   "Big Boy done gone n killed a white man."

540   Sanders stopped short, then came forward, his face thrust out, his mouth open. His lips moved several times before he could speak.

541   "A *white* man?"

542   "They gonna kill me; they gonna kill me!" Big Boy cried, running to the old man.

543   "Saul, cant we git im erway somewhere?"

544 "Here now, take it easy; take it easy," said Sanders, holding Big Boy's wrists.

545 "They gonna kill me; they gonna lynch me!"

546 Big Boy slipped to the floor. They lifted him to a stool. His mother held him closely, pressing his head to her bosom.

547 "Whut we gonna do?" asked Sanders.

548 "Ah done sent for Brother Jenkins n Elder Peters."

549 Sanders leaned his shoulders against the wall. Then, as the full meaning of it came to him, he exclaimed:

550 "Theys gonna git a mob! . . ." His voice broke off and his eyes fell on the shotgun.

551 Feet came pounding on the steps. They turned toward the door. Lucy ran in crying. Jenkins followed. The old man met him in the middle of the room, taking his hand.

552 "Wes in bad trouble here, Brother Jenkins. Big Boy's done gone n killed a white man. Yuh-alls gotta hep me . . ."

553 Jenkins looked hard at Big Boy.

554 "Elder Peters says hes comin," said Lucy.

555 "When all this happen?" asked Jenkins.

556 "Near bout a hour ergo, now," said the old man.

557 "Whut we gonna do?" asked Jenkins.

558 "Ah wanna wait till Elder Peters come," said the old man helplessly.

559 "But we gotta work fas ef we gonna do anythin," said Sanders. "We'll git in trouble jus standin here like this."

560 Big Boy pulled away from his mother.

561 "Pa, lemma go now! Lemma go now!"

562 "Be still, Big Boy!"

563 "Where kin yuh go?"

564 "Ah could ketch a freight!"

565 "Thas *sho* death!" said Jenkins, "They'll be watchin em all!"

566 "Kin yuh-all hep me wid some money?" the old man asked.

567 They shook their heads.

568 "Saul, whut kin we do? Big Boy cant stay here."

569 There was another knock at the door.

570 The old man backed stealthily to the shotgun.

571 "Lucy, go!"

572 Lucy looked at him, hesitating.

573 "Ah better go," said Jenkins.

574 It was Elder Peters. He came in hurriedly.

575 "Good evenin, everybody!"

576   "How yuh, Elder?"

577   "Good evenin."

578   "How yuh today?"

579   Peters looked around the crowded kitchen.

580   "Whuts the matter?"

581   "Elder, wes in deep trouble," began the old man. "Big Boy n some mo boys . . ."

582   ". . . Lester n Buck n Bobo . . ."

583   ". . . wuz over on ol man Harveys place swimmin . . ."

584   "N he don like us niggers *none*," said Peter's emphatically. He widened his legs and put his thumbs in the armholes of his vest.

585   ". . . n some white woman . . ."

586   "Yeah?" said Peters, coming closer.

587   ". . . comes erlong n the boys tries t git their cloes where they done lef em under a tree. Waal, she started screamin n all, see? Reckon she thought the boys wuz after her. Then a white man in a soljers suit shoots two of em . . ."

588   ". . . Lester n Buck . . ."

589   "Huummm," said Peters. "Tha wuz old man Harveys son."

590   "Harveys son?"

591   "Yuh mean the one that wuz in the Army?"

592   "Yuh mean Jim?"

593   "Yeah," said Peters. "The papers said he wuz here fer a vacation from his regiment. N tha woman the boys saw wuz jus erbout his wife . . ."

594   They stared at Peters. Now that they knew what white person had been killed, their fears became definite.

595   "N whut else happened?"

596   "Big Boy shot the man . . ."

597   "Harveys *son?*"

598   "He had t, Elder. He wuz gonna shoot im ef he didnt . . ."

599   "Lawd!" said Peters. He looked around and put his hat back on.

600   "How long ergo wuz this?"

601   "Mighty near an hour, now, Ah reckon."

602   "Do the white folks know yit?"

603   "Don know, Elder."

604   "Yuh-all better git this boy outta here right now," said Peters. "Cause ef yuh don theres gonna be a lynchin . . ."

605   "Where kin Ah go, Elder?" Big Boy ran up to him.

606   They crowded around Peters. He stood with his legs wide apart, looking up at the ceiling.

607   "Mabbe we kin hide im in the church till he kin git erway," said Jenkins.

608   Peters' lips flexed.

609   "Naw, Brother, thall never do! Theyll git im there sho. N anyhow, ef they ketch im there itll ruin us all. We gotta git the boy outta town . . ."

610   Sanders went up to the old man.

611   "Lissen," he said in a whisper. "Mah son, Will, the one whut drives for the Magnolia Express Comny, is takin a truck o goods t Chicawgo in the mawnin. If we kin hide Big Boy somewhere till then, we kin put him on the truck . . ."

612   "Pa, please, lemme go wid Will when he goes in the mawnin," Big Boy begged.

613   The old man stared at Sanders.

614   "Yuh reckon thas safe?"

615   "Its the only thing yuh *kin* do," said Peters.

616   "But where we gonna hide im till then?"

617   "Whut time yo boy leavin out in the mawnin?"

618   "At six."

619   They were quiet, thinking. The water kettle on the stove sang.

620   "Pa, Ah knows where Will passes erlong wid the truck out on Bullards Road. Ah kin hide in one of them ol kilns . . ."

621   "Where?"

622   "In one of them kilns we built . . ."

623   "But they'll git yuh there," wailed the mother.

624   "But there ain no place else for im t go."

625   "Theres some holes big enough fer me t git in n stay till. Will comes erlong," said Big Boy. "Please, Pa, lemme go fo they ketches me . . ."

626   "Let im go!"

627   "Please, Pa . . ."

628   The old man breathed heavily.

629   "Lucy, git his things!"

630   "Saul, theyll git im out there!" wailed the mother, grabbing Big Boy.

631   Peters pulled her away.

632   "Sister Morrison, ef yuh don let im go n git erway from here hes gonna be caught shos theres a Gawd in Heaven!"

633   Lucy came running with Big Boy's shoes and pulled them on his feet. The old man thrust a battered hat on his head. The mother

went to the stove and dumped the skillet of corn pone into her apron. She wrapped it, and unbuttoning Big Boy's overalls, pushed it into his bosom.

634 "Heres something fer yuh t eat; n pray, Big Boy, cause thas all anybody kin do now . . ."

635 Big Boy pulled to the door, his mother clinging to him.

636 "Let im go, Sister Morrison!"

637 "Run fas, Big Boy!"

638 Big Boy raced across the yard, scattering the chickens. He paused at the fence and hollered back:

639 "Tell Bobo where Ahm hidin n tell im t c mon!"

IV

640 He made for the railroad, running straight toward the sunset. He held his left hand tightly over his heart, holding the hot pone of corn bread there. At times he stumbled over the ties, for his shoes were tight and hurt his feet. His throat burned from thirst; he had had no water since noon.

641 He veered off the track and trotted over the crest of a hill, following Bullard's Road. His feet slipped and slid in the dust. He kept his eyes straight ahead, fearing every clump of shrubbery, every tree. He wished it were night. If he could only get to the kilns without meeting anyone. Suddenly a thought came to him like a blow. He recalled hearing the old folks tell tales of blood-hounds, and fear made him run slower. None of them had thought of that. Spose blood-houns wuz put on his trail? Lawd! Spose a whole pack of em, foamin n howlin, tore im t pieces? He went limp and his feet dragged. Yeah, thas whut they wuz gonna send after im, blood-houns! N then thered be no way fer im t dodge! Why hadnt Pa let im take tha shotgun? He stopped. He oughta go back n git tha shotgun. And then when the mob came he would take some with him.

642 In the distance he heard the approach of a train. It jarred him back to a sharp sense of danger. He ran again, his big shoes sopping up and down in the dust. He was tired and his lungs were bursting from running. He wet his lips, wanting water. As he turned from the road across a plowed field he heard the train roaring at his heels. He ran faster, gripped in terror.

643 He was nearly there now. He could see the black clay on the sloping hillside. Once inside a kiln he would be safe. For a little while, at least. He thought of the shotgun again. If he only had something!

Someone to talk to . . . Thas right! Bobo! Bobod be wid im. Hed almost fergot Babo. Bobod bringa gun; he knowed he would. N tergether they could kill the whole mob. Then in the mawning theyd git inter Will's truck n go far erway, t Chicawgo . . .

644   He slowed to a walk, looking back and ahead. A light wind skipped over the grass. A beetle lit on his cheek and he brushed it off. Behind the dark pines hung a red sun. Two bats flapped against that sun. He shivered, for he was growing cold; the sweat on his body was drying.

645   He stopped at the foot of the hill, trying to choose between two patches of black kilns high above him. He went to the left, for there lay the ones he, Bobo, Lester, and Buck had dug only last week. He looked around again; the landscape was bare. He climbed the embankment and stood before a row of black pits sinking four and five feet deep into the earth. He went to the largest and peered in. He stiffened when his ears caught the sound of a whir. He ran back a few steps and poised on his toes. Six foot of snake slid out of the pit and went into coil. Big Boy looked around wildly for a stick. He ran down the slope, peering into the grass. He stumbled over a tree limb. He picked it up and tested it by striking it against the ground.

646   Warily, he crept back up the slope, his stick poised. When about seven feet from the snake he stopped and waved the stick. The coil grew tighter, the whir sounded louder, and a flat head reared to strike. He went to the right, and the flat head followed him, the blue-black tongue darting forth; he went to the left, and the flat head followed him there too.

647   He stopped, teeth clenched. He had to kill this snake. Jus had t kill im! This wuz the safest pit on the hillside. He waved the stick again, looking at the snake before, thinking of a mob behind. The flat head reared higher. With stick over shoulder, he jumped in, swinging. The stick sang through the air, catching the snake on the side of the head, sweeping him out of coil. There was a brown writhing mass. Then Big Boy was upon him, pounding blows home, one on top of the other. He fought viciously, his eyes red, his teeth bared in a snarl. He beat till the snake lay still; then he stomped it with his heel, grinding its head into the dirt.

648   He stopped, limp, wet. The corners of his lips were white with spittle. He spat and shuddered.

649   Cautiously, he went to the hole and peered. He longed for a match. He imagined whole nests of them in there waiting. He put the stick into the hole and waved it around. Stooping, he peered again. It mus be awright. He looked over the hillside, his eyes coming back

to the dead snake. Then he got to his knees and backed slowly into the hole.

650   When inside he felt there must be snakes about him, ready to strike. It seemed he could see and feel them there, waiting tensely in coil. In the dark he imagined long, white fangs ready to sink into his neck, his side, his legs. He wanted to come out, but kept still. Shucks, he told himself, ef there wuz any snakes in here they sho woulda done bit me by now. Some of his fear left, and he relaxed.

651   With elbows on ground and chin on palms, he settled. The clay was cold to his knees and thighs, but his bosom was kept warm by the hot pone of corn bread. His thirst returned and he longed for a drink. He was hungry, too. But he did not want to eat the corn pone. Naw, not now. Mabbe after erwhile, after Bobo came. Then theyd both eat the corn pone.

652   The view from his hole was fringed by the long tufts of grass. He could see all the way to Bullard's Road, and even beyond. The wind was blowing, and in the east the first touch of dusk was rising. Every now and then a bird floated past, a spot of wheeling black printed against the sky. Big Boy sighed, shifted his weight, and chewed at a blade of grass. A wasp droned. He heard number nine, far away and mournful.

653   The train made him remember how they had dug these kilns on long hot summer days, how they had made boilers out of big tin cans, filled them with water, fixed stoppers for steam, cemented them in holes with wet clay, and built fires under them. He recalled how they had danced and yelled when a stopper blew out of a boiler, letting out a big spout of steam and a shrill whistle. There were times when they had the whole hillside blazing and smoking. Yeah, yuh see, Big Boy wuz Casey Jones n wuz speedin it down the gleamin rails of the Southern Pacific. Bobo had number two on the Santa Fe. Buck wuz on the Illinoy Central. Lester the Nickel Plate. Lawd, how they sheveled the wood in! The boiling water would almost jar the cans loose from the clay. More and more pine-knots and dry leaves would be piled under the cans. Flames would grow so tall they would have to shield, their eyes. Sweat would pour off their faces. Then, suddenly, a peg would shoot high into the air, and

654   Pssseeeezzzzzzzzzzzzzzzz . . .

655   Big Boy sighed and stretched out his arm, quenching the flames and scattering the smoke. Why didnt Bobo c mon? He looked over the fields; there was nothing but dying sunlight. His mind drifted back to the kilns. He remembered the day when Buck, jealous of his

winning, had tried to smash his kiln. Yeah, that ol sonofabitch! Naw, Lawd! He didnt go t say tha! Whut wu he thinkin erbout? Cussin the dead! Yeah, po ol Buck wuz dead now. N Lester too. Yeah, it wuz awright fer Buck t smash his kiln. Sho. N he wished he hadnt socked ol Buck so hard tha day. He wuz sorry fer Buck now. N he sho wished he hadnt cussed po ol Bucks ma, neither. Tha wuz sinful! Mabbe Gawd would git im fer that? But he didnt go t do it! Po Buck! Po Lester! Hed never treat anybody like tha ergin, never . . .

656   Dusk was slowly deepening. Somewhere, he could not tell exactly where, a cricket took up a fitful song. The air was growing soft and heavy. He looked over the fields, longing for Bobo . . .

657   He shifted his body to ease the cold damp of the ground, and thought back over the day. Yeah, hed been dam right erbout not wantin t go swimmin. N ef hed followed his right min hed neverve gone n got inter all this trouble. At first hed said naw. But shucks, somehow hed just went on wid the res. Yeah he shoulda went on t school tha mawnin, like Ma told im t do. But, hell, who wouldnt git tireda awways drivin a guy t school! Tha wuz the big trouble awways drivin a guy t school. He wouldnt be in all this trouble now if it wuznt fer that Gawddam school! Impatiently, he took the grass out of his mouth and threw it away, demolishing the little red school house . . .

658   Yeah, if they had all kept still n quiet when tha ol white woman showed-up, mabbe shedve went on off. But yuh never kin tell erbout these white folks. Mabbe she wouldntve went. Mabbe tha white man woulda killed all of em! All *fo* of em! Yeah, yuh never kin tell erbout white folks. Then, ergin, mabbe tha white woman woulda went on off n laffed. Yeah, mabbe tha white man woulda said: *Yuh nigger bastards git t hell outta here! Yuh know Gawdam well yuh don berlong here!* N then they woulda grabbed their cloes n run like all hell . . . He blinked the white man away. Where wuz Bobo? Why didnt he hurry up n c mon?

659   He jerked another blade and chewed. Yeah, ef Pa had only let im have tha shotgun! He could stan off a whole mob wid a shotgun. He looked at the ground as he turned a shotgun over in his hands. Then he leveled it at an advancing white man. *Boooom!* The man curled up. Another came. He reloaded quickly, and let him have what the other had got. He too curled up. Then another came. He got the same medicine. Then the whole mob swirled around him, and he blazed away, getting as many as he could. They closed in; but, by Gawd, he had done his part, hadnt he? N the newspapersd say: NIGGER KILLS DOZEN OF MOB BEFO LYNCHED! Er mabbe theyd

say: TRAPPED NIGGER SLAYS TWENTY BEFO KILLED! He
smiled a little. Tha wouldnt be so bad, would it? Blinking the newspaper away, he looked over the fields. Where wuz Bobo? Why didnt
he hurry up n c mon?

660 He shifted, trying to get a crick out of his legs. Shucks, he wuz gettin tireda this. N it wuz almos dark now. Yeah, there wuz a little bit-
tie star way over yonder in the eas. Mabbe tha white man wuznt
dead? Mabbe they wuznt even lookin fer im? Mabbe he could go back
home now? Naw, better wait erwhile. Thad be bes. But, Lawd, ef he
only had some water! He could hardly swallow, his throat was so
dry. Gawddam them white folks! Thas all they wuz good fer, t run
a nigger down lika rabbit! Yeah, they git yuh in a corner n then they
let yuh have it. A thousan of em! He shivered, for the cold of the
clay was chilling his bones. Lawd, spose they found im here in this
hole? N wid nobody t help im? . . . But ain no use in thinkin erbout
tha; wait till trouble come fo yuh start fightin it. But if tha mob came
one by one hed wipe em all out. Clean up the whole bunch. He caught
one by the neck and choked him long and hard, choked him till his
tongue and eyes popped out. Then he jumped upon his chest and
stomped him like he had stomped that snake. When he had finished
with one, another came. He choked him too. Choked till he sank
slowly to the ground, gasping . . .

661 "Hoalo!"

662 Big Boy snatched his fingers from the white man's neck and looked
over the fields. He saw nobody. Had someone spied him? He was sure
that somebody had hollered. His heart pounded. But, shucks, nobody
couldnt see im here in this hole . . . But mabbe theyd seen im when
he wuz comin n had laid low n wuz now closin in on im! Praps they
wuz signalin fer the others? Yeah, they wuz creepin up on im! Mabbe
he oughta git up n run . . . Oh! Mabbe tha wuz Bobo! Yeah, Bobo!
He oughta clim out n see if Bobo wuz lookin fer im . . . He stiffened.

663 "Hoalo!"

664 "Hoalo!"

665 "Wheres yuh?"

666 "Over here on Bullards Road!"

667 "C mon over!"

668 "Awright!"

669 He heard footsteps. Then voices came again, low and far away this
time.

670 "Seen anybody?"

671 "Naw. Yuh?"

672   "Naw."

673   "Yuh reckon they got erway?"

674   "Ah dunno. Its hard t tell."

675   "Gawddam them sonofabitchin niggers!"

676   "We oughta kill ever black bastard in this country!"

677   "Waal, Jim got two of em, anyhow."

678   "But Bertha said there wuz *fo!*"

679   "Where in hell they hidin?"

680   "She said one of em wuz named Big Boy, or somethin like tha."

681   "We went t his shack lookin fer im."

682   "Yeah?"

683   "But we didnt fin im."

684   "These niggers stick tergether; they don never tell on each other."

685   "We looked all thu the shack n couldnt fin hide ner hair of im. Then
we drove the ol woman n man out n set the shack on fire . . ."

686   "Jeesus! Ah wished Ah coulda been there!"

687   "Yuh shoulda heard the ol nigger woman howl . . ."

688   "Hoalo!"

689   "C mon over!"

690   Big Boy eased to the edge and peeped. He saw a white man with
a gun alung over his shoulder running down the slope. Wuz they
gonna search the hill? Lawd, there wuz no way fer im t git erway now;
he wuz caught! he shoulda knowed theyd git im here. N he didnt hava
thing, notta thing t fight wid. Yeah, soon as the blood-houns came
theyd fin im. Lawd, have mercy! Theyd lynch im right here on the
hill . . . Theyd git im n tie im t a stake n burn im erlive! Lawd!
Nobody but the good Lawd could hep im now, nobody . . .

691   He heard more feet running. He nestled deeper. His chest ached.
Nobody but the good Lawd could hep now. They wuz crowdn all
round im n when they hada big crowd theyd close in on im. Then
itd be over . . . The good Lawd would have t hep im, cause nobody
could hep im now, nobody . . .

692   And then he went numb when he remembered Bobo. Spose
Bobod come now? Hed be caught sho! Both of em would be caught!
Theyd make Bobo tell where he wuz! Bobo oughts not try to come
now. Somebody oughta tell im . . . But there wuz nobody; there
wuz no way . . .

693   He eased slowly back to the opening. There was a large group of
men. More were coming. Many had guns. Some had coils of rope slung
over shoulders.

694   "Ah tell yuh they still here, somewhere . . ."

695 "But we looked all over!"

696 "What t hell! Wouldnt do t let em glt erway!"

697 "Naw. Ef they git erway notta woman in this town would be safe."

698 "Say, whuts tha yuh got?"

699 "Er pillar."

700 "Fer whut?"

701 "Feathers, fool!"

702 "Chris! Thiall be hot if we kin ketch them niggers!"

703 "Ol Anderson said he wuz gonna bringa barrela tar!"

704 "Ah got some gasolin in mah car if yuh need it."

705 Big Boy had no feelings now. He was waiting. He did not wonder if they were coming after him. He just waited. He did not wonder about Bobo. He rested his cheek against the cold clay, waiting.

706 A dog barked. He stiffened. It barked again. He balled himself into a knot at the bottom of the hole, waiting. Then he heard the patter of dog feet.

707 "Look!"

708 "Whuts he got?"

709 "Its a snake!"

710 "Yeah, the dogs foun a snake!"

711 "Gee, its a big one!"

712 "Shucks, Ah wish he could fin one of them sonofabitchin niggers!"

713 The voices sank to low murmurs. Then he heard number twelve, its bell tolling and whistle crying as it slid along the rails. He flattened himself against the clay. Someone was singing:

We'll hang ever nigger t a sour apple tree . . .

714 When the song ended there was hard laughter. From the other side of the hill he heard the dog barking furiously. He listened. There was more than one dog now. There were many and they were barking their throats out.

715 "Hush. Ah hear them dogs!"

716 "When theys barkin like tha theys foun somethin!"

717 "Here they come over the hill!"

718 "WE GOT IM! WE GOT IM!"

719 There came a roar. Tha must be Bobo; tha mus be Bobo . . . In spite of his fear, Big Boy looked. The road, and half of the hillside across the road, were covered with men. A few were at the top of the hill, stenciled against the sky. He could see dark forms moving up the slopes. They were yelling.

720   "By Gawd, we got im!"

721   "C mon!"

722   "Where is he?"

723   "Theyre bringin im over the hill!"

724   "Ah got a rope fer im!"

725   "Say, somebody go n git the others!"

726   "Where is he? Cant we see im, Mister?"

727   "They say Berthas comin, too."

728   "Jack! Jack! Don leave me! Ah wanna see im!"

729   "Theyre bringin im over the hill, sweetheart!"

730   "AH WANNA BE THE FIRS T PUT A ROPE ON THA BLACK BASTARDS NECK!"

731   "Les start the fire!"

732   "Heat the tar!"

733   "Ah got some chains t chain im."

734   "Bring im over this way!"

735   "Chris, Ah wished Ah hada drink . . ."

736   Big Boy saw men moving over the hill. Among them was a long dark spot. Tha mus be Bobo; tha mus be Bobo theys carryin . . . Theyll git im here. He oughta git up n run. He clamped his teeth and ran his hand across his forehead, bringing it away wet. He tried to swallow, but could not; his throat was dry.

737   They had started the song again:

     We'll hang ever nigger t a sour apple tree . . .

738   There were women singing now. Their voices made the song round and full. Song waves rolled over the top of pine trees. The sky sagged low, heavy with clouds. Wind was rising. Sometimes cricket cries cut surprisingly across the mob song. A dog had gone to the utmost top of the hill. At each lull of the song his howl floated full into the night.

739   Big Boy shrank when he saw the first flame light the hillside. Would they see im here? Then he remembered you could not see into the dark if you were standing in the light. As flames leaped higher he saw two men rolling a barrel up the slope.

740   "Say, gimme a han here, will yuh?"

741   "Awright, heave!"

742   "C mon! Straight up! Git t the other end!"

743   "Ah got the feathers here in this pillar!"

744   "BRING SOME MO WOOD!"

745   Big Boy could see the barrel surrounded by flames. The mob fell back, forming a dark circle. Theyd fin im here! He had a wild impulse to climb out and fly across the hills. But his legs would not move. He stared hard, trying to find Bobo. His eyes played over a long, dark spot near the fire. Fanned by wind, flames leaped higher. He jumped. That dark spot had moved. Lawd, thas Bobo; thas Bobo . . .

746   He smelt the scent of tar, faint at first, then stronger. The wind brought it full into his face, then blew it away. His eyes burned and he rubbed them with his knuckles. He sneezed.

747   "LES GIT SOURVINEERS!"

748   He saw the mob close in around the fire. Their faces were hard and sharp in the light of the flames. More men and women were coming over the hill. The long, dark spot was smudged out.

749   "Everybody git back!"

750   "Look! Hes gotta finger!"

751   "C MON! GIT THE GALS BACK FROM THE FIRE!"

752   "He's got one of his ears, see?"

753   "Whuts the matter!"

754   "A woman fell out! Fainted, Ah reckon . . ."

755   The stench of tar permeated the hillside. The sky was black and the wind was blowing hard.

756   "HURRY UP N BURN THE NIGGER FO IT RAINS!"

757   Big Boy saw the mob fall back, leaving a small knot of men about the fire. Then, for the first time, he had a full glimpse of Bobo. A black body flashed in the light. Bobo was struggling, twisting; they were binding his arms and legs.

758   When he saw them tilt the barrel he stiffened. A scream quivered. He knew the tar was on Bobo. The mob fell back. He saw a tar-drenched body glistening and turning.

759   "THE BASTARDS GOT IT!"

760   There was a sudden quiet. Then he shrank violently as the wind carried, like a flurry of snow, a widening spiral of white feathers into the night. The flames leaped tall as the trees. The scream came again. Big Boy trembled and looked. The mob was running down the slopes, leaving the fire clear. Then he saw a writhing white mass cradled in yellow flame, and heard screams, one on top of the other, each shriller and shorter than the last. The mob was quiet now, standing still, looking up the slopes at the writhing white mass gradually growing black, growing black in a cradle of yellow flame.

761   "PO ON MO GAS!"

762   "Gimme a lif, will yuh!"

763   Two men were struggling, carrying between them a heavy can. They set it down, tilted it, leaving it so that the gas would trickle down to the hollowed earth around the fire.

764   Big Boy slid back into the hole, his face buried in clay. He had no feelings now, no fears. He was numb, empty, as though all blood had been drawn from him. Then his muscles flexed taut when he heard a faint patter. A tiny stream of cold water seeped to his knees, making him push back to a drier spot. He looked up; rain was beating in the grass.

765   "It's rainin!"

766   "C mon, les git t town!"

767   ". . . don worry, when the fire git thu wid im hell be gone . . ."

768   "Wait, Charles! Don leave me; its slippery here . . ."

769   "Ahll take some of yuh ladies back in mah car . . ."

770   Big Boy heard the dogs barking again, this time closer. Running feet pounded past. Cold water chilled his ankles. He could hear rain-drops steadily hissing.

771   Now a dog was barking at the mouth of the hole, barking furiously, sensing a presence there. He balled himself into a knot and clung to the bottom, his knees and shins buried in water. The bark came louder. He heard paws scraping and felt the hot scent of dog breath on his face. Green eyes glowed and drew nearer as the barking, muffled by the closeness of the hole, beat upon his eardrums. Backing till his shoulders pressed against the clay, he held his breath. He pushed out his hands, his fingers stiff. The dog yawped louder, advancing, his bark rising sharp and thin. Big Boy rose to his knees, his hands before him. Then he flattened out still more against the bottom, breathing lungsful of hot dog scent, breathing it slowly, hard, but evenly. The dog came closer, bringing hotter dog scent. Big Boy could go back no more. His knees were slipping and slopping in the water. He braced himself, ready. Then, he never exactly knew how—he never knew whether he had lunged or the dog had lunged—they were together, rolling in the water. The green eyes were beneath him, between his legs. Dognails bit into his arms. His knees slipped backward and he landed full on the dog; the dog's breath left in a heavy gasp. Instinctively, he fumbled for the throat as he felt the dog twisting between his knees. The dog snarled, long and low, as though gathering strength. Big Boy's hands traveled swiftly over the dog's back, groping for the throat. He felt dognails again and saw green eyes, but his fingers had found the throat. He choked, feeling his fingers sink; he choked, throwing back his head and stiffening his arms. He

felt the dog's body heave, felt dognails digging into his loins. With strength flowing from fear, he closed his fingers, pushing his full weight on the dog's throat. The dog heaved again, and lay still . . . Big Boy heard the sound of his own breathing filling the hole, and heard shouts and footsteps above him going past.

772 For a long time he held the dog, held it long after the last footstep had died out, long after the rain had stopped.

V

773 Morning found him still on his knees in a puddle of rain-water, staring at the stiff body of a dog. As the air brightened he came to himself slowly. He held still for a long time, as though waking from a dream, as though trying to remember.

774 The chug of a truck came over the hill. He tried to crawl to the opening. His knees were stiff and a thousand needle-like pains shot from the bottom of his feet to the calves of his legs. Giddiness made his eyes blur. He pulled up and looked. Through brackish light he saw Will's truck standing some twenty-five yards away, the engine running. Will stood on the running board, looking over the slopes of the hill.

775 Big Boy scuffled out, falling weakly in the wet grass. He tried to call to Will, but his dry throat would make no sound. He tried again.

776 "Will!"

777 Will heard, answering:

778 "Big Boy, c mon!"

779 He tried to run, and fell. Will came, meeting him in the tall grass.

780 "C mon," Will said, catching his arm.

781 They struggled to the truck.

782 "Hurry up!" said Will, pushing him onto the running-board.

783 Will pushed back a square trapdoor which swung above the back of the driver's seat. Big Boy pulled through, landing with a thud on the bottom. On hands and knees he looked around in the semi-darkness.

784 "Wheres Bobo?"

785 Big Boy stared.

786 "Wheres Bobo?"

787 "They got im."

788 "When?"

789 "Las night."

790 "The mob?"

791 Big Boy pointed in the direction of a charred sapling on the slope of the opposite hill. Will looked. The trapdoor fell. The engine purred,

the gears whined, and the truck lurched forward over the muddy road, sending Big Boy on his side.

792   For a while he lay as he had fallen, on his side, too weak to move. As he felt the truck swing around a curve he straightened up and rested his back against a stack of wooden boxes. Slowly, he began to make out objects in the darkness. Through two long cracks fell thin blades of daylight. The floor was of smooth steel, and cold to his thighs. Splinters and bits of sawdust danced with the rumble of the truck. Each time they swung around a curve he was pulled over the floor; he grabbed at corners of boxes to steady himself. Once he heard the crow of a rooster. It made him think of home, of ma and pa. He thought he remembered hearing somewhere that the house had burned, but could not remember where . . . It all seemed unreal now.

793   He was tired. He dozed, swaying with the lurch. Then he jumped awake. The truck was running smoothly, on gravel. Far away he heard two short blasts from the Buckeye Lumber Mill. Unconsciously, the thought sang through his mind: Its six erclock . . .

794   The trapdoor swung in. Will spoke through a corner of his mouth.

795   "How yuh comin?"

796   "Awright."

797   "How they git Bobo?"

798   "He wuz comin over the hill."

799   "Whut they do?"

800   "They burnt im . . . Will, Ah wan some water; mah throats like fire . . ."

801   "Well git some when we pas a fillin station."

802   Big Boy leaned back and dozed. He jerked awake when the truck stopped. He heard Will get out. He wanted to peep through the trapdoor, but was afraid. For a moment, the wild fear he had known in the hole came back. Spose theyd search n fin im? He quieted when he heard Will's footsteps on the running board. The trapdoor pushed in. Will's hat came through, dripping.

803   "Take it, quick!"

804   Big Boy grabbed, spilling water into his face. The truck lurched. He drank. Hard cold lumps of brick rolled into his hot stomach. A dull pain made him bend over. His intestines seemed to be drawing into a tight knot. After a bit it eased, and he sat up, breathing softly.

805   The truck swerved. He blinked his eyes. The blades of daylight had turned brightly golden. The sun had risen.

306 The truck sped over the asphalt miles, sped northward, jolting him, shaking out of his bosom the crumbs of corn bread, making them dance with the splinters and sawdust in the golden blades of sunshine.

807 He turned on his side and slept.

Zora Neale Hurston

(1891–1960)

For biographical information, see page 71. The following is a chapter from the novel Their Eyes Were Watching God *(1937), Hurston's most celebrated and popular work. Examining the interior journey of Janie Crawford, this novel attests to her growth from adolescence to adulthood, specifically through her reclamation of voice. In this scene, Hurston recounts the life and work of Janie and her third husband, bluesman Vergible (Tea Cake) Woods, as they participate in the agrarian culture of the "muck," the Florida everglades.*

Their Eyes Were Watching God

1 To Janie's strange eyes, everything in the Everglades was big and new. Big Lake Okechobee, big beans, big cane, big weeds, big everything. Weeds that did well to grow waist high up the state were eight and often ten feet tall down there. Ground so rich that everything went wild. Volunteer cane just taking the place. Dirt roads so rich and black that a half mile of it would have fertilized a Kansas wheat field. Wild cane on either side of the road hiding the rest of the world. People wild too.

2 "Season don't open up till last of September, but we had tuh git heah ahead uh time tuh git us uh room," Tea Cake explained. "Two weeks from now, it'll be so many folks heah dey won't be lookin' fuh rooms, dey'll be jus' looking fuh somewhere tuh sleep. Now we got uh chance tuh git uh room at de hotel, where dey got uh bath tub. Yuh can't live on de muck 'thout yuh take uh bath every day. Do dat muck'll itch yuh lak ants. 'Tain't but one place round heah wid uh bath tub. 'Tain't nowhere near enough rooms."

3   "Whut we gointuh do round heah?"

4   "All day Ah'm pickin' beans. All night Ah'm pickin' mah box and rollin' dice. Between de beans and de dice Ah can't lose. Ah'm gone right now tuh pick me uh job uh work wid de best man on de muck. Before de rest of 'em gits heah. You can always git jobs round heah in de season, but not wid de right folks."

5   "When do de job open up, Tea Cake? Everybody round here look lak dey waitin' too."

6   "Dat's right. De big men haves uh certain time tuh open de season jus' lak in everything else. Mah bossman didn't get sufficient seed. He's out huntin' up uh few mo' bushels. Den we'se gointuh plantin'."

7   "Bushels?"

8   "Yeah, bushels. Dis ain't no game fuh pennies. Po' man ain't got no business at de show."

9   The very next day he burst into the room in high excitement. "Boss done bought out another man and want me down on de lake. He got houses fuh de first ones dat git dere. Less go!"

10   They rattled nine miles in a borrowed car to the quarters that squatted so close that only the dyke separated them from great, sprawling Okechobee. Janie fussed around the shack making a home while Tea Cake planted beans. After hours they fished. Every now and then they'd run across a party of Indians in their long, narrow dugouts calmly winning their living in the trackless ways of the 'Glades. Finally the beans were in. Nothing much to do but wait to pick them. Tea Cake picked his box a great deal for Janie, but he still didn't have enough to do. No need of gambling yet. The people who were pouring in were broke. They didn't come bringing money, they were coming to make some.

11   "Tell yuh whut, Janie, less buy us some shootin' tools and go huntin' round heah."

12   "Dat would be fine, Tea Cake, exceptin' you know Ah can't shoot. But Ah'd love tuh go wid *you*."

13   "Oh, you needs tuh learn how. 'Tain't no need uh you not knowin' how tuh handle shootin' tools. Even if you didn't never find no game, it's always some trashy rascal dat needs uh good killin'," he laughed. "Less go intuh Palm Beach and spend some of our money."

14   Every day they were practising. Tea Cake made her shoot at little things just to give her good aim. Pistol and shot gun and rifle. It got so the others stood around and watched them. Some of the men would beg for a shot at the target themselves. It was the most exciting thing on the muck. Better than the jook and the pool-room

unless some special band was playing for a dance. And the thing that got everybody was the way Janie caught on. She got to the place she could shoot a hawk out of a pine tree and not tear him up. Shoot his head off. She got to be a better shot than Tea Cake. They'd go out any late afternoon and come back loaded down with game. One night they got a boat and went out hunting alligators. Shining their phosphorescent eyes and shooting them in the dark. They could sell the hides and teeth in Palm Beach besides having fun together till work got pressing.

15   Day by day now, the hordes of workers poured in. Some came limping in with their shoes and sore feet from walking. It's hard trying to follow your shoe instead of your shoe following you. They came in wagons from way up in Georgia and they came in truck loads from east, west, north and south. Permanent transients with no attachments and tired looking men with their families and dogs in flivvers. All night, all day, hurrying in to pick beans. Skillets, beds, patched up spare inner tubes all hanging and dangling from the ancient cars on the outside and hopeful humanity, herded and hovered on the inside, chugging on to the muck. People ugly from ignorance and broken from being poor.

16   All night now the jooks clanged and clamored. Pianos living three lifetimes in one. Blues made and used right on the spot. Dancing, fighting, singing, crying, laughing, winning and losing love every hour. Work all day for money, fight all night for love. The rich black earth clinging to bodies and biting the skin like ants.

17   Finally no more sleeping places. Men made big fires and fifty or sixty men slept around each fire. But they had to pay the man whose land they slept on. He ran the fire just like his boarding place—for pay. But nobody cared. They made good money, even to the children. So they spent good money. Next month and next year were other times. No need to mix them up with the present.

18   Tea Cake's house was a magnet, the unauthorized center of the "job." The way he would sit in the doorway and play his guitar made people stop and listen and maybe disappoint the jook for that night. He was always laughing and full of fun too. He kept everybody laughing in the bean field.

19   Janie stayed home and boiled big pots of black-eyed peas and rice. Sometimes baked big pans of navy beans with plenty of sugar and hunks of bacon laying on top. That was something Tea Cake loved so no matter if Janie had fixed beans two or three times during the week, they had baked beans again on Sunday. She always had some

kind of dessert too, as Tea Cake said it give a man something to taper off on. Sometimes she'd straighten out the two-room house and take the rifle and have fried rabbit for supper when Tea Cake got home. She didn't leave him itching and scratching in his work clothes, either. The kettle of hot water was already waiting when he got in.

20 Then Tea Cake took to popping in at the kitchen door at odd hours. Between breakfast and dinner, sometimes. Then often around two o'clock he'd come home and tease and wrestle with her for a half hour and slip on back to work. So one day she asked him about it.

21 "Tea Cake, whut you doin' back in de quarters when everybody else is still workin'?"

22 "Come tuh see 'bout you. De boogerman liable tuh tote yuh off whilst Ah'm gone."

23 "'Taint't no boogerman got me tuh study 'bout. Maybe you think Ah ain't treatin' yuh right and you watchin' me."

24 "Naw, naw, Janie. Ah *know* better'n dat. But since you got dat in yo' head, Ah'll have tuh tell yuh de real truth, so yuh can know. Janie, Ah gits lonesome out dere all day 'thout yuh. After dis, you betta come git uh job uh work out dere lak de rest uh de women — so Ah won't be losin' time comin' home."

25 "Tea Cake, you'se uh mess! Can't do 'thout me dat lil time."

26 "'Tain't no lil time. It's near 'bout all day."

27 So the very next morning Janie got ready to pick beans along with Tea Cake. There was a suppressed murmur when she picked up a basket and went to work. She was already getting to be a special case on the muck. It was generally assumed that she thought herself too good to work like the rest of the women and that Tea Cake "pomped her up tuh dat." But all day long the romping and playing they carried on behind the boss's back made her popular right away. It got the whole field to playing off and on. Then Tea Cake would help get supper afterwards.

28 "You don't think Ah'm tryin' tuh git outa takin' keer uh yuh, do yuh, Janie, 'cause Ah ast yuh tuh work long side uh me?" Tea Cake asked her at the end of her first week in the field.

29 "Ah naw, honey. Ah laks it. It's mo' nicer than settin' round dese quarters all day. Clerkin' in dat store wuz hard, but heah, we ain't got nothin' tuh do but do our work and come home and love."

30 The house was full of people every night. That is, all around the doorstep was full. Some were there to hear Tea Cake pick the box; some came to talk and tell stories, but most of them came to get into whatever game was going on or might go on. Sometimes Tea Cake lost

heavily, for there were several good gamblers on the lake. Sometimes he won and made Janie proud of his skill. But outside of the two jooks, everything on that job went on around those two.

31   Sometimes Janie would think of the old days in the big white house and the store and laugh to herself. What if Eatonville could see her now in her blue denim overalls and heavy shoes? The crowd of people around her and a dice game on her floor! She was sorry for her friends back there and scornful of the others. The men held big arguments here like they used to do on the store porch. Only here, she could listen and laugh and even talk some herself if she wanted to. She got so she could tell big stories herself from listening to the rest. Because she loved to hear it, and the men loved to hear themselves, they would "woof" and "boogerboo" around the games to the limit. No matter how rough it was, people seldom got mad, because everything was done for a laugh. Everybody loved to hear Ed Dockery, Bootyny, and Sop-de-Bottom in a skin game. Ed Dockery was dealing one night and he looked over at Sop-de-Bottom's card and he could tell Sop thought he was going to win. He hollered, "Ah'll break up *dat* settin' uh eggs." Sop looked and said, "Root de peg." Bootyny asked, "What are you goin' tuh do? Do do!" Everybody was watching that next card fall. Ed got ready to turn. "Ah'm gointuh sweep out hell and burn up de broom." He slammed down another dollar. "Don't oversport yourself, Ed," Bootyny challenged. "You gittin' too yaller." Ed caught hold of the corner of the card. Sop dropped a dollar. "Ah'm gointuh shoot in de hearse, don't keer how sad de funeral be." Ed said, "You see how this man is teasin' hell?" Tea Cake nudged Sop not to bet. "You gointuh git caught in uh bullet storm if you don't watch out." Sop said, "Aw 'tain't nothin' tuh dat bear but his curly hair. Ah can look through muddy water and see dry land." Ed turned off the card and hollered, "Zachariah, Ah says come down out dat sycamore tree. You can't do no business." Nobody fell on that card. Everybody was scared of the next one. Ed looked around and saw Gabe standing behind his chair and hollered, "Move, from over me, Gabe! You too black. You draw heat! Sop, you wanta pick up dat bet whilst you got uh chance?" "Naw, man, Ah wish Ah had uh thousandleg tuh put on it." "So yuh won't lissen, huh? Dumb niggers and free schools. Ah'm gointuh take and teach yuh. Ah'll main-line but Ah won't side-track." Ed flipped the next card and Sop fell and lost. Everybody hollered and laughed. Ed laughed and said, "Git off de muck! You ain't nothin'. Dat's all! Hot boilin' water won't help

yuh none." Ed kept on laughing because he had been so scared before. "Sop, Bootyny, all y'all dat lemme win yo' money: Ah'm sending it straight off to Sears and Roebuck and buy me some clothes, and when Ah turn out Christmas day, it would take a doctor to tell me how near Ah is dressed tuh death."

Gloria Naylor

(1950–)

Gloria Naylor was born January 25, 1950, in New York City to recent Southern migrants, Mississippi cotton sharecroppers who vowed that their children would not be born in the South. Naylor received a bachelor's degree in English from Brooklyn College and a master's degree in Afro-American Studies from Yale University. Naylor has taught at several universities, including George Washington University, Princeton University, and New York University. She has written five novels, The Women of Brewster Place *(1982),* Linden Hills *(1985),* Mama Day *(1988),* Bailey's Café *(1992), and* The Men of Brewster Place *(1998). Included in this chapter are the opening pages of* Mama Day, *a novel set in Willow Springs, a fictional island off the coast of South Carolina and Georgia. Beginning with the story of Sapphira Wade, the matriarch of Willows Springs, Naylor attests to the importance of the ancestors, whose lives are indelibly present in this island community.*

Mama Day

1 Willow Springs. Everybody knows but nobody talks about the legend of Sapphira Wade. A true conjure woman: satin black, biscuit cream, red as Georgia clay: depending upon which of us takes a mind to her. She could walk through a lightning storm without being touched; grab a bolt of lightning in the palm of her hand; use the heat of lightning to start the kindling going under her medicine pot: depending upon which of us takes a mind to her. She turned the moon into salve, the stars into a swaddling cloth, and healed the wounds of every creature walking up on two or down on four. It ain't about right or wrong, truth or lies; it's about a slave woman who brought a whole new meaning to both them words, soon as you cross over here from beyond the bridge. And somehow, some way, it happened in

1823: she smothered Bascombe Wade in his very bed and lived to tell the story for a thousand days. 1823: married Bascombe Wade, bore him seven sons in just a thousand days, to put a dagger through his kidney and escape the hangman's noose, laughing in a burst of flames. 1823: persuaded Bascombe Wade in a thousand days to deed all his slaves every inch of land in Willow Springs, poisoned him for his trouble, to go on and bear seven sons—by person or persons unknown. Mixing it all together and keeping everything that done shifted down through the holes of time, you end up with the death of Bascombe Wade (there's his tombstone right out by Chevy's Pass), the deeds to our land (all marked back to the very year), and seven sons (ain't Miss Abigail and Mama Day the granddaughters of that seventh boy?). The wild card in all this is the thousand days, and we guess if we put our heads together we'd come up with something—which ain't possible since Sapphira Wade don't live in the part of our memory we can use to form words.

2   But ain't a soul in Willow Springs don't know that little dark girls, hair all braided up with colored twine, got their "18 & 23's coming down" when they lean too long over them back yard fences, laughing at the antics of little dark boys who got the nerve to be "breathing 18 & 23" with mother's milk still on their tongues. And if she leans there just a mite too long or grins a bit too wide, it's gonna bring a holler straight through the dusty screen door. "Get your bow-legged self 'way from my fence, Johnny Blue. Won't be no 'early 18 & 23's' coming here for me to rock. I'm still raising her." Yes, the *name* Sapphira Wade is never breathed out of a single mouth in Willow Springs. But who don't know that old twisted-lip manager at the Sheraton Hotel beyond the bridge, offering Winky Browne only twelve dollars for his whole boatload of crawdaddies—"tried to 18 & 23 him," if he tried to do a thing? We all sitting here, a hop, skip, and one Christmas left before the year 2000, and ain't nobody told him niggers can read now? Like the menus in his restaurant don't say a handful of crawdaddies sprinkled over a little bowl of crushed ice is almost twelve dollars? Call it shrimp cocktail, or whatever he want—we can count, too. And the price of everything that swims, crawls, or lays at the bottom of The Sound went up in 1985, during the season we had that "18 & 23 summer" and the bridge blew down. Folks didn't take their lives in their hands out there in that treacherous water just to be doing it—ain't that much 18 & 23 in the world.

3   But that old hotel manager don't make no never mind. He's the least of what we done had to deal with here in Willow Springs.

Malaria. Union soldiers. Sandy soil. Two big depressions. Hurricanes. Not to mention these new real estate developers who think we gonna sell our shore land just because we ain't fool enough to live there. Started coming over here in the early '90s, talking "vacation paradise," talking "pic-ture-ess." Like Winky said, we'd have to pick their ass out the bottom of the marsh first hurricane blow through here again. See, they just thinking about building where they ain't got no state taxes—never been and never will be, 'cause Willow Springs ain't in no state. Georgia and South Carolina done tried, though—been trying since right after the Civil War to prove that Willow Springs belong to one or the other of them. Look on any of them old maps they hurried and drew up soon as the Union soldiers pulled out and you can see that the only thing connects us to the mainland is a bridge—and even that gotta be rebuilt after every big storm. (They was talking about steel and concrete way back, but since Georgia and South Carolina couldn't claim the taxes, nobody wanted to shell out for the work. So we rebuild it ourselves when need be, and build it how we need it—strong enough to last till the next big wind. Only need a steel and concrete bridge once every seventy years or so. Wood and pitch is a tenth of the cost and serves us a good sixty-nine years—matter of simple arithmetic.) But anyways, all forty-nine square miles curves like a bow, stretching toward Georgia on the south end and South Carolina on the north, and right smack in the middle where each foot of our bridge sits is the dividing line between them two states.

4   So who it belong to? It belongs to us—clean and simple. And it belonged to our daddies, and our daddies before them, and them too—who at one time all belonged to Bascombe Wade. And when they tried to trace him and how he got it, found out he wasn't even American. Was Norway-born or something, and the land had been sitting in his family over there in Europe since it got explored and claimed by the Vikings—imagine that. So thanks to the conjuring of Sapphira Wade we got it from Norway or theres about, and if taxes owed, it's owed to them. But ain't no Vikings or anybody else from over in Europe come to us with the foolishness that them folks out of Columbia and Atlanta come with—we was being un-American. And the way we saw it, America ain't entered the question at all when it come to our land: Sapphira was African-born, Bascombe Wade was from Norway, and it was the 18 & 23'ing that went down between them two put deeds in our hands. And we wasn't even Americans when we got it—was slaves. And the laws about slaves not owning nothing in

Georgia and South Carolina don't apply, 'cause the land wasn't then—
and isn't now—in either of them places. When there was lots of cotton here, and we baled it up and sold it beyond the bridge, we paid
our taxes to the U.S. of A. And we keeps account of all the fishing
that's done and sold beyond the bridge, all the little truck farming.
And later when we had to go over there to work or our children went,
we paid taxes out of them earnings. We pays taxes on the telephone
lines and electrical wires run over The Sound. Ain't nobody here
about breaking the law. But Georgia and South Carolina ain't seeing the shine off a penny for our land, our homes, our roads, or our
bridge. Well, they fought each other up to the Supreme Court about
the whole matter, and it came to a draw. We guess they got so tired
out from that, they decided to leave us be—until them developers
started swarming over here like sand flies at a Sunday picnic.

5   Sure, we coulda used the money and weren't using the land. But
like Mama Day told 'em (we knew to send 'em straight over there
to her and Miss Abigail), they didn't come huffing and sweating all
this way in them dark gaberdine suits if they didn't think our land
could make them a bundle of money, and the way we saw it, there
was enough land—shoreline, that is—to make us all pretty comfortable. And calculating on the basis of all them fancy plans they had
in mind, a million an acre wasn't asking too much. Flap, flap, flap—
Lord, didn't them jaws and silk ties move in the wind. The land
wouldn't be worth that if they couldn't *build* on it. Yes, suh, she told
'em, and they couldn't build on it unless we *sold* it. So we get ours
now, and they get theirs later. You shoulda seen them coattails flapping back across The Sound with all their lies about "community
uplift" and "better jobs." 'Cause it weren't about no them now and
us later—was them now and us never. Hadn't we seen it happen back
in the '80s on St. Helena, Daufuskie, and St. John's? And before that
in the '60s on Hilton Head? Got them folks' land, built fences around
it first thing, and then brought in all the builders and high-paid managers from mainside—ain't nobody on them islands benefited. And
the only dark faces you see now in them "vacation paradises" is the
ones cleaning the toilets and cutting the grass. On their own land,
mind you, their own land. Weren't gonna happen in Willow Springs.
'Cause if Mama Day say no, everybody say no. There's 18 & 23, and
there's 18 & 23—and nobody was gonna trifle with Mama Day's,
'cause she know how to use it—her being a direct descendant of Sap-
hira Wade, piled on the fact of springing from the seventh son of a
seventh son—uh, uh. Mama Day say no, everybody say no. No point

in making a pile of money to be guaranteed the new moon will see you scratching at fleas you don't have, or rolling in the marsh like a mud turtle. And if some was waiting for her to die, they had a long wait. She says she ain't gonna. And when you think about it, to show up in one century, make it all the way through the next, and have a toe inching over into the one approaching *is* about as close to eternity anybody can come.

6   Well, them developers upped the price and changed the plans, changed the plans and upped the price, till it got to be a game with us. Winky bought a motorboat with what they offered him back in 1987, turned it in for a cabin cruiser two years later, and says he expects to be able to afford a yacht with the news that's waiting in the mail this year. Parris went from a new shingle roof to a split-level ranch and is making his way toward adding a swimming pool and greenhouse. But when all the laughing's done, it's the principle that remains. And we done learned that anything coming from beyond the bridge gotta be viewed real, real careful. Look what happened when Reema's boy—the one with the pear-shaped head—came hauling himself back from one of those fancy colleges mainside, dragging his notebooks and tape recorder and a funny way of curling up his lip and clicking his teeth, all excited and determined to put Willow Springs on the map.

7   We was polite enough—Reema always was a little addle-brained—so you couldn't blame the boy for not remembering that part of Willow Spring's problems was that it got put on some maps right after the War Between the States. And then when he went around asking us about 18 & 23, there weren't nothing to do but take pity on him as he rattled on about "ethnography," "unique speech patterns," "cultural preservation," and whatever else he seemed to be getting so much pleasure out of while talking into his little gray machine. He was all over the place—What 18 & 23 mean? What 18 & 23 mean? And we all told him the God-honest truth: it was just our way of saying something. Winky was awful, though, he even spit tobacco juice for him. Sat on his porch all day, chewing up the boy's Red Devil premium and spitting so the machine could pick it up. There was enough fun in that to take us through the fall and winter when he had hauled himself back over The Sound to wherever he was getting what was supposed to be passing for an education. And he sent everybody he'd talked to copies of the book he wrote, bound all nice with our name and his signed on the first page. We couldn't hold Reema down, she was so proud. It's good thing she didn't read

it. None of us made it much through the introduction, but that said it all: you see, he had come to the conclusion after "extensive field work" (ain't never picked a boll of cotton or head of lettuce in his life—Reema spoiled him silly), but he done still made it to the conclusion that 18 & 23 wasn't 18 & 23 at all—was really 81 & 32, which just so happened to be the lines of longitude and latitude marking off where Willow Springs sits on the map. And we were just so damned dumb that we turned the whole thing around.

8   Not that he called it being dumb, mind you, called it "asserting our cultural identity," "inverting hostile social and political parameters." 'Cause, see, being we was brought here as slaves, we had no choice but to look at everything upside-down. And then being that we was isolated off here on this island, everybody else in the country went on learning good English and calling things what they really was—in the dictionary and all that—while we kept on calling things ass-backwards. And he thought that was just so wonderful and marvelous, etcetera, etcetera . . . Well, after that crate of books came here, if anybody had any doubts about what them developers was up to, if there was just a tinge of seriousness behind them jokes about the motorboats and swimming pools that could be gotten from selling a piece of land, them books squashed it. The people who ran the type of schools that could turn our children into raving lunatics—and then put his picture on the back of the book so we couldn't even deny it was him—didn't mean us a speck of good.

9   If the boy wanted to know what 18 & 23 meant, why didn't he just ask? When he was running around sticking that machine in everybody's face, we was sitting right here—every one of us—and him being one of Reema's, we woulda obliged him. He coulda asked Cloris about the curve in her spine that came from the planting season when their mule broke its leg, and she took up the reins and kept pulling the plow with her own back. Winky woulda told him about the hot tar that took out the corner of his right eye the summer we had only seven days to rebuild the bridge so the few crops we had left after the storm could be gotten over before rot sat in. Anybody woulda carried him through the fields we had to stop farming back in the '80s to take outside jobs—washing cars, carrying groceries, cleaning house—anything—cause it was leave the land or lose it during the Silent Depression. Had more folks sleeping in city streets and banks foreclosing on farms than in the Great Depression before that.

10   Naw, he didn't really want to know what 18 & 23 meant, or he woulda asked. He woulda asked right off where Miss Abigail Day was

staying, so we coulda sent him down the main road to that little yellow house where she used to live. And she woulda given him a tall glass of ice water or some cinnamon tea as he heard about Peace dying young, then Hope and Peace again. But there was the child of Grace—the grandchild, a girl who went mainside, like him, and did real well. Was living outside of Charleston now with her husband and two boys. So she visits a lot more often than she did when she was up in New York. And she probably woulda pulled out that old photo album, so he coulda seen some pictures of her grandchild, Cocoa, and then Cocoa's mama, Grace. And Miss Abigail flips right through to the beautiful one of Grace resting in her satin-lined coffin. And as she walks him back out to the front porch and points him across the road to a silver trailer where her sister, Miranda, lives, she tells him to grab up and chew a few sprigs of mint growing at the foot of the steps—it'll help kill his thirst in the hot sun. And if he'd known enough to do just that, thirsty or not, he'd know when he got to that silver trailer to stand back a distance calling *Mama, Mama Day*, to wait for her to come out and beckon him near.

11   He'da told her he been sent by Miss Abigail and so, more likely than not, she lets him in. And he hears again about the child of Grace, her grandniece, who went mainside, like him, and did real well. Was living outside of Charleston now with her husband and two boys. So she visits a lot more often than she did when she was up in New York. Cocoa is like her very own, Mama Day tells him, since she never had no children.

12   And with him carrying that whiff of mint on his breath, she surely woulda walked him out to the side yard, facing that patch of dogwood, to say she has to end the visit a little short 'cause she has some gardening to do in the other place. And if he'd had the sense to offer to follow her just a bit of the way—then and only then—he hears about that summer fourteen years ago when Cocoa came visiting from New York with her first husband. Yes, she tells him, there was a first husband—a stone city boy. How his name was George. But how Cocoa left, and he stayed. How it was the year of the last big storm that blew her pecan trees down and even caved in the roof of the other place. And she woulda stopped him from walking just by a patch of oak: she reaches up, takes a bit of moss for him to put in them closed leather shoes—they're probably sweating his feet something terrible, she tells him. And he's to sit on the ground, right there, to untie his shoes and stick in the moss. And then he'd see through the low bush that old graveyard just down the slope. And when he looks back up, she

woulda disappeared through the trees; but he's to keep pushing the moss in them shoes and go on down to that graveyard where he'll find buried Grace, Hope, Peace, and Peace again. Then a little ways off a grouping of seven old graves, and a little ways off seven older again. All circled by them live oaks and hanging moss, over a rise from the tip of The Sound.

13   Everything he needed to know coulda been heard from that yellow house to that silver trailer to that graveyard. Be too late for him to go that route now, since Miss Abigail's been dead for over nine years. Still, there's an easier way. He could just watch Cocoa any one of these times she comes in from Charleston. She goes straight to Miss Abigail's to air out the rooms and unpack her bags, then she's across the road to call out at Mama Day, who's gonna come to the door of the trailer and wave as Cocoa heads on through the patch of dogwoods to that oak grove. She stops and puts a bit of moss in her open-toe sandals, then goes on past those graves to a spot just down the rise toward The Sound, a little bit south of that circle of oaks. And if he was patient and stayed off a little ways, he'd realize she was there to meet up with her first husband so they could talk about that summer fourteen years ago when she left, but he stayed. And as her and George are there together for a good two hours or so—neither one saying a word—Reema's boy coulda heard from them everything there was to tell about 18 & 23.

14   But on second thought, someone who didn't know how to ask wouldn't know how to listen. And he coulda listened to them the way you been listening to us right now. Think about it: ain't nobody really talking to you. We're sitting here in Willow Springs, and you're God-knows-where. It's August 1999—ain't but a slim chance it's the same season where you are. Uh, huh, listen. Really listen this time: the only voice is your own. But you done just heard about the legend of Sapphira Wade, though nobody here breathes her name. You done heard it the way we know it, sitting on our porches and shelling June peas, quieting the midnight cough of a baby, taking apart the engine of a car—you done heard it without a single living soul really saying a word. Pity, though, Reema's boy couldn't listen, like you, to Cocoa and George down by them oaks—or he woulds left here with quite a story.

Maya Angelou

(1928–)

Born Marguerite Johnson on April 4, 1928, in St. Louis, Missouri, Maya Angelou spent the formative years of her life in Stamps, Arkansas, where her grandmother and uncle raised her and her brother, Bailey. Angelou has turned to the material of her life to create vivid, detailed autobiographical installments, including I Know Why the Caged Bird Sings *(1970),* Gather Together in My Name *(1974), the* Heart of a Woman *(1981), and, most recently,* A Song Flung Up to Heaven *(2002). In these books, Angelou deftly recounts her childhood experiences, her work in the Civil Rights Movement, and her many occupations, including dancer, actor, editor for the* Arab Observer *in Cairo, Egypt, and writer for the* Ghanaian Times. *In addition to her autobiographical work, Angelou has written numerous volumes of poetry, including* Just Give Me a Cool Drink of Water 'fore I Diiie *(1971) (nominated for a Pulitzer Prize) and the much-celebrated collection,* And Still I Rise *(1976). Angelou wrote and presented a poem, "On the Pulse of the Morning," at President Clinton's 1993 inauguration. She was only the second poet—after Robert Frost in 1961—to have an official role in such a ceremony. Angelou is a popular speaker who holds the Reynolds Professorship of American Studies at Wake Forest University in North Carolina. The following excerpt is from her second published autobiography,* Gather Together in My Name. *Angelou recounts the climate of racism that marked her formative years in Stamps, Arkansas, and deftly compares this reality to the romantic myths tied to that region.*

Gather Together in My Name

1   There is a much-loved region in the American fantasy where pale white women float eternally under black magnolia trees, and white men with soft hands brush wisps of wisteria from the creamy shoulders of their lady loves. Harmonious black music drifts like perfume through this precious air, and nothing of a threatening nature intrudes.

2   The South I returned to, however, was flesh-real and swollen-belly poor. Stamps, Arkansas, a small hamlet, had subsisted for hundreds of years on the returns from cotton plantations, and until World War

I, a creaking lumbermill. The town was halved by railroad tracks, the swift Red River and racial prejudice. Whites lived on the town's small rise (it couldn't be called a hill), while blacks lived in what had been known since slavery as "the Quarters."

3   After our parents' divorce in California, our father took us from Mother, put identification and destination tags on our wrists, and sent us alone, by train, to his mother in the South. I was three and my brother four when we first arrived in Stamps. Grandmother Henderson accepted us, asked God for help, then set about raising us in His way. She had established a country store around the turn of the century, and we spent the Depression years minding the store, learning Bible verses and church songs, and receiving her undemonstrative love.

4   We lived a good life. We had some food, some laughter and Momma's quiet strength to lean against. During World War II the armed services drew the town's youth, black and white, and Northern war plants lured the remaining hale and hearty. Few, if any, blacks or poor whites returned to claim their heritage of terror and poverty. Old men and women and young children stayed behind to tend the gardens, the one paved block of stores and the long-accepted way of life.

5   In my memory, Stamps is a place of light, shadow, sounds and entrancing odors. The earth smell was pungent, spiced with the odor of cattle manure, the yellowish acid of the ponds and rivers, the deep pots of greens and beans cooking for hours with smoked or cured pork. Flowers added their heavy aroma. And above all, the atmosphere was pressed down with the smell of old fears, and hates, and guilt.

6   On this hot and moist landscape, passions clanged with the ferocity of armored knights colliding. Until I moved to California at thirteen I had known the town, and there had been no need to examine it. I took its being for granted and now, five years later, I was returning, expecting to find the shield of anonymity I had known as a child.

7   Along with other black children in small Southern villages, I had accepted the total polarization of the races as a psychological comfort. Whites existed, as no one denied, but they were not present in my everyday life. In fact, months often passed in my childhood when I only caught sight of the thin hungry po' white trash (sharecroppers), who lived sadder and meaner lives than the blacks I knew. I had no idea that I had outgrown childhood's protection until I arrived back in Stamps.

8   Momma took my son in one arm and folded the other around me. She held us for one sweet crushing moment. "Praise God Almighty you're home safe."

9   She was already moving away to keep her crying private.

10   "Turned into a little lady. Sure did." My Uncle Willie examined me with his quiet eyes and reached for the baby. "Let's see what you've got there."

11   He had been crippled in early childhood, and his affliction was never mentioned. The right side of his body had undergone severe paralysis, but his left arm and hand were huge and powerful. I laid the baby in the bend of his good arm.

12   "Hello, baby. Hello. Ain't he sweet?" The words slurred over his tongue and out of the numb lips. "Here, take him." His healthy muscles were too strong for a year-old wriggler.

13   Momma called from the kitchen, "Sister, I made you a little something to eat."

14   We were in the Store; I had grown up in its stronghold. Just seeing the shelves loaded with weenie sausages and Brown Plug chewing tobacco, salmon and mackerel and sardines all in their old places softened my heart and tears stood at the ready just behind my lids. But the kitchen, where Momma with her great height bent to pull cakes from the wood-burning stove and arrange the familiar food on well-known plates, erased my control and the tears slipped out and down my face to plop onto the baby's blanket.

15   The hills of San Francisco, the palm trees of San Diego, prostitution and lesbians and the throat hurting of Curly's departure disappeared into a never-could-have-happened land. I was home.

16   "Now what you crying for?" Momma wouldn't look at me for fear my tears might occasion her own. "Give the baby to me, and you go wash your hands. I'm going to make him a sugar tit. You can set the table. Reckon you remember where everything is."

17   The baby went to her without a struggle and she talked to him without the cooing most people use with small children. "Man. Just a little man, ain't you? I'm going to call you Man and that's that."

18   Momma and Uncle Willie hadn't changed. She still spoke softly and her voice had a little song in it.

19   "Bless my soul, Sister, you come stepping up here looking like your daddy for the world."

20   Christ and Church were still the pillars of her life.

21   "The Lord my God is a rock in a weary land. He is a great God. Brought you home, all in one piece. Praise His name."

22   She was, as ever, the matriarch. "I never did want you children to go to California. Too fast that life up yonder. But then, you all's their children, and I didn't want nothing to happen to you, while you're in my care. Jew was getting a little too big for his britches."

23   Five years before, my brother had seen the body of a black man pulled from the river. The cause of death had not been broadcast, but Bailey (Jew was short for Junior) had seen that the man's genitals had been cut away. The shock caused him to ask questions that were dangerous for a black boy in 1940 Arkansas. Momma decided we'd both be better off in California where lynchings were unheard of and a bright young Negro boy could go places. And even his sister might find a niche for herself.

24   Despite the sarcastic remarks of Northerners, who don't know the region (read Easterners, Westerners, North Easterners, North Westerners, Midwesterners), the South of the United States can be so impellingly beautiful that sophisticated creature comforts diminish in importance.

25   For four days I waited on the curious in the Store, and let them look me over. I was that rarity, a Stamps girl who had gone to the fabled California and returned. I could be forgiven a few siditty airs. In fact, a pretension to worldliness was expected of me, and I was too happy to disappoint.

26   When Momma wasn't around, I stood with one hand on my hip and my head cocked to one side and spoke of the wonders of the West and the joy of being free. Any listener could have asked me: if things were so grand in San Francisco, what had brought me back to a dusty mote of Arkansas? No one asked, because they all needed to believe that a land existed somewhere, even beyond the Northern Star, where Negroes were treated as people and whites were not the all-powerful ogres of their experience.

27   For the first time the farmers acknowledged my maturity. They didn't order me back and forth along the shelves but found subtler ways to make their wants known.

28   "You all have any long-grain rice, Sister?"

29   The hundred-pound sack of rice sat squidged down in full view.

30   "Yes, ma'am, I believe we do."

31   "Well then, I'll thank you for two pounds."

32   "Two pounds? Yes, ma'am."

33   I had seen the formality of black adult equals all my youth but had never considered that a time would come when I, too, could participate. The customs are as formalized as an eighteenth-century minuet, and a child at the race's knee learns the moves and twirls by osmosis and observation.

34   Values among Southern rural blacks are not quite the same as those existing elsewhere. Age has more worth than wealth, and religious piety more value than beauty.

35   There were no sly looks over my fatherless child. No cutting insinuations kept me shut away from the community. Knowing how closely my grandmother's friends hewed to the Bible, I was surprised not to be asked to confess my evil ways and repent. Instead, I was seen in the sad light which had been shared and was to be shared by black girls in every state in the country. I was young, yes, unmarried, yes— but I was a mother, and that placed me nearer to the people.

36   I was flattered to receive such acceptance from my betters (seniors) and strove mightily to show myself worthy.

37   Momma and Uncle Willie noted my inclusion into the adult stratum, and on my fourth day they put up no resistance when I said I was going for a night on the town. Since they knew Stamps, they knew that any carousing I chose to do would be severely limited. There was only one "joint" and the owner was a friend of theirs.

38   Age and travel had certainly broadened me and obviously made me more attractive. A few girls and boys with whom I'd had only generalities in common, all my life, asked me along for an evening at Willie Williams' café. The girls were going off soon to Arkansas Mechanical and Technical College to study Home Economics and the boys would be leaving for Tuskegee Institute in Alabama to learn how to farm. Although I had no education, my California past and having a baby made me equal to an evening with them.

39   When my escorts walked into the darkened Store, Momma came from the kitchen, still wearing her apron, and joined Uncle Willie behind the counter.

40   "Evening, Mrs. Henderson. Evening, Mr. Willie."

41   "Good evening, children." Momma gathered herself into immobility.

42   Uncle Willie leaned against the wall. "Evening, Philomena, and Harriet and Johnny Boy and Louis. How you all this evening?"

43   Just by placing their big still bodies in the Store at that precise time, my grandmother and uncle were saying, "Be good. Be very very good. Somebody is watching you."

44   We squirmed and grinned and understood.

45   The music reached out for us when we approached the halfway point. A dark throbbing bass line whonked on the air lanes, and our bodies moved to tempo. The steel guitar urged the singer to complain

> *Well, I ain't got no*
> *special reason here.*
> *No, I ain't got no*
> *special reason here.*

*I'm going leave
'cause I don't feel welcome here . . ."*

46   The Dew Drop In café was a dark square outline, and on its
wooden exterior, tin posters of grinning white women divinely suggested Coca-Cola, R.C. Cola and Dr Pepper for complete happiness.
Inside the one-room building, blue bulbs hung down precariously
close to dancing couples, and the air moved heavily like stagnant
water.

47   Our entrance was noted but no one came rushing over to welcome me or ask questions. That would come, I knew, but certain formalities had first to be observed. We all ordered Coca-Cola, and a
pint bottle of sloe gin appeared by magic. The music entered my
body and raced along my veins with the third syrupy drink. Hur-
ray, I was having a good time. I had never had the chance to learn
the delicate art of flirtation, so now I mimicked the other girls at the
table. Fluttering one hand over my mouth, while laughing as hard
as I could. The other hand waved somewhere up and to my left as
if I and it had nothing to do with each other.

48   "Marguerite?"

49   I looked around the table and was surprised that everyone was
gone. I had no idea how long I had sat there laughing and smirking
behind my hand. I decided they had joined the dancing throng and
looked up to search for my, by now, close but missing friends.

50   "Marguerite." L.C. Smith's face hung above me like the head of
a bodyless brown ghost.

51   "L.C., how are you?" I hadn't seen him since my return, and as
I waited for his answer a wave of memory crashed in my brain. He
was the boy who had lived on the hill behind the school who rode
his own horse and at fifteen picked as much cotton as the grown men.
Despite his good looks he was never popular. He didn't talk unless
forced. His mother had died when he was a baby, and his father drank
moonshine, even during the week. The girls said he was womanish,
and the boys that he was funny that way.

52   I commenced to giggle and flutter and he took my hand.

53   "Come on. Let's dance."

54   I agreed and caught the edge of the table to stand. Half erect, I
noticed that the building moved. It rippled and buckled as if a nest
of snakes were mating beneath the floors. I was concerned, but the
sloe gin had numbed my brain and I couldn't panic. I held on to the
table and L.C.'s hand, and tried to straighten myself up.

55   "Sit down. I'll be right back." He took his hand away and I plopped back into the chair. Sometime later he was back with a glass of water.

56   "Come on. Get up." His voice was raspy like old corn shucks. I set my intention on getting up and pressed against the iron which had settled in my thighs.

57   "We're going to dance?" My words were thick and cumbersome and didn't want to leave my mouth.

58   "Come on." He gave me his hand and I stumbled up and against him and he guided me to the door.

59   Outside, the air was only a little darker and a little cooler, but it cleared one corner of my brain. We were walking in the moist dirt along the pond, and the café was again a distant outline. With soberness came a concern for my virtue. Maybe he wasn't what they said.

60   "What are you going to do?" I stopped and faced him, readying myself for his appeal.

61   "It's not me. It's you. You're going to throw up." He spoke slowly. "You're going to put your finger down your throat and tickle, then you can puke."

62   With his intentions clear, I regained my pose.

63   "But I don't want to throw up. I'm not in the least—"

64   He closed a hand on my shoulder and shook me a little. "I say, put your finger in your throat and get that mess out of your stomach."

65   I became indignant. How could he, a peasant, a nobody, presume to lecture me? I snatched my shoulder away.

66   "Really, I'm fine. I think I'll join my friends," I said and turned toward the café.

67   "Marguerite." It was no louder than his earlier tone but had more force than his hand.

68   "Yes?" I had been stopped.

69   "They're not your friends. They're laughing at you." He had misjudged. They couldn't be laughing at me. Not with my sophistication and city ways.

70   "Are you crazy?" I sounded like a San Francisco-born debutante.

71   "No. You're funny to them. You got away. And then you came back. What for? And with what to show for your travels?" His tone was as soft as the Southern night and the pond lapping. "You come back swaggering and bragging that you've just been to paradise and you're wearing the very clothes everybody here wants to get rid of."

72   I hadn't stopped to think that while loud-flowered skirts and embroidered white blouses caused a few eyebrows to be raised in San Diego, in Stamps they formed the bulk of most girl's wardrobes.

73   L.C. went on, "They're saying you must be crazy. Even people in Texarkana dress better than you do. And you've been all the way to California. They want to see you show your butt outright. So they gave you extra drinks of sloe gin."

74   He stopped for a second, then asked, "You don't drink, do you?"

75   "No." He had sobered me.

76   "Go on, throw up. I brought some water so you can rinse your mouth after."

77   He stepped away as I began to gag. The bitter strong fluid gurgled out of my throat, burning my tongue. And the thought of nausea brought on new and stronger contractions.

78   After the cool water we walked back past the joint, and the music, still heavy, throbbed like gongs in my head. He left the glass by the porch and steered me in the direction of the Store.

79   His analysis had confused me and I couldn't understand why I should be the scapegoat.

80   He said, "They want to be free, free from this town, and crackers, and farming, and yes-sirring and no-sirring. You never were very friendly, so if you hadn't gone anywhere, they wouldn't have liked you any more. I was born here, and will die here, and they've never liked me." He was resigned and without obvious sorrow.

81   "But, L.C., why don't you get away?"

82   "And what would my poppa do? I'm all he's got." He stopped me before I could answer, and went on, "Sometimes I bring home my salary and he drinks it up before I can buy food for the week. Your grandmother knows. She lets me have credit all the time."

83   We were nearing the Store and he kept talking as if I weren't there. I knew for sure that he was going to continue talking to himself after I was safely in my bed.

84   "I've thought about going to New Orleans or Dallas, but all I know is how to chop cotton, pick cotton and hoe potatoes. Even if I could save the money to take Poppa with me, where would I get work in the city? That's what happened to him, you know? After my mother died he wanted to leave the house, but where could he go? Sometimes when he's drunk two bottles of White Lightning, he talks to her. " 'Reenie, I can see you standing there. How come you didn't take me with you, Reenie? I ain't got no place to go, Reenie. I want to be with you, Reenie.' And I act like I don't even hear him."

85   We had reached the back door of the Store. He held out his hand.

86   "Here, chew these Sen-sen. Sister Henderson ought not know you've been drinking. Good night, Marguerite. Take it easy."

87   And he melted into the darker darkness. The following year I heard that he had blown his brains out with a shotgun on the day of his father's funeral.

Billie Holiday

(1915–1959)

Considered by many to be the greatest jazz vocalist of all time, Lady Day, as she was known, is a musical legend. Born Eleanora Fagan on April 7, 1915, in Baltimore, Maryland, Holiday's early life was marked by poverty and parental abandonment. She began her career singing in brothels and after-hour clubs in Brooklyn and Harlem, but in 1933 she was discovered by John Hammond, a talent scout, who arranged for the singer to record with such jazz greats as Benny Goodman and Count Basie. While Holiday recorded numerous songs, two of the most famous are "Strange Fruit" and "God Bless the Child." In addition to her musical career, much has been made of the tragedies of her personal life, including drug addiction and jail time. This is chronicled in her autobiography, Lady Sings the Blues, *published in 1956 and co-authored with William Dufty.*

Strange Fruit

Southern trees bear a strange fruit
Blood on the leaves, blood at the root
Black bodies swinging in the Southern breeze
Strange fruit hanging from the poplar trees
5 Pastoral scene of the gallant South
The bulging eyes and the twisted mouth
Scent of magnolia sweet and fresh
Then the sudden smell of burning flesh
Here is a fruit for the crows to pluck
10 For the rain to gather, for the wind to suck
For the sun to rot, for the tree to drop
Here is a strange and bitter crop.

Arrested Development

In 1992, Arrested Development released their debut album, 3 Years, 5 Months and 2 Days in the Life Of . . . *and quickly emerged as a popular alternative rap group, with a spiritual sound that blended blues, soul, and hip-hop. The album, which sold more than four million copies, focused on African American history and culture, and was widely acclaimed, winning Grammys for Best Rap Album and Best New Artist. The group's leader and songwriter, Todd Thomas (Speech), grew up in Milwaukee and spent summers with his grandmother in rural Tennessee. He returned to the South to study at the Art Institute of Atlanta and while there formed the band in the late 1980s. In 1994, the band released their final album,* Zingalamaduni.

Tennessee

VERSE ONE: SPEECH

Lord I've really been real stressed
Down and out, losin ground
Although I am black and proud
Problems got me pessimistic
5 Brothers and sisters keep messin up
Why does it have to be so damn tuff?
I don't know where I can go
To let these ghosts out of my skull
My grandmas past, my brothers gone
10 I never at once felt so alone
I know you're supposed to be my steering wheel
Not just my spare tire (home)
But lord I ask you (home)
To be my guiding force and truth (home)
15 For some strange reason it had to be (home)
He guided me to Tennessee (home)

CHORUS

Take me to another place
Take me to another land

Make me forget all that hurts me
20 Let me understand your plan

VERSE TWO

Lord it's obvious we got a relationship
Talkin to each other every night and day
Although you're superior over me
We talk to each other in a friendship way

25 Then outta nowhere you tell me to break
Outta the country and into more country
Past Dyesburg into Ripley
Where the ghost of childhood haunts me

Walk the roads my forefathers walked
30 Climbed the trees my forefathers hung from
Ask those trees for all their wisdom
They tell me my ears are so young (home)
Go back to from whence you came (home)
My family tree my family name (home)
35 For some strange reason it had to be (home)
He guided me to Tennessee (home)

CHORUS

VERSE THREE

Now I see the importance of history
Why people be in the mess that they be
Many journeys to freedom made in vain
40 By brothers on the corner playin ghetto games
I ask you lord why you enlightened me
Without the enlightment of all my folks
He said cuz I set myself on a quest for truth
And he was there to quench my thirst
45 But I am still thirsty . . .
The lord allowed me to drink some more
He said what I am searchin for are
The answers to all which are in front of me

The ultimate truth started to get blurry
50   For some strange reason it had to be
It was all a dream about Tennessee

CHORUS

Writing Assignments

1. As discussed in the introduction to this chapter, the South is a recurring theme in African American literature. However, the treatment of the South differs considerably from author to author. Compare and contrast the excerpt from Maya Angelou's *Gather Together in My Name* and Richard Wright's "Big Boy Leaves Home." How is the South presented? How might the South be read not only spatially, but also symbolically in these works?

2. Toomer's haunting evocation of the South, where brutality, bloodshed, and loss are paired with lyrical elegies of dusk, female beauty, and Georgia night skies, underlies the tension of *Cane*. Select a recurring symbol from "Karintha," "Georgia Dusk," and "Blood-Burning Moon," such as cane, dusk, or ashes, and trace it through the pieces, paying particular attention to how it accumulates textual meaning. How does this symbol indicate the tensions in Toomer's portrait of the South?

3. How do ritual acts of violence punctuate the works in this chapter? How are the portrayals of such violence similar? What is the overall effect of each episode on the work as a whole?

4. Listen to both "Strange Fruit" and "Tennessee" and compare and contrast their representations of the South as a location of memory, brutality, and home. How is landscape a site of history in these works? Do some background research on Billie Holiday and her performance of this famous song. Do you think that Arrested Development's song does similar political work?

CHAPTER FOUR

FOLKLORE

All cultures have folk traditions, namely those stories, songs, legends, behaviors, and material artifacts that circulate and are known to their people regardless of economic strata, gender, or geography. Folklore is critical for understanding culture because the sustaining folk texts reveal mores, beliefs, customs, and histories. Indeed, the currency of folk material suggests its importance to the group, for as Frantz Fanon explains in *Black Skin, White Masks*, "When a story flourishes in the heart of a folklore it is because in one way or another it expresses an aspect of the 'spirit of the group.'" Thus, in this chapter we turn our attention to the rich and varied folk culture of African Americans, a unique tradition informed by West African, Caribbean, and Euro-American cultural performances and texts. Although there are numerous sources that directly link African American folk tradition to other cultural folk practices, it is imperative to recognize that Africans in the United States created a distinct folk tradition, or what Toni Morrison has called a "third thing": cultural practices that are neither African nor white American. As she notes, Africans in the United States created, among other things, new music, new ways of speaking, and innovative psychological methods to deal with oppression.

Given the immense body of work collected under the rubric of African American folk culture, we have focused on a few oral expressions that have been modified over time, and their manifestations in the literature. In addition, this chapter specifically examines three archetypal folk characters—tricksters, badmen, and midwives—as they highlight indigenous cultural folkways.

The frequency with which the trickster figure appears in African American folktales and literature suggests the ritualized nature of its employment in the tradition. Tricksters, who can take either human or animal form, are wily characters who use wit to outmaneuver others for self-serving ends. While tricksterism is not restricted to African American texts (consider the coyote of Native American tales or the antebellum Confidence Man of Anglo American letters), the centrality of the trickster figure in the tradition's orature and literature is undeniable. Indeed, one of the leading critics of African American literature, Henry Louis Gates, Jr., in *The Signifying Monkey: A Theory of Afro-American Literature*, reads the African American expressive tradition through the African trickster figure Esu-Elegbara, who is a messenger of the gods in Yoruba culture and a consummate linguist. This trickster figure is the master of various kinds of wordplay, including double entendres, irony, indirection, satire, disruption, open-endedness, and ambiguity, and he can act as both translator and medium. As Gates explains, Esu's variations in the African Diaspora include Legba in Benin, Exu in Brazil, Echu-Elegua in Cuba, and Papa Legba in Haiti. The incarnation of this trickster in the United States is the Signifying Monkey, the seemingly weak figure from African American folk culture who has no overt power but who is able, through his gift for language, to outsmart and outwit his more formidable opponents. The tale of the Signifying Monkey is included in this chapter and elucidates the paradigm of tricksterism in African American literature. The trickster is a profoundly subversive figure, for his language play often disrupts the status quo and as a result enhances the trickster's chances of surviving in what are adverse if not life-threatening situations.

Animal tricksters, who inhabited many slave stories, were complicated figures that sometimes emerged as selfish, cruel, and devoid of communal spirit. Other tricksters, though, are clear symbols for powerless groups who subvert hierarchical structures through the verbal art of signifying. These stories were sometimes based on real-life circumstances, as animals were anthropomorphized as slaves and masters. While these animal tales were dismissed as merely humorous anecdotes, some were profoundly revelatory of plantation hierarchy. Certain tales spoke to the captives' survival tactics, which included tricks such as cheating, lying, stealing, feigning illness, and pretending to misunderstand orders, which allowed slaves a measure of freedom. Therefore, trickster narratives in which characters engage in role-playing and demonstrate their verbal dexterity are not confined to slave tales, but continue to be employed as tools with which characters confront the dominant culture. In this chapter, trickster tales are elucidated through the writing of Charles Chesnutt and Ishmael Reed, published decades apart. Both Uncle Julius McAdoo from Chesnutt's short story collection, *The Conjure Woman* (1899), and Raven Quickskill from Reed's *Flight to Canada* (1976) are masters at deception, who though seemingly naïve, promote their own self-interests while offering shrewd and incisive critiques of slavery.

Related to the trickster figure is the "badman," who, rather than relying on wit and persuasion to outsmart his opponent, as the trickster does, often exploits his brawn, violence, and sexuality. Indeed, these folk heroes have been memorialized in songs, ballads, and, especially, toasts, which are long narrative poems of rhyming couplets that are generally coarse and obscene. These folk poems have been particularly popular with African American males, and many scholars find the lyrics of contemporary rap artists to have traces of toasts, in both form and content. Geneva Smitherman argues that toasts "let it all hang out. The hero is fearless, defiant, openly rebellious, and full of braggadocio about his masculinity, sexuality, fighting ability, and general badness. Narrated in first person, this epic folk style is a tribute—that is, a 'toast'—to this superbad, omnipotent black hustler, pimp, player, killer who is mean to the max."

Although most scholars agree that the exploits of the badman arose during the post-bellum South, traces of this folk hero are found in slave tales involving the male captive who fought back against his oppressor and was perpetually punished, or who resisted the will of his captors and fled. Clearly, these men were revered for their overt displays of courage, suggesting their status as forerunners to the badmen of African American folk culture. The popularity of this folk hero lies in his subversiveness. He is disdainful of social conventions, boldly stands up to white authority, breaks rules, violates taboos, and, perhaps most important, is not intimidated by the law, the police, or even the devil, who often figures in the folklore as an adversary the badman defeats. Despite the fact that his exploits are self-serving and sometimes at the expense of his community members (including African American women, who are often sexually objectified), this figure continues to endure, some folklorists conjecture, because of the continued disproportion of power in American society. Therefore, this folk hero's badness, even though hyperbolic, is honored and admired because it suggests an alternative to racial oppression and submission.

In this chapter, the badmen are embodied in such legendary figures as Stagolee, Shine, Railroad Bill, and John Henry. Even though the latter two figures are believed to be based on real-life people and situations, all of these figures have become mythic through the extensive retelling of their tales over time. Stagolee, who is also known as Stackolee, Stackerlee, Stackalee, Stacker Lee, and Staggerlee, is perhaps the most notorious badman in the tradition and thus a paradigm of violence and toughness. Likewise, Railroad Bill is a folk hero whose violence is exacted on both the white and Black communities. Railroad Bill is a figure based upon the life of Morris Slater, who in Alabama, in 1893, shot and killed a police officer and escaped on a freight train. For three years, before he was murdered, he robbed trains and "sold" food at gunpoint to poor African Americans who lived along the tracks. This figure, even as he turned against his own people, fought against the larger system; therefore, his actions were embellished and immortalized in story and song.

Shine and John Henry demonstrate their badness in less violent ways. Shine, who is the most trickster-like figure of the group, relies on verbal wit, intelligence, and physical endurance; therefore, despite the fact that he occupies the most menial position on the ill-fated *Titanic*, he emerges as the lone survivor. Likewise, John Henry's physical prowess enables him to triumph over the white man's technology. Unlike Railroad Bill, who terrorizes his own people, John Henry is a popular folk icon who represents the power of his entire race. It is widely believed that the John Henry legend was based on the building of the Chesapeake and Ohio Railroad in West Virginia in the 1870s, where African American workers toiled under brutal conditions. Laboring in unbearable heat, thick smoke, and dangerous conditions of falling rock and dynamite explosions, John Henry symbolized workers and their plight to stay viable in the face of mechanization and increased industrialization. Although John Henry dies at the end of the story, his victory over the steam drill is most resonant in the tale. This chapter includes the folktale, along with two revisions: Melvin Tolson's "The Birth of John Henry" (1965) and an excerpt from Colson Whitehead's novel *John Henry Days* (2001). Paralleling modern society with the industrial age, Whitehead's novel attests to the continuing relevance of this legendary rail worker's plight.

Our last folk hero type, illustrated in this chapter by Ntozake Shange's *Sasafrass, Cypress & Indigo* (1982) and Tina McElroy Ansa's *Baby of the Family* (1989), is the midwife, who is a healer/conjure woman. Historically, this figure was revered in the African American community, for as the medicine woman she would tend not only to pregnant women, but also to the sick and the dying. Although conjurers were both men and women, midwives historically were female, a fact shared by numerous cultures around the world. The midwife brought with her to America a substantial knowledge of health and the curative properties of herbs and roots. Generally denied conventional medical care, the African American community in the antebellum South relied on the wisdom of the midwife and treated her with due respect.

Beyond administering medicinal treatments, the conjurer was called upon to perform a variety of social functions for the community, and as an herbalist this often included concocting remedies for love, revenge, childbirth, financial reward, and punishment. "Conjuring" refers to an entire folk system that is a blend of Christian and African-based religions. At its core is a belief in the mystic and spiritual world, which is illustrated most profoundly in the Indigo section of *Sasafrass, Cypress & Indigo*. As a young woman with "too much South in her," Indigo's spirit is connected to ancestral ways, and as an adult she becomes a midwife. Likewise, *Baby of the Family* is also set in the South in the middle of the twentieth century. Ansa portrays the persistence of folk traditions in the face of modern-day society. A skilled and esteemed nurse, who was once a country midwife, works in a fully equipped hospital and witnesses the birth of a child with a caul, a thin embryonic membrane covering the head of some newborns. Many folk beliefs surround the caul (or veil): In African American culture, the caul signifies that the child possesses special powers, including an ability to communicate with ghosts and spirits. Although the midwife-cum-nurse performs all of the necessary folk rituals and traditions on the baby, the infant's mother refuses to participate, and as a result the novel illustrates the consequences of dismissing African American folk practices as merely old-fashioned superstitions. Reading *Baby of the Family* as a cautionary tale, it is appropriate that we end the chapter with this piece of fiction, for it suggests that folk customs are an enduring and edifying cultural practice that continue to inspire and inform the African American community and its literary canon.

Further Reading:

Brown, Cecil. *Stagolee Shot Billy*. Cambridge, MA: Harvard University Press, 2003.

Courlander, Harold, ed. *A Treasury of Afro-American Folklore*. New York: Crown Publishers, 1975.

Dance, Daryl Cumber, ed. *From My People: 400 Years of African American Folklore*. New York: W. W. Norton & Company, 2002.

Dundes, Alan., ed. *Mother Wit from the Laughing Barrel: Readings in the Interpretation of Afro-American Folklore.* Englewood Cliffs, NJ: Prentice Hall, 1972.

Ellison, Ralph Waldo. *Shadow and Act.* New York: Random House, 1964.

Fanon, Franz. Trans. Charles Lam Markmann. *Black Skin, White Masks.* New York: Grove Press, 1967.

Gates, Henry Louis Jr. *The Signifying Monkey: A Theory of African-American Literary Criticism.* New York: Oxford, 1988.

Hurston, Zora Neale. *Mules and Men.* Philadelphia: J. B. Lippincott Company, 1935.

Lee, Valerie. *Granny Midwives & Black Women Writers: Double-Dutched Readings.* New York: Routledge, 1996.

Levine, Lawrence W. *Black Culture and Black Consciousness: Afro-American Folk Thought from Slavery to Freedom.* New York: Oxford, 1977.

Smitherman, Geneva. *Talkin and Testifyin: The Language of Black America.* Boston: Houghton Mifflin, 1977.

Thomas, H. Nigel. *From Folklore to Fiction: A Study of Folk Heroes and Rituals in the Black American Novel.* New York: Greenwood Press, 1988.

Anonymous

The Signifying Monkey
Traditional

The Monkey and the Lion got to talkin' one day.
Monkey say, "There's a bad cat livin' down your way."
He say, "You take this fellow to be your friend,
But the way he talks about you is a sin;
5 He say folks say you king, and that may be true,
But he can whip the daylights outta you.
And somethin' else I forgot to say:
He talks about your mother in a hell of a way."
Monkey say, "His name is Elephant, and he's not your friend."
10 Lion say, "He don't need to be 'cause today will be his end."

Say like a ball of fire and a streak of heat,
The old Lion went rolling down the street.
That Lion let out a terrible sneeze,
And knocked the damned giraffe to his everlastin' knees.
15 Now he saw Elephant sittin' under a tree,
And he say, "Now you bring your big black butt to me."
The Elephant looked at 'im out the corner of his eyes,
And say, "Now little punk, go play with somebody your size."
The Lion let out a roar and reared up six feet tall,
20 Elephant just kicked him in the belly and laughed to see him fall.
Now they fought all night and they fought all day;
And I don't know how in the hell that Lion ever got away.
But the Lion was draggin' back through the jungle more dead than
    alive,
And that's when that Monkey start that signifying.
25 He say, "Hey-y-y-y, Mr. Lion, you don't look so swell;
Look to me like you caught a whole lotta hell!
You call yourself a king and a ace,
It's gon' take ninety yards o' sailcloth to patch yo' face.
Now git on out from under my tree,
30 before I decide to drop my drawers and pee.
Stop, don't let me hear you roar,
or I'll come down outta this tree and beat your tail some more.
Say the damn old Lion was sitting down there crying,
And the Monkey just *kept* signifying.
35 And then Monkey started jumpin' around
And his foot slipped and he fell down.
Like a ball of fire and a streak of heat,
The old Lion was on him with all four feet.
Say the Monkey looked up with tears in his eyes,
40 And say, "Mr. Lion, I apologize!
Now, good buddy, in this jungle friends are few;
You know I was only playin' wit' you."
Monkey looked at Lion and saw he wasn't gon' get away,
So he decided to think of a bold damn play.
45 He say, "Mr. Lion, you ain't raisin' no hell,
Everybody in the jungle saw me when I fell.
Now if you let me up like a real man should,
I'll kick your butt all over these woods."
The old Lion looked at 'im and jumped back for a hell of a fight.

50 And in a split second the Monkey was damn near outta sight.
He jumped up in a tree higher than any human eye can see,
And say, "You dumb mammyjammer, don't you ever mess wid
    me!"

Charles Chesnutt

(1858–1932)

*Charles Waddell Chesnutt was born June 20, 1858, in Cleveland,
Ohio, but he was raised in Fayetteville, North Carolina. Chesnutt went
to schools founded by the Freedmen's Bureau and became an assistant
principal for an African American school before his twentieth birthday.
In 1884, Chesnutt returned with his wife and family to Cleveland,
where he became a legal stenographer. Chesnutt's first short story,
"The Goophered Grapevine," was published in the* Atlantic Monthly *in
1887 and became part of his first collection of short stories,* The Conjure Woman *(1899). In this volume, Uncle Julius McAdoo, an ex-slave
who resides on a former plantation, tells stories that are infused with
Southern folklore, rituals, and traditions. On the surface, this volume
appears to be merely part of the local color tradition, but, as "Goophered Grapevine" and "Po' Sandy," the two stories reprinted below
attest,* The Conjure Woman *illustrates Chesnutt's critique of the brutality inherent in chattel slavery. In the fall of 1899, Chesnutt published a second collection,* The Wife of His Youth and Other Stories of
the Color Line, *and in following years he published novels that directly examined and critiqued racial problems in the postwar South,
including* The House Behind the Cedars *(1900),* The Marrow of Tradition *(1901), and* The Colonel's Dream *(1905).*

The Goophered Grapevine

1 Some years ago my wife was in poor health, and our family doctor, in
whose skill and honesty I had implicit confidence, advised a change
of climate. I shared, from an unprofessional standpoint, his opinion
that the raw winds, the chill rains, and the violent changes of tem-
perature that characterized the winters in the region of the Great
Lakes tended to aggravate my wife's difficulty, and would undoubtedly shorten her life if she remained exposed to them. The doctor's

advice was that we seek, not a temporary place of sojourn, but a permanent residence, in a warmer and more equable climate. I was engaged at the time in grape-culture in northern Ohio, and, as I liked the business and had given it much study, I decided to look for some other locality suitable for carrying it on. I thought of sunny France, of sleepy Spain, of Southern California, but there were objections to them all. It occurred to me that I might find what I wanted in some one of our own Southern States. It was a sufficient time after the war for conditions in the South to have become somewhat settled; and I was enough of a pioneer to start a new industry, if I could not find a place where grape-culture had been tried. I wrote to a cousin who had gone into the turpentine business in central North Carolina. He assured me, in response to my inquiries, that no better place could be found in the South than the State and neighborhood where he lived; the climate was perfect for health, and, in conjunction with the soil, ideal for grape-culture; labor was cheap, and land could be bought for a mere song. He gave us a cordial invitation to come and visit him while we looked into the matter. We accepted the invitation, and after several days of leisurely travel, the last hundred miles of which were up a river on a sidewheel steamer, we reached our destination, a quaint old town, which I shall call Patesville, because, for one reason, that is not its name. There was a red brick market-house in the public square, with a tall tower, which held a four-faced clock that struck the hours, and from which there pealed out a curfew at nine o'clock. There were two or three hotels, a court-house, a jail, stores, offices, and all the appurtenances of a county seat and a commercial emporium; for while Patesville numbered only four or five thousand inhabitants, of all shades of complexion, it was one of the principal towns in North Carolina, and had a considerable trade in cotton and naval stores. This business activity was not immediately apparent to my unaccustomed eyes. Indeed, when I first saw the town, there brooded over it a calm that seemed almost sabbatic in its restfulness, though I learned later on that underneath its somnolent exterior the deeper currents of life—love and hatred, joy and despair, ambition and avarice, faith and friendship—flowed not less steadily than in livelier latitudes.

2   We found the weather delightful at that season, the end of summer, and were hospitably entertained. Our host was a man of means and evidently regarded our visit as a pleasure, and we were therefore correspondingly at our ease, and in a position to act with the coolness of judgment desirable in making so radical a change in our lives. My

cousin placed a horse and buggy at our disposal, and himself acted as our guide until I became somewhat familiar with the country.

3   I found that grape-culture, while it had never been carried on to any great extent, was not entirely unknown in the neighborhood. Several planters there-abouts had attempted it on a commercial scale, in former years, with greater or less success; but like most Southern industries, it had felt the blight of war and had fallen into desuetude.

4   I went several times to look at a place that I thought might suit me. It was a plantation of considerable extent, that had formerly belonged to a wealthy man by the name of McAdoo. The estate had been for years involved in litigation between disputing heirs, during which period shiftless cultivation had well-nigh exhausted the soil. There had been a vineyard of some extent on the place, but it had not been attended to since the war, and had lapsed into utter neglect. The vines—here partly supported by decayed and broken-down trellises, there twining themselves among the branches of the slender saplings which had sprung up among them—grew in wild and unpruned luxuriance, and the few scattered grapes they bore were the undisputed prey of the first comer. The site was admirably adapted to grape-raising; the soil, with a little attention, could not have been better; and with the native grape, the luscious scuppernong, as my main reliance in the beginning, I felt sure that I could introduce and cultivate successfully a number of other varieties.

5   One day I went over with my wife to show her the place. We drove out of the town over a long wooden bridge that spanned a spreading mill-pond, passed the long whitewashed fence surrounding the county fair-ground, and struck into a road so sandy that the horse's feet sank to the fetlocks. Our route lay partly up hill and partly down, for we were in the sand-hill county; we drove past cultivated farms, and then by abandoned fields grown up in scrub-oak and short-leaved pine, and once or twice through the solemn aisles of the virgin forest, where the tall pines, well-nigh meeting over the narrow road, shut out the sun, and wrapped us in cloistral solitude. Once, at a cross-roads, I was in doubt as to the turn to take, and we sat there waiting ten minutes—we had already caught some of the native infection of restfulness—for some human being to come along, who could direct us on our way. At length a little negro girl appeared, walking straight as an arrow, with a piggin full of water on her head. After a little patient investigation, necessary to overcome the child's shyness, we learned what we wished to know, and at the end of about five miles from the town reached our destination.

6   We drove between a pair of decayed gateposts—the gate itself had long since disappeared—and up a straight sandy lane, between two lines of rotting rail fence, partly concealed by jimson-weeds and briers, to the open space where a dwelling-house had once stood, evidently a spacious mansion, if we might judge from the ruined chimneys that were still standing, and the brick pillars on which the sills rested. The house itself, we had been informed, had fallen a victim to the fortunes of war.

7   We alighted from the buggy, walked about the yard for a while, and then wandered off into the adjoining vineyard. Upon Annie's complaining of weariness I led the way back to the yard, where a pine log, lying under a spreading elm, afforded a shady though somewhat hard seat. One end of the log was already occupied by a venerable-looking colored man. He held on his knees a hat full of grapes, over which he was smacking his lips with great gusto, and a pile of grapeskins near him indicated that the performance was no new thing. We approached him at an angle from the rear, and were close to him before he perceived us. He respectfully rose as we drew near, and was moving away, when I begged him to keep his seat.

8   "Don't let us disturb you," I said. "There is plenty of room for us all."

9   He resumed his seat with somewhat of embarrassment. While he had been standing, I had observed that he was a tall man, and, though slightly bowed by the weight of years, apparently quite vigorous. He was not entirely black, and this fact, together with the quality of his hair, which was about six inches long and very bushy, except on the top of his head, where he was quite bald, suggested a slight strain of other than negro blood. There was a shrewdness in his eyes, too, which was not altogether African, and which, as we afterwards learned from experience, was indicative of a corresponding shrewdness in his character. He went on eating the grapes, but did not seem to enjoy himself quite so well as he had apparently done before he became aware of our presence.

10   "Do you live around here?" I asked, anxious to put him at his ease.

11   "Yas, suh. I lives des ober yander, behine de nex' san'-hill, on de Lumberton plank-road."

12   "Do you know anything about the time when this vineyard was cultivated?"

13   "Lawd bless you, suh, I knows all about it. Dey ain' na'er a man in dis settlement w'at won' tell you ole Julius McAdoo 'uz bawn en raise' on dis yer same plantation. Is you de Norv'n gemman w'at's gwine ter buy de ole vimya'd?"

14   "I am looking at it," I replied; "but I don't know that I shall care to buy unless I can be reasonably sure of making something out of it."

15   "Well, suh, you is a stranger ter me, en I is a stranger ter you, en we is bofe strangers ter one anudder, but 'f I 'uz in yo' place, I would n' buy dis vimya'd."

16   "Why not?" I asked.

17   "Well, I dunno whe'r you b'lieves in cunj'in'er not,—some er de w'ite folks don't, er says dey don't,—but de truf er de matter is dat dis yer ole vimya'd is goophered."

18   "Is what?" I asked, not grasping the meaning of this unfamiliar word.

19   "Is goophered,—cunju'd, bewitch'."

20   He imparted this information with such solemn earnestness, and with such an air of confidential mystery, that I felt somewhat interested, while Annie was evidently much impressed, and drew closer to me.

21   "How do you know it is bewitched?" I asked.

22   "I would n' spec' fer you ter b'lieve me 'less you know all 'bout de fac's. But ef you en young miss dere doan' min' lis'nin' ter a ole nigger run on a minute er two w'ile you er restin', I kin 'splain to you how it all happen'."

23   We assured him that we would be glad to hear how it all happened, and he began to tell us. At first the current of his memory—or imagination—seemed somewhat sluggish; but as his embarrassment wore off, his language flowed more freely, and the story acquired perspective and coherence. As he became more and more absorbed in the narrative, his eyes assumed a dreamy expression, and he seemed to lose sight of his auditors, and to be living over again in monologue his life on the old plantation.

24   "Ole Mars Dugal' McAdoo," he began, "bought dis place long many years befo' de wah, en I 'member well w'en he sot out all dis yer part er de plantation in scuppernon's. De vimes growed monst'us fas', en Mars Dugal' made a thousan' gallon er scuppernon' wine eve'y year.

25   "Now, ef dey's an'thing a nigger lub, nex' ter 'possum, en chick'n, en watermillyums, it 's scuppernon's. Dey ain' nuffin dat kin stan' up side'n de scuppernon' fer sweetness; sugar ain't a suckumstance ter scuppernon'. W'en de season is nigh 'bout ober, en de grapes begin ter swivel up des a little wid de wrinkles er ole age,—w'en de skin git sof' en brown,—den de scuppernon' make you smack yo' lip en roll yo' eye en wush fer mo'; so I reckon it ain' very 'stonishin' dat niggers lub scuppernon'.

26   "Dey wuz a sight er niggers in de naberhood er de vimya'd. Dere wuz ole Mars Henry Brayboy's niggers, en ole Mars Jeems McLean's niggers, en Mars Dugal's own niggers; den dey wuz a settlement er free niggers en po' buckrahs down by de Wim'l'ton Road, en Mars Dugal' had de only vimya'd in de naberhood. I reckon it ain' so much so nowadays, but befo' de wah, in slab'ry times, a nigger did n' mine goin' fi' er ten mile in a night, w'en dey wuz sump'n good ter eat at de yuther een'.

27   "So atter a w'ile Mars Dugal' begin ter miss his scuppernon's. Co'se he 'cuse' de niggers er it, but dey all 'nied it ter de las'. Mars Dugal' sot spring guns en steel traps, en he en de oberseah sot up nights once't er twice't, tel one night Mars Dugal'—he 'uz a monst'us keer-less man—got his leg shot full er cow-peas. But somehow er nudder dey could n' nebber ketch none er de niggers. I dunner how it hap-pen, but it happen des like I tell you, en de grapes kep' on a-goin' des de same.

28   "But bimeby ole Mars Dugal' fix' up a plan ter stop it. Dey wuz a cunjuh 'oman livin' down 'mongs' de free niggers on de Wim'l'ton Road, en all de darkies fum Rockfish ter Beaver Crick wuz feared er her. She could wuk de mos' powerfulles' kin' er goopher,—could make people hab fits, er rheumatiz, er make 'em des dwinel away en die; en dey say she went out ridin' de niggers at night, fer she wuz a witch 'sides bein' a cunjuh 'oman. Mars Dugal' hearn 'bout Aun' Peggy's doin's, en begun ter 'flect whe'r er no he could n' git her ter he'p him keep de niggers off'n de grapevimes. One day in de spring er de year, ole miss pack' up a basket er chick'n en poun'-cake, en a bottle er scuppernon' wine, en Mars Dugal' tuk it in his buggy en driv ober ter Aun' Peggy's cabin. He tuk de basket in, en had a long talk wid Aun' Peggy.

29   "De nex' day Aun' Peggy come up ter de vimya'd. De niggers seed her slippin' 'roun', en dey soon foun' out what she 'uz doin' dere. Mars Dugal' had hi'ed her ter goopher de grapevimes. She sa'ntered 'roun' 'mongs' de vimes, en tuk a leaf fum dis one, en a grape-hull fum dat one, en a grape-seed fum anudder one; en den a little twig fum here, en a little pinch er dirt fum dere,—en put it all in a big black bottle, wid a snake's toof en a speckle' hen's gall en some ha'rs fum a black cat's tail, en den fill' de bottle wid scuppernon' wine. W'en she got de goopher all ready en fix', she tuk'n went out in de woods en buried it under de root uv a red oak tree, en den come back en tole one er de niggers she done goopher de grapevimes, en a'er a nigger w'at eat dem grapes 'ud be sho ter die inside'n twel' mont's.

30   "Atter dat de niggers let de scuppernon's 'lone, en Mars Dugal' did n' hab no 'casion ter fine no mo' fault; en de season wuz mos' gone, w'en a strange gemman stop at de plantation one night ter see Mars Dugal' on some business; en his coachman, seein' de scuppernon's growin' so nice en sweet, slip 'roun' behine de smoke-house, en et all de scuppernon's he could hole. Nobody did n' notice it at de time, but dat night, on de way home, de gemman's hoss runned away en kill' de coachman. W'en we hearn de noos, Aun' Lucy, de cook, she up 'n say she seed de strange nigger eat'n' er de scuppernon's behine de smoke-house; en den we knowed de goopher had b'en er wukkin'. Den one er de nigger chilluns runned away fum de quarters one day, en got in de scuppernon's, en died de nex' week. W'ite folks say he die' er de fevuh, but de niggers knowed it wuz de goopher. So you k'n be sho de darkies did n' hab much ter do wid dem scuppernon' vimes.

31   "W'en de scuppernon' season 'uz ober fer dat year, Mars Dugal' foun' he had made fifteen hund'ed gallon er wine; en one er de niggers hearn him laffin' wid de oberseah fit ter kill, en sayin' dem fifteen hund'ed gallon er wine wuz monst'us good intrus' on de ten dollars he laid out on de vimya'd. So I 'low ez he paid Aun' Peggy ten dollars fer to goopher de grapevimes.

32   "De goopher did n' wuk no mo' tel de nex' summer, w'en 'long to'ds de middle er de season one er de fiel' han's died; en ez dat lef' Mars Dugal' sho't er han's, he went off ter town fer ter buy anudder. He fotch de noo nigger home wid 'im. He wuz er ole nigger, er de color er a gingy-cake, en ball ez a hoss-apple on de top er his head. He wuz a peart ole nigger, do', en could do a big day's wuk.

33   "Now it happen dat one er de niggers on de nex' plantation, one er ole Mars Henry Brayboy's niggers, had runned away de day befo', en tuk ter de swamp, en ole Mars Dugal' en some er de yuther nabor w'ite folks had gone out wid dere guns en dere dogs fer ter he'p 'em hunt fer de nigger; en de han's on our own plantation wuz all so flusterated dat we fuhgot ter tell de noo han' 'bout de goopher on de scuppernon' vimes. Co'se he smell de grapes en see de vimes, an atter dahk er fus' thing he done wuz ter slip off ter de grapevimes 'dout sayin' nuffin ter nobody. Nex' mawnin' he tole some er de niggers 'bout de fine bait er scuppernon' he et de night befo'.

34   "W'en dey tole 'im 'bout de goopher on de grapevimes, he 'uz dat tarrified dat he turn pale, en look des like he gwine ter die right in his tracks. De oberseah come up en axed w'at 'uz de matter; en w'en dey tole 'im Henry be'n eatin' er de scuppernon's, en got de goopher on 'im, be gin Henry a big drink er w'iskey, en 'low dat de nex'

rainy day he take 'im ober ter Aun' Peggy's, en see ef she would n' take de goopher off'n him, seein' ez he did n' know nuffin erbout it tel he done et de grapes.

35 "Sho nuff, it rain de nex' day, en de oberseah went ober ter Aun' Peggy's wid Henry. En Aun' Peggy say dat bein' ez Henry did n' know 'bout de goopher, en et de grapes in ign'ance er de conseq'ences, she reckon she mought be able fer ter take de goopher off'n him. So she fotch out er bottle wid some cunjuh medicine in it, en po'd some out in a go'd fer Henry ter drink. He manage ter git it down; he say it tas'e like whiskey wid sump'n bitter in it. She 'lowed dat 'ud keep de goopher off'n him tel de spring; but w'en de sap begin ter rise in de grapevimes he ha' ter come en see her ag'in, en she tell him w'at e's ter do.

36 "Nex' spring, w'en de sap commence' ter rise in de scuppernon' vime, Henry tuk a ham one night. Whar'd he git de ham? *I* doan know; dey wa'n't no hams on de plantation 'cep'n' w'at 'uz in de smoke-house, but *I* never see Henry 'bout de smoke-house. But ez I wuz a-sayin', he tuk de ham ober ter Aun' Peggy's; en Aun' Peggy tole 'im dat w'en Mars Dugal' begin ter prune de grapevimes, he mus' go en take'n scrape off de sap whar it ooze out'n de cut een's er de vimes, en 'n'int his ball head wid it; en ef he do dat once't a year de goopher would n' wuk agin 'im long ez he done it. En bein' ez he fotch her de ham, she fix' it so he kin eat all de scuppernon' he want.

37 "So Henry 'n'int his head wid de sap out'n de big grapevime des ha'f way 'twix' de quarters en de big house, en de goopher nebber wuk agin him dat summer. But de beatenes' thing you eber see happen ter Henry. Up ter dat time he wuz ez ball ez a sweeten' 'tater, but des ez soon ez de young leaves begun ter come out on de grapevimes, de ha'r begun ter grow out on Henry's head, en by de middle er de summer he had de bigges' head er ha'r on de plantation. Befo' dat, Henry had tol'able good ha'r 'roun' de aidges, but soon ez de young grapes begun ter come, Henry's ha'r begun to quirl all up in little balls, des like dis yer reg'lar grapy ha'r, en by de time de grapes got ripe his head look des like a bunch er grapes. Combin' it did n' do no good; he wuk at it ha'f de night wid er Jim Crow,* en think he git it straighten' out, but in de mawnin' de grapes 'ud be dere des de same. So he gin it up, en tried ter keep de grapes down by havin' his ha'r cut sho't.

---

*A small card, resembling a currycomb in construction, and used by negroes in the rural districts instead of a comb.

38   "But dat wa'n't de quares' thing 'bout de goopher. When Henry come ter de plantation, he wuz gittin' a little ole an stiff in de j'ints. But dat summer he got des ez spry en libely ez any young nigger on de plantation; fac', he got so biggity dat Mars Jackson, de oberseah, ha' ter th'eaten ter whip 'im, ef he did n' stop cuttin' up his didos en behave hisse'f. But de mos' cur'ouses' thing happen' in de fall, when de sap begin ter go down in de grapevimes. Fus', when de grapes 'uz gethered, de knots begun ter straighten out'n Henry's ha'r; en w'en de leaves begin ter fall, Henry's ha'r 'mence' ter drap out; en when de vimes 'uz bar', Henry's head wuz baller 'n it wuz in de spring, en he begin ter git ole en stiff in de j'ints ag'in, en paid no mo' 'tention ter de gals dyoin' er de whole winter. En nex' spring, w'en he rub de sap on ag'in, he got young ag'in, en so soopl en libely dat none er de young niggers on de plantation could n' jump, ner dance, ner hoe ez much cotton ez Henry. But in de fall er de year his grapes 'mence' ter straighten out, en his j'ints ter git stiff, en his ha'r drap off, en de rheumatiz begin ter wrastle wid 'im.

39   "Now, ef you 'd 'a' knowed ole Mars Dugal' McAdoo, you 'd 'a' knowed dat it ha' ter be a mighty rainy day when he could n' fine sump'n fer his niggers ter do, en it ha' ter be a mighty little hole he could n' crawl thoo, en ha' ter be a monst'us cloudy night when a dollar git by him in de dahkness; en w'en he see how Henry git young in de spring en ole in de fall, he 'lowed ter hisse'f ez how he could make mo' money out'n Henry dan by wukkin' him in de cotton-fiel'. 'Long de nex' spring, atter de sap 'mence' ter rise, en Henry 'n'int 'is head en sta'ted fer ter git young en soopl, Mars Dugal' up 'n tuk Henry ter town, en sole 'im fer fifteen hunder' dollars. Co'se de man w'at bought Henry did n' know nuffin 'bout de goopher, en Mars Dugal' did n' see no 'casion fer ter tell 'im. Long to'ds de fall, w'en de sap went down, Henry begin ter git ole ag'in same ez yuzhal, en his noo marster begin ter git skeered les'n he gwine ter lose his fifteen-hunder'-dollar nigger. He sent fer a mighty fine doctor, but de med'cine did n' 'pear ter do no good; de goopher had a good holt. Henry tole de doctor 'bout de goopher, but he doctor des laff at 'im.

40   "One day in de winter Mars Dugal' went ter town, en wuz santerin' 'long de Main Street, when who should he meet but Henry's noo marster. Dey said 'Hoddy,' en Mars Dugal' ax 'im ter hab a seegyar; en atter dey run on awhile 'bout de craps en de weather, Mars Dugal' ax 'im, sorter keerless, like ez ef he des thought of it,—

41   " 'How you like de nigger I sole you las' spring?'

42 "Henry's marster shuck his head en knock de ashes off'n his see-gyar.

43 " 'Spec' I made a bad bahgin when I bought dat nigger. Henry done good wuk all de summer, but sence de fall set in he 'pears ter be sorter pinin' away. Dey ain' nuffin pertickler de matter wid 'im—leastways de doctor say so—'cep'n' a tech er de rheumatiz; but his ha'r is all fell out, en ef he don't pick up his strenk mighty soon, I spec' I 'm gwine ter lose 'im.'

44 "Dey smoked on awhile, en bimeby ole mars say, 'Well, a bahgin 's a bahgin, but you en me is good fren's, en I doan wan' ter see you lose all de money you paid fer dat nigger; en ef w'at you say is so, en I ain't 'sputin' it, he ain't wuf much now. I 'spec's you wukked him too ha'd dis summer, er e'se de swamps down here don't agree wid de san'-hill nigger. So you des lemme know, en ef he gits any wusser I'll be willin' ter gib yer five hund'ed dollars fer 'im, en take my chances on his livin'.'

45 "Sho 'nuff, when Henry begun ter draw up wid de rheumatiz en it look like he gwine ter die fer sho, his noo marster sen' fer Mars Dugal', en Mars Dugal' gin him what he promus, en brung Henry home ag'in. He tuk good keer uv 'im dyoin' er de winter,—give 'im w'iskey ter rub his rheumatiz, en terbacker ter smoke, en all he want ter eat,—'caze a nigger w'at he could make a thousan' dollars a year off'n did n' grow on eve'y huckleberry bush.

46 "Nex' spring, w'en de sap ris en Henry's ha'r commence' ter sprout, Mars Dugal' sole 'im ag'in, down in Robeson County dis time; en he kep' dat sellin' business up fer five year er mo'. Henry nebber say nuffin 'bout de goopher ter his noo marsters, 'caze he know he gwine ter be tuk good keer uv de nex' winter, w'en Mars Dugal' buy him back. En Mars Dugal' made 'nuff money off'n Henry ter buy anudder plantation ober on Beaver Crick.

47 "But 'long 'bout de een' er dat five year dey come a stranger ter stop at de plantation. De fus' day he 'uz dere he went out wid Mars Dugal' en spent all de mawnin' lookin' ober de vimya'd, en atter dinner dey spent all de evenin' playin' kya'ds. De niggers soon 'skiver' dat he wuz a Yankee, en dat he come down ter Norf C'lina fer ter l'arn de w'ite folks how to raise grapes en make wine. He promus Mars Dugal' he c'd make de grapevimes b'ar twice't ez many grapes, en dat de noo winepress he wuz a-sellin' would make mo' d'n twice't ez many gallons er wine. En ole Mars Dugal' des drunk it all in, des 'peared ter be bewitch' wid dat Yankee. W'en de darkies see dat Yankee runnin' 'roun' de vimya'd en diggin' under de grapevimes, dey

shuk dere heads, en 'lowed dat dey feared Mars Dugal' losin' his min'.
Mars Dugal' had all de dirt dug away fum under de roots er all de
scuppernon' vimes, an' let 'em stan' dat away fer a week er mo'.
Den dat Yankee made de niggers fix up a mixtry er lime en ashes en
manyo, en po' it 'roun' de roots er de grapevimes. Den he 'vise Mars
Dugal' fer ter trim de vimes close't, en Mars Dugal' tuck 'n done
eve'ything de Yankee tole him ter do. Dyoin' all er dis time, mind yer,
dis yer Yankee wuz libbin' off'n de fat er de lan', at de big house,
en playin' kya'ds wid Mars Dugal' eve'y night; en dey say Mars Dugal'
los' mo'n a thousan' dollars dyoin' er de week dat Yankee wuz a-
ruinin' de grapevimes.

48 "W'en de sap ris nex' spring, ole Henry 'n'inted his head ez yuzhal,
en his ha'r 'mence' ter grow des de same ez it done eve'y year. De
scuppernon' vimes growed monst's fas', en de leaves wuz greener en
thicker dan dey eber be'n dyoin' my remem'ance; en Henry's ha'r
growed out thicker dan eber, en he 'peared ter git younger 'n younger,
en soopler 'n soopler; en seein' ez he wuz sho't er han's dat spring,
havin' tuk in consid'able noo groun', Mars Dugal' 'cluded he would
n' sell Henry 'tel he git de crap in en de cotton chop'. So he kep' Henry
on de plantation.

49 "But 'long 'bout time fer de grapes ter come on de scuppernon'
vimes, dey 'peared ter come a change ober 'em; de leaves withered en swivel' up, en de young grapes turn' yaller, en bimeby
eve'ybody on de plantation could see dat de whole vimya'd wuz
dyin'. Mars Dugal' tuk'n water de vimes en done all he could, but
't wa'n' no use: dat Yankee had done bus' de watermillyum. One
time de vimes picked up a bit, en Mars Dugal' 'lowed dey wuz
gwine ter come out ag'in; but dat Yankee done dug too close under
de roots, en prune de branches too close ter de vime, en all dat lime
en ashes done burn' de life out'n de vimes, en dey des kep' a-with-
'in' en a-swivelin'.

50 "All dis time de goopher wuz a-wuk-kin'. When de vimes sta'ted
ter wither, Henry 'mence' ter complain er his rheumatiz; en when
de leaves begin ter dry up, his ha'r 'mence' ter drap out. When de
vimes fresh' up a bit, Henry 'd git peart ag'in, en when de vimes
wither' ag'in, Henry 'd git ole ag'in, en des kep' gittin' mo' en mo' fit-
ten fer nuffin; he des pined away, en pined away, en fine'ly tuk ter his
cabin; en when de big vime whar he got de sap ter 'n'int his head
withered en turned yaller en died, Henry died too, — des went out
sorter like a cannel. Dey did n't 'pear ter be nuffin de matter wid
'im, 'cep'n' de rheumatiz, but his strenk des dwinel' away 'tel he did

n' hab ernuff lef' ter draw his bref. De goopher had got de under holt, en th'owed Henry dat time fer good en all.

51   "Mars Dugal' tuk on might'ly 'bout losin' his vimes en his nigger in de same year; en he swo' dat ef he could git holt er dat Yankee he'd wear 'im ter a frazzle, en den chaw up de frazzle; en he'd done it, too, for Mars Dugal' 'uz a monst'us brash man w'en he once git started. He sot de vimya'd out ober ag'in, but it wuz th'ee er fo' year befo' de vimes got ter b'arin' any scuppernon's.

52   "W'en de wah broke out, Mars Dugal' raise' a comp'ny, en went off ter fight de Yankees. He say he wuz mighty glad dat wah come, en he des want ter kill a Yankee fer eve'y dollar he los' 'long er dat grape-raisin' Yankee. En I 'spec' he would 'a' done it, too, ef de Yankees had n' s'picioned sump'n, en killed him fus'. Atter de s'render ole miss move' ter town, de niggers all scattered 'way fum de plantation, en de vimya'd ain' be'n cultervated sence."

53   "Is that story true?" asked Annie doubtfully, but seriously, as the old man concluded his narrative.

54   "It's des ez true ez I'm a-settin' here, miss. Dey's a easy way ter prove it : I kin lead de way right ter Henry's grave ober yander in de plantation bury-in'-groun'. En I tell yer w'at, marster, I would n' 'vise you to buy dis yer ole vimya'd, 'caze de goopher's on it yit, en dey ain' no tellin' w'en it's gwine ter crap out."

55   "But I thought you said all the old vines died."

56   "Dey did 'pear ter die, but a few un 'em come out ag'in, en is mixed in 'mongs' de yuthers. I ain' skeered ter eat de grapes, 'caze I knows de old vimes fum de noo ones; but wid strangers dey ain' no tellin' w'at mought happen. I would n' 'vise yer ter buy dis vimya'd."

57   I bought the vineyard, nevertheless, and it has been for a long time in a thriving condition, and is often referred to by the local press as a striking illustration of the opportunities open to Northern capital in the development of Southern industries. The luscious scuppernong holds first rank among our grapes, though we cultivate a great many other varieties, and our income from grapes packed and shipped to the Northern markets is quite considerable. I have not noticed any developments of the goopher in the vineyard, although I have a mild suspicion that our colored assistants do not suffer from want of grapes during the season.

58   I found, when I bought the vineyard, that Uncle Julius had occupied a cabin on the place for many years, and derived a respectable revenue from the product of the neglected grapevines. This, doubtless, accounted for his advice to me not to buy the vineyard, though

whether it inspired the goopher story I am unable to state. I believe, however, that the wages I paid him for his services as coachman, for I gave him employment in that capacity, were more than an equivalent for anything he lost by the sale of the vineyard.

Po' Sandy

1   On the northeast corner of my vineyard in central North Carolina, and fronting on the Lumberton plank-road, there stood a small frame house, of the simplest construction. It was built of pine lumber, and contained but one room, to which one window gave light and one door admission. Its weather-beaten sides revealed a virgin innocence of paint. Against one end of the house, and occupying half its width, there stood a huge brick chimney: the crumbling mortar had left large cracks between the bricks; the bricks themselves had begun to scale off in large flakes, leaving the chimney sprinkled with unsightly blotches. These evidences of decay were but partially concealed by a creeping vine, which extended its slender branches hither and thither in an ambitious but futile attempt to cover the whole chimney. The wooden shutter, which had once protected the unglazed window, had fallen from its hinges, and lay rotting in the rank grass and jimson-weeds beneath. This building, I learned when I bought the place, had been used as a schoolhouse for several years prior to the breaking out of the war, since which time it had remained unoccupied, save when some stray cow or vagrant hog had sought shelter within its walls from the chill rains and nipping winds of winter.

2   One day my wife requested me to build her a new kitchen. The house erected by us, when we first came to live upon the vineyard, contained a very conveniently arranged kitchen; but for some occult reason my wife wanted a kitchen in the back yard, apart from the dwelling-house, after the usual Southern fashion. Of course I had to build it.

3   To save expense, I decided to tear down the old schoolhouse, and use the lumber, which was in a good state of preservation, in the construction of the new kitchen. Before demolishing the old house, however, I made an estimate of the amount of material contained in it, and found that I would have to buy several hundred feet of lumber additional, in order to build the new kitchen according to my wife's plan.

4   One morning old Julius McAdoo, our colored coachman, harnessed the gray mare to the rockaway, and drove my wife and me over to the sawmill from which I meant to order the new lumber. We drove down the long lane which led from our house to the plank-road; following the plank-road for about a mile, we turned into a road running through the forest and across the swamp to the sawmill beyond. Our carriage jolted over the half-rotted corduroy road which traversed the swamp, and then climbed the long hill leading to the sawmill. When we reached the mill, the foreman had gone over to a neighboring farmhouse, probably to smoke or gossip, and we were compelled to await his return before we could transact our business. We remained seated in the carriage, a few rods from the mill, and watched the leisurely movements of the mill-hands. We had not waited long before a huge pine log was placed in position, the machinery of the mill was set in motion, and the circular saw began to eat its way through the log, with a loud whir which resounded throughout the vicinity of the mill. The sound rose and fell in a sort of rhythmic cadence, which, heard from where we sat, was not unpleasing, and not loud enough to prevent conversation. When the saw started on its second journey through the log, Julius observed, in a lugubrious tone, and with a perceptible shudder:—

5   "Ugh! but dat des do cuddle my blood!"

6   "What's the matter, Uncle Julius?" inquired my wife, who is of a very sympathetic turn of mind. "Does the noise affect your nerves?"

7   "No, Mis' Annie," replied the old man, with emotion, "I ain' narvous; but dat saw, a-cuttin' en grindin' thoo dat stick er timber, en moanin', en groanin,' en sweekin', kyars my 'memb'ance back ter ole times, en 'min's me er po' Sandy." The pathetic intonation with which he lengthened out the "po' Sandy" touched a responsive chord in our own hearts.

8   "And who was poor Sandy?" asked my wife, who takes a deep interest in the stories of plantation life which she hears from the lips of the older colored people. Some of these stories are quaintly humorous; others wildly extravagant, revealing the Oriental cast of the negro's imagination; while others, poured freely into the sympathetic ear of a Northern-bred woman, disclose many a tragic incident of the darker side of slavery.

9   "Sandy," said Julius, in reply to my wife's question, "was a nigger w'at useter b'long ter ole Mars Marrabo Mc-Swayne. Mars Marrabo's place wuz on de yuther side'n de swamp, right nex' ter yo' place. Sandy wuz a monst'us good nigger, en could do so many

things erbout a plantation, en alluz 'ten' ter his wuk so well, dat
w'en Mars Marrabo's chilluns growed up en married off, dey all un
'em wanted dey daddy fer ter gin 'em Sandy fer a weddin' present.
But Mars Marrabo knowed de res' would n' be satisfied ef he gin
Sandy ter a'er one un 'em; so w'en dey wuz all done married, he fix
it by 'lowin' one er his chilluns ter take Sandy fer a mont' er so, en
den ernudder for a mont' er so, en so on dat erway tel dey had all had
'im de same lenk er time; en den dey would all take him roun' ag'in,
'cep'n' oncet in a w'ile w'en Mars Marrabo would len' 'im ter some
er his yuther kinfolks 'roun' de country, w'en dey wuz short er han's;
tel bimeby it go so Sandy did n' hardly knowed whar he wuz gwine
ter stay fum one week's een' ter de yuther.

10   "One time w'en Sandy wuz lent out ez yushal, a spekilater come
erlong wid a lot er niggers, en Mars Marrabo swap' Sandy's wife off
fer a noo 'oman. W'en Sandy come back, Mars Marrabo gin 'im a dollar, en 'lowed he wuz monst'us sorry fer ter break up de fambly, but
de spekilater had gin 'im big boot, en times wuz hard en money skase,
en so he wuz bleedst ter make de trade. Sandy tuk on some 'bout
losin' his wife, but he soon seed dey want no use cryin' ober spilt mer-
lasses; en bein' ez he lacked de looks er de noo 'oman, he tuk up
wid her atter she'd be'n on de plantation a mont' er so.

11   "Sandy en his noo wife got on mighty well tergedder, en de niggers all 'mence' ter talk about how lovin' dey wuz. W'en Tenie wuz
tuk sick oncet, Sandy useter set up all night wid 'er, en den go ter wuk
in de mawnin' des lack he had his reg'lar sleep; en Tenie would 'a'
done anythin' in de worl' for her Sandy.

12   "Sandy en Tenie had n' be'n libbin' tergedder fer mo' d'n two
mont's befo' Mars Marrabo's old uncle, w'at libbed down in Robeson County, sent up ter fin' out ef Mars Marrabo could n' len' 'im
er hire 'im a good han' fer a mont' er so. Sandy's marster wuz one
er dese yer easy-gwine folks w'at wanter please eve'ybody, en he says
yas, he could len' 'im Sandy. En Mars Marrabo tol' Sandy fer ter git
ready ter go down ter Robeson nex' day, fer ter stay a mont' er so.

13   "It wuz monst'us hard on Sandy fer ter take 'im 'way fum Tenie.
It wuz so fur down ter Robeson dat he did n' hab no chance er comin'
back ter see her tel de time wuz up; he would n' 'a' mine comin' ten
er fifteen mile at night ter see Tenie, but Mars Marrabo's uncle's plantation wuz mo' d'n forty mile off. Sandy wuz mighty sad en cas' down
atter w'at Mars Marrabo tol' 'im, en he says ter Tenie, sezee:—

14   " 'I'm gittin' monst'us ti'ed er dish yer gwine roun' so much. Here
I is lent ter Mars Jeems dis mont', en I got ter do so-en-so; en ter Mars

Archie de nex' mont', en I got ter do so-en-so; den I got ter go ter Miss Jinnie's: en hit's Sandy dis en Sandy dat, en Sandy yer en Sandy dere, tel it 'pears ter me I ain' got no home, ner no marster, ner no mistiss, ner no nuffin. I can't eben keep a wife: my yuther ole 'oman wuz sol' away widout my gittin' a chance fer ter tell her good-by; en now I got ter go off en leab you, Tenie, en I dunno whe'r I'm eber gwine ter see you ag'in er no. I wisht I wuz a tree, er a stump, er a rock, er sump'n w'at could stay on de plantation fer a w'ile.'

15   "Atter Sandy got thoo talkin', Tenie did n' say naer word, but des sot dere by de fier, studyin' en studyin'. Bimeby she up'n' says:—

16   " 'Sandy, is I eber tol' you I wuz a cunjuh 'oman?'

17   "Co'se Sandy had n' nebber dremp' er nuffin lack dat, en he made a great 'miration w'en he hear w'at Tenie say. Bimeby Tenie went on:—

18   " 'I ain' goophered nobody, ner done no cunjuh wuk, fer fifteen year er mo'; en w'en I got religion I made up my mine I would n' wuk no mo' goopher. But dey is some things I doan b'lieve it's no sin fer ter do; en ef you doan wanter be sent roun' fum pillar ter pos', en ef you doan wanter go down ter Robeson, I kin fix things so you won't haf ter. Ef you'll des say de word, I kin turn you ter w'ateber you wanter be, en you kin stay right whar you wanter, ez long ez you mineter.'

19   "Sandy say he doan keer; he's will-in' fer ter do anythin' fer ter stay close ter Tenie. Den Tenie ax 'im ef he doan wanter be turnt inter a rabbit.

20   "Sandy say, 'No, de dogs mought git atter me.'

21   " 'Shill I turn you ter a wolf?' sez Tenie.

22   " 'No, eve'ybody's skeered er a wolf, en I doan want nobody ter be skeered er me.'

23   " 'Shill I turn you ter a mawkin'-bird?'

24   " 'No, a hawk mought ketch me. I wanter be turnt inter sump'n w'at 'll stay in one place.'

25   " 'I kin turn you ter a tree,' sez Tenie. 'You won't hab no mouf ner years, but I kin turn you back oncet in a w'ile, so you kin git sump'n ter eat, en hear w'at 's gwine on.'

26   "Well, Sandy say dat 'll do. En so Tenie tuk 'im down by de aidge er de swamp, not fur fum de quarters, en turnt 'im inter a big pine-tree, en sot 'im out 'mongs' some yuther trees. En de nex' mawnin', ez some er de fiel' han's wuz gwine long dere, dey seed a tree w'at dey did n' 'member er habbin' seed befo'; it wuz monst'us quare, en dey wuz bleedst ter 'low dat dey had n' 'membered right, er e'se one er de saplin's had be'n growin' monst'us fas'.

27 "W'en Mars Marrabo 'skiver' dat Sandy wuz gone, he 'lowed Sandy had runned away. He got de dogs out, but de las' place dey could track Sandy ter wuz de foot er dat pine-tree. En dere de dogs stood en barked, en bayed, en pawed at de tree, en tried ter climb up on it; en w'en dey wuz tuk roun' thoo de swamp ter look fer de scent, dey broke loose en made fer dat tree ag'in. It wuz de beat-enis' thing de w'ite folks eber hearn of, en Mars Marrabo 'lowed dat Sandy must 'a' clim' up on de tree en jump' off on a mule er sump'n, en rid fur ernuff fer ter spile de scent. Mars Marrabo wanted ter 'cuse some er de yuther niggers er heppin' Sandy off, but dey all 'nied it ter de las'; en eve'ybody knowed Tenie sot too much sto' by Sandy fer ter he'p 'im run away whar she could n' nebber see 'im no mo'.

28 "W'en Sandy had be'n gone long ernuff fer folks ter think he done got clean away, Tenie useter go down ter de woods at night en turn 'im back, en den dey 'd slip up ter de cabin en set by de fire en talk. But dey ha' ter be monst'us keerful, er e'se somebody would 'a' seed 'em, en dat would 'a' spile' de whole thing; so Tenie alluz turnt Sandy back in de mawnin' early, befo' anybody wuz a-stirrin'.

29 "But Sandy did n' git erlong widout his trials en tribberlations. One day a woodpecker come erlong en 'mence' ter peck at de tree; en de nex' time Sandy wuz turnt back he had a little roun' hole in his arm, des lack a sharp stick be'n stuck in it. Atter dat Tenie sot a sparrer-hawk fer ter watch de tree; en w'en de woodpecker come erlong nex' mawnin' fer ter finish his nes', he got gobble' up mos''fo' he stuck his bill in de bark.

30 "Nudder time, Mars Marrabo sent a nigger out in de woods fer ter chop tuppentime boxes. De man chop a box in dish yer tree, en hack' de bark up two er th'ee feet, fer ter let de tuppentime run. De nex' time Sandy wuz turnt back he had a big skyar on his lef' leg, des lack it be'n skunt; en it tuk Tenie nigh 'bout all night fer ter fix a mix-try ter kyo it up. Atter dat, Tenie sot a hawnet fer ter watch de tree; en w'en de nigger come back ag'in fer ter cut ernudder box on de yuther side'n de tree, de hawnet stung 'im so hard dat de ax slip en cut his foot nigh 'bout off.

31 "W'en Tenie see so many things happenin' ter de tree, she 'cluded she 'd ha' ter turn Sandy ter sump'n e'se; en atter studyin' de mat-ter ober, en talkin' wid Sandy one ebenin', she made up her mine fer ter fix up a goopher mixtry w'at would turn herse'f en Sandy ter foxes, er sump'n, so dey could run away en go some'rs whar dey could be free en lib lack w'ite folks.

32   "But dey ain' no tellin' w'at 's gwine ter happen in dis worl'. Tenie
had got de night sot fer her en Sandy ter run away, w'en dat ve'y
day one er Mars Marrabo's sons rid up ter de big house in his buggy,
en say his wife wuz monst'us sick, en he want his mammy ter len' 'im
a 'oman fer ter nuss his wife. Tenie's mistiss say sen' Tenie; she wuz
a good nuss. Young mars wuz in a tarrible hurry fer ter git back home.
Tenie wuz washin' at de big house dat day, en her mistiss say she
should go right 'long wid her young marster. Tenie tried ter make
some 'scuse fer ter git away en hide 'tel night, w'en she would have
eve'ything fix' up fer her en Sandy; she say she wanter go ter her
cabin fer ter git her bonnet. Her mistiss say it doan matter 'bout de
bonnet; her head-hank-cher wuz good ernuff. Den Tenie say she wanter git her bes' frock; her mistiss say no, she doan need no mo' frock,
en w'en dat one got dirty she could git a clean one whar she wuz
gwine. So Tenie had ter git in de buggy en go 'long wid young Mars
Dunkin ter his plantation, w'ich wuz mo' d'n twenty mile away; en
dey wa'n't no chance er her seein' Sandy no mo' 'tel she come back
home. De po' gal felt monst'us bad 'bout de way things wuz gwine
on, en she knowed Sandy mus' be a wond'rin' why she did n' come
en turn 'im back no mo'.

33   "W'iles Tenie wuz away nussin' young Mars Dunkin's wife, Mars
Marrabo tuk a notion fer ter buil' 'im a noo kitchen; en bein' ez
he had lots er timber on his place, he begun ter look 'roun' fer a
tree ter hab de lumber sawed out'n. En I dunno how it come to
be so, but he happen fer ter hit on de ve'y tree w'at Sandy wuz turnt
inter. Tenie wuz gone, en dey wa'n't nobody ner nuffin fer ter watch
de tree.

34   "De two men w'at cut de tree down say dey nebber had sech a time
wid a tree befo': dey axes would glansh off, en did n' 'pear ter make
no progress thoo de wood; en of all de creakin', en shakin', en wob-
blin' you eber see, dat tree done it w'en it commence' ter fall. It wuz
de beatenis' thing!

35   "W'en dey got de tree all trim' up, dey chain it up ter a timber
waggin, en start fer de sawmill. But dey had a hard time gittin' de log
dere: fus' dey got stuck in de mud w'en dey wuz gwine crosst de
swamp, en it wuz two er th'ee hours befo' dey could git out. W'en dey
start' on ag'in, de chain kep' a-comin' loose, en dey had ter keep a-
stoppin' en a-stoppin' fer ter hitch de log up ag'in. W'en dey commence' ter climb de hill ter de sawmill, de log broke loose, en roll
down de hill en in 'mongs' de trees, en hit tuk nigh 'bout half a day
mo' ter git it haul' up ter de sawmill.

36   "De nex' mawnin' atter de day de tree wuz haul' ter de sawmill, Tenie come home. W'en she got back ter her cabin, de fus' thing she done wuz ter run down ter de woods en see how Sandy wuz gittin' on. W'en she seed de stump standin' dere, wid de sap runnin' out'n it, en de limbs layin' scattered roun', she nigh 'bout went out'n her min'. She run ter her cabin, en got her goopher mixtry, en den follered de track er de timber waggin ter de sawmill. She knowed Sandy could n'lib mo' d'n a minute er so ef she turnt him back, fer he wuz all chop' up so he 'd 'a' be'n bleedst ter die. But she wanted ter turn 'im back long ernuff fer ter 'splain ter 'im dat she had n' went off a-purpose, en lef' 'im ter be chop' down en sawed up. She did n' want Sandy ter die wid no hard feelin's to'ds her.

37   "De han's at de sawmill had des got de big log on de kerridge, en wuz startin' up de saw, w'en dey seed a 'oman runnin' up de hill, all out er bref, cryin' en gwine on des lack she wuz plumb 'stracted. It wuz Tenie; she come right inter de mill, en th'owed herse'f on de log, right in front er de saw, a-hollerin' en cryin' ter her Sandy ter fergib her, en not ter think hard er her, fer it wa'n't no fault er hern. Den Tenie 'membered de tree did n' hab no years, en she wuz gittin' ready fer ter wuk her goopher mixtry so ez ter turn Sandy back, w'en de mill-hands kotch holt er her en tied her arms wid a rope, en fasten' her to one er de posts in de sawmill; en den dey started de saw up ag'in, en cut de log up inter bo'ds en scantlin's right befo' her eyes. But it wuz mighty hard wuk; fer of all de sweekin', en moanin', en groanin', dat log done it w'iles de saw wuz a-cuttin' thoo it. De saw wuz one er dese yer ole-timey, up-en-down saws, en hit tuk longer dem days ter saw a log 'en it do now. Dey greased de saw, but dat did n' stop de fuss; hit kep' right on, tel fin'ly dey got de log all sawed up.

38   "W'en de oberseah w'at run de sawmill come fum breakfas', de han's up en tell him 'bout de crazy 'oman—ez dey s'posed she wuz— w'at had come runnin' in de sawmill, a-hollerin' en gwine on, en tried ter th'ow herse'f befo' de saw. En de oberseah sent two er th'ee er de han's fer ter take Tenie back ter her marster's plantation.

39   "Tenie 'peared ter be out'n her min' fer a long time, en her marster ha' ter lock her up in de smoke-'ouse 'tel she got ober her spells. Mars Marrabo wuz monst'us mad, en hit would 'a' made yo' flesh crawl fer ter hear him cuss, 'caze he say de spekilater w'at he got Tenie fum had fooled 'im by wukkin' a crazy 'oman off on him. W'iles Tenie wuz lock up in de smoke-'ouse, Mars Marrabo tuk 'n' haul de lumber fum de sawmill, en put up his noo kitchen.

40   "W'en Tenie got quiet' down, so she could be 'lowed ter go 'roun' de plantation, she up'n' tole her marster all erbout Sandy en de pine-tree; en w'en Mars Marrabo hearn it, he 'lowed she wuz de wuss 'stracted nigger he eber hearn of. He did n' know w'at ter do wid Tenie: fus' he thought he 'd put her in de po'-house; but fin'ly, seein' ez she did n' do no harm ter nobody ner nuffin, but des went 'roun' moanin', en groanin', en shakin' her head, he 'cluded ter let her stay on de plantation en nuss de little nigger chilluns w'en dey mammies wuz ter wuk in de cotton-fiel'.

41   "De noo kitchen Mars Marrabo buil' wuz n' much use, fer it had n' be'n put up long befo' de niggers 'mence' ter notice quare things erbout it. Dey could hear sump'n moanin' en groanin' 'bout de kitchen in de night-time, en w'en de win' would blow dey could hear sump'n a-hollerin' en sweekin' lack it wuz in great pain en sufferin'. En it got so atter a w'ile dat it wuz all Mars Marrabo's wife could do ter git a 'oman ter stay in de kitchen in de daytime long ernuff ter do de cookin'; en dey wa'n't naer nigger on de plantation w'at would n' rudder take forty dan ter go 'bout dat kitchen atter dark,—dat is, 'cep'n' Tenie; she did n' 'pear ter min' de ha'nts. She useter slip 'roun' at night, en set on de kitchen steps, en lean up agin de do'-jamb, en run on ter herse'f wid some kine er foolishness w'at nobody could n' make out; fer Mars Marrabo had th'eaten' ter sen' her off'n de plantation ef she say anything ter any er de yuther niggers 'bout de pine-tree. But somehow er 'nudder de niggers foun' out all erbout it, en dey all knowed de kitchen wuz ha'nted by Sandy's sperrit. En bimeby hit got so Mars Marrabo's wife herse'f wuz skeered ter go out in de yard atter dark.

42   "W'en it come ter dat, Mars Marrabo tuk en to' de kitchen down, en use' de lumber fer ter buil' dat ole school'ouse w'at you er talkin' 'bout pullin' down. De school'ouse wuz n' use' 'cep'n' in de daytime, en on dark nights folks gwine 'long de road would hear quare soun's en see quare things. Po' ole Tenie useter go down dere at night, en wan-der 'roun' de school'ouse; en de niggers all 'lowed she went fer ter talk wid Sandy's sperrit. En one winter mawnin', w'en one er de boys went ter school early fer ter start de fire, w'at should he fin' but po' ole Tenie, layin' on de flo', stiff, en col', en dead. Dere did n' 'pear ter be nuffin pertickler de matter wid her,—she had des grieve' herse'f ter def fer her Sandy. Mars Marrabo did n' shed no tears. He thought Tenie wuz crazy, en dey wa'n't no tellin' w'at she mought do nex'; en dey ain' much room in dis worl' for crazy w'ite folks, let 'lone a crazy nigger.

43   "Hit wa'n't long atter dat befo' Mars Marrabo sol' a piece er his track er lan' ter Mars Dugal' McAdoo,— *my* ole marster,—en dat's how

de ole school-'ouse happen to be on yo' place. W'en de wah broke out, de school stop', en de ole school'ouse be'n stannin' empty ever sence,— dat is, 'cep'n' fer de ha'nts. En folks sez dat de ole school'ouse, er any yuther house w'at got any er dat lumber in it w'at wuz sawed out'n de tree w'at Sandy wuz turnt inter, is gwine ter be ha'nted tel de las' piece er plank is rotted en crumble' inter dus'."

44 Annie had listened to this gruesome narrative with strained attention.

45 "What a system it was," she exclaimed, when Julius had finished, "under which such things were possible!"

46 "What things?" I asked, in amazement. "Are you seriously considering the possibility of a man's being turned into a tree?"

47 "Oh, no," she replied quickly, "not that;" and then she murmured absently, and with a dim look in her fine eyes; "Poor Tenie!"

48 We ordered the lumber, and returned home. That night, after we had gone to bed, and my wife had to all appearances been sound asleep for half an hour, she startled me out of an incipient doze by exclaiming suddenly,—

49 "John, I don't believe I want my new kitchen built out of the lumber in that old schoolhouse."

50 "You would n't for a moment allow yourself," I replied, with some asperity, "to be influenced by that absurdly impossible yarn which Julius was spinning to-day?"

51 "I know the story is absurd," she replied dreamily, "and I am not so silly as to believe it. But I don't think I should ever be able to take any pleasure in that kitchen if it were built out of that lumber. Besides, I think the kitchen would look better and last longer if the lumber were all new."

52 Of course she had her way. I bought the new lumber, though not without grumbling. A week or two later I was called away from home on business. On my return, after an absence of several days, my wife remarked to me,—

53 "John, there has been a split in the Sandy Run Colored Baptist Church, on the temperance question. About half the members have come out from the main body, and set up for themselves. Uncle Julius is one of the seceders, and he came to me yesterday and asked if they might not hold their meetings in the old schoolhouse for the present."

54 "I hope you did n't let the old rascal have it," I returned, with some warmth. I had just received a bill for the new lumber I had bought.

55 "Well," she replied, "I couldn't refuse him the use of the house for so good a purpose."

56   "And I'll venture to say," I continued, "that you subscribed something toward the support of the new church?"

57   She did not attempt to deny it.

58   "What are they going to do about the ghost?" I asked, somewhat curious to know how Julius would get around this obstacle.

59   "Oh," replied Annie, "Uncle Julius says that ghosts never disturb religious worship, but that if Sandy's spirit *should* happen to stray into meeting by mistake, no doubt the preaching would do it good."

Anonymous

Railroad Bill

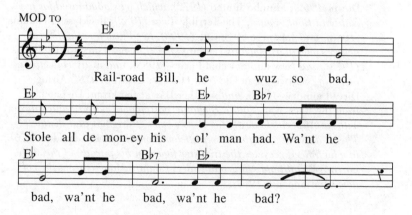

Railroad Bill, he wuz so bad,
Stole all de money his ol' man had.
Wa'nt he bad, wa'nt he bad, wa'nt he bad?

Railroad Bill, he went down Souf,
5 Shot all de teef outen a constable's mouf.
Wa'nt he bad, wa'nt he bad, wa'nt he bad?

Railroad Bill, he sot on a fence,
Called his gal a brownskin wench,
Wa'nt he bad, wa'nt he bad, wa'nt he bad?

10 Railroad Bill run his train so fas',
Couldn't see de postes as dey passed.
Wa'nt he fas', wa'nt he fas', wa'nt he fas'?

Ishmael Reed

(1938–)

On February 22, 1938, Ishmael Reed was born in Chattanooga, Tennessee, but he grew up in a working-class neighborhood in Buffalo, New York. Reed graduated from high school in 1956, then attended the University of Buffalo, without completing a degree. He joined the writing staff of an African American newspaper, Empire Star Weekly, *where he began writing pieces about the Civil Rights movement, which included an interview with Malcolm X. Shortly thereafter, Reed relocated to New York City, helping to establish an underground newspaper,* East Village Other, *and became active in the Black Arts Movement. In 1967 Reed relocated to California and published his first novel,* The Free-Lance Pallbearers, *which has been followed by numerous additional novels, including* Yellow Black Radio Broke-Down *(1969);* Mumbo Jumbo *(1972), which was nominated for a National Book Award;* The Terrible Twos *(1982);* Reckless Eyeballing *(1986); and* Japanese by Spring *(1993). Reed also has published poetry collections, such as* Conjure *(1972),* A Secretary to the Spirits *(1978), and* New and Selected Poems *(1988), and essay collections, including* Shrovetide in Old New Orleans: Essays *(1978),* Airing Dirty Laundry *(1993), and* Another Day at the Front: Dispatches from the Race War *(2003). Blending postmodern parody and satire with an Afrocentric aesthetic, Reed's voice is original and distinct. This is illustrated in the excerpt below from* Flight to Canada *(1976), in which Reed recycles the trickster figure in his parody of the slave narrative tradition. "Railroad Bill, A Conjure Man" is from the volume* Chattanooga *(1974).*

Railroad Bill, A Conjure Man

A HOODOO SUITE

Railroad Bill, a conjure man
Could change hisself to a tree
He could change hisself to a

Lake, a ram, he could be
5 What he wanted to be

When a man-hunt came he became
An old slave shouting boss
He went thataway. A toothless
Old slave standing next to a
10 Hog that laughed as they
Galloped away.
Would laugh as they galloped
Away

Railroad Bill was a conjure man
15 He could change hisself to a bird
He could change hisself to a brook
A hill he could be what he wanted
To be

One time old Bill changed hisself
20 To a dog and led a pack on his
Trail. He led the hounds around
And around. And laughed a-wagging
His tail. And laughed
A-wagging his tail

25 Morris Slater was from Escambia
County, he went to town a-toting
A rifle. When he left that
Day he was bounty.
Morris Slater was Railroad Bill
30 Morris Slater was Railroad Bill

Railroad Bill was an electrical
Man he could change hisself into
Watts. He could up his voltage
Whenever he pleased
35 He could, you bet he could
He could, you bet he could

Now look here boy hand over that
Gun, hand over it now not later
I needs my gun said Morris Slater
40 The man who was Railroad Bill

I'll shoot you dead you SOB
let me be whatever I please
The policeman persisted he just
Wouldn't listen and was buried the
45 Following eve. Was buried the
Following eve. Many dignitaries
Lots of speech-making.

Railroad Bill was a hunting man
Never had no trouble fetching game
50 He hid in the forest for those
Few years and lived like a natural
King. Whenever old Bill would
Need a new coat he'd sound out his
Friend the Panther. When Bill got
55 Tired of living off plants the
Farmers would give him some hens.
In swine-killing time the leavings of
Slaughter. They'd give Bill the
Leavings of slaughter. When he
60 needed love their fine Corinas
They'd lend old Bill their daughters

Railroad Bill was a conjure man he
Could change hisself to a song. He
Could change hisself to some blues
65 Some reds he could be what he wanted
To be

E. S. McMillan said he'd get old
Bill or turn in his silver star
Bill told the Sheriff you best
70 Leave me be said the outlaw from
Tombigbee. Leave me be warned
Bill in 1893

Down in Yellowhammer land
By the humming Chattahoochee
75 Where the cajun banjo pickers
Strum. In Keego, Volina, and
Astoreth they sing the song of
How come

Bill killed McMillan but wasn't
80 Willin rather reason than shoot
A villain. Rather reason than
Shoot McMillan

"Railroad Bill was the worst old coon
Killed McMillan by the light of the
85 *Moon*
Was lookin for Railroad Bill
Was lookin for Railroad Bill"

Railroad Bill was a gris-gris man
He could change hisself to a mask
90 A Ziba, a Zulu
A Zambia mask. A Zaramo
Doll as well
One with a necklace on it
A Zaramo doll made of wood

95 I'm bad, I'm bad said Leonard
McGowin. He'll be in hell and dead he
          Said in 1896
Shot old Bill at Tidmore's store
This was near Atmore that Bill was
100   Killed in 1896.
He was buying candy for some children
Procuring sweets for the farmers' kids

Leonard McGowin and R. C. John as
Cowardly as they come. Sneaked up
105 On Bill while he wasn't lookin.
Ambushed old Railroad Bill
Ambushed the conjure man. Shot him
In the back. Blew his head off.

Well, lawmen came from miles around
110 All smiles the lawmen came.
They'd finally got rid of
Railroad Bill who could be what
He wanted to be

Wasn't so the old folks claimed
115 From their shacks in the Wawbeek

Wood. That aint our Bill in that
old coffin, that aint our man
You killed. Our Bill is in the
Dogwood flower and in the grain
120 We eat
See that livestock grazing there
That Bull is Railroad Bill
The mean one over there near the
Fence, that one is Railroad Bill

125 Now Hollywood they's doing old
Bill they hired a teacher from
Yale. To treat and script and
Strip old Bill, this classics
Professor from Yale.
130 He'll take old Bill the conjure
Man and give him a-na-ly-sis. He'll
Put old Bill on a leather couch
And find out why he did it.
Why he stole the caboose and
135 Avoided nooses why Bill raised so
Much sand.
He'll say Bill had a complex
He'll say it was all due to Bill's
Mother. He'll be playing the
140 Dozens on Bill, this
Professor from Yale

They'll make old Bill a neurotic
Case these tycoons of the silver
Screen. They'll take their cue
145 From the teacher from Yale they
Gave the pile of green
A bicycle-riding dude from Yale
Who set Bill for the screen
Who set Bill for the screen

150 They'll shoot Bill zoom Bill and
Pan old Bill until he looks plain
Sick. Just like they did old Nat
The fox and tried to do Malik

Just like they did Jack Johnson
155 Just like they did Jack Johnson

But it wont work what these hacks
Will do, these manicured hacks from
Malibu cause the people will see
That aint our Bill but a haint of
160 The silver screen. A disembodied
Wish of a Yalie's dream

Our Bill is where the camellia
Grows and by the waterfalls. He's
Sleeping in a hundred trees and in
165 A hundred skies. That cumulus
That just went by that's Bill's
Old smiling face. He's having a joke
On Hollywood
He's on the varmint's case.

170 Railroad Bill was a wizard. And
His final trick was tame. Wasn't
Nothing to become some celluloid
And do in all the frames.
And how did he manage technology
175 And how did Bill get so modern?
He changed hisself to a production
Assistant and went to work with
The scissors.
While nobody looked he scissored
180 Old Bill he used the scissors.

Railroad Bill was a conjure man
He could change hisself to the end.
He could outwit the chase and throw
Off the scent he didn't care what
185 They sent. He didn't give a damn what
They sent.
Railroad Bill was a conjure man
Railroad Bill was a star he could change
Hisself to the sun, the moon
190 Railroad Bill was free
Railroad Bill was free

Flight to Canada

Dear Massa Swille:
What it was?
I have done my Liza Leap
& am safe in the arms
5 of Canada, so
Ain't no use your Slave
Catchers waitin on me
At Trailways
I won't be there

10 I flew in non-stop
Jumbo jet this A.M. Had
Champagne
Compliments of the Cap'n
Who announced that a
15 Runaway Negro was on the
Plane. Passengers came up
And shook my hand
& within 10 min. I had
Signed up for 3 anti-slavery
20 Lectures. Remind me to get an
Agent

Traveling in style
Beats craning your neck after
The North Star and hiding in
25 Bushes anytime, Massa
Besides, your Negro dogs
Of Hays & Allen stock can't
Fly

By now I s'pose that
30 Yellow Judas Cato done tole
You that I have snuck back to
The plantation 3 maybe 4 times
Since I left the first time

Last visit I slept in
35 Your bed and sampled your
Cellar. Had your prime

Quadroon give me
She-Bear. Yes, yes

　　You was away at a
40　Slave auction at Ryan's Mart
In Charleston & so I knowed
You wouldn't mind
Did you have a nice trip, Massa?

　　I borrowed your cotton money
45　to pay for my ticket & to get
Me started in this place called
Saskatchewan Brrrrrr!
It's cold up here but least
Nobody is collaring hobbling gagging
50　Handcuffing yoking chaining & thumbscrewing
You like you is they hobby horse

　　The Mistress Ms. Lady
Gived me the combination
To your safe, don't blame
55　The feeble old soul, Cap'n
I told her you needed some
More money to shop with &
You sent me from Charleston
To get it. Don't worry
60　Your employees won't miss
It & I accept it as a
Down payment on my back
Wages

　　I must close now
65　Massa, by the time you gets
This letter old Sam will have
Probably took you to the
Deep Six

　　That was rat poison I left
70　In your Old Crow

　　　　　　　　Your boy
　　　　　　　　Quickskill

1

1   *Little did I know when I wrote the poem "Flight to Canada" that there were so many secrets locked inside its world. It was more of a reading than a writing. Everything it said seems to have caught up with me. Other things are running away. The black in my hair is running away. The bad spirits who were in me left a long time ago. The devil who was catching up with me is slipping behind and losing ground. What a war it was!*

2   *Lincoln. Harriet Beecher Stowe. Douglass. Jeff Davis and Lee. Me, 40s, and Stray Leechfield. Robin and Judy. Princess Quaw Quaw Tralaralara. Mammy Barracuda. Cato the Graffado.* Yankee Jack. Pompey. Bangalang. It affected us all one way or the other.*

3   *"So you're the little woman who started the big war," Lincoln was supposed to have said. Received Harriet Beecher Stowe in the White House, only to have her repay his courtesy by spreading the rumor that he was illiterate. They were always spreading rumors about Lincoln. That he and his son Todd were drunks. That Mrs. Lincoln was mad. That he was a womanizer. That his mother Nancy Hanks was a slut. The Confederates said that he was a "nigger." Who is to say what is fact and what is fiction?*

4   *Old Harriet. Naughty Harriet. Accusing Lord Byron of pornography. She couldn't take to Lincoln. She liked Nobility. Curious. The woman who was credited with ruining the Planters was a toady to Nobility, just as they were. Strange, history. Complicated, too. It will always be a mystery, history. New disclosures are as bizarre as the most bizarre fantasy.*

5   *Harriet caught some of it. She popularized the American novel and introduced it to Europe.* Uncle Tom's Cabin. *Writing is strange, though. That story caught up with her. The story she "borrowed" from Josiah Henson. Harriet only wanted enough money to buy a silk dress. The paper mills ground day and night. She'd read Josiah Henson's book. That Harriet was alert.* The Life of Josiah Henson, Formerly a Slave. *Seventy-seven pages long. It was short, but it was his. It was all he had. His story. A man's story is his gris-gris, you know. Taking his story is like taking his gris-gris. The thing that is himself. It's like robbing a man of his Etheric Double. People pine away. It baffles the doctors the way some people pine away for no reason. For no reason? Somebody has made off with their Etheric Double, has crept into the hideout of themselves and taken all they*

---

*Sometimes spelled Griffado.

found there. Human hosts walk the streets of the cities, their eyes hollow, the spirit gone out of them. Somebody has taken their story.

6   *Josiah Henson went away and fell in love with wood. Nobody could take his wood. His walnut boards. He took his walnut boards to England and exhibited them at the Crystal Palace. Met the young Queen Victoria.*

7   *Nobody could take away his Dawn, his settlement in Canada.*

8   *Harriet gave Josiah credit in her* The Key to Uncle Tom's Cabin. *What was the key to her Cabin? Strange woman, that Harriet. Josiah would never have thought of waging a plot-toting suit against her. Couldn't afford one anyway. Besides, he was bad at figures. His Dawn went broke because he was trusting and bad at figures. It's unfortunate when a man's Dawn goes broke, leaving him hopeless and frustrated. When I see those two men in* The New York Times *in a booth in a fancy restaurant —two bulb-faced jaded men, sitting there, rich as Creole Candy, discussing the money they're going to make from the musical version of* Uncle Tom's Cabin, *and they have those appetizers in front of them and three kinds of wine—when I see that, and when I see their agent in* National Era *swimming in the ocean with his chow dog, I wonder why won't the spirits go out to Long Island and touch him. Touch him for what he did to Josiah Henson. Touch him like they touched Harriet.*

9   *Harriet paid. Oh yes, Harriet paid. When you take a man's story, a story that doesn't belong to you, that story will get you. Harriet made enough money on someone else's plot to buy thousands of silk dresses and a beautiful home, "One of those spacious frame mansions of bland and hospitable mien which the New England joiners knew so well how to build." A Virginia plantation in New England.*

10   *Henson had to sell Dawn, his settlement, to pay his creditors. Is there no sympathy in Nature? Dawn, that's a pretty name. Are people lost because the gods have deserted when they said they never would? They promised they never would. Are they concealing themselves to spite the mean-minded, who are too unimaginative to recognize the new forms they've given themselves? Are they rebuking us for our stupidity? They are mean and demanding. They want to be fed. But before you can feed you have to recognize. They told Josiah Henson to behave with "gentlemanly dignity." But the common people knew. Guede knew. Guede is here. Guede is in New Orleans. Guede got people to write parodies and minstrel shows about Harriet. How she made all that money. Black money. That's what they called it. The money stained her hands.*

11   *When Lord Byron came out of the grave to get her, the cartoon showed Harriet leaving her dirty stains all over Byron's immaculate and idealized white statue. Did Josiah Henson do this? The man so identified with Uncle Tom that his home in Dresden, Canada, is called Uncle Tom's Museum? Did Tom have the power the Brazilians say he has? Does he know "roots"? Umbanda.* Pretos Velhos, Pai Tomas, Pai Tomas. *The "curer." Did Tom make Byron's ghost rise out of his undead burial place of Romance and strangle Harriet's reputation, so that one biographer entitled a chapter dealing with the scandal "Catastrophe"? Do the old African and Indian gods walk the land as the old one said they would, too proud to reveal themselves to the mean-minded? The mean-minded who won't pay attention. Too hard-headed and mean-minded to see. Harriet's HooDoo book. "I was an instrument of the Lord." HooDoo writing.*

12   *Do the lords still talk? Do the lords still walk? Are they writing this book? Will they go out to Long Island and touch these men who were musing in the restaurant about the money they were going to make on the musical comedy* Uncle Tom's Cabin? *Will they get the old mummy grip?*

13   *Harriet said that Byron was fucking his sister. She said that she'd gotten it from her friend Lady Byron, who she felt had been slandered by Countess Guiccioli, Byron's last mistress and the tramp of the Tuilleries Gardens. Harriet accused Byron and his half-sister Augusta Leigh of sharing lustful embrace. Is that why Harriet, the spinster, referred to Lord Byron as a "brilliant seductive genius"? Watch what you put down on the page, Harriet. Did Harriet want to trade places with Augusta Leigh and transform Byron into her brother, Henry? History sure is complicated, or can you, like Stray Leechfield, cash your way out of history?*

14   *Why isn't Edgar Allan Poe recognized as the principal biographer of that strange war? Fiction, you say? Where does fact begin and fiction leave off? Why does the perfectly rational, in its own time, often sound like mumbo-jumbo? Where did it leave off for Poe, prophet of a civilization buried alive, where, according to witnesses, people were often whipped for no reason. No reason? Will we ever know, since there are so few traces left of the civilization the planters called "the fairest civilization the sun ever shown upon," and the slaves called "Satan's Kingdom." Poe got it all down. Poe says more in a few stories than all of the volumes by historians. Volumes about that war. The Civil War. The Spirit War. Douglass, Tubman and Bibb all believing in*

omens, consulting conjure and carrying unseen amulets on their persons. Lincoln, the American Christ, who died on Good Friday. Harriet saying that God wrote Uncle Tom's Cabin. *Which God? Some gods will mount any horse. Even the spinster schoolteacher crawling like an animal from the sightseeing bus toward an Umbanda temple with no a priori beliefs, as they say.*

15 Dressed in white planter's pants, white waistcoat and white shoes, Raven Quickskill dines alone at the end of a long white Virginia table.

16 He has just consumed a good old Southern meal of plum pudding, wild duck, oyster soup and Madeira wine, the kind of meal Kentucky generals used to sup at Jeff Davis' "white house" in Montgomery before the South was reduced to corn bread and molasses. All of the boarders had left the Castle for the weekend. All fifty of them. Craftsmen from all over the South: blacksmiths, teachers, sculptors, writers. Uncle Robin had become exultant when Quickskill first made the suggestion. He hadn't been able to figure his way out of his inheritance.

17 He and Judy traveled a lot. Now they were in the Ashanti Holy Land. Their last trip out they had brought back some serpents. They had given Quickskill the whole first floor of their Castle. It was airy and had big spacious rooms. Mountains, meadows, and the Atlantic Ocean could be seen through the windows. Quickskill would write Uncle Robin's story in such a way that, using a process the old curers used, to lay hands on the story would be lethal to the thief. That way his Uncle Robin would have the protection that Uncle Tom (Josiah Henson) didn't. (Or did he merely use another technique to avenge his story? Breathing life into Byron.)

18 Raven has the Richmond newspaper spread out in front of him. Princess Quaw Quaw has been arrested carrying a fifteen-foot balance pole, two American flags at each end, while walking on the steel cables of the Golden Gate Bridge. In the photo, crowds were hurling pellets at the officers for interfering with Quaw Quaw's act. She was beginning to become an international event, and the media speculated about her every action. She was becoming the female Blondin, a characterization she resented. "Why don't they call him the male Quaw Quaw Tralaralara?" she once protested in an interview.

19 This is not to say that she became a media bug. She insisted on her privacy and occasionally there were photos of her wandering about her husband's yacht, nude, wearing sun-glasses, as he docked off Trinidad, Majorca or Sausalito.

20   The note she had left Quickskill on the dresser of the Eagle Hotel had read merely, "Gone South," with her signature scrawled underneath.

21   He had sent a note to her in care of her agent:

> Dear Quaw Quaw Wherever or Whoever:
>   Maybe one day people of your class will realize that people of my class must grovel, worm and root our way through life fending off the bad birds so we've little time to take those we love under our wing. And that we become like mythical Goofus birds, invented by lumbermen I think, who fly backwards and build their nests upside down. We get smashed and our endings are swift.

And she wrote back:

> Dear Raven:
>   And I thought our people were bad, worshipping Bears, Turtles, Ravens, Coyotes and Eagles, but your people worship any old thing or make an "object of reverence" of just about any "new things," as in that HooDoo expression you once taught me, "Only Ghosts Hate New Things," and then that morning I saw you, in our berth, on the steamer, Lake Erie mumbling before it, the typewriter was sitting there and seemed to be crouched like a black frog with white clatter for teeth. You thought I was asleep.

22   And it went on that way until one day she signed a letter "See you soon." And that was that. She'd be back. She always came back. And they always had quarrels about "the human condition," as her Columbia Professors would say.

23   "Flight to Canada" was the problem. It made him famous but had also tracked him down. It had pointed to where he, 40s and Stray Leechfield were hiding. It was their bloodhound, this poem "Flight to Canada." It had tracked him down just as his name had. The name his mother gave him before she went away into the Fog Woman. It had dogged him. "Evil Dogs Us." Yes, indeed. His poem flew just as his name had flown. Raven. A scavenger to some, a bringer of new light to others. The one who makes war against the Ganooks of this world. As quick on his opponents as a schooner on a slaver. "Flight to Canada" had given him enough mint to live on. "Flight to Canada" had taken him all the way to the White

House, where he shook hands with Abe the Player, as history would call him.

24 He had never gotten along with Uncle Robin in slavery, but away from slavery they were the best of friends. He would try to live up to the confidence Robin had in him by writing a good book. "You put witchery on the word," Robin said. He would try to put witchery on the word.

25 Uncle Robin had turned down an offer from Jewett and Company of Boston's best-known writer and had put his story in the hands of Quickskill: "Now you be careful with my story," Robin said. "Treat that story as precious as old Swille treated his whips." They both knew what that meant.

26 Bangalang came into the room from the kitchen. She was about to leave to return to the Frederick Douglass Houses where she and her husband lived. His carriage was outside waiting for her.

27 "Is there anything else I can get for you?" she asked Quickskill.

28 "No," he said, and then, "Bangalang?"

29 "Yes, Quickskill?"

30 She had gotten a little grey. They had all gotten a little grey.

31 "Do you hear from Mammy Barracuda and Cato the Graffado?"

32 "Last I heard, she sang before the last reunion of Confederate Soldiers. They—"

33 "What happened, Bangalang?" She'd begun to laugh.

34 "She sang a chorus from 'Dixie.' Well, I have to tell you when she got to those lines that go 'Will run away—Missus took a decline, oh / Her face was de color ob bacon-rine-oh!', the old soldiers took Mammy on their shoulders and marched her out from the convention hall. Cato was leading the parade like a cheerleader, I'm telling you. Well, if you need something else, there's an apple pie in the kitchen." She turned and walked out.

35 Curious. Even in the Confederate anthem there was a belle fading away and losing her color. What was this fascination with declining belles in the South? What was the South all about? I'll have to include all of this in my story, Quickskill thought.

36 Quickskill drank his coffee. He had a swell. His belly was up again. He spent so much time in thought, he forgot about his stomach. That was the writing business all right. He'd been writing since he could remember; his "Flight to Canada" was to him what blacks were to old Abe.

37 "Abe Lincoln's last card or Rouge et Noir" was the caption under the wood engraving printed in *Punch* magazine. It showed Lincoln

beating a Confederate with his ace of spades. Inside the card's black spade was the grinning Negro. The engraving was by Sir John Tenniel, a Royalist. He'd have to write all of this in Robin's story.

38   Raven was the first one of Swille's slaves to read, the first to write and the first to run away. Master Hugh, the bane of Frederick Douglass, said, "If you give a nigger an inch, he'll take an ell. If you teach him how to read, he'll want to know how to write. And this accomplished, he'll be running away with himself."

39   Master Hugh could have taught Harriet Beecher Stowe a thing or two.

Anonymous

Stagolee
Traditional

Back in thirty-two when times was hard,
Stag had two forty-fives and a marked deck o' cards.
He had a pin-striped suit and a old messed-up hat,
He had a twenty-nine Ford and owed payments on that.
5 Stag thought he'd take a walk down on Vampire Street,
There where all them slick and ba-a-d dudes meet.
He wade through filth and he wade through mud,
He come to a crib they call the Bucket o' Blood.
He called to the bartender for something to eat.
10 Bartender gave 'im a muddly glass o' water and a stale piece o'
    meat.
He say, "Bartender, Bartender, you don't realize who I am!"
Bartender say, "Frankly speaking, Mister, I don't give damn."
But just then (the bartender hadn't realized what he had said)
Stag pumped two forty-five slugs in his mammyjamming head.
15 And in walked this ho [whore] and say, "Oh, no! Oh, no! He can't
    be dead!"
Stag say, "Then you get back there, ho, and mend them holes in
    his mammyjamming head."

In walked that bad mammyjammer they call Billy Lyons.
He say, "Where, oh, where may that bad man be?"

Stag say, "Excuse me, Mister, but my name is Stagolee."
20 Ho come up there and say, "Stag, please—"
Stag slapped that ho down to her mammyjamming knees.
And then old Slick Willie John, he turned out the lights,
And when the lights came on Billy Lyons was layin' at rest
With two of Stagolee's forty-five slugs pumped in his chest.
25 Somebody say, "Stag, oh Stag, you know that ain't right.
One o' us tell Mrs. Lyons 'bout this old fight."
Stag went to Mrs. Lyons, say, "Miz Lyons, Miz Lyons, you know
    what I've done?
I went out there and killed your last and only son."
Mrs. Lyons looked at Stag, say, "Stag, Stag, you know that can't be
    true!
30 You and Billy been good friends for the last year or two."
He say, "Look, woman, if you don't believe what I said,
Go down there and count them holes in his mammyjamming head."
And in walked the rollers [police];
They picked up Stag and carried him to court.
35 Judge told Stag, say, "Stag, I been wanting you for a long time."
Say, "I'm gon' give you twenty years."
Stag looked up at the Judge, say, "Twenty years! Twenty years
    ain't no time.
I got a brother in Sing Sing doing one ninety-nine."

And then a ho walked in and to the courtroom's surprise
40 She pulled out two long forty-fives.
Stag grabbed one and shot his way to the courtroom do',
Tipping his hat to all the ladies once mo'.

The Sinking of the *Titanic*

It was a hell of day in the merry month of May
When the great *Titanic* was sailing away.
The captain and his daughter was there too,
And old black Shine, he didn't need no crew.
5 Shine was downstairs eating his peas
When the motherfucking water come up to his knees.
He said, "Captain, Captain, I was downstairs eating my peas
When the water come up to my knees."

He said, "Shine, Shine, set your black ass down.
10 I got ninety-nine pumps to pump the water down."
Shine went downstairs looking through space.
That's when the water came up to his waist.
He said, "Captain, Captain, I was downstairs looking through space,
That's when the water came up to my waist."
15 He said, "Shine, Shine set your black ass down.
I got ninety-nine pumps to pump the water down."
Shine went downstairs, he ate a piece of bread.
That's when the water came above his head.
He said, "Captain, Captain, I was downstairs eating my bread
20 And the motherfucking water came above my head."
He said, "Shine, Shine, set your black ass down.
I got ninety-nine pumps to pump the water down."
Shine took off his shirt, took a dive. He took one stroke
And the water pushed him like it pushed a motorboat.
25 The Captain said, "Shine, Shine, save poor me.
I'll give you more money than any black man see."
Shine said, "Money is good on land or sea.
Take off your shirt and swim like me."
That's when the Captain's daughter came on deck;
30 Hands on her pussy, and drawers 'round her neck.
Says, "Shine, Shine, save poor me.
Give you more pussy than any black man see."
Shine said, "Pussy ain't nothing but meat on the bone,
You may fuck it or suck it or leave it alone.
35 I like cheese but I ain't no rat.
I like pussy, but not like that." '
And Shine swum on.
He said, "I hope you meet up with a whale."
Old Shine, he swim mighty fine.
40 Shine met up with a whale.
The whale said, "Shine, Shine, you swim mighty fine,
But if you miss one stroke, your black ass is mine."
Shine said, "You may be king of the ocean, king of the sea,
But you got to be a swimming motherfucker to outswim me."
45 And Shine swum on.
Now when the news got to the port, the great *Titanic* had sunk,
You won't believe this, but old Shine was on the corner, damn near
      drunk.

—Philadelphia

Etheridge Knight

(1931–1991)

On April 19, 1931, Etheridge Knight was born in Corinth, Mississippi. As one of seven children, Knight dropped out of school and spent his adolescence in pool halls and poker games. In this environment he became versed in the language of street poetry, which is imprinted in his published work. In 1947, Knight enlisted in the army and served in Korea, where he acquired a drug addiction. In 1960, Knight was arrested for robbery, served a prison sentence in the Indiana State Prison, and was released eight years later. He published his first volume, Poems from Prison *(1968), that year and married poet Sonia Sanchez. Shortly thereafter, Knight taught at the University of Pittsburgh, the University of Hartford, and Lincoln University. Knight received a Guggenheim Fellowship in 1974 following his second volume,* Belly Songs and Other Poems *(1973). Despite the fact that he struggled with his drug habit throughout his life, Knight was an important voice in the Black Arts Movement. The following selection is from* Poems from Prison.

I Sing of Shine

And, yeah, brothers,
while white/america sings about the unsink
able molly brown
(who was hustling the titanic
5   when it went down)
I sing to thee of Shine
the stoker who was hip
enough to flee the fucking ship
and let the white folks drown
10 with screams on their lips
jumped his black ass into the dark sea, Shine did,
broke free from the straining steel.
yeah, I sing of Shine
and how the millionaire banker stood on the deck
15 and pulled from his pocket a million dollar check
saying Shine Shine save poor me
and I'll give you all the money a black boy needs—
how Shine looked at the money and then at the sea
and said jump in muthafucka and swim like me—
20 and Shine swam on—Shine swam on—

how the banker's daughter ran naked on the deck
with her pinktits trembling and her pants roun her neck
screaming Shine Shine save poor me
and I'll give you all the cunt a black boy needs—
25 how Shine said now cunt is good and that's no jive
but you got to swim not fuck to stay alive—
then Shine swam past a preacher afloat on a board
crying save me nigger Shine in the name of the Lord—
how the preacher grabbed Shine's arm and broke his stroke—
30 how Shine pulled his shank and cut the preacher's throat—
and Shine swam on—all alone.
And when the news hit shore that the titanic had sunk
Shine was up in Harlem damn near drunk—
and dancing in the streets.
35 yeah, damn near drunk and dancing in the streets.

Anonymous

John Henry

When John Henry was a little fellow,
    You could hold him in the palm of your hand,
He said to his pa, "When I grow up
    I'm gonna be a steel-driving man.
5   Gonna be a steel-driving man."

When John Henry was a little baby,
    Setting on his mammy's knee,
He said "The Big Bend Tunnel on the C.&O. Road
    Is gonna be the death of me,
10   Gonna be the death of me."

One day his captain told him,
    How he had bet a man
That John Henry would beat his steam drill down,
    Cause John Henry was the best in the land,
15   John Henry was the best in the land.

John Henry kissed his hammer,
    White man turned on steam,

Shaker held John Henry's trusty steel,
 Was the biggest race the world had ever seen,
20 Lord, biggest race the world ever seen.

John Henry on the right side
 The steam drill on the left,
"Before I'll let your steam drill beat me down,
 I'll hammer my fool self to death,
25 Hammer my fool self to death."

John Henry walked in the tunnel,
 His captain by his side,
The mountain so tall, John Henry so small,
 He laid down his hammer and he cried,
30 Laid down his hammer and he cried.

Captain heard a mighty rumbling,
 Said "The mountain must be caving in,
John Henry said to the captain,
 "It's my hammer swinging in de wind,
35 My hammer swinging in de wind."

John Henry said to his shaker,
 "Shaker, you'd better pray;
For if ever I miss this piece of steel,
 Tomorrow'll be your burial day,
40 Tomorrow'll be your burial day."

John Henry said to his shaker,
 "Lordy, shake it while I sing,
I'm pulling my hammer from my shoulders down,
 Great Gawdamighty, how she ring,
45 Great Gawdamighty, how she ring!"

John Henry said to his captain,
 "Before I ever leave town,
Gimme one mo' drink of dat tom-cat gin,
 And I'll hammer dat steam driver down,
50 I'll hammer dat steam driver down."

John Henry said to his captain,
 "Before I ever leave town,
Gimme a twelve-pound hammer wid a whale-bone handle,
 And I'll hammer dat steam driver down,
55 I'll hammer dat steam drill on down."

John Henry said to his captain,
  "A man ain't nothin' but a man,
But before I'll let dat steam drill beat me down,
  I'll die wid my hammer in my hand,
60   Die wid my hammer in my hand."

The man that invented the steam drill
  He thought he was mighty fine,
John Henry drove down fourteen feet,
  While the steam drill only made nine,
65   Steam drill only made nine.

"Oh, lookaway over yonder, captain,
  You can't see like me,"
He gave a long and loud and lonesome cry,
  "Lawd, a hammer be the death of me,
70   A hammer be the death of me!"

John Henry had a little woman,
  Her name was Polly Ann,
John Henry took sick, she took his hammer,
  She hammered like a natural man,
75   Lawd, she hammered like a natural man.

John Henry hammering on the mountain
  As the whistle blew for half-past two,
The last words his captain heard him say,
  "I've done hammered my insides in two,
80   Lawd, I've hammered my insides in two."

The hammer that John Henry swung
  It weighed over twelve pound,
He broke a rib in his left hand side
  And his intrels fell on the ground,
85   And his intrels fell on the ground.

John Henry, O, John Henry,
  His blood is running red,
Fell right down with his hammer to the ground,
  Said, "I beat him to the bottom but I'm dead,
90   Lawd, beat him to the bottom but I'm dead."

When John Henry was laying there dying,
  The people all by his side,
The very last words they heard him say,

"Give me a cool drink of water 'fore I die,
95   Cool drink of water 'fore I die."

John Henry had a little woman,
    The dress she wore was red,
She went down the track, and she never looked back,
    Going where her man fell dead,
100   Going where her man fell dead.

John Henry had a little woman,
    The dress she wore was blue,
Do very last words she said to him,
    "John Henry, I'll be true to you,
105   John Henry, I'll be true to you."

"Who's gonna shoes yo' little feet,
    Who's gonna glove yo' hand,
Who's gonna kiss yo' pretty, pretty cheek,
    Now you done lost yo' man?
110   Now you done lost yo' man?"

"My mammy's gonna shoes my little feet,
    Pappy gonna glove my hand,
My sister's gonna kiss my pretty, pretty cheek,
    Now I done lost my man,
115   Now I done lost my man."

They carried him down by the river,
    And buried him in the sand,
And everybody that passed that way,
    Said, "There lies that steel-driving man,
120   There lies a steel-driving man."

They took John Henry to the river,
    And buried him in the sand,
And every locomotive come a-roaring by,
    Says "There lies that steel-drivin' man,
125   Lawd, there lies a *steel*-drivin' man."

Some say he came from Georgia,
    And some from Alabam,
But it's wrote on the rock at the Big Bend Tunnel,
    That he was an East Virginia man,
130   Lord, Lord, an East Virginia man.

Melvin Tolson
(1898–1966)

Melvin B. Tolson was born February 6, 1898, in Moberly, Missouri. Tolson, who lived in many small Midwestern towns, briefly attended Fisk University, graduated from Lincoln University in Pennsylvania in 1923, and shortly thereafter took a teaching position at Wiley College in Texas. While on sabbatical from Wiley College, Tolson received his master's degree in comparative literature from Columbia University, where he met prominent Harlem Renaissance figures. This experience was instrumental in Tolson's writing career; he wrote his master's thesis on the Harlem Renaissance and began Harlem Gallery *a poetry collection published in 1965. His first major poem, "Dark Symphony," won the 1939 national poetry contest sponsored by the Chicago American Negro Exposition. This poem was included in Tolson's first published collection,* Rendezvous with America *(1944), which was well reviewed. Many of his novels and plays written during this period have yet to be published or are lost altogether. In 1947, Tolson left Wiley College for a teaching position at Langston University in Oklahoma, and he was named the poet laureate of Liberia. For Liberia's centennial celebration in 1956, Tolson wrote his most impressive work,* Libretto for the Republic of Liberia, *an eight-section, modernist epic poem, for which he is best known.*

The Birth of John Henry

The night John Henry is born an ax
    of lightning splits the sky,
and a hammer of thunder pounds the earth,
    and the eagles and panthers cry!

5   John Henry—he says to his Ma and Pa:
        "Get a gallon of barleycorn.
    I want to start right, like a he-man child,
        the night that I am born!"

Says: "I want some ham hocks, ribs, and jowls,
10   a pot of cabbage and greens;
    some hoecakes, jam, and buttermilk,
        a platter of pork and beans!"

John Henry's Ma—she wrings her hands,
    and his Pa—he scratches his head.

15   John Henry—he curses in giraffe-tall words,
       flops over, and kicks down the bed.

    He's burning mad, like a bear on fire—
       so he tears to the riverside.
As he stoops to drink, Old Man River gets scared
20   and runs upstream to hide!

    Some say he was born in Georgia—O Lord!
       Some say in Alabam.
But it's writ on the rock at the Big Bend Tunnel:
    "Lousyana was my home. So scram!"

Colson Whitehead

(1969–)

Born in New York City in 1969, Colson Whitehead received his BA in 1991 from Harvard University. Prior to the publication of his first novel, he worked for several years as a freelance journalist and as a television critic for The Village Voice. *His acclaimed first novel,* The Intuitionist *(1998), a racial allegory that has been compared to Toni Morrison's* The Bluest Eye *and Ralph Ellison's* Invisible Man, *was an Ernest Hemingway/PEN Award finalist. His second novel,* John Henry Days *(2001), excerpted below, centers around the unveiling of a commemorative stamp to honor this immortal folk hero. Whitehead, who writes novels of extraordinary scope, takes on history, myth, popular culture, and racism as he satirizes the American landscape. Winner of a 2002 MacArthur Fellowship, Whitehead currently lives in Brooklyn, New York.*

John Henry Days

1 Yes, her father would have loved it and probably would have stormed the microphone to make a speech. And perhaps they would have let him speak. First the mayor, then the man from the Post Office, and then her father takes the podium to deliver a few remarks. She's heard each sentence before, ten years before or fifteen years, he stitches the stiff threads of ancient and favorite rants into one bitter shroud for John Henry the man and his times. He runs over the allotted

time and people shift in their seats, strangling the necks of napkin birds in their laps. Mr. Street has not even approached his point, whatever that may be. One or two repeated sentences, the blurred edges of phrases make the people wonder if he is drunk and they listen more closely following this lapse—is he drunk or crazy. Obviously he feels for John Henry keenly but there is a pace to the night, when they will drink and when they will eat and who will speak and that boy at the end who will sing. The mayor wonders if they need this man's collection of artifacts as much as he thought they did. Maybe they can hire someone to make things out of plaster and call them replicas of the genuine article. The tourists will have already paid their entrance fee and tourists never feel completely ripped off at tourist places, no matter how much they have been misled. The tourists are glad to be out of the house, and the real is so hard to come by these days, they understand and expect these deceptions. Maybe if the kitchen staff brings out the food, the guests will slowly get up to get something to eat, and Mr. Street will get the message.

2   Pamela sits in a plastic chair outside her motel room, legs crossed, right hand cupping her left elbow, expelling colonies of smoke from her mouth at regular intervals. The smoke lights out into the dark lands and swirls away by forces into diasporic scattering. She looks down into the foiled maw of her pack and counts the cigarettes, placing her nervousness and resulting hunger for smokes on one hand, and the dwindling number of smokes and her imprisonment at the hotel on the other hand. She is stuck at the hotel until morning, which would be fine if she were sleeping. But she can't sleep, even though she turned the picture of John Henry walking down railroad tracks to face the wall. Rather than making her feel at home—her parents' house had been crammed with mawkish pictures like that—the motel picture bullied her into ruinous confessions. She dragged a chair from the empty pool and sits outside her door, smoking, sometimes watching the crackling blue death of insects in the coils of the bug trap, sometimes watching her cigarette tip wither to ash. Sometimes the face of the choking man at dinner creeps up, his thrashing body and bulging eyes, and she shivers.

3   Talcott. She had heard the name thousands of times over the years, her father shaping the name as paradise or proving ground or just another town on a map depending on his mood. How far is she from the town itself? She still hasn't seen it. The Motor Lodge is on the outskirts and the Millhouse Inn is part of the town of Pipestem. The black laborers on the C&O weren't allowed in town,

she remembers that factoid from her father's sermons, they lived in shanties near the work camps and were allowed into town only for one hour on Friday afternoons to buy supplies. She wondered if any of their shanty town remained, and if it was part of the weekend's festivities. Take a walk through John Henry Town! Here's the man's very own lean-to, notice the spaces between planks allowing nice cross-ventilation in the summertime, and the tar-paper roof protecting a full 35 percent of the abode from the rain and snow. No, it isn't here. If it were, her father would have put it on a flatbed and driven it up to their apartment as part of his collection. Probably would have slept in it too, poured some scotch into a clay jar and sat inside there at night, tapping his foot to some old work song and sipping from the jug of 'shine. Where they lived after they walked away from the plantations, pieces of paper signed by a magistrate in their hands, to trade tobacco and cotton for the currency of the industrial South. Coal and steel. And layin' the line.

4   *Layin' the line*, out of her father's mouth, became this all-purpose non sequitur that testified to balance in the world, whether the matter be existential or quotidian. Stub a toe? Layin' the line. Passing grades in chemistry? Layin' the line. Summer heartbreak, a backed-up toilet, walking pneumonia, winning three bucks in Lotto. Layin' the line, girl. You were layin' the line whatever you did, trudging through dust until you returned to it.

5   It began, like most obsessions, as a harmless interest. She was six, her family returning from Delaware from a visit with her grandparents when her mother noticed an antique store by the side of the highway. They stopped. It was a good point to stretch their legs. While Pamela provoked to no avail the scarred old tomcat perched on a barrel, its green eyes squinting timeless feline reproach, and her mother peered through a glass counter at what can only be described as the heirlooms of the damned, her father discovered something in the recesses of the musty store, past a neighborhood of decapitated street signs named for trees native to North America. It was a ceramic figure about three feet tall, its base a short expanse of railroad track supporting a hunched black man with a hammer poised to slam a railroad spike that jutted from the track precociously. Her father prowled around the object like a wrestler. Sections of it were chipped away, a bit from the man's cranium, a crescent of his cheek, exposing the crude white matter beneath. Her father called Pamela and her mother over to that corner of the roadside antique store, where lawn jockeys of variegated expression and purpose gathered, arms tired.

The figure of John Henry layin' the line was surrounded on all sides by small men in red outfits hefting the strange burden of gold rings. The hammer's impending but stalled convergence with the spike had a spooky presence to it and Pamela felt a chill: it was a fragment of something larger fallen from above, eternal forces glimpsed for a second. She asked her father what it was. He told her it was John Henry, and John Henry sat in the backseat with her all the way back to Harlem, swaddled in her favorite red blanket, her blanket.

6   She exhales smoke into the night air, aiming for a denomination of gnats a few yards away. So it is sibling rivalry, she thinks. John Henry took her blanket. It started with that. At first she and her mother made fun of the little creature. Her father placed it in the doorway next to the umbrella stand so that it was the first thing you saw when you unlocked the three locks, that tumbling line of security, pushed in the slow door and entered their apartment. Sometimes they'd talk in his voice, a deep "How do you do?" and chuckle at their stupid joke. The hardware store thrived, it was on a corner with a lot of traffic and had a domain. Mr. Street hung his shingle at the right time, at the right place, and he joked with the handymen who did odd jobs in the neighborhood, he swept down on homeowners and renters as they dozed along the aisles looking for something to unstop the drain or punish the truant hinge, understanding exactly when their postures intimated defeat before the long and stocked shelves of Street Hardware. A man of his age and success could use a hobby. Model airplanes, collecting stamps, or John Henry: he had earned the solace of taking his mind off things. And as the pictures of Mrs. Street's family came down to make room for framed, faded sheet music and photographs of the Big Bend Tunnel and woodcuts of a hero, she thought, the man has earned it.

7   She hears laughter from down the row of rooms. It is one in the morning. Pamela breaks the rules of cigarette rationing she set a few minutes before and lights another Newport while still exhaling the smoke from its predecessor. Then how do you trace the course of an addiction. It is a child. It feeds off nurture and care, it learns how to crawl and learns cunning and suddenly it is its own being, willful and scheming every second at survival.

8   The hobby grew. The traces of its development were savored and polished by Mr. Street, he talked to the artifacts when no one was around, or he thought no one was around, or he thought everyone was asleep and he had John Henry to himself. Chronicles of mechanical production. Yellowed and tattered handwritten drafts of ballads,

nibbled and yellowed published versions of the ballads for drawing room amateurs, early sound recordings—one hundred twenty versions of the song and counting. Ink scratched into paper at midnight by hopeful songsmiths under lantern flicker; Yellen&Company Music printed sheet music, a tavern favorite in some localities; the recordings, expression of those written notes, piled up in their sleeves in alphabetical order, subcategorized by region. Fat 78s preserving the croaks of bluesmen who chronicled the showdown at C&O's Big Bend Tunnel, dainty 45s from sixties English bands that garnished the fable with paisley chords and frenetic sitar of the psychedelic sound, eight-track tapes of Johnny Cash on pills singing of John Henry, C-60 bootleg cassettes of Johnny Cash on pills singing of John Henry. Recording equipment necessary for the 3 A.M. playback of said recordings.

9   Mr. Street made weekend pilgrimages to antiquities shows and fairs, he wrote to terse P.O. boxes in the back of obscure magazines unavailable on any newsstand. Certainly not in their neighborhood. He assembled John Henry. A playbill from the Broadway show and the original score. The very trousers and shirt Paul Robeson wore during the show's troubled and truncated run. Did Mr. Street decline the temptation to wear the clothes from time to time? Pamela cannot find any way he could have. Hammers. Ten-pound and twenty-pound sledges in pairs. He rubbed brown oil into their handles with one of her old T-shirts, loving the wood as it was said John Henry did, to keep the wood limber, to allow it to absorb the shock of each blow. A grizzled old geezer from Charleston showed up at their apartment one Sunday night and opened a suitcase containing five of what he claimed were actual drill bits used by the Big Bend Tunnel crew, long rusted javelins with mashed plug ends. Her father bought them all, the new school clothes could wait, and hung them over the mantel, five fingers of a railroad hand.

10   At one point he proclaimed, over a pot of string beans entwined with bloated flats of bacon, his artifacts the largest collection of John Henry in the world. None stepped forward to dispute his claim. Some houses smelled of dogs or cats. The Street household smelled of her father's rotting mania and the sour reek of Pamela's and her mother's snuffed lives. He tried to acquire one of Palmer Hayden's famous paintings of John Henry, a piece of the Harlem Renaissance. The owners wouldn't budge. Like he had the money. He settled for a poster and in the dining room John Henry sprawled dead on his back, surrounded by the witnesses of his feat, arms

spread wide like Christ's and his hammer in his hand, he died with his hammer in his hand. One time her father disappeared for two weeks to hunt down an old Adirondack hermit he'd heard of, to tape record from the man's drooling lips a variant of the John Henry ballad, which had been told to him by his grandfather, supposedly a Big Bend worker who had toiled with John Henry. Her father had cleaned out the receipts from the hardware store for the trip, leaving Pamela and her mother with no money and the Street women ate tuna fish and macaroni and cheese for two weeks. The tape turned out to be unintelligible, the old hermit muttered dementia but if you listened hard enough, and her father did with all his life, you could hear the big man's name.

11   The air is cool. This is the country. She hears steps down the cement walkway. Pamela sees it is the writer, the one who choked at dinner. He walks slowly and timorously, as if on a listing deck. He looks up from the ground and sees her, lifts a hand. "Still up?" he asks.

12   "How are you feeling?" She blows out smoke through her nostrils.

13   "Better," he mumbles. He raises the soda can. "This should help," he says. He doesn't sound as if he believes it.

14   "That was pretty scary."

15   His eyes dip down again. "Well, the guy saw what was going on and knew what to do." They give their names to each other and he apologizes for his colleagues' behavior in the van. He tells her they get a little excited sometimes.

16   "No problem," she says. "I lived next to a fraternity house in college." He smiles at this and she offers him a cigarette.

17   "My throat," he says, shaking his head. He asks her what brought her down here.

18   "My father collected John Henry material," she says. "It was his hobby. They want to buy it for a museum they're planning." She is entirely truthful.

19   "Must be a big collection," the writer says.

20   "It is," she answers and she lights another cigarette. One of the rooms down the line opens and the man with the eye patch pokes his head out. He yells out the man's name and waves his arm in circles.

21   "Maybe I'll see you tomorrow," he says.

22   "Probably."

23   Tomorrow she has an appointment to meet Mayor Cliff to hear his personal appeal. She has already decided not to give it to them.

Ntozake Shange

(1948–)

Born Paulette Williams on October 18, 1948, in Trenton, New Jersey, Ntozake Shange (whose first and last name translate as "she who brings her own things" and "she who walks with lions," respectively) enjoyed a comfortable childhood. As the oldest of four children born to Eloise Owens Williams, a psychiatric social worker, and Paul T. Williams, a surgeon, Shange was introduced at an early age to jazz, blues, and literature ranging from Paul Laurence Dunbar to T. S. Eliot. Shange received a BA from Barnard College in 1970 and an MA in American Studies from UCLA in 1973. Shange's work is characterized by a strong feminist voice. Her debut, for colored girls who have considered suicide/when the rainbow is enuf, *which she labels a "choreopoem" (a poem that integrates word and dance), was first produced in 1975, won the 1977 Obie and Outer Critics Circle awards, and received Tony, Grammy, and Emmy nominations. It is the second play by an African American woman to reach Broadway. Although this remains her most celebrated work, Shange has written poetry, essays, and novels, including* Nappy Edges *(1978),* A Daughter's Geography *(1983),* Betsey Brown *(1985),* The Love Space Demands: A Continuous Saga *(1991), and* Sassafrass, Cypress & Indigo *(1982), an experimental novel that incorporates recipes, charms, and spells as it weaves together the lives of Hilda Effania and her three daughters. The story of the youngest daughter, Indigo, is excerpted below.*

Sassafrass, Cypress & Indigo

1   Where there is a woman there is magic. If there is a moon falling from her mouth, she is a woman who knows her magic, who can share or not share her powers. A woman with a moon falling from her mouth, roses between her legs and tiaras of Spanish moss, this woman is a consort of the spirits.

2   Indigo seldom spoke. There was a moon in her mouth. Having a moon in her mouth kept her laughing. Whenever her mother tried to pull the moss off her head, or clip the roses round her thighs, Indigo was laughing.

3   "Mama, if you pull 'em off, they'll just grow back. It's my blood. I've got earth blood, filled up with the Geechees long gone, and the sea."

4   Sitting among her dolls, Indigo looked quite mad. As a small child, she stuffed socks with red beans, raw rice, sawdust or palm leaves. Tied ribbons made necks, so they could have heads and torsos. Then eyes from carefully chosen buttons or threads, hair from yarns specially dyed by her sisters and her mama, dresses of the finest silk patches, linen shoes and cotton underskirts, satin mitts or gloves embroidered with the delight of a child's hand. These creatures were still her companions, keeping pace with her changes, her moods and dreams, as no one else could. Indigo heard them talking to her in her sleep. Sometimes when someone else was talking, Indigo excused herself—her dolls were calling for her. There was so much to do. Black people needed so many things. That's why Indigo didn't tell her mama what all she discussed with her friends. It had nothing to do with Jesus. Nothing at all. Even her mama knew that, and she would shake her head the way folks do when they hear bad news, murmuring, "Something's got hold to my child, I swear. She's got too much South in her."

5   The South in her, the land and salt-winds, moved her through Charleston's streets as if she were a mobile sapling, with the gait of a well-loved colored woman whose lover was the horizon in any direction. Indigo imagined tough winding branches growing from her braids, deep green leaves rustling by her ears, doves and macaws flirting above the nests they'd fashioned in the secret, protected niches way high up in her headdress. When she wore this Carolinian costume, she knew the cobblestone streets were really polished oyster shells, covered with pine needles and cotton flowers. She made herself, her world, from all that she came from. She looked around her at the wharf. If there was nobody there but white folks, she made them black folks. In the grocery, if the white folks were buying up all the fresh collards and okra, she made them disappear and put the produce on the vegetable wagons that went round to the Colored. There wasn't enough for Indigo in the world she'd been born to, so she made up what she needed. What she thought the black people needed.

> *Access to the moon.*
> *The power to heal.*
> *Daily visits with the spirits.*

MOON JOURNEYS
cartography by Indigo

Find an oval stone that's very smooth. Wash it in rosewater, 2 times. Lay it out to dry in the night air where no one goes. When dry, hold stone tightly in the right hand, caress entire face with the left hand. Repeat the same action with the stone in the left hand. Without halting the movement, clasp left stone-filled hand with the right. Walk to a tree that houses a spirit-friend. Sit under the tree facing the direction of your mother's birthplace. Hold your hands between your bosom, tight. Take 5 quick breaths and 3 slow ones. Close your eyes. You are on your way.

ALTERNATIVE MODES OF MOON JOURNEYS
(Winter travel/Inclement weather)

In a thoroughly cleaned bathroom with the window open, burn magnolia incense, preferably, but cinnamon will do. In a hand-kerchief handled by some other woman in your family (the further back the better), put chamomile, an undamaged birth-wort leaf, and Lady's Fern. Tie this with a ribbon from your own hair. Kiss the sachet 3 times. Drop it gently into a tub of warm water that will cover all your body. Place two white burning candles at either end of the tub. Float one fully opened flower in the water. Get in the tub while tickling the water in circles with the petals of the flower. Lie in the tub, with flower over your heart. Close your eyes. You are on your way.

6   Not all black people wanted to go to the moon. But some did. Aunt Haydee had gone to the moon a lot. She'd told Indigo about the marvelous parties there were in the very spots the white people put flags and jumped up and down erratically. They never did learn how to dance. Been round black folks all these years and still don't have sense enough to keep in rhythm. But there they were walking on the moon, like nothing ever went on up there. Like women didn't sidle up to lunar hills every month. Like seas of menses could be held back by

a rocket launcher. Like the Colored might disappear with the light
of the moon.

7   "We ain't goin' anywhere, are we?" Indigo sat some of the dolls on
the inside of her thigh. Her very favorites she sat in her lap. Indigo
had made every kind of friend she wanted. African dolls filled with
cotton root bark, so they'd have no more slave children. Jamaican
dolls in red turbans, bodies formed with comfrey leaves because
they'd had to work on Caribbean and American plantations and their
bodies must ache and be sore. Then there were the mammy dolls that
Indigo labored over for months. They were almost four feet high, with
big gold earrings made from dried sunflowers, and tits of uncleaned
cotton. They smelled of fennel, peach leaves, wild ginger, wild yams.
She still crawled up into their arms when she was unavoidably lonely,
anxious that no living black folks would talk to her the way her dolls
and Aunt Haydee did.

8   Everybody said she was just too ornery to hold a decent conversation. But that wasn't true. What was true was that Indigo had
always had to fight Cypress and Sassafrass just to get them to listen
to her. They thought they were so grown. So filled up with white folks'
ways. They didn't want to hear about the things Aunt Haydee knew.
Indigo watched her mother over huge vats of dyes, carrying newly
spun yarn from the pots to the lines and back again. Sassafrass,
throwing shuttles back and forth and back and forth. Cypress tying
off cloth, carrying the cloth to the stairway where she began the
appliqués the family was famous for. There was too much back and
forth going on for anybody to engage little Indigo in conversations
about the haints and the Colored. If the rhythm was interrupted, Sassafrass would just stare at the loom. Cypress would look at her work
and not know where to start or what gauge her stitches were. Mama
would burn herself with some peculiarly tinted boiling water. Everybody would be mad and not working, so Indigo was sent to talk to the
dolls. All the dolls in the house became hers. And the worlds Sassafrass wandered in her weaving, and those Cypress conjured through
her body, were lost to Indigo, who handled three-way conversations
with her cloth companions all alone.

9   A girl-child with her dolls is unlikely to arouse attention anywhere,
same as little boys with footballs or Davy Crockett hats. So Indigo
would sneak from the place she'd been put (the corridor around the
back porch), and take her friends out visiting. Old ladies loved for
Indigo and Company to pass by. They would give her home-made

butter cookies or gingerbread. They offered teas and chocolates, as well as the Scriptures and the legends of their lives. Indigo only had colored dolls and only visited colored ladies. She didn't like Miz Fitzhugh, who fawned over Cypress and Sassafrass like they were 'most white. No, Mrs. Yancey with the low, secret voice and seventeen million hundred braids was Indigo's friend. And Sister Mary Louise who kept a garden of rose bushes and herbs was Indigo's cut-buddy, down to the Colored Methodist Episcopal Church.

10   Streets in Charleston wind the way old ladies' fingers crochet as they unravel the memories of their girlhoods. One thing about a Charlestonian female is her way with little things. The delicacy of her manner. The force of ritual in her daily undertakings. So what is most ordinary is made extraordinary. What is hard seems simple. Indigo listened to their tales, the short and long ones, with a mind to make herself a doll whose story that was, or who could have helped out. When her father died, Indigo had decided it was the spirit of things that mattered. The humans come and go. Aunt Haydee said spirits couldn't be gone, or the planet would fall apart.

11   The South in her.

12   Rumor was that Mrs. Yancey had a way with white folks. They couldn't deny her anything. That's what folks said . . . that she must honey up to them; leastways, smile a lot. That was the only way the beautiful things she had in her house could be accounted for. Mrs. Yancey couldn't have bought such lace, or that silver tea service. Imagine a colored woman having afternoon tea and crumpets with all that silver. Indigo always carried her doll-friend Miranda over to Mrs. Yancey's. Miranda had better manners than some of her other dolls. Miranda was always clean, too, in a red paisley pinafore and small black sandals. Indigo let Miranda use her parasol to protect her from the sun. What proper young woman would come visiting faint and perspiring? Only some of Indigo's more country dolls would have marched to Mrs. Yancey's with the outdoors all over them.

13   Indigo walked up to Mrs. Yancey's front porch, pulled her slip up, and fussed with the hair sticking out of her braids. She'd rinsed her hands off, but re-doing her hair for a short chat seemed to make too much of a regular outing. Besides, Miranda was really dressed up. Indigo had decorated her bonnet with dandelions, and sprayed some of her mama's perfume under her arms and behind her knees. When she was ready, Indigo rang the bell and waited. Sure enough, Mrs.

Yancey was coming to the door. She wore slippers with the heels all beat down that made a sound like Bill Bojangles when he did the soft shoe. Opening the bright white door, while pulling the apron from around her neck, Mrs. Yancey bent down to kiss Indigo on the cheek.

14   "Now ain't you looking mighty fresh today, Indigo. And Miranda must be going to a social, all decked out, huh?"

15   "No, M'am. We just thought you might want some company. I was talking to Miranda and she told me you were thinking on us real hard."

16   "Y'all come in and make yourselves at ease in the parlor. Miranda must gotta second sense. She always knows when I wanna see my little girls."

17   Mrs. Yancey's house smelled like collard greens and corn bread, even when she fried oysters and made red sauce. Indigo nudged Miranda.

18   "Can ya smell that? Mrs. Yancey's house smells good, doesn't it?" Her house felt good, too. There were so many soft places to sit and smell other things. Mrs. Yancey liked to make pillows. Oval pillows, square pillows, rectangles, triangles, shapes that had no names but were scented, soft, huggable pillows. These pillows were covered with satins and silks, and embroidered in blinding scarlets and golds, and set off with laces, tassels, and cords. Mrs. Yancey told Miranda that she made the pillows now because all her life she had been living between a rock and a hard place. Even though she didn't really need any more, something called her to keep sewing herself comforts. Miranda asked Mrs. Yancey the questions that Indigo considered too forward. Why, one time when Miranda and Indigo were having a bit of pineapple-upside-down cake with their tea, and Mrs. Yancey was talking about how the white folks drove down the Colored, drove the Colored to drink and evil ways, drove decent young gals into lives of sin, chasing them up and down the back stairways from Allendale to Hilton Head, Miranda blurted:

19   "Well, how come the white people give you so many things? If they so hard-hearted and low-down, why you smile up to 'em?"

20   Indigo was embarrassed, and gave Miranda a good whack 'cross the face.

21   "She didn't mean that, M'am."

22   "Yes, she did, Indigo. She did, and it ain't correct to be slapping on no free somebody. You keep your hands to yourself and listen to what I gotta say."

23   Indigo settled back in the love seat, almost disappearing in all the pillows. Miranda finally relaxed and lay next to her, listening.

24 "Folks in these parts got sucha low idea of the women of the race. They can't imagine how I come by what I come by 'less they weigh my reputation down with they dirty, filthy minds."

25 "Oh, no M'am, didn't nobody say you did that!" Indigo shot up out of the pillows, dragging Miranda with her to Mrs. Yancey's lap.

26 "That's not what I mean, sweetheart. Those be shooting words. I was suggesting that whoever be announcing that I grin up in the faces of these folks is out of they minds. All I do is go round the house that I be cleaning, waxing, dusting, ironing, sweeping . . . my regular chores. And if I come 'cross something that I gotta yen for, I say to the Mrs., 'I sho' do like that.' Then I stare at her, but with my eyes a lil bit going down and in a crooked direction. I look at what it was I wanted and look back at the white lady. I tell my soul to get all in what I want. Next thing you know the white lady can't think of no reason why she should have whatever that is. And she turn round asking me don't I want it, and of course I want it 'cause I done put all my soul in it. And I gotta have my soul in order to come on back round here to my house."

27 Indigo and Miranda thought about what Mrs. Yancey had said for days, but not nearly so much as they did about Mrs. Yancey and Mr. Henderson, also known as Uncle John the junk man. He was looking bad most of the time. Indigo figured that before she was born, Uncle John would have been called a fine looking man. Mrs. Yancey found no fault with that. Yet every time Uncle John would come round in his horse and wagon with things everybody didn't want, Mrs. Yancey would shudder, like the ugliness of whatall he carted startled her. She'd purse her lips, put her hands on her hips, whisper that cursing whisper Indigo had told Miranda about, or she would throw open her screen door and shout:

28 "John Henderson get that nasty mess out my face, get on away from my door with your trash, you hear me!"

29 Then she'd slam the door shut, brush her hands on her apron and pat her braids, as if she was making sure that nothing about her was as out of order as everything about Uncle John. Still, one day after she had shouted the daylights out the window for Uncle John to go on where ever it was that he laid his pitiful head, he came creeping up the steps.

30 Miranda and Indigo peeked out the window, being careful to stay behind the curtains. Uncle John was a slight man, copper colored. Indigo explained to Miranda that that was the Indian in him. His eyes had a sly look, like the eyes of those boys that came tearing after

Cypress after school; giggling eyes, and a mouth fitting a proud man. Mrs. Yancey looked more like Sister Mary Louise to Indigo. Here she was prancing around, twitching, putting her hair this way and that, because Uncle John was at the door. That didn't make no sense. No sense at all.

31 Uncle John had to push the bell three times. Finally, Mrs. Yancey slowly opened the wood door, leaving the screen door quite shut.

32 "Well, John Henderson, what are you doing on my front porch, looking how you look?"

33 She was right. Uncle John was a mite unkempt: white fuzzies curled from his ear, beneath his chin; his jacket was fraying at the lapels, and his shoes were covered with dirt. Mrs. Yancey hoped it was dirt, anyway. Uncle John, on the other hand, didn't pay no mind to Mrs. Yancey. He just looked at her with those giggling eyes and said:

34 "I been passing by here more frequent than I usedta, M'am. I'm not a young man no more, an' I been thinking how you collects nice things jus' like I do, an' how you still too smart looking to stay off by yourself all the time. I'm fixing to come calling in the nigh future if you don't mind?"

35 "John Henderson, you don't even have a place to live. You don't take baths, or shave. And you think you gonna grace my house with your I-don't-care-'bout-nothing-self. You don't even have a place to live."

36 "I'll just pass by round dinner time, awright." That's all he said, though he was grinning even as he patted his horse, Yoki. He must have been saying sweet things, because Yoki neighed, seemed to blush, and then they were gone.

37 Miranda had not said much about Mrs. Yancey and Uncle John, but Indigo figured that the way Mrs. Yancey carried on after he left that she set more store by him than she let on. That's why Indigo stole out of her mother's house quickly after their dinner of okra, rice and ham hocks, to see if Uncle John really came back, like he said he would. She carried Marie-Hélène with her, along with Miranda, because Marie-Hélène was so frail that she didn't get out much.

38 Indigo was really glad both her doll-friends were with her. Otherwise she would never have believed what she saw. Uncle John was there all right. Going up Mrs. Yancey's walk like he would have to, but he was in a tuxedo and top hat. The spats on his shoes gleamed in the lavender sky. He kept his pace up and his back straight with the help of an ebony cane with a gold handle. Plus, when Mrs. Yancey came to the door, her hair wasn't in braids. It was all over the place like those women in the pictures over bars, the mermaids covering their privates, with their

hair flowing like seaweed everywhere. She wasn't wearing her slippers, either. She had on high heels and a pale blue dress chiseled onto her form like white on rice. Mrs. Yancey took Uncle John's arm; they virtually floated off the porch, down the walk to the corner.

39   Indigo kept hearing Mrs. Yancey say, "Uncle John you don't even have a place to live." Everybody knew Uncle John lived in his wagon, but nobody had ever seen what Indigo saw. Uncle John went over to his wagon, pulled out a fine easy chair and set it by the curb, then motioned for Mrs. Yancey to have a seat. Next thing Indigo knew, he had spread a Persian rug in the middle of the street, set a formal table, pulled out a wine bucket, and started dinner on the stove at the back of his wagon. Yoki was all dressed up with flowers woven through her mane and violet feathers tied on her hooves. Uncle John put candles on the table, and pinned a corsage to Mrs. Yancey's dress. She kept looking around like she thought being in the middle of the street in Uncle John's living room was not really safe, when out of nowhere the guys from the Geechee Capitans, a motorcycle gang of disrepute led by Pretty Man, came speeding down the street. Mrs. Yancey 'most jumped to her roof. Uncle John didn't exhibit much concern about these young ruffians on their huffing, humming bikes. He looked up, waved his hand, and the Geechee Capitans, who had never done a good turn by anybody in the city of Charleston, South Carolina, made road blocks on either side of Uncle John's parlor-in-the-middle-of-the-street.

40   Marie-Hélène told Indigo she thought she would faint. Miranda was speechless. Indigo tried to accept the Geechee Capitans, clad in leather jackets with crossed switchblades painted on their backs, pork-pie hats and black boots, guarding her friend Mrs. Yancey, who was having dinner with Uncle John the junk man in the street. Indigo stayed behind the bushes by the Johnsons' house as long as she could, looking. When Uncle John pulled out a Victrola, played a Fletcher Henderson 78, and asked Mrs. Yancey to dance, Indigo knew it was time to go home. There was too much magic out in the night. Indigo felt the moon in her mouth, singing. The South in her.

SUITORS WITH THE MOON'S BLESSING

Fill a glass that sparkles in sunlight with pure spring water. Place one sprig of fresh mint in the water, and a mouthful of honey. Take your middle finger gently round the curve of your lips as you imagine your beloved might. Kiss the edges of the

finger. Take a breath so deep your groin senses it. Hold your
breath while envisioning your beloved's face. Release the
breath still picturing your beloved. Then with the kissed finger, make a circle round the rim of the glass 12 times, each
time repeating your beloved's name. Each time seeing your
beloved filled with joy. Close your eyes. Let your beloved fill
your heart. Bring the glass to your lips. Drink the gladness that
shall be yours.

IF YOUR BELOVED HAS EYES FOR ANOTHER

Sleep on your left side with 6 white roses by your head. Fill
your pillow with 2 handfuls of damiana leaves. Do this 3 days
in a row. On the fourth day, use one handful of the damiana
leaves to make tea. Drink 2 cups; one at dawn, the other at
dusk. The other handful of damiana leaves should be mixed
with cubeb berries, wrapped in a red or blue piece of cotton
(use red if you have passions for your beloved. Use blue if
you merely desire fidelity). With the damiana-cubeb berry-
filled pouch anywhere on your person in the presence of your
beloved, your way shall be had.

SEEKING NOTHING/GIVING THANKS FOR LUNAR GIFTS

(Full moon required)

Bathe casually in a bath scented with cinnamon and vanilla.
Wash hair with raspberry tea. Rinse thoroughly, being sure
your hands have touched every part of your body as your
beloved might. Without adornment of any kind, jewelry or
clothing, go to the outside. Lie fully open to the sky, widely,
naked. Think of your beloved. Smell your beloved. Allow the
Moon to share with you the pleasures your beloved brings you.
Hold back nothing. Your thanks are mightily received. (May
be executed in the company of your beloved, if he or she stands
open over you, or if he or she lies as you lie at least 6 inches

from you.) Before rising, you must have surrendered all you know of your beloved to the Moon, or your beloved shall have no more to offer you. (Very advanced. Wait if not sure.)

41 ". . . 'And your sons will become shepherds in the wilderness.' Numbers 14:33. I think that's enough for you to meditate on tonight, Indigo."

42 "But that doesn't have anything to do with me, Sister Mary Louise!" Indigo squirmed in her seat where she was helping Sister Mary Louise select the flowers for the Little Shepherd of Judea, C.M.E. Church's Young People's Meeting.

43 "Don't blaspheme, Indigo. The Lord don't take kindly to senseless babblin'."

44 "I'm not babbling, Sister, really. I'm a girl, that's all. I want to know what I'm supposed to do." Indigo pushed the roses from this side to that, nimbly avoiding the thorns, handling buds with caring alacrity. This one will do. This one will not. Bruised flowers had no place on the altar in Christ's House. Sister Mary Louise was heartened when Indigo came round. Those other two, the one who went off to the North and the other one shaking her ass all the time, they had never learned how to touch flowers or the ways of the Lord. Sister Mary Louise with no children in her house invited Indigo, but not Indigo's doll friends, to be among her flowers, to join in singing the praises of the Lord Almighty whose blessings are so bountiful we can never give thanks enough, and to bake breads.

45 "You can take those loaves out the oven, and behave like a good Christian girl, that's what you can do."

46 Indigo looked at the roses and then at her friend, Mary Louise Murray, who must have been around roses too long. Her face shone like petals with veins glowing, like the opals she wore in her ears. One big plait lay smack in the middle of her head, wound round and round; serpents in the garden. Pale green eyes rushed from her face whenever the Holy Spirit took her, if her bushes were dewy and the sun just coming up. Indigo had a reluctant soul, to Sister Mary's mind. Not that Indigo was a bad child, only she'd been exposed to so many heathenish folks, pagans out there on those islands.

47 "Christian girls don't do nothing but bake bread?" Indigo peered into the oven. The heat beat her face till she frowned. "Not ready yet," she said, and carefully let the oven door fit back in its latch. Sister Mary Louise was tickled.

48   "No. Indigo, we don't just bake bread. We tend after beauty in the world. The flowers and the children." For all her Godfearing ways, Sister Mary Murray had been known to get the spirit outside of Church. Sometimes, when she was walking to the fish market or delivering breads, she'd be singing "I Ain't Got Weary Yet," or "Didn't My Lord Deliver Daniel," and she would just get happy in the street. This was not exemplary behavior for a Deaconess. At many a sermon she would be called forth to testify about how the Devil seized her in broad daylight, taking on the movements of the Holy Spirit, tempting the sinner in her. Other folks believed that being without children is what drove Sister Mary to have these fits in public. It only happened when some young boy from the country was within ten feet of her, broad shouldered and raw. Other folks figured that Sister Mary Louise sipped a little bit, and got to feeling so good she couldn't stand it. Indigo knew that Sister Mary Louise was in fact a Christian woman. Sister didn't allow any dolls that could talk in her house.

49   "No haints coming in my house. What do you imagine the Lord God Jesus Christ would think, if I set my table for haints?" That's what she'd said to Indigo.

50   Now Indigo was angry. The bread wasn't ready. Sister's saying little girls make bread and take care of beauty. Indigo thought her stomach was going to jump out of her mouth and knock over all the flowers, stomp the breads, and let hell aloose in Sister Mary's big white kitchen, where Jesus looked down from every wall. The Last Supper. The Annunciation. From way up on Mt. Calvary, there he was waiting for "his sons to shepherd." Indigo was so mad she felt lightheaded; hot all over.

51   "Sister Mary Louise, when I talked to Miranda she didn't want to bake nothing."

52   "I told you awready. You too big to be talking to dolls. Good Lord, Indigo, look at yourself." Indigo tried to focus on Sister Mary's face. But she only saw a glimmering. She tried to look at herself, and kept blinking her eyes, rubbing her palms over them, to get some focus. She saw something spreading out of her in a large scarlet pool at her feet. Sister Mary jumped up and down.

53   "Indigo the Lord's called you to be a woman. Look on High for His Blessing. Look I say. Look to Jesus, who has "blessed you this day.' " Indigo fell down on her knees like Sister Mary had. And listened and swayed in her growing scarlet lake to the voice of this green-eyed woman singing for the heavens: "Trouble In Mind," "Done

Made My Vow," and "Rise and Shine," so that Indigo would know "among whom was Mary Magdalene."

54 "Speak, child, raise your voice that the Lord May Know You as the Woman You Are."

55 Then Sister Mary Louise rose, her thin body coated with Indigo's blood. She gently took off Indigo's clothes, dropped them in a pail of cold water. She bathed Indigo in a hot tub filled with rose petals: white, red, and yellow floating around a new woman. She made Indigo a garland of flowers, and motioned for her to go into the back yard.

56 "There in the garden, among God's other beauties, you should spend these first hours. Eve's curse threw us out the garden. But like I told you, women tend to beauty and children. Now you can do both. Take your blessing and let your blood flow among the roses. Squat like you will when you give birth. Smile like you will when God chooses to give you a woman's pleasure. Go now, like I say. Be not afraid of your nakedness."

57 Then Sister Mary shut the back door. Indigo sat bleeding among the roses, fragrant and filled with grace.

MARVELOUS MENSTRUATING MOMENTS

(As Told by Indigo to Her Dolls as She Made Each and Every One of Them a Personal Menstruation Pad of Velvet)

A. Flowing:

When you first realize your blood has come, smile; an honest smile, for you are about to have an intense union with your magic. This is a private time, a special time, for thinking and dreaming. Change your bedsheet to the ones that are your favorite. Sleep with a laurel leaf under your head. Take baths in wild hyssop, white water lilies. Listen for the voices of your visions; they are nearby. Let annoying people, draining worries, fall away as your body lets what she doesn't need go from her. Remember that you are a river; your banks are red honey where the Moon wanders.

B. For Disturbance of the Flow:

Don't be angry with your body if she is not letting go of her blood. Eat strawberries, make strawberry tea with the leaves to facilitate the flow. To increase the flow, drink squaw weed tea. For soothing before your blood flows, drink some black snakeroot or valerian tea. For cramps, chew wild ginger.

58   "Indigo, I don't want to hear another word about it, do you understand me. I'm not setting the table with my Sunday china for fifteen dolls who got their period today!"

59   "But, Mama, I promised everybody we'd have a party because we were growing up and could be more like women. That's what Sister Mary Louise said. She said that we should feast and celebrate with our very best dresses and our very favorite foods."

60   "Sister Mary Louise needs to get herself married 'fore she's lost what little of her mind she's got left. I don't want you going round that simple woman's house. You take my good velvet from 'tween those dolls' legs. Go to the store and buy yourself some Kotex. Then you come back here and pack those creatures up. Put them in the attic. Bring yourself back here and I'm going to tell you the truth of what you should be worrying about now you sucha grown woman."

61   "Mama, I can't do that. I can't put them away. I'll have nobody to talk to. Nobody at all."

62   "Indigo, you're too big for this nonsense. Do like I say, now."

63   "Mama. What if I stopped carrying Miranda in the street with me, and left my other friends upstairs all the time, could I leave 'em out then, could I? Please Mama, I know they're dollies. I really do. Sassafrass and Cypress kept all the things they made when they were little, didn't they?"

64   "That's a lie. Don't you have all their dolls? I can't believe a girl as big as you, wearing a training bra and stockings to school, can't think of nothing but make-believe. But if you promise me that you going to leave them in your room and stop asking me to sing to 'em, feed 'em, and talk with 'em, you can leave them out. Now go on to the store."

65   Indigo left her lesson book on the kitchen table, went to her mother tearing collards by the sink, and gave her a big hug. Her mother's apron always smelled like cinnamon and garlic no matter how many times it was washed. It smelled of times like this when her mother felt a surge in her bosom like her nipples were exploding with milk again, leaving her damp and sweet, but now it was Indigo's tears that softened her spirit.

66   "Indigo, you're my littlest baby, but you make it hard for me sometimes, you know that."

67   "Mama, I can make it easier today 'cause I aweady know what it is you were gonna tell me when I came back from the store."

68   "You do, do you?"

69   "Yeah, you were going to tell me that since I became a woman, boys were gonna come round more often, 'cause they could follow the trail of stars that fall from between my legs after dark."

70   "What?"

71   "The stars that fall from 'tween my legs can only be seen by boys who are pure of mind and strong of body."

72   "Indigo, listen to me very seriously. This is Charleston, South Carolina. Stars don't fall from little colored girls' legs. Little boys don't come chasing after you for nothing good. White men roam these parts with evil in their blood, and every single thought they have about a colored woman is dangerous. You have gotta stop living this make-believe. Please, do that for your mother."

73   "Every time I tell you something, you tell me about white folks. 'White folks say you can't go here—white folks say you can't do this—you can't do that.' I didn't make up white folks, what they got to do with me? I ain't white. My dolls ain't white. I don't go round bothering white folks!"

74   "That's right, they come round bothering us, that's what I'm trying to tell you . . ."

75   "Well if they bothering you so much, you do something about 'em."

76   "Is that some sass comin' out your mouth?"

77   "No, M'am. It's just I don't understand why any ol' white person from outta nowhere would want to hurt us. That's all."

78   Indigo moved to her mother, with a seriousness about her that left the kitchen emptied of all its fullness and aroma.

79   "I love you so much, Mama. & you are a grown colored woman. Some white man could just come hurt you, any time he wants, too? Oh I could just kill 'em, if they hurt you, Mama. I would. I would just kill anybody who hurt you."

80   Holding her child as tight as she could, as close into herself as she could, the mother whispered as softly as she could, as lovingly as she could: "Well, then we'll both be careful & look after each. Won't we?"

81   Indigo sort of nodded her head, but all she remembered was that even her mother was scared of white folks, and that she still wrote out the word Kotex on a piece of torn paper wrapped up in a dollar bill to give to Mr. Lucas round to the pharmacy. This, though Indigo insisted Mr. Lucas must know what it is, 'cause he ordered it for his store so all the other colored women could have it when they needed it. After all, even her mother said, this bleeding comes without fail to every good girl once a month. Sometimes her mother made no sense

at all, Indigo thought with great consternation. On the other hand, as a gesture of goodwill & in hopes that her littlest girl would heed her warnings, the mother allowed Indigo one more public jaunt with Miranda, who was, according to Indigo, fraught with grief that their outings were to be curtailed.

82   Weeping willows curled up from the earth, reaching over Indigo & Miranda on this their last walk in a long friendship, a simple, laughing friendship. Miranda thought the weeping willows were trying to hug them, to pull them up to the skies where whether you were real or not didn't matter. Indigo, in her most grown-up voice, said, "No, they want us to feel real special on this day, that's all." Miranda wasn't convinced, and neither was Indigo, who managed to take the longest walk to the drugstore that her family had ever known.

83   After following the willows' trellises till there were no more, Indigo reverently passed by Mrs. Yancey's, back round to Sister Mary Louise's, down to the wharf where she & Miranda waved to her father who was living in the sea with mermaids, & then 'cross to the railroad tracks looking for Uncle John. Indigo liked colored folks who worked with things that took 'em some place: colored folks on ships, trains, trolleys, & horses. Yoki was a horse. Uncle John did go places, and after that night with Mrs. Yancey in the street, Indigo figured him mighty powerful.

84   In between two lone railroad cars was Uncle John's wagon. Sequestered from ill-wishers & the wind, there he was chatting away with the air, the cars, or Yoki. Sometimes men of Color disappear into the beauty of the light, especially toward day's end. It's like clouds take on color & get down on the ground & talk to you, or the stars jump in some black man's body & shine all over you. Uncle John was looking like that to Indigo's mind, just brushing away, leaving Yoki's coat glimmering like dusk.

85   "Good evening, Uncle John."

86   "Humph." Mr. Henderson turned round knowing full well who'd come calling, but not wanting to let on. "Oh. If it ain't my girl Indigo. & who's that ya got witcha?"

87   "This is Miranda. We're going to Mr. Lucas' to pick up something." Indigo was quite careful not to say what she was going to the drugstore for, 'cause her mother had said not to say anything to anybody.

88   "Indigo, Mr. Lucas' place way off from heah, don't ya think?"

89   "Well, Uncle John, that's some of it, but not all of it."

90 Laying down his brush, pulling a stool from the other side of a fire where he was cooking either a chicken or a pigeon, Uncle John motioned for Indigo to take a seat.

91 "Some of it, but t'aint all of it, ya say? Well, I would be guessin' the rest of it be a matter for discussion."

92 "Yes, Uncle John. I want you to tell me something. I'm asking you 'cause you been doin' what suits your own mind since I was born."

93 "No, long fo' that, chile."

94 "Well, anyway, I want to keep on talkin' with all my dolls. You know they my very best friends." Indigo was talking so fast now, Uncle John started walking in a circle around her so as to understand better. "& Mama wants me to put 'em way 'cause now I am a woman&who will I talk to? I can't seem to get on with the chirren in the school I go ta. I don't like real folks near as much." Indigo had jumped off the stool with Miranda in her arms, much like a woman daring someone to touch her child. Uncle John stood still for a minute, looking at the shadows of the rail cars on Yoki's back.

95 "Indigo, times catch up on everybody. Me & Yoki heah been catched up by trains & grocery stores. Now you bein' catched up by ya growin' up. That's what ya mama's tryin' to say to ya. Ya gotta try to be mo' in this world. I know, it don't suit me either."

96 Miranda was crying, nestled in Indigo's elbow. Uncle John mumbled to himself, & climbed in his wagon. Indigo stayed put. Folks said that sometimes, when Uncle John had said all he had to say, he got in his wagon & that was that. Other times folks said Uncle John would get in his wagon & come back out with something to keep your life moving along sweeter. So Indigo didn't move a muscle. Miranda prayed some good would come of all this. They still hadn't gone to Mr. Lucas'. Indigo could hear Uncle John humming to himself, fumbling in that wagon. He was looking for something for her so she could keep talkin' & not have to be with them real folks & all their evil complicated ways of doing. The last of the day's sun settled on Indigo's back, warmed the taut worry out of her limbs, & sat her back down on the stool, jabbering away to Miranda.

97 "See, you thought that I was gonna just go on & do what Mama said & never play witya no more or go explore & make believe. See, see, ya didn't have no faith. What's that Sister Mary Louise is all the time sayin'?"

98 "Oh ye of lil faith . . ." Miranda rejoined.

99   Uncle John didn't come out of his wagon first. A fiddle did. Uncle John was holding it, of course, but he poked the fiddle out, then one leg, his backside, and the other leg, his precious greying head, and the last arm with a bow in his grasp. Indigo & Miranda were suspicious.

100   "What we need a violin for?" Miranda sniggled.

101   "Hush, Miranda, Uncle John knows what he's doin'. Just wait a minute, will ya?"

102   Uncle John sure nuf had intentions to give this fiddle to Indigo. His face was beaming, arms wide open, with the fiddle & bow tracing the horizons, moving toward Indigo who was smiling with no reason why.

103   "Indigo, this heah is yo' new talkin' friend."

104   "A fiddle, Uncle John?" Indigo tried to hide her disappointment, but Miranda hit her in her stomach. "Uh, that's not what I need, Uncle John." She sat back on the stool like she'd lost her backbone. Uncle John was a bit taken back, but not swayed.

105   "Listen now, girl. I'ma tell ya some matters of the reality of the unreal. In times blacker than these," Uncle John waved the violin & the bow toward the deepening night, "when them slaves was ourselves & we couldn't talk free, or walk free, who ya think be doin' our talkin' for us?"

106   "White folks, of course," snapped Indigo.

107   Uncle John's face drew up on his bones like a small furious fire. His back shot up from his legs like a mahogany log.

108   "Whatchu say, gal?? I caint believe ya tol' me some white folks was doin' our talkin'. Now, if ya want me to help ya, don't say nary another word to me till I'm tellin' ya I'm finished. Now, listen. Them whites what owned slaves took everythin' was ourselves & didn't even keep it fo' they own selves. Just threw it on away, ya heah. Took them drums what they could, but they couldn't take our feet. Took them languages what we speak. Took off wit our spirits & left us wit they Son. But the fiddle was the talkin' one. The fiddle be callin' our gods what left us/be givin' back some devilment & hope in our bodies worn down&lonely over these fields & kitchens. Why white folks so dumb, they was thinkin' that if we didn't have nothin' of our own, they could come controllin', meddlin', whippin' our sense on outta us. But the Colored smart, ya see. The Colored got some wits to em, you & me, we ain't the onliest ones be talkin' wit the unreal. What ya think music is, whatchu think the blues be, & them get happy church musics is about, but talkin' wit the unreal what's mo' real than most folks ever gonna know."

109   With that Uncle John placed the fiddle in the middle of his left arm & began to make some conversations with Miranda & Indigo. Yes, conversations. Talkin' to em. Movin' to an understandin' of other worlds. Puttin' the rhythm in a good sit down & visit. Bringin' the light out a good cry. Chasing the night back round yonder. Uncle John pulled that bow, he bounced that bow, let the bow flirt with those strings till both Miranda & Indigo were most talkin' in tongues. Like the slaves who were ourselves had so much to say, they all went on at once in the voices of the children: this child, Indigo.

110   When Indigo first tried to hold the fiddle under her neck like the children in the orchestra at school, Uncle John just chuckled, looked away. When she had it placed nearer her armpit & closer to her heart, with the bow tucked indelicately in her palm, he said, "Now talk to us, girl." Indigo hesitated, pulled the bow toward the A string, took a breath, & stopped. "I don't know how to play a violin, Uncle John."

111   "Yeah, ya do. Tell Miranda somethin' on that fiddle. 'Cause after today, ya won't be able to reach out to her like ya do now. Ya gonna haveta call her out, wit that fiddle."

112   Indigo looked at Miranda lying on the stool & then back at Uncle John whose eyes were all over her face, the fiddle, the bow.&in a moment like a fever, Indigo carried that bow cross those fiddle strings till Miranda knew how much her friend loved her, till the slaves who were ourselves made a chorus round the fire, till Indigo was satisfied she wasn't silenced. She had many tongues, many spirits who loved her, real & unreal.

113   The South in her.

114   It was already so late Mr. Lucas had started to lock up his shop. Only the lights in the very back were still on. Indigo held onto her violin with its musty case religiously, & she beat on the doors of the pharmacy like somebody possessed. "Please open up, Mr. Lucas. It's a emergency," she shouted. Mr. Lucas, portly & honey brown, peered out the door thru the lettering: Lucas' Pharmacy, Oldest Negro Drugstore in Charleston, S.C. Between the "S" & the "C" there was Indigo's face, churning & shouting. Mr. Lucas opened up remarking, "An emergency is somebody dyin' or a woman who needs some Kotex." Indigo was stunned. "Hi, Mr. Lucas, how'd you know that?"

115   "Oh, I been in this business a long time, Indigo. Tell your mother she almost missed me this time."

116   "Oh, it's not for Mama, it's for me." All of a sudden Indigo blushed & shrank. She'd gone & done what her mother had asked her please not to do. Mr. Lucas took a step toward Indigo, like he was looking

for the woman in her. He'd seen younger girls than Indigo who were busy having babies. He'd even seen girls more comely in a grown-woman manner than she who didn't bleed at all. But here was this girl with this child body & woman in her all at once. It was difficult for Mr. Lucas to just go & get the Kotex. He wanted to keep looking at this girl, this woman. He wanted to know what she felt like.

117   Indigo heard somebody talking to her. She saw Mr. Lucas coming toward her & somebody talking to her. Telling her to get the Kotex & get home quick. Get the Kotex & get home quick. Indigo ran to the back of the store, grabbed the blue box, stuffed it under her arm with Miranda & whipped thru the aisles with Mr. Lucas behind her, lumbering, quiet. The fiddle was knocking all kinds of personal hygiene products off shelves: toothpaste, deodorant, shaving cream. Indigo almost dropped it, but she held tighter, moved faster, heard somebody telling her to get home quick. She got to the doors, started to look back & didn't. She just opened the door as best she could without letting go of anything & ran out.

118   Mr. Lucas stood in the back of his pharmacy, looking at his S.C. Certification, his diploma from Atlanta University. He knew he might be in some trouble. Didn't know what had got hold to him. Every once in a while, he saw a woman with something he wanted. Something she shouldn't have. He didn't know what it was, an irreverence, an insolence, like the bitch thought she owned the moon.

119   "Yeah, that's right." Mr. Lucas relaxed. "The whole town knows that child's crazed. If she says a thing, won't a soul put no store in it."

120   The South in her.

TO RID ONESELF OF THE SCENT OF EVIL*

by Indigo

(Traditional Method)
        Though it may cause some emotional disruptions, stand absolutely still & repeat the offender's name till you are overwhelmed with the memory of your encounter. Take two deep slow breaths, on a 7 count. Then, waving your arms & hands

---

*(Violence or purposeful revenge should not be considered in most cases. Only during wars of national liberation, to restore the honor of the race, or to redress calamitous personal & familial trauma, may we consider brute force/annihilation.)

all about you, so your atmosphere may again be clean, say the name of the offender softly. Each time blowing your own breath into the world that we may all benefit from your renewal. Then in a hot place (your kitchen or out of doors) cover yourself in warm clay poultices. Let them dry on you, taking the poisons of the offender out of your body & spirit. Run a steaming shower over your body, allowing all grime & other to fall from you without using your hands or a cloth. Then, run yourself a new tub full of warm water filled with angelica & chamomile. Bring to your bath a tall clear glass of spring water wherein floats one closed white rose. Lying in your fragrant bath, sip the rose's water, for you are again among nature's flowers.

(For Modern Times)

Drink a strong mix of lemon tea&honey. This, if you've not cheated, should bring sweat to your brow. This is the poison the offender has left lurking. As you sweat, draw a bath that sends steam up toward your face, if you are on your knees. Take a piece of silk or cotton to which you feel attached & that bodes of happier times. Fill it with caraway seeds. Tie it with a ribbon that is your oldest female relative's favorite color. Float it in your bath. Stand naked over your tub. Kiss your right shoulder. Then your left. Step breathing briskly into the water. You shall be cleaned of all the offender's toxic presence.

121   Indigo did not tell her mother about Mr. Lucas being so evil, nor did she mention that her new fiddle could talk. These notions would bring her mother's ire up & out. Nowadays Indigo minded what she said & to whom. Some folks you tell some things, some folks you don't. With the dolls all lined up in her room now, no longer going calling, coming down for dinner, Indigo kept her window open all the time. She told her mother this was just for health reasons. Why New England people sleep with the windows open in snow: gives the body & spirit strength. Now, her mother didn't want her own windows open, but it seemed like Indigo was making more reasonable connections. The windows in the child's room stayed open.

122   Indigo invited the Moon in to sing to her doll-companions, mute though they were. She thought they had trouble sleeping. When the night air danced about them, leaving the shivers of that embrace, Indigo would take out her violin & play the way she learned. Letting

the instrument speak right up. Giving another space to all the feelings her little girl's body could not always contain. The talking music aroused the dolls to celebrate. Indigo sat in her window, working with her fiddle, telling everybody, the wind & all his brothers, what was on her mind, the turmoil in the spirit realm, the luxuriant realities she meandered in her sleep. Whenever she wanted to pray, she let her fiddle talk. Whenever she was angry, here came the fiddle. All the different ways of handling a violin & bow came to Indigo as she needed. They came: *legato, staccato, andante, forte, fortissimo, piano, allegro, presto.*

123 "Indigo, we're going to have to talk about this violin." Indigo was startled by her mother's nocturnal visit. The breeze felt good on her face. Indigo turned gently from the soft rumble of a sea-town night to her mother.

124 "Oh, I'm so glad, Mama. I wanted to talk to you about the fiddle some more, but I was afraid you . . ."

125 "Why Indigo, how could you think I wouldn't find somebody to give you lessons. I gave Sassafrass every weaving lesson she asked for, sent Cypress to New York for her dancing. Why wouldn't I give you violin lessons? Surely, there's one brave soul in Charleston who'll take this terrible-playing child of mine."

126 Indigo looked at her mother for a long while. Her mother feeling very proud of her daughter who'd tried to teach herself how to play the fiddle, who'd given up talking out of her head, talking only to her dolls. She glanced at her child's handiwork, Marie-Hélène, Miranda, Susie-Q, Candace, Lilli, fingering their hats and petticoats delicately. Now Indigo was involved with music which she would be as diligent&loving about as she had about her dolls, her companions, as she called them. The mother looked over to Indigo still sitting in the window. Not a word did she say, there in the window with her violin in an acceptable rest position.

127 "Now Indigo, what do you say to real violin lessons & closing that window so our neighbors can be spared this racket till you've learned a bit more?" Approaching her daughter with some glee, the mother stopped when Indigo turned her back, stood up, & began making those strange, erratic, annoying non-songs she played each night, that Miz Fitzhugh had complained about twice, along with the Daltons. Even Mr. Epps who lived three doors down & across the street had stopped by on his way to the post office to say, "Please do something about those noises from your house, or I'll have to call the constable round this way."

128   No, Indigo would not have her way this time. She wasn't going to be run out of her own home cause Indigo was playing a violin. She had to have some lessons 'cause these folks didn't realize the passion her daughter had for the violin.

129   "Indigo, I promise you. I'll get you the best teacher I can find." Indigo stopped slowly, C#, fifth position, D string.

130   "Mama, I'm happy with how the fiddle's talk . . . sounding now. I don't want any lessons at all. I just want to play." Thinking her mother was relieved, Indigo left the window. She put the violin away, even closed the gingham curtains. Indigo smiled up at her mama, who had a most curious expression. No matter what she did, Indigo was always beyond her reason. A good girl, yet out of reach.

131   "Mama, what's wrong? I said you don't have to get me lessons. I'm just fine."

132   "Indigo, you may have those lessons whenever you like & I mean that. But until you decide to take them, I can't allow you to make that noise in my house. I've got enough trouble on my hands without having every neighbor I've got thinking we got banshees living in here at night. Besides, Miz Fitzhugh, herself, even mentioned to me how unpleasant your violin-playing actually is, right now. I don't mean to say you won't be a wonderful musician in the future. But, Indigo, you may not submit the whole world to your will. No lessons, no violin playing under this roof."

133   Indigo sat back on her bed 'tween Candace & Marie-Hélène, who whispered: "Listen, I've gotta idea, Indigo."

134   "Mama, would you be mad if I played it someplace else? Outside, somewhere?"

135   Imagining she could use a nice hot toddy, the mother was going out Indigo's door, when she turned round to say that Indigo could take the violin anywhere out of the neighborhood & make any noise she liked 'cause then she would have to talk to the strangers beseeching her: "Please, get a lesson, girl," which is precisely what her mother had said.

136   Indigo patted the violin by her bed exactly where Aunt Haydee kept her shotgun. "No, Mama, that's not what's gonna happen." She kissed Miranda good-night & went to sleep. Her mother left a glass of cider & a deep chocolate on Indigo's night stand. It was midnight & the Moon was full.

137   Sister Mary Louise put Indigo & her violin behind the shed where she kept her gardening tools—shovels, vitamins for roses & violets,

peat moss, watering cans, heavy gloves, rakes, & strings. Too much of the Holy Ghost came out of Indigo & that fiddle. Sister Mary Louise swore even she couldn't stand that much spirit every day. "Back there behind the shed, Indigo, is just fine. Come anytime ya like. If I feel callt, I'ma come on out & listen." That's what Sister Mary Louise had decided about that. "Good for the plants. Too much order, too much gentility'll make my flowers more prim than glorious. We all need a lil wildness." So here came Indigo every day after school plying her new medium out back.

138   Indigo wanted to sound like the sparrows & wrens. She mimicked the jays & peckers. Conversing with gulls was easy 'cause they saw her daddy's soul every day. Indigo had mastered the hum of dusk, the crescendoes of the cicadas, swamp rushes in light winds, thunder at high tide, & her mother's laughter down the hall. Uncle John told her one time when they were frying porgies by his wagon that he'd got this feeling in his waking up that Indigo was dwelling dangerous on the misery of the slaves who were ourselves, & this feeling directed him to march her toward the beauty of this world & the joys of the those come before us. Indigo couldn't get enough. No creature that moved escaped Indigo's attention. If the fiddle talked, it also rumbled, cawed, rustled, screamed, sighed, sirened, giggled, stomped, & sneered. Every once in a while Indigo even played songs. Some colored singing, Tina Turner, B. B. King, Etta James: they songs. This was a secret. Indigo had some pride & couldn't admit to those who claimed she made noise all the time that she'd found out the difference 'tween her free communion with the universe, primal, unrelenting flights, & melody. She played these softly, for herself. Then she'd blush, hurriedly put the fiddle back into the case, the Colored & Romance having got the best of her. Young boys were alien to her. She didn't want to be a fool in love, have something terrible getta holdt to her. When she'd had enough of "sweetheart," "babee," & "please, please, please," Indigo yelped, "Oh Sister Mary Louise, you missed that."

139   There was something moving up her leg, something that was not supposed to be there. Indigo looked down, lost a little fear, just a twig. How was a twig going up & down the inside of her leg, tickling her like the "sweet-hearts" & "babees" she'd been playing. Indigo looked cautiously behind her where two brown-skinned boys leaned over Sister Mary Louise's fence.

140   "Get that twig from 'tween my legs."

141   "We just tryin' to get ya attention. Ya so busy fiddlin' ya don't see nobody. Where ya learn to play like that, gal?"

142   "My name ain't 'gal' & I taught myself. Now go on 'way & leave me be, please." Indigo hoped they hadn't heard her playing songs, but her wild sounds. She hadda hunch it was them Romance riffs that brought these fellas by the shed. Nobody ever came behind Sister Mary Louise's house. There were devils, Mandingo giants, quadroon elves, & wayward ghosts in her shed.

143   "What's your name, sweetheart?" the taller boy asked. This one in worn jeans particularly frayed at the edges the way the Geechee Capitans wore theirs when they went crabbing. His head was shaved to keep from the ringworm, Indigo surmised. But the boy had such a pretty head. It was not flat in the back, a pancake head, nor was it all forced up above his eyes, a waterhead. No, this boy had a pretty nutmeg head. He was still slipping that stick round Indigo's ankle though, & she'd told him to stop. The other boy was real stocky, a flathead, but high cheekbones. Indigo recognized the blood of that colored family married Chinese. They all looked like that. Still there was no doubt she'd told them to leave her be & they didn't. Indigo closed her eyes tight like she was fixing to run or scream; instead she said: "*Falcon come in this fiddle. Falcon come in this fiddle. Leopard come in this fiddle. Leopard come in this fiddle. I'm on the prey. I'm on the prey.*" 'Fore she knew it, Indigo was so busy bowing the daylights & jungles out her violin, she didn't notice the two boys duck down on the other side of the fence. When she opened her eyes, she realized she'd stood her ground. & that stick was no longer 'tween her legs. She smiled a tiny smile, peered over the fence, tapped the tall boy's shin with the tip of the bow.

144   "What's your name, sweetheart?" Indigo chirped, so fulla herself. The boys brushed the sand from their knees, grinned self-consciously.

145   "I'm Spats," the tall boy answered, " & this here is Crunch. We Junior Geechee Capitans."

146   Indigo held her tongue. "Why imagine that. Y'all Junior G.C. Ain't that somethin'. I'm Indigo."

147   Spats jumped over the fence first. He reached for Indigo's fiddle. She pulled it away gracefully. "I can't let anyone touch my instrument. It's bad luck." Spats shrugged his shoulders. "Hey, whatever ya say. Ain't that right, Crunch?" Crunch hanging tough in the alleyway was hardly enthusiastic. A girl with a violin had got him down on his knees in broad daylight.

148   "What the hell was ya doin' on that damn thing?" Crunch grumbled, messing with his elbows, his thick crop of black hair meeting his furrowed indignant brow.

149 "I was fightin' back in my own way. That's what I was doin'. & you know it. Come puttin' a stick 'tween my legs like I ain't got no better sense than to let you do it 'cause you boys. Um-humph. Uncle John, he spoke to me on that. He said, 'Indigo, when trouble come, get your fiddle.' "

150 Spats & Crunch stared at each other. How could a girl know Uncle John? What was Uncle John doing giving some girl all his advice & counsel? Why their seniors, the real Geechee Capitans, held counsel with Uncle John. Very impressed, a little riled, the two boys folded their arms cross their chests & began a culturally recognized & universally feared ritual: The Geechee Capitan Cock Walk. Spats took off his sweatshirt with no sleeves, a slit down the middle, turned inside-out anyway, threw it on the ground. Crunch peeled his black tee-shirt from his ample torso, threw it on the ground. They clapped their hands. Clap. Clapclap. Clap. Spit on the ground, once to the east & once to the west. Then they walked in a circle round Indigo. Slow-n-don't-mess-round clockwise. Slow-n-this-might-be-the-last-time counter clock-wise. Again. Humph. Again. Humph. Clap. Clapclap. Clap.

151 Indigo'd been round long enough to know that she was either being initiated or 'bout to die. Crunch was not too excited 'bout the powers of her fiddlin'. Spats was probably more physical than his slight frame intimated. Indigo held her breath. Next thing was gonna happen, was somebody'd break the rhythm & whoever that was had better be on the case or die.

152 Spats moved first, fast. Had Indigo on his small shoulders 'fore Crunch could move all of himself anywhere. There was still the pos-sibility that Crunch might plow into them or belly-whip 'em to a tum-ble. Spats glanced up at Indigo, who was delighted to be such a prize & safe. Crunch kept his flat face straight: "Awright man, she in." Indigo jumped offa Spats, jubilant. The real world was workin' its way up. Crunch didn't like that she was a girl, but whoever could scare a G.C., even the Jr. G.C.'s, had the right to be initiated or die. Plus, a somebody who was already a G.C. hadta put his honor on the line: to really save the person from all the rest, or do harm to the person in the face of all the other G.C.'s. Now it was also true there were only two mem-bers of the Jr. Geechee Capitans, Spats & Crunch. That's 'cause they hadn't met anybody could fight as well as they could. Till Indigo. Crunch really didn't like that she was a girl. Spats liked that.

153 Indigo had a moon in her mouth after all. With Spats & Crunch to run with, her workings, as she called them, were more down to earth. Indigo's specialities were other worlds, fiddling. Spats concentrated

on hands, deft, light knife throwing-get-a-watch-offa-wrist, agile hands. Crunch, himself, was moved by yearnings to tear-the-damn-place-down, your place, you anybody he hadda hankering to. Awesome trio. The immediate problem was how to identify Indigo as a Jr. G.C. Spats almost slapped the devil out of Crunch when he said, "Man, that's impossible. She a girl, how she gonna look like us?" Spats snarled, "Ain't nothin' impossible for a Geechee Cap-i-tan." With that the two assembled Indigo's uniform. 'Cause she wouldn't look right in a inside-out sweatshirt or in cut-offs like theirs, they decided on a hat. Spats stole a Stetson, the smallest one he saw in Kerreson's. They didn't like the Colored to try the hats on anyway. Crunch beat up some yellow hincty boy who was playing ball on King Street & took a fine leather belt off him. Then they decorated it with switchblade handles & a strap for Indigo to carry her fiddle round. What Geechee Capitan would walk round without having both hands free? In her new get-up Indigo was a fierce-looking lil sister. She stuffed her braids up in her Stetson, dark brown & tilted over her left eye. Spats, Crunch, & Indigo, all agreed that she was now presentable. Nevertheless, Crunch felt something was missing.

154 "Hey, Spats, I know what's wrong! She ain't gotta real name. Ya know, a name particular to us!" Indigo had always liked her name. There was nothing wrong with her name. She was particularly herself. She changed the nature of things. She colored & made richer what was blank & plain. The slaves who were ourselves knew all about indigo & Indigo herself. Besides there was great danger in callin' someone out their name. Spirits get confused, bring you something meant for someone else. Folks get upset, move with wrath instead of grace, when callt by a name not blessed & known on earth. Indigo was not hot on this new name business. After some discussion, Crunch accepted a shortening of Indigo to "Digo." Spats had learned enough to know that in another language, Spanish to be exact, "digo" had something to do with "to say" & to his mind, Digo was really sayin' somethin'. If she chose to get on her fiddle, ya best mind what she say.

155 The South in her.

156 Coming down Chad Street or running thru the Yards, the Jr. G.C.'s served notice that the colored children were manifestations of the twentieth century. No mythology in the Old Slave Mart approached their realities. Nothing in the Calhoun House reminded them of themselves. Catfish Row was so old-fashioned, dusted pastel frame houses

where hominy-grits, oysters, & okra steamed each evening. Crap games went on as usual in the tiny alleyways, edged by worn porches where grandmas made believe they didn't have any idea all that was goin' on. Yet they'd smile if somebody had a high streak of luck, sending yelps & bass guffaws over the roofs. Here Digo, Crunch, & Spats performed, mixing the skills of modern wayward children with the past-times of the more traditional colored iconoclasts.

157   They especially liked to go round to Sneed's. Now, Sneed's was a bakery; fresh breads, muffins, cakes, & cookies every day. But the reasons the Jr. G.C.'s spent so much time there was that Sneed's was connected to a winding complex of underground rooms where gambling, cockfights, and a twenty-four-hour social room entertained the most adventurous of Charleston's colored subterraneans. Spats' brother, Pretty Man, made sure that the transactions in the various gaming activities stayed calm. Whenever possible, Pretty Man believed that money should change hands in his favor, calmly, of course.

158   Actually, the bakers in their high white hats & flour-covered aprons carried more than dough downstairs directly under the ovens. They took the daily numbers receipts down to The Caverns, as they were called, & came back up to the muffins & turnovers with a possible change of life-style for a confirmed pastry-gourmet. Indigo didn't mind the numbers. She played a few from time to time. That meant new dress-up clothes, Eudoxa strings for the violin, a Sunday chapeau for Mama, and spending change for the spirits who still kept Indigo's company late at night.

NUMBERS FOR PROSPERITY & FURTHERED INDEPENDENCE OF THE RACE
by Indigo

164—if searching for hearth & home, more secure familial relations.

626—if desirous of a journey to one's true home, spiritual or physical, play once a week for a month.

208—if in need of immediate assistance for ordinary amenities, play only on Monday.

176—if seeking a larger dwelling for one's family, this works, in conjunction with 164.

508—if yearning for retreat & personal solitude, play on five consecutive Wednesdays.

141—if conflicted by the stresses of racism, play twice a week for five years.

999—to be freed from debilitating relations, fiscal or otherwise, daily.

REALIZING SPIRITS' HINTS/WHAT YOUR DREAMS CAN DO FOR YOU

by Indigo

If you see a gull flying over your house, there is a 7 in your combination. If the gull swoops downward, there is also a 2. If the gull flies toward the moon, there is a 9.

If your Mother is burning something on the stove, and you cannot get up to warn her, play I. If she is burning up something, and you are able to warn her, play 7. If what your Mother is cooking & burning is your favorite dish, that's a 123, in combination.

If there is a lover of yours kissing your best friend in your house, there are two 3's in your number. If you are angry about this, your number is 353. If you find it amusing, your number is 333.

If you keep falling down in your dream, there's surely an 8 in your number. If where you are falling is never reached or is unknown, add a 1. If you fall somewhere, change that to 6.

GENERAL NOTES

Flowers—719/ A car—520/ Fires—882/ Beds—231/ The Christ Child—777/ The Crucifix—111/ Judas (someone you know or Iscariot)—001/ A deceased grandmother—803/ A deceased grandfather—902/ Mulberry bushes—756/ Maggots—395/ Guns—246.

159   Pretty Man hired Spats & Crunch to clean up after the cockfights. To carry the screeching bleeding birds on outside & kill'em, if need be, was Spats' job. Taking the razors off their feet was Crunch's. Indigo stayed away from the ring after the first time. She'd watched these men shouting out for their favorite to slay the other. All this money waving in their hands, collected by Pretty Man, who must have been a mathematical genius. He kept all the odds, paid out, collected what was due him, without taking his eyes off the match. Indigo felt a steely vengeance growing in her spirit. Grown men laughing at dying animals. She felt birds hovering above her eyes. She moved the razors off the roosters. Put them in the palms of the onlookers. Let them cut each other to shreds, she thought. Let them know the havoc of pain. Spats & Crunch had suspicions 'bout Indigo's powers, but couldn't believe she'd gone & done something like this.

160   The cocks stalked the ring quietly. The men round the ring leaped over one another, flailing their razored palms at throats, up & down backs, backsides, ankles. Such a conglomeration of footwear swung over the side of the ring: high-top sneakers, lizard loafers, wing-tips, galoshes, work boots. Indigo stood by the door watching this bloodletting. Silent. Pretty Man surveyed the situation. Put the evilest eye he could gather up on Indigo, who startled under the power of his gaze. That was all it took. The men slowly came back to themselves. Looked about, puzzled. Put their hats back on. Shook the sawdust from themselves. Wondered where all this blood in the stands came from. The wounds had closed, no scars. Indigo was not malevolent. Yet Pretty Man would not tolerate such shenanigans in his place.

161   Without exchanging words, Pretty Man & Indigo came up with an arrangement. She was, after all, a Geechee Capitan, too. From that point on Indigo spent her time at Sneed's in the "social room," playing her fiddle. Since you could only buy liquor in bottles from sunup till sundown, coming over to Sneed's social room for a glass of beer or a shot of whiskey just made common sense to high-livers in Charleston.

162   Table service, some gambling, and that child on the fiddle were a gratifying combination after work for the family folks, and before work for the night labor force.

163   Indigo didn't change her style of playing. She still went after what she was feeling. But now she'd look at somebody. Say a brown-skinned man with a scar on his cheek, leathery hands, and a tiredness in his eyes. Then she'd bring her soul all up in his till she'd ferreted out the most lovely moment in that man's life. & she played that. You could tell from looking that as Indigo let notes fly from the fiddle, that man's

scar wasn't quite so ugly; his eyes filling with energy, a tenderness tapping from those fingers now, just music. The slaves who were ourselves aided Indigo's mission, connecting soul & song, experience & unremembered rhythms. Pretty Man was relieved. Indigo'd found her a place. He could tell Uncle John there'd be no more wanton juvenile Circe in these parts. There was coming for sure a woman in charge of her powers. Training was what she was wanting.

164 Pretty Man didn't know how Indigo played what she played, but he did know she had a gift. Spats had mentioned how the girl couldn't play in her house 'less she agreed to take lessons. So a teacher for Indigo was out of the question. There's more than one way to skin a cat, & Pretty Man hadn't gotten this far 'cause of a lack of imagination. No. There was something real simple that he could do. Pretty Man liked the simple things in life: money, a good woman, respect. Mabel, his girl, was a simple sweet woman who helped out in the social room. Pretty Man sent Mabel in her tight straight red skirt out in the streets looking for any records with violin playing on 'em. They were gonna replace the jukebox for a while. "Yes," he said to himself, "Digo gonna play it by ear, here, for a time. For some time."

165 Mabel, who was as dutiful as a southern girl could be, came back from all the record stores with a peculiar assortment of violin melodies & violinists. Yehudi Menuhin plays Bartók, *Violin Concerto #2*. Papa John Creach. *Duke Ellington's Jazz Violin Session* with Svend Asmussen, Stéphane Grappelli, Ray Nance, & Billy Strayhorn. Heifetz plays Bach, *Unaccompanied Sonatas & Partitas*. Plus Stuff Smith. "I got one of every violiner they had," Mabel cooed. Pretty Man looked at each album. Nodded his head. "Get these on that ol' jukebox for me, okay?" It was done.

166 Pretty Man offered Indigo a dollar for every one of the tunes she learned to play by ear, or to play as the record played. Pretty Man called everything from Bach to Ellington a tune. If it was Smith's "Blues in the Dungeon," that was a tune. Just as Bartók's 2nd movement, *andante tranquillo*, was a tune. Indigo didn't jump at the chance to change her aesthetic. In fact, she told Pretty Man there was no sense at all in playing something that somebody else could already play. But Spats & Crunch had a meeting on the matter, determined that Indigo's pursuits would mightily enhance the Jr. G.C. treasury. Even Indigo didn't argue 'gainst that. Imagine all the finery & catfish the Jr. Geechee Capitans could offer the not-so-well-off Colored, now Christmas was coming. Indigo, indeed, had made her presence felt in the small gang since her initiation. Give gifts to those who

should know love. Give hell to those who take us lightly. New mottos. New priorities emerging for the Geechee Capitans.

167   Pretty Man gave Mabel change for the jukebox, whenever Indigo was training. Indigo didn't do badly. Yet the nuance & dexterity of the masters occasionally eluded her, her personal rhythms running contrary to theirs. The octaves she chose, not the ones sounded by Creach or Heifetz. Then, too, one time she forgot she wasn't to take solos during Ellington's "Tricky Licks" and played all on top of Ray Nance. Pretty Man was impressed by Indigo's determination to rise up to the challenge. Mabel was concerned, 'cause folks used to the child's fiddlin' till they souls spoke, were getting cantankerous, leaving early, not leaving tips, being genuinely unpleasant. Missing something.

168   Late one afternoon when the social room was usually crowded with menfolks & womenfolks, going on 'bout the Colored, the day's doings, and what might be in the cards, Mabel watched. Nothing going on but Indigo & that jukebox. Violins. Violins. Violins, white folks done come up from they grave to drive the Colored out of a nice spot, they spot. 'All this fiddlin' was makin' folks unhappy, not wanting no drinks, not wanting the hush puppies, greens, & catfish Mabel prepared with so much spice. All them empty tables. All them fiddles. It was better before, when the girl played her own mind. There was a fullness to conversation then. Plus, Pretty Man spoke to her 'bout more than how was Indigo playing. "What's the girl doing on her fiddle these days?" he'd ask. Like all Mabel had to do was remember each time she'd heard "Blues in C" or "Arabian Song, No. 42." No. No. Mabel looked at Indigo sitting by the jukebox, listening, fingering, humming. No more. Mabel pulled the plug out the wall. Took a step toward Indigo. "Indigo, give me that fiddle. Right this minute, do you hear me? Pretty Man don't want no more fiddlin' round heah. Now, c'mon, give it heah." Indigo moved quick, like moonlight. "Spats. Crunch. *G.C. in trouble. G.C. in trouble.*" Indigo let the force of her own style of fiddle-fightin' come to the fore. Such a war-cry bouncing in the social room where hips & bosoms used to shake. Mabel was overwhelmed by her mission to have things be the way they used to be, not understanding that Indigo's existence made that impossible.

169   Spats & Crunch came running. Spats threw chairs in fronta Mabel's every step. Crunch kept Mabel's grabbing hands off Indigo's face & fiddle. Mabel took on the attributes of a lioness, prowling, growling. It was everything the boys could do to save Indigo; her hair or her fiddle.

170   Mabel proceeded to attack the boys with her nails, her heels, her teeth, her voice. She callt on everybody: Moses & her mother.

"Jesus, get that fiddle out my life." Spats had some scratches. Crunch was generally a mess. They were all a little scared. Mabel was shouting for Pretty Man. Pretty Man was Mabel's man. They were in a lot of trouble.

171   Spats thought they should get on outta Sneed's. "My brother ain't gonna stand for us fightin' his woman." Fiddle in arm, Indigo clammered thru the caverns, Spats & Crunch beside her. "We in for it now. Damn we might haveta hide out, when Pretty Man know what we done!" Crunch's hearing wasn't subtle enough to catch Mabel's screams. Pretty Man having one of his tempers. Indigo slowed down. "We ain't the ones haveta run nowhere." Spats was impatient. "We got ta keep movin'." Crunch was already gone. Spats tried pulling Indigo by her free arm. "Digo, c'mon. We cain't let Pretty Man catch us. Let's go." Indigo shook her head. "No, I'ma go back & see to Mabel." & Spats was gone.

172   Indigo felt The Caverns for the first time. The air was dark, heavy. The baking breads wafted thru her nostrils, leaden. Her fiddle, as she let it fall over her side, weighed down on her spirit. Shame crawled up her cheeks. She was going to see about Mabel. Mabel had gotten in trouble 'cause of Indigo's fiddle, 'cause Indigo was a Geechee Capitan. Mabel was just some woman. One day Indigo would be a woman, too. The shame etched tears down her face, pushed her back toward the social room. Fear dashed her 'gainst the wall in the dark, when Pretty Man, as pretty as ever, briskly went up to the bakery. He was putting his shirt back in his pants as he walked, straightening himself up. Indigo wisht the switchblade handles on her violin case were knives. She'd have them all land in his back, but she didn't want to hurt anybody else. The Colored had been hurt enough already.

173   The Caverns began to moan, not with sorrow but in recognition of Indigo's revelation. The slaves who were ourselves had known terror intimately, confused sunrise with pain, & accepted indifference as kindness. Now they sang out from the walls, pulling Indigo toward them. Indigo ran her hands along the walls, to get the song, getta hold to the voices. Instead her fingers grazed cold, hard metal rings. Rust covered her palms & fingers. She kept following the rings. Chains. Leg irons. The Caverns revealed the plight of her people, but kept on singing. The tighter Indigo held the chains in her hands, the less shame was her familiar. Mabel's tiny woeful voice hovered over the blood thick chorus of The Caverns. Indigo knew her calling. The Colored had hurt enough already.

EMERGENCY CARE OF OPEN WOUNDS/WHEN IT HURTS
by Indigo

Calmly rinse the wound with copious amounts of cold tap water. This will significantly reduce the possibilities of infection. If available, use clean linen applied firmly against the wound to inhibit bleeding. If the pressure is not adequate, do it again. Another method allows the bottom of a stainless-steel saucepan to be applied to the wound. The cold of the pan reduces swelling as well as bleeding. A poultice of mandrake berries can be of great use also, until further care can be offered.

EMERGENCY CARE OF WOUNDS THAT CANNOT BE SEEN

Hold the victim gently. Rock in the manner of a quiet sea. Hum softly from your heart. Repeat the victim's name with love. Offer a brew of red sunflower to cleanse the victim's blood & spirit. Fasting & silence for a time refurbish the victim's awareness of her capacity to nourish & heal herself. New associations should be made with caution, more caring for herself.

174   Indigo carefully wrapped her dolls in sheets of white cotton she'd borrowed from her mother's weaving rooms. To the left of the moon she'd painted on her wall was a growing mound of white ovals with little cloth feet sticking out. The sun was fading. Fine tints of orange lingered on the edges of the dolls' heads, which all pointed to the east. Indigo had wrapped Marie-Hélène & Miranda last. Hugging them both, kissing their fore-heads, holding them at arms' length to get one final glimpse of those who had been her closest friends. After a final curtsey to the shrouded companions, Indigo played what she remembered of Bartók. Each note demanding precision, honesty, and depth.

175   Lord, this child is a miracle, thought her mother, Hilda Effania, as she listened & watched from the door. She'd stolen up the back stairs as quickly as she could when she'd heard *real* music

coming from Indigo's room. Yet now she felt a regret that she'd forbidden the child her willful desire to play her soul. It was true like Aunt Haydee said, "A youngun'll come up with what you want, when ya leave 'em the room to find it." Indigo finished all the lyrical fragments she could from heart, plus she'd added a tag from "Cotton Tail." Bowing very formally, *legato*, Indigo turned to put her fiddle in its case. She saw her mother, hesitated, and stammered, "Mama, I think it's time I stopped playing with dolls, don't you?"

176   "Well, I do recall sayin' something like that one of those terribly busy days, when I already had my hands full. Musta been the day you wanted a 'period' dinner . . ."

177   "No, a menstruation dinner, Mama."

178   "That's right, I do believe I tol' you to pack 'em up in the attic." Hilda Effania bit her lips, smuggled a smile out of her concern for her child. "Indigo, you don't haveta bury the girls. I think they look wonderful here in your room. As long as I can remember, you've gone to bed with your dollies. No matter how angry I was when I said what I said, you know I don't hold a soul to my every word. You keep your dolls as long as you want. Why, I think at least Miranda can come to Christmas dinner." Hilda Effania wanted Indigo to lose this forlorn curve in her back, the sadness in her gaze. But Indigo was resolute.

179   "No, Mama. I don't think they're quite dead, they're just resting, I think." Indigo looked up at her mama wanting very much. All she said was: "Mama, I couldn't bear for them to grow up. I couldn't stand it, Mama. I just couldn't."

180   Hilda Effania really didn't know what was the matter. She knew to hold Indigo close to her, to say her name over & over till the child was ready to talk.

181   "Mama, it's hard, isn't it?"

182   "What's hard, Indigo?"

183   "Being a grown colored woman is hard, ain't it? Just like you tol' me. Just 'cause I haveta grow up, my dolls don't haveta. I can save them. Mama, let's take them to the attic. You & me. I don't even wanta invite Mrs. Yancey, though Miranda will miss her. Just you & me, let's do something very special."

184   Hilda Effania sat Indigo down on the bed with her. She rocked her baby in her arms, patted her back, hummed a tune as she made it up.

185   "I don't know that it's all that hard to be a full-grown colored woman, Indigo. I can imagine not wanting your friends to grow up,

though. If they grow up, eventually, they will haveta go. But, you know they could stay little girls forever."

186   "How, Mama?"

187   "You know it's Christmas time, & there's hundreds of other little girls, oh tiny little girls, who'd take real good care of Miranda, Marie-Hélène & all the rest of them. & you & I know there's no dollies in the whole world quite like these." Hilda Effania tried so hard not to laugh. She had flashes of Indigo stealing rice from the kitchen, buttons from the sewing room, bits of satin from patterns for Miz Fitzhugh's ball gowns. "Like I was saying, Indigo, there's no dollies like this anywhere on the earth."

188   "You mean, give 'em away to strangers?" Indigo asked, indignant.

189   "You said they weren't dead, just resting," Hilda Effania responded, while she put Indigo's Stetson on her head. "You know, for a man's hat, that's pretty sharp, Indigo."

190   Indigo pulled the hat off her head, thought a second. Stood in front of her mother with a desperate air.

191   "Mama, I'll make the other lil girls new dollies, honest I will. I promise. But I want you & me to have a ceremony for my dollies & let em rest till I have a baby, or till Cypress or Sassafrass has a baby. Please Mama, I want them to stay with the family."

192   It was true. After Indigo there'd be no more babies in the family till one of her girls was grown enough to bring one home. Hilda Effania couldn't agree more with Indigo's familial fervor. After all, she was devoted to her daughters. Now, Indigo, all of 12, was saving her most treasured possessions for the daughters to come. This made sense to Hilda Effania, who'd seen those other two grow up much too fast. This was the day that Indigo caught up with them.

193   "Okay, what sort of ceremony do you want to have?"

194   "I want you to sing some holy song, while I carry them one by one to the attic. That's what I wanta do, Mama. Then I wanta come downstairs & help you make the gumbo for when Cypress & Sassafrass come home. Can I, please?" Indigo was excited, beginning & ending the largest segment of her life.

195   Hilda Effania changed her clothes once she got in the spirit of things. She put on a crêpe dress with pearls & black velvet round the shoulders, a little lipstick, some mascara. At her suggestion, Indigo put on her white taffeta Communion dress. Hilda Effania stationed herself at the foot of the second-floor stairs leading to the attic. Indigo solemnly carried each doll up the curving steps, as her mother's voice rose behind her to the rafters:

"Jesus lover of my soul
Hide me, oh my Savior
Hide me till the storm of life is past
While the stormy waters roll
While the tempest still is high."

* * *

196   The last time Aunt Haydee opened her mouth, she'd asked Indigo to play some rough blues on that fiddle. That was just before Ella Mae's twins arrived. Indigo'd been rubbing Aunt Haydee's hands on the porch by the scrub pines. The sea breeze left her face loved & clear. Aunt Haydee's hands, the same ones delivered hundreds of brown little babies, yellow tykes, screaming black tiny ol' things, those hands were aching, ugly, unmoving now. Indigo told Aunt Haydee her own stories: how the crocodile got his tail; where the rabbit learned to jump; how the wolf couldn't be trusted. Aunt Haydee rocked in her chair. Now this chair had belonged to Aunt Carrie who was the mother to Aunt Susie Marie whose sister married that half-breed from Allendale, moved all the way to New York City & was killt in a barroom brawl where the Colored carried on.

197   Ella Mae's delivery was quite ordinary. Everybody came out head first. Nothing was missing on either one. Johnny Orpheus held Ella Mae's left leg, while Indigo raised the right so the babies had a free path. Ella Mae didn't tear. She made a few yells that Christ would have heard in the other world, but Aunt Haydee kept on murmuring that Ella Mae was a good strong gal, strong gal, birthing two at a time like this.

198   "Be proud of yourself, Ella Mae. I ain't never done none of this. Not a child to my name & I can see whatta trial you been thru & how the Lord's gonna set a bounty of goodness upon ya. I can see it, Ella Mae. Don't push too hard now. Jesus don't want nothing coming express."

199   Indigo'd studied violin with the white woman Miz Fitzhugh sent every summer, but she concentrated more on learning what Aunt Haydee knew. Giving birth, curing women folks & their loved ones. At first Aunt Haydee only allowed Indigo to play her fiddle to soothe the women in labor, but soon the mothers, the children, sought Indigo for relief from elusive disquiet, hungers of the soul. Aunt Haydee was no fool. She watched Indigo playing the fiddle one evening as the

tide came in. It'd been a long time since a colored woman on Difuskie moved the sea. Some say it was back in slavery time.

200   *Blue Sunday*, that was her name 'cause she was born on a Sunday & as black as pitch. *Blue Sunday* was the favorite of Master Fitzhugh, but everytime he came near her the sea would getta fuming, swinging whips of salt water round the house where the white folks lived. This went on for years till *Blue Sunday* was so grown even Master Fitzhugh knew she'd have to breed or lose him money. He liked the way her bosom was barely visible, how her hips defined that coarse scratchy garb field hands wore. He'd sent her silks, even a corset from France, but *Blue Sunday*'d tied these round a hog she left in his library. When he whipped her in fronta all the slaves before the indigo harvest, all she did was laugh. No scars, no blood appeared on her back. He threw her to the overseers, two po' white trash hooligans decent white folks wouldn't look at. When they were through with her she was still a virgin. Master Fitzhugh took her, unconscious, to his bed. When he penetrated her, she turned into a crocodile. As a crocodile, *Blue Sunday* was benign. Her only struggle was to remain unconquered. Master Fitzhugh was left with one leg, but otherwise quite himself. The Fitzhughs no longer cultivated indigo as a cash crop. *Blue Sunday* was never seen again by any white person, but women of color in labor called on her and heard her songs when they risked mothering free children.

201   Now this is what the folks said. What actually transpired when the sea was rough & a woman was in labor was that Aunt Haydee pleaded with *Blue Sunday* to "Please, give this child life, please, give this child the freedom you know." Then Indigo would play her fiddle, however the woman wanted. Once Hilda Effania came to get Indigo after Sister Liza Anne had been in labor for 48 hours, but Indigo'd fiddled her own mother out the cabin. There was nothing could come between Indigo, Aunt Haydee, & new people of color. Hilda gave up. Miz Fitzhugh gave up. When Aunt Haydee died, right after Ella Mae's twins first suckled, Indigo just picked up her fiddle. Aunt Haydee went to Our Lord on a melody only Indigo or *Blue Sunday* could know.

202   Johnny Orpheus tried to give Indigo a few dollars for his two boys, Muhammed & Ali, but Indigo declined. She'd lost Aunt Haydee, which meant we'd all lost touch with a thirst for freedom. Indigo would have tossed Aunt Haydee's ashes to the waves sauntering up to the cabin every now & then, but she decided to carry Aunt Haydee home in a funny bluish jar Uncle John'd given her when she was small. Uncle John had told her that colored trapeze artists usedta spit

into that jar or be strung up by their heels. Now that was a long time ago, but that's what he said.

203   No one had ever expected it, but that child from Charleston, that Indigo, moved into Aunt Haydee's tabby hut, just like she belonged there. It wasn't that she didn't have gifted hands or a tenderness that could last a lifetime. It was just folks weren't sure where she came from or how she came to be among them. Charleston was far away.

204   Indigo knew, holding Aunt Haydee's ashes in her arms, she'd not be back for a long while. Charleston wasn't her home, any more than *Blue Sunday* hadn't suffered. In Martinique with the other black people, Indigo could have carried her aunt's ashes on a ferry, but 'tween Difuskie & Charleston she was lucky to be on more than a canoe.

205   She spent little time on it, but she was concerned. Her sisters were artists. Would they understand she just wanted where they came from to stay alive? Hilda Effania knew Indigo had an interest in folklore. Hilda Effania had no idea that Indigo was the folks.

206   Somebody said that the day Indigo left Difuskie, 2,000 *Blue Sundays* came out dancing to Scott Joplin, drinking moonshine, & showing their legs. Indigo never denied this, but she kept a drawer fulla silk stockings that had not a run, & she'd never been one to miss a dance, when the aqua-blue men strode up from the sea, the slaves who were ourselves.

Tina McElroy Ansa
(1949–)

A native of Macon, Georgia, and the youngest of five children, Tina McElroy Ansa was born in November 1949. Her childhood was steeped in storytelling and reading. Ansa was educated in Catholic schools and graduated from Spelman College, in Atlanta, Georgia, in 1971 with a major in English. She initially worked as a journalist for the Atlanta Constitution *and the* Charlotte Observer. *Subsequently, she has written four novels that are set in the fictive town of Mulberry, Georgia, and are resplendent in African American folklore. Ansa's debut novel,* Baby of the Family *(1989), excerpted below, considers the role of the supernatural in the lives of a modern family. The* New York Times *named this novel a Notable Book of the Year, and a film version is slated for production. To date, Ansa has also published* Ugly Ways *(1993),* The Hand I Fan With *(1996), and* You Know Better *(2002). Ansa currently lives with her husband on St. Simon Island in Georgia.*

Baby of the Family

BIRTH

1   A hush swallowed the hot little room as the mother shuddered one last time, pushed down hard, and bore her third child, her baby girl, into the world.

2   "Awww," the doctor's and nurses' sighs floated on the hot humid air of the room like a hymn.

3   "Well, well, well. You got you a lucky baby here." Dr. Williams was red in the face, as if he had been doing all the work himself. He held the newborn child up for the nurses and the mother to see. "Yeah, a mighty special child."

4   Nellie, the mother, wasn't a bit surprised by the doctor's words. She had known this child would be different the moment she felt its head break through her vagina and enter the world. It was a special sensation, unlike those of the births of her two sons.

5   Around the time her water had broken the evening before, the mild November temperatures had suddenly dropped into the thirties. But now it was torrid in the tiny delivery room. Everyone there was as soaked with sweat as the mother who lay panting and grunting on the hospital table.

6   To Nellie everything in the delivery room seemed to be covered by a spotless white material: the nurses, the doctor, the table she lay on, her own body. Even the walls and ceiling were painted a white white that reflected the sharp glare of the round overhead light. The glare made her eyes ache, but Nellie was so glad to be in the last stages of labor—a hard, long, wrenching labor such as she had never experienced before—that she didn't mind the light.

7   The labor pains had gone on all night, and with the rising of the sun her baby was born.

8   "Yeah, a mighty special little girl, Mrs. Mac," Dr. Williams repeated.

9   As if she weren't the center of attention already, the doctor's statement made all eyes in the small hot room fix on the newborn child even more intently. In her first seconds in this world, the little girl seemed to bask in the glow from the eyes of her mother, her physician, and two nurses—a tiny cynosure.

10 "This one came with a veil over her face. Yes indeed, it's a sure sign that she's a lucky one, yes indeedy."

11   Wide arcs of perspiration marked the doctor's armpits, and the white surgical gown he wore over his tight little round belly was stained front and back with his sweat.

12   When Nellie rose up on her elbows, the sweat at the roots of her auburn-tinted hair and on her brow rolled down into her eyes and stung them a little. But she was so anxious to see her little girl that she hurriedly blinked the salty drops away as if they were tears and craned her neck to see around the younger nurse who had moved in for a closer look. Still blowing and puffing from the exertion of the birth, the mother was forgotten in the excitement of the newborn child. She looked at her longed-for girl over the sparkling white cotton cloth draping her knees. At first sight of the infant, Nellie drew in her breath so sharply that the shot of oxygen made her a little dizzy.

13   The baby, whom she planned to call Lena after her own grandmother, lay in the doctor's outstretched hands. Her wrinkled skin was hardly any color at all and her tiny legs and arms made circles in the air as she wiggled about. She began a soft sweet whimper that made the doctor and nurses smile at each other as if the child had performed a trick.

14   It surprised her mother that Lena could cry at all. Over her entire head, as if draped there by a band of angels, lay a thin membrane that rose and fell away from the child's sweet face with each breath she took. It looked almost like the white stockings the nurses in the room wore.

15   Although at first Nellie's gasp sounded like one of fear, it was really an expression of wonder. She herself was an only child and had learned everything she knew about babies when her own children were born. She had never seen an infant with a caul before.

16   The veil over her daughter's face gave the little girl a ghostly appearance. Nellie almost expected her to rise from Dr. Williams's large rubber-gloved hands and float around the small steamy room like a newborn apparition.

17   "Oh, my precious, precious," she crooned to the child lying a few feet away from her in the doctor's hands. She longed to reach over and take the baby in her arms, but she was so fatigued that even the thought of lifting her arms made her eyes roll around in her head.

18   Everyone in the delivery room was still. The doctor and the two nurses, grinning under their white surgical masks, stood around as if they were part of a Christmas tableau. Arriving with a veil over her face, the child brought with her a touch of the supernatural into a place that owed so much to the scientific. The doctor was reluctant

to break the spell that had settled on them all there in the hot, antiseptic little room.

19 The fact that St. Luke's Hospital existed at all in the small Georgia town of Mulberry in 1949 was spectacular in itself. Nellie had thought so each time she went there for a doctor's visit or a child's emergency or to visit a sick friend. She knew that when black people went downtown to the large county hospital, they had to use a back entrance and sit in a dingy back room until a surly white nurse got around to them and shunted them off to the colored ward and rooms, where everything, even the sheets, looked used.

20 But a stay at St. Luke's, no matter how serious the complaint, was a life-affirming experience. Nothing but black folks—the doctor, the nurses, the receptionist, the aides, the orderlies, the patients, the families—all black folks. And the sick and injured got nothing but the best the staff could give.

21 Being private it cost more than the public county hospital. Even a stay in the wards at St. Luke's cost almost as much as a private room on the colored floor of the public hospital. But Nellie didn't know anyone able to scrape up the money who didn't try to get into St. Luke's first.

22 Dr. Williams, once a poor ashy-legged boy in Mulberry, had made two promises to himself when he returned home from working and scuffling his way through medical school: one was that he would help another black Mulberry boy through medical school if the boy promised to come back home and practice there; the other was that he would have a real hospital in his hometown for his own folks one day. After years in a lucrative and busy practice as the only black doctor in town, he had fulfilled both promises. His first wife's nephew would be graduating from Meharry in the spring. And this little hospital—just a one-story white wooden building with a wide front porch, on a paved residential street in the black part of town—was the other.

23 And exactly as the doctor—now graying at the temples and thickening at the waist—had planned as a young man, his hospital had as much modern equipment as he could acquire. There was an old but functioning incubator in the delivery room, an X-ray room behind the nurses' station, and a small laboratory in the basement next to the laundry, where the hospital's nurses did all their own routine tests.

24 Dr. Williams only hired nurses from the top of their classes at Tuskegee Institute. The examining rooms and main operating room had such up-to-date equipment that he was sometimes reluctant to

let the white doctors from the county hospital come for a tour, for fear of their jealousy.

25   For weeks the whole town had talked of the time Dr. Williams had stormed out the front door of the hospital in the dead of winter, leaving his hat and overcoat behind, in a fury about the death of another black premature baby. "That's the last baby we're going to lose because we don't have an incubator!" old Nurse Bloom told folks he had shouted as he jumped into his shiny black Ford and drove off into the night. Two days later a crate arrived from Boston, Massachusetts, with a used incubator inside.

26   "Don't be asking me a lot of questions 'bout this stuff," he'd tell his staff when a new piece of equipment arrived unexpectedly. "Just read those specifications and make sure you all know how to work it. You all smart people, that's why you're here."

27   But this early morning Dr. Williams gave no thought to the techniques he had learned at Meharry. Seeming to forget his usual delivery-room procedure, formed over nearly a quarter century of practice, he turned the next two minutes into a ritualized dance that had nothing to do with modern medicine.

28   Standing at the foot of the delivery table so the mother could see what was going on, the doctor turned with the baby in his outstretched hands to Nurse Bloom, the older of the two women in white, walked three steps over to her, and proffered his bundle, still steaming from the womb. Wiggling and squirming and fighting the air with her tiny fists, little Lena stretched her body out to its full length and threw her head back, seeming to strain against the veil.

29   Nurse Bloom, acting as if the gods were watching her every move, reached out, her elasticized fingers trembling a little. Starting at the base of the child's neck where the thin membrane began, the nurse gently pulled the caul from the baby's face until she had uncovered her miniature features, the crown of her round head, and her mat of thick tightly curled hair.

30   In the nurse's slim hands, wrinkled under her rubber gloves from age and innumerable scrubbings in hot soapy water, the veil gave no resistance. It came away from the child's head evenly, with a faint hiss, disengaging at the nape of the tiny girl's neck where her hair grew to a little V.

31   Now it was the young nurse who gasped as she watched the procedure for the first time. Old Nurse Bloom, feeling the gossamer weight of the caul in her finely etched hands, had to stifle a bubble rising in her throat and call on all her years of training and

self-discipline to fight the giddiness that was about to overwhelm her in the windowless room. Turning away from the others, she walked to the far side of the room, dropped the limp membrane into a shining silver pan, and deftly slipped the receptacle onto a shelf under one of the white tables there. Beneath the white mask that covered her nose and mouth, her wrinkled lips moved to a chant she spoke in her head.

32   The sound of the caul hitting the metal pan and the pan sliding across the metal shelf were the only noises in the room besides the soft mewling of the baby squirming in the doctor's big hands. The atmosphere in the stark delivery room reminded Nellie of a joyous yet reverent occasion—a baptism or a wake. "Let's get this baby cleaned up and in her mother's arms where she belong," Dr. Williams barked. But when he handed the child over to the older nurse, it was with a gentleness that few of the staff of the small hospital had ever seen in the harried physician. And Nellie thought his whole stance, which had stiffened while he issued his order, had suddenly relaxed again as he watched the old nurse take the newborn baby into her hands.

33   Nurse Bloom hadn't giggled in years. Now, like a young girl accepting a prize at the county fair, she carried the child to the metal table and silver pan of clear water with a smile playing around the corners of her mouth. Lying next to the pan of warm water was a stack of bleached white towels neatly folded into squares by the younger nurse's aide.

34   The old woman dipped the baby's body into the pan of warm water, washing the blood and afterbirth from the infant's face, throat, chest, arms, legs, behind, and feet as she crooned softly to the child.

35   "Oh, what a special baby. What a sweet little lucky pretty baby girl. Yes, that's what you are, all right. That's what you are. A sweet little lucky baby girl. Yes, you are, 'cause you come to this world right to the person who know all about you, who know everything to do for you. Uh-huh, this old lady right here washing your new little behind know just what to do for a pretty, lucky little baby girl like you."

36   Nurse Bloom was standing on the other side of the room from where the mother lay on the cloth-covered table, her feet still in the stirrups; with her knees poking up in the air, Nellie looked like a capital M. She couldn't quite make out what Nurse Bloom was saying, but the old nurse cooed so sweetly to tiny Lena that to the mother's ear each word sounded like a tablespoon of rich warm Alaga syrup poured over the child's soft new body.

37   Dr. Williams and the other nurse looked on silently, smiling like godparents. They stood there at the foot of Nellie's table with their hands hanging limply by their sides as if they had nothing else to do but admire Lena.

38   Well, damn, they just gonna forget completely about me, Nellie thought, and let her elbows slip down the smooth sheet covering the surgical table and her tired body fall back on its padded surface. She closed her eyes against the bright light shining directly into her face, and before she knew anything she had fallen into a deep, peaceful slumber.

39   When she awoke, the first thing she noticed was the strawberry-ice-cream-pink walls. They were such a contrast to all the glaringly stark whiteness she had been surrounded by in the delivery room that for a moment she thought she must still be dreaming. But when she heard Christine Williams's rich throaty laughter floating down the hall outside her private room, she remembered where she was and allowed herself to drift back to sleep.

40   Christine was the reason her room was pink instead of the antiseptic white of most rooms in the small hospital. Even the narrow white iron hospital bed in which she had just spent nearly twelve hours of labor had been replaced by a brand-new pink one.

41   Christine, Dr. Williams's second wife, had insisted that some color was needed for the women's private rooms and wards.

42   "Ya'll just wait," the tall slender woman with the elegant pompadour hairstyle had promised as she stuck her head into each room one evening. "I'm gonna get your butts out of these old white iron beds and into some pretty pastel ones to match your new walls before this time tomorrow."

43   And everybody believed her, too. All the next morning, the nurses and staff could hardly do their work for running to the windows and doors each time they heard the gears of a truck grinding outside. The staff had been as excited about the promised delivery of the pink, blue, and peach beds as the patients were. If Christine Williams said they would be there, they would be there.

44   Christine was the type of woman whom people just naturally flocked to and trusted. More than one patient had teased Dr. Williams that the only reason his hospital did such good business was because his wife ran it.

45   When Edward, Nellie's second son, had been born at St. Luke's Hospital, Nellie had seen Christine send twice to the drugstore down the street for tobacco for an old man on the ward who couldn't even afford to pay for it. When he complained about it not being his brand,

Christine just laughed at the old fool's crotchetiness and promised to get it right the next time.

46   Everyone knew that Dr. Williams owned the hospital. But they also understood that his wife, a woman much younger than he, who strolled the halls and rooms all times of day and night dressed to kill in taupe gabardine suits and neutral-colored silk blouses, was the heart of the private establishment that black people in Mulberry considered a privilege to get well in.

47   Most of the hospital—the wards, private rooms, and operating rooms—was laid out on one floor, but at the end of the hall was a staircase that led downstairs to the basement. This was Miss Sallie Mae's domain. She was the cook for the hospital and ran the large basement kitchen like a minor dictator. Reluctantly she shared the basement with the laundry, the lab, and the hospital's owner himself, whose office was at the very rear of the building.

48   "Leave this room the way it is," Nurse Bloom told the orderly the moment he entered the delivery room. "I'll take care of it myself."

VEIL

49   As soon as Nurse Bloom had seen that Nellie was comfortably on her way back to her private room with a nurse and the orderly by her gurney, she cradled the infant Lena in her arms and headed for the nursery and the process that all newborns at St. Luke's Hospital went through.

50   The old nurse never put Lena down, from the time she washed the newborn baby until she laid her in her bassinet among the other babies in the hospital nursery. Nurse Bloom saw to it herself that Lena was weighed, measured, and footprinted. Then the old nurse pinned her first diaper on her and set her down in her crib.

51   The whole process wouldn't have taken as long as it did if Nurse Bloom had been left alone to finish her business. But she wasn't. Every nurse, nurse's aide, and cleaning woman in the place kept slipping away from her duties to come get a look at the new baby, the one born with a veil over her face. Even Miss Sallie Mae from down in the kitchen hoisted her wide heavy frame up the back steps to see Lena and cluck her tongue over the special child.

52   "Would you look at that little one come to this earth with a veil over her face? Gon' be a wise child," Miss Sallie Mae pronounced, then headed right back downstairs, sniffing all the way as if she smelled something burning.

53   The cook's place was immediately filled by two young nurse's aides. "Oh, look, isn't she pretty? I've never seen one come with a veil over its face before. You can't even tell where it was," one young woman said.

54   "She already got a head full of hair," the other replied. "Lord, I shore hope she ain't tender-headed, 'cause I bet it's gonna be a chore and a half to comb it."

55   "I wish she'd open her eyes. You know it's supposed to be good luck for a child like that to look at you. That's what I always heard. She supposed to be a lucky child herself."

56   "My grandmama always said a child like that was kin to being a witch."

57   "A witch?"

58   "Yeah, but not a evil witch, just a person with special powers. I had a cousin who was born with a caul over her whole body that folks used to come to from all over south Georgia to see 'cause she could read 'em. Tell 'em they future."

59   "That's right, they do supposed to have special powers. They supposed to be able to tell you things. But the biggest power is they able to see ghosts."

60   "You right about that. I knew a woman in the country who had three children—a boy and two girls—who was all born with cauls over they faces. And she say they used to see ghosts all the time. Say they used to play with 'em as children."

61   "For real?"

62   "That's what she told me. And she didn't have no reason to lie on her own children. She said they used to play with them ghosts when they was small. But said as they got older, they grew real scared."

63   "All of you talking that silliness about ghosts and haunts and spirits," an older nurse cut in. "But you're overlooking the real thing that this child's caul is a sign of. It's a sure sign that this child is special. That caul is a gift from God, that's what it is. This little girl has been chosen by God as a special person on this earth. She can't hardly help but do something great in this life because God has touched her in the womb."

64   Nurse Bloom just let them talk. She didn't confirm or dispute what they said. She acted as if they weren't there and kept crooning to little Lena as she weighed and measured her, "Oh, yes, sweet baby, Nurse Bloom gonna take care of this sweet little thing. No need to worry atall. Old Nurse Bloom know what she doing, sugar."

65   The whole process took less than half an hour. Nurse Bloom kept
an eye on the clock over the nurses' station to make sure. When she
finished with Lena and laid her on her stomach in her crib, the
nurse glanced at the clock on the wall again and shot the women
gathered around the baby a meaningful look. They got the message
immediately and scattered like baby chicks out of the nursery back
to their duties.

66   Nurse Bloom stood in the hall and watched the women disappear
into doorways. Then she turned to the left and headed back to the
nurses' station.

67   "Let Mrs. Mac have her baby as soon as she wakes up," she told
the nurse behind the desk. "And I don't want anyone to bother me for
at least an hour. I'm taking a break." She turned with a slight smile
on her wrinkled face and headed down the hall to the delivery room,
where the piece of membrane lay drying out in its metal tray.

68   When Nurse Bloom had been a midwife in the country, she had
never let a caul sit for more than a few minutes before preserving it
for the child. Now that she worked in a hospital, she had to adjust her
ritual to fit into the modern mode. But there were still some things
that she would not give in on.

69   I'm not the one to be changing some things that have always been,
she would tell herself when, on occasion, she bent hospital procedure and slipped a sharp knife under the bed of a narrowhipped
woman who was having a hard time having her baby.

70   The old nurse stopped at the door to the hot little delivery room.
She was about to ask the powers who controlled such things to look
on this newborn child kindly and let pass what must pass. She took
the white starched cap off her head and the white leather oxfords
off her feet and laid them on the black-and-white square-tiled
linoleum floor by the door.

71   The atmosphere inside the room was alive. She glanced around
quickly to make sure nothing had been disturbed. Satisfied that everything was as she had left it, Nurse Bloom padded over to the table
against the far wall with the pan of water on top and pulled out the
pan with Lena's caul resting there where she had dropped it.

72   Picking up the thin membrane sent shivers through the nurse's
stocky body and set her teeth on edge. The caul had begun to stiffen
and dry out a bit in the room's heat. Without hesitating, Nurse Bloom
dropped the drying membrane into the still-warm bloody water in the
round metal pan beside her on the table. The caul immediately loosened and spread out on the surface of the pinkish water.

73 With a satisfied little grunt the woman picked up the pan of water and headed out the door. She was surprised at first to find the hall deserted at this time of morning. But then, she thought, a child had been born in this hospital with a veil over her face. Nothing much that happened this November day was going to surprise her much. She turned to the left and hurried toward the back staircase, careful not to slosh the water from the pan onto the floor. At the foot of the stairs she made a sharp right and slipped into the laundry room.

74 The heat of the room nearly knocked Nurse Bloom off her feet. The big white industrial dryer in a far corner was kept running most of the time, and even the linoleum floor was damp and warm under the nurse's stockinged feet. The only person in the single large laundry room was Ted, the orderly who had helped take Lena's mother back to her room.

75 "Ted, I need you to go up and scrub the small O.R.," Nurse Bloom told the orderly, who sat with his feet stretched out in front of him taking a break. "Please see to it that that room is spotless and antiseptic before you leave it. You know what to do. And when you finish that, collect all the soiled linens from the closet upstairs and sort them for pickup. Then you can go to lunch."

76 Ted pulled himself up from his comfortable seat and wondered what he had done to deserve Nurse Bloom's attention. Efficiency was a prized commodity at St. Luke's, and he had tried to keep in step with the hospital's policy since he had begun working there two years before. But all this jumping back and forth! First leave the O.R. the way it is, then clean up the O.R. right away. Don't touch those linens; collect and sort those linens right now. Ted frowned. I'll have to have a talk with Mrs. Williams, he thought. Still, all he said was, "Yes, ma'am." He was so steamed that he didn't even notice she wasn't wearing her cap or her shoes.

77 The nurse watched Ted leave the room, then walked over to the long wooden table where the aides folded the clean dry clothes and linens. Except for a large roll of white butcher's paper on a holder that was used to keep its surface clean, the table was clear. She put the metal pan she was holding down on the smooth paper surface. The caul, still floating on the top of the water, waved around in the pan like a jellyfish. She reached over the pan, pulled off a length of the heavy white paper, and tore it off from the roll. Then she spread the paper on the tabletop and smoothed down its curling ends with her hands.

78 She had to smile at her hospital efficiency. For years in the country, where she was called Mother Bloom, she had conducted this same ritual time and time again but not with all these conveniences.

79   "But I guess I been in the city too long," Nurse Bloom said to herself with a cackle. In her three years at Saint Luke's, she had found the most efficient way to preserve a child's veil. Until she returned to her people's home in the country when she retired, she planned to continue doing it this way.

80   She took the caul from the baby's bath water and spread it out as smoothly and evenly as possible on the paper. She didn't hurry. In all the years that she had done this—Must be forty at least, she thought—no one had ever burst in and disrupted her. And she believed that events, once set in motion, continued on the road intended for them.

81   Carefully she picked up the paper with the caul, placed it on the hot clean surface of the dryer, and stepped back with an air of satisfaction. Now she had to dispose of the water she had first bathed Lena in. She had no intention of pouring it down the drain of the deep double porcelain sink in the corner of the laundry room. The pipes connected to that drain led to the city sewerage system, where the child's bath water would be mingled with all kinds of waste. And Lena's first bath water, in which Nurse Bloom had soaked her birth caul, was, like the child, special. It deserved special treatment.

82   The nurse picked up the pan, headed out of the room into the basement hall, and padded in her stockinged feet toward the back stairs leading outside.

83   The freezing temperatures of the night before, when she had come on duty, had mellowed into a crisp autumn day with a pristine blue sky and the smell of old leaves in the air. What a good day to be born, she thought as she walked over to the rosebushes lining the rear wall of the building beside the door. She clucked her tongue and shook her head sadly. Every time she saw the poor sickly-looking things, she got a picture of Mrs. Williams in one of her pretty suits squatting down in the dirt with Ted the orderly to see what was ailing the bushes that had looked stunted and yellow and refused to grow ever since the two had planted them.

84   Let's see what this baby's water can do for Mrs. Williams's poor little roses, Nurse Bloom said to herself as she sprinkled the base of the plants with the pinkish water. I wouldn't be surprised if those things aren't flourishing next spring.

85   Back in the building, the laundry room was still empty. When she reached the dryer, the air escaping from inside felt so good blowing on

the front of her body that she stood there awhile with her eyes closed, letting the warm dry heat blow up under her dress on her thighs.

86   Before she knew it, she was singing to herself a rhyme she had sung as a girl: "Uncle Ted got this, Uncle Ted got that, Uncle Ted got a dick long as a baseball bat." She thought about Amos, a boy who used to live next to her folks' farm when she was a girl. He was the first boy she ever opened her legs to and he used to blow his hot breath on her thighs, too.

87   "Lord, have mercy," the old woman said aloud, as she shook herself all over and stepped out of the direct blast of the dryer's heat. "What's the matter with me? I hadn't thought about that little old nappy-headed boy in years. Must be this child's caul making me remember such things. There's all kinds of powers in this here caul. I can tell."

88   She reached over and touched the dried and wrinkled membrane and wasn't a bit surprised to see her hands shaking. Along the edges of the caul, the paper had turned a pale beige and left faint water marks. In the center the caul itself had dried and puckered into tiny peaks and valleys. The whole sheet of paper resembled an ancient map of some unexplored territory.

89   "It's done," the nurse said softly and lifted the caul with the paper and took it back to the folding table. Then she headed across the hall to Miss Sallie Mae's steamy kitchen that smelled of fresh vegetables—turnip greens and rutabagas and pole beans—cooking in a little fatback, and juices and roast beef and chicken baking in the oven. Nurse Bloom had the nose of a hound, Ted the orderly always complained.

90   No one paid any attention as she took down a pretty blue-and-white-flowered china teapot, just big enough to hold about two cups of water, and a small sharp knife from the shelf where the nurses kept their personal eating things. On her way out the door, she looked over at the stove to make sure the big copper tea kettle was whistling gently, as it usually was, on a back burner.

91   When she reentered the laundry room, she walked over to the dried caul on the table, swiftly cut a piece of it about the size of her palm away from the paper, rolled the stiff section of skin up, and dropped it in the teapot. Then she hurried back across the hall to Miss Sallie Mae's kitchen and poured a stream of hot water into the teapot from the steaming kettle. She was finished and out of the kitchen before the workers noticed her.

92   Returning to the laundry room, the nurse placed the hot teapot on
the table and ran her hands over the dried caul once more. Then she
deftly folded the sheet of white paper with the caul inside nine times,
until it was reduced to a rectangle no bigger than her fist. She slipped
it into her pocket along with the small knife and headed back up
the stairs with the warm teapot in her hand.

93   When she nearly slipped on the freshly mopped floor that smelled
of disinfectant, she stopped and looked down at her bare feet. Frowning at the dirty footprints she had left on Ted the orderly's clean floor,
she turned in her tracks and went back down the hall to the delivery room. He won't like it one bit, she said to herself. But he'll have
to go back over this floor again with the mop.

94   As soon as she had slipped her dirty feet into her white oxfords
and set her cap neatly over the spot where her graying nappy hair
was pulled back into a bun at the back of her head, she was ready
to go.

95   "I'm back on duty," she told the nurse at the station near the nursery as she passed by on her way to the infants' supply closet. When
she glanced at the clock over the nurse's head, she was surprised to
see that only forty-five minutes had passed since her trip to the laundry room. It seemed like she had spent hours down there. But it
always did. In the country, when she had dried babies' cauls over a
red-hot brick, the ritual had seemed to take all day.

96   Now she was moving with such smooth efficiency that she could
almost feel her body humming. She took a glass baby bottle down
from the shelf and poured the warm caul tea into it. When the pot
was drained of everything but the wet, limp piece of caul itself, Nurse
Bloom put the pot back on the table, screwed the nipple lid on the
bottle, and held the bottle up to the light.

97   Ignoring the nurse who sat at the station pretending to look
through some papers, Nurse Bloom headed out the door and placed
the teapot and small knife from her pocket into her satchel among her
personal things in the hall closet.

98   "I can take care of that when I get home," Nurse Bloom muttered to herself as she returned to the nursery. Passing through, she
noticed that Lena's bassinet, like most of the others, was empty of
its little occupant.

99   That's even better, she thought as she went back to the nursery
closet, picked up the baby bottle of caul tea still warm and undisturbed on the counter, and headed for Nellie's room. I'll let her mother
give it to her. That's the way it should be anyway.

TEA

100   When the old nurse entered Nellie's room, the new mother was holding Lena in the crook of her arm, which rested on the fluffy white pillow at her shoulder, watching her little girl suck greedily at her breast. While Lena drank, Nellie was doing what every new mother does. She had stripped the infant naked and was checking her over, head to toe. She was fingering Lena's little seashell ears, counting her fingers and toes, pinching her nose to see her breathe through her mouth, bending her arms at the elbow, kissing the tips of her tiny fingernails.

101   Nurse Bloom starting smiling as soon as she entered the room. "She got everything she supposed to have?"

102   Nellie just gave a sheepish grin in reply. This room, a vision in pink, was one of the prettiest private rooms in the hospital. Bright morning sunlight poured into the tall window on the east wall and flooded the foot of the new pink hospital bed with dust beams. A large green vase of red roses stood on the bedside table right by the window.

103   Maybe I'll cut some of those last lavender chrysanthemums from the front yard and bring them in here, Nurse Bloom thought as she looked around the room for some nicety she could add to make Lena's first home even prettier.

104   She approached Nellie's bed playfully. She was still grinning the way she had in the delivery room. But at that point the caterwauling of some other woman's baby from down the hall began to get on her nerves. She stopped a few feet from the foot of Nellie's bed and said, "I'll be right back." Then she turned on her heels and charged out of the room and down the hall to the women's ward. There a young mother, still in her teens, was sharing the ward with three other women; the teenager hugged her crying child to her breast and eyed the nurse suspiciously.

105   "If you don't keep that crying youngun quiet, I'm gonna throw him in the trash can," Nurse Bloom barked.

106   "Oh, please, ma'am, don't throw my baby in the trash can," the mother pleaded as she gripped her bundle of joy tighter in her rail-thin arms.

107   The old nurse just looked at the woman cringing in her pastel-blue bed a moment and sucked her teeth in exasperation. "Girl," she said finally, "don't you know I wouldn't go around throwing babies in the garbage can?"

108   The young mother wasn't so sure. She clutched her child tighter, which made the baby cry all the more. Nurse Bloom stormed across the black-and-white linoleum floor of the ward and silently took the child from the mother's grasp.

109   "Lie back," the nurse ordered as she rocked the baby in her arms, quieting the infant instantly.

110   The young mother obeyed. The nurse expertly flipped the child over in her hands and gently laid him on his mother's stomach, his face between the girl's pitiful little titties.

111   "Now, put your hand on your baby's back and pat and soothe him instead of being a frantic Frances," Nurse Bloom instructed as she marched out of the room.

112   "Young fool girls don't know nothing about babies but how to get them," she muttered venomously as she walked back down the hall to Nellie's room. When she entered, she turned to Lena and her mother with a new face of kindness replacing the face of anger she had worn a second earlier.

113   "Now, where's that sweet little girl baby who came to us with a veil over her face," the hoary nurse purred. "I got something for that little girl."

114   The old woman felt as frisky as she had in the delivery room when the child had been born. She waved the bottle of clear tea back and forth before the child's eyes as if it were a toy.

115   Nellie tried to look interested, but she was still tired from the long, difficult labor and delivery, and she resented this intrusion on the first minutes she and her baby girl had together.

116   "I'm naming her Lena," Nellie said in an effort to be polite as the nurse lifted a straight-back chair from its place by the wall, brought it over to the side of the bed, and sat down.

117   "Well now, ain't that a pretty name?" Nurse Bloom said in a singsong voice that cracked in her throat. "I got something for that baby named Lena. In fact I've got two things, one for the baby and one for the mama."

118   "What's that, Nurse Bloom?" the mother asked.

119   "Nellie," the nurse said familiarly, lowering her voice as if others were in the room. "I guess you know you got a special child here. You were aware enough to see she came here with a veil over her face?"

120   "I sure did," Nellie said proudly as Lena began to fret a bit and her mother's nipple slipped out of her mouth. "Oh-oh, did you lose it, sweetheart? Here you go. Now, don't be in such a hurry."

121   "I sure did," she repeated to the nurse, who sat by the side of the bed smiling down at the feeding baby.

122   "Well, I don't know you all that well. I never knew your people, 'cept your aunt that ran the barber shop, so I don't know how much you know about things like veils over babies' faces and such." Nurse Bloom let the statement hang in the air like a question.

123   "To tell you the truth, Nurse Bloom," Nellie said, "not a whole lot."

124   "Well, there's no reason to worry, 'cause I know all about that kind of thing. Your little girl coming here to this world with a caul over her face means something, Nellie. It means she's a very special child."

125   "She certainly is, Nurse Bloom. I been hoping and praying for a little girl each time I got pregnant. That's what I always wanted since I was a little girl myself. But I had two boys first, and now it is almost five years since the last one. I was beginning to think I wasn't gonna have me my own baby girl."

126   "Oh, I know she's special to you, 'specially since you wanted a girl and all. But what I mean is she's special in her own right. That caul she was born with over her face was more than a piece of thin skin, you know. That caul was a sign that your little girl got a link with all kinds of things, all kinds of powers that the rest of us ordinary people don't have."

127   "Oh, Nurse Bloom, I have to tell you, I've never been one to believe in all those old-timey ideas," Nellie said with a smile. She didn't want to offend the woman who was sounding so sincere. "I guess I'm just not a superstitious type of person."

128   Nurse Bloom's face fell a little, but she leaned in closer, rested her elbow on Nellie's bed, and continued.

129   "Oh, this isn't superstitions I'm talking about, dear," she said. "What I'm talking about is what really is. I've been in this world almost sixty years and I know of what I speak."

130   "Well, Nurse Bloom . . ." Nellie began slowly.

131   "Now, just listen to me, Nellie," the nurse said, sounding a bit more like her normal stern self. "There's all kinds of things in this world that people call superstitions because they don't understand them or they don't fit neatly into their way of thinking nowadays, but that doesn't mean that these things are just some crazy mumbo-jumbo of ignorant country people."

132   This was not going anything like the nurse had thought it would. She had been sure the mother would be thrilled that her baby had a nurse right in this hospital who knew so much about her and the

veil over her face and what it all meant. Instead Nellie was acting like she didn't appreciate what she had.

133 Lena whimpered a bit and let her mother's nipple fall out of her mouth again, but her tiny lips continued to make sucking motions in the air.

134 "Is this baby still hungry?" Nellie asked in a baby voice as she began to heave herself up on the pillow in preparation for turning the infant around to her other breast.

135 Nurse Bloom stood up quickly and gently took Lena from her mother's arms. "Let me give you a hand there with that pretty little hungry thing," she said as she turned the baby around and laid her with her head against her mother's unnursed breast.

136 Seeing the old nurse handle her little girl with such care fairly melted Nellie's heart. After she took her nipple and rubbed it against Lena's soft cheek to get her to start nursing there, she looked up at Nurse Bloom with softer eyes.

137 "I didn't mean to imply that you were country or ignorant, Nurse Bloom," the mother said sincerely. "Everybody knows how much everyone around here looks up to you."

138 "Well, I *am* country—spent almost all of my life there," the nurse answered, herself softening. "But I sho' ain't ignorant. I brought more babies into this world as a midwife than you can shake a stick at, and I learned a thing or two in the process. When I tell you your child is special, I mean it, and I know what I'm talking about."

139 Nellie didn't say anything, but she looked interested.

140 "Nellie, a child born with a veil over its face is an unusual thing. It don't happen every day, or every month for that matter. And believe me when I say it, it means something."

141 "What's it mean, Nurse Bloom?" Nellie asked.

142 "It means that little Lena is not like your other children and never will be. She is gonna be very wise and wise in ways we don't always appreciate. Nellie, that veil over her face means she has a link to that other world that most of us just pretend don't exist. Well, it does. I know you've heard tell that a child born with a caul over its face can see ghosts."

143 "I have heard that," Nellie said slowly.

144 "Well, it's true. When people talk about ghosts, they usually think of spirits of dead people. It's just not that simple. Of course there are spirits of dead people that still wander the earth. But there are two kinds of ghosts, one is the peaceful and harmless kind that appear before you just the way they were on earth, natural-like, and they can

be helpful, too. Then there's the other kind, and they can scare you plenty. Some of them look like death itself, some don't have any heads or any feet, or their heads are turned around on their shoulders."

145   Nurse Bloom saw Nellie's eyes begin to widen, and she wondered what kind of family this smart-looking young woman came from that she hadn't heard all this at some time in her life. But the old nurse didn't want to scare her now that she had her attention and, seemingly, her respect.

146   "Oh, don't you worry any about your little girl, now. What I have in this bottle will take care of any problems she would ever have in that area." The nurse waved the bottle again like a rattle before Lena, who was absorbed in her mother's tit.

147   "You see, I made a little tea for the child that will blind her to any of those scary kinds of ghosts, so she won't be terrorized by those spirits. Now, she was born with a veil over her face, so the child is gonna see some ghosts—you can't get away from that—but at least after she drink this tea, it will just be the harmless kind she'll see. Nothing that'll ever scare her."

148   The nurse smiled as if she had just accomplished an act of charity. When she reached out and gave the mother the bottle of caul tea, she was beaming. Nellie felt that there was little she could do but accept the bottle with a smile. The woman seemed so proud of what she was doing for Lena, Nellie knew she could never tell the nurse what foolishness she thought all this talk was.

149   She stood the bottle on the bed, propped up next to her waist, and kept smiling at Nurse Bloom, who acted like she wasn't anywhere near ready to leave. The old woman sat in the straight-backed chair looking at Nellie and Lena with all the self-importance of a grandmother.

150   "Now, don't let that bottle tip over and drip all that good tea out on the bed there before little Lena gets to drink it," Nurse Bloom said a little nervously. "It won't do her no good on that sheet."

151   "Don't worry," Nellie said as she steadied the bottle next to her body. "It'll be fine right where it is."

152   "You mean, it'll be fine there until you give it to the child," Nurse Bloom prompted.

153   "Uh-huh," said the mother vaguely, then added quickly, "So my baby being born with a caul over her face really sets her apart, does it?"

154   "There's all kinds of things connected with being born with a veil over your face," the nurse said, happy to impart her knowledge. "When I was handling this caul of hers downstairs I could feel some

mighty power in it. Shoot, Lena may be able to read people, see things, do all kinds of things."

155   "Handling it? Why would you be handling it at all?" Nellie wanted to know suddenly.

156   "Well, you don't think I would just dry something like that in a big clump the way it fell, do you?" Nurse Bloom asked. "Nosiree. This caul is a special thing. Let me tell you, I sure am glad that you decided to have your baby at this here hospital instead of over at the big county place where them white nurses take their time about getting you in and then rush you out. Shoot, one of the cleaning women up there told me that when a child is born with a veil over its face up there, they just take it and throw it away in the trash." The old nurse clutched her chest in distress at the thought.

157   "Thank God, there's no such goings-on in this hospital, not as long as I'm here," she continued proudly. "Naw, I gave little Lena's caul the right attention, spread it out on this white paper." She reached in her pocket.

158   Nellie was repelled by the idea of this woman playing around with the caul she had last seen over her baby girl's face. Nellie had a weak stomach. She would always tell people, "Uh, don't show me that, I've got a weak stomach, always did." Or she'd tell her sons, "Boys, one of you run in the fish house right quick and get me some pretty mullet. You know I can't go in that fish house and smell all those fishy odors. I've got a weak stomach and will throw up in a minute."

159   She had just in the last year been able to clean chitterlings at the kitchen sink without getting sick to her stomach as she fingered the slimy greasy membranes and picked them clean of dirt and hair and flecks of paper. Now she imagined Lena's veil like the sink full of chitterlings—thirty pounds of them, for the whole family—sloshing and slithering around, sliding away through her fingers when she tried to pick up a piece of the intestines.

160   At the thought, she had to bring the flat of her fist quickly to her mouth and press it there firmly. She took deep breaths through her nose over her bent index finger.

161   "Now, don't go getting overexcited, little mother." Nurse Bloom reached for the back of Nellie's head and gently bent it forward onto her chest. "Now, just breathe deeply. Take it slow, now—just in and out. Slow, now—in and out." She massaged the back of the new mother's neck.

162   The antiseptic smell of Nurse Bloom's uniform snapped Nellie right out of her sick-to-the-stomach spell. She pushed her head back

and shoved the nurse away with one motion. Nurse Bloom sat back down and continued talking.

163   "See, that dizzy spell just passed. Now, like I was saying, I dried the caul all nice and neat on a piece of white paper for your little girl. You understand that you must keep this caul for your child until she is grown. That's important. She may never do anything with it but take it out once in a while and look at it, or she may need it right away, but it has to be kept, just the same. So until she's grown, you're gonna have to keep this in some very safe place. If it's lost or misplaced, it will make the child forgetful."

164   Nurse Bloom felt as if she were trying to cram a lifetime of common sense into a few minutes. This whole confrontation with the new mother was setting her on edge, ready to jump at the least thing. She didn't know when she had last felt so tense.

165   "But then I guess I don't have to tell you everything at once, do I?" she asked Nellie, as she tried to fight the nervousness that was overwhelming her. "We all live right here in Mulberry, don't we? Now, if you ever have any questions you know you can just come to me."

166   She paused. The only reason Nellie could see for pausing was for effect. It seemed a rather dramatic gesture. Then, the old nurse reached in her pocket and pulled out the thick rectangle of white paper.

167   Lord, I got more gris-gris, as mama's mama used to call it, in this room than Madame Hand out on Highway 17, Nellie thought. But there is no way I am going to go around handling my child's birth veil.

168   "Oh, Nurse Bloom, I can't believe you went to all this trouble," she said.

169   "Wasn't no trouble at all, child. It was my pleasure. You have to know that," Nurse Bloom said. "Here. Here's the caul in this paper. Here, take it, it's for you to protect and keep safe."

170   Nellie lay there a long moment just looking at the thick paper the nurse was offering her. She had the half-sick smile on her face that she used when she couldn't come up with a social lie quickly enough. Now what must I do? she wondered. If I take this piece of skin from this woman, I bet she'll be asking me about it every time I step foot in this place, expecting me to keep up with some old-fashioned foolishness like it made any difference in my baby girl's life. But if I don't take it, I'll hurt her feelings and she'll let me lay up in this bed and rot before she'll answer my buzzer again. What must I do?

171   Nurse Bloom stood there smiling, with the white rectangle of paper extended toward the new mother. "Go on, Nellie," she insisted, "take it."

172   Nellie shifted Lena a little bit up on her breast to stall for more time, but she couldn't think of any way out of taking the paper. She bit her lip and took the paper between two fingers and gingerly laid it on the bedside table.

173   "Now, you just be sure to give her that little bit of water in that bottle for me. Give it her a couple of minutes after she finish feeding. Then she'll take it right along, so don't worry 'bout that—I never seen one child turn it down yet."

174   Nurse Bloom slapped her chubby knees and stood up as if she were finished, then said, "Now, don't just leave that caul sitting right there."

175   "Would you put it in my overnight bag for me?" Nellie asked the nurse with a smile. Nellie wanted to touch the thing as little as possible.

176   Nurse Bloom did as she was asked and smiled in return. Then, reluctantly, she headed toward the door. "Just buzz when you're ready for us to come get that little prize for you. As a matter of fact, I'll come get her myself." And the old nurse disappeared out the door.

177   Nellie heaved a sigh of relief and held the bottle of nearly clear liquid up to the sunlight. She was surprised to see strains of color floating through the water. "What in the world...?" she muttered to herself as the sunbeam that sparkled through the water disappeared behind a cloud and the colors in the water vanished, too. She shook off the chilled feeling the disappearing sun gave her and kissed her baby girl lightly on the top of the head.

178   "Nurse Bloom is a sweet woman, going to all this trouble for my baby, yes, she is, for my sweet little Lena." Nellie looked down at the baby at her breast, who seemed to stop sucking and listen. "But if she thinks I'm gonna give my baby girl any of this old-fashioned potion shit—God only knows what's in it—she better think again. Just imagine, Lena, a grown intelligent woman like that believing in ghosts."

179   As she cooed to Lena, Nellie unscrewed the cap of the glass bottle, lifted off the nippled top, and slowly poured the precious water into the vase of roses her husband had had waiting for her when she awoke after being rolled back in from the delivery room.

180   "But there's no reason anybody but us needs to know anything about this, not anybody—not Nurse Bloom, not your grandmama, especially not Grandmama, you know how she is about all this old-timey stuff, she's almost as bad as Nurse Bloom. It'll be our little secret, our first secret, my baby girl."

181   The modern new mother screwed the lid back on the empty bottle and put it on the table next to her bed.

182   "I'll burn that thing as soon as I get home." Nellie wrinkled her nose as she glanced at the stiff white paper with the baby's caul inside sticking out of her cosmetic case. She brushed her lips across the top of Lena's head. Then mother and daughter fell asleep before Nellie had a chance to buzz for the nurse.

Writing Assignments

1.   Stagolee, Shine, John Henry, and Railroad Bill are major heroes in African American folktales. What characteristics unite these heroes? Why do you suppose these figures have survived in legend and song? Do you believe they continue to serve a social and cultural function?

2.   In *Baby of the Family*, Ansa juxtaposes folkloric practices with modern scientific technology. Carefully analyze the language used to describe both the hospital setting and Nurse Bloom's ritual. Do you find that the text privileges one set of healing practices over the other? Does Ansa believe it is possible for the ancient to co-exist with the modern?

3.   In Reed's *Flight to Canada*, Raven Quickskill asks, "Where does fact begin and fiction leave off?" Using Reed's text and Chesnutt's short stories, discuss the relationship between truth and fiction. What are the implications of destabilizing the paradigm of truth? To what ends do the protagonists in the narratives exploit the tension between fact and fiction?

4.   Analyze the unconventional narrative style of Ntozake Shange's *Sassafrass, Cypress & Indigo*. What is the significance of Shange's inclusion of spells, healing rituals, and incantations in the narrative? Does it disturb or enhance your reading? Explore in detail whether this is an effective strategy for showcasing folkloric sensibilities.

5.   The importance of folklore is evident in African American literature, as many authors turn to this source in their writing. Analyze the John Henry tale and the modern revisions by Tolson and Whitehead. How do the authors revisit the folktale? What particular aspects do they expand upon in their retellings? How do you interpret these narrative choices?

CHAPTER FIVE

EXPRESSIONS OF BLUES AND JAZZ

Blues and jazz are among the most important cultural influences, nationally and internationally, of the past 100 years. Not only have they shaped the direction of musical output around the globe, they have had a profound impact on visual and literary art, particularly that of African Americans. The blues, the older of the two forms, derive from or are closely related to African American folk music like work songs and incorporate descriptions of a vast range of Black experiences. Expressly secular, raw, and, in "low down dirty" versions, quite profane, the blues embrace the vicissitudes of life with special attention to the hard times. In some sense, to keep it real, as the popular saying goes, is to keep it like the blues. Not a music of resignation or ultimate despair, as some may imagine, the blues are better thought of as poignant and sobering recognition that there will always be more obstacles to overcome. Commenting on the blues, James Cone asserts that, "They are not propositional truths *about* the Black experience. Rather they are the essential ingredients that define the *essence* of the Black experience. And to understand them, it is necessary to view the blues as *a state of mind in relation to the Truth of the Black experience.*"

The blues performer, a survivor who may be regarded as an optimist based upon his or her fundamental belief in art, has been a testament to human endurance in the face of continual struggle. To testify has been the blues singer's essential mission. As the narrator declares in "Sonny's Blues" (1957), James Baldwin's well-known short story, "While the tale of how we suffer, and how we are delighted, and how we may triumph is never new, it always must be heard. There isn't any other tale to tell, it's the only light we've got in all this darkness." A blues ethos is thus a key marker of African American identity.

Jazz stems from several musical sources, including ragtime, marching bands, and European symphonies. It is associated most closely, however, with the blues. There are two main reasons for this. One, jazz musicians have been keenly interested in the "blue notes," that is, the "flattening" of notes on the standard eight-point musical scale by playing them at a pitch below what is considered normal. Such flattening of the third and seventh notes is deemed to be a primary trait of the blues, although the fifth note often is played in a similar fashion, as suggested by the Langston Hughes poem "Flatted Fifths" (1951). Jazz musicians have continually experimented with the blue notes, flattening additional notes, as well, and developed rhythmic and harmonic complexity beyond, though still frequently based on, the framework of the blues. Two, improvisation is an integral feature of both musical forms. Blues or jazz musicians are not expected to play a song the same way all the time. Such performance could even be negatively regarded. What is favored is an assertion of individuality and dynamism by the artist, a sign of active, ongoing engagement with or interpretation of the surrounding environment whether in terms of the audience, other members of a band, or the social and political circumstances to which he or she bears witness.

Jazz developed at the dawn of the twentieth century, while conventional wisdom has it that the blues began to appear during the earlier post-Reconstruction period as artists were responding to a new freedom that was bitterly compromised by a resurgent and virulent racism marked by the end of Reconstruction efforts. To illustrate the dominant politics of the times, scholars point to the withdrawal of federal troops from the South in 1877, where they had been stationed to safeguard the political rights of African Americans, and the 1883 Supreme Court ruling overturning the Civil Rights Act of 1875. However, Delridge Hunter posits a much earlier date for the origin of the blues, arguing passionately that the blues were the first Black music to appear in what became the United States. Challenging what he terms the Blues Orthodoxy, he claims that the blues evolved early in the antebellum period and were related to African songs called *engung*. Work, he correctly points out, is a task, not a genre. Work songs, it follows, though often cited as a source of the blues, were actually blues songs adapted to the demands of labor.

Whatever the case, both the blues and jazz had become wildly popular by the 1920s. Although frowned upon by some African Americans as the "devil's music" at worst, or crude at best, these musical forms, with their vitality and spontaneity, would inspire numerous African American writers in terms of both content and form.

Hughes was the first writer to receive wide acclaim using blues structures, which he did from the 1920s to the end of his career. A typical example is the following stanza from his "Midwinter Blues" (1926):

> Don't know's I mind his goin'
> But he left me when the coal was low
> Don't know's I mind his goin'
> But he left me when the coal was low
> Now, if a man loves a woman
> That ain't no time to go.

One can see the connection between Hughes's poem and W. C. Handy's "St. Louis Blues" (1914), perhaps the most popular of blues songs:

> Gypsy done tol' me, "Don't you wear no black"
> Yes, she done tol' me, "Don't you wear no black.
> Go to St. Louis, you can win him back."

The classic, or 12-bar, blues pattern is evident in Handy's composition. The three-line stanza consists of a first line that is repeated, or at least nearly so, as the second line; these are followed by a completely different third line, resulting in a line pattern of *aab*. But because the end words of the lines all rhyme, the rhyme scheme of the classic stanza is *aaa*. Four bars, or measures, are accorded to each line, meaning 12 bars per stanza, though the singing is usually done more quickly than four bars in each line, leaving room for improvisation. A third feature of a classic blues is a *caesura*, or pause, within each line. This usually occurs in the middle of a line (medial caesura) or near the beginning (initial caesura). Sometimes the pause is marked by punctuation, as is the case with the medial caesuras in the stanza from "St. Louis Blues." The stops in Hughes's poem are accomplished by creating six lines based on the basic three-line form.

As one might expect, the blues are generally rendered in African American Vernacular English, which is most true to the down-to-earth lives of blues people. In "St. Louis Blues," we see the softening of a consonant cluster (*tol'* as opposed to *told*) and the use of the completive "done" (*done tol'*). The latter construction is used as a more emphatic statement of action than the roughly equivalent *has told*. Both consonant simplification and the completive "done" are systematic features of African American Vernacular English. Representation of the sound and syntax is also evident in the following stanza from Bessie Smith's "Backwater Blues" (1927):

> Backwater blues done cause me to pack mah things an' go
> Backwater blues done cause me to pack mah things an' go
> Cause mah house fell down an' I cain' live there no mo'

Sterling Brown was a second major poet who seriously engaged the blues tradition, as demonstrated by poems like "Ma Rainey" (1930) and "The New St. Louis Blues" (1931). Later poets like Quincy Troupe and Mari Evans have worked in a similar fashion. Some of the writers included in this chapter and, as mentioned previously, James Baldwin, also incorporated the blues into their work.

Jazz has been no less influential for writers. Poets like Hughes, Ted Joans, Bob Kaufman, Jayne Cortez, Sterling Plumpp, Yusuf Komunyakaa, Angela Jackson, and Brian Gilmore have celebrated in their works an array of jazz artists, including Charlie Parker, John Coltrane, Miles Davis, Billie Holiday, Cecil Taylor, Von Freeman, Thelonius Monk, and Duke Ellington. In many instances, the poets have tried to capture on page the tempo, spontaneity, rhythmic complexity, and group interplay of jazz performance. Xam Wilson Cartiér's *Be-Bop, Re-Bop* (1987), an excerpt of which is included in this chapter, is a notable experiment in fiction.

Further Reading:

Cone, James H. *The Spirituals and the Blues: An Interpretation.* New York: Seabury Press, 1972.

Ellison, Ralph. *Shadow and Act.* New York: Random House, 1964.

Hunter, Delridge L. *The Lyric Poet: A Blues Continuum.* Brooklyn, N.Y.: Caribbean Diaspora Press, 2001.

Jones, LeRoi. *Blues People: Negro Music in White America.* New York: Morrow, 1963.

Murray, Albert. *Stomping the Blues.* New York: McGraw-Hill, 1976.

Powell, Richard J. *The Blues Aesthetic: Black Culture and Modernism.* Washington, D.C.: Washington Project for the Arts, 1989.

Southern, Eileen. *The Music of Black Americans: A History.* New York: W.W. Norton, 1971.

Tracy, Stephen C. *Langston Hughes & the Blues.* Urbana: University of Illinois Press, 1988.

W. C. Handy

(1873–1958)

*William Christopher Handy was born on November 16, 1873,
in Florence, Alabama. He began his professional career in 1896
when he joined Mahara's Minstrels as a cornet player. Later, he
led bands that were based in Clarksdale, Mississippi, and Memphis,
Tennessee. In 1909, he was hired by Memphis mayoral candidate
Edward Crump and composed "Mr. Crump," a campaign song.
The title was changed to "Memphis Blues," and in 1912, it was
among the first blues compositions to be made available as sheet
music. Handy published two music collections,* Blues: An Anthology
(1926) and Book of Negro Spirituals *(1938). Handy became
widely known as "Father of the Blues," which is the title of his
autobiography, published in 1941. "St. Louis Blues" (1914) is his
most popular composition.*

St. Louis Blues

I hate to see de evenin' sun go down
I hate to see de evenin' sun go down
Cause mah baby, he done lef' dis town

Feelin' tomorrow lak I feel today
5 Feelin' tomorrow lak I feel today
I'll pack mah trunk, an' make mah getaway

St. Louis woman wid her diamon' rings
Pulls dat man aroun' by her apron strings
'Twant for powder an' for store-bought hair
10 De man I love would not gone nowhere

Got de St. Louis blues, jes as blue as I can be
Dat man got a heart lak a rock cast in de sea
Or else he wouldn't have gone so far from me

Been to de gypsy to get mah fortune tol'
15 To de gypsy, done got mah fortune tol'
Cause I'm most wild 'bout mah jelly roll

Gypsy done tol' me, "Don't you wear no black"
Yes, she done tol' me, "Don't you wear no black.
Go to St. Louis, you can win him back"

20 Help me to Cairo; make St. Louis by mahself
Git to Cairo, find mah ol' frien', Jeff
Gwine to pin mahself close to his side
If I flag his train, I sho can ride

I loves dat man lak a schoolboy loves his pie
25 Lak a Kentucky Colonel loves his mint an' rye
I'll love mah baby till de day I die

You ought to see dat stovepipe brown o' mine
Lak he owns de Dimon' Joseph line
He'd make a cross-eyed 'oman go stone blind

30 Blacker than midnight, teeth lak flags of truce
Blackest man in de whole St. Louis
Blacker de berry, sweeter is de juice. . . .

A black headed gal make a freight train jump de track
Said, a black headed gal make a freight train jump de track
35 But a long tall gal makes a preacher "Ball de Jack"

Lawd, a blond headed woman makes a good man leave the town
I said, blond headed woman makes a good man leave the town
But a red headed woman make a boy slap his papa down. . . .

Bessie Smith

(1894–1937)

Promoted as the "Empress of the Blues," Bessie Smith was born in Chattanooga, Tennessee, on April 15, 1894. Growing up in poverty, she was singing on street corners before she was 10 years old. Her brother Clarence became a dancer in a traveling vaudeville troupe. In 1912, Bessie Smith also was hired as a dancer by the show, which included Ma Rainey. Smith began recording for Columbia Record Company in 1923, receiving a flat fee for each recording. Her record sales were in the millions, but she received no share of the royalties generated. Smith took to the road frequently, often

*organizing her own variety show. She retained a loyal fan base
even after her recording career ended in 1931 due to the Great
Depression. Smith was killed in an automobile accident on September 26, 1937. "Backwater Blues," the following selection, was first
recorded in 1927.*

Backwater Blues*

When it rain five days an' de skies turned dark as night
When it rain five days an' de skies turned dark as night
Then trouble taken place in the lowland that night

I woke up this mornin', can't even get outa mah do'
5 I woke up this mornin', can't even get outa mah do'
That's enough trouble to make a po' girl wonder where she wanta go

Then they rowed a little boat about five miles 'cross the pond
They rowed a little boat about five miles 'cross the pond
I packed all mah clothes, th'owed 'em in, an' they rowed me along

10 When it thunder an' a-lightnin', an' the wind begin to blow
When it thunder an' a-lightnin', an' the wind begin to blow
An' thousan' people ain' got no place to go

Then I went an' stood up on some high ol' lonesome hill
I went an' stood up on some high ol' lonesome hill
15 An' looked down on the house where I used to live

Backwater blues done cause me to pack mah things an' go
Backwater blues done cause me to pack mah things an' go
Cause mah house fell down an' I cain' live there no mo'

O-o-o-oom, I cain' move no mo'
20 O-o-o-oom, I cain' move no mo'
There ain' no place fo' a po' ol' girl to go

*By Bessie Smith (1895–1937); first recorded in 1927.

Langston Hughes

(1902–1967)

A central figure of the Harlem Renaissance and perhaps the best-known writer in the African American literary tradition, James Mercer Langston Hughes was born on February 1, 1902, in Joplin, Missouri. He grew up in Lawrence, Kansas, and Cleveland, Ohio. A precocious poet, Hughes was already publishing and receiving considerable attention when he entered Columbia University in 1921. After a year in college, he left to focus on his writing. He worked on ships and sailed to various sites overseas. Hughes then attended and graduated from Lincoln University in Pennsylvania. He is remembered best for faithfully exploring the mass culture of African Americans and rendering such experience with flourishes of brilliance, in language both simple and profound. At home in several genres, he was a fiction writer, a playwright, a songwriter, a journalist, an autobiographer, and a translator, as well as a poet. Among his dozens of books are the novel Not Without Laughter *(1930); the short story collection* The Ways of White Folks *(1934); the autobiographies* The Big Sea *(1940) and* I Wonder as I Wander *(1956); the poetry volumes* The Weary Blues *(1926),* Fine Clothes to the Jew *(1927),* The Dream Keeper *(1932),* A New Song *(1938),* Shakespeare in Harlem *(1942),* One-Way Ticket *(1949),* Montage of a Dream Deferred *(1951),* Ask Your Mama: 12 Moods for Jazz *(1961), and the posthumously released* The Panther and the Lash *(1967). Of the following poems—all of which have been taken from* The Collected Poems of Langston Hughes *(1996)—"The Weary Blues" was first published in book form in* The Weary Blues; *"Midwinter Blues" first appeared in book form in* Fine Clothes to the Jew, *and this version of "Ma Man" is also from* Fine Clothes to the Jew; *"Wide River" was first published in book form in* The Dream Keeper; *"Flatted Fifths" first appeared in* Montage of a Dream Deferred, *but Hughes changed a line or two and this exact version appears in* Selected Poems of Langston Hughes *(1959); "Jam Session" first appeared in* Montage of a Dream Deferred; *and "The Backlash Blues" is from* The Panther and the Lash.

The Weary Blues

Droning a drowsy syncopated tune,
Rocking back and forth to a mellow croon,
   I heard a Negro play.
Down on Lenox Avenue the other night
5 By the pale dull pallor of an old gas light

He did a lazy sway. . . .
He did a lazy sway. . . .
To the tune o' those Weary Blues.
With his ebony hands on each ivory key
10 He made that poor piano moan with melody.
    O Blues!
Swaying to and fro on his rickety stool
He played that sad raggy tune like a musical fool.
    Sweet Blues!
15 Coming from a black man's soul.
    O Blues!
In a deep song voice with a melancholy tone
I heard that Negro sing, that old piano moan—
    "Ain't got nobody in all this world,
20   Ain't got nobody but ma self.
    I's gwine to quit ma frownin'
    And put ma troubles on the shelf."

Thump, thump, thump, went his foot on the floor.
He played a few chords then he sang some more—
25   "I got the Weary Blues
    And I can't be satisfied.
    Got the Weary Blues
    And can't be satisfied—
    I ain't happy no mo'
30   And I wish that I had died."
And far into the night he crooned that tune.
The stars went out and so did the moon.
The singer stopped playing and went to bed
While the Weary Blues echoed through his head.
He slept like a rock or a man that's dead.

Midwinter Blues

In the middle of the winter,
Snow all over the ground.
In the middle of the winter,
Snow all over the ground—
5 'Twas the night befo' Christmas
My good man turned me down.

Don't know's I'd mind his goin'
But he left me when the coal was low.
Don't know's I'd mind his goin'
10 But he left when the coal was low.
Now, if a man loves a woman
That ain't no time to go.

He told me that he loved me
But he must a been tellin' a lie.
15 He told me that he loved me.
He must a been tellin' a lie.
But he's the only man I'll
Love till the day I die.

I'm gonna buy me a rose bud
20 An' plant it at my back door,
Buy me a rose bud,
Plant it at my back door,
So when I'm dead they won't need
No flowers from the store.

Ma Man

When ma man looks at me
He knocks me off ma feet.
When ma man looks at me
He knocks me off ma feet.
5 He's got those 'lectric-shockin' eyes an'
De way he shocks me sho is sweet.

Wide River

Ma baby lives across de river
An' I ain't got no boat.
She lives across de river.
I ain't got no boat.
5 I ain't a good swimmer
An' I don't know how to float.

Wide, wide river
'Twixt ma love an' me.
Wide, wide river
10 'Twixt ma love an' me.'
I never knowed how
Wide a river can be.

Got to cross that river
An' git to ma baby somehow.
15 Cross that river,
Git to ma baby somehow—
Cause if I don't see ma baby
I'll lay down an' die right now.

Flatted Fifths

Little cullud boys with beards
re-bop be-bop mop and stop.

Little cullud boys with fears,
frantic, kick their draftee years
5   into flatted fifths and flatter beers
that at a sudden change become
sparkling Oriental wines
rich and strange
silken bathrobes with gold twines
10 and Heilbroner, Crawford,
Nat-undreamed-of Lewis combines
in silver thread and diamond notes
on trade-marks inside
Howard coats.

15 Little cullud boys in berets
oop pop-a-da
horse a fantasy of days
ool ya koo
and dig all plays.

Jam Session

Letting midnight
out on bail
    pop-a-da
having been
5 detained in jail
      oop-pop-a-da
for sprinkling salt
on a dreamer's tail
    pop-a-da

The Backlash Blues

Mister Backlash, Mister Backlash,
Just who do you think I am?
Tell me, Mister Backlash,
Who do you think I am?
5 You raise my taxes, freeze my wages,
Send my son to Vietnam.

You give me second-class houses,
Give me second-class schools,
Second-class houses
10 And second-class schools.
You must think us colored folks
Are second-class fools.

When I try to find a job
To earn a little cash,
15 Try to find myself a job
To earn a little cash,
All you got to offer
Is a white backlash.

But the world is big,
20 The world is big and round,
Great big world, Mister Backlash,
Big and bright and round—
And it's full of folks like me who are
Black, Yellow, Beige, and Brown.

25 Mister Backlash, Mister Backlash,
   What do you think I got to lose?
   Tell me, Mister Backlash,
   What you think I got to lose?
   I'm gonna leave you, Mister Backlash,
30 Singing your mean old backlash blues.

   You're the one,
   Yes, you're the one
   Will have the blues.

Ma Rainey

(1886–1939)

The daughter of minstrel performers Thomas and Ella Pridgett,
Gertrude Pridgett "Ma" Rainey was born April 26, 1886, in Columbus,
Georgia. In 1904, after working in several stage shows, she married
entertainer William "Pa" Rainey (thus her nickname). They performed
as "Rainey and Rainey" until 1916. Ma Rainey began recording in
1923 for Paramount Records and was largely responsible for the com-
mercial success of the company. Her raw style and creative energy—as
well as sexually suggestive lyrics that were cutting-edge even by blues
standards—make her a legend in the blues tradition.

See, See Rider

See See Rider, see what you done done!
   Lord, Lord, Lord!
You made me love you, now your gal done come.
You made me love you, now your gal done come.

5 I'm goin' away, baby, I won't be back till fall.
   Lord, Lord, Lord!
Goin' away, baby, won't be back till fall.
If I find me a good man, I won't be back at all.

I'm gonna buy me a pistol just as long as I am tall.
10   Lord, Lord, Lord!

Kill my man and catch the Cannon Ball.
If he won't have me, he won't have no gal at all.

See See Rider, where did you stay last night?
    Lord, Lord, Lord!
15 Your shoes ain't buttoned, clothes don't fit you right.
You didn't come home till the sun was shinin' bright.

Sissy Blues

I dreamed last night I was far from harm
Woke up and found my man in a sissy's arms

"Hello, Central, it's 'bout to run me wild
Can I get that number, or will I have to wait a while?"

5 Some are young, some are old
My man says sissy's got good jelly roll

My man got a sissy, his name is Miss Kate
He shook that thing like jelly on a plate

Now all the people ask me why I'm all alone
10 A sissy shook that thing and took my man from me

Prove It on Me Blues

Went out last night, had a great big fight,
Everything seemed to go on wrong;
I looked up, to my surprise,
The gal I was with was gone.

5 Where she went, I don't know,
I mean to follow everywhere she goes;
Folks said I'm crooked, I didn't know where she took it,
I want the whole world to know:

They say I do it, ain't nobody caught me,
10 Sure got to prove it on me;
Went out last night with a crowd of my friends,
They must've been women, 'cause I don't like no men.

It's true I wear a collar and a tie,
Make the wind blow all the while;
15 They say I do it, ain't nobody caught me,
They sure got to prove it on me.

Say I do it, ain't nobody caught me,
Sure got to prove it on me;
I went out last night with a crowd of my friends,
20 They must've been women, 'cause I don't like no men.

Wear my clothes just like a fan,
Talk to the gals just like any old man;
'Cause they say I do it, ain't nobody caught me,
Sure got to prove it on me.

Sterling Brown

(1901–1989)

Sterling Allen Brown was born on May 1, 1901, in Washington, D.C. His father, Sterling Nelson Brown, was a theology professor at Howard University, where Sterling himself would later teach for 40 years. Brown received a bachelor's degree from Williams College in 1922 and a master's degree from Harvard in 1923. After Harvard, Brown spent time teaching in the South, including a three-year stint at the Virginia Seminary in Lynchburg, Virginia. During this period, he became keenly interested in African American folklore and infused his own work with vernacular expressions. His first volume of poetry, Southern Road, was published in 1932. Although he received critical praise, Brown could not find a publisher for his second book of poems. Turning to work in criticism, he published Negro Poetry and Drama *(1938),* The Negro in American Fiction *(1938), and edited, with Arthur P. Davis and Ulysses Lee,* The Negro Caravan *(1941), an important anthology. Brown eventually published* The Last Ride of Wild Bill and Eleven Narrative Poems *(1975) and* The Collected Poems of Sterling Brown *(1980).*

Ma Rainey
(Ma Rainey, "Mother of the Blues," 1886–1939)

1

When Ma Rainey
Comes to town,
Folks from anyplace
Miles aroun'
5 From Cape Girardeau,
Poplar Bluff,
Flocks in to hear
Ma do her stuff;
Comes flivverin' in,
10 Or ridin' mules,
Or packed in trains,
Picknickin' fools . . .
That's what it's like
Fo' miles on down,
15 To New Orleans delta
An' Mobile town,
When Ma hits
Anywheres aroun'.

2

Dey comes to hear Ma Rainey from de little river settlements,
20 From blackbottom cornrows and from lumber camps;
Dey stumble in de hall, je' a-laughin' an' a-cacklin',
Cheerin' lak roarin' water, lak wind in river swamps.

An' some jokers keeps deir laughs a-goin' in de crowded aisles,
An' some folk sits dere waitin' wid' deir aches an' miseries,
25 Till Ma comes out before dem, a-smilin' gold-toofed smiles,
An' Long Boy ripples minors on de black an' yellow keys.

3

O Ma Rainey,
Sing yo' song;
Now you's back
30 Whah you belong,
Git way inside us,
Keep us strong . . .
O Ma Rainey,
Li'l an' low,
35 Sing us 'bout de hard luck
Roun' our do';
Sing us 'bout de lonesome road
We mus' go . . .

4

I talked to a fellow, an' the fellow say,
40 'She jes' catch hold of us, somekindaway.
She sang Backwater Blues one day:
—'IT RAINED FO' DAYS AN' DE SKIES WAS DARK AS NIGHT,
      TROUBLE TAKEN PLACE IN DE LOWLANDS AT NIGHT.
      THUNDERED AN' LIGHTENED AN' THE STORM BEGIN TO ROLL
45   THOUSAN'S OF PEOPLE AIN'T GOT NO PLACE TO GO.
      DEN I WENT AN' STOOD UPON SOME HIGH OL' LONESOME HILL,
      AN' LOOKED DOWN ON THE PLACE WHERE I USED TO LIVE.

'An' den de folks, dey natchally bowed dey heads an' cried,
Bowed dey heavy heads, shet dey moufs up tight an' cried,
50 An' Ma lef' de stage, an' followed some of de folks outside.'

Dere wasn't much more de fellow say:
She jes' gits hold of us dataway.

New St. Louis Blues

MARKET STREET WOMAN

Market Street woman is known fuh to have dark days,
Market Street woman noted fuh to have dark days,
Life do her dirty in a hundred onery ways.

Let her hang out de window and watch de busy worl' go pas',
5 Hang her head out de window and watch de careless worl' go pas',
Maybe some good luck will come down Market Street at las'

Put paint on her lips, purple powder on her choklit face,
Paint on her lips, purple powder on her choklit face,
Take mo' dan paint to change de luck of dis dam place.

10 Gettin' old and ugly, an' de sparks done lef' her eye,
Old an' ugly an' de fire's out in her eye,
De men may see her, but de men keeps passin' by—

Market Street woman have her hard times, oh my Lawd,
Market Street woman have her hard times, oh my Lawd,
15 Let her git what she can git, 'fo dey lays her on de coolin' board.

TORNADO BLUES

Black wind come a-speedin' down de river from de Kansas plains,
Black wind come a-speedin' down de river from de Kansas plains,
Black wind come a-roarin' like a flock of giant aeroplanes—

Destruction was a-drivin' it and close behind was Fear,
20 Destruction was a-drivin' it and hand in hand with Fear,
Grinnin' Death and skinny Sorrow was a-bringin' up de rear.

Dey got some ofays, but dey mostly got de Jews an' us,
Got some ofays, but mostly got de Jews an' us,
Many po' boys castle done settled to a heap o' dus'.

25 Newcomers dodge de mansions, and knocked on de po' folks' do',
Dodged most of the mansions, and knocked down de po' folks' do',
Never know us po' folks so popular befo'—

Foun' de moggidge unpaid, foun' de insurance long past due,
Moggidge unpaid, de insurance very long past due,
30 All de homes we wukked so hard for goes back to de Fay and Jew.

De Black wind evil, done done its dirty work an' gone,
Black wind evil, done done its dirty work an' gone,
Lawd help de folks what de wind ain't had no mercy on.

LOW DOWN

So low down bummin' cut plug from de passers by,
35 So low down bummin' cut plug from de passers by,
When a man bum tobacco ain't much lef' to do but die. . . .

Bone's gittin' brittle, an' my brain won't low no rest,
Bone's gittin' brittle, an' my brain won't let me rest,
Death drivin' rivets overtime in my scooped out chest.

40 Woman done quit me, my boy lies fast in jail,
Woman done quit me, pa'dner lies fast in jail,
Kin bum tobacco but I cain't bum de jack for bail.

Church don't help me, 'cause I ain't got no Sunday clothes,
Church don't help me, got no show off Sunday clothes,
45 Preachers and deacons, don't look to get no help from those.

Wouldn't mind dyin' but I ain't got de jack fo' toll,
Wouldn't mind dyin' but I'd have to bum de jack fo' toll,
Some dirty joker done put a jinx on my po' soul.

Dice are loaded, an' de deck's all marked to hell,
50 Dice are loaded, de deck's all marked to hell,
Whoever runs dis gamble sholy runs it well.

Quincy Troupe

(1939–)

*Born in New York City on July 22, 1939, and raised in St. Louis,
Quincy Troupe was a member of the Watts Writers' Workshop, an
important group that emerged in Los Angeles during the 1960s. Sub-
sequently, he taught writing and literature for many years at the City
University of New York and the University of California, San Diego. He
twice won the title of Heavyweight Champion of Poetry at the World
Poetry Bout in Taos, New Mexico. His poetry volumes include* Embryo
(1972), Snake-Back Solos *(1978),* Skulls Along the River *(1984),*
Weather Reports *(1991),* Avalanche *(1996),* Choruses *(1999), and*
Trancircularities: New and Selected Poems *(2002). Troupe edited, with
Rainer Schulte,* Giant Talk: An Anthology of Third World Writing
(1975). He also wrote two books about jazz legend Miles Davis, Miles:
The Autobiography *(co-authored, 1989) and* Miles and Me *(2000).*

River Town Packin House Blues;
for Sterling Brown

Big Tom was a black nigguh man,
cold & black,
eye say Big Tom was a black nigguh man,
black steel flesh,
5   standin like a gladiator, soaked in
animal blood, bits of flesh,
wringin wet,
standin at the center of death,
buzzards hoverin,
10 swingin his hammer called death,
260 workdays,
swingin his hammer named death

Big Tom was a black packin houseman,
thirty years,
15 eye say Big Tom was a black packin houseman,
loved them years,
& swang his hammer like ol John Henry
poundin nails,
swang that hammer twenty years
20 crushin skulls
of cows & pigs screamin fear,
the man underneath slit their throats,
twenty years,
the man underneath slit their throats
25 Big Tom was a 'prentice for ten long years,
watchin death,
eye say Big Tom was 'prentice for ten long years,
smellin death,
was helper to a fat white man,
30 who got slow,
was helper to a fat white man,
who swang a hammer
till he couldnt do it no mo,

so he taught Big Tom how to kill
35 with a hammer,
he taught Big Tom how to kill

& twenty years of killin
is a lot to bring home,
eye say twenty years of killin
40 is a lot to bring home,
& drinkin too much gin & whiskey
can make a gentle/man blow
dont chu know
eye say drinkin too much
45 gin & whiskey
can make a good man
sho nuff blow,
dont chu know

Big Tom beat his wife after killin all day,
50 his six chillun too,
eye say Tom beat his wife after killin all day,
his young chillun too,
beat em so awful bad, he beat em right out dey shoes,
screamin blues,
55 eye say he beat em so awful bad
he made a redeyed hungry alley rat spread the news
'bout dues
these black/ blues people was payin, couldnt even bite em,
cause of the dues
60 these black/ blues people was payin

Big Tom killed six men, maimed a couple a hundred,
& never served a day,
eye say Big Tom killed six men, maimed a couple a
hundred,
65 never in jail one day,
the figures coulda been higher, but the smart ones,
they ran away,
eye say the number that was maimed, or dead, coulda
been higher,
70 but the smart ones,
they ran away, swallowin pride, saved from the graveyard,
another day,

the smart ones,
they ran away

75 Big Tom, workin all day, thirty years,
uh huh, sweatin heavy
Big Tom swingin his hamma, all right, twenty summers
outta love
Big Tom killin for pay,
80 Uh huh, twenty autumns, outta need,
Big Tom dealin out murders, like a houseman, all night,
in the painyards, outta false pride,
Big Tom drinkin heavy, uh huh,
laughing loose in taverns,
85 Big Tom loose
in Black communities, death fights cancels light,
& Big Tom keeps on, stumblin

& twenty years of killin
is too much to bring home to love,
90 eye say twenty years of killin
is too much to bring home to love,
& drinkin heavy gin & whiskey
can make a strong man fall in mud,
eye say drinkin too much/ gin & whiskey
95 can make a good man have bad blood
dont chu know
can make a strong
man have
bad blood

100 Big Black Tom was a cold nigguh man,
strong & black,
eye say Big Black Tom was a cold nigguh man,
hard steel flesh,
& stood like a gladiator, soaked in blood,
105 bits of flesh,
soakin wet,
stood at the center, in the middle of death,
sweatin vultures,
swingin his hamma called death, 260 workdays,
110 twenty years,
like ol John Henry,
eye say swingin his hammer named death

Mari Evans

A poet, an essayist, and a dramatist, Mari Evans was born in Toledo, Ohio. An important voice concerning African American cultural and political experiences, she first drew major attention when she produced and directed the television show The Black Experience, *which was broadcast from 1968–1973 by WTTV in Indianapolis. Evans also created* Eyes *(1979), a musical based on Zora Neale Hurston's* Their Eyes Were Watching God, *and edited* Black Women Writers, 1950–1980: A Critical Evaluation *(1984). Her poetry volumes include* Where Is All the Music? *(1968),* I Am a Black Woman *(1970),* Nightstar: 1973–1978 *(1981), and* A Dark and Splendid Mass *(1992).*

Liberation Blues

Woke up this morning, feeling sad and blue
I woke up worried, feeling sad and blue
Thinking 'bout my baby
And what he's put me through
5   Thinking how he done me
How he put me down last night
Thinking how he done me
He didn't do me right

Didn't fix no breakfast, had no appetite
10 Couldn't eat for thinking
How he hurt my heart last night
Thinking how he done me
He didn't do me right

I get up early in the mornin
15 Work hard each and every day
I bring home all my money
An yet he play
Ho ho pretty daddy, hurt my heart last night
Thinking how he done me
20 He didn't do me right

Reached for my work clothes, hangin on the rack
Then I decided I would put them muthus back

Thinking 'bout my baby
How he put me down last night
25 Thinking how he done me
He didn't do me right

Called and got a reservation
Kiss this house and him goodbye
Got me a reservation
30 Kiss this house and him goodbye
I don't have to stay and take it
I don't have to stay and cry

Never thought I'd leave him
Never believed the day would come
35 But this is not the first time
My baby's done the things he's done
Cryin shame the way he done me
All a y'all there last night
Saw the way he done me
40 He didn't do me right

I'm gone.

Lee Morgan

His blue yearnings   his
hoarse staccato screams a
stratospheric reaching
    pristine flight,
5   A personal anguish, naked
and intense
        Her single shot
antiphonous
        His love
10 blasted into some abyss
Elusive as any grace note he
could not be possessed
His last round breathing

poignantly on key
15 reverberating into infinity
the disbelief the silence
The held note's echo gone
The wooden platform's dust
     a gentle settling
20   A reluctant tag

  discordant
    final

James Baldwin

(1924–1987)

*James Arthur Baldwin, one of the preeminent African American
writers of the twentieth century, was born in Harlem on August 2,
1924. He had a troubled relationship with his stepfather, David
Baldwin, who was a preacher. Baldwin became an evangelist himself at the age of 14 and proved to be more popular in the pulpit
than his stepfather. But neither his preaching career nor his devout
faith lasted for long. At Clinton High School in the Bronx, Baldwin
belonged to the school's literary club, which was supervised by
Countee Cullen. He began publishing reviews and essays in the mid-
1940s. Feeling stifled in the United States as an openly gay Black
man, he moved to France in 1948, remaining there for most of his
life. Beginning in the late 1950s, however, he traveled often between
the two countries. Achieving distinction as a fiction writer, an essayist, and a dramatist, Baldwin challenged racial and sexual oppression in his work (sometimes including controversial descriptions of
sexual relations) and is largely remembered as an eloquent
spokesperson for the Civil Rights movement. His novels include* Go
Tell It on the Mountain *(1953),* Giovanni's Room *(1956),* Another
Country *(1962),* Tell Me How Long the Train's Been Gone *(1968),* If
Beale Street Could Talk *(1974), and* Just Above My Head *(1979).
Baldwin is perhaps better known for his essay collections* Notes of a
Native Son *(1955),* Nobody Knows My Name *(1961), and* The Fire
Next Time *(1963). Baldwin's other works include the successful
Broadway plays* The Amen Corner *(1955) and* Blues for Mister
Charlie *(1964), and the story collection* Going to Meet the Man
(1965). "Sonny's Blues" first appeared in Partisan Review *in 1957.*

Sonny's Blues

1   I read about it in the the paper, in the subway, on my way to work. I read it, and I couldn't believe it, and I read it again. Then perhaps I just stared at it, at the newsprint spelling out his name, spelling out the story. I stared at it in the swinging lights of the subway car, and in the faces and bodies of the people, and in my own face, trapped in the darkness which roared outside.

2   It was not to be believed and I kept telling myself that, as I walked from the subway station to the high school. And at the same time I couldn't doubt it. I was scared, scared for Sonny. He became real to me again. A great block of ice got settled in my belly and kept melting there slowly all day long, while I taught my classes algebra. It was a special kind of ice. It kept melting, sending trickles of ice water all up and down my veins, but it never got less. Sometimes it hardened and seemed to expand until I felt my guts were going to come spilling out or that I was going to choke or scream. This would always be at a moment when I was remembering some specific thing Sonny had once said or done.

3   When he was about as old as the boys in my classes his face had been bright and open, there was a lot of copper in it; and he'd had wonderfully direct brown eyes, and great gentleness and privacy. I wondered what he looked like now. He had been picked up, the evening before, in a raid on an apartment downtown, for peddling and using heroin.

4   I couldn't believe it: but what I mean by that is that I couldn't find any room for it anywhere inside me. I had kept it outside me for a long time. I hadn't wanted to know. I had had suspicions, but I didn't name them, I kept putting them away. I told myself that Sonny was wild, but he wasn't crazy. And he'd always been a good boy, he hadn't ever turned hard or evil or disrespectful, the way kids can, so quick, so quick, especially in Harlem. I didn't want to believe that I'd ever see my brother going down, coming to nothing, all that light in his face gone out, in the condition I'd already seen so many others. Yet it had happened and here I was, talking about algebra to a lot of boys who might, every one of them for all I knew, be popping off needles every time they went to the head. Maybe it did more for them than algebra could.

5   I was sure that the first time Sonny had ever had horse, he couldn't have been much older than these boys were now. These

boys, now, were living as we'd been living then, they were growing up with a rush and their heads bumped abruptly against the
low ceiling of their actual possibilities. They were filled with rage.
All they really knew were two darknesses, the darkness of their
lives, which was now closing in on them, and the darkness of the
movies, which had blinded them to that other darkness, and in
which they now, vindictively, dreamed, at once more together than
they were at any other time, and more alone.

6   When the last bell rang, the last class ended, I let out my breath.
It seemed I'd been holding it for all that time. My clothes were wet—
I may have looked as though I'd been sitting in a steam bath, all
dressed up, all afternoon. I sat alone in the classroom a long time. I
listened to the boys outside, downstairs, shouting and cursing and
laughing. Their laughter struck me for perhaps the first time. It was
not the joyous laughter which—God knows why—one associates with
children. It was mocking and insular, its intent was to denigrate. It
was disenchanted, and in this, also, lay the authority of their curses.
Perhaps I was listening to them because I was thinking about my
brother and in them I heard my brother. And myself.

7   One boy was whistling a tune, at once very complicated and very
simple, it seemed to be pouring out of him as though he were a bird,
and it sounded very cool and moving through all that harsh, bright
air, only just holding its own through all those other sounds.

8   I stood up and walked over to the window and looked down
into the courtyard. It was the beginning of the spring and the sap
was rising in the boys. A teacher passed through them every now
and again, quickly, as though he or she couldn't wait to get out of
that courtyard, to get those boys out of their sight and off their
minds. I started collecting my stuff. I thought I'd better get home
and talk to Isabel.

9   The courtyard was almost deserted by the time I got downstairs.
I saw this boy standing in the shadow of a doorway, looking just like
Sonny. I almost called his name. Then I saw that it wasn't Sonny,
but somebody we used to know, a boy from around our block. He'd
been Sonny's friend. He'd never been mine, having been too young
for me, and, anyway, I'd never liked him. And now, even though he
was a grown-up man, he still hung around that block, still spent hours
on the street corners, was always high and raggy. I used to run into
him from time to time and he'd often work around to asking me for
a quarter or fifty cents. He always had some real good excuse, too,
and I always gave it to him, I don't know why.

10 But now, abruptly, I hated him. I couldn't stand the way he looked at me, partly like a dog, partly like a cunning child, I wanted to ask him what the hell he was doing in the school courtyard.

11 He sort of shuffled over to me, and he said, "I see you got the papers. So you already know about it."

12 "You mean about Sonny? Yes, I already know about it. How come they didn't get you?"

13 He grinned. It made him repulsive and it also brought to mind what he'd looked like as a kid. "I wasn't there. I stay away from them people."

14 "Good for you." I offered him a cigarette and I watched him through the smoke. "You come all the way down here just to tell me about Sonny?"

15 "That's right." He was sort of shaking his head and his eyes looked strange, as though they were about to cross. The bright sun deadened his damp dark brown skin and it made his eyes look yellow and showed up the dirt in his kinked hair. He smelled funky. I moved a little away from him and I said, "Well, thanks. But I already know about it and I got to get home."

16 "I'll walk you a little ways," he said. We started walking. There were a couple of kids still loitering in the courtyard and one of them said goodnight to me and looked strangely at the boy beside me.

17 "What're you going to do?" he asked me. "I mean, about Sonny?"

18 "Look. I haven't seen Sonny for over a year, I'm not sure I'm going to do anything. Anyway, what the hell *can* I do?"

19 "That's right," he said quickly, "ain't nothing you can do. Can't much help old Sonny no more, I guess."

20 It was what I was thinking and so it seemed to me he had no right to say it.

21 "I'm surprised at Sonny, though," he went on—he had a funny way of talking, he looked straight ahead as though he were talking to himself—"I thought Sonny was a smart boy, I thought he was too smart to get hung."

22 "I guess he thought so too," I said sharply, "and that's how he got hung. And now about you? You're pretty goddamn smart, I bet."

23 Then he looked directly at me, just for a minute. "I ain't smart," he said. "If I was smart, I'd have reached for a pistol a long time ago."

24 "Look. Don't tell *me* your sad story, if it was up to me, I'd give you one." Then I felt guilty—guilty, probably, for never having supposed that the poor bastard *had* a story of his own, much less a sad one, and I asked, quickly, "What's going to happen to him now?"

25   He didn't answer this. He was off by himself some place. "Funny thing," he said, and from his tone we might have been discussing the quickest way to get to Brooklyn, "when I saw the papers this morning, the first thing I asked myself was if I had anything to do with it. I felt sort of responsible."

26   I began to listen more carefully. The subway station was on the corner, just before us, and I stopped. He stopped, too. We were in front of a bar and he ducked slightly, peering in, but whoever he was looking for didn't seem to be there. The juke box was blasting away with something black and bouncy and I half watched the barmaid as she danced her way from the juke box to her place behind the bar. And I watched her face as she laughingly responded to something someone said to her, still keeping time to the music. When she smiled one saw the little girl, one sensed the doomed, still-struggling woman beneath the battered face of the semi-whore.

27   "I never *give* Sonny nothing," the boy said finally, "but a long time ago I come to school high and Sonny asked me how it felt." He paused, I couldn't bear to watch him, I watched the barmaid, and I listened to the music which seemed to be causing the pavement to shake. "I told him it felt great." The music stopped, the barmaid paused and watched the juke box until the music began again. "It did."

28   All this was carrying me some place I didn't want to go. I certainly didn't want to know how it felt. It filled everything, the people, the houses, the music, the dark, quicksilver barmaid, with menace; and this menace was their reality.

29   "What's going to happen to him now?" I asked again.

30   "They'll send him away some place and they'll try to cure him." He shook his head. "Maybe he'll even think he's kicked the habit. Then they'll let him loose"—he gestured, throwing his cigarette into the gutter. "That's all."

31   "What do you mean, that's *all?*"

32   But I knew what he meant.

33   "I *mean*, that's *all*." He turned his head and looked at me, pulling down the corners of his mouth. "Don't you know what I mean?" he asked, softly.

34   "How the hell *would* I know what you mean?" I almost whispered it, I don't know why.

35   "That's right," he said to the air, "how would *he* know what I mean?" He turned toward me again, patient and calm, and yet I somehow felt him shaking, shaking as though he were going to fall

apart. I felt that ice in my guts again, the dread I'd felt all afternoon; and again I watched the barmaid, moving about the bar, washing glasses, and singing. "Listen. They'll let him out and then it'll just start all over again. That's what I mean."

36 "You mean—they'll let him out. And then he'll just start working his way back in again. You mean he'll never kick the habit. Is that what you mean?"

37 "That's right," he said, cheerfully. "*You* see what I mean."

38 "Tell me," I said it last, "why does he want to die? He must want to die, he's killing himself, why does he want to die?"

39 He looked at me in surprise. He licked his lips. "He don't want to die. He wants to live. Don't nobody want to die, ever."

40 Then I wanted to ask him—too many things. He could not have answered, or if he had, I could not have borne the answers. I started walking. "Well, I guess it's none of my business."

41 "It's going to be rough on old Sonny," he said. We reached the subway station. "This is your station?" he asked. I nodded. I took one step down. "Damn!" he said, suddenly. I looked up at him. He grinned again. "Damn it if I didn't leave all my money home. You ain't got a dollar on you, have you? Just for a couple of days, is all."

42 All at once something inside gave and threatened to come pouring out of me. I didn't hate him any more. I felt that in another moment I'd start crying like a child.

43 "Sure," I said. "Don't sweat." I looked in my wallet and didn't have a dollar, I only had a five. "Here," I said. "That hold you?"

44 He didn't look at it—he didn't want to look at it. A terrible, closed look came over his face, as though he were keeping the number on the bill a secret from him and me. "Thanks," he said, and now he was dying to see me go. "Don't worry about Sonny. Maybe I'll write him or something."

45 "Sure," I said. "You do that. So long."

46 "Be seeing you," he said. I went on down the steps.

47 And I didn't write Sonny or send him anything for a long time. When I finally did, it was just after my little girl died, he wrote me back a letter which made me feel like a bastard.

48 Here's what he said:

> Dear brother,
> You don't know how much I needed to hear from you. I wanted to write you many a time but I dug how much I must have hurt you and so I didn't write. But now I feel like a man

who's been trying to climb up out of some deep, real deep and funky hole and just saw the sun up there, outside. I got to get outside.

I can't tell you much about how I got here. I mean I don't know how to tell you. I guess I was afraid of something or I was trying to escape from something and you know I have never been very strong in the head (smile). I'm glad Mama and Daddy are dead and can't see what's happened to their son and I swear if I'd known what I was doing I would never have hurt you so, you and a lot of other fine people who were nice to me and who believed in me.

I don't want you to think it had anything to do with me being a musician. It's more than that. Or maybe less than that. I can't get anything straight in my head down here and I try not to think about what's going to happen to me when I get outside again. Sometime I think I'm going to flip and *never* get outside and sometime I think I'll come straight back. I tell you one thing, though, I'd rather blow my brains out than go through this again. But that's what they all say, so they tell me. If I tell you when I'm coming to New York and if you could meet me, I sure would appreciate it. Give my love to Isabel and the kids and I was sure sorry to hear about little Gracie. I wish I could be like Mama and say the Lord's will be done, but I don't know it seems to me that trouble is the one thing that never does get stopped and I don't know what good it does to blame it on the Lord. But maybe it does some good if you believe it.

Your brother,
Sonny

49   Then I kept in constant touch with him and I sent him whatever I could and I went to meet him when he came back to New York. When I saw him many things I thought I had forgotten came flooding back to me. This was because I had begun, finally, to wonder about Sonny, about the life that Sonny lived inside. This life, whatever it was, had made him older and thinner and it had deepened the distant stillness in which he had always moved. He looked very unlike my baby brother. Yet, when he smiled, when we shook hands, the baby brother I'd never known looked out from the depths of his private life, like an animal waiting to be coaxed into the light.

50   "How you been keeping?" he asked me.

51   "All right. And you?"

52   "Just fine." He was smiling all over his face. "It's good to see you again."

53   "It's good to see you."

54   The seven years' difference in our ages lay between us like a chasm: I wondered if these years would ever operate between us as a bridge. I was remembering, and it made it hard to catch my breath, that I had been there when he was born; and I had heard the first words he had ever spoken. When he started to walk, he walked from our mother straight to me. I caught him just before he fell when he took the first steps he ever took in this world.

55   "How's Isabel?"

56   "Just fine. She's dying to see you."

57   "And the boys?"

58   "They're fine, too. They're anxious to see their uncle."

59   "Oh, come on. You know they don't remember me."

60   "Are you kidding? Of course they remember you."

61   He grinned again. We got into a taxi. We had a lot to say to each other, far too much to know how to begin.

62   As the taxi began to move, I asked, "You still want to go to India?"

63   He laughed. "You still remember that. Hell, no. This place is Indian enough for me."

64   "It used to belong to them," I said.

65   And he laughed again. "They damn sure knew what they were doing when they got rid of it."

66   Years ago, when he was around fourteen, he'd been all hipped on the idea of going to India. He read books about people sitting on rocks, naked, in all kinds of weather, but mostly bad, naturally, and walking barefoot through hot coals and arriving at wisdom. I used to say that it sounded to me as though they were getting away from wisdom as fast as they could. I think he sort of looked down on me for that.

67   "Do you mind," he asked, "if we have the driver drive alongside the park? On the west side—I haven't seen the city in so long."

68   "Of course not," I said. I was afraid that I might sound as though I were humoring him, but I hoped he wouldn't take it that way.

69   So we drove along, between the green of the park and the stony, lifeless elegance of hotels and apartment buildings, toward the vivid, killing streets of our childhood. These streets hadn't changed, though housing projects jutted up out of them now like rocks in the middle of a boiling sea. Most of the houses in which we had grown up had

vanished, as had the stores from which we had stolen, the basements in which we had first tried sex, the rooftops from which we had hurled tin cans and bricks. But houses exactly like the houses of our past yet dominated the landscape, boys exactly like the boys we once had been found themselves smothering in these houses, came down into the streets for light and air and found themselves encircled by disaster. Some escaped the trap, most didn't. Those who got out always left something of themselves behind, as some animals amputate a leg and leave it in the trap. It might be said, perhaps, that I had escaped, after all, I was a school teacher; or that Sonny had, he hadn't lived in Harlem for years. Yet, as the cab moved uptown through streets which seemed, with a rush, to darken with dark people, and as I covertly studied Sonny's face, it came to me that what we both were seeking through our separate cab windows was that part of ourselves which had been left behind. It's always at the hour of trouble and confrontation that the missing member aches.

70   We hit 110th Street and started rolling up Lenox Avenue. And I'd known this avenue all my life, but it seemed to me again, as it had seemed on the day I'd first heard about Sonny's trouble, filled with a hidden menace which was its very breath of life.

71   "We almost there," said Sonny.

72   "Almost." We were both too nervous to say anything more.

73   We live in a housing project. It hasn't been up long. A few days after it was up it seemed uninhabitably new, now, of course, it's already rundown. It looks like a parody of the good, clean, faceless life—God knows the people who live in it do their best to make it a parody. The beat-looking grass lying around isn't enough to make their lives green, the hedges will never hold out the streets, and they know it. The big windows fool no one, they aren't big enough to make space out of no space. They don't bother with the windows, they watch the TV screen instead. The playground is most popular with the children who don't play at jacks, or skip rope, or roller skate, or swing, and they can be found in it after dark. We moved in partly because it's not too far from where I teach, and partly for the kids; but it's really just like the houses in which Sonny and I grew up. The same things happen, they'll have the same things to remember. The moment Sonny and I started into the house I had the feeling that I was simply bringing him back into the danger he had almost died trying to escape.

74   Sonny has never been talkative. So I don't know why I was sure he'd be dying to talk to me when supper was over the first night. Everything went fine, the oldest boy remembered him, and the

youngest boy liked him, and Sonny had remembered to bring something for each of them; and Isabel, who is really much nicer than I am, more open and giving, had gone to a lot of trouble about dinner and was genuinely glad to see him. And she's always been able to tease Sonny in a way that I haven't. It was nice to see her face so vivid again and to hear her laugh and watch her make Sonny laugh. She wasn't, or, anyway, she didn't seem to be, at all uneasy or embarrassed. She chatted as though there were no subject which had to be avoided and she got Sonny past his first, faint stiffness. And thank God she was there, for I was filled with that icy dread again. Everything I did seemed awkward to me, and everything I said sounded freighted with hidden meaning. I was trying to remember everything I'd heard about dope addiction and I couldn't help watching Sonny for signs. I wasn't doing it out of malice. I was trying to find out something about my brother. I was dying to hear him tell me he was safe.

75   "Safe!" my father grunted, whenever Mama suggested trying to move to a neighborhood which might be safer for children. "Safe, hell! Ain't no place safe for kids, nor nobody."

76   He always went on like this, but he wasn't, ever, really as bad as he sounded, not even on weekends, when he got drunk. As a matter of fact, he was always on the lookout for "something a little better," but he died before he found it. He died suddenly, during a drunken weekend in the middle of the war, when Sonny was fifteen. He and Sonny hadn't ever got on too well. And this was partly because Sonny was the apple of his father's eye. It was because he loved Sonny so much and was frightened for him, that he was always fighting with him. It doesn't do any good to fight with Sonny. Sonny just moves back, inside himself, where he can't be reached. But the principal reason that they never hit it off is that they were so much alike. Daddy was big and rough and loud-talking, just the opposite of Sonny, but they both had—that same privacy.

77   Mama tried to tell me something about this, just after Daddy died. I was home on leave from the army.

78   This was the last time I ever saw my mother alive. Just the same, this picture gets all mixed up in my mind with pictures I had of her when she was younger. The way I always see her is the way she used to be on a Sunday afternoon, say, when the old folks were talking after the big Sunday dinner. I always see her wearing pale blue. She'd be sitting on the sofa. And my father would be sitting in the easy chair, not far from her. And the living room would be full of church folks and relatives. There they sit, in chairs all around the living room, and

the night is creeping up outside, but nobody knows it yet. You can see the darkness growing against the windowpanes and you hear the street noises every now and again, or maybe the jangling beat of a tambourine from one of the churches close by, but it's real quiet in the room. For a moment nobody's talking, but every face looks darkening, like the sky outside. And my mother rocks a little from the waist, and my father's eyes are closed. Everyone is looking at something a child can't see. For a minute they've forgotten the children. Maybe a kid is lying on the rug, half asleep. Maybe somebody's got a kid in his lap and is absent-mindedly stroking the kid's head. Maybe there's a kid, quiet and big-eyed, curled up in a big chair in the corner. The silence, the darkness coming, and the darkness in the faces frightens the child obscurely. He hopes that the hand which strokes his forehead will never stop—will never die. He hopes that there will never come a time when the old folks won't be sitting around the living room, talking about where they've come from, and what they've seen, and what's happened to them and their kinfolk.

79   But something deep and watchful in the child knows that this is bound to end, is already ending. In a moment someone will get up and turn on the light. Then the old folks will remember the children and they won't talk any more that day. And when light fills the room, the child is filled with darkness. He knows that every time this happens he's moved just a little closer to that darkness outside. The darkness outside is what the old folks have been talking about. It's what they've come from. It's what they endure. The child knows that they won't talk any more because if he knows too much about what's happened to *them*, he'll know too much too soon, about what's going to happen to *him*.

80   The last time I talked to my mother, I remember I was restless. I wanted to get out and see Isabel. We weren't married then and we had a lot to straighten out between us.

81   There Mama sat, in black, by the window. She was humming an old church song, *Lord, you brought me from a long ways off.* Sonny was out somewhere. Mama kept watching the streets.

82   "I don't know," she said, "if I'll ever see you again, after you go off from here. But I hope you'll remember the things I tried to teach you."

83   "Don't talk like that," I said, and smiled. "You'll be here a long time yet."

84   She smiled, too, but she said nothing. She was quiet for a long time. And I said, "Mama, don't you worry about nothing. I'll be writing all the time, and you be getting the checks. . . ."

85   "I want to talk to you about your brother," she said, suddenly. "If anything happens to me he ain't going to have nobody to look out for him."

86   "Mama," I said, "ain't nothing going to happen to you *or* Sonny. Sonny's all right. He's a good boy and he's got good sense."

87   "It ain't a question of his being a good boy," Mama said, "nor of his having good sense. It ain't only the bad ones, nor yet the dumb ones that gets sucked under." She stopped, looking at me. "Your Daddy once had a brother," she said, and she smiled in a way that made me feel she was in pain. "You didn't never know that, did you?"

88   "No," I said, "I never knew that," and I watched her face.

89   "Oh, yes," she said, "your Daddy had a brother." She looked out of the window again. "I know you never saw your Daddy cry. But *I* did—many a time, through all these years."

90   I asked her, "What happened to his brother? How come nobody's ever talked about him?"

91   This was the first time I ever saw my mother look old.

92   "His brother got killed," she said, "when he was just a little younger than you are now. I knew him. He was a fine boy. He was maybe a little full of the devil, but he didn't mean nobody no harm."

93   Then she stopped and the room was silent, exactly as it had sometimes been on those Sunday afternoons. Mama kept looking out into the streets.

94   "He used to have a job in the mill," she said, "and, like all young folks, he just liked to perform on Saturday nights. Saturday nights, him and your father would drift around to different place, go to dances and things like that, or just sit around with people they knew, and your father's brother would sing, he had a fine voice, and play along with himself on his guitar. Well, this particular Saturday night, him and your father was coming home from some place, and they were both a little drunk and there was a moon that night, it was bright like day. Your father's brother was feeling kind of good, and he was whistling to himself, and he had his guitar slung over his shoulder. They was coming down a hill and beneath them was a road that turned off from the highway. Well, your father's brother, being always kind of frisky, decided to run down this hill, and he did, with that guitar banging and clanging behind him, and he ran across the road, and he was making water behind a tree. And your father was sort of amused at him and he was still coming down the hill, kind of slow. Then he heard a car motor and that same minute his brother stepped from behind the

tree, into the road, in the moonlight. And he started to cross the road. And your father started to run down the hill, he says he don't know why. This car was full of white men. They was all drunk, and when they seen your father's brother they let out a great whoop and holler and they aimed the car straight at him. They was having fun, they just wanted to scare him, the way they do sometimes, you know. But they was drunk. And I guess the boy, being drunk, too, and scared, kind of lost his head. By the time he jumped it was too late. Your father says he heard his brother scream when the car rolled over him, and he heard the wood of that guitar when it give, and he heard them strings go flying, and he heard them white men shouting, and the car kept on a-going and it ain't stopped till this day. And, time your father got down the hill, his brother weren't nothing but blood and pulp."

95 Tears were gleaming on my mother's face. There wasn't anything I could say.

96 "He never mentioned it," she said, "because I never let him mention it before you children. Your Daddy was like a crazy man that night and for many a night thereafter. He says he never in his life seen anything as dark as that road after the lights of that car had gone away. Weren't nothing, weren't nobody on that road, just your Daddy and his brother and that busted guitar. Oh, yes. Your Daddy never did really get right again. Till the day he died he weren't sure but that every white man he saw was the man that killed his brother."

97 She stopped and took out her handkerchief and dried her eyes and looked at me.

98 "I ain't telling you all this," she said, "to make you scared or bitter or to make you hate nobody. I'm telling you this because you got a brother. And the world ain't changed."

99 I guess I didn't want to believe this. I guess she saw this in my face. She turned away from me, toward the window again, searching those streets.

100 "But I praise my Redeemer," she said at last, "that He called your Daddy home before me. I ain't saying it to throw no flowers at myself, but, I declare, it keeps me from feeling too cast down to know I helped your father get safely through this world. Your father always acted like he was the roughest, strongest man on earth. And everybody took him to be like that. But if he hadn't had *me* there—to see his tears!"

101 She was crying again. Still, I couldn't move. I said, "Lord, Lord, Mama, I didn't know it was like that."

102   "Oh, honey," she said, "there's a lot that you don't know. But you are going to find it out." She stood up from the window and came over to me. "You got to hold on to your brother," she said, "and don't let him fall, no matter what it looks like is happening to him and no matter how evil you gets with him. You going to be evil with him many a time. But don't you forget what I told you, you hear?"

103   "I won't forget," I said. "Don't you worry, I won't forget. I won't let nothing happen to Sonny."

104   My mother smiled as though she were amused at something she saw in my face. Then, "You may not be able to stop nothing from happening. But you got to let him know you's *there*."

105   Two days later I was married, and then I was gone. And I had a lot of things on my mind and I pretty well forgot my promise to Mama until I got shipped home on a special furlough for her funeral.

106   And, after the funeral, with just Sonny and me alone in the empty kitchen, I tried to find out something about him.

107   "What do you want to do?" I asked him.

108   "I'm going to be a musician," he said.

109   For he had graduated, in the time I had been away, from dancing to the juke box to finding out who was playing what, and what they were doing with it, and he had bought himself a set of drums.

110   "You mean, you want to be a drummer?" I somehow had the feeling that being a drummer might be all right for other people but not for my brother Sonny.

111   "I don't think," he said, looking at me very gravely, "that I'll ever be a good drummer. But I think I can play a piano."

112   I frowned. I'd never played the role of the older brother quite so seriously before, had scarcely ever, in fact, *asked* Sonny a damn thing. I sensed myself in the presence of something I didn't really know how to handle, didn't understand. So I made my frown a little deeper as I asked: "What kind of musician do you want to be?"

113   He grinned. "How many kinds do you think there are?"

114   "Be *serious*," I said.

115   He laughed, throwing his head back, and then looked at me. "I *am* serious."

116   "Well, then, for Christ's sake, stop kidding around and answer a serious question. I mean, do you want to be a concert pianist, you want to play classical music and all that, or—or what?" Long before I finished he was laughing again. "For Christ's *sake*, Sonny!"

117   He sobered, but with difficulty. "I'm sorry. But you sound so— *scared!*" and he was off again.

118   "Well, you may think it's funny now, baby, but it's not going to be so funny when you have to make your living at it, let me tell you *that*." I was furious because I knew he was laughing at me and I didn't know why.

119   "No," he said, very sober now, and afraid, perhaps, that he'd hurt me, "I don't want to be a classical pianist. That isn't what interests me. I mean"—he paused, looking hard at me, as though his eyes would help me to understand, and then gestured helplessly, as though perhaps his hand would help—"I mean, I'll have a lot of studying to do, and I'll have to study *everything*, but, I mean, I want to play *with*—jazz musicians." He stopped. "I want to play jazz," he said.

120   Well, the word had never before sounded as heavy, as real, as it sounded that afternoon in Sonny's mouth. I just looked at him and I was probably frowning a real frown by this time. I simply couldn't see why on earth he'd want to spend his time hanging around nightclubs, clowning around on bandstands, while people pushed each other around a dance floor. It seemed—beneath him, somehow. I had never thought about it before, had never been forced to, but I suppose I had always put jazz musicians in a class with what Daddy called "good-time people."

121   "Are you *serious?*"

122   "Hell, *yes*, I'm serious."

123   He looked more helpless than ever, and annoyed, and deeply hurt.

124   I suggested, helpfully: "You mean—like Louis Armstrong?"

125   His face closed as though I'd struck him. "No. I'm not talking about none of that old-time, down home crap."

126   "Well, look, Sonny, I'm sorry, don't get mad. I just don't altogether get it, that's all. Name somebody—you know, a jazz musician you admire."

127   "Bird."

128   "Who?"

129   "Bird! Charlie Parker! Don't they teach you nothing in the goddamn army?"

130   I lit a cigarette. I was surprised and then a little amused to discover that I was trembling. "I've been out of touch," I said. "You'll have to be patient with me. Now. Who's this Parker character?"

131   "He's just one of the greatest jazz musicians alive," said Sonny, sullenly, his hands in his pockets, his back to me. "Maybe *the* greatest," he added, bitterly, "that's probably why *you* never heard of him."

132   "All right," I said, "I'm ignorant. I'm sorry. I'll go out and buy all the cat's records right away, all right?"

133   "It don't," said Sonny, with dignity, "make any difference to me. I don't care what you listen to. Don't do me no favors."

134   I was beginning to realize that I'd never seen him so upset before. With another part of my mind I was thinking that this would probably turn out to be one of those things kids to through and that I shouldn't make it seem important by pushing it too hard. Still, I didn't think it would do any harm to ask: "Doesn't all this take a lot of time? Can you make a living at it?"

135   He turned back to me and half leaned, half sat, on the kitchen table. "Everything takes time," he said, "and—well, yes, sure, I can make a living at it. But what I don't seem to be able to make you understand is that it's the only thing I want to do."

136   "Well, Sonny," I said, gently, "you know people can't always do exactly what they *want* to do—"

137   "*No*, I don't know that," said Sonny, surprising me. "I think people *ought* to do what they want to do, what else are they alive for?"

138   "You getting to be a big boy," I said desperately, "it's time you started thinking about your future."

139   "I'm thinking about my future," said Sonny, grimly. "I think about it all the time."

140   I gave up. I decided, if he didn't change his mind, that we could always talk about it later. "In the meantime," I said, "you got to finish school." We had already decided that he'd have to move in with Isabel and her folks. I knew this wasn't the ideal arrangement because Isabel's folks are inclined to be dicty and they hadn't especially wanted Isabel to marry me. But I didn't know what else to do. "And we have to get you fixed up at Isabel's."

141   There was a long silence. He moved from the kitchen table to the window. "That's a terrible idea. You know it yourself."

142   "Do you have a *better* idea?"

143   He just walked up and down the kitchen for a minute. He was as tall as I was. He had started to shave. I suddenly had the feeling that I didn't know him at all.

144   He stopped at the kitchen table and picked up my cigarettes. Looking at me with a kind of mocking, amused defiance, he put one between his lips. "You mind?"

145   "You smoking already?"

146   He lit the cigarette and nodded, watching me through the smoke. "I just wanted to see if I'd have the courage to smoke in front of you." He grinned and blew a great cloud of smoke to the ceiling. "It was easy." He looked at my face. "Come on, now. I bet you was smoking at my age, tell the truth."

147   I didn't say anything but the truth was on my face, and he laughed. But now there was something very strained in his laugh. "Sure. And I bet that ain't all you was doing."

148   He was frightening me a little. "Cut the crap," I said. "We already decided that you was going to go and live at Isabel's. Now what's got into you all of a sudden?"

149   "*You* decided it," he pointed out. "*I* didn't decide nothing." He stopped in front of me, leaning against the stove, arms loosely folded. "Look, brother. I don't want to stay in Harlem no more, I really don't." He was very earnest. He looked at me, then over toward the kitchen window. There was something in his eyes I'd never seen before, some thoughtfulness, some worry all his own. He rubbed the muscle of one arm. "It's time I was getting out of here."

150   "Where do you want to *go*, Sonny?"

151   "I want to join the army. Or the navy, I don't care. If I say I'm old enough, they'll believe me."

152   Then I got mad. It was because I was so scared. "You must be crazy. You goddamn fool, what the hell do you want to go and join the *army* for?"

153   "I just told you. To get out of Harlem."

154   "Sonny, you haven't even finished *school*. And if you really want to be a musician, how do you expect to study if you're in the *army?*"

155   He looked at me, trapped, and in anguish. "There's ways. I might be able to work out some kind of deal. Anyway, I'll have the G.I. Bill when I come out."

156   "*If* you come out." We stared at each other. "Sonny, please. Be reasonable. I know the setup is far from perfect. But we got to do the best we can."

157   "I ain't learning nothing in school," he said. "Even when I go." He turned away from me and opened the window and threw his cigarette out into the narrow alley. I watched his back. "At least, I ain't learning nothing you'd want me to learn." He slammed the window so hard I thought the glass would fly out, and turned back to me. "And I'm sick of the stink of these garbage cans!"

158   "Sonny," I said, "I know how you feel. But if you don't finish school now, you're going to be sorry later that you didn't." I grabbed him by the shoulders. "And you only got another year. It ain't so bad. And I'll come back and I swear I'll help you do *whatever* you want to do. Just try to put up with it till I come back. Will you please do that? For me?"

159   He didn't answer and he wouldn't look at me.

160   "Sonny. You hear me?"

161   He pulled away. "I hear you. But you never hear anything *I* say."

162   I didn't know what to say to that. He looked out of the window and then back at me. "OK," he said, and sighed. "I'll try."

163   Then I said, trying to cheer him up a little, "They got a piano at Isabel's. You can practice on it."

164   And as a matter of fact, it did cheer him up for a minute. "That's right," he said to himself. "I forgot that." His face relaxed a little. But the worry, the thoughtfulness, played on it still, the way shadows play on a face which is staring into the fire.

165   But I thought I'd never hear the end of that piano. At first, Isabel would write me, saying how nice it was that Sonny was so serious about his music and how, as soon as he came in from school, or wherever he had been when he was supposed to be at school, he went straight to that piano and stayed there until suppertime. And, after supper, he went back to that piano and stayed there until everybody went to bed. He was at the piano all day Saturday and all day Sunday. Then he bought a record player and started playing records. He'd play one record over and over again, all day long sometimes, and he'd improvise along with it on the piano. Or he'd play one section of the record, one chord, one change, one progression, then he'd do it on the piano. Then back to the record. Then back to the piano.

166   Well, I really don't know how they stood it. Isabel finally confessed that it wasn't like living with a person at all, it was like living with sound. And the sound didn't make any sense to her, didn't make any sense to any of them—naturally. They began, in a way, to be afflicted by this presence that was living in their home. It was as though Sonny were some sort of god, or monster. He moved in an atmosphere which wasn't like theirs at all. They fed him and he ate, he washed himself, he walked in and out of their door; he certainly wasn't nasty or unpleasant or rude, Sonny isn't any of those things; but it was as though he were all wrapped up in some cloud, some fire, some vision all his own; and there wasn't any way to reach him.

167   At the same time, he wasn't really a man yet, he was still a child, and they had to watch out for him in all kinds of ways. They certainly couldn't throw him out. Neither did they dare to make a great scene about that piano because even they dimly sensed, as I sensed, from so many thousands of miles away, that Sonny was at that piano playing for his life.

168   But he hadn't been going to school. One day a letter came from the school board and Isabel's mother got it—there had, apparently, been other letters but Sonny had torn them up. This day, when Sonny came in, Isabel's mother showed him the letter and asked where he'd been spending his time. And she finally got it out of him that he'd been down in Greenwich Village, with musicians and other characters, in a white girl's apartment. And this scared her and she started to scream at him and what came up, once she began—though she denies it to this day—was what sacrifices they were making to give Sonny a decent home and how little he appreciated it.

169   Sonny didn't play the piano that day. By evening, Isabel's mother had calmed down but then there was the old man to deal with, and Isabel herself. Isabel says she did her best to be calm but she broke down and started crying. She says she just watched Sonny's face. She could tell, by watching him, what was happening with him. And what was happening was that they penetrated his cloud, they had reached him. Even if their fingers had been a thousand times more gentle than human fingers ever are, he could hardly help feeling that they had stripped him naked and were spitting on that nakedness. For he also had to see that his presence, that music, which was life or death to him, had been torture for them and that they had endured it, not at all for his sake, but only for mine. And Sonny couldn't take that. He can take it a little better today than he could then but he's still not very good at it and, frankly, I don't know anybody who is.

170   The silence of the next few days must have been louder than the sound of all the music ever played since time began. One morning, before she went to work, Isabel was in his room for something and she suddenly realized that all of his records were gone. And she knew for certain that he was gone. And he was. He went as far as the navy would carry him. He finally sent me a postcard from some place in Greece and that was the first I knew that Sonny was still alive. I didn't see him any more until we were both back in New York and the war had long been over.

171   He was a man by then, of course, but I wasn't willing to see it. He came by the house from time to time, but we fought almost every time we met. I didn't like the way he carried himself, loose and dreamlike all the time, and I didn't like his friends, and his music seemed to be merely an excuse for the life he led. It sounded just that weird and disordered.

172   Then we had a fight, a pretty awful fight, and I didn't see him for months. By and by I looked him up, where he was living, in a

furnished room in the Village, and I tried to make it up. But there were lots of other people in the room and Sonny just lay on his bed, and he wouldn't come downstairs with me, and he treated these other people as though they were his family and I weren't. So I got mad and then he got mad, and then I told him that he might just as well be dead as live the way he was living. Then he stood up and he told me not to worry about him any more in life, that he *was* dead as far as I was concerned. Then he pushed me to the door and the other people looked on as though nothing were happening, and he slammed the door behind me. I stood in the hallway, staring at the door. I heard somebody laugh in the room and then the tears came to my eyes. I started down the steps, whistling to keep from crying, I kept whistling to myself, *You going to need me, baby, one of these cold, rainy days.*

173   I read about Sonny's trouble in the spring. Little Grace died in the fall. She was a beautiful little girl. But she only lived a little over two years. She died of polio and she suffered. She had a slight fever for a couple of days, but it didn't seem like anything and we just kept her in bed. And we would certainly have called the doctor, but the fever dropped, she seemed to be all right. So we thought it had just been a cold. Then, one day, she was up, playing, Isabel was in the kitchen fixing lunch for the two boys when they'd come in from school, and she heard Grace fall down in the living room. When you have a lot of children you don't always start running when one of them falls, unless they start screaming or something. And, this time, Grace was quiet. Yet, Isabel says that when she heard that *thump* and then that silence, something happened in her to make her afraid. And she ran to the living room and there was little Grace on the floor, all twisted up, and the reason she hadn't screamed was that she couldn't get her breath. And when she did scream, it was the worst sound, Isabel says, that she'd ever heard in all her life, and she still hears it sometimes in her dreams. Isabel will sometimes wake me up with a low, moaning, strangled sound and I have to be quick to awaken her and hold her to me and where Isabel is weeping against me seems a mortal wound.

174   I think I may have written Sonny the very day that little Grace was buried. I was sitting in the living room in the dark, by myself, and I suddenly thought of Sonny. My trouble made his real.

175   One Saturday afternoon, when Sonny had been living with us, or, anyway, been in our house, for nearly two weeks, I found myself wandering aimlessly about the living room, drinking from a can of

beer, and trying to work up the courage to search Sonny's room. He was out, he was usually out whenever I was home, and Isabel had taken the children to see their grandparents. Suddenly I was standing still in front of the living room window, watching Seventh Avenue. The idea of searching Sonny's room made me still. I scarcely dared to admit to myself what I'd be searching for. I didn't know what I'd do if I found it. Or if I didn't.

176   On the sidewalk across from me, near the entrance to a barbecue joint, some people were holding an old-fashioned revival meeting. The barbecue cook, wearing a dirty white apron, his conked hair reddish and metallic in the pale sun, and a cigarette between his lips, stood in the doorway, watching them. Kids and older people paused in their errands and stood there, along with some older men and a couple of very tough-looking women who watched everything that happened on the avenue, as though they owned it, or were maybe owned by it. Well, they were watching this, too. The revival was being carried on by three sisters in black, and a brother. All they had were their voices and their Bibles and a tambourine. The brother was testifying and while he testified two of the sisters stood together, seeming to say, amen, and the third sister walked around with the tambourine outstretched and a couple of people dropped coins into it. Then the brother's testimony ended and the sister who had been taking up the collection dumped the coins into her palm and transferred them to the pocket of her long black robe. Then she raised both hands, striking the tambourine against the air, and then against one hand, and she started to sing. And the two other sisters and the brother joined in.

177   It was strange, suddenly, to watch, though I had been seeing these street meetings all my life. So, of course, had everybody else down there. Yet, they paused and watched and listened and I stood still at the window. *"Tis the old ship of Zion,"* they sang, and the sister with the tambourine kept a steady, jangling beat, *"it has rescued many a thousand!"* Not a soul under the sound of their voices was hearing this song for the first time, not one of them had been rescued. Nor had they seen much in the way of rescue work being done around them. Neither did they especially believe in the holiness of the three sisters and the brother, they knew too much about them, knew where they lived, and how. The woman with the tambourine, whose voice dominated the air, whose face was bright with joy, was divided by very little from the woman who stood watching her, a cigarette between her heavy, chapped lips, her hair a cuckoo's nest,

her face scarred and swollen from many beatings, and her black eyes glittering like coal. Perhaps they both knew this, which was why, when, as rarely, they addressed each other, they addressed each other as Sister. As the singing filled the air the watching, listening faces underwent a change, the eyes focusing on something within; the music seemed to soothe a poison out of them; and time seemed, nearly, to fall away from the sullen, belligerent, battered faces, as though they were fleeing back to their first condition, while dreaming of their last. The barbecue cook half shook his head and smiled, and dropped his cigarette and disappeared into his joint. A man fumbled in his pockets for change and stood holding it in his hand impatiently, as though he had just remembered a pressing appointment further up the avenue. He looked furious. Then I saw Sonny, standing on the edge of the crowd. He was carrying a wide, flat notebook with a green cover, and it made him look, from where I was standing, almost like a schoolboy. The coppery sun brought out the copper in his skin, he was very faintly smiling, standing very still. Then the singing stopped, the tambourine turned into a collection plate again. The furious man dropped in his coins and vanished, so did a couple of the women, and Sonny dropped some change in the plate, looking directly at the woman with a little smile. He started across the avenue, toward the house. He has a slow, loping walk, something like the way Harlem hipsters walk, only he's imposed on this his own half-beat. I had never really noticed it before.

178   I stayed at the window, both relieved and apprehensive. As Sonny disappeared from my sight, they began singing again. And they were still singing when his key turned in the lock.

179   "Hey," he said.

180   "Hey, yourself. You want some beer?"

181   "No. Well, maybe." But he came up to the window and stood beside me, looking out. "What a warm voice," he said.

182   They were singing *If I could only hear my mother pray again!*

183   "Yes," I said, "and she can sure beat that tambourine."

184   "But what a terrible song," he said, and laughed. He dropped his notebook on the sofa and disappeared into the kitchen. "Where's Isabel and the kids?"

185   "I think they went to see their grandparents. You hungry?"

186   "No." He came back into the living room with his can of beer. "You want to come some place with me tonight?"

187   I sensed, I don't know how, that I couldn't possibly say no. "Sure. Where?"

188   He sat down on the sofa and picked up his notebook and started leafing through it. "I'm going to sit in with some fellows in a joint in the Village."

189   "You mean, you're going to play, tonight?"

190   "That's right." He took a swallow of his beer and moved back to the window. He gave me a sidelong look. "If you can stand it."

191   "I'll try," I said.

192   He smiled to himself and we both watched as the meeting across the way broke up. The three sisters and the brother, heads bowed, were singing *God be with you till we meet again.* The faces around them were very quiet. Then the song ended. The small crowd dispersed. We watched the three women and the lone man walk slowly up the avenue.

193   "When she was singing before," said Sonny, abruptly, "her voice reminded me for a minute of what heroin feels like sometimes—when it's in your veins. It makes you feel sort of warm and cool at the same time. And distant. And—and sure." He sipped his beer, very deliberately not looking at me. I watched his face. "It makes you feel—in control. Sometimes you've got to have that feeling."

194   "Do you?" I sat down slowly in the easy chair.

195   "Sometimes." He went to the sofa and picked up his notebook again. "Some people do."

196   "In order," I asked, "to play?" And my voice was very ugly, full of contempt and anger.

197   "Well"—he looked at me with great, troubled eyes, as though, in fact, he hoped his eyes would tell me things he could never otherwise say—"they *think* so. And *if* they think so—!"

198   "And what do *you* think?" I asked.

199   He sat on the sofa and put his can of beer on the floor. "I don't know," he said, and I couldn't be sure if he were answering my question or pursuing his thoughts. His face didn't tell me. "It's not so much to *play.* It's to *stand* it, to be able to make it at all. On any level." He frowned and smiled: "In order to keep from shaking to pieces."

200   "But these friends of yours," I said, "they seem to shake themselves to pieces pretty goddamn fast."

201   "Maybe." He played with the notebook. And something told me that I should curb my tongue, that Sonny was doing his best to talk, that I should listen. "But of course you only know the ones that've gone to pieces. Some don't—or at least they haven't *yet* and that's just about all *any* of us can say." He paused. "And then there are some who just live, really, in hell, and they know it and they see

what's happening and they go right on. I don't know." He sighed, dropped the notebook, folded his arms. "Some guys, you can tell from the way they play, they on something *all* the time. And you can see that, well, it makes something real for them. But of course," he picked up his beer from the floor and sipped it and put the can down again, "they *want* to, too, you've got to see that. Even some of them that say they don't—*some*, not all."

202   "And what about you?" I asked—I couldn't help it. "What about you? Do *you* want to?"

203   He stood up and walked to the window and remained silent for a long time. Then he sighed. "Me," he said. Then: "While I was downstairs before, on my way here, listening to that woman sing, it struck me all of a sudden how much suffering she must have had to go through—to sing like that. It's *repulsive* to think you have to suffer that much."

204   I said: "But there's no way not to suffer—is there, Sonny?"

205   "I believe not," he said and smiled, "but that's never stopped anyone from trying." He looked at me. "Has it?" I realized, with this mocking look, that there stood between us, forever, beyond the power of time or forgiveness, the fact that I had held silence—so long!—when he had needed human speech to help him. He turned back to the window. "No, there's no way not to suffer. But you try all kinds of ways to keep from drowning in it, to keep on top of it, and to make it seem—well, like *you*. Like you did something, all right, and now you're suffering for it. You know?" I said nothing. "Well you know," he said, impatiently, "why *do* people suffer? Maybe it's better to do something to give it a reason, *any* reason."

206   "But we just agreed," I said, "that there's no way not to suffer. Isn't it better, then, just to—take it?"

207   "But nobody just takes it," Sonny cried, "that's what I'm telling you! *Everybody* tries not to. You're just hung up on the *way* some people try—it's not *your* way!"

208   The hair on my face began to itch, my face felt wet. "That's not true," I said, "that's not true. I don't give a damn what other people do, I don't even care how they suffer. I just care how *you* suffer." And he looked at me. "Please believe me," I said, "I don't want to see you—die—trying not to suffer."

209   "I won't," he said, flatly, "die trying not to suffer. At least, not any faster than anybody else."

210   "But there's no need," I said, trying to laugh, "is there? in killing yourself."

211   I wanted to say more, but I couldn't. I wanted to talk about will power and how life could be—well, beautiful. I wanted to say that

it was all within; but was it? or, rather, wasn't that exactly the trouble? And I wanted to promise that I would never fail him again. But it would all have sounded—empty words and lies.

212 So I made the promise to myself and prayed that I would keep it.

213 "It's terrible sometimes, inside," he said, "that's what's the trouble. You walk these streets, black and funky and cold, and there's not really a living ass to talk to, and there's nothing shaking, and there's no way of getting it out—that storm inside. You can't talk it and you can't make love with it, and when you finally try to get with it and play it, you realize *nobody's* listening. So *you've* got to listen. You got to find a way to listen."

214 And then he walked away from the window and sat on the sofa again, as though all the wind had suddenly been knocked out of him. "Sometimes you'll do *anything* to play, even cut your mother's throat." He laughed and looked at me. "Or your brother's." Then he sobered. "Or your own." Then: "Don't worry. I'm all right now and I think I'll *be* all right. But I can't forget—where I've been. I don't mean just the physical place I've been, I mean where I've *been*. And *what* I've been."

215 "What have you been, Sonny?" I asked.

216 He smiled—but sat sideways on the sofa, his elbow resting on the back, his fingers playing with his mouth and chin, not looking at me. "I've been something I didn't recognize, didn't know I could be. Didn't know anybody could be." He stopped, looking inward, looking helplessly young, looking old. "I'm not talking about it now because I feel *guilty* or anything like that—maybe it would be better if I did, I don't know. Anyway, I can't really talk about it. Not to you, not to anybody," and now he turned and faced me. "Sometimes, you know, and it was actually when I was most *out* of the world, I felt that I was in it, that I was *with* it, really, and I could play or I didn't really have to *play*, it just came out of me, it was there. And I don't know how I played, thinking about it now, but I know I did awful things, those times, sometimes, to people. Or it wasn't that I *did* anything to them—it was that they weren't real." He picked up the beer can; it was empty; he rolled it between his palms: "And other times—well, I needed a fix, I needed to find a place to lean, I needed to clear a space to *listen*—and I couldn't find it, and I—went crazy, I did terrible things to *me*, I was terrible *for* me." He began pressing the beer can between his hands, I watched the metal begin to give. It glittered, as he played with it, like a knife, and I was afraid he would cut himself, but I said nothing. "Oh well. I can never tell you. I was all by myself at the bottom of something, stinking and sweating and crying and shaking, and I

smelled it, you know? *my* stink, and I thought I'd die if I couldn't get away from it and yet, all the same, I knew that everything I was doing was just locking me in with it. And I didn't know," he paused, still flattening the beer can, "I didn't know, I still *don't* know, something kept telling me that maybe it was good to smell your own stink, but I didn't think that *that* was what I'd been trying to do—and—who can stand it?" and he abruptly dropped the ruined beer can, looking at me with a small, still smile, and then rose, walking to the window as though it were the lodestone rock. I watched his face, he watched the avenue. "I couldn't tell you when Mama died—but the reason I wanted to leave Harlem so bad was to get away from drugs. And then, when I ran away, that's what I was running from—really. When I came back, nothing had changed, *I* hadn't changed, I was just—older." And he stopped, drumming with his fingers on the windowpane. The sun had vanished, soon darkness would fall. I watched his face. "It can come again," he said, almost as though speaking to himself. Then he turned to me. "It can come again," he repeated. "I just want you to know that."

217   "All right," I said, at last. "So it can come again, All right."

218   He smiled, but the smile was sorrowful. "I had to try to tell you," he said.

219   "Yes," I said. "I understand that."

220   "You're my brother," he said, looking straight at me, and not smiling at all.

221   "Yes," I repeated, "yes. I understand that."

222   He turned back to the window, looking out. "All that hatred down there," he said, "all that hatred and misery and love. It's a wonder it doesn't blow the avenue apart."

223   We went to the only nightclub on a short, dark street, down-town. We squeezed through the narrow, chattering, jampacked bar to the entrance of the big room, where the bandstand was. And we stood there for a moment, for the lights were very dim in this room and we couldn't see. Then, "Hello, boy," said a voice and an enormous black man, much older than Sonny or myself, erupted out of all that atmospheric lighting and put an arm around Sonny's shoulder. "I been sitting right here," he said, "waiting for you."

224   He had a big voice, too, and heads in the darkness turned toward us.

225   Sonny grinned and pulled a little away, and said, "Creole, this is my brother. I told you about him."

226   Creole shook my hand. "I'm glad to meet you, son," he said, and it was clear that he was glad to meet me *there*, for Sonny's sake. And

he smiled, "You got a real musician in *your* family," and he took his arm from Sonny's shoulder and slapped him, lightly, affectionately, with the back of his hand.

227   "Well. Now I've heard it all," said a voice behind us. This was another musician, and a friend of Sonny's, a coal-black, cheerful-looking man, built close to the ground. He immediately began confiding to me, at the top of his lungs, the most terrible things about Sonny, his teeth gleaming like a light-house and his laugh coming up out of him like the beginning of an earthquake. And it turned out that everyone at the bar knew Sonny, or almost everyone; some were musicians, working there, or nearby, or not working, some were simply hangers-on, and some were there to hear Sonny play. I was introduced to all of them and they were all very polite to me. Yet, it was clear that, for them, I was only Sonny's brother. Here, I was in Sonny's world. Or, rather: his kingdom. Here, it was not even a question that his veins bore royal blood.

228   They were going to play soon and Creole installed me, by myself, at a table in a dark corner. Then I watched them, Creole, and the little black man, and Sonny, and the others, while they horsed around, standing just below the bandstand. The light from the bandstand spilled just a little short of them and, watching them laughing and gesturing and moving about, I had the feeling that they, nevertheless, were being most careful not to step into that circle of light too suddenly: that if they moved into the light too suddenly, without thinking, they would perish in flame. Then, while I watched, one of them, the small, black man, moved into the light and crossed the bandstand and started fooling around with his drums. Then—being funny and being, also, extremely ceremonious—Creole took Sonny by the arm and led him to the piano. A woman's voice called Sonny's name and a few hands started clapping. And Sonny, also being funny and being ceremonious, and so touched, I think, that he could have cried, but neither hiding it nor showing it, riding it like a man, grinned, and put both hands to his heart and bowed from the waist.

229   Creole then went to the bass fiddle and a lean, very bright-skinned brown man jumped up on the bandstand and picked up his horn. So there they were, and the atmosphere on the bandstand and in the room began to change and tighten. Someone stepped up to the microphone and announced them. Then there were all kinds of murmurs. Some people at the bar shushed others. The waitress ran around, frantically getting in the last orders, guys and chicks got closer to each other, and the lights on the bandstand, on the quartet, turned to a

kind of indigo. Then they all looked different there. Creole looked
about him for the last time, as though he were making certain that all
his chickens were in the coop, and then he—jumped and struck the
fiddle. And there they were.

230   All I know about music is that not many people ever really hear
it. And even then, on the rare occasions when something opens within,
and the music enters, what we mainly hear, or hear corroborated, are
personal, private, vanishing evocations. But the man who creates the
music is hearing something else, is dealing with the roar rising from the
void and imposing order on it as it hits the air. What is evoked in him,
then, is of another order, more terrible because it has no words, and triumphant, too, for that same reason. And his triumph, when he triumphs, is ours. I just watched Sonny's face. His face was troubled, he
was working hard, but he wasn't with it. And I had the feeling that,
in a way, everyone on the bandstand was waiting for him, both waiting for him and pushing him along. But as I began to watch Creole, I
realized that it was Creole who held them all back. He had them on
a short rein. Up there, keeping the beat with his whole body, wailing
on the fiddle, with his eyes half closed, he was listening to everything,
but he was listening to Sonny. He was having a dialogue with Sonny.
He wanted Sonny to leave the shoreline and strike out for the deep
water. He was Sonny's witness that deep water and drowning were
not the same thing—he had been there, and he knew. And he wanted
Sonny to know. He was waiting for Sonny to do the things on the keys
which would let Creole know that Sonny was in the water.

231   And, while Creole listened, Sonny moved, deep within, exactly
like someone in torment. I had never before thought of how awful
the relationship must be between the musician and his instrument.
He has to fill it, this instrument, with the breath of life, his own.
He has to make it do what he wants it to do. And a piano is just
a piano. It's made out of so much wood and wires and little hammers and big ones, and ivory. While there's only so much you can
do with it, the only way to find this out is to try; to try and make
it do everything.

232   And Sonny hadn't been near a piano for over a year. And he
wasn't on much better terms with his life, not the life that stretched
before him now. He and the piano stammered, started one way, got
scared, stopped; started another way, panicked, marked time, started
again; then seemed to have found a direction, panicked again, got
stuck. And the face I saw on Sonny I'd never seen before. Everything had been burned out of it, and, at the same time, things usually

hidden were being burned in, by the fire and fury of the battle which was occurring in him up there.

233 Yet, watching Creole's face as they neared the end of the first set, I had the feeling that something had happened, something I hadn't heard. Then they finished, there was scattered applause, and then, without an instant's warning, Creole started into something else, it was almost sardonic, it was *Am I Blue*. And, as though he commanded, Sonny began to play. Something began to happen. And Creole let out the reins. The dry, low, black man said something awful on the drums, Creole answered, and the drums talked back. Then the horn insisted, sweet and high, slightly detached perhaps, and Creole listened, commenting now and then, dry, and driving, beautiful and calm and old. Then they all came together again, and Sonny was part of the family again. I could tell this from his face. He seemed to have found, right there beneath his fingers, a damn brand-new piano. It seemed that he couldn't get over it. Then, for awhile, just being happy with Sonny, they seemed to be agreeing with him that brand-new pianos certainly were a gas.

234 Then Creole stepped forward to remind them that what they were playing was the blues. He hit something in all of them, he hit something in me, myself, and the music tightened and deepened, apprehension began to beat the air. Creole began to tell us what the blues were all about. They were not about anything very new. He and his boys up there were keeping it new, at the risk of ruin, destruction, madness, and death, in order to find new ways to make us listen. For, while the tale of how we suffer, and how we are delighted, and how we may triumph is never new, it always must be heard. There isn't any other tale to tell, it's the only light we've got in all this darkness.

235 And this tale, according to that face, that body, those strong hands on those strings, has another aspect in every country, and a new depth in every generation. Listen, Creole seemed to be saying, listen. Now these are Sonny's blues. He made the little black man on the drums know it, and the bright, brown man on the horn. Creole wasn't trying any longer to get Sonny in the water. He was wishing him Godspeed. Then he stepped back, very slowly, filling the air with the immense suggestion that Sonny speak for himself.

236 Then they all gathered around Sonny and Sonny played. Every now and again one of them seemed to say, amen. Sonny's fingers filled the air with life, his life. But that life contained so many others. And Sonny went all the way back, he really began with the spare, flat statement of the opening phrase of the song. Then he began to make

it his. It was very beautiful because it wasn't hurried and it was no longer a lament. I seemed to hear with what burning he had made it his, with what burning we had yet to make it ours, how we could cease lamenting. Freedom lurked around us and I understood, at last, that he could help us to be free if we would listen, that he would never be free until we did. Yet, there was no battle in his face now. I heard what he had gone through, and would continue to go through until he came to rest in earth. He had made it his: that long line, of which we knew only Mama and Daddy. And he was giving it back, as everything must be given back, so that, passing through death, it can live forever. I saw my mother's face again, and felt, for the first time, how the stones of the road she had walked on must have bruised her feet. I saw the moonlit road where my father's brother died. And it brought something else back to me, and carried me past it, I saw my little girl again and felt Isabel's tears again, and I felt my own tears begin to rise. And I was yet aware that this was only a moment, that the world waited outside, as hungry as a tiger, and that trouble stretched above us, longer than the sky.

237   Then it was over. Creole and Sonny let out their breath, both soaking wet, and grinning. There was a lot of applause and some of it was real. In the dark, the girl came by and I asked her to take drinks to the bandstand. There was a long pause, while they talked up there in the indigo light and after awhile I saw the girl put a Scotch and milk on top of the piano for Sonny. He didn't seem to notice it, but just before they started playing again, he sipped from it and looked toward me, and nodded. Then he put it back on top of the piano. For me, then, as they began to play again, it glowed and shook above my brother's head like the very cup of trembling.

Ted Joans

(1928–2003)

Poet, musician, painter, and sculptor Ted Joans was born on July 4, 1928, in Cairo, Illinois. His father, a riverboat entertainer, gave Ted a trumpet and sent him out into the world when he was still a youth. After receiving a bachelor's degree in fine arts from Indiana University, he moved to New York City's Greenwich Village in 1951 and was a part of the literary avant-garde that included Allen Ginsberg and LeRoi Jones (Amiri Baraka). Joans traveled widely in Europe and Africa. His poetry books include Jazz Poems *(1959),* All of T. J. and No More *(1961),* Black

Pow-Wow: Jazz Poems *(1969)*, Afrodisia: New Poems *(1970)*, The Aard-
vark-Watcher: Der Erdferkelforscher *(1980), a bilingual volume, and*
Teducation: Selected Poems 1949–1999 *(1999)*.

Jazz Is . . .

dedicated to Cecil Taylor

a scream / can scare / awake or shake one UP!!
to joy's highest pitch / forth deep into fathoms where / boss
bass sounds rumble / round riffs repeat rhythms / there. . . . .
a shout is what / that's about / five or groove / right on
5 across the bridge / work and rework them changes / catch
this bit / here   not   steady / ready? accidentally fell in
and out of those fast changing bars / discovering and
uncovering / dare a devil phrases / skipping the last
measure at last minute / plenty plenty soul stirred down in
10 it in it in it / git up git up / let up off that there click /
away heres what I gotta say / forcing fierce fragments /
out side of me into machine voice / tearing away its
mathematice of so-called so believed and preached music /
a moan may cause tears / reminds or just shatters / the
15 mask is down on its knees / now to disguise the non melody
in me / out of me / free / glad to be / keep in touch with
your axe / truth streaming across the earth / worming its
way / out beyond the seas / mountains / fields / and graveyard
giggles / sad at first burst / bigger blacker blacks
20 to be had / biggest barriers broken / sound pounding is
swings / let freedom swing one more again / bright
explosions hammer human hang-ups dark moods massage
the guilt / gas leak of pleasure / marvelous images
surround / brain tissues / discarding manmade forbidden
25 issues / these beats blending and bending / back to black /
and forth to forward march / beats heat increased / to
arouse what's really there / down inside / soul sacks / a
black sound / a black sound / leaps / or glides / into the
ear / of the digger (a listener who stirs) and like water and
30 air / Jazz is . . . . .

good for the soul

Jazz Is My Religion

Jazz is my religion   and it alone do I dig   the jazz clubs are
my house of worship   and sometimes the concert halls but some
holy places are too commercial (like churches)   so I don't dig the
sermons there   I buy jazz sides to dig in solitude   Like man/ Harlem,
5 Harlem USA Used to be a jazz heaven where most of the jazz
sermons were preached   but now-a-days due to chacha cha and
rotten rock'n'roll alotta good jazzmen have sold their souls   but jazz
is still my religion   because I know and feel the message it brings
like Reverend Dizzy Gillespie / Brother Bird and Basie / Uncle
10 Armstrong/ Minister Monk / Deacon Miles Davis / Rector Rollins/
Priest Ellington / His Funkness Horace Silver / and the great
John COLTRANE   and Cecil Taylor   They Preach A Sermon
That Always Swings!!   Yeah jazz is MY religion   Jazz is my story
it was my mom's and pop's   and their moms and pops from the
15 days of Buddy Bolden who swung them blues to Charlie Parker and
Ornette Coleman's extension of Bebop   Yeah jazz is my religion
Jazz is a unique musical religion the sermons spread happiness and
joy   to be able to dig and swing inside   what a wonderful feeling
jazz is / YEAH BOY!! JAZZ is my religion and dig this: it wasn't for
20 us to choose because they created it for a damn good reason   as   a
weapon to battle our blues! JAZZ is my religion   and its
international   all the   way   JAZZ is just an Afroamerican music
and like us it's here to stay   So remember that JAZZ is my religion
but it can be your religion too but JAZZ is a truth that   is always
25 black and blue   Halleluiah I love JAZZ so   Halleluiah I dig JAZZ so
Yeah JAZZ   IS   MY   RELIGION

Him the Bird

in memory of Babs Gonzales

Once upon a time a few years ago now
There was a young café-au-lait colored bird
Who blew sax   and his earth name   was   CHARLES PARKER

He mounted a small bandstand in Greenwich Village
5 And blew through Bob Reisner's Open Door where
Bohemian whores used to sit with big-assed business
Men talking trade backed Bird's funky lore

He lived at flophouse on Barrow Street and froze
With a Moslem and me   during that winter of my time '53
10 Eating canned beans   sardines   sipping wine and drinking tea

He blew for young Hebrew in Mafia-owned joint
Where sat James Dean with Weegee and some technicolored
     chicks

He blew for kicks and a few measly bills
15 Those solos he took on borrowed alto
Sax gave everybody their jazz-as-religious thrills

He blew his born in the Village and wailed for the world
He died a pauper although now his every
Effort on wax will sell   So the BIRD is gone and
20 In the outer world he cooks   therefore women and
Men like me will always have the BIRD influence in
Their   music   paintings   and poetry books

Bird Lives   Bird Lives   Bird Lives   Bird Lives!!

1958

Bob Kaufman

(1925–1986)

*Born on April 18, 1925, in New Orleans, Bob Kaufman was a cru-
cial figure among the Beat poets. After a long tenure as a merchant
marine, he settled in San Francisco in the late 1950s. He became
well known in San Francisco's North Beach and, while in New York,
in Greenwich Village. He published the broadside* Abomunist
Manifesto *in 1959. Some of Kaufman's other poetry is included in*
Solitudes Crowded with Loneliness *(1965),* Golden Sardine *(1967),
and* The Ancient Rain: Poems 1956–1978 *(1981).* Cranial Guitar:
Selected Poems by Bob Kaufman, *edited by Gerald Nicosia, was
published in 1996. Kaufman was known to take vows of silence for
political reasons; reportedly, he held to one vow for a decade.
The following selections are found in* Golden Sardine.

His Horn

Swinging horn softly confirming
Anguished cries of eternal losers
Whose gifts outgrow their presence.
We hear this lonesome Saxworld dweller
5 Swing higher—
Defiantly into a challenge key
Screamed over a heartbeat
Shouting at all beat seekers
To vanish into soft sounds of jazz
10 And walk with him to smoky ends
While his jazz walks forever
Across our parched heartstrings.

O-JAZZ-O

Where the string
At
Some point,
Was some umbilical jazz,
5 Or perhaps,
In memory,
A long lost bloody cross,
Buried in some steel calvary.
In what time
10 For whom do we bleed,
Lost notes, from some jazzman's
Broken needle.
Musical tears from lost
Eyes.
15 Broken drumsticks, why?
Pitter patter, boom dropping
Bombs in the middle
Of my emotions
My father's sound
20 My mother's sound,
Is love,
Is life.

Amiri Baraka

(1934–)

*For biographical information about Amiri Baraka, see page 221.
"AM/TRAK" is a part of the poetic outpouring by many in tribute to
the stellar saxophonist John Coltrane; it appeared in the book*
AM/TRAK *(1979).*

AM/TRAK

1

Trane,
Trane,
History Love Scream Oh
Trane, Oh
5   Trane, Oh
Scream History Love
Trane

2

Begin on by a Philly night club
or the basement of a cullut chuhch
10   walk the bars my man for pay
honk the night lust of money
oh
blow—
scream history love
15   Rabbit, Cleanhead, Diz
Big Maybelle, Trees in the shining night forest

Oh
blow
love, history

20   Alcohol we submit to thee
3x's consume our lives
our livers quiver under yr poison hits
eyes roll back in stupidness

The navy, the lord, niggers,
25   the streets
all converge a shitty symphony
of screams
   to come
   dazzled invective
30   Honk Honk Honk, "I am here
to love
it." Let me be fire-mystery
air feeder beauty."

Honk
35   Oh
scream—Miles
comes.

3

Hip band alright
sum up life in the slick
40   street part of the
world, oh,
blow,
if you cd
nigger
45   man

Miles wd stand back and negative check
oh, he dug him—Trane
But Trane clawed at the limits of cool
slandered sanity
50   with his tryin to be born
raging
shit
    Oh
    blow,
55   yeh go do it
       honk, scream
       uhuh yeh—history
           love
           blue clipped moments

60   of intense feeling.
   "Trane you blows too long."
   Screaming niggers drop out yr solos
   Bohemian nights, the "heavyweight champ"
   smacked him
65 in the face
   his eyes sagged like a spent
   dick, hot vowels escaped the metal clone of his soul
   fucking saxophone
   tell us shit tell us tell us!

4

70 There was nothing left to do but
   be where monk cd find him
   that crazy
   mother fucker
            duh duh-duh duh-duh duh
75   duh duh
            duh duh-duh duh-duh duh
            duh duh
            duh duh-duh duh-duh duh
            duh duh
80   duh Duuuuuuuuuuhhhhhh
   Can you play this shit? (Life asks
   Come by and listen

   & at the 5 Spot Bach, Mulatto ass Beethoven
   & even Duke, who has given America its hip tongue
85 checked
   checked
   Trane stood and dug
   Crazy monk's shit
   Street gospel intellectual mystical survival codes
90 Intellectual street gospel funk modes
   Tink a ling put downs of dumb shit
   pink pink a cool bam groove note air breath
   a why I'm here
   a why I aint
95 & who is you-ha-you-ha-you-ha

Monk's shit
Blue Cooper 5 Spot
was the world busting
on piano bass drums&tenor

100 This was Coltrane's College. A Ph motherfuckin d
sitting at the feet, elbows
& funny grin
Of Master T Sphere
too cool to be a genius
105 he was instead
Thelonius
with Comrades Shadow
on tubs, lyric Wilbur
who hipped us to electric futures
110 & the monster with the horn.

5

From the endless sessions
money lord hovers oer us
capitalism beats our ass
dope & juice wont change it
115 Trane, blow, oh scream
yeh, anyway.

There then came down in the ugly streets of us
inside the head & tongue
of us
120 a man
black blower of the now
The vectors from all sources—slavery, renaissance
bop charlie parker,
nigger absolute super-sane screams against reality
125 course through him
AS SOUND!
"Yes, it says
this is now in your screaming
recognize the truth
130 recognize reality
& even check me (Trane)

who blows it
Yes it says
Yes &
135 Yes again   Convulsive multi orgasmic
                  Art
                  Protest

&finally, brother, you took you were
       (are we gathered to dig this?
140   electric wind find us finally
       on red records of the history of ourselves)

The cadre came together
the inimitable 4 who blew the pulse of then, exact
The flame the confusion the love of
145 whatever the fuck there was
       to love
Yes it says
blow, oh honk-scream (bahhhhhhh-wheeeeeeee)

(If Don Lee thinks I am imitating him in this poem,
150 this is only payback for his imitating me—we
are brothers, even if he is a backward cultural nationalist
motherfucker—Hey man only socialism brought by revolution
can win)
                  Trane was the spirit of the 60's
155   He was Malcolm X in New Super Bop Fire
                  Baaahhhhh
                  Wheeeeeee . . . Black Art!!!
Love
History
160   On The Bar Tops of Philly
in the Monkish College of *Express*
in the cool Grottoes of Miles Davis Funnytimery
Be
Be
165 Be reality
Be reality alive in motion in flame to change (You Knew It!)
                              to change!!
            (All you reactionaries listening
            Fuck you, Kill you
170   get outta here!!!)

Jimmy Garrison, bass, McCoy Tyner, piano, Captain Marvel Elvin
on drums, the number itself—the precise saying
all of it in it afire aflame talking saying being doing meaning
Meditations
175 *Expressions*
A Love Supreme
(I lay in solitary confinement, July 67
Tanks rolling thru Newark
& whistled all I knew of Trane
180 my knowledge heartbeat
& he was *dead*
they
said.

And yet last night I played *Meditations*
185 & it told me what to do
Live, you crazy mother
fucker!
Live!
  & organize
190 yr shit
  as rightly
  burning!

Sonia Sanchez

(1934–)

Among the most moving and in-demand poets, Sonia Sanchez (originally Wilsonia Benita Driver) was born in Birmingham, Alabama, on September 9, 1934. Her mother died while Sanchez was still an infant. At the age of nine, she moved to New York City with her father, who was a musician. Sanchez graduated from Hunter College in 1955 and worked on behalf of political groups like The Congress of Racial Equality (CORE). She was involved in the founding of the nation's first department of African American Studies, at San Francisco State University in 1968. Sanchez has been in the front rank of African American poetry for more than three decades. Her volumes include We a BaddDDD People *(1970),* Love Poems *(1973),* A Blues Book for Blue Black Magical Woman *(1974),* I've Been a Woman *(1978),* homegirls & handgrenades *(1984),* Under a Soprano Sky *(1987),* Wounded in the House of a Friend *(1995),* Does Your House Have Lions? *(1997),* Like the Singing Coming Off the

Drums *(1998), and* Shake Loose My Skin: New and Selected Poems
(1999). The following poem is from We a BaddDDD People.

a/coltrane/poem

my favorite things
　　　　　　is u/blowen
　　　　　　　　　yo/favorite/things.
stretchen the mind
5　　　　　　till it bursts past the con/fines of
solo/en melodies.
　　　　　　　to the many/solos
of the
　　mind/spirit.
10　　　are u sleepen　　(to be
　　　are u sleepen　　　sung
　　　brotha john　　　softly)
　　　brotha john
　　　　　　where u have gone to.
15　　　no mornin bells
　　　are ringen here. only the quiet
aftermath of assassinations.
　　　　　　but i saw yo/murder/
the massacre
20　　　　of all blk/musicians. planned
in advance.
　　　　　yrs befo u blew away our passsst
　　and showed us our futureeeeee
　　screech screeech screeeeech screeech
25　　a/love/supreme, alovesupreme a lovesupreme.
　　　A LOVE SUPREME
scrEEEccCHHHHH screeeeEEECHHHHHHH
　　sCReeeEEECHHHHHH SCREEEEECCCCHHHH
　　SCREEEEEEEECCCHHHHHHHHHHHH
30　　a lovesupremealovesupremealovesupreme for our blk
people.
　　　BRING IN THE WITE/MOTHA/fuckas
　　　ALL THE MILLIONAIRES/BANKERS/ol
MAIN/LINE/ASS/RISTOCRATS (ALL

35   THEM SO-CALLED BEAUTIFUL
   PEOPLE)
     WHO HAVE KILLED
   WILL CONTINUE TO
      KILL US WITH
40   THEY CAPITALISM/18% OWNERSHIP
   OF THE WORLD.
       YEH. U RIGHT
 THERE U ROCKEFELLERS. MELLONS
   VANDERBILTS
45   FORDS.
        yeh.
  GITem.
     PUSHem/PUNCHem/STOMPem. THEN
   LIGHT A FIRE TO
50   THEY pilgrim asses.
   TEAROUT THEY eyes.
      STRETCH they necks
 till no mo
    raunchy sounds of MURDER/
55   POVERTY/STARVATION

       come from they
  throats.
screeeeeeeeeeeeeeeeeeeCHHHHHHHHHHH
SCREEEEEEEEEEEEEEECHHHHHHHHHHH
60 screeEEEEEEEEEEEEEEEEEEEEEEEEEE
EECCCCHHHHHHH
SCREEEEEEEEEEEEEEEEEEEEEEEEEEEEEE
   EEEEEECHHHHHHHHHH
BRING IN THE WITE/LIBERALS ON THE SOLO
65 SOUND OF YO/FIGHT IS MY FIGHT
      SAXOPHONE.
       TORTURE
 THEM FIRST AS THEY HAVE
      TORTURED US WITH
70 PROMISES/
   PROMISES, IN WITE/AMURICA. WHEN
 ALL THEY WUZ DOEN
     WAS HAVEN FUN WITH THEY
 ORGIASTIC DREAMS OF BLKNESS.
75   (JUST SOME MO

CRACKERS FUCKEN OVER OUR MINDS.)
                         MAKE THEM
SCREEEEEEAM
       FORGIVE ME. IN SWAHILI.
80 DON'T ACCEPT NO MEA CULPAS.
                        DON'T WANT TO
                        HEAR
BOUT NO EUROPEAN FOR/GIVE/NESS.
DEADDYINDEADDYINDEADDYINWITEWESTERN
85   SHITTTTTT
(softly   da-dum-da da da da da da da da da/da-dum-da
till it   da da da da da da da da da
builds   da-dum- da da da
up)   da-dum. da. da. da. this is a part of my
90   favorite things.
         da dum da da da da da da
         da da da da
         da dum da da da da da da
         da da da da
95   da dum da da da da
            da dum da da da da – – – – –
(to be   rise up blk/ people
sung   de dum da da da da
slowly   move straight in yo/blkness
100 to tune   da dum da da da da
of my   step over the wite/ness
favorite   that is yesssss terrrrrr day
things.)   weeeeeeee are toooooooday.
(f   da dum
105 a   da da da (stomp, stomp) da da da
s   da dum
t   da da da (stomp, stomp) da da da
e   da dum
r)   da da da (stomp) da da da dum (stomp)
110   weeeeeeeee (stomp)
               areeeeeeeee (stomp)
                    areeeeeeeee (stomp, stomp)
       tooooooday   (stomp.
         day   stomp.
115   day   stomp.
         day   stomp.
         day   stomp!)

```
(soft      rise up blk/people. rise up blk/people
chant)     RISE.&BE. What u can.
120        MUST BE.BE.BE.BE.BE.BE.BE-E-E-E-E-BE-E-E-E-E-E-
```

                      yeh. john coltrane.
my favorite things is u.
                          showen us life/
                                    liven.
125 a love supreme.
                for each
            other
        if we just
lisssssssSSSTEN.

Jayne Cortez

(1936–)

Poet and performance artist Jayne Cortez was born May 10, 1936, in Fort Huachuca, Arizona, but grew up in the Watts section of Los Angeles. After a six-year marriage to saxophonist Ornette Coleman, she began writing poetry and studying drama. After working in the South for the Student Nonviolent Coordinating Committee (SNCC), she returned to co-found the Watts Repertory Theater. Cortez moved to New York City in the early 1970s. Her poetry volumes include Pisstained Stairs and the Monkey Man's Wares *(1969),* Festivals and Funerals *(1971),* Mouth on Paper *(1977),* Coagulations: New and Selected Poems *(1984), and* Somewhere in Advance of Nowhere *(1996). Cortez has made several recordings, including, with the Firespitters Band,* Taking the Blues Back Home: Poetry & Music *(1996). The following selections appear in* Jazz Fan Looks Back *(2002).*

Into This Time

(for Charles Mingus)

Into this time
of steel feathers blowing from hearts
into this turquoise flame time in the mouth
into this sonic boom time in the conch

5 into this musty stone-fly time sinking into
the melancholy buttocks of dawn
sinking into lacerated whelps
into gun holsters
into breast bones
10 into a manganese field of uranium nozzles
into a nuclear tube full of drunk rodents
into the massive vein of one interval
into one moment's hair plucked down into
the timeless droning fixed into
15 long pauses
fixed into a lash of ninety-eight minutes screeching into
the internal heat of an ice ball melting time into
a configuration of commas on strike
into a work force armed with a calendar of green wings
20 into a collection of nerves
into magnetic mucus
into tongueless shrines
into water pus of a silver volcano
into the black granite face of Morelos
25 into the pigeon toed dance of Mingus
into a refuge of air bubbles
into a cylinder of snake whistles
into clusters of slow spiders
into spade fish skulls
30 into rosin coated shadows of women wrapped in live iguanas
into coins into crosses into St. Martin De Porres
into the pain of this place changing pitches beneath
fingers swelling into
night shouts
35 into day trembles
into month of precious bloods flowing into
this fiesta of sadness year
into this city of eternal spring
into this solo
40 on the road of young bulls
on the street of lost children
on the avenue of dead warriors
on the frisky horse tail fuzz zooming
into ears of every madman
45 stomping into every new composition

everyday of the blues
penetrating into this time

This time of loose strings in low tones
pulling boulders of Olmec heads into the sun
50 into tight wires uncoiling from body of a strip teaser on the table
into half-tones wailing between snap and click
of two castanets smoking into
scales jumping from tips of sacrificial flints
into frogs yodeling across grieving cults
55 yodeling up into word stuffed smell of flamingo stew
into wind packed fuel of howling dog throats slit into
this January flare of aluminum dust falling into
laminated stomach of a bass violin rubbed into red ashes
rubbed into the time sequence of
60 this time of salmonella leaking from eyeballs of a pope
into this lavender vomit time in the chest into
this time plumage of dried bats in the brain into
this wallowing time weed of invisible wakes on cassettes into
this off-beat time syncopation in a leopard skin suit
65 into this radiated protrusion of time in the desert into
this frozen cheek time of dead infants in the cellar
into this time flying with the rotten bottoms of used tuxedos
into this purple brown grey gold minus zero time trilling into
a lime stone crusted Yucatan belching
70 into fifty six medallions shaking
into armadillo drums thumping
into tambourines of fetishes rattling
into an oil slick of poverty symbols flapping
into flat-footed shuffle of two birds advancing
75 into back spine of luminous impulses tumbling
into metronomes of colossal lips ticking
into a double zigzag of callouses splitting
into foam of electric snow flashing into this time
of steel feathers blowing from hearts
80 into this turquoise flame time in the mouth into
this sonic boom time in the conch
into this musty stone fly time sinking into
the melancholy buttocks of dawn

Solo Finger Solo

When evening goes down into its jelly jelly jelly
into drain pipe cuts and stitches and vaccinations
protruding from arms

And spirit of the five by five man pushes
5 his sweet potatoes in the air
feather daddy leaps into a falcon of tropical bird squats
rubber legs swing into off-beat onijos onijos
then into your solo finger solo
the blues chantress jumps up and
10 repeats her nasal volcanic chant calling

Count Basie   Count Basie   Count Basie

And Count Basie
you burn through this timbale of goose flesh rhythms
a drop of iodine on your starfish lips
15 the intonation of your kiss of melodica trilling
into a labyrinth of one o'clock jumps
into corpuscle flashes of the blues torpedo
the erupting volcano of the blues shouters chanting your name

Count Basie   Count Basie   take em to Chicago Count Basie

20 And Count Basie
you punctuate this strong bourbon mist of gamma globulin breath
a mixture of chords like serpentariums coiling
from the deep everglades of your body
and when the luscious screams of three headed root doctors split
25 Kansas City reeds in unison with this triple tapping
double stopping slow grinding loosey butt night swinging
with the blues chantress
erupting volcano of the blues torpedoes chanting your name

Count Basie
30 you reach through the bottom of the music
way down beneath cross rhythm vamps
below air stream of the lowest octave
into depths of a sacred drum
and Count Basie Count Basie Count Basie
35 how powerful and dignified and exquisite and direct and sharp
your solo finger solo is

Xam Wilson Cartiér

(1949–)

Born in Missouri in 1949, novelist, musician, dancer, and artist Xam Wilson Cartiér moved to San Francisco as a young adult to pursue the arts. After writing several successful scripts, she published the novel Be-Bop, Re-Bop (1987). The novel portrays the narrator's reflections on her childhood in the 1950s, an experience greatly influenced by her musician father, Double. The opening pages are included below. Cartiér's second novel is Muse-Echo Blues (1991).

Be-Bop, Re-Bop

BE-BOP, RE-BOP & ALL THOSE OBLIGATOS

1 The liquor was flowing, everyone had a plate, folks had visited all the way back to the kitchen. . . . We were just settling into the spirit of Double's funeral wake when Vole took it in mind to drive all the guests from the house.

2 For some reason of crisis insanity and because my first reaction to mayhem is to staple down the madness to some detail of order, I've begun to take stock of the folks in the room, to estimate the number of floating mourners who've made their way past the living room rut to the recondite sanctum in the rear of the house. There are twenty-four people poised at candid angles as far back through the room as the eye can see, including five men: two family friends and three co-workers of Double's whom I've seen two or three times. The women, role models around me, are fine-feathered birds flown from flighty Saks and Montaldos, the *haute couture* rooms. We're all, all of us are musing over inscrutable chalices of highballs, including me in spasmodic sweet-sixteenhood, thanks to the blessing of mother-gone-from-the-room, but now Vole's back, so here's my solo, about to be crimped. . . .

3 Vole had been resting in the bedroom away from it all when Mona threw out, "Some folks might've called him irresponsible and impulsive, but one thing about Double is, he might have been practically back down to where he started when he died, but now there was a man who could keep going when the chips were down no matter *what*

it took. If it took a Tom, he'd be one, and he has his own good reasons too, he must have, considering what he stooped to just to hold on to that trifling job in parcel post. It was the best thing he'd ever lucked up on."

4   She sucked her teeth and shook her head.

5   "Truth is the light," somebody said.

6   "Let it shine," somebody else said.

7   "Now *some* folks might have said Double was a dreamer with no firm sense of direction;" Mona went on, "they'd have said he was good for nothing but dead-end dreams . . . but I know better! though Double *had* him some dreams, at least til Vole started to stay on his back—she rode him all the time you know, though let it be said, Double needed some get-up and go. Don't talk about the dead, but youall know what I mean, you can't live a man's life for him; you've got to let him breathe. Vole knows that—maybe she's got another opinion—but well, you all know the story: You don't miss your water til your well runs dry!"

8   She raised her glass to the tune of the assents around her.

9   "Well, well, well." Vole appeared in the doorway looking store-rack crisp in her undefiled black dress, faille skirt riding impossible curves of her paragon legs. She raised that tight tan face, angled those high-carved cheekbones, fast-focused those radar eyes from their dusty socket-shadows. Her fingers draped the knob of the door like a mannequin's hand but for the fingernails, which she trimmed stoically in ruthless crescents. We're all looking over at her, ruffled in our own different ways, with reactions ranging from bitterness to outrage. Where are Vole's tears anyway? I'm thinking—and where's the crash of her gloom? There she stands, intact and unacceptable as usual. Her sometime pal Mona is one juror in particular who gives Vole the eye; Mona's response to Vole at the moment is disappointment that the convicted widow's alive and well.

10 "Having fun?" Vole flings at Mona over under-musical silence and rustling nudges, just as Mona's in process of leaning her emerald suede vested chest toward the woman beside her, in bracing gesture of *uh-oh*. . . .

11 "Now Vole, just calm down, honey," Mona dodges, the defense is pushed out of her instantly and she rolls on automatically: "Death is always hard, we know that, and it's hardest on the widow, yes, it always is, it's the shock, and—"

12 "What do you know?" Vole cut her off at the pass of her sass. "Just what in the *hell* do you know?" And I tense, since I feel Vole building

to an open storm of her closet feelings; already she's lapsed into what she calls *vulgar language in public*, brazenly defying the Salt Away Box (this being a cylindrical empty salt box that we keep family fines in; whoever cursed had to pay). "I'm tired, but I ain't crazy," Vole goes on with further indication of no-holds barredness, her lapse into "slang" as she calls it. "I'm tired but I ain't crazy enough to think you actually give a damn about anybody's grief, least of all mine, or do I *look* like a fool? Tell me anything!" Vole's leaning forward now with arms crossed across her chest, a hanging judge, waiting. . . .

13   "Uh—" starts Mona. . . .

14   "Yeah, 'uh,'" says Vole relentlessly, leaning further toward defendant—"Come on, tell me anything, just front me right off. I'm supposed to be under the influence of widowhood, so you can't go wrong. Come on, don't let me stop your show since you know so much. Knock yourself out, come on; make like I'm not here.

15   "Look at you," Vole sneers on, "in your weep motif. You never did a damn thing for Double while he was alive, or for any of the rest of us" (here she gestures maternally toward me), "and you know it. But you take plenty time to rake us through with your mouth, mouth almighty, fatmouth queen, brilliantine—"

16   ("God*damn*" goes someone's hushed catharsis; all of us onlookers had been swept into the spirit of Vole's testimony)—

17   "Well surprise, fools"—Vole turns to the room at large—"I can read you like a book. But don't let that throw you—" With this last you can hear a crew of voices arming with mumbles for self-defense just in case, be prepared, but look! There's Vole, on everyone's case already . . . here she comes, snatching plates of food and drinks from visitors ("Here I'll take that"), rushing out of the room mechanically then back again now with armloads of hats and coats which she flings in a heap on the couch and returns for the rest.

18   "*If it took a Tom, he'd be one. . . .*" It's this I consider during the following frantic interval; I try not to, but can't help but think it, this peanut butter thought that sticks to the roof of my immature mind . . . I think of the time only last week, when Double had lost his post office gig and Vole and I had passed him talking on the wallphone in the hall. . . .

19   "Well, do you take colored?" Double had mouthed this then in mealy manner, or so it seemed to the both of us, Vole headed one way and I another, so that *What?* we stop and stare at each other, then both jump in at once—

20   "Do they do what?" Vole challenges Double and then walks away with no further display, a mystery to teenage me at the time, and I stay on to follow her words with a cop-bust frown of disgust aimed at Double, this at know-all black-and-white stage of analysis development, righteous adolescence. To tom or not to tom—seemed perfectly clear to me. . . .

21   Aw Double, I thought at the wake then that day, there it is, so my hump of shock and let-down can sink to its rest in the pit of my stomach—Was our case really so critical then that we were all the way down to our tommery? I asked myself again and again all through that week, near the time of your seemed-to-be sin when I thought I knew the answer, one answer: *Hell no! You can be down to death, and not down to tom!* Yet—this I know now—what could you do, standing limp with livelihood soon to be lost, as you knew, to the rake of unfeeling circumstance? What's more I'm human too and've whipped out my own slave-kerchief in time of distress, "It's reflex survival," I fibbed to myself until then when that day at your wake all your contrivance (just venial connivance, not mortal!)—all your contrivance comes floodingly clear and wet comprehension, it courses a trail through the heat of my face.

22   Militant memories: For months, years after his passing Double would appear through my sleep to bump a lesser dream, still bopping with the armed resistance of his dedication to "jazz"—which he said was "two, say three broad crooked jumps off to the side of the mainstream straight and narrow, out to where sound becomes sight, as it should be!"

23   When I think of Double that day at his wake, I see him standing beside the radio with his forefinger crooking for me to run over and check out this riff or those taps or that vamp or these changes. This I'd casually stroll up to do with cool beyond my childish years; my thumbs would be tucked in pinafore straps under fat kinky braids that laid on my chest.

24   *"And how's Daddy's masterpiece comin along?"*

25   *"Aw, I can't kick."*

26   *"Well say hey, whatcha know?"*

27   *"Aw, you got the go!"*

28   *"So tell me, what's to it?"*

29   *"Nothin to it but to do it!"*

30   *"Mean to say YOU can do the do?"*

31   *"Can Ella Fitz cut a scat?. . . . Then, don't hand me that!"*

32   *"Can Eisenhower dance? Say HEY—not a chance!"*

33   *"Hey now. And how!"*

34 My smallfry face at Double's knee. Abracadabra afternoons! And
    every day, on the way home from kindergarten at BookerTWashing-
    ton School, there's hopeful harmony of Double and me, two hipsters
    vocaleesing to wide-angle sound up front in the Studebaker.
35 *"Oop bop shabam, buh do be do,*
36 *We like to boogie, woogie, re-bop and be-bop it too!"*

37 Yet Double has died. But why call it *death*, when in the scheme
    of simple reality, I should be and am convinced by the age of six-
    teen (time of no questions) that his passing, like his music, is more
    process than product by nature—that Double's demise has the
    matrix-free flow of an on-the-spot bop change. So since I know he's
    still bopping nearby in time to the tune of temporality, while Vole's
    handing out the coats and hats at his wake, I shake the scheme of
    my dream and seize the opportunity to come up with a note of rel-
    evant reality for the mourn-watchers.
38 "A side of Fats, anyone?" I call out, surrounded by scotchsip-
    pers' eyebrows jumping like spastic grass-hoppers. "Ain't Misbe-
    havin" has popped into mind like the miracle of the gramophone.
    So *apropos!* Talk about chromatic consciousness—why it's the final
    flipside! Besides, it was Double's favorite jam, so I put it on the hi-
    fi and turn it to crescendo. Then's when Vole turns to face me so
    suddenly that distress bends distended in our corner of the cosmos—
    rapport needs no words in light of the sight of Vole rushing toward
    me with her hand upraised, the hand which she uses to spin me in
    place for a heartfelt lindy hop, steps of which I fall into by rote due
    to Double's diligent teaching—and Vole and I, hey, well we dance past
    all woe for a whirlaround while!

DOUBLE OR NOTHING AND ALL THAT JAZZ

39 Double's death was a personal nuclear disaster that radiated negative
    energy in all directions, from was-peaceful past to fallout-filled future.
    For one thing, death hit Double so all of a sudden that it seemed too
    contaminating to absorb. I found myself starting to envy folks whose
    folks had died of lingering cancer or any other dress-rehearsal dis-
    ease; at least they'd had a fair cool-down period: Death had said *All
    right, here's the cue for my solo,* and the grieved-to-be had been able
    to say, *"Goddamn! Why him?"* til they wore themselves out in a nat-
    ural way. All their guilt and blues had had a chance to sift around

til it settled in place, not like me and my lump that still pulsates, ooz-ing poison gas at random.

40　　Yet Double/dear Papa was dead all right—though his death began my siege of dreaming for months, years after his passing that he still was standing beside the chifforobe with one foot resting on the radi-ator, singing the "Monkey Song" as I called it in kidhood, about one of the world's perennial agitators, this one anthropoid and clinging to the back of a wily buzzard who, pragmatist that he was, was bent on devouring the monkey dead or alive.

> . . . *Loosen up, said the buzzard,*
> *you're chokin me. . . .*
> *Loosen up your grip .*
> *and I'll set you free.*
>
> *The monkey looked the buzzard*
> *right dead in the eye:*
> *"Your story's very touchin—*
> *but I know it's a lie!"*

41　　When I think of Double, I hear him tapping his feet in time to the beat of developing melody, humming or scat-singing, winging his way through music of process, running through tonal tongue-to-tooth changes with curled fingers striding, flying off ivories in thin air. He'd turn to me in mid-riff with a question in the movement of his eyebrows—

42　　"Young Fats," I'd answer with head cocked to doubledare side. "Young Fats, early Stride!"

43　　Then came a pause, and next, his applause for diligent growth on the part of a smallfry. *"Whoo-whee! The kid's on the ball! What say? SKIN me, my friend!"*

44　　And I'll do it again! I'm kneehigh at the time and filing the bulk of Double's sagacity for future reference, though already I've soaked up weight enough to hold my own in our name-that-tone champion finals. Fact is, I'm still spongy with pride when Double takes me aside to show me a dog-eared copy of a nineteenth-century abolitionist's knotted dialectic on the "marvelous complication" and "curious rhythmic effect" of a "strong musical network" which defied all due deployment of whitefolks' wit.

45　　"See?" Double said then. "They never can manage to hook up our music to its source in the ghetto, be it concrete or cotton. Their bright idea has always been to rip up our music and chop it off at the roots, grimreaper style, just like they do their turnips. They keep the leaves and scrap the soul of the taste in the turnip!"

46   Our music. It's Double's top doctrine. And by default and devotion, I'm his ace apostle. Which's why later that same afternoon near the noon of it all, when Double's working his graveyard shift so's my daily caretaker while Vole social works her days away, Double and I've been jitterbugging up a storm all over the front room and now we're seated respectfully on the throw rug in the corner, watching the combination radio, a dome-shaped mahogany Mahal for the sounds coming through. We're as intent as if we can see through to the carrier crystal inside the box, major and minor soul-sensors that we are—watching as if the animated armoire is a t.v., which is further down the line of dreamed-up illusion. But movement seems to materialize suddenly from the radio bowels, and a wildroot-dampened lilliputian, dapper ofay dollhouse doll, steps up to a miniature microphone between two fat black vacuum tubes.

47   "You said it!" he enlightens, as we look on unamazed. "That was *Scrapple From The Apple!*" Then he turns to flash a bright white turnip smile at all of us here in the jimcrow balcony.

48   But look! Here comes wonder-worker Ladyday, tipping onstage from the wings, wearing her wiltless gardenia and sizzling sequins and mellow phantom pain, pulling free for a while from her private prison with grief disguised as a series of croons:

49   . . . *I don't stay out late . . .* (Yeah, Billie!) *. . . don't care to go . . . 'm'home about eight . . . just me an my ray-dee-oe . . .*

50   She knocks us out. Kills us. Absolutely! And Double's now in process of snatching me up into a topheavy foxtrot, with his scratchy cheek to cheek. . . . We're riding out on a riff, right on up to the rickety railing in the redbrick hallway, don't-give-a-damn gliding right on down to the front door with its held-back reality demons. Then back we swing toward the tune, in a serious gravity sweep to the source. A dip; we part. Brief shadow of a simple separation.

51   Why is it that time is so upbeat discreet, cuts no slack in its tempo for our schemes unredeemed? The illusion of endings in this world. Addictive fantasy.

52   *Wait, Time, don't you see? At just 43 he was kicked into infinity by an off-the-rack/black/heart attack/and I was only/I'm still trying to improvise/to finishingtouch-up the rest of his life/in the riffs and the runs (BOPBOP/A-REE BOP!) of the chase through the (BOOGEDY/ BOOGEDY/BOPBOPBOP) neo-blue/everblack/labyrinth life*
        of my dreams!

A MATTER OF TASTE

53   According to norm and nevermind Hoyle, Double had cooked dinner such as it was—canned lima beans (a gruesome family favorite to my kid's taste at the time), fried chicken which he'd paprikaed down in spots where the brown was missing, thick beige gravy, canned spinach: dark green and the top of it sprinkled with shocking yellow and white boiled egg pieces for contrast in the spirit of Double's aesthete's touch, and canned dairy-case rolls: innocent looking fakes with a telltale smell.

54   To date I'd lost weight to the size of a child two years younger and two-thirds as tall as myself, according to the chart painted on the pediatrician's scale where I did my on-the-spot research while waiting for the doctor to come and check me over. I remember being called upon to explain my weight loss—afterall, I'd been getting enough to eat yet here I was in bold sad shape, the upstanding child of a mother who could articulate the doctor to shame—and me just standing there thinking, inwardly test-running my tale of excuse since it beat me too, I knew I was to blame, but *Give me time enough*, I'm thinking: *I'll come up with something. . . .* Which's when the doctor decrees that to spark my appetite I only can have milk at the end of my meals, a diabolical punishment tailor-made to fit. Milk is my favorite food, and I use it religiously as a sacrosanct supplement to everything on my plate.

55   But after we'd eaten dinner that day—Double'd had to get up repeatedly to round up Muz from the bedroom where she'd retreated time and time again during the course of our meal; she'd take a bite of spinach and stray away mysteriously with no explanation, to take care of business of her own, apparently mental—she had to get her worrying done, it seemed; I couldn't tell at the time. At any rate, after dinner Double was on his way to the bedroom with a dish of ice cream for Muz, his beloved Vole, who was off to herself again by this time, sequestered once more. The ice cream was vanilla, her favorite, with chocolate sauce on top. I just had dug down into my own bowl of it—in those days we all were ice cream junkies driven by fumbling nutrition-hunting instinct—when I decided to creep up to the door of their room so as to lay in wait for Double's return. When he appeared, I'd planned to startle him with all my might just on general principles, a kid's priorities. So there I was in the hall, flattened against the wall near the door with my dish of ice cream setting on the floor beside me, when I heard Vole say in quick-severed silence, ". . . so what's this you've brought me, the consolation prize?"

56   Then I could hear Double's careful drawl, "You . . . think . . . of the damndest things!"

57   "You think of the damndest answers," said Vole. "Now come up with one for this mess that we're in!"

58   "Look," Double said. "How do you think it makes *me* feel? I'm used to pullin my own weight around here!"

59   "Well buddy," said Vole, "the full load just shifted to my side of the wagon. So you'd best to manage those reins with all your spunk!"

60   "I'm workin on it!"

61   "He's working on it," Vole sighed. "What a relief!"

62   "Well what do you expect me to do? I can't just rush in and—"

63   "Heaven forbid you should *rush!*"

64   "Just what am I suposed to do? Answer me that!"

65   "You can protest it, that's what! How many times do I have to tell you—"

66   "That's what *I* want to know!" Double sliced in. "How many times can I look forward to hearin this same jack again and again? I mean how many times can we go round the mulberry bush and still stay sane?"

67   Vole stopped for a moment; she had to regroup or recoup her lost lather before she continued pursuit of the issue.

68   "When are you going to confront this thing and deal with it?" she said, straight ahead. "If you're waiting for a cue, *here! Take this one!"*

69   "I told you, I'm waitin til—"

70   "The man's '*waiting*,' " Vole said in a weird tone of awe.

71   " 'You stand when it's *time* to stand!' Remember that line?"

72   "That was an entirely different situation!"

73   "Was it?" said Double. "What do you take me for? I'm not go' let a clown like Crimshaw badmouth me, call me outa my name, get all up in my face an get away with it. I should've jumped down his throat on the spot—but naw!" He shook his head heroically. "What makes you so sure I'm way off base, when you don't even know what happened?"

74   "I know what's happened." Vole jerked to face Double. "What's happened is from now on, every Friday your paycheck will be missing in action from the post office roll, and nine years of seniority's washed down the drain in a matter of indiscreet minutes!"

75   "Ain't that a scream?" Double said as if to himself. "I was '*indiscreet*'? How do you think I got suspended from duty? You think I lost some kind *manners* competition? Well I want you to know, Emily Post wasn't at the scene of the shit—an if she hadda been there, she wouldn't of given a hot hump in hell!"

76   "There's no need to be crude," Vole said with disgust. "Use your head instead of your heart for one solid second. Try it on for size! What I'm saying is—Man, this is like pulling teeth!—What I'm tryin to get across to you is the simple fact that there's an established line of recourse for a situation like this." She stopped for a while to stockpile strained patience. "There's such a thing as a grievance hearing. All you have to do is file a formal complaint. Just take your case to the grievance committee. That's what they're there for!"

77   "Yeah, *solid!*" Double said with weird late elation. "Sure thing. Take it up with Crim's Klan pals at the top. Thanks for the tip!"

78   "You don't know that," Vole said. "You don't know a thing about that white man! So don't start cooking up hold-me-backs to stop yourself before you get started!"

79   "You must think I'm a full-fledged fool," Double said in a terminal tone. "Be for real! If I take this thing up with the brass in the office . . . Hell, Crim's their main boy! He does their biddin an then some. They love his dirty draws!"

80   "There's no need—"

81   "If I turned the searchlight on Crim, they'd go ahead and fire me so fast it'd make your head swim."

82   *When he went into work at three A.M. that morning, it had been like any other day—He spotted Aldrich first off as usual, short, chunky Aldrich practicing postal zone schemes, sorting a stack of 3X5 cards and pitching them into the wood slatted envelope rack as fast as he could.*

83   *Across the room was lanky, slap-happy Sky Chief, hanging up his coat at the locker. ("What's up, man?" "Aw, sky's the limit!") And down near the time clock was long Arvis. ("Hey Arvis, what you know good?" "Ask me again at 12 o'clock noon.") And here—just follow the scent of the Maxwell House—was P.Q., with his freckles and grin.*

84   *"Hey, hey, cool Papa," Double said, "tell me somethin slick."*

85   *"Old Crimshaw won't be in today," said P.Q. "He got hit by a truck and dragged fifty miles on a new-tarred road."*

86   *"On the level?"*

87   *"Naw, but I can dream, can't I?"*

88   And yeah, bringing up the rear of the ranks as the men filed into the mailroom beyond was red-eyed Too Short Perkins, always late ("Thass cuz I got places to see an women to do"). . . . And up ahead, with his hostile cigar chewed to a sorry state of disaster was old tight-jaw Crimshaw with his narrow pink self, lookin at his watch and smilin that same slippery smile.

89   *"Step right in, boys. We're all waiting for you." He pointed to a hill of overstuffed mailbags at the warehouse end of the room where five or six black handlers worked, heaving five-foot sacks from truck to loading dock. "Hey, budd. You, pal." Crimshaw grinned at Double. "Go give em a hand. On the double."*

90   *Double waited for a moment, undecided.*

91   *"Get the lead out, boy. Hop to it!"*

92   *The other men had begun to fan forward in different directions, dragging sacks to their posts at the sorting racks.*

93   *"Thought you didn't want me workin parcel post," Double said to Crimshaw who was walking toward the trucks.*

94   *"I want you working where I want you working." Crimshaw turned and grinned. "You got any objection to this job?"*

95   *"Not if it's got no objection to me—" Before he could think he had said it, and still he didn't know what had happened next. Too Short said that Crimshaw pushed the loaded mail cart at Double on purpose—he had to brace his shoulders against it and shove it with his foot to get it to roll at that speed. Aldrich said Crimshaw tripped and fell onto the cart so couldn't stop himself from crashing into Double before Double jumped and slammed it back at Crim. P.Q. said Crimshaw's guardian devil gave him the strength to ram the cart into Double's knee. ("Man, Satan's like that. You oughta know that from workin wit Crim!")*

96   There was strange restless silence before Vole replied. "Is that what's scaring you to death? What have you got to lose?" She stopped for a while, then threw out in a rush as if dammed up too long with a gush of her feelings now at high tide: "You hold your *own* self back! Well you do! Look at Johnson and that senseless P.Q. They've still got their salaries, haven't they? Of course! With all their jive and who-shot-john, they've still got their salaries and they know enough to keep them! Both those niggers'll be shuckin and jivin all the way to the retirement office!"

97   With this last, I'm aghast; I've never heard Vole talk like this before—something's up here that's new and it's out of control—but wait, listen up, Double's speaking again—

98   "Look, I hate to say this, cuz it gives me brick-wall-itis even to *think* of runnin back through this again—But WHAT DID I SAY, Woman?! Didn't I say I'll think of somethin?"

99   "That was this afternoon," Vole cracked back, "a lifetime ago!"

100   Then, as Vole goes on to rant to herself ("THERE'S SUCH A
THING AS TIME TO ACT!") I hear Double begin to speak clearly
with vigor, though Vole seems not to hear or care to dig his monotribe,
just pursues her own line of gripe as if she's alone while Double leans
into his peeve with full speed, without need of her audience. . . .

101   *"Got-DAMN, Woman! I'm used to standin on my own two feet! You
think I'm lookin FORWARD to you bringin in the only bread an all
that lip to go with it?"*

102   Oh God, his speech problem, like mine to this day, it's genetic—
Can't help but shoot back with his bent sense of humor of course;
as he sees it, it's just the thing for encounters with the low-humored
who're bent forever on Keeping It Down for all time, constipating
the world. Double was Double in time of crisis, believed in being himself at all times and so refused to adjust his output to responses
around him . . . said other folks' ideas could ooze in any direction they
pleased, but they'd have to flow around him being him. And he was
right on so many levels, simple human interaction levels, where our
understanding is so tainted by relationship stain that love exchange
disintegrates by force of erosion on so many ridiculous levels: money
problems, dead romance, adhoc hearing and speech problems of
lover-combatants—so many levels completely absurd and hidden
from view til they're stacked like early morning pancakes, perverse.

103   Vole and Double would be having one of their verbal skirmishes
that always meant a t.k.o. in Vole's favor—she'd jab below the belt
with rapid one-two retorts while Double stood with guard down, letting himself be pummeled to pulp except to say *"Right! You're
ALWAYS right!"* his cursory defense in an ongoing call-and-wicked-
response bout forever in motion, blow-trading on with no regard for
ringsiders like me. I'd be shrinking behind a closed door nearby, waiting like ten-year-old Job for their word tryst to escalate into siege warfare, waiting with bubbling visions of Vole and Double sickening
finally of stunted word struggle, so falling on each other with tangible axes and hammers to hack to finis—My green psyche and neon
fantasy exploded their struggle to a crashing violent final resolution
time and time again, unlike these insufferable anti-climaxes. . . .

104   But this time Double charges out of their discord room and heads
straight to the hi-fi (*where he's stashed his machete?*) as I'm watching undetected, bracing for action, since in my role of innocent
bystander I expect to be fatally involved by circumstance. But Double's got method in his madness, it turns out, so by the time I step into

the room behind him, he's just opened the record bin to pull out a razorless record album . . . and he's holding the record gingerly between his palms in order to read the label. . . . Now he's slipping it onto the turntable. . . .

105 Then all in a jiff there's a musical fitting finale to all our confusion—not a crash-boom! symphonic finale, but a jazz trickle from the heart into heart-thumping ad-infinitum. Of all twisted endings, before my very ears "My Funny Valentine" eases through Miles Davis' instrumental mute into the room around us, weaving liquid lines of reconciliation between Double and Vole, between me and Double and Vole, between man, woman, child, and bleak city, crazy country, road-to-hell world, well-meaning universe—A meeting of the minds of shooting stars slapping five through fluid tactical space looking on. Meanwhile Vole feels the summons and so is making her way to join Double and me and the three of us are standing motionless, time dies, and each of us is lit by need for radical redemption. We're just there, corny, shining at each other til Double blasts out, "All right, huddle time!" and we grab for each other and start to hug, all in a bunch.

Sterling Plumpp
(1940–)

Poet and lyricist Sterling Plumpp was born in Clinton, Mississippi, on January 30, 1940. After finishing high school in Jackson, Mississippi, he spent time at St. Benedict's College and in the army. He moved to Chicago in 1962 and has since become a familiar and revered figure on the literary and music scenes. Plumpp teaches in the creative writing program at Chicago State University. His poetry books include Half Black, Half Blacker *(1970),* The Mojo Hands Call, I Must Go *(1982),* Hornman *(1995),* Ornate with Smoke *(1998).* Blues Narratives *(1999), and* Velvet Be-Bop Kente Cloth *(2003). The first two poems are from* Ornate with Smoke.

Law Giver in the Wilderness

Coltrane
takes the night
train to Small's Paradise

Lost in urban
5　renewal landscapes

From Von I learn Be
Bop is the under
ground language of the spirit
and you play where some
10　body picks in a wind
ukelele quartet: baby don't you
wanna go back to that same old place

sweet home Chicago

And I
15　visit you in the Bird
House in tornadic
corridors of wind
but not before I
find you up
20　where you sit in the pent
house of the grand upper
room and I get Mahalia

to take me there in octaves of
her Gospel Commuter of Hallelujahs
25　Prez and Coleman and Jug all
ways take down in the basement
on silences between night

trains and Coltranes just
before the break of day
30　light years where I am Ewart
bound and hire a dirigible
and a five-year-old Didgeridoo-rag
time for my voice

You are a be
35　bopper popping the shoe
shine rag in ear
phones of tomorrows where twelve
Gabriels audition in Bowie's
triumphs in night
40　shadows of special futures
he riffs just for a

thrill and Satchmo's trumpet
wrapped in green onions

From Von
45 I learn the saxophone
is a tenor law
giver in the wilderness of
loneliness where he presides
over ballads dueling the sun
50 shine for bragging rights
in the torrid sky
lines of Chi
town chitlin switch
boards where all the hear
55 say is one big party
line

He
takes twelve bar
bells of blues
60 and fans his
self-proposed adventures in
to theories
of physical touches and gate
ways he inscribes on platinum
65 nodes of his fingers

adjusting moods to his scotch
or cognac or vodka or bourbon memories
misty in B-flat
lands where Jesse James
70 mows his lawn and Billy the kid
napped laughter of his wife in
laws jumps from glass
house to glass
house
75 to house parties
even in the New Apartment

From Von
I learn

Ornate With Smoke

Remaking:
a distinguished breakage.

The
fountain of language
5 discoursing with every
day feet. In postures of
wings. Stem of a tongue
rising from debris of a
Trane ornate with smoke.

10 Short
bursts of air signify. A century of
silence recoiled
in tenor moments you
revive. Velvet totems of faces
15 you wear. Ricocheted touches.
Jamming with masks of iron
and thunder tap
dancing with rattling
feats of rhythms.

20 You
have been here
before.

And I

know you from hemorrhages of light
25 years. I hear Miles
down hives of the Be
bopping itch to create.

Avalanches I prepare.
Atoms I raise.
30 Clouds I mime.
Montages of demons I translate.

I pursue languages of my foot
step children of swing in Dixie
land or at Minton's.

35 Dissonance
is a ventriloquist calling
my speech from dry bones
through silent drums. Down to McCall's
voice.

40 Is the do
rag common
denominator of riffing paths
through nights of bone mountains.

I chew terrible bubble gum
45 bo arrows of speech.
I order from Mingus's catalogs
of tonight at noon
or Ornette's tomorrow.
Tonight is
50 the night I be
head youth.

Cryptic dialogues of alien
greetings in chords are slaps on my back
water blues. I drink muddy
55 logic sleep in cold
train's box
cars of innovative ceilings. I adjust.

I do
not need to sign an agreement of
60 unity with a foreign
language. In order to speak my mother
tongue.

I
come from death and after
65 thoughts. Of another life on chromatic planes of
How I Got Over and No Hiding Place and Strange
Fruits. I pick from vine
yards of Birds and Counts and Dukes and Poppa
Got Brand New Bags of maps.
70 I file in my imagination.

I
find staples of my diet in hors d'oeuvres.
On kaleidoscopic menus of chance

and my axe leases an apartment
75 from tenements of pain
and begin teaching sultry
liaisons with a geography.
Circumscribed by holy
rollers and the mighty rock
80 church inventions of shouts.
In the face of bleeding ulcers of
forecasts of rain on my days.

A generation robbed.
Of its cacophony
85 is illiterate.

I got black cat
a combs in dread
locks of the Rubic
on off nights I back
90 stroke to back
beats of Handy melodies
I feel and shout:

Yo
rub a belly of dialects
95 I name with windows I
open with riffs of a good
morning glory
I offer

Nommo auction clocks
100 for me
Nommo auction clocks
for me
Nommo auction clocks
for me

105 I watch my shadow perform
at rodeo stations of the cross
my dreams rise from membranes of
thieves to sing

Nommo auction clocks
110 for me

I am an old seventy-eight
My forty-fives are empty
The thirty-third and
one third degree of
115 my father's masonry
spins meandering in unemployment
lines

Nommo
Nommo
120 Nommo

I am responsible for language
I live
in The A Cappella Dew
Drop Inn
125 where I hear years of silences
shift into drive

As Malachi, the Calysonian of Rhythms,
pastes his colors betwixt
between pulses of blood
130 on the corner of jive and Mister Down
Child

The Judge
gives me ninety-nine
years on Parchment Farm
135 and I harvest signatures of dust
jackets I wear

I wake
in little E
we we hours of screaming

140 Give me
a glass of Rum
boogie at Basin
Street car salvage
missions

145 I am locked out
done lost McKie's

Throw me
out my juke boxer
shorts so I can improvise
150 this ring

By
the dawn's early Light
Henry Huffing and puffing
to heal
155 some brother inflicted
by white
rejection but exhibiting
symptoms of cancer

I wear
160 a Crown
Propeller on my little finger
for good lucky
strikes down lanes of white
approval but I fail

165 I find VeeJay data
bases in the Regal voices do
woping and motowning high
ways I travel
till the Sun
170 Ra boats of oarsmen
orchestrate paradigms of high
hat blues talking trash
in broken accents of salutations
in other galaxies

175 where I staff light
years for the good
times

I am just Da
homey a long ways
180 from my home
land
lords

I build settlement
hospices for old days

185 Yo
    rub a dialect
    I bring from sounds I heave
    Yo
    rub a language I sling
190 betwen rocks I use
    as pillows

    I am just Da
    homey a long ways
    from home
195 I am just Da
    homey a long ways
    from home

    Strike
    a match to hear my sound
200 Strike
    a match to hear my sound

    I am broke and alone
    I am always prism bound

Riffs

(for Birthday Girl 8/18)

1.

    Blues is a cliChé
    Guevara Journey on Grandma
    Rainey mother witted Martin Luther King
    Oliver crawling king snake Jelly Roll
5 over Beethoven rock
    Church believers' Malcolm X
    Ray reading glasses
    of white lightening
    bugs kneeling at black
10 male sessions of moans
    in the back yard

bird house
party hearty Saturday night
time is the riff time
15 Gabriel blows to Prosser breezes
Denmark inhales in Vesey lungs
while swatting a gnat
Turner premonition from prayers
he encounters in the bath tub
20 man puts underground
hog generation's Be Bop rib
tips of fingers trumpeting misty
crescendos silhouetted in altotudes of a
dizzy atmosphere autumn leaves
25 falling round misterioso midnights
in Tunisia.

2.

Jazz is impromptu gumbo
yo yo dialects on the string
beans my momma cooks
30 with green onions and ham
bones hip cats use to hand
jive sambas in Rio Harlem
diasporic resistance tones
against big house buoys
35 who wanna define what said
before big Fred's dazzling Jig
saw cross cuts paths
to freedom or places
                Green Dolphin Street
40 cars run under
water going up North in
side somebody's horn
Yeah! Inside somebody's horn.

Riffing till a safe space
45 is born

Jazz, archivist of the spirit
documenting possibility.

3.

Rap is just a forty four
I draw from my hip
50   hop monolog
book of memory to fire
silver bullets at yo mama
peg legged morality
merry Christmas without
55   guided mistletoe
jam sandwich and catch
up on the roof
      or below on some funky funky broad

way steps between Motown
60   house boys chasing James Brown
stone rhythms down
turf where shadows take the A

Trane up
starladders to a love
65   Supreme's   where have our love gone hitch
winging it to Heideo
high five long years working
           in the steel

mildewed conversations
70   with yesterday
light saving time and I am a blind
                alley
cat in polite company
      memos.

My History

1.

Every day since I was five
I climb Mount McKinley
      Morganfield
hollers to breathe stations of the cross

5 roads where Ogun and Shango wrestle Robert
Johnson till Muddy Waters
moan down streams of consciousness
to flood overtures I cannot understand

I was born in the delta, my mother's
10 tears, the river, Muddy Waters color
              with mud slide
guitar callings for heaven, Lord
callings for mojo voices to claim space
for my homeless spirituals
15 coming to carry me home, swing low
swing low.

2.

My history is a junk
        yard Bird *Dog*
on memory, B-Flat
20 landscapes, musical fire side
shadow boxing monologues
resurrected by blue devils
from ghetto nuanced crevices
where my blood resides

25 Every day I have collard green
Dolphin Street, side order of Dolphy
dish of bass
clarinetted fish bones   and salad of autumn leaves
of grass   out to lunch
30 with imagination

Blues is my history

3.

My history   fragment of cries
and laughter I corral
in dreams   spiritual factory
35 worker of myth I believe
I'll dust my broom in
side self definition
My history   loneliest

moment I know inventing
40 when facts say I don't exist
but I build my self from junk,
artists, people collecting scraps
to quilt worlds, quilt identity
built from paths to self.

4.

45 I journey when there is no way
to go anywhere. I invented,
like Bird, riff landscapes over
time in my time in pauses
I Be Bop the knocks against
50 my name. I Be Bop.

Religion prevents me
from defining boundaries of my mortality
and borders of my infinite choices
to invent myself
55 whatever my life is
I will invent its parameters
whatever black hole that
shall swallow me I will
invent its a voice

60 I am a poet opening
worlds inside closed fists
I sing to wake demons whom
I incarcerate in song
I am a dreamer, a dreamer
65 a junk man with tools to invent
from his collectibles.

5.

My wounds, fertile fields,
where I implant my dreams
the women I love, roads
70 I wander, good whisky
I drink, and satisfaction
I get from peace of mind

piece of junk I invent
arias from.

6.

75 Blues, uncorked limits
of spirituality, unmeasured
territory of imagination
surveyed and furrowed by poets
who sleep with African gods inside head
80 lines in their eyes.

Blues, place where you got
nowhere to run to and
you can't run from.
Existential echoes spelling
85 my name   Something or
somebody blocking the muddy
road to the door of heaven.
I break down with riffs
Be bopping claims to be

90 Because every day since I was five
I climb Mount McKinley
        Morganfield
hollers to breathe stations of the cross
roads where Shango and Ogun wrestle Robert
95 Johnson till Muddy Waters
moan down streams of consciousness
to flood overtures I cannot understand.

Yusef Komunyakaa
(1947–)

*A native of Bogalusa, Louisiana, Yusef Komunyakaa was born on April
29, 1947. A Vietnam veteran and a professor at Princeton University,
he won the Pulitzer Prize for poetry for his 1993 book of poetry,* Neon
Vernacular: New and Selected Poems. *His other poetry volumes include*
Copacetic *(1984),* I Apologize for the Eyes in My Head *(1986),* Dien
Cai Dau *(1988),* February in Sydney *(1989),* Magic City *(1992),* Talk
Dirty to the Gods *(2000), and* Pleasure Dome: New and Selected

Poems *(2001)*. *With Sascha Feinstein, Komunyakaa edited* The Jazz
Poetry Anthology *(1991) and* The Second Set *(1996)*. *The following
"Elegy for Thelonious" is from* Copacetic, *and "February in Sydney" is
from the volume of the same name.*

Elegy for Thelonious

Damn the snow.
Its senseless beauty
pours a hard light
through the hemlock.
5 Thelonious is dead. Winter
drifts in the hourglass;
notes pour from the brain cup.
Damn the alley cat
wailing a muted dirge
10 off Lenox Ave.
Thelonious is dead.
Tonight's a lazy rhapsody of shadows
swaying to blue vertigo
& metaphysical funk.
15 Black trees in the wind.
Crepuscule with Nellie
plays inside the bowed head.
"Dig the Man Ray of piano!"
O Satisfaction,
20 hot fingers blur
on those white rib keys.
Coming on the Hudson.
Monk's Dream.
The ghost of bebop
25 from 52nd Street,
footprints in the snow.
Damn February.
Let's go to Minton's
& play "modern malice"
30 till daybreak. Lord,

there's Thelonious
wearing that old funky hat
pulled down over his eyes.

February in Sydney

Dexter Gordon's tenor sax
plays "April in Paris"
inside my head all the way back
on the bus from Double Bay.
5 *Round Midnight*, the '50's,
cool cobblestone streets
resound footsteps of Bebop
musicians with whiskey-laced voices
from a boundless dream in French.
10 Bud, Prez, Webster & The Hawk,
their names run together
like mellifluous riffs.
Painful gods jive talk through
bloodstained reeds & shiny brass
15 where music is an anesthetic.
Unreadable faces from the human void
float like torn pages across the bus
windows. An old anger drips into my throat,
& I try thinking something good,
20 letting the precious bad
settle to the salty bottom.
Another scene keeps repeating itself:
I emerge from the dark theatre,
passing a woman who grabs her red purse
25 & hugs it to her like a heart attack.
Tremolo. Dexter comes back to rest
behind my eyelids. A loneliness
lingers like a silver needle
under my black skin,
30 as I try to feel how it is
to scream for help through a horn.

Angela Jackson

(1951–)

Poet, fiction writer, and playwright Angela Jackson was born in Greenville, Mississippi, on July 25, 1951. She grew up in Chicago and attended Northwestern University, intending to become a doctor until she was inspired to pursue a writing career by visiting professors Margaret Walker and Hoyt Fuller. Her poetry volumes include Voo Doo/Love Magic *(1974),* Solo in the Boxcar Third Floor E *(1985),* Dark Legs and Silk Kisses: The Beatitudes of the Spinners *(1993),* And All These Roads Be Luminous: Poems Selected and New *(1998). "Billie in Silk" appears in* Dark Legs and Silk Kisses; *"Make/n My Music" appears in* Voo Doo/Love Magic.

Billie in Silk

I have nothing to say to you, Billie Holiday.
You do not look at me when I try to speak to you.
You cannot look me in the eye. Your eyes
look elsewhere.
5 Your steamy mouth sewn up with red tears
is poised to speak
to someone.
The orchid in your hair grows, grows like
a spider turning herself inside out.
10 The shadow hangs
into your eye.

I have smiled the way you
do not smile.
I was just out of love,
15 and cold.
I was naked, beyond caring.
My smile, like yours, was a wry line
beside my steamy mouth.
My eyes, like yours, didn't look at me,
20 I only saw the fall
from
grace.

(You lay down with music in the leaves.
You wrapped him in leaves, in sheets.
25   Your legs lindyed around him. Young
then old. Do not be deceived. The
thunder of the spider is no small
thing. You had your way with music,
and ate him. The memory hot
30   in your belly. Ours.)

You never want to let her leave.
She. The voice deceives.
You could hurt it.
It would kill you
35   *too.*
The dragline seeking
curving above Surprise.
Below
Just so.
40   *Size is not the issue.*
Volume not
the question. A hairline
fracture in the Silence
in which nothing rests.
45   *The voice deceives.*
Every thing
swings.

I have something to say to you, Billie Holiday.
Sew up your breathing, then send it back to me.
50 Fluent and ruminating the source of such anguish.

Look into my eyes.

If only it were not so lonely to be black and bruised
by an early-morning dream
that lifts the mouth to sing.

55 Here is an orchid, spideresque-petaled, glorious,
full of grace.

My mouth is on fire. Let it burn.

Make/n My Music

     my colored child/hood wuz mostly music
        celebrate/n be/n young an Black (but we din know it)
           scream/n up the wide alleys
       an holler/n afta the walla-mellon-man.

5   sun-rest time
      my mama she wuz yell/n
         (all ova the block
             sang/n fa us
      ta git our butts in
10   side.

     we grew up run/n jazz rhythms
        an watch/n mr. wiggins downstairs
           knock the blues up side   his woman's
                      head
15 we rocked.   an the big boys they snuck
    an rolled   dice / in the hallways at nite.

    i mean. we laughed love. an the teen
        agers they jus slow dragged thru smokey
                     tunes.
20   life wuz a ordinary miracle an
        have/n fun wuzn no temptation

        we just dun it.
    an u know
    i think we grew. thru them spirit-uals
25   the saint-tified folks wud git happy off
        of even if we *wuz* just clown/n
        when we danced the grizzly bear an
        felt good when the reverend
        the black cadillac said:

30   let the holy ghost come in
        side you

    that music make you/feel sooo/ good!

    any how   i wuz a little colored girl
        then . . .

35 so far
my Black woman/hood ain't been noth/n but music

    i found billie
        holiday   an learned
                how
40   to cry.

Brian Gilmore

(1962–)

Brian Gilmore was born and raised in Washington, D. C. He grew up to pursue both poetry and legal studies. He has performed legal work for the homeless and is currently Legislative Counsel at the City Council for the District of Columbia. His poetry collections are Elvis Presley Is Alive and Well and Living in Harlem *(1993) and* Jungle Nights & Soda Fountain Rags *(1999), a book-length poem from which the following selection is excerpted.*

d.c.-harlem suite

1. *WASHINGTON, D.C.*

the boy who painted
signs was blessed
from birth.
played baseball
5 piano
and hung out all over
the city where he was born,
ward place washington, d.c.
rent party regular
10 down with the
blues
buddy bolden
bunk johnson
intrigued with this

15 newfangled
new orleans
negro music
called

"jasssss. . ."

20 composing soda fountain rags
longing to know luckie
the lion
and
louis brown
25 getting all the basics from
doc perry and henry grant
jamming these beats in simulated juke
joints with broken down eighty eights
for entertainment.
30 giving him
enough guts to
cut father james p
on "carolina shout",
learning some left hand
35 incantations
right hand rhythms
stride style extempore with an
orchestra looming in his mind
the blessed boy is
40 quickly declared royalty
and the only signs
he gonna paint now
are those tunes he bangs out
on broken down eighty eights
45 in smoke filled pool halls
long into the night. . .

*2. DC/HARLEM
(ALTERNATE TAKE)*

i got a scholarship.
gonna learn how to paint classics.
i'm a colorful guy

50 wear regal clothes
i'm gonna give the world
beautiful night portraits.
people.
places.
55 hearts that break and mend.
negro worlds that reek
of grits and gravy.
cities full of fancy cars.
perfumed ladies
60 dressed carefully for church.
postal workers.
pool sharks.
domestics.
dancers.

65 but
i wanna play piano.
make mood my medium
rhythm my rhapsody.
harmony
70 swinging
swaying my
urban indigo
canvas
conveying
75 the colored
relics
of my youth.

howard theatre hanger
headed for harlem
80 make my living
brushing
broad strokes
producing
passionate paintings
85 musical murals
a sumptuous
universe
of sensous
melody

90 telling
emotional
tales
of old black
women with
95 wrinkled saddened faces
educated men
driving taxis down
american streets
full of
100 forgotten dreams
that are now
just sleepless nights
years and years
of the same old
105 blues tune
played
on juke boxes
in familiar places
where the drinks
110 are cold
women are pretty
music is hotter
than neighborhoods
we crowd
115 during summer days
in the western world
where my piano
has become my paint brush. . .

3. HARLEM
(FOR JAMES P. JOHNSON, WILLIE "THE LION" SMITH,
LUCKIE ROBERTS, & FATS WALLER)

"sensational sonny" greer
120 from
jersey
gonna take
them washingtonians
to harlem

125 show the blessed boy
what the tough
east coast piano school
can do for him
get him roasted
130 by ragtime's righteous roll call in
all night jam sessions
full of whiskey
cigarettes
and black as night bawdy house music

135 these washingtonians
stagger around from place
to place like
the new music they play
bellies never full.
140 hearts real hungry.
they in search of an
authentic street sound yelling loud
and fierce these days from
the big easy

145 after a few months of
improvising for meals
they are back on the train
to washington
begging
150 for the smell
and taste of momma daisy's best
biscuits and some deep fried mackarel
the boy who paints signs
gonna sop his biscuits up with gravy
155 pretend it
is that stride style
he still perfecting.

4. BUBBER
(FOR BUBBER MILEY)

james miley
playing plumber

160 unclogging drains
turning his trumpet into
a toilet
his blowing into a bordello
he some low down
165 dirty mean old mamie smith
hound dog
growling
gut bucket blues shouts.
we was a polite dance band
170 until bubber got us drunk
with the dismals.
with a groove that gangsters
might like, with some conjuring
like king oliver.
175 with a message
that moans, groans and
testifies with a wah wah
wah wah east st. louis
toodle-o-boogie.
180 black and tan.
black beauty.
black and white keys on a
black baby grand behind him
blasting out hot and bothered hop heads
185 that bloom blue bubbles
and birmingham breakdowns
doing the voom voom
and wobbling all the
way to washington
190 and if you need a
creole love call
the best drain man in town
can stomp out your troubles
or make you dance the night away
195 with just a plunger.

5. COTTON
(FOR KING OLIVER)

-east st. louis toodle-oo-
out of the swamp.
out of the fields.
on the hot dusty roads.
stumbling towards
200 the train headed uptown.
them wiseguys got steady work.
tuxedos.
tails,
shiny shoes.
205 swinging stomps and
vamps out of vaudeville.

the prettiest high yellow chorus girls
tempt the tans in gowns and risque threads,
exotic aura of far away places,
210 the wiseguys don't like the kid at first,
they can't fight off his charm,
must be that "jungle" noise,

the gangsters wanted king joe,
joe didn't have this kid's luck (or irving mills),
215 that famous folk sound got on
a fancy suit now.
with nightly radio
visits the whole notion waits for.
prohibition is the decree.
220 only tans can get tanked up here.
the boy who already captured new england
soon will own harlem.

the world can hardly wait

Writing Assignments

1. Compare and contrast the blues poetry of two writers chosen from among Langston Hughes, Sterling Brown, Quincy Troupe, Mari Evans, and Sterling Plumpp. What are the similarities and differences among the language and rhythmic patterns they utilize? In terms of both content and style, how are their works similar or dissimilar to lyrics by Bessie Smith, Robert Johnson, and Ma Rainey?

2. Compare and contrast Hughes's "The Weary Blues" and Baldwin's "Sonny's Blues." For example, how does each author describe the blues? What is the social and psychological function of the music in each literary piece? Which narrative details, if any, unite the two works?

3. Analyze the ways in which the excerpts from *Corregidora* and *Be-Bop, Re-Bop* can be read, respectively, as blues and jazz texts. Compare and contrast theme, language, character, mood, and social context. What do you take to be the message of each selection?

4. Several musicians, such as Ma Rainey, Charlie Parker, John Coltrane, Ella Fitzgerald, Billie Holiday, Thelonius Monk, and Duke Ellington, are mentioned prominently in this chapter. Research the backgrounds of at least three such musicians and report on their cultural and social significance. How does your research influence your reading of some of the poems in this chapter?

CHAPTER SIX

STORIES OF MIGRATION

Migration is one of the dominant themes in the African American artistic tradition. Treatments of migration can be found in spirituals, blues songs, folktales, visual artworks, and literary texts. Movement, both forced and chosen, has been a major factor in determining the contours of African American culture. During the antebellum period, movement was severely limited, as enslaved peoples were not permitted the choice of where or how they would live and were often required to carry passes simply to move outside of plantation boundaries. Even free African Americans in the South were restricted when attempting to cross state lines. After the abolition of the international slave trade in 1808, there was still a great deal of forced domestic migration. In fact, the laws prohibiting the international slave trade did not eradicate the importation of Africans to the Americas, but they further created a sense of labor shortage that slave traders capitalized on, selling captives to the deep South and West in unprecedented numbers. In this way, forced dislocation and the consequent familial separation for African Americans actually increased as a result of these laws.

Therefore, the ability to choose one's destination is a marker of freedom in African American culture and has found expression in a number of venues. One of the most prominent migratory experiences in African American culture and literature is the post-Reconstruction movement from the rural South to urban northern centers. The Great Migration, as it is often labeled, refers to the first wave of mass migration, from 1915–1940, and is considered one of the largest American internal migrations to date. The heaviest flow of this migration occurred after the onset of World War I. From 1916–1919, approximately half a million African Americans left their Southern homes, and another million followed in the 1920s.

A series of incidents and conditions led to this mass migration. In the decade before World War I, a boll weevil infestation devastated cotton crops. The boll weevil, which originated in Mexico, is a small insect that attacks cotton plants; the damage it wreaked on crop yields during that period was as high as 50 percent. Many Southern African American sharecroppers were hit hard by these losses. In addition to the boll weevil infestation, a series of floods in the Mississippi Valley in the late nineteenth century compounded farmers' economic crises, often resulting in staggering levels of unemployment.

Another major factor that led to the first migration was wartime industry, which generated a great need for laborers who could work in factories in Northern industrial centers. As the flow of European immigration halted during World War I, and as many white soldiers were fighting overseas, the jobs that once had been closed to African Americans now welcomed this Southern migrant population. Some employment organizations sent agents to the South to recruit workers by promoting labor conditions in Northern mills and factories. These businesses' promise of higher wages was certainly a strong motivation for African Americans to relocate, for the money differential between similar jobs in the South and North was considerable. For example, female domestics in Chicago earned on average $2 a day, which was what they could expect to earn for a week's worth of work in the South, and unskilled factory workers could earn as much as $5 per day in the North.

While all of these factors certainly created conditions that made it more amenable for Blacks to uproot and move North, the need for wartime labor and harsh economic conditions cannot alone explain this massive relocation. Much of the movement North undoubtedly was spurred by the oppressive social conditions of the South. From injustices in the court system to all forms of mistreatment, sanctioned through either laws or customs, African American lives in the South were circumscribed by institutionalized forms of white racism.

Of all of the horrors, lynching was the emblematic act of Southern terror, and men and women were lynched for a variety of reasons, including trying to vote, testifying against whites in court, seeking alternative employment, and being "disrespectful" to whites. African American men, who made up the majority of lynching victims, were often charged with the crime of raping white women, and, while the vast majority of these cases were based on trumped-up changes, protecting white womanhood was a rallying cry that prompted masses of whites to gather for grotesque lynching and burning spectacles. Statistics indicate that between 1890 and 1917, two to three African Americans were lynched and burned every week in the American South. As demographic studies reveal, a great number of African Americans would flee to the North after a highly public lynching, making this phenomenon a significant factor in migration. This raises another important issue, namely, that urban migration was at times spontaneous and without structured leadership—although white resistance to African American migration could be quite organized. Many white Southerners were outraged by this enormous flight by the African American population; at times, they refused to sell railroad tickets to African American customers. Despite this resistance, many people did leave the South, ironically occupying segregated railroad cars that epitomized their living conditions there.

Many of the oppressive conditions for African Americans in the South were the result of the United States' Supreme Court's 1896 decision in *Plessy v. Ferguson*, which affirmed the constitutionality of laws that mandated separate but equal accommodations for African Americans. These segregation statutes were commonly known as "Jim Crow" laws and extended to all areas of life in the South, including schools, buses, hospitals, bank windows, elevators, and trains. Indeed, the Jim Crow train cars were connected to baggage cars that were dirty and filled with exhaust. Despite these unsanitary conditions, the railway cars often were so crowded that some passengers had to stand in the aisles throughout the journey. In the South, the dining car was closed to African American travelers, as were restroom facilities. Despite these restraints, many people persevered, and some passengers marked the momentous crossing of the Mason-Dixon line by singing, praying, and rejoicing for their new lives.

The use of trains as a symbol for freedom was especially significant during slavery, as the network of freed and escaped African Americans and white abolitionists who provided temporary shelter to them, and the secret routes that spanned from the deep South to Canada, was known as the "Underground Railroad." While not a literal railroad, this important association aided fugitive slaves in their often-harrowing journey to the North and Canada by providing cover despite the dangers involved. Some historians have posited that participants in the Underground Railroad communicated secret messages of escape and meetings to one another through the lyrics of spirituals that thematize movement, such as "There's a great camp meeting in the Promised Land." In fact, migration is, as noted in Chapter Two, a recurrent theme in African American spirituals.

These longings for freedom through movement, so pronounced in earlier years, are central concerns throughout the twentieth century as well. As evidenced in blues songs and migration novels, the African American expressive tradition has continued to focus on travel, yet this treatment is anything but monolithic. Although many works retain the impulse to travel as a marker of freedom and agency, as the selections in this chapter attest, there were losses associated with relocation. Whereas Ma Rainey's "Traveling Blues" revoices the train as the primary means of movement and reinforces the act of travel as potentially liberating, she has no particular destination in mind, and thus it is the mere fact of movement, not any vision of an ideal location at the end of her journey, that assures her of freedom. By contrast, "Far Away Blues" suggests that travel itself constitutes the blues. Unlike the aimless journeying in Ma Rainey's song, Bessie and Clara Smith address Northern migration as potentially damaging and cite it as a source of solitude and despair. In fact, many treatments of Northern migration in the African American tradition are characterized by expressions of communal displacement. This is particularly true of Paul Laurence Dunbar's *The Sport of the Gods* (1901), which is generally considered the first major migration novel. The story chronicles Southern injustices while revealing the pernicious effects of New York City on the moral character of the Hamilton family, which results in a reverse migration back to the South.

Likewise, we see a rather complicated treatment of Harlem, as a primary destination of migration in the early twentieth century, with the inclusion of pieces by Alain Locke and Toni Morrison. "The New Negro," the title essay of Locke's 1925 anthology, captures the tenor of the New Negro Movement, or what we now label the Harlem Renaissance. Although the essay reveals Locke's elitist position, as it speaks both to and for the concerns of the educated classes, Locke clearly recognizes that it is the migrants who are changing Harlem into a "race capital," a virtual Mecca for African Diasporic people. Morrison's *Jazz* (1991), also representing 1920s Harlem, balances Locke's optimistic view with a critique of urban social conditions of the time. Harlem, referred to merely as the "City" in Morrison's novel, is at once a site of freedom for migrants Joe and Violet Trace and the source of their alienation and estrangement. Ralph Ellison, too, offers an expression of migration as a complicated and at times contradictory ritual. In *Invisible Man* (1952), Ellison deftly uses the motif of food as a marker of home and identity and thus explores migration as an act of dislocation. Given the exigencies of Southern life in the nineteenth century and early twentieth century, it is reasonable to conclude that the move from South to North was coterminous with a desire to forget the past and claim new, often citified personas. Thus, it is noteworthy that in the passage from *Invisible Man* included here, it is food from home—yams—that materializes for the migrants the costs associated with migration.

We end this chapter with a selection from Arthur Flowers's *Another Good Loving Blues* (1993) because it showcases a salient migratory experience that was contained below the Mason-Dixon border. This is an important narrative of migration because it charts the move from the rural to the urban South, which itself represented a radical shift of lifestyle, culture, and home.

Further Reading:

Adero, Malaika, ed. *Up South: Stories, Studies, and Letters of this Century's African-American Migrations.* New York: The New Press, 1993.

Griffin, Farah Jasmine. *"Who Set You Flowin'?": The African-American Migration Narrative.* New York: Oxford, 1995.

Grossman, James R. *Land of Hope: Chicago, Black Southerners and the Great Migration.* Chicago: The University of Chicago Press, 1989.

LeMann, Nicholas. *The Promised Land: The Great Black Migration and How it Changed America.* New York: Knopf, 1991.

Litwack, Leon F. *Trouble in Mind: Black Southerners in the Age of Jim Crow.* New York: Vintage Books, 1998.

Stepto, Robert. *From Behind the Veil: A Study of Afro-American Narrative.* 2nd ed. Chicago: University of Illinois Press, 1991.

Wright, Richard. 1941. *12 Million Black Voices.* New York: Thunder's Mouth Press, 1988.

Paul Laurence Dunbar

(1872–1906)

For biographical information on Dunbar see page 62 (Chapter One). Following is Dunbar's The Sport of the Gods, *a seminal novel in African American letters that tells the story of the Hamilton family's struggle to survive in Harlem during the turn of the twentieth century.*

The Sport of the Gods

THE HAMILTONS

1 Fiction has said so much in regret of the old days when there were plantations and overseers and masters and slaves, that it was good to come upon such household as Berry Hamilton's, if for no other reason than that it afforded a relief from the monotony of tiresome iteration.

2 The little cottage in which he lived with his wife, Fannie, who was housekeeper to the Oakleys, and his son and daughter, Joe and Kit, sat back in the yard some hundred paces from the mansion of his employer. It was somewhat in the manner of the old cabin in the quarters, with which usage as well as tradition had made both master and servant familiar. But, unlike the cabin of the elder day, it was a neatly furnished, modern house, the home of a typical, good-living negro. For twenty years Berry Hamilton had been butler for Maurice Oakley. He was one of the many slaves who upon their accession to freedom had not left the South, but had wandered from place to place in their own beloved section, waiting, working, and struggling to rise with its rehabilitated fortunes.

3 The first faint signs of recovery were being seen when he came to Maurice Oakley as a servant. Through thick and thin he remained with him, and when the final upward tendency of his employer began his fortunes had increased in like manner. When, having married, Oakley bought the great house in which he now lived, he left the little servant's cottage in the yard, for, as he said laughingly, "There is no telling when Berry will be following my example and be taking a wife unto himself."

4 His joking prophecy came true very soon. Berry had long had a tenderness for Fannie, the housekeeper. As she retained her post under the new Mrs. Oakley, and as there was a cottage ready to his hand, it promised to be cheaper and more convenient all around to get married. Fannie was willing, and so the matter was settled.

5 Fannie had never regretted her choice, nor had Berry ever had cause to curse his utilitarian ideas. The stream of years had flowed pleasantly and peacefully with them. Their little sorrows had come, but their joys had been many.

6 As time went on, the little cottage grew in comfort. It was replenished with things handed down from "the house" from time to time and with others bought from the pair's earnings.

7   Berry had time for his lodge, and Fannie time to spare for her own house and garden. Flowers bloomed in the little plot in front and behind it; vegetables and greens testified to the housewife's industry.

8   Over the door of the little house a fine Virginia creeper bent and fell in graceful curves, and a cluster of insistent morning-glories clung in summer about its stalwart stock.

9   It was into this bower of peace and comfort that Joe and Kitty were born. They brought a new sunlight into the house and a new joy to the father's and mother's hearts. Their early lives were pleasant and carefully guarded. They got what schooling the town afforded, but both went to work early, Kitty helping her mother and Joe learning the trade of barber.

10   Kit was the delight of her mother's life. She was a pretty, cheery little thing, and could sing like a lark. Joe too was of a cheerful disposition, but from scraping the chins of aristocrats came to imbibe some of their ideas, and rather too early in life bid fair to be a dandy. But his father encouraged him, for, said he, "It's de p'opah thing fu' a man what waits on quality to have quality mannahs an' to waih quality clothes."

11   "'Tain't no use to be a-humo'in' dat boy too much, Be'y," Fannie had replied, although she did fully as much "humo'in'" as her husband; "hit sho' do mek' him biggety, an' a biggety po' niggah is a 'bomination befo' de face of de Lawd; but I know 'tain't no use a-talkin' to you, fu' you plum boun' up in dat Joe."

12   Her own eyes would follow the boy lovingly and proudly even as she chided. She could not say very much, either, for Berry always had the reply that she was spoiling Kit out of all reason. The girl did have the prettiest clothes of any of her race in the town, and when she was to sing for the Benefit of the A. M. E. church or for the benefit of her father's society, the Tribe of Benjamin, there was nothing too good for her to wear. In this too they were aided and abetted by Mrs. Oakley, who also took a lively interest in the girl.

13   So the two doting parents had their chats and their jokes at each other's expense and went bravely on, doing their duties and spoiling their children much as white fathers and mothers are wont to do.

14   What the less fortunate negroes of the community said of them and their offspring is really not worth while. Envy has a sharp tongue, and when has not the aristocrat been the target for the plebeian's sneers?

15   Joe and Kit were respectively eighteen and sixteen at the time when the preparations for Maurice Oakley's farewell dinner to his brother Francis were agitating the whole Hamilton household. All

of them had a hand in the work: Joe had shaved the two men; Kit had helped Mrs. Oakley's maid; the mother had fretted herself weak over the shortcomings of a cook that had been in the family nearly as long as herself, while Berry was stern and dignified in anticipation of the glorious figure he was to make in serving.

16   When all was ready, peace again settled upon the Hamiltons. Mrs, Hamilton, in the whitest of white aprons, prepared to be on hand to annoy the cook still more; Kit was ready to station herself where she could view the finery; Joe had condescended to promise to be home in time to eat some of the good things, and Berry—Berry was gorgeous in his evening suit with the white waistcoat, as he directed the nimble waiters hither and thither.

A FAREWELL DINNER

17   Maurice Oakley was not a man of sudden or violent enthusiasms. Conservatism was the quality that had been the foundation of his fortunes at a time when the disruption of the country had involved most of the men of his region in ruin.

18   Without giving any one ground to charge him with being lukewarm or renegade to his cause, he had yet so adroitly managed his affairs that when peace came he was able quickly to recover much of the ground lost during the war. With a rare genius for adapting himself to new conditions, he accepted the changed order of things with a passive resignation, but with a stern determination to make the most out of any good that might be in it.

19   It was a favorite remark of his that there must be some good in every system, and it was the duty of the citizen to find out that good and make it pay. He had done this. His house, his reputation, his satisfaction, were all evidences that he had succeeded.

20   A childless man, he bestowed upon his younger brother, Francis, the enthusiasm he would have given to a son. His wife shared with her husband this feeling for her brother-in-law, and with him played the rôle of parent, which had otherwise been denied her.

21   It was true that Francis Oakley was only a half-brother to Maurice, the son of a second and not too fortunate marriage, but there was no halving of the love which the elder man had given to him from childhood up.

22   At the first intimation that Francis had artistic ability, his brother had placed him under the best masters in America, and later, when the promise of his youth had begun to blossom, he sent him to Paris,

although the expenditure just at that time demanded a sacrifice which might have been the ruin of Maurice's own career. Francis's promise had never come to entire fulfillment. He was always trembling on the verge of a great success without quite plunging into it. Despite the joy which his presence gave his brother and sister-in-law, most of his time was spent abroad, where he could find just the atmosphere that suited his delicate, artistic nature. After a visit of two months he was about returning to Paris for a stay of five years. At last he was going to apply himself steadily and try to be less the dilettante.

23   The company which Maurice Oakley brought together to say good-bye to his brother on this occasion was drawn from the best that this fine old Southern town afforded. There were colonels there at whose titles and the owners' rights to them no one could laugh; there were brilliant women there who had queened it in Richmond, Baltimore, Louisville, and New Orleans, and every Southern capital under the old régime, and there were younger ones there of wit and beauty who were just beginning to hold their court. For Francis was a great favorite both with men and women. He was a handsome man, tall, slender, and graceful. He had the face and brow of a poet, a pallid face framed in a mass of dark hair. There was a touch of weakness in his mouth, but this was shaded and half hidden by a full mustache that made much forgivable to beauty-loving eyes.

24   It was generally conceded that Mrs. Oakley was a hostess whose guests had no awkward half-hour before dinner. No praise could be higher than this, and tonight she had no need to exert herself to maintain this reputation. Her brother-in-law was the life of the assembly; he had wit and daring, and about him there was just that hint of charming danger that made him irresistible to women. The guests heard the dinner announced with surprise,—an unusual thing, except in this house.

25   Both Maurice Oakley and his wife looked fondly at the artist as he went in with Claire Lessing. He was talking animatedly to the girl, having changed the general trend of the conversation to a manner and tone directed more particularly to her. While she listened to him, her face glowed and her eyes shone with a light that every man could not bring into them.

26   As Maurice and his wife followed him with their gaze, the same thought was in their minds, and it had not just come to them. Why could not Francis marry Claire Lessing and settle in America, instead of going back ever and again to that life in the Latin Quarter? They did not believe that it was a bad life or a dissipated one, but from

the little that they had seen of it when they were in Paris, it was at least a bit too free and unconventional for their traditions. There were, too, temptations which must assail any man of Francis's looks and talents. They had perfect faith in the strength of his manhood, of course; but could they have had their way, it would have been their will to hedge him about so that no breath of evil invitation could have come nigh to him.

27   But this younger brother, this half ward of theirs, was an unruly member. He talked and laughed, rode and walked, with Claire Lessing with the same free abandon, the same show of uninterested good comradeship, that he had used towards her when they were boy and girl together. There was not a shade more of warmth or self-consciousness in his manner towards her than there had been fifteen years before. In fact, there was less, for there had been a time, when he was six and Claire three, that Francis, with a boldness that the lover of maturer years tries vainly to attain, had announced to Claire that he was going to marry her. But he had never renewed this declaration when it came time that it would carry weight with it.

28   They made a fine picture as they sat together tonight. One seeing them could hardly help thinking on the instant that they were made for each other. Something in the woman's face, in her expression perhaps, supplied a palpable lack in the man. The strength of her mouth and chin helped the weakness of his. She was the sort of woman who, if ever he came to a great moral crisis in his life, would be able to save him if she were near. And yet he was going away from her, giving up the pearl that he had only to put out his hand to take.

29   Some of these thoughts were in the minds of the brother and sister now.

30   "Five years does seem a long while," Francis was saying, "but if a man accomplishes anything, after all, it seems only a short time to look back upon."

31   "All time is short to look back upon. It is the looking forward to it that counts. It doesn't, though, with a man, I suppose. He's doing something all the while."

32   "Yes, a man is always doing something, even if only waiting, but waiting is such unheroic business."

33   "That is the part that usually falls to a woman's lot. I have no doubt that some dark-eyed mademoiselle is waiting for you now."

34   Francis laughed and flushed hotly. Claire noted the flush and wondered at it. Had she indeed hit upon the real point? Was that the reason that he was so anxious to get back to Paris? The thought

struck a chill through her gaiety. She did not want to be suspicious, but what was the cause of that tell-tale flush? He was not a man easily disconcerted; then why so to-night? But her companion talked on with such innocent composure that she believed herself mistaken as to the reason for his momentary confusion.

35   Someone cried gayly across the table to her: "Oh, Miss Claire, you will not dare to talk with such little awe to our friend when he comes back with his ribbons and his medals. Why, we shall all have to bow to you, Frank!"

36   "You're wronging me, Esterton," said Francis. "No foreign decoration could ever be to me as much as the flower of approval from the fair women of my own State."

37   "Hear!" cried the ladies.

38   "Trust artists and poets to pay pretty compliments, and this wily friend of mine pays his at my expense."

39   "A good bit of generalship, that, Frank," an old military man broke in. "Esterton opened the breach and you at once galloped in. That's the highest art of war."

40   Claire was looking at her companion. Had he meant the approval of the women, or was it one woman that he cared for? Had the speech had a hidden meaning for her? She could never tell. She could not understand this man who had been so much to her for so long, and yet did not seem to know it; who was full of romance and fire and passion, and yet looked at her beauty with the eyes of a mere comrade. She sighed as she rose with the rest of the women to leave the table.

41   The men lingered over their cigars. The wine was old and the stories new. What more could they ask? There was a strong glow in Francis Oakley's face, and his laugh was frequent and ringing. Some discussion came up which sent him running up to his room for a bit of evidence. When he came down it was not to come directly to the dining-room. He paused in the hall and dispatched a servant to bring his brother to him.

42   Maurice found him standing weakly against the railing of the stairs. Something in his air impressed his brother strangely.

43   "What is it, Francis?" he questioned, hurrying to him.

44   "I have just discovered a considerable loss," was the reply in a grieved voice.

45   "If it is no worse than loss, I am glad; but what is it?"

46   "Every cent of money that I had to secure my letter of credit is gone from my bureau."

47   "What? When did it disappear?"

48   "I went to my bureau to-night for something and found the money gone; then I remembered that when I opened it two days ago I must have left the key in the lock, as I found it to-night."

49   "It's a bad business, but don't let's talk of it now. Come, let's go back to our guests. Don't look so cut up about it, Frank, old man. It isn't as bad as it might be, and you mustn't show a gloomy face to-night."

50   The younger man pulled himself together, and reentered the room with his brother. In a few minutes his gaiety had apparently returned.

51   When they rejoined the ladies, even their quick eyes could detect in his demeanour no trace of the annoying thing that had occurred. His face did not change until, with a wealth of fervent congratulations, he had bade the last guest good-bye.

52   Then he turned to his brother. "When Leslie is in bed, come into the library. I will wait for you there," he said, and walked sadly away.

53   "Poor, foolish Frank," mused his brother, "as if the loss could matter to him."

THE THEFT

54 Frank was very pale when his brother finally came to him at the appointed place. He sat limply in his chair, his eyes fixed upon the floor.

55 "Come, brace up now, Frank, and tell me about it."

56 At the sound of his brother's voice he started and looked up as though he had been dreaming.

57 "I don't know what you'll think of me, Maurice," he said; "I have never before been guilty of such criminal carelessness."

58 "Don't stop to accuse yourself. Our only hope in this matter lies in prompt action. Where was the money?"

59 "In the oak cabinet and lying in the bureau drawer. Such a thing as a theft seemed so foreign to this place that I was never very particular about the box. But I did not know until I went to it to-night that the last time I had opened it I had forgotten to take the key out. It all flashed over me in a second when I saw it shining there. Even then I didn't suspect anything. You don't know how I felt to open that cabinet and find all my money gone. It's awful."

60 "Don't worry. How much was there in all?"

61 "Nine hundred and eighty-six dollars, most of which, I am ashamed to say, I had accepted from you."

62 "You have no right to talk that way, Frank; you know I do not begrudge a cent you want. I have never felt that my father did quite

right in leaving me the bulk of the fortune; but we won't discuss that now. What I want you to understand, though, is that the money is yours as well as mine, and you are always welcome to it."

63   The artist shook his head. "No, Maurice," he said, "I can accept no more from you. I have already used up all my own money and too much of yours in this hopeless fight. I don't suppose I was ever cut out for an artist, or I'd have done something really notable in this time, and would not be a burden upon those who care for me. No, I'll give up going to Paris and find some work to do."

64   "Frank, Frank, be silent. This is nonsense. Give up your art? You shall not do it. You shall go to Paris as usual. Leslie and I have perfect faith in you. You shall not give up on account of this misfortune. What are the few paltry dollars to me or to you?"

65   "Nothing, nothing, I know. It isn't the money, it's the principle of the thing."

66   "Principle be hanged! You go back to Paris tomorrow, just as you had planned. I do not ask it, I command it."

67   The younger man looked up quickly.

68   "Pardon me, Frank, for using those words and at such a time. You know how near my heart your success lies, and to hear you talk of giving it all up makes me forget myself. Forgive me, but you'll go back, won't you?"

69   "You are too good, Maurice," said Frank impulsively, "and I will go back, and I'll try to redeem myself."

70   "There is no redeeming of yourself to do, my dear boy; all you have to do is to mature yourself. We'll have a detective down and see what we can do in this matter."

71   Frank gave a scarcely perceptible start. "I do so hate such things," he said; "and, anyway, what's the use? They'll never find out where the stuff went to."

72   "Oh, you need not be troubled in this matter. I know that such things must jar on your delicate nature. But I am a plain hard-headed business man, and I can attend to it without distaste."

73   "But I hate to shove everything unpleasant off on you. It's what I've been doing all my life."

74   "Never mind that. Now tell me, who was the last person you remember in your room?"

75   "Oh, Esterton was up there awhile before dinner. But he was not alone two minutes."

76   "Why, he would be out of the question anyway. Who else?"

77   "Hamilton was up yesterday."

78 "Yes, for a while. His boy, Joe, shaved me, and Jack was up for a while brushing my clothes."

79 "Then it lies between Jack and Joe?"

80 Frank hesitated.

81 "Neither one was left alone, though."

82 "Then only Hamilton and Esterton have been alone for any time in your room since you left the key in your cabinet?"

83 "Those are the only ones of whom I know anything. What others went in during the day, of course, I know nothing about. It couldn't have been either Esterton or Hamilton."

84 "Not Esterton, no."

85 "And Hamilton is beyond suspicion."

86 "No servant is beyond suspicion."

87 "I would trust Hamilton anywhere," said Frank stoutly, "and with anything."

88 "That's noble of you, Frank, and I would have done the same, but we must remember that we are not in the old days now. The negroes are becoming less faithful and less contented, and more's the pity, and a deal more ambitious, although I have never had any unfaithfulness on the part of Hamilton to complain of before."

89 "Then do not condemn him now."

90 "I shall not condemn any one until I have proof positive of his guilt or such clear circumstantial evidence that my reason is satisfied."

91 "I do not believe that you will ever have that against old Hamilton."

92 "This spirit of trust does you credit, Frank, and I very much hope that you may be right. But as soon as a negro like Hamilton learns the value of money and begins to earn it, at the same time he begins to covet some easy and rapid way of securing it. The old negro knew nothing of the value of money. When he stole, he stole hams and bacon and chickens. These were his immediate necessities and the things he valued. The present laughs at this tendency without knowing the cause. The present negro resents the laugh, and he has learned to value other things than those which satisfy his belly."

93 Frank looked bored.

94 "But pardon me for boring you. I know you want to go to bed. Go ahead and leave everything to me."

95 The young man reluctantly withdrew, and Maurice went to the telephone and rung up the police station.

96 As Maurice had said, he was a plain, hard-headed business man, and it took very few words for him to put the Chief of Police in possession of the principal facts of the case. A detective was detailed to take charge

of the case, and was started immediately, so that he might be upon the ground as soon after the commission of the crime as possible.

97   When he came he insisted that if he was to do anything he must question the robbed man and search his room at once. Oakley protested, but the detective was adamant. Even now the presence in the room of a man uninitiated into the mysteries of criminal methods might be destroying the last vestige of a really important clue. The master of the house had no alternative save to yield. Together they went to the artist's room. A light shone out through the crack under the door.

98   "I am sorry to disturb you again, Frank, but may we come in?"

99   "Who is with you?"

100   "The detective."

101   "I did not know he was to come to-night."

102   "The chief thought it better."

103   "All right in a moment."

104   There was a sound of moving around, and in a short time the young fellow, partly undressed, opened the door.

105   To the detective's questions he answered in substance what he had told before. He also brought out the cabinet. It was a strong oak box, uncarven, but bound at the edges with brass. The key was still in the lock, where Frank had left it on discovering his loss. They raised the lid. The cabinet contained two compartments, one for letters and a smaller one for jewels and trinkets.

106   "When you opened this cabinet, your money was gone?"

107   "Yes."

108   "Were any of your papers touched?"

109   "No."

110   "How about your jewels?"

111   "I have but few and they were elsewhere."

112   The detective examined the room carefully, its approaches, and the hall-ways without. He paused knowingly at a window that overlooked the flat top of a porch.

113   "Do you ever leave this window open?"

114   "It is almost always so."

115   "Is this porch on the front of the house?"

116   "No, on the side."

117   "What else is out that way?"

118   Frank and Maurice looked at each other. The younger man hesitated and put his hand to his head. Maurice answered grimly, "My butler's cottage is on that side and a little way back."

119   "Uh huh! and your butler is, I believe, the Hamilton whom the young gentleman mentioned some time ago."

120   "Yes."

121   Frank's face was really very white now. The detective nodded again.

122   "I think I have a clue," he said simply. "I will be here again to-morrow morning."

123   "But I shall be gone," said Frank.

124   "You will hardly be needed, anyway."

125   The artist gave a sigh of relief. He hated to be involved in unpleasant things. He went as far as the outer door with his brother and the detective. As he bade the officer good-night and hurried up the hall, Frank put his hand to his head again with a convulsive gesture, as if struck by a sudden pain.

126   "Come, come, Frank, you must take a drink now and go to bed," said Oakley.

127   "I am completely unnerved."

128   "I know it, and I am no less shocked than you. But we've got to face it like men."

129   They passed into the dining room, where Maurice poured out some brandy for his brother and himself. "Who would have thought it?" he asked, as he tossed his own down.

130   "Not I. I had hoped against hope up until the last that it would turn out to be a mistake."

131   "Nothing angers me so much as being deceived by the man I have helped and trusted. I should feel the sting of all this much less if the thief had come from the outside, broken in, and robbed me, but this, after all these years, is too low."

132   "Don't be hard on a man, Maurice; one never knows what prompts him to do a deed. And this evidence is all circumstantial."

133   "It is plain enough for me. You are entirely too kindhearted, Frank. But I see that this thing has worn you out. You must not stand here talking. Go to bed, for you must be fresh for to-morrow morning's journey to New York."

134   Frank Oakley turned away towards his room. His face was haggard, and he staggered as he walked. His brother looked after him with a pitying and affectionate gaze.

135   "Poor fellow," he said, "he is so delicately constructed that he cannot stand such shocks as these"; and then he added: "To think of that black hound's treachery! I'll give him all that the law sets down for him."

136   He found Mrs. Oakley asleep when he reached the room, but he awakened her to tell her the story. She was horror-struck. It was

hard to have to believe this awful thing of an old servant, but she agreed with him that Hamilton must be made an example of when the time came. Before that, however, he must not know that he was suspected.

137   They fell asleep, he with thoughts of anger and revenge, and she grieved and disappointed.

FROM A CLEAR SKY

138   The inmates of the Oakley house had not been long in their beds before Hamilton was out of his and rousing his own little household.

139   "You, Joe," he called to his son, "git up f'om daih an' come right hyeah. You got to he'p me befo' you go to any shop dis mo'nin'. You, Kitty, stir yo' stumps, miss. I know yo' ma's a-dressin' now. Ef she ain't, I bet I'll be aftah huh in a minute, too. You all layin' 'roun', snoozin' w'en you all des' pint'ly know dis is de mo'nin' Mistah Frank go 'way f'om hyeah."

140   It was a cool Autumn morning, fresh and dewwashed. The sun was just rising, and a cool clear breeze was blowing across the land. The blue smoke from the "house," where the fire was already going, whirled fantastically over the roofs like a belated ghost. It was just the morning to doze in comfort, and so thought all of Berry's household except himself. Loud was the complaining as they threw themselves out of bed. They maintained that it was an altogether unearthly hour to get up. Even Mrs. Hamilton added her protest, until she suddenly remembered what morning it was, when she hurried into her clothes and set about getting the family's breakfast.

141   The good-humour of all of them returned when they were seated about their table with some of the good things of the night before set out, and the talk ran cheerily around.

142   "I do declaih," said Hamilton, "you all's as bad as dem white people was las' night. De way dey waded into dat food was a caution." He chuckled with delight at the recollection.

143   "I reckon dat's what dey come fu'. I wasn't payin' so much 'tention to what dey eat as to de way dem women was dressed. Why, Mis' Jedge Hill was des' mo'n go'geous."

144   "Oh, yes, ma, an' Miss Lessing wasn't no ways behin' her," put in Kitty.

145   Joe did not condescend to join in the conversation, but contented himself with devouring the good things and aping the manners of the young men whom he knew had been among last night's guests.

146 "Well, I got to be goin'," said Berry, rising. "There'll be early breakfas' at de 'house' dis mo'nin', so's Mistah Frank kin ketch de fus' train."

147 He went out cheerily to his work. No shadow of impending disaster depressed his spirits. No cloud obscured his sky. He was a simple, easy man, and he saw nothing in the manner of the people whom he served that morning at breakfast save a natural grief at parting from each other. He did not even take the trouble to inquire who the strange white man was who hung about the place.

148 When it came time for the young man to leave, with the privilege of an old servitor Berry went up to him to bid him good-bye. He held out his hand to him, and with a glance at his brother, Frank took it and shook it cordially. "Good-bye, Berry," he said. Maurice could hardly restrain his anger at the sight, but his wife was moved to tears at her brother-in-law's generosity.

149 The last sight they saw as the carriage rolled away towards the station was Berry standing upon the steps waving a hearty farewell and god-speed.

150 "How could you do it, Frank?" gasped his brother, as soon as they had driven well out of hearing.

151 "Hush, Maurice," said Mrs. Oakley gently; "I think it was very noble of him."

152 "Oh, I felt sorry for the poor fellow," was Frank's reply. "Promise me you won't be too hard on him, Maurice. Give him a little scare and let him go. He's possibly buried the money, anyhow."

153 "I shall deal with him as he deserves."

154 The young man sighed and was silent the rest of the way.

155 "Whether I fail or succeed, you will always think well of me, Maurice?" he said in parting; "and if I don't come up to your expectations, well—forgive me—that's all."

156 His brother wrung his hand. "You will always come up to my expectations, Frank," he said. "Won't he, Leslie?"

157 "He will always be our Frank, our good, generous-hearted, noble boy. God bless him!"

158 The young fellow bade them a hearty good-bye, and they, knowing what his feelings must be, spared him the prolonging of the strain. They waited in the carriage, and he waved to them as the train rolled out of the station.

159 "He seems to be sad at going," said Mrs. Oakley.

160   "Poor fellow, the affair of last night has broken him up considerably, but I'll make Berry pay for every pang of anxiety that my brother has suffered."

161   "Don't be revengeful, Maurice; you know what brother Frank asked of you."

162   "He is gone and will never know what happens, so I may be as revengeful as I wish."

163   The detective was waiting on the lawn when Maurice Oakley returned. They went immediately to the library, Oakley walking with the firm, hard tread of a man who is both exasperated and determined, and the officer gliding along with the cat-like step which is one of the attributes of his profession.

164   "Well?" was the impatient man's question as soon as the door closed upon him.

165   "I have some more information that may or may not be of importance."

166   "Out with it; maybe I can tell."

167   "First, let me ask you if you had any reason to believe that your butler had any resources of his own, say to the amount of three or four hundred dollars?"

168   "Certainly not. I pay him thirty dollars a month, and his wife fifteen dollars, and with keeping up his lodges and the way he dresses that girl, he can't save very much."

169   "You know that he has money in the bank?"

170   "No."

171   "Well, he has. Over eight hundred dollars."

172   "What? Berry? It must be the pickings of years."

173   "And yesterday it was increased by five hundred more."

174   "The scoundrel!"

175   "How was your brother's money, in bills?"

176   "It was in large bills and gold, with some silver."

177   "Berry's money was almost all in bills of a small denomination and silver."

178   "A poor trick; it could easily have been changed."

179   "Not such a sum without exciting comment."

180   "He may have gone to several places."

181   "But he had only a day to do it in."

182   "Then someone must have been his accomplice."

183   "That remains to be proven."

184   "Nothing remains to be proven. Why, it's as clear as day that the money he has is the result of a long series of peculations, and that this last is the result of his first large theft."

185   "That must be made clear to the law."

186   "It shall be."

187   "I should advise, though, no open proceedings against this servant until further evidence to establish his guilt is found."

188   "If the evidence satisfies me, it must be sufficient to satisfy any ordinary jury. I demand his immediate arrest."

189   "As you will, sir. Will you have him called here and question him, or will you let me question him at once?"

190   "Yes."

191   Oakley struck the bell, and Berry himself answered it.

192   "You're just the man we want," said Oakley, shortly.

193   Berry looked astonished.

194   "Shall I question him," asked the officer, "or will you?"

195   "I will. Berry, you deposited five hundred dollars at the bank yesterday?"

196   "Well, suh, Mistah Oakley," was the grinning reply, "ef you ain't de beatenes' man to fin' out things I evah seen."

197   The employer half rose from his chair. His face was livid with anger. But at a sign from the detective he strove to calm himself.

198   "You had better let me talk to Berry, Mr. Oakley," said the officer.

199   Oakley nodded. Berry was looking distressed and excited. He seemed not to understand it at all.

200   "Berry," the officer pursued, "you admit having deposited five hundred dollars in the bank yesterday?"

201   "Sut'ny. Dey ain't no reason why I shouldn't admit it, 'ceptin' erroun' ermong dese jealous niggahs."

202   "Uh huh! well, now, where did you get this money?"

203   "Why, I wo'ked fu' it, o' co'se, whaih you s'pose I got it? 'Tain't drappin' off trees, I reckon, not roun' dis pa't of de country."

204   "You worked for it? You must have done a pretty big job to have got so much money all in a lump?"

205   "But I didn't git it in a lump. Why, man, I've been savin' dat money fu' mo'n fo' yeahs."

206   "More than four years? Why didn't you put it in the bank as you got it?"

207   "Why, mos'ly it was too small, an' so I des' kep' it in a ol' sock. I tol' Fannie dat some day ef de bank didn't bus' wid all de res' I had, I'd put it in too. She was alus sayin' it was too much to have layin'

'roun' de house. But I des' tol' huh dat no robber wasn't goin' to bothah de po' niggah down in de ya'd wid de rich white man up at de house. But fin'lly I listened to huh an' sposited it yistiddy."

208   "You're a liar! you're a liar, you black thief!" Oakley broke in impetuously. "You have learned your lesson well, but you can't cheat me. I know where that money came from."

209   "Calm yourself, Mr. Oakley, calm yourself."

210   "I will not calm myself. Take him away. He shall not stand here and lie to me."

211   Berry had suddenly turned ashen.

212   "You say you know whaih dat money come f'om? Whaih?"

213   "You stole it, you thief, from my brother Frank's room."

214   "Stole it! My Gawd, Mistah Oakley, you believed a thing lak dat aftah all de yeahs I been wid you?"

215   "You've been stealing all along."

216   "Why, what shell I do?" said the servant helplessly. "I tell you, Mistah Oakley, ask Fannie. She'll know how long I been a-savin' dis money."

217   "I'll ask no one."

218   "I think it would be better to call his wife, Oakley."

219   "Well, call her, but let this matter be done with soon."

220   Fannie was summoned, and when the matter was explained to her, first gave evidences of giving way to grief, but when the detective began to question her, she calmed herself and answered directly just as her husband had.

221   "Well posted," sneered Oakley. "Arrest that man."

222   Berry had begun to look more hopeful during Fannie's recital, but now the ashen look came back into his face. At the word "arrest" his wife collapsed utterly, and sobbed on her husband's shoulder.

223   "Send the woman away."

224   "I won't go," cried Fannie stoutly; "I'll stay right hyeah by my husband. You sha'n't drive me away f'om him."

225   Berry turned to his employer. "You b'lieve dat I stole f'om dis house aftah all de yeahs I've been in it, aftah de caih I took of yo' money an' yo' valybles, aftah de way I've put you to bed f'om many a dinnah, an' you woke up to fin' all yo' money safe? Now, can you b'lieve dis?"

226   His voice broke, and he ended with a cry.

227   "Yes, I believe it, you thief, yes. Take him away."

228   Berry's eyes were bloodshot as he replied, "Den, damn you! damn you! ef dat's all dese yeahs counted fu', I wish I had a-stoled it."

229   Oakley made a step forward, and his man did like-wise, but the officer stepped between them.

230   "Take that damned hound away, or, by God! I'll do him violence!"

231   The two men stood fiercely facing each other, then the handcuffs were snapped on the servant's wrist.

232   "No, no," shrieked Fannie, "you mustn't, you mustn't. Oh, my Gawd! he ain't no thief. I'll go to Mis' Oakley. She nevah will believe it." She sped from the room.

233   The commotion had called a crowd of curious servants into the hall. Fannie hardly saw them as she dashed among them, crying for her mistress. In a moment she returned, dragging Mrs. Oakley by the hand.

234   "Tell 'em, oh, tell 'em, Miss Leslie, dat you don't believe it. Don't let 'em 'rest Berry."

235   "Why, Fannie, I can't do anything. It all seems perfectly plain, and Mr. Oakley knows better than any of us, you know."

236   Fannie, her last hope gone, flung herself on the floor, crying, "O Gawd! O Gawd! he's gone fu' sho'!"

237   Her husband bent over her, the tears dropping from his eyes. "Nevah min', Fannie," he said, "nevah min'. Hit's boun' to come out all right."

238   She raised her head, and seizing his manacled hands pressed them to her breast, wailing in a low monotone, "Gone! gone!"

239   They disengaged her hands, and led Berry away.

240   "Take her out," said Oakley sternly to the servants; and they lifted her up and carried her away in a sort of dumb stupor that was half a swoon.

241   They took her to her little cottage, and laid her down until she could come to herself and the full horror of her situation burst upon her.

THE JUSTICE OF MEN

242   The arrest of Berry Hamilton on the charge preferred by his employer was the cause of unusual commotion in the town. Both the accuser and the accused were well known to the citizens, white and black— Maurice Oakley as a solid man of business, and Berry as an honest, sensible negro, and the pink of good servants. The evening papers had a full story of the crime, which closed by saying that the prisoner had amassed a considerable sum of money, it was very likely from a long series of smaller peculations.

243   It seems a strange irony upon the force of right living, that this man, who had never been arrested before, who had never even been suspected of wrong-doing, should find so few who even at the first telling doubted the story of his guilt. Many people began to remember things that had looked particularly suspicious in his dealings. Some others said, "I didn't think it of him." There were only a few who dared to say, "I don't believe it of him."

244   The first act of his lodge, "The Tribe of Benjamin," whose treasurer he was, was to have his accounts audited, when they should have been visiting him with comfort, and they seemed personally grieved when his books were found to be straight. The A. M. E. church, of which he had been an honest and active member, hastened to disavow sympathy with him, and to purge itself of contamination by turning him out. His friends were afraid to visit him and were silent when his enemies gloated. On every side one might have asked, Where is charity? and gone away empty.

245   In the black people of the town the strong influence of slavery was still operative, and with one accord they turned away from one of their own kind upon whom had been set the ban of the white people's displeasure. If they had sympathy, they dared not show it. Their own interests, the safety of their own positions and firesides, demanded that they stand aloof from the criminal. Not then, not now, nor has it ever been true, although it has been claimed, that negroes either harbor or sympathise with the criminal of their kind. They did not dare to do it before the sixties. They do not dare to do it now. They have brought down as a heritage from the days of their bondage both fear and disloyalty. So Berry was unbefriended while the storm raged around him. The cell where they had placed him was kind to him, and he could not hear the envious and sneering comments that went on about him. This was kind, for the tongues of his enemies were not.

246   "Tell me, tell me," said one, "you needn't tell me dat a bird kin fly so high dat he don' have to come down some time. An' w'en he do light, honey, my Lawd, how he flop!"

247   "Mistah Rich Niggah," said another. "He wanted to dress his wife an' chillen lak white folks, did he? Well, he foun' out, he foun' out. By de time de jedge git thoo wid him he won't be hol'in' his haid so high."

248   "W'y, dat gal o' his'n," broke in old Isaac Brown indignantly, "w'y, she wouldn' speak to my gal; Minty, when she met huh on de street. I reckon she come down off'n huh high hoss now."

249   The fact of the matter was that Minty Brown was no better than she should have been, and did not deserve to be spoken to. But none of this was taken into account either by the speaker or the hearers. The man was down, it was time to strike.

250   The women too joined their shrill voices to the general cry, and were loud in their abuse of the Hamiltons and in disparagement of their high-toned airs.

251   "I knowed it, I knowed it," mumbled one old crone, rolling her bleared and jealous eyes with glee. "W'enevah you see niggahs gittin' so high dat dey own folks ain' good enough fu' 'em, look out."

252   "W'y, la, Aunt Chloe, I knowed it too. Dem people got so owdacious proud dat dey wouldn't walk up to de collection table no mo' at chu'ch, but allus set an' waited twell de basket was passed erroun'."

253   "Hit's de livin' trufe, an' I's been seein' it all 'long. I ain't said nuffin', but I knowed what 'uz gwine to happen. Ol' Chloe ain't lived all dese yeahs fu' nuffin', an' ef she got de gif' o' secon' sight, 'tain't fu' huh to say."

254   The women suddenly became interested in this half assertion, and the old hag, seeing that she had made the desired impression, lapsed into silence.

255   The whites were not neglecting to review and comment on the case also. It had been long since so great a bit of wrong-doing in a negro had given them cause for speculation and recrimination.

256   "I tell you," said old Horace Talbot, who was noted for his kindliness towards people of colour. "I tell you, I pity that darky more than I blame him. Now, here's my theory." They were in the bar of the Continental Hotel, and the old gentleman sipped his liquor as he talked. "It's just like this." The North thought they were doing a great thing when they come down here and freed all the slaves. They thought they were doing a great thing, and I'm not saying a word against them. I give them the credit for having the courage of their convictions. But I maintain that they were all wrong, now, in turning these people loose upon the country the way they did, without knowledge of what the first principle of liberty was. The natural result is that these people are irresponsible. They are unacquainted with the ways of our higher civilisation, and it'll take them a long time to learn. You know Rome wasn't built in a day. I know Berry and I've known him for a long while, and a politer, likelier darky than him you would have to go far to find. And I haven't the least doubt in the world that he took that money absolutely without a thought of wrong, sir, absolutely. He

saw it. He took it, and to his mental process, that was the end of it. To him there was no injury inflicted on any one, there was no crime committed. His elemental reasoning was simply this: This man has more money than I have; here is some of his surplus,—I'll just take it. Why, gentlemen, I maintain that that man took that money with the same innocence of purpose with which one of our servants a few years ago would have appropriated a stray ham."

257   "I disagree with you entirely, Mr. Talbot," broke in Mr. Beach-field Davis, who was a mighty hunter.—"Make mine the same, Jerry, only add a little syrup.—I disagree with you. It's simply total deprav-ity, that's all. All niggers are alike, and there's no use trying to do any-thing with them. Look at that man, Dodson, of mine. I had one of the finest young hounds in the State. You know that white pup of mine, Mr. Talbot, that I bought from Hiram Gaskins? Mighty fine breed. Well, I was spendin' all my time and patience trainin' that dog in the daytime. At night I put him in that nigger's care to feed and bed. Well, do you know, I came home the other night and found that black rascal gone? I went out to see if the dog was properly bedded, and by Jove, the dog was gone too. Then I got suspicious. When a nig-ger and a dog go out together at night, one draws certain conclusions. I thought I had heard bayin' way out towards the edge of the town. So I stayed outside and watched. In about an hour here came Dodson with a possum hung over his shoulder and my dog trottin' at his heels. He'd been possum huntin' with my hound—with the finest hound in the State, sir. Now, I appeal to you all, gentlemen, if that ain't total depravity, what is total depravity?"

258   "Not total depravity, Beachfield, I maintain, but the very irre-sponsibility of which I have spoken. Why, gentlemen, I foresee the day when these people themselves shall come to us Southerners of their own accord and ask to be re-enslaved until such time as they shall be fit for freedom." Old Horace was nothing if not logical.

259   "Well, do you think there's any doubt of the darky's guilt?" asked Colonel Saunders hesitatingly. He was the only man who had ever thought of such a possibility. They turned on him as if he had been some strange, unnatural animal.

260   "Any doubt!" cried Old Horace.

261   "Any doubt!" exclaimed Mr. Davis.

262   "Any doubt!" almost shrieked the rest. "Why, there can be no doubt. Why, Colonel, what are you thinking of? Tell us who has got the money if he hasn't? Tell us where on earth the nigger got the money he's been putting in the bank? Doubt? Why, there isn't the least doubt about it."

263   "Certainly, certainly," said the Colonel, "but I thought, of course, he might have saved it. There are several of those people, you know, who do a little business and have bank accounts."

264   "Yes, but they are in some sort of business. This man makes only thirty dollars a month. Don't you see?"

265   The Colonel saw, or said he did. And he did not answer what he might have answered, that Berry had no rent and no board to pay. His clothes came from his master, and Kitty and Fannie looked to their mistress for the larger number of their supplies. He did not call to their minds that Fannie herself made fifteen dollars a month, and that for two years Joe had been supporting himself. These things did not come up, and as far as the opinion of the gentlemen assembled in the Continental bar went, Berry was already proven guilty.

266   As for the prisoner himself, after the first day when he had pleaded "Not guilty" and been bound over to the Grand Jury, he had fallen into a sort of dazed calm that was like the stupor produced by a drug. He took little heed of what went on around him. The shock had been too sudden for him, and it was as if his reason had been for the time unseated. That it was not permanently overthrown was evidenced by his waking to the most acute pain and grief whenever Fannie came to him. Then he would toss and moan and give vent to his sorrow in passionate complaints.

267   "I didn't tech his money, Fannie, you know I didn't. I wo'ked fu' every cent of dat money, an' I saved it myself. Oh, I'll nevah be able to git a job ag'in. Me in de lock-up—me, aftah all dese yeahs!"

268   Beyond this, apparently, his mind could not go. That his detention was anything more than temporary never seemed to enter his mind. That he would be convicted and sentenced was as far from possibility as the skies from the earth. If he saw visions of a long sojourn in prison, it was only as a nightmare half consciously experienced and which with the struggle must give way before the waking.

269   Fannie was utterly hopeless. She had laid down whatever pride had been hers and gone to plead with Maurice Oakley for her husband's freedom, and she had seen his hard, set face. She had gone upon her knees before his wife to cite Berry's long fidelity.

270   "Oh, Mis' Oakley," she cried, "ef he did steal de money, we've got enough saved to mek it good. Let him go! let him go!"

271   "Then you admit that he did steal?" Mrs. Oakley had taken her up sharply.

272   "Oh, I didn't say dat; I didn't mean dat."

273   "That will do, Fannie. I understand perfectly. You should have confessed that long ago."

274   "But I ain't confessin'! I ain't! He didn't—"

275   "You may go."

276   The stricken woman reeled out of her mistress's presence, and Mrs. Oakley told her husband that night, with tears in her eyes, how disappointed she was with Fannie,—that the woman had known it all along, and had only just confessed. It was just one more link in the chain that was surely and not too slowly forging itself about Berry Hamilton.

277   Of all the family Joe was the only one who burned with a fierce indignation. He knew that his father was innocent, and his very helplessness made a fever in his soul. Dandy as he was, he was loyal, and when he saw his mother's tears and his sister's shame, something rose within him that had it been given play might have made a man of him, but, being crushed, died and rotted, and in the compost it made all the evil of his nature flourished. The looks and gibes of his fellow-employees at the barber-shop forced him to leave his work there. Kit, bowed with shame and grief, dared not appear upon the streets, where the girls who had envied her now hooted at her. So the little family was shut in upon itself away from fellowship and sympathy.

278   Joe went seldom to see his father. He was not heartless; but the citadel of his long desired and much vaunted manhood trembled before the sight of his father's abject misery. The lines came round his lips, and lines too must have come round his heart. Poor fellow, he was too young for this forcing process, and in the hothouse of pain he only grew an acrid, unripe cynic.

279   At the sitting of the Grand Jury Berry was indicted. His trial followed soon, and the town turned out to see it. Some came to laugh and scoff, but these, his enemies, were silenced by the spectacle of his grief. In vain the lawyer whom he had secured showed that the evidence against him proved nothing. In vain he produced proof of the slow accumulation of what the man had. In vain he pleaded the man's former good name. The judge and the jury saw otherwise. Berry was convicted. He was given ten years at hard labour.

280   He hardly looked as if he could live out one as he heard his sentence. But Nature was kind and relieved him of the strain. With a cry as if his heart were bursting, he started up and fell forward on his face unconscious. Some one, a bit more brutal than the rest, said, "It's five dollars' fine every time a nigger faints," but no one laughed. There was something too portentous, too tragic in the degradation of this man.

281   Maurice Oakley sat in the court-room, grim and relentless. As soon as the trial was over, he sent for Fannie, who still kept the cottage in the yard.

282   "You must go," he said. "You can't stay here any longer. I want none of your breed about me."

283   And Fannie bowed her head and went away from him in silence.

284   All the night long the women of the Hamilton household lay in bed and wept, clinging to each other in their grief. But Joe did not go to sleep. Against all their entreaties, he stayed up. He put out the light and sat staring into the gloom with hard, burning eyes.

OUTCASTS

285 What particularly irritated Maurice Oakley was that Berry should to the very last keep up his claim of innocence. He reiterated it to the very moment that the train which was bearing him away pulled out of the station. There had seldom been seen such an example of criminal hardihood, and Oakley was hardened thereby to greater severity in dealing with the convict's wife. He began to urge her more strongly to move, and she, dispirited and humiliated by what had come to her, looked vainly about her for the way to satisfy his demands. With her natural protector gone, she felt more weak and helpless than she had thought it possible to feel. It was hard enough to face the world. But to have to ask something of it was almost more than she could bear.

286   With the conviction of her husband the last five hundred dollars had been confiscated as belonging to the stolen money, but their former deposit remained untouched. With this she had the means at her disposal to tide over their present days of misfortune. It was not money she lacked, but confidence. Some inkling of the world's attitude towards her, guiltless though she was, reached her and made her afraid.

287   Her desperation, however, would not let her give way to fear, so she set forth to look for another house. Joe and Kit saw her go as if she were starting on an expedition into a strange country. In all their lives they had known no home save the little cottage in Oakley's yard. Here they had toddled as babies and played as children and been happy and care-free. There had been times when they had complained and wanted a home off by themselves, like others whom they knew. They had not failed, either, to draw unpleasant comparisons between their mode of life and the old

plantation quarters system. But now all this was forgotten, and there were only grief and anxiety that they must leave the place and in such a way.

288 Fannie went out with little hope in her heart, and a short while after she was gone Joe decided to follow her and make an attempt to get work.

289 "I'll go an' see what I kin do, anyway, Kit. 'Tain't much use, I reckon, trying to get into a bahbah shop where they shave white folks, because all the white folks are down on us. I'll try one of the colored shops."

290 This was something of a condescension for Berry Hamilton's son. He had never yet shaved a black chin or put shears to what he termed "naps," and he was proud of it. He thought, though, that after the training he had received from the superior "Ton-sorial Parlours" where he had been employed, he had but to ask for a place and he would be gladly accepted.

291 It is strange how all the foolish little vaunting things that a man says in days of prosperity wax a giant crop around him in the days of his adversity. Berry Hamilton's son found this out almost as soon as he had applied at the first of the coloured shops for work.

292 "Oh, no, suh," said the proprietor, "I don't think we got anything fu' you to do; you're a white man's bahbah. We don't shave nothin' but niggahs hyeah, an' we shave 'em in de light o' day an' on de groun' flo'."

293 "W'y, I hyeah you say dat you couldn't git a paih of sheahs thoo a niggah's naps. You ain't been practisin' lately, has you?" came from the back of the shop, where a grinning negro was scraping a fellow's face.

294 "Oh, yes, you're done with burr-heads, are you? But burr-heads are good enough fu' you now."

295 "I think," the proprietor resumed, "that I hyeahed you say you wasn't fond o' grape pickin'. Well, Josy, my son, I wouldn't begin it now, 'specially as anothah kin' o' pickin' seems to run in yo' fambly."

296 Joe Hamilton never knew how he got out of that shop. He only knew that he found himself upon the street outside the door, tears of anger and shame in his eyes, and the laughs and taunts of his tormentors still ringing in his ears.

297 It was cruel, of course it was cruel. It was brutal. But only he knew how just it had been. In his moments of pride he had said all those things, half in fun and half in earnest, and he began to wonder how he could have been so many kinds of a fool for so long without realizing it.

298   He had not the heart to seek another shop, for he knew that what would be known at one would be equally well known at all the rest. The hardest thing that he had to bear was the knowledge that he had shut himself out of all the chances that he now desired. He remembered with a pang the words of an old negro to whom he had once been impudent, "Nevah min', boy, nevah min', you's bo'n, but you ain't daid!"

299   It was too true. He had not known then what would come. He had never dreamed that anything so terrible could overtake him. Even in his straits, however, desperation gave him a certain pluck. He would try for something else for which his own tongue had not disqualified him. With Joe, to think was to do. He went on to the Continental Hotel, where there were almost always boys wanted to "run the bells." The clerk looked him over critically. He was a bright, spruce-looking young fellow, and the man liked his looks.

300   "Well, I guess we can take you on," he said. "What's your name?"

301   "Joe," was the laconic answer. He was afraid to say more.

302   "Well, Joe, you go over there and sit where you see those fellows in uniform, and wait until I call the head bellman."

303   Young Hamilton went over and sat down on a bench which ran along the hotel corridor and where the bellman were wont to stay during the day awaiting their calls. A few of the blue-coated Mercuries were there. Upon Joe's advent they began to look askance at him and to talk among themselves. He felt his face burning as he thought of what they must be saying. Then he saw the head bellman talking to the clerk and looking in his direction. He saw him shake his head and walk away. He could have cursed him. The clerk called to him.

304   "I didn't know," he said,—"I didn't know that you were Berry Hamilton's boy. Now, I've got nothing against you myself. I don't hold you responsible for what your father did, but I don't believe our boys would work with you. I can't take you on."

305   Joe turned away to meet the grinning or contemptuous glances of the bellmen on the seat. It would have been good to be able to hurl something among them. But he was helpless.

306   He hastened out of the hotel, feeling that every eye was upon him, every finger pointing at him, every tongue whispering, "There goes Joe Hamilton, whose father went to the penitentiary the other day."

307   What should he do? He could try no more. He was prescribed, and the letters of his ban were writ large throughout the town, where all who ran might read. For a while he wandered aimlessly about and then turned dejectedly homeward. His mother had not yet come.

308   "Did you get a job?" was Kit's first question.

309   "No," he answered bitterly, "no one wants me now."

310   "No one wants you? Why, Joe—they—they don't think hard of us, do they?"

311   "I don't know what they think of ma and you, but they think hard of me, all right."

312   "Oh, don't you worry; it'll be all right when it blows over."

313   "Yes, when it all blows over; but when'll that be?"

314   "Oh, after a while, when we can show 'em we're all right."

315   Some of the girl's cheery hopefulness had come back to her in the presence of her brother's dejection, as a woman always forgets her own sorrow when some one she loves is grieving. But she could not communicate any of her feeling to Joe, who had been and seen and felt, and now sat darkly waiting his mother's return. Some presentiment seemed to tell him that, armed as she was with money to pay for what she wanted and asking for nothing without price, she would yet have no better tale to tell than he.

316   None of these forebodings visited the mind of Kit, and as soon as her mother appeared on the threshold she ran to her, crying, "Oh, where are we going to live, ma?"

317   Fannie looked at her for a moment, and then answered with a burst of tears, "Gawd knows, child, Gawd knows."

318   The girl stepped back astonished. "Why, why!" and then with a rush of tenderness she threw her arms about her mother's neck. "Oh, you're tired to death," she said; "that's what's the matter with you. Never mind about the house now. I've got some tea made for you, and you just take a cup."

319   Fannie sat down and tried to drink her tea, but she could not. It stuck in her throat, and the tears rolled down her face and fell into the shaking cup. Joe looked on silently. He had been out and he understood.

320   "I'll go out to-morrow and do some looking around for a house while you stay at home an' rest, ma."

321   Her mother looked up, the maternal instinct for the protection of her daughter at once aroused. "Oh, no, not you, Kitty," she said.

322   Then for the first time Joe spoke: "You'd just as well tell Kitty now, ma, for she's got to come across it anyhow."

323   "What you know about it? Whaih you been to?"

324   "I've been out huntin' work. I've been to Jones's bahbah shop an' to the Continental Hotel." His lightbrown face turned brick red with anger and shame at the memory of it. "I don't think I'll try any more."

325   Kitty was gazing with wide and saddening eyes at her mother.

326   "Were they mean to you too, ma?" she asked breathlessly.

327   "Mean? Oh Kitty! Kitty! you don't know what it was like. It nigh killed me. Thaih was plenty of houses an' owned by people I've knowed fu' yeahs, but not one of 'em wanted to rent to me. Some of 'em made excuses 'bout one thing er t'other, but de res' come right straight out an' said dat we'd give a neighbourhood a bad name ef we moved into it. I've almos' tramped my laigs off. I've tried every decent place I could think of, but nobody wants us."

328   The girl was standing with her hands clenched nervously before her. It was almost more than she could understand.

329   "Why, we ain't done anything," she said. "Even if they don't know any better than to believe that pa was guilty, they know we ain't done anything."

330   "I'd like to cut the heart out of a few of 'em," said Joe in his throat.

331   "It ain't goin' to do no good to look at it that away, Joe," his mother replied. "I know hit's ha'd, but we got to do de bes' we kin."

332   "What are we goin' to do?" cried the boy fiercely. "They won't let us work. They won't let us live anywhaih. Do they want us to live on the levee an' steal, like some of 'em do?"

333   "What are we goin' to do?" echoed Kitty helplessly. "I'd go out ef I thought I could find anythin' to work at."

334   "Don't you go anywhaih, child. It 'ud only be worse. De niggah men dat ust to be bowin' an' scrapin' to me an' tekin' off dey hats to me laughed in my face. I met Minty—an' she slurred me right in de street. Dey'd do worse fu' you."

335   In the midst of the conversation a knock came at the door. It was a messenger from the "House," as they still called Oakley's home, and he wanted them to be out of the cottage by the next afternoon, as the new servants were coming and would want the rooms.

336   The message was so curt, so hard and decisive, that Fannie was startled out of her grief into immediate action.

337   "Well, we got to go," she said, rising wearily.

338   "But where are we goin'?" wailed Kitty in affright. "There's no place to go to. We haven't got a house. Where'll we go?"

339   "Out o' town someplace as fur away from this damned hole as we kin git." The boy spoke recklessly in his anger. He had never sworn before his mother before.

340   She looked at him in horror. "Joe, Joe," she said, "you're mekin' it wuss. You're mekin' it ha'dah fu' me to baih when you talk dat a-way. What you mean? Whaih you think Gawd is?"

341   Joe remained sullenly silent. His mother's faith was too stalwart for his comprehension. There was nothing like it in his own soul to interpret it.

342   "We'll git de secon'-han' dealah to tek ouah things tomorrer, an' then we'll go away some place, up No'th maybe."

343   "Let's go to New York," said Joe.

344   "New Yo'k?"

345   They had heard of New York as a place vague and far away, a city that, like Heaven, to them had existed by faith alone. All the days of their lives they had heard of it, and it seemed to them the center of all the glory, all the wealth, and all the freedom of the world. New York. It had an alluring sound. Who would know them there? Who would look down upon them?

346   "It's a mighty long ways off fu' me to be sta'tin' at dis time o' life."

347   "We want to go a long ways off."

348   "I wonder what pa would think of it if he was here," put in Kitty.

349   "I guess he'd think we was doin' the best we could."

350   "Well, den, Joe," said his mother, her voice trembling with emotion at the daring step they were about to take, "you set down an' write a lettah to yo' pa, an' tell him what we goin' to do, an' to-morrer—to-morrer—we'll sta't."

351   Something akin to joy came into the boy's heart as he sat down to write the letter. They had taunted him, had they? They had scoffed at him. But he was going where they might never go, and some day he would come back holding his head high and pay them sneer for sneer and jibe for jibe.

352   The same night the commission was given to the furniture dealer who would take charge of their things and sell them when and for what he could.

353   From his window the next morning Maurice Oakley watched the wagon emptying the house. Then he saw Fannie come out and walk about her little garden, followed by her children. He saw her as she wiped her eyes and led the way to the side gate.

354   "Well, they're gone," he said to his wife. "I wonder where they're going to live?"

355   "Oh, some of their people will take them in," replied Mrs. Oakley languidly.

356   Despite the fact that his mother carried with her the rest of the money drawn from the bank, Joe had suddenly stepped into the place of the man of the family. He attended to all the details of their getting away with a promptness that made it seem untrue that he had never

been more than thirty miles from his native town. He was eager and excited. As the train drew out of the station, he did not look back upon the place which he hated, but Fannie and her daughter let their eyes linger upon it until the last house, the last chimney, and the last spire faded from their sight, and their tears fell and mingled as they were whirled away toward the unknown.

IN NEW YORK

357 To the provincial coming to New York for the first time, ignorant and unknown, the city presents a notable mingling of the qualities of cheeriness and gloom. If he have any eye at all for the beautiful, he cannot help experiencing a thrill as he crosses the ferry over the river filled with plying craft and catches the first sight of the spires and buildings of New York. If he have the right stuff in him, a something will take possession of him that will grip him again every time he returns to the scene and will make him long and hunger for the place when he is away from it. Later, the lights in the busy streets will bewilder and entice him. He will feel shy and helpless amid the hurrying crowds. A new emotion will take his heart as the people hasten by him,—a feeling of loneliness, almost of grief, that with all of these souls about him he knows not one and not one of them cares for him. After a while he will find a place and give a sigh of relief as he settles away from the city's sights behind his cosey blinds. It is better here, and the city is cruel and cold and unfeeling. This he will feel, perhaps, for the first half-hour, and then he will be out in it all again. He will be glad to strike elbows with the bustling mob and be happy at their indifference to him, so that he may look at them and study them. After it is all over, after he has passed through the first pangs of strangeness and homesickness, yes, even after he has got beyond the stranger's enthusiasm for the metropolis, the real fever of love for the place will begin to take hold upon him. The subtle, insidious wine of New York will begin to intoxicate him. Then, if he be wise, he will go away, any place,—yes, he will even go over to Jersey. But if he be a fool, he will stay and stay on until the town becomes all in all to him; until the very streets are his chums and certain buildings and corners his best friends. Then he is hopeless, and to live elsewhere would be death. The Bowery will be his romance, Broadway his lyric, and the Park his pastoral, the river and the glory of it all his epic, and he will look down pityingly on all the rest of humanity.

358   It was the afternoon of a clear October day that the Hamiltons reached New York. Fannie had some misgivings about crossing the ferry,

but once on the boat these gave way to speculations as to what they should find on the other side. With the eagerness of youth to take in new impressions, Joe and Kitty were more concerned with what they saw about them than with what their future would hold, though they might well have stopped to ask some such questions. In all the great city they knew absolutely no one, and had no idea which way to go to find a stopping-place.

359   They looked about them for some coloured face, and finally saw one among the porters who were handling the baggage. To Joe's inquiry he gave them an address, and also proffered his advice as to the best way to reach the place. He was exceedingly polite, and he looked hard at Kitty. They found the house to which they had been directed, and were a good deal surprised at its apparent grandeur. It was a four-storied brick dwelling on Twenty-seventh Street. As they looked from the outside, they were afraid that the price of staying in such a place would be too much for their pockets. Inside, the sight of the hard, gaudily upholstered installment-plan furniture did not disillusion them, and they continued to fear that they could never stop at this fine place. But they found Mrs. Jones, the proprietress, both gracious and willing to come to terms with them.

360   As Mrs. Hamilton—she began to be Mrs. Hamilton now, to the exclusion of Fannie—would have described Mrs. Jones, she was a "big yellow woman." She had a broad good-natured face and a tendency to run to bust.

361   "Yes," she said, "I think I could arrange to take you. I could let you have two rooms, and you could use my kitchen until you decided whether you wanted to take a flat or not. I has the whole house myself, and I keeps roomers. But latah on I could fix things so's you could have the whole third floor of you wanted to. Most o' my gent'men's railroad gent'men, they is. I guess it must 'a' been Mr. Thomas that sent you up here."

362   "He was a little bright man down at de deepo."

363   "Yes, that's him. That's Mr. Thomas. He's always lookin' out to send someone here, because he's been here three years hisself an' he kin recommend my house."

364   It was a relief to the Hamiltons to find Mrs. Jones so gracious and home-like. So the matter was settled, and they took up their abode with her and sent for their baggage.

365   With the first pause in the rush that they had experienced since starting away from home, Mrs. Hamilton began to have time for reflection, and their condition seemed to her much better as it was.

Of course, it was hard to be away from home and among strangers, but the arrangement had this advantage,—that no one knew them or could taunt them with their past trouble. She was not sure that she was going to like New York. It had a great name and was really a great place, but the very bigness of it frightened her and made her feel alone, for she knew that there could not be so many people together without a deal of wickedness. She did not argue the complement of this, that the amount of good would also be increased, but this was because to her evil was the very present factor in her life.

366   Joe and Kit were differently affected by what they saw about them. The boy was wild with enthusiasm and with a desire to be a part of all that the metropolis meant. In the evening he saw the young fellows passing by dressed in their spruce clothes, and he wondered with a sort of envy where they could be going. Back home there had been no place much worth going to, except church and one or two people's houses. But these young fellows seemed to show by their manners that they were neither going to church nor a family visiting. In the moment that he recognized this, a revelation came to him,—the knowledge that his horizon had been very narrow, and he felt angry that it was so. Why should those fellows be different from him? Why should they walk the streets so knowingly, so independently, when he knew not whither to turn his steps? Well, he was in New York, and now he would learn. Some day some greenhorn from the South should stand at a window and look out envying him, as he passed, red-cravated, patent-leathered, intent on some goal. Was it not better, after all, that circumstances had forced them thither? Had it not been so, they might all have stayed home and stagnated. Well, thought he, it's an ill wind that blows nobody good, and somehow, with a guilty under-thought, he forgot to feel the natural pity for his father, toiling guiltless in the prison of his native State.

367   Whom the Gods wish to destroy they first make mad. The first sign of the demoralization of the provincial who comes to New York is his pride at his insensibility to certain impressions which used to influence him at home. First, he begins to scoff, and there is no truth in his views nor depth in his laugh. But by and by, from mere pretending, it becomes real. He grows callous. After that he goes to the devil very cheerfully.

368   No such radical emotions, however, troubled Kit's mind. She too stood at the windows and looked down into the street. There was a sort of complacent calm in the manner in which she viewed the girls'

hats and dresses. Many of them were really pretty, she told herself, but for the most part they were not better than what she had down home. There was a sound quality in the girl's make-up that helped her to see through the glamour of mere place and recognise worth for itself. Or it may have been the critical faculty, which is prominent in most women, that kept her from thinking a five-cent cheese-cloth any better in New York than it was at home. She had a certain self-respect which made her value herself and her own traditions higher than her brother did his.

369   When later in the evening the porter who had been kind to them came in and was introduced as Mr. William Thomas, young as she was, she took his open admiration for her with more coolness than Joe exhibited when Thomas offered to show him something of the town some day or night.

370   Mr. Thomas was a loquacious little man with a confident air born of an intense admiration of himself. He was the idol of a number of servant-girls' hearts, and altogether a decidedly dashing back-area-way Don Juan.

371   "I tell you, Miss Kitty," he burst forth, a few minutes after being introduced, "they ain't no use talkin', N' Yawk'll give you a shakin' up 'at you won't soon forget. It's the only town on the face of the earth. You kin bet your life they ain't no flies on N' Yawk. We git the best shows here, we git the best concerts—say now, what's the use o' my callin' it all out?—we simply git the best of everything."

372   "Great place," said Joe wisely, in what he thought was going to be quite a man-of-the-world manner. But he burned with shame the next minute because his voice sounded so weak and youthful. Then too the oracle only said "Yes" to him, and went on expatiating to Kitty on the glories of the metropolis.

373   "D' jever see the statue o' Liberty? Great thing, the statue o' Liberty. I'll take you 'round some day. An' Cooney Island—oh, my, now that's the place; and talk about fun! That's the place for me."

374   "La, Thomas," Mrs. Jones put in, "how you do run on! Why, the strangers'll think they'll be talked to death before they have time to breathe."

375   "Oh, I guess the folks understan' me. I'm one o' them kin' o' men' at believe in whooping things up right from the beginning. I'm never strange with anybody. I'm a N' Yawker, I'll tell you, from the word go. I say, Mis' Jones, let's have some beer, an' we'll have some music purty soon. There's a fellah in the house 'at plays 'Rag-time' out o' sight."

376   Mr. Thomas took the pail and went to the corner. As he left the room, Mrs. Jones slapped her knee and laughed until her bust shook like jelly.

377   "Mr. Thomas is a case, sho'," she said; "but he likes you all, an' I'm mighty glad of it, fu' he's mighty curious about the house when he don't like the roomers."

378   Joe felt distinctly flattered, for he found their new acquaintance charming. His mother was still a little doubtful, and Kitty was sure she found the young man "fresh."

379   He came in pretty soon with his beer, and a half-dozen crabs in a bag.

380   "Thought I'd bring home something to chew. I always like to eat something with my beer."

381   Mrs. Jones brought in the glasses, and the young man filled one and turned to Kitty.

382   "No, thanks," she said with a surprised look.

383   "What, don't you drink beer? Oh, come now, you'll get out o' that."

384   "Kitty don't drink no beer," broke in her mother with mild resentment. "I drinks it sometimes, but she don't. I reckon maybe de chillen better go to bed."

385   Joe felt as if the "chillen" had ruined all his hopes, but Kitty rose.

386   The ingratiating "N' Yawker" was aghast.

387   "Oh, let 'em stay," said Mrs. Jones heartily; "a little beer ain't goin' to hurt 'em. Why, sakes, I know my father gave me beer from the time I could drink it, and I knows I ain't none the worse fu' it."

388   "They'll git out o' that, all right, if they live in N' Yawk," said Mr. Thomas, as he poured out a glass and handed it to Joe. "You neither?"

389   "Oh, I drink it," said the boy with an air, but not looking at his mother.

390   "Joe," she cried to him, "you must ricollect you ain't at home. What 'ud yo' pa think?" Then she stopped suddenly, and Joe gulped his beer and Kitty went to the piano to relieve her embarrassment.

391   "Yes, that's it, Miss Kitty, sing us something," said the irrepressible Thomas, "an' after while we'll have that fellah down that plays 'Rag-time.' He's out o' sight, I tell you."

392   With the pretty shyness of girlhood, Kitty sang one or two little songs in the simple manner she knew. Her voice was full and rich. It delighted Mr. Thomas.

393   "I say, that's singin' now, I tell you," he cried. "You ought to have some o' the new songs. D' jever hear 'Baby, you got to leave'? I tell you, that's a hot one. I'll bring you some of 'em. Why, you could git

a job on the stage easy with that voice o' yourn. I got a frien' in one o' the comp'nies an' I'll speak to him about you."

394   "You ought to git Mr. Thomas to take you to the th'atre some night. He goes lots."

395   "Why, yes, what's the matter with to-morrer night? There's a good coon show in town. Out o' sight. Let's all go."

396   "I ain't nevah been to nothin' lak dat, an' I don't know," said Mrs. Hamilton.

397   "Aw, come, I'll git the tickets an' we'll all go. Great singin', you know. Whatd' you say?"

398   The mother hesitated, and Joe filled the breach.

399   "We'd all like to go," he said. "Ma, we'll go if you ain't too tired."

400   "Tired? Pshaw, you'll furgit all about your tiredness when Smithkins gits on the stage. Y' ought to hear him sing. 'I bin huntin' fu' wo'k'! You'd die laughing."

401   Mrs. Hamilton made no further demur, and the matter was closed.

402   Awhile later the "Rag-time" man came down and gave them a sample of what they were to hear the next night. Mr. Thomas and Mrs. Jones two-stepped, and they sent a boy after some more beer. Joe found it a very jolly evening, but Kit's and the mother's hearts were heavy as they went up to bed.

403   "Say," said Mr. Thomas when they had gone, "that little girl's a peach, you bet; a little green, I guess, but she'll ripen in the sun."

An Evening Out

404   Fannie Hamilton, tired as she was, sat long into the night with her little family discussing New York;—its advantages and disadvantages, its beauty and its ugliness, its morality and immorality. She had somewhat receded from her first position, that it was better being here in the great strange city than being at home where the very streets shamed them. She had not liked the way that their fellow lodger looked at Kitty. It was bold, to say the least. She was not pleased, either, with their new acquaintance's familiarity. And yet, he had said no more than some stranger, if there could be such a stranger, would have said down home. There was a difference, however, which she recognized. Thomas was not the provincial who puts every one on a par with himself, nor was he the metropolitan who complacently patronises the whole world. He was trained out of the one and not up to the other. The intermediate only succeeded in being offensive. Mrs. Jones' assurance as to her guest's fine qualities did not do all that

might have been expected to reassure Mrs. Hamilton in the face of the difficulties of the gentleman's manner.

405   She could not, however, lay her finger on any particular point that would give her the reason for rejecting his friendly advances. She got ready the next evening to go to the theatre with the rest. Mr. Thomas at once possessed himself of Kitty and walked on ahead, leaving Joe to accompany his mother and Mrs. Jones,—an arrangement, by the way, not altogether to that young gentleman's taste. A good many men bowed to Thomas in the street, and they turned to look enviously after him. At the door of the theatre they had to run the gantlet of a dozen pairs of eyes. Here, too, the party's guide seemed to be well known, for some one said, before they passed out of hearing, "I wonder who that little light girl is that Thomas is with tonight? He's a hot one for you."

406   Mrs. Hamilton had been in a theatre but once before in her life, and Joe and Kit but a few times oftener. On those occasions they had sat far up in the peanut gallery in the place reserved for people of colour. This was not a pleasant, cleanly, nor beautiful locality, and by contrast with it, even the garishness of the cheap New York theatre seemed fine and glorious.

407   They had good seats in the first balcony, and here their guide had shown his managerial ability again, for he had found it impossible, or said so, to get all the seats together, so that he and the girl were in the row in front and to one side of where the rest sat. Kitty did not like the arrangement, and innocently suggested that her brother take her seat while she went back to her mother. But her escort overruled her objections easily, and laughed at her so frankly that from very shame she could not urge them again, and they were soon forgotten in her wonder at the mystery and glamour that envelops the home of the drama. There was something weird to her in the alternate spaces of light and shade. Without any feeling of its ugliness, she looked at the curtain as at a door that should presently open between her and a house of wonders. She looked at it with the fascination that one always experiences for what either brings near or withholds the unknown.

408   As for Joe, he was not bothered by the mystery or the glamour of things. But he had suddenly raised himself in his own estimation. He had gazed steadily at a girl across the aisle until she had smiled in response. Of course, he went hot and cold by turns, and the sweat broke out on his brow, but instantly he began to swell. He had made a decided advance in knowledge, and he swelled with the consciousness that already he was coming to be a man of the world. He looked

with a new feeling at the swaggering, sporty young negroes. His attitude towards them was not one of humble self-deprecation any more. Since last night he had grown, and felt that he might, that he would, be like them, and it put a sort of chuckling glee into his heart.

409   One might find it in him to feel sorry for this small-souled, warped being, for he was so evidently the jest of Fate, if it were not that he was so blissfully, so conceitedly, unconscious of his own nastiness. Down home he had shaved the wild young bucks of the town, and while doing it drunk in eagerly their unguarded narrations of their gay exploits. So he had started out with false ideals as to what was fine and manly. He was afflicted by a sort of moral and mental astigmatism that made him see everything wrong. As he sat there tonight, he gave to all he saw a wrong value and upon it based his ignorant desires.

410   When the men of the orchestra filed in and began tuning their instruments, it was the signal for an influx of loiterers from the door. There were a large number of coloured people in the audience, and because members of their own race were giving the performance, they seemed to take a proprietary interest in it all. They discussed its merits and demerits as they walked down the aisle in much the same tone that the owners would have used had they been wondering whether the entertainment was going to please the people or not.

411   Finally the music struck up one of the numerous negro marches. It was accompanied by the rhythmic patting of feet from all parts of the house. Then the curtain went up on a scene of beauty. It purported to be a grove to which a party of picnickers, the ladies and gentlemen of the chorus, had come for a holiday, and they were telling the audience all about it in crescendos. With the exception of one, who looked like a faded kid glove, the men discarded the grease paint, but the women under their make-ups ranged from pure white, pale yellow, and sickly greens to brick reds and slate grays. They were dressed in costumes that were not primarily intended for picnic going. But they could sing, and they did sing, with their voices, their bodies, their souls. They threw themselves into it because they enjoyed and felt what they were doing, and they gave almost a semblance of dignity to the tawdry music and inane words.

412   Kitty was enchanted. The airily dressed women seemed to her like creatures from fairy-land. It is strange how the glare of the footlights succeeds in deceiving so many people who are able to see through other delusions. The cheap dresses on the street had not fooled Kitty for an instant, but take the same cheese-cloth, put a little water starch into it, and put it on the stage, and she could see only chiffon.

413   She turned around and nodded delightedly at her brother, but he did not see her. He was lost, transfixed. His soul was floating on a sea of sense. He had eyes and ears and thoughts only for the stage. His nerves tingled and his hands twitched. Only to know one of those radiant creatures, to have her speak to him, smile at him! If ever a man was intoxicated, Joe was. Mrs. Hamilton was divided between shame at the clothes of some of the women and delight with the music. Her companion was busy pointing out who this and that actress was, and giving jelly-like appreciation to the doings on the stage.

414   Mr. Thomas was the only cool one in the party. He was quietly taking stock of his young companion,—of her innocence and charm. She was a pretty girl, little and dainty, but well developed for her age. Her hair was very black and wavy, and some strain of the South's chivalric blood, which is so curiously mingled with the African in the veins of most coloured people, had tinged her skin to an olive hue.

415   "Are you enjoying yourself?" he leaned over and whispered to her. His voice was very confidential and his lips near her ear, but she did not notice.

416   "Oh, yes," she answered, "this is grand. How I'd like to be an actress and be up there!"

417   "Maybe you will some day."

418   "Oh, no, I'm not smart enough."

419   "We'll see," he said wisely; "I know a thing or two."

420   Between the first and second acts a number of Thomas's friends strolled up to where he sat and began talking, and again Kitty's embarrassment took possession of her as they were introduced one by one. They treated her with a half-courteous familiarity that made her blush. Her mother was not pleased with the many acquaintances that her daughter was making, and would have interfered had not Mrs. Jones assured her that the men clustered about their host's seat were some of the "best people in town." Joe looked at them hungrily, but the man in front with his sister did not think it necessary to include the brother or the rest of the party in his miscellaneous introductions.

421   One brief bit of conversation which the mother overheard especially troubled her.

422   "Not going out for a minute or two?" asked one of the men, as he was turning away from Thomas.

423   "No, I don't think I'll go out to-night. You can have my share."

424   The fellow gave a horse laugh and replied, "Well, you're doing a great piece of work, Miss Hamilton, whenever you can keep old Bill

from goin' out an' lushin' between acts. Say, you got a good thing; push it along."

425   The girl's mother half rose, but she resumed her seat, for the man was going away. Her mind was not quiet again, however, until the people were all in their seats and the curtain had gone up on the second act. At first she was surprised at the enthusiasm over just such dancing as she could see any day from the loafers on the street corners down home, and then, like a good, sensible, humble woman, she came around to the idea that it was she who had always been wrong in putting too low a value on really worthy things. So she laughed and applauded with the rest, all the while trying to quiet something that was tugging at her way down in her heart.

426   When the performance was over she forced her way to Kitty's side, where she remained in spite of all Thomas's palpable efforts to get her away. Finally he proposed that they all go to supper at one of the coloured cafés.

427   "You'll see a lot o' the show people," he said.

428   "No, I reckon we'd bettah go home," said Mrs. Hamilton decidedly. "De chillen ain't ust to stayin' up all hours o' nights, an' I ain't anxious fu' 'em to git ust to it."

429   She was conscious of a growing dislike for this man who treated her daughter with such a proprietary air. Joe winced again at "de chillen."

430   Thomas bit his lip, and mentally said things that are unfit for publication. Aloud he said, "Mebbe Miss Kitty'ud like to go an' have a little lunch."

431   "Oh, no, thank you," said the girl; "I've had a nice time and I don't care for a thing to eat."

432   Joe told himself that Kitty was the biggest fool that it had ever been his lot to meet, and the disappointed suitor satisfied himself with the reflection that the girl was green yet, but would get bravely over that.

433   He attempted to hold her hand as they parted at the parlor door, but she drew her fingers out of his clasp and said, "Good-night; thank you," as if he had been one of her mother's old friends.

434   Joe lingered a little longer.

435   "Say, that was out o' sight," he said.

436   "Think so?" asked the other carelessly.

437   "I'd like to get out with you some time to see the town," the boy went on eagerly.

438   "All right, we'll go some time. So long."

439   "So long."

440   Some time. Was it true? Would he really take him out and let
him meet stage people? Joe went to bed with his head in a whirl. He
slept little that night for thinking of his heart's desire.

HIS HEART'S DESIRE

441   Whatever else his visit to the theatre may have done for Joe, it inspired
him with a desire to go to work and earn money of his own, to be
independent both of parental help and control, and so be able to
spend as he pleased. With this end in view he set out to hunt for work.
It was a pleasant contrast to his last similar quest, and he felt it with
joy. He was treated everywhere he went with courtesy, even when
no situation was forthcoming. Finally he came upon a man who was
willing to try him for an afternoon. From the moment the boy rightly
considered himself engaged, for he was master of his trade. He began
his work with heart elate. Now he had within his grasp the possibility of being all that he wanted to be. Now Thomas might take him out
at any time and not be ashamed of him.

442   With Thomas, the fact that Joe was working put the boy in an
entirely new light. He decided that now he might be worth cultivating. For a week or two he had ignored him, and, proceeding upon the
principle that if you give corn to the old hen she will cluck to her
chicks, had treated Mrs. Hamilton with marked deference and kindness. This had been without success, as both the girl and her mother
held themselves politely aloof from him. He began to see that his hope
of winning Kitty's affections lay, not in courting the older woman
but in making a friend of the boy. So on a certain Saturday night
when the Banner Club was to give one of its smokers, he asked Joe
to go with him. Joe was glad to, and they set out together. Arrived,
Thomas left his companion for a few moments while he attended,
as he said, to a little business. What he really did was to seek out
the proprietor of the club and some of its hangers on.

443   "I say," he said, "I've got a friend with me tonight. He's got some
dough on him. He's fresh and young and easy."

444   "Whew!" exclaimed the proprietor.

445   "Yes, he's a good thing, but push it along kin' o' light at first; he
might get skittish."

446   "Thomas, let me fall on your bosom and weep," said a young man
who, on account of his usual expression of innocent gloom, was called
Sadness. "This is what I've been looking for for a month. My hat

was getting decidedly shabby. Do you think he would stand for a touch on the first night of our acquaintance?"

447   "Don't you dare! Do you want to frighten him off? Make him believe that you've got coin to burn and that it's an honour to be with you."

448   "But, you know, he may expect a glimpse of the gold."

449   "A smart man don't need to show nothin'. All he's got to do is to act."

450   "Oh, I'll act; we'll all act."

451   "Be slow to take a drink from him."

452   "Thomas, my boy, you're an angel. I recognise that more and more every day, but bid me do anything else but that. That I refuse: It's against nature"; and Sadness looked more mournful than ever.

453   "Trust old Sadness to do his part," said the portly proprietor; and Thomas went back to the lamb.

454   "Nothin' doin' so early," he said; "let's go an' have a drink."

455   They went, and Thomas ordered.

456   "No, no, this is on me," cried Joe, trembling with joy.

457   "Pshaw, your money's counterfeit," said his companion with fine generosity. "This is on me, I say. Jack, what'll you have yourself?"

458   As they stood at the bar, the men began strolling up one by one. Each in his turn was introduced to Joe. They were very polite. They treated him with a pale, dignified, high-minded respect that menaced his pocket-book and possessions. The proprietor, Mr. Turner, asked him why he had never been in before. He really seemed much hurt about it, and on being told that Joe had only been in the city for a couple of weeks expressed emphatic surprise, even disbelief, and assured the rest that any one would have taken Mr. Hamilton for an old New Yorker.

459   Sadness was introduced last. He bowed to Joe's "Happy to know you, Mr. Williams."

460   "Better known as Sadness," he said, with an expression of deep gloom. "A distant relative of mine once had a great grief. I have never recovered from it."

461   Joe was not quite sure how to take this; but the others laughed and he joined them, and then, to cover his own embarrassment, he did what he thought the only correct and manly thing to do,—he ordered a drink.

462   "I don't know as I ought to," said Sadness.

463   "Oh, come on," his companions called out, "don't be stiff with a stranger. Make him feel at home."

464   "Mr. Hamilton will believe me when I say that I have no intention of being stiff, but duty is duty. I've got to go down town to pay

a bill, and if I get too much aboard, it wouldn't be safe walking around with money on me."

465   "Aw, shut up, Sadness," said Thomas. "My friend Mr. Hamilton 'll feel hurt if you don't drink with him."

466   "I cert'n'y will," was Joe's opportune remark, and he was pleased to see that it caused the reluctant one to yield.

467   They took a drink. There was quite a line of them. Joe asked the bartender what he would have. The men warmed towards him. They took several more drinks with him and he was happy. Sadness put his arm about his shoulder and told him, with tears in his eyes, that he looked like a cousin of his that had died.

468   "Aw, shut up, Sadness!" said someone else. "Be respectable."

469   Sadness turned his mournful eyes upon the speaker. "I won't," he replied. "Being respectable is very nice as a diversion, but it's tedious if done steadily." Joe did not quite take this, so he ordered another drink.

470   A group of young fellows came in and passed up the stairs. "Shearing another lamb?" said one of them significantly.

471   "Well, with that gang it will be well done."

472   Thomas and Joe left the crowd after a while, and went to the upper floor, where, in a long, brilliantly lighted room, tables were set out for drinking-parties. At one end of the room was a piano, and a man sat at it listlessly strumming some popular air. The proprietor joined them pretty soon', and steered them to a table opposite the door.

473   "Just sit down here, Mr. Hamilton," he said, "and you can see everybody that comes in. We have lots of nice people here on smoker nights, especially after the shows are out and the girls come in."

474   Joe's heart gave a great leap, and then settled as cold as lead. Of course, those girls wouldn't speak to him. But his hopes rose as the proprietor went on talking to him and to no one else. Mr. Turner always made a man feel as if he were of some consequence in the world, and men a good deal older than Joe had been fooled by his manner. He talked to one in a soft, ingratiating way, giving his whole attention apparently. He tapped one confidentially on the shoulder, as who should say, "My dear boy, I have but two friends in the world, and you are both of them."

475   Joe, charmed and pleased, kept his head well. There is a great deal in heredity, and his father had not been Maurice Oakley's butler for so many years for nothing.

476   The Banner Club was an institution for the lower education of negro youth. It drew its pupils from every class of people and from

every part of the country. It was composed of all sorts and conditions of men, educated and uneducated, dishonest and less so, of the good, the bad, and the—unexposed. Parasites came there to find victims, politicians for votes, reporters for news, and artists of all kinds for colour and inspiration. It was the place of assembly for a number of really bright men, who after days of hard and often unrewarded work came there and drank themselves drunk in each other's company, and when they were drunk talked of the eternal verities.

477   The Banner was only one of a kind. It stood to the stranger and the man and woman without connections for the whole social life. It was a substitute—poor, it must be confessed—to many youths for the home life which is so lacking among certain classes in New York.

478   Here the rounders congregated, or came and spent the hours until it was time to go forth to bout or assignation. Here too came sometimes the curious who wanted to see something of the other side of life. Among these, white visitors were not infrequent,—those who were young enough to be fascinated by the bizarre, and those who were old enough to know that it was all in the game. Mr. Skaggs, of the New York *Universe*, was one of the former class and a constant visitor,—he and a "lady friend" called "Maudie," who had a penchant for dancing to "Rag-time" melodies as only the "puffessor" of such a club can play them. Of course, the place was a social cess-pool, generating a poisonous miasma and reeking with the stench of decayed and rotten moralities. There is no defense to be made for it. But what do you expect when false idealism and fevered ambition come face to face with catering cupidity?

479   It was into this atmosphere that Thomas had introduced the boy Joe, and he sat there now by his side, firing his mind by pointing out the different celebrities who came in and telling highly flavoured stories of their lives or doings. Joe heard things that had never come within the range of his mind before.

480   "Aw, there's Skaggsy an' Maudie—Maudie's his girl, y' know, an' he's a reporter on the N' Yawk *Universe*. Fine fellow, Skaggsy."

481   Maudie—a portly, voluptuous-looking brunette—left her escort and went directly to the space by the piano. Here she was soon dancing with one of the coloured girls who had come in.

482   Skaggs started to sit down alone at a table, but Thomas called him, "Come over here, Skaggsy."

483   In the moment that it took the young man to reach them, Joe wondered if he would ever reach that state when he could call that white man Skaggsy and the girl Maudie. The new-comer set all of that at ease.

484   "I want you to know my friend, Mr. Hamilton, Mr. Skaggs."

485   "Why, how d' ye do, Hamilton? I'm glad to meet you. Now, look a here; don't you let old Thomas here string you about me bein' any old 'Mr!' Skaggs. I'm Skaggsy to all of my friends. I hope to count you among 'em."

486   It was such a supreme moment that Joe could not find words to answer, so he called for another drink.

487   "Not a bit of it," said Skaggsy, "not a bit of it. When I meet my friends I always reserve to myself the right of ordering the first drink. Waiter, this is on me. What'll you have, gentlemen?"

488   They got their drinks, and then Skaggsy leaned over confidentially and began talking.

489   "I tell you, Hamilton, there ain't an ounce of prejudice in my body. Do you believe it?"

490   Joe said that he did. Indeed Skaggsy struck one as being aggressively unprejudiced.

491   He went on: "You see, a lot o' fellows say to me, 'What do you want to go down to that nigger club for?' That's what they call it,— 'nigger club.' But I say to 'em, 'Gentlemen, at that nigger club, as you choose to call it, I get more inspiration than I could get at any of the greater clubs in New York.' I've often been invited to join some of the swell clubs here, but I never do it. By Jove! I'd rather come down here and fellowship right in with you fellows. I like coloured people, anyway. It's natural. You see, my father had a big plantation and owned lots of slaves,—no offense, of course, but it was the custom of that time,—and I've played with little darkies ever since I could remember."

492   It was the same old story that the white who associates with negroes from volition usually tells to explain his taste.

493   The truth about the young reporter was that he was born and reared on a Vermont farm, where his early life was passed in fighting for his very subsistence. But this never troubled Skaggsy. He was a monumental liar, and the saving quality about him was that he calmly believed his own lies while he was telling them, so no one was hurt, for the deceiver was as much a victim as the deceived. The boys who knew him best used to say that when Skaggs got started on one of his debauches of lying, the Recording Angel always put on an extra clerical force.

494   "Now look at Maudie," he went on; "would you believe it that she was of a fine, rich family, and that the coloured girl she's dancing with

now used to be her servant? She's just like me about that. Absolutely no prejudice."

495   Joe was wide-eyed with wonder and admiration, and he couldn't understand the amused expression on Thomas's face, nor why he surreptitiously kicked him under the table.

496   Finally the reporter went his way, and Joe's sponsor explained to him that he was not to take in what Skaggsy said, and that there hadn't been a word of truth in it. He ended with, "everybody knows Maudie, and that colored girl is Mamie Lacey, and never worked for anybody in her life. Skaggsy's a good fellah, all right, but he's the biggest liar in N' Yawk."

497   The boy was distinctly shocked. He wasn't sure but Thomas was jealous of the attention the white man had shown him and wished to belittle it. Anyway, he did not thank him for destroying his romance.

498   About eleven o'clock, when the people began to drop in from the plays, the master of ceremonies opened proceedings by saying that "The free concert would now begin, and he hoped that all present, ladies included, would act like gentlemen, and not forget the waiter. Mr. Meriweather will now favour us with the latest coon song, entitled 'Come back to yo' Baby, Honey.' "

499   There was a patter of applause, and a young negro came forward, and in a strident, music-hall voice, sung or rather recited with many gestures the ditty. He couldn't have been much older than Joe, but already his face was hard with dissipation and foul knowledge. He gave the song with all the rank suggestiveness that could be put into it. Joe looked upon him as a hero. He was followed by a little, brownskinned fellow with an immature Vandyke beard and a lisp. He sung his own composition and was funny; how much funnier than he himself knew or intended, may not even be hinted at. Then, while an instrumentalist, who seemed to have a grudge against the piano, was hammering out the opening bars of a march, Joe's attention was attracted by a woman entering the room, and from that moment he heard no more of the concert. Even when the master of ceremonies announced with an air that, by special request, he himself would sing "Answer,"—the request was his own,—he did not draw the attention of the boy away from the yellow-skinned divinity who sat at a near table, drinking whiskey straight.

500   She was a small girl, with fluffy dark hair and good features. A tiny foot peeped out from beneath her rattling silk skirts. She was a good-looking young woman and daintily made, though her face was

no longer youthful, and one might have wished that with her complexion she had not run to silk waists in magenta.

501   Joe, however, saw no fault in her. She was altogether lovely to him, and his delight was the more poignant as he recognized in her one of the girls he had seen on the stage a couple of weeks ago. That being true, nothing could keep her from being glorious in his eyes,—not even the grease-paint which adhered in unneat patches to her face, nor her taste for whiskey in its unreformed state. He gazed at her in ecstasy until. Thomas, turning to see what had attracted him, said with a laugh, "Oh, it's Hattie Sterling. Want to meet her?"

502   Again the young fellow was dumb. Just then Hattie also noticed his intent look, and nodded and beckoned to Thomas.

503   "Come on," he said, rising.

504   "Oh, she didn't ask for me," cried Joe, tremulous and eager.

505   His companion went away laughing.

506   "Who's your young friend?" asked Hattie.

507   "A fella from the South."

508   "Bring him over here."

509   Joe could hardly believe in his own good luck, and his head, which was getting a bit weak, was near collapsing when his divinity asked him what he'd have? He began to protest, until she told the waiter with an air of authority to make it a little "'skey." Then she asked him for a cigarette, and began talking to him in a pleasant, soothing way between puffs.

510   When the drinks came, she said to Thomas, "Now, old man, you've been awfully nice, but when you get your little drink, you run away like a good little boy. You're superfluous."

511   Thomas answered, "Well, I like that," but obediently gulped his whiskey and withdrew, while Joe laughed until the master of ceremonies stood up and looked sternly at him.

512   The concert had long been over and the room was less crowded when Thomas sauntered back to the pair.

513   "Well, good-night," he said. "Guess you can find your way home, Mr. Hamilton"; and he gave Joe a long wink.

514   "Goo'-night," said Joe, woozily, "I be a' ri'. Goo'-night."

515   "Make it another 'skey," was Hattie's farewell remark.

516   It was late the next morning when Joe got home. He had a headache and a sense of triumph that not even his illness and his mother's reproof could subdue.

517   He had promised Hattie to come often to the club.

A VISITOR FROM HOME

518 Mrs. Hamilton began to question very seriously whether she had done the best thing in coming to New York as she saw her son staying away more and more and growing always farther away from her and his sister. Had she known how and where he spent his evenings, she would have had even greater cause to question the wisdom of their trip. She knew that although he worked he never had any money for the house, and she foresaw the time when the little they had would no longer suffice for Kitty and her. Realising this, she herself set out to find something to do.

519 It was a hard matter, for wherever she went seeking employment, it was always for her and her daughter, for the more she saw of Mrs. Jones, the less she thought it well to leave the girl under her influence. Mrs. Hamilton was not a keen woman, but she had a mother's intuitions, and she saw a subtle change in her daughter. At first the girl grew wistful and then impatient and rebellious. She complained that Joe was away from them so much enjoying himself, while she had to be housed up like a prisoner. She had receded from her dignified position, and twice of an evening had gone out for a car-ride with Thomas; but as that gentleman never included the mother in his invitation, she decided that her daughter should go no more, and she begged Joe to take his sister out sometimes instead. He demurred at first, for he now numbered among his city acquirements a fine contempt for his woman relatives. Finally, however, he consented, and took Kit once to the theatre and once for a ride. Each time he left her in the care of Thomas as soon as they were out of the house, while he went to find or to wait for his dear Hattie. But his mother did not know all this, and Kit did not tell her. The quick poison of the unreal life about her had already begun to affect her character. She had grown secretive and sly. The innocent longing which in a burst of enthusiasm she had expressed that first night at the theatre was growing into a real ambition with her, and she dropped the simple old songs she knew to practise the detestable coon ditties which the stage demanded.

520 She showed no particular pleasure when her mother found the sort of place they wanted, but went to work with her in sullen silence. Mrs. Hamilton could not understand it all, and many a night she wept and prayed over the change in this child of her heart. There were times when she felt that there was nothing left to work or fight for. The letters from Berry in prison became fewer and fewer. He was sinking into the dull, dead routine of his life. Her own letters to him fell

off. It was hard getting the children to write. They did not want to be bothered, and she could not write for herself. So in the weeks and months that followed she drifted farther away from her children and husband and all the traditions of her life.

521   After Joe's first night at the Banner Club he had kept his promise to Hattie Sterling and had gone often to meet her. She had taught him much, because it was to her advantage to do so. His greenness had dropped from him like a garment, but no amount of sophistication could make him deem the woman less perfect. He knew that she was much older than he, but he only took this fact as an additional sign of his prowess in having won her. He was proud of himself when he went behind the scenes at the theatre or waited for her at the stage door and bore her off under the admiring eyes of a crowd of gapers. And Hattie? She liked him in a half-contemptuous, half-amused way. He was a good-looking boy and made money enough, as she expressed it, to show her a good time, so she was willing to overlook his weakness and his callow vanity.

522   "Look here," she said to him one day, "I guess you'll have to be moving. There's a young lady been inquiring for you to-day, and I won't stand for that."

523   He looked at her, startled for a moment, until he saw the laughter in her eyes. Then he caught her and kissed her. "What're you givin' me?" he said.

524   "It's a straight tip, that's what."

525   "Who is it?"

526   "It's a girl named Minty Brown from your home."

527   His face turned brick-red with fear and shame. "Minty Brown!" he stammered.

528   Had that girl told all and undone him? But Hattie was going on about her work and evidently knew nothing.

529   "Oh, you needn't pretend you don't know her," she went on banteringly. "She says you were great friends down South, so I've invited her to supper. She wants to see you."

530   "To supper!" he thought. Was she mocking him? Was she restraining her scorn of him only to make his humiliation the greater after a while? He looked at her, but there was no suspicion of malice in her face, and he took hope.

531   "Well, I'd like to see old Minty," he said. "It's been many a long day since I've seen her."

532   All that afternoon, after going to the barber-shop, Joe was driven by a tempest of conflicting emotions. If Minty Brown had not told

his story, why not? Would she yet tell, and if she did, what would happen? He tortured himself by questioning if Hattie would cast him off. At the very thought his hand trembled, and the man in the chair asked him if he hadn't been drinking.

533   When he met Minty in the evening, however, the first glance at her reassured him. Her face was wreathed in smiles as she came forward and held out her hand.

534   "Well, well, Joe Hamilton," she exclaimed, "if I ain't right-down glad to see you! How are you?"

535   "I'm middlin', Minty. How's yourself?" He was so happy that he couldn't let go of her hand.

536   "An' jes' look at the boy! Ef he ain't got the impidence to be waihin' a mustache too. You must 'a' been lettin' the cats lick yo' upper lip. Didn't expect to see me in New York, did you?"

537   "No, indeed. What you doin' here?"

538   "Oh, I got a gent'man friend what's a porter, an' his run's been changed so that he comes hyeah, an' he told me, if I wanted to come he'd bring me thoo fur a visit, so, you see, hyeah I am. I allus was mighty anxious to see this hyeah town. But tell me, how's Kit an' yo' ma?"

539   "They're both right well." He had forgotten them and their scorn of Minty.

540   "Whaih do you live? I'm comin' roun' to see 'em."

541   He hesitated for a moment. He knew how his mother, if not Kit, would receive her, and yet he dared not anger this woman, who had his fate in the hollow of her hand.

542   She saw his hesitation and spoke up. "Oh, that's all right. Let by-gones be by-gones. You know I ain't the kin' o' person that holds a grudge ag'in anybody."

543   "That's right, Minty, that's right," he said, and gave her his mother's address. Then he hastened home to prepare the way for Minty's coming. Joe had no doubt but that his mother would see the matter quite as he saw it, and be willing to temporise with Minty; but he had reckoned without his host. Mrs. Hamilton might make certain concessions to strangers on the score of expediency, but she absolutely refused to yield one iota of her dignity to one whom she had known so long as an inferior.

544   "But don't you see what she can do for us, ma? She knows people that I know, and she can ruin me with them."

545   "I ain't never bowed my haid to Minty Brown an' I ain't a-goin' to do it now," was his mother's only reply.

546 "Oh, ma," Kitty put in, "you don't want to get talked about up here, do you?"

547 "We'd jes' as well be talked about fu' somep'n we didn't do as fu' somep'n we did do, an' it wouldn' be long befo' we'd come to dat if we made frien's wid dat Brown gal. I ain't a-goin' to do it. I'm ashamed o' you, Kitty, fu' wantin' me to."

548 The girl began to cry, while her brother walked the floor angrily.

549 "You'll see what'll happen," he cried; "you'll see."

550 Fannie looked at her son, and she seemed to see him more clearly than she had ever seen him before,—his foppery, his meanness, his cowardice.

551 "Well," she answered with a sigh, "it can't be no wuss den what's already happened."

552 "You'll see, you'll see," the boy reiterated.

553 Minty Brown allowed no wind of thought to cool the fire of her determination. She left Hattie Sterling's soon after Joe, and he was still walking the floor and uttering dire forebodings when she rang the bell below and asked for the Hamiltons.

554 Mrs. Jones ushered her into her fearfully upholstered parlour, and then puffed up stairs to tell her lodgers that there was a friend there from the South who wanted to see them.

555 "Tell huh," said Mrs. Hamilton, "dat dey ain't no one hyeah wants to see huh."

556 "No, no," Kitty broke in.

557 "Heish," said her mother; "I'm goin' to boss you a little while yit."

558 "Why, I don't understan' you, Mis' Hamilton," puffed Mrs. Jones. "She's a nice-lookin' lady, an' she said she knowed you at home."

559 "All you got to do is to tell dat ooman jes' what I say."

560 Minty Brown downstairs had heard the little colloquy, and, perceiving that something was amiss, had come to the stairs to listen. Now her voice, striving hard to be condescending and sweet, but growing harsh with anger, floated up from below:

561 "Oh, nevah min', lady, I ain't anxious to see 'em. I jest called out o' pity, but I reckon dey 'shamed to see me 'cause de ol' man's in penitentiary an' dey was run out o' town."

562 Mrs. Jones gasped, and then turned and went hastily downstairs.

563 Kit burst out crying afresh, and Joe walked the floor muttering beneath his breath, while the mother sat grimly watching the outcome. Finally they heard Mrs. Jones' step once more on the stairs. She came in without knocking, and her manner was distinctly unpleasant.

564   "Mis' Hamilton," she said, "I've had a talk with the lady downstairs, an' she's tol' me everything. I'd be glad if you'd let me have my rooms as soon as possible."

565   "So you goin' to put me out on de wo'd of a stranger?"

566   "I'm kin' o' sorry, but everybody in the house heard what Mis' Brown said, an' it'll soon be all over town, an' that 'ud ruin the reputation of my house."

567   "I reckon all dat kin be 'splained."

568   "Yes, but I don't know that anybody kin 'splain your daughter allus being with Mr. Thomas, who ain't even divo'ced from his wife." She flashed a vindictive glance at the girl, who turned deadly pale and dropped her head in her hands.

569   "You daih to say dat, Mis' Jones, you dat fust interduced my gal to dat man and got huh to go out wid him? I reckon you'd bettah go now."

570   And Mrs. Jones looked at Fannie's face and obeyed.

571   As soon as the woman's back was turned, Joe burst out, "There, there! see what you've done with your damned foolishness."

572   Fannie turned on him like a tigress. "Don't you cuss hyeah befo' me; I ain't nevah brung you up to it, an' I won't stan' it. Go to dem whaih you larned it, an whaih de wo'ds soun' sweet." The boy started to speak, but she checked him. "Don't you daih to cuss ag'in or befo' Gawd dey'll be somep'n fu' one o' dis fambly to be rottin' in jail fu'!"

573   The boy was cowed by his mother's manner. He was gathering his few belongings in a bundle.

574   "I ain't goin' to cuss," he said sullenly, "I'm goin' out o' your way."

575   "Oh, go on," she said, "go on. It's been a long time sence you been my son. You on yo' way to hell, an' you is been fu' lo dese many days."

576   Joe got out of the house as soon as possible. He did not speak to Kit nor look at his mother. He felt like a cur, because he knew deep down in his heart that he had only been waiting for some excuse to take this step.

577   As he slammed the door behind him, his mother flung herself down by Kit's side and mingled her tears with her daughter's. But Kit did not raise her head.

578   "Dey ain't nothin' lef' but you now, Kit"; but the girl did not speak, she only shook with hard sobs.

579   Then her mother raised her head and almost screamed, "My Gawd, not you, Kit!" The girl rose, and then dropped unconscious in her mother's arms.

580   Joe took his clothes to a lodging-house that he knew of, and then went to the club to drink himself up to the point of going to see Hattie after the show.

BROKEN HOPES

581   What Joe Hamilton lacked more than anything else in the world was some one to kick him. Many a man who might have lived decently and become a fairly respectable citizen has gone to the dogs for the want of some one to administer a good resounding kick at the right time. It is corrective and clarifying.

582   Joe needed especially its clarifying property, for though he knew himself a cur, he went away from his mother's house feeling himself somehow aggrieved, and the feeling grew upon him the more he thought of it. His mother had ruined his chance in life, and he could never hold up his head again. Yes, he had heard that several of the fellows at the club had shady reputations, but surely to be the son of a thief or a supposed thief was not like being the criminal himself.

583   At the Banner he took a seat by himself, and, ordering a cocktail, sat glowering at the few other lonely members who had happened to drop in. There were not many of them, and the contagion of unsociability had taken possession of the house. The people sat scattered around at different tables, perfectly unmindful of the bartender, who cursed them under his breath for not "getting together."

584   Joe's mind was filled with bitter thoughts. How long had he been away from home? he asked himself. Nearly a year. Nearly a year passed in New York, and he had come to be what he so much desired,—a part of its fast life,—and now in a moment an old woman's stubbornness had destroyed all that he had builded.

585   What would Thomas say when he heard it? What would the other fellows think? And Hattie? It was plain that she would never notice him again. He had no doubt but that the malice of Minty Brown would prompt her to seek out all of his friends and make the story known. Why had he not tried to placate her by disavowing sympathy with his mother? He would have had no compunction about doing so, but he had thought of it too late. He sat brooding over his trouble until the bartender called with respectful sarcasm to ask if he wanted to lease the glass he had.

586   He gave back a silly laugh, gulped the rest of the liquor down, and was ordering another when Sadness came in. He came up directly to Joe and sat down beside him. "Mr. Hamilton says 'Make it two,

Jack,"' he said with easy familiarity. "Well, what's the matter, old man? You're looking glum."

587 "I feel glum."

588 "The divine Hattie hasn't been cutting any capers, has she? The dear old girl hasn't been getting hysterical at her age? Let us hope not."

589 Joe glared at him. Why in the devil should this fellow be so sadly gay when he was weighted down with sorrow and shame and disgust?

590 "Come, come now, Hamilton, if you're sore because I invited myself to take a drink with you, I'll withdraw the order. I know the heroic thing to say is that I'll pay for the drinks myself, but I can't screw my courage up to the point of doing so unnatural a thing."

591 Young Hamilton hastened to protest. "Oh, I know you fellows now well enough to know how many drinks to pay for. It ain't that."

592 "Well, then, out with it. What is it? Haven't been up to anything, have you?"

593 The desire came to Joe to tell this man the whole truth, just what was the matter, and so to relieve his heart. On the impulse he did. If he had expected much from Sadness he was disappointed, for not a muscle of the man's face changed during the entire recital.

594 When it was over, he looked at his companion critically through a wreath of smoke. Then he said: "For a fellow who has had for a full year the advantage of the education of the New York clubs, you are strangely young. Let me see, you are nineteen or twenty now— yes. Well, that perhaps accounts for it. It's a pity you weren't born older. It's a pity that most men aren't. They wouldn't have to take so much time and lose so many good things learning. Now, Mr. Hamilton, let me tell you, and you will pardon me for it, that you are a fool. Your case isn't half as bad as that of nine-tenths of the fellows that hang around here. Now, for instance, my father was hung."

595 Joe started and gave a gasp of horror.

596 "Oh yes, but it was done with a very good rope and by the best citizens of Texas, so it seems that I really ought to be very grateful to them for the distinction they conferred upon my family, but I am not. I am ungratefully sad. A man must be very high or very low to take the sensible view of life that keeps him from being sad. I must confess that I have aspired to the depths without ever being fully able to reach them.

597 "Now look around a bit. See that little girl over there? That's Viola. Two years ago she wrenched up an iron stool from the floor of a lunchroom, and killed another woman with it. She's nineteen,—just about

your age, by the way. Well, she had friends with a certain amount of pull. She got out of it, and no one thinks the worse of Viola. You see, Hamilton, in this life we are all suffering from fever, and no one edges away from the other because he finds him a little warm. It's dangerous when you're not used to it; but once you go through the parching process, you become inoculated against further contagion. Now, there's Barney over there, as decent a fellow as I know; but he has been indicted twice for pocket-picking. A half-dozen fellows whom you meet here every night have killed their man. Others have done worse things for which you respect them less. Poor Wallace, who is just coming in, and who looks like a jaunty rag-picker, came here about six months ago with about two thousand dollars, the proceeds from the sale of a house his father had left him. He'll sleep in one of the club chairs to-night, and not from choice. He spent his two thousand learning. But, after all, it was a good investment. It was like buying an annuity. He begins to know already how to live on others as they have lived on him. The plucked bird's beak is sharpened for other's feathers. From now on Wallace will live, eat, drink, and sleep at the expense of others, and will forget to mourn his lost money. He will go on this way until, broken and useless, the poorhouse or the potter's field gets him. Oh, it's a fine, rich life, my lad. I know you'll like it. I said you would the first time I saw you. It has plenty of stir in it, and a man never gets lonesome. Only the rich are lonesome. It's only the independent who depend upon others."

598 Sadness laughed a peculiar laugh, and there was a look in his terribly bright eyes that made Joe creep. If he could only have understood all that the man was saying to him, he might even yet have turned back. But he didn't. He ordered another drink. The only effect that the talk of Sadness had upon him was to make him feel wonderfully "in it." It gave him a false bravery, and he mentally told himself that now he would not be afraid to face Hattie.

599 He put out his hand to Sadness with a knowing look. "Thanks, Sadness," he said, "you've helped me lots."

600 Sadness brushed the proffered hand away and sprung up. "You lie," he cried, "I haven't; I was only fool enough to try"; and he turned hastily away from the table.

601 Joe looked surprised at first, and then laughed at his friend's retreating form. "Poor old fellow," he said, "drunk again. Must have had something before he came in."

602 There was not a lie in all that Sadness had said either as to their crime or their condition. He belonged to a peculiar class,—one that

grows larger and larger each year in New York and which has imitators in every large city in this country. It is a set which lives, like the leech, upon the blood of others,—that draws its life from the veins of foolish men and immoral women, that prides itself upon its well-dressed idleness and has no shame in its voluntary pauperism. Each member of the class knows every other, his methods and his limitations, and their loyalty one to another makes of them a great hulking, fashionably uniformed fraternity of indolence. Some play the races a few months of the year; others, quite as intermittently, gamble at "shoestring" politics, and waver from party to party as time or their interests seem to dictate. But mostly they are like the lilies of the field.

603   It was into this set that Sadness had sarcastically invited Joe, and Joe felt honored. He found that all of his former feelings had been silly and quite out of place; that all he had learned in his earlier years was false. It was very plain to him now that to want a good reputation was the sign of unpardonable immaturity, and that dishonor was the only real thing worthwhile. It made him feel better.

604   He was just rising bravely to swagger out to the theatre when Minty Brown came in with one of the club-men he knew. He bowed and smiled, but she appeared not to notice him at first, and when she did she nudged her companion and laughed.

605   Suddenly his little courage began to ooze out, and he knew what she must be saying to the fellow at her side, for he looked over at him and grinned. Where now was the philosophy of Sadness? Evidently Minty had not been brought under its educating influences, and thought about the whole matter in the old, ignorant way. He began to think of it too. Somehow old teachings and old traditions have an annoying way of coming back upon us in the critical moments of life, although one has long ago recognised how much truer and better some newer ways of thinking are. But Joe would not allow Minty to shatter his dreams by bringing up these old notions. She must be instructed.

606   He rose and went over to her table.

607   "Why, Minty," he said, offering his hand, "you ain't mad at me, are you?"

608   "Go on away f'om hyeah," she said angrily; "I don't want none o' thievin' Berry Hamilton's fambly to speak to me."

609   "Why, you were all right this evening."

610   "Yes, but jest out o' pity, an' you was nice' cause you was afraid I'd tell on you. Go on now."

611   "Go on now," said Minty's young man; and he looked menacing.

612 Joe, what little self-respect he had gone, slunk out of the room and needed several whiskeys in a neighbouring saloon to give him courage to go to the theatre and wait for Hattie, who was playing in vaudeville houses pending the opening of her company.

613 The closing act was just over when he reached the stage door. he was there but a short time, when Hattie tripped out and took his arm. Her face was bright and smiling, and there was no suggestion of disgust in the dancing eyes she turned up to him. Evidently she had not heard, but the thought gave him no particular pleasure, as it left him in suspense as to how she would act when she should hear.

614 "Let's go somewhere and get some supper," she said; "I'm as hungry as I can be. What are you looking so cut up about?"

615 "Oh, I ain't feelin' so very good."

616 "I hope you ain't lettin' that long-tongued Brown woman bother your head, are you?"

617 His heart seemed to stand still. She did know, then.

618 "Do you know all about it?"

619 "Why, of course I do. You might know she'd come to me first with her story."

620 "And you still keep on speaking to me?"

621 "Now look here, Joe, if you've been drinking, I'll forgive you; if you ain't, you go on and leave me. Say, what do you take me for? Do you think I'd throw down a friend because somebody else talked about him? Well, you don't know Hat Sterling. When Minty told me that story, she was back in my dressing-room, and I sent her out o' there a-flying, and with a tongue-lashing that she won't forget for a month o' Sundays."

622 "I reckon that was the reason she jumped on me so hard at the club." He chuckled. He had taken heart again. All that Sadness had said was true, after all, and people thought no less of him. His joy was unbounded.

623 "So she jumped on you hard, did she? The cat!"

624 "Oh, she didn't say a thing to me."

625 "Well, Joe, it's just like this. I ain't an angel, you know that, but I do try to be square, and whenever I find a friend of mine down on his luck, in his pocketbook or his feelings, why, I give him my flipper. Why, old chap, I believe I like you better for the stiff upper lip you've been keeping under all this."

626 "Why, Hattie," he broke out, unable any longer to control himself, "you're—you're—"

627 "Oh, I'm just plain Hat Sterling, who won't throw down her friends. Now come on and get something to eat. If that thing is at the club, we'll go there and show her just how much her talk amounted to. She thinks she's the whole game, but I can spot her and then show her that she ain't one, two, three."

628 When they reached the Banner, they found Minty still there. She tried on the two the same tactics that she had employed so successfully upon Joe alone. She nudged her companion and tittered. But she had another person to deal with. Hattie Sterling stared at her coldly and indifferently, and passed on by her to a seat. Joe proceeded to order supper and other things in the nonchalant way that the woman had enjoined upon him. Minty began to feel distinctly uncomfortable, but it was her business not to be beaten. She laughed outright. Hattie did not seem to hear her. She was beckoning Sadness to her side. He came and sat down.

629 "Now look here," she said, "you can't have any supper because you haven't reached the stage of magnificent hunger to make a meal palatable to you. You've got so used to being nearly starved that a meal don't taste good to you under any other circumstances. You're in on the drinks, though. Your thirst is always available.—Jack," she called down the long room to the bartender, "make it three.— Lean over here, I want to talk to you. See that woman over there by the wall? No, not that one,—the big light woman with Griggs. Well, she's come here with a story trying to throw Joe down, and I want you to help me do her."

630 "Oh, that's the one that upset our young friend, is it?" said Sadness, turning his mournful eyes upon Minty.

631 "That's her. So you know about it, do you?"

632 "Yes, and I'll help do her. She mustn't touch one of the fraternity, you know." He kept his eyes fixed upon the outsider until she squirmed. She could not at all understand this serious conversation directed at her. She wondered if she had gone too far and if they contemplated putting her out. It made her uneasy.

633 Now, this same Miss Sterling had the faculty of attracting a good deal of attention when she wished to. She brought it into play to-night, and in ten minutes, aided by Sadness, she had a crowd of jolly people about her table. When, as she would have expressed it, "everything was going fat," she suddenly paused and, turning her eyes full upon Minty, said in a voice loud enough for all to hear,—

634 "Say, boys, you've heard that story about Joe, haven't you?"

635   They had.

636   "Well, that's the one that told it; she's come here to try to throw him and me down. Is she going to do it?"

637   "Well, I guess not!" was the rousing reply, and every face turned towards the now frightened Minty. She rose hastily and, getting her skirts together, fled from the room, followed more leisurely by the crestfallen Griggs. Hattie's laugh and "Thank you, fellows," followed her out.

638   Matters were less easy for Joe's mother and sister than they were for him. A week or more after this, Kitty found him and told him that Minty's story had reached their employers and that they were out of work.

639   "You see, Joe," she said sadly, "we've took a flat since we moved from Mis' Jones', and we had to furnish it. We've got one lodger, a race-horse man, an' he's mighty nice to ma an' me, but that ain't enough. Now we've got to do something."

640   Joe was so smitten with sorrow that he gave her a dollar and promised to speak about the matter to a friend of his.

641   He did speak about it to Hattie.

642   "You've told me once or twice that your sister could sing. Bring her down here to me, and if she can do anything, I'll get her a place on the stage," was Hattie's answer.

643   When Kitty heard it she was radiant, but her mother only shook her head and said, "De las' hope, de las' hope."

"ALL THE WORLD'S A STAGE"

644   Kitty proved herself Joe's sister by falling desperately in love with Hattie Sterling the first time they met. The actress was very gracious to her, and called her "child" in a pretty, patronizing way, and patted her on the check.

645   "It's a shame that Joe hasn't brought you around before. We've been good friends for quite some time."

646   "He told me you an' him was right good friends."

647   Already Joe took on a new importance in his sister's eyes. He must be quite a man, she thought, to be the friend of such a person as Miss Sterling.

648   "So you think you want to go on the stage, do you?"

649   "Yes, 'm, I thought it might be right nice for me if I could."

650   "Joe, go out and get some beer for us, and then I'll hear your sister sing."

651   Miss Sterling talked as if she were a manager and had only to snap her fingers to be obeyed. When Joe came back with the beer, Kitty drank a glass. She did not like it, but she would not offend her hostess. After this she sang, and Miss Sterling applauded her generously, although the young girl's nervousness kept her from doing her best. The encouragement helped her, and she did better as she became more at home.

652   "Why, child, you've got a good voice. And, Joe, you've been keeping her shut up all this time. You ought to be ashamed of yourself."

653   The young man had little to say. He had brought Kitty almost under a protest, because he had no confidence in her ability and thought that his "girl" would disillusion her. It did not please him now to find his sister so fully under the limelight and himself "up stage."

654   Kitty was quite in a flutter of delight; not so much with the idea of working as with the glamour of the work she might be allowed to do.

655   "I tell you, now," Hattie Sterling pursued, throwing a brightly stockinged foot upon a chair, "your voice is too good for the chorus. Gi' me a cigarette, Joe. Have one, Kitty?—I'm goin' to call you Kitty. It's nice and homelike, and then we've got to be great chums, you know."

656   Kitty, unwilling to refuse anything from the sorceress, took her cigarette and lighted it, but a few puffs set her off coughing.

657   "Tut, tut, Kitty, child, don't do it if you ain't used to it. You'll learn soon enough."

658   Joe wanted to kick his sister for having tried so delicate an art and failed, for he had not yet lost all of his awe of Hattie.

659   "Now, what I was going to say," the lady resumed after several contemplative puffs, "is that you'll have to begin in the chorus any way and work your way up. It wouldn't take long for you, with your looks and voice, to put one of the 'up and ups' out o' the business. Only hope it won't be me. I've had people I've helped try to do it often enough."

660   She gave a laugh that had just a touch of bitterness in it, for she began to recognize that although she had been on the stage only a short time, she was no longer the all-conquering Hattie Sterling, in the first freshness of her youth.

661   "Oh, I wouldn't want to push anybody out," Kit expostulated.

662   "Oh, never mind, you'll soon get bravely over that feeling, and even if you didn't it wouldn't matter much. The thing has to happen. Somebody's got to go down. We don't last long in this life: it soon wears us out, and when we're worn out and sung out, danced out and played out, the manager has no further use for us; so he reduces us to the ranks or kicks us out entirely."

663   Joe here thought it time for him to put in a word.

664   "Get out, Hat," he said contemptuously; "you're good for a dozen years yet."

665   She didn't deign to notice him, save so far as a sniff goes.

666   "Don't you let what I say scare you, though, Kitty. You've got a good chance, and maybe you'll have more sense than I've got, and at least save money—while you're in it. But let's get off that. It makes me sick. All you've got to do is to come to the opera-house tomorrow and I'll introduce you to the manager. He's a fool, but I think we can make him do something for you."

667   "Oh, thank you, I'll be around to-morrow, sure."

668   "Better come about ten o'clock. There's a rehearsal tomorrow, and you'll find him there. Of course, he'll be pretty rough, he always is at rehearsals, but he'll take to you if he thinks there's anything in you and he can get it out."

669   Kitty felt herself dismissed and rose to go. Joe did not rise.

670   "I'll see you later, Kit," he said; "I ain't goin' just yet. Say," he added, when his sister was gone, "you're a hot one. What do you want to give her all that con for? She'll never get in."

671   "Joe," said Hattie, "don't you get awful tired of being a jackass? Sometimes I want to kiss you, and sometimes I feel as if I had to kick you. I'll compromise with you now by letting you bring me some more beer. This got all stale while your sister was here. I saw she didn't like it, and so I wouldn't drink any more for fear she'd try to keep up with me."

672   "Kit is a good deal of a jay yet," Joe remarked wisely.

673   "Oh, yes, this world is full of jays. Lots of 'em have seen enough to make 'em wise, but they're still jays, and don't know it. That's the worst of it. They go around thinking they're it, when they ain't even in the game. Go on and get the beer."

674   And Joe went, feeling vaguely that he had been sat upon.

675   Kit flew home with joyous heart to tell her mother of her good prospects. She had burst into the room, crying, "Oh, ma, ma, Miss Hattie thinks I'll do to go on the stage. Ain't it grand?"

676   She did not meet with the expected warmth of response from her mother.

677   "I do' know as it'll be so gran'. F'om what I see of dem stage people dey don't seem to 'mount to much. De way dem gals shows demse'ves is right down bad to me. Is you goin' to dress lak dem we seen dat night?"

678   Kit hung her head.

679   "I guess I'll have to."

680   "Well, ef you have to, I'd ruther see you daid any day. Oh, Kit, my little gal, don't do it, don't do it. Don't you go down lak yo' brothah Joe. Joe's gone."

681   "Why, ma, you don't understand. Joe's somebody now. You ought to 've heard how Miss Hattie talked about him. She said he's been her friend for a long while."

682   "Her frien', yes, an' his own inimy. You needn' pattern aftah dat gal, Kit. She ruint Joe, an' she's aftah you now."

683   "But nowadays everybody thinks stage people respectable up here."

684   "Maybe I'm ol'-fashioned, but I can't believe in any ooman's lady-ship when she shows herse'f lak dem gals does. Oh, Kit, don't do it. Ain't you seen enough? Don't you know enough already to stay away f'om dese hyeah people? Dey don't want nothin' but to pull you down an' den laugh at you w'en you's dragged in de dust."

685   "You mustn't feel that away, ma. I'm doin' it to help you."

686   "I do' want no sich help. I'd ruther starve."

687   Kit did not reply, but there was no yielding in her manner.

688   "Kit," her mother went on, "dey's somep'n I ain't nevah tol' you dat I'm goin' to tell you now. Mistah Gibson ust to come to Mis' Jones's lots to see me befo' we moved hyeah, an' he's been talkin' 'bout a good many things to me." She hesitated. "He say dat I ain't noways ma'ied to my po' husban', dat a pen'tentiary sentence is de same as a divo'ce, an' if Be'y should live to git out, we'd have to ma'y ag'in. I wouldn't min' dat, Kit, but he say dat at Be'y's age dey ain't much chanst of his livin' to git out, an' hyeah I'll live all dis time alone, an' den have no one to tek keer o' me w'en I git ol'. He wants me to ma'y him, Kit. Kit, I love yo' fathah; he's my only one. But Joe, he's gone, an' ef yo go, befo' Gawd I'll tell Tawm Gibson yes."

689   The mother looked up to see just what effect her plea would have on her daughter. She hoped that what she said would have the desired result. But the girl turned around from fixing her neck-ribbon before the glass, her face radiant. "Why, it'll be splendid. He's such a nice man, an' race-horse men 'most always have money. Why don't you marry him, ma? Then I'd feel that you was safe an' settled, an' that you wouldn't be lonesome when the show was out of town."

690   "You want me to ma'y him an' desert yo' po' pa?"

691   "I guess what he says is right, ma. I don't reckon we'll ever see pa again an' you got to do something. You got to live for yourself now."

692   Her mother dropped her head in her hands. "All right," she said, "I'll do it; I'll ma'y him. I might as well go de way both my chillen's

gone. Po' Be'y, po' Be'y. Ef you evah do come out, Gawd he'p you to baih what you'll fin'." And Mrs. Hamilton rose and tottered from the room, as if the old age she anticipated had already come upon her.

693   Kit stood looking after her, fear and grief in her eyes. "Poor ma," she said, "an' poor pa. But I know, an' I know it's for the best."

694   On the next morning she was up early and practising hard for her interview with the managing star of "Martin's Blackbirds."

695   When she arrived at the theatre, Hattie Sterling met her with frank friendliness.

696   "I'm glad you came early, Kitty," she remarked, "for maybe you can get a chance to talk with Martin before he begins rehearsal and gets all worked up. He'll be a little less like a bear then. But even if you don't see him before then, wait, and don't get scared if he tries to bluff you. His bark is a good deal worse than his bite."

697   When Mr. Martin came in that morning, he had other ideas than that of seeing applicants for places. His show must begin in two weeks, and it was advertised to be larger and better than ever before, when really nothing at all had been done for it. The promise of this advertisement must be fulfilled. Mr. Martin was late, and was out of humour with every one else on account of it. He came in hurried, fierce, and important.

698   "Mornin', Mr. Smith, mornin', Mrs. Jones. Ha, ladies and gentlemen, all here?"

699   He shot every word out of his mouth as if the after-taste of it were unpleasant to him. He walked among the chorus like an angry king among his vassals, and his glance was a flash of insolent fire. From his head to his feet he was the very epitome of self-sufficient, brutal conceit.

700   Kitty trembled as she noted the hush that fell on the people at his entrance. She felt like rushing out of the room. She could never face this terrible man. She trembled more as she found his eyes fixed upon her.

701   "Who's that?" he asked, disregarding her, as if she had been a stick or a stone.

702   "Well, don't snap her head off. It's a girl friend of mine that wants a place," said Hattie. She was the only one who would brave Martin.

703   "Humph. Let her wait. I ain't got no time to hear any one now. Get yourselves in line, you all who are on to that first chorus, while I'm getting into my sweat-shirt."

704   He disappeared behind a screen, whence he emerged arrayed, or only half arrayed, in a thick absorbing shirt and a thin pair of woolen trousers. Then the work began. The man was indefatigable. He was

like the spirit of energy. He was in every place about the stage at once, leading the chorus, showing them steps, twisting some awkward girl into shape, shouting, gesticulating, abusing the pianist.

705   "Now, now," he would shout, "the left foot on that beat. Bah, bah, stop! You walk like a lot of tin soldiers. Are your joints rusty? Do you want oil? Look here, Taylor, if I didn't know you, I'd take you for a truck. Pick up your feet, open your mouths, and move, move, move! Oh!" and he would drop his head in despair. "And to think that I've got to do something with these things in two weeks—two weeks!" Then he would turn to them again with a sudden reaccession of eagerness. "Now, at it again, at it again! Hold that note, hold it! Now whirl, and on the left foot. Stop that music, stop it! Miss Coster, you'll learn that step in about a thousand years, and I've got nine hundred and ninety-nine years and fifty weeks less time than that to spare. Come here and try that step with me. Don't be afraid to move. Step like a chicken on a hot griddle!" And some blushing girl would come forward and go through the step alone before all the rest.

706   Kitty contemplated the scene with a mind equally divided between fear and anger. What should she do if he should so speak to her? Like the others, no doubt, smile sheepishly and obey him. But she did not like to believe it. She felt that the independence which she had known from babyhood would assert itself, and that she would talk back to him, even as Hattie Sterling did. She felt scared and discouraged, but every now and then her friend smiled encouragingly upon her across the ranks of moving singers.

707   Finally, however, her thoughts were broken in upon by hearing Mr. Martin cry: "Oh, quit, quit, and go rest yourselves, you ancient pieces of hickory, and let me forget you for a minute before I go crazy. Where's that new girl now?"

708   Kitty rose and went toward him, trembling so that she could hardly walk.

709   "What can you do?"

710   "I can sing," very faintly.

711   "Well, if that's the voice you're going to sing in, there won't be many that'll know whether it's good or bad. Well, let's hear something. Do you know any of these?"

712   And he ran over the titles of several songs. She knew some of them, and he selected one. "Try this. Here, Tom, play it for her."

713   It was an ordeal for the girl to go through. She had never sung before at anything more formidable than a church concert, where only her immediate acquaintances and townspeople were present. Now

to sing before all these strange people, themselves singers, made her
feel faint and awkward. But the courage of desperation came to her,
and she struck into the song. At the first her voice wavered and threatened to fail her. It must not. She choked back her fright and forced
the music from her lips.

714   When she was done, she was startled to hear Martin burst into a
raucous laugh. Such humiliation! She had failed, and instead of
telling her, he was bringing her to shame before the whole company.
The tears came into her eyes, and she was about giving way when she
caught a reassuring nod and smile from Hattie Sterling, and seized
on this as a last hope.

715   "Haw, haw, haw!" laughed Martin, "haw, haw haw! The little one
was scared, see? She was scared, d' you understand? But did you see
the girl she went at it with? Just took the bit in her teeth and got away.
Haw, haw, haw! Now, that's what I like. If all you girls had that spirit,
we could do something in two weeks. Try another one, girl."

716   Kitty's heart had suddenly grown light. She sang the second one
better because something within her was singing.

717   "Good!" said Martin, but he immediately returned to his cold
manner. "You watch these girls close and see what they do, and tomorrow be prepared to go into line and move as well as sing."

718   He immediately turned his attention from her to the chorus, but
no slight that he could inflict upon her now could take away the sweet
truth that she was engaged and tomorrow would begin work. She
wished she could go over and embrace Hattie Sterling. She thought
kindly of Joe, and promised herself to give him a present out of her
first month's earnings.

719   On the first night of the show pretty little Kitty Hamilton was
pointed out as a girl who wouldn't be in the chorus long. The mother,
who was soon to be Mrs. Gibson, sat in the balcony, a grieved, pained
look on her face. Joe was in a front row with some of the rest of his
gang. He took many drinks between the acts, because he was proud.

720   Mr. Thomas was there. He also was proud, and after the performance he waited for Kitty at the stage door and went forward to meet
her as she came out. The look she gave him stopped him, and he let
her pass without a word.

721   "Who'd 'a' thought," he mused, "that the kid had that much
nerve? Well, if they don't want to find out things, what do they come
to N' Yawk for? It ain't nobody's old Sunday-school picnic. Guess I
got out easy, anyhow."

722   Hattie Sterling took Joe home in a hansom.

723   "Say," she said, "if you come this way for me again, it's all over, see? Your little sister's a comer, and I've got to hustle to keep up with her."

724   Joe growled and fell asleep in his chair. One must needs have a strong head or a strong will when one is the brother of a celebrity and would celebrate the distinguished one's success.

THE OAKLEYS

725   A year after the arrest of Berry Hamilton, and at a time when New York had shown to the eyes of his family so many strange new sights, there were few changes to be noted in the condition of affairs at the Oakley place. Maurice Oakley was perhaps a shade more distrustful of his servants, and consequently more testy with them. Mrs. Oakley was the same acquiescent woman, with unbounded faith in her husband's wisdom and judgment. With complacent minds both went their ways, drank their wine, and said their prayers, and wished that brother Frank's five years were past. They had letters from him now and then, never very cheerful in tone, but always breathing the deepest love and gratitude to them.

726   His brother found deep cause for congratulation in the tone of these epistles.

727   "Frank is getting down to work," he would cry exultantly. "He is past the first buoyant enthusiasm of youth. Ah, Leslie, when a man begins to be serious, then he begins to be something." And her only answer would be, "I wonder, Maurice, if Claire Lessing will wait for him?"

728   The two had frequent questions to answer as to Frank's doing and prospects, and they had always bright things to say of him, even when his letters gave them no such warrant. Their love for him made them read large between the lines, and all they read was good.

729   Between Maurice and his brother no word of the guilty servant ever passed. They each avoided it as an unpleasant subject. Frank had never asked and his brother had never proffered aught of the outcome of the case.

730   Mrs. Oakley had once suggested it. "Brother ought to know," she said, "that Berry is being properly punished."

731   "By no means," replied her husband. "You know that it would only hurt him. He shall never know if I have to tell him."

732   "You are right, Maurice, you are always right. We must shield Frank from the pain it would cause him. Poor fellow! he is so sensitive."

733   Their hearts were still steadfastly fixed upon the union of this younger brother with Claire Lessing. She had lately come into a fortune,

and there was nothing now to prevent it. They would have written Frank to urge it, but they both believed that to try to woo him away from his art was but to make him more wayward. That any woman could have power enough to take him away from this jealous mistress they very much doubted. But they could hope, and hope made them eager to open every letter that bore the French postmark. Always it might contain news that he was coming home, or that he had made a great success, or, better, some inquiry after Claire. A long time they had waited, but found no such tidings in the letters from Paris.

734   At last, as Maurice Oakley sat in his library one day, the servant brought him a letter more bulky in weight and appearance than any he had yet received. His eyes glistened with pleasure as he read the postmark. "A letter from Frank," he said joyfully, "and an important one, I'll wager."

735   He smiled as he weighed it in his hand and caressed it. Mrs. Oakley was out shopping, and as he knew how deep her interest was, he hesitated to break the seal before she returned. He curbed his natural desire and laid the heavy envelope down on the desk. But he could not deny himself the pleasure of speculating as to its contents.

736   It was such a large, interesting-looking package. What might it contain? It simply reeked of possibilities. Had any one banteringly told Maurice Oakley that he had such a deep vein of sentiment, he would have denied it with scorn and laughter. But here he found himself sitting with the letter in his hand and weaving stories as to its contents.

737   First, now, it might be a notice that Frank had received the badge of the Legion of Honour. No, no, that was too big, and he laughed aloud at his own folly, wondering the next minute, with half shame, why he laughed, for did he, after all, believe anything was too big for that brother of his? Well, let him begin, anyway, away down. Let him say, for instance, that the letter told of the completion and sale of a great picture. Frank had sold small ones. He would be glad of this, for his brother had written him several times of things that were a-doing, but not yet of anything that was done. Or, better yet, let the letter say that some picture, long finished, but of which the artist's pride and anxiety had forbidden him to speak, had made a glowing success, the success it deserved. This sounded well, and seemed not at all beyond the bounds of possibility. It was an alluring vision. He saw the picture already. It was a scene from life, true in detail to the point of very minuteness, and yet with something spiritual in it that lifted it above the mere copy of the commonplace. At the Salon it would be hung on the line, and people would stand before it admiring its

workmanship and asking who the artist was. He drew on his memory of old reading. In his mind's eye he saw Frank, unconscious of his own power or too modest to admit it, stand unknown among the crowds around his picture waiting for and dreading their criticisms. He saw the light leap to his eyes as he heard their words of praise. He saw the straightening of his narrow shoulders when he was forced to admit that he was the painter of the work. Then the windows of Paris were filled with his portraits. The papers were full of his praise, and brave men and fair women met together to do him homage. Fair women, yes, and Frank would look upon them all and see reflected in them but a tithe of the glory of one woman, and that woman Claire Lessing. He roused himself and laughed again as he tapped the magic envelope.

738   "My fancies go on and conquer the world for my brother," he muttered. "He will follow their flight one day and do it himself."

739   The letter drew his eyes back to it. It seemed to invite him, to beg him even. "No, I will not do it; I will wait until Leslie comes. She will be as glad to hear the good news as I am."

740   His dreams were taking the shape of reality in his mind, and he was believing all that he wanted to believe.

741   He turned to look at a picture painted by Frank which hung over the mantel. He dwelt lovingly upon it, seeing in it the touch of a genius.

742   "Surely," he said, "this new picture cannot be greater than that, though it shall hang where kings can see it and this only graces the library of my poor house. It has the feeling of a woman's soul with the strength of a man's heart. When Frank and Claire marry, I shall give it back to them. It is too great a treasure for a clod like me. Heigho, why will women be so long a-shopping?"

743   He glanced again at the letter, and his hand went out involuntarily towards it. He fondled it, smiling.

744   "Ah, Lady Leslie, I've a mind to open it to punish you for staying so long."

745   He essayed to be playful, but he knew that he was trying to make a compromise with himself because his eagerness grew stronger than his gallantry. He laid the letter down and picked it up again. He studied the postmark over and over. He got up and walked to the window and back again, and then began fumbling in his pockets for his knife. No, he did not want it; yes, he did. He would just cut the envelope and make believe he had read it to pique his wife; but he would not read it. Yes, that was it. He found the knife and slit the paper. His fingers trembled as he touched the sheets that protruded. Why would

not Leslie come? Did she not know that he was waiting for her? She ought to have known that there was a letter from Paris to-day, for it had been a month since they had had one.

746   There was a sound of footsteps without. He sprang up, crying, "I've been waiting so long for you!" A servant opened the door to bring him a message. Oakley dismissed him angrily. What did he want to go down to the Continental for to drink and talk politics to a lot of muddle-pated fools when he had a brother in Paris who was an artist and a letter from him lay unread in his hand? His patience and his temper were going. Leslie was careless and unfeeling. She ought to come; he was tired of waiting.

747   A carriage rolled up the driveway and he dropped the letter guiltily, as if it were not his own. He would only say that he had grown tired of waiting and started to read it. But it was only Mrs. Davis's footman leaving a note for Leslie about some charity.

748   He went back to the letter. Well, it was his. Leslie had forfeited her right to see it as soon as he. It might be mean, but it was not dishonest. No, he would not read it now, but he would take it and show her that he had exercised his self-control in spite of her short-comings. He laid it on the desk once more. It leered at him. He might just open the sheets enough to see the lines that began it, and read no further. Yes, he would do that. Leslie could not feel hurt at such a little thing.

749   The first line had only "Dear Brother." "Dear Brother"! Why not the second? That could not hold much more. The second line held him, and the third, and the fourth, and as he read on, unmindful now of what Leslie might think or feel, his face turned from the ruddy glow of pleasant anxiety to the pallor of grief and terror. He was not half-way through it when Mrs. Oakley's voice in the hall announced her coming. He did not hear her. He sat staring at the page before him, his lips apart and his eyes staring. Then, with a cry that echoed through the house, crumpling the sheets in his hand, he fell forward fainting to the floor, just as his wife rushed into the room.

750   "What is it?" she cried. "Maurice! Maurice!"

751   He lay on the floor staring up at the ceiling, the letter clutched in his hands. She ran to him and lifted up his head, but he gave no sign of life. Already the servants were crowding to the door. She bade one of them to hasten for a doctor, others to bring water and brandy, and the rest to be gone. As soon as she was alone, she loosed the crumpled sheets from his hand, for she felt that this must have been the cause of her husband's strange attack. Without a thought of wrong,

for they had no secrets from each other, she glanced at the opening lines. Then she forgot the unconscious man at her feet and read the letter through to the end.

752   The letter was in Frank's neat hand, a little shaken, perhaps, by nervousness.

"DEAR BROTHER," it ran, "I know you will grieve at receiving this, and I wish that I might bear your grief for you, but I cannot, though I have as heavy a burden as this can bring to you. Mine would have been lighter to-day, perhaps, had you been more straight-forward with me. I am not blaming you, however, for I know that my hypocrisy made you believe me possessed of a really soft heart, and you thought to spare me. Until yesterday, when in a letter from Esterton he casually mentioned the matter, I did not know that Berry was in prison, else this letter would have been written sooner. I have been wanting to write it for so long, and yet have been too great a coward to do so.

"I know that you will be disappointed in me, and just what that disappointment will cost you I know; but you must hear the truth. I shall never see your face again, or I should not dare to tell it even now. You will remember that I begged you to be easy on your servant. You thought it was only my kindness of heart. It was not; I had a deeper reason. I knew where the money had gone and dared not tell. Berry is an innocent as yourself—and I—well, it is a story, and let me tell it to you.

"You have had so much confidence in me, and I hate to tell you that it was all misplaced. I have no doubt that I should not be doing it now but that I have drunken absinthe enough to give me the emotional point of view, which I shall regret to-morrow. I do not mean that I am drunk. I can think clearly and write clearly, but my emotions are extremely active.

"Do you remember Claire's saying at the table that night of the farewell dinner that some dark-eyed mademoiselle was waiting for me? She did not know how truly she spoke, though I fancy she saw how I flushed when she said it: for I was already in love—madly so.

"I need not describe her. I need say nothing about her, for I know that nothing I say can ever persuade you to forgive her for taking me from you. This has gone on since I first came here, and I dared not tell you, for I saw whither your eyes had turned. I loved this girl, and she both inspired and hindered my work. Perhaps I would have been successful had I not met her, perhaps not.

"I love her too well to marry her and make of our devotion a stale, prosy thing of duty and compulsion. When a man does not marry a woman, he must keep her better than he would a wife. It costs. All that you gave me went to make her happy.

"Then, when I was about leaving you, the catastrophe came. I wanted much to carry back to her. I gambled to make more. I would surprise her. Luck was against me. Night after night I lost. Then, just before the dinner, I woke from my frenzy to find all that I had was gone. I would have asked you for more, and you would have given it; but that strange, ridiculous something which we misname Southern honour, that honour which strains at a gnat and swallows a camel, withheld me, and I preferred to do worse. So I lied to you. The money from my cabinet was not stolen save by myself. I am a liar and a thief, but your eyes shall never tell me so.

"Tell the truth and have Berry released. I can stand it. Write me but one letter to tell me of this. Do not plead with me, do not forgive me, do not seek to find me, for from this time I shall be as one who has perished from the earth; I shall be no more.

> "Your brother,
>
> "FRANK."

753 By the time the servants came they found Mrs. Oakley as white as her lord. But with firm hands and compressed lips she ministered to his needs pending the doctor's arrival. She bathed his face and temples, chafed his hands, and forced the brandy between his lips. Finally he stirred and his hands gripped.

754 "The letter!" he gasped.

755 "Yes, dear. I have it; I have it."

756 "Give it to me," he cried. She handed it to him. He seized it and thrust it into his breast.

757 "Did—did—you read it?"

758 "Yes, I did not know—"

759 "Oh, my God, I did not intend that you should see it. I wanted the secret for my own. I wanted to carry it to my grave with me. Oh, Frank, Frank, Frank!"

760   "Never mind, Maurice. It is as if you alone knew it."

761   "It is not, I say, it is not!"

762   He turned upon his face and began to weep passionately, not like a man, but like a child whose last toy has been broken.

763   "Oh, my God," he moaned, "my brother, my brother!"

764   " 'Sh, dearie, think—it's—it's—Frank."

765   "That's it, that's it—that's what I can't forget. It's Frank,—Frank, my brother."

766   Suddenly he sat up and his eyes stared straight into hers.

767   "Leslie, no one must ever know what is in this letter," he said calmly.

768   "No one shall, Maurice; come, let us burn it."

769   "Burn it? No, no," he cried, clutching at his breast. "It must not be burned. What! burn my brother's secret? No, no, I must carry it with me,—carry it with me to the grave."

770   "But, Maurice—"

771   "I must carry it with me."

772   She saw that he was overwrought, and so did not argue with him.

773   When the doctor came, he found Maurice Oakley in bed, but better. The medical man diagnosed the case and decided that he had received some severe shock. He feared too for his heart, for the patient constantly held his hands pressed against his bosom. In vain the doctor pleaded; he would not take them down, and when the wife added her word, the physician gave up, and after prescribing, left, much puzzled in mind.

774   "It's a strange case," he said; "there's something more than the nervous shock that makes him clutch his chest like that, and yet I have never noticed signs of heart trouble in Oakley. Oh, well, business worry will produce anything in anybody."

775   It was soon common talk about the town about Maurice Oakley's attack. In the seclusion of his chamber he was saying to his wife:

776   "Ah, Leslie, you and I will keep the secret. No one shall ever know."

777   "Yes, dear, but—but—what of Berry?"

778   "What of Berry?" he cried, starting up excitedly. "What is Berry to Frank? What is that nigger to my brother? What are his sufferings to the honor of my family and name?"

779   "Never mind, Maurice, never mind, you are right."

780   "It must never be known, I say, if Berry has to rot in jail."

781   So they wrote a lie to Frank, and buried the secret in their breasts, and Oakley wore its visible form upon his heart.

FRANKENSTEIN

782 Five years is but a short time in the life of a man, and yet many things may happen therein. For instance, the whole way of a family's life may be changed. Good natures may be made into bad ones and out of a soul of faith grow a spirit of unbelief. The independence of respectability may harden into the insolence of defiance, and the sensitive cheek of modesty into the brazen face of shamelessness. It may be true that the habits of years are hard to change, but this is not true of the first sixteen or seventeen years of a young person's life, else Kitty Hamilton and Joe could not so easily have become what they were. It had taken barely five years to accomplish an entire metamorphosis of their characters. In Joe's case even a shorter time was needed. He was so ready to go down that it needed but a gentle push to start him, and once started, there was nothing within him to hold him back from the depths. For his will was as flabby as his conscience, and his pride, which stands to some men for conscience, had no definite aim or direction.

783   Hattie Sterling had given him both his greatest impulse for evil and for good. She had at first given him his gentle push, but when she saw that his collapse would lose her a faithful and useful slave she had sought to check his course. Her threat of the severance of their relations had held him up for a little time, and she began to believe that he was safe again. He went back to the work he had neglected, drank moderately, and acted in most things as a sound, sensible being. Then, all of a sudden, he went down again, and went down badly. She kept her promise and threw him over. Then he became a hanger-on at the clubs, a genteel loafer. He used to say in his sober moments that at last he was one of the boys that Sadness had spoken of. He did not work, and yet he lived and ate and was proud of his degradation. But he soon tired of being separated from Hattie, and straightened up again. After some demur she received him upon his former footing. It was only for a few months. He fell again. For almost four years this had happened intermittently. Finally he took a turn for the better that endured so long that Hattie Sterling gave him her faith. Then the woman made her mistake. She warmed to him. She showed him that she was proud of him. He went forth at once to celebrate his victory. He did not return to her for three days. Then he was battered, unkempt, and thick of speech.

784   She looked at him in silent contempt for a while as he sat nursing his aching head.

785   "Well, you're a beauty," she said finally with cutting scorn. "You ought to be put under a glass case and placed on exhibition."

786   He groaned and his head sunk lower. A drunken man is always disarmed.

787   His helplessness, instead of inspiring her with pity, inflamed her with an unfeeling anger that burst forth in a volume of taunts.

788   "You're the thing I've given up all my chances for—you, a miserable, drunken jay, without a jay's decency. No one had ever looked at you until I picked you up and you've been strutting around ever since, showing off because I was kind to you, and now this is the way you pay me back. Drunk half the time and half drunk the rest. Well, you know what I told you the last time you got 'loaded'? I mean it too. You're not the only star in sight, see?"

789   She laughed meanly and began to sing, "You'll have to find another baby now."

790   For the first time he looked up, and his eyes were full of tears—tears both of grief and intoxication. There was an expression of a whipped dog on his face.

791   "Do'—Ha'ie, do'—" he pleaded, stretching out his hands to her.

792   Her eyes blazed back at him, but she sang on insolently, tauntingly.

793   The very inanity of the man disgusted her, and on a sudden impulse she sprang up and struck him full in the face with the flat of her hand. He was too weak to resist the blow, and, tumbling from the chair, fell limply to the floor, where he lay at her feet, alternately weeping aloud and quivering with drunken, hiccoughing sobs.

794   "Get up!" she cried; "get up and get out o' here. You sha'n't lay around my house."

795   He had already begun to fall into a drunken sleep, but she shook him, got him to his feet, and pushed him outside the door. "Now, go, you drunken dog, and never put your foot inside this house again."

796   He stood outside, swaying dizzily upon his feet and looking back with dazed eyes at the door, then he muttered: "Pu' me out, wi' you? Pu' me out, damn you! Well, I ki' you. See 'f I don't;" and he half walked, half fell down the street.

797   Sadness and Skaggsy were together at the club that night. Five years had not changed the latter as to wealth or position or inclination, and he was still a frequent visitor at the Banner. He always came in alone now, for Maudie had gone the way of all the half-world,

and reached depths to which Mr. Skaggs's job prevented him from following her. However, he mourned truly for his lost companion, and to-night he was in a particularly pensive mood:

798   Some one was playing rag-time on the piano, and the dancers were wheeling in time to the music. Skaggsy looked at them regretfully as he sipped his liquor. It made him think of Maudie. He sighed and turned away.

799   "I tell you, Sadness," he said impulsively, "dancing is the poetry of motion."

800   "Yes," replied Sadness, "and dancing in rag-time is the dialect poetry."

801   The reporter did not like this. It savoured of flippancy, and he was about entering upon a discussion to prove that Sadness had no soul, when Joe, with bloodshot eyes and dishevelled clothes, staggered in and reeled towards them.

802   "Drunk again," said Sadness. "Really, it's a waste of time for Joe to sober up. Hullo there!" as the young man brought up against him; "take a seat." He put him in a chair at the table. "Been lushin' a bit, eh?"

803   "Gi' me some'n' drink."

804   "Oh, a hair of the dog. Some men shave their dogs clean, and then have hydrophobia. Here, Jack!"

805   They drank, and then, as if the whiskey had done him good, Joe sat up in his chair.

806   "Ha'ie's throwed me down."

807   "Lucky dog! You might have known it would have happened sooner or later. Better sooner than never."

808   Skaggs smoked in silence and looked at Joe.

809   "I'm goin' to kill her."

810   "I wouldn't if I were you. Take old Sadness's advice and thank your stars that you're rid of her."

811   "I'm goin' to kill her." He paused and looked at them drowsily. Then, bracing himself up again, he broke out suddenly, "Say, d' ever tell y' 'bout the ol' man? He never stole that money. Know he di' n'."

812   He threatened to fall asleep now, but the reporter was all alert. He scented a story.

813   "By Jove!" he exclaimed, "did you hear that? Bet the chap stole it himself and's letting the old man suffer for it. Great story, ain't it? Come, come, wake up here. Three more, Jack. What about your father?"

814   "Father? Who's father. Oh, do' bother me. What?"

815   "Here, here, tell us about your father and the money. If he didn't steal it, who did?"

816   "Who did? Tha' 's it, who did? Ol' man di' n' steal it, know he di' n'."

817   "Oh, let him alone, Skaggsy, he don't know what he's saying."

818   "Yes, he does, a drunken man tells the truth."

819   "In some cases," said Sadness.

820   "Oh, let me alone, man. I've been trying for years to get a big sensation for my paper, and if this story is one, I'm a made man."

821   The drink seemed to revive the young man again, and by bits Skaggs was able to pick out of him the story of his father's arrest and conviction. At its close he relapsed into stupidity, murmuring, "She throwed me down."

822   "Well," sneered Sadness, "you see drunken men tell the truth, and you don't seem to get much guilt out of our young friend. You're disappointed, aren't you?"

823   "I confess I am disappointed, but I've got an idea, just the same."

824   "Oh, you have? Well, don't handle it carelessly; it might go off." And Sadness rose. The reporter sat thinking for a time and then followed him, leaving Joe in a drunken sleep at the table. There he lay for more than two hours. When he finally awoke, he started up as if some determination had come to him in his sleep. A part of the helplessness of his intoxication had gone, but his first act was to call for more whiskey. This he gulped down, and followed with another and another. For a while he stood still, brooding silently, his red eyes blinking at the light. Then he turned abruptly and left the club.

825   It was very late when he reached Hattie's door, but he opened it with his latch-key, as he had been used to do. He stopped to help himself to a glass of brandy, as he had so often done before. Then he went directly to her room. She was a light sleeper, and his step awakened her.

826   "Who is it?" she cried in affright.

827   "It's me." His voice was steadier now, but grim.

828   "What do you want? Didn't I tell you never to come here again? Get out or I'll have you taken out."

829   She sprang up in bed, glaring angrily at him.

830   His hands twitched nervously, as if her will were conquering him and he were uneasy, but he held her eye with his own.

831   "You put me out to-night," he said.

832   "Yes, and I'm going to do it again. You're drunk."

833   She started to rise, but he took a step towards her and she paused. He looked as she had never seen him look before. His face was ashen

and his eyes like fire and blood. She quailed beneath the look. He took another step towards her.

834 "You put me out to-night," he repeated, "like a dog."

835 His step was steady and his tone was clear, menacingly clear. She shrank back from him, back to the wall. Still his hands twitched and his eye held her. Still he crept slowly towards her, his lips working and his hands moving convulsively.

836 "Joe, Joe!" she said hoarsely, "what's the matter? Oh, don't look at me like that."

837 The gown had fallen away from her breast and showed the convulsive fluttering of her heart.

838 He broke into a laugh, a dry, murderous laugh, and his hands sought each other while the fingers twitched over one another like coiling serpents.

839 "You put me out—you—you, and you made me what I am." The realisation of what he was, of his foulness and degradation, seemed just to have come to him fully. "You made me what I am, and then you sent me away. You let me come back, and now you put me out."

840 She gazed at him fascinated. She tried to scream and she could not. This was not Joe. This was not the boy that she had turned and twisted about her little finger. This was a terrible, terrible man or a monster.

841 He moved a step nearer her. His eyes fell to her throat. For an instant she lost their steady glare and then she found her voice. The scream was checked as it began. His fingers had closed over her throat just where the gown had left it temptingly bare. They gave it the caress of death. She struggled. They held her. Her eyes prayed to his. But his were the fire of hell. She fell back upon her pillow in silence. He had not uttered a word. He held her. Finally he flung her from him like a rag, and sank into a chair. And there the officers found him when Hattie Sterling's disappearance had become a strange thing.

"DEAR, DAMNED, DELIGHTFUL TOWN"

842 When Joe was taken, there was no spirit or feeling left in him. He moved mechanically, as if without sense or volition. The first impression he gave was that of a man over-acting insanity. But this was soon removed by the very indifference with which he met everything concerned with his crime. From the very first he made no effort to exonerate or to vindicate himself. He talked little and only in a dry, stupefied way. He was as one whose soul is dead, and perhaps it was;

for all the little soul of him had been wrapped up in the body of this one woman, and the stroke that took her life had killed him too.

843 The men who examined him were irritated beyond measure. There was nothing for them to exercise their ingenuity upon. He left them nothing to search for. Their most damning question he answered with an apathy that showed absolutely no interest in the matter. It was as if someone whom he did not care about had committed a crime and he had been called to testify. The only thing which he noticed or seemed to have any affection for was a little pet dog which had been hers and which they sometimes allowed to be with him after the life sentence had been passed upon him and when he was awaiting removal. He would sit for hours with the little animal in his lap, caressing it dumbly. There was a mute sorrow in the eyes of both man and dog, and they seemed to take comfort in each other's presence. There was no need of any sign between them. They had both loved her, had they not? So they understood.

844 Sadness saw him and came back to the Banner, torn and unnerved by the sight. "I saw him," he said with a shudder, "and it'll take more whiskey than Jack can give me in a year to wash the memory of him out of me. Why, man, it shocked me all through. It's a pity they didn't send him to the chair. It couldn't have done him much harm and would have been a real mercy."

845 And so Sadness and all the club, with a muttered "Poor devil!" dismissed him. He was gone. Why should they worry? Only one more who had got into the whirlpool, enjoyed the sensation for a moment, and then swept dizzily down. There were, indeed, some who for an earnest hour sermonised about it and said, "Here is another example of the pernicious influence of the city on untrained negroes. Oh, is there no way to keep these people from rushing away from the small villages and country districts of the South up to the cities, where they cannot battle with the terrible force of a strange and unusual environment? Is there no way to prove to them that woollen-shirted, brown-jeaned simplicity is infinitely better than broad-clothed degradation?" They wanted to preach to these people that good agriculture is better than bad art,—that it was better and nobler for them to sing to God across the Southern fields than to dance for rowdies in the Northern halls. They wanted to dare to say that the South has its faults no one condones them—and its disadvantages, but that even what they suffered from these was better than what awaited them in the great alleys of New York. Down there, the bodies were restrained, and they chafed; but here the soul would fester, and they would be content.

846   This was but for an hour, for even while they exclaimed they knew that there was no way, and that the stream of young negro life would continue to flow up from the South, dashing itself against the hard necessities of the city and breaking like waves against a rock,—that, until the gods grew tired of their cruel sport, there must still be sacrifices to false ideals and unreal ambitions.

847   There was one heart, though, that neither dismissed Joe with gratuitous pity nor sermonised about him. The mother heart had only room for grief and pain. Already it had borne its share. It had known sorrow for a lost husband, tears at the neglect and brutality of a new companion, shame for a daughter's sake, and it had seemed already filled to overflowing. And yet the fates had put in this one other burden until it seemed it must burst with the weight of it.

848   To Fannie Hamilton's mind now all her boy's shortcomings became as naught. He was not her wayward, erring, criminal son. She only remembered that he was her son, and wept for him as such. She forgot his curses, while her memory went back to the sweetness of his baby prattle and the soft words of his tenderer youth. Until the last she clung to him, holding him guiltless, and to her thought they took to prison, not Joe Hamilton, a convicted criminal, but Joey, Joey, her boy, her firstborn,—a martyr.

849   The pretty Miss Kitty Hamilton was less deeply impressed. The arrest and subsequent conviction of her brother was quite a blow. She felt the shame of it keenly, and some of the grief. To her, coming as it did just at a time when the company was being strengthened and she more importantly featured than ever, it was decidedly inopportune, for no one could help connecting her name with the affair.

850   For a long time she and her brother had scarcely been upon speaking terms. During Joe's frequent lapses from industry he had been prone to "touch" his sister for the wherewithal to supply his various wants. When, finally, she grew tired and refused to be "touched," he rebuked her for withholding that which, save for his help, she would never have been able to make. This went on until they were almost entirely estranged. He was wont to say that "now his sister was up in the world, she had got the big head," and she to retort that her brother "wanted to use her for a 'soft thing.' "

851   From the time that she went on the stage she had begun to live her own life, a life in which the chief aim was the possession of good clothes and the ability to attract the attention which she had learned to crave. The greatest sign of interest she showed in her brother's affair was, at first, to offer her mother money to secure a lawyer.

But when Joe confessed all, she consoled herself with the reflection that perhaps it was for the best, and kept her money in her pocket with a sense of satisfaction. She was getting to be so very much more Joe's sister. She did not go to see her brother. She was afraid it might make her nervous while she was in the city, and she went on the road with her company before he was taken away.

852 Miss Kitty Hamilton had to be very careful about her nerves and her health. She had had experiences, and her voice was not as good as it used to be, and her beauty had to be aided by cosmetics. So she went away from New York, and only read of all that happened when someone called her attention to it in the papers.

853 Berry Hamilton in his Southern prison knew nothing of all this, for no letters had passed between him and his family for more than two years. The very cruelty of destiny defeated itself in this and was kind.

SKAGGS'S THEORY

854 There was, perhaps, more depth to Mr. Skaggs than most people gave him credit for having. However it may be, when he got an idea into his head, whether it were insane or otherwise, he had a decidedly tenacious way of holding to it. Sadness had been disposed to laugh at him when he announced that Joe's drunken story of his father's troubles had given him an idea. But it was, nevertheless, true, and that idea had stayed with him clear through the exciting events that followed on that fatal night. He thought and dreamed of it until he had made a working theory. Then one day, with a boldness that he seldom assumed when in the sacred Presence, he walked into the office and laid his plans before the editor. They talked together for some time, and the editor seemed hard to convince.

855 "It would be a big thing for the paper," he said, "if it only panned out; but it is such a rattle-brained, harum-scarum thing. No one under the sun would have thought of it but you, Skaggs."

856 "Oh, it's bound to pan out. I see the thing as clear as day. There's no getting around it."

857 "Yes, it looks plausible, but so does all fiction. You're taking a chance. You're losing time. If it fails—"

858 "But if it succeeds?"

859 "Well, go and bring back a story. If you don't, look out. It's against my better judgment anyway. Remember I told you that."

860 Skaggs shot out of the office, and within an hour and a half had boarded a fast train for the South.

861   It is almost a question whether Skaggs had a theory or whether he had told himself a pretty story and, as usual, believed it. The editor was right. No one else would have thought of the wild thing that was in the reporter's mind. The detective had not thought of it five years before, nor had Maurice Oakley and his friends had an inkling, and here was one of the New York *Universe's* young men going miles to prove his idea about something that did not at all concern him.

862   When Skaggs reached the town which had been the home of the Hamiltons, he went at once to the Continental Hotel. He had as yet formulated no plan of immediate action and with a fool's or a genius' belief in his destiny he sat down to await the turn of events. His first move would be to get acquainted with some of his neighbours. This was no difficult matter, as the bar of the Continental was still the gathering-place of some of the city's choice spirits of the old régime. Thither he went, and his convivial cheerfulness soon placed him on terms of equality with many of his kind.

863   He insinuated that he was looking around for business prospects. This proved his open-sesame. Five years had not changed the Continental frequenters much, and Skaggs's intention immediately brought Beachfield Davis down upon him with the remark, "If a man wants to go into business, business for a gentleman, suh, Gad, there's no finer or better paying business in the world than breeding blooded dogs—that is, if you get a man of experience to go in with you."

864   "Dogs, dogs," drivelled old Horace Talbot, "Beachfield's always talking about dogs. I remember the night we were all discussing that Hamilton nigger's arrest, Beachfield said it was a sign of total depravity because his man hunted 'possums with his hound." The old man laughed inanely. The hotel whiskey was getting on his nerves.

865   The reporter opened his eyes and his ears. He had stumbled upon something, at any rate.

866   "What was it about some nigger's arrest, sir?" he asked respectfully.

867   "Oh, it wasn't anything much. Only an old and trusted servant robbed his master, and my theory—"

868   "But you will remember, Mr. Talbot," broke in Davis, "that I proved your theory to be wrong and cited a conclusive instance."

869   "Yes, a 'possum-hunting dog."

870   "I am really anxious to hear about the robbery, though. It seems such an unusual thing for a negro to steal a great amount."

871   "Just so, and that was part of my theory. Now—"

872   "It's an old story and a long one, Mr. Skaggs, and one of merely local repute," interjected Colonel Saunders. "I don't think it could possibly interest you, who are familiar with the records of the really great crimes that take place in a city such as New York."

873   "Those things do interest me very much, though. I am something of a psychologist, and I often find the smallest and most insignificant-appearing details pregnant with suggestion. Won't you let me hear the story, Colonel?"

874   "Why, yes, though there's little in it save that I am one of the few men who have come to believe that the negro, Berry Hamilton, is not the guilty party."

875   "Nonsense! nonsense!" said Talbot; "of course Berry was guilty, but, as I said before, I don't blame him. The negroes—"

876   "Total depravity," said Davis. "Now look at my dog—"

877   "If you will retire with me to the further table I will give you whatever of the facts I can call to mind."

878   As unobtrusively as they could, they drew apart from the others and seated themselves at a more secluded table, leaving Talbot and Davis wrangling, as of old, over their theories. When the glasses were filled and the pipes going, the Colonel began his story, interlarding it frequently with comments of his own.

879   "Now, in the first place, Mr. Skaggs," he said when the tale was done, "I am lawyer enough to see for myself how weak the evidence was upon which the negro was convicted, and later events have done much to confirm me in the opinion that he was innocent."

880   "Later events?"

881   "Yes." The Colonel leaned across the table and his voice fell to a whisper. "Four years ago a great change took place in Maurice Oakley. It happened in the space of a day, and no one knows the cause of it. From a social, companionable man, he became a recluse, shunning visitors and dreading society. From an open-hearted, unsuspicious neighbour, he became secretive and distrustful of his own friends. From an active business man, he has become a retired brooder. He sees no one if he can help it. He writes no letters and receives none, not even from his brother, it is said. And all of this came about in the space of twenty-four hours."

882   "But what was the beginning of it?"

883   "No one knows, save that one day he had some sort of nervous attack. By the time the doctor was called he was better, but he kept clutching his hand over his heart. Naturally, the physician wanted to examine him there, but the very suggestion of it seemed to throw him

into a frenzy; and his wife too begged the doctor, an old friend of the family, to desist. Maurice Oakley had been as sound as a dollar, and no one of the family had had any tendency to heart affection."

884   "It is strange."

885   "Strange it is, but I have my theory."

886   "His actions are like those of a man guarding a secret."

887   "Sh! His negro laundress says that there is an inside pocket in his undershirts."

888   "An inside pocket?"

889   "Yes."

890   "And for what?" Skaggs was trembling with eagerness.

891   The Colonel dropped his voice lower.

892   "We can only speculate," he said; "but, as I have said, I have my theory. Oakley was a just man, and in punishing his old servant for the supposed robbery it is plain that he acted from principle. But he is also a proud man and would hate to confess that he had been in the wrong. So I believed that the cause of his first shock was the finding of the money that he supposed gone. Unwilling to admit this error, he lets the misapprehension go on, and it is the money which he carries in his secret pocket, with a morbid fear of its discovery, that has made him dismiss his servants, leave his business, and refuse to see his friends."

893   "A very natural conclusion, Colonel, and I must say that I believe you. It is strange that others have not seen as you have seen and brought the matter to light."

894   "Well, you see, Mr. Skaggs, none are so dull as the people who think they think. I can safely say that there is not another man in this town who has lighted upon the real solution of this matter, though it has been openly talked of for so long. But as for bringing it to light, no one would think of doing that. It would be sure to hurt Oakley's feelings, and he is of one of our best families."

895   "Ah, yes, perfectly right."

896   Skaggs had got all that he wanted; much more, in fact, than he had expected. The Colonel held him for a while yet to enlarge upon the views that he had expressed.

897   When the reporter finally left him, it was with a cheery "Good-night, Colonel. If I were a criminal, I should be afraid of that analytical mind of yours!"

898   He went upstairs chuckling. "The old fool!" he cried as he flung himself into a chair. "I've got it! I've got it! Maurice Oakley must see me, and then what?" He sat down to think out what he should do

tomorrow. Again, with his fine disregard of ways and means, he determined to trust to luck, and as he expressed it, "brace old Oakley."

899 Accordingly he went about nine o'clock the next morning to Oakley's house. A gray-haired, sad-eyed woman inquired his errand.

900 "I want to see Mr. Oakley," he said.

901 "You cannot see him. Mr. Oakley is not well and does not see visitors."

902 "But I must see him, madam; I am here upon business of importance."

903 "You can tell me just as well as him. I am his wife and transact all of his business."

904 "I can tell no one but the master of the house himself."

905 "You cannot see him. It is against his orders."

906 "Very well," replied Skaggs, descending one step; "it is his loss, not mine. I have tried to do my duty and failed. Simply tell him that I came from Paris."

907 "Paris?" cried a queruious voice behind the woman's back. "Leslie, why do you keep the gentleman at the door? Let him come in at once."

908 Mrs. Oakley stepped from the door and Skaggs went in. Had he seen Oakley before he would have been shocked at the change in his appearance; but as it was, the nervous, white-haired man who stood shiftily before him told him nothing of an eating secret long carried. The man's face was gray and haggard, and deep lines were cut under his staring, fish-like eyes. His hair tumbled in white masses over his pallid forehead, and his lips twitched as he talked.

909 "You're from Paris, sir, from Paris?" he said. "Come in, come in."

910 His motions were nervous and erratic. Skaggs followed him into the library, and the wife disappeared in another direction.

911 It would have been hard to recognize in the Oakley of the present the man of a few years before. The strong frame had gone away to bone, and nothing of his old power sat on either brow or chin. He was as a man who trembled on the brink of insanity. His guilty secret had been too much for him, and Skaggs's own fingers twitched as he saw his host's hands seek the breast of his jacket every other moment.

912 "It is there the secret is hidden," he said to himself, "and whatever it is, I must have it. But how—how? I can't knock the man down and rob him in his own house." But Oakley himself proceeded to give him his first cue.

913 "You—you—perhaps have a message from my brother—my brother who is in Paris. I have not heard from him for some time."

914   Skaggs's mind worked quickly. He remembered the Colonel's story. Evidently the brother had something to do with the secret. "Now or never," he thought. So he said boldly, "Yes, I have a message from your brother."

915   The man sprung up, clutching again at his breast. "You have? you have? Give it to me. After four years he sends me a message! Give it to me!"

916   The reporter looked steadily at the man. He knew that he was in his power, that his very eagerness would prove traitor to his discretion.

917   "Your brother bade me to say to you that you have a terrible secret, that you bear it in your breast—there—there. I am his messenger. He bids you to give it to me."

918   Oakley had shrunken back as if he had been struck.

919   "No, no!" he gasped, "no, no! I have no secret."

920   The reporter moved nearer him. The old man shrunk against the wall, his lips working convulsively and his hand tearing at his breast as Skaggs drew nearer. He attempted to shriek, but his voice was husky and broke off in a gasping whisper.

921   "Give it to me, as your brother commands."

922   "No, no, no! It is not his secret; it is mine. I must carry it here always, do you hear? I must carry it till I die. Go away! Go away!"

923   Skaggs seized him. Oakley struggled weakly, but he had no strength. The reporter's hand sought the secret pocket. He felt a paper beneath his fingers. Oakley gasped hoarsely as he drew it forth. Then raising his voice gave one agonized cry, and sank to the floor frothing at the mouth. At the cry rapid foot-steps were heard in the hallway, and Mrs. Oakley threw open the door.

924   "What is the matter?" she cried.

925   "My message has somewhat upset your husband," was the cool answer.

926   "But his breast is open. Your hand has been in his bosom. You have taken something from him. Give it to me, or I shall call for help."

927   Skaggs had not reckoned on this, but his wits came to the rescue.

928   "You dare not call for help," he said, "or the world will know!"

929   She wrung her hands helplessly, crying, "Oh, give it to me, give it to me. We've never done you any harm."

930   "But you've harmed someone else; that is enough."

931   He moved towards the door, but she sprang in front of him with the fierceness of a tigress protecting her young. She attacked him with teeth and nails. She was pallid with fury, and it was all he could do to protect himself and yet not injure her. Finally, when her anger had taken

her strength, he succeeded in getting out. He flew down the hallway and out of the front door, the woman's screams following him. He did not pause to read the precious letter until he was safe in his room at the Continental Hotel. Then he sprang to his feet, crying, "Thank God! thank God! I was right, and the *Universe* shall have a sensation. The brother is the thief, and Berry Hamilton is an innocent man. Hurrah! Now, who is it that has come on a wild-goose chase? Who is it that ought to handle his idea carefully? Heigho, Saunders my man, the drinks'll be on you, and old Skaggsy will have done some good in the world."

A YELLOW JOURNAL

932 Mr. Skaggs had no qualms of conscience about the manner in which he had come by the damaging evidence against Maurice Oakley. It was enough for him that he had it. A corporation, he argued, had no soul, and therefore no conscience. How much less, then, should so small a part of a great corporation as himself be expected to have them?

933   He had his story. It was vivid, interesting, dramatic. It meant the favour of his editor, a big thing for the *Universe*, and a fatter lining for his own pocket. He sat down to put his discovery on paper before he attempted anything else, although the impulse to celebrate was very strong within him.

934   He told his story well, with an eye to every one of its salient points. He sent an alleged picture of Berry Hamilton as he had appeared at the time of his arrest. He sent a picture of the Oakley home and of the cottage where the servant and his family had been so happy. There was a strong pen-picture of the man, Oakley, grown haggard and morose from carrying his guilty secret, of his confusion when confronted with the supposed knowledge of it. The old Southern city was described, and the opinions of its residents in regard to the case given. It was there—clear, interesting, and strong. One could see it all as if every phase of it were being enacted before one's eyes. Skaggs surpassed himself.

935   When the editor first got hold of it he said "Huh!" over the opening lines,—a few short sentences that instantly pricked the attention awake. He read on with increasing interest. "This is good stuff," he said at the last page. "Here's a chance for the *Universe* to look into the methods of Southern court proceedings. Here's a chance for a spread."

936   The *Universe* had always claimed to be the friend of all poor and oppressed humanity, and every once in a while it did something to

substantiate its claim, whereupon it stood off and said to the public, "Look you what we have done, and behold how great we are, the friend of the people!" The *Universe* was yellow. It was very so. But it had power and keenness and energy. It never lost an opportunity to crow, and if one was not forthcoming, it made one. In this way it managed to do a considerable amount of good, and its yellowness became forgivable, even commendable. In Skaggs's story the editor saw an opportunity for one of its periodical philanthropies. He seized upon it. With headlines that took half a page, and with cuts authentic and otherwise, the tale was told, and the people of New York were greeted next morning with the announcement of—

"A Burning Shame!
A Poor and Innocent Negro
made to Suffer
For a Rich Man's Crime!
Great Expose by the 'Universe'!
A 'Universe' Reporter to the Rescue!
The Whole Thing to be Aired that the
People May Know!"

937   Then Skaggs received a telegram that made him leap for joy. He was to do it. He was to go to the capital of the State. He was to beard the Governor in his den, and he, with the force of a great paper behind him, was to demand for the people the release of an innocent man. Then there would be another write-up and much glory for him and more shekels. In an hour after he had received his telegram he was on his way to the Southern capital.

938   Meanwhile in the house of Maurice Oakley there were sad times. From the moment that the master of the house had fallen to the floor in impotent fear and madness there had been no peace within his doors. At first his wife had tried to control him alone, and had humoured the wild babblings with which he woke from his swoon. But these changed to shrieks and cries and curses, and she was forced to throw open the doors so long closed and call in help. The neighbours and her old friends went to her assistance, and what the reporter's story had not done, the ravings of the man accomplished; for, with a show of matchless cunning, he continually clutched at his breast, laughed, and babbled his secret openly. Even then they would have smothered it in silence, for the honour of one of their best

families; but too many ears had heard, and then came the yellow journal bearing all the news in emblazoned headlines.

939   Colonel Saunders was distinctly hurt to think that his confidence had been imposed on, and that he had been instrumental in bringing shame upon a Southern name.

940   "To think, suh," he said generally to the usual assembly of choice spirits,—"to think of that man's being a reporter, such a common, ordinary reporter, and that I sat and talked to him as if he were a gentleman!"

941   "You're not to be blamed, Colonel," said old Horace Talbot. "You've done no more than any other gentleman would have done. The trouble is that the average Northerner has no sense of honour, suh, no sense of honour. If this particular man had had, he would have kept still, and everything would have gone on smooth and quiet. Instead of that, a distinguished family is brought to shame, and for what? To give a nigger a few more years of freedom when, likely as not, he don't want it; and Berry Hamilton's life in prison has proved nearer the ideal reached by slavery than anything he has found since emancipation. Why, suhs, I fancy I see him leaving his prison with tears of regret in his eyes."

942   Old Horace was inanely eloquent for an hour over his pet theory. But there were some in the town who thought differently about the matter, and it was their opinions and murmurings that backed up Skaggs and made it easier for him when at the capital he came into contact with the official red tape.

943   He was told that there were certain forms of procedure, and certain times for certain things, but he hammered persistently away, the murmurings behind him grew louder, while from his sanctum the editor of the *Universe* thundered away against oppression and high-handed tyranny. Other papers took it up and asked why this man should be despoiled of his liberty any longer? And when it was replied that the man had been convicted, and that the wheels of justice could not be stopped or turned back by the letter of a romantic artist or the ravings of a madman, there was a mighty outcry against the farce of justice that had been played out in this man's case.

944   The trial was reviewed; the evidence again brought up and examined. The dignity of the State was threatened. At this time the State did the one thing necessary to save its tottering reputation. It would not surrender, but it capitulated, and Berry Hamilton was pardoned.

945   Berry heard the news with surprise and a half-bitter joy. He had long ago lost hope that justice would ever be done to him. He marvelled

at the word that was brought to him now, and he could not understand the strange cordiality of the young white man who met him at the warden's office. Five years of prison life had made a different man of him. He no longer looked to receive kindness from his fellows, and he blinked at it as he blinked at the unwonted brightness of the sun. The lines about his mouth where the smiles used to gather had changed and grown stern with the hopelessness of years. His lips drooped pathetically, and hard treatment had given his eyes a lowering look. His hair, that had hardly shown a white streak, was as white as Maurice Oakley's own. His erstwhile quick wits were dulled and imbruted. He had lived like an ox, working without inspiration or reward, and he came forth like an ox from his stall. All the higher part of him he had left behind, dropping it off day after day through the wearisome years. He had put behind him the Berry Hamilton that laughed and joked and sang and believed, for even his faith had become only a numbed fancy.

946   "This is a very happy occasion, Mr. Hamilton," said Skaggs, shaking his hand heartily.

947   Berry did not answer. What had this slim, glib young man to do with him? What had any white man to do with him after what he had suffered at their hands?

948   "You know you are to go to New York with me?"

949   "To New Yawk? What fu'?"

950   Skaggs did not tell him that, now that the *Universe* had done its work, it demanded the right to crow to its heart's satisfaction. He said only, "You want to see your wife, of course?"

951   Berry had forgotten Fannie, and for the first time his heart thrilled within him at the thought of seeing her again.

952   "I ain't hyeahed f'om my people fu' a long time. I didn't know what had become of 'em. How's Kit an' Joe?"

953   "They're all right," was the reply. Skaggs couldn't tell him, in this the first hour of his freedom. Let him have time to drink the sweetness of that all in. There would be time afterwards to taste all of the bitterness.

954   Once in New York, he found that people wished to see him, some fools, some philanthropists, and a great many reporters. He had to be photographed—all this before he could seek those whom he longed to see. They printed his picture as he was before he went to prison and as he was now, a sort of before-and-after-taking comment, and in the morning that it all appeared, when the *Universe* spread itself to tell

the public what it had done and how it had done it, they gave him his wife's address.

955   It would be better, they thought, for her to tell him herself all that happened. No one of them was brave enough to stand to look in his eyes when he asked for his son and daughter, and they shifted their responsibility by pretending to themselves that they were doing it for his own good: that the blow would fall more gently upon him coming from her who had been his wife. Berry took the address and inquired his way timidly, hesitatingly, but with a swelling heart, to the door of the flat where Fannie lived.

WHAT BERRY FOUND

956   Had not Berry's years of prison life made him forget what little he knew of reading, he might have read the name Gibson on the door-plate where they told him to ring for his wife. But he knew nothing of what awaited him as he confidently pulled the bell. Fannie herself came to the door. The news the papers held had not escaped her, but she had suffered in silence, hoping that Berry might be spared the pain of finding her. Now he stood before her, and she knew him at a glance, in spite of his haggard countenance.

957   "Fannie," he said, holding out his arms to her, and all of the pain and pathos of long yearning was in his voice, "don't you know me?"

958   She shrank away from him, back in the hall-way.

959   "Yes, yes, Be'y, I knows you. Come in."

960   She led him through the passage-way and into her room, he following with a sudden sinking at his heart. This was not the reception he had expected from Fannie.

961   When they were within the room he turned and held out his arms to her again, but she did not notice them. "Why, is you 'shamed o' me?" he asked brokenly.

962   "'Shamed? No! Oh, Be'y," and she sank into a chair and began rocking to and fro in her helpless grief.

963   "What's de mattah, Fannie? Ain't you glad to see me?"

964   "Yes, yes, but you don't know nothin', do you? Dey lef' me to tell you?"

965   "Lef' you to tell me? What's de mattah? Is Joe or Kit daid? Tell me."

966   "No, not daid. Kit dances on de stage fu' a livin', an', Be'y, she ain't de gal she ust to be. Joe—Joe—Joe—he's in pen'tentiary fu' killin' a ooman."

967   Berry started forward with a cry, "My Gawd! my Gawd! my little gal! my boy!"

968   "Dat ain't all," she went on dully, as if reciting a rote lesson; "I ain't yo' wife no mo'. I's ma'ied ag'in. Oh Be'y, Be'y, don't look at me lak dat. I couldn't he'p it. Kit an' Joe lef' me, an' dey said de pen'tentiary divo'ced you an' me, an' dat you'd nevah come out nohow. Don't look at me lak dat, Be'y."

969   "You ain't my wife no mo'? Hit's a lie, a damn lie! You is my wife. I's a innocent man. No pen'tentiary kin tek you erway f'om me. Hit's enough what dey've done to my chillen." He rushed forward and seized her by the arm. "Dey sha'n't do no mo', by Gawd! dey sha'n't, I say!" His voice had risen to a fierce roar, like that of a hurt beast, and he shook her by the arm as he spoke.

970   "Oh, don't, Be'y, don't, you hu't me. I couldn't he'p it."

971   He glared at her for a moment, and then the real force of the situation came full upon him, and he bowed his head in his hands and wept like a child. The great sobs came up and stuck in his throat.

972   She crept up to him fearfully and laid her hand on his head.

973   "Don't cry, Be'y," she said; "I done wrong, but I loves you yit."

974   He seized her in his arms and held her tightly until he could control himself. Then he asked weakly, "Well, what am I goin' to do?"

975   "I do' know, Be'y, 'ceptin' dat you'll have to leave me."

976   "I won't! I'll never leave you again," he replied doggedly.

977   "But, Be'y, you mus'. You'll only mek it ha'der on me, an' Gibson'll beat me ag'in."

978   "Ag'in!"

979   She hung her head: "Yes."

980   He gripped himself hard.

981   "Why cain't you come on off wid me, Fannie? You was mine fus'."

982   "I couldn't. He would fin' me anywhaih I went to."

983   "Let him fin' you. You'll be wid me, an' we'll settle it, him an' me."

984   "I want to, but oh, I can't, I can't," she wailed. "Please go now, Be'y, befo' he gits home. He's mad anyhow, 'cause you're out."

985   Berry looked at her hard, and then said in a dry voice, "An' so I got to go an' leave you to him?"

986   "Yes, you mus'; I'm his'n now."

987   He turned to the door, murmuring, "My wife gone, Kit a nobody, an' Joe, little Joe, a murderer, an' then I—I—ust to pray to Gawd an' call him 'Ouah Fathah.' " He laughed hoarsely. It sounded like nothing Fannie had ever heard before.

988   "Don't, Be'y, don't say dat. Maybe we don't un'erstan'."

989 Her faith still hung by a slender thread, but his had given way in that moment.

990 "No, we don't un'erstan'," he laughed as he went out of the door. "We don't un'erstan'."

991 He staggered down the steps, blinded by his emotions, and set his face towards the little lodging that he had taken temporarily. There seemed nothing left in life for him to do. Yet he knew that he must work to live, although the effort seemed hardly worth while. He remembered now that the *Universe* had offered him the under janitorship in its building. He would go and take it, and some day, perhaps—He was not quite sure what the "perhaps" meant. But as his mind grew clearer he came to know, for a sullen, fierce anger was smoldering in his heart against the man who through lies had stolen his wife from him. It was anger that came slowly, but gained in fierceness as it grew.

992 Yes, that was it, he would kill Gibson. It was no worse than his present state. Then it would be father and son murderers. They would hang him or send him back to prison. Neither would be hard now. He laughed to himself.

993 And this was what they had let him out of prison for? To find out all this. Why had they not left him there to die in ignorance? What had he to do with all these people who gave him sympathy? What did he want of their sympathy? Could they give him back one tithe of what he had lost? Could they restore to him his wife or his son or his daughter, his quiet happiness or his simple faith?

994 He went to work for the *Universe*, but night after night, armed, he patrolled the sidewalk in front of Fannie's house. He did not know Gibson, but he wanted to see them together. Then he would strike. His vigils kept him from his bed, but he went to the next morning's work with no weariness. The hope of revenge sustained him, and he took a savage joy in the thought that he should be the dispenser of justice to at least one of those who had wounded him.

995 Finally he grew impatient and determined to wait no longer, but to seek his enemy in his own house. He approached the place cautiously and went up the steps. His hand touched the bell-pull. He staggered back.

996 "Oh, my Gawd!" he said.

997 There was crape on Fannie's bell. His head went round and he held to the door for support. Then he turned the knob and the door opened. He went noiselessly in. At the door of Fannie's room he halted, sick with fear. He knocked, a step sounded within, and his wife's face looked out upon him. He could have screamed aloud with relief.

998   "It ain't you!" he whispered huskily.

999   "No, it's him. He was killed in a fight at the race-track. Some o' his friends are settin' up. Come in."

1000   He went in, a wild, strange feeling surging at his heart. She showed him into the death-chamber.

1001   As he stood and looked down upon the face of his enemy, still, cold, and terrible in death, the recognition of how near he had come to crime swept over him, and all his dead faith sprang into new life in a glorious resurrection. He stood with clasped hands, and no word passed his lips. But his heart was crying, "Thank God! thank God! this man's blood is not on my hands."

1002   The gamblers who were sitting up with the dead wondered who the old fool was who looked at their silent comrade and then raised his eyes as if in prayer.

1003   When Gibson was laid away, there were no formalities between Berry and his wife; they simply went back to each other. New York held nothing for them now but sad memories. Kit was on the road, and the father could not bear to see his son; so they turned their faces southward, back to the only place they could call home. Surely the people could not be cruel to them now, and even if they were, they felt that after what they had endured no wound had power to give them pain.

1004   Leslie Oakley heard of their coming, and with her own hands reopened and refurnished the little cottage in the yard for them. There the white-haired woman begged them to spend the rest of their days and be in peace and comfort. It was the only amend she could make. As much to satisfy her as to settle themselves, they took the cottage, and many a night thereafter they sat together with clasped hands listening to the shrieks of the madman across the yard and thinking of what he had brought to them and to himself.

1005   It was not a happy life, but it was all that was left to them, and they took it up without complaint, for they knew they were powerless against some Will infinitely stronger than their own.

Ma Rainey

(1886–1939)

For biographical information on Ma Rainey see page 463 (Chapter Five). Ma Rainey's performance of "Traveling Blues," reprinted below, allowed the audience to feel the power of travel as a means to increased freedom. It was also one of Ma Rainey's favorite songs.

Traveling Blues

(Composer unknown)

Train's at the station, I heard the whistle blow
The train's at the station, I heard the whistle blow
I done bought my ticket and I don't know where I'll go

I went to the depot, looked up and down the board
5 I went to the depot, looked up and down the board
I asked the ticket agent, "Is my town on this road?"

The ticket agent said, "Woman, don't sit and cry."
The ticket agent said, "Woman, don't you sit and cry."
The train blows at this station, but she keeps on passing by.

10 I hear my daddy calling some other woman's name
I hear my daddy calling some other woman's name
I know he don't need me, but I'm gonna answer just the same

I'm dangerous and blue, can't stay here no more
I'm dangerous and blue, can't stay here no more
15 Here come my train, folk, and I've got to go.

Bessie Smith

(1894–1937)

For biographical information on Bessie Smith see page 456.

Clara Smith

(1894–1935)

Born in Spartanburg, South Carolina, in 1894, Clara Smith began singing professionally throughout the South while she was still a teenager. By 1923, she was singing in Harlem clubs, and she later opened her own theatrical club, which was very successful. Smith, who worked with famous jazz musicians, including Louis Armstrong, is known for her low-down interpretations of the blues. During the 1920s, she was regarded as the chief musical rival of Bessie Smith (no relation), and this tension was manifest in some of the duets the women performed, most notably "My Man Blues." The rivals, both Southerners, joined forces to record "Far Away Blues," one of Bessie Smith's least successful recordings.

Far Away Blues

We left our southern home and wandered north to roam
Like birds, went seekin' a brand new field of corn
We don't know why we are here
But we're up here just the same
5 And we are just the lonesomest girls that's ever been born

Some of these days we are going far away
Some of these days we are going far away
Where we have got a lots of friends and don't have no roof rent to pay

Oh, there'll come a day when from us you'll hear no news
10 Oh, there'll come a day when from us you'll hear no news
The you will know that we have died from those lonesome far
away blues.

Alain Locke

(1886–1954)

Alain Locke, known as the architect of the Harlem Renaissance, was born on September 13, 1886, in Philadelphia, to schoolteachers Pliny Ishmael Locke and Mary Hawkins Locke, and he enjoyed an upper-middle-class life. After graduating with an undergraduate degree in philosophy from Harvard, he became the first African American Rhodes scholar (1907), attending Oxford University and the University of Berlin, and he received his PhD from Harvard in 1918. Locke, who was a professor at Howard University for more than 40 years, is best known for his edited collection, The New Negro *(1925), the title essay of which is reprinted below. This famous anthology grew out of the March 1925 issue of* Survey Graphic *magazine. At the time of its publication,* The New Negro *was hailed for charting the artistic, political, and philosophical dimensions of the New Negro movement. Locke is remembered as one of the most important intellectuals of the twentieth century.*

The New Negro

1   In the last decade something beyond the watch and guard of statistics has happened in the life of the American Negro and the three norns who have traditionally presided over the Negro problem have a changeling in their laps. The Sociologist, the Philanthropist, the Race-leader are not unaware of the New Negro, but they are at a loss to account for him. He simply cannot be swathed in their formulæ. For the younger generation is vibrant with a new psychology; the new spirit is awake in the masses, and under the very eyes of the professional observers is transforming what has been a perennial problem into the progressive phases of contemporary Negro life.

2   Could such a metamorphosis have taken place as suddenly as it has appeared to? The answer is no; not because the New Negro is not here, but because the Old Negro had long become more of a myth than a man. The Old Negro, we must remember, was a creature of moral debate and historical controversy. His has been a stock figure perpetuated as an historical fiction partly in innocent sentimentalism, partly in deliberate reactionism. The Negro himself has contributed his share to this through a sort of protective social mimicry forced upon him by the adverse circumstances of dependence. So for generations in the mind of America, the Negro has been more of a formula than a human being—a something to be argued about, condemned or defended, to be "kept down," or "in his place," or "helped up," to be worried with or worried over, harassed or patronized, a social bogey or a social burden. The thinking Negro even has been induced to share this same general attitude, to focus his attention on controversial issues, to see himself in the distorted perspective of a social problem. His shadow, so to speak, has been more real to him than his personality. Through having had to appeal from the unjust stereotypes of his oppressors and traducers to those of his liberators, friends and benefactors he has had to subscribe to the traditional positions from which his case has been viewed. Little true social or self-understanding has or could come from such a situation.

3   But while the minds of most of us, black and white, have thus burrowed in the trenches of the Civil War and Reconstruction, the actual march of development has simply flanked these positions, necessitating a sudden reorientation of view. We have not been watching

in the right direction; set North and South on a sectional axis, we have not noticed the East till the sun has us blinking.

4   Recall how suddenly the Negro spirituals revealed themselves; suppressed for generations under the stereotypes of Wesleyan hymn harmony, secretive, half-ashamed, until the courage of being natural brought them out—and behold, there was folk-music. Similarly the mind of the Negro seems suddenly to have slipped from under the tyranny of social intimidation and to be shaking off the psychology of imitation and implied inferiority. By shedding the old chrysalis of the Negro problem we are achieving something like a spiritual emancipation. Until recently, lacking self-understanding, we have been almost as much of a problem to ourselves as we still are to others. But the decade that found us with a problem has left us with only a task. The multitude perhaps feels as yet only a strange relief and a new vague urge, but the thinking few know that in the reaction the vital inner grip of prejudice has been broken.

5   With this renewed self-respect and self-dependence, the life of the Negro community is bound to enter a new dynamic phase, the buoyancy from within compensating for whatever pressure there may be of conditions from without. The migrant masses, shifting from countryside to city, hurdle several generations of experience at a leap, but more important, the same thing happens spiritually in the life-attitudes and self-expression of the Young Negro, in his poetry, his art, his education and his new outlook, with the additional advantage, of course, of the poise and greater certainty of knowing what it is all about. From this comes the promise and warrant of a new leadership. As one of them has discerningly put it:

> *We have tomorrow*
> *Bright before us*
> *Like a flame.*
>
> *Yesterday, a night-gone thing*
> *A sun-down name.*
>
> *And dawn today*
> *Broad arch above the road we came.*
> *We march!*

6   This is what, even more than any "most creditable record of fifty years of freedom," requires that the Negro of to-day be seen through other than the dusty spectacles of past controversy. The day of

"aunties," "uncles" and "mammies" is equally gone. Uncle Tom and Sambo have passed on, and even the "Colonel" and "George" play barnstorm rôles from which they escape with relief when the public spotlight is off. The popular melodrama has about played itself out, and it is time to scrap the fictions, garret the bogeys and settle down to a realistic facing of facts.

7   First we must observe some of the changes which since the traditional lines of opinion were drawn have rendered these quite obsolete. A main change has been, of course, that shifting of the Negro population which has made the Negro problem no longer exclusively or even predominantly Southern. Why should our minds remain sectionalized, when the problem itself no longer is? Then the trend of migration has not only been toward the North and the Central Midwest, but city-ward and to the great centers of industry—the problems of adjustment are new, practical, local and not peculiarly racial. Rather they are an integral part of the large industrial and social problems of our present-day democracy. And finally, with the Negro rapidly in process of class differentiation, if it ever was warrantable to regard and treat the Negro *en masse* it is becoming with every day less possible, more unjust and more ridiculous.

8   In the very process of being transplanted, the Negro is becoming transformed.

9   The tide of Negro migration, northward and city-ward, is not to be fully explained as a blind flood started by the demands of war industry coupled with the shutting off of foreign migration, or by the pressure of poor crops coupled with increased social terrorism in certain sections of the South and Southwest. Neither labor demand, the boll-weevil nor the Ku Klux Klan is a basic factor, however contributory any or all of them may have been. The wash and rush of this human tide on the beach line of the northern city centers is to be explained primarily in terms of a new vision of opportunity, of social and economic freedom, of a spirit to seize, even in the face of an extortionate and heavy toll, a chance for the improvement of conditions. With each successive wave of it, the movement of the Negro becomes more and more a mass movement toward the larger and the more democratic chance—in the Negro's case a deliberate flight not only from countryside to city, but from medieval America to modern.

10   Take Harlem as an instance of this. Here in Manhattan is not merely the largest Negro community in the world, but the first concentration in history of so many diverse elements of Negro life. It has attracted the African, the West Indian, the Negro American; has

brought together the Negro of the North and the Negro of the South; the man from the city and the man from the town and village; the peasant, the student, the business man, the professional man, artist, poet, musician, adventurer and worker, preacher and criminal, exploiter and social outcast. Each group has come with its own separate motives and for its own special ends, but their greatest experience has been the finding of one another. Proscription and prejudice have thrown these dissimilar elements into a common area of contact and interaction. Within this area, race sympathy and unity have determined a further fusing of sentiment and experience. So what began in terms of segregation becomes more and more, as its elements mix and react, the laboratory of a great race-welding. Hitherto, it must be admitted that American Negroes have been a race more in name than in fact, or to be exact, more in sentiment than in experience. The chief bond between them has been that of a common condition rather than a common consciousness; a problem in common rather than a life in common. In Harlem, Negro life is seizing upon its first chances for group expression and self-determination. It is— or promises at least to be—a race capital. That is why our comparison is taken with those nascent centers of folk-expression and self-determination which are playing a creative part in the world today. Without pretense to their political significance, Harlem has the same rôle to play for the New Negro as Dublin has had for the New Ireland or Prague for the New Czechoslovakia.

11   Harlem, I grant you, isn't typical—but it is significant, it is prophetic. No sane observer, however sympathetic to the new trend, would contend that the great masses are articulate as yet, but they stir, they move, they are more than physically restless. The challenge of the new intellectuals among them is clear enough—the "race radicals" and realists who have broken with the old epoch of philanthropic guidance, sentimental appeal and protest. But are we after all only reading into the stirrings of a sleeping giant the dreams of an agitator? The answer is in the migrating peasant. It is the "man farthest down" who is most active in getting up. One of the most characteristic symptoms of this is the professional man, himself migrating to recapture his constituency after a vain effort to maintain in some Southern corner what for years back seemed an established living and clientele. The clergyman following his errant flock, the physician or lawyer trailing his clients, supply the true clues. In a real sense it is the rank and file who are leading, and the leaders who are following. A transformed and transforming psychology permeates the masses.

12   When the racial leaders of twenty years ago spoke of developing race-pride and stimulating race-consciousness, and of the desirability of race solidarity, they could not in any accurate degree have anticipated the abrupt feeling that has surged up and now pervades the awakened centers. Some of the recognized Negro leaders and a powerful section of white opinion identified with "race work" of the older order have indeed attempted to discount this feeling as a "passing phase," an attack of "race nerves" so to speak, an "aftermath of the war," and the like. It has not abated, however, if we are to gauge by the present tone and temper of the Negro press, or by the shift in popular support from the officially recognized and orthodox spokesmen to those of the independent, popular, and often radical type who are unmistakable symptoms of a new order. It is a social disservice to blunt the fact that the Negro of the Northern centers has reached a stage where tutelage, even of the most interested and well-intentioned sort, must give place to new relationships, where positive self-direction must be reckoned with in ever increasing measure. The American mind must reckon with a fundamentally changed Negro.

13   The Negro too, for his part, has idols of the tribe to smash. If on the one hand the white man has erred in making the Negro appear to be that which would excuse or extenuate his treatment of him, the Negro, in turn, has too often unnecessarily excused himself because of the way he has been treated. The intelligent Negro of to-day is resolved not to make discrimination an extenuation for his shortcomings in performance, individual or collective; he is trying to hold himself at par, neither inflated by sentimental allowances nor depreciated by current social discounts. For this he must know himself and be known for precisely what he is, and for that reason he welcomes the new scientific rather than the old sentimental interest. Sentimental interest in the Negro has ebbed. We used to lament this as the falling off of our friends; now we rejoice and pray to be delivered both from self-pity and condescension. The mind of each racial group has had a bitter weaning, apathy or hatred on one side matching disillusionment or resentment on the other; but they face each other to-day with the possibility at least of entirely new mutual attitudes.

14   It does not follow that if the Negro were better known, he would be better liked or better treated. But mutual understanding is basic for any subsequent coöperation and adjustment. The effort toward this will at least have the effect of remedying in large part what has been the most unsatisfactory feature of our present stage of race relationships in America, namely the fact that the more intelligent and

representative elements of the two race groups have at so many points got quite out of vital touch with one another.

15   The fiction is that the life of the races is separate, and increasingly so. The fact is that they have touched too closely at the unfavorable and too lightly at the favorable levels.

16   While inter-racial councils have sprung up in the South, drawing on forward elements of both races, in the Northern cities manual laborers may brush elbows in their everyday work, but the community and business leaders have experienced no such interplay or far too little of it. These segments must achieve contact or the race situation in America becomes desperate. Fortunately this is happening. There is a growing realization that in social effort the co-operative basis must supplant long-distance philanthropy, and that the only safeguard for mass relations in the future must be provided in the carefully maintained contacts of the enlightened minorities of both race groups. In the intellectual realm a renewed and keen curiosity is replacing the recent apathy; the Negro is being carefully studied, not just talked about and discussed. In art and letters, instead of being wholly caricatured, he is being seriously portrayed and painted.

17   To all of this the New Negro is keenly responsive as an augury of a new democracy in American culture. He is contributing his share to the new social understanding. But the desire to be understood would never in itself have been sufficient to have opened so completely the protectively closed portals of the thinking Negro's mind. There is still too much possibility of being snubbed or patronized for that. It was rather the necessity for fuller, truer self-expression, the realization of the unwisdom of allowing social discrimination to segregate him mentally, and a counter-attitude to cramp and fetter his own living—and so the "spite-wall" that the intellectuals built over the "color-line" has happily been taken down. Much of this reopening of intellectual contacts has centered in New York and has been richly fruitful not merely in the enlarging of personal experience, but in the definite enrichment of American art and letters and in the clarifying of our common vision of the social tasks ahead.

18   The particular significance in the re-establishment of contact between the more advanced and representative classes is that it promises to offset some of the unfavorable reactions of the past, or at least to re-surface race contacts somewhat for the future. Subtly the conditions that are molding a New Negro are molding a new American attitude.

19   However, this new phase of things is delicate; it will call for less charity but more justice; less help, but infinitely closer understanding. This is indeed a critical stage of race relationships because of the likelihood, if the new temper is not understood, of engendering sharp group antagonism and a second crop of more calculated prejudice. In some quarters, it has already done so. Having weaned the Negro, public opinion cannot continue to paternalize. The Negro today is inevitably moving forward under the control largely of his own objectives. What are these objectives? Those of his outer life are happily already well and finally formulated, for they are none other than the ideals of American institutions and democracy. Those of his inner life are yet in process of formation, for the new psychology at present is more of a consensus of feeling than of opinion, of attitude rather than of program. Still some points seem to have crystallized.

20   Up to the present one may adequately describe the Negro's "inner objectives" as an attempt to repair a damaged group psychology and reshape a warped social perspective. Their realization has required a new mentality for the American Negro. And as it matures we begin to see its effects; at first, negative, iconoclastic, and then positive and constructive. In this new group psychology we note the lapse of sentimental appeal, then the development of a more positive self-respect and self-reliance; the repudiation of social dependence, and then the gradual recovery from hyper-sensitiveness and "touchy" nerves, the repudiation of the double standard of judgment with its special philanthropic allowances and then the sturdier desire for objective and scientific appraisal; and finally the rise from social disillusionment to race pride, from the sense of social debt to the responsibilities of social contribution, and offsetting the necessary working and commonsense acceptance of restricted conditions, the belief in ultimate esteem and recognition. Therefore the Negro to-day wishes to be known for what he is, even in his faults and shortcomings, and scorns a craven and precarious survival at the price of seeming to be what he is not. He resents being spoken of as a social ward or minor, even by his own, and to being regarded a chronic patient for the sociological clinic, the sick man of American Democracy. For the same reasons, he himself is through with those social nostrums and panaceas, the so-called "solutions" of his "problem," with which he and the country have been so liberally dosed in the past. Religion, freedom, education, money—in turn, he has ardently hoped for and peculiarly trusted these things; he still believes in them, but not in blind trust that they alone will solve his life-problem.

21   Each generation, however, will have its creed, and that of the present is the belief in the efficacy of collective effort, in race co-operation. This deep feeling of race is at present the mainspring of Negro life. It seems to be the outcome of the reaction to proscription and prejudice; an attempt, fairly successful on the whole, to convert a defensive into an offensive position, a handicap into an incentive. It is radical in tone, but not in purpose and only the most stupid forms of opposition, misunderstanding or persecution could make it otherwise. Of course, the thinking Negro has shifted a little toward the left with the world-trend, and there is an increasing group who affiliate with radical and liberal movements. But fundamentally for the present the Negro is radical on race matters, conservative on others, in other words, a "forced radical," a social protestant rather than a genuine radical. Yet under further pressure and injustice iconoclastic thought and motives will inevitably increase. Harlem's quixotic radicalisms call for their ounce of democracy to-day lest to-morrow they be beyond cure.

22   The Negro mind reaches out as yet to nothing but American wants, American ideas. But this forced attempt to build his Americanism on race values is a unique social experiment, and its ultimate success is impossible except through the fullest sharing of American culture and institutions. There should be no delusion about this. American nerves in sections unstrung with race hysteria are often fed the opiate that the trend of Negro advance is wholly separatist, and that the effect of its operation will be to encyst the Negro as a benign foreign body in the body politic. This cannot be—even if it were desirable. The racialism of the Negro is no limitation or reservation with respect to American life; it is only a constructive effort to build the obstructions in the stream of his progress into an efficient dam of social energy and power. Democracy itself is obstructed and stagnated to the extent that any of its channels are closed. Indeed they cannot be selectively closed. So the choice is not between one way for the Negro and another way for the rest, but between American institutions frustrated on the one hand and American ideals progressively fulfilled and realized on the other.

23   There is, of course, a warrantably comfortable feeling in being on the right side of the country's professed ideals. We realize that we cannot be undone without America's undoing. It is within the gamut of this attitude that the thinking Negro faces America, but with variations of mood that are if anything more significant than the attitude itself. Sometimes we have it taken with the defiant ironic challenge of McKay:

> *Mine is the future grinding down to-day*
> *Like a great landslip moving to the sea,*
> *Bearing its freight of débris far away*
> *Where the green hungry waters restlessly*
> *Heave mammoth pyramids, and break and roar*
> *Their eeric challenge to the crumbling shore.*

Sometimes, perhaps more frequently as yet, it is taken in the fervent and almost filial appeal and counsel of Weldon Johnson's:

> *O Southland, dear Southland!*
> *Then why do you still cling*
> *To an idle age and a musty page,*
> *To a dead and useless thing?*

But between defiance and appeal, midway almost between cynicism and hope, the prevailing mind stands in the mood of the same author's *To America*, an attitude of sober query and stoical challenge:

> *How would you have us, as we are?*
> *Or sinking 'neath the load we bear,*
> *Our eyes fixed forward on a star,*
> *Or gazing empty at despair?*
>
> *Rising or falling? Men or things?*
> *With dragging pace or footsteps fleet?*
> *Strong, willing sinews in your wings,*
> *Or tightening chains about your feet?*

24   More and more, however, an intelligent realization of the great discrepancy between the American social creed and the American social practice forces upon the Negro the taking of the moral advantage that is his. Only the steadying and sobering effect of a truly characteristic gentleness of spirit prevents the rapid rise of a definite cynicism and counter-hate and a defiant superiority feeling. Human as this reaction would be, the majority still deprecate its advent, and would gladly see it forestalled by the speedy amelioration of its causes. We wish our race pride to be a healthier, more positive achievement than a feeling based upon a realization of the shortcomings of others. But all paths toward the attainment of a sound social attitude have been difficult; only a relatively few enlightened minds have been able as the phrase puts it "to rise above" prejudice. The ordinary man has

had until recently only a hard choice between the alternatives of supine and humiliating submission and stimulating but hurtful counter-prejudice. Fortunately from some inner, desperate resourcefulness has recently sprung up the simple expedient of fighting prejudice by mental passive resistance, in other words by trying to ignore it. For the few, this manna may perhaps be effective, but the masses cannot thrive upon it.

25   Fortunately there are constructive channels opening out into which the balked social feelings of the American Negro can flow freely.

26   Without them there would be much more pressure and danger than there is. These compensating interests are racial but in a new and enlarged way. One is the consciousness of acting as the advance-guard of the African peoples in their contact with Twentieth Century civilization; the other, the sense of a mission of rehabilitating the race in world esteem from that loss of prestige for which the fate and conditions of slavery have so largely been responsible. Harlem, as we shall see, is the center of both these movements; she is the home of the Negro's "Zionism." The pulse of the Negro world has begun to beat in Harlem. A Negro newspaper carrying news material in English, French and Spanish, gathered from all quarters of America, the West Indies and Africa has maintained itself in Harlem for over five years. Two important magazines, both edited from New York, maintain their news and circulation consistently on a cosmopolitan scale. Under American auspices and backing, three pan-African congresses have been held abroad for the discussion of common interests, colonial questions and the future co-operative development of Africa. In terms of the race question as a world problem, the Negro mind has leapt, so to speak, upon the parapets of prejudice and extended its cramped horizons. In so doing it has linked up with the growing group consciousness of the dark-peoples and is gradually learning their common interests. As one of our writers has recently put it: "It is imperative that we understand the white world in its relations to the non-white world." As with the Jew, persecution is making the Negro international.

27   As a world phenomenon this wider race consciousness is a different thing from the much asserted rising tide of color. Its inevitable causes are not of our making. The consequences are not necessarily damaging to the best interests of civilization. Whether it actually brings into being new Armadas of conflict or argosies of cultural exchange and enlightenment can only be decided by the attitude of the dominant races in an era of critical change. With the American Negro, his new internationalism is primarily an effort to recapture

contact with the scattered peoples of African derivation. Garveyism may be a transient, if spectacular, phenomenon, but the possible rôle of the American Negro in the future development of Africa is one of the most constructive and universally helpful missions that any modern people can lay claim to.

28   Constructive participation in such causes cannot help giving the Negro valuable group incentives, as well as increased prestigé at home and abroad. Our greatest rehabilitation may possibly come through such channels, but for the present, more immediate hope rests in the revaluation by white and black alike of the Negro in terms of his artistic endowments and cultural contributions, past and prospective. It must be increasingly recognized that the Negro has already made very substantial contributions, not only in his folk-art, music especially, which has always found appreciation, but in larger, though humbler and less acknowledged ways. For generations the Negro has been the peasant matrix of that section of America which has most undervalued him, and here he has contributed not only materially in labor and in social patience, but spiritually as well. The South has unconsciously absorbed the gift of his folk-temperament. In less than half a generation it will be easier to recognize this, but the fact remains that a leaven of humor, sentiment, imagination and tropic nonchalance has gone into the making of the South from a humble, unacknowledged source. A second crop of the Negro's gifts promises still more largely. He now becomes a conscious contributor and lays aside the status of a beneficiary and ward for that of a collaborator and participant in American civilization. The great social gain in this is the releasing of our talented group from the arid fields of controversy and debate to the productive fields of creative expression. The especially cultural recognition they win should in turn prove the key to that revaluation of the Negro which must precede or accompany any considerable further betterment of race relationships. But whatever the general effect, the present generation will have added the motives of self-expression and spiritual development to the old and still unfinished task of making material headway and progress. No one who understandingly faces the situation with its substantial accomplishment or views the new scene with its still more abundant promise can be entirely without hope. And certainly, if in our lifetime the Negro should not be able to celebrate his full initiation into American democracy, he can at least, on the warrant of these things, celebrate the attainment of a significant and satisfying new phase of group development, and with it a spiritual Coming of Age.

Toni Morrison

(1931–)

*For biographical information about Toni Morrison see page 36
(Chapter One). In the following excerpt from Morrison's sixth novel,*
Jazz, *she captures the excitement and fear that accompanied the
Southerners' migration. Focusing specifically on Joe and Violet Trace,
who "train-danced" their way into Harlem, Morrison explores the per-
ils of city life.*

Jazz

1   They met in Vesper County, Virginia, under a walnut tree. She had
been working in the fields like everybody else, and stayed past picking time to live with a family twenty miles away from her own. They
knew people in common; and suspected they had at least one relative in common. They were drawn together because they had been put
together, and all they decided for themselves was when and where
to meet at night.

2   Violet and Joe left Tyrell, a railway stop through Vesper County,
in 1906, and boarded the colored section of the Southern Sky. When
the train trembled approaching the water surrounding the City, they
thought it was like them: nervous at having gotten there at last, but terrified of what was on the other side. Eager, a little scared, they did
not even nap during the fourteen hours of a ride smoother than a rocking cradle. The quick darkness in the carriage cars when they shot
through a tunnel made them wonder if maybe there was a wall ahead
to crash into or a cliff hanging over nothing. The train shivered with
them at the thought but went on and sure enough there was ground
up ahead and the trembling became the dancing under their feet. Joe
stood up, his fingers clutching the baggage rack above his head. He felt
the dancing better that way, and told Violet to do the same.

3   They were hanging there, a young country couple, laughing and
tapping back at the tracks, when the attendant came through, pleasant but unsmiling now that he didn't have to smile in this car full
of colored people.

4   "Breakfast in the dining car. Breakfast in the dining car. Good
morning. Full breakfast in the dining car." He held a carriage blanket over his arm and from underneath it drew a pint bottle of milk,

which he placed in the hands of a young woman with a baby asleep across her knees. "Full breakfast."

5   He never got his way, this attendant. He wanted the whole coach to file into the dining car, now that they could. Immediately, now that they were out of Delaware and a long way from Maryland there would be no green-as-poison curtain separating the colored people eating from the rest of the diners. The cooks would not feel obliged to pile extra helpings on the plates headed for the curtain; three lemon slices in the iced tea, two pieces of coconut cake arranged to look like one— to take the sting out of the curtain; homey it up with a little extra on the plate. Now, skirting the City, there were no green curtains; the whole car could be full of colored people and everybody on a first-come first-serve basis. If only they would. If only they would tuck those little boxes and baskets underneath the seat; close those paper bags, for once, put the bacon-stuffed biscuits back into the cloth they were wrapped in, and troop single file through the five cars ahead on into the dining car, where the table linen was at least as white as the sheets they dried on juniper bushes; where the napkins were folded with a crease as stiff as the ones they ironed for Sunday dinner; where the gravy was as smooth as their own, and the biscuits did not take second place to the bacon-stuffed ones they wrapped in cloth. Once in a while it happened. Some well-shod woman with two young girls, a preacherly kind of man with a watch chain and a rolled-brim hat might stand up, adjust their clothes and weave through the coaches toward the tables, foamy white with heavy silvery knives and forks. Presided over and waited upon by a black man who did not have to lace his dignity with a smile.

6   Joe and Violet wouldn't think of it—paying money for a meal they had not missed and that required them to sit still at, or worse, separated by, a table. Not now. Not entering the lip of the City dancing all the way. Her hip bones rubbed his thigh as they stood in the aisle unable to stop smiling. They weren't even there yet and already the City was speaking to them. They were dancing. And like a million others, chests pounding, tracks controlling their feet, they stared out the windows for first sight of the City that danced with them, proving already how much it loved them. Like a million more they could hardly wait to get there and love it back.

7   Some were slow about it and traveled from Georgia to Illinois, to the City, back to Georgia, out to San Diego and finally, shaking their heads, surrendered themselves to the City. Others knew right away that it was for them, this City and no other. They came on a whim

because there it was and why not? They came after much planning, many letters written to and from, to make sure and know how and how much and where. They came for a visit and forgot to go back to tall cotton or short. Discharged with or without honor, fired with or without severance, dispossessed with or without notice, they hung around for a while and then could not imagine themselves anywhere else. Others came because a relative or hometown buddy said, Man, you best see this place before you die; or, We got room now, so pack your suitcase and don't bring no high-top shoes.

8   However they came, when or why, the minute the leather of their soles hit the pavement—there was no turning around. Even if the room they rented was smaller than the heifer's stall and darker than a morning privy, they stayed to look at their number, hear themselves in an audience, feel themselves moving down the street among hundreds of others who moved the way they did, and who, when they spoke, regardless of the accent, treated language like the same intricate, malleable toy designed for their play. Part of why they loved it was the specter they left behind. The slumped spines of the veterans of the 27th Battalion betrayed by the commander for whom they had fought like lunatics. The eyes of thousands, stupefied with disgust at having been imported by Mr. Armour, Mr. Swift, Mr. Montgomery Ward to break strikes then dismissed for having done so. The broken shoes of two thousand Galveston longshoremen that Mr. Mallory would never pay fifty cents an hour like the white ones. The praying palms, the raspy breathing, the quiet children of the ones who had escaped from Springfield Ohio, Springfield Indiana, Greensburg Indiana, Wilmington Delaware, New Orleans Louisiana, after raving whites had foamed all over the lanes and yards of home.

9   The wave of black people running from want and violence crested in the 1870s; the '80s; the '90s but was a steady stream in 1906 when Joe and Violet joined it. Like the others, they were country people, but how soon country people forget. When they fall in love with a city, it is for forever, and it is like forever. As though there never was a time when they didn't love it. The minute they arrive at the train station or get off the ferry and glimpse the wide streets and the wasteful lamps lighting them, they know they are born for it. There, in a city, they are not so much new as themselves: their stronger, riskier selves. And in the beginning when they first arrive, and twenty years later when they and the City have grown up, they love that part of themselves so much they forget what loving other people was like—if they ever knew, that is. I don't

mean they hate them, no, just that what they start to love is the way a person is in the City; the way a schoolgirl never pauses at a stoplight but looks up and down the street before stepping off the curb; how men accommodate themselves to tall buildings and wee porches, what a woman looks like moving in a crowd, or how shocking her profile is against the backdrop of the East River. The restfulness in kitchen chores when she knows the lamp oil or the staple is just around the corner and not seven miles away; the amazement of throwing open the window and being hypnotized for hours by people on the street below.

10 Little of that makes for love, but it does pump desire. The woman who churned a man's blood as she leaned all alone on a fence by a country road might not expect even to catch his eye in the City. But if she is clipping quickly down the big-city street in heels, swinging her purse, or sitting on a stoop with a cool beer in her hand, dangling her shoe from the toes of her foot, the man, reacting to her posture, to soft skin on stone, the weight of the building stressing the delicate, dangling shoe, is captured. And he'd think it was the woman he wanted, and not some combination of curved stone, and a swinging, high-heeled shoe moving in and out of sunlight. He would know right away the deception, the trick of shapes and light and movement, but it wouldn't matter at all because the deception was part of it too. Anyway, he could feel his lungs going in and out. There is no air in the City but there is breath, and every morning it races through him like laughing gas brightening his eyes, his talk, and his expectations. In no time at all he forgets little pebbly creeks and apple trees so old they lay their branches along the ground and you have to reach down or stoop to pick the fruit. He forgets a sun that used to slide up like the yolk of a good country egg, thick and red-orange at the bottom of the sky, and he doesn't miss it, doesn't look up to see what happened to it or to stars made irrelevant by the light of thrilling, wasteful street lamps.

11 That kind of fascination, permanent and out of control, seizes children, young girls, men of every description, mothers, brides, and barfly women, and if they have their way and get to the City, they feel more like themselves, more like the people they always believed they were. Nothing can pry them away from that; the City is what they want it to be: thriftless, warm, scary and full of amiable strangers. No wonder they forget pebbly creeks and when they do not forget the sky completely think of it as a tiny piece of information about the time of day or night.

12   But I have seen the City do an unbelievable sky. Redcaps and
dining-car attendants who wouldn't think of moving out of the City
sometimes go on at great length about country skies they have seen
from the windows of trains. But there is nothing to beat what the
City can make of a nightsky. It can empty itself of surface, and more
like the ocean than the ocean itself, go deep, starless. Close up on
the tops of buildings, near, nearer than the cap you are wearing,
such a citysky presses and retreats, presses and retreats, making me
think of the free but illegal love of sweethearts before they are discovered. Looking at it, this nightsky booming over a glittering city,
it's possible for me to avoid dreaming of what I know is in the ocean,
and the bays and tributaries it feeds: the two-seat aeroplanes, nose
down in the muck, pilot and passenger staring at schools of passing bluefish; money, soaked and salty in canvas bags, or waving
their edges gently from metal bands made to hold them forever.
They are down there, along with yellow flowers that eat water bee-
tles and eggs floating away from thrashing fins; along with the children who made a mistake in the parents they chose; along with slabs
of Carrara pried from unfashionable buildings. There are bottles
too, made of glass beautiful enough to rival stars I cannot see above
me because the citysky has hidden them. Otherwise, if it wanted
to, it could show me stars cut from the lamé gowns of chorus girls,
or mirrored in the eyes of sweethearts furtive and happy under the
pressure of a deep, touchable sky.

13   But that's not all a citysky can do. It can go purple and keep an
orange heart so the clothes of the people on the streets glow like
dance-hall costumes. I have seen women stir shirts into boiled starch
or put the tiniest stitches into their hose while a girl straightens the
hair of her sister at the stove, and all the while heaven, unnoticed and
as beautiful as an Iroquois, drifts past their windows. As well as the
windows where sweethearts, free and illegal, tell each other things.

14   Twenty years after Joe and Violet train-danced on into the City,
they were still a couple but barely speaking to each other, let alone
laughing together or acting like the ground was a dance-hall floor.
Convinced that he alone remembers those days, and wants them back,
aware of what it looked like but not at all of what it felt like, he coupled himself elsewhere. He rented a room from a neighbor who knows
the exact cost of her discretion. Six hours a week he has purchased.
Time for the citysky to move from a thin ice blue to purple with a
heart of gold. And time enough, when the sun sinks, to tell his new
love things he never told his wife.

Ralph Ellison

(1913–1994)

Named for Ralph Waldo Emerson, Ralph Waldo Ellison was born on March 1, 1913, in Oklahoma City, Oklahoma, to Lewis Alfred and Ida Millsap Ellison, who moved from the South to Oklahoma in order to provide better opportunities for their two sons. Educated in segregated schools, Ellison graduated from high school in 1931 and attended Tuskegee Institute in Alabama, where he continued his conservatory training and study of music theory from 1933 to 1936. Ellison became interested in modern literature at Tuskegee, and before he could complete an undergraduate degree, he left the school for New York City, where he participated in the Federal Writers' Project and met such notables as Richard Wright, Langston Hughes, and Alain Locke. Ellison lectured on African American folklore and music and taught at many universities, including Columbia, Princeton, and New York University, where he taught for many years and was named the Albert Schweitzer Professor of the Humanities. Ellison published collections of essays and stories, including Shadow and Act *(1964) and* Going to the Territory *(1986), as well as one novel,* Invisible Man *(1952), for which he won the National Book Award in 1953.* Invisible Man, *considered Ellison's magnum opus, is a richly textured bildungsroman (a novel about the moral and psychological growth of the main character) replete with allusions to African American folklore, history, and culture.* Invisible Man *remains one of the most significant novels in the American literary tradition. After Ellison's death, a second, unfinished novel,* Juneteenth *(1999), was published.*

Invisible Man

1 At first I had turned away from the window and tried to read but my mind kept wandering back to my old problems and, unable to endure it any longer, I rushed from the house, extremely agitated but determined to get away from my hot thoughts into the chill air.

2 At the entrance I bumped against a woman who called me a filthy name, only causing me to increase my speed. In a few minutes I was several blocks away, having moved to the next avenue and downtown. The streets were covered with ice and soot-flecked snow and from above a feeble sun filtered through the haze. I walked with my head down, feeling the biting air. And yet I was hot, burning with an inner

fever. I barely raised my eyes until a car, passing with a thudding of skid chains whirled completely around on the ice, then turned cautiously and thudded off again.

3   I walked slowly on, blinking my eyes in the chill air, my mind a blur with the hot inner argument continuing. The whole of Harlem seemed to fall apart in the swirl of snow. I imagined I was lost and for a moment there was an eerie quiet. I imagined I heard the fall of snow upon snow. What did it mean? I walked, my eyes focused into the endless succession of barber shops, beauty parlors, confectioneries, luncheonettes, fish houses, and hog maw joints, walking close to the windows, the snowflakes lacing swift between, simultaneously forming a curtain, a veil, and stripping it aside. A flash of red and gold from a window filled with religious articles caught my eye. And behind the film of frost etching the glass I saw two brashly painted plaster images of Mary and Jesus surrounded by dream books, love powders, God-Is-Love signs, money-drawing oil and plastic dice. A black statue of a nude Nubian slave grinned out at me from beneath a turban of gold. I passed on to a window decorated with switches of wiry false hair, ointments guaranteed to produce the miracle of whitening black skin. "You too can be truly beautiful," a sign proclaimed. "Win greater happiness with whiter complexion. Be outstanding in your social set."

4   I hurried on, suppressing a savage urge to push my fist through the pane. A wind was rising, the snow thinning. Where would I go? To a movie? Could I sleep there? I ignored the windows now and walked along, becoming aware that I was muttering to myself again. Then far down at the corner I saw an old man warming his hands against the sides of an odd-looking wagon, from which a stove pipe reeled off a thin spiral of smoke that drifted the odor of baking yams slowly to me, bringing a stab of swift nostalgia. I stopped as though struck by a shot, deeply inhaling, remembering, my mind surging back, back. At home we'd bake them in the hot coals of the fireplace, had carried them cold to school for lunch; munched them secretly, squeezing the sweet pulp from the soft peel as we hid from the teacher behind the largest book, the *World's Geography*. Yes, and we'd loved them candied, or baked in a cobbler, deep-fat fried in a pocket of dough, or roasted with pork and glazed with the well-browned fat; had chewed them raw—yams and years ago. More yams than years ago, though the time seemed endlessly expanded, stretched thin as the spiraling smoke beyond all recall.

5   I moved again. "Get yo' hot, baked Car'lina yam," he called. At the corner the old man, wrapped in an army overcoat, his feet covered

with gunny sacks, his head in a knitted cap, was puttering with a stack of paper bags. I saw a crude sign on the side of the wagon proclaiming YAMS, as I walked flush into the warmth thrown by the coals that glowed in a grate underneath.

6   "How much are your yams?" I said, suddenly hungry.

7   "They ten cents and they sweet," he said, his voice quavering with age. "These ain't none of them binding ones neither. These here is real, sweet, yaller yams. How many?"

8   "One," I said, "If they're that good, one should be enough."

9   He gave me a searching glance. There was a tear in the corner of his eye. He chuckled and opened the door of the improvised oven, reaching gingerly with his gloved hand. The yams, some bubbling with syrup, lay on a wire rack above glowing coals that leaped to low blue flame when struck by the draft of air. The flash of warmth set my face aglow as he removed one of the yams and shut the door.

10   "Here you are, suh," he said, starting to put the yam into a bag.

11   "Never mind the bag, I'm going to eat it. Here . . ."

12   "Thanks." He took the dime. "If that ain't a sweet one, I'll give you another one free of charge."

13   I knew that it was sweet before I broke it; bubbles of brown syrup had burst the skin.

14   "Go ahead and break it," the old man said. "Break it and I'll give you some butter since you gon' eat it right here. Lots of folks takes 'em home. They got their own butter at home."

15   I broke it, seeing the sugary pulp steaming in the cold.

16   "Hold it over here," he said. He took a crock from a rack on the side of the wagon. "Right here."

17   I held it, watching him pour a spoonful of melted butter over the yam and the butter seeping in.

18   "Thanks."

19   "You welcome. And I'll tell you something."

20   "What's that?" I said.

21   "If that ain't the best eating you had in a long time, I give you your money back."

22   "You don't have to convince me," I said. "I can look at it and see it's good."

23   "You right, but everything what looks good ain't necessarily good," he said. "But these is."

24   I took a bite, finding it as sweet and hot as any I'd ever had, and was overcome with such a surge of homesickness that I turned away

to keep my control. I walked along, munching the yam, just as suddenly overcome by an intense feeling of freedom—simply because I was eating while walking along the street. It was exhilarating. I no longer had to worry about who saw me or about what was proper. To hell with all that, and as sweet as the yam actually was, it became like nectar with the thought. If only someone who had known me at school or at home would come along and see me now. How shocked they'd be! I'd push them into a side street and smear their faces with the peel. What a group of people we were, I thought. Why, you could cause us the greatest humiliation simply by confronting us with something we liked. Not *all* of us, but so many. Simply by walking up and shaking a set of chitterlings or a well-boiled hog maw at them during the clear light of day! What consternation it would cause! And I saw myself advancing upon Bledsoe, standing bare of his false humility in the crowded lobby of Men's House, and seeing him there and him seeing me and ignoring me and me enraged and suddenly whipping out a foot or two of chitterlings, raw, uncleaned and dripping sticky circles on the floor as I shake them in his face, shouting:

25   "Bledsoe, you're a shameless chitterling eater! I accuse you of relishing hog bowels! Ha! And not only do you eat them, you sneak and eat them in *private* when you think you're unobserved! You're a sneaking chitterling lover! I accuse you of indulging in a filthy habit, Bledsoe! Lug them out of there, Bledsoe! Lug them out so we can see! I accuse you before the eyes of the world!" And he lugs them out, yards of them, with mustard greens, and racks of pigs' ears, and pork chops and black-eyed peas with dull accusing eyes.

26   I let out a wild laugh, almost choking over the yam as the scene spun before me. Why, with others present, it would be worse than if I had accused him of raping an old woman of ninety-nine years, weighing ninety pounds . . . blind in one eye and lame in the hip! Bledsoe would disintegrate, disinflate! With a profound sigh he'd drop his head in shame. He'd lose caste. The weekly newspapers would attack him. The captions over his picture: *Prominent Educator Reverts to Field-Niggerism!* His rivals would denounce him as a bad example for the youth. Editorials would demand that he either recant or retire from public life. In the South his white folks would desert him; he would be discussed far and wide, and all of the trustees' money couldn't prop up his sagging prestige. He'd end up an exile washing dishes at the Automat. For down South he'd be unable to get a job on the honey wagon.

27   This is all very wild and childish, I thought, but to hell with being ashamed of what you liked. No more of that for me. I am what I am! I wolfed down the yam and ran back to the old man and handed him twenty cents. "Give me two more," I said.

28   "Sho, all you want, long as I got 'em. I can see you a serious yam eater, young fellow. You eating them right away?"

29   "As soon as you give them to me," I said.

30   "You want 'em buttered?"

31   "Please."

32   "Sho, that way you can get the most out of 'em. Yessuh," he said, handing over the yams, "I can see you one of these old-fashioned yam eaters."

33   "They're my birthmark," I said. "I yam what I am!"

34   "Then you must be from South Car'lina," he said with a grin.

35   "South Carolina nothing, where I come from we really go for yams."

36   "Come back tonight or tomorrow if you can eat some more," he called after me. "My old lady'll be out here with some hot sweet potato fried pies."

37   Hot fried pies, I thought sadly, moving away. I would probably have indigestion if I ate one—now that I no longer felt ashamed of the things I had always loved, I probably could no longer digest very many of them. What and how much had I lost by trying to do only what was expected of me instead of what I myself had wished to do? What a waste, what a senseless waste! But what of those things which you actually didn't like, not because you were not supposed to like them, not because to dislike them was considered a mark of refinement and education—but because you actually found them distasteful? The very idea annoyed me. How could you know? It involved a problem of choice. I would have to weigh many things carefully before deciding and there would be some things that would cause quite a bit of trouble, simply because I had never formed a personal attitude toward so much. I had accepted the accepted attitudes and it had made life seem simple . . .

38   But not yams, I had no problem concerning them and I would eat them whenever and wherever I took the notion. Continue on the yam level and life would be sweet—though somewhat yellowish. Yet the freedom to eat yams on the street was far less than I had expected upon coming to the city. An unpleasant taste bloomed in my mouth now as I bit the end of the yam and threw it into the street; it had been frost-bitten.

39   The wind drove me into a side street where a group of boys had
set a packing box afire. The gray smoke hung low and seemed to
thicken as I walked with my head down and eyes closed, trying to
avoid the fumes. My lungs began to pain; then emerging, wiping
my eyes and coughing, I almost stumbled over it: It was piled in a
jumble along the walk and over the curb into the street, like a lot
of junk waiting to be hauled away. Then I saw the sullen-faced
crowd, looking at a building where two white men were totting out
a chair in which an old woman sat; who, as I watched, struck at them
feebly with her fists. A motherly-looking old woman with her head
tied in a handkerchief, wearing a man's shoes and a man's heavy blue
sweater. It was startling: The crowd watching silently, the two white
men lugging the chair and trying to dodge the blows and the old
woman's face streaming with angry tears as she thrashed at them
with her fists. I couldn't believe it. Something, a sense of foreboding,
filled me, a quick sense of uncleanliness.

40   "Leave us alone," she cried, "leave us alone!" as the men pulled
their heads out of range and sat her down abruptly at the curb, hurrying back in the building.

41   What on earth, I thought, looking above me. What on earth? The old
woman sobbed, pointing to the stuff piled along the curb. "Just look what
they doing to us. Just look," looking straight at me. And I realized that
what I'd taken for junk was actually worn household furnishings.

42   "Just look at what they're doing," she said, her teary eyes upon
my face.

43   I looked away embarrassed, staring into the rapidly growing
crowd. Faces were peering sullenly from the windows above. And now
as the two men reappeared at the top of the steps carrying a battered chest of drawers, I saw a third man come out and stand behind
them, pulling at his ear as he looked out over the crowd.

44   "Shake it up, you fellows," he said, "shake it up. We don't have
all day."

45   Then the men came down with the chest and I saw the crowd
give way sullenly, the men trudging through, grunting and putting the
chest at the curb, then returning into the building without a glance to
left or right.

46   "Look at that," a slender man near me said. "We ought to beat the
hell out of those paddies!"

47   I looked silently into his face, taut and ashy in the cold, his eyes
trained upon the men going up the steps.

48   "Sho, we ought to stop 'em," another man said, "but ain't that much nerve in the whole bunch."

49   "There's plenty nerve," the slender man said. "All they need is someone to set it off. All they need is a leader. You mean *you* don't have the nerve."

50   "Who me?" the man said. "Who me?"

51   "Yes, you."

52   "Just look," the old woman said, "just look," her face still turned toward mine. I turned away, edging closer to the two men.

53   "Who are those men?" I said, edging closer.

54   "Marshals or something. I don't give a damn who they is."

55   "Marshals, hell," another man said. "Those guys doing all the toting ain't nothing but trusties. Soon as they get through they'll lock 'em up again."

56   "I don't care who they are, they got no business putting these old folks out on the sidewalk."

57   "You mean they're putting them out of their apartment?" I said. "They can do that up *here?*"

58   "Man, where *you* from?" he said, swinging toward me. "What does it look they puttin' them out of, a Pullman car? They being evicted!"

59   I was embarrassed; others were turning to stare. I had never seen an eviction. Someone snickered.

60   "Where did *he* come from?"

61   A flash of heat went over me and I turned. "Look, friend," I said, hearing a hot edge coming into my voice. "I asked a civil question. If you don't care to answer, don't, but don't try to make me look ridiculous."

62   "Ridiculous? Hell, all scobos is ridiculous. Who the hell is you?"

63   "Never mind, I am who I am. Just don't beat up your gums at me," I said, throwing him a newly acquired phrase.

64   Just then one of the men came down the steps with an armful of articles, and I saw the old woman reach up, yelling, "Take your hands off my Bible!" And the crowd surged forward.

65   The white man's hot eyes swept the crowd. "Where, lady?" he said. "I don't see any Bible."

66   And I saw her snatch the Book from his arms, clutching it fiercely and sending forth a shriek. "They can come in your home and do what they want to you," she said. "Just come stomping and jerk your life up by the roots! But this here's the last straw. They ain't going to bother with my Bible!"

67   The white man eyed the crowd. "Look, lady," he said, more to the rest of us than to her, "I don't want to do this, I *have* to do it. They sent me up here to do it. If it was left to me, you could stay here till hell freezes over . . ."

68   "These white folks, Lord. These white folks," she moaned, her eyes turned toward the sky, as an old man pushed past me and went to her.

69   "Hon, Hon," he said, placing his hand on her shoulder. "It's the agent, not these gentlemen. He's the one. He says it's in the bank, but you know he's the one. We've done business with him for over twenty years."

70   "Don't tell me," she said. "It's all the white folks, not just one. They all against us. Every stinking low-down one of them."

71   "She's right!" a hoarse voice said. "She's right! They *all* is!"

72   Something had been working fiercely inside me, and for a moment I had forgotten the rest of the crowd. Now I recognized a self-consciousness about them, as though they, we, were ashamed to witness the eviction, as though we were all unwilling intruders upon some shameful event; and thus we were careful not to touch or stare too hard at the effects that lined the curb; for we were witnesses of what we did not wish to see, though curious, fascinated, despite our shame, and through it all the old female, mind-plunging crying.

73   I looked at the old people, feeling my eyes burn, my throat tighten. The old woman's sobbing was having a strange effect upon me—as when a child, seeing the tears of its parents is moved by both fear and sympathy to cry. I turned away, feeling myself being drawn to the old couple by a warm, dark, rising whirlpool of emotion which I feared. I was wary of what the sight of them crying there on the sidewalk was making me begin to feel. I wanted to leave, but was too ashamed to leave, was rapidly becoming too much a part of it to leave.

74   I turned aside and looked at the clutter of household objects which the two men continued to pile on the walk. And as the crowd pushed me I looked down to see looking out of an oval frame a portrait of the old couple when young, seeing the sad, stiff dignity of the faces there; feeling strange memories awakening that began an echoing in my head like that of a hysterical voice stuttering in a dark street. Seeing them look back at me as though even then in that nineteenth-century day they had expected little, and this with a grim, unillusioned pride that suddenly seemed to me both a reproach and a warning. My eyes fell upon a pair of crudely carved and polished bones, "knocking bones," used to accompany music at country

dances, used in black-face minstrels; the flat ribs of a cow, a steer or sheep, flat bones that gave off a sound, when struck, like heavy castanets (had he been a minstrel?) or the wooden block of a set of drums. Pots and pots of green plants were lined in the dirty snow, certain to die of the cold; ivy, canna, a tomato plant. And in a basket I saw a straightening comb, switches of false hair, a curling iron, a card with silvery letters against a background of dark red velvet, reading "God Bless Our Home"; and scattered across the top of a chiffonier were nuggets of High John the Conqueror, the lucky stone; and as I watched the white men put down a basket in which I saw a whiskey bottle filled with rock candy and camphor, a small Ethiopian flag, a faded tintype of Abraham Lincoln, and the smiling image of a Hollywood star torn from a magazine. And on a pillow several badly cracked pieces of delicate china, a commemorative plate celebrating the St. Louis World's Fair . . . I stood in a kind of daze, looking at an old folded lace fan studded with jet and mother-of-pearl.

75   The crowd surged as the white men came back, knocking over a drawer that spilled its contents in the snow at my feet. I stooped and starting replacing the articles: a bent Masonic emblem, a set of tarnished cuff links, three brass rings, a dime pierced with a nail hole so as to be worn about the ankle on a string for luck, an ornate greeting card with the message "Grandma, I love you" in childish scrawl; another card with a picture of what looked like a white man in black-face seated in the door of a cabin strumming a banjo beneath a bar of music and the lyric "Going back to my old cabin home"; a useless inhalant, a string of bright glass beads with a tarnished clasp, a rabbit foot, a celluloid baseball scoring card shaped like a catcher's mitt, registering a game won or lost years ago; an old breast pump with rubber bulb yellowed with age, a worn baby shoe and a dusty lock of infant hair tied with a faded and crumpled blue ribbon. I felt nauseated. In my hand I held three lapsed life insurance policies with perforated seals stamped "Void"; a yellowing newspaper portrait of a huge black man with the caption: MARCUS GARVEY DEPORTED.

76   I turned away, bending and searching the dirty snow for anything missed by my eyes, and my fingers closed upon something resting in a frozen footstep: a fragile paper, coming apart with age, written in black ink grown yellow. I read: FREE PAPERS. *Be it known to all men that my negro, Primus Provo, has been freed by me this sixth day of August, 1859. Signed: John Samuels. Macon.* . . . I folded it quickly, blotting out the single drop of melted snow which glistened on the yellowed page, and dropped it back into the drawer. My hands

were trembling, my breath rasping as if I had run a long distance or come upon a coiled snake in a busy street. *It has been longer than that, further removed in time,* I told myself, and yet I knew that it hadn't been. I replaced the drawer in the chest and pushed drunkenly to the curb.

77   But it wouldn't come up, only a bitter spurt of gall filled my mouth and splattered the old folk's possessions. I turned and stared again at the jumble, no longer looking at what was before my eyes, but inwardly-outwardly, around a corner into the dark, far-away-and-long-ago, not so much of my own-memory as of remembered words, of linked verbal echoes, images, heard even when not listening at home. And it was as though I myself was being dispossessed of some painful yet precious thing which I could not bear to lose; something confounding, like a rotted tooth that one would rather suffer indefinitely than endure the short, violent eruption of pain that would mark its removal. And with this sense of dispossession came a pang of vague recognition: this junk, these shabby chairs, these heavy, old-fashioned pressing irons, zinc wash tubs with dented bottoms—all throbbed within me with more meaning than there should have been: *And why did I, standing in the crowd, see like a vision my mother banging wash on a cold windy day, so cold that the warm clothes froze even before the vapor thinned and hung stiff on the line, and her hands white and raw in the skirt-swirling wind and her gray bead bare to the darkened sky—why were they causing me discomfort so far beyond their intrinsic meaning as objects? And why did I see them now, as behind a veil that threatened to lift, stirred by the cold wind in the narrow street?*

Arthur Flowers

(1950–)

Literary blues man Arthur Flowers was born in Memphis, Tennessee, in 1950, but has spent the majority of his adulthood in New York City. Flowers attended the Harlem Writers Guild workshop for more than a decade, and out of this experience Flowers cofounded the New Renaissance Writer's Guild in New York and a literary workshop in Memphis called the Griot Shop. Flowers's writing is steeped in the cultural landscape of his youth, highlighting the blues and jazz scene in Memphis's Beale Street, hoodoo, and oral traditions. Flowers's first novel, De Mojo Blues: De Quest of HighJohn de Conquerer *(1985), has autobiographical resonance, as he, like the protagonist, is a Vietnam War veteran. His second novel,* Another Good Loving Blues *(1993), excerpted below, places the romantic relationship between a blues man and a hoodoo woman in the context of the Great Migration. Flowers currently teaches creative writing at Syracuse University.*

Another Good Loving Blues

IF BEALE STREET COULD TALK

1 Like all the really good things in life, Melvira Dupree and Lucas Bodeen finally made it to Beale Street. They crossed over the bridge by wagon one bright Saturday morning. Once across the river Melvira was faced with the stolid brick squares of Memphis' budding eight-story skyline. On the otherside of the river, Arkansas dressed the delta horizon in the bright shades of autumn and Melvira Dupree knew she was leaving something behind. They caught a trolley up Main to Beale. Melvira was fascinated. Memphis. She may be leaving something behind but she knows already that mysteries await her here, buried somewhere under all the unfamiliar cars and big brick buildings right up on each other. Trolley cars, hordes of people, every single one of them in a hurry. They got off the trolley at Beale and walked; Bodeen wanted to walk. "This is it," he told her with grinning excitement, "Beale Street."

2   Beale Street. About a mile of street running from the riverbank deep into the heart of Memphis. From the levee to Front Street was strictly rivertown, a wild and wooly section crowded with rooming houses and hog-nosed cafés for burly roustabouts and rivermen. Front Street was strictly cotton. Baled on the sidewalk, weighed in the store-fronts, sold at the cotton marts. Between Front and Second you got your pawnshops and your dry goods stores. Already the countryfolk were coming in from the fields and farms of Tennessee, Mississippi and Arkansas, parking their horses, wagons and Fords in the old Wagon Yard over on Second and Beale, hunting down overalls, boots, dresses, plows and harness and the cherished gifts of unnecessary lace, hand mirrors or red suspenders from Schwabs. Melvira was fascinated, a hick from the sticks, mouth open and big-eyed. Wow, look

at all the people. Bodeen laughed at her. "Girl you as bad as all the rest of these country Negroes. Be cool, you with Lucas Bodeen now."

3 They turned down Hernando, a little side street off Beale, and knocked on the door of a large white two-story building with a line of steps leading up the side to a second-story balcony.

4 A big pretty solid woman in a long print dress came to the door.

5 "Lord help us all," she murmured with a pretty smile, "Lucas Bodeen is back in town." Her unruly laughter seemed to shake both her and the house. She and Bodeen hugged and danced into the street. They danced around pedestrians, totally unconcerned with the spectacle, so obviously pleased to see each other that Melvira couldn't help a twinge of jealousy at the obviously old and weathered intimacy between them. They finally ended up where they started, all tired and winded.

6 "Got a place for me Jackie J.?"

7 Jackie looked at Melvira and stepped back from Lucas.

8 "Rooms scarce Bodeen, so many folks coming through town these days. But you know Jackie J. gon always look out for you. You come on in here boy, who is this with you, she yours? You with this man honey? He a good ole boy, but he need domestication bad."

9 Jackie looked Melvira over with a curious eye and nodded sagely. "I spec you just might be the one to tame him though."

10 Glancing occasionally at Melvira, she led them up the steps to the second floor and gave Bodeen the key. "Pay me every week on Sunday. None of your stuff now Bodeen. You pays me this time." She slapped Bodeen's butt and he growled playfully, "Watch it now Jackie, you know I got a low threshold."

11 "You watch him good now girl," Jackie said affectionately as she left them. "The gals in this town just loves theyself some SweetLuke Bodeen."

12 Nice little place, big and airy. Facing Hernando. Two big windows and a little wood framed balcony. Lace curtains and a four-poster bed on the far wall. By the window, a chair for sitting, a small round table with a pitcher and a large bowl on it. Jackie always made sure he had a place to lay his head. They went back all the way. But this was nicer than usual, probably Melvira's doing.

13 Being that it was Saturday evening, Bodeen wanted to drop off their bags and go right out, but Melvira made him help her clean up the place first. Make it livable, make it theirs. By the time they got the place to Melvira's satisfaction it was dark out, but Saturday night found them strolling the street with all Beale Street's other stalkers

of the night. Mostly working folk out for a good time, gardeners and maids, clerks and countryfolk in big grins and loud finery. But it was the fast-life crowd that ruled at night; the Beale Streeters were out in force. Predators. The gamblers and rounders, the easy riders and their fast-life women, all strolling to and fro amongst the dives and dance hall palaces. And music. Music coming from everywhere. From every joint and on every corner they was doing the blues. It was like the blues were a part of the air she breathed.

14 My boy Bodeen was in pig heaven, home sweet Beale Street. Noplace in the world I'd rather be.

15 "Over there," he said proudly, "is PeeWees. Professor Handy wrote the *Beale Street Blues* there. And over there is the Hole-in-the-Wall. And over there is the Monarch, see, the big one there. They call it the Castle of Missing Men cause there's a funeral parlor right behind it and when folks get killed they just get drug out back for the undertaker to pick up in the morning."

16 "You telling me truth Bodeen?"

17 "Truth?" He laughed, one of his best. "Who cares if its true or not, it sounds good don't it?"

18 On every corner they stop and listen to the street musicians, Bodeen running down pedigree. A jug band played at the edge of Church's Park.

19 "Chatmon boys from down Bolton way, whole family of them, they do good blues."

20 On Beale and Fourth there was a blind harp player, with black shades and a weaving head. Played a mean harp, but he didn't have but one line that he sang over and over:

> *Every good man need a real good woman*
> *Every good woman need a real good man.*

21 "Gabriel," said Bodeen with a smile. "Best harp in the city, but long as I knowed him he ain't played but that one line."

22 As they walked through the streets, weaving amongst the crowded press of folks, Melvira felt herself getting caught up in the excitement, a taste of what Bodeen felt about this Beale Street of his. Life in abundance. She hadn't really wanted to come, but now that she was out here they had a real good Beale Street of a time, going from spot to spot, dancing, listening to the blues and meeting Bodeen's old friends. Mostly women. They were in the Monarch: a fancy place, she had never conceived of anything remotely like it, cushioned seats built into

the mirrored wall and a brass-railed mahogany bar, and people, people, people, when a pretty babybrown woman in a red sequined dress suddenly appeared out of the press of folks around them.

23 "SweetLuke Bodeen, I didn't know you were back in town."

24 The woman draped herself all over him.

25 "Hey Mamie, long time no see," he said absently. A piano player had caught his interest. A little wasted-looking guy with a New Orleans quiff haircut. Eyes squinted up from the smoke of a cigarette in the side of his mouth. Playing jazz off a score in front of him. It was the score that had Bodeen's attention.

26 "You the one been gone, I ain't heard from you since the last time you were in Memphis."

27 She glanced at Melvira and they spoke in the secret language of women. Mine, said Dupree. Mamie smiled lazily and undraped herself from Bodeen. Patted him on his cheek and moved on.

28 "See you around Bodeen."

29 "Who is that, SweetLuke?" asked Melvira.

30 "I don't know," he said, "but they call that music he playing Jass down in New Orleans. Ain't nothing but some warmed-over blues, I don't think much gon come out of it myself."

31 Lies and propaganda. He had played a little of that Jazz himself during one of his early New Orleans sojourns. Played with boys like mad Buddy Bolden and smooth Jelly Roll Morton and wasn't half as contemptuous as he sounded. Those New Orleans boys did some good work. Trained musicians a lot of them. He had been there when they started it. Had sneered cause it wasn't the blues; he liked the power of the word with his music. Bodeen remembered back when there wasn't no such thing as the blues, or jazz. He was a young boy then, about 15, maybe 16, new to Memphis, living off his wits and fascinated with the piano. They were playing rag-time back then. He'd haunt the places that they were playing it and watch the old guys' fingering. Then he'd go try to play the same thing on a log or a fence railing. There was this little place off Fourth where they had a player piano. Put a nickel in and pump away at the pedals. Follow the fingering. He put in many a nickel. Got so he could make a tune on a real piano and played whenever he could, more heart than skill. First they didn't even have to pay him, just let him play. Had all kinds of makework jobs, but nothing serious. Rather starve than do something other than learn how to play the piano better every day. Quit a good job in a minute to go make 15 cents a night playing piano.

32   Soon as he was good enough to get by, he went out on the road. Played jukes and pineywoods logging camps, anywhere he could, but his first real gig and true love was playing the riverboats. Stayed with the *Stacker Lee* for almost a year, big pretty double-decker steamboat, prettiest thing on the river. Boy loved getting paid to travel up and down the river playing piano. Thats when he picked up his love for Stetsons, brocaded vests and blouse-sleeved shirts. And a new sound. It was traveling up and down the river that he began to notice this new thing coming out of the roustabouts and the rivermen, started hearing it on the levees and in the logging camps and fields. He saw the way it was moving folk, and thats what he liked to do, move folk with his music.

33   They wasn't calling it the blues then, wasn't no such thing then as the blues. They were calling it cottonfield music and rivermusic, backcountry music, and one day down Tutwiler way he heard it called the blues, and he knew thats what he wanted to do, the blues, and thats what he wanted to be, a bluesman. By the time he got back to Memphis thats what he was calling himself, bluesman.

34   About 1906, 1907 maybe, he was playing piano over to PeeWees one night and he was doing his regular rag-time and the kind of partymusic that folks was accustomed to, but late that night he commence to playing some blues for them. Most of them didn't known where he was coming from and half of them didn't care. He got more perplexed frowns than he got approval. It's always rough on the cutting edge. They pretty much booed him off the stage that first night, hurt his feelings bad, liketa made him cry. Got into a big argument with some fool, made him so mad he almost pulled his pistol and killed somebody. But he came back the second night to do it again, and there was folks there who had come back to hear him do it again. And there were some who had heard Luke Bodeen was playing some of those blues they had been hearing about. They were a lot nicer to him that night. Ole PeeWee Virgilio, a stroking that handlebar mustache of his like he did whenever he saw a chance to profit, asked him what was it? "The blues," and where did he learn to play it? "the river." Asked him to come on back and play some more of it.

35   For a long while wasn't but him and about four or five other guys that could play that music. But by and by more and more folks come to ask for it, by name now, "Play the blues for me pianoman." Before you knew it every guitar and piano player on Beale was playing the blues, some of them better than him. Then Professor Handy put em on paper and the blues were born.

36 Put em on paper.

37 Now they had been playing em all along, but it wasn't till it was put down on paper that it became real for a lot of folk. Bodeen watched the jazz fella playing off the sheetmusic and thought about it some. Back when he started hardly anybody could read music. Bodeen played by ear, could play anything he heard once. But he couldn't read a lick. He had been playing a long time not to know how to read music. Blues have gone through a lot of changes since he started. Couldn't get by these days playing what he used to play back when he started, or even what he was playing the last time he was in town. A man had to keep up or fall behind.

38 "Excuse me baby," he said, rising up from the table, "be right back."

39 He went to the piano and watched the little guy play. Eyebrows lined, he tried to match the fingering with the sheetmusic. Melvira knew something was bothering him and watched him closely until he got involved in a poker game and she could focus on all the activity around her. So much going on. People all around her, ain't nothing in the world more interesting to a hoodoo than people. Memphis was going to be real enlightening. All this time she thought that she was knowledgeable sitting out there in the middle of nowhere. And this was just part of the world. It was humbling, how much she didn't know, how far she had to go. Her eyes were systematically sweeping the place, intently filing patterns and process, when Bodeen broke the bank. In the old days a gambling man that broke the bank was expected to set up the house till his winnings run out, or at least (lets be real here) till his extra winnings run out.

40 It was in the backroom of the Monarch that Bodeen did the trick, and before Melvira knew it she was on her first gravy train, grabbing Bodeen around his hips, her own grabbed by some big rascal behind her. Bodeen lead the delta snake-dancing line around the front room and on out into the street. First stop Hammitt's place. They set up the house, picked up some new believers, snake-danced through and on to the next place, picking up more folks at every spot. Had a real good time. Melvira laughed so hard her stomach was hurting and her mouth was tired. At one point Bodeen was so full of the feeling that he stopped and turned in the middle of the street. Melvira snake-danced right on into him and the rest of the line collapsed on itself, folks falling all over each other. Bodeen pulled her close and kissed her soundly while the rest of the gravy train cheered such a rousing display of spontaneous passion. O yes o yes, a good time was had by all.

41   Melvira Dupree let her hair down that night and it was sweated all down her back when Sunday's dawn found them flopping onto the bed still dressed and totally exhausted. Outside, Beale Street, so busy and alive that night, was now quiet and still, the air a Sunday morning crisp. They heard some muted morning sounds. Trolleys rolling through the streets. The bells of the many churches of Beale calling out the faithful. Somewhere close they heard Gabriel's harp. Mellow morning music now but the same old lyrics,

> *Every good man need a real good woman*
> *Every good woman need a real good man.*

42   Melvira laid her head on Bodeen's chest, exhausted, sated. A thick tendril of her loose hair tickled his nose and he stroked it out of the way with an affectionate hand.

43   "Enjoy yourself?" Bodeen asked her, half asleep, still stroking her hair.

44   "Not half as much as you did."

45   He snuggled into the warmth. Glad she was there. The sheet was fresh and clean, the room nice and homey. A woman's touch. Fell asleep without realizing it until the bed suddenly sprang and he popped his eyes open. Arms braced to either side of him, Melvira was looking down on him, thick mane of hair brushed back and tamed under a floppy hat. She was washed and dressed in her Sunday best and he raised a questioning eyebrow.

46   "Church," she said.

47   Melvira had been a regular churchgoing woman back in Sweetwater. Bodeen didn't understand why a hoodoo went to church in the first place.

48   "Church? What kinda hoodoo are you anyway?"

49   "Many roads to God Lucas Bodeen."

50   "What?"

51   "It feels good. You coming?"

52   He shook his head and settled deeper into the bed. Far as Luke Bodeen was concerned he had just got back from Church.

53   In 1919 Beale Street was still Beale Street, in spite of periodic *Cleanup Beale* campaigns. The first one was right after the election of Boss Crump in 1909. Prohibition had been decreed in Tennessee, but Crump didn't hardly enforce it; claimed it would cause more trouble than it was worth. Not to mention interfere with his colored votes.

Boss Crump was ousted the first time by reformers in 1916 and they immediately called themselves cleaning up Beale. Beale survived. Another cleanup movement in 1919 by the Citizens Movement and Mayor Paine slowed it up some but not measurably so. Federal Prohibition had been passed in 1917 but not enacted yet.

54 So, in 1919, Beale was still Beale. But it wasn't just the honkytonk strip between Fourth and Hernando. By 1919 Beale Street was a community. There were quite a few colored Memphis communities growing from the steady stream coming in from the delta during the Great Migration, springing up wherever they could find land nobody else wanted, marginal land like over in the bayou and down along the levee with the river for back yard, but these hardy little communities took root and thrived. Places like Douglas and Orange Mound and Beale Street. Beale Street was the heart of colored Memphis. The majority of Beale Street folk never set foot in a juke or a honkytonk or a fancy joint in their lives. Colored families shopped, paid bills, visited doctor and dentist, ate, got their hair done and went to church. As many churches as there were gin joints. This was Melvira's world. Now ole Bodeen, he never left the Beale Strip. Thats where the blues where and the congregations that appreciated them. But Melvira was fascinated with the new colored communities. Melvira had business to take care of.

Writing Assignments

1. Read Alain Locke's "New Negro," paying particular attention to its tone. Try to define the New Negro according to Locke's essay. How does Locke characterize socio-economic issues? Compare his tone to Toni Morrison's in *Jazz*. How does Morrison portray New York City in the 1920s?

2. Because of the great demographic shift from the rural South to the urban North, the notion of home and displacement is a major theme in this chapter. How does Dunbar characterize home in *The Sport of the Gods*? What role does the Northern city play in shaping the lives of the Hamilton family?

3. Read the essay by Toni Morrison entitled "City Limits, Village Values" (not collected in this chapter), then state whether you agree with her comments about the importance of establishing a village in the city and explain your perspective. Do any of the texts in this chapter

illustrate Morrison's notion of the village? If so, do those works have a positive take on city life?

4. Research African American newspapers such as the *Pittsburgh Courier* and the *Chicago Defender* and locate letters to the editors that were written in the early twentieth century by Southerners or other recent migrants. Copy two of those letters and discuss the thoughts and feelings that African Americans expressed in them about the move from the South to the North. Are these sentiments reflected in any of the selections in this chapter?

CHAPTER SEVEN

URBAN LANDSCAPES

As a counterpoint to the rural South, the urban experience is fundamental to African American literary expression. As the chapter on the South attests, many writers return in their work to a rural Southern location as a kind of ancestral homeland. However, there is an equally strong, decidedly urban current in the African American literary tradition. The city, regardless of geography, is an overwhelming presence in African American life and letters. While the rural South often emerges as the past (through memory or through journeys down home), the urban location is routinely constructed as the present, the now. This is not to suggest that the portrayal of the city is merely a current literary phenomenon. In fact, given the exigencies of antebellum society, the city was equated with freedom even in the eighteenth and nineteenth centuries. This predominantly hopeful portrayal of city life in slave narratives is evidenced in what is clearly the most famous, *The Narrative of the Life of Frederick Douglass* (1845), in which Douglass suggested that the city is a place of restoration for African Americans. Other early writers and leaders, including W. E. B. Du Bois and James Weldon Johnson, followed suit, promoting the city as a site of freedom and deliverance.

During the first few decades of the twentieth century, cities all around the country, including New York, Detroit, Chicago, Philadelphia, and Pittsburgh, were epicenters of excitement and renewal. Nonetheless, urban centers were often contradictory spaces. Henry Louis Gates, Jr. sheds light on the gap between the promise of the Harlem Renaissance and the socio-economic reality of the 1920s and 30s: "What *does* seem curious about the Harlem Renaissance is that its creation occurred precisely as Harlem was turning into the great American slum. The death-rate in Harlem was 42 percent higher than in other parts of the city. The infant mortality rate in 1928 was twice as high in Harlem as it was in the rest of New York. The tuberculosis death-rate was four times as high as that among the white population. The unemployment rate, according to Adam Clayton Powell Jr., was 50 percent higher." A. Robert Lee, considering Harlem's cultural depictions, observes: "The only *fact* about Harlem . . . may be its intractability, its undiminished refusal to be accommodated by any single explanation. That, one supposes and readily celebrates, accounts for why there have been so many Harlems on the mind—be they expressed in the novel or in any of the abundant other forms inspired by the enduring black First City of America."

Even during that widely celebrated urban experience in letters, the Harlem Renaissance, city life was rendered as complicated and confounding. Richard Wright's documentary of city conditions, *12 Million Black Voices* (1941), provides compelling photographs that feature individual and family existence both in the city streets and in the interior landscape of tenements, churches, and other domestic quarters. Exploring the state of Northern industrial centers, Wright argues that the jobs "were low-paying, menial and exhaustive." The Depression hit especially hard for city dwellers who were already living close to the poverty line.

Post-Depression city life, which is the focus of this chapter, is as paradoxical as the hardship and promise of the 1930s. African American city literature is often bleak, but also captures the cautious optimism and energy of the urban experience. The tempo of city life— quicker, energized, and stylized—finds a literary analogue in African American urban writing. While urban despair is omnipresent, so too is the power of urban centers, cities transformed by industry and technology, and energized by a vibrant street culture. The literary city, in short, is not a monolithic entity; it is a combination of seemingly paradoxical forces that vacillate between elegies of glamour and portraits of isolation and alienation.

Given the hardships associated with city life, there is an understandable desire to escape the pressures of urban living, which often manifest in drug abuse and crime. Nathan McCall's *Makes Me Wanna Holler* (1994) theorizes about the rage resulting from America's racial and class hierarchy and how the street promises to fill this void. Responding directly to Marvin Gaye's famous song "Inner City Blues" in the title of his memoir, McCall locates the city as the source of devastation, describing how the urban streets lure young boys into a debilitating cycle of drugs, violence, and prison. Likewise, John Edgar Wideman's conversation with his brother Robby in *Brothers and Keepers* (1984), a combination auto-biography/biography, explores how the streets of Homewood, a poor neighborhood in Pittsburgh, infuenced each man's escape—John's as a Rhodes scholar and college professor, and Robby's as an inmate in a Pennsylvania prison.

Beyond escape, mere survival is a paramount concern, as Wanda Coleman's "Fast Eddie" (1998) illustrates. In this poem, Coleman questions the delinquent status so readily branded on African American youth as she explores the life of a young victim of domestic abuse, who tries in vain to ease the poverty of his family's life through a paper delivery route. In fact, many pieces collected here chronicle the difficulty of making ends meet. Terry McMillan's *Mama* (1987) reveals the drudgery of domestic work; Walter Mosley's "The Thief" (1998) examines the life of an ex-con who tries to survive by collecting cans. Keith Gilyard's "The Hatmaker" (1993), Rita Dove's "My Mother Enters the Work Force" (1999), and Lamont B. Steptoe's "Seamstress" (2001) pay tribute to the struggle of women whose tireless work in the textile industry provided for their families.

Survival, though, is complicated by the systemized brutality visited on the poor and the disfranchised. Coleman's poem "Low English" (2001) sounds a resonant theme throughout the selections in this chapter, namely racial profiling and police brutality. This becomes particularly poignant in her poem "South Central Los Angeles Deathtrip 1982" (2001), where police harassment turns into a ritualized killing of innocent victims. Steptoe continues this conversation in "Spooked" (1994) by questioning the racial stereotyping of Black violence: "it wasn't me / or my people / who looted and murdered / Nations of Red folks / stole the land / from sea to shining sea."

Despite the failure of America's cities to adequately provide for many of its urban dwellers, the pleasures of street life are stressed by numerous texts in the chapter, including Gilyard's "Anyone Heard from Manuel?" (2001). In the first stanza, the view of the city creates an outlook of excitement, fraternity, and community. The poem is a meditation on the life and fate of Manuel, a man accused of armed robberies, and his friends, whose lives reflect some of the strictures of urban society. Sliding between Manuel's jail sentence and the community's imprisonment, Gilyard concretizes the suffocating enclosure of the urban grid: "knew my street plus the next one / plus the next one led nowhere near / a big show i could star in." The reader confronts the reality of this urban blight while nevertheless realizing that youthful fun is also portrayed.

Whether in slave narratives, Harlem Renaissance literature, contemporary poetry, or hip-hop, the city emerges (though not unproblematically) as a place of potential freedom, a site of promised opportunity and citizenship. Moving beyond both the early construct of the city as a redemptive force and the migrants' initial stages of disillusionment, the literary city is a multitude of forces. While none of these works offer a romanticized notion of the city, each offers eloquent discourse on the city's paradoxical nature, revealing the city as a palpable experience that leaves its mark, one way or another, on the characters' lives.

Further Reading

Gates, Henry Louis, Jr. "Harlem on Our Minds." *Rhapsodies in Black: Art of the Harlem Renaissance.* Eds. Richard J. Powell and David A. Bailey. Berkeley: University of California Press, 1997.

Gooding-Williams, Robert, ed. *Reading Rodney King, Reading Urban Uprising.* New York: Routledge, 1993.

Hakutani, Yoshinobu, and Robert Butler, eds. *The City in African-American Literature.* Cranbury: Associated UP, 1995.

Jaye, Michael C., and Ann Chalmers Watts, eds. *Literature and the Urban Experience: Essays on the City and Literature.* New Brunswick: Rutgers UP, 1981.

Lee, A. Robert. "Harlem on My Mind: Fictions of a Black Metropolis." *The American City: Cultural and Literary Perspectives.* Ed. Graham Clarke. New York: St. Martin's Press, 1988.

Scruggs, Charles. *Sweet Home: Invisible Cities in the Afro-American Novel.* Baltimore: Johns Hopkins UP, 1993.

Wright, Richard. 1941. *12 Million Black Voices.* New York: Thunder's Mouth Press, 1988.

Nathan McCall

(1955–)

Nathan McCall was raised in Portsmouth, Virginia. After being sent to prison at the age of 20 for an armed robbery, he began an intellectual quest that was fueled by reading Richard Wright and others. McCall subsequently earned a bachelor's degree in journalism from Norfolk State University and worked for the Virginia Pilot-Ledger Star, *the* Atlanta Journal-Constitution, *and the* Washington Post. *While employed as a reporter at the* Post, *he published his best-selling memoir,* Makes Me Wanna Holler: A Young Black Man in America *(1994). McCall published a second book,* What's Going On: Personal Essays *(1997), and has served as a journalism professor at Emory University. The following selection, which is the conclusion of* Makes Me Wanna Holler, *chronicles McCall's arrival in Washington, D.C., to assume his job with the* Post, *and reveals his thoughts about problems old and new.*

Makes Me Wanna Holler

1   My arrival in D.C. was more than just a good career move. It put me closer to a ghost of the past I needed to confront. Her name was Carolyn, and even though I hadn't seen or talked with her since I was eighteen, she'd haunted me for years. Back during the days when the fellas and I were running trains and raising hell, I met Carolyn at a local amusement park. We rapped and got together one night when my parents were out of town. For me, it was supposed to be a quick hit-and-forget, a slam-bam-thankyou-ma'am. I picked her up on a designated corner, took her to my house, and got over. A month later, Carolyn told me she was pregnant.

2   "No way," I told her. We'd only been together that once. I figured that given the case with which I'd gotten her into bed, other dudes had likely done the same. When she insisted she was pregnant by me, I thought up a scheme to duck the blame: The fellas and I would run a train, to try to create confusion about paternity. Naively, we figured that if a number of guys said they had trained a girl, she couldn't possibly know who was the father of her child.

3   One night, I had Carolyn meet me at the Zeus Club in Douglas Park. Using my stepfather's car, I took her for a cruise, with my friend

Greg riding shotgun. A group of the fellas followed inconspicuously in a different car. On the way to the lake, where we planned to run the train, Carolyn noticed the other car. She got hysterical and began to scream. "Nathan, stop the car and let me out!"

4   I said, "Be cool, girl. It'll be all right."

5   "Nathan, if you don't stop the car, I'm gonna jump."

6   I tried to scare her by accelerating. But the next thing I knew, Carolyn, who was sitting in the front passenger seat, opened the door, jumped from the car, and landed in the street, smashing her head against the pavement. The car behind us swerved sharply and barely avoided running over her. I pulled to the side of the road and ran back to where Carolyn lay motionless. The impact had knocked her unconscious. She went into convulsions, spewing foam from her mouth and trembling, like she was having a seizure.

7   Of course the guys in the other car split. After helping us load Carolyn into the backseat of my stepfather's car, they left Greg and me to handle it alone. We drove her back crosstown near her sister's house, parked in a wooded area, and tried unsuccessfully to bring her to. She really needed medical care. Greg said, "We better take her to the hospital."

8   I was too scared. "We can't, man. If we take her to the hospital, they gonna call the fuzz."

9   You never know what you're capable of doing until confronted with that kind of irrational, crazy fear. Several times before, fear had driven me to do foolish things with potential consequences far severer than the fate I was trying to avoid. That night, I concluded we had no option left except the most desperate. I told Greg, "If anybody finds out what happened to her, we goin' to jail. We gotta kill her, man. We ain't got no choice. . . . We can throw her in those bushes over there."

10   Years later, Greg told me he'd had no intention of going through with my idea, but that night he looked like he was willing. All I know is, I'd decided it was something I *had* to do and I was feeling desperate enough to carry it out.

11   As we talked, an elderly woman walked up from nowhere and passed the car. Noticing Carolyn lying motionless in the backseat, she stopped and asked, "Is anything wrong?" Moving closer to the car, she spoke again, pointing to the backseat. "Wha's the matter wit dat chile?"

12   "Uh, nothin's wrong, ma'am. She just had a little too much to drink and we were trying to help her get herself together before we took her home."

13   "You sure she all right?" The woman was still peering into the car, straining in the pitch dark to get a better look.

14   "Yeah, she'll be all right. She just needs some fresh air. That's all. . . . We gonna take her home."

15   "All right. If ya'll need help with anything, come and knock on my door." She pointed toward a lone house set off from the road, back in the woods. It was strange: I hadn't noticed that house when we first parked out there.

16   After the woman left, it was clear that killing Carolyn was out of the question. The woman had seen our faces. She saw our car. Greg looked at Carolyn and said, "We gotta take her home now."

17   I said, "I ain't taking her. I don't want her people to see me."

18   Greg left me on a corner and took her alone, rang the doorbell, and told Carolyn's sister she'd had too much to drink. Then he returned and picked me up.

19   A few days later, my folks got a telephone call from Carolyn's parents. She had been hospitalized. Her father said she had told them she'd been out with me. He wanted an explanation and hinted he might call the cops. With my mother and stepfather, I went to their house to explain. Sitting in the living room with the four stern-faced adults, I made up an account of what went down. They listened calmly, then talked among themselves. Carolyn's parents seemed disinclined to drag the police into it. They were decent, hardworking people, much like my own parents. They asked me to leave the room. I don't know what was said. All I knew or cared about was that I got off the hook.

20   Some months later, Carolyn delivered a baby girl. I never saw the child before I was sent to the joint. After I got out of prison, Carolyn moved to Washington, and we lost contact.

21   But not entirely. Toward the end of my stay in Atlanta, I learned my mother had been in touch with Carolyn from time to time in those intervening years. My mother and my stepfather had taken diapers and other supplies to Carolyn when the child was very young. Carolyn had written letters to me and sent them to my mother's address. Mama never showed them to me. She kept the letters until she got one just as I was about to leave Atlanta. She sent it to me.

22   After I got settled in D.C., I did what I'd thought of doing for years. I got in touch with Carolyn and made arrangements to see her and her daughter in their place in northeast Washington. By then, her daughter was about eighteen, two years older than Monroe.

23 It was a trip seeing Carolyn after all those years. Short, petite, and coffee-brown, she looked the same, right down to the gold tooth that sparkled in her mouth. She was warm and cordial. I wondered how she could bring herself to forgive me for what I'd done to her. She never said anything about it, though, and acted like it had never happened.

24 Carolyn introduced me to Cheryl, her daughter, and I didn't know whether to hug her, kiss her, or shake her hand. She seemed reticent, too. I sensed she wanted to reach out but was afraid to take the risk. As we talked, I searched her face for traces of myself. There were none. She had her mother's wide nose and thick eyebrows, and she was darker-complexioned than either of us.

25 Looking at her, I wondered, *How could I have gone so long without trying to resolve this matter?* Even as I asked myself that question, I half knew the answer: I was afraid to face the guilt it would bring if it turned out that I'd had other fatherhood responsibilities I'd neglected to face. It would force me to accept the fact that despite all my efforts to be different from my blood father, J.L., I was more like him than I realized.

26 Cheryl and I got together a few times after that first visit. I told her about my life and what I had been like when I met her mother. I was up-front with her. I told her I was unsure if she was mine, but that I intended to find out. "As soon as we get some blood tests done, we'll take it from there."

27 I sought advice from friends and family, and even talked with a counselor about it. All of them told me, "Leave it alone. There's little you can do for her now, at her age."

28 But I'd resolved to try to do what was right if the tests proved positive. Maybe I'd let her come live with me and make a new start. She'd dropped out of school in the ninth or tenth grade and wasn't doing much more with her life than hanging out and fighting. I talked to her about returning to school. It was evident from her blank expression and one-word responses that her concept of the value of an education was as vague as mine had once been. Thinking about my own past, I told her, "Anybody can rise above their station in life."

29 We didn't get a chance to see what she could do if given a shot at improving her life. Cheryl, who went back and forth to Portsmouth in impulsive fits, got pregnant by an unemployed hometown boy. She insisted on having the baby and making it on her own.

30 She gave birth to a baby girl in Washington. I went to the hospital after work one day to visit her. A nurse stopped me at the entrance

to the maternity ward and said, "The baby can only have visits from its parents and grandparents. Who are you?"

31   I said, "My name is Nathan McCall."

32   "Oh, you're the grandfather?"

33   "Well, uh, uh . . . yeah."

34   "Go on in." She walked away.

35   I stood there a second, stunned. *Grandfather? I'm only thirty-six.*

36   I entered the room, where Cheryl was in bed, cradling her newborn baby like it was a play doll. Carolyn was there, along with a few other women I didn't know. The baby's father was nowhere to be found. The women chatted gaily about the sweetness of motherhood.

37   I remained quiet the entire time. I kept thinking about that nurse calling me a grandfather. I thought about the blood tests that we needed to take. I thought about something else that was bugging me: It seemed I was still investing a lot of energy trying to straighten out all the crazy things I'd done in the past.

38   When it was my turn to hold the baby, I couldn't pretend to share the joy the others felt. I kept looking into that baby's innocent eyes and thinking about the hell in store for her. *Another fatherless black child*, I thought. *These cycles. These cycles keep repeating themselves.*

39   One day, while I was sitting at my desk at work, a letter arrived from the Lorton prison, just outside of D.C. It was from an inmate who said he'd seen my byline in the newspaper. He wanted to know if I was the same Nathan McCall who once did time with him at Southampton. I recognized the name right off. It was Mahdee, a homeboy from Portsmouth who was once part of the group of prison intellectuals I hung with at Southampton.

40   I took the letter home, reread it a few times, and considered what to do. It was clear that Mahdee's letter was a plea for contact and support. I wrote him back, then went to see him.

41   The prison was comprised of several institutions that warehoused a total of nearly ten thousand inmates—about 96 percent of them black. Lorton made Southampton look like kindergarten. The place was so massive it looked like a small rural town. They even had street names within the complex. It broke my heart to see all that black talent and energy wasting away.

42   A few minutes after I got into the visiting room, Mahdee walked in, grinned broadly, and rushed over to the table to shake my hand. "Good to see you, my man. Thanks for comin' all the way out here to visit me."

43   It had been about ten years since I'd seen Mahdee. Tall and lean, he looked basically the same, but I couldn't help noticing that something about him was different. Of course, he was older—about thirty-five now—but age was not the only factor in the change. The stress lines on his face indicated that this latest prison bid was rougher on him than the one before. Of course, there was the added strain of doing time so far away from home. That meant he seldom got visits from friends and family, and had to make do on the prison yard without protection from homeboys to watch his back.

44   We talked for a good while. He said he'd served nine years on a forty-year sentence and was due for parole in one more year. "I've gotten a trade in brick masonry and plan to get a job workin' with a construction company when I get out. All I need is a union card and I'm on my way."

45   He went on. "I'm thinkin' 'bout relocatin' D.C. I been writin' the sister of an inmate who lives in my dorm, and she wants me to come live with her and her four kids when I get out. I figure it shouldn't take me long to get on my feet. . . . I'm goin' straight this time, man. I can't afford to take another fall."

46   I sat there, listening quietly and thinking all the while, *Cycles. I've heard all this before.* My old buddy from Southampton, Jim, and I talked about the cycles all the time. We'd get on the phone and talk long-distance about the brothers we knew who had gotten out, been killed, or sent back to the joint. At least two of the guys who were at Southampton with us had since committed other crimes and been sent to the electric chair. I was sure that many of those cats had every intention of doing what they said they would when they were released. But once they got out and confronted the harsh realities of the streets, they were overwhelmed, sucked back into cycles they seemed unable to fend off.

47   That's what had happened to Mahdee. He was sharp at Southampton. An understudy of Jim's, he'd gotten involved in Islam and become well-read and disciplined. I think he had a near photographic memory. Once, I gave him a philosophical essay to read so he could join us in the next day's discussion on the prison yard. He came back and ran it down almost verbatim. The cat really had it together—when he was locked up.

48   When Jim and I got out, we'd continued going back to the joint to visit Mahdee to help him get through the rest of his bid. But after he got out, he began to change. He crept gradually back into the fast lane. At Southampton, he'd looked healthy and his skin was clear, but after he got back into drugs and hustling on the street his skin

looked greasy and his face was gaunt. He even tossed aside his Muslim name and went back to using his old street name, Li'l Willie.

49   One night in 1982, Mahdee came with some friends to my house in Portsmouth. They were flying high as kites and talking pure trash. They stayed awhile, then I told them I had things to do. When I walked them to the door, I pulled Mahdee aside and said, "Slow down, man. You movin' kinda fast."

50   He looked at me through reddened eyes and said, "Don't worry, Nate. I got it under control."

51   A short time later, Jim called and told me the news. Mahdee and another guy had gotten busted. They drove from Portsmouth to D.C., stuck up somebody, and were caught. I thought, *All that promise gone down the drain—again.*

52   I thought about all that as I sat there in 1991 listening to Mahdee run down his plans. I thought about his life—how he'd spent most of it in and out of the joint. I thought about how he'd blown several opportunities to straighten himself out. After about an hour, I left.

53   I wrote him once or twice after that visit, but I never went back. I couldn't bring myself to look Mahdee in the eye and tell him I no longer believed he'd do what he said he would. When Jim asked me why I hadn't been back to see my homeboy, I told him that I no longer held out much hope for Mahdee. "I'm not sure he's as committed as he says he is."

54   Several months after that visit, we lost contact. Mahdee was transferred to another institution farther away from D.C., then he eventually made parole again.

55   I often reflected on what made the difference between Mahdee and me. We were similar in many ways. Although we both had done bad things, we were basically well-intentioned dudes trying to find our way in the world. I concluded that the distinction between us came down to some things that were simple and, at the same time, very complex:

56   Mahdee and his siblings had been raised by their mother in the Jeffry Wilson projects, a neighborhood of mostly single mothers and shiftless men who hung around. Life there hadn't convinced Mahdee that there was another way. None of the grand assertions that people make about human potential were ever concrete to him. Whenever he got out of prison, he went back to Jeffry Wilson and hung out, even after his family finally moved away. I think he felt unwelcome anywhere else—the world outside his neighborhood had never opened its doors to let him see what he could really be and do.

57   But I'd come from a stronger, intact family and a neighborhood where there were lots of hardworking, right-doing black men and women whose lives demonstrated that there were many alternatives to life in the streets. There had always been some older person—a teacher, a neighbor, a relative—to encourage me when I'd faltered or fallen down. Even when I chose the gutter, I'd always had a frame of reference for a better life.

58   That had made all the difference in the world.

59   It made a difference, too, when it came time for me to pass along the kind of support that had been given me. A few months after I moved to D.C., Liz called from California. "I'm sending Monroe to you."

60   I said nothing, waiting to hear more. Actually, I'd been expecting that phone call for some time. Once before when Liz had called, she'd sounded frustrated. Monroe had gotten into trouble. He and some other boys tried to steal some things from a record shop and got caught.

61   There had been other, more subtle signs of trouble in the previous year: Monroe was becoming more defiant toward Liz and aloof toward his stepfather and two half brothers. He was behaving in a way that nobody understood. But I understood, and I knew it was time for him to come to me.

62   Every time I mentioned it to Liz, she'd go off: "You must be crazy. You didn't do anything for him when he was very young, now you're trying to say you want to get custody of him?!"

63   She was right. But her refusal to hand him over was based on her judgment of the guy she'd known in the past. She hadn't seen much of me in the eleven years since I'd gotten out of prison, and she had no idea how much I'd changed.

64   But Monroe wanted to see more of me, just like I'd hungered for my old man when I was a boy. It was hard strengthening the bond when we lived two thousand miles apart. Our relationship was restricted largely to the telephone. That drove me up the wall sometimes and made me feel helpless and inept.

65   I was sure that if I had him with me I could compete with the pressures he'd get from school and neighborhood peers. But with little say in the matter, I resigned myself to do what I could during the summers, when he visited me in Atlanta. We did the usual things that fathers and sons do. We played basketball and went to the movies. But we also talked, shared, and hugged. We talked a lot about the streets so he wouldn't get a glorified perspective from uninformed peers. I'd take him bike-riding through the streets and point out drug

dealers and prostitutes. I told him everything about my past, including the experience with doing time. I even drove him to Southampton a few times and ran down, in graphic detail, the horrors of prison. Of course, we talked a lot about racial matters, too. One summer, when he was about fifteen, I took Monroe to apply for a job at the Six Flags Over Georgia amusement park. It reminded me of my frustrating times job-hunting when I was a teen. All the white kids his age were working in air-conditioned buildings, and the black kids were given outdoor jobs cleaning up the amusement park. I told him, "You may as well get ready. This is what you're going to have to contend with *all your life*."

66 In July 1989, after Monroe had spent another summer vacation with me, he asked if he could live with me instead of returning home. I sensed a desperation in him that I hadn't seen before. When I talked with Liz about it again, her response was the same: "No way."

67 I didn't want to start another war with her, yet I didn't want Monroe to think I had turned my back on him. When it was time for him to return to California, we struck a deal. I told him to give it another try. "If it isn't working out for you by the midsemester mark, call me and I'll send you a ticket." I had no idea how soon I'd see him again.

68 When Liz called a few months later, she said she'd found a letter that Monroe was composing to her. In the letter, he explained why he wanted to live with me. "He said he feared that if he didn't live with you before graduating from school, he might never get a chance to get to know you well," Liz said. "That's what convinced me to let him come to you."

69 I resisted the temptation to gloat. Her voice was already shaky. Monroe was her firstborn, and she felt she was losing him.

70 By December, Monroe was standing in a terminal at Washington National Airport, waiting for his luggage. Right away, he entered the eleventh grade, starting his new life and settling into my tiny one-bedroom apartment, where he slept on the living-room couch.

71 Suddenly, my life was no longer my own. I had a teenage son, and three immediate goals: to help him prepare for his future, whatever he chose; to keep him away from macho pressures to hang in the streets; and to keep him alive in a city where young black males treat each other like targets on a shooting range.

72 I was really concerned because of our schedules. Monroe got out of school at three in the afternoon. I got off work at seven—on a good day. Most days, I worked until nine or ten and, if I could get a cab,

got home by eleven. I was uneasy with all the time Monroe would spend alone.

73   At work, I constantly got visions of some gang member approaching my son, asking for money or his clothing, then pointing a gun to his head and firing, just for the hell of it. I came up with strategies to minimize the risks: I made sure he came nowhere to being sharply dressed in school. No expensive sneakers or flashy clothes that might entice jealous dudes to go after him. I drilled him on ways to handle different street scenarios and coached him on how to respond if approached by hoods. "If somebody asks you for your coat, don't put up a fuss. Just take it off and hand it to them without a word. We can always get you another coat," I said.

74   Although I schooled him on practically every potential situation that came to mind, it still wasn't enough to calm my nerves. Every time I read a news story about some teenage boy being gunned down over some senseless shit, I got visions of my son in subway encounters or neighborhood brawls.

75   My fears about his safety forced me to come to grips with a troubling reality: As much as I ranted about white folks' messing with us, I felt more threatened—physically—by my own people and the powerful self-hatred driving them.

76   Eventually, I took a final precaution to ease my mind. I got Monroe out of the path of the urban storm and moved to Arlington, just across the river, where the violence seemed less intense.

77   I still worried about him and sensed that the cultural pull of pseudomacho hip-hop fads was even more powerful than the things that once influenced me. I began to see signs of that after he met and started hanging with some cats at a local basketball court: He bopped with a more pronounced pimp and started letting his baggy jeans fall lower on his behind; he suddenly became resistant to doing household chores and took on that arrogant body language that teenagers use as their coded way of telling their parents to go to hell.

78   Finally, when things started getting out of hand, I had to yoke him, Cavalier Manor–style, break down the macho facade so he'd be real clear on what manhood was and was *not* about. It didn't take a whole lot more to bring him around. I think it helped that Liz and his stepfather had instilled in him a foundation of decency.

79   After that, we talked a lot about serious things, including girls, sex, and other matters of the heart. I learned from those rap sessions that little had changed on the streets since I was there. He came into my

bedroom late one night and asked, "Is it all right to take it from a girl if you take her out and she won't give it up?"

80   I guessed it was something he'd heard in bathroom rap with other dudes, and I flashed back to those street-corner discussions that had shaped my views. After he posed the question, I paused a long while before I said anything. I wondered, *What can I say to him now? How can I tell him not to do things that I have done?*

81   Finally, I told him about the things we did to girls while growing up and explained how much I regretted it now. I couldn't bring myself to preach to him, but I presented the issue in a way that hit close to home. Monroe was always paranoid about guys hungrily eyeing Liz in public. So I used her as an example of the danger in viewing other females—girls *and* women—as pieces of meat. I asked him, "How would you feel if somebody decided that they could rape your mother just because she won't give it up?"

82   He paused. "I'd be mad."

83   "Then think about it that way with other girls."

84   He said he understood.

85   That's how we got through everything: talking, communicating, doing something my parents' generation hadn't been taught to do. I often wondered during those talks with Monroe how I might have turned out if I'd had somebody I could talk to about everything.

86   When Monroe graduated from high school in 1991, my parents drove up from Portsmouth and Liz flew in from California to see him march. He walked down the aisle, got his diploma, and became my parents' first grandchild to graduate from high school. We threw a cookout and invited his friends. As I watched them playing music, laughing, and jonin', I saw a cycle that brought back memories. I wondered if Monroe was as fearful of facing the hostile white world as I'd been on my graduation day. Watching him, I felt a lot of things. Mostly, though, I felt glad that Monroe was not in trouble and was college-bound. I felt proud and confident that he'd skip the rite of passage to prison that I went through.

* * *

87   I wish there were more successes like Monroe to point to. I wish that somehow, brothers everywhere would reach down deep and summon the will to defy the inner hatred driving them to self-destruct. But everywhere I see them giving in, and I am reminded of it especially when I go home.

88   Sure, there are some among the old crew who are doing all right: Greg kicked his drug habit, got married, and is living clean. Ton, the high school football great and heavyweight thumper, is a Navy chaplain now. Shell Shock works at the shipyard. My brother Dwight got married and settled down. Turkey is hanging: Once he was hustling; now he's got a real job. Nutbrain got married and is giving it a real shot on the straight side. "Nate," he said in a recent phone call, "I been working for a year. Ain't that *strange?*" And me, I'm just a tourist in the white mainstream.

89   But ours are the quiet triumphs you seldom hear about, the ones overshadowed by the ugly, depressing things.

90   These days, my visits home have become occasions for mourning, soul-searching, and anger. On one visit, I saw a story splashed across the top of the newspaper about the police busting up a twenty-million-dollar narcotics ring. Listed in the article were several people I've known most of my life. I sighed. It wasn't the first time that day I'd been hit with negative news about the neighborhood. And it wasn't the last. Before that day ended, family members and people I met on the streets told me tale after tale of homeboys, young black men like me, living lives mired in lunacy.

91   Every day in D.C., I read dismal accounts of blacks murdered over trivia—drugs, a coat, a pair of sneakers, pocket change. The people in these stories are faceless to me. I peruse the accounts with detached sadness, then turn the page.

92   But in my hometown, the names conjure images of real people who lived down the street, around the corner, on the next block. My trips to Cavalier Manor provide a distressingly close-up view of black America's running tragedy. When I'm there, it dawns on me over and over again that this "endangered species" thing is no empty phrase.

93   Most of the dudes I grew up with are either in prison, dead, drug zombies, or nickel-and-dime hustlers. Some are racing full-throttle toward self-destruction. Others have already plunged into the abyss: Kenny Banks got life for dealing drugs, Frog got shot in Lincoln Park, Lep just got sprung from a three-year bid, and Shane was recently sent to prison. He shot a man several times, execution-style. He got life.

94   Of the ten families living on my street when I was growing up that had young males in their households, four—including my own—have had one or more of those young men serve time.

95   Often, when I go home, I prepare with a pep talk to myself and a pledge to focus on the positive—to spend time with family and old friends who are doing well, and to seek out opportunities to lend a

compassionate car to those not so well off. I know I will see former buddies, old hoods, hanging on the same corners where I left them years ago. I see in them how far I've come. I'm not sure what they see in me. In exchanges that are sometimes awkward, they recount their hard knocks. I say little about my establishment job or the new life I've found. What should I say? Get a job? Go to college? Adopt my middle-class success strategies? The fact is, I know what they've been through. And I understand what they face. I took the plunge myself, many times.

96 Many people are puzzled about the culture of violence pervading black communities; it's so foreign to them. Some wonder if there is something innately wrong with black males. And when all else fails, they reach for the easy responses: Broken homes. Misplaced values. Impoverished backgrounds.

97 I can answer with certainty only about myself. My background and those of my running partners don't fit all the convenient theories, and the problems among us are more complex than something we can throw jobs, social programs, or more policemen at.

98 Shane and I and the others in our loosely knit gang started out like most other kids. Yet somewhere between adolescence and adulthood, something inside us changed. Our hearts hardened, and many of us went on to share the same fates as the so-called disadvantaged.

99 I'm not exactly sure why, but I've got a good idea. A psychologist friend once explained that our fates are linked partly to how we perceive our choices in life. Looking back, I see that the reality may well have been that possibilities for us were abundant. But in Cavalier Manor, we perceived our choices as being somewhat limited.

100 When I read about shootings in urban areas and at home, I often flash back to scenes in which I played a part. It's hard for me now to believe I was once very much a part of that world, and harder still sometimes for me to adapt to the one I crossed over into. My new life is still a struggle, harsher in some ways than the one I left. At times I feel suspended in a kind of netherworld, belonging fully neither to the streets nor to the establishment.

101 I have come to believe two things that might seem contradictory: Some of our worst childhood fears *were* true—the establishment *is* teeming with racism. Yet I also believe whites are as befuddled about race as we are, and they're as scared of us as we are of them. Many of them are seeking solutions, just like us.

102 I am torn by a different kind of anger now. I resent suggestions that blacks enjoy being "righteous victims." And when people ask,

"What is wrong with black men?," it makes me want to lash out. When I hear that question, I am reminded of something Malcolm X once said: "I have no mercy or compassion in me for a society that will crush people and then penalize them for not being able to stand up under the weight."

103   Sometimes I wonder how I endured when so many others were crushed. I was not special. And when I hear the numbing statistics about black men, I often think of guys I grew up with who were smarter and more talented than me, but who will never realize their potential. Nutbrain, a mastermind in the ways of the streets, had the kind of raw intellect that probably could not be gauged in achievement tests. Shane, who often breezed effortlessly through tests in school, could have done anything he wanted with his life had he known what to do. Now he has *no* choices.

104   When Shane was caught in a police manhunt several years ago, I considered volunteering as a character witness but dismissed the notion because I knew there was no way to tell his jury what I had been unable to articulate to a judge at my own trial. How could I explain our anger and alienation from the rest of the world? Where was our common language?

105   Most people, I'm sure, would regard Shane's fate with the same detachment I feel when reading crime reports about people I don't know. But I hurt for Shane, who will likely spend the rest of his days behind bars and who must live with the agony of having taken a life. I hurt more for Shane's mother, who has now seen two of her four sons go to prison. A divorcee, she now delivers newspapers in Cavalier Manor.

106   I saw her recently after she tossed a paper onto my parents' doorstep. Her hair had grayed considerably. We hugged and chatted. She seemed proud that I had turned my life around, but I felt guilty and wondered again why I got a second chance and her sons did not. After an awkward silence, I got Shane's prison address from her and said good-bye. I wrote to him and he wrote me back. I broke down and cried when I read the letter:

> Yo Nate,
>   I am sorry that I didn't get back with you before now. I am fine and everything is going well with me. I know that you are still doing well. I am proud of you, Nate. . . .
>   Now I have my mind in the right frame of thinking with this long-term bid of mine. But I did what I had to do. (There

was more to it than appeared in the papers.) Anyway I will
keep in touch with you from now on. I am really heavy in the
Qur'an now. And I am truly a warrior from the spirit within
me. I know what and where my life will lead me from here
on. Peace be with you, Brother.

Later,
Shane

107   For those who'd like answers, I have no pithy social formulas to
end black-on-black violence. But I do know that I see a younger,
meaner generation out there now—more lost and alienated than we
were, and placing even less value on life. We were at least touched
by role models; this new bunch is totally estranged from the black
mainstream. Crack has taken the drug game to a more lethal level
and given young blacks far more economic incentive to opt for the
streets.

108   I've come to fear that of the many things a black man can die
from, the first may be rage—his own or someone else's. For that reason, I seldom stick around when I stop on the block. One day not long
ago, I spotted a few familiar faces hanging out at the old haunt, the
7-Eleven. I wheeled into the parking lot, strode over, and high-fived
the guys I knew. Within moments, I sensed that I was in danger. I
felt hostile stares from those I didn't know.

109   I was frightened by these younger guys, who now controlled my
former turf. I eased back to my car and left, because I knew this:
that if they saw the world as I once did, they believed they had nothing to lose, including life itself.

110   It made me wanna holler and throw up both my hands.

John Edgar Wideman
(1941–)

*Born June 14, 1941, in Washington, D.C., John Edgar Wideman was
raised in the Pittsburgh, Pennsylvania, neighborhood of Homewood,
the setting for much of his fiction. Wideman, who was the eldest of five
children, excelled at both academics and athletics in high school,
emerging as the class president and valedictorian. Attending the University of Pennsylvania on a Benjamin Franklin Scholarship, Wideman
became a Phi Beta Kappa and in 1963 was named a Rhodes scholar,
becoming only the second African American to be so honored (Alain*

*Locke, 55 years earlier, was the first). In 1966, he graduated from
Oxford University and thereafter held academic appointments at the
University of Pennsylvania and the University of Wyoming. Currently,
he is a professor of English at the University of Massachusetts at
Amherst. After publishing* A Glance Away *(1967), his first novel, at the
age of 26, Wideman has produced such works of fiction as* Hurry
Home *(1969),* The Lynchers *(1973),* Damballah *(1981),* Hiding Place
(1981), Sent for You Yesterday *(1984),* Reuben *(1987),* Philadelphia
Fire *(1990),* The Cattle Killing *(1996), and* Two Cities: A Love Story
*(1998). Wideman also has published autobiographical works, includ-
ing* Brothers and Keepers *(1984), which is excerpted below,*
Fatheralong: A Meditation on Fathers and Sons *(1994), and* Hoop
Roots *(2001). For more than 30 years, Wideman has been hailed as an
innovative writer whose technique, vision, and craft have been rewarded
with two PEN/Faulkner Awards.*

Brothers and Keepers

1   At about the time I was beginning to teach Afro-American literature
at the University of Pennsylvania, back home on the streets of Pittsburgh Robby was living through the changes in black culture and
consciousness I was reading about and discussing with my students
in the quiet of the classroom. Not until we began talking together in
prison did I learn about that side of his rebelliousness. *Black Fire* was
a book I used in my course. It was full of black rage and black dreams
and black love. In the sixties when the book was published, young
black men were walking the streets with, as one of the *Black Fire* writers put it, dynamite growing out of their skulls. I'd never associated
Robby with the fires in Homewood and in cities across the land, never
envisioned him bobbing in and out of the flames, a constant danger
to himself, to everyone around him because "dynamite was growing
out of his skull." His plaited naps hadn't looked like fuses to me. I
was teaching, I was trying to discover words to explain what was happening to black people. That my brother might have something to say
about these matters never occurred to me. The sad joke was, I never
even spoke to Robby. Never knew until years later that he was the one
who could have told me much of what I needed to hear.

2   It was a crazy summer. The summer of '68. We fought the cops
in the streets. I mean sure nuff punch-out fighting like in them Wild

West movies and do. Shit. Everybody in Homewood up on Homewood Avenue duking with the cops. Even the little weeny kids was there, standing back throwing rocks. We fought that whole summer. Cop cars all over the place and they'd come jumping out with night sticks and fists balled up. They wore leather jackets and gloves and sometimes they be wearing them football helmets so you couldn't go upside they heads without hurting your hand. We was rolling. Steady fighting. All you need to be doing was walking down the avenue and here they come. Screeching the brakes. Pull up behind you and three or four cops come busting out the squad car ready to rumble. Me and some the fellas just minding our business walking down Homewood and this squad car pulls up. Hey, you. Hold it. Stop where you are, like he's talking to some silly kids or something. All up in my face. What you doing here, like I ain't got no right to be on Homewood Avenue, and I been walking on Homewood Avenue all my life an ain't no jive police gon get on my case just cause I'm walking down the avenue. Fuck you, pig. Ain't none your goddamn business, pig. Well, you know it's on then. Cop come running at Henry and Henry ducks down on one knee and jacks the mother-fucker up. Throw him clean through that big window of Murphy's five-and-dime. You know where I mean. Where Murphy's used to be. Had that cop snatched up in the air and through that window before he knew what hit him. Then it's on for sure. We rolling right there in the middle of Homewood Avenue.

3   That's the way it was. Seem like we was fighting cops everyday. Funny thing was, it was just fighting. Wasn't no shooting or nothing like that. Somebody musta put word out from Downtown. You can whip the niggers' heads but don't be shooting none of em. Yeah. Cause the cops would get out there and fight but they never used no guns. Might bust your skull with a nightstick but they wasn't gon shoot you. So the word must have been out. Cause you know if it was left to the cops they would have blowed us all away. Somebody said don't shoot and we figured that out so it was stone rock 'n' roll and punch-up time.

4   Sometimes I think the cops dug it too. You know like it was exercise or something. Two or three carloads roll up and it's time to get it on. They was looking for trouble. You could tell. You didn't have to yell pig or nothing. Just be minding your business and here they come piling out the car ready to go ten rounds. I got tired of fighting cops. And getting whipped on. We had some guys go up on the rooves. Brothers was gon waste the motherfuckers from up there when they go riding down the street but shit, wasn't no sense bringing guns

into it long as they wasn't shooting at us. Brothers didn't play in those days. We was organized. Cops jump somebody and in two minutes half of Homewood out there on them cops' ass. We was organized and had our own weapons and shit. Rooftops and them old boarded-up houses was perfect for snipers. Dudes had pistols and rifles and shotguns. You name it. Wouldna believed what the brothers be firing if it come to that but it didn't come to that. Woulda been stone war in the streets. But the shit didn't come down that way. Maybe it woulda been better if it did. Get it all out in the open. Get the killing done wit. But the shit didn't hit the fan that summer. Least not that way.

5   Lemme see. I woulda been in eleventh grade. One more year of Westinghouse left after the summer of '68. We was the ones started the strike. Right in the halls of good old Westinghouse High School. Like I said, we had this organization. There was lots of organizations and clubs and stuff like that back then but we had us a mean group. Like, if you was serious business you was wit us. Them other people was into a little bit of this and that, but we was in it all the way. We was gon change things or die trying. We was known as bad. Serious business, you know. If something was coming down they always wanted us wit them. See, if we was in it, it was some mean shit. Had to be. Cause we didn't play. What it was called was Together. Our group. We was so bad we was having a meeting once and one the brothers bust in. Hey youall. Did youall hear on the radio Martin Luther King got killed? One the older guys running the meeting look up and say, We don't care nothing bout that ass-kissing nigger, we got important business to take care of. See, we just knew we was into something. Together was where it was at. Didn't nobody dig what King putting down. We wasn't about begging whitey for nothing and we sure wasn't taking no knots without giving a whole bunch back. After the dude come in hollering and breaking up the meeting we figured we better go on out in the street anyway cause we didn't want no bullshit. You know. Niggers running wild and tearing up behind Martin Luther King getting wasted. We was into planning. Into organization. When the shit went down we was gon be ready. No point in just flying around like chickens with they heads cut off. I mean like it ain't news that whitey is offing niggers. So we go out the meeting to cool things down. No sense nobody getting killed on no humbug.

6   Soon as we got outside you could see the smoke rising off Homewood Avenue. Wasn't that many people out and Homewood burning already, so we didn't really know what to do. Walked down to

Hamilton and checked it out around in there and went up past the A & P. Say to anybody we see, Cool it. Cool it, brother. Our time will come. It ain't today, brother. Cool it. But we ain't really got no plan. Didn't know what to do, so me and Henry torched the Fruit Market and went on home.

7   Yeah. I was a stone mad militant. Didn't know what I was saying half the time and wasn't sure what I wanted, but I was out there screaming and hollering and waving my arms around and didn't take no shit from nobody. Mommy and them got all upset cause I was in the middle of the school strike. I remember sitting down and arguing with them many a time. All they could talk about was me messing up in school. You know. Get them good grades and keep your mouth shut and mind your own business. Trying to tell me white folks ain't all bad. Asking me where would niggers be if it wasn't for good white folks. They be arguing that mess at me and they wasn't about to hear nothing I had to say. What it all come down to was be a good nigger and the white folks take care of you. Now I really couldn't believe they was saying that. Mommy and Geral got good sense. They ain't nobody's fools. How they talking that mess? Wasn't no point in arguing really, cause I was set in my ways and they sure was set in theirs. It was the white man's world and wasn't no way round it or over it or under it. Got to get down and dance to the tune the man be playing. You know I didn't want to hear nothing like that, so I kept on cutting classes and fucking up and doing my militant thing every chance I got.

8   I dug being a militant cause I was good. It was something I could do. Rap to people. Whip a righteous message on em. People knew my name. They'd listen. And I'd steady take care of business. This was when Rap Brown and Stokely and Bobby Seale and them on TV. I identified with those cats. Malcolm and Eldridge and George Jackson. I read their books. They was Gods. That's who I thought I was when I got up on the stage and rapped at the people. It seemed like things was changing. Like no way they gon turn niggers round this time.

9   You could feel it everywhere. In the streets. On the corner. Even in jive Westinghouse High people wasn't going for all that old, tired bullshit they be laying on you all the time. We got together a list of demands. Stuff about the lunchroom and a black history course. Stuff like that and getting rid of the principal. We wasn't playing. I mean he was a mean nasty old dude. Hated niggers. No question about that. He wouldn't listen to nobody. Didn't care what was going on. Everybody hated him. We told them people from the school board his ass

had to go first thing or we wasn't coming back to school. It was a strike, see. Started in Westinghouse, but by the end of the week it was all over the city. Langley and Perry and Fifth Avenue and Schenley. Sent messengers to all the schools, and by the end of the week all the brothers and sisters on strike. Shut the schools down all cross the city, so they knew we meant business. Knew they had to listen. The whole Board of Education came to Westinghouse and we told the principal to his face he had to go. The nasty old motherfucker was sitting right there and we told the board, He has to go. The man hates us and we hate him and his ass got to go. Said it right to his face and you ought to seen him turning purple and flopping round in his chair. Yeah. We got on his case. And the thing was they gave us everything we asked for. Yes . . . Yes . . . Yes. Everything we had on the list. Sat there just as nice and lied like dogs. Yes. We agree. Yes. You'll have a new principal. I couldn't believe it. Didn't even have to curse them out or nothing. Didn't even raise my voice cause it was yes to this and yes to that before the words out my mouth good.

10   We's so happy we left that room with the Board and ran over to the auditorium and in two minutes it was full and I'm up there screaming. We did it. We did it. People shouting back Right on and Work out and I gets that whole auditorium dancing in they seats. I could talk now. Yes, I could. And we all happy as could be, cause we thought we done something. We got the black history course and got us a new principal and, shit, wasn't nothing we couldn't do, wasn't nothing could stop us that day. Somebody yelled, Party, and I yelled back, Party, and then I told them, Everybody come on up to Westinghouse Park. We gon stone party. Wasn't no plan or nothing. It all just started in my head. Somebody shouted party and I yelled Party and the next thing I know we got this all-night jam going. We got bands and lights and we partied all night long. Ima tell you the truth now. Got more excited bout the party than anything else. Standing up there on the stage I could hear the music and see the niggers dancing and I'm thinking, Yeah. I'm thinking bout getting high and tipping round, checking out the babes and grooving on the sounds. Got me a little reefer and sipping out somebody's jug of sweet wine and the park's full of bloods and I'm in heaven. That's the way it was too. We partied all night long in Westinghouse Park. Cops like to shit, but wasn't nothing they could do. This was 1968. Wasn't nothing they could do but surround the park and sit out there in they cars while we partied. It was something else. Bands and bongos and

niggers singing, *Oh bop she bop* everywhere in the park. Cops sat out in them squad cars and Black Marias, but wasn't nothing they could do. We was smoking and drinking and carrying on all night and they just watched us, just sat in the dark and didn't do a thing. We broke into the park building to get us some lectricity for the bands and shit. And get us some light. Broke in the door and took what we wanted, but them cops ain't moved an inch. It was our night and they knew it. Knew they better leave well enough alone. We owned Westinghouse Park that night. Thought we owned Homewood.

11   In a way the party was the end. School out pretty soon after that and nobody followed through. We come back to school in the fall and they got cops patrolling the halls and locks on every door. You couldn't go in or out the place without passing by a cop. They had our ass then. Turned the school into a prison. Wasn't no way to get in the auditorium. Wasn't no meetings or hanging out in the halls. They broke up all that shit. That's when having police in the schools really got started. When it got to be a regular everyday thing. They fixed us good. Yes, yes, yes, when we was sitting down with the Board, but when we come back to school in September everything got locks and chains on it.

12   We was just kids. Didn't really know what we wanted. Like I said. The party was the biggest thing to me. I liked to get up and rap. I was a little Stokely, a little Malcolm in my head but I didn't know shit. When I look back I got to admit it was mostly just fun and games. Looking for a way to get over. Nothing in my head. Nothing I could say I really wanted. Nothing I wanted to be. So they lied through their teeth. Gave us a party and we didn't know no better, didn't know we had to follow through, didn't know how to keep our foot in they ass.

13   Well, you know the rest. Nothing changed. Business as usual when we got back in the fall. Hey, hold on. What's this? Locks on the dorm. Cops in the halls. Big cops with big guns. Hey, man, what's going down? But it was too late. The party was over and they wasn't about to give up nothing no more. We had a black history class, but wasn't nobody eligible to take it. Had a new principal, but nobody knew him. Nobody could get to him. And he didn't know us. Didn't know what we was about except we was trouble. Troublemakers; and he had something for that. Boot your ass out in a minute. Give your name to the cops and you couldn't get through the door cause everybody had to have an I.D. Yeah. That was a new one. Locks and I.D.'s and cops. Wasn't never our school. They

made it worse instead of better. Had our chance, then they made
sure we wouldn't have no more chances.

14   It was fun while it lasted. Some good times, but they was over in
a minute and then things got worser and worser. Sixty-eight was when
the dope came in real heavy too. I mean you could always get dope
but it seems like they flooded Homewood. Easy as buying a quart
of milk. Could cop your works in a drugstore. Dope was everywhere
that summer. Cats ain't never touched the stuff before got into dope
and dope got into them. A bitch, man. It came in like a flood.

15   Me. I start to using heavy that summer. Just like everybody else
I knew. The shit was out there and it was good and cheap, so why not?
What else we supposed to be doing? It was part of the fun. The good
times. The party.

16   We lost it over the summer, but I still believe we did something hip
for a bunch of kids. The strike was citywide. We shut the schools
down. All the black kids was with us. The smart ones. The dumb
ones. It was hip to be on strike. To show our asses. We had them
honkies scared. Got the whole Board of Education over to Westinghouse High. We lost it, but we had them going, Bruh. And I was in
the middle of it. Mommy and them didn't understand. They thought
I was just in trouble again. The way I always was, Daddy said one
his friends works Downtown told him they had my name down there.
Had my name and the rest of the ringleaders'. He said they were
watching me. They had my name Downtown and I better be cool. But
I wasn't scared. Always in trouble, always doing wrong. But the strike
was different. I was proud of that. Proud of getting it started, proud
of being one the ringleaders. The mad militant. Didn't know exactly
what I was doing, but I was steady doing it.

17   The week the strike started, think it was Tuesday, could have
been Monday but I think it was Tuesday, cause the week before
was when some the students went to the principal's office and said
the student council or some damn committee or something wanted
to talk to him about the lunchroom and he said he'd listen but he
was busy till next week, so it could have been Monday, but I think
it was Tuesday cause knowing him he'd put it off long as he could.
Anyway, Mr. Lindsay sitting in the auditorium. Him and vice-prin-
cipal Meers and the counselor, Miss Kwalik. They in the second or
third row sitting back and the speakers is up on stage behind the
mike but they ain't using it. Just talking to the air really, cause I
slipped in one the side doors and I'm peeping what's going on. And

ain't nothing going on. Most the time the principal whispering to Miss Kwalik and Mr. Meers. Lindsay got a tablet propped up on his knee and writes something down every now and then but he ain't really listening to the kids on stage. Probably just taking names cause he don't know nobody's name. Taking names and figuring how he's gon fuck over the ones doing the talking. You. You in the blue shirt, Come over here. Don't none them know your name less you always down in the office cause you in trouble or you one the kiss-ass, nicey-nice niggers they keep for flunkies and spies. So he's taking names or whatever, and every once in a while he says something like, Yes. That's enough now. Who's next? Waving the speakers on and off and the committee, or whatever the fuck they calling theyselves, they ain't got no better sense than to jump when he say jump. Half of them so scared they stuttering and shit. I know they glad when he wave them off the stage cause they done probably forgot what they up there for.

18   Well, I get sick of this jive real quick. Before I know it I'm up on the stage and I'm tapping the mike and can't get it turned on so I goes to shouting. Talking trash loud as I can. Damn this and damn that and Black Power and I'm somebody. Tell em ain't no masters and slaves no more and we want freedom and we want it now. I'm stone preaching. I'm chirping. Get on the teachers, get on the principal and everybody else I can think of. Called em zookeepers. Said they ran a zoo and wagged my finger at the chief zookeeper and his buddies sitting down there in the auditorium. Told the kids on the stage to go and get the students. You go here. You go there. Like I been giving orders all my life. Cleared the stage in a minute. Them chairs scraped and kids run off and it's just me up there all by my own-self. I runs out of breath. I'm shaking, but I'm not scared. Then it gets real quiet. Mr. Lindsay stands up. He's purple and shaking worse than me. Got his finger stabbing at me now. Shoe's on the other foot now. Up there all by myself now and he's doing the talking.

19   Are you finished? I hope you're finished cause your ass is grass. Come down from there this instant. You've gone too far this time, Wideman. Get down from there. I want you in my office immediately.

20   They's all three up now, Mr. Lindsay and Miss Kwalik and Meers, up and staring up at me like I'm stone crazy. Like I just pulled out my dick and peed on the stage or something. Like they don't believe it. And to tell the truth I don't hardly believe it myself. One minute I'm watching them kids making fools of theyselves, next minute I'm

bad-mouthing everything about the school and giving orders and telling Mr. Lindsay to his face he ain't worth shit. Now the whiteys is up and staring at me like I'm a disease, like I'm Bad Breath or Okey Doke the damn fool and I'm looking round and it's just me up there. Don't know if the other kids is gone for the students like I told them or just run away cause they scared.

21   Ain't many times in life I felt so lonely. I'm thinking bout home. What they gon say when Mr. Lindsay calls and tells them he kicked my ass out for good. Cause I had talked myself in a real deep hole. Like, Burn, baby burn. We was gon run the school our way or burn the motherfucker down. Be our school or wasn't gon be no school. Yeah, I was yelling stuff like that and I was remembering it all. Cause it was real quiet in there. Could of heard a pin drop in the balcony. Remembering everything I said and then starting to figure how I was gon talk myself out this one. Steady scheming and just about ready to cop a plea. I's sorry boss. Didn't mean it, Boss. I was just kidding. Making a joke. Ha. Ha. I loves this school and loves you Mr. Lindsay. My head's spinning and I'm moving away from the mike but just at that very minute I hears the kids busting into the balcony. It's my people. It's sure nuff them. They bust in the balcony and I ain't by myself no more. I'm hollering again and shaking a power fist and I tells Mr. Lindsay:

22   You get out. You leave.

23   I'm king again. He don't say a word. Just splits with his flunkies. The mike starts working and that's when the strike begins.

24   Your brother was out there in the middle of it. I was good, too. Lot of the time I be thinking bout the party afterward, my heart skipping forward to the party, but I was willing to work. Be out front. Take the weight. Had the whole city watching us, Bruh.

Eugene B. Redmond

(1937–)

Eugene B. Redmond was born on December 1, 1937, in St. Louis, Missouri. His family moved across the river to East St. Louis, Illinois, when he was six months old. Redmond has authored or edited numerous volumes of poetry, collections of diverse writings, and plays for stage and television. He has edited the posthumously published works of Henry Dumas, for whose estate Redmond serves as literary executor. In the 1960s, he spent two years as Teacher-Counselor and Poet-in-Residence at Southern Illinois University's Experiment in Higher Education in East St. Louis, where he was a colleague of Dumas, Joyce Ladner, and Katherine Dunham. He is currently at work on a multi-year epic poem about Dunham, his longtime friend and mentor. Redmond received an American Book Award for The Eye in the Ceiling: Selected Poems *(1993). Other collections of his poetry include* Sentry of the Four Golden Pillars *(1970),* River of Bones and Flesh and Blood *(1971),* Songs from an Afro-Phone *(1972),* Consider Loneliness as These Things *(1974), and* Blues-Ode to the ForeDreamers & Other Poems *(2001). He was named Poet Laureate of East St. Louis in 1976, the same year that he published his best-selling critical history,* Drumvoices: The Mission of Afro-American Poetry. *Currently, he is professor of English, Chairman of the Creative Writing Committee, and editor of* Drumvoices Revue *(of which he is the founding editor) at Southern Illinois University-Edwardsville.*

City Night Storm

For L. Wendell Rivers

Dark winds kiss the walls
And split on the blades of corners;
The burning eyes of the city dance
In a thousand rusting skulls.

5 Twisting trees listen to
The pulses of tired streets;
And birds miss their landings.

A fleeing garbage can suddenly
Scares a sleeping cat; and a drunk,
10 Held upright by the headwind,
Slouches into daylight.

The condescending moon says nothing,
But coasts half-seen along night's ceiling;
And the angry, chilling breath rushes over
15 *Darkness, like water over a fall.*

We're Tight, Soul-Tight—
Like Lincolnites

(Occasioned by the 45ᵗʰ Reunion of the East St. Louis (Illinois) Lincoln
High School Class of 1957)

It wasn't Elmore James, Muddy Waters or Howlin' Wolf growling
　"Dust My Broom"
Or Big Mama Thornton driving a "Hound Dog" from Big Sister's
　door
Or the Coasters crooning "Charlie Brown" from hi-fis & juke boxes
　at the Green House or Masonic Hall . . .
It was Lincolnite Amos Leon Thomas, expanding/contracting
　against wall lockers in the boys room—

5　　　　"Who did they kill?
　　　　Emmett Bobo Till"—

anticipating the quietly explosive Freedom Ride of Rosa Parks,
Montgomery's dauntless seamstress,
as Shock Troupes of "We Shall Overcome"
10 invaded the Evil Kingdom of Orval Faubus on the Planet Arkansas.

And, baby, ain't no Friend *tight* as a Fifties' Friend: we were
　Lincolnite-*tight*, *tight* as Dick's hatband,
frontporch-*tight*, virgin-*tight*, *tight* as our slave-ship ancestors,
　jazz-*tight*, Billy Eckstine-*tight*, blood-*tight*.
Bluesplendently tight in The Age of Metropolitan Opera's Marian
　Anderson, Charlie Parker & Sputnik,
Chuck Berry & Nobel Laureate Ralph Bunche, Little Richard & Joe
　Louis, Amos n' Andy & Elvis,
15 Dorothy Dandridge & Thurgood Marshall, American Bandstand &
　Ruth Brown, coalsheds, crawlspaces &
outhouses, Monroe & Hitchcock, & hydrogen/bomb/shelters built
　in the shadows of Khrushchev-fear. The
Age of Pioneers & Frontiers, rib tips & wing tips, the sexy-breathy
　snarl of Eartha Kitt & Julie London.

1957 in the sunglassed city of copper-river-smiles, packing-house-
　hips & rail-road-legs—

& we were *Miles Ahead* with Homeboy Trumpeters Miles & Raleigh
 McDonald,
20 "Move/d On Up a Little Higher" by Mahalia Jackson, make-
 shifting—like Wesbury Bascom,
 Jesse Owens, Althea Gipson, Spike Perkins & Sugar Ray
 Robinson—
 from chump change to Sam Cooke's seismic "gonna come" *change*,
 dap as Sammy Davis in "Mr. Wonderful," keen as the news-eye of
 John Hicks & John Kirkpatrick,
 feasting like King Satchmo on smothered, fried or barbecued
 gospel bird after sermonic Sundays.

25 Sons—& daughters, too—shone everyday at Lincoln—carrier of
 Hughes-Quinn's dream-bright baton—
 unless someone "had"—or "missed"—a "monthly"—in endless
 glistening bi-lingual halls
 of gossip, Latin, algebra, Muzzy, French, hooky, nooky & dice
 games: hundred-yard dash halls
 winging eastward to shop classes, a winning season of hoops, lunch
 stampedes & drill-field;
 westward to silver-brassy boom-booms of band room &
 homemakers drunk on acappela ala
30 Billie/Ethel/Ella/Clara/Dinah . . . near a hall-end avenue of
 fashion & culture brimming with talent shows
 gracing star-bound Grace Bumbry, "Moody's Mood for Love," pep
 rallies & Ike Turner
 crossing the tracks between the Manhattan Club & Lincoln on a
 flotilla of guitars
 where Boss Ross ("two-weeks") Miller, jingling like keys and
 dangling from suspenders,
 punctuated oscillations of Ike's pelvis with "no no no no no no no
 no no!!!!"

35 O Lincoln Academy of Arts Sciences Athletics where teenage
 orators, crooners & instrumentalists
 like Joseph Enlow unleashed "Honky-Tonk," "The Creation," "Too
 Young," "The Great Pretender,"
 "The Raven," "Mama," our namesake's "Gettysburg Address,"
 "Mona Lisa," "If," "The Signifying
 Monkey," "Lift Every Voice and Sing," "You Saw Me Crying in the
 Chapel," "I Believe," "Thanatopsis,"

"One Mint Julep," "Hiawatha," "Earth Angel," "Tweedle Dee,"
    "Walk On," "Everyday I Have the Blues,"
40 "Jim Dandy," "In the Still of the Night," "Hoochie Coochie Man,"
    "Sixty-Minute Man" . . .

    "O who lit Montgomery's sparks?
    That dauntless seamstress Rosa Parks!"

O Beckoning two-story skyscraper on a neighborhood Highway, 2-
    buildings & 69-years removed
from your 1888 beginnings (at 6th & St. Louis Avenue) when
    classy-sassy "1957" exited your
45 hypnotic bosom bounded by Catfish River Sippi & Fireworks
    Station, sandwiched by pedal-pushing
visions & multi-part harmonies of John Robinson and John
    DeShields Projects, concentric-sound spicings
of Goose Hill, Polack Town, Popeye's/Ringside's/Yates's Pool Halls,
    Rush City & Denverside
(backyard watermelon farms, onion groves, bean vines, goat
    dominions & chicken coops),
omnipresent Jesuses in statuesque or storefront sanctuaries,
50 15th Street's south-marching continuum of commercial hives:
Broadway Brady Bond Piggott Boismenue Russell, Harlem &
    Deluxe Theaters,
hamlets & harbors & hangouts of Alorton Centreville Eagle Park
    The Island,
Midtown shores of Virginia Place & Brother Joe Mays's Dynasty,
Sykes Drugs & Daisy's Floral Shop of boutonnières, corsages,
    carnations & peppermint pickles,
55 Scotia's post-prom Shrimps, Deadman's Curve to Brooklyn—&
    Young's & Garrett's, Dabney's due south on
Market, McDonald's & Shorty Humphrey's Rockway for after-a-
    game banana splits & sundaes,
Chuck-ducking with Berry & swiveling with B.B.'s Lucille at the
    Cosmo,
petticoat dreams/bobbysocks'd-bubblegum/divas whose first
    French Kiss lit up the Southend like Xmas
(steamy Tigerettes purring in pushbutton Dodges, under black
    bridges & in Franklin & Lincoln Parks),
60 fellas graduating from brogans to biscuit mouth Staceys
    (surrounded by a river of white threads),
from coveralls to charcoals & pinstripes & belt-in-the-back
    bennies,

from spitballs to brass knucks & razors & zip guns
(while ex-virgins, longing for their hit-it & quit-it heroes, were left
    cryin' momma a river . . .)—

       "Who did they kill?
65   Emmett 'Bobo' Till!"

Lincoln Land of rail-road-legs & packing-house-hips,
party-lines/hi-fi's/jukeboxes/drive-ins,
brothers fathers boyfriends bound for or back from Korea,
sisters mothers girlfriends bounding from kitchens to typewriters to
    civil service to loneliness,
70 alumni launching into the worlds Jackson & Tennessee State,
    Omaha & Chicago "killing floors,"
Lincoln U. & SIU, Naptown & Virginia Union, armed forces, jail &
    alcohol & oblivion . . .

Destiny gave Fifty-Seveners its best & worst shots. Turned its
    beauty & its backside to us.
Through warts, triumphs, heart- & brain-break, we sparkle *tight*
    like true Lincolnites.
Two score & five years ago, as we emerged from the Lincoln Oven,
75 baked & ready for the Whirl to decorate us with icings, trimmings
    & dangers;
we were bequeathed the baton of Elwood Buchanan, Scotia
    Thomas Calhoun,
Marion Officer, Eugene Haynes, Jr., Miles Davis, Wyvetter Hoover
    Younge, Donald McHenry,
Reginald Petty & Barbara Ann Teer—
a baton we passed to Eugene Foley, Portia Hunt, Peggy Gregory,
    Wesley McNeese,
80 Reginald Thomas, Jackie Joyner-Kersee, Homer Bush, LaFonso
    Ellis, Erika Johnson. Russell Gunn,
Vicki Hubbard & Darius Miles . . . extending the hand-off into a
    natal cord-Continuum . . .
our own children & their children & . . . let the story, like the
    CIRCLE of the ring shout, never be unbroken.

SO, Say Hey! Hey! Classmates! We're Phine & Phoxxy as New
    Money,
Straddling Two Millennia, Two Centuries, Two Decades & some
    change.

85 *Tight*, Soul-*tight*, Blood-*tight* like *Lincolnites!*

Indigenous Daughter Awake in the Dreams of Nana

For Peggy Ann Newman—on the occasion of her 55th Birthday, June 30, 2000

indigenous daughter's heart spoke through her eyes
upon her dream-brilliant arrival
   curled like a pearl
in the womb of wartime East Saint Louis
5 whose Gregoryan chants,
syncopated stitches of a homespun pastiche,
emerged from gardens, green thumbs, cigar trees, clean dirt
yards,
train whistles, bard Dunbar's School, hymns & street corner
10 oracles

who, from her 14th street fo'c'sle,
scoped the hives of jive & ethics of sweat
floating between 13th Street, Boismenue & Colas Avenues

navigated dutiful daughter-hours
15 through oceans of dictionaries, bibles & dishwater

girlwhirled in the family gyre
of activists, composers, educators, polyglots & farmers
—several Milky Ways from Ladue—
she became Bond Avenue's Valedictorian,
20 sandwiched between Miles & Jackie at Lincoln High,
then hurdled the Mississippi & climbed
the Phi Beta Kappa staircase at Washington University

began exploring God's sleeping provinces,
looking for hidden countries of opportunity

25 became daughter-mother & astute parent
scholar-mother & astute parent
lawyer-mother & astute parent
le grand mother & astute nana

with seed & thread she sewed credos
30 of tolerance into mosaics of commitment,
volunteering her heart to bi-state & bi-cultural causes,
forbid that the River be a divide—
but an arterial song of reciprocal transfusions

spiritual homebody circling her son/s—& their gardens—
35 & stitching petite stems of love
into the fabric of newly encountered spheres

quilted families by hand & washed them in joy-boiled tears
before pegging them to the stars
& ecstatically flying to remotely accessible
40 heights of music, drama, opera, jazz . . .
but remained un-at-home in airplanes

versatile defender of underlived lives,
nana,
empowered flower from the garden of King Alfred & Queen Mary,

45 nana,
whose heart, cuddling a bouquet of green thumbs,
speaks through her eyes
speaks through her eyes

Choreo-Empress' Leg-a-cy Lands on East Saint Earth, 2nd Take

homage to Katherine Dunham, age 90 plus

#1

1967: descendant descends to black arts movement

Touchdown: East Saint Earth:
maze of Port Au Princely slinks:
choreojazzopera.

#2

5   *routes de passage*

Hambone's "Minnehaha"—
Katherine's choreoper-ah!—
"Sally Walker" to "L'Ag Ya!"

#3

1925 bus ride recalls east saint louis race riots of 1917

10   Yanvalou lurched past
East Boogie's charred memories,
tomb of Lovejoy's Alton.

#4

joliet, chicago, port au prince

Lady Diaspora
15   hurdled AME's prayer bench,
ball & jack'd Damballah.

#5

christening of the drumpriestess

Between death & dawn
snakes, stilts & tambourines
20   chased rum-drunk zombies.

#6

1967: dumas & dunham return to east saint louis

Fox/goddess & Ankh Dumas
orbited Arkansippi,
Blood Island & Cotton Club.

#7

25   *fleshing dreams & homages at the barre*

Pelvic motors buzzed
Queen's Court in Milesville, drumscoped
"East Saint Louis Toodle-oo."

#8

star of dakar domiciles in east boogie

30 From tin & wombwood, Mor Thiam,
her Wolof prince/protégé,
fleshed djembe miracle.

#9

feasts of art & revolution

Labanotations
35 rioted in Katherine's
God-spacious girdle.

#10

90th birthday celebration in Milesvile

Lords of London legs
flew her Vodou chariot
40 thru nine decades & change.

Wishing . . .

that deaf jams ignite a def love,
deaf wars beget def peace, rulers imbibe
freedom-sweet serum ala caged bird café
trent-numbed dreams scale grooves of blues
5 before lott-ery yields home/grown nine-elevens
dressed in bomb-ware of third whirls,
that outside traders make end-runs 'round
enron's offense: rattle conch/us chattel—to battle!,
that patient plurals . . . kwanzaa ramadan xmas . . . prevail,
10 & litany of britney w/jelly of nelly
rise yeast-like—like Billie/s of duke,
dre(a)ds of scott, miles of jackie, lions
of east-saint-leon, deaf jams fencing
def love, deaf wars' rebirth . . . def peace . . .

Terry McMillan
(1951–)

Among the most popular African American authors, Terry McMillan was born on October 18, 1951, in Port Huron, Michigan. She earned a bachelor's degree from the University of California, Berkeley, and a master's degree from Columbia University. Upon the publication of her first novel, Mama *(1987), she tirelessly promoted the work, mailing some 3,000 letters to bookstores, universities, and other organizations. Her campaign was successful and, as a result,* Mama *went into a third printing in less than two months. The novel was a critical success as well; McMillan received an American Book Award in 1988. Subsequent novels include* Disappearing Acts *(1989),* Waiting to Exhale *(1992), and* How Stella Got Her Groove Back *(1996), each of which has been adapted to film. McMillan also has written the novel* A Day Late A Dollar Short *(2001) and edited* Breaking Ice: An Anthology of Contemporary African-American Fiction *(1990). The following selection is the third chapter from* Mama, *wherein Mildred Peacock talks with her oldest daughter, Freda, as they move about Point Haven, Michigan.*

Mama

1   Even after the first year had passed and Mildred's endurance had sunk below sea level, she didn't have a single regret about divorcing Crook. She'd been fired from Diamond Crystal Salt because she'd called in sick too many times in the few short months she'd worked there. It was boring work to Mildred anyway. All she did from seven to three in the afternoon was add a free-flowing agent to the fine-grained salt so it wouldn't cake up from the humidity. It didn't make any sense to her. She always had to put a few grains of rice in her salt shaker when it caked up anyway, so what was the point?

2   It was mostly the kids who'd gotten sick, not her. Bad colds. Mumps. Measles. Then Freda started her period in the middle of her science class and threw up all over the bathroom floor when she got home. Now, Mildred was back out in Huronville on her knees six days a week, cleaning the Hales', Grahams', and Callingtons' houses.

3   Mildred hated cleaning up behind white folks (behind anybody, really), but it was steady work and most of the time they left her alone in the house and she was able to work at her own pace. Nobody was standing over her shoulder the way they had when she worked at Big Boy's and the Shingle, breathing out commands or hinting at what she should do next. Here she did everything the way she felt like doing it. Quickly.

4   One morning, after six months of listening to Freda beg her, Mildred let Freda come with her to see the rich folks' houses on the condition that Freda would help her clean, do something besides get in her way.

5   When they pulled up in the Mercury, Freda acted like she was getting out of a limousine. She walked proudly through the oak doors.

6   "Ooooooo, Mama, can you believe this?" Freda asked, as she glided through one room after another.

7   "Just don't touch nothing, girl, this shit ain't fake. Everything in here is real, and it's expensive. We barely had enough gas to get out here so you know we can't pay for nothing if you break it."

8   Freda promised her she wouldn't touch anything, but as soon as Mildred went about her business, Freda's fingers slid over the bronze and brass and alabaster. She was awestruck. When she heard the vacuum cleaner in the other room, she flopped down in the middle of the white couch and spread her arms across the back. Her bright black eyes scanned the airy room. She tried to guess how high the ceiling was. Fifteen or twenty feet? A chandelier with at least five thousand tiny lights glistened in the sun streaming through the tall windows. A fireplace big enough for her to walk in stood in the center of the room. Freda wondered how many times it had been lit, and if they roasted marshmallows or weenies there in the winter-time. What a way to live, she thought. She closed her eyes, let her head fall back on the couch, and imagined six of her best girlfriends lying by the fireplace in flannel nightgowns, eating popcorn and dreaming out loud about their prospective boy-friends. They were having a great time in Freda's house, and how they envied her. They loved her slumber parties because there was always plenty of everything to eat and her house was always spotless.

9   "Freda, what you doing in there, girl? You too quiet, and I know when you quiet you up to something. I told you not to touch nothing, didn't I?"

10   "I didn't touch nothing, Mama. I'm coming." Freda walked toward the yellow and white kitchen, where Mildred was running hot water into a tin pail.

11   "I'm hungry, Mama. Can I have something to eat?"

12   "Look in the icebox, girl." When Freda opened the door, her eyes zigzagged across each shelf. She had never seen so much food in a refrigerator. There were pickles and olives, a big leafy head of lettuce, stacks and stacks of lunch meat, and three different kinds of bread. There was fresh fruit—oranges and apples and grapes. Everything was neatly housed in plastic containers. But there was something so orderly about this refrigerator, Freda didn't feel comfortable about touching anything. Something was missing: it lacked a wholesome smell. She'd noticed it was missing in the rest of the house, too. That smell that meant somebody really lived here, tracked up the floors, burnt something on the stove every now and then. There was no smell of heat coming from the radiators, or any signs that rubber boots and wet mittens ever dried over them. Her own house smelled rich from fried chicken and collard greens and corn bread, from Pine-Sol and washing powder and Windex and Aero Wax and the little coned incense Mildred burned after she'd finished giving the house a good cleaning.

13   Freda decided she wasn't hungry and closed the refrigerator. Mildred hollered from the living room for her to go upstairs and start cleaning the bathroom. Freda slowly made her way up the winding staircase to the blue tiled bathroom in the hallway. The towels were folded neatly across the silver racks and looked like they had never been used. The blue bathtub was shining like a satin bedspread. Nothing in here needed cleaning. Freda pulled down her slacks to use the toilet, then remembered her mama had told her never to use a toilet when she didn't know the owners. So she put her hands on the seat and let her small behind support itself in midair. When she'd finished, she washed her hands, dried them on her slacks, and ran back downstairs.

14   "I'm done, Mama."

15   "Good. You may think we playing house, but I'm counting dollars and cents. All I gotta do now is wax this floor and we through. Look in that pantry over there and get the duster and swish it across the furniture in the front room and dining room, even if don't nothing look dusty."

16   While Freda was dusting, the real reason they were there finally hit her. Cleaning. She wondered just how long her mama would have

to do this kind of work. Until something better came along? Like a new husband for her and a new daddy for them? One who could afford them all. When Freda finished, she stood in the doorway watching Mildred work on her hands and knees. She saw the sweat oozing down Mildred's temples, which made her red headrag look like it was soaked in fresh blood. Freda didn't like seeing her mama like this. Didn't care how much money she was getting for it. And on the way home, Freda tried to figure out the best way to tell her mama that one day if she had anything to do with it, she would see to it that Mildred wouldn't have to work so hard to get so little.

17   "Mama, guess what," she said, as they drove down the winding road along the river. It was a clear fall afternoon, the kind that children are anxious to go out and play in, and come home sniffling and hungry, their fingers too stiff to unbutton their own coats.

18   "What?" replied Mildred, only half paying attention.

19   "I'ma be rich when I grow up and I'ma buy us a better and bigger house than the Hales' and you ain't gon' have to scrub no floors for no white folks."

20   "That's what I need to hear, chile. I sure wish you was grown now. But you got plenty of time to be worrying about millions of thangs. Take your mama's word for it. And you don't have to worry about me. I *know* I ain't gon' be on my knees for the rest of my life. I got way too much sense for that. This is what I gotta do right now so I don't have to ask nobody for nothing. Ain't no sense in me whining like some chessy cat. This ain't killing me. Women've done worse thangs to earn a living, and this may not be the bottom for me."

21   Mildred pulled up to a stoplight and reached for her purse to get a cigarette. The light changed so she handed the purse to Freda.

22   "Light me a cigarette, would you?"

23   Freda found the pack of Tareytons [Mildred'd quit L&Ms right after she and Crook had broken up because they reminded her of him], and lit it. Freda thought of inhaling that first puff, but decided against it. She handed it to Mildred.

24   "One thang I do know," Mildred continued, "and you can mark my words. Y'all ain't never gon' have to worry about eating, that's for damn sure. It may not be steak and onions and mashed potatoes and gravy, but you won't go hungry. And y'all ain't gon' never be caught looking like no damn orphans, either. If I can't give you what you need, you ain't gon' get it, and I don't care if I have to beg, borrow, or steal, every last one of y'all is going to college. I

mean it. All y'all got good sense, and I'ma make sure you stretch it to the fullest."

25   Mildred took two quick puffs on the cigarette and tossed it out the window. Freda listened intently. She loved it when her mama went off on a tangent like this.

26   "And baby, let me tell you something so you can get this straight. That big fancy house ain't the only thang in life worth striving for. Decency. A good husband. Some healthy babies. Peace of mind. Them is the thangs you try to get out of life. Everything else'll fall in place. It always do. You hear me?"

27   "Yeah, I hear you, Mama," she said.

28   "What'd you say?"

29   "I mean yes. But I'm still gon' be rich anyway, 'cause from what I see being poor don't get you nowhere and just about everybody we know except white people is poor. Why is that, Mama?"

30   " 'Cause niggahs is stupid, that's why. They thank they can get something for nothing and that that God they keep praying to every Sunday is gon' rush down from the sky and save 'em. But look at 'em. What it takes is real hard work. Ain't nobody gon' give you nothing in this world unless you work for it. I don't care what they tell you in church. One thang is true, and this is the tricky part. White folks own every damn thang 'cause they was here first and took it all. They don't like to see niggahs getting ahead and when they feel like it, they can stop you and make it just that much harder. But with all you learn in them books at school, least you can do is learn how to get around some shit like that. Anybody can see through something that's crystal clear. Just keep your eyes open and don't believe everythang—naw, don't believe half the shit people tell you 'cause don't nobody know everythang. Not even your mama. Believe me, I ain't gon' steer you too far off in the wrong direction. Mark my words. If y'all just learn to thank for yourself, don't take nobody's bullshit, I won't have to worry about you. I don't care if they white, purple, or green. Always remember that you just as good as the next person. How many times I told y'all that? All you gotta do is believe it."

31   Mildred pressed her foot down on the accelerator and the car jutted forward in spurts. They began to see smaller houses ahead. Freda didn't like Point Haven and dreamed of leaving after she graduated. She had no idea where she would go, but she knew that there had

to be a better place to live than here. Mildred had never given any thought to living anywhere else.

32   Most people who didn't live within a seventy-five-mile radius had never even heard of Point Haven. It was in the thumb of Michigan, and from a hundred feet above, the town would look like a blanket of gray and black stripes spread out beside Lake Huron. Most of the streets were pressed black dirt with rocks still stuck beneath it. There were so many trees and fields that no one appreciated them, except in hot sticky summers. There were blueberry, blackberry, elderberry, and strawberry patches in back yards and miles of woods.

33   And there was plenty of water, which meant good fishing, something the black folks cherished most about the town. They could never catch enough pickerel, catfish, perch, or sheepshead to satisfy their insatiable appetites for fillets dipped in egg batter and yellow cornmeal, dropped in hot grease, and smothered with Louisiana hot sauce.

34   A lot of people had drowned from undertows in the St. Clair River, where they often fished. Folks swore the currents came from Canada, which they could see when standing at the shore. Even when the sanctified preacher put on his white robe and walked through waves and over stones to baptize people, he wouldn't go out too far. Once he dropped his Bible in the water after dipping Melinda Pinkerton backward into salvation and a wave clipped his sleeve, sweeping his Bible away. He didn't try to go after it, either.

35   There were three residential sections in Point Haven. Half of the black population lived in South Park by the railroad tracks or near the small factories on the outskirts of town. In South Park there were five churches, one bank, two grocery stores, one Laundromat, one bar, and four liquor stores. Coming from Detroit, you reached South Park first, and the first impression people got was that this place looked like a ghost town. It was. Full of black ghosts who crept quietly up and down the mostly unpaved streets, with no place to go besides the Shingle. If you were under twenty-one, there was roller-skating twice a week, uptown at the McKinley Auditorium, but this was only in the summer. Uptown consisted of only three main streets, which housed stores that sold all the same items, only at different prices. There was no building in the entire town more than four stories,

except the YMCA and the telephone company. They were six stories. There was one movie house, three drive-ins, three beaches, a softball field, and, in the fall, football games at the high school. In the winter there was outdoor ice skating but everybody's main source of entertainment was TV.

36   Word was that all the rickety houses along Twenty-fourth Street were going to be torn down to make room for an industrial park. Supposedly it was already in the planning stages, but the colored people didn't believe this for a minute. They had lived here too long, some for as many as three generations. Surely the city wasn't going to tear down the houses that most of them had scrimped and scraped to buy. Where would they go, anyway? There was also supposed to be a plan to build a housing project smack dab in the middle of South Park, but this too they thought was all talk. After all, nothing had been built in this town since the library and state office building uptown, and that was where white people lived.

37   Mid Town was where the so-called in-between black folks lived. These people weren't altogether poor because most of them had never received a welfare check, or if they had, they'd been working steadily enough to consider themselves middle class. Many of them were now buying instead of renting, and there were some white folks scattered in their neighborhood, but everybody called them white trash.

38   As you continued north on Twenty-fourth Street, past Mid Town, you began to see aluminum siding and the houses were set back farther from the street. The front yards became longer and wider and this was a sure sign you were entering the allwhite neighborhoods. There was no name for this area. Directly behind it was the highway, which veered off to the left and led to Strawberry Lane, where middle-class white folks who thought they were upper class lived. The only black folks you ever saw up there were the ones who cleaned house, raked leaves, or picked up trash. Black people called this redneck country. These white folks didn't actually hate colored people, they just didn't like being too close to them. People like the Leonards, who ran the NAACP chapter, the Colemans, whose family was full of schoolteachers, or the Halls, who both had Ph.D's in psychology, couldn't buy a house in this neighborhood without fearing for their lives.

39   Even farther north was the North End. It was only ten minutes from Sarnia, Ontario. Here was a mixture of everybody: poor, not-so-poor, middle- and upper-middle-class black and white folks, all of whom considered themselves better than everybody else in town.

40   Half the reading and writing population of the Point—black and white—worked in factories. One, Prest-o-Lite, was in South Park. They manufactured spark plugs, shocks, and points for diesel trucks, and some car parts that were shipped to major car manufacturers near Detroit, like Ford, General Motors, and Chrysler. The women usually did day work, like Mildred, and the men worked for the Department of Sanitation, like Crook had. Or they were on welfare. Those on welfare looked for opportunities in all employable cracks and crevices but once they found jobs, many of them realized that their welfare checks were steadier and went a lot further. So a lot of them stopped looking altogether and spent their afternoons watching soap operas and gossiping.

Rita Dove

(1952–)

Rita Dove was born in Akron, Ohio, on August 28, 1952. She graduated from Miami University of Ohio, attended the University of Tubingen as a Fulbright scholar, and earned a master's degree at the University of Iowa. Dove's works include the poetry volumes The Yellow House on the Corner *(1980),* Museum *(1983),* Thomas and Beulah *(1986),* Grace Notes *(1989),* Selected Poems *(1993),* Mother Love *(1995), and* On the Bus with Rosa Parks *(1999); it is this last title from which the following poems are drawn. Dove received the Pulitzer Prize for poetry in 1987 for* Thomas and Beulah, *making her the second African American (after Gwendolyn Brooks) to win the award. In 1993, she was appointed to a two-year term as the Poet Laureate of the United States, the youngest person and first African American to be so honored. Dove has also published a collection of short fiction,* Fifth Sunday *(1985), from which the story "The Zulus" is taken. She also has published the novel* Through the Ivory Gate *(1992) and the verse drama* The Darker Face of the Earth *(1994). Since 1989, Dove has been Commonwealth Professor of English at the University of Virginia.*

The Zulus

1 Like their name, they soared on the dark edges of adventure and superstition—young men on heavy Japanese machines, custom-made leather jackets rippling over their chests and across the backs, at the shoulders the biker's name and their trademark, a flaming spear and a skull, stitched in silver and crimson. They poured through the streets of a dying city, honking and shouting to the uninitiated behind curtains. *Where were you when the lights went out?* they sang, *in Buffalo, Pittsburgh, Cleveland, Chi-town, Motown, Gary Indiana . . .* for they had been to all these places which belched along the glittery soiled neckline of North America.

2 They were high-school age, though some had dropped out. Parents warned their daughters away: *if nothing else, think of your family.* The members of the High School Honor Society officially shunned them. Girls tittered nervously whenever one of them sauntered down the corridor.

3 Which was why, when I heard that Swoop had asked Caroline Mosley to the Prom, I laughed. Actually, I snorted. It was absurd. His real name was Leander Swope, but everybody called him Swoop because that's the sound the basketball net made whenever he was there for the handoff. Like a kiss, his shots were perfect. Swoop! The crowd went wild.

4 Leander Swope may have been a thing of beauty on the court, but in classes he was just another beetle-browed athlete, dimwitted and sullen. Rumor had it that the two diagonal gouges on his left cheek were dug there by a girl's fingernails as she tried to defend herself. But I knew those scars were the marks of dishonor—the brand for those brave enough to undergo the initiation into the Zulus.

5 And Caroline? Caroline was beyond reproach. When everyone in fourth grade had to give a demonstration speech, Caroline brought in a mop and dustcloths and explained how one cleaned a house. As the youngest daughter of a broken home, I guess she had had lots of practice. She was dimpled and was fun to be around; although she had lots of boyfriends, they all spoke well of her. The girls liked her, too.

6 "The men in this town are spoiled," she would say. "Somehow they got it into their heads that they're a blessing to us all, and they run around with their noses in the stratosphere. Have you ever heard of

a guy expecting the girl to call him up before? They'll stand there bold as day and scribble their phone number on a greasy slip of paper. And when another girl tries to steal him, he expects you to fight for him! Look at them—a bunch of the sorriest mangy dogs around. When are these gals going to do something for themselves? Look at the women in this town—aren't they some of the prettiest women you've ever seen?" We looked around. It was true.

7 And when her father discovered Black Power and moved into an apartment where he could put up his H. Rap Brown posters and entertain turbanned sisters under black lights, Caroline went on as if nothing had happened. And we followed her lead. After all, we knew nothing about divorces and too many children. We were friends, but we never spoke much about personal matters.

8 So when I heard about Swoop and Caroline, I didn't ask her if it was true. I waited . . . and when Prom night came, watched with the others in amazement as the band opened with a fanfare of saxes and Swoop and Caroline appeared in matching baby blue, looking like the plastic dolls on a wedding cake.

9 It was not to be comprehended, but we didn't have time to ponder. We had to pack for college. We were already in the world of Shetland sweaters and meal tickets.

10 The summer after our first year at college, we saw Caroline again. She was working at Pittsburgh Plate Glass; Swoop had lost his job at the potato chip factory. She hadn't changed at all—she laughed at our descriptions of the "educated turkeys" we'd dated and gave us an update on the exploits of our former Homecoming queen. She giggled as she told us how her mother nearly caught her and Lee buck naked on the leather E-Z chair in the basement. We had all lost our virginity that year, so we tried not to make a big deal of it, but inside we were shocked. It was something you didn't talk about.

11 In August the announcement came: a garden wedding. DeeDee, Caroline's older sister, met three of us in a movie and offered the services of her boyfriend—a tall dark-skinned dude with a diamond stud in one ear—for driving us to the wedding, since it was on the north side of town. DeeDee was what we called "fast." She had very fine features and slightly slanted black eyes set in a heart-shaped face the color of pale coffee, and it seems everything she wore was calculated to hide her beauty—she tacked on false eyelashes and fake clover-leafed "beauty marks;" she dyed her hair a different shade

every month (this time it was the color of sherry) and poked heavy gold hoops through her ears.

12   On the day of the wedding a blossom-white convertible spun into the driveway and out he unfolded, long limbs resplendent in royal blue with a lavender silk shirt. He arranged us with all due courtesy in the leather upholstery and spun off again. After a year with no opportunity to dress up, we had outdone ourselves—there were even white gloves tucked in the side pockets of our purses. But our hair! DeeDee's friend's convertible had no mercy. In collective dismay we felt our upsweep tugged loose, the curls swept from a pageboy, a silk gardenia flapping indignantly on the last bobby pin.

13   The garden was nothing more than a hastily mown lawn. Folding chairs had been set up in the back yard and the side lot, surrounded by a latticed fence, bordered on a dead-end street. The path between the folding chairs led up to a wicker arbor laced with vines and studded with blue carnations.

14   We took our places on the side designated for "friends of the bride" and waited for the music. A quarter of an hour passed. People began to whisper: Lee was mad because he couldn't invite his motorcycle buddies; someone had forgotten the marriage license; Lee was inside watching baseball on T.V. and wouldn't come out until the game was over. From the window behind us could be heard muted voices, interrupted by sporadic cheering. Poor Caroline! What an ending for the most admired girl in the city, one who owed it to herself to do better. And for what—Love? Here, in a backyard where roses drooped, babies squawled, bees attacked and here and there a dandelion showed its impertinent proletarian head? No, it wasn't possible.

15   The voices stopped and the mothers—Lee's in pale blue and Caroline's in yellow—marched down the aisle and seated themselves in the front row. The bridegroom and the minister appeared at the arbor; Leander looked surprisingly handsome in a light blue tuxedo with a cream-colored ruffled shirt. The beautiful, whorish DeeDee skimmed by, followed by an entourage of blue silks and unfamiliar faces, concluding with the intolerably cute ring bearer with his plump pillow.

16   A white cloth was rolled out, and in its wake came Caroline—the old Caroline, with a spray of blue and white flowers and the dimples held in check. Her father, aware of his uselessness, tried to look inconspicuous. When the Lohengrin—which had been assaulting us from a stereo at the back of the house—stopped, the babies started

up again. In a short while it was over, and without having heard a word we made our way to the adjoining yard where the tables were stacked with plates of ham and chicken.

17   There was nothing left to say. It was done. Caroline presented a dimpled cheek and looked genuinely happy. We looked for a hostess but none was introduced.

18   Some guests had already lined up for a second piece of cake when a low-pitched noise grew above the general hum of voices. It was a fuzzy rumble that sharpened as it drew nearer, stopping all conversation, inspiring even the babies to silence. When it seemed the sound could come no nearer, the first of them appeared, helmets flashing the gilt insignia of the Zulus, a spear and a skull. They drove up the dead-end street and parked their bikes along the fence, clustering in a dark glittering knot. Swoop greeted them with a shout, and they clapped him on the back. They wouldn't come in but they would have some cake—which Swoop passed over the fence in crumbling chunks while Caroline, a rose among thorns, stood by smiling.

Maple Valley Branch Library, 1967

For a fifteen-year-old there was plenty
to do: Browse the magazines,
slip into the Adult Section to see
what vast *tristesse* was born of rush-hour traffic,
5   décolletés, and the plague of too much money.
There was so much to discover—how to
lay out a road, the language of flowers,
and the place of women in the tribe of Moost.
There were equations elegant as a French twist,
10 fractal geometry's unwinding maple leaf;

I could follow, step-by-step, the slow disclosure
of a pineapple Jell-O mold—or take
the path of Harold's purple crayon through
the bedroom window and onto a lavender
15 spill of stars. Oh, I could walk any aisle
and smell wisdom, put a hand out to touch

the rough curve of bound leather,
the harsh parchment of dreams.

As for the improbable librarian
20 with her salt and paprika upsweep,
her British accent and sweater clip
(mom of a kid I knew from school)—
I'd go up to her desk and ask for help
on bareback rodeo or binary codes,
25 phonics, Gestalt theory,
lead poisoning in the Late Roman Empire,
the play of light in Dutch Renaissance painting;
I would claim to be researching
pre-Columbian pottery or Chinese foot-binding,
30 but all I wanted to know was:
Tell me what you've read that keeps
that half smile afloat
above the collar of your impeccable blouse.

So I read *Gone with the Wind* because
35 it was big, and haiku because they were small.
I studied history for its rhapsody of dates,
lingered over Cubist art for the way
it showed all sides of a guitar at once.
All the time in the world was there, and sometimes
40 all the world on a single page.
As much as I could hold
on my plastic card's imprint I took,

greedily: six books, six volumes of bliss,
the stuff we humans are made of:
45 words and sighs and silence,
ink and whips, Brahma and cosine,
corsets and poetry and blood sugar levels—
I carried it home, past five blocks of aluminum siding
and the old garage where, on its boarded-up doors,
50 someone had scrawled:

I CAN EAT AN ELEPHANT
IF I TAKE SMALL BITES.

Yes, I said, to no one in particular: *That's*
what I'm gonna do!

My Mother Enters the Work Force

The path to ABC Business School
was paid for by a lucky sign:
ALTERATIONS, QUALIFIED SEAMSTRESS INQUIRE WITHIN.
Tested on sleeves, hers
5 never puckered—puffed or sleek,
leg-o' mutton or raglan—
they barely needed the damp cloth
to steam them perfect.

Those were the afternoons. Evenings
10 she took in piecework, the treadle machine
with its locomotive whir
traveling the lit path of the needle
through quicksand taffeta
or velvet deep as a forest.
15 *And now and now* sang the treadle,
I know, I know. . . .

And then it was day again, all morning
at the office machines, their clack and chatter
another journey—rougher,
20 that would go on forever
until she could break a hundred words
with no errors—ah, and then

no more postponed groceries,
and that blue pair of shoes!

Wanda Coleman

(1946–)

*Born in 1946, poet and fiction writer Wanda Coleman was raised in the
Watts section of Los Angeles. After the famed Watts rebellion in 1965,
Coleman joined several organizations that were established to guide
African American youth. Despite being a young welfare mother, Cole-
man was determined to become a writer. She worked as a secretary, an*

*editor, a journalist, and a scriptwriter before eventually receiving cre-
ative writing awards from the National Endowment of the Arts, the
Guggenheim Foundation, and the California Arts Council. Her books
include* Heavy Daughter Blues: Poems & Stories 1968–1986 *(1987)*, A
War of Eyes & Other Stories *(1988)*, American Sonnets *(1994)*,
Bathwater Wine *(1998)*, Mambo Hips & Make Believe: A Novel *(1999)*,
and Mercurochrome: New Poems *(2001). "Fast Eddie," "Flight of the
California Condor (2)," and "Dominoes" are from* Bathwater Wine.
*"Low English," "Sears Life," and "South Central Los Angeles Deathtrip
1982" are from* Mercurochrome.

Fast Eddie

hair shaved to the scalp like poboys do
those bourgeois kids made fun of his face

marked

those crude scars would appear overnight
5   graphemes of violent strokes like tribal initiation
eschara straggling his cheek, jaw or noggin/tracks
from rites of passage via paternal rage,
a drunk and reeking darkness hemmed in
by a whiteness never to be overcome

10 we made a junior gang of ourselves
Eddie's main squeeze, his best buddy Red and me
hanging tough in our spot between the bungalows
and the music building, necking the robin's blue
out of that afternoon sky, holding hands so tightly
15 it registered in our groins

while the lucky caught their beautywinks
Eddie rose before the sun and went breakfastless
into a cold morning, tossed newspapers up on
porches where another world enjoyed joe full tass
20 or fresh squoze orange juice with eggs bacon toast

Eddie workin' that Schwinn, ridin' bronco
bustin' the air

bringin' all he earned home to help defray the cost of
barely livin'

25 before he was branded delinquent
and expelled for shootin' craps

dear Eddie, how's the world treatin' you?
did you survive long enough to survive Nam? would
they have wanted you anyway, seein' how you were so short
in height and temper? i think about us lots these days
30 *especially when some fool says the word happy*

ever-and-always, Red's Girl

Flight of the California Condor (2)

mass migration began in the 50s
we observed their withdrawal and kept note

we lived in their midst
the ones in the house on our left, a strange pair
5   they always crossed their yard on tiptoe
as children, my brother and i watched them
through the thick barrier of morning glory vines
and peach trees
the female always wore an expression of dread
10 and kept peeking over her shoulders
in our direction
the male seemed less afraid but nevertheless
cautious. one time they saw us watching
and stood stark still, frozen
15 in the light of our
amazed inquiry

in 1956
they were all over the elementary school
grounds
20 but within two years they were all going
and by 1958 when i graduated
most were gone. i didn't miss them
but wondered where they had gotten to
and why

25 when we traveled north, south, west or east
away from our home
we saw that there were plenty of them
and even as the face of our neighborhood blackened
there were still two nests of them stubbornly
30 resistant, but these were elderly survivors
and eventually died out

by 1961 it was apparent. something was amiss
i was in junior high school.
again, they were everywhere. i claimed two
35 in friendship. but one spring there were rumors
and the yellow buses came
and they all got on, including my two friends
and went off to visit the new school
and when they returned they told me they were
40 moving onward after the summer
we'd be friends no more

by 1964 they had all gone from the throbbing
black heart of the city
there were a few unable to flee due to some
45 circumstance of age or economy. and by this time
we were no longer concerned with their leaving
for the swallows were returning from Mexico

after the Revolt of August 1965
they were rarer still. only a few stubborn
50 species remained: the blue-coated throat choker,
the red-fisted money grubber, the purple-livered
land snatcher, the green-beaked dope dabbler and
the magenta-throated street strutter

it is claimed by some
55 that one day they will all
virtually disappear
and by others
that this carnivorous bird of prey
will persist
60 not only in our destruction
but in its own

Dominoes

she breaks her back while he's
sittin' out yonder under
the shade tree with his cronies playin'
layin' ivory double down. and so much beer
5 risin' before it passes thru
his kidneys he damned near look as pregnant as her
she got angry breasts and her hips are
liable to join the action. but
she can usually find him when she needs to

10 rattlin' them dots like another kind
of death while she's busy stretchin' eagles
till she's screamin' with 'em
flustered when he comes in like nuthin' and
hands her a small wad of winnings,
15 hating when he loses the little
pocket change, the lack of wealth makin'
them equals but her back more equal
than others and determined to
have sumpthin' more than the piss-ant
20 doled out between a want and a wish. thinkin'
how love's fruit is long overripe. his
johnny-so-long lips that used to
thrill her cold as yesterday's grits and
stinkin' of disappointment. yet
25 his touch still moves her tears to resist
the common dust and she walks the city
without fret. and she keeps that job.

she breaks her back thru the years
that don't fit, like the clothes she's
30 birthin' out of, got that baby
kickin' around down in there and she's
afraid to be happy about it, worried
he'll pull up roots, move on to find another
hard-dreamin' fool perhaps prettier, with
35 a head as strong as her back,

sheet-smart and heavy-hipped, willin' to
take sex in exchange for idleness, to
trade that empty heart for a full
bed, a river of six packs and the savvy
40 frivolity of black men slammin' bones

Low English

i saw a squad car pull up outside
the grocery store as i was
leaving it. i had just bought a pack
of Big Red Gum and some Zig-Zag
5   rolling papers. i knew they'd take
one look at me and stop me.
i lived in the neighborhood and all i
needed was the embarrassment
of being patted down in front of every
10 toothy snot-nosed nubbin-headed gossip-monger
for blocks. i wanted to vomit.
here i come walking out of the store with
nothing but my purse, scantily dressed
because it's 96° in the skimpy shade
15 and these grinning donut holes are
gonna jack me up right here on the
goddamned street just so my palms
can fry on the hood of their Crown Vic

the operating stereotype that
20 i'm a working girl instead of a woman
who works for her living—the gum
is for a friend, the papers purchased
at my about-to-be ex-husband's request

there go all my plans for later

25 they began stepping out of their ride
the way authority steps.
i was about to make their morning
if not the entire day.

i had important business,
30 my fake attitude said. yeah, we
can guess, said their salacious sham
smiles. i began walking toward
the bus stop pretending like i had
intended to do so all along.
35 my heart was jitterbugging
against my scalp. "o miss, we'd like
to have a word." i pretended to
look for a bus, to be impatient. and
then i looked at them. "you! come
40 over here," ordered the pretty
one. "we've got something hanging
for your big ugly black ass"

Sears Life

it makes me nervous to go into a store
because i never know if i'm going to
come out. have you noticed how much
they look like prisons these days? no display
5 windows anymore. all that cold soulless
lighting—as atmospheric as county jail—and
all that ground-breaking status-quo
shattering rock 'n' roll reduced to neuron
pablum and piped in over the escalators.
10 breaks my rebel heart. and i especially
hate the aroma of fresh-nuked popcorn
rushing my nose, throwing my stomach
off balance. eyes follow me everywhere
like i'm a neon sign that shouts shoplifter.
15 and so many snide counter rats want to
service me, it almost makes me feel rich
and royal. that's why i rarely bother to
browse. i go straight to the department
of object of conjecture, make my decision
20 quick, throw down the cash and split

one time i had barely left this store
when i heard somebody yelling stop! stop!
i turned around and this dough-fleshed
armed security guard was waving me down.
25 i waited while he caught his breath and
demanded to search my purse i stared him
into his socks. we're outside the store,
i reminded him. if you search me, you'd
better find some goddamned something.
30 he took a minute to examine my eyes, turned
around and went back to his job, snorting
dust and coondogging teenage loiterers

South Central Los Angeles Deathtrip 1982

1

jes another X marking it

dangling gold chains & pinky rings
nineteen. done in black leather & defiance
teeth white as halogen lamps, skin dark as a threat

5 they spotted him taking in the night
made for the roust
arrested him on "suspicion of"
they say he became violent
they say he became combative in the rear seat of
10 that sleek zebra maria. they say
it took a chokehold to restrain him
and then they say he died of asphyxiation
on the spot

summarized in the coroner's report
15 as the demise of one
more nondescript dustbunny
ripped on phencyclidine

(which justified their need to
leave his hands cuffed behind his back
20 long after rigor mortis set in)

2

stress had damaged his thirty-nine-year-old mind
more than he could admit but he was trying
to make life work as well as it could
for a father with three children praying
25 dad will pull through

where the butcher knife came from
no one's sure. they say
he held off ten riot squad patrol cars
for forty-five minutes outside that 109th Street
30 church. they say the cops had stopped him
because they didn't like his looks.
they say something fragile inside his head
snapped. they say it took twenty rounds of ammo
to bring him down they say he took five
35 gunshot pellets & thirteen bullets
they say that was a lot of outrage over
a case of misconstrued identity

3

she was fed up that day with
everything. now here they come turning off
40 the damned gas so she went and
chased the service rep
from the yard before he could carry out the
disconnection order. by the time
police officers arrived she had lost what was
45 left of her common sense
had grabbed up & brandished an eleven-inch
boning knife to back up her mouth.
the two officers complained she threw
that knife at them. and they were so terrified
50 they didn't consider a wounding. they
simply emptied both guns into

the thirty-nine-year-old hefty female.
it took twelve shots to
subdue all that treataniggahthis
55   and whitesonofabitchesthat,
they said, and kill it

4

strangely he was dodging & ducking,
    bouncing & rolling,
    tipping & slipping
60   (as if dangling from the end of it)
in and out of traffic in front of the sheriff's
station, embarrassing them, causing a modest jam
    for no apparent reason
therefore they arrested the twenty-six-year-old
65   descendant of slaves and booked him for
this queer behavior, their spokesman said
    because there weren't
enough terrorists, assassins or irate taxpayers
to keep them busy that Wednesday afternoon.
70   he was handcuffed
and left alone in his cell and fell inexplicably
into unconsciousness in a mere three hours,
    they said. he was
rushed to a nearby hospital still in cuffs
75   where he died within twenty-two minutes

cause of demise as unknown as ever

5

without evidence to support the supposition
they swore the twenty-one-year-old
consumer was involved in the robbery of the
80   popular Manchester Avenue chicken shack,
and not just another hungry-but-innocent bystander
he was assumed guilty, if not the brainiac
perhaps the getaway driver. he was captured during
the fray before questions could be asked or

85 players & slayers identified. that he was unarmed
was not a pertinent issue. that he was ignorant
decidedly was. they handcuffed him and made
him lay on the ground in the middle of the fray
where, unfortunately, his ignorance got
90 him killed by police gunfire. they say an officer
yelled freeze and this inexperienced
young black hoodlum being unfamiliar with the
procedure of how one freezes while being held face down
on the sidewalk, hands cuffed behind one's back
95 could not do so. therefore the inability to freeze
under these conditions cost him his life

6

exhausted after working the nightshift
he was so dead on his feet he couldn't
hear 'em ramming in his door, so they broke into
100 the sepia-toned man's apartment by mistake
(it was supposed to be the one downstairs).
officers swarmed his bed as he opened his eyes,
officers were on him like maggots on foul meat.
nevertheless he managed to free himself long
105 enough to run into the bathroom where
he was ultimately subdued without ever knowing why

the coroner reported this
as death due to heart attack
brought on by advanced arteriosclerosis
110 in a twenty-eight-year-old black male

7

he was bound for college but was caught
standing on a street corner blocks from home
maybe, like they say, he had recently scored some
dope (which could not be found) or maybe
115 minutes earlier he'd been snacking on that ham
sandwich mama made for her nineteen-year-old
sure is handsome fine young black man.

maybe there was nothing to it at all, not even
that missing piece of aluminum foil the officers
120 claim they saw him pull out of his trousers

sudden-like

as they happened to be cruising past. it made
a mysterious metallic gleam

which they mistook for the glint of steel
125 which is why there was all that draw-and-fire
which is why

mama went to his funeral instead of his graduation

8

all of twenty-six, the ebony diabetic had
no steady job and lived with his parents.
130 he was a young man with mental & physical
problems. he began to act strangely, they say
although no one noticed him brandishing
that piece of radiator fan belt or that
kitchen knife in the middle of the street.
135 perhaps some car somewhere had broken down
certainly, he had, enough to make the sheriff's
deputies approach with caution and order him
to freeze. he turned toward them and even
though he was fourteen feet away from them his
140 turning toward them inspired so much fear
in the armed men one of them emptied his
Smith & Wesson service revolver into the
young diabetic who died from three slugs

9

that night Bob came blamming on her door.
145 she had just gotten home from working
the register at the club and her feet were
killing her, now here come some numbskull
sayhisnameis Bob knocking the damn door
in with some okey-doke about "here come da

150 police. hide me quick!" so she got something
for Bob's jive probably-drunk ass, that .22
caliber rifle she uses regularly to scare off
the riffraff. then she cracked the door a taste
but before she could make her melodrama move
155 it slammed open and she was blinded by the
flash as she took a shot in her left breast.
the bullet entered her right rib cage and killed
the 8 1/2-month-old baby she was carrying.
all this behind a supposedtobe drug bust where
160 no drugs were found by the officers in charge

jes another X marking it

Lamont B. Steptoe
(1949–)

Lamont B. Steptoe was born in Pittsburgh, Pennsylvania, on February 9, 1949. The third child of four, he was brought up in a single-parent household by his mother, Maybelle Dawson Steptoe Boyd. He is the author of nine collections of poetry, which include Crimson River *(1984),* American Morning/Mourning *(1990),* Mad Minute *(1993),* Catfish & Neckbone Jazz *(1994),* Dusty Road *(1995),* Uncle's South China Sea Blue Nightmare *(1995), and* In the Kitchens of the Masters *(1997). Currently a resident of Philadelphia, Steptoe has read widely both nationally and internationally, and is an activist concerning environmental, human rights, and gay/bisexual issues.*

Window Shopping

us po' Black boys
walked the streets of the 1950's
Pittsburgh business district
on Sundays
5 dazzled by the attire
of the white dummies
in the department store windows
the "Stacy Adams" shoes

the "Brooks Brothers" suits
10 the "Stetson" hats
belonged on "our" bodies
those silk ascots
those gold cuff links
would be ours
15 if we could but sell enough papers
hock enough "pop" bottles
run enough errands
beg and borrow long enough
With those shoes, those suits
20 those fine button downed shirts
would come beautiful women and love
and sports cars
and a house on a hill overlooking the sea
and wonderful kids
25 and everything glorious
just like in the movies
and we would forget
our dark painful roots
mired in poverty and racism
30 in a steel town
that used "niggers" like "iron ore"
in the blast furnace of life

Kennywood

Kennywood and Westview parks
were Pittsburgh's Disneyland
Momma filled many a shoebox
with sandwiches for a days outing
5 Getting there was as much fun
as being there
The streetcar rocked and rolled
like an amusement ride high above the river
wide eyed and chattering us Black kids
10 were jazzed with joy
our minds filled with popcorn, cotton candy,
hotdogs and ice cream

O' Momma
it was the best time of our lives
15   the ozone smell of the bumper cars
and roller coasters
were the odors of heaven
Howdy Doody was everywhere
What did it matter
20   they didn't want "niggers"
in the pool?

Three Legged Chairs

make the poem like the 'hood
couches and three legged chairs at the curb
scrawled graffiti on abandoned buildings
fetid damp smell emanating from dark cellars
5   two story homes run down like bad teeth
make the poem like the 'hood
litter the language with busted wine bottles
scatter old mattresses
people with scrawny cats
10   color the streetlights blue
have all the trees stagger like human drunks
let the wind forever sound like gunshots and sirens
somewhere in all of this children play and bleed
some escape with bullets in the back
15   some escape into the church or mental wards
some escape at the wheel of the word
some run, jump, dance into beauty and fame golden name
most go to graves embittered, enraged, unknown and
screaming

Spooked

on the streets
spooked white women
clutch dey purses tighter

when i appear
5 (some even run)
snap automatic locks
at stop lights
when i cross the street
hell
10 it wasn't me
or my people
who looted and murdered
Nations of Red folks
stole the land
15 from sea to shining sea

Seamstress

for Guadalupe León

she stitched for years on machines the whirr in her ears forever
the needle a blur a blinding blur she stitched and sewed sewed
and stitched the whirr in her ears in her blood in her bones the work
was necessary and numbing numbing and necessary she joined and
5 seamed seamed and joined stitching and stitching and stitching
stitching the father to the house the house to the father the son to
the
world the job to the cross stitching forever stitching the whirr of the
machine in her bones in her dreams in the Puerto Rican dishes she
prepared the whirr of the machine there always there stitching her
son to
10 school to railroads of light joining and seaming finally left to stitch
her
husband to death even in retirement stitching her life to
grandchildren
grandchildren to God stitching joining seaming Spanish to English
Carribbean beauty to Philadelphia barrio stitching joining seaming
her
15 spirit to God her bones to her land her dust her sunrise her rhythmic
nights of Afro-Taino-Spanish blues

A Ghosted Blues

for Etheridge Knight

"You know Lamont, you gonna have to be gettin'
out there on the road one day."
ETHERIDGE KNIGHT

Time has moved on
leaving the poet stone cold dead
in an Indianapolis graveyard
Still his voice echoes in my ears
5 and memories of shared moments
drift by like the lingering storm clouds
overhead draped against a canvas of blue
if he walks Naptowns streets
he's an unseen visitor from the underworld
10 a ghosted blues of yesterdays
Is he as lonely as I missing him?
Or does he move in an entourage
of the vanished telling tales like the wind wails
O' Etheridge
15 Is your rest rest or test
a complicated mathematics for genius and prophets?
Out there in that "far away country"
dreaming a future of what it's in the been done gone
mastering the science of death like a game of poker
20 played with a dealer of bones
Your Momma in a house of stars
wishing you well
wishing you well

Mursalata Muhammad
(1969–)

Mursalata Muhammad was born on May 30, 1969, in Detroit, Michi-
gan. Her writing is influenced both by the impromptu jazz jam ses-
sions her parents often hosted during her childhood and by rap music.
Muhammad is a faculty member at Grand Rapids Community College;

her work has been featured in several publications, including From Totems to Hip Hop: A Multicultural Anthology of Poetry Across the Americas, 1900–2002, *edited by Ishmael Reed (2003).*

Detroit

like most over-peopled places, I'm a toilet
I stand before you w/o façade
I aint got no identity hang-ups

My Northside harbors
5 once-upon-a gangsters left with only grandiose stories
  Negro heydays of singin & dancin, pushin & pimpin
They aint got nothing on Eastside young-blooded killers
  some don't know they fates so
  they still ask "what's up" and play ball wit cha
10 My Southside should have a neon sign
  "Welcome to Wetback/Hispanic/Latino Land"
  where the only thing separating them from the hood is a
    maybe Spanish accent
Bow-tied F.O.I accost you on the Westside
  with fruit/bean pies/Muhammad Speaks
15 enough Malcolm X impersonation to remind one what they
    used to be

All over I breed:
  People who've forgone living any american greeting card lines
    opting to hone skills that make survival a most profitable
    commodity
  Women who don't love & those that do until it
20   breaks noses, detaches retinas, kicks fetuses from wombs
  Crime that's 100% equal opportunity
    accompanied by un-sexist police ass kickins
That said
Give me my props:
25 I once had Paradise in an Alley
  Now I got Joe Louis' fist hovering above the place white
    men meet

Street Play

slowly u enter my mind
despite resistance of reluctant
married memories
making smooth Godiva-edible
5   images

revealing a form
underneath the football jersey
amply solid & yellow-brown
wet w/body moisture
10 I can never make of the numbers
face it "I" become small
realizing that doesn't matter
against a silouette of u
in my head
15 sweating palms
bring me back
to street races
laughing faces
as we play
20 run & jump
Pac-Man moments
keep us occupied
until motherly voices
interrupt the fun
25 w/their romeo-juliet
callings for us to part
back in time when our
vocabulary
did not allow us
30 to name the joy
we brought one another

& we indulged ourselves
in chocolate
without fear of consequences
35 I remember as now
remnants of u slip

out my ear
roll down my body
settling in unexpected
40 places

Women at the House of Braids Discuss Flo Jo

While sleeping
Electrical impulses
Overtook her brain &
An epileptic seizure became
5 the only material faster than Flo Jo
I heard she used to chase jackrabbits
Chase em girl, she passed them and she was only 6!
Her real name is Delorez, I like Flo-Jo better
Yeah that do say it bett
10 **When I read she was number 7 of eleve**n kids, hell you got to
be fast
Specially growing up in L.A. public housing
It don't make no difference where you live, if you poor or you
black, if you smart, you know you got to be fast!
Newspapers speculate
15 How she left the race
"Drugs" "steroids" "what really made her fast"
"Flo Jo's Dead: but how?"
They always trying to pick a sista apart dissect every nook n
cranny
always looking for something
20 Hell, football players blow up on na fields, an dey write natural
causes
Girl, you a trip
After all their *in-ves-ti-ga-tion* they end up with nothing
Yeah but Flo Jo's still dead

That's true, but she aint dead like they wanted her to be
25 '84 officials used her nails
To deny her a spot
On the relay team
With spirit she returned
In '88 to leave
30 Little girls
Records to chase
100 in 10.49
200 in 21.34
you got to admit her game was tight   **She had some**
    nails, na didn't she?
35   Yeah and in '88 she painted one red, one white, one blue
but the fourth one was Gold
they some ignant asses, telling a sista her nails too long
       Can't nobody show one leg like Flo Jo!
   She gave Seoul, Soul
40 *She knew how to bring it*
          And leave it in record books

Keith Gilyard

(1952–)

Born on February 24, 1952, in Harlem, Keith Gilyard lived in New York City for more than 40 years. He earned degrees from the City University of New York, Columbia University, and NYU. He began writing professionally while enrolled in writing workshops at the Langston Hughes Community Library & Cultural Center in Queens. His previous books include Voices of the Self: A Study of Language Competence *(1991), an education memoir for which he received an American Book Award;* Let's Flip the Script: An African American Discourse on Language, Literature, and Learning *(1996); and the poetry collections* American Forty: Poems *(1993),* Poemographies *(2001), and* How I Figure *(2003). In addition, Gilyard edited* Spirit & Flame: An Anthology of Contemporary African American Poetry *(1997). "The Hatmaker" is taken from* American Forty; *"Anyone Heard from Manuel?" is taken from* Poemographies.

The Hatmaker

(for Mary Lewis Gilyard)

I.

cold metal snake down
A snake
E snake
F snake
5 cold metal subway down
to the district
to make hats

fingers flipping through felt
rifling through ribbon
10 paste sequins mesh feathers
hard tight straw
didn't matter what style

hats since 1947

dark eyed dark faced momma
15 swept north of georgia on new hope
swept up to new york
new york, harbor of hope
swept to this big puzzle town
this half lit skyscraper town
20 this dazzle & dark mixed town
this dazzle & dull mixed town
this big rubik's cube town

swept north
brown georgia girl
25 fingers molding material
into hats to sit atop
empty heads of ladies who could never
have her grace

hats since 1947
30 hats since 1947

didn't matter what style
she didn't wear em much nohow

machines sucking hats from her fingers
sucked hats of pain from her fingers

35 didn't matter

sew on saturday

didn't matter

do overtime

didn't matter what style

40 she had youth to pour into hats in '47
youth into hats 38 years ago
just a new mover making this move
trying to beat this big puzzle town
beat this big 1947 jackie robinson town
45 hats since jackie was rookie of the year
hats to go see the black comet lose his
but not his head
big fun loving nerve wracked georgia boy
with flashy feet

50 fun loving georgia girl fan
with working fingers

hats since 1947
machines spilling hats since 1947

didn't matter what style
55 she didn't much wear em nohow

hustle bustle out hats
sewing machine foot stomp dance
hats for ladies in all styles

bosses doing finger tap dance
60 on the cash register
machine hum register jingle dance

great worker mary you are
good hatmaking girl you are

never sick
65 foot pedal machine stomp dance
since '47

tried to keep an eye on this big puzzle town
tried to get feet rooted in this
slippery as a seal's back
70 big puzzle town

metal snake down
struggling & sewing & struggling
wiggling out hats since '47
fingers shedding hats since '47
75 didn't matter what style

hats don't keep off much chill nohow
in this cold metal big puzzle town

II

as long as too many women of thick fingered greed
or thin fingered vanity
80 scooped them up
and kept retailers happy
hats dripped from her brow

motherhood wore a hat
her children wore hats on their backs
85 hats on their backs in this cold metal town
hats on their backs and knew
a brown georgia hatmaking girl would never
let them down

hats had her up at six
90 in bed by ten
then nine
then eight
even seven

hats in some pleasant dreams
95 hats in her greatest nightmares

hats since 1947
hats since 1947

hats get heavy since '47
hundreds of thousands of hats get
100 real heavy since '47
keeping four children in hats
gets real heavy

children get heavy

especially that son on the run
105 hardheaded boy
that do it his way boy
that in one ear out the other pants leg ripping
too hard on shoes boy
that disrupt class street running drug seeking
110 jail peeping sense leaking
boy

III

maybe worked on a million hats since 1947
maybe a million heads wearing her fingers since '47
heads bobbing to the rhythm
115 of sewing machine madness

hats since 1947
hats since 1947

never mattered what style
she never wore em much nohow

120 fingers as wheels on limousines
a hard driving answer for this town
a hard driven answer for this town
a hard children in hats answer
for this big puzzle town
125 a can't cover all bases but
i'm doing the best i can answer
for this cold metal big puzzle town

hats since 1947
hats since 1947

130 didn't matter what style
never really for her nohow

and the boy could not go hatless
wore her pride as his main skimmer in this town
wore his mother as answer
135 in this big puzzle town
wears her even now on this
cold bitter night in this
cold metal town
this big puzzle
140 cold metal
snake metal
machine mad
son of a hatmaker's town

this son of a hatmaker's town

anyone heard from manuel?

I.

in the jump of july
in the boogie down of 1973
main ingredient blue magic manu dibango
flipping old sly stone
5 summer fun in the hot times

we'll continue the revolution with you
after we smoke these blunts
that we pass from car to car on the
fuck the police
10 grand central parkway
at 70 miles per hour faster
than we're reading *black panther muhammad speaks*

riis beach in the wee hours
what's left of the dom
15 and the electric circus
on eighth street east village
where two of us

hooked up with three
that time

20 basic recipe for small group freedom:
one acquittal on a larceny beef
add one reversal of a bank robbery conviction
stir in the convictions of one college junior
a pinch of a parolee after burglaries
25 a flight back from vietnam
a bus ride back from rehab in the south

mix assorted others in well
but has anyone heard from manuel?

II.

he smiled the parabolic beauty
30 of inverted rainbows
danced our streets winking at stars
into karate and stealing cars
but we heard heavy news now
armed robbery spree across states
35 of shock
even for us

grapevine say it was vickie the vet
too fast a jet
who with her experience and rhythm set
40 youngblood on that cocaine express
white lady autobahn
10k aculpulco pit stop junkets
before the big crash of
a reunion's full moon

III.

45 i heard delaware wants him after new york
i heard pennsylvania and ohio too
i heard indiana
naw, it wasn't no indiana
i heard connecticut
50 coulda been connecticut

and jersey
how much time he looking at
one day every day
like all of us
55 you know what i mean
you punk ass muthafucka
all them states
they might not be able to count that high
all them states
60 he could start his own country
well it is nation time
pass that wine
pour some for manuel
i heard he wrote del
65 sounding like a five percenter
they all turn something
in a cell
that ain't all percent bad
maybe i'll try to write
70 you know you ain't
nobody better to get your back though
more nerve than g. gordon liddy
like when he tried to get that oldsmobile
from the dealership lot
75 and the guard woke up and shot
he had to wear casts on both arms
wasn't quite like that
you wasn't there
you wasn't either
80 needed more consciousness with that heart
he wasn't political
didn't play the part
maybe he'll become manuel x
six years like malcolm if he lucky
85 if he lucky he beats everything
man, he ain't beating all them states

IV.

lawyer said my case
was harder than calculus

hope he smart then
90 nobody ever said i was
you don't have to ace an IQ test
to get here
but i was bright
in my own mind anyway about
95 geography and entertainment
knew my street plus the next one
plus the next one led nowhere near
a big show i could star in
and she glowed dangerously
100 like a leading lady
wiggled and i pulled out my pistol
all over

V.

everybody here hopes at least once
for music beyond smokey
105 beyond the music of slamming locks
maybe a miracle
like their mental manipulation of molecules
could enable them to walk through a wall
or the court could grant a do over like
110 when we couldn't resolve a dispute
in a stickball game after comic books that
won't work now even for mothers
who shouldn't suffer

VI.

if indeed my sister queen
115 you should come to visit
to meet one of your black brother warriors who
has fallen to the white man's trickery
do not
i repeat
120 do not
come down here "improperly" dressed
in the she devil's (white woman's)
indecent mini skirt or other garments that

expose your beautiful blackness
125 which is shameful and disrespectful
not only to yourself
but to other black people who
know and recognize
what black dignity is all about
130 as salaam alaikum

VII.

when they gon bounce that tricky sucker
from the white house
when the war gon end
when you gon finish school
135 when you gon start
they attacking affirmative action
they don't talk about the quota system in prison
they need some prison affirmative action
for white folks beginning with nixon
140 and you yourself for messing
with that young girl seventeen
just talking to her
yeah dick language
no really, it's her mind
145 you mean the one tied to her behind
y'all tired as fat ass elvis presley
where the reefer
y'all trying to make it deeper
than melvin franklin can sing
150 o.j. gon get two thousand yards this season
juice on the loose
you better hope loose for afeni shakur
i heard she had a little boy

VIII.

i heard manuel knocked out a c.o.
155 i heard he threw him off the tier
sentenced him to a wheelchair

facing twenty more just for that
what he got on the robberies
his brother can't get the story straight because
160 he playing too much of that rock guitar and
running with acid heads gon bug him out
moms don't have the info either
seen her hanging around some chemicals
and dudes
165 she don't need
she used to do little league for us
but check the squad now
the double play combination combined
for thirty years
170 no funny shit like
abbott and costello

who's on first
got three and a half to seven
what's on second
175 got four and a half to nine
third base is dead
as well as the pitcher
the catcher caught ten with the feds
and manuel slugging it out in his head
180 i heard the solution now is by elijah

IX.

i learn this dumping ground
time drips but the action is fast
sometimes quicker than a makeshift machete
snatching breath

X.

185 a lot of boredom though
they buckle black spirits with routine
they planned it that way
we didn't have knowledge of self

XI.

i'm in the hole more than not
190 folks say settle down
i have settled for too little
already

XII.

designated troublemaker
i'm always moved around
195 i know they plan to bury me
for sure

XIII.

never say you can't do all the time
they always say
don't worry son
200 just do all that you can

XIV.

to have a nightmare before a life
seems backward
what's a judge or c.o. up against that
whatever the facts

XV.

205 sonny stayed around
getting married
you know i'm down
you going
i like the sound
210 and you kept that young girl too
she kept me
keith would laugh at that one
i heard he left town

he'll be back
215 we're in his blood
to the last pound

XVI.

ordinary john found another corner
became hitched to
a second heroin habit
220 backed out of the store with the loot
when they popped him
then yelled halt
which naturally he did

the second fall is always harder

XVII.

225 they come back all the time dashing about
i don't even try to block them anymore
the thoughts
my son has a father
that's pretty good i guess
230 i tell my younger brother
to get himself together
take a good look at life
he says he looks at me and
figures he ain't that bad
235 so what the hell he says
our mother is worse

XVIII.

i remember we were playing touch football.
and keith was trying to throw me passes and
was getting them blocked by big tall benny
240 jumping too high so
he asked me to quarterback
and drill benny right in the chest
hard as i could

if he tried that block shit with me
245 benny knew like he was in our huddle
that i did it on purpose and
glared and glared
but that's all he dared
with the two of us
250 tight as we were

XIX.

i really stretched him that time
asking him to drive that car i stashed
i mean he was in college
moving on
255 had to be sweating
especially when the fire engine
rolled up behind him
must have flashed him back
to his own arrests

260 i didn't dig it at the moment
because even i couldn't drive two cars
at the same time
but i do understand why

he quit halfway

265 i never bothered him again

XX.

man, i heard they turned down the disco music
in pippin's because folks wanted to hear
the telecast of *roots*
i was down there the week after

270 kunte kinte and kizzy on the dance floor
did make more sense than the peanut farmer in d.c.
sipping champagne with the shah of iran and
getting hostaged out of an election by reagan as
the ayatollah hung in effigy in trees
275 with yellow ribbons growing from the branches

man, iran ain't the enemy but i'll take dutch
because that means the eighties gon be
like the sixties and such
black folks gon act right on
280 right up
upright
though not on this corner tonight
with these young kids running wild
amid the rise of disorganized crime

XXI.

285 ketchup is a vegetable
AIDS is stronger than the sixties virus
economy is depressed
so am i and the price of life
billie sang "strange fruit"
290 but this is a strange crop grown for jail
on the campaign trail
jesse jackson couldn't talk them out of it

XXII.

mandela gon be out before manuel
you ever get clear on that c.o. story
295 it's fuzzy but i know he ain't home yet
you mean he ain't released
home is another story
what about all them states
you mean all that ohio and indiana stuff
300 wasn't indiana
i heard it was indiana
some guys were saying that
some states i don't remember
how long has it been
305 ten eleven years
nah, my son is 19
manuel been gon longer
damn
i remember early '73 i think

310 when all of us would chill
    manuel would be in my car
    which died that same year
    and he was already gone by then
    so you remember all that
315 some of it
    you too old
    ain't no too old

XXIII.

    if you don't die
    you might get magic
320 better than johnson
    maybe not dying is the magic
    and i am going home
    i suppose it's home
    if anyone remembers
325 i got spiritual
    not organized
    no more
    just my own thing i'm into
    just me keeping strong
330 ideas that will get a man through
    i heard many things too
    deep in the night
    afro-blue

XXIV.

    barely familiar face
335 doing masonry in front of a house
    i knew from long ago

    barely knew the boulevard
    where i heard that manuel was home

    i asked the face i knew but name i didn't

340 and manuel emerged calmly

    serenely

said i looked exactly the same and
he recognized me better than his own mug shot
from twenty-four years ago
345 working all angles
that was impossible enough to be true

Walter Mosley
(1952–)

A resident of New York City, Walter Mosley was born in Los Angeles on January 12, 1952. He first achieved popularity with the appearance of his Easy Rawlins mystery novels, the first of which, Devil in a Blue Dress *(1990), was made into a major motion picture of the same title (1995). Other books in the series include* A Red Death *(1991),* White Butterfly *(1992),* Black Betty *(1994),* A Little Yellow Dog *(1996), the prequel* Gone Fishin', *(1997),* Bad Boy Brawly Brown *(2002), and* Six Easy Pieces *(2002). Mosley's other works include a blues novel,* R L's Dream *(1995); a science fiction novel,* Blue Light *(1998); and a third novel,* A Man in the Basement *(2004). He has introduced a second mystery series, with the titles* Fearless Jones *(2001) and* Fear Itself *(2003). In 1997, Mosley introduced the character Socrates Fortlow in a collection of stories titled* Always Outnumbered, Always Outgunned. *"The Thief," reprinted below, is from that collection.* Always Outnumbered, Always Outgunned *was also made into a film, and a second group of Socrates Fortlow stories,* Walkin' the Dog, *was published in 1999.*

The Thief

{1.}

1   Iula's grill sat on aluminum stilts above an open-air, fenced-in auto garage on Slauson. Socrates liked to go to the diner at least once a month on a Tuesday because they served meat loaf and mustard greens on Tuesdays at Iula's. The garage was run by Tony LaPort, who had rented the diner out to Iula since before their marriage; it was a good arrangement for Tony so he still leased to her eight years after their divorce.

2   Tony had constructed the restaurant when he was in love and so it was well built. The diner was made from two large yellow school buses that Tony had welded together—side by side. One bus held the counter where the customers sat, while the other one held the kitchen and storage areas. The banistered stairway that led up to the door was aluminum also. When Iula closed for the night she used a motor-driven hoist to lift the staircase far up off the street. Then she'd go through the trapdoor down a wooden ladder to Tony's work space, let herself out through the wire gate, and set the heavy padlocks that Tony used to keep thieves out.

3   If the locks failed to deter an enterprising crook there was still Tina to contend with. Tina was a hundred-pound mastiff who hated everybody in the world except Iula and Tony. Tina sat right by the gate all night long, paws crossed in a holy prayer that some fool might want to test her teeth.

4   She was waiting that afternoon as Socrates approached the aluminum stairs. She growled in a low tone and Socrates found himself wondering if he would have a chance to crush the big dog's windpipe before she could tear out his throat. It was an idle thought; the kind of question that men discussed when they were in prison. In prison, studying for survival was the only real pastime.

5   How many ways were there to kill a man? What was more dangerous in a close fight—a gun or a knife? How long could you hold your breath underwater if there were policemen looking for you on the shore? Will God really forgive any sin?

6   Thinking about killing that dog was just habit for Socrates. The habit of twenty-seven years behind bars out of fifty-eight.

7   As he climbed the aluminum staircase he thought again about how well built it was. He liked the solid feeling that the light metal gave. He was happy because he could smell the mustard greens.

8   He could almost taste that meat loaf.

{2.}

9   "Shet that do'!" Iula shouted, her back turned to Socrates. "Damn flies like t'eat me up in here."

10   "Shouldn't cook so damn good you don't want no notice, I." Socrates slammed shut the makeshift screen door and walked up the stepwell into the bus.

11   The diner was still empty at four-thirty. Socrates came early because he liked eating alone. He went to the stool nearest Iula and

sat down. The musical jangle of coins came from the pockets of his army jacket.

12   "You been collectin' cans again?" Iula had turned around to admire her customer. Her face was a deep amber color splattered with dark freckles, especially around her nose. She was wide-hipped and large-breasted. Three gold teeth decorated her smile. And she was smiling at Socrates. She put a fist on one hip and pushed her apron out, making an arc that brushed her side of the counter.

13   Socrates was looking at her breasts. Tony had once told him that the first time he saw those titties they were standing straight up, nipples pointing left and right.

14   "Yeah, I," he said, in answer to her question. "I got me a route now. Got three barmen keep the bottles an' cans on the side for me. All I gotta do is clean up outside for them twice a week. I made seventeen dollars just today."

15   "Ain't none these young boys out here try an' take them bottles from you, Mr. Fortlow?"

16   "Naw. Gangbanger be ashamed t'take bottles in a sto'. An' you know as long as I got my black jeans and khaki I don't got no color t'get them young bulls mad. If you know how t'handle them they leave you alone."

17   "I'ont care what you say," Iula said. "Them boys make me sick wit' all that rap shit they playin' an' them guns an' drugs."

18   "I seen worse," Socrates said. "You know these three men live in a alley off'a Crenshaw jump me today right after I got my can money."

19   "They did?"

20   "Uh-huh. Fools thought they could take me." Socrates held out his big black hand. The thick fingers were the size of large cigars. When he made a fist the knuckles rode high like four deadly fins.

21   Iula was impressed.

22   "They hurt you?" she asked.

23   Socrates looked down at his left forearm. There, near the wrist, was a sewn-up tear and a dark stain.

24   "What's that?" Iula cried.

25   "One fool had a bottle edge. Huh! He won't try an' cut me soon again."

26   "Did he break the skin?"

27   "Not too much."

28   "You been to a doctor, Mr. Fortlow?"

29   "Naw. I went home an' cleaned it out. Then I sewed up my damn coat. I cracked that boy's arm 'cause he done ripped my damn coat."

30   "You better get down to the emergency room," Iula said. "That could get infected."

31   "I cleaned it good."

32   "But you could get lockjaw."

33   "Not me. In the penitentiary they gave you a tetanus booster every year. You might get a broke jaw in jail but you ain't never gonna get no lockjaw."

34   Socrates laughed and set his elbows on the counter. He cleared his throat and looked at Iula watching him. Behind her was the kitchen and a long frying grill. There were big pots of beef and tomato soup, mashed potatoes, braised short ribs, stewed chicken, and mustard greens simmering on the stove. The meat loaves, Socrates knew from experience, were in bread pans in the heating pantry above the ovens.

35   It was hot in Iula's diner.

36   Hotter under her stare.

37   She put her hand on Socrates' arm.

38   "You shouldn't be out there hustlin' bottles, Mr. Fortlow," she said. Her voice was like the rustling of coarse blankets.

39   "I got t'eat. An' you know jobs don't grow on trees, I. Anyway, I got a bad temper. I might turn around one day and break a boss man's nose."

40   Iula laid her finger across his knucklebones.

41   "You could work here," she said. "There's room enough for two behind this here counter."

42   Iula turned her head to indicate what she meant. In doing so she revealed her amber throat. It was a lighter shade than her face.

43   He remembered another woman, just a girl really, and her delicate neck. That woman died by the same hand Iula stroked. She died and hadn't done a thing to deserve even a bruise. He had killed her and was a little sorrier every day; every day for thirty-five years. He got sadder but she was still dead. She was dead and he was still asking himself why.

44   "I don't know," he said.

45   "What?"

46   "I don't know what to say, I."

47   "What is there to say?" she demanded. "All you could say is yeah. You ain't got hardly a dime. You need a job. And the Lord knows I could use you too."

48   "I got to think about it," he said.

49   "Think about it?" Just that fast Iula was enraged. "Think about it? Here I am offerin' you a way outta that hole you in. Here I am

offerin' you a life. An' you got to think about it? Look out here in the streets around you, Mr. Fortlow. Ain't no choice out there. Ain't nuthin' t'think about out there."

50   Socrates didn't have to look around to see the boarded-up businesses and stores; the poor black faces and brown faces of the men and women who didn't have a thing. Iula's diner and Tony's garage were the only working businesses on that block.

51   And he hated bringing bottles and cans to the Ralph's supermarket on Crenshaw. To get there he had to walk for miles pulling as many as three grocery carts linked by twisted wire coat hangers. And when he got there they always made him wait; made him stand outside while they told jokes and had coffee breaks. And then they checked every can. They didn't have to do that. He knew what they took and what they didn't. He came in twice a week with his cans and bottles and nobody ever found one Kessler's Root Beer or Bubble-Up in the lot. But they checked every one just the same. And they never bothered to learn his name. They called him "Pop" or "old man." They made him wait and checked after him like he was some kind of stupid animal.

52   But he took it. He took it because of that young girl's neck; because of her boyfriend's dead eyes. Those young people in Ralph's were stupid and arrogant and mean—but he was evil. That's what Socrates thought.

53   That's what he believed.

54   "Well?" Iula asked.

55   "I'd . . . I'd like some meat loaf, Iula. Some meat loaf with mashed potatoes and greens."

56   From the back of her throat Iula hissed, "Damn you!"

{3.}

57   Socrates felt low but that didn't affect his appetite. He'd learned when he was a boy that the next meal was never a promise; only a fool didn't eat when he could.

58   He laced his mashed potatoes and meat loaf with pepper sauce and downed the mustard greens in big noisy mouthfuls. When he was finished he looked behind the counter hoping to catch Iula's eye. Iula would usually give Socrates seconds while smiling and complimenting him on the good appetite he had.

59   "You eat good but you don't let it turn to fat," she'd say, admiring his big muscles.

60   But now she was mad at him for insulting her offer. Why should she feed the kitty when there wasn't chance to win the pot?

61   "I," Socrates said.

62   "What you want?" It was more a dare than a question.

63   "Just some coffee, babe," he said.

64   Iula slammed the mug down and flung the Pyrex coffeepot so recklessly that she spilled half of what she poured. But Socrates didn't mind. He was still hungry and so finished filling the mug with milk from two small serving pitchers on the counter.

65   He had eleven quarters in his right-hand jacket pocket. Two dollars and fifty cents for the dinner and twenty-five cents more for Iula's tip. That was a lot of money when all you had to your name was sixty-eight quarters, four dimes, three nickels, and eight pennies. It was a lot of money but Socrates was still hungry—and that meat loaf smelled better than ever.

66   Iula used sage in her meat loaf. He couldn't make it himself because all he had at home was a hot plate and you can't make meat loaf on a hot plate.

67   "Iula!"

68   Socrates turned to see the slim young man come up into the bus. He was wearing an electric-blue exercise suit, zipped up to the neck, and a bright yellow headband.

69   "Wilfred." There were still no seconds in Iula's voice.

70   "How things goin'?" the young man asked.

71   "Pretty good if you don't count for half of it."

72   "Uh-huh," he answered, not having heard. "An' where's Tony today?"

73   "It's Tuesday, ain't it?"

74   "Yeah."

75   "Then Tony's down at Christ Congregational settin' up for bingo."

76   Wilfred sat himself at the end of the counter, five stools away from Socrates. He caught the older man's eye and nodded—as black men do.

77   Then he said, "I done built me up a powerful hunger today, Iula. I got two hollow legs to fill."

78   "What you want?" she asked, not at all interested in the story he was obviously wanting to tell.

79   "You got a steak back there in the box?"

80   "Shit." She would have spit on the floor if she wasn't in her own restaurant.

81   "Okay. Okay. I tell you what. I want some stewed chicken, some braised ribs, an' two thick slabs' a meat loaf on one big plate."

82   "That ain't on the menu."

83   "Charge me a dinner for each one then."

84   Iula's angry look changed to wonder. "You only get one slice of meat loaf with a dinner."

85   "Then ring it up twice, honey. I got mad money for this here meal."

86   Iula stared until Wilfred pulled out a fan of twenty-dollar bills from his pocket. He waved the fan at her and said, "Don't put no vegetables on that shit. You know I'm a workin' man—I needs my strength. I need meat."

87   Iula moved back into the kitchen to fill Wilfred's order.

88   Socrates sipped his coffee.

89   "Hey, brother," Wilfred said.

90   Socrates looked up at him.

91   "How you doin'?" the young man offered.

92   "Okay, I guess."

93   "You guess?"

94   "It depends."

95   "Depends on what?"

96   "On what comes next."

97   When Wilfred smiled, Socrates could see that he was missing one of his front teeth.

98   "You jus' livin' minute t'minute, huh?" the young man said.

99   "That's about it."

100   "I used to be like that. Used to be. That is till I fount me a good job." Wilfred sat back as well as he could on the stool and stared at Socrates as if expecting to be asked a question.

101   Socrates took another sip of coffee. He was thinking about another helping of meat loaf and his quarters, about Iula's nipples, and that long-ago dead girl. He didn't have any room for what was on the young man's mind.

102   Iula came out then with a platter loaded down with meats. It was a steaming plate looking like something out of the dreams Socrates had had when he was deep inside of his jail sentence.

103   "Put it over there, Iula." Wilfred was pointing to the place next to Socrates. He got up from his stool and went to sit behind the platter.

104   He was a tall man, in his twenties. He'd shaved that morning and had razor bumps along his jaw and throat. His clothes were bulky and Socrates wondered why. He was thin and well built. Obviously

from *the hood*—Socrates could tell that from the hunger he brought to his meal.

105   "What's your name, man?" Wilfred asked.

106   "Socrates."

107   "Socrates? Where'd you get a name like that?"

108   "We was poor and country. My mother couldn't afford school so she figured that if she named me after somebody smart then maybe I'd get smart."

109   "I knew it was somebody famous. You see?" Wilfred said, full of pride. "I ain't no fool. I know shit too. I got it up here. My name is Wilfred."

110   Socrates breathed in deeply the smells from Wilfred's plate. He was still hungry—having walked a mile for every two dollars he'd made that day.

111   His stomach growled like an angry dog.

112   "What you eatin', Socco?" Wilfred asked. Before giving him a chance to answer he called out to Iula, "What's my brother eatin', Iula? Bring whatever it is out to 'im. I pay for that too."

113   While Iula put together Socrates's second plate, Wilfred picked up a rib and sucked the meat from the bone.

114   He grinned and said, "Only a black woman could cook like this."

115   Socrates didn't know about that but he was happy to see the plate Iula put before him.

{4.}

116 Socrates didn't pick up his fork right away. Instead he regarded his young benefactor and said, "Thank you."

117   "That's okay, brother. Eat up."

118   Halfway through his second meal Socrates' hunger eased a bit. Wilfred had demolished his four dinners and pushed his plate away.

119   "You got some yams back there?" he called out to Iula.

120   "Yeah," she answered. She had gone to a chair in her kitchen to rest and smoke a cigarette before more customers came.

121   "Bring out a big plate for me an' my friend here."

122   Iula brought out the food without saying a word to Socrates. But he wasn't worried about her silence.

123   He came around on Tuesdays, when Tony was gone, because he wanted Iula for something; a girlfriend, a few nights in bed, maybe more, maybe. He hadn't touched a woman since before prison.

124   And now he was afraid of what his hands could do.

125   Iula was petulant but she didn't understand how scared he was even to want her.

126   She wanted a man up there on stilts with her to lift tubs of shortening that she couldn't budge. She wanted a man to sit down next to her in the heat that those stoves threw off.

127   If he came up there he'd probably get fat.

128   "What you thinkin' about, brother?" Wilfred asked.

129   "That they ain't nuthin' for free."

130   "Well . . . maybe sometime they is."

131   "Maybe," Socrates said. "But I don't think so."

132   Wilfred grinned.

133   Socrates asked, "What kinda work you do, Wilfred?"

134   "I'm self-employed. I'm a businessman."

135   "Oh yeah? What kinda business?"

136   Wilfred smiled and tried to look coy. "What you think?"

137   "I'd say a thief," Socrates answered. He speared a hot yam and pushed it in his mouth.

138   Wilfred's smile widened but his eyes went cold.

139   "You got sumpin' against a man makin' a livin'?" he asked.

140   "Depends."

141   "Pends on what?"

142   "On if it's wrong or not."

143   "Stealin's stealin', man. It's all the same thing. You got it—I take it."

144   "If you say so."

145   "That's what I do say," Wilfred said. "Stealin's right for the man takin' an' wrong fo' the man bein' took. That's all they is to it."

146   Socrates decided that he didn't like Wilfred. But his stomach was full and he'd become playful. "But if a man take some bread an' he's hungry, starvin'," he said. "That's not wrong to nobody. That's good sense."

147   "Yeah. You right," Wilfred conceded. "But s'pose you hungry for a good life. For a nice house with a bathtub an' not just some shower. S'pose you want some nice shoes an' socks don't bust out through the toe the first time you wear' em?"

148   "That depends too."

149   "'Pends on what? What I want don't depend on a damn thing." Wilfred's smile was gone now.

150   "Maybe not. I mean maybe the wantin' don't depend on nuthin' but how you get it does, though."

151   "Like what you mean?"

152   "Well let's say that there's a store sellin' this good life you so hungry for. They got it in a box somewhere. Now you go an' steal it. Well, I guess that's okay. That means the man got the good life give it up to you. That's cool."

153   "Shit," Wilfred said. "If they had a good life in a box you know I steal me hunnert'a them things. I be right down here on Adams sellin' 'em for half price."

154   "Uh-huh. But they don't have it in a box now do they?"

155   "What you tryin' t'say, man?" Wilfred was losing patience. He was, Socrates thought, a kind benefactor as long as he didn't have to see a man eye to eye.

156   "I'm sayin' that this good life you talkin' 'bout stealin' comes outta your own brother's house. Either you gonna steal from a man like me or you gonna steal from a shop where I do my business. An' ev'ry time I go in there I be payin' for security cameras an' security guards an' up-to-the-roof insurance that they got t'pay off what people been stealin'. An' they gonna raise the prices higher'n a motherfucker to pay the bills, wit' a little extra t'pay us back for you stealin'."

157   Socrates thought that Wilfred might get mad. He half expected the youth to pull out a gun. But Socrates wasn't worried about a gun in those quarters. He was stronger than Wilfred, and, as he had learned in prison, a strong arm can beat a gun up close.

158   But Wilfred wasn't mad. He laughed happily. He patted Socrates on the shoulder, feeling his hard muscle, and said, "You got a good tongue there, brother. You good as a preacher, or a cop, when it comes to talkin' that talk."

159   Wilfred stood up and Socrates swiveled around on his seat, ready for the fight.

160   Iula sensed the tension and came out with a cigarette dangling from her lips.

161   Wilfred stripped off his exercise jacket and stepped out of the gaudy nylon pants. Underneath he was wearing a two-piece tweed suit with a brown suede vest. His silk tie showed golden-and-green clouds with little flecks of red floating here and there. His shirt was white as Sunday's clothesline.

162   "What you think?" Wilfred asked his audience.

163   Iula grunted and turned back to her kitchen. He was too skinny for her no matter what he had on.

164   "Come here," Wilfred said to Socrates. "Look out here in the street."

165   Socrates went to the bus window and crouched down to look outside. There was a new tan car, a foreign job, parked out there. Socrates didn't know the model but it looked like a nice little car.

166   "That's my ride," Wilfred said.

167   "Where it take you?" Socrates asked.

168   "Wherever I wanna go," Wilfred answered. "But mostly I hit the big malls an' shoppin' centers up in West Hollywood, Beverly Hills, Santa Monica, and what-have-you.

169   "I get one'a my girlfriends to rent me a car. Then I get all dressed up like this an' put on a runnin' suit, or maybe some funky clothes like you got on, over that. An' I always got me a hat or a headband or somethin'. You know they could hardly ever pick you out of a lineup if you had sumpin' on yo' head."

170   Socrates had learned that in jail too.

171   "I grab 'em in the parkin' lot." Wilfred sneered with violent pleasure. "I put my knife up hard against they necks an' tell'em they dead. You know I don't care if I cut 'em up a li'l bit. Shit. I had one young Jap girl peed on herself."

172   Wilfred waited for a laugh or something. When it didn't come the jaunty young man went back to his seat.

173   "You don't like it," Wilfred said. "Too bad."

174   "I don't give a damn what you do, boy," Socrates answered. He sat back down and scooped up the last bit of gravy in his spoon. "I cain't keep a fool from messin' up."

175   "I ain't no fool, old man. I don't mess up neither. I get they money an' cut 'em up some so they call a doctor fo' they call the cops. Then I run an' th'ow off my niggah clothes. When the cops come I'm in my suit, in my car comin' home. An' if they stop me I look up all innocent an' lie an' tell'em that I work for A&M Records. I tell'em that I'm a manager in the mailroom over there. No sir, I don't fuck up at all."

176   "Uh-huh," Socrates said. He put a yam in his mouth after dipping it in the honey butter sauce at the bottom of the dish; it was just about the best thing he had ever tasted.

177   "Mothahfuckah, you gonna sit there an' dis me with yo' mouth fulla the food I'm buyin'?" Wilfred was amazed.

178   "You asked me an' I told ya," Socrates said. "I don't care what you do, boy. But that don't mean I got to call it right."

179   "What you talkin' 'bout, man? I ain't stealin' from no brother. I ain't stealin' where no po' brother live. I'm takin' the good life from people who got it—just like you said."

180 "You call my clothes funky, din't ya, boy?"

181 "Hey, man. I din't mean nuthin'."

182 "Yes you did," Socrates said. "You think I'm funky an' smelly an' I ain't got no feelin's. That's what you think. You don't see that I keep my socks darned an' my clothes clean. You don't see that you walkin' all over me like I was some piece'a dog shit. An' you don't care. You just put on a monkey suit an' steal a few pennies from some po' woman's purse. You come down here slummin', flashin' your twenty-dollar bills, talkin' all big. But when you all through people gonna look at me like I'm shit. They scared'a me 'cause you out there pretendin' that you're me robbin' them."

183 Wilfred held up his hands in a false gesture of surrender and laughed. "You too deep for me, brother," he said. He was smiling but alert to the violence in the older man's words. "Way too deep."

184 "You the one shovelin' it, man. You the one out there stealin' from the white man an' blamin' me. You the one wanna be like them in their clothes. You hatin' them an' dressed like the ones you hate. You don't even know who the hell you is!"

185 Socrates had to stop himself from striking Wilfred. He was shaking, scared of his own hands again.

186 "I know who I am all right, brother," Wilfred said. "And I'm a damn sight better'n you."

187 "No you not," Socrates said. A sense of calm came over him. "No you not. You just dressin' good, eatin' like a pig. But when the bill come due I'm the one got t'pay it. Me an' all the rest out here."

188 "All right, fine!" Wilfred shouted. "But the only one right now payin' fo' somethin' is me. I'm the one got you that food you been eatin'. But if you don't like it then pay for it yourself."

189 Iula came out again. Socrates noted the pot of steaming water she carried.

190 "I do you better than that, boy," Socrates said. "I'll pay for yo' four dinners too."

191 "What?" Wilfred and Iula both said.

192 "All of it," Socrates said. "I'll pay for it all."

193 "You a new fool, man," Wilfred said.

194 Socrates stood up and then bent down to pick up Wilfred's stickup clothes from the floor.

195 "You always got to pay, Wilfred. But I'll take this bill. I'll leave the one out there for you."

196 Wilfred faked a laugh and took the clothes from Socrates.

197 "Get outta here, man," Socrates said.

198   For a moment death hung between the two men. Wilfred was full of violence and pride and Socrates was sick of violent and prideful men.

199   "I don't want no trouble in here now!" Iula shouted when she couldn't take the tension anymore.

200   Wilfred smiled again and nodded. "You win, old man," he said. "But you crazy though."

201   "Just get outta here," Socrates said. "Go."

202   Wilfred considered for the final time doing something. He was probably faster than the older man. But it was a small space and strength canceled out speed in close quarters.

203   Socrates read all of that in Wilfred's eyes. Another young fool, he knew, who thought freedom was out the back door and in the dark.

204   Wilfred turned away slowly, went down the stairwell, then down the aluminum staircase to the street.

205   Socrates watched the tan car drive off.

{5.}

206   "You're insane, Socrates Fortlow, you know that?" Iula said. She was standing on her side of the counter in front of seventeen stacks of four quarters each.

207   "You got to pay for your dinner, I."

208   "But why you got to pay for him? He had money."

209   "That was just a loan, I. But the interest was too much for me."

210   "You ain't responsible fo' him."

211   "You wrong there, baby. I'm payin' for niggahs like that ev'ry day. Just like his daddy paid for me."

212   "You are a fool."

213   "But I'm my own fool, I."

214   "I don't get it," she said. "If you so upstandin' an' hardworkin' an' honest—then why don't you wanna come here an' work fo' me? Is it 'cause I'm a woman? 'Cause you don't wanna work fo' no woman?"

215   Socrates was feeling good. He had a full stomach. The muscles in his arms relaxed now that he didn't have to fight. There was an ache in his forearm where he'd been cut, but, as the prison doctor used to say, pain was just a symptom of life.

216   Socrates laughed.

217   "You're a woman all right, I. I know you had that boilin' water out there t'save me from Wilfred. You a woman all right, and I'm gonna be comin' back here every Tuesday from now on. I'm gonna come see

you and we gonna talk too, Momma. Yeah. You gonna be seein' much more'a me."

218   He got up and kissed her on the cheek before leaving. When his lips touched her skin a sound came from the back of her throat. Socrates heard that satisfied hum in his dreams every night for a month.

{6.}

219 Socrates only had four dimes, three nickels, and eight pennies left to his name. If he took a bus he'd be broke, but he was just as happy to walk. On the way home he thought about finding a job somewhere. Some kind of work, he thought, where you didn't have to bleed and die for your meal.

Writing Assignments

1. As discussed in the chapter introduction, themes of survival and escape are central concerns in African American urban fiction. After reading the works in this chapter, make a list of other recurrent themes. What do they suggest about the effects of urban daily living on city inhabitants?

2. Choose three poets and examine the metaphors each employs to capture city life. Why, for example, do so many poets personify the city?

3. Walter Mosley's "The Thief" and Rita Dove's "The Zulus" end rather ambiguously. What is significant about the lack of traditional closure in these works, and how might the urban consciousness of the works explain this narrative choice?

4. In Nathan McCall's *Makes Me Wanna Holler*, Keith Gilyard's "Anyone Heard from Manuel?," and Wanda Coleman's "South Central Los Angeles Deathtrip 1982," the urban landscape is contaminated by police brutality and biased judicial systems. How do these enactments of state-sanctioned violence severely qualify the scope of possibilities promised by the city? Considering the perils of the street, how do these works treat the American dream?

CHAPTER EIGHT

A STRAND OF SOCIAL PROTEST

All African American literature to some extent challenges racism. At the very least, it stands as testament to Black humanity in a society where the possibilities of Black selfhood have been often contested, suppressed, or denied. Thus, there is an element of protest in every story, play, poem, or essay penned by an African American. What we mean in this chapter by the term *protest literature* is the expression in literary works by African Americans, often aimed primarily at the conscience of white readers, of explicit political grievances with respect to racist oppression in this country. More narrowly, we focus on a particular strand of writing inaugurated by Richard Wright, whose name is often synonymous with such work. Not all critics, African American or otherwise, have celebrated Black protest writing. Some have felt that it focuses too much on stereotypes, environmental determinism, and the mindsets of white people. It has been furthermore argued that the result of such writing is a reduction in the variety and complexity of the African American experiences presented to the public. Notwithstanding these criticisms, writers working in the protest vein have produced some of the most important and powerful works in the African American literary tradition.

In 1940, with the publication of his first novel, *Native Son*, Wright was well on his way to becoming the most prominent African American writer of his generation. In the story of Bigger Thomas, he demonstrated with unflinching vividness the raw and brutal effects of racism on the development of African American youth. Bigger is overly fearful, yet prone to violence. He is inarticulate in the face of his social superiors, yet totally obsessed with white presence. He explains to his friend that white folks do not live on the other side of town, but inside him: "Right down here in my stomach." His environment determines his actions. He can imagine no way around the tragic end he eventually meets.

Despite the fact that Bigger was too psychologically damaged to have ever thrived, he remains an unsympathetic figure, ultimately, because of his own embrace of murder. He represents, therefore, a departure from a host of Black casualties in African American literature—which was Wright's intent. In an essay titled "How 'Bigger' Was Born" (1940), which appeared in subsequent editions of the novel, the author recounts how the moral issues he presented were too clear-cut in his first book, a short-story collection titled *Uncle Tom's Children* (1938). He mused that he had written stories about Black victims that "even bankers' daughters could read and weep over and feel good about." He then resolved that his next book would not open itself to simplistic or sentimental interpretation.

As the most celebrated African American writer and a proponent of naturalism or environmentalism, Wright was an obvious target for Black writers who objected to the type of social protest literature he created. Indeed, a two-essay response by James Baldwin, which effectively ended the friendship between the two writers, appears sometimes to have become as famous as Wright's novel. In "Everybody's Protest Novel" (1949), which actually deals more with Harriet Beecher's Stowe's *Uncle Tom's Cabin* (1852) than with *Native Son*, Baldwin suggests that writers move beyond the stereotypes of the protest vehicle to portray complexity and ambiguity in their characters. Baldwin believed that if categories became more important than individuals to writers, then the fiction such writers produced would be psychologically shallow. He elaborates upon these points in "Many Thousands Gone" (1951), in which complains once again that *Native Son* is psychologically and socially underdeveloped because readers are mainly restricted to Bigger's perceptions and are not given an in-depth look at the African American community. Baldwin calls for writers to recreate their own experiences as opposed to dealing in types.

Baldwin seems to contend that tales like Wright's are never worth telling. The argument is ironic because Ralph Ellison, in "A World and a Jug" (1963/1964), observes that Baldwin, once established, seemed to be "out-Wrighting Wright." Ellison, in fact, also has been associated with criticism of *Native Son*, but his remarks are far less antagonistic than Baldwin's. He makes clear his appreciation for Wright's accomplishment and states forcefully that social protest, in and of itself, is not a problem for African American writers. The question was, as always for Ellison, how well the work was crafted. Ellison does call for diverse depictions of African American life, and he does comment mischievously that, "Wright could imagine Bigger, but Bigger could not possibly imagine Richard Wright. Wright saw to that." But he defends Wright's artistic vision.

The appearance of *Native Son*, then, was a watershed in terms of both the literary and critical output it sparked. Although there would continue to be calls for characters more richly textured and community-oriented, there is little doubt that Bigger's presence and perceptions are impressive and influential artistic achievements. Rather than seeing Bigger's viewpoint as a flaw, writer Charles Johnson argues in his critical monograph that it is the strength of the book. As he says in *Being and Race*, Wright's story "remains one of our most phenomenologically successful novels."

Other authors responded to Wright in their own literary stylings. Chester Himes was perhaps the first, with his novel *If He Hollers Let Him Go (1945)*. During the story, the protagonist, Bob Jones, actually engages in a debate about the merits of *Native Son*. Jones has been to college; thus, he reads literature and is capable of articulating the opinion that Bigger Thomas is a good character to demonstrate the effects of racist oppression and indicate the need for social revolution. Although Jones is much advanced beyond Bigger Thomas intellectually, he nonetheless shares the same fear and rage because of domination by whites. His environment proves more potent than his intellect, and his reactions to the continual humiliation he is subjected to by whites are, like Bigger's, dysfunctional.

Ann Petry's *The Street* (1946) is another novel that has been linked, understandably, to *Native Son*. Lutie Johnson, the heroine, is trapped by her surroundings, namely, the street on which she lives and its attendant activities. Both are rendered in descriptive fullness. Johnson is a more developed character than Bigger Thomas or Bob Jones. Rather than engaging in a series of irrational acts, she logically charts a reasonable course of action for herself and her son Bub. However, ghetto oppression causes her downfall nonetheless. Her murder of Boots Smith, who himself is scarred physically and psychologically, is clarifying for Lutie as she sheds all her illusions about her chances for success as a poor Black woman in American society. But for this price she loses her son, who was her main reason for struggling as diligently as she did. In the end, all poor African Americans succumb to the street, or so it appears. At the end of *The Street*, Lutie Johnson leaves Harlem for Chicago, which is hardly a bright prospect. She travels westward in resignation, no longer even asking, as Langston Hughes put it in his poem "Tell Me" (1951), "Why should it be *my* dream/deferred/overlong?"

Although Himes and Petry make significant gestures to *Native Son,* Lorraine Hansberry is the writer who drew from the novel most elaborately in her play *A Raisin in the Sun* (1959). The title comes from Hughes's "Harlem [2]" (1951), his poetic wondering about the fate of a deferred dream: "Does it dry up/like a raisin in the sun?" Indeed, much of Hughes's poetry could have served as a model of social protest. He had certainly been at it long enough, much longer than Wright. But Wright's abundant fingerprints on Hansberry's play are unmistakable. The Youngers, like the Thomases, live on the south side of Chicago. Walter Lee Younger, like Bigger, has a job as a chauffeur. The difference in age between Bigger and Walter is virtually the same as the time span between the publication of Wright's novel and the completion of Hansberry's script. Therefore, in a sense, Bigger would be Walter's age had he lived. Both the play and the novel open early in the morning. The first sounds in both are the ringing of an alarm clock followed by the urging of a woman to get males of the family in motion. Travis's encounter with a rat echoes Bigger's. And the reader should consider the homophonic resonance of *sun* and *son,* the contribution of Hughes notwithstanding.

The crucial differences are Hansberry's focus on a family and the fact that the play does not end tragically. The Youngers are surviving, even beginning to prosper, as a unit. They transcend the limitations of their environment and trade it in for a new one. Thus, the play ends on a note of optimism, albeit a very guarded one. Hansberry adds additional wrinkles to the conception of Black social protest discussed in this chapter. Beneatha's ambitions to be a doctor range beyond the aspirations of many other female characters; Asagai's Afrocentrism hints at other forms of socialization beyond the urban ghetto. Walter Lee possesses much of the rage that earlier protest characters are consumed by, but he is able to redeem himself within acceptable norms. Yet the criticism of a racist power structure is announced clearly in Hansberry's play. Her borrowing of and then extending what was by then standard protest fare, by incorporating new elements, is part of her artistic power and genius.

Further Reading

Baldwin, James. *Notes of a Native Son.* Boston: Beacon Press, 1955.

Ellison, Ralph. *The Collected Essays of Ralph Ellison.* Ed. John F. Callahan. New York:Modern Library, 1995.

Johnson, Charles. *Being & Race: Black Writing Since 1970.* Bloomington: Indiana University Press, 1988.

Richard Wright
(1908–1960)

For biographical information about Richard Wright, see page 341.
Native Son, a story detailing the explosive life of Bigger Thomas,
is Wright's most celebrated novel. When it was published in 1940,
it sold more than two hundred thousand copies in less than a
month and drew comparisons to the fiction of Theodore Dreiser
and John Steinbeck.

Native Son

1   *Brrrrrrrüüüüüüüüüüüüüüinng!*

2   An alarm clock clanged in the dark and silent room. A bed spring creaked. A woman's voice sang out impatiently:

3   "Bigger, shut that thing off!"

4   A surly grunt sounded above the tinny ring of metal. Naked feet swished dryly across the planks in the wooden floor and the clang ceased abruptly.

5   "Turn on the light, Bigger."

6   "Awright," came a sleepy mumble.

7   Light flooded the room and revealed a black boy standing in a narrow space between two iron beds, rubbing his eyes with the backs of his hands. From a bed to his right the woman spoke again:

8   "Buddy, get up from there! I got a big washing on my hands today and I want you all out of here."

9   Another black boy rolled from bed and stood up. The woman also rose and stood in her nightgown.

10   "Turn your heads so I can dress," she said.

11   The two boys averted their eyes and gazed into a far corner of the room. The woman rushed out of her nightgown and put on a pair of step-ins. She turned to the bed from which she had risen and called:

12   "Vera! Get up from there!"

13   "What time is it, Ma?" asked a muffled, adolescent voice from beneath a quilt.

14   "Get up from there, I say!"

15   "O.K., Ma."

16   A brown-skinned girl in a cotton gown got up and stretched her arms above her head and yawned. Sleepily, she sat on a chair and fumbled with her stockings. The two boys kept their faces averted while their mother and sister put on enough clothes to keep them from feeling ashamed; and the mother and sister did the same while the boys dressed. Abruptly, they all paused, holding their clothes in their hands, their attention caught by a light tapping in the thinly plastered walls of the room. They forgot their conspiracy against shame and their eyes strayed apprehensively over the floor.

17   "There he is again, Bigger!" the woman screamed, and the tiny, one-room apartment galvanized into violent action. A chair toppled as the woman, half-dressed and in her stocking feet, scrambled breathlessly upon the bed. Her two sons, barefoot, stood tense and motionless, their eyes searching anxiously under the bed and chairs. The girl ran into a corner, half-stooped and gathered the hem of her slip into both of her hands and held it tightly over her knees.

18   "Oh! Oh!" she wailed.

19   "There he goes!"

20   The woman pointed a shaking finger. Her eyes were round with fascinated horror.

21   "Where?"

22   "I don't see 'im!"

23   "Bigger, he's behind the trunk!" the girl whimpered.

24   "Vera!" the woman screamed. "Get up here on the bed! Don't let that thing *bite* you!"

25   Frantically, Vera climbed upon the bed and the woman caught hold of her. With their arms entwined about each other, the black mother and the brown daughter gazed open-mouthed at the trunk in the corner.

26   Bigger looked round the room wildly, then darted to a curtain and swept it aside and grabbed two heavy iron skillets from a wall above a gas stove. He whirled and called softly to his brother, his eyes glued to the trunk.

27   "Buddy!"

28   "Yeah?"

29   "Here; take this skillet."

30   "O.K."

31   "Now, get over by the door!"

32   "O.K."

33   Buddy crouched by the door and held the iron skillet by its handle, his arm flexed and poised. Save for the quick, deep breathing

of the four people, the room was quiet. Bigger crept on tiptoe toward the trunk with the skillet clutched stiffly in his hand, his eyes dancing and watching every inch of the wooden floor in front of him. He paused and, without moving an eye or muscle, called:

34   "Buddy!"

35   "Hunh?"

36   "Put that box in front of the hole so he can't get out!"

37   "O.K."

38   Buddy ran to a wooden box and shoved it quickly in front of a gaping hole in the molding and then backed again to the door, holding the skillet ready. Bigger eased to the trunk and peered behind it cautiously. He saw nothing. Carefully, he stuck out his bare foot and pushed the trunk a few inches.

39   "There he is!" the mother screamed again.

40   A huge black rat squealed and leaped at Bigger's trouser-leg and snagged it in his teeth, hanging on.

41   "Goddamn!" Bigger whispered fiercely, whirling and kicking out his leg with all the strength of his body. The force of his movement shook the rat loose and it sailed through the air and struck a wall. Instantly, it rolled over and leaped again. Bigger dodged and the rat landed against a table leg. With clenched teeth, Bigger held the skillet; he was afraid to hurl it, fearing that he might miss. The rat squeaked and turned and ran in a narrow circle, looking for a place to hide; it leaped again past Bigger and scurried on dry rasping feet to one side of the box and then to the other, searching for the hole. Then it turned and reared upon its hind legs.

42   "Hit 'im, Bigger!" Buddy shouted.

43   "Kill 'im!" the woman screamed.

44   The rat's belly pulsed with fear. Bigger advanced a step and the rat emitted a long thin song of defiance, its black beady eyes glittering, its tiny forefeet pawing the air restlessly. Bigger swung the skillet; it skidded over the floor, missing the rat, and clattered to a stop against a wall.

45   "Goddamn!"

46   The rat leaped. Bigger sprang to one side. The rat stopped under a chair and let out a furious screak. Bigger moved slowly backward toward the door.

47   "Gimme that skillet, Buddy," he asked quietly, not taking his eyes from the rat.

48   Buddy extended his hand. Bigger caught the skillet and lifted it high in the air. The rat scuttled across the floor and stopped again

at the box and searched quickly for the hole; then it reared once more and bared long yellow fangs, piping shrilly, belly quivering.

49   Bigger aimed and let the skillet fly with a heavy grunt. There was a shattering of wood as the box caved in. The woman screamed and hid her face in her hands. Bigger tiptoed forward and peered.

50   "I got 'im," he muttered, his clenched teeth bared in a smile. "By God, I got 'im."

51   He kicked the splintered box out of the way and the flat black body of the rat lay exposed, its two long yellow tusks showing distinctly. Bigger took a shoe and pounded the rat's head, crushing it, cursing hysterically:

52   "You sonofa*bitch!*"

53   The woman on the bed sank to her knees and buried her face in the quilts and sobbed:

54   "Lord, Lord, have mercy. . . ."

55   "Aw, Mama," Vera whimpered, bending to her. "Don't cry. It's dead now."

56   The two brothers stood over the dead rat and spoke in tones of awed admiration.

57   "Gee, but he's a big bastard."

58   "That sonofabitch could cut your throat."

59   "He's over a foot long."

60   "How in hell do they get so big?"

61   "Eating garbage and anything else they can get."

62   "Look, Bigger, there's a three-inch rip in your pantleg."

63   "Yeah; he was after me, all right."

64   "Please, Bigger, take 'im out," Vera begged.

65   "Aw, don't be so scary," Buddy said.

66   The woman on the bed continued to sob. Bigger took a piece of newspaper and gingerly lifted the rat by its tail and held it out at arm's length.

67   "Bigger, take 'im out," Vera begged again.

68   Bigger laughed and approached the bed with the dangling rat, swinging it to and fro like a pendulum, enjoying his sister's fear.

69   "Bigger!" Vera gasped convulsively; she screamed and swayed and closed her eyes and fell headlong across her mother and rolled limply from the bed to the floor.

70   "Bigger, for God's sake!" the mother sobbed, rising and bending over Vera. "Don't do that! Throw that rat out!"

71   He laid the rat down and started to dress.

72   "Bigger, help me lift Vera to the bed," the mother said.

73   He paused and turned round.

74   "What's the matter?" he asked, feigning ignorance.

75   "Do what I asked you, will you, boy?"

76   He went to the bed and helped his mother lift Vera. Vera's eyes were closed. He turned away and finished dressing. He wrapped the rat in a newspaper and went out of the door and down the stairs and put it into a garbage can at the corner of an alley. When he returned to the room his mother was still bent over Vera, placing a wet towel upon her head. She straightened and faced him, her cheeks and eyes wet with tears and her lips tight with anger.

77   "Boy, sometimes I wonder what makes you act like you do."

78   "What I do now?" he demanded belligerently.

79   "Sometimes you act the biggest fool I ever saw."

80   "What you talking about?"

81   "You scared your sister with that rat and she *fainted!* Ain't you got no sense at *all?*"

82   "Aw, I didn't know she was that scary."

83   "Buddy!" the mother called.

84   "Yessum."

85   "Take a newspaper and spread it over that spot."

86   "Yessum."

87   Buddy opened out a newspaper and covered the smear of blood on the floor where the rat had been crushed. Bigger went to the window and stood looking out abstractedly into the street. His mother glared at his back.

88   "Bigger, sometimes I wonder why I birthed you," she said bitterly.

89   Bigger looked at her and turned away.

90   "Maybe you oughtn't've. Maybe you ought to left me where I was."

91   "You shut your sassy mouth!"

92   "Aw, for Chrissakes!" Bigger said, lighting a cigarette.

93   "Buddy, pick up them skillets and put 'em in the sink," the mother said.

94   "Yessum."

95   Bigger walked across the floor and sat on the bed. His mother's eyes followed him.

96   "We wouldn't have to live in this garbage dump if you had any manhood in you," she said.

97   "Aw, don't start that again."

98   "How you feel, Vera?" the mother asked.

99   Vera raised her head and looked about the room as though expecting to see another rat.

100 "Oh, Mama!"

101 "You poor thing!"

102 "I couldn't help it. Bigger scared me."

103 "Did you hurt yourself?"

104 "I bumped my head."

105 "Here; take it easy. You'll be all right."

106 "How come Bigger acts that way?" Vera asked, crying again.

107 "He's just crazy," the mother said. "Just plain dumb black crazy."

108 "I'll be late for my sewing class at the Y.W.C.A.," Vera said.

109 "Here; stretch out on the bed. You'll feel better in a little while," the mother said.

110 She left Vera on the bed and turned a pair of cold eyes upon Bigger.

111 "Suppose you wake up some morning and find your sister dead? What would you think then?" she asked. "Suppose those rats cut our veins at night when we sleep? Naw! Nothing like that ever bothers you! All you care about is your own pleasure! Even when the relief offers you a job you won't take it till they threaten to cut off your food and starve you! Bigger, honest, you the most no-countest man I ever seen in all my life!"

112 "You done told me that a thousand times," he said, not looking round.

113 "Well, I'm telling you agin! And mark my word, some of these days you going to set down and *cry*. Some of these days you going to wish you had made something out of yourself, instead of just a tramp. But it'll be too late then."

114 "Stop prophesying about me," he said.

115 "I prophesy much as I please! And if you don't like it, you can get out. We can get along without you. We can live in one room just like we living now, even with you gone," she said.

116 "Aw, for Chrissakes!" he said, his voice filled with nervous irritation.

117 "You'll regret how you living some day," she went on. "If you don't stop running with that gang of yours and do right you'll end up where you never thought you would. You think I don't know what you boys is doing, but I do. And the gallows is at the end of the road you traveling, boy. Just remember that." She turned and looked at Buddy. "Throw that box outside, Buddy."

118 "Yessum."

119 There was silence. Buddy took the box out. The mother went behind the curtain to the gas stove. Vera sat up in bed and swung her feet to the floor.

120 "Lay back down, Vera," the mother said.

121   "I feel all right now, Ma. I got to go to my sewing class."

122   "Well, if you feel like it, set the table," the mother said, going behind the curtain again. "Lord, I get so tired of this I don't know what to do," her voice floated plaintively from behind the curtain.

123   "All I ever do is try to make a home for you children and you don't care."

124   "Aw, Ma," Vera protested. "Don't say that."

125   "Vera, sometimes I just want to lay down and quit."

126   "Ma, please don't say that."

127   "I can't last many more years, living like this."

128   "I'll be old enough to work soon, Ma."

129   "I reckon I'll be dead then. I reckon God'll call me home."

130   Vera went behind the curtain and Bigger heard her trying to comfort his mother. He shut their voices out of his mind. He hated his family because he knew that they were suffering and that he was powerless to help them. He knew that the moment he allowed himself to feel to its fulness how they lived, the shame and misery of their lives, he would be swept out of himself with fear and despair. So he held toward them an attitude of iron reserve; he lived with them, but behind a wall, a curtain. And toward himself he was even more exacting. He knew that the moment he allowed what his life meant to enter fully into his consciousness, he would either kill himself or someone else. So he denied himself and acted tough.

131   He got up and crushed his cigarette upon the window sill. Vera came into the room and placed knives and forks upon the table.

132   "Get ready to eat, you-all," the mother called.

133   He sat at the table. The odor of frying bacon and boiling coffee drifted to him from behind the curtain. His mother's voice floated to him in song.

> *Life is like a mountain railroad*
> *With an engineer that's brave*
> *We must make the run successful*
> *From the cradle to the grave. . . .*

134   The song irked him and he was glad when she stopped and came into the room with a pot of coffee and a plate of crinkled bacon. Vera brought the bread in and they sat down. His mother closed her eyes and lowered her head and mumbled,

135   "Lord, we thank Thee for the food You done placed before us for the nourishment of our bodies. Amen." She lifted her eyes and without

changing her tone of voice, said, "You going to have to learn to get up earlier than this, Bigger, to hold a job."

136 He did not answer or look up.

137 "You want me to pour you some coffee?" Vera asked.

138 "Yeah."

139 "You going to take the job, ain't you, Bigger?" his mother asked.

140 He laid down his fork and stared at her.

141 "I told you last night I was going to take it. How many times you want to ask me?"

142 "Well, don't bite her head off," Vera said. "She only asked you a question."

143 "Pass the bread and stop being smart."

144 "You know you have to see Mr. Dalton at five-thirty," his mother said.

145 "You done said that ten times."

146 "I don't want you to forget, son."

147 "And you know how you can forget," Vera said.

148 "Aw, lay off Bigger," Buddy said. "He told you he was going to take the job."

149 "Don't tell 'em nothing," Bigger said.

150 "You shut your mouth, Buddy, or get up from this table," the mother said. "I'm not going to take any stinking sass from you. One fool in the family's enough."

151 "Lay off, Ma," Buddy said.

152 "Bigger's setting here like he ain't glad to get a job," she said.

153 "What you want me to do? Shout?" Bigger asked.

154 "Oh, Bigger!" his sister said.

155 "I wish you'd keep your big mouth out of this!" he told his sister.

156 "If you get that job," his mother said in a low, kind tone of voice, busy slicing a loaf of bread, "I can fix up a nice place for you children. You could be comfortable and not have to live like pigs."

157 "Bigger ain't decent enough to think of nothing like that," Vera said.

158 "God, I wish you-all would let me eat," Bigger said.

159 His mother talked on as though she had not heard him and he stopped listening.

160 "Ma's talking to you, Bigger," Vera said.

161 "So *what?*"

162 "Don't be that way, Bigger!"

163 He laid down his fork and his strong black fingers gripped the edge of the table; there was silence save for the tinkling of his brother's fork against a plate. He kept staring at his sister till her eyes fell.

164   "I wish you'd let me eat," he said again.

165   As he ate he felt that they were thinking of the job he was to get that evening and it made him angry; he felt that they had tricked him into a cheap surrender.

166   "I need some carfare," he said.

167   "Here's all I got," his mother said, pushing a quarter to the side of his plate.

168   He put the quarter in his pocket and drained his cup of coffee in one long swallow. He got his coat and cap and went to the door.

169   "You know, Bigger," his mother said, "if you don't take that job the relief'll cut us off. We won't have any food."

170   "I told you I'd take it!" he shouted and slammed the door.

171   He went down the steps into the vestibule and stood looking out into the street through the plate glass of the front door. Now and then a street car rattled past over steel tracks. He was sick of his life at home. Day in and day out there was nothing but shouts and bickering. But what could he do? Each time he asked himself that question his mind hit a blank wall and he stopped thinking. Across the street directly in front of him, he saw a truck pull to a stop at the curb and two white men in overalls got out with pails and brushes. Yes, he could take the job at Dalton's and be miserable, or he could refuse it and starve. It maddened him to think that he did not have a wider choice of action. Well, he could not stand here all day like this. What was he to do with himself? He tried to decide if he wanted to buy a ten-cent magazine, or go to a movie, or go to the poolroom and talk with the gang, or just loaf around. With his hands deep in his pockets, another cigarette slanting across his chin, he brooded and watched the men at work across the street. They were pasting a huge colored poster to a signboard. The poster showed a white face.

172   "That's Buckley!" He spoke softly to himself. "He's running for State's Attorney again." The men were slapping the poster with wet brushes. He looked at the round florid face and wagged his head. "I bet that sonofabitch rakes off a million bucks in graft a year. Boy, if I was in his shoes for just one day I'd *never* have to worry again."

173   When the men were through they gathered up their pails and brushes and got into the truck and drove off. He looked at the poster: the white face was fleshy but stern, one hand was uplifted and its index finger pointed straight out into the street at each passer-by. The poster showed one of those faces that looked straight at you when you looked at it and all the while you were walking and turning your head to look at it it kept looking unblinkingly back at you until you got

so far from it you had to take your eyes away, and then it stopped, like a movie blackout. Above the top of the poster were tall red letters: YOU CAN'T WIN!

174 He snuffed his cigarette and laughed silently. "You crook," he mumbled, shaking his head. "You let whoever pays *you* off win!" He opened the door and met the morning air. He went along the sidewalk with his head down, fingering the quarter in his pocket. He stopped and searched all of his pockets; in his vest pocket he found a lone copper cent. That made a total of twenty-six cents, fourteen cents of which would have to be saved for carfare to Mr. Dalton's; that is, if he decided to take the job. In order to buy a magazine and go to the movies he would have to have at least twenty cents more. "Goddammit, I'm always broke!" he mumbled.

175 He stood on the corner in the sunshine, watching cars and people pass. He needed more money; if he did not get more than he had now he would not know what to do with himself for the rest of the day. He wanted to see a movie; his senses hungered for it. In a movie he could dream without effort; all he had to do was lean back in a seat and keep his eyes open.

176 He thought of Gus and G.H. and Jack. Should he go to the poolroom and talk with them? But there was no use in his going unless they were ready to do what they had been long planning to do. If they could, it would mean some sure and quick money. From three o'clock to four o'clock in the afternoon there was no policeman on duty in the block where Blum's Delicatessen was and it would be safe. One of them could hold a gun on Blum and keep him from yelling; one could watch the front door; one could watch the back; and one could get the money from the box under the counter. Then all four of them could lock Blum in the store and run out through the back and duck down the alley and meet an hour later, either at Doc's poolroom or at the South Side Boys' Club, and split the money.

177 Holding up Blum ought not take more than two minutes, at the most. And it would be their last job. But it would be the toughest one that they had ever pulled. All the other times they had raided newsstands, fruit stands, and apartments. And, too, they had never held up a white man before. They had always robbed Negroes. They felt that it was much easier and safer to rob their own people, for they knew that white policemen never really searched diligently for Negroes who committed crimes against other Negroes. For months they had talked of robbing Blum's, but had not been able to bring themselves to do it. They had the feeling that the robbing of Blum's

would be a violation of ultimate taboo; it would be a trespassing into territory where the full wrath of an alien white world would be turned loose upon them; in short, it would be a symbolic challenge of the white world's rule over them; a challenge which they yearned to make, but were afraid to. Yes; if they could rob Blum's, it would be a real hold-up, in more senses than one. In comparison, all of their other jobs had been play.

178   "Good-bye, Bigger."

179   He looked up and saw Vera passing with a sewing kit dangling from her arm. She paused at the corner and came back to him.

180   "Now, what you want?"

181   "Bigger, please. . . . You're getting a good job now. Why don't you stay away from Jack and Gus and G.H. and keep out of trouble?"

182   "You keep your big mouth out of my business!"

183   "But, Bigger!"

184   "Go on to school, will you!"

185   She turned abruptly and walked on. He knew that his mother had been talking to Vera and Buddy about him, telling them that if he got into any more trouble he would be sent to prison and not just to the reform school, where they sent him last time. He did not mind what his mother said to Buddy about him. Buddy was all right. Tough, plenty. But Vera was a sappy girl; she did not have any more sense than to believe everything she was told.

186   He walked toward the poolroom. When he got to the door he saw Gus half a block away, coming toward him. He stopped and waited. It was Gus who had first thought of robbing Blum's.

187   "Hi, Bigger!"

188   "What you saying, Gus?"

189   "Nothing. Seen G.H. or Jack yet?"

190   "Naw. You?"

191   "Naw. Say, got a cigarette?"

192   "Yeah."

193   Bigger took out his pack and gave Gus a cigarette; he lit his and held the match for Gus. They leaned their backs against the red-brick wall of a building, smoking, their cigarettes slanting white across their black chins. To the east Bigger saw the sun burning a dazzling yellow. In the sky above him a few big white clouds drifted. He puffed silently, relaxed, his mind pleasantly vacant of purpose. Every slight movement in the street evoked a casual curiosity in him. Automatically, his eyes followed each car as it whirred over the smooth black asphalt. A woman came by and he watched the gentle sway of her

body until she disappeared into a doorway. He sighed, scratched his chin and mumbled,

194 "Kinda warm today."

195 "Yeah," Gus said.

196 "You get more heat from this sun than from them old radiators at home."

197 "Yeah; them old white landlords sure don't give much heat."

198 "And they always knocking at your door for money."

199 "I'll be glad when summer comes."

200 "Me too," Bigger said.

201 He stretched his arms above his head and yawned; his eyes moistened. The sharp precision of the world of steel and stone dissolved into blurred waves. He blinked and the world grew hard again, mechanical, distinct. A weaving motion in the sky made him turn his eyes upward; he saw a slender streak of billowing white blooming against the deep blue. A plane was writing high up in the air.

202 "Look!" Bigger said.

203 "What?"

204 "That plane writing up there," Bigger said, pointing.

205 "Oh!"

206 They squinted at a tiny ribbon of unfolding vapor that spelled out the word: USE. . . . The plane was so far away that at times the strong glare of the sun blanked it from sight.

207 "You can hardly see it," Gus said.

208 "Looks like a little bird," Bigger breathed with childlike wonder.

209 "Them white boys sure can fly," Gus said.

210 "Yeah," Bigger said, wistfully. "They get a chance to do everything."

211 Noiselessly, the tiny plane looped and veered, vanishing and appearing, leaving behind it a long trail of white plumage, like coils of fluffy paste being squeezed from a tube; a plume-coil that grew and swelled and slowly began to fade into the air at the edges. The plane wrote another word: SPEED. . . .

212 "How high you reckon he is?" Bigger asked.

213 "I don't know. Maybe a hundred miles; maybe a thousand."

214 "I could fly one of them things if I had a chance," Bigger mumbled reflectively, as though talking to himself.

215 Gus pulled down the corners of his lips, stepped out from the wall, squared his shoulders, doffed his cap, bowed low and spoke with mock deference:

216 "Yessuh."

217 "You go to hell," Bigger said, smiling.

218   "Yessuh," Gus said again.

219   "I *could* fly a plane if I had a chance," Bigger said.

220   "If you wasn't black and if you had some money and if they'd let you go to that aviation school, you *could* fly a plane," Gus said.

221   For a moment Bigger contemplated all the "ifs" that Gus had mentioned. Then both boys broke into hard laughter, looking at each other through squinted eyes. When their laughter subsided, Bigger said in a voice that was half-question and half-statement:

222   "It's funny how the white folks treat us, ain't it?"

223   "It better be funny," Gus said.

224   "Maybe they right in not wanting us to fly," Bigger said. "Cause if I took a plane up I'd take a couple of bombs along and drop 'em as sure as hell. . . ."

225   They laughed again, still looking upward. The plane sailed and dipped and spread another word against the sky: GASOLINE. . . .

226   "Use Speed Gasoline," Bigger mused, rolling the words slowly from his lips. "God, I'd like to fly up there in that sky."

227   "God'll let you fly when He gives you your wings up in heaven," Gus said.

228   They laughed again, reclining against the wall, smoking, the lids of their eyes drooped softly against the sun. Cars whizzed past on rubber tires. Bigger's face was metallically black in the strong sunlight. There was in his eyes a pensive, brooding amusement, as of a man who had been long confronted and tantalized by a riddle whose answer seemed always just on the verge of escaping him, but prodding him irresistibly on to seek its solution. The silence irked Bigger; he was anxious to do something to evade looking so squarely at this problem.

229   "Let's play 'white,'" Bigger said, referring to a game of play-acting in which he and his friends imitated the ways and manners of white folks.

230   "I don't feel like it," Gus said.

231   "General!" Bigger pronounced in a sonorous tone, looking at Gus expectantly.

232   "Aw, hell! I don't want to play," Gus whined.

233   "You'll be court-martialed," Bigger said, snapping out his words with military precision.

234   "Nigger, you nuts!" Gus laughed.

235   "General!" Bigger tried again, determinedly.

236   Gus looked wearily at Bigger, then straightened, saluted and answered:

237   "Yessuh."

238   "Send your men over the river at dawn and attack the enemy's left flank," Bigger ordered.

239   "Yessuh."

240   "Send the Fifth, Sixth, and Seventh Regiments," Bigger said, frowning. "And attack with tanks, gas, planes, and infantry."

241   "Yessuh!" Gus said again, saluting and clicking his heels.

242   For a moment they were silent, facing each other, their shoulders thrown back, their lips compressed to hold down the mounting impulse to laugh. Then they guffawed, partly at themselves and partly at the vast white world that sprawled and towered in the sun before them.

243   "Say, what's a 'left flank'?" Gus asked.

244   "I don't know," Bigger said. "I heard it in the movies."

245   They laughed again. After a bit they relaxed and leaned against the wall, smoking. Bigger saw Gus cup his left hand to his ear, as though holding a telephone receiver; and cup his right hand to his mouth, as though talking into a transmitter.

246   "Hello," Gus said.

247   "Hello," Bigger said. "Who's this?"

248   "This is Mr. J. P. Morgan speaking," Gus said.

249   "Yessuh, Mr. Morgan," Bigger said; his eyes filled with mock adulation and respect.

250   "I want you to sell twenty thousand shares of U.S. Steel in the market this morning," Gus said.

251   "At what price, suh?" Bigger asked.

252   "Aw, just dump 'em at any price," Gus said with casual irritation. "We're holding too much."

253   "Yessuh," Bigger said.

254   "And call me at my club at two this afternoon and tell me if the President telephoned," Gus said.

255   "Yessuh, Mr. Morgan," Bigger said.

256   Both of them made gestures signifying that they were hanging up telephone receivers; then they bent double, laughing.

257   "I bet that's *just* the way they talk," Gus said.

258   "I wouldn't be surprised," Bigger said.

259   They were silent again. Presently, Bigger cupped his hand to his mouth and spoke through an imaginary telephone transmitter.

260   "Hello."

261   "Hello," Gus answered. "Who's this?"

262   "This is the President of the United States speaking," Bigger said.

263   "Oh, yessuh, Mr. President," Gus said.

264   "I'm calling a cabinet meeting this afternoon at four o'clock and you, as Secretary of State, *must* be there."

265   "Well, now, Mr. President," Gus said, "I'm pretty busy. They raising sand over there in Germany and I got to send 'em a note. . . ."

266   "But this is important," Bigger said.

267   "What you going to take up at this cabinet meeting?" Gus asked.

268   "Well, you see, the niggers is raising sand all over the country," Bigger said, struggling to keep back his laughter. "We've got to do something with these black folks. . . ."

269   "Oh, if it's about the niggers, I'll be right there, Mr. President," Gus said.

270   They hung up imaginary receivers and leaned against the wall and laughed. A street car rattled by. Bigger sighed and swore.

271   "Goddammit!"

272   "What's the matter?"

273   "They don't let us do *nothing*."

274   "Who?"

275   "The *white* folks."

276   "You talk like you just now finding that out," Gus said.

277   "Naw. But I just can't get used to it," Bigger said. "I swear to God I can't. I know I oughtn't think about it, but I can't help it. Every time I think about it I feel like somebody's poking a red-hot iron down my throat. Goddammit, look! We live here and they live there. We black and they white. They got things and we ain't. They do things and we can't. It's just like living in jail. Half the time I feel like I'm on the outside of the world peeping in through a knot-hole in the fence. . . ."

278   "Aw, ain't no use feeling that way about it. It don't help none," Gus said.

279   "You know one thing?" Bigger said.

280   "What?"

281   "Sometimes I feel like something awful's going to happen to me," Bigger spoke with a tinge of bitter pride in his voice.

282   "What you mean?" Gus asked, looking at him quickly. There was fear in Gus's eyes.

283   "I don't know. I just feel that way. Every time I get to thinking about me being black and they being white, me being here and they being there, I feel like something awful's going to happen to me. . . ."

284   "Aw, for Chrissakes! There ain't nothing you can do about it. How come you want to worry yourself? You black and they make the laws. . . ."

285   "Why they make us live in one corner of the city? Why don't they let us fly planes and run ships. . . ."

286   Gus hunched Bigger with his elbow and mumbled good-naturedly, "Aw, nigger, quit thinking about it. You'll go nuts."

287   The plane was gone from the sky and the white plumes of floating smoke were thinly spread, vanishing. Because he was restless and had time on his hands, Bigger yawned again and hoisted his arms high above his head.

288   "Nothing ever happens," he complained.

289   "What you want to happen?"

290   "Anything," Bigger said with a wide sweep of his dingy palm, a sweep that included all the possible activities of the world.

291   Then their eyes were riveted; a slate-colored pigeon swooped down to the middle of the steel car tracks and began strutting to and fro with ruffled feathers, its fat neck bobbing with regal pride. A street car rumbled forward and the pigeon rose swiftly through the air on wings stretched so taut and sheer that Bigger could see the gold of the sun through their translucent tips. He tilted his head and watched the slate-colored bird flap and wheel out of sight over the edge of a high roof.

292   "Now, if I could only do that," Bigger said.

293   Gus laughed.

294   "Nigger, you nuts."

295   "I reckon we the only things in this city that can't go where we want to go and do what we want to do."

296   "Don't think about it," Gus said.

297   "I can't help it."

298   "That's why you feeling like something awful's going to happen to you," Gus said. "You think too much."

299   "What in hell can a man do?" Bigger asked, turning to Gus.

300   "Get drunk and sleep it off."

301   "I can't. I'm broke."

302   Bigger crushed his cigarette and took out another one and offered the package to Gus. They continued smoking. A huge truck swept past, lifting scraps of white paper into the sunshine; the bits settled down slowly.

303   "Gus?"

304   "Hunh?"

305   "You know where the white folks live?"

306   "Yeah," Gus said, pointing eastward. "Over across the 'line'; over there on Cottage Grove Avenue."

307   "Naw; they don't," Bigger said.

308   "What you mean?" Gus asked, puzzled. "Then, where do they live?"

309   Bigger doubled his fist and struck his solar plexus.

310   "Right down here in my stomach," he said.

311   Gus looked at Bigger searchingly, then away, as though ashamed.

Chester Himes

(1909–1984)

Chester Himes was born into a middle-class family on July 29, 1909, in Jefferson, Missouri. His family relocated fairly often because his father taught at various industrial schools in the South. The Himes family eventually arrived in Cleveland, Ohio, where Himes was drawn to elements of street life. He enrolled at Ohio State University but completed only one semester. In 1928, he was convicted of robbery. He began his literary career while serving seven years in prison. Himes is often praised for his vivid depictions of racism and alienation. His books include the naturalist novels If He Hollers Let Him Go *(1945),* Lonely Crusade *(1947),* Cast the First Stone *(1952),* The Third Generation *(1954), and* The Primitive *(1955); the detective novels* For Love of Imabelle *(1957),* The Crazy Kill *(1959),* Cotton Comes to Harlem *(1965), and* Blind Man with a Pistol *(1969); and the two-volume autobiography* The Quality of Hurt: The Autobiography of Chester Himes *(1972) and* My Life of Absurdity: The Autobiography of Chester Himes *(1976). In 1953, Himes moved to Europe, living in France and then Spain. The following selection, taken from* If He Hollers Let Him Go, *details the visit of Bob Jones, a laborer who is struggling in the racist environment of wartime Los Angeles, to the home of his girlfriend.*

If He Hollers Let Him Go

CHAPTER X

1   Dr. Harrison answered my ring. He was dressed in a brown flannel smoking jacket with a black velvet collar. He waved a soggy cigar butt in his left hand, stuck out his right.

2   'Hello, Robert, it's good to see you, boy.'

3   We shook hands; his felt dry, lifeless, and his mouth looked nasty. I said, 'It's good to see you, Doctor.'

4   He closed the door behind me and steered me into his study.

5   'You're just in time to join me in a nip.'

6   'Well, thanks,' I said. I always felt a sharp sense of embarrassment around him. I didn't like him, didn't respect him, didn't have anything to say to him, didn't like to listen to him. But he always cornered me off for a conversation and I didn't know how to get out of it short of blasting him one.

7   He went over to his bar. 'What'll it be, Scotch?'

8   'Scotch is fine,' I said. 'A little water.'

9   'A gentleman's drink,' he said, mixing it. 'Now I prefer rye.' Then he noticed I was standing and said: 'Sit down, sit down. As Bertha says, "We're all coloured folks." You know Bertha Gowing, head of the South Side Clinic?'

10   'No, I don't,' I said, taking the drink and sitting down.

11   'A fine person, charming personality, very capable, very capable,' he said, returning to his easy chair across from me. He waved at the Pittsburgh *Courier* on the floor. 'I was just reading about our fighter pilots in Italy; they're achieving a remarkable record.'

12   I said, 'That's right.'

13   'Makes the old man wish he was young again,' he went on. 'Think of it, the first time in the history of our nation that Negro boys have served as pilots. We can thank Roosevelt for that.'

14   'That's right.' I said. My mind was on Alice. I wondered how she was going to react to seeing me.

15   'The Nazi pilots say they'd rather engage any two white pilots than one of our Negro boys,' he said.

16   'Yeah, they're some tough customers,' I said.

17   'I was talking to Blakely the other day, and he said we should send them a cablegram saying, "The eyes of the world are on you." You know Blakely Moore, the young attorney who fought that restricted covenant case for the Du Barrys?'

18   'No, I don't,' I said.

19   'Bright young man,' he said. 'Has a wonderful future. I attended his birth.' He took a sip of rye. 'Well, how is your work progressing, Robert? I understand you have been made a supervisor.'

20   I stole a look at him, looked away. 'Well, not exactly a supervisor. I'm what they call a leaderman.'

21   'A leaderman, eh? I'm always intrigued by the titles applied to industrial workers. Now what is a leaderman?'

22   'I just have charge of a small crew of workers,' I said.

23   'But you're in authority?' he insisted.

24 'Well . . . ' To hell with trying to explain it, I thought, and said, 'Yes.'

25 'That's what I like to see,' he said. 'Our Negro boys in authority. It proves that we can do it if we are given the opportunity.'

26 A little bit of that went a long way. 'How's everything with you, Doctor?' I asked, changing the conversation. My vocal cords were getting tight.

27 'I keep pretty busy,' he chuckled. 'Walter and I were just talking the other day about the tremendous change that's taken place in Los Angeles—'

28 'Yes, it has,' I cut in rapidly. 'The city's really growing up.' If he asked me if I knew Walter Somebody-or-other I was subject to tell him to go to hell. 'Is Alice in?' I asked before he could get it out.

29 'I'll see,' he said, getting up. 'You know, this house is so arranged we can go for days without running into each other.' He went into the hallway and called, 'Alice!'

30 After a moment she replied from upstairs, 'Yes?'

31 'Robert is here.'

32 'Oh!' A pause. Then, 'Tell him to come right up.'

33 He turned to me. 'You can go right up, Robert.'

34 'Thanks,' I said.

35 He stopped me to shake hands again. 'It was nice seeing you, Robert.' He always made it a point to let me know he didn't have anything against me, even if I didn't belong to his class.

36 'It was nice seeing you too, Doctor,' I said.

37 Alice was waiting for me at the head of the spiral stairway. 'How are you, dear?' she greeted. Her cool contralto voice was under wraps and her eyes were controlled. She wore a scarlet velvet housecoat and her cheeks were slightly rouged. I couldn't help but think she was a regal-looking chick.

38 ''Lo, baby,' I said, kissing at her.

39 She dodged. 'Don't!'

40 'All right, if that's the way—' I broke it off, looking beyond her into the sitting room. 'Goddamn, you've got company,' I accused. I was ready to turn and go.

41 But she said quickly, 'Oh, you'll like them,' took me by the hand and led me into her sitting-room.

42 It was a large pleasant room with a love seat and three armchairs done in flowered chintz. There were white scatter rugs on the polished oak floor and white organdie curtains at the double windows facing the street. Her bedroom was to the rear.

43   'You know Polly Johnson,' she said, and I said, 'Hello, Polly,' to
a sharp-faced, bright yellow woman with a mannish haircut, dressed
in a green slack suit.

44   'Hi, Bob, how's tricks?' she said around her cigarette.

45   'And Arline,' Alice went on. 'Arline Wilson.'

46   'Hello, Arline,' I said. She was a big sloppy dame in a wrinkled
print dress with her black hair pulled tight in a knot at the back of
her head, giving her a surprised, sweaty look. I imagine she thought
it made her look childish. She was a schoolteacher.

47   'Here's that man again,' she said. I gave her a quick, startled look;
she was too old for that, I thought.

48   'And this is Cleotine Dobbs,' Alice said of the third dame. 'Miss
Dobbs, Mr. Jones.'

49   I shook hands with her. 'How do you do, Miss Dobbs.'

50   She was a long, angular, dark woman dressed in an Eastern suit.
She was strictly out of place in that light bright clique.

51   'Cleo has just come to our city to direct the Downtown Settlement House,' Alice said sweetly. 'She's a Chicago gal.'

52   'That's fine,' I said, figuring on how to escape. Then to Alice: 'I
really can't stay. I just dropped by to say hello.'

53   'Oh hush, Bob, and sit down,' she said. 'You know you haven't got
a thing to do.'

54   I gave her a lidded look. 'Don't be too sure,' I said.

55   She put her hands on my shoulders and pushed me down on the
other half of the love seat with Cleo, the dark dame.

56   'That's right, girl, don't let a man get away from us,' Arline said.
I sneaked another look at her.

57   'Maybe Bob's afraid of all us women,' Polly said. 'We must look
like dames on the make.' She had a blunt, sharp-tongued manner that
could soon irritate me.

58   'Although God knows I haven't started picking them up off the
street,' Arline said, and she and Polly crossed glances.

59   'I'm overwhelmed,' I choked, then got my voice under better
control.

60   'We were just discussing the problems that confront the social
worker in Little Tokyo,' Cleo said, coming to my rescue, I supposed.
'I was saying that first of all there must be some organization within
the community through which a programme of integration may be
instituted into the broader pattern of the community. There must be
adequate provisions for health care, adequate educational resources

and opportunities for recreation,' she enumerated. She sounded as if she'd just gotten her Doctor's.

61 'What they need down there more than anything else is public housing.' Polly said bluntly. 'Have you seen some of those places that those people live in? Twelve people in a single room and not even any running water.' I remembered then that she worked with the housing authority. 'That place is a rat hole. Without adequate housing you can't even start any programme of integration.'

62 I sat there with my hands clasped in my lap, looking from one speaker to another with a forced interested smile, wondering what the hell had brought all of this on and getting tighter every second.

63 'Housing takes time,' Arline put in. She had the soft manner of the appeaser. 'And you know how they'll do even if they build a development down there; they'll allocate about one-fourth to Negroes and the rest to whites and Mexicans.'

64 'Mexicans are white in California,' Polly said.

65 'I know,' Arline said. 'That's what I mean. What they should really do is to stop all these Southern Negroes from coming into the city.'

66 By now I was tense, on edge; what they were saying didn't have any meaning for me—just some cut-rate jive in social workers' phraseology that proved a certain intellectualism, I supposed. But I didn't have to listen to it; I was going to get the hell out.

67 'But these people are already here,' Cleo pointed out. 'The ghetto's already formed. The problem now is how best to integrate the people of this ghetto into the life of the community.' She turned to me; I'd been silent long enough, 'What do you think, Mr. Jones?'

68 'About what?' I asked.

69 She threw a look at me. 'I mean what is your opinion as to the problem arising from conditions in Little Tokyo?'

70 Well, sister, you're asking for it, I thought. Aloud I said. 'Well, now, I think we ought to kill the coloured residents and eat them. In that way we'll not only solve the race problem but alleviate the meat shortage as well.'

71 There was a shocked silence for an instant, then Polly broke into a raucous laugh. Alice said softly, 'Bob!'

72 All I wanted was for them to get the hell out of there so I could be alone with Alice, but I lightened up a little out of common courtesy. 'All kidding aside,' I said, 'if I knew any solution for the race problem I'd use it for myself first of all.'

73   'But this isn't just a problem of race,' Cleo insisted. 'It's a ghetto problem involving a class of people with different cultures and traditions at a different level of education.'

74   'Different from what?' I said.

75   'The mayor's organizing a committee to investigate conditions down there,' Arline said. 'Blakely Moore is on it.'

76   'Would you gals like a drink?' Alice asked, and at their quick nods, turned to me, 'Bob dear . . .'

77   I went down to the kitchen with her for the rum-and-coke setups, glad to get a breather. 'Can't you get rid of 'em?' I asked. 'I want to talk to you, baby.'

78   She put her arms about me and kissed me. 'Be nice, darling,' she said. 'Tom's coming by and they want to meet him.'

79   'Tom who?' I asked, but she just smiled.

80   'You'll like him,' she said. 'He's something like you.'

81   The drinks got them gossipy.

82   'Herbie Washington has married a white girl.'

83   'No!'

84   'I don't believe it!'

85   'Who is she?' Alice asked.

86   'She's white,' I muttered to myself. 'Ain't that enough?' They didn't even hear me.

87   'Nobody knows,' Arline said. 'Some girl he met at one of Melba's parties.'

88   That started Cleo off. 'I can't understand these Negro men marrying these white tramps,' she said. You wouldn't, I thought, black as you are. 'Chicago's full of it. Just as soon as some Negro man starts to getting a little success he runs and marries a white woman. No decent self-respecting Negro man would marry one of those white tramps these Negroes marry.'

89   'I wouldn't say that exactly,' Polly injected. 'I know of Negro men married to decent white women—as decent as you and I.' She was taking up for herself—her father was a Negro married to a white woman.

90   But Cleo didn't know that. 'Nothing but tramps!' she stormed, getting excited about it. The veneer came off and she looked and talked just like any other Southern girl who'd never been farther than grammar school. 'Nobody but a white tramp would marry a nigger!' she shouted, almost hitting me in the mouth with her gesticulations. 'And nobody but a nigger tramp would have 'em. I was at a party in Chicago and saw one of our supposed-to-be leading Negro actors sitting up there making love to some white tramp's eyebrows.'

91   I laughed out loud. 'To her eyebrows?' I said. 'Now I'd like to see that.'

92   Polly and Arline were exchanging strange looks, as if to say, 'Where did this creature come from?' And Alice looked positively pricked.

93   But Cleo didn't pay any attention to any of us; she went on beating up her chops, looking wild and agitated. 'One of my teachers at Chicago U, was talking 'bout some girl 'bout your colour'—she indicated Alice—'and I just up and told him that it was an insult to mention light Negroes' colour to 'em; it was 'most the same as calling 'em bastards, saying their mamas had been slipping off in the bushes with white men. . . . '

94   Alice looked horrified; I knew she'd never be invited there again. But it tickled me. It was all I could do to keep from falling out laughing.

95   'Just as soon as a Negro marries one of them they start going down,' Cleo went on vehemently. 'Decent Negro people won't accept them in their homes—'

96   The doorbell chimed and Alice went down to answer it. Cleo was still raving when Alice ushered a tall, nice-looking, well-dressed white fellow into the room. He had sandy hair and a pleasant smile and looked like a really nice guy. But he was white, and I was antagonistic from the start.

97   'This is Tom Leighton, one of my co-workers,' she introduced him about.

98   For a moment there was an embarrassed silence; then the dames became intellectual again.

99   'Perhaps Mr. Leighton can give us some suggestions on our Little Tokyo problem,' Polly prompted, and they had it and gone.

100   Leighton said something that didn't make any sense at all to me, and Cleo gushed. 'Oh, that's it! That's just the thing!' I jerked a look at her; she'd blown coy to the point of simpering. I thought, well, whataya know; this white animosity didn't go as far as the men.

101   Finally, when they got through kicking Little Tokyo around, Leighton turned his bright friendly smile to me. 'Did I understand Miss Harrison to say you were an attorney?'

102   'No, I'm a shipyard worker,' I said.

103   'Oh, I'm sorry,' he apologized.

104   I let him dangle. There was another embarrassed silence.

105   Then Alice said, 'Bob's going into law after the war. He's fighting on our production front now.'

106   Leighton gave me another of his bright friendly smiles. 'I imagine it's a very interesting occupation,' he said.

107   'It's a killer,' I said. He blinked a little.

108   'Tom has just finished reading *Strange Fruit*,' Alice said. 'He thought it was fascinating.'

109   Something about the way she pronounced his name made me throw a quick searching glance at her, started me to wondering what her relations were with Leighton. I began watching both of them under lowered lids, half ashamed for the crazy suspicion that had come into my mind, jealous of the guy against my will. I'd seen so many light-complexioned Negro women absolutely pure nuts about white men, it scared me to think that Alice might be like that herself. I started thinking again of some excuse to get away.

110   He was saying, 'I was particularly interested in the characterization of Nonnie.'

111   You would, I thought, since she was so goddamned crazy about a white man.

112   'I didn't like Nonnie at all,' Polly said. 'I can't even imagine a Negro girl who's been to college doing any of the things Nonnie was supposed to do.'

113   'That was it,' Alice said, 'She didn't do anything.'

114   Watching her furtively, I began getting so tight inside I could hardly breathe. She might be having an affair with Leighton sure enough, I thought. She wouldn't count that, just like she wouldn't count that stuff at Stella's. She'd probably be proud of it, I thought; probably feel that I shouldn't resent it even if I found out. . . .

115   Arline was saying, 'Oh, I know a girl just like Nonnie. She's a good friend of mine—at least I went to school with her—and she's just like Nonnie.'

116   'Did you read the book, Mr. Jones?' Leighton asked.

117   'Yes, I did,' I said, and dropped it.

118   He waited for me, and when he saw I wasn't coming he said by way of appeasement, 'Of course I think that Richard Wright makes the point better in *Native Son*.'

119   'Oh, but what Lillian Smith does is condemn the white Southerner,' Arline said. 'All Wright did was write a vicious crime story.'

120   'Personally, I think the white Southerner doesn't mind being just like Lillian Smith portrays him,' I said.

121   'I think Richard Wright is naïve,' Polly said.

122   'Aren't we all?' I said.

123   '*Native Son* turned my stomach,' Arline said. 'It just proved what the white Southerner has always said about us; that our men are rapists and murderers.'

124   'Well, I will agree that the selection of Bigger Thomas to prove the point of Negro oppression was an unfortunate choice,' Leighton said.

125   'What do you think, Mr. Jones?' Cleo asked.

126   I said, 'Well, you couldn't pick a better person than Bigger Thomas to prove the point. But after you prove it, then what? Most white people I know are quite proud of having made Negroes into Bigger Thomases.'

127   There was another silence and everybody looked at me. 'Take me for instance,' I went on. 'I've got a job as leaderman at a shipyard. I'm supposed to have a certain amount of authority over the ordinary workers. But I'm scared to ask a white woman to do a job. All she's got to do is say I insulted her and I'm fired.'

128   Leighton looked concerned. 'Is that so?' he said. 'I didn't realize relations between white and coloured were that strained in our industries.'

129   'Of course Bob's problem is more or less individual,' Alice apologized. 'He's really temperamentally unsuited for industrial work. As soon as he enters into a profession his own problem will be solved.'

130   'Yes, I can understand that,' Leighton said. 'But as far as the problem of the Negro industrial worker is concerned, I feel that it is not so much racial as it is the problem of the masses. As soon as the masses, including all of our minority groups, have achieved economic security, racial problems will reach a solution of their own accord.' He turned to me. 'Won't you agree with me to that extent, Mr. Jones?'

131   'No,' I said. 'It's a state of mind. As long as the white folks hate me and I hate them we can earn the same amount of money, live side by side in the same kind of house, and fight every day.'

132   He got one of those condescending, indulgent smiles. 'Then how would you suggest effecting a solution to a minority group problem?'

133   'I don't know about any other minority group problem,' I said, 'but the only solution to the Negro problem is a revolution. We've got to make white people respect us and the only thing white people have ever respected is force.'

134   'But do you think a revolution by Negro people could be successful?' he asked in that gentle tone of voice used on an unruly child.

135   But I tried to keep my head. 'Not unless there were enough white people on our side,' I said.

136   'By the same token,' he argued, 'if there were enough white people on your side there wouldn't be any need for a revolution.'

137   'There's a lot of 'em who don't do anything but talk. If we had a revolution it'd force you to act, either for us or against us—personally, I wouldn't give a goddamn which way.'

138   'Suppose your revolution failed?' he asked.

139   'That'd be all right, too,' I said. 'At least we'd know where we stood.'

140   His smile became more indulgent, his voice more condescending. 'I think that you will discover that the best course for Negroes to take at this time is to participate and co-operate in the general uprising of the masses all over the world.'

141   'Are you a Communist?' I asked him.

142   Everybody else looked shocked, but he didn't even flinch. 'No, not that I have anything against the Communists, but I believe in the same, sensible way of doing things. And there's just one solution for the Negro—'

143   All of a sudden I burnt up. I'd been trying to get away from the white folks to begin with. And I wasn't going to have this peckerwood coming down here among my people, playing a great white god, sitting on his ass, solving the Negro problem with a flow of diction and making me look like a goddamned fool in front of my girl, when all I could do around his people was to be a flunkey and get kicked in the mouth. And what was more, his goddamned condescending smile was getting under my skin.

144   I cut him off with a sudden violent gesture and jumped to my feet. That broke it up.

Ann Petry

(1908–1997)

Known mostly as a fiction writer, Ann Petry was born on October 12, 1908, in Old Saybrook, Connecticut. She was a member of the only African American family in town. After attaining a degree from the University of Connecticut, she worked as a pharmacist in drugstores owned by her family in Old Saybrook and Lyme. But she also wrote stories, and she moved to New York City in 1938 to pursue writing full time. After publishing several stories, she was encouraged to apply for a Houghton Mifflin fellowship that carried a $2,400 prize and publication. She was awarded the prize in 1945. Her first novel, The Street, *was published the next year and became a best-seller. Petry was the first African American woman with book sales surpassing one million copies; approximately two million copies of the novel have been sold to date. Other books by Petry include the novels* The Narrows *(1953) and* Country Place *(1947), as well as* Miss Muriel and Other Stories *(1971). The following selection is the concluding chapter of* The Street

(1946), in which the protagonist, Lutie Johnson, attempts to borrow money to hire a lawyer for her young son, Bub, who has been arrested for stealing.

The Street

CHAPTER 18

1 IT WAS BEGINNING to snow when Lutie left the beauty parlour. The flakes were fine, small; barely recognizable as snow. More like rain, she thought, except that rain didn't sting one's face like these sharp fragments.

2 In a few more minutes it would be dark. The outlines of the buildings were blurred by long shadows. Lights in the houses and at the street corners were yellow blobs that made no impression on the ever-lengthening shadows. The small, fine snow swirled past the yellow lights in a never-ending rapid dancing that was impossible to follow and the effort made her dizzy.

3 The noise and confusion in the street were pleasant after the stillness that hung about the curtained booths of the beauty shop. Buses and trucks roared to a stop at the corners. People coming home from work jostled against her. There was the ebb and flow of talk and laughter; punctuated now and then by the sharp scream of brakes.

4 The children swarming past her added to the noise and the confusion. They were everywhere—rocking back and forth on the traffic rails in front of the post-office, stealing rides on the backs of the crosstown buses, drumming on the sides of dust bins with broomsticks, sitting in small groups in doorways, playing on the steps of the houses, writing on the pavement with coloured chalk, bouncing balls against the sides of the buildings. They turned a deaf ear to the commands shrilling from the windows all up and down the street. 'You Tommie, Jimmie, Billie, can't you see it's snowin'? Come in out the street.'

5 The street was so crowded that she paused frequently in order not to collide with a group of children, and she wondered if these were the things that Bub had done after school. She tried to see the street with his eyes and couldn't because the crap game in progress in the middle of the block, the scraps of obscene talk she heard as she passed

the poolroom, the tough young boys with their caps on backward who swaggered by, were things that she saw with the eyes of an adult and reacted to from an adult's point of view. It was impossible to know how this street looked to eight-year-old Bub. It may have appealed to him or it may have frightened him.

6   There was a desperate battle going on in front of the house where she lived. Kids were using bags of garbage from the bins lined up along the curb as ammunition. The bags had broken open, covering the pavement with litter, filling the air with a strong, rancid smell.

7   Lutie picked her way through orange skins, coffee grounds, chicken bones, fish bones, toilet paper, potato peelings, wilted kale, skins of baked sweet potatoes, pieces of newspaper, broken gin bottles, broken whisky bottles, a man's discarded felt hat, an old pair of trousers. Perhaps Bub had taken part in this kind of warfare, she thought, even as she frowned at the rubbish under her feet; possibly a battle would have appealed to some unsatisfied spirit of adventure in him, so that he would have joined these kids, overlooking the stink of the garbage in his joy in the conflict just as they were doing.

8   Mrs. Hedges was leaning far out of her window, urging the contestants on.

9   'That's right, Jimmie,' Mrs. Hedges cried. 'Hit him on the head.' And then as the bag went past its mark, 'Aw, shucks, boy, what's the matter with your aim?'

10   She caught sight of Lutie and knowing that she was home earlier than when she went to work, immediately deduced that she had been somewhere to see Bub or see about him. 'Did you see Bub?' she asked.

11   'Yes. For a little while.'

12   'Been to the beauty parlour, ain't you?' Mrs. Hedges studied the black curls shining under the skull cap on Lutie's head. 'Looks right nice,' she said.

13   She leaned a little farther out of the window. 'Bub being in trouble you probably need some money. A friend of mine, a Mr. Junto—a very nice white gentleman, dearie—'

14   Her voice trailed off because Lutie turned away abruptly and disappeared through the house door. Mrs. Hedges scowled after her. After all, if you needed money you needed money and why anyone would act like that when it was offered to them she couldn't imagine. She shrugged her shoulders and turned her attention back to the battle going on under her window.

15   As Lutie climbed the stairs, she deliberately accentuated the clicking of the heels of her shoes on the treads because the sharp sound
helped relieve the hard resentment she felt; it gave expression to the
anger flooding through her.

16   At first, she merely fumed at the top of her mind about a white
gentleman wanting to sleep with a coloured girl. A nice white gentleman
who's a little cold around the edges wants to sleep with a nice warm
coloured girl. All of it nice—nice gentleman, nice girl; one's coloured and
the other's white, so it's a coloured girl and a white gentleman.

17   Then she began thinking about Junto—specifically about Junto.
Junto hadn't wanted her paid for singing. Mrs. Hedges knew Junto.
Boots Smith worked for Junto. Junto's squat-bodied figure, as she had
seen it reflected in the sparkling mirror in his Bar and Grill, established itself in her mind; and the anger in her grew and spread directing itself first against Junto and Mrs. Hedges and then against the
street that had reached out and taken Bub and then against herself
for having been partly responsible for Bub's stealing.

18   Inside her flat she stood motionless, assailed by the deep, uncanny
silence that filled it. It was a too sharp contrast to the noise in the street.
She turned on the radio and then turned it off again, because she kept
listening, straining to hear something under the sound of the music.

19   The creeping, silent thing that she had sensed in the theatre, in the
beauty parlour, was here in her living room. It was sitting on the
lumpy studio couch.

20   Before it had been formless, shapeless, a fluid moving mass—
something disembodied that she couldn't see, could only sense. Now,
as she stared at the couch, the thing took on form, substance. She
could see what it was.

21   It was Junto. Grey hair, grey skin, short body, thick shoulders.
He was sitting on the studio couch. The blue-glass coffee table was
right in front of him. His feet were resting, squarely, firmly, on the
congoleum rug.

22   If she wasn't careful she would scream. She would start screaming and never be able to stop, because there wasn't anyone there.
Yet she could see him and when she didn't see him she could feel his
presence. She looked away and then looked back again. Sometimes
he was there when she looked and sometimes he wasn't.

23   She stared at the studio couch until she convinced herself there
had never been anyone there. Her eyes were playing tricks on her
because she was upset, nervous. She decided that a warm bath would
make her relax.

24 But in the bath she started trembling so that the water was agitated. Perhaps she ought to phone Boots and tell him that she wouldn't come tonight. Perhaps by tomorrow she would be free of this mounting, steadily increasing anger and this hysterical fear that made her see things that didn't exist, made her feel things that weren't there.

25 Yet less than half an hour later she was dressing, putting on the short, flared black coat; pulling on a pair of white gloves. As she thrust her hands into the gloves, she wondered when she had made the decision to go anyway; what part of her mind had already picked out the clothes she would wear, even to these white gloves, without her ever thinking about it consciously. Because, of course, if she didn't go tonight, Boots might change his mind.

26 When she rang the bell of Boots' flat, he opened the door instantly as though he had been waiting for her.

27 'Hello, baby,' he said, grinning. 'Sure glad you got here. I got a friend I want you to meet.'

28 Only two of the lamps in the living room were lit. They were the tall ones on each side of the davenport. They threw a brilliant light on the squat white man sitting there. He got up when he saw Lutie and stood in front of the imitation fireplace, leaning his elbow on the mantel.

29 Lutie stared at him, not certain whether this was Junto in the flesh or the imaginary one that had been on the studio couch in her apartment. She closed her eyes and then opened them and he was still there, standing by the fireplace. His squat figure partly blocked out the orange-red glow from the electric logs. She turned her head away and then looked toward him. He was still there, standing by the fireplace.

30 Boots established him as Junto in the flesh. 'Mr. Junto, meet Mrs. Johnson. Lutie Johnson.'

31 Lutie nodded her head. A figure in a mirror turned thumbs down and as he gestured the playground for Bub vanished, the nice new furniture disappeared along with the big airy rooms. 'A nice white gentleman.' 'Need any extra money.' She looked away from him, not saying anything.

32 'I want to talk to you, baby,' Boots said. 'Come on into the bedroom'—he pointed toward a door, started toward it, turned back and said, 'We'll be with you in a minute, Junto.'

33 Boots closed the bedroom door, sat down on the edge of the bed, leaning his head against the headboard.

34   'If you'll give me the money now, I'll be able to get it to the lawyer before he closes his office tonight,' she said abruptly. This room was like the living room, it had too many lamps in it, and in addition there were too many mirrors so that she saw him reflected on each of the walls—his legs stretched out, his expression completely indifferent. There was the same soft, sound-absorbing carpet on the floor.

35   'Take your coat off and sit down, baby,' he said lazily.

36   She shook her head. She didn't move any farther into the room, but stood with her back against the door, aware that there was no sound from the living room where Junto waited. She had brought that awful silence in here with her.

37   'I can't stay,' she said sharply. 'I only came to get the money.'

38   'Oh, yes—the money,' he said. He sounded as though he had just remembered it. 'You can get the money easy, baby. I figured it out.' He half-closed his eyes. 'Junto's the answer. He'll give it to you. Just like that'—he snapped his fingers.

39   He paused for a moment as though he were waiting for her to say something, and when she made no comment he continued: 'All you got to do is be nice to him. Just be nice to him as long as he wants and the two hundred bucks is yours. And bein' nice to Junto pays better than anything else I know.'

40   She heard what he said, knew exactly what he meant, and her mind skipped over his words and substituted other words. She was back in the big shabby ballroom at the Casino, straining to hear a thin thread of music that kept getting lost in the babble of voices, in the clink of glasses, in the bursts of laughter, so that she wasn't certain the music was real. Sometimes it was there and then again it was drowned out by the other sounds.

41   The faint, drifting melody went around and under the sound of Boots' voice and the words that he had spoken then blotted out what he had just said.

42   'Baby, this is just experience. Be months before you can earn money at it.'

43   'Nothing happened, baby. What makes you think something happened?'

44   'I don't have all the say-so. The guy who owns the Casino—guy named Junto—says you ain't ready yet.'

45   'Christ! he owns the joint.'

46   The guy named Junto owned the Bar and Grill, too. Evidently his decision that she wasn't to be paid for singing had been based on his desire to sleep with her; and he had concluded that, if she

had to continue living in that house where his friend Mrs. Hedges lived or in one just like it, she would be a pushover.

47 And now the same guy, named Junto, was sitting outside on a sofa, just a few feet away from this door, and she thought, I would like to kill him. Not just because he happens to be named Junto, but because I can't even think straight about him or anybody else any more. It is as though he were a piece of that dirty street itself, tangible, close at hand, within reach.

48 She could still hear that floating, drifting tune. It was inside her head and she couldn't get it out. Boots was staring at her, waiting for her to say something, waiting for her answer. He and Junto thought they knew what she would say. If she hummed that fragment of melody aloud, she would get rid of it. It was the only way to make it disappear; otherwise it would keep going around and around in her head. And she thought, I must be losing my mind, wanting to hum a tune and at the same time thinking about killing that man who is sitting, waiting, outside.

49 Boots said, 'Junto's a good guy. You'll be surprised how much you'll take to him.'

50 The sound of her own voice startled her. It was hoarse, loud, furious. It contained the accumulated hate and the accumulated anger from all the years of seeing the things she wanted slip past her without her ever having touched them.

51 She shouted, 'Get him out of here! Get him out of here! Get him out of here quick!'

52 And all the time she was thinking, Junto has a brick in his hand. Just one brick. The final one needed to complete the wall that had been building up around her for years, and when that one last brick was shoved in place, she would be completely walled in.

53 'All right. All right. Don't get excited.' Boots got up from the bed, pushed her away from the door and went out, slamming it behind him.

54 'Sorry, Junto,' Boots said. 'She's mad as hell. No use your waiting.'

55 'I heard her,' Junto said sourly. 'And if this is something you planned, you'd better unplan it.'

56 'You heard her, didnya?'

57 'Yes. But you still could have planned it.' Junto said. He walked toward the foyer. At the door he turned to Boots. 'Well?' he said.

58 'Don't worry, Mack,' Boots said coldly. 'She'll come around. Come back about ten o'clock.'

59 He closed the door quietly behind Junto. He hadn't intended to in the beginning, but he was going to trick him and Junto would never

know the difference. Sure, Lutie would sleep with Junto, but he was going to have her first. He thought of the thin curtains blowing in the wind. Yeah, he can have the leavings. After all, he's white and this time a white man can have a black man's leavings.

60 Junto had pushed him hard, threatened him, nagged him about Lutie Johnson. This would be his revenge. He locked the door leading to the foyer and put the key in his pocket. Then he headed toward the kitchenette in the back of the flat. He'd fix a drink for Lutie and one for himself.

61 The murmur of their voices came to Lutie in the bedroom. She couldn't hear what they said and she waited standing in front of the door, listening for some indication that Junto had gone.

62 As soon as Junto left, she would go home. But she had to make certain he had gone, because if she walked outside there and saw him she would try to kill him. The thought frightened her. This was no time to get excited or to get angry. She had to be calm and concentrate on how to keep Bub from going to the reform school.

63 She'd been so angry just now she had forgotten that she still had to get two hundred dollars to take to the lawyer. Pop might have some ideas. Yes, he'd have ideas. He always had them. But she was only kidding herself if she thought any of them would yield two hundred dollars.

64 There was the sound of a door closing, and then silence. She looked out into the living room. It was empty. She could hear the clinking sound of glasses from somewhere in the back of the flat.

65 And then Boots entered the room carrying a tray. Ice tinkled in tall glasses. A bottle of soda and a bottle of whisky teetered precariously on the tray as he walked toward her.

66 'Here, baby,' he said. 'Have a drink and get yourself together.'

67 She stood in front of the fireplace, holding the glass in her hand, not drinking it, just holding it. She could feel its coldness through her glove. She would go and talk to Pop. He'd lived three steps in front of the law for so long, he just might have a friend who was a lawyer and if Pop had ever done the friend any favours he might take Bub's case on the promise of weekly payments from her.

68 And she ought to go now. Why was she standing here holding this glass of liquor that she didn't want and had no intention of drinking? Because you're still angry, she thought, and you haven't anyone to vent your anger on and you're halfway hoping Boots will say something or do something that will give you an excuse to blow up in a thousand pieces.

69   'Whyn't you sit down?' Boots said.

70   'I've got to go.' And yet she didn't move. She stayed in front of the fireplace watching him as he sat on the sofa, sipping his drink.

71   Occasionally he glanced up at her and she saw the scar on his cheek as a long thin line that looked darker than she had remembered it. And she thought he's like these streets that trap all of us—vicious, dangerous.

72   Finally he said, 'Listen, you want to get the little bastard out of jail, don't yah? What you being so fussy about?'

73   She put the glass down on a table. Some of the liquor slopped over, oozing down the sides of the glass, and as she looked at it, it seemed as though something had slopped over inside her head in the same fashion, was oozing through her so that she couldn't think.

74   'Skip it,' she said.

75   Her voice was loud in the room. That's right, she thought, skip it. Let's all skip together, children. All skip together. Up the golden stairs. Skipping hand in hand up the golden stairs.

76   'Just skip it,' she repeated.

77   She had to get out of here, now, and quickly. She mustn't stand here any longer looking down at him like this, because she kept thinking that he represented everything she had fought against. Yet she couldn't take her eyes away from the ever-darkening scar that marred the side of his face; and as she stared at him, she felt she was gazing straight at the street with its rows of old houses, its piles of garbage, its swarms of children.

78   'Junto's rich as hell,' Boots said. 'What you got to be so particular about? There ain't a dame in town who wouldn't give everything they got for a chance at him.' And he thought, Naw, she ain't acting right. And she was all that stood between him and going back to portering or some other lousy, stinking job where he would carry his hat in his hand all day and walk on his head, saying 'Yessir, yessir, yessir.'

79   She moved away from the fireplace. There wasn't any point in answering him. She couldn't even think straight, couldn't even see straight. She kept thinking about the street, kept seeing it.

80   All those years, going to grammar school, going to high school, getting married, having a baby, going to work for the Chandlers, leaving Jim because he got himself another woman—all those years she'd been heading straight as an arrow for that street or some other street just like it. Step by step she'd come, growing up, working, saving, and finally getting a flat on a street that nobody could have beaten. Even if she hadn't talked to Bub about money all the time, he would have

got into trouble sooner or later, because the street looked after him
when she wasn't around.

81   'Aw, what the hell!' Boots muttered. He put his glass down on
the table in front of the sofa, got up and by moving swiftly blocked
her progress to the door.

82   'Let's talk it over,' he said. 'Maybe we can work out something.'

83   She hesitated. There wasn't anything to work out or talk over
unless he meant he would lend her the money with no strings
attached. And if he was willing to do that, she would be a fool not
to accept it. Pop was a pretty feeble last resort.

84   'Come on, baby,' he said. 'Ten minutes' talk will straighten it out'
And she went back to stand in front of the fireplace.

85   'Ain't no point in your getting mad, baby. We can still be friends,'
he said softly, and put his arm around her waist.

86   He was standing close to her. She smelt faintly sweet and he pulled
her closer. She tried to back away from him and he forced her still closer,
held her hands behind her back, pulling her ever closer and closer.

87   As he kissed her, he felt a hot excitement swell up in him that made
him forget all the logical, reasoned things he had meant to say; for
her skin was soft under his mouth and warm. He fumbled with the
fastenings of her coat, his hand groping toward her breasts.

88   'Aw, Christ, baby,' he whispered. 'Junto can get his afterward.'
And the rhythm of the words sank into him, seemed to correspond
with the rhythm of his desire for her so that he had to say them again.
'Let him get his afterward. I'll have mine first.'

89   She twisted out of his arms with a sudden, violent motion that
nearly sent him off balance. The anger surging through her wasn't
directed solely at him. He was there at hand; he had tricked her into
staying an extra few minutes in this room with him, because she
thought he was going to lend her the money she so urgently needed;
and she was angry with him for that and for being a procurer for
Junto and for assuming that she would snatch at an opportunity to
sleep with either or both of them. This quick surface anger helped
to swell and became a part of the deepening stream of rage that had
fed on the hate, the frustration, the resentment she had toward the
pattern her life had followed.

90   So she couldn't stop shouting, and shouting wasn't enough. She
wanted to hit out at him, to reduce him to a speechless mass of flesh,
to destroy him completely, because he was there in front of her and
she could get at him and in getting at him she would find violent
outlet for the full sweep of her wrath.

91   Words tumbled from her throat. 'You no good bastard!' she
shouted. 'You can tell Junto I said if he wants a whore to get one from
Mrs. Hedges. And the same thing goes for you. Because I'd just as
soon get in bed with a rattlesnake—I'd just as soon—'

92   And he reached out and slapped her across the face. And as she
stood there in front of him, trembling with anger, her face smart-
ing, he slapped her again.

93   'I don't take that kind of talk from dames,' he said, 'Not even good-
looking ones like you. Maybe after I beat the hell out of you a coupla
times, you'll begin to like the idea of sleeping with me and with Junto.'

94   The blood pounding in her head blurred her vision so that she saw
not one Boots Smith but three of him; and behind these three figures the room was swaying, shifting, and changing with a wavering
motion. She tried to separate the three blurred figures and it was
like trying to follow the course of heat waves as they rose from a pavement on a hot day in August.

95   Despite this unstable triple vision of him, she was scarcely aware
of him as an individual. His name might have been Brown or Smith
or Wilson. She might never have seen him before, might have known
nothing about him. He happened to be within easy range at the
moment he set off the dangerous accumulation of rage that had been
building in her for months.

96   When she remembered there was a heavy iron candlestick on the
mantelpiece just behind her, her vision cleared; the room stopped
revolving and Boots Smith became one person, not three. He was
the person who had struck her, her face still hurt from the blow; he
had threatened her with violence and with a forced relationship with
Junto and with himself. These things set off her anger, but as she
gripped the iron candlestick and brought it forward in a swift motion
aimed at his head, she was striking, not at Boots Smith, but at a
handy, anonymous figure—a figure which her angry resentment
transformed into everything she had hated, everything she had fought
against, everything that had served to frustrate her.

97   He was so close to her that she struck him on the side of the head
before he saw the blow coming. The first blow stunned him. And
she struck him again and again, using the candlestick as though it
were a club. He tried to back away from her and stumbled over the
sofa and sprawled there.

98   A lifetime of pent-up resentment went into the blows. Even after
he lay motionless, she kept striking him, not thinking about him,
not even seeing him. First she was venting her rage against the dirty,

crowded street. She saw the rows of dilapidated old houses; the small dark rooms; the long steep flights of stairs; the narrow dingy passages; the little lost girls in Mrs. Hedges' apartment; the smashed homes where the women did drudgery because their men had deserted them. She saw all of these things and struck at them.

99   Then the limp figure on the sofa became, in turn, Jim and the slender girl she'd found him with; became the insult in the moisteyed glances of white men on the subway; became the unconcealed hostility in the eyes of white women; became the greasy, lecherous man at the Crosse School for Singers; became the gaunt Super pulling her down, down into the basement.

100   Finally, and the blows were heavier, faster, now, she was striking at the white world which thrust black people into a walled enclosure from which there was no escape; and at the turn of events which had forced her to leave Bub alone while she was working so that he now faced a reform school, now had a police record.

101   She saw the face and head of the man on the sofa through waves of anger in which he represented all these things and she was destroying them.

102   She grew angrier as she struck him, because he seemed to be eluding her behind a red haze that obscured his face. Then the haze of red blocked his face out completely. She lowered her arm, peering at him, trying to locate his face through the redness that concealed it.

103   The room was perfectly still. There was no sound in it except her own hoarse breathing. She let the candlestick fall out of her hand. It landed on the thick rug with a soft clump and she started to shiver.

104   He was dead. There was no question about it. No one could live with a head battered in like that. And it wasn't a red haze that had veiled his face. It was blood.

105   She backed away from the sight of him, thinking that if she took one slow step at a time, just one slow step at a time, she could get out of here, walking backward, step by step. She was afraid to turn her back on that still figure on the sofa. It had become a thing. It was no longer Boots Smith, but a thing on a sofa.

106   She stumbled against a chair and sat down in it, shivering. She would never get out of this room. She would never, never get out of here. For the rest of her life she would be here with this awful faceless thing on the sofa. Then she forced herself to get up, to start walking backward again.

107   The hall door was closed because she backed right into it. Just a few more steps and she would be out. She fumbled for the knob.

The door was locked. She didn't believe it and rattled it. She felt for a key. There was none. It would, she was certain, be in Boots Smith's pocket and she felt a faint stirring of anger against him. He had deliberately locked the door because he hadn't intended to let her out of here.

108   The anger went as quickly as it came. She had to go back to that motionless, bloody figure on the sofa. The stillness in the room made her feel as though she was wading through water, wading waist-deep toward the couch, and the water swallowed up all sound. It tugged against her, tried to pull her back.

109   The key was in his pocket. In her haste she pulled all the things out of his pocket—a handkerchief, a wallet, book matches, and the key. She held on to the key, but the other things went out of her hand because as she drew away from him she thought he moved. And all the stories she had ever heard about the dead coming back to life, about the dead talking, about the dead walking, went through her mind; making her hands shake so that she couldn't control them.

110   As she moved hurriedly away from the couch, she almost stepped on the wallet. She picked it up and looked inside. It bulged with money. He could have given her two hundred dollars and never missed it.

111   The two hundred dollars she needed was right there in her hand. She could take it to the lawyer tonight. Or could she?

112   For the first time the full implication of what she had done swept over her. She was a murderess. And the smartest lawyer in the world couldn't do anything for Bub, not now, not when his mother had killed a man. A kid whose mother was a murderess didn't stand any chance at all. Everyone he came in contact with would believe that sooner or later he, too, would turn criminal. The Court wouldn't parole him in her care either, because she was no longer a fit person to bring him up.

113   She couldn't stop the quivering that started in her stomach, that set up a spasmodic contracting of her throat so that she felt as though her breath had been cut off. The only thing she could do was to go away and never come back, because the best thing that could happen to Bub would be for him never to know that his mother was a murderess. She took half the bills out of the wallet, stuffed them into her purse, left the wallet on the sofa.

114   Getting back to the hall door was worse this time. The four corners of the room were alive with silence—deepening pools of an ominous silence. She kept turning her head in an effort to see all of the

room at once; kept fighting against a desire to scream. Hysteria mounted in her because she began to believe that at any moment the figure on the sofa might disappear into one of these pools of silence and then emerge from almost any part of the room, to bar her exit.

115   When she finally turned the key in the door, crossed the small hall, and reached the outside landing, she had to lean against the wall for a long moment before she could control the shaking of her legs, but the contracting of her throat was getting worse.

116   She saw that the white gloves she was wearing were streaked with dust from the candlestick. There was a smear of blood on one of them. She ripped them off and put them in her coat pocket, and as she did it she thought she was acting as though murder was something with which she was familiar. She walked down the stairs instead of taking the elevator, and the thought recurred.

117   When she left the building, it was snowing hard. The wind blew the snow against her face, making her walk faster as she approached the entrance to the Eighth Avenue subway.

118   She thought confusedly of the best place for her to go. It had to be a big city. She decided that Chicago was not too far away and it was big. It would swallow her up. She would go there.

119   On the subway she started shivering again. Had she killed Boots by accident? The awful part of it was she hadn't even seen him when she was hitting him like that. The first blow was deliberate and provoked, but all those other blows weren't provoked. There wasn't any excuse for her. It hadn't even been self-defence. This impulse to violence had been in her for a long time, growing, feeding, until finally she had blown up in a thousand pieces. Bub must never know what she had done.

120   In Pennsylvania Station she bought a ticket for Chicago. 'One way?' the ticket man asked.

121   'One way,' she echoed. Yes, a one-way ticket, she thought. I've had one since the day I was born.

122   The train was at the platform. People flowed and spilled through the gates like water running over a dam. She walked in the middle of the crowd.

123   The coaches filled up rapidly. People with bags and hatboxes and bundles and children moved hastily down the aisles, almost falling into the seats in their haste to secure a place to sit.

124   Lutie found a seat midway in the coach. She sat down near the window. Bub would never understand why she had disappeared. He

was expecting to see her tomorrow. She had promised him she would come. He would never know why she had deserted him and he would be bewildered and lost without her.

125   Would he remember that she loved him? She hoped so, but she knew that for a long time he would have that half-frightened, worried look she had seen on his face the night he was waiting for her at the subway.

126   He would probably go to a reform school. She looked out of the train window, not seeing the last-minute passengers hurrying down the ramp. The constriction of her throat increased. So he will go to a reform school, she repeated. He'll be better off there. He'll be better off without you. That way he may have some kind of chance. He didn't have the ghost of a chance on that street. The best you could give him wasn't good enough.

127   As the train started to move, she began to trace a design on the window. It was a series of circles that flowed into each other. She remembered that when she was in the primary school the children were taught to get the proper slant to their writing, to get the feel of a pen in their hands, by making these same circles.

128   Once again she could hear the flat, exasperated voice of the teacher as she looked at the circles Lutie had produced. 'Really,' she said, 'I don't know why they make us bother to teach your people to write.'

129   Her finger moved over the glass, around and around. The circles showed up plainly on the misty surface. The woman's statement was correct, she thought. What possible good has it done to teach people like me to write?

130   The train crept out of the tunnel, gathered speed as it left the city behind. Snow whispered against the windows. And as the train roared into the darkness, Lutie tried to think out by what twists and turns of fate she had landed on this train. Her mind baulked at the task. All she could think was, it was that street. It was that goddamned street.

131   The snow fell softly on the street. It muffled sound. It sent people scurrying homeward, so that the street was soon deserted, empty, quiet. And it could have been any street in the city, for the snow laid a delicate film over the pavement, over the brick of the tired, old buildings; gently obscuring the grime and the garbage and the ugliness.

Langston Hughes

(1902–1967)

For biographical information, please see page 458. The following poems appear in Hughes's Montage of a Dream Deferred *(1951). They also are included in* Selected Poems of Langston Hughes *(1959). In the later volume, "Harlem [2]" is retitled "Dream Deferred."*

Tell Me

Why should it be *my* loneliness,
Why should it be *my* song,
Why should it be *my* dream
  deferred
5   overlong?

Harlem [2]

What happens to a dream deferred?

Does it dry up
like a raisin in the sun?
Or fester like a sore—
5   And then run?
Does it stink like rotten meat?
Or crust and sugar over—
like a syrupy sweet?

Maybe it just sags
10   like a heavy load.

Or does it explode?

Lorraine Hansberry

(1930–1965)

On May 19, 1930, in Chicago, Lorraine Hansberry was born into a relatively prosperous family. Her parents, Carl Hansberry and Nan Perry, despite their affluence, preached social activism and civic responsibility. Visitors to the Hansberry home included W. E. B. Du Bois, Paul Robeson, and Langston Hughes. Hansberry attended the University of Wisconsin, where she became active and a leader in the Young Progressive Association, a leftist student organization. She left school after her sophomore year and moved to New York City, becoming a writer for Robeson's newspaper, Freedom. *She left the paper in 1953 to devote herself more fully to her creative work. The task became easier, financially, when her husband Robert Nemiroff wrote the hit song "Cindy Oh Cindy" (1956). Hansberry's signature work,* A Raisin in the Sun, *the first play by an African American produced on Broadway, ran for 538 appearances after it opened at the Ethel Barrymore Theater on March 11, 1959. The powerful portrayal of the Younger family's attempt to transcend the effects of racism, a work partly based on an incident from Hansberry's childhood (her family was attacked after moving into a white neighborhood), earned Hansberry the 1959 New York Drama Critics Circle Award. She was the first African American and the youngest person to be so honored. Hansberry's other works include* The Sign in Sidney Brustein's Window *(1964) and the posthumously published* To Be Young, Gifted and Black: Lorraine Hansberry in Her Own Words *(1969). The latter work was edited by Nemiroff, who, although he and Hansberry had divorced, had become her literary executor. Hansberry died, at the age of thirty-four, of pancreatic cancer on January 12, 1965.*

A Raisin in the Sun

The action of the play is set
in Chicago's Southside, sometime between
World War II and the present.

Act I
Scene One: Friday morning.
Scene Two: The following morning.

Act II
Scene One: Later, the same day.
Scene Two: Friday night, a few weeks later.
Scene Three: Moving day, one week later.

Act III
An hour later.

ACT I

Scene One

The YOUNGER *living room would be a comfortable and well-ordered room if it were not for a number of indestructible contradictions to this state of being. Its furnishings are typical and undistinguished and their primary feature now is that they have clearly had to accommodate the living of too many people for too many years—and they are tired. Still, we can see that at some time, a time probably no longer remembered by the family (except perhaps for* MAMA*), the furnishings of this room were actually selected with care and love and even hope—and brought to this apartment and arranged with taste and pride.*

That was a long time ago. Now the once loved pattern of the couch upholstery has to fight to show itself from under acres of crocheted doilies and couch covers which have themselves finally come to be more important than the upholstery. And here a table or a chair has been moved to disguise the worn places in the carpet; but the carpet has fought back by showing its weariness, with depressing uniformity, elsewhere on its surface.

Weariness has, in fact, won in this room. Everything has been polished, washed, sat on, used, scrubbed too often. All pretenses but living itself have long since vanished from the very atmosphere of this room.

Moreover, a section of this room, for it is not really a room unto itself, though the landlord's lease would make it seem so, slopes backward to provide a small kitchen area, where the family prepares the meals that are eaten in the living room proper, which must also serve as dining room. The single window that has been provided for these "two" rooms is located in this kitchen area. The sole natural light the family may enjoy in the course of a day is only that which fights its way through this little window.

At left, a door leads to a bedroom which is shared by mama and her daughter, BENEATHA. *At right, opposite, is a second room (which in the beginning of the life of this apartment was probably a breakfast room) which serves as a bedroom for* WALTER *and his wife,* RUTH.
Time: Sometime between World War II and the present.
Place: Chicago's Southside.
At Rise: It is morning dark in the living room. TRAVIS *is asleep on the make-down bed at center. An alarm clock sounds from within the bedroom at right, and presently* RUTH *enters from that room and closes the door behind her. She crosses sleepily toward the window. As she passes her sleeping son she reaches down and shakes him a little. At the window she raises the shade and a dusky Southside morning light comes in feebly. She fills a pot with water and puts it on to boil. She calls to the boy, between yawns, in a slightly muffled voice.*
RUTH *is about thirty. We can see that she was a pretty girl, even exceptionally so, but now it is apparent that life has been little that she expected, and disappointment has already begun to hang in her face. In a few years, before thirty-five even, she will be known among her people as a "settled woman."*
She crosses to her son and gives him a good, final, rousing shake.

RUTH Come on now, boy, it's seven thirty! *(Her son sits up at last, in a stupor of sleepiness)* I say hurry up, Travis! You ain't the only person in the world got to use a bathroom! *(The child, a sturdy, handsome little boy of ten or eleven, drags himself out of the bed and almost blindly takes his towels and "today's clothes" from drawers and a closet and goes out to the bathroom, which is in an outside hall and which is shared by another family or families on the same floor.* RUTH *crosses to the bedroom door at right and opens it and calls in to her husband)* Walter Lee! . . . It's after seven thirty! Lemme see you do some waking up in there now! *(She waits)*. You better get up from there, man! It's after seven thirty I tell you. *(She waits again)* All right, you just go ahead and lay there and next thing you know Travis be finished and Mr. Johnson'll be in there and you'll be fussing and cussing round here like a madman! And be late too! *(She waits, at the end of patience)* Walter Lee—it's time for you to GET UP!

(She waits another second and then starts to go into the bedroom, but is apparently satisfied that her husband has begun to get up. She stops, pulls the door to, and returns

*to the kitchen area. She wipes her face with a moist cloth
and runs her fingers through her sleep-disheveled hair in a
vain effort and ties an apron around her housecoat. The
bedroom door at right opens and her husband stands in
the doorway in his pajamas, which are rumpled and
mismated. He is a lean, intense young man in his middle
thirties, inclined to quick nervous movements and erratic
speech habits—and always in his voice there is a quality
of indictment)*

WALTER   Is he out yet?

RUTH   What you mean *out*? He ain't hardly got in there good yet.

WALTER   (*Wandering in, still more oriented to sleep than to a new
day*) Well, what was you doing all that yelling for if I can't even
get in there yet? (*Stopping and thinking*) Check coming today?

5   **RUTH**   They *said* Saturday and this is just Friday and I hopes to
God you ain't going to get up here first thing this morning and
start talking to me 'bout no money—'cause I 'bout don't want to
hear it.

WALTER   Something the matter with you this morning?

RUTH   No—I'm just sleepy as the devil. What kind of eggs you want?

WALTER   Not scrambled. (RUTH *starts to scramble eggs*) Paper
come? (RUTH *points impatiently to the rolled up* Tribune *on the
table, and he gets it and spreads it out and vaguely reads the front
page*) Set off another bomb yesterday.

RUTH   (*Maximum indifference*) Did they?

10   **WALTER**   (*Looking up*) What's the matter with you?

RUTH   Ain't nothing the matter with me. And don't keep asking me
that this morning.

WALTER   Ain't nobody bothering you. (*Reading the news of the day
absently again*) Say Colonel McCormick is sick.

RUTH   (*Affecting tea-party interest*) Is he now? Poor thing.

WALTER   (*Sighing and looking at his watch*) Oh, me. (*He waits*)
Now what is that boy doing in that bathroom all this time? He just
going to have to start getting up earlier. I can't be being late to
work on account of him fooling around in there.

15   **RUTH**   (*Turning on him*) Oh, no he ain't going to be getting up no
earlier no such thing! It ain't his fault that he can't get to bed
no earlier nights 'cause he got a bunch of crazy good-for-nothing clowns sitting up running their mouths in what is supposed
to be his bedroom after ten o'clock at night . . .

WALTER That's what you mad about, ain't it? The things I want to talk about with my friends just couldn't be important in your mind, could they?

(He rises and finds a cigarette in her handbag on the table and crosses to the little window and looks out, smoking and deeply enjoying this first one)

RUTH *(Almost matter of factly, a complaint too automatic to deserve emphasis)* Why you always got to smoke before you eat in the morning?

WALTER *(At the window)* Just look at 'em down there . . . Running and racing to work . . . *(He turns and faces his wife and watches her a moment at the stove, and then, suddenly)* You look young this morning, baby.

RUTH *(Indifferently)* Yeah?

20 **WALTER** Just for a second—stirring them eggs. Just for a second it was—you looked real young again. *(He reaches for her; she crosses away. Then, drily)* It's gone now—you look like yourself again!

RUTH Man, if you don't shut up and leave me alone.

WALTER *(Looking out to the street again)* First thing a man ought to learn in life is not to make love to no colored woman first thing in the morning. You all some eeeevil people at eight o'clock in the morning.

(TRAVIS appears in the hall doorway, almost fully dressed and quite wide awake now, his towels and pajamas across his shoulders. He opens the door and signals for his father to make the bathroom in a hurry)

TRAVIS *(Watching the bathroom)* Daddy, come on!

(WALTER gets his bathroom utensils and flies out to the bathroom)

RUTH Sit down and have your breakfast, Travis.

25 **TRAVIS** Mama, this is Friday. *(Gleefully)* Check coming tomorrow, huh?

RUTH You get your mind off money and eat your breakfast.

TRAVIS *(Eating)* This is the morning we supposed to bring the fifty cents to school.

RUTH Well, I ain't got no fifty cents this morning.

TRAVIS Teacher say we have to.

30 **RUTH** I don't care what teacher say. I ain't got it. Eat your breakfast, Travis.

TRAVIS I *am* eating.

RUTH Hush up now and just eat!

*(The boy gives her an exasperated look for her lack of
understanding, and eats grudgingly)*

TRAVIS You think Grandmama would have it?

RUTH No! And I want you to stop asking your grandmother for
money, you hear me?

35 **TRAVIS** *(Outraged)* Gaaaleee! I don't ask her, she just gimme it
sometimes!

RUTH Travis Willard Younger—I got too much on me this morning to be—

TRAVIS Maybe Daddy—

RUTH *Travis!*

*(The boy hushes abruptly. They are both quiet and tense
for several seconds)*

TRAVIS *(Presently)* Could I maybe go carry some groceries in front
of the supermarket for a little while after school then?

40 **RUTH** Just hush, I said. *(Travis jabs his spoon into his cereal bowl
viciously, and rests his head in anger upon his fists)* If you through
eating, you can get over there and make up your bed.

*(The boy obeys stiffly and crosses the room, almost
mechanically, to the bed and more or less folds the bedding
into a heap, then angrily gets his books and cap)*

TRAVIS *(Sulking and standing apart from her unnaturally)* I'm gone.

RUTH *(Looking up from the stove to inspect him automatically)*
Come here. *(He crosses to her and she studies his head)* If you
don't take this comb and fix this here head, you better! (TRAVIS
*puts down his books with a great sigh of oppression, and crosses
to the mirror. His mother mutters under her breath about his
"slubbornness")* 'Bout to march out of here with that head looking just like chickens slept in it! I just don't know where you get
your slubborn ways . . . And get your jacket, too. Looks chilly
out this morning.

TRAVIS *(With conspicuously brushed hair and jacket)* I'm gone.

RUTH Get carfare and milk money—*(Waving one finger)*—and not
a single penny for no caps, you hear me?

45 **TRAVIS**   *(With sullen politeness)* Yes'm.

> *(He turns in outrage to leave. His mother watches after him as in his frustration he approaches the door almost comically. When she speaks to him, her voice has become a very gentle tease)*

RUTH   *(Mocking; as she thinks he would say it)* Oh, Mama makes me so mad sometimes, I don't know what to do! *(She waits and continues to his back as he stands stock-still in front of the door)* I wouldn't kiss that woman good-bye for nothing in this world this morning! *(The boy finally turns around and rolls his eyes at her, knowing the mood has changed and he is vindicated; he does not, however, move toward her yet)* Not for nothing in this world! *(She finally laughs aloud at him and holds out her arms to him and we see that it is a way between them, very old and practiced. He crosses to her and allows her to embrace him warmly but keeps his face fixed with masculine rigidity. She holds him back from her presently and looks at him and runs her fingers over the features of his face. With utter gentleness—)* Now—whose little old angry man are you?

TRAVIS   *(The masculinity and gruffness start to fade at last)* Aw gaalee—Mama . . .

RUTH   *(Mimicking)* Aw gaaaaalleeeee, Mama! *(She pushes him, with rough playfulness and finality, toward the door)* Get on out of here or you going to be late.

TRAVIS   *(In the face of love, new aggressiveness)* Mama, could I *please* go carry groceries?

50 **RUTH**   Honey, it's starting to get so cold evenings.

WALTER   *(Coming in from the bathroom and drawing a make-believe gun from a make-believe holster and shooting at his son)* What is it he wants to do?

RUTH   Go carry groceries after school at the supermarket.

WALTER   Well, let him go . . .

TRAVIS   *(Quickly, to the ally)* I *have* to—she won't gimme the fifty cents . . .

55 **WALTER**   *(To his wife only)* Why not?

RUTH   *(Simply, and with flavor)* 'Cause we don't have it.

WALTER   *(To RUTH only)* What you tell the boy things like that for? *(Reaching down into his pants with a rather important gesture)* Here, son—

(He hands the boy the coin, but his eyes are directed to his wife's. TRAVIS *takes the money happily)*

TRAVIS Thanks, Daddy.

(He starts out. RUTH *watches both of them with murder in her eyes.* WALTER *stands and stares back at her with defiance, and suddenly reaches into his pocket again on an afterthought)*

WALTER (*Without even looking at his son, still staring hard at his wife*). In fact, here's another fifty cents . . . Buy yourself some fruit today—or take a taxicab to school or something!

60 **TRAVIS** Whoopee—

(He leaps up and clasps his father around the middle with his legs, and they face each other in mutual appreciation; slowly WALTER LEE *peeks around the boy to catch the violent rays from his wife's eyes and draws his head back as if shot)*

WALTER You better get down now—and get to school, man.

TRAVIS *(At the door)* O.K. Good-bye.

(He exits)

WALTER *(After him, pointing with pride)* That's *my* boy. *(She looks at him in disgust and turns back to her work).* You know what I was thinking 'bout in the bathroom this morning?

RUTH No.

65 **WALTER** How come you always try to be so pleasant!

RUTH What is there to be pleasant 'bout!

WALTER You want to know what I was thinking 'bout in the bathroom or not!

RUTH I know what you thinking 'bout.

WALTER *(Ignoring her)* 'Bout what me and Willy Harris was talking about last night.

70 **RUTH** *(Immediately—a refrain)* Willy Harris is a good-for-nothing loudmouth.

WALTER Anybody who talks to me has got to be a good-for-nothing loudmouth, ain't he? And what you know about who is just a good-for-nothing loudmouth? Charlie Atkins was just a "good-for-nothing loudmouth" too, wasn't he! When he wanted me to go in the dry-cleaning business with him. And now—he's grossing a hundred thousand a year. A hundred thousand dollars a year! You still call *him* a loudmouth!

RUTH *(Bitterly)* Oh, Walter Lee . . .

(She folds her head on her arms over the table)

WALTER *(Rising and coming to her and standing over her)* You tired, ain't you? Tired of everything. Me, the boy, the way we live—this beat-up hole—everything. Ain't you? *(She doesn't look up, doesn't answer)* So tired—moaning and groaning all the time, but you wouldn't do nothing to help, would you? You couldn't be on my side that long for nothing, could you?

RUTH Walter, please leave me alone.

75 **WALTER** A man needs for a woman to back him up . . .

RUTH Walter—

WALTER Mama would listen to you. You know she listen to you more than she do me and Bennie. She think more of you. All you have to do is just sit down with her when you drinking your coffee one morning and talking 'bout things like you do and—*(He sits down beside her and demonstrates graphically what he thinks her methods and tone should be)*—you just sip your coffee, see, and say easy like that you been thinking 'bout that deal Walter Lee is so interested in, 'bout the store and all, and sip some more coffee, like what you saying ain't really that important to you—And the next thing you know, she be listening good and asking you questions and when I come home—I can tell her the details. This ain't no fly-by-night proposition, baby. I mean we figured it out, me and Willy and Bobo.

RUTH *(With a frown)* Bobo?

WALTER Yeah. You see, this little liquor store we got in mind cost seventy-five thousand and we figured the initial investment on the place be 'bout thirty thousand, see. That be ten thousand each. Course, there's a couple of hundred you got to pay so's you don't spend your life just waiting for them clowns to let your license get approved—

80 **RUTH** You mean graft?

WALTER *(Frowning impatiently)* Don't call it that. See there, that just goes to show you what women understand about the world. Baby, don't *nothing* happen for you in this world 'less you pay *somebody* off!

RUTH Walter, leave me alone! *(She raises her head and stares at him vigorously—then says, more quietly)* Eat your eggs, they gonna be cold.

WALTER *(Straightening up from her and looking off)* That's it. There you are. Man say to his woman: I got me a dream. His woman say: Eat your eggs. *(Sadly, but gaining in power)* Man say: I got to take hold of this here world, baby! And a woman will say: Eat your eggs and go to work. *(Passionately now)* Man say: I got to change my life, I'm choking to death, baby! And his woman say—*(In utter anguish as he brings his fists down on his thighs)*—Your eggs is getting cold!

RUTH *(Softly)* Walter, that ain't none of our money.

85 **WALTER** *(Not listening at all or even looking at her)* This morning, I was lookin' in the mirror and thinking about it . . . I'm thirty-five years old; I been married eleven years and I got a boy who sleeps in the living room—*(Very, very quietly)*—and all I got to give him is stories about how rich white people live . . .

RUTH Eat your eggs, Walter.

WALTER *(Slams the table and jumps up)*—DAMN MY EGGS— DAMN ALL THE EGGS THAT EVER WAS!

RUTH Then go to work.

WALTER *(Looking up at her)* See—I'm trying to talk to you 'bout myself—*(Shaking his head with the repetition)*—and all you can say is eat them eggs and go to work.

90 **RUTH** *(Wearily)* Honey, you never say nothing new. I listen to you every day, every night and every morning, and you never say nothing new. *(Shrugging)* So you would rather *be* Mr. Arnold than be his chauffeur. So—I would *rather* be living in Buckingham Palace.

WALTER That is just what is wrong with the colored woman in this world . . . Don't understand about building their men up and making 'em feel like they somebody. Like they can do something.

RUTH *(Drily, but to hurt)* There *are* colored men who do things.

WALTER No thanks to the colored woman.

RUTH Well, being a colored woman, I guess I can't help myself none.

> *(She rises and gets the ironing board and sets it up and attacks a huge pile of rough-dried clothes, sprinkling them in preparation for the ironing and then rolling them into tight fat balls)*

95 **WALTER** *(Mumbling)* We one group of men tied to a race of women with small minds!

> *(His sister BENEATHA enters. She is about twenty, as slim and intense as her brother. She is not as pretty as her*

sister-in-law, but her lean, almost intellectual face has a handsomeness of its own. She wears a bright-red flannel nightie, and her thick hair stands wildly about her head. Her speech is a mixture of many things; it is different from the rest of the family's insofar as education has permeated her sense of English—and perhaps the Midwest rather than the South has finally—at last—won out in her inflection; but not altogether, because over all of it is a soft slurring and transformed use of vowels which is the decided influence of the Southside. She passes through the room without looking at either ruth or walter and goes to the outside door and looks, a little blindly, out to the bathroom. She sees that it has been lost to the Johnsons. She closes the door with a sleepy vengeance and crosses to the table and sits down a little defeated)

BENEATHA   I am going to start timing those people.

WALTER   You should get up earlier.

BENEATHA   *(Her face in her hands. She is still fighting the urge to go back to bed)* Really—would you suggest dawn? Where's the paper?

WALTER   *(Pushing the paper across the table to her as he studies her almost clinically, as though he has never seen her before)* You a horrible-looking chick at this hour.

100 **BENEATHA**   *(Drily)* Good morning, everybody.

WALTER   *(Senselessly)* How is school coming?

BENEATHA   *(In the same spirit)* Lovely. Lovely. And you know, biology is the greatest. *(Looking up at him)* I dissected something that looked just like you yesterday.

WALTER   I just wondered if you've made up your mind and everything.

BENEATHA   *(Gaining in sharpness and impatience)* And what did I answer yesterday morning—and the day before that?

105 **RUTH**   *(From the ironing board, like someone disinterested and old)* Don't be so nasty, Bennie.

BENEATHA   *(Still to her brother)* And the day before that and the day before that!

WALTER   *(Defensively)* I'm interested in you. Something wrong with that? Ain't many girls who decide—

WALTER   and BENEATHA   *(In unison)* —"to be a doctor."

(Silence)

WALTER   Have we figured out yet just exactly how much medical school is going to cost?

110 **RUTH**   Walter Lee, why don't you leave that girl alone and get out of here to work?

BENEATHA   *(Exits to the bathroom and bangs on the door)* Come on out of there, please!

(She comes back into the room)

WALTER   *(Looking at his sister intently)* You know the check is coming tomorrow.

BENEATHA   *(Turning on him with a sharpness all her own)* That money belongs to Mama, Walter, and it's for her to decide how she wants to use it. I don't care if she wants to buy a house or a rocket ship or just nail it up somewhere and look at it. It's hers. Not ours—*hers.*

WALTER   *(Bitterly)* Now ain't that fine! You just got your mother's interest at heart, ain't you, girl? You such a nice girl—but if Mama got that money she can always take a few thousand and help you through school too—can't she?

115 **BENEATHA**   I have never asked anyone around here to do anything for me!

WALTER   No! And the line between asking and just accepting when the time comes is big and wide—ain't it!

BENEATHA   *(With fury)* What do you want from me, Brother—that I quit school or just drop dead, which!

WALTER   I don't want nothing but for you to stop acting holy 'round here. Me and Ruth done made some sacrifices for you—why can't you do something for the family?

RUTH   Walter, don't be dragging me in it.

120 **WALTER**   You are in it—Don't you get up and go work in somebody's kitchen for the last three years to help put clothes on her back?

RUTH   Oh, Walter—that's not fair . . .

WALTER   It ain't that nobody expects you to get on your knees and say thank you, Brother; thank you, Ruth; thank you, Mama—and thank you, Travis, for wearing the same pair of shoes for two semesters—

BENEATHA   *(Dropping to her knees)* Well—I do—all right?—thank everybody! And forgive me for ever wanting to be anything at all! *(Pursuing him on her knees across the floor)* FORGIVE ME, FORGIVE ME, FORGIVE ME!

RUTH   Please stop it! Your mama'll hear you.

125 **WALTER**   Who the hell told you you had to be a doctor? If you so crazy 'bout messing 'round with sick people—then go be a nurse like other women—or just get married and be quiet . . .

BENEATHA   Well—you finally got it said . . . It took you three years but you finally got it said. Walter, give up; leave me alone—it's Mama's money.

WALTER   *He was my father, too!*

BENEATHA   So what? He was mine, too—and Travis' grandfather—but the insurance money belongs to Mama. Picking on me is not going to make her give it to you to invest in any liquor stores—*(Underbreath, dropping into a chair)*—and I for one say, God bless Mama for that!

WALTER   *(To* RUTH*)* See—did you hear? Did you hear!

130 **RUTH**   Honey, please go to work.

WALTER   Nobody in this house is ever going to understand me.

BENEATHA   Because you're a nut.

WALTER   Who's a nut?

BENEATHA   You—you are a nut. Thee is mad, boy.

135 **WALTER**   *(Looking at his wife and his sister from the door, very sadly).* The world's most backward race of people, and that's a fact.

BENEATHA   *(Turning slowly in her chair)* And then there are all those prophets who would lead us out of the wilderness—*(*WALTER *slams out of the house)*—into the swamps!

RUTH   Bennie, why you always gotta be pickin' on your brother? Can't you be a little sweeter sometimes? *(Door opens.* WALTER *walks in. He fumbles with his cap, starts to speak, clears throat, looks everywhere but at* RUTH*, Finally:)*

WALTER   *(To* RUTH*)* I need some money for carfare.

RUTH   *(Looks at him, then warms; teasing, but tenderly)* Fifty cents? *(She goes to her bag and gets money)* Here—take a taxi!

*(*WALTER *exits.* MAMA *enters. She is a woman in her early sixties, full-bodied and strong. She is one of those women of a certain grace and beauty who wear it so unobtrusively that it takes a while to notice. Her dark-brown face is surrounded by the total whiteness of her hair, and, being a woman who has adjusted to many things in life and overcome many, more, her face is full of strength. She has, we can see, wit and faith of a kind that keep her eyes lit and full of interest and expectancy. She is, in a word, a beautiful woman. Her bearing is perhaps most like the noble bearing of the women of the Hereros of Southwest Africa—rather as if she imagines that as she walks she still*

bears a basket or a vessel upon her head. Her speech, on the other hand, is as careless as her carriage is precise—she is inclined to slur everything—but her voice is perhaps not so much quiet as simply soft)

140 **MAMA** Who that 'round here slamming doors at this hour?

(She crosses through the room, goes to the window, opens it, and brings in a feeble little plant growing doggedly in a small pot on the windowsill. She feels the dirt and puts it back out)

RUTH That was Walter Lee. He and Bennie was at it again.

MAMA My children and they tempers. Lord, if this little old plant don't get more sun than it's been getting it ain't never going to see spring again. *(She turns from the window)* What's the matter with you this morning, Ruth? You looks right peaked. You aiming to iron all them things? Leave some for me. I'll get to 'em this afternoon. Bennie honey, it's too drafty for you to be sitting 'round half dressed. Where's your robe?

BENEATHA In the cleaners.

MAMA Well, go get mine and put it on.

145 **BENEATHA** I'm not cold, Mama, honest.

MAMA I know—but you so thin . . .

BENEATHA *(Irritably)* Mama, I'm not cold.

MAMA *(Seeing the make-down bed as* TRAVIS *has left it)* Lord have mercy, look at that poor bed. Bless his heart—he tries, don't he?

(She moves to the bed TRAVIS *has sloppily made up)*

RUTH No—he don't half try at all 'cause he knows you going to come along behind him and fix everything. That's just how come he don't know how to do nothing right now—you done spoiled that boy so.

150 **MAMA** *(Folding bedding)* Well—he's a little boy. Ain't supposed to know 'bout housekeeping. My baby, that's what he is. What you fix for his breakfast this morning?

RUTH *(Angrily)* I feed my son, Lena!

MAMA I ain't meddling—*(Underbreath; busy-bodyish)* I just noticed all last week he had cold cereal, and when it starts getting this chilly in the fall a child ought to have some hot grits or something when he goes out in the cold—

RUTH *(Furious)* I gave him hot oats—is that all right!

MAMA I ain't meddling. *(Pause)* Put a lot of nice butter on it? (RUTH *shoots her an angry look and does not reply*) He likes lots of butter.

155 **RUTH** *(Exasperated)* Lena—

MAMA *(To* BENEATHA. MAMA *is inclined to wander conversationally sometimes)* What was you and your brother fussing 'bout this morning?

BENEATHA It's not important, Mama.

(She gets up and goes to look out at the bathroom, which is apparently free, and she picks up her towels and rushes out)

MAMA What was they fighting about?

RUTH Now you know as well as I do.

160 **MAMA** *(Shaking her head)* Brother still worrying hisself sick about that money?

RUTH You know he is.

MAMA You had breakfast?

RUTH Some coffee.

MAMA Girl, you better start eating and looking after yourself better. You almost thin as Travis.

165 **RUTH** Lena—

MAMA Un-hunh?

RUTH What are you going to do with it?

MAMA Now don't you start, child. It's too early in the morning to be talking about money. It ain't Christian.

RUTH It's just that he got his heart set on that store—

170 **MAMA** You mean that liquor store that Willy Harris want him to invest in?

RUTH Yes—

MAMA We ain't no business people, Ruth. We just plain working folks.

RUTH Ain't nobody business people till they go into business. Walter Lee say colored people ain't never going to start getting ahead till they start gambling on some different kinds of things in the world—investments and things.

MAMA What done got into you, girl? Walter Lee done finally sold you on investing.

175 **RUTH** No. Mama, something is happening between Walter and me. I don't know what it is—but he needs something—something I can't give him anymore. He needs this chance, Lena.

MAMA *(Frowning deeply)* But liquor, honey—

RUTH Well—like Walter say—I spec people going to always be drinking themselves some liquor.

MAMA Well—whether they drinks it or not ain't none of my business. But whether I go into business selling it to 'em *is*, and I don't want that on my ledger this late in life. *(Stopping suddenly and studying her daughter-in-law)* Ruth Younger, what's the matter with you today? You look like you could fall over right there.

RUTH I'm tired.

180 **MAMA** Then you better stay home from work today.

RUTH I can't stay home. She'd be calling up the agency and screaming at them, "My girl didn't come in today—send me somebody! My girl didn't come in!" Oh, she just have a fit . . .

MAMA Well, let her have it. I'll just call her up and say you got the flu—

RUTH *(Laughing)* Why the flu?

MAMA 'Cause it sounds respectable to 'em. Something white people get, too. They know 'bout the flu. Otherwise they think you been cut up or something when you tell 'em you sick.

185 **RUTH** I got to go in. We need the money.

MAMA Somebody would of thought my children done all but starved to death the way they talk about money here late. Child, we got a great big old check coming tomorrow.

RUTH *(Sincerely, but also self-righteously)* Now that's your money. It ain't got nothing to do with me. We all feel like that—Walter and Bennie and me—even Travis.

MAMA *(Thoughtfully, and suddenly very far away)* Ten thousand dollars—

RUTH Sure is wonderful.

190 **MAMA** Ten thousand dollars.

RUTH You know what you should do, Miss Lena? You should take yourself a trip somewhere. To Europe or South America or someplace—

MAMA *(Throwing up her hands at the thought)* Oh, child!

RUTH I'm serious. Just pack up and leave! Go on away and enjoy yourself some. Forget about the family and have yourself a ball for once in your life—

MAMA *(Drily)* You sound like I'm just about ready to die. Who'd go with me? What I look like wandering 'round Europe by myself?

195 **RUTH** Shoot—these here rich white women do it all the time. They don't think nothing of packing up they suitcases and piling on one of them big steamships and—swoosh!—they gone, child.

MAMA Something always told me I wasn't no rich white woman.

RUTH Well—what are you going to do with it then?

MAMA I ain't rightly decided. *(Thinking. She speaks now with emphasis)* Some of it got to be put away for Beneatha and her schoolin'—and ain't nothing going to touch that part of it. Nothing. *(She waits several seconds, trying to make up her mind about something, and looks at* RUTH *a little tentatively before going on)* Been thinking that we maybe could meet the notes on a little old two-story somewhere, with a yard where Travis could play in the summertime, if we use part of the insurance for a down payment and everybody kind of pitch in. I could maybe take on a little day work again, few days a week—

RUTH *(Studying her mother-in-law furtively and concentrating on her ironing, anxious to encourage without seeming to)* Well, Lord knows, we've put enough rent into this here rat trap to pay for four houses by now . . .

200 **MAMA** *(Looking up at the words "rat trap" and then looking around and leaning back and sighing—in a suddenly reflective mood—)* "Rat trap"—yes, that's all it is. *(Smiling)* I remember just as well the day me and Big Walter moved in here. Hadn't been married but two weeks and wasn't planning on living here no more than a year. *(She shakes her head at the dissolved dream)* We was going to set away, little by little, don't you know, and buy a little place out in Morgan Park. We had even picked out the house. *(Chuckling a little)* Looks right dumpy today. But Lord, child, you should know all the dreams. I had 'bout buying that house and fixing it up and making me a little garden in the back—*(She waits and stops smiling)* And didn't none of it happen.

(Dropping her hands in a futile gesture)

RUTH *(Keeps her head down, ironing)* Yes, life can be a barrel of disappointments, sometimes.

MAMA Honey, Big Walter would come in here some nights back then and slump down on that couch there and just look at the rug, and look at me and look at the rug and then back at me—and I'd know he was down then . . . really down. *(After a second very long and thoughtful pause; she is seeing back to times that only she can see)* And then, Lord, when I lost that baby—little Claude—I almost thought I was going to lose Big Walter too. Oh, that man grieved hisself! He was one man to love his children.

RUTH Ain't nothin' can tear at you like losin' your baby.

MAMA I guess that's how come that man finally worked hisself to death like he done. Like he was fighting his own war with this here world that took his baby from him.

205 **RUTH** He sure was a fine man, all right. I always liked Mr. Younger.

MAMA Crazy 'bout his children! God knows there was plenty wrong with Walter Younger—hard-headed, mean, kind of wild with women—plenty wrong with him. But he sure loved his children. Always wanted them to have something—be something. That's where Brother gets all these notions, I reckon. Big Walter used to say, he'd get right wet in the eyes sometimes, lean his head back with the water standing in his eyes and say, "Seem like God didn't see fit to give the black man nothing but dreams—but He did give us children to make them dreams seems worth while." *(She smiles)* He could talk like that, don't you know.

RUTH Yes, he sure could. He was a good man, Mr. Younger.

MAMA Yes, a fine man—just couldn't never catch up with his dreams, that's all.

> (BENEATHA *comes in, brushing her hair and looking up to the ceiling, where the sound of a vacuum cleaner has started up)*

BENEATHA What could be so dirty on that woman's rugs that she has to vacuum them every single day?

210 **RUTH** I wish certain young women 'round here who I could name would take inspiration about certain rugs in a certain apartment I could also mention.

BENEATHA *(Shrugging)* How much cleaning can a house need, for Christ's sakes.

MAMA *(Not liking the Lord's name used thus)* Bennie!

RUTH Just listen to her—just listen!

BENEATHA Oh, God!

215 **MAMA** If you use the Lord's name just one more time—

BENEATHA *(A bit of a whine)* Oh, Mama—

RUTH Fresh—just fresh as salt, this girl!

BENEATHA *(Drily)* Well—if the salt loses its savor—

MAMA Now that will do. I just ain't going to have you 'round here reciting the scriptures in vain—you hear me?

220 **BENEATHA** How did I manage to get on everybody's wrong side by just walking into a room?

RUTH If you weren't so fresh—

BENEATHA Ruth, I'm twenty years old.

MAMA What time you be home from school today?

BENEATHA Kind of late. *(With enthusiasm)* Madeline is going to start my guitar lessons today.

*(*MAMA *and* RUTH *look up with the same expression)*

225 **MAMA** Your *what* kind of lessons?

BENEATHA Guitar.

RUTH Oh, Father!

MAMA How come you done taken it in your mind to learn to play the guitar?

BENEATHA I just want to, that's all.

230 **MAMA** *(Smiling)* Lord, child, don't you know what to do with yourself? How long it going to be before you get tired of this now—like you got tired of that little play-acting group you joined last year? *(Looking at* RUTH*)* And what was it the year before that?

RUTH The horseback-riding club for which she bought that fifty-five-dollar riding habit that's been hanging in the closet ever since!

MAMA *(To* BENEATHA*)* Why you got to flit so from one thing to another, baby?

BENEATHA *(Sharply)* I just want to learn to play the guitar. Is there anything wrong with that?

MAMA Ain't nobody trying to stop you. I just wonders sometimes why you has to flit so from one thing to another all the time. You ain't never done nothing with all that camera equipment you brought home—

235 **BENEATHA** I don't flit! I—I experiment with different forms of expression—

RUTH Like riding a horse?

BENEATHA —People have to express themselves one way or another.

MAMA What is it you want to express?

BENEATHA *(Angrily)* Me! (MAMA *and* RUTH *look at each other and burst into raucous laughter)* Don't worry—I don't expect you to understand.

240 **MAMA** *(To change the subject)* Who you going out with tomorrow night?

BENEATHA *(With displeasure)* George Murchison again.

MAMA *(Pleased)* Oh—you getting a little sweet on him?

RUTH You ask me, this child ain't sweet on nobody but herself— *(Underbreath)* Express herself!

(They laugh)

BENEATHA Oh—I like George all right, Mama. I mean I like him
enough to go out with him and stuff, but—

245 **RUTH** *(For devilment)* What does *and stuff* mean?

BENEATHA Mind your own business.

MAMA Stop picking at her now, Ruth. *(She chuckles—then a suspicious sudden look at her daughter as she turns in her chair for
emphasis)* What DOES it mean?

BENEATHA *(Wearily)* Oh, I just mean I couldn't ever really be serious about George. He's—he's so shallow.

RUTH Shallow—what do you mean he's shallow? He's *rich!*

250 **MAMA** Hush, Ruth.

BENEATHA I know he's rich. He knows he's rich, too.

RUTH Well—what other qualities a man got to have to satisfy you,
little girl?

BENEATHA You wouldn't even begin to understand. Anybody who
married Walter could not possibly understand.

MAMA *(Outraged)* What kind of way is that to talk about your
brother?

255 **BENEATHA** Brother is a flip—let's face it.

MAMA *(To* RUTH, *helplessly)* What's a flip?

RUTH *(Glad to add kindling)* She's saying he's crazy.

BENEATHA Not crazy. Brother isn't really crazy yet—he—he's an
elaborate neurotic.

MAMA Hush your mouth!

260 **BENEATHA** As for George. Well. George looks good—he's got a
beautiful car and he takes me to nice places and, as my sister-
in-law says, he is probably the richest boy I will ever get to know
and I even like him sometimes—but if the Youngers are sitting
around waiting to see if their little Bennie is going to tie up the
family with the Murchisons, they are wasting their time.

RUTH You mean you wouldn't marry George Murchison if he asked
you someday? That pretty, rich thing? Honey, I knew you was odd—

BENEATHA No I would not marry him if all I felt for him was what
I feel now. Besides, George's family wouldn't really like it.

MAMA Why not?

BENEATHA Oh, Mama—The Murchisons are honest-to-God-real-
live-rich colored people, and the only people in the world who
are more snobbish than rich white people are rich colored people. I thought everybody knew that. I've met Mrs. Murchison.
She's a scene!

265 **MAMA** You must not dislike people 'cause they well off, honey.

BENEATHA Why not? It makes just as much sense as disliking people 'cause they are poor, and lots of people do that.

RUTH *(A wisdom-of-the-ages manner. To* MAMA*)* Well, she'll get over some of this—

BENEATHA Get over it? What are you talking about, Ruth? Listen, I'm going to be a doctor. I'm not worried about who I'm going to marry yet—if I ever get married.

MAMA *and* RUTH *If!*

270 **MAMA** Now, Bennie—

BENEATHA Oh, I probably will . . . but first I'm going to be a doctor, and George, for one, still thinks that's pretty funny. I couldn't be bothered with that. I am going to be a doctor and everybody around here better understand that!

MAMA *(Kindly)* 'Course you going to be a doctor, honey, God willing.

BENEATHA *(Drily)* God hasn't got a thing to do with it.

MAMA Beneatha—that just wasn't necessary.

275 **BENEATHA** Well—neither is God. I get sick of hearing about God.

MAMA Beneatha!

BENEATHA I mean it! I'm just tired of hearing about God all the time. What has He got to do with anything? Does he pay tuition?

MAMA You 'bout to get your fresh little jaw slapped!

RUTH That's just what she needs, all right!

280 **BENEATHA** Why? Why can't I say what I want to around here, like everybody else?

MAMA It don't sound nice for a young girl to say things like that— you wasn't brought up that way. Me and your father went to trouble to get you and Brother to church every Sunday.

BENEATHA Mama, you don't understand. It's all a matter of ideas, and God is just one idea I don't accept. It's not important. I am not going out and be immoral or commit crimes because I don't believe in God. I don't even think about it. It's just that I get tired of Him getting credit for all the things the human race achieves through its own stubborn effort. There simply is no blasted God— there is only man and it is *he* who makes miracles!

*(*MAMA *absorbs this speech, studies her daughter and rises slowly and crosses to* BENEATHA *and slaps her powerfully across the face. After, there is only silence and the daughter*

drops her eyes from her mother's face, and mama is very tall before her)

MAMA Now—you say after me, in my mother's house there is still God. *(There is a long pause and* BENEATHA *stares at the floor wordlessly.* MAMA *repeats the phrase with precision and cool emotion)* In my mother's house there is still God.

BENEATHA In my mother's house there is still God.

(A long pause)

285 **MAMA** *(Walking away from* BENEATHA, *too disturbed for triumphant posture. Stopping and turning back to her daughter)* There are some ideas we ain't going to have in this house. Not long as I am at the head of this family.

BENEATHA Yes, ma'am.

*(*MAMA *walks out of the room)*

RUTH *(Almost gently, with profound understanding)* You think you a woman, Bennie—but you still a little girl. What you did was childish—so you got treated like a child.

BENEATHA I see. *(Quietly)* I also see that everybody thinks it's all right for Mama to be a tyrant. But all the tyranny in the world will never put a God in the heavens!

(She picks up her books and goes out. Pause)

RUTH *(Goes to* MAMA*'s door)* She said she was sorry.

290 **MAMA** *(Coming out, going to her plant)* They frightens me, Ruth. My children.

RUTH You got good children, Lena. They just a little off sometimes—but they're good.

MAMA No—there's something come down between me and them that don't let us understand each other and I don't know what it is. One done almost lost his mind thinking 'bout money all the time and the other done commence to talk about things I can't seem to understand in no form or fashion. What is it that's changing, Ruth.

RUTH *(Soothingly, older than her years)* Now . . . you taking it all too seriously. You just got strong-willed children and it takes a strong woman like you to keep 'em in hand.

MAMA *(Looking at her plant and sprinkling a little water on it)* They spirited all right, my children. Got to admit they got spirit—

Bennie and Walter. Like this little old plant that ain't never had enough sunshine or nothing—and look at it . . .

(She has her back to RUTH, *who has had to stop ironing and lean against something and put the back of her hand to her forehead)*

295 **RUTH** *(Trying to keep* MAMA *from noticing)* You . . . sure . . . loves that little old thing, don't you? . . .

MAMA Well, I always wanted me a garden like I used to see sometimes at the back of the houses down home. This plant is close as I ever got to having one. *(She looks out of the window as she replaces the plant)* Lord, ain't nothing as dreary as the view from this window on a dreary day, is there? Why ain't you singing this morning, Ruth? Sing that "No Ways Tired." That song always lifts me up so—*(She turns at last to see that* RUTH *has slipped quietly to the floor, in a state of semiconsciousness).* Ruth! Ruth honey—what's the matter with you . . . Ruth!

Curtain

Scene Two

It is the following morning; a Saturday morning, and house cleaning is in progress at the YOUNGERS. *Furniture has been shoved hither and yon and* MAMA *is giving the kitchen-area walls a washing down.* BENEATHA, *in dungarees, with a handkerchief tied around her face, is spraying insecticide into the cracks in the walls. As they work, the radio is on and a Southside disk-jockey program is inappropriately filling the house with a rather exotic saxophone blues.* TRAVIS, *the sole idle one, is leaning on his arms, looking out of the window.*

TRAVIS Grandmama, that stuff Bennie is using smells awful. Can I go downstairs, please?

MAMA Did you get all them chores done already? I ain't seen you doing much.

TRAVIS Yes'm—finished early. Where did Mama go this morning?

300 **MAMA** *(Looking at* BENEATHA*)* She had to go on a little errand.

(The phone rings. BENEATHA *runs to answer it and reaches it before* WALTER, *who has entered from bedroom)*

TRAVIS Where?

MAMA To tend to her business.

BENEATHA Haylo . . . *(Disappointed)* Yes, he is. *(She tosses the phone to* WALTER, *who barely catches it)* It's Willie Harris again.

WALTER *(As privately as possible under* MAMA's *gaze)* Hello, Willie. Did you get the papers from the lawyer? . . . No, not yet. I told you the mailman doesn't get here till ten-thirty . . . No, I'll come there . . . Yeah! Right away. *(He hangs up and goes for his coat)*

305 **BENEATHA** Brother, where did Ruth go?

WALTER *(As he exits)* How should I know!

TRAVIS Aw come on, Grandma. Can I go outside?

MAMA Oh, I guess so. You stay right in front of the house though, and keep a good lookout for the postman.

TRAVIS Yes'm. *(He darts into bedroom for stickball and bat, reenters, and sees* BENEATHA *on her knees spraying under sofa with behind upraised. He edges closer to the target, takes aim, and lets her have it. She screams)* Leave them poor little cockroaches alone, they ain't bothering you none! *(He runs as she swings the spray gun at him viciously and playfully)* Grandma! Grandma!

310 **MAMA** Look out there, girl, before you be spilling some of that stuff on that child!

TRAVIS *(Safely behind the bastion of* MAMA) That's right—look out, now! *(He exits)*

BENEATHA *(Drily)* I can't imagine that it would hurt him—it has never hurt the roaches.

MAMA Well, little boys' hides ain't as tough as Southside roaches. You better get over there behind the bureau. I seen one marching out of there like Napoleon yesterday.

BENEATHA There's really only one way to get rid of them, Mama—

315 **MAMA** How?

BENEATHA Set fire to this building! Mama, where did Ruth go?

MAMA *(Looking at her with meaning)* To the doctor, I think.

BENEATHA The doctor? What's the matter? *(They exchange glances)* You don't think—

MAMA *(With her sense of drama)* Now I ain't saying what I think. But I ain't never been wrong 'bout a woman neither.

(The phone rings)

320 **BENEATHA** *(At the phone)* Hay-lo . . . *(Pause, and a moment of recognition)* Well—when did you get back! . . . And how was it? . . . Of course I've missed you—in my way . . . This morning? No . . . house cleaning and all that and Mama hates it if I let people come over when the house is like this . . . You *have?* Well, that's

different . . . What is it—Oh, what the hell, come on over . . . Right, see you then. *Arrivederci.*

(She hangs up)

MAMA *(Who has listened vigorously, as is her habit)* Who is that you inviting over here with this house looking like this? You ain't got the pride you was born with!

BENEATHA Asagai doesn't care how houses look, Mama—he's an intellectual.

MAMA *Who?*

BENEATHA Asagai—Joseph Asagai. He's an African boy I met on campus. He's been studying in Canada all summer.

325 **MAMA** What's his name?

BENEATHA Asagai, Joseph. Ah-sah-guy . . . He's from Nigeria.

MAMA Oh, that's the little country that was founded by slaves way back . . .

BENEATHA No, Mama—that's Liberia.

MAMA I don't think I never met no African before.

330 **BENEATHA** Well, do me a favor and don't ask him a whole lot of ignorant questions about Africans. I mean, do they wear clothes and all that—

MAMA Well, now, I guess if you think we so ignorant 'round here maybe you shouldn't bring your friends here—

BENEATHA It's just that people ask such crazy things. All anyone seems to know about when it comes to Africa is Tarzan—

MAMA *(Indignantly)* Why should I know anything about Africa?

BENEATHA Why do you give money at church for the missionary work?

335 **MAMA** Well, that's to help save people.

BENEATHA You mean save them from *heathenism*—

MAMA *(Innocently)* Yes.

BENEATHA I'm afraid they need more salvation from the British and the French.

(RUTH comes in forlornly and pulls off her coat with dejection. They both turn to look at her)

RUTH *(Dispiritedly)* Well, I guess from all the happy faces—everybody knows.

340 **BENEATHA** You pregnant?

MAMA Lord have mercy, I sure hope it's a little old girl. Travis ought to have a sister.

*(*BENEATHA *and* RUTH *give her a hopeless look for this grandmotherly enthusiasm)*

BENEATHA How far along are you?

RUTH Two months.

BENEATHA Did you mean to? I mean did you plan it or was it an accident?

345 **MAMA** What do you know about planning or not planning?

BENEATHA Oh, Mama.

RUTH *(Wearily)* She's twenty years old, Lena.

BENEATHA Did you plan it, Ruth?

RUTH Mind your own business.

350 **BENEATHA** It is my business—where is he going to live, on the roof? *(There is silence following the remark as the three women react to the sense of it)* Gee—I didn't mean that, Ruth, honest. Gee, I don't feel like that at all. I—I think it is wonderful.

RUTH *(Dully)* Wonderful.

BENEATHA Yes—really. *(There is a sudden commotion from the street and she goes to the window to look out)* What on earth is going on out there? These kids. *(There are, as she throws open the window, the shouts of children rising up from the street. She sticks her head out to see better and calls out)* TRAVIS! TRAVIS . . . WHAT ARE YOU DOING DOWN THERE? *(She sees)* Oh Lord, they're chasing a rat!

*(*RUTH *covers her face with hands and turns away)*

MAMA *(Angrily)* Tell that youngun to get himself up here, at once!

BENEATHA TRAVIS . . . YOU COME UPSTAIRS . . . AT ONCE!

355 **RUTH** *(Her face twisted)* Chasing a rat. . . .

MAMA *(Looking at* RUTH, *worried)* Doctor say everything going to be all right?

RUTH *(Far away)* Yes—she says everything is going to be fine . . .

MAMA *(Immediately suspicious)* "She"—What doctor you went to?

*(*RUTH *just looks at* MAMA *meaningfully and* MAMA *opens her mouth to speak as* TRAVIS *bursts in)*

TRAVIS *(Excited and full of narrative, coming directly to his mother)* Mama, you should of seen the rat . . . Big as a cat, honest! *(He shows an exaggerated size with his hands)* Gaaleee, that rat was really cuttin' and Bubber caught him with his heel and the janitor, Mr. Barnett, got him with a stick—and then they got him in a corner and—BAM! BAM! BAM!—and he was still jumping around and bleeding like everything too—there's rat blood all over the street—

(RUTH reaches out suddenly and grabs her son without even looking at him and clamps her hand over his mouth and holds him to her. MAMA crosses to them rapidly and takes the boy from her)

360 **MAMA** You hush up now . . . talking all that terrible stuff. . . . *(TRAVIS is staring at his mother with a stunned expression. BENEATHA comes quickly and takes him away from his grandmother and ushers him to the door)*

BENEATHA You go back outside and play . . . but not with any rats. *(She pushes him gently out the door with the boy straining to see what is wrong with his mother)*

MAMA *(Worriedly hovering over RUTH)* Ruth honey—what's the matter with you—you sick?

(RUTH has her fists clenched on her thighs and is fighting hard to suppress a scream that seems to be rising in her)

BENEATHA What's the matter with her, Mama?

MAMA *(Working her fingers in RUTH's shoulders to relax her)* She be all right. Women gets right depressed sometimes when they get her way. *(Speaking softly, expertly, rapidly)* Now you just relax. That's right . . . just lean back, don't think 'bout nothing at all . . . nothing at all—

365 **RUTH** I'm all right . . .

(The glassy-eyed look melts and then she collapses into a fit of heavy sobbing. The bell rings)

BENEATHA Oh, my God—that must be Asagai.

MAMA *(To RUTH)* Come on now, honey. You need to lie down and rest awhile . . . then have some nice hot food.

(They exit, RUTH'S weight on her mother-in-law. BENEATHA, herself profoundly disturbed, opens the door to admit a rather dramatic-looking young man with a large package)

ASAGAI Hello, Alaiyo—

BENEATHA *(Holding the door open and regarding him with pleasure)* Hello . . . *(Long pause)* Well—come in. And please excuse everything. My mother was very upset about my letting anyone come here with the place like this.

370 **ASAGAI** *(Coming into the room)* You look disturbed too . . . Is something wrong?

BENEATHA *(Still at the door, absently)* Yes . . . we've all got acute ghetto-itis. *(She smiles and comes toward him, finding a cigarette and sitting)* So—sit down! No! Wait! *(She whips the spray gun off sofa where she had left it and puts the cushions back. At last perches on arm of sofa. He sits)* So, how was Canada?

ASAGAI *(Shrugging)* Were you born with it like that?

BENEATHA *(Reaching up to touch it)* No . . . of course not.

(She looks back to the mirror, disturbed)

ASAGAI *(Smiling)* How then?

375 **BENEATHA** You know perfectly well how . . . as crinkly as yours . . . that's how.

ASAGAI And it is ugly to you that way?

BENEATHA *(Quickly)* Oh, no—not ugly . . . *(More slowly, apologetically)* But it's so hard to manage when it's, well—raw.

ASAGAI And so to accommodate that—you mutilate it every week?

BENEATHA It's not mutilation!

380 **ASAGAI** *(Laughing aloud at her seriousness)* Oh . . . please! I am only teasing you because you are so very serious about these things. *(He stands back from her and folds his arms across his chest as he watches her pulling at her hair and frowning in the mirror)* Do you remember the first time you met me at school? . . . *(He laughs)* You came up to me and you said—and I thought you were the most serious little thing I had ever seen—you said: *(He imitates her)* "Mr. Asagai—I want very much to talk with you. About Africa. You see, Mr. Asagai, I am looking for my *identity!*"

(He laughs)

BENEATHA *(Turning to him, not laughing)* Yes—

(Her face is quizzical, profoundly disturbed)

ASAGAI *(Still teasing and reaching out and taking her face in his hands and turning her profile to him)* Well . . . it is true that this is not so much a profile of a Hollywood queen as perhaps a queen of the Nile— *(A mock dismissal of the importance of the question)* But what does it matter? Assimilationism is so popular in your country.

BENEATHA *(Wheeling, passionately, sharply).* I am not an assimilationist!

ASAGAI *(The protest hangs in the room for a moment and* ASAGAI *studies her, his laughter fading)* Such a serious one. *(There is a pause)* So—you like the robes? You must take excellent care of them—they are from my sister's personal wardrobe.

385 **BENEATHA** *(With incredulity)* You—you sent all the way home—for me?

ASAGAI *(With charm)* For you—I would do much more . . . Well, that is what I came for, I must go.

BENEATHA Will you call me Monday?

ASAGAI Yes . . . We have a great deal to talk about. I mean about identity and time and all that.

BENEATHA Time?

390 **ASAGAI** Yes. About how much time one needs to know what one feels.

BENEATHA You see! You never understood that there is more than one kind of feeling which can exist between a man and a woman—or, at least, there should be.

ASAGAI *(Shaking his head negatively but gently)* No. Between a man and a woman there need be only one kind of feeling. I have that for you . . . Now even . . . right this moment . . .

BENEATHA I know—and by itself—it won't do. I can find that anywhere.

ASAGAI For a woman it should be enough.

395 **BENEATHA** I know—because that's what it says in all the novels that men write. But it isn't. Go ahead and laugh—but I'm not interested in being someone's little episode in America or—*(With feminine vengeance)*—one of them! (ASAGAI *has burst into laughter again*) That's funny as hell, huh!

ASAGAI It's just that every American girl I have known has said that to me. White—black—in this you are all the same. And the same speech, too!

BENEATHA *(Angrily)* Yuk, yuk, yuk!

ASAGAI It's how you can be sure that the world's most liberated women are not liberated at all. You all talk about it too much!

(MAMA *enters and is immediately all social charm because of the presence of a guest).*

BENEATHA Oh—Mama—this is Mr. Asagai.

400 **MAMA** How do you do?

ASAGAI *(Total politeness to an elder)* How do you do, Mrs. Younger. Please forgive me for coming at such an outrageous hour on a Saturday.

MAMA Well, you are quite welcome. I just hope you understand that our house don't always look like this. *(Chatterish)* You must come again. I would love to hear all about—*(Not sure of the name)*— your country. I think it's so sad the way our American Negroes don't know nothing about Africa 'cept Tarzan and all that. And all that money they pour into these churches when they ought to be helping you people over there drive out them French and Englishmen done taken away your land.

(The mother flashes a slightly superior look at her daughter upon completion of the recitation)

ASAGAI *(Taken aback by this sudden and acutely unrelated expression of sympathy)* Yes . . . yes . . .

MAMA *(Smiling at him suddenly and relaxing and looking him over)* How many miles is it from here to where you come from?

405 **ASAGAI** Many thousands.

MAMA *(Looking at him as she would* WALTER*)* I bet you don't half look after yourself, being away from your mama either. I spec you better come 'round here from time to time to get yourself some decent home-cooked meals . . .

ASAGAI *(Moved)* Thank you. Thank you very much. *(They are all quiet, them—)* Well . . . I must go. I will call you Monday, Alaiyo.

MAMA What's that he call you?

ASAGAI Oh—"Alaiyo." I hope you don't mind. It is what you would call a nickname, I think. It is a Yoruba word. I am a Yoruba.

410 **MAMA** *(Looking at* BENEATHA*)* I—I thought he was from— *(Uncertain)*

ASAGAI *(Understanding)* Nigeria is my country. Yoruba is my tribal origin—

BENEATHA You didn't tell us what Alaiyo means . . . for all I know, you might be calling me Little Idiot or something . . .

ASAGAI Well . . . let me see . . . I do not know how just to explain it . . . The sense of a thing can be so different when it changes languages.

BENEATHA You're evading.

415 **ASAGAI** No—really it is difficult . . . *(Thinking)* It means . . . it means One for Whom Bread—Food—Is Not Enough. *(He looks at her)* Is that all right?

BENEATHA *(Understanding, softly)* Thank you.

MAMA *(Looking from one to the other and not understanding any of it)* Well . . . that's nice . . . You must come see us again—Mr.—

ASAGAI Ah-sah-guy . . .

MAMA Yes . . . Do come again.

420 **ASAGAI** Good-bye.

(He exits)

MAMA *(After him)* Lord, that's a pretty thing just went out here! *(Insinuatingly, to her daughter)* Yes, I guess I see why we done commence to get so interested in Africa 'round here. Missionaries my aunt Jenny!

(She exits)

BENEATHA Oh, Mama! . . .

(She picks up the Nigerian dress and holds it up to her in front of the mirror again. She sets the headdress on haphazardly and then notices her hair again and clutches at it and then replaces the headdress and frowns at herself. Then she starts to wriggle in front of the mirror as she thinks a Nigerian woman might. TRAVIS *enters and stands regarding her)*

TRAVIS What's the matter, girl, you cracking up?

BENEATHA Shut up.

(She pulls the headdress off and looks at herself in the mirror and clutches at her hair again and squinches her eyes as if trying to imagine something. Then, suddenly, she gets her raincoat and kerchief and hurriedly prepares for going out)

425 **MAMA** *(Coming back into the room)* She's resting now. Travis, baby, run next door and ask Miss Johnson to please let me have a little kitchen cleanser. This here can is empty as Jacob's kettle.

TRAVIS I just came in.

MAMA Do as you told. *(He exits and she looks at her daughter)* Where you going?

BENEATHA *(Halting at the door)* To become a queen of the Nile!

(She exits in a breathless blaze of glory. RUTH *appears in the bedroom doorway)*

MAMA Who told you to get up?

430 **RUTH** Ain't nothing wrong with me to be lying in no bed for. Where did Bennie go?

MAMA *(Drumming her fingers)* Far as I could make out—to Egypt. *(RUTH just looks at her)* What time is it getting to?

RUTH Ten twenty. And the mailman going to ring that bell this morning just like he done every morning for the last umpteen years.

(TRAVIS comes in with the cleanser can)

TRAVIS She say to tell you that she don't have much.

MAMA *(Angrily)* Lord, some people I could name sure is tight-fisted! *(Directing her grandson)* Mark two cans of cleanser down on the list there. If she that hard up for kitchen cleanser, I sure don't want to forget to get her none!

435 **RUTH** Lena—maybe the woman is just short on cleanser—

MAMA *(Not listening)*—Much baking powder as she done borrowed from me all these years, she could of done gone into the baking business!

(The bell sounds suddenly and sharply and all three are stunned—serious and silent—mid-speech. In spite of all the other conversations and distractions of the morning, this is what they have been waiting for, even TRAVIS who looks helplessly from his mother to his grandmother. RUTH is the first to come to life again)

RUTH *(To TRAVIS)* Get down them steps, boy!

(TRAVIS snaps to life and flies out to get the mail)

MAMA *(Her eyes wide, her hand to her breast)* You mean it done really come?

RUTH *(Excited)* Oh, Miss Lena!

440 **MAMA** *(Collecting herself)* Well . . . I don't know what we all so excited about 'round here for. We known it was coming for months.

RUTH That's a whole lot different from having it come and being able to hold it in your hands . . . a piece of paper worth ten thousand dollars . . . *(TRAVIS bursts back into the room. He holds the envelope high above his head, like a little dancer, his face is radiant and he is breathless. He moves to his grandmother with sudden slow ceremony and puts the envelope into her hands. She*

accepts it, and then merely holds it and looks at it) Come on!
Open it . . . Lord have mercy, I wish Walter Lee was here!

TRAVIS Open it, Grandmama!

MAMA *(Staring at it)* Now you all be quiet. It's just a check.

RUTH Open it . . .

445 **MAMA** *(Still staring at it)* Now don't act silly . . . We ain't never been
no people to act silly 'bout no money—

RUTH *(Swiftly)* We ain't never had none before—OPEN IT!

*(*MAMA *finally makes a good strong tear and pulls out the
thin blue slice of paper and inspects it closely. The boy and
his mother study it raptly over* MAMA'S *shoulders)*

MAMA *Travis! (She is counting off with doubt)* Is that the right number of zeros?

TRAVIS Yes'm . . . ten thousand dollars. Gaalee, Grand-mama, you
rich.

MAMA *(She holds the check away from her, still looking at it.
Slowly her face sobers into a mask of unhappiness)* Ten thousand dollars. *(She hands it to* RUTH*)* Put it away somewhere,
Ruth. *(She does not look at* RUTH*; her eyes seem to be seeing
something somewhere very far off)* Ten thousand dollars they
give you. Ten thousand dollars.

450 **TRAVIS** *(To his mother, sincerely)* What's the matter with Grandmama—don't she want to be rich?

RUTH *(Distractedly)* You go on out and play now, baby. (TRAVIS
exits. MAMA *starts wiping dishes absently, humming intently to
herself.* RUTH *turns to her, with kind exasperation)* You've gone
and got yourself upset.

MAMA *(Not looking at her)* I spec if it wasn't for you all . . . I would
just put that money away or give it to the church or something.

RUTH Now what kind of talk is that. Mr. Younger would just be
plain mad if he could hear you talking foolish like that.

MAMA *(Stopping and staring off)* Yes . . . he sure would. *(Sighing)*
We got enough to do with that money, all right. *(She halts then,
and turns and looks at her daughter-in-law hard;* RUTH *avoids her
eyes and* MAMA *wipes her hands with finality and starts to speak
firmly to* RUTH*)* Where did you go today, girl?

455 **RUTH** To the doctor.

MAMA *(Impatiently)* Now, Ruth . . . you know better than that. Old
Doctor Jones is strange enough in his way but there ain't nothing 'bout him make somebody slip and call him "she"—like you
done this morning.

RUTH Well, that's what happened—my tongue slipped.

MAMA You went to see that woman, didn't you?

RUTH *(Defensively, giving herself away)* What woman you talking about?

460 **MAMA** *(Angrily)* That woman who—

(WALTER *enters in great excitement)*

WALTER Did it come?

MAMA *(Quietly)* Can't you give people a Christian greeting before you start asking about money?

WALTER *(To* RUTH) Did it come? *(*RUTH *unfolds the check and lays it quietly before him, watching him intently with thoughts of her own.* WALTER *sits down and grasps it close and counts off the zeros)* Ten thousand dollars—*(He turns suddenly, frantically to his mother and draws some papers out of his breast pocket)* Mama—look. Old Willy Harris put everything on paper—

MAMA Son—I think you ought to talk to your wife . . . I'll go on out and leave you alone if you want—

465 **WALTER** I can talk to her later—Mama, look—

MAMA Son—

WALTER WILL SOMEBODY PLEASE LISTEN TO ME TODAY!

MAMA *(Quietly)* I don't 'low no yellin' in this house, Walter Lee, and you know it—*(*WALTER *stares at them in frustration and starts to speak several times)* And there ain't going to be no investing in no liquor stores.

WALTER But, Mama, you ain't even looked at it:

470 **MAMA** I don't aim to have to speak on that again.

(A long pause)

WALTER You ain't looked at it and you don't aim to have to speak on that again? You ain't even looked at it and *you* have decided— *(Crumpling his papers)* Well, *you* tell that to my boy tonight when you put him to sleep on the living-room couch . . . *(Turning to* MAMA *and speaking directly to her)* Yeah—and tell it to my wife, Mama, tomorrow when she has to go out of here to look after somebody else's kids. And tell it to *me*, Mama, every time we need a new pair of curtains and I have to watch *you* go out and work in somebody's kitchen. Yeah, you tell me then!

*(*WALTER *starts out)*

RUTH Where you going?

WALTER I'm going out!

RUTH Where?

475 **WALTER** Just out of this house somewhere—

RUTH *(Getting her coat)* I'll come too.

WALTER I don't want you to come!

RUTH I got something to talk to you about, Walter.

WALTER That's too bad.

480 **MAMA** *(Still quietly)* Walter Lee—*(She waits and he finally turns and looks at her)* Sit down.

WALTER I'm a grown man, Mama.

MAMA Ain't nobody said you wasn't grown. But you still in my house and my presence. And as long as you are—you'll talk to your wife civil. Now sit down.

RUTH *(Suddenly)* Oh, let him go on out and drink himself to death! He makes me sick to my stomach! *(She flings her coat against him and exits to bedroom)*

WALTER *(Violently flinging the coat after her)* And you turn mine too, baby! *(The door slams behind her)* That was my biggest mistake—

485 **MAMA** *(Still quietly)* Walter, what is the matter with you?

WALTER Matter with me? Ain't nothing the matter with *me!*

MAMA Yes there is. Something eating you up like a crazy man. Something more than me not giving you this money. The past few years I been watching it happen to you. You get all nervous acting and kind of wild in the eyes—*(WALTER jumps up impatiently at her words)* I said sit there now, I'm talking to you!

WALTER Mama—I don't need no nagging at me today.

MAMA Seem like you getting to a place where you always tied up in some kind of knot about something. But if anybody ask you 'bout it you just yell at 'em and bust out the house and go out and drink somewheres. Walter Lee, people can't live with that. Ruth's a good, patient girl in her way—but you getting to be too much. Boy, don't make the mistake of driving that girl away from you.

490 **WALTER** Why—what she do for me?

MAMA She loves you.

WALTER Mama—I'm going out. I want to go off somewhere and be by myself for a while.

MAMA I'm sorry 'bout your liquor store, son. It just wasn't the thing for us to do. That's what I want to tell you about—

WALTER I got to go out, Mama—

(He rises)

495 **MAMA** It's dangerous, son.

WALTER What's dangerous?

MAMA When a man goes outside his home to look for peace.

WALTER (*Beseechingly*) Then why can't there never be no peace in this house then?

MAMA You done found it in some other house?

500 **WALTER** No—there ain't no woman! Why do women always think there's a woman somewhere when a man gets restless. (*Picks up the check*) Do you know what this money means to me? Do you know what this money can do for us? (*Puts it back*) Mama— Mama—I want so many things . . .

MAMA Yes, son—

WALTER I want so many things that they are driving me kind of crazy . . . Mama—look at me.

MAMA I'm looking at you. You a good-looking boy. You got a job, a nice wife, a fine boy and—

WALTER A job. (*Looks at her*) Mama, a job? I open and close car doors all day long. I drive a man around in his limousine and I say, "Yes, sir; no, sir; very good, sir; shall I take the Drive, sir?" Mama, that ain't no kind of job . . . that ain't nothing at all. (*Very quietly*) Mama, I don't know if I can make you understand.

505 **MAMA** Understand what, baby?

WALTER (*Quietly*) Sometimes it's like I can see the future stretched out in front of me—just plain as day. The future, Mama. Hanging over there at the edge of my days. Just waiting for me—a big, looming blank space—full of *nothing*. Just waiting for *me*. But it don't have to be. (*Pause. Kneeling beside her chair*) Mama— sometimes when I'm downtown and I pass them cool, quiet-looking restaurants where them white boys are sitting back and talking 'bout things . . . sitting there turning deals worth millions of dollars . . . sometimes I see guys don't look much older than me—

MAMA Son—how come you talk so much 'bout money?

WALTER (*With immense passion*) Because it is life, Mama!

MAMA (*Quietly*) Oh—(*Very quietly*) So now it's life. Money is life. Once upon a time freedom used to be life—now it's money. I guess the world really do change . . .

510 **WALTER** No—it was always money, Mama. We just didn't know about it.

MAMA No . . . something has changed. (*She looks at him*) You something new, boy. In my time we was worried about not being lynched and getting to the North if we could and how to stay alive and still have a pinch of dignity too . . . Now here come you and Beneatha—talking 'bout things we ain't never even thought about hardly, me and your daddy. You ain't satisfied or proud of nothing we done. I mean that you had a home; that we kept you out of trouble till you was grown; that you don't have to ride to work on the back of nobody's streetcar—You my children—but how different we done become.

WALTER (*A long beat. He pats her hand and gets up*) You just don't understand, Mama, you just don't understand.

MAMA Son—do you know your wife is expecting another baby? (WALTER *stands, stunned, and absorbs what his mother has said*) That's what she wanted to talk to you about. (WALTER *sinks down into a chair*) This ain't for me to be telling—but you ought to know. (*She waits*) I think Ruth is thinking 'bout getting rid of that child.

WALTER (*Slowly understanding*) No—no—Ruth wouldn't do that.

515 **MAMA** When the world gets ugly enough—a woman will do anything for her family. *The part that's already living.*

WALTER You don't know Ruth, Mama, if you think she would do that.

(RUTH *opens the bedroom door and stands there a little limp*)

RUTH (*Beaten*) Yes I would too, Walter. (*Pause*) I gave her a five-dollar down payment.

(*There is total silence as the man stares at his wife and the mother stares at her son*)

MAMA (*Presently*) Well—(*Tightly*) Well—son, I'm waiting to hear you say something . . . (*She waits*) I'm waiting to hear how you be your father's son. Be the man he was . . . (*Pause. The silence shouts*) Your wife say she going to destroy your child. And I'm waiting to hear you talk like him and say we a people who give children life, not who destroys them—(*She rises*) I'm waiting to see you stand up and look like your daddy and say we done give up one baby to poverty and that we ain't going to give up nary another one . . . I'm waiting.

WALTER Ruth—(*He can say nothing*)

520 **MAMA** If you a son of mine, tell her! (WALTER *picks up his keys and his coat and walks out. She continues, bitterly*) You . . . you are a disgrace to your father's memory. Somebody get me my hat!

Curtain

ACT II

Scene One

Time: Later the same day.

At rise: RUTH *is ironing again. She has the radio going. Presently* BENEATHA*'s bedroom door opens and* RUTH*'s mouth falls and she puts down the iron in fascination.*

RUTH What have we got on tonight!

BENEATHA *(Emerging grandly from the doorway so that we can see her thoroughly robed in the costume Asagai brought)* You are looking at what a well-dressed Nigerian woman wears—*(She parades for* RUTH, *her hair completely hidden by the headdress; she is coquettishly fanning herself with an ornate oriental fan, mistakenly more like Butterfly than any Nigerian that ever was)* Isn't it beautiful? *(She promenades to the radio and, with an arrogant flourish, turns off the good loud blues that is playing)* Enough of this assimilationist junk! (RUTH *follows her with her eyes as she goes to the phonograph and puts on a record and turns and waits ceremoniously for the music to come up. Then, with a shout—)* OCOMOGOSIAY!

> *(*RUTH *jumps. The music comes up, a lovely Nigerian melody.* BENEATHA *listens, enraptured, her eyes far away— "back to the past." She begins to dance.* RUTH *is dumbfounded)*

RUTH What kind of dance is that?

BENEATHA A folk dance.

525 **RUTH** *(Pearl Bailey)* What kind of folks do that, honey?

BENEATHA It's from Nigeria. It's a dance of welcome.

RUTH Who you welcoming?

BENEATHA The men back to the village.

RUTH Where they been?

530 **BENEATHA** How should I know—out hunting or something. Anyway, they are coming back now . . .

RUTH Well, that's good.

BENEATHA *(With the record)*

Alundi, alundi

Alundi alunya

Jop pu a jeepua

Ang gu sooooooooooo

Ai yai yae . . .
Ayehaye—alundi . . .

> *(*WALTER *comes in during this performance; he has obviously been drinking. He leans against the door heavily and watches his sister, at first with distaste. Then his eyes look off—"back to the past"—as he lifts both his fists to the roof, screaming)*

WALTER   YEAH . . . AND ETHIOPIA STRETCH FORTH HER HANDS AGAIN! . . .

RUTH   *(Drily, looking at him)* Yes—and Africa sure is claiming her own tonight. *(She gives them both up and starts ironing again)*

535   WALTER   *(All in a drunken, dramatic shout)* Shut up! . . . I'm digging them drums . . . them drums move me! . . . *(He makes his weaving way to his wife's face and leans in close to her)* In my heart of hearts—*(He thumps his chest)*—I am much warrior!

RUTH   *(Without even looking up)* In your heart of hearts you are much drunkard.

WALTER   *(Coming away from her and starting to wander around the room, shouting)* Me and Jomo . . . *(Intently, in his sister's face. She has stopped dancing to watch him in this unknown mood)* That's my man, Kenyatta. *(Shouting and thumping his chest)* FLAMING SPEAR! HOT DAMN! *(He is suddenly in possession of an imaginary spear and actively spearing enemies all over the room)* OCOMOGOSIAY . . .

BENEATHA   *(To encourage* WALTER, *thoroughly caught up with this side of him)* OCOMOGOSIAY, FLAMING SPEAR!

WALTER   THE LION IS WAKING . . . OWIMOWEH! *He pulls his shirt open and leaps up on the table and gestures with his spear)*

540   BENEATHA   OWIMOWEH!

WALTER   *(On the table, very far gone, his eyes pure glass sheets. He sees what we cannot, that he is a leader of his people, a great chief, a descendant of Chaka, and that the hour to march has come)* Listen, my black brothers—

BENEATHA   OCOMOGOSIAY!

WALTER   —Do you hear the waters rushing against the shores of the coastlands—

BENEATHA   OCOMOGOSIAY!

545   WALTER   —Do you hear the screeching of the cocks in yonder hills beyond where the chiefs meet in council for the coming of the mighty war—

BENEATHA OCOMOGOSIAY!

(And now the lighting shifts subtly to suggest the world of WALTER*'s* imagination, and the mood shifts from pure comedy. It is the inner WALTER speaking: the Southside chauffeur has assumed an unexpected majesty)

WALTER —Do you hear the beating of the wings of the birds flying low over the mountains and the low places of our land—

BENEATHA OCOMOGOSIAY!

WALTER —Do you hear the singing of the women, singing the war songs of our fathers to the babies in the great houses? Singing the sweet war songs! *(The doorbell rings)* OH, DO YOU HEAR, MY BLACK BROTHERS!

550 **BENEATHA** *(Completely gone)* We hear you, Flaming Spear—

(RUTH shuts off the phonograph and opens the door. GEORGE MURCHISON enters)

WALTER Telling us to prepare for the GREATNESS OF THE TIME! *(Lights back to normal. He turns and sees* GEORGE*)* Black Brother!

(He extends his hand for the fraternal clasp)

GEORGE Black Brother, hell!

RUTH *(Having had enough, and embarrassed for the family)* Beneatha, you got company—what's the matter with you? Walter Lee Younger, get down off that table and stop acting like a fool . . .

(WALTER comes down off the table suddenly and makes a quick exit to the bathroom)

RUTH He's had a little to drink . . . I don't know what her excuse is.

555 **GEORGE** *(To* BENEATHA*)* Look honey, we're going *to* the theatre— we're not going to be *in* it . . . so go change, huh?

(BENEATHA looks at him and slowly, ceremoniously lifts her hands and pulls off the headdress. Her hair is close-cropped and unstraightened. GEORGE freezes mid-sentence and RUTH*'s* eyes all but fan out of her head)

GEORGE What in the name of—

RUTH *(Touching* BENEATHA*'s hair)* Girl, you done lost your natural mind!? Look at your head!

GEORGE What have you done to your head—I mean your hair!

BENEATHA Nothing—except cut it off.

560 **RUTH** Now that's the truth—it's what ain't been done to it! You expect this boy to go out with you with your head all nappy like that?

BENEATHA *(Looking at* GEORGE*)* That's up to George. If he's ashamed of his heritage—

GEORGE Oh, don't be so proud of yourself, Bennie—just because you look eccentric.

BENEATHA How can something that's natural be eccentric?

GEORGE That's what being eccentric means—being natural. Get dressed.

565 **BENEATHA** I don't like that, George.

RUTH Why must you and your brother make an argument out of everything people say?

BENEATHA Because I hate assimilationist Negroes!

RUTH Will somebody please tell me what assimila-who-ever means!

GEORGE Oh, it's just a college girl's way of calling people Uncle Toms—but that isn't what it means at all.

570 **RUTH** Well, what does it mean?

BENEATHA *(Cutting* GEORGE *off and staring at him as she replies to* RUTH*)* It means someone who is willing to give up his own culture and submerge himself completely in the dominant, and in this case *oppressive* culture!

GEORGE Oh, dear, dear, dear! Here we go! A lecture on the African past! On our Great West African Heritage! In one second we will hear all about the great Ashanti empires; the great Songhay civilizations; and the great sculpture of Bénin—and then some poetry in the Bantu—and the whole monologue will end with the word *heritage!* *(Nastily)* Let's face it, baby, your heritage is nothing but a bunch of raggedy-assed spirituals and some grass huts!

BENEATHA GRASS HUTS! (RUTH *crosses to her and forcibly pushes her toward the bedroom)* See there . . . you are standing there in your splendid ignorance talking about people who were the first to smelt iron on the face of the earth! (RUTH *is pushing her through the door)* The Ashanti were performing surgical operations when the English—(RUTH *pulls the door to, with* BENEATHA *on the other side, and smiles graciously at* GEORGE. BENEATHA *opens the door and shouts the end of the sentence defiantly at* GEORGE*)*—were still tattooing themselves with blue dragons! *(She goes back inside)*

RUTH Have a seat, George *(They both sit.* RUTH *folds her hands rather primly on her lap, determined to demonstrate the civilization of the family)* Warm, ain't it? I mean for September. *(Pause)*

Just like they always say about Chicago weather: If it's too hot
or cold for you, just wait a minute and it'll change. *(She smiles
happily at this cliché of clichés)* Everybody say it's got to do with
them bombs and things they keep setting off. *(Pause)* Would you
like a nice cold beer?

575 **GEORGE**   No, thank you. I don't care for beer. *(He looks at his
watch)* I hope she hurries up.

RUTH   What time is the show?

GEORGE   It's an eight-thirty curtain. That's just Chicago, though. In
New York standard curtain time is eight forty.

(He is rather proud of this knowledge)

RUTH   *(Properly appreciating it)* You get to New York a lot?

GEORGE   *(Offhand)* Few times a year.

580 **RUTH**   Oh—that's nice. I've never been to New York.

*(*WALTER *enters. We feel he has relieved himself, but the edge
of unreality is still with him)*

WALTER   New York ain't got nothing Chicago ain't. Just a bunch
of hustling people all squeezed up together—being "Eastern."

(He turns his face into a screw of displeasure)

GEORGE   Oh—you've been?

WALTER   *Plenty* of times.

RUTH   *(Shocked at the lie)* Walter Lee Younger!

585 **WALTER**   *(Staring her down)* Plenty! *(Pause)* What we got to drink
in this house? Why don't you offer this man some refreshment.
(To GEORGE*)* They don't know how to entertain people in this
house, man.

GEORGE   Thank you—I don't really care for anything.

WALTER   *(Feeling his head; sobriety coming)* Where's Mama?

RUTH   She ain't come back yet.

WALTER   *(Looking* MURCHISON *over from head to toe, scrutinizing his
carefully casual tweed sports jacket over cashmere V-neck sweater
over soft eyelet shirt and tie, and soft slacks, finished off with white
buckskin shoes)* Why all you college boys wear them faggoty-looking white shoes?

590 **RUTH**   Walter Lee! *(*GEORGE MURCHISON *ignores the remark)*

WALTER   *(To* RUTH*)* Well, they look crazy as hell—white shoes, cold
as it is.

RUTH   *(Crushed)* You have to excuse him—

WALTER No he don't! Excuse me for what? What you always excusing me for! I'll excuse myself when I needs to be excused! *(A pause)* They look as funny as them black knee socks Beneatha wears out of here all the time.

RUTH It's the college *style*, Walter.

595 **WALTER** Style, hell. She looks like she got burnt legs or something!

RUTH Oh, Walter—

WALTER *(An irritable mimic)* Oh, Walter! Oh, Walter! *(To* MURCHISON*)* How's your old man making out? I understand you all going to buy that big hotel on the Drive? *(He finds a beer in the refrigerator, wanders over to* MURCHISON, *sipping and wiping his lips with the back of his hand, and straddling a chair backwards to talk to the other man)* Shrewd move. Your old man is all right, man. *(Tapping his head and half winking for emphasis)* I mean he knows how to operate. I mean he thinks *big*, you know what I mean, I mean for a *home*, you know? But I think he's kind of running out of ideas now. I'd like to talk to him. Listen, man, I got some plans that could turn this city upside down. I mean think like he does. *Big*. Invest big, gamble big, hell, lose *big* if you have to, you know what I mean. It's hard to find a man on this whole Southside who understands my kind of thinking—you dig? *(He scrutinizes* MURCHISON *again, drinks his beer, squints his eyes and leans in close, confidential, man to man)* Me and you ought to sit down and talk sometimes, man. Man, I got me some ideas . . .

GEORGE *(With boredom)* Yeah—sometimes we'll have to do that, Walter.

WALTER *(Understanding the indifference, and offended)* Yeah—well, when you get the time, man. I know you a busy little boy.

600 **RUTH** Walter, please—

WALTER *(Bitterly, hurt)* I know ain't nothing in this world as busy as you colored college boys with your fraternity pins and white shoes . . .

RUTH *(Covering her face with humiliation)* Oh, Walter Lee—

WALTER I see you all all the time—with the books tucked under your arms—going to your *(British A—a mimic)* "clahsses." And for what! What the hell you learning over there? Filling up your heads—*(Counting off on his fingers)*—with the sociology and the psychology—but they teaching you how to be a man? How to take over and run the world? They teaching you how to run a rubber plantation or a steel mill? Naw—just to talk proper and read books and wear them faggoty-looking white shoes . . .

GEORGE *(Looking at him with distaste, a little above it all)* You're all wacked up with bitterness, man.

605 **WALTER** *(Intently, almost quietly, between the teeth, glaring at the boy)* And you—ain't you bitter, man? Ain't you just about had it yet? Don't you see no stars gleaming that you can't reach out and grab? You happy?—You contented son-of-a-bitch—you happy? You got it made? Bitter? Man, I'm a volcano. Bitter? Here I am a giant—surrounded by ants! Ants who can't even understand what it is the giant is talking about.

RUTH *(Passionately and suddenly)* Oh, Walter—ain't you with nobody!

WALTER *(Violently)* No! 'Cause ain't nobody with me! Not even my own mother!

RUTH Walter, that's a terrible thing to say!

*(*BENEATHA *enters, dressed for the evening in a cocktail dress and earrings, hair natural)*

GEORGE Well—hey—*(Crosses to* BENEATHA; *thoughtful, with emphasis, since this is a reversal)* You look great!

610 **WALTER** *(Seeing his sister's hair for the first time)* What's the matter with your head?

BENEATHA *(Tired of the jokes now)* I cut it off, Brother.

WALTER *(Coming close to inspect it and walking around her)* Well, I'll be damned. So that's what they mean by the African bush . . .

BENEATHA Ha ha. Let's go, George.

GEORGE *(Looking at her)* You know something? I like it. It's sharp. I mean it really is. *(Helps her into her wrap)*

615 **RUTH** Yes—I think so, too. *(She goes to the mirror and starts to clutch at her hair)*

WALTER Oh no! You leave yours alone, baby. You might turn out to have a pin-shaped head or something!

BENEATHA See you all later.

RUTH Have a nice time.

GEORGE Thanks. Good night. *(Half out the door, he re-opens it. To* WALTER*)* Good night, Prometheus!

*(*BENEATHA *and* GEORGE *exit)*

620 **WALTER** *(To* RUTH*)* Who is Prometheus?

RUTH I don't know. Don't worry about it.

WALTER *(In fury, pointing after* GEORGE*)* See there—they get to a point where they can't insult you man to man—they got to go talk about something ain't nobody never heard of!

RUTH How do you know it was an insult? *(To humor him)* Maybe Prometheus is a nice fellow.

WALTER Prometheus! I bet there ain't even no such thing! I bet that simple-minded clown—

625 **RUTH** Walter—

(She stops what she is doing and looks at him)

WALTER *(Yelling)* Don't start!

RUTH Start what?

WALTER Your nagging! Where was I? Who was I with? How much money did I spend?

RUTH *(Plaintively)* Walter Lee—why don't we just try to talk about it . . .

630 **WALTER** *(Not listening)* I been out talking with people who understand me. People who care about the things I got on my mind.

RUTH *(Wearily)* I guess that means people like Willy Harris.

WALTER Yes, people like Willy Harris.

RUTH *(With a sudden flash of impatience)* Why don't you all just hurry up and go into the banking business and stop talking about it!

WALTER Why? You want to know why? 'Cause we all tied up in a race of people that don't know how to do nothing but moan, pray and have babies!

(The line is too bitter even for him and he looks at her and sits down)

635 **RUTH** Oh, Walter . . . *(Softly)* Honey, why can't you stop fighting me?

WALTER *(Without thinking)* Who's fighting you? Who even cares about you?

(This line begins the retardation of his mood)

RUTH Well—*(She waits a long time, and then with resignation starts to put away her things)* I guess I might as well go on to bed . . . *(More or less to herself)* I don't know where we lost it . . . but we have . . . *(Then, to him)* I—I'm sorry about this new baby, Walter. I guess maybe I better go on and do what I started . . . I guess I just didn't realize how bad things was with us . . . I guess I just didn't really realize—*(She starts out to the bedroom and stops)* You want some hot milk?

WALTER   Hot milk?

RUTH   Yes—hot milk.

640 **WALTER**   Why hot milk?

RUTH   'Cause after all that liquor you come home with you ought to have something hot in your stomach.

WALTER   I don't want no milk.

RUTH   You want some coffee then?

WALTER   No, I don't want no coffee. I don't want nothing hot to drink. *(Almost plaintively)* Why you always trying to give me something to eat?

645 **RUTH**   *(Standing and looking at him helplessly)* What else can I give you, Walter Lee Younger?

(She stands and looks at him and presently turns to go out again. He lifts his head and watches her going away from him in a new mood which began to emerge when he asked her "Who cares about you?")

WALTER   It's been rough, ain't it, baby? *(She hears and stops but does not turn around and he continues to her back)* I guess between two people there ain't never as much understood as folks generally thinks there is. I mean like between me and you—*(She turns to face him)* How we gets to the place where we scared to talk softness to each other. *(He waits, thinking hard himself)* Why you think it got to be like that? *(He is thoughtful, almost as a child would be)* Ruth, what is it gets into people ought to be close?

RUTH   I don't know, honey. I think about it a lot.

WALTER   On account of you and me, you mean? The way things are with us. The way something done come down between us.

RUTH   There ain't so much between us, Walter . . . Not when you come to me and try to talk to me. Try to be with me . . . a little even.

650 **WALTER**   *(Total honesty)* Sometimes . . . sometimes . . . I don't even know how to try.

RUTH   Walter—

WALTER   Yes?

RUTH   *(Coming to him, gently and with misgiving, but coming to him)* Honey . . . life don't have to be like this. I mean sometimes people can do things so that things are better . . . You remember how we used to talk when Travis was born . . . about the way we were going to live . . . the kind of house . . . *(She is stroking his head)* Well, it's all starting to slip away from us . . .

(He turns her to him and they look at each other and kiss, tenderly and hungrily. The door opens and MAMA *enters—* WALTER *breaks away and jumps up. A beat)*

WALTER Mama, where have you been?

655 **MAMA** My—them steps is longer than they used to be. Whew! *(She sits down and ignores him)* How you feeling this evening, Ruth?

*(*RUTH *shrugs, disturbed at having been interrupted and watching her husband knowingly)*

WALTER Mama, where have you been all day?

MAMA *(Still ignoring him and leaning on the table and changing to more comfortable shoes)* Where's Travis?

RUTH I let him go out earlier and he ain't come back yet. Boy, is he going to get it!

WALTER Mama!

660 **MAMA** *(As if she has heard him for the first time)* Yes, son?

WALTER Where did you go this afternoon?

MAMA I went downtown to tend to some business that I had to tend to.

WALTER What kind of business?

MAMA You know better than to question me like a child, Brother.

665 **WALTER** *(Rising and bending over the table)* Where were you, Mama? *(Bringing his fists down and shouting)* Mama, you didn't go do something with that insurance money, something crazy?

(The front door opens slowly, interrupting him, and TRAVIS *peeks his head in, less than hopefully)*

TRAVIS *(To his mother)* Mama, I—

RUTH "Mama I" nothing! You're going to get it, boy! Get on in that bedroom and get yourself ready!

TRAVIS But I—

MAMA Why don't you all never let the child explain hisself.

670 **RUTH** Keep out of it now, Lena.

*(*MAMA *clamps her lips together, and* RUTH *advances toward her son menacingly)*

RUTH A thousand times I have told you not to go off like that—

MAMA *(Holding out her arms to her grandson)* Well—at least let me tell him something. I want him to be the first one to hear . . . Come here, Travis. *(The boy obeys, gladly)* Travis—*(She takes him by the shoulder and looks into his face)*—you know that money we got in the mail this morning?

TRAVIS Yes'm—

MAMA Well—what you think your grandmama gone and done with that money?

675 **TRAVIS** I don't know, Grandmama.

MAMA *(Putting her finger on his nose for emphasis).* She went out and she bought you a house! *(The explosion comes from WALTER at the end of the revelation and he jumps up and turns away from all of them in a fury. MAMA continues, to TRAVIS)* You glad about the house? It's going to be yours when you get to be a man.

TRAVIS Yeah—I always wanted to live in a house.

MAMA All right, gimme some sugar then—*(TRAVIS puts his arms around her neck as she watches her son over the boy's shoulder. Then, to TRAVIS, after the embrace)* Now when you say your prayers tonight, you thank God and your grandfather—'cause it was him who give you the house—in his way.

RUTH *(Taking the boy from MAMA and pushing him toward the bedroom)* Now you get out of here and get ready for your beating.

680 **TRAVIS** Aw, Mama—

RUTH Get on in there—*(Closing the door behind him and turning radiantly to her mother-in-law)* So you went and did it!

MAMA *(Quietly, looking at her son with pain)* Yes, I did.

RUTH *(Raising both arms classically)* PRAISE GOD! *(Looks at WALTER a moment, who says nothing. She crosses rapidly to her husband)* Please, honey—let me be glad . . . you be glad too. *(She has laid her hands on his shoulders, but he shakes himself free of her roughly, without turning to face her)* Oh Walter . . . a home . . . a home. *(She comes back to MAMA)* Well—where is it? How big is it? How much it going to cost?

MAMA Well—

685 **RUTH** When we moving?

MAMA *(Smiling at her)* First of the month.

RUTH *(Throwing back her head with jubilance)* Praise God!

MAMA *(Tentatively, still looking at her son's back turned against her and RUTH)* It's—it's a nice house too . . . *(She cannot help speaking directly to him. An imploring quality in her voice, her manner, makes her almost like a girl now)* Three bedrooms—nice big one

for you and Ruth. . . . Me and Beneatha still have to share our
room, but Travis have one of his own—and *(With difficulty)* I figure if the—new baby—is a boy, we could get one of them double-decker outfits . . . And there's a yard with a little patch of
dirt where I could maybe get to grow me a few flowers . . . And
a nice big basement . . .

RUTH Walter honey, be glad—

690 MAMA *(Still to his back, fingering things on the table)* 'Course I
don't want to make it sound fancier than it is . . . It's just a plain
little old house—but it's made good and solid—and it will be *ours.*
Walter Lee—it makes a difference in a man when he can walk
on floors that belong to *him* . . .

RUTH Where is it?

MAMA *(Frightened at this telling)* Well—well—it's out there in
Clybourne Park—

> *(*RUTH'S *radiance fades abruptly, and* WALTER *finally turns
> slowly to face his mother with incredulity and hostility)*

RUTH Where?

MAMA *(Matter-of-factly)* Four o six Clybourne Street, Clybourne Park.

695 RUTH Clybourne Park? Mama, there ain't no colored people living
in Clybourne Park.

MAMA *(Almost idiotically)* Well, I guess there's going to be some now.

WALTER *(Bitterly)* So that's the peace and comfort you went out and
bought for us today!

MAMA *(Raising her eyes to meet his finally)* Son—I just tried to find
the nicest place for the least amount of money for my family.

RUTH *(Trying to recover from the shock)* Well—well—'course I
ain't one never been 'fraid of no crackers, mind you—but—well,
wasn't there no other houses nowhere?

700 MAMA Them houses they put up for colored in them areas way
out all seem to cost twice as much as other houses. I did the best
I could.

RUTH *(Struck senseless with the news, in its various degrees of goodness and trouble, she sits a moment, her fists propping her chin in
thought, and then she starts to rise, bringing her fists down with
vigor, the radiance spreading from cheek to cheek again).* Well
—well!—All I can say is—if this is my time in life—MY TIME—
to say good-bye—(And she builds with momentum as she starts to
circle the room with an exuberant, almost tearfully happy*

release)—to these goddamned cracking walls!—*(She pounds, the walls)* —and these marching roaches!—*(She wipes at an imaginary army of marching roaches)*—and this cramped little closet which ain't now or never was no kitchen! . . . then I say it loud and good, HALLELUJAH! AND GOOD-BYE MISERY . . . I DON'T NEVER WANT TO SEE YOUR UGLY FACE AGAIN! *(She laughs joyously, having practically destroyed the apartment, and flings her arms up and lets them come down happily, slowly, reflectively, over her abdomen, aware for the first time perhaps that the life therein pulses with happiness and not despair)* Lena?

MAMA *(Moved, watching her happiness)* Yes, honey?

RUTH *(Looking off)* Is there—is there a whole lot of sunlight?

MAMA *(Understanding)* Yes, child, there's a whole lot of sunlight.

(Long pause)

705 **RUTH** *(Collecting herself and going to the door of the room* TRAVIS *is in)* Well—I guess I better see 'bout Travis. *(To* MAMA*)* Lord, I sure don't feel like whipping nobody today!

(She exits)

MAMA *(The mother and son are left alone now and the mother waits a long time, considering deeply, before she speaks)* Son—you— you understand what I done, don't you? *(*WALTER *is silent and sullen)* I—I just seen my family falling apart today . . . just falling to pieces in front of my eyes . . . We couldn't of gone on like we was today. We was going backwards 'stead of forwards—talking 'bout killing babies and wishing each other was dead . . . When it gets like that in life—you just got to do something different, push on out and do something bigger . . . *(She waits)* I wish you say something, son . . . I wish you'd say how deep inside you you think I done the right thing—

WALTER *(Crossing slowly to his bedroom door and finally turning there and speaking measuredly)* What you need me to say you done right for? You the head of this family. You run our lives like you want to. It was your money and you did what you wanted with it. So what you need for me to say it was all right for? *(Bitterly, to hurt her as deeply as he knows is possible)* So you butchered up a dream of mine—you—who always talking 'bout your children's dreams . . .

MAMA Walter Lee—

(He just closes the door behind. MAMA *sits alone, thinking heavily)*

Curtain

Scene Two

Time: Friday night. A few weeks later.
At rise: Packing crates mark the intention of the family to move.
BENEATHA *and* GEORGE *come in, presumably from an evening out again.*

GEORGE   O.K. . . . O.K., whatever you say . . . *(They both sit on the couch. He tries to kiss her. She moves away)* Look, we've had a nice evening; let's not spoil it, huh? . . .

(He again turns her head and tries to nuzzle in and she turns away from him, not with distaste but with momentary lack of interest; in a mood to pursue what they were talking about)

710 **BENEATHA**   I'm *trying* to talk to you.
GEORGE   We always talk.
BENEATHA   Yes—and I love to talk.
GEORGE   *(Exasperated; rising)* I know it and I don't mind it some-times . . . I want you to cut it out, see—The moody stuff, I mean. I don't like it. You're a nice-looking girl . . . all over. That's all you need, honey, forget the atmosphere. Guys aren't going to go for the atmosphere—they're going to go for what they see. Be glad for that. Drop the Garbo routine. It doesn't go with you. As for myself, I want a nice—*(Groping)*—simple *(Thoughtfully)*—sophisticated girl . . . not a poet—O.K.?

(He starts to kiss her, she rebuffs him again and he jumps up)

BENEATHA   Why are you angry, George?
715 **GEORGE**   Because this is stupid! I don't go out with you to discuss the nature of "quiet desperation" or to hear all about your thoughts—because the world will go on thinking what it thinks regardless—
BENEATHA   Then why read books? Why go to school?
GEORGE   *(With artificial patience, counting on his fingers)* It's sim-ple. You read books—to learn facts—to get grades—to pass the

course—to get a degree. That's all—it has nothing to do with thoughts.

(A long pause)

BENEATHA I see. *(He starts to sit)* Good night, George.

*(*GEORGE *looks at her a little oddly, and starts to exit. He meets* MAMA *coming in)*

GEORGE Oh—hello, Mrs. Younger.

720 **MAMA** Hello, George, how you feeling?

GEORGE Fine—fine, how are you?

MAMA Oh, a little tired. You know them steps can get you after a day's work. You all have a nice time tonight?

GEORGE Yes—a fine time. A fine time.

MAMA Well, good night.

725 **GEORGE** Good night. *(He exits.* MAMA *closes the door behind her)* Hello, honey. What you sitting like that for?

BENEATHA I'm just sitting.

MAMA Didn't you have a nice time?

BENEATHA No.

MAMA No? What's the matter?

730 **BENEATHA** Mama, George is a fool—honest. *(She rises)*

MAMA *(Hustling around unloading the packages she has entered with. She stops)* Is he, baby?

BENEATHA Yes.

*(*BENEATHA *makes up* TRAVIS' *bed as she talks)*

MAMA You sure?

BENEATHA Yes.

735 **MAMA** Well—I guess you better not waste your time with no fools.

*(*BENEATHA *looks up at her mother, watching her put groceries in the refrigerator. Finally she gathers up her things and starts into the bedroom. At the door she stops and looks back at her mother)*

BENEATHA Mama—

MAMA Yes, baby—

BENEATHA Thank you.

MAMA For what?

740 **BENEATHA** For understanding me this time.

(She exits quickly and the mother stands, smiling a little, looking at the place where BENEATHA just stood. RUTH enters)

RUTH Now don't you fool with any of this stuff, Lena—
MAMA Oh, I just thought I'd sort a few things out. Is Brother here?
RUTH Yes.
MAMA *(With concern)* Is he—
745 **RUTH** *(Reading her eyes)* Yes.

(MAMA is silent and someone knocks on the door. MAMA and RUTH exchange weary and knowing glances and RUTH opens it to admit the neighbor, MRS. JOHNSON,* who is a rather squeaky wide-eyed lady of no particular age, with a newspaper under her arm)

MAMA *(Changing her expression to acute delight and a ringing cheerful greeting)* Oh—hello there, Johnson.
JOHNSON *(This is a woman who decided long ago to be enthusiastic about EVERYTHING in life and she is inclined to wave her wrist vigorously at the height of her exclamatory comments)* Hello there, yourself! H'you this evening, Ruth?
RUTH *(Not much of a deceptive type)* Fine, Mis' Johnson, h'you?
JOHNSON Fine. *(Reaching out quickly, playfully, and patting RUTH'S stomach)* Ain't you starting to poke out none yet! *(She mugs with delight at the overfamiliar remark and her eyes dart around looking at the crates and packing preparation; MAMA'S face is a cold sheet of endurance)*. Oh, ain't we getting ready 'round here, though! Yessir! Lookathere! I'm telling you the Youngers is really getting ready to "move on up a little higher!"—Bless God!
750 **MAMA** *(A little drily, doubting the total sincerity of the Blesser)* Bless God.
JOHNSON He's good, ain't He?
MAMA Oh yes, He's good.
JOHNSON I mean sometimes He works in mysterious ways . . . but He works, don't He!
MAMA *(The same)* Yes, he does.
755 **JOHNSON** I'm just soooooo happy for y'all. And this here child— *(About RUTH)* looks like she could just pop open with happiness, don't she. Where's all the rest of the family?

---

*This character and the scene of her visit were cut from the original production and early editions of the play.

MAMA Bennie's gone to bed—

JOHNSON Ain't no . . . *(The implication is pregnancy)* sickness done hit you—I hope . . . ?

MAMA No—she just tired. She was out this evening.

JOHNSON *(All is a coo, an emphatic coo)* Aw—ain't that lovely. She still going out with the little Murchison boy?

760 **MAMA** *(Drily)* Ummmm huh.

JOHNSON That's lovely. You sure got lovely children, Younger. Me and Isaiah talks all the time 'bout what fine children you was blessed with. We sure do.

MAMA Ruth, give Mis' Johnson a piece of sweet potato pie and some milk.

JOHNSON Oh honey, I can't stay hardly a minute—I just dropped in to see if there was anything I could do. *(Accepting the food easily)* I guess y'all seen the news what's all over the colored paper this week . . .

MAMA No—didn't get mine yet this week.

765 **JOHNSON** *(Lifting her head and blinking with the spirit of catastrophe)* You mean you ain't read 'bout them colored people that was bombed out their place out there?

> *(*RUTH *straightens with concern and takes the paper and reads it.* JOHNSON *notices her and feeds commentary)*

JOHNSON Ain't it something how bad these here white folks is getting here in Chicago! Lord, getting so you think you right down in Mississippi! *(With a tremendous and rather insincere sense of melodrama)* 'Course I thinks it's wonderful how our folks keeps on pushing out. You hear some of these Negroes 'round here talking 'bout how they don't go where they ain't wanted and all that— but not me, honey! *(This is a lie)* Wilhemenia Othella Johnson goes anywhere, any time she feels like it! *(With head movement for emphasis)* Yes I do! Why if we left it up to these here crackers, the poor niggers wouldn't have nothing—*(She clasps her hand, over her mouth)* Oh, I always forgets you don't 'low that word in your house.

MAMA *(Quietly, looking at her)* No—I don't 'low it.

JOHNSON *(Vigorously again)* Me neither! I was just telling Isaiah yesterday when he come using it in front of me—I said, "Isaiah, it's just like Mis' Younger says all the time—"

MAMA Don't you want some more pie?

770 **JOHNSON** No—no thank you; this was lovely. I got to get on over home and have my midnight coffee. I hear some people say it don't let them sleep but I finds I can't close my eyes right lessen I done had that laaaast cup of coffee . . . *(She waits. A beat. Undaunted)* My Goodnight coffee, I calls it!

MAMA *(With much eye-rolling and communication between herself and* RUTH*)* Ruth, why don't you give Mis' Johnson some coffee.

*(*RUTH *gives* MAMA *an unpleasant look for her kindness)*

JOHNSON *(Accepting the coffee)* Where's Brother tonight?

MAMA He's lying down.

JOHNSON Mmmmmm, he sure gets his beauty rest, don't he? Good-looking man. Sure is a good-looking man! *(Reaching out to pat* RUTH'S *stomach again)* I guess that's how come we keep on having babies around here. *(She winks at* MAMA*)* One thing 'bout Brother, he always know how to have a *good* time. And soooooo ambitious! I bet it was his idea y'all moving out to Clybourne Park. Lord—I bet this time next month y'all's names will have been in the papers plenty—*(Holding up her hands to mark off each word of the headline she can see in front of her)* "NEGROES INVADE CLYBOURNE PARK—BOMBED!"

775 **MAMA** *(She and* RUTH *look at the woman in amazement)* We ain't exactly moving out there to get bombed.

JOHNSON Oh, honey—you know I'm praying to God every day that don't nothing like that happen! But you have to think of life like it is—and these here Chicago peckerwoods is some baaaad peckerwoods.

MAMA *(Wearily)* We done thought about all that Mis' Johnson.

*(*BENEATHA *comes out of the bedroom in her robe and passes through to the bathroom.* MRS. JOHNSON *turns)*

JOHNSON Hello there, Bennie!

BENEATHA *(Crisply)* Hello, Mrs. Johnson.

780 **JOHNSON** How is school?

BENEATHA *(Crisply)* Fine, thank you. *(She goes out.)*

JOHNSON *(Insulted)* Getting so she don't have much to say to nobody.

MAMA The child was on her way to the bathroom.

JOHNSON I know—but sometimes she act like ain't got time to pass the time of day with nobody ain't been to college. Oh—I ain't criticizing her none. It's just—you know how some of our young people gets when they get a little education. *(*MAMA *and* RUTH *say nothing, just look at her)* Yes—well. Well, I guess I better get on home. *(Unmoving)* 'Course I can understand how she must be proud and everything—being the only one in the family to make something of herself. I know just being a chauffeur ain't never satisfied Brother none. He shouldn't feel like that, though. Ain't nothing wrong with being a chauffeur.

785 **MAMA** There's plenty wrong with it.

JOHNSON What?

MAMA Plenty. My husband always said being any kind of a servant wasn't a fit thing for a man to have to be. He always said a man's hands was made to make things, or to turn the earth with—not to drive nobody's car for 'em—or—*(She looks at her own hands)* carry they slop jars. And my boy is just like him—he wasn't meant to wait on nobody.

JOHNSON *(Rising, somewhat offended)* Mmmmmmmmm. The Youngers is too much for me! *(She looks around)* You sure one proud-acting bunch of colored folks. Well—I always thinks like Booker T. Washington said that time—"Education has spoiled many a good plow hand"—

MAMA Is that what old Booker T. said?

790 **JOHNSON** He sure did.

MAMA Well, it sounds just like him. The fool.

JOHNSON *(Indignantly)* Well—he was one of our great men.

MAMA Who said so?

JOHNSON *(Nonplussed)* You know, me and you ain't never agreed about some things, Lena Younger. I guess I better be going—

795 **RUTH** *(Quickly)* Good night.

JOHNSON Good night. Oh—*(Thrusting it at her)* You can keep the paper! *(With a trill)* 'Night.

MAMA Good night, Mis' Johnson.

*(*MRS. JOHNSON *exits)*

RUTH If ignorance was gold . . .

MAMA Shush. Don't talk about folks behind their backs.

800 **RUTH** You do.

MAMA I'm old and corrupted. (BENEATHA *enters)* You was rude to Mis' Johnson, Beneatha, and I don't like it at all.

BENEATHA *(At her door)* Mama, if there are two things we, as a people, have got to overcome, one is the Ku Klux Klan—and the other is Mrs. Johnson. *(She exits)*

MAMA Smart aleck.

(The phone rings)

RUTH I'll get it.

805 **MAMA** Lord, ain't this a popular place tonight.

RUTH *(At the phone)* Hello—Just a minute. *(Goes to door)* Walter, it's Mrs. Arnold. *(Waits. Goes back to the phone. Tense)* Hello. Yes, this is his wife speaking . . . He's lying down now. Yes . . . well, he'll be in tomorrow. He's been very sick. Yes—I know we should have called, but we were so sure he'd be able to come in today. Yes—yes, I'm very sorry. Yes . . . Thank you very much. *(She hangs up.* WALTER *is standing in the doorway of the bedroom behind her)* That was Mrs. Arnold.

WALTER *(Indifferently)* Was it?

RUTH She said if you don't come in tomorrow that they are getting a new man . . .

WALTER Ain't that sad—ain't that crying sad.

810 **RUTH** She said Mr. Arnold has had to take a cab for three days . . . Walter, you ain't been to work for three days! *(This is a revelation to her)* Where you been, Walter Lee Younger? *(*WALTER *looks at her and starts to laugh)* You're going to lose your job.

WALTER That's right . . . *(He turns on the radio)*

RUTH Oh, Walter, and with your mother working like a dog every day—

(A steamy, deep blues pours into the room)

WALTER That's sad too—Everything is sad.

MAMA What you been doing for these three days, son?

815 **WALTER** Mama—you don't know all the things a man what got leisure can find to do in this city . . . What's this—Friday night? Well—Wednesday I borrowed Willy Harris' car and I went for a drive . . . just me and myself and I drove and drove . . . Way out . . . way past South Chicago, and I parked the car and I sat and looked at the steel mills all day long. I just sat in the car and looked at them big black chimneys for hours. Then I drove back and I went to the Green Hat. *(Pause)* And Thursday—Thursday I borrowed the car again and I got in it and I pointed it the other way and I drove the other way—for hours—way, way up to Wisconsin, and I looked at the farms. I just drove and looked at the farms. Then I drove back and I went to the Green Hat. *(Pause)* And today—today I didn't get the car. Today I just walked. All

over the Southside. And I looked at the Negroes, and they looked at me and finally I just sat down on the curb at Thirty-ninth and South Parkway and I just sat there and watched the Negroes go by. And then I went to the Green Hat. You all sad? You all depressed? And you know where I am going right now—

(RUTH *goes out quietly*)

MAMA Oh, Big Walter, is this the harvest of our days?

WALTER You know what I like about the Green Hat? I like this lit-tle cat they got there who blows a sax . . . He blows. He talks to me. He ain't but 'bout five feet tall and he's got a conked head and his eyes is always closed and he's all music—

MAMA *(Rising and getting some papers out of her handbag)* Walter—

WALTER And there's this other guy who plays the piano . . . and they got a sound. I mean they can work on some music . . . They got the best little combo in the world in the Green Hat . . . You can just sit there and drink and listen to them three men play and you realize that don't nothing matter worth a damn, but just being there—

820 **MAMA** I've helped do it to you, haven't I, son? Walter I been wrong.

WALTER Naw—you ain't never been wrong about nothing, Mama.

MAMA Listen to me, now. I say I been wrong, son. That I been doing to you what the rest of the world been doing to you. *(She turns off the radio)* Walter—*(She stops and he looks up slowly at her and she meets his eyes pleadingly)* What you ain't never under-stood is that I ain't got nothing, don't own nothing, ain't never really wanted nothing that wasn't for you. There ain't nothing as precious to me . . . There ain't nothing worth holding on to, money, dreams, nothing else—if it means—if it means it's going to destroy my boy. *(She takes an envelope out of her handbag and puts it in front of him and he watches her without speaking or moving)* I paid the man thirty-five hundred dollars down on the house. That leaves sixty-five hundred dollars. Monday morning I want you to take this money and take three thousand dollars and put it in a savings account for Beneatha's medical schooling. The rest you put in a checking account—with your name on it. And from now on any penny that come out of it or that go in it is for you to look after. For you to decide. *(She drops her hands a lit-tle helplessly)* It ain't much, but it's all I got in the world and I'm putting it in your hands. I'm telling you to be the head of this fam-ily from now on like you supposed to be.

WALTER *(Stares at the money)* You trust me like that, Mama?

MAMA I ain't never stop trusting you. Like I ain't never stop loving you.

(She goes out, and WALTER *sits looking at the money on the table. Finally, in a decisive gesture, he gets up, and, in mingled joy and desperation, picks up the money. At the same moment,* TRAVIS *enters for bed)*

825 **TRAVIS** What's the matter, Daddy? You drunk?

WALTER *(Sweetly, more sweetly than we have ever known him)* No, Daddy ain't drunk. Daddy ain't going to never be drunk again. . . .

TRAVIS Well, good night, Daddy.

(The FATHER *has come from behind the couch and leans over, embracing his son)*

WALTER Son, I feel like talking to you tonight.

TRAVIS About what?

830 **WALTER** Oh, about a lot of things. About you and what kind of man you going to be when you grow up. . . . Son—son, what do you want to be when you grow up?

TRAVIS A bus driver.

WALTER *(Laughing a little)* A what? Man, that ain't nothing to want to be!

TRAVIS Why not?

WALTER 'Cause, man—it ain't big enough—you know what I mean.

835 **TRAVIS** I don't know then. I can't make up my mind. Sometimes Mama asks me that too. And sometimes when I tell her I just want to be like you—she says she don't want me to be like that and sometimes she says she does. . . .

WALTER *(Gathering him up in his arms)* You know what, Travis? In seven years you going to be seventeen years old. And things is going to be very different with us in seven years, Travis. . . . One day when you are seventeen I'll come home—home from my office downtown somewhere—

TRAVIS You don't work in no office, Daddy.

WALTER No—but after tonight. After what your daddy gonna do tonight, there's going to be offices—a whole lot of offices. . . .

TRAVIS What you gonna do tonight, Daddy?

840 **WALTER** You wouldn't understand yet, son, but your daddy's gonna make a transaction . . . a business transaction that's going to change

our lives. . . . That's how come one day when you 'bout seventeen years old I'll come home and I'll be pretty tired, you know what I mean, after a day of conferences and secretaries getting things wrong the way they do . . . 'cause an executive's life is hell, man— *(The more he talks the farther away he gets)* And I'll pull the car up on the driveway . . . just a plain black Chrysler, I think, with white walls—no—black tires. More elegant. Rich people don't have to be flashy . . . though I'll have to get something a little sportier for Ruth—maybe a Cadillac convertible to do her shopping in. . . . And I'll come up the steps to the house and the gardener will be clipping away at the hedges and he'll say, "Good evening, Mr. Younger." And I'll say, "Hello, Jefferson, how are you this evening?!" And I'll go inside and Ruth will come downstairs and meet me at the door and we'll kiss each other and she'll take my arm and we'll go up to your room to see you sitting on the floor with the catalogues of all the great schools in America around you. . . . All the great schools in the world! And—and I'll say, all right son—it's your seventeenth birthday, what is it you've decided? . . . Just tell me where you want to go to school and you'll *go*. Just tell me, what it is you want to be—and you'll *be* it. . . . Whatever you want to be—Yessir! *(He holds his arms open for* TRAVIS*)* You just name it, son . . . *(*TRAVIS *leaps into them)* and I hand you the world!

*(*WALTER'S *voice has risen in pitch and hysterical promise and on the last line he lifts* TRAVIS *high)*

Blackout

Scene Three

Time: Saturday, moving day, one week later.

Before the curtain rises, RUTH'S *voice, a strident, dramatic church alto, cuts through the silence.*

It is, in the darkness, a triumphant surge, a penetrating statement of expectation: "Oh, Lord, I don't feel no ways tired! Children, oh, glory hallelujah!"

As the curtain rises we see that RUTH *is alone in the living room, finishing up the family's packing. It is moving day. She is nailing crates and tying cartons.* BENEATHA *enters, carrying a guitar case, and watches her exuberant sister-in-law.*

RUTH Hey!

BENEATHA *(Putting away the case)* Hi.

RUTH *(Pointing at a package)* Honey—look in that package there and see what I found on sale this morning at the South Center. *(RUTH gets up and moves to the package and draws out some curtains)* Lookahere—handturned hems!

BENEATHA How do you know the window size out there?

845 **RUTH** *(Who hadn't thought of that)* Oh—Well, they bound to fit something in the whole house. Anyhow, they was too good a bargain to pass up. *(RUTH slaps her head, suddenly remembering something)* Oh, Bennie—I meant to put a special note on that carton over there. That's your mama's good china and she wants 'em to be very careful with it.

BENEATHA I'll do it.

(BENEATHA finds a piece of paper and starts to draw large letters on it)

RUTH You know what I'm going to do soon as I get in that new house?

BENEATHA What?

RUTH Honey—I'm going to run me a tub of water up to here . . . *(With her fingers practically up to her nostrils)* And I'm going to get in it—and I am going to sit . . . and sit . . . and sit in that hot water and the first person who knocks to tell me to hurry up and come out—

850 **BENEATHA** Gets shot at sunrise.

RUTH *(Laughing happily)* You said it, sister! *(Noticing how large* BENEATHA *is absent-mindedly making the note)* Honey, they ain't going to read that from no airplane.

BENEATHA *(Laughing herself)* I guess I always think things have more emphasis if they are big, somehow.

RUTH *(Looking up at her and smiling)* You and your brother seem to have that as a philosophy of life. Lord, that man—done changed so 'round here. You know—you know what we did last night? Me and Walter Lee?

BENEATHA What?

855 **RUTH** *(Smiling to herself)* We went to the movies. *(Looking at* BENEATHA *to see if she understands)* We went to the movies. You know the last time me and Walter went to the movies together?

BENEATHA No.

RUTH   Me neither. That's how long it been. *(Smiling again)* But we went last night. The picture wasn't much good, but that didn't seem to matter. We went—and we held hands.

BENEATHA   Oh, Lord!

RUTH   We held hands—and you know what?

860 **BENEATHA**   What?

RUTH   When we come out of the show it was late and dark and all the stores and things was closed up . . . and it was kind of chilly and there wasn't many people on the streets . . . and we was still holding hands, me and Walter.

BENEATHA   You're killing me.

> *(WALTER enters with a large package. His happiness is deep in him; he cannot keep still with his newfound exuberance. He is singing and wiggling and snapping his fingers. He puts his package in a corner and puts a phonograph record, which he has brought in with him, on the record player. As the music, soulful and sensuous, comes up he dances over to* RUTH *and tries to get her to dance with him. She gives in at last to his raunchiness and in a fit of giggling allows herself to be drawn into his mood. They dip and she melts into his arms in a classic, body-melding "slow drag")*

BENEATHA   *(Regarding them a long time as they dance, then drawing in her breath for a deeply exaggerated comment which she does not particularly mean)* Talk about—oldddddddddd-fashionedddddddd—Negroes!

WALTER   *(Stopping momentarily)* What kind of Negroes? *(He says this in fun. He is not angry with her today, nor with anyone. He starts to dance with his wife again)*

865 **BENEATHA**   Old-fashioned.

WALTER   *(As he dances with* RUTH*)* You know, when these New Negroes have their convention—*(Pointing at his sister)*—that is going to be the chairman of the Committee on Unending Agitation. *(He goes on dancing, then stops)* Race, race, race! . . . Girl, I do believe you are the first person in the history of the entire human race to successfully brainwash yourself. *(*BENEATHA *breaks up and he goes on dancing. He stops again, enjoying his tease)* Damn, even the N double A C P takes a holiday sometimes! *(*BENEATHA *and* RUTH *laugh. He dances with* RUTH *some more and starts to laugh and stops and pantomimes someone over an operating table).* I can just see that chick someday looking down at some poor cat on an operating table and before she starts to slice him, she says . . . *(Pulling his sleeves back maliciously)* "By the way, what are your views on civil rights down there? . . . "

(He laughs at her again and starts to dance happily. The bell sounds)

BENEATHA Sticks and stones may break my bones but . . . words will never hurt me!

*(*BENEATHA *goes to the door and opens it as* WALTER *and* RUTH *go on with the clowning.* BENEATHA *is somewhat surprised to see a quiet-looking middle-aged white man in a business suit holding his hat and a briefcase in his hand and consulting a small piece of paper)*

MAN Uh—how do you do, miss. I am looking for a Mrs.—*(He looks at the slip of paper)* Mrs. Lena Younger? *(He stops short, struck dumb at the sight of the oblivious* WALTER *and* RUTH*)*

BENEATHA *(Smoothing her hair with slight embarrassment)* Oh— yes, that's my mother. Excuse me *(She closes the door and turns to quiet the other two)* Ruth! Brother! *(Enunciating precisely but soundlessly: "There's a white man at the door!")* They stop dancing, RUTH *cuts off the phonograph,* BENEATHA *opens the door. The man casts a curious quick glance at all of them)* Uh—come in please.

870 **MAN** *(Coming in)* Thank you.

BENEATHA My mother isn't here just now. Is it business?

MAN Yes . . . well, of a sort.

WALTER *(Freely, the Man of the House)* Have a seat. I'm Mrs. Younger's son. I look after most of her business matters.

*(*RUTH *and* BENEATHA *exchange amused glances)*

MAN *(Regarding* WALTER, *and sitting)* Well—My name is Karl Lindner . . .

875 **WALTER** *(Stretching out his hand)* Walter Younger. This is my wife—*(*RUTH *nods politely)*—and my sister.

LINDNER How do you do.

WALTER *(Amiably, as he sits himself easily on a chair, leaning forward on his knees with interest and looking expectantly into the newcomer's face)* What can do for you, Mr. Lindner!

LINDNER *(Some minor shuffling of the hat and briefcase on his knees)* Well—I am a representative of the Clybourne Park Improvement Association—

WALTER *(Pointing)* Why don't you sit your things on the floor?

880 **LINDNER** Oh—yes. Thank you. *(He slides the briefcase and hat under the chair)* And as I was saying—I am from the Clybourne Park Improvement Association and we have had it brought to our attention at the last meeting that you people—or at least your mother—has bought a piece of residential property at—*(He digs for the slip of paper again)*—four o six Clybourne Street . . .

WALTER That's right. Care for something to drink? Ruth, get Mr. Lindner a beer.

LINDNER *(Upset for some reason)* Oh—no, really. I mean thank you very much, but no thank you.

RUTH *(Innocently)* Some coffee?

LINDNER Thank you, nothing at all.

*(*BENEATHA *is watching the man carefully)*

885 **LINDNER** Well, I don't know how much you folks know about our organization. *(He is a gentle man; thoughtful and somewhat labored in his manner)* It is one of these community organizations set up to look after—oh, you know, things like block upkeep and special projects and we also have what we call our New Neighbors Orientation Committee . . .

BENEATHA *(Drily)* Yes—and what do they do?

LINDNER *(Turning a little to her and then returning the main force to* WALTER*)* Well—it's what you might call a sort of welcoming committee, I guess. I mean they, we—I'm the chairman of the committee—go around and see the new people who move into the neighborhood and sort of give them the lowdown on the way we do things out in Clybourne Park.

BENEATHA *(With appreciation of the two meanings, which escape* RUTH *and* WALTER*)* Un-huh.

LINDNER And we also have the category of what the association calls— *(He looks elsewhere)*—uh—special community problems . . .

890 **BENEATHA** Yes—and what are some of those?

WALTER Girl, let the man talk.

LINDNER *(With understated relief)* Thank you. I would sort of like to explain this thing in my own way. I mean I want to explain to you in a certain way.

WALTER Go ahead.

LINDNER Yes. Well. I'm going to try to get right to the point. I'm sure we'll all appreciate that in the long run.

895 **BENEATHA** Yes.

WALTER Be still now!

LINDNER Well—

RUTH *(Still innocently)* Would you like another chair—you don't look comfortable.

LINDNER *(More frustrated than annoyed)* No, thank you very much. Please. Well—to get right to the point I—*(A great breath, and he is off at last)* I am sure you people must be aware of some of the incidents which have happened in various parts of the city when colored people have moved into certain areas—*(BENEATHA exhales heavily and starts tossing a piece of fruit up and down in the air)* Well—because we have what I think is going to be a unique type of organization in American community life—not only do we deplore that kind of thing—but we are trying to do something about it. *(BENEATHA stops tossing and turns with a new and quizzical interest to the man)* We feel—*(gaining confidence in his mission because of the interest in the faces of the people he is talking to)*—we feel that most of the trouble in this world, when you come right down to it—*(He hits his knee for emphasis)*—most of the trouble exists because people just don't sit down and talk to each other.

900 **RUTH** *(Nodding as she might in church, pleased with the remark)* You can say that again, mister.

LINDNER *(More encouraged by such affirmation).* That we don't try hard enough in this world to understand the other fellow's problem. The other guy's point of view.

RUTH Now that's right.

(BENEATHA and WALTER merely watch and listen with genuine interest)

LINDNER Yes—that's the way we feel out in Clybourne Park. And that's why I was elected to come here this afternoon and talk to you people. Friendly like, you know, the way people should talk to each other and see if we couldn't find some way to work this thing out. As I say, the whole business is a matter of *caring* about the other fellow. Anybody can see that you are a nice family of folks, hard working and honest I'm sure. (BENEATHA *frowns slightly, quizzically, her head tilted regarding him)* Today everybody knows what it means to be on the outside of *something*. And of course, there is always somebody who is out to take advantage of people who don't always understand.

WALTER What do you mean?

905 **LINDNER** Well—you see our community is made up of people who've worked hard as the dickens for years to build up that little community. They're not rich and fancy people; just hard-working, honest people who don't really have much but those little homes and a dream of the kind of community they want to raise their children in. Now, I don't say we are perfect and there is a lot wrong in some of the things they want. But you've got to admit that a man, right or wrong, has the right to want to have the neighborhood he lives in a certain kind of way. And at the moment the overwhelming majority of our people out there feel that people get along better, take more of a common interest in the life of the community, when they share a common background. I want you to believe me when I tell you that race prejudice simply doesn't enter into it. It is a matter of the people of Clybourne Park believing, rightly or wrongly, as I say, that for the happiness of all concerned that our Negro families are happier when they live in their *own* communities.

BENEATHA *(With a grand and bitter gesture)* This, friends, is the Welcoming Committee!

WALTER *(Dumbfounded, looking at* LINDNER*)* Is this what you came marching all the way over here to tell us?

LINDNER Well, now we've been having a fine conversation. I hope you'll hear me all the way through.

WALTER *(Tightly)* Go ahead, man.

910 **LINDNER** You see—in the face of all the things I have said, we are prepared to make your family a very generous offer . . .

BENEATHA Thirty pieces and not a coin less!

WALTER Yeah?

LINDNER *(Putting on his glasses and drawing a form out of the briefcase)* Our association is prepared, through the collective effort of our people, to buy the house from you at a financial gain to your family.

RUTH Lord have mercy, ain't this the living gall!

915 **WALTER** All right, you through?

LINDNER Well, I want to give you the exact terms of the financial arrangement—

WALTER We don't want to hear no exact terms of no arrangements. I want to know if you got any more to tell us 'bout getting together?

LINDNER *(Taking off his glasses)* Well—I don't suppose that you feel . . .

WALTER Never mind how I feel—you got any more to say 'bout how people ought to sit down and talk to each other? . . . Get out of my house, man.

(He turns his back and walks to the door)

920 **LINDNER** *(Looking around at the hostile faces and reaching and assembling his hat and briefcase)* Well—I don't understand why you people are reacting this way. What do you think you are going to gain by moving into a neighborhood where you just aren't wanted and where some elements—well—people can get awful worked up when they feel that their whole way of life and everything they've ever worked for is threatened.

WALTER Get out.

LINDNER *(At the door, holding a small card)* Well—I'm sorry it went like this.

WALTER Get out.

LINDNER *(Almost sadly regarding* WALTER*)* You just can't force people to change their hearts, son.

(He turns and put his card on a table and exits. WALTER *pushes the door to with stinging hatred, and stands looking at it.* RUTH *just sits and* BENEATHA *just stands. They say nothing.* MAMA *and* TRAVIS *enter)*

925 **MAMA** Well—this all the packing got done since I left out of here this morning. I testify before God that my children got all the energy of the *dead!* What time the moving men due?

BENEATHA Four o'clock. You had a caller, Mama.

(She is smiling, teasingly)

MAMA Sure enough—who?

BENEATHA *(Her arms folded saucily)* The Welcoming Committee.

*(*WALTER *and* RUTH *giggle)*

MAMA *(Innocently)* Who?

930 **BENEATHA** The Welcoming Committee. They said they're sure going to be glad to see you when you get there.

WALTER *(Devilishly)* Yeah, they said they can't hardly wait to see your face.

(Laughter)

MAMA *(Sensing their facetiousness)* What's the matter with you all?

WALTER Ain't nothing the matter with us. We just telling you 'bout the gentleman who came to see you this afternoon. From the Clybourne Park Improvement Association.

MAMA What he want?

935 **RUTH** *(In the same mood as* BENEATHA *and* WALTER*)* To welcome you, honey.

WALTER He said they can't hardly wait. He said the one thing they don't have, that they just *dying* to have out there is a fine family of fine colored people! *(To* RUTH *and* BENEATHA*)* Ain't that right!

RUTH *(Mockingly)* Yeah! He left his card—

BENEATHA *(Handing card to* MAMA*)* In case.

*(*MAMA *reads and throws it on the floor—understanding and looking off as she draws her chair up to the table on which she has put her plant and some sticks and some cord)*

MAMA Father, give us strength. *(Knowingly—and without fun)* Did he threaten us?

940 **BENEATHA** Oh—Mama—they don't do it like that any more. He talked Brotherhood. He said everybody ought to learn how to sit down and hate each other with good Christian fellowship.

(She and WALTER *shake hands to ridicule the remark)*

MAMA *(Sadly)* Lord, protect us . . .

RUTH You should hear the money those folks raised to buy the house from us. All we paid and then some.

BENEATHA What they think we going to do—eat 'em?

RUTH No, honey, marry 'em.

945 **MAMA** *(Shaking her head)* Lord, Lord, Lord . . .

RUTH Well—that's the way the crackers crumble. *(A beat)* Joke.

BENEATHA *(Laughingly noticing what her mother is doing)* Mama, what are you doing?

MAMA Fixing my plant so it won't get hurt none on the way . . .

BENEATHA Mama, you going to take *that* to the new house?

950 **MAMA** Un-huh—

BENEATHA That raggedy-looking old thing?

MAMA *(Stopping and looking at her)* It expresses ME!

RUTH *(With delight, to* BENEATHA*)* So there, Miss Thing! *(*WALTER *comes to* MAMA *suddenly and bends down behind her and squeezes her in his arms with all his strength. She is overwhelmed by the suddenness of it and, though delighted, her manner is like that of* RUTH *and* TRAVIS*)*

MAMA Look out now, boy! You make me mess up my thing here!

955 **WALTER** *(His face lit, he slips down on his knees beside her, his arms still about her)* Mama . . . you know what it means to climb up in the chariot?

MAMA *(Gruffly, very happy)* Get on away from me now . . .

RUTH *(Near the gift-wrapped package, trying to catch* WALTER's *eye)* Psst—

WALTER What the old song say, Mama . . .

RUTH Walter—Now?

(She is pointing at the package)

960 **WALTER** *(Speaking the lines, sweetly, playfully, in his mother's face)* I got wings . . . you got wings . . .
All God's children got wings . . .

MAMA Boy—get out of my face and do some work . . .

WALTER When I get to heaven gonna put on my wings,
Gonna fly all over God's heaven . . .

BENEATHA *(Teasingly, from across the room)* Everybody talking 'bout heaven ain't going there!

WALTER *(To* RUTH, *who is carrying the box across to them)* I don't know, you think we ought to give her that . . . Seems to me she ain't been very appreciative around here.

MAMA *(Eyeing the box, which is obviously a gift)* What is that?

965 **WALTER** *(Taking it from* RUTH *and putting it on the table in front of* MAMA) Well—what you all think? Should we give it to her?

RUTH Oh—she was pretty good today.

MAMA I'll good you—

(She turns her eyes to the box again)

BENEATHA Open it, Mama.

(She stands up, looks at it, turns and looks at all of them, and then presses her hands together and does not open the package)

WALTER *(Sweetly)* Open it, Mama. It's for you. (MAMA *looks in his eyes. It is the first present in her life without its being Christmas. Slowly she opens her package and lifts out, one by one, a brand-new sparkling set of gardening tools.* WALTER *continues, prodding)* Ruth made up the note—read it . . .

970 **MAMA** *(Picking up the card and adjusting her glasses)* "To our own Mrs. Miniver—Love from Brother, Ruth and Beneatha." Ain't that lovely . . .

TRAVIS *(Tugging at his father's sleeve)* Daddy, can I give her mine now?

WALTER All right, son. *(TRAVIS flies to get his gift)*

MAMA Now I don't have to use my knives and forks no more . . .

WALTER Travis didn't want to go in with the rest of us, Mama. He got his own. *(Somewhat amused)* We don't know what it is . . .

975 **TRAVIS** *(Racing back in the room with a large hatbox and putting it in front of his grandmother)* Here!

MAMA Lord have mercy, baby. You done gone and bought your grandmother a hat?

TRAVIS *(very proud)* Open it!

(She does and lifts out an elaborate, but very elaborate, wide gardening hat, and all the adults break up at the sight of it)

RUTH Travis, honey, what is that?

TRAVIS *(Who thinks it is beautiful and appropriate)* It's a gardening hat! Like the ladies always have on in the magazines when they work in their gardens.

980 **BENEATHA** *(Giggling fiercely)* Travis—we were trying to make Mama Mrs. Miniver—not Scarlett O'Hara!

MAMA *(Indignantly)* What's the matter with you all! This here is a beautiful hat! *(Absurdly)* I always wanted me one just like it!

(She pops it on her head to prove it to her grandson, and the hat is ludicrous and considerably oversized)

RUTH Hot dog! Go, Mama!

WALTER *(Doubled over with laughter)* I'm sorry, Mama—but you look like you ready to go out and chop you some cotton sure enough!

(They all laugh except MAMA, out of deference to TRAVIS' feelings)

MAMA *(Gathering the boy up to her)* Bless your heart—this is the prettiest hat I ever owned—(WALTER, RUTH *and* BENEATHA *chime in—noisily, festively and insincerely congratulating* TRAVIS *on his* *gift)* What are we all standing around here for? We ain't finished packin' yet. Bennie, you ain't packed one book.

(The bell rings)

985 **BENEATHA** That couldn't be the movers . . . it's not hardly two good yet—

(BENEATHA goes into her room. MAMA *starts for door)*

WALTER *(Turning, stiffening)* Wait—wait—I'll get it.

(He stands and looks at the door)

MAMA You expecting company, son?

WALTER *(Just looking at the door)* Yeah—yeah . . .

(MAMA looks at RUTH, and they exchange innocent and unfrightened glances)

MAMA *(Not understanding)* Well, let them in, son.

990 **BENEATHA** *(From her room)* We need some more string.

MAMA TRAVIS —you run to the hardware and get me some string cord.

(MAMA goes out and WALTER turns and looks at RUTH. TRAVIS goes to a dish for money)

RUTH Why don't you answer the door, man?

WALTER *(Suddenly bounding across the floor to embrace her)* 'Cause sometimes it hard to let the future begin! *(Stooping down in her face)*

I got wings! You got wings!

All God's children got wings!

(He crosses to the door and throws it open. Standing there is a very slight little man in a not too prosperous business suit and with haunted frightened eyes and a hat pulled down tightly, brim up, around his forehead. TRAVIS *passes between the men and exits.* WALTER *leans deep in the man's face, still in his jubilance)*

When I get to heaven gonna put on my wings,

Gonna fly all over God's heaven . . .

(The little man just stares at him)

Heaven—

(Suddenly he stops and looks past the little man into the empty hallway) Where's Willy, man?

BOBO He ain't with me.

995 **WALTER** *(Not disturbed)* Oh—come on in. You know my wife.

BOBO *(Dumbly, taking off his hat)* Yes—h'you, Miss Ruth.

RUTH *(Quietly, a mood apart from her husband already, seeing* BOBO*)* Hello, Bobo.

WALTER You right on time today . . . Right on time. That's the way! *(He slaps* BOBO *on his back)* Sit down . . . lemme hear.

> *(*RUTH *stands stiffly and quietly in back of them, as though somehow she senses death, her eyes fixed on her husband)*

BOBO *(His frightened eyes on the floor, his hat in his hands)* Could I please get a drink of water, before I tell you about it, Walter Lee?

> *(*WALTER *does not take his eyes off the man.* RUTH *goes blindly to the tap and gets a glass of water and brings it to* BOBO*)*

1000 **WALTER** There ain't nothing wrong, is there?

BOBO Lemme tell you—

WALTER Man—didn't nothing go wrong?

BOBO Lemme tell you—Walter Lee. *(Looking at* RUTH *and talking to her more than to* WALTER*)* You know how it was. I got to tell you how it was. I mean first I got to tell you how it was all the way . . . I mean about the money I put in, Walter Lee . . .

WALTER *(With taut agitation now)* What about the money you put in?

1005 **BOBO** Well—it wasn't much as we told you—me and Willy—*(He stops)* I'm sorry, Walter. I got a bad feeling about it. I got a real bad feeling about it . . .

WALTER Man, what you telling me about all this for? . . . Tell me what happened in Springfield . . .

BOBO Springfield.

RUTH *(Like a dead woman)* What was supposed to happen in Springfield?

BOBO *(To her)* This deal that me and Walter went into with Willy— Me and Willy was going to go down to Springfield and spread some money 'round so's we wouldn't have to wait so long for the liquor license . . . That's what we were going to do. Everybody said that was the way you had to do, you understand, Miss Ruth?

1010 **WALTER** Man—what happened down there?

BOBO *(A pitiful man, near tears)* I'm trying to tell you, Walter.

WALTER *(Screaming at him suddenly)* THEN TELL ME, GOD-DAMMIT . . . WHAT'S THE MATTER WITH YOU?

BOBO   Man . . . I didn't go to no Springfield, yesterday.

WALTER   *(Halted, life hanging in the moment)* Why not?

1015 **BOBO**   *(The long way, the hard way to tell)* 'Cause I didn't have no reasons to . . .

WALTER   Man, what are you talking about!

BOBO   I'm talking about the fact that when I got to the train station yesterday morning—eight o'clock like we planned . . . Man— *Willy didn't never show up.*

WALTER   Why . . . where was he . . . where is he?

BOBO   That's what I'm trying to tell you . . . I don't know . . . I waited six hours . . . I called his house . . . and I waited . . . six hours . . . I waited in that train station six hours . . . *(Breaking into tears)* That was all the extra money I had in the world . . . *(Looking up at* WALTER *with the tears running down his face)* Man, *Willy is gone.*

1020 **WALTER**   Gone, what you mean Willy is gone? Gone where? You mean he went by himself. You mean he went off to Springfield by himself—to take care of getting the license—*(Turns and looks anxiously at* RUTH*)* You mean maybe he didn't want too many people in on the business down there? *(Looks to* RUTH *again, as before)* You know Willy got his own ways. *(Looks back to* BOBO*)* Maybe you was late yesterday and he just went on down there without you. Maybe—maybe—he's been callin' you at home tryin' to tell you what happened or something. Maybe—maybe—he just got sick. He's somewhere—he's got to be somewhere. We just got to find him—me and you got to find him. *(Grabs* BOBO *senselessly by the collar and starts to shake him)* We got to!

BOBO   *(In sudden angry, frightened agony)* What's the matter with you, Walter! *When a cat take off with your money he don't leave you no road maps!*

WALTER   *(Turning madly, as though he is looking for* WILLY *in the very room)* Willy! . . . Willy . . . don't do it . . . Please don't do it . . . Man, not with that money . . . Man, please, not with that money . . . Oh, God . . . Don't let it be true . . . *(He is wandering around, crying out for* WILLY *and looking for him or perhaps for help from God)* Man . . . I trusted you . . . Man, I put my life in your hands . . . *(He starts to crumple down on the floor as* RUTH *just covers her face in horror.* MAMA *opens the door and comes into the room, with* BENEATHA *behind her)* Man . . . *(He starts to pound the floor with his fists, sobbing wildly)* THAT MONEY IS MADE OUT OF MY FATHER'S FLESH—

BOBO *(Standing over him helplessly)* I'm sorry, Walter . . . *(Only* WALTER's *sobs reply.* BOBO *puts on his hat)* I had my life staked on this deal, too . . .

> *(He exits)*

MAMA *(To* WALTER*)* Son—*(She goes to him, bends down to him; talks to his bent head)* Son . . . Is it gone? Son, I gave you sixty-five hundred dollars. Is it gone? All of it? Beneatha's money too?

1025 **WALTER** *(Lifting his head slowly)* Mama . . . I never . . . went to the bank at all . . .

MAMA *(Not wanting to believe him)* You mean . . . your sister's school money . . . you used that too . . . Walter? . . .

WALTER Yessss! All of it . . . It's all gone . . .

> *(There is total silence.* RUTH *stands with her face covered with her hands;* BENEATHA *leans forlornly against a wall, fingering a piece of red ribbon from the mother's gift.* MAMA *stops and looks at her son without recognition and then, quite without thinking about it, starts to beat him senselessly in the face.* BENEATHA *goes to them and stops it)*

BENEATHA Mama!

> *(*MAMA *stops and looks at both of her children and rises slowly and wanders vaguely, aimlessly away from them)*

MAMA I seen . . . him . . . night after night . . . come in . . . and look at that rug . . . and then look at me . . . the red showing in his eyes . . . the veins moving in his head . . . I seen him grow thin and old before he was forty . . . working and working and working like somebody's old horse . . . killing himself . . . and you—you give it all away in a day—*(She raises her arms to strike him again)*

1030 **BENEATHA** Mama—

MAMA Oh, God . . . *(She looks up to Him)* Look down here—and show me the strength.

BENEATHA Mama—

MAMA *(Folding over)* Strength . . .

BENEATHA *(Plaintively)* Mama . . .

1035 **MAMA** Strength!

Curtain

Act III

An hour later.

At curtain, there is a sullen light of gloom in the living room, gray light not unlike that which began the first scene of Act One. At left we can see WALTER *within his room, alone with himself. He is stretched out on the bed, his shirt out and open, his arms under his head. He does not smoke, he does not cry out, he merely lies there, looking up at the ceiling, much as if he were alone in the world.*

In the living room BENEATHA *sits at the table, still surrounded by the now almost ominous packing crates. She sits looking off. We feel that this is a mood struck perhaps an hour before, and it lingers now, full of the empty sound of profound disappointment. We see on a line from her brother's bedroom the sameness of their attitudes. Presently the bell rings and* BENEATHA *rises without ambition or interest in answering. It is* ASAGAI, *smiling broadly, striding into the room with energy and happy expectation and conversation.*

ASAGAI I came over . . . I had some free time. I thought I might help with the packing. Ah, I like the look of packing crates! A household in preparation for a journey! It depresses some people . . . but for me . . . it is another feeling. Something full of the flow of life, do you understand? Movement, progress . . . It makes me think of Africa.

BENEATHA Africa!

ASAGAI What kind of a mood is this? Have I told you how deeply you move me?

BENEATHA He gave away the money, Asagai . . .

1040 **ASAGAI** Who gave away what money?

BENEATHA The insurance money. My brother gave it away.

ASAGAI Gave it away?

BENEATHA He made an investment! With a man even Travis wouldn't have trusted with his most worn-out marbles.

ASAGAI And it's gone?

1045 **BENEATHA** Gone!

ASAGAI I'm very sorry . . . And you, now?

BENEATHA Me? . . . Me? . . . Me, I'm nothing . . . Me. When I was very small . . . we used to take our sleds out in the wintertime and the only hills we had were the ice-covered stone steps of some houses down the street. And we used to fill them in with snow and make them smooth and slide down them all day . . . and it was very dangerous, you know . . . far too steep . . . and sure enough one day a kid named Rufus came down too fast and hit the sidewalk and we saw his face just split open right there in front of us . . . And I remember standing there looking at his bloody open face thinking that was the end of Rufus. But the ambulance came and they took him to the hospital and they fixed the broken bones and they sewed it all up . . . and the next time I saw Rufus he just had a little line down the middle of his face . . . I never got over that . . .

ASAGAI What?

BENEATHA That that was what one person could do for another, fix him up—sew up the problem, make him all right again. That was the most marvelous thing in the world . . . I wanted to do that. I always thought it was the one concrete thing in the world that a human being could do. Fix up the sick, you know—and make them whole again. This was truly being God . . .

1050 **ASAGAI** You wanted to be God?

BENEATHA No—I wanted to cure. It used to be so important to me. I wanted to cure. It used to matter. I used to care. I mean about people and how their bodies hurt . . .

ASAGAI And you've stopped caring?

BENEATHA Yes—I think so.

ASAGAI Why?

1055 **BENEATHA** (*Bitterly*) Because it doesn't seem deep enough, close enough to what ails mankind! It was a child's way of seeing things—or an idealist's.

ASAGAI Children see things very well sometimes—and idealists even better.

BENEATHA I know that's what you think. Because you are still where I left off. You with all your talk and dreams about Africa! You still think you can patch up the world. Cure the Great Sore of Colonialism—(*Loftily, mocking it*) with the Penicillin of Independence—!

ASAGAI Yes!

BENEATHA Independence *and then what?* What about all the crooks and thieves and just plain idiots who will come into power and steal and plunder the same as before—only now they will be black and do it in the name of the new Independence—WHAT ABOUT THEM?!

1060 **ASAGAI** That will be the problem for another time. First we must get there.

BENEATHA And where does it end?

ASAGAI End? Who even spoke of an end? To life? To living?

BENEATHA An end to misery! To stupidity! Don't you see there isn't any real progress, Asagai, there is only one large circle that we march in, around and around, each of us with our own little picture in front of us—our own little mirage that we think is the future.

ASAGAI That is the mistake.

1065 **BENEATHA** What?

ASAGAI What you just said about the circle. It isn't a circle—it is simply a long line—as in geometry, you know, one that reaches into infinity. And because we cannot see the end—we also cannot see how it changes. And it is very odd but those who see the changes—who dream, who will not give up—are called idealists . . . and those who see only the circle we call *them* the "realists"!

BENEATHA Asagai, while I was sleeping in that bed in there, people went out and took the future right out of my hands! And nobody asked me, nobody consulted me—they just went out and changed my life!

ASAGAI Was it your money?

BENEATHA What?

1070 **ASAGAI** Was it your money he gave away?

BENEATHA It belonged to all of us.

ASAGAI But did you earn it? Would you have had it at all if your father had not died?

BENEATHA No.

ASAGAI Then isn't there something wrong in a house—in a world—where all dreams, good or bad, must depend on the death of a man? I never thought to see *you* like this, Alaiyo. You! Your brother made a mistake and you are grateful to him so that now you can give up the ailing human race on account of it! You talk about what good is struggle, what good is anything! Where are we all going and why are we bothering!

1075 **BENEATHA** AND YOU CANNOT ANSWER IT!

ASAGAI (*Shouting over her*) I LIVE THE ANSWER! (*Pause*) In my village at home it is the exceptional man who can even read a newspaper . . . or who ever sees a book at all. I will go home and much of what I will have to say will seem strange to the people of my village. But I will teach and work and things will happen, slowly and swiftly. At times it will seem that nothing changes at all . . . and then again the sudden dramatic events which make history leap into the future. And then quiet again. Retrogression even. Guns, murder, revolution. And I even will have moments when I wonder if the quiet was not better than all that death and hatred. But I will look about my village at the illiteracy and disease and ignorance and I will not wonder long. And perhaps . . . perhaps I will be a great man . . . I mean perhaps I will hold on to the substance of truth and find my way always with the right course . . . and perhaps for it. I will be butchered in my bed some night by the servants of empire . . .

BENEATHA *The martyr!*

ASAGAI (*He smiles*) . . . or perhaps I shall live to be a very old man, respected and esteemed in my new nation . . . And perhaps I shall hold office and this is what I'm trying to tell you, Alaiyo: Perhaps the things I believe now for my country will be wrong and outmoded, and I will not understand and do terrible things to have things my way or merely to keep my power. Don't you see that there will be young men and women—not British soldiers then, but my own black countrymen—to step out of the shadows some evening and slit my then useless throat? Don't you see they have always been there . . . that they always will be. And that such a thing as my own death will be an advance? They who might kill me even . . . actually replenish all that I was.

BENEATHA Oh, Asagai, I know all that.

1080 **ASAGAI** Good! Then stop moaning and groaning and tell me what you plan to do.

BENEATHA Do?

ASAGAI I have a bit of a suggestion.

BENEATHA What?

ASAGAI (*Rather quietly for him*) That when it is all over—that you come home with me—

1085 **BENEATHA** (*Staring at him and crossing away with exasperation*) Oh—Asagai—at this moment you decide to be romantic!

ASAGAI (*Quickly understanding the misunderstanding*) My dear, young creature of the New World—I do not mean across the city— I mean across the ocean: home—to Africa.

BENEATHA (*Slowly understanding and turning to him with murmured amazement*) To Africa?

ASAGAI Yes! . . . (*Smiling and lifting his arms playfully*) Three hundred years later the African Prince rose up out of the seas and swept the maiden back across the middle passage over which her ancestors had come—

BENEATHA (*Unable to play*) To—to Nigeria?

1090 **ASAGAI** Nigeria. Home. *(Coming to her with genuine romantic flippancy)* I will show you our mountains and our stars; and give you cool drinks from gourds and teach you the old songs and the ways of our people—and, in time, we will pretend that—*(Very softly)*—you have only been away for a day. Say that you'll come *(He swings her around and takes her full in his arms in a kiss which proceeds to passion)*

BENEATHA *(Pulling away suddenly)* You're getting me all mixed up—

ASAGAI Why?

BENEATHA Too many things—too many things have happened today. I must sit down and think. I don't know what I feel about anything right this minute.

(She promptly sits down and props her chin on her fist)

ASAGAI *(Charmed)* All right, I shall leave you. No—don't get up. *(Touching her, gently, sweetly)* Just sit awhile and think . . . Never be afraid to sit awhile and think. *(He goes to door and looks at her)* How often I have looked at you and said, "Ah—so this is what the New World hath finally wrought . . . "

(He exits. BENEATHA sits on alone. Presently WALTER enters from his room and starts to rummage through things, feverishly looking for something. She looks up and turns in her seat).

1095 **BENEATHA** *(Hissingly)* Yes—just look at what the New World hath wrought! . . . Just look! *(She gestures with bitter disgust)* There he is! *Monsieur le petit bourgeois noir*—himself! There he is— Symbol of a Rising Class! Entrepreneur! Titan of the system! *(WALTER ignores her completely and continues frantically and destructively looking for something and hurling things to floor and tearing things out of their place in his search. BENEATHA ignores the eccentricity of his actions and goes on with the monologue of insult)* Did you dream of yachts on Lake Michigan, Brother? Did you see yourself on that Great Day sitting down at the Conference Table, surrounded by all the mighty bald-headed men in America? All halted, waiting, breathless, waiting for your pronouncements on industry? Waiting for you—Chairman of the Board! *(WALTER finds what he is looking for—a small piece of white paper—and pushes it in his pocket and puts on his coat and rushes out without ever having looked at her. She shouts after him)* I look at you and I see the final triumph of stupidity in the world!

(The door slams and she returns to just sitting again. RUTH *comes quickly out of* MAMA'S *room)*

RUTH Who was that?

BENEATHA Your husband.

RUTH Where did he go?

BENEATHA Who knows—maybe he has an appointment at U.S. Steel.

1100 **RUTH** *(Anxiously, with frightened eyes)* You didn't say nothing bad to him, did you?

BENEATHA Bad? Say anything bad to him? No—I told him he was a sweet boy and full of dreams and everything is strictly peachy keen, as the ofay kids say!

*(*MAMA *enters from her bedroom. She is lost, vague, trying to catch hold, to make some sense of her former command of the world, but it still eludes her. A sense of waste overwhelms her gait; a measure of apology rides on her shoulders. She goes to her plant, which has remained on the table, looks at it, picks it up and takes it to the window-sill and sits it outside, and she stands and looks at it a long moment. Then she closes the window, straightens her body with effort and turns around to her children)*

MAMA Well—ain't it a mess in here, though? *(A false cheerfulness, a beginning of something)* I guess we all better stop moping around and get some work done. All this unpacking and everything we got to do. *(*RUTH *raises her head slowly in response to the sense of the line; and* BENEATHA *in similar manner turns very slowly to look at her mother)* One of you all better call the moving people and tell 'em not to come.

RUTH Tell 'em not to come?

MAMA Of course, baby. Ain't no need in 'em coming all the way here and having to go back. They charges for that too. *(She sits down, fingers to her brow, thinking)* Lord, ever since I was a little girl, I always remembers people saying, "Lena—Lena Eggleston, you aims too high all the time. You needs to slow down and see life a little more like it is. Just slow down some." That's what they always used to say down home—"Lord, that Lena Eggleston is a high-minded thing. She'll get her due one day!"

1105 **RUTH** No, Lena . . .

MAMA Me and Big Walter just didn't never learn right.

RUTH   Lena, no! We gotta go, Bennie—tell her . . . *(She rises and crosses to* BENEATHA *with her arms out-stretched.* BENEATHA *doesn't respond)* Tell her we can still move . . . the notes ain't but a hundred and twenty-five a month. We got four grown people in this house—we can work . . .

MAMA   *(To herself)* Just aimed too high all the time—

RUTH   *(Turning and going to* MAMA *fast—the words pouring out with urgency and desperation)* Lena—I'll work . . . I'll work twenty hours a day in all the kitchens in Chicago . . . I'll strap my baby on my back if I have to and scrub all the floors in America and wash all the sheets in America if I have to—but we got to MOVE! We got to get OUT OF HERE!!

*(*MAMA *reaches out absently and pats* RUTH'S *hand)*

1110 **MAMA**   No—I sees things differently now. Been thinking 'bout some of the things we could do to fix this place up some. I seen a secondhand bureau over on Maxwell Street just the other day that could fit right there. *(She points to where the new furniture might go.* RUTH *wanders away from her)* Would need some new handles on it and then a little varnish and it look like something brand-new. And—we can put up them new curtains in the kitchen . . . Why this place be looking fine. Cheer us all up so that we forget trouble ever come . . . *(To* RUTH*)* And you could get some nice screens to put up in your room 'round the baby's bassinet . . . *(She looks at both of them, pleadingly)* Sometimes you just got to know when to give up some things . . . and hold on to what you got . . .

*(*WALTER *enters from the outside, looking spent and leaning against the door, his coat hanging from him)*

MAMA   Where you been, son?

WALTER   *(Breathing hard)* Made a call.

MAMA   To who, son?

WALTER   To The Man. *(He heads for his room)*

1115 **MAMA**   What man, baby?

WALTER   *(Stops in the door)* The Man, Mama. Don't you know who The Man is?

RUTH   Walter Lee?

WALTER   *The Man.* Like the guys in the streets say—The Man. Captain Boss—Mistuh Charley . . . Old Cap'n Please Mr. Bossman . . .

BENEATHA   *(Suddenly)* Lindner!

1120 **WALTER** That's right! That's good. I told him to come right over.

BENEATHA *(Fiercely, understanding)* For what? What do you want to see him for!

WALTER *(Looking at his sister)* We going to do business with him.

MAMA What you talking 'bout, son?

WALTER Talking 'bout life, Mama. You all always telling me to see life like it is. Well—I laid in there on my back today . . . and I figured it out. Life just like it is. Who gets and who don't get. *(He sits down with his coat on and laughs)* Mama, you know it's all divided up. Life is. Sure enough. Between the takers and the "tooken." *(He laughs)* I've figured it out finally. *(He looks around at them)* Yeah. Some of us always getting "tooken." *(He laughs)* People like Willy Harris, they don't never get "tooken." And you know why the rest of us do? 'Cause we all mixed up. Mixed up bad. We get to looking 'round for the right and the wrong; and we worry about it and cry about it and stay up nights trying to figure out 'bout the wrong and the right of things all the time . . . And all the time, man, them takers is out there operating, just taking and taking. Willy Harris? Shoot—Willy Harris don't even count. He don't even count in the big scheme of things. But I'll say one thing for old Willy Harris . . . he's taught me something. He's taught me to keep my eye on what counts in this world. Yeah— *(Shouting out a little)* Thanks, Willy!

1120 **RUTH** What did you call that man for, Walter Lee?

WALTER Called him to tell him to come on over to the show. Gonna put on a show for the man. Just what he wants to see. You see, Mama, the man came here today and he told us that them people out there where you want us to move—well they so upset they willing to pay us *not* to move! *(He laughs again)* And—and oh, Mama you would of been proud of the way me and Ruth and Bennie acted. We told him to get out . . . Lord have mercy! We told the man to get out! Oh, we was some proud folks this afternoon, yeah. *(He lights a cigarette)* We were still full of that old-time stuff . . .

RUTH *(Coming toward him slowly)* You talking 'bout taking them people's money to keep us from moving in that house?

WALTER I ain't just talking 'bout it, baby—I'm telling you that's what's going to happen!

BENEATHA Oh, God! Where is the bottom! Where is the real honest-to-God bottom so he can't go any farther!

1130 **WALTER** See—that's the old stuff. You and that boy that was here today. You all want everybody to carry a flag and a spear and sing some marching songs, huh? You wanna spend your life looking into things and trying to find the right and the wrong part, huh? Yeah. You know what's going to happen to that boy someday—he'll find himself sitting in a dungeon, locked in forever—and the takers will have the key! Forget it, baby! There ain't no causes—there ain't nothing but taking in this world, and he who takes most is smartest—and it don't make a damn bit of difference *how.*

MAMA You making something inside me cry, son. Some awful pain inside me.

WALTER Don't cry, Mama. Understand. That white man is going to walk in that door able to write checks for more money than we ever had. It's important to him and I'm going to help him . . . I'm going to put on the show, Mama.

MAMA Son—I come from five generations of people who was slaves and sharecroppers—but ain't nobody in my family never let nobody pay 'em no money that was a way of telling us we wasn't fit to walk the earth. We ain't never been that poor. *(Raising her eyes and looking at him)* We ain't never been that— dead inside.

BENEATH Well—we are dead now. All the talk about dreams and sunlight that goes on in this house. It's all dead now.

1135 **WALTER** What's the matter with you all! I didn't make this world! It was give to me this way! Hell, yes, I want me some yachts someday! Yes, I want to hang some real pearls 'round my wife's neck. Ain't she supposed to wear no pearls? Somebody tell me—tell me, who decides which women is suppose to wear pearls in this world. I tell you I am a *man*—and I think my wife should wear some pearls in this world!

> *(This last line hangs a good while and walter begins to move about the room. The word "Man" has penetrated his consciousness; he mumbles it to himself repeatedly between strange agitated pauses as he moves about)*

MAMA Baby, how you going to feel on the inside?

WALTER Fine! . . . Going to feel fine . . . a man . . .

MAMA You won't have nothing left then, Walter Lee.

WALTER *(Coming to her)* I'm going to feel fine, Mama. I'm going to look that son-of-a-bitch in the eyes and say—*(He falters)*—and say, "All right, Mr. Lindner—*(He falters even more)*—that's *your* neighborhood out there! You got the right to keep it like you want!

You got the right to have it like you want! Just write the check and—the house is yours." And—and I am going to say—*(His voice almost breaks)* "And you—you people just put the money in my hand and you won't have to live next to this bunch of stinking niggers! . . ." *(He straightens up and moves away from his mother, walking around the room)* And maybe—maybe I'll just get down on my black knees . . . *(He does so;* RUTH *and* BENNIE *and* MAMA *watch him in frozen horror)* "Captain, Mistuh, Bossman— *(Groveling and grinning and wringing his hands in profoundly anguished imitation of the slow-witted movie stereotype)* A-hee-hee-hee! Oh, yassuh boss! Yasssssuh! Great white—*(Voice breaking, he forces himself to go on)*—Father, just gi' ussen de money, fo' God's sake, and we's—we's ain't gwine come out deh and dirty up yo' white folks neighborhood . . ." *(He breaks down completely)* And I'll feel fine! Fine! FINE! *(He gets up and goes into the bedroom)*

1140 **BENEATHA** That is not a man. That is nothing but a toothless rat.

MAMA Yes—death done come in this here house. *(She is nodding, slowly, reflectively)* Done come walking in my house on the lips of my children. You what supposed to be my beginning again. You—what supposed to be my harvest. *(To* BENEATHA*)* You—you mourning your brother?

BENEATHA He's no brother of mine.

MAMA What you say?

BENEATHA I said that that individual in that room is no brother of mine.

1145 **MAMA** That's what I thought you said. You feeling like you better than he is today? *(BENEATHA does not answer)* Yes? What you tell him a minute ago? That he wasn't a man? Yes? You give him up for me? You done wrote his epitaph too—like the rest of the world? Well, who give you the privilege?

BENEATHA Be on my side for once! You saw what he just did, Mama! You saw him—down on his knees. Wasn't it you who taught me to despise any man who would do that? Do what he's going to do?

MAMA Yes—I taught you that. Me and your daddy. But I thought I taught you something else too . . . I thought I taught you to love him.

BENEATHA Love him? There is nothing left to love.

MAMA There is *always* something left to love. And if you ain't learned that, you ain't learned nothing. *(Looking at her)* Have you cried for that boy today? I don't mean for yourself and for the family 'cause we lost the money. I mean for him: what he been through and what it done to him. Child, when do you think is the time to love somebody the most? When they done good and made things easy for everybody? Well then, you ain't through learning—because that ain't the time at all. It's when he's at his lowest and can't believe in hisself 'cause the world done whipped him so! When you starts measuring somebody, measure him right, child, measure him right. Make sure you done taken into account what hills and valleys he come through before he got to wherever he is.

*(*TRAVIS *bursts into the room at the end of the speech, leaving the door open)*

1150 **TRAVIS** Grandmama—the moving men are downstairs! The truck just pulled up.

MAMA *(Turning and looking at him)* Are they, baby? They downstairs?

*(She sighs and sits. *LINDNER *appears in the doorway. He peers in and knocks lightly, to gain attention, and comes in. All turn to look at him)*

LINDNER *(Hat and briefcase in hand)* Uh—hello . . .

*(*RUTH *crosses mechanically to the bedroom door and opens it and lets it swing open freely and slowly as the lights come up on *WALTER *within, still in his coat, sitting at the far corner of the room. He looks up and out through the room to* lindner*)*

RUTH He's here.

*(A long minute passes and *WALTER *slowly gets up)*

LINDNER *(Coming to the table with efficiency, putting his briefcase on the table and starting to unfold papers and unscrew fountain pens)* Well, I certainly was glad to hear from you people. (*WALTER *has begun the trek out of the room, slowly and awkwardly, rather like a small boy, passing the back of his sleeve across his mouth from time to time)* Life can really be so much simpler than people let it be most of the time. Well—with whom do I negotiate? You, Mrs. Younger, or your son here? (*MAMA *sits with her hands folded on her lap and her eyes closed as *WALTER *advances.* TRAVIS *goes closer to* LINDNER *and looks at the papers curiously)* Just some official papers, sonny.

1155 **RUTH** Travis, you go downstairs—

MAMA *(Opening her eyes and looking into* WALTER'S*)* No. Travis, you stay right here. And you make him understand what you doing, Walter Lee. You teach him good. Like Willy Harris taught you. You show where our five generations done come to *(*WALTER *looks from her to the boy, who grins at him innocently)* Go ahead, son— *(She folds her hands and closes her eyes)* Go ahead.

WALTER *(At last crosses to* LINDNER, *who is reviewing the contract)* Well, Mr. Lindner. *(*BENEATHA *turns away)* We called you—*(There is a profound, simple groping quality in his speech)*—because, well, me and my family *(He looks around and shifts from one foot to the other)* Well—we are very plain people . . .

LINDNER Yes—

WALTER I mean—I have worked as a chauffeur most of my life— and my wife here, she does domestic work in people's kitchens. So does my mother. I mean—we are plain people . . .

1160 **LINDNER** Yes, Mr. Younger—

WALTER *(Really like a small boy, looking down at his shoes and then up at the man)* And—uh—well, my father, well, he was a laborer most of his life. . . .

LINDNER *(Absolutely confused)* Uh, yes—yes, I understand. *(He turns back to the contract)*

WALTER *(A beat; staring at him)* And my father—*(With sudden intensity)* My father almost *beat a man to death* once because this man called him a bad name or something, you know what I mean?

LINDNER *(Looking up, frozen)* No, no, I'm afraid I don't—

1165 **WALTER** *(A beat. The tension hangs; then* WALTER *steps back from it)* Yeah, Well—what I mean is that we come from people who had a lot of *pride*. I mean—we are very proud people. And that's my sister over there and she's going to be a doctor—and we are very proud—

LINDNER Well—I am sure that is very nice, but—

WALTER What I am telling you is that we called you over here to tell you that we are very proud and that this—*(Signaling to* TRAVIS*)* Travis, come here. *(*TRAVIS *crosses and* WALTER *draws him before him facing the man)* This is my son, and he makes the sixth generation our family in this country. And we have all thought about your offer—

LINDNER Well, good . . . good—

WALTER   And we have decided to move into our house because my father—my father—he earned it for us brick by brick. *(MAMA has her eyes closed and is rocking back and forth as though she were in church, with her head nodding the Amen yes)* We don't want to make no trouble for nobody or fight no causes, and we will try to be good neighbors. And that's *all* we got to say about that. *(He looks the man absolutely in the eyes)* We don't want your money. *(He turns and walks away)*

1170 **LINDNER**   *(Looking around at all of them)* I take it then—that you have decided to occupy . . .

BENEATHA   That's what the man said.

LINDNER   *(To* MAMA *in her reverie)* Then I would like to appeal to you, Mrs. Younger. You are older and wiser and understand things better I am sure . . .

MAMA   I am afraid you don't understand. My son said we was going to move and there ain't nothing left for me to say. *(Briskly)* You know how these young folks is nowadays, mister. Can't do a thing with 'em! *(As he opens his mouth, she rises)* Good-bye.

LINDNER   *(Folding up his materials)* Well—if you are that final about it . . . there is nothing left for me to say. *(He finishes, almost ignored by the family, who are concentrating on* WALTER LEE. *At the door* LINDNER *halts and looks around)* I sure hope you people know what you're getting into.

(He shakes his head and exits)

1175 **RUTH**   *(Looking around and coming to life)* Well, for God's sake—if the moving men are here—LET'S GET THE HELL OUT OF HERE!

MAMA   *(Into action)* Ain't it the truth! Look at all this here mess. Ruth, put Travis' good jacket on him . . . Walter Lee, fix your tie and tuck your shirt in, you look like somebody's hoodlum! Lord have mercy, where is my plant? *(She flies to get it amid the general bustling of the family, who are deliberately trying to ignore the nobility of the past moment)* You all start on down . . . Travis child, don't go empty-handed . . . Ruth, where did I put that box with my skillets in it? I want to be in charge of it myself . . . I'm going to make us the biggest dinner we ever ate tonight . . . Beneatha, what's the matter with them stockings? Pull them things up, girl . . .

(The family starts to file out as two moving men appear and begin to carry out the heavier pieces of furniture, bumping into the family as they move about)

BENEATHA Mama, Asagai asked me to marry him today and go to Africa—

MAMA *(In the middle of her getting-ready activity)* He did? You ain't old enough to marry nobody—*(Seeing the moving men lifting one of her chairs precariously)* Darling, that ain't no bale of cotton, please handle it so we can sit in it again! I had that chair twenty-five years . . .

(The movers sigh with exasperation and go on with their work)

BENEATHA *(Girlishly and unreasonably trying to pursue the conversation)* To go to Africa, Mama—be a doctor in Africa . . .

1180 **MAMA** *(Distracted)* Yes, baby—

WALTER *Africa!* What he want you to go to Africa for?

BENEATHA To practice there . . .

WALTER Girl, if you don't get all them silly ideas out your head! You better marry yourself a man with some loot . . .

BENEATHA *(Angrily, precisely as in the first scene of the play)* What have you got to do with who I marry!

1185 **WALTER** Plenty. Now I think George Murchison—

BENEATHA *George Murchison!* I wouldn't marry him if he was Adam and I was Eve!

(WALTER and BENEATHA go out yelling at each other vigorously and the anger is loud and real till their voices diminish. RUTH stands at the door and turns to MAMA and smiles knowingly)

MAMA *(Fixing her hat at last)* Yeah—they something all right, my children . . .

RUTH Yeah—they're something. Let's go, Lena.

MAMA *(Stalling, starting to look around at the house)* Yes—I'm coming. Ruth—

1190 **RUTH** Yes?

MAMA *(Quietly, woman to woman)* He finally come into his manhood today, didn't he? Kind of like a rainbow after the rain . . .

RUTH *(Biting her lip lest her own pride explode in front of MAMA)* Yes, Lena.

(WALTER's voice calls for them raucously)

WALTER *(Off stage)* Y'all come on! These people charges by the hour, you know!

MAMA   (*Waving* RUTH *out vaguely*) All right, honey—go on down. I be down directly.
(RUTH *hesitates, then exits.* MAMA *stands, at last alone in the living room, her plant on the table before her as the lights start to come down. She looks around at all the walls and ceilings and suddenly, despite herself, while the children call below, a great heaving thing rises in her and she puts her fist to her mouth to stifle it, takes a final desperate look, pulls her coat about her, pats her hat and goes out. The lights dim down. The door opens and she comes back in, grabs her plant, and goes out for the last time)*

Curtain

Writing Assignments

1. Read the two essays by James Baldwin—"Everybody's Protest Novel" and "Many Thousands Gone"—referred to in the introduction to this chapter. Both are included in *Notes of a Native Son*. Explain whether you agree with his comments about the psychological limits of protest literature, particularly his remarks about *Native Son*. Which elements of Wright's prose, either in the opening chapter or the entire novel, lead you to support or contradict Baldwin's view?

2. Discuss your response to the portrayal of Bob Jones, Himes's character in *If He Hollers Let Him Go*. Also consider the social circumstances described in the novel. What is your take, for example, on the conversation among Jones, Alice Harrison, and her friends?

3. In Ann Petry's *The Street*, Lutie Johnson remembers her primary school teacher's remark, that "I don't know why they make us bother to teach your people to write." Address the teacher's remark in the context of the novel and the broader world. How does the remark relate to the climactic action in *The Street*? How does the fact that Lutie Johnson is female figure into your analysis?

4. Lena Younger considers her husband, Big Walter, a fine man who "just couldn't never catch up with his dreams, that's all." All the major characters in *A Raisin in the Sun*—Lena, Walter Lee, Ruth,

Beneatha, and Asagai—are in pursuit of dreams and hoping to avoid Big Walter's fate. Toward which character or vision do you have the most sympathy? Explain why. As you develop your argument, comment on the decision to move to Clybourne Park as a solution to the family's problems and as a model of action for other African Americans.

CHAPTER NINE

JEREMIADS

In addition to studying folklore, fiction, poetry, song, and drama, scholars have devoted much attention to African American essays and oratory because such expressions also have been crucial methods by which people of African descent in the United States have asserted their humanity and agitated for social change. Relying upon a fundamental belief in the power of the Word and remaining cognizant of the myths that many Americans hold dear, Black essayists and orators have fashioned unique methods to rally both African American and wider audiences to combat white supremacy. A pervasive form of persuasion in African American letters, a form that is the focus of this chapter, is the *African American jeremiad*.

The term *jeremiad* derives from the Old Testament prophet Jeremiah, who foretold the fall of Judah to the Babylonians and the destruction of the temple in Jerusalem, acts that occurred because his people had strayed from the Mosaic covenant. Jeremiah warned about trouble in the immediate future, though his long-range forecast for the Hebrews was positive. Jeremiah, in the view of some scholars, is also the author of Lamentations. Thus, *jeremiad* has come to mean an extended lament or prediction of calamity. The word became connected to concepts of public discourse when it was used to describe the sermons often delivered by Puritan ministers, beginning in the seventeenth century, whereby they warned their congregations of the grave consequences that would follow from violations of the religious and social ideal. This type of speech, the *American jeremiad*, in turn, was bound to the identity formation of the Puritans, who saw themselves as a chosen people. For example, John Winthrop, the first governor of the Massachusetts

Bay Colony, described New England as a shining City on the Hill, selected by God to be a model of liberty and social virtue. But Winthrop
warned that if the settlers betrayed their divine mission, then they
would be dealt with harshly by the Almighty. These ideas were at the
core of what became known as America's civil religion. The accompanying rituals and symbols include the Declaration of Independence, the
Constitution, Thanksgiving dinners, and Fourth of July celebrations.
For many colonists, their victory in the American Revolutionary War
was a providential sign that they were justified in their belief about their
righteous and privileged status. When people seemed to be departing
from the so-called proper path, they were exhorted, often through some
version of the American jeremiad, to rectify their behavior. The
American jeremiad, then, as David Howard-Pitney explains in *The
Afro-American Jeremiad*, has three components: "the citing of the
promise; criticism of *declension* or retrogressing from the promise; and a
resolving *prophecy* that society will shortly complete its mission and redeem the promise." The idea was also that if the promise were not redeemed, then the society would face doom.

Of course, Blacks keenly noted the discrepancy between the stated
ideal of social grace and their enslaved condition. They were victims of
the tyrannical power exerted by those who purported to be beacons of
virtue. The enslaved and their sympathizers sincerely felt that, as the
folk saying has it, God don't like ugly. Given their circumstances, including their exposure to evangelical Protestantism, Blacks begin to
view themselves as a chosen people as well. After all, the story of
Exodus was a much closer match to their reality of bondage than to the
lives of white people. Metaphorically, Blacks were the Israelites; the
Promised Land, freedom, was their destiny. If America were to live up
to the ideal of liberty for all, it could only come through a just reckoning
with its Black inhabitants, its chosen redeemers. When given opportunities to publicly air their grievances, Blacks drew tremendous rhetorical
force from the national backsliding on the question of social equality.
The African American jeremiad, therefore, is a shrewd variation of the
American one. Blacks are cast as a chosen people *within* the parameters
of the nation's archetypal civil myth—so, they are deemed to be a chosen people in the midst of a chosen people. The speaker or writer employing this form addresses a double audience whose destinies are woven tightly together. Although not the focus of this chapter, African
American fiction has exhibited a jeremiadic impulse as well, with a focus on apocalypticism. Whatever the broader literary genre, however,
the African American jeremiad gestures toward the "end of an oppressive

sociopolitical system and the establishment of a new world order where racial justice prevails," as Maxine Lavon Montgomery writes in *The Apocalypse and African-American Fiction*. Activists who have used the African American jeremiad include David Walker, Frederick Douglass, Booker T. Washington, W. E. B. Du Bois, Ida B. Wells-Barnett, Mary McLeod Bethune, Martin Luther King, Jr., and, in contemporary times, Cornel West. This is not to say these writers and speakers used or have wielded the form in a pure dimension or exclusively. There are various degrees and shadings of the African American jeremiad. The promise or prophecy may be stated quite boldly or issued with some measure of reserve. In addition, various speakers and writers, some of whom show up in a different chapter in this very anthology, have opted for other forms as well, sometimes in the same text. Furthermore, ideological distinctions exist among speakers and writers like those listed above. All have been Black cultural nationalists to some extent; they had to have been in order to fill the role of a Black Jeremiah. However, some have been more politically accommodationist or integrationist or militant than others. Douglass, Du Bois, King, and, perhaps now, West have utilized the African American jeremiad most fully and consistently. But the essential point is that all the speakers and writers represented in this chapter have habitually reaffirmed a desire to see Black liberation as part of an era when America truly lives up to the tenets of its civil religion. They have wanted African Americans to reap the full benefits the larger "chosen" identity.

Walker provided an early and powerful version of the African American jeremiad. In his 1829 *Appeal*, he bluntly indicts mainstream hypocrisy and prophesizes retribution for the fact of slavery. He warns in his pamphlet that "unless you speedily alter your course, *you* and your *Country are gone!!!!!!*" Douglass, too, criticized the ideas and actions of slaveholders and their cohorts. Writing in his newspaper *The North Star* in 1848, after the election of slaveholder Zachary Taylor to the Presidency of the United States, he presents a classic example of the African American jeremiad complete with a clear articulation of promise, declension, and prophecy:

> As a people, you claim for yourselves a higher civilization—a purer morality—a deeper religious faith—a larger love of liberty, and a broader philanthropy, than any other nation on the globe. In a word, you claim yours to be a model Republic, and promise, by the force and excellence of your institutions, and the purity and brightness of your example, to

overthrow the thrones and despotisms of the old world, and
substitute your own in their stead. Your missionaries are
found in the remotest parts of the globe, while our land
swarms with churches and religious institutions. In words of
Religion and Liberty, you are abundant and preeminent. You
have long desired to get rid of the odium of being regarded as
pro-slavery, and have even insisted that the charge of pro-
slavery made against you was a slander and that those who
made it were animated by wild and fanatical spirit. To make
your innocence apparent, you have now had a fair opportunity. The issue for freedom or slavery has been clearly submitted to you, and you have deliberately chosen slavery.

Douglass closes by forecasting that, without appropriate changes, "the
sun of this guilty nation must go down in blood." Both Walker and
Douglass were proven correct by the Civil War, an event viewed by
many abolitionists as God's judgment on the South.

In the early twentieth century, fighting a persistent racism that still
compromised the American promise, Du Bois addressed the 1906
Niagara convention, telling the participants that "the battle we wage
is not for ourselves but for all true Americans. It is a fight for ideals,
lest this, our common fatherland, false to its founding, become in
truth the land of the thief and the home of the Slave." Six decades
later, at the 1963 March on Washington, King, with nonpareil elo-
quence, would also highlight the participation of African Americans in
the struggle not merely for Black progress but for America's soul.
Using the classic structure of the African American jeremiad, King
contrasts the perceived destiny of the nation (its promissory note) with
its shortcomings with respect to African Americans (insufficient
funds). He argues, portending doom, that "the whirlwinds of revolt
will continue to shake the foundations of our nation until the bright
day of justice emerges." He stresses, though, highly aware of his double audience, that his vision is "a dream deeply rooted in the
American dream." King's rhetorical formula, an old one culturally by
then, began cohering for him personally at least as early as 1955. In
his speech at the Holt Street Baptist at the outset of the Montgomery
bus boycott, he asserts that "if we are wrong, justice is a lie." And his
jeremiad extended beyond 1963. He writes in his 1967 book, *Where
Do We Go from Here?*, "Giving our ultimate allegiance to the empire of
justice, we must be that colony of dissenters to imbue our nation with
the ideals of a higher and nobler order. So in dealing with our particular

dilemma, we will challenge this nation to deal with its larger dilemma." Again, this is evidence of the notion of a chosen people operating as part of an even larger group of chosen people.

West continues the classic tradition of the African American jeremiad, emphasizing its prophetic aspect. In "A Twilight Civilization" (1996), he urges us "to strive with genuine compassion, personal integrity, and human decency to fight for radical democracy in the face of the frightening abyss—or terrifying inferno—of the twenty-first century."

Washington, Wells-Barnett, and Bethune incorporated elements of the African American jeremiad in their oratory, although they were not examples of its classic expression. In Washington's case, he was most connected to the establishment and, to the dismay of many Black activists, he sought to accommodate his practice to the existing social pattern. He believed in America's destiny to become the model society. The language he uses to express his hope for "a new heaven and a new earth" at the close of his 1895 speech at the Atlanta exposition is drawn directly from Revelations 21:1. Despite considerable evidence that racism was an intractable feature of American life, Washington viewed it as a trend that would dissipate when the economic condition of Blacks improved. He thus focused on Black self-help initiatives. While many African American speakers offered different messages to exclusively Black as opposed to other audiences, Washington was much more the exhorter and castigator, more of a typical Jeremiah, with Blacks. In fact, his deference toward the white power structure would be a source of the major criticism leveled against him. Without agitating for political rights, critics wondered, how were economic gains to be protected?

Wells-Barnett asked some version of this question repeatedly. Although a rather forceful speaker, her written style resembled more that of the social scientist or investigative reporter than a fiery orator. She does manage certain prophetic phrases in *Mob Rule in New Orleans* (1900) like "when this conscience wakes and speaks out in thunder tones, as it must." Furthermore, she includes in her pamphlet a poem by James Russell Lowell that is an American jeremiad in verse. But Wells-Barnett probably understood that jeremiads had been a masculine vehicle and that if she appropriated the form fully it might have raised some side issues that would have distracted attention from her basic message. Bethune, somewhat an insider and also female, operated in a manner similar to Wells-Barnett. She was not a full-fledged Jeremiah but made rhetorical use of the American promise and civil religion, as indicated by the opening of "Certain Unalienable Rights" (1944).

The African American jeremiad has proved to be an effective mechanism for effecting civil and legal reform, particularly when the target has been the Southern caste system. When tackling issues of economic fairness, those employing the form have been far less effective. America has been more willing, as Howard-Pitney reminds us, to bend about manners than money. This suggests that for the future empowerment of African Americans, other forms of discourse need to be used as well, although the African American jeremiad, for better or worse, will remain an important rhetorical device.

Further Reading

Albanese, Catherine. *Sons of the Fathers: The Civil Religion of the American Revolution*. Philadelphia: Temple UP, 1976.

Bercovitch, Sacvan. *The American Jeremiad*. Madison: University of Wisconsin Press, 1978.

Howard-Pitney, David. *The Afro-American Jeremiad: Appeals for Justice in America*. Philadelphia: Temple UP, 1990.

Montgomery, Maxine Lavon. *The Apocalypse in African-American Fiction*. Gainesville: University Press of Florida, 1996.

Moses, Wilson Jeremiah. *Black Messiahs and Uncle Toms: Social and Literary Manipulations of a Religious Myth*. University Park: Pennsylvania State UP, 1982.

Tuveson, Ernest Lee. *Redeemer Nation: The Idea of America's Millennial Role*. Chicago: University of Chicago Press, 1968.

David Walker

(1785–1830)

Born to a free woman in Wilmington, North Carolina, on September 28, 1785, David Walker was thus free under the customs of the South; children assumed the condition of their mothers. He apparently traveled widely as a young man and eventually settled in Boston in the mid-1820s. A dedicated activist, Walker sheltered fugitive slaves, joined the Massachusetts General Colored Association, and served as an agent for the first African American newspaper, Freedom's Journal. In September 1829, he published the first edition of David Walker's Appeal in Four Articles; Together with a Preamble, to the Coloured Citizens of the World, but in Particular and Very Expressly, to Those of the United States of America. *This militant rejection of slavery and colonialism prompted a vehemently hostile reaction by whites in both the North and the South. A bounty was offered on him in Georgia—ten thousand dollars alive, one thousand dollars dead. Walker died under mysterious circumstances on June 28, 1830, less than a year after the first appearance of the* Appeal. *Many suspect that he was poisoned.*

Appeal, &c.

ARTICLE III.

Our Wretchedness in Consequence of the Preachers of the Religion of Jesus Christ.

1 Religion, my brethren, is a substance of deep consideration among all nations of the earth. The Pagans have a kind, as well as the Mahometans, the Jews and the Christians. But pure and undefiled religion, such as was preached by Jesus Christ and his apostles, is hard to be found in all the earth. God, through his instrument, Moses, handed a dispensation of his Divine will, to the children of Israel after they had left Egypt for the land of Canaan or of Promise, who through hypocrisy, oppression and unbelief, departed from the faith.—He then, by his apostles, handed a dispensation of his, together with the will of Jesus Christ, to the Europeans in Europe, who, in open violation of which, have made *merchandise* of us, and it does appear as though they take this very dispensation to aid them in their *infernal* depredations upon us. Indeed, the way in which religion was and is conducted by the Europeans and their descendants, one might believe it was a plan fabricated by themselves and the *devils* to *oppress* us. But hark! My master has taught me better than to believe it—he has taught me that his gospel as it was preached by himself and his apostles remains the same, notwithstanding Europe has tried to mingle blood and oppression with it.

2 It is well known to the Christian world, that Bartholomew Las Casas, that very very notoriously avaricious Catholic priest or preacher, and adventurer with Columbus in his second voyage, proposed to his countrymen, the Spaniards in Hispaniola to import the Africans from the Portuguese settlement in Africa, to dig up gold

and silver, and work their plantations for them, to effect which, he made a voyage thence to Spain, and opened the subject to his master, Ferdinand then in declining health, who listened to the plan: but who died soon after, and left it in the hand of his successor Charles V.* This wretch, ("Las Casas, the Preacher,") succeeded so well in his plans of oppression, that in 1503, the first blacks had been imported into the new world. Elated with this success, and stimulated by sordid avarice only, he importuned Charles V. in 1511, to grant permission to a Flemish merchant to import 4000 blacks at one time.** Thus we see, through the instrumentality of a pretended preacher of the gospel of Jesus Christ our common master, our wretchedness first commenced in America—where it has been continued from 1503, to this day, 1829. A period of three hundred and twenty-six years. But two hundred and nine, from 1620—when twenty of our fathers were brought into Jamestown, Virginia, by a Dutch man of war, and sold off like brutes to the highest bidders; and there is not a doubt in my mind, but that tyrants are in hope to perpetuate our miseries under them and their children until the final consummation of all things.—But if they do not get dreadfully deceived, it will be because God has forgotten them.

3   The Pagans, Jews and Mahometans try to make proselytes to their religions, and whatever human beings adopt their religions they extend to them their protection. But Christian Americans, not only hinder their fellow creatures, the Africans, but thousands of them *will absolutely beat a coloured person nearly to death, if they catch him on his knees, supplicating the throne of grace.* This barbarous cruelty was by all the heathen nations of antiquity, and is by the Pagans, Jews and Mahometans of the present day, left entirely to Christian Americans to inflict on the Africans and their descendants, that their cup which is nearly full may be completed. I have known tyrants or

---

*See Butler's *History of the United States,* vol. 1, page 24.—See also, page 25.

**It is not unworthy of remark, that the Portuguese and Spaniards, were among, if not the very first Nations upon Earth, about three hundred and fifty or sixty years ago—But see what those *Christians* have come to now in consequence of afflicting our fathers and us, who have never molested, or disturbed them or any other of the white *Christians,* but have they received one quarter of what the Lord will yet bring upon them, for the murders they have inflicted upon us?—They have had, and in some degree have now, sweet times on our blood and groans, the time however, of bitterness have sometime since commenced with them—There is a God the Maker and preserver of all things, who will as sure as the world exists, give all his creatures their just recompense of reward in this and in the world to come,—we may fool or deceive, and keep each other in the most profound ignorance, beat murder and keep each other out of what is our lawful rights, or the rights of man, yet it is impossible for us to deceive or escape the Lord Almighty.

usurpers of human liberty in different parts of this country to take their fellow creatures, the coloured people, and beat them until they would scarcely leave life in them; what for? Why they say "The black devils had the audacity to be found *making prayers and supplications to the God who made them!!!!*"

4   Yes, I have known small collections of coloured people to have convened together, for no other purpose than to worship God Almighty, in spirit and in truth, to the best of their knowledge; when tyrants, calling themselves *patrols*, would also convene and wait almost in breathless silence for the poor coloured people to commence singing and praying to the Lord our God, as soon as they had commenced, the wretches would burst in upon them and drag them out and commence beating them as they would rattlesnakes—many of whom, they would beat so unmercifully, that they would hardly be able to crawl for weeks and sometimes for months. Yet the American ministers send out missionaries to convert the heathen, while they keep us and our children sunk at their feet in the most abject ignorance and wretchedness that ever a people was afflicted with since the world began. Will the Lord suffer this people to proceed much longer? Will he not stop them in their career? Does he regard the heathens abroad, more than the heathens among the Americans? Surely the Americans must believe that God is partial, notwithstanding his Apostle Peter, declared before Cornelius and others that he has no respect to persons, but in every nation he that feareth God and worketh righteousness is accepted with him—"The word," said he, "which God sent unto the children of Israel, preaching peace, by Jesus Christ, (he is Lord of all)."* Have not the Americans the Bible in their hands? Do they believe it? Surely they do not. See how they treat us in open violation of the Bible!!

5   They no doubt will be greatly offended with me, but if God does not awaken them, it will be, because they are superior to other men, as they have represented themselves to be. Our divine Lord and Master said, "all things whatsoever ye would that men should do unto you, do ye even so unto them." But an American minister, with the Bible in his hand, holds us and our children in the most abject slavery and wretchedness. Now I ask them, would they like for us to hold them and their children in abject slavery and wretchedness? No says one, that never can be done—you are too abject and ignorant

*See Acts of the Apostles, chap. xv.–25–27.

to do it—you are not men—you were made to be slaves to us, to dig up gold and silver for us and our children. Know this, my dear sirs, that although you treat us and our children now, as you do your domestic beast—yet the final result of all future events are known but to God Almighty alone, who rules in the armies of heaven and among the inhabitants of the earth, and who dethrones one earthly king and sits up another, as it seemeth good in his holy sight. We may attribute these vicissitudes to what we please, but the God of armies and of justice rules in heaven and in earth and the whole American people shall see and know it yet to their satisfaction.

6   I have known pretended preachers of the gospel of my Master, who not only held us as their natural inheritance, but treated us with as much rigor as any Infidel or Deist in the world—just as though they were intent only on taking our blood and groans to glorify the Lord Jesus Christ. The wicked and ungodly, seeing their preachers treat us with so much cruelty, they say: our preachers, who must be right, if any body are, treat them like brutes, and why cannot we?—They think it is no harm to keep them in slavery and put the whip to them, and why cannot we do the same!—They being preachers of the gospel of Jesus Christ, if it were any harm, they would surely preach against their oppression and do their utmost to erase it from the country; not only in one or two cities, but one continual cry would be raised in all parts of this confederacy, and would cease only with the complete overthrow of the system of slavery, in every part of the country.

7   But how far the American preachers are from preaching against slavery and oppression, which have carried their country to the brink of a precipice; to save them from plunging down the side of which, will hardly be affected, will appear in the sequel of this paragraph, which I shall narrate just as it transpired. I remember a Camp Meeting in South Carolina, for which I embarked in a Steam Boat at Charleston, and having been five or six hours on the water, we at last arrived at the place of hearing, where was a very great concourse of people, who were no doubt, collected together to hear the word of God, (that some had collected barely as spectators to the scene, I will not here pretend to doubt, however, that is left to themselves and their God.)

8   Myself and boat companions, having been there a little while, we were all called up to hear; I among the rest went up and took my seat—being seated, I fixed myself in a complete position to hear the word of my Saviour and to receive such as I thought was authenticated by the Holy Scriptures; but to my no ordinary astonishment,

our Reverend gentleman got up and told us (coloured people) that slaves must be obedient to their masters—must do their duty to their masters or be whipped—the whip was made for the backs of fools, &c. Here I pause for a moment, to give the world time to consider what was my surprise, to hear such preaching from a minister of my Master, whose very gospel is that of peace and not of blood and whips, as this pretended preacher tried to make us believe. What the American preachers can think of us, I aver this day before my God, I have never been able to define. They have newspapers and monthly periodicals, which they receive in continual succession, but on the pages of which, you will scarcely ever find a paragraph respecting slavery, which is ten thousand times more injurious to this country than all the other evils put together; and which will be the final overthrow of its government, unless something is very speedily done; for their cup is nearly full.—Perhaps they will laugh at or make light of this; but I tell you Americans! that unless you speedily alter your course, *you* and your *Country are gone!!!!!!* For God Almighty will tear up the very face of the earth!!!

9   Will not that very remarkable passage of Scripture be fulfilled on Christian Americans? Hear it Americans!! "He that is unjust, let him be unjust still:—and he which is filthy let him be filthy still: and he that is righteous, let him be righteous still: and he that is holy, let him be holy still."* I hope that the Americans may hear, but I am afraid that they have done us so much injury, and are so firm in the belief that our Creator made us to be an inheritance to them for ever, that their hearts will be hardened, so that their destruction may be sure. This language, perhaps is too harsh for the American's delicate ears. But Oh Americans! Americans!! I warn you in the name of the Lord, (whether you will hear, or forbear,) to repent and reform, or you are ruined!!!

10   Do you think that our blood is hidden from the Lord, because you can hide it from the rest of the world, by sending our missionaries, and by your charitable deeds to the Greeks, Irish, &c? Will he not publish your secret crimes on the housetop? Even here in Boston, pride and prejudice have got to such a pitch, that in the very houses erected to the Lord, they have built little places for the reception of coloured people, where they must sit during meeting, or keep away from the house of God, and the preachers say nothing about it—much less go into the hedges and highways seeking the lost sheep of the

---

*See Revelation, chap. xxii. II.

house of Israel, and try to bring them in to their Lord and Master. There are not a more wretched, ignorant, miserable, and abject set of beings in all the world, than the blacks in the Southern and Western sections of this country, under tyrants and devils. The preachers of America cannot see them, but they can send out missionaries to convert the heathens, notwithstanding Americans! unless you speedily alter your course of proceeding, if God Almighty does not stop you, I say it in his name, that you may go on and do as you please for ever, both in time and eternity—never fear any evil at all!!!!!!!!

11   ADDITION.—The preachers and people of the United States form societies against Free Masonry and Intemperance, and write against Sabbath breaking, Sabbath mails, Infidelity, &c. &c. But the fountain head,* compared with which, all those other evils are comparatively nothing, and from the bloody and murderous head of which, they receive no trifling support, is hardly noticed by Americans. This is a fair illustration of the state of society in this country—it shows what a bearing *avarice* has upon a people, when they are nearly given up by the Lord to a hard heart and a reprobate mind, in consequence of afflicting their fellow creatures. God suffers some to go on until they are ruined for ever!!!!! Will it be the case with the whites of the United States of America?—We hope not—we would not wish to see them destroyed notwithstanding, they have and do now treat us more cruel than any people have treated another, on this earth since it came from the hands of its Creator (with the exceptions of the French and the Dutch, they treat us nearly, as bad as the Americans of the United States.) The will of God must however, in spite of us, *be done.*

12   The English are the best friends the coloured people have upon earth. Though they have oppressed us a little and have colonies now in the West Indies, which oppress us *sorely.*—Yet notwithstanding they (the English) have done one hundred times more for the melioration of our condition, than all the other nations of the earth put together. The blacks cannot but respect the English as a nation, notwithstanding they have treated us a little cruel.

13   There is no intelligent *black man* who knows any thing, but esteems a real Englishman, let him see him in what part of the world he will—for they are the greatest benefactors we have upon earth. We have here and there, in other nations, good friends. But as a nation, the English are our friends.

---

*Slavery and oppression.

14   How can the preachers and people of America believe the Bible? Does it teach them any distinction on account of man's colour? Hearken, Americans! to the injunctions of our Lord and Master, to his humble followers.

15   *And Jesus came and spake unto them, saying all power is given unto me in Heaven and in earth.

Go ye, therefore, and teach all nations, baptizing them in the name of the Father, and of the Son, and of the Holy Ghost.

Teaching them to observe all things whatsoever I have commanded you; and lo, I am with you always, even unto the end of the world. Amen.

16   I declare, that the very face of these injunctions appear to be of God and not of man. They do not show the slightest degree of distinction. "Go ye therefore," (says my divine Master) "and teach all nations," (or in other words, all people) "baptizing them in the name of the Father, and of the Son, and of the Holy Ghost." Do you understand the above, Americans?

17   We are a people, notwithstanding many of you doubt it. You have the Bible in your hands, with this very injunction.—Have you been to Africa, teaching the inhabitants thereof the words of the Lord Jesus? "Baptizing them in the name of the Father, and of the Son, and of the Holy Ghost." Have you not, on the contrary, entered among us, and learnt us the art of throat-cutting, by setting us to fight, one against another, to take each other as prisoners of war, and sell to you for small bits of calicoes, old swords, knives, &c. to make slaves for you and your children? This being done, have you not brought us among you, in chains and handcuffs, like brutes, and treated us with all the cruelties and rigour your ingenuity could invent, consistent with the laws of your country, which (for the blacks) are tyrannical enough? Can the American preachers appeal unto God, the Maker and Searcher of hearts, and tell him, with the Bible in their hands, that they make no distinction on account of men's colour? Can they say, O God! thou knowest all things—thou knowest that we make no distinction between thy creatures, to whom we preach thy Word? Let them answer the Lord; and if they cannot do it in the affirmative, have they not departed from the Lord Jesus Christ, their master?

---

*See St. Matthew's Gospel, chap. xxviii. 18, 19, 20. After Jesus was risen from the dead.

18   But some may say, that they never had, or were in possession of a religion, which made no distinction, and of course they could not have departed from it. I ask you then, in the name of the Lord, of what kind can your religion be? Can it be that which was preached by our Lord Jesus Christ from Heaven? I believe you cannot be so wicked as to tell him that his Gospel was that of *distinction*. What can the American preachers and people take God to be? Do they believe his words? If they do, do they believe that he will be mocked? Or do they believe, because they are whites and we blacks, that God will have respect to them? Did not God make us all as it seemed best to himself? What right, then, has one of us to despise another, and to treat him cruel, on account of his colour, which none, but the God who made it can alter? Can there be a greater absurdity in nature, and particularly in a free republican country?

19   But the Americans, having introduced slavery among them, their hearts have become almost seared, as with an hot iron, and God has nearly given them up to believe a lie in preference to the truth!!! And I am awfully afraid that pride, prejudice, avarice and blood, will, before long prove the final ruin of this happy republic, or land of *liberty!!!!* Can any thing be a greater mockery of religion than the way in which it is conducted by the Americans?

20   It appears as though they are bent only on daring God Almighty to do his best—they chain and handcuff us and our children and drive us around the country like brutes, and go into the house of the God of justice to return him thanks for having aided them in their infernal cruelties inflicted upon us. Will the Lord suffer this people to go on much longer, taking his holy name in vain? Will he not stop them, PREACHERS and all? O Americans! Americans!! I call God—I call angels—I call men, to witness, that your DESTRUCTION *is at hand*, and will be speedily consummated unless you REPENT.

Frederick Douglass

(1818–1895)

For biographical information, see page 241.

The Blood of the Slave on the Skirts of the Northern People*

1   A victim of your power and oppression, humbly craves your attention to a few words, (in behalf of himself and three millions of his brethren, whom you hold in chains and slavery,) with respect to the election just completed. In doing so, I desire to be regarded as addressing you individually and collectively. If I should seem severe, remember that the iron of slavery has pierced and rankled in my heart, and that I not only smart under the recollection of a long and cruel enslavement, but am even now passing my life in a country, and among a people, whose prejudices against myself and people subjects me to a thousand poisonous stings. If I speak harshly, my excuse is, that I speak in fetters of your own forging. Remember that oppression hath the power to make even a wise man mad.

2   In the selection of your national rulers just completed, you have made another broad mark on the page of your nation's history, and have given to the world and the coming generation a certain test by which to determine your present integrity as a people. That actions speak louder than words—that within the character of the representative may be seen that of the constituency—that no people are better than their laws of lawmakers—that a stream cannot rise higher than its source—that a sweet fountain cannot send forth bitter water, and that a tree is to be known by its fruits, are truisms; and in their light let us examine the character and pretensions of your boasted Republic.

3   As a people, you claim for yourselves a higher civilization—a purer morality—a deeper religious faith—a larger love of liberty, and a broader philanthropy, than any other nation on the globe. In a word, you claim yours to be a model Republic, and promise, by the force and excellence of your institutions, and the purity

*The North Star, November 17, 1848

and brightness of your example, to overthrow the thrones and despotisms of the old world, and substitute your own in their stead. Your missionaries are found in the remotest parts of the globe, while our land swarms with churches and religious institutions. In words of Religion and Liberty, you are abundant and preeminent. You have long desired to get rid of the odium of being regarded as pro-slavery, and have even insisted that the charge of pro-slavery made against you was a slander and that those who made it were animated by wild and fanatical spirit. To make your innocence apparent, you have now had a fair opportunity. The issue for freedom or slavery has been clearly submitted to you, and you have deliberately chosen slavery.

4   General Taylor and General Cass were the chosen and admitted Southern and slavery candidates for the Presidency. Martin Van Buren, though far from being an abolitionist, yet in some sort represented the Anti-Slavery idea of the North, in a political form— him you have rejected, and elected a slaveholder to rule over you in his stead. When the question was whether New Mexico and California shall be Free or Slave States, you have rejected him who was solemnly pledged to maintain their freedom, and have chosen a man whom you knew to be pledged, by his position, to the maintenance of slavery. By your votes, you have said that slavery is better than freedom—that war is better than peace, and that cruelty is better than humanity. You have given your sanction to slave rule and slavery propagandism, and interposed whatever of moral character and standing you possess, to shield the reputation of slaveholders generally. You have said, that to be a man-stealer is no crime—to traffic in human flesh shall be a passport, rather than a barrier to your suffrages. To slaveholders you have said, Chain up your men and women, and before the bloody lash drive them to new fields of toil in California and New Mexico. To the slave in his chains you have said, Be content in your chains, and if you dare to gain your freedom by force, whether in New Mexico or California, in numbers indicated by our votes, our muskets shall find you out. In a word, you have again renewed your determination to support the Constitution of the United States, in its parts of freedom to the whites, and slavery, to the blacks. If General Taylor's slaves run away, you have promised again to return them to bondage. While General Taylor is the well-known robber of three hundred human beings of all their hard earnings, and is coining their hard

earnings into gold, you have conferred upon him an office worth twenty-five thousand dollars a year, and the highest honor within your power. By this act, you have endorsed his character and history. His murders in Mexico—his "blood-hound" cruelty in the Florida war—his awful profanity, together with the crimes attendant upon a slave plantation, such as theft, robbery, murder, and adultery, you have sanctioned as perfectly consistent with your morality, humanity, liberty, religion and civilization. You have said that the most available and suitable person in all this great nation, to preside over this model Republic, is a warrior, slaveholder, swearer, and bloodhound importer.—During the campaign just ended, your leaders have dubbed this man-stealer as an *honest man*, and many of you have shouted over the lie, as being a truth, thus destroying all moral distinctions. To talk of a veracious liar, a pious blasphemer, a righteous robber, a candid hypocrite, a sober drunkard, or a humane cannibal, would be quite as just and rational as to call an admitted man-stealer an honest man. Yet in the wildness of a wicked enthusiasm, you have given your countenance and support to this.

5   Now is it too much to say that you have made his crimes your own, and that the blood of the slave is on your garments? You have covered his theft with honesty, his blasphemy with piety, and, as far as in your power, you have rendered the blows intended to destroy slavery nugatory and innoxious. Before high heaven and the world, you are responsible for the blood of the slave. You may shut your eyes to the fact, sport over it, sleep over it, dance over it, and sing psalms over it, but so sure as there is a God of Justice and an unerring Providence, just so sure will the blood of the bondman be required at your hands.—An opportunity was presented to you by which you could have fixed an indelible mark of your utter detestation of slavery, and given a powerful blow to that bitter curse. This you have failed to do. When Christ and Barabbas were presented, you have cried out in your madness, Give us Barabbas the robber, in preference to Christ, the innocent. The perishing slave, with uplifted hands and bleeding hearts, implored you, in the name of the God you profess to serve, and the humanity you profess to cherish, not to add this mill-stone to the weight already crushing his heart and hopes. But he has appealed in vain. You have turned a deaf ear to his cries, hardened your hearts to his appeal, turned your back upon his sorrows, and united with the tyrant to

perpetuate his enslavement. The efforts made in your presence to impress you with the awful sin of slavery, and to awaken you to a sense of your duty to the oppressed, have thus far been unavailing. You continue to fight against God, and declare that *injustice* exalteth a nation, and that sin is an *honor* to any people.

6   Do you really think to circumvent God?—Do you suppose that you can go on in your present career of injustice and political profligacy undisturbed? Has the law of righteous retribution been repealed from the statutes of the Almighty? Or what mean ye that ye bruise and bind my people? Will justice sleep forever? Oh, that you would lay these things to heart! Oh, that you would consider the enormity of your conduct, and seek forgiveness at the hands of a merciful Creator. Repent of this wickedness, and bring forth fruit meet for repentance, by delivering the despoiled out of the hands of the despoiler.

7   You may imagine that you have now silenced the annoying cry of abolition—that you have sealed the doom of the slave—that abolition is stabbed and dead; but you will find your mistake. You have stabbed, but the cause is not dead. Though down and bleeding at your feet, she shall rise again, and going before you, shall give you no rest till you break every yoke and let the oppressed go free. The Anti-Slavery Societies of the land will rise up and spring to action again, sending forth from the press and on the voice of the living speaker, words of burning truth, to alarm the guilty, to unmask the hypocrite, to expose the frauds of political parties, and rebuke the spirit of a corrupt and sin-sustaining church and clergy. Slavery will be attacked in its stronghold—the compromises of the Constitution, and the cry of disunion shall be more fearlessly proclaimed, till slavery be abolished, the Union dissolved, or the sun of this guilty nation must go down in blood.—F. D.

Emancipation, Racism, and the Work Before Us: An Address Delivered in Philadelphia, Pennsylvania, On 4 December 1863

1   Ladies and Gentlemen: I confess at the outset to have felt a very profound desire to utter a word at some period during the present meeting. As it has been repeatedly said here, it has been a meeting of reminiscences. I shall not attempt to treat you to any of my own in what I have now to say, though I have some in connection with the labors of this Society, and in connection with my experience as an American slave, that I might not inappropriately bring before you on this occasion. I desire to be remembered among those having a word to say at this meeting, because I began my existence as a free man in this country with this association, and because I have some hopes or apprehensions, whichever you please to call them, that we shall never, as a Society, hold another decade meeting.

2   I well remember the first time I ever listened to the voice of the honored President of this association, and I have some recollection of the feelings of hope inspired by his utterances at that time.* Under the inspiration of those hopes, I looked forward to the abolition of slavery as a certain event in the course of a very few years. So clear were his utterances, so simple and truthful, and so adapted. I conceived, to the human heart were the principles and doctrines propounded by him, that I thought five years at any rate would be all that would be required for the abolition of slavery. I thought it was only necessary for the slaves, or their friends, to lift up the hatchway of slavery's internal hold, to uncover the bloody scenes of American thraldom, and give the nation a peep into its horrors, its deeds of deep damnation, to arouse them to almost phrensied opposition

*In his third autobiography. Douglass recollects having first heard William Lloyd Garrison president of the American Anti-Slavery Society from 1843 to 1865, speak early in 1839 Douglass, *Life and Times*, 213–14.

to this foul curse. But I was mistaken. I had not been five years pelted by the mob, insulted by the crowds, shunned by the church, denounced by the ministry, ridiculed by the press, spit upon by the loafers, before I became convinced that I might perhaps live, struggle, and die, and go down to my grave, and the slaves of the South yet remain in their chains.

3   We live to see a better hope to-night. I participate in the profound thanksgiving expressed by all, that we do live to see this better day. I am one of those who believe that it is the mission of this war to free every slave in the United States. I am one of those who believe that we should consent to no peace which shall not be an abolition peace. I am, moreover, one of those who believe that the work of the American Anti-Slavery Society will not have been completed until the black men of the South, and the black men of the North, shall have been admitted fully and completely into the body politic of America. I look upon slavery as going the way of all the earth.* It is the mission of the war to put it down. But a mightier work than the abolition of slavery now looms up before the Abolitionist. This Society was organized, if I remember rightly, for two distinct objects; one was the emancipation of the slave, and the other the elevation of the colored people. When you have taken the chains off the slave, as I believe we shall do, we shall find a harder resistance to the second purpose of this great association than we have found even upon slavery itself.

4   I am hopeful, but while I am hopeful I am thoughtful withal. If I lean to either side of the controversy to which we have listened to-day, I lean to that side which implies caution, which implies apprehension, which implies a consciousness that our work is not done. Protest, affirm, hope, glorify as we may, it cannot be denied that abolitionism is still unpopular in the United States. It cannot be denied that this war is at present denounced by its opponents as an abolition war; and it is equally clear that it would not be denounced as an abolition war, if abolitionism were not odious. It is equally clear that our friends. Republicans, Unionists, Loyalists,** would not spin out elaborate explanations, and denials that this is the character of the war,

---

*Douglass quotes from Josh. 23:14: "And, behold this day I *am* going the way of all the earth."
**In an attempt to broaden support for the Lincoln administration during the Civil War, Republican politicians in several regions adopted new labels for their party. In the Ohio Valley and Middle Atlantic states an electoral coalition of Republicans and Democratic politicians who favored vigorous prosecution of the war campaigned under the banner of the "Union party." In the Border states pro-administration candidates preferred the patriotic-sounding Unionist or Loyalist labels to "Republican," which still carried an antislavery connotation in that region. The convention that nominated Lincoln for a second term in 1864 exchanged the name Republican for "National Union party." Mathews, *Dictionary of Americanisms*, 2: 1006, 1796–98.

if abolition were popular. Men accept the term Abolitionist with qualifications. They do not come out square and open-handed, and affirm themselves to be Abolitionists. As a general rule, we are attempting to explain away the charge that this is an abolition war. I hold that it is an abolition war, because slavery has proved itself stronger than the Constitution. It has proved itself stronger than the Union, and has forced upon us the necessity of putting down slavery in order to save the Union, and in order to save the Constitution. (Applause.)

5   I look at this as an abolition war instead of being a Union war, because I see that the lesser is included in the greater, and that you cannot have the lesser until you have the greater. You cannot have the Union, the Constitution, and republican institutions, until you have stricken down that damning curse, and put it beyond the pale of the Republic. For, while it is in this country, it will make your Union impossible; it will make your Constitution impossible. I therefore call this just what the Democrats have charged it with being, an abolition war. Let us emblazon it on our banners, and declare before the world that this is an abolition war, (applause), that it will prosper precisely in proportion as it takes upon itself this character. (Renewed applause.)

6   My respected friend, Mr. Purvis, called attention to the existence of prejudice against color in this country.* This gives me great cause for apprehension, if not for alarm. I am afraid of this powerful element of prejudice against color. While it exists, I want the voice of the American Anti-Slavery Society to be continually protesting, continually exposing it. While it can be said that in this most anti-slavery city in the Northern States of our Union, in the city of Philadelphia, the city of Brotherly Love, in the city of churches, the city of piety,** that the most genteel and respectable colored lady or gentleman may be kicked out of your commonest street car, we are in danger of a compromise. While it can be said that black men, fighting bravely for this country, are asked to take $7 per month, while the government lays down as a

*According to the *National Anti-Slavery Standard*. Robert Purvis, the first speaker at the 4 December evening session, "delivered an impassioned address, dwelling mainly upon the proscriptive spirit of caste, which, in defiance of the fundamental principles of the American government deprives the colored man of his political, educational and social rights, and often exposes him to insult and outrage." *NASS*, 12, 26 December 1863.
**Douglass describes Philadelphia by several of its nicknames. In 1681 William Penn selected the Greek noun *philadelphia*, meaning literally "brotherly love," for the name of his new colony's capital. The nickname "City of Churches" became attached to Philadelphia because of the large number of religious edifices lowering above its early nineteenth-century skyline. Alexander, *Nicknames and Sobriquets*, 189; George R. Stewart, *American Place-Names: A Concise and Selective Dictionary for the Continental United States of America* (New York, 1970), 370.

rule or criterion of pay a complexional one, we are in danger of a compromise. While to be radical is to be unpopular, we are in danger of a compromise. While we have a large minority, called Democratic, in every State of the North, we have a powerful nucleus for a most infernal reaction in favor of slavery. I know it is said that we have recently achieved vast political victories. I am glad of it. I value those victories, however, more for what they have prevented than for what they have actually accomplished. I should have been doubly sad at seeing any one of these States wheel into line with the Peace Democracy.* But, however it may be in the State of Pennsylvania, I know that you may look for abolition in the creed of any party in New York with a microscope, and you will not find a single line of anti-slavery there. The victories were Union victories, victories to save the Union in such ways as the country may devise to save it.** But whatever may have been the meaning of these majorities in regard to the Union, we know one thing, that the minorities, at least, mean slavery. They mean submission. They mean the degradation of the colored man. They mean everything but open rebellion against the Federal government in the South. But the mob, the rioters in the city of New York, convert that city into a hell, and its lower orders into demons, and dash out the brains of little children against the curbstones;*** and they mean anything and everything that the Devil

*The term *Peace Democrat* originated in the highly partisan rhetoric of Northern politics during the Civil War. By 1863 some northern Democrats such as Clement Vallandigham of Ohio and Fernando Wood of New York publicly endorsed an armistice to end hostilities and negotiations to restore the Union. Republicans used these statements to brand the bulk of Democrats with favoring peace at any price. Denying that anything short of Union military victory could reunite the nation, the Republicans accused the Peace Democrats of being at best tools of at worst traitors Mathews, *Dictionary of Americanisms*, 2: 1212; Silbey. *Respectable Minority*, 92, 100 05, 166

**Douglass characterizes the spirit of the 1863 campaign in New York. On 2 September 1863 a Union party state convention representing the Republicans and a small number of prowar Democrats met in Syracuse to nominate candidates and adopt a platform. The convention's original declaration of principles was silent on the controversial issue of emancipation. At the very end of the proceedings, an additional resolution was added to the party's platform endorsing Lincoln's Emancipation Proclamation "as a war measure, thoroughly legal and justifiable." In the subsequent campaign, however, Unionist nominees generally ignored the slavery question and stressed their party's support for a vigorous prosecution of the war. New York *Daily Tribune*. 3 September 1863; New York *Times*, 3 September 1863: Flick, *History of New York*. 7: 116–17.

***In March 1863, when it had become clear that recruitment could not keep pace with Union army requirements. Congress passed a conscription act. Legal attempts by Democratic politicians such as New York governor Horatio Seymour to block enforcement of the draft failed, and the drawing of names began in New York City on 11 July 1863. Two days later a mob composed mainly of foreign-born laborers sacked the city's draft headquarters and looted and turned homes and businesses. A major target of the mob was the city's black population. Rioters lynched at least a dozen blacks, burned a black orphanage, and plundered and terrorized black neighborhoods. Local authorities proved unable to quell the violence, and Federal troops fresh from the Gettysburg battlefield had to be rushed to New York City. Order was not restored until 16 July. James McCague. *The Second Rebellion: The Story of the New York City Draft Riots of 1863* (New York, 1968): Eugene Converse Murdock, *Patriotism Limited, 1862–1865. The Civil War Draft and the Bounty System* ([Kent. Ohio], 1967), 63–80.

exacts at their hands. While we had in this State a majority of but 15,000 over this pro-slavery Democratic party, they have a mighty minority, a dangerous minority.* Keep in mind when these minorities were gotten. Powerful as they are, they were gotten when slavery, with bloody hands, was stabbing at the very heart of the nation itself. With all that disadvantage, they have piled up these powerful minorities.

7   We have work to do, friends and fellow-citizens, to look after these minorities. The day that shall see Jeff Davis fling down his Montgomery Constitution,** and call home his Generals, will be the most trying day to the virtue of this people that this country has ever seen. When the slaveholders shall give up the contest, and ask for re-admission into the Union, then, as Mr. Wilson has told us, we shall see the trying time in this country.*** Your Democracy will clamor for peace and for restoring the old order of things, because that old order of things was the life of the Democratic party. "You do take away mine house, when you take away the prop that sustains my house," and the support of the Democratic party we all know to be slavery. The Democratic party is for war for slavery: it is for peace for slavery; it is for the *habeas corpus* for slavery; it is against the *habeas corpus* for slavery; it was for the Florida war for slavery; it was for the Mexican war for slavery; it is for jury trial for traitors for slavery; it is against jury trial for men claimed as fugitive slaves for slavery. It has but one principle, one master; and it is guided, governed and directed by it. I say that with this party among us, flaunting its banners in our faces, with the New York *World* scattered broadcast over the North, with the New York *Express*, with the mother and father and devil of them all, the New York *Herald*, (applause), with those papers flooding our land, and coupling the term Abolitionist with all manner of coarse

*In October 1863 Republican Andrew G. Curtin was reelected governor of Pennsylvania by a vote of 269,506 to 254,171 over Democratic candidate George W. Woodward. Sobel and Raimo, *Biographical Directory of Governors*, 3: 1310–11; William II Egle, ed., *Andrew Gregg Curtin: His Life and Services* (Philadelphia, 1895). 159–66
**On 11 March 1861, after five weeks of deliberations at Montgomery, Alabama, the Provisional Congress of the Confederate States of America unanimously adopted a permanent constitution for their new government. Thomas, *Confederate Nation*. 57–58, 62–66; Eaton, *Southern Confederacy*, 43–44.
***Senator Henry Wilson of Massachusetts preceded Douglass in addressing the American Anti-Slavery Society convention. In the remarks to which Douglass alludes, Wilson warned the abolitionists not to believe that the Emancipation Proclamation had won the battle against slavery. Wilson declared: "We are to be tried—the government is to be tried. . . . Yet, while we are to be tried. I believe we shall remain firm, true, and faithful, and that we shall triumph." *Lib.*, 25 December 1863; *NASS*, 26 December 1863; American Anti-Slavery Society, *Proceedings . . . at Its Third Decade*. 102–10.

epithets,* in all our hotels, at all our crossings, our highways, and byways, and railways, all over the country, there is work to be done— a good deal of work to be done.

8   I have said that our work will not be done until the colored man is admitted a full member in good and regular standing into the American body politic. Men have very nice ideas about the body politic where I have travelled: and they don't like the idea of having the negro in the body politic. He may remain in this country, for he will be useful as a laborer, valuable perhaps in time of trouble as a helper; but to make him a full and complete citizen, a legal voter, that would be contaminating the body politic. I was a little curious, some years ago, to find out what sort of a thing this body politic was; and I was very anxious to know especially about what amount of baseness, brutality, coarseness, ignorance, and bestiality, could find its way into the body politic; and I was not long in finding it out. I took my stand near the little hole through which the body politic put its votes. (Laughter.) And first among the mob, I saw Ignorance, unable to read its vote, asking *me* to read it, by the way, (great laughter), depositing its vote in the body politic. Next I saw a man stepping up to the body politic, casting in his vote, having a black eye, and another one ready to be blacked, having been engaged in a street fight. I saw, again, Pat, fresh from the Emerald Isle, with the delightful brogue peculiar to him, stepping up—not walking, but leaning upon the arms of two of his friends, unable to stand, passing into the body politic! I came to the conclusion that this body politic was, after all, not quite so pure a body as the representation of its friends would lead us to believe.

9   I know it will be said that I ask you to make the black man a voter in the South. Yet you are for having brutality and ignorance introduced into the ballot-box. It is said that the colored man is ignorant, and therefore he shall not vote. In saying this, you lay down a

*The New York *World* had been an independent religious newspaper until purchased by a committee of Democratic party leaders in September 1862. The prestige of its sponsors and the talent of its young editor, Manton Marble, quickly attracted a national readership for the *World*. Although heavily partisan, the *World* gave editorial support in a vigorous prosecution of the war The New York *Evening Express*, founded in 1836 by James and Erastus Brooks, shifted political allegiance in the 1850s from the Whigs to the Know Nothings and finally to the Democrats. During the Civil War the *Express* criticized the Lincoln administration and supported the Peace Democrat's position. Since its founding in 1835, the New York *Herald*, under the editorship of James Gordon Bennett, had become one of the most influential newspapers in the country. In 1860 the *Herald* endorsed Stephen A. Douglas and called for sectional compromise in the secession crisis. Although critical of the administration's emancipation policy and its arbitrary arrests of opponents, the *Herald* gave qualified support to Lincoln's reelection in 1864. Harper, *Lincoln and the Press*. 252 61.318 24. Silbey, *Respectable Minority*, 64.65; Randall, *Constitutional Problems under Lincoln*, 487–88, *ACAB*. 1 : 386–87; *DAB*. 2: 195–99.

rule for the black man that you apply to no other class of your citizens. I will hear nothing of degradation nor of ignorance against the black man. If he knows enough to be hanged, he knows enough to vote. If he knows an honest man from a thief, he knows much more than some of our white voters. If he knows as much when sober as an Irishman knows when drunk, he knows enough to vote. If he knows enough to take up arms in defence of this government, and bare his breast to the storm of rebel artillery, he knows enough to vote. (Great applause.)

10   Away with this talk of the want of knowledge on the part of the negro! I am about as big a negro as you will find anywhere about town; and any man that does not believe I know enough to vote, let him try it. I think I can convince him that I do. Let him run for office in my district, and solicit my vote, and I will show him.

11   All I ask, however, in regard to the blacks, is that whatever rule you adopt, whether of intelligence or wealth, as the condition of voting, you should apply it equally to the black man. Do that, and I am satisfied, and eternal justice is satisfied. Liberty, fraternity, equality, are satisfied; and the country will move on harmoniously.

12   Mr. President, I have a patriotic argument in favor of insisting upon the immediate enfranchisement of the slaves of the South; and it is this. When this rebellion shall have been put down, when the arms shall have fallen from the guilty hand of traitors, you will need the friendship of the slaves of the South, of those millions there. Four or five million men are not of inconsiderable importance at anytime; but they will be doubly important when you come to reorganize and reestablish republican institutions in the South. Will you mock those bondmen by breaking their chains with one hand, and with the other giving their rebel masters the elective franchise and robbing them of theirs? I tell you the negro is your friend. But you will make him not only your friend in sentiment and heart by enfranchising him, you will thus make him your best defender, your best protector against the traitors and the descendants of those traitors who will inherit the hate, the bitter revenge which shall crystalize all over the South, and seek to circumvent the government that they could not throw off. You will need the black man there as a watchman and patrol; and you may need him as a soldier. You may need him to uphold in peace, as he is now upholding in war, the star-spangled banner. (Applause.) I wish our excellent friend, Senator Wilson, would bend his energies to this point as well as the other—to let the negro have a vote. It will be helping him from the jaws of the wolf. We are surrounded by those

who, like the wolf, will use their jaws, if you give the elective franchise to the descendants of the traitors, and keep it from the black man. We ought to be voters there! We ought to be members of Congress! (Applause.) You may as well make up your minds that you have got to see something dark down that way! There is no way to get rid of it. I am a candidate already! (Applause.)

13   For twenty-five years, Mr. President, you know that when I got as far South as Philadelphia, I felt that I was rubbing against my prison wall, and could not go any further. I dared not go over yonder into Delaware.* Twenty years ago, when I attended the first Decade meeting of this Society, as I came along the vales and hills of Gettysburg, my good friends, the anti-slavery people along there, warned me to remain in the house during the daytime and travel in the night, lest I should be kidnapped, and carried over into Maryland. My good friend Dr. Fussell was one of the number who did not think it safe for me to attend an anti-slavery meeting along the borders of this State.** I can go down there now. I have been to Washington to see the President; and as you were not there, perhaps you may like to know how the President of the United States received a black man at the White House.*** I will tell you how he received me—just as you have seen one gentleman receive another! (great applause); with a hand and a voice well-balanced between a kind cordiality and a respectful reserve. I tell you I felt big there. (Laughter.) Let me tell you how I got to him; because every body can't get to him. He has to be a little guarded in admitting spectators. The manner in getting to him gave me an idea that the cause was rolling on. The stairway

---

*Douglass escaped from slavery in 1838 and did not reenter a slave state until passing through Delaware and Maryland on his way to Washington, D.C., in July 1863 Quarles. *I.D.* 210 11.

**On his way to the Diennial Convention of the American Anti-Slavery Society held in Philadelphia on 4–7 December 1843. Douglass lectured in Pittsburgh and several other Pennsylvania towns. No record exists of the warnings that Douglass remembers having received while on this tour. His reference to, a Dr. Fussell is probably to either Bartholomew Fussell of York, Pennsylvania, or Edwin Fussell of Pendleton, Indiana, both Hicksite Quakers and physicians. Bartholomew Fussell was one of the founders of the American Anti-Slavery Society in 1833. His nephew, Edwin (?–1882), was a Garrisonian abolitionist who had braved a mob in Pendleton when he had hosted Douglass in his home that previous September. In 1844, Edwin moved to the Philadelphia area, where he continued to practice medicine. *NASS,* 14 December 1843; *Lib.,* 15, 22 December 1843; Holland, *Frederick Douglass,* 95–96.

***In the company of Senator Samuel C. Pomeroy of Kansas. Douglass had an interview with Lincoln at the White House on 10 August 1863. Douglass's account of this meeting appears in Allen Thorndike Rice, ed., *Reminiscences of Abraham Lincoln by Distinguished Men of His Time* (New York, 1886). 187–89, and in Douglass, *Life and Times,* 381–84. Douglass to George L. Steams, 12 August 1863. Abraham Harker Scrap Book, PHI: Tyler Dennett, ed., *Lincoln and the Civil War in the Diaries and Letters of John Max* (New York, 1939), 79: Quarles, *Lincoln and the Negro,* 168.

was crowded with applicants. Some of them looked eager; and I have no doubt some of them had a purpose in being there, and wanted to see the President for the good of the country! They were white, and as I was the only dark spot among them. I expect[ed] to have a wait at least half a day; I have heard of men waiting a week; but in two minutes after I sent in my card, the messenger came out, and respectfully invited "Mr. Douglass" in, I could hear, in the eager multitude outside, as they saw me pressing and elbowing my way through, the remark, "Yes, damn it, I knew they would let the nigger through," in a kind of despairing voice—a Peace Democrat, I suppose, (Laughter.) When I went in, the President was sitting in his usual position. I was told, with his feet in different parts of the room, taking it easy. (Laughter.) Don't put this down, Mr. Reporter, I pray you; for I am going down there again to-morrow. (Laughter.) As I came in and approached him, the President began to rise, and he continued to rise until he stood over me (laughter); and he reached out his hand and said, "Mr. Douglass, I know you; I have read about you, and Mr. Seward* has told me about you;" putting me quite at ease at once.

14 Now you will want to know how I was impressed by him. I will tell you that, too. He impressed me as being just what every one of you have been in the habit of calling him—an honest man. (Applause.) I never met with a man, who, on the first blush, impressed me more entirely with his sincerity, with his devotion to his country, and with his determination to save it at all hazards. (Applause.) He told me (I think he did me more honor than I deserve), that I had made a little speech somewhere in New York, and it had got into the papers, and among the things I had said was this: That if I were called upon to state what I regarded as the most sad and most disheartening feature in our present political and military situation, it would not be the various disasters experienced by our armies and our navies, on flood and field, but it would be the tardy, hesitating and vacillating policy of the President of the United States;** and the President said to me, "Mr. Douglass, I have been charged with being tardy, and the like;" and he went on, and partly admitted that he might seem slow; but he said, "I am charged with vacillating; but, Mr. Douglass, I do

---

*William H. Seward.
**Although Douglass criticized Lincoln in many speeches early in the war, this particular reference is to his lecture delivered at Boston's Tremont Temple on 5 February 1862 and again at New York City's Cooper Institute on 12 February 1862. *DM*, 4 : 613–16 (March 1862); New York *Daily Tribune*, 13 February 1862.

not think that charge can be sustained; I think it cannot be shown that when I have once taken a position, I have ever retreated from it." (Applause.) That I regarded as the most significant point in what he said during our interview. I told him that he had been somewhat slow in proclaiming equal protection to our colored soldiers and prisoners; and he said that the country needed talking up to that point.* He hesitated in regard to it when he felt that the country was not ready for it. He knew that the colored man throughout this country was a despised man, a hated man, and he knew that if he at first came out with such a proclamation, all the hatred which is poured on the head of the negro race would be visited on his Administration. He said that there was preparatory work needed, and that that preparatory work had been done. And he added, "Remember this, Mr. Douglass; remember that Milliken's Bend, Port Hudson, and Fort Wagner are recent events; and that these were necessary to prepare the way for this very proclamation of mine."** I thought it was reasonable; but I came to the conclusion that while Abraham Lincoln will not go down to posterity as Abraham the Great, or as Abraham the Wise, or as Abraham the Eloquent, although he is all three, wise, great, and eloquent, he will go down to posterity, if the country is saved, as Honest Abraham, (applause): and going down thus, his name may be written anywhere in this wide world of ours side by side with that of Washington, without disparaging the latter. (Cheers.)

15   But we are not to be saved by the captain this time, but by the crew. We are not to be saved by Abraham Lincoln, but by that power behind the throne, greater than the throne itself. You and I and all of us have this matter in hand. Men talk about saving the Union, and restoring the Union as it was. They delude themselves with the miserable idea that that old Union can be brought to life again. That old Union, whose canonized bones we so quietly inurned under the

*On 30 July 1863 Lincoln signed an order pledging the U.S. government to "give the same protection to all its soldiers, and if the enemy shall sell or enslave anyone because of his color, the offense shall be punished by retaliation upon the enemy's prisoners in our possession" Basler, *Collected Works of Lincoln*, 6 : 357.

**Lincoln's reference was to three battles in 1863 in which black Union troops demonstrated their courage and military competence. On 27 May 1863 two black regiments raised in Louisiana made repeated charges, despite heavy casualties, on Confederate fortifications at Port Hudson in that state. On 7 June 1863 two other black Louisiana regiments repulsed a Confederate attack on their camp at Milliken's Bend in hand-to-hand combat. On the night of 18–19 July 1863, the black Fifty-fourth Massachusetts Infantry Regiment sustained 247 casualties while spearheading an unsuccessful attack on Fort Wagner, South Carolina. The complimentary official reports of the black soldiers performance in these battles helped to erase much of the widespread doubt about the wisdom of black enlistment. Quarles, *Negro in the Civil War*, 12–21, 214–25; Cornish, *Sable Arm*, 142–156; Boatner, *Civil War Dictionary*, 301, 663.

shattered walls of Sumter, can never come to life again. It is dead, and you cannot put life into it. The first shot fired at the walls of Sumter caused it to fall as dead as the body of Julius Caesar when stabbed by Brutus.* We do not want it. We have outlived the old Union. We had outlived it long before the rebellion came to tell us—I mean the Union under the old pro-slavery interpretation of it—and had become ashamed of it. The South hated it with our anti-slavery interpretation, and the North hated it with the Southern interpretation of its requirements. We had already come to think with horror of the idea of being called upon here in our churches and literary societies, to take up arms and go down South, and pour the leaden death into the breasts of the slaves, in case they should rise for liberty; and the better part of the people did not mean to do it. They shuddered at the idea of so sacrilegious a crime. They had already become utterly disgusted with the idea of playing the part of blood-hounds for the slave-masters, and watch-dogs for the plantations. They had come to detest the principle upon which the slaveholding States had a larger representation in Congress than the free States. They had come to think that the little finger of dear old John Brown was worth more to the world than all the slaveholders in Virginia put together. (Applause.) What business, then, have we to fight for the old Union? We are not fighting for it. We are fighting for something incomparably better than the old Union. We are fighting for unity; unity of object, unity of institutions, in which there shall be no North, no South, no East, no West, no black, no white, but a solidarity of the nation, making every slave free, and every free man a voter. (Great applause.)

Booker T. Washington

(1856–1915)

Born into slavery on April 5, 1856, in Franklin County, Virginia (now West Virginia), Booker Taliaferro Washington, perhaps the most controversial of race leaders because of his often accommodationist stance, succeeded Frederick Douglass as the premier African American spokesperson. Washington was unmatched in his ability to attract financial support from white philanthropies, especially after he delivered his

---

*Douglass alludes to the murder of Roman general Julius Caesar by Marcus Julius Brutus in the Senate on the Ides of March 44 n.c. William Smith, ed., *Dictionary of Greek and Roman Biography and Mythology*, 3 vols. (Boston, 1849), 1 : 510, 539, 553–54.

famous "Speech at the Atlanta Exposition," known popularly as the Atlanta Compromise, at the Cotton States and International Exposition in September 1895. He received an honorary degree from Harvard in 1897. Washington founded Tuskegee Institute in 1881 and presided over the school until his death on November 14, 1915. His works include The Future of the American Negro *(1899) and the autobiography* Up from Slavery *(1901).*

Speech at the Atlanta Exposition

1 Mr. President and Gentlemen of the Board of Directors and Citizens:

2   One-third of the population of the South is of the Negro race. No enterprise seeking the material, civil, or moral welfare of this section can disregard this element of our population and reach the highest success. I but convey to you, Mr. President and Directors, the sentiment of the masses of my race when I say that in no way have the value and manhood of the American Negro been more fittingly and generously recognized than by the managers of this magnificent exposition at every stage of its progress. It is a recognition that will do more to cement the friendship of the two races than any occurrence since the dawn of our freedom.

3   Not only this, but the opportunity here afforded will awaken among us a new era of industrial progress. Ignorant and inexperienced, it is not strange that in the first years of our new life we began at the top instead of at the bottom; that a seat in Congress or the state legislature was more sought than real estate or industrial skill; that the political convention or stump speaking had more attractions than starting a dairy farm or truck garden.

4   A ship lost at sea for many days suddenly sighted a friendly vessel. From the mast of the unfortunate vessel was seen a signal: "Water, water; we die of thirst!" The answer from the friendly vessel at once came back: "Cast down your bucket where you are" A second time the signal, "Water, water, send us water!" ran up from the distressed vessel, and was answered: "Cast down your bucket where you are." And a third and fourth signal for water was answered: "Cast down your bucket where you are." The captain of the distressed vessel, at last heeding the injunction, cast down his bucket, and it came up full of fresh, sparkling water from the mouth of the Amazon River.

5   To those of my race who depend on bettering their condition in a foreign land or who underestimate the importance of cultivating friendly relations with the Southern white man, who is their next-door neighbor. I would say: Cast down your bucket where you are; cast it down in making friends, in every manly way, of the people of all races by whom we are surrounded. Cast it down in agriculture, mechanics, in commerce, in domestic service, and in the professions. And in this connection it is well to bear in mind that whatever other sins the South may be called to bear, when it comes to business, pure and simple, it is in the South that the Negro is given a man's chance in the commercial world, and in nothing is this exposition more eloquent than in emphasizing this chance.

6   Our greatest danger is that, in the great leap from slavery to freedom, we may overlook the fact that the masses of us are to live by the productions of our hands and fail to keep in mind that we shall prosper in proportion as we learn to dignify and glorify common labor, and put brains and skill into the common occupations of life shall prosper in proportion as we learn to draw the line between the superficial and the substantial, the ornamental gewgaws of life and the useful. No race can prosper till it learns that there is as much dignity in tilling a field as in writing a poem. It is at the bottom of life we must begin, and not at the top. Nor should we permit our grievances to overshadow our opportunities.

7   To those of the white race who look to the incoming of those of foreign birth and strange tongue and habits for the prosperity of the South, were I permitted I would repeat what I say to my own race, "Cast down your bucket where you are." Cast it down among the 8 million Negroes whose habits you know, whose fidelity and love you have tested in days when to have proved treacherous meant the ruin of your firesides. Cast down your bucket among these people who have, without strikes and labor wars, tilled your fields, cleared your forests, builded your railroads and cities, and brought forth treasures from the bowels of the earth and helped make possible this magnificent representation of the progress of the South. Casting down your bucket among my people, helping and encouraging them as you are doing on these grounds, and, with education of head, hand, and heart, you will find that they will buy your surplus land, make blossom the waste places in your fields, and run your factories.

8   While doing this, you can be sure in the future, as in the past, that you and your families will be surrounded by the most patient, faithful, law-abiding, and unresentful people that the world has seen. As we have proved our loyalty to you in the past, in nursing your children,

watching by the sickbed of your mothers and fathers, and often following them with tear-dimmed eyes to their graves, so in the future, in our humble way, we shall stand by you with a devotion that no foreigner can approach, ready to lay down our lives, if need be, in defense of yours: interlacing our industrial, commercial, civil, and religious life with yours in a way that shall make the interests of both races one. In all things that are purely social we can be as separate as the fingers, yet one as the hand in all things essential to mutual progress.

9   There is no defense or security for any of us except in the highest intelligence and development of all. If anywhere there are efforts tending to curtail the fullest growth of the Negro, let these efforts be turned into stimulating, encouraging, and making him the most useful and intelligent citizen. Effort or means so invested will pay a thousand percent interest. These efforts will be twice blessed—"blessing him that gives and him that takes."

10   There is no escape, through law of man or God, from the inevitable:

> *The laws of changeless justice bind*
> *Oppressor with oppressed;*
> *And close as sin and suffering joined*
> *We march to fate abreast*

11   Nearly 16 millions of hands will aid you in pulling the load upward, or they will pull against you the load downward. We shall constitute one-third and more of the ignorance and crime of the South, or one-third its intelligence and progress; we shall contribute one-third to the business and industrial prosperity of the South, or we shall prove a veritable body of death, stagnating, depressing, retarding every effort to advance the body politic.

12   Gentlemen of the exposition, as we present to you our humble effort at an exhibition of our progress, you must not expect overmuch. Starting thirty years ago with ownership here and there in a few quilts and pumpkins and chickens (gathered from miscellaneous sources), remember: the path that has led from these to the invention and production of agricultural implements, buggies, steam engines, newspapers, books, statuary, carving, paintings, the management of drugstores and banks, has not been trodden without contact with thorns and thistles. While we take pride in what we exhibit as a result of our independent efforts, we do not for a moment forget that our part in this exhibition would fall far short of your expectations but for the constant help that has come to our educational life, not only from the Southern states but

especially from Northern philanthropists who have made their gifts a constant stream of blessing and encouragement.

13   The wisest among my race understand that the agitation of questions of social equality is the extremest folly and that progress in the enjoyment of all the privileges that will come to us must be the result of severe and constant struggle rather than of artificial forcing. No race that has anything to contribute to the markets of the world is long in any degree ostracized. It is important and right that all privileges of the law be ours, but it is vastly more important that we be prepared for the exercise of these privileges. The opportunity to earn a dollar in a factory just now is worth infinitely more than the opportunity to spend a dollar in an opera house.

14   In conclusion, may I repeat that nothing in thirty years has given us more hope and encouragement and drawn us so near to you of the white race as this opportunity offered by the exposition; and here bending, as it were, over the altar that represents the results of the struggles of your race and mine, both starting practically empty-handed three decades ago, I pledge that, in your effort to work out the great and intricate problem which God has laid at the doors of the South, you shall have at all times the patient, sympathetic help of my race; only let this be constantly in mind that, while from representations in these buildings of the product of field, of forest, of mine, of factory, letters, and art, much good will come—yet far above and beyond material benefits will be that higher good, that let us pray God will come in a blotting out of sectional differences and racial animosities and suspicions, in a determination to administer absolute justice, in a willing obedience among all classes to the mandates of law. This, coupled with our material prosperity, will bring into our beloved South a new heaven and a new earth.

The Future of the American Negro

1   One of the main problems as regards the education of the Negro is how to have him use his education to the best advantage after he has secured it. In saying this, I do not want to be understood as implying that the problem of simple ignorance among the masses has been

settled in the South; for this is far from true. The amount of ignorance still prevailing among the Negroes, especially in the rural districts, is very large and serious. But I repeat, we must go farther if we would secure the best results and most gratifying returns in public good for the money spent than merely to put academic education in the Negro's head with the idea that this will settle everything.

2   In his present condition it is important, in seeking after what he terms the ideal, that the Negro should not neglect to prepare himself to take advantage of the opportunities that are right about his door. If he lets these opportunities slip, I fear they will never be his again. In saying this, I mean always that the Negro should have the most thorough mental and religious training; for without it no race can succeed. Because of his past history and environment and present condition it is important that he be carefully guided for years to come in the proper use of his education. Much valuable time has been lost and money spent in vain, because too many have not been educated with the idea of fitting them to do well the things which they could get to do. Because of the lack of proper direction of the Negro's education, some good friends of his, North and South, have not taken that interest in it that they otherwise would have taken. In too many cases where merely literary education alone has been given the Negro youth, it has resulted in an exaggerated estimate of his importance in the world, and an increase of wants which his education has not fitted him to supply.

3   But, in discussing this subject, one is often met with the question, Should not the Negro be encouraged to prepare himself for any station in life that any other race fills? I would say, Yes; but the surest way for the Negro to reach the highest positions is to prepare himself to fill well at the present time the basic occupations. This will give him a foundation upon which to stand while securing what is called the more exalted positions. The Negro has the right to study law; but success will come to the race sooner if it produces intelligent, thrifty farmers, mechanics, and housekeepers to support the lawyers. The want of proper direction of the use of the Negro's education results in tempting too many to live mainly by their wits, without producing anything that is of real value to the world. Let me quote examples of this.

4   Hayti, Santo Domingo, and Liberia, although among the richest countries in natural resources in the world, are discouraging examples of what must happen to any people who lack industrial or technical training. It is said that in Liberia there are no wagons,

wheelbarrows, or public roads, showing very plainly that there is a painful absence of public spirit and thrift. What is true of Liberia is also true in a measure of the republics of Hayti and Santo Domingo. The people have not yet learned the lesson of turning their education toward the cultivation of the soil and the making of the simplest implements for agricultural and other forms of labour.

5   Much would have been done toward laying a sound foundation for general prosperity if some attention had been spent in this direction. General education itself has no bearing on the subject at issue, because, while there is no well-established public school system in either of these countries, yet large numbers of men of both Hayti and Santo Domingo have been educated in France for generations. This is especially true of Hayti. The education has been altogether in the direction of *belles lettres*, however, and practically little in the direction of industrial and scientific education.

6   It is a matter of common knowledge that Hayti has to send abroad even to secure engineers for her men-of-war, for plans for her bridges and other work requiring technical knowledge and skill. I should very much regret to see any such condition obtain in any large measure as regards the coloured people in the South, and yet this will be our fate if industrial education is much longer neglected. We have spent much time in the South in educating men and women in letters alone, too, and must now turn our attention more than ever toward educating them so as to supply their wants and needs. It is more lamentable to see educated people unable to support themselves than to see uneducated people in the same condition. Ambition all along this line must be stimulated.

7   If educated men and women of the race will see and acknowledge the necessity of practical industrial training and go to work with a zeal and determination, their example will be followed by others, who are now without ambition of any kind.

8   The race cannot hope to come into its own until the young coloured men and women make up their minds to assist in the general development along these lines. The elder men and women trained in the hard school of slavery, and who so long possessed all of the labour, skilled and unskilled, of the South, are dying out; their places must be filled by their children, or we shall lose our hold upon these occupations. Leaders in these occupations are needed now more than ever.

9   It is not enough that the idea be inculcated that coloured people should get book learning; along with it they should be taught that

book education and industrial development must go hand in hand. No race which fails to do this can ever hope to succeed. Phillips Brooks gave expression to the sentiment: "One generation gathers the material, and the next generation builds the palaces." As I understand it, he wished to inculcate the idea that one generation lays the foundation for succeeding generations. The rough affairs of life very largely fall to the earlier generation, while the next one has the privilege of dealing with the higher and more aesthetic things of life. This is true of all generations, of all peoples; and, unless the foundation is deeply laid, it is impossible for the succeeding one to have a career in any way approaching success. As regards the coloured men of the South, as regards the coloured men of the United States, this is the generation which, in a large measure, must gather the material with which to lay the foundation for future success.

10   Some time ago it was my misfortune to see a Negro sixty-five years old living in poverty and filth. I was disgusted, and said to him, "If you are worthy of your freedom, you would surely have changed your condition during the thirty years of freedom which you have enjoyed." He answered: "I do want to change. I want to do something for my wife and children; but I do not know how,—I do not know what to do." I looked into his lean and haggard face, and realised more deeply than ever before the absolute need of captains of industry among the great masses of the coloured people.

11   It is possible for a race or an individual to have mental development and yet be so handicapped by custom, prejudice, and lack of employment as to dwarf and discourage the whole life. This is the condition that prevails among the race in many of the large cities of the North; and it is to prevent this same condition in the South that I plead with all the earnestness of my heart. Mental development alone will not give us what we want, but mental development tied to hand and heart training will be the salvation of the Negro.

12   In many respects the next twenty years are going to be the most serious in the history of the race. Within this period it will be largely decided whether the Negro will be able to retain the hold which he now has upon the industries of the South or whether his place will be filled by white people from a distance. The only way he can prevent the industrial occupations slipping from him in all parts of the South, as they have already in certain parts, is for all educators, ministers, and friends of the race to unite in pushing forward in a whole-souled manner the industrial or business development of the Negro, whether in school or out of school. Four times as many young men

and women of the race should be receiving industrial training. Just now the Negro is in a position to feel and appreciate the need of this in a way that no one else can. No one can fully appreciate what I am saying who has not walked the streets of a Northern city day after day seeking employment, only to find every door closed against him on account of his colour, except in menial service. It is to prevent the same thing taking place in the South that I plead. We may argue that mental development will take care of all this. Mental development is a good thing. Gold is also a good thing, but gold is worthless without an opportunity to make itself touch the world of trade. Education increases greatly an individual's wants. It is cruel in many cases to increase the wants of the black youth by mental development alone without, at the same time, increasing his ability to supply these increased wants in occupations in which he can find employment.

13   The place made vacant by the death of the old coloured man who was trained as a carpenter during slavery, and who since the war had been the leading contractor and builder in the Southern town, had to be filled. No young coloured carpenter capable of filling his place could be found. The result was that his place was filled by a white mechanic from the North, or from Europe, or from elsewhere. What is true of carpentry and house building in this case is true, in a degree, in every skilled occupation; and it is for professional service. Whether they receive the training of the hand while pursuing their academic training or after their academic training is finished, or whether they will get their literary training in an industrial school or college, are questions which each individual must decide for himself. No matter how or where educated, the educated men and women must come to the rescue of the race in the effort to get and hold its industrial footing. I would not have the standard of mental development lowered one whit; for, with the Negro, as with all races, mental strength is the basis of all progress. But I would have a large measure of this mental strength reach the Negroes' actual needs through the medium of the hand. Just now the need is not so much for the common carpenters, brick masons, farmers, and laundry women as for industrial leaders who, in addition to their practical knowledge, can draw plans, make estimates, take contracts; those who understand the latest methods of truck-gardening and the science underlying practical agriculture; those who understand machinery to the extent that they can operate steam and electric laundries, so that our women can hold on to the laundry work in the South, that is so fast drifting into the hands of others in the large cities and towns.

14   Having tried to show in previous chapters to what a condition
the lack of practical training has brought matters in the South, and
by the examples in this chapter where this state of things may go if
allowed to run its course, I wish now to show what practical training, even in its infancy among us, has already accomplished.

15   I noticed, when I first went to Tuskegee to start the Tuskegee Normal and Industrial Institute, that some of the white people about there
rather looked doubtfully at me; and I thought I could get their influence by telling them how much algebra and history and science and
all those things I had in my head, but they treated me about the same
as they did before. They didn't seem to care about the algebra, history, and science that were in my head only. Those people never even
began to have confidence in me until we commenced to build a large
three-story brick building, and then another and another, until now
we have forty buildings which have been erected largely by the labour
of our students; and to-day we have the respect and confidence of
all the white people in that section.

16   There is an unmistakable influence that comes over a white man
becoming true of common labour. I do not mean to say that all of the
skilled labour has been taken out of the Negro's hands; but I do mean
to say that in no part of the South is he so strong in the matter of skilled
labour as he was twenty years ago, except possibly in the country districts and the smaller towns. In the more northern of the Southern cities,
such as Richmond and Baltimore, the change is most apparent; and
it is being felt in every Southern city. Wherever the Negro has lost
ground industrially in the South, it is not because there is prejudice
against him as a skilled labourer on the part of the native Southern
white man; the Southern white man generally prefers to do business
with the Negro mechanic rather than with a white one, because he is
accustomed to do business with the Negro in this respect. There is
almost no prejudice against the Negro in the South in matters of business, so far as the native whites are concerned; and here is the entering wedge for the solution of the race problem. But too often, where the
white mechanic or factory operative from the North gets a hold, the
trades-union soon follows, and the Negro is crowded to the wall.

17   But what is the remedy for this condition? First, it is most important that the Negro and his white friends honestly face the facts as
they are; otherwise the time will not be very far distant when the
Negro of the South will be crowded to the ragged edge of industrial
life as he is in the North. There is still time to repair the damage and
to reclaim what we have lost.

18   I stated in the beginning that industrial education for the Negro
has been misunderstood. This has been chiefly because some have
gotten the idea that industrial development was opposed to the
Negro's higher mental development. This has little or nothing to do
with the subject under discussion; we should no longer permit such
an idea to aid in depriving the Negro of the legacy in the form of
skilled labour that was purchased by his forefathers at the price of
two hundred and fifty years of slavery. I would say to the black boy
what I would say to the white boy. Get all the mental development
that your time and pocket-book will allow of,—the more, the better; but the time has come when a larger proportion—not all, for we
need professional men and women—of the educated coloured men
and women should give themselves to industrial or business life. The
professional class will be helped in so far as the rank and file have
an industrial foundation, so that they can pay when he sees a black
man living in a two-story brick house that has been paid for. I need
not stop to explain. It is the tangible evidence of prosperity. You know
Thomas doubted the Saviour after he had risen from the dead; and
the Lord said to Thomas, "Reach hither thy finger, and behold my
hands; and reach hither thy hand, and thrust it into my side." The
tangible evidence convinced Thomas.

19   We began, soon after going to Tuskegee, the manufacture of
bricks. We also started a wheelwright establishment and the manufacture of good wagons and buggies; and the white people came to
our institution for that kind of work. We also put in a printing plant,
and did job printing for the white people as well as for the blacks.

20   By having something that these people wanted, we came into contact with them, and our interest became interlinked with their interest, until to-day we have no warmer friends anywhere in the country
than we have among the white people of Tuskegee. We have found by
experience that the best way to get on well with people is to have
something that they want, and that is why we emphasise this Christian Industrial Education.

21   Not long ago I heard a conversation among three white men something like this. Two of them were berating the Negro, saying the Negro
was shiftless and lazy, and all that sort of thing. The third man listened
to their remarks for some time in silence, and then he said: "I don't
know what your experience has been; but there is a 'nigger' down our
way who owns a good house and lot with about fifty acres of ground.
His house is well furnished, and he has got some splendid horses and
cattle. He is intelligent and has a bank account. I don't know how the

'niggers' are in your community, but Tobe Jones is a gentleman. Once, when I was hard up, I went to Tobe Jones and borrowed fifty dollars; and he hasn't asked me for it yet. I don't know what kind of 'niggers' you have down your way, but Tobe Jones is a gentleman."

22   Now what we want to do is to multiply and place in every community these Tobe Joneses; and, just in so far as we can place them throughout the South this race question will disappear.

23   Suppose there was a black man who had business for the railroads to the amount of ten thousand dollars a year. Do you suppose that, when that black man takes his family aboard the train, they are going to put him into a Jim Crow car and run the risk of losing that ten thousand dollars a year? No, they will put on a Pullman palace car for him.

24   Some time ago a certain coloured man was passing through the streets of one of the little Southern towns, and he chanced to meet two white men on the street. It happened that this coloured man owns two or three houses and lots, has a good education and a comfortable bank account. One of the white men turned to the other, and said: "By Gosh! It is all I can do to keep from calling that 'nigger' Mister." That's the point we want to get to.

25   Nothing else so soon brings about right relations between the two races in the South as the commercial progress of the Negro. Friction between the races will pass away as the black man, by reason of his skill, intelligence, and character, can produce something that the white man wants or respects in the commercial world. This is another reason why at Tuskegee we push industrial training. We find that as every year we put into a Southern community coloured men who can start a brickyard, a saw-mill, a tin-shop, or a printing-office,—men who produce something that makes the white man partly dependent upon the Negro instead of all the dependence being on the other side,—a change for the better takes place in the relations of the races. It is through the dairy farm, the truck-garden, the trades, the commercial life, largely, that the Negro is to find his way to respect and confidence.

26   What is the permanent value of the Hampton and Tuskegee system of training to the South, in a broader sense? In connection with this, it is well to bear in mind that slavery unconsciously taught the white man that labour with the hands was something fit for the Negro only, and something for the white man to come into contact with just as little as possible. It is true that there was a large class of poor white people who laboured with the hands, but they did it because they were not able to secure Negroes to work for them; and these poor whites were constantly trying to imitate the slaveholding class in

escaping labour, as they, too, regarded it as anything but elevating. But the Negro, in turn, looked down upon the poor whites with a certain contempt because they had to work. The Negro, it is to be borne in mind, worked under constant protest, because he felt that his labour was being unjustly requited; and he spent almost as much effort in planning how to escape work as in learning how to work. Labour with him was a badge of degradation. The white man was held up before him as the highest type of civilisation, but the Negro noted that this highest type of civilisation himself did little labour with the hand. Hence he argued that, the less work he did, the more nearly he would be like the white man. Then, in addition to these influences, the slave system discouraged labour-saving machinery. To use labour-saving machinery, intelligence was required; and intelligence and slavery were not on friendly terms. Hence the Negro always associated labour with toil, drudgery, something to be escaped. When the Negro first became free, his idea of education was that it was something that would soon put him in the same position as regards work that his recent master had occupied. Out of these conditions grew the habit of putting off till to-morrow and the day after the duty that should be done promptly to-day. The leaky house was not repaired while the sun shone, for then the rain did not come through While the rain was falling, no one cared to expose himself to stop the rain. The plough, on the same principle, was left where the last furrow was run, to rot and rust in the field during the winter. There was no need to repair the wooden chimney that was exposed to the fire, because water could be thrown on it when it was on fire. There was no need to trouble about the payment of a debt to-day, because it could be paid as well next week or next year. Besides these conditions, the whole South at the close of the war was without proper food, clothing, and shelter,—was in need of habits of thrift and economy and of something laid up for a rainy day.

27   To me it seemed perfectly plain that here was a condition of things that could not be met by the ordinary process of education. At Tuskegee we became convinced that the thing to do was to make a careful, systematic study of the condition and needs of the South, especially the Black Belt, and to bend our efforts in the direction of meeting these needs, whether we were following a well-beaten track or were hewing out a new path to meet conditions probably without a parallel in the world. After eighteen years of experience and observation, what is the result? Gradually, but surely, we find that all through the South the disposition to look upon labour as a disgrace

is on the wane; and the parents who themselves sought to escape work are so anxious to give their children training in intelligent labour that every institution which gives training in the handicrafts is crowded, and many (among them Tuskegee) have to refuse admission to hundreds of applicants. The influence of Hampton and Tuskegee is shown again by the fact that almost every little school at the remotest crossroad is anxious to be known as an industrial school, or, as some of the coloured people call it, an "industrous" school.

28   The social lines that were once sharply drawn between those who laboured with the hands and those who did not are disappearing. Those who formerly sought to escape labour, now when they see that brains and skill rob labour of the toil and drudgery once associated with it, instead of trying to avoid it, are willing to pay to be taught how to engage in it. The South is beginning to see labour raised up, dignified and beautified, and in this sees its salvation. In proportion as the love of labour grows, the large idle class, which has long been one of the curses of the South, disappears. As people become absorbed in their own affairs, they have less time to attend to everybody's else business.

29   The South is still an undeveloped and unsettled country, and for the next half-century and more the greater part of the energy of the masses will be needed to develop its material resources. Any force that brings the rank and file of the people to have a greater love of industry is therefore especially valuable. This result industrial education is surely bringing about. It stimulates production and increases trade,—trade between the races; and in this new and engrossing relation both forget the past. The white man respects the vote of a coloured man who does ten thousand dollars' worth of business; and, the more business the coloured man has, the more careful he is how he votes.

30   Immediately after the war there was a large class of Southern people who feared that the opening of the free schools to the freedmen and the poor whites—the education of the head alone—would result merely in increasing the class who sought to escape labour, and that the South would soon be overrun by the idle and vicious. But, as the results of industrial combined with academic training begin to show themselves in hundreds of communities that have been lifted up, these former prejudices against education are being removed. Many of those who a few years ago opposed Negro education are now among its warmest advocates.

31   This industrial training, emphasising, as it does, the idea of economic production, is gradually bringing the South to the point where it is feeding itself. After the war, what profit the South made out of

the cotton crop it spent outside of the South to purchase food supplies,—meat, bread, canned vegetables, and the like,—but the improved methods of agriculture are fast changing this custom. With the newer methods of labour, which teach promptness and system and emphasise the worth of the beautiful, the moral value of the well-painted house, the fence with every paling and nail in its place, is bringing to bear upon the South an influence that is making it a new country in industry, education, and religion.

32   It seems to me I cannot do better than to close this chapter on the needs of the Southern Negro by quoting from a talk given to the students at Tuskegee:

33   "I want to be a little more specific in showing you what you have to do and how you must do it.

34   "One trouble with us is—and the same is true of any young people, no matter of what race or condition—we have too many stepping-stones. We step all the time, from one thing to another. You find a young man who is learning to make bricks; and, if you ask him what he intends to do after learning the trade, in too many cases he will answer, 'Oh, I am simply working at this trade as a stepping-stone to something higher.' You see a young man working at the brick-mason's trade, and he will be apt to say the same thing. And young women learning to be milliners and dressmakers will tell you the same. All are stepping to something higher. And so we always go on, stepping somewhere, never getting hold of anything thoroughly. Now we must stop this stepping business, having so many stepping stones. Instead, we have got to take hold of these important industries, and stick to them until we master them thoroughly. There is no nation so thorough in their education as the Germans. Why? Simply because the German takes hold of a thing, and sticks to it until he masters it. Into it he puts brains and thought from morning to night. He reads all the best books and journals bearing on that particular study, and he feels that nobody else knows so much about it as he does.

35   "Take any of the industries I have mentioned, that of brick-making, for example. Any one working at that trade should determine to learn all there is to be known about making bricks; read all the papers and journals bearing upon the trade; learn not only to make common hand-bricks, but pressed bricks, fire-bricks,—in short, the finest and best bricks there are to be made. And, when you have learned all you can by reading and talking with other people, you should travel from one city to another, and learn how the best bricks are made. And then, when you go into business for yourself, you will

make a reputation for being the best brick-maker in the community; and in this way you will put yourself on your feet, and become a helpful and useful citizen. When a young man does this, goes out into one of these Southern cities and makes a reputation for himself, that person wins a reputation that is going to give him a standing and position. And, when the children of that successful brick-maker come along, they will be able to take a higher position in life. The grandchildren will be able to take a still higher position. And it will be traced back to that grandfather who, by his great success as a brick-maker, laid a foundation that was of the right kind.

36   "What I have said about these two trades can be applied with equal force to the trades followed by women. Take the matter of millinery. There is no good reason why there should not be, in each principal city in the South, at least three or four competent coloured women in charge of millinery establishments. But what is the trouble?

37   "Instead of making the most of our opportunities in this industry, the temptation, in too many cases, is to be music-teachers, teachers of elocution, or something else that few of the race at present have any money to pay for, or the opportunity to earn money to pay for, simply because there is no foundation. But, when more coloured people succeed in the more fundamental occupations, they will then be able to make better provision for their children in what are termed the higher walks of life.

38   "And, now, what I have said about these important industries is especially true of the important industry of agriculture. We are living in a country where, if we are going to succeed at all, we are going to do so largely by what we raise out of the soil. The people in those backward countries I have told you about have failed to give attention to the cultivation of the soil, to the invention and use of improved agricultural implements and machinery. Without this no people can succeed. No race which fails to put brains into agriculture can succeed; and, if you want to realize the truth of this statement, go with me into the back districts of some of our Southern States, and you will find many people in poverty, and yet they are surrounded by a rich country.

39   "A race, like an individual, has got to have a reputation. Such a reputation goes a long way toward helping a race or an individual; and, when we have succeeded in getting such a reputation, we shall find that a great many of the discouraging features of our life will melt away.

40   "Reputation is what people think we are, and a great deal depends on that. When a race gets a reputation along certain lines, a great

many things which now seem complex, difficult to attain, and are most discouraging, will disappear.

41   "When you say that an engine is a Corliss engine, people understand that that engine is a perfect piece of mechanical work, perfect as far as human skill and ingenuity can make it perfect. You say a car is a Pullman car. That is all; but what does it mean? It means that the builder of that car got a reputation at the outset for thorough, perfect work, for turning out everything in first-class shape. And so with a race. You cannot keep back very long a race that has the reputation for doing perfect work in everything that it undertakes. And then we have got to get a reputation for economy. Nobody cares to associate with an individual in business or otherwise who has a reputation for being a trifling spendthrift, who spends his money for things that he can very easily get along without, who spends his money for clothing, gewgaws, superficialities, and other things, when he has not got the necessaries of life. We want to give the race a reputation for being frugal and saving in everything. Then we want to get a reputation for being industrious. Now, remember these three things: Get a reputation for being skilled. It will not do for a few here and there to have it: the race must have the reputation. Get a reputation for being so skilful, so industrious, that you will not leave a job until it is as nearly perfect as any one can make it. And then we want to make a reputation for the race for being honest,—honest at all times and under all circumstances. A few individuals here and there have it, a few communities have it; but the race as a mass must get it.

42   "You recall that story of Abraham Lincoln, how, when he was postmaster at a small village, he had left on his hands $1.50 which the government did not call for. Carefully wrapping up this money in a handkerchief, he kept it for ten years. Finally, one day, the government agent called for this amount; and it was promptly handed over to him by Abraham Lincoln, who told him that during all those ten years he had never touched a cent of that money. He made it a principle of his life never to use other people's money. That trait of his character helped him along to the Presidency. The race wants to get a reputation for being strictly honest in all its dealings and transactions,—honest in handling money, honest in all its dealings with its fellow-men.

43   "And then we want to get a reputation for being thoughtful. This I want to emphasise more than anything else. We want to get a reputation for doing things without being told to do them every time.

If you have work to do, think about it so constantly, investigate and read about it so thoroughly, that you will always be finding ways and means of improving that work. The average person going to work becomes a regular machine, never giving the matter of improving the methods of his work a thought. He is never at his work before the appointed time, and is sure to stop the minute the hour is up. The world is looking for the person who is thoughtful, who will say at the close of work hours: 'Is there not something else I can do for you? Can I not stay a little later, and help you?'

44   "Moreover, it is with a race as it is with an individual: it must respect itself if it would win the respect of others. There must be a certain amount of unity about a race, there must be a great amount of pride about a race, there must be a great deal of faith on the part of a race in itself. An individual cannot succeed unless he has about him a certain amount of pride,—enough pride to make him aspire to the highest and best things in life. An individual cannot succeed unless that individual has a great amount of faith in himself.

45   "A person who goes at an undertaking with the feeling that he cannot succeed is likely to fail. On the other hand, the individual who goes at an undertaking, feeling that he can succeed, is the individual who in nine cases out of ten does succeed. But, whenever you find an individual that is ashamed of his race, trying to get away from his race, apologising for being a member of his race, then you find a weak individual. Where you find a race that is ashamed of itself, that is apologising for itself, there you will find a weak, vacillating race. Let us no longer have to apologise for our race in these or other matters. Let us think seriously and work seriously: then, as a race, we shall be thought of seriously, and therefore, seriously respected."

Ida B. Wells-Barnett
(1862–1931)

Ida B. Wells-Barnett was born in Holly Springs, Mississippi, on July 16, 1862. At the age of 16 having lost her parents and her youngest brother to a yellow fever epidemic, she became a schoolteacher to support her six younger siblings. She moved to Memphis in 1884, where she continued to teach before losing her job in 1891 because of her militant writings. A top-notch investigative journalist, she bought an interest in Free Speech and Headlight *newspaper. Wells-Barnett was*

*forced to leave Memphis under threat, however, after she wrote an
exposé about lynching. She continued to write in the North, remaining
an ardent activist who championed the causes of African Americans
and women. She lectured widely in both the United States and
abroad. Her pamphlets include* Southern Horrors: Lynch Law in All
Its Phases *(1892);* A Red Record: Tabulated Statistics and Alleged
Causes of Lynchings in the United States *(1892), from which the following reading is taken;* Mob Rule in New Orleans *(1900), from which
the second reading is taken; and* The Arkansas Race Riot *(1922).*

A Red Record

CHAPTER X: THE REMEDY

1 It is a well established principle of law that every wrong has a remedy. Herein rests our respect for law. The Negro does not claim that
all of the one thousand black men, women and children, who have
been hanged, shot and burned alive during the past ten years, were
innocent of the charges made against them. We have associated too
long with the white man not to have copied his vices as well as his
virtues. But we do insist that the punishment is not the same for
both classes of criminals. In lynching, opportunity is not given the
Negro to defend himself against the unsupported accusations of
white men and women. The word of the accuser is held to be true
and the excited blood-thirsty mob demands that the rule of law be
reversed and instead of proving the accused to be guilty, the victim of their hate and revenge must prove himself innocent. No evidence he can offer will satisfy the mob; he is bound hand and foot
and swung into eternity. Then to excuse its infamy, the mob almost
invariably reports the monstrous falsehood that its victim made a
full confession before he was hanged.

2   With all military, legal and political power in their hands, only two
of the lynching States have attempted a check by exercising the power
which is theirs. Mayor Trout, of Roanoke, Virginia, called out the militia in 1893, to protect a Negro prisoner, and in so doing nine men
were killed and a number wounded. Then the mayor and militia withdrew, left the negro to his fate and he was promptly lynched. The
business men realized the blow to the town's financial interests, called
the mayor home, [and] the grand jury indicted and prosecuted the

ringleaders of the mob. They were given light sentences, the highest being one of twelve months in State prison. The day he arrived at the penitentiary, he was pardoned by the governor of the State.

3 The only other real attempt made by the authorities to protect a prisoner of the law, and which was more successful, was that of Gov. McKinley, of Ohio, who sent the militia to Washington Courthouse, O., in October, 1894, and five men were killed and twenty wounded in maintaining the principle that the law must be upheld.

4 In South Carolina, in April, 1893, Gov. Tillman aided the mob by yielding up to be killed, a prisoner of the law, who had voluntarily placed himself under the Governor's protection. Public sentiment by its representatives has encouraged Lynch Law, and upon the revolution of this sentiment we must depend for its abolition.

5 Therefore, we demand a fair trial by law for those accused of crime, and punishment by law after honest conviction. No maudlin sympathy for criminals is solicited, but we do ask that the law shall punish all alike. We earnestly desire those that control the forces which make public sentiment to join with us in the demand. Surely the humanitarian spirit of this country which reaches out to denounce the treatment of the Russian Jews, the Armenian Christians, the laboring poor of Europe, the Siberian exiles and the native women of India—will no longer refuse to lift its voice on this subject. If it were known that the cannibals or the savage Indians had burned three human beings alive in the past two years, the whole of Christendom would be roused, to devise ways and means to put a stop to it. Can you remain silent and inactive when such things are done in our own community and country? Is your duty to humanity in the United States less binding?

6 What can you do, reader, to prevent lynching, to thwart anarchy and promote law and order throughout our land?

7 1st. You can help disseminate the facts contained in this book by bringing them to the knowledge of every one with whom you come in contact, to the end that public sentiment may be revolutionized. Let the facts speak for themselves, with you as a medium.

8 2d. You can be instrumental in having churches, missionary societies, Y.M.C.A.'s, W.C.T.U.'s and all Christian and moral forces in connection with your religious and social life, pass resolutions of condemnation and protest every time a lynching takes place; and see that they are sent to the place where these outrages occur.

9 3d. Bring to the intelligent consideration of Southern people the refusal of capital to invest where lawlessness and mob violence hold

sway. Many labor organizations have declared the resolution that they would avoid lynch infested localities as they would the pestilence when seeking new homes. If the South wishes to build up its waste places quickly, there is no better way than to uphold the majesty of the law by enforcing obedience to the same, and meting out the same punishment to all classes of criminals, white as well as black. "Equality before the law," must become a fact as well as a theory before America is truly the "land of the free and the home of the brave."

10   4th. Think and act on independent lines in this behalf, remembering that after all, it is the white man's civilization and the white man's government which are on trial. This crusade will determine whether that civilization can maintain itself by itself, or whether anarchy shall prevail; whether this Nation shall write itself down a success at self government, or in deepest humiliation admit its failure complete; whether the precepts and theories of Christianity are professed and practiced by American white people as Golden Rules of thought and action, or adopted as a system of morals to be preached to heathen until they attain to the intelligence which needs the system of Lynch Law.

11   5th. Congressman Blair offered a resolution in the House of Representatives, August, 1894. The organized life of the country can speedily make this a law by sending resolutions to Congress indorsing Mr. Blair's bill and asking Congress to create the commission. In no better way can the question be settled, and the Negro does not fear the issue. The following is the resolution:

12   "Resolved, By the House of Representatives and Senate in congress assembled, That the committee on labor be instructed to investigate and report the number, location and date of all alleged assaults by males upon females throughout the country during the ten years last preceding the passing of this joint resolution, for or on account of which organized but unlawful violence has been inflicted or attempted to be inflicted. Also to ascertain and report all facts of organized but unlawful violence to the person, with the attendant facts and circumstances, which have been inflicted upon accused persons alleged to have been guilty of crimes punishable by due process of law which have taken place in any part of the country within the ten years last preceding the passage of this resolution. Such investigation shall be made by the usual methods and agencies of the Department of Labor, and report made to Congress as soon as the work can be satisfactorily done, and the sum of $25,000, or so much thereof as may be necessary, is hereby appropriated to pay the expenses out of any money in the treasury not otherwise appropriated."

13   The belief has been constantly expressed in England that in the United States, which has produced Wm. Lloyd Garrison, Henry Ward Beecher, James Russell Lowell, John G. Whittier and Abraham Lincoln there must be those of their descendants who would take hold of the work of inaugurating an era of law and order. The colored people of this country who have been loyal to the flag believe the same, and strong in that belief have begun this crusade. To those who still feel they have no obligation in the matter, we commend the following lines of Lowell on "Freedom."

> *Men! whose boast it is that ye*
> *Come of fathers brave and free,*
> *If there breathe on earth a slave*
> *Are ye truly free and brave?*
> *If ye do not feel the chain,*
> *When it works a brother's pain,*
> *Are ye not base slaves indeed,*
> *Slaves unworthy to be freed?*
>
> *Women! who shall one day bear*
> *Sons to breathe New England air,*
> *If ye hear without a blush,*
> *Deeds to make the roused blood rush*
> *Like red lava through your veins,*
> *For your sisters now in chains,—*
> *Answer! are ye fit to be*
> *Mothers of the brave and free?*
>
> *Is true freedom but to break*
> *Fetters for our own dear sake,*
> *And, with leathern hearts, forget*
> *That we owe mankind a debt?*
> *No! true freedom is to share*
> *All the chains our brothers wear,*
> *And, with heart and hand, to be*
> *Earnest to make others free!*
>
> *There are slaves who fear to speak*
> *For the fallen and the weak;*
> *They are slaves who will not choose*
> *Hatred, scoffing, and abuse,*
> *Rather than in silence shrink*
> *From the truth they needs must think;*
> *They are slaves who dare not be*
> *In the right with two or three.*

A Field for Practical Work

14 The very frequent inquiry made after my lectures by interested friends is, "What can I do to help the cause?" The answer always is, "Tell the world the facts." When the Christian world knows the alarming growth and extent of outlawry in our land, some means will be found to stop it.

15 The object of this publication is to tell the facts, and friends of the cause can lend a helping hand by aiding in the distribution of these books. When I present our cause to a minister, editor, lecturer, or representative of any moral agency, the first demand is for facts and figures. Plainly, I can not then hand out a book with a twenty-five cent tariff on the information contained. This would be only a new method in the book agents' art. In all such cases it is a pleasure to submit this book for investigation, with the certain assurance of gaining a friend to the cause.

16 There are many agencies which may be enlisted in our cause by the general circulation of the facts herein contained. The preachers, teachers, editors and humanitarians of the white race, at home and abroad, must have facts laid before them, and it is our duty to supply these facts. The Central Anti-Lynching League, Room 9, 128 Clark St., Chicago, has established a Free Distribution Fund, the work of which can be promoted by all who are interested in this work.

17 Anti-lynching leagues, societies and individuals can order books from this fund at agents' rates. The books will be sent to their order, or, if desired, will be distributed by the League among those whose co-operative aid we so greatly need. The writer hereof assures prompt distribution of books according to order, and public acknowledgment of all orders through the public press.

Mob Rule in New Orleans*

INTRODUCTION

1 Immediately after the awful barbarism which disgraced the State of Georgia in April of last year, during which time more than a dozen

*Originally self-published in 1900 in Chicago.
IDA B. WELLS-BARNETT.
Chicago, Sept. 1, 1900.

colored people were put to death with unspeakable barbarity, I published a full report showing that Sam Hose, who was burned to death during that time, never committed a criminal assault, and that he killed his employer in self-defense.

2   Since that time I have been engaged on a work not yet finished, which I interrupt now to tell the story of the mob in New Orleans, which, despising all law, roamed the streets day and night, searching for colored men and women, whom they beat, shot and killed at will.

3   In the account of the New Orleans mob I have used freely the graphic reports of the New Orleans Times-Democrat and the New Orleans Picayune. Both papers gave the most minute details of the week's disorder. In their editorial comment they were at all times most urgent in their defense of law and in the strongest terms they condemned the infamous work of the mob.

4   It is no doubt owing to the determined stand for law and order taken by these great dailies and the courageous action taken by the best citizens of New Orleans, who rallied to the support of the civic authorities, that prevented a massacre of colored people awful to contemplate.

5   For the accounts and illustrations taken from the above-named journals, sincere thanks are hereby expressed.

6   The publisher hereof does not attempt to moralize over the deplorable condition of affairs shown in this publication, but simply presents the facts in a plain, unvarnished, connected way, so that he who runs may read. We do not believe that the American people who have encouraged such scenes by their indifference will read unmoved these accounts of brutality, injustice and oppression. We do not believe that the moral conscience of the nation—that which is highest and best among us—will always remain silent in face of such outrages, for God is not dead, and His Spirit is not entirely driven from men's hearts.

7   When this conscience wakes and speaks out in thunder tones, as it must, it will need facts to use as a weapon against injustice, barbarism and wrong. It is for this reason that I carefully compile, print and send forth these facts. If the reader can do no more, he can pass this pamphlet on to another, or send to the bureau addresses of those to whom he can order copies mailed.

8   Besides the New Orleans case, a history of burnings in this country is given, together with a table of lynchings for the past eighteen years. Those who would like to assist in the work of disseminating these facts, can do so by ordering copies, which are furnished at greatly reduced rates for gratuitous distribution. The bureau has no funds and is entirely dependent upon contributions from friends and members in carrying on the work.

W. E. B. Du Bois

(1868–1963)

*For biographical information about Du Bois, see page 56. During his
long and prolific career, Du Bois was associated, at various times,
with integrationism, pan-Africanism, and radical socialism. His
shifts in thinking prove exasperating for some critics, but he consistently and incessantly worked to improve the lives of African Americans. The following selections reflect some of his clearest uses of
the African American jeremiad. "The Niagara Movement" was
delivered in 1906; "Awake America" appeared in the* Crisis *in
1917; the third selection is excerpted from* The Autobiography
of W. E .B. Du Bois *(1968).*

The Niagara Movement

1   The men of the Niagara movement coming from the toil of the year's
hard work and pausing a moment from the earning of their daily bread
turn toward the nation and again ask in the name of ten million the
privilege of a hearing. In the past year the work of the Negro hater
has flourished in the land. Step by step the defenders of the rights of
American citizens have retreated. The work of stealing the black man's
ballot has progressed and the fifty and more representatives of stolen
votes still sit in the nation's capital. Discrimination in travel and public accommodation has so spread that some of our weaker brethren
are actually afraid to thunder against color discrimination as such and
are simply whispering for ordinary decencies.

2   Against this the Niagara Movement eternally protests. We will
not be satisfied to take one jot or tittle less than our full manhood
rights. We claim for ourselves every single right that belongs to a free-
born American, political, civil and social; and until we get these rights
we will never cease to protest and assail the ears of America. The battle we wage is not for ourselves alone but for all true Americans. It
is a fight for ideals, lest this, our common fatherland, false to its
founding, become in truth the land of the thief and the home of the
Slave—a by-word and a hissing among the nations for its sounding
pretentions and pitiful accomplishment.

3   Never before in the modern age has a great and civilized folk threatened to adopt so cowardly a creed in the treatment of its fellow-citizens

born and bred on its soil. Stripped of verbiage and subterfuge and in its naked nastiness the new American creed says: Fear to let black men even try to rise lest they become the equals of the white. And this is the land that professes to follow Jesus Christ. The blasphemy of such a course is only matched by its cowardice.

4   In detail our demands are clear and unequivocal. First, we would vote; with the right to vote goes everything: Freedom, manhood, the honor of your wives, the chastity of your daughters, the right to work, and the chance to rise, and let no man listen to those who deny this.

5   We want full manhood suffrage, and we want it now, henceforth and forever.

6   Second. We want discrimination in public accommodation to cease. Separation in railway and street cars, based simply on race and color, is un-American, undemocratic, and silly. We protest against all such discrimination.

7   Third. We claim the right of freemen to walk, talk, and be with them that wish to be with us. No man has a right to choose another man's friends, and to attempt to do so is an impudent interference with the most fundamental human privilege.

8   Fourth. We want the laws enforced against rich as well as poor; against Capitalist as well as Laborer; against white as well as black. We are not more lawless than the white race, we are more often arrested, convicted and mobbed. We want justice even for criminals and out-laws. We want the Constitution of the country enforced. We want Congress to take charge of Congressional elections. We want the Fourteenth amendment carried out to the letter and every State disfranchised in Congress which attempts to disfranchise its rightful voters. We want the Fifteenth amendment enforced and No State allowed to base its franchise simply on color.

9   The failure of the Republican Party in Congress at the session just closed to redeem its pledge of 1904 with reference to suffrage conditions at the South seems a plain, deliberate, and premeditated breach of promise, and stamps that party as guilty of obtaining votes under false pretense.

10   Fifth. We want our children educated. The school system in the country districts of the South is a disgrace and in few towns and cities are the Negro schools what they ought to be. We want the national government to step in and wipe out illiteracy in the South. Either the United States will destroy ignorance or ignorance will destroy the United States.

11   And when we call for education we mean real education. We believe in work. We ourselves are workers, but work is not necessarily education. Education is the development of power and ideal. We want our children trained as intelligent human beings should be, and we will fight for all time against any proposal to educate black boys and girls simply as servants and underlings, or simply for the use of other people. They have a right to know, to think, to aspire.

12   These are some of the chief things which we want. How shall we get them? By voting where we may vote, by persistent, unceasing agitation; by hammering at the truth, by sacrifice and work.

13   We do not believe in violence, neither in the despised violence of the raid nor the lauded violence of the soldier, nor the barbarous violence of the mob, but we do believe in John Brown, in that incarnate spirit of justice, that hatred of a lie, that willingness to sacrifice money, reputation, and life itself on the altar of right. And here on the scene of John Brown's martyrdom we reconsecrate ourselves, our honor, our property to the final emancipation of the race which John Brown died to make free.

14   Our enemies, triumphant for the present, are fighting the stars in their courses. Justice and humanity must prevail. We live to tell these dark brothers of ours—scattered in counsel, wavering and weak—that no bribe of money or notoriety, no promise of wealth or fame, is worth the surrender of a peoples' manhood or the loss of a man's self-respect. We refuse to surrender the leadership of this race to cowards and trucklers. We are men; we will be treated as men. On this rock we have planted our banners. We will never give up, though the trump of doom find us still fighting.

15   And we shall win. The past promised it, the present foretells it. Thank God for John Brown! Thank God for Garrison and Douglass! Sumner and Phillips, Nat Turner and Robert Gould Shaw, and all the hallowed dead who died for freedom! Thank God for all those to-day, few though their voices be, who have not forgotten the divine brother-hood of all men white and black, rich and poor, fortunate and unfortunate.

16   We appeal to the young men and women of this nation, to those whose nostrils are not yet befouled by greed and snobbery and racial narrowness: Stand up for the right, prove yourselves worthy of your heritage and whether born north or south dare to treat men as men. Cannot the nation that has absorbed ten million foreigners into its political life without catastrophe absorb ten million Negro Americans

into that same political life at less cost than their unjust and illegal exclusion will involve?

17　Courage brothers! The battle for humanity is not lost or losing. All across the skies sit signs of promise. The Slav is raising in his might, the yellow millions are tasting liberty, the black Africans are writhing toward the light, and everywhere the laborer, with ballot in his hand, is voting open the gates of Opportunity and Peace. The morning breaks over blood-stained hills. We must not falter, we may not shrink. Above are the everlasting stars.

Awake America

1　Let us enter this war for Liberty with clean hands. May no blood-smeared garments bind our feet when we rise to make the world safe for Democracy. The New Freedom cannot survive if it means Waco, Memphis and East St. Louis. We cannot lynch 2,867 untried black men and women in thirty-one years and pose successfully as leaders of civilization. Rather let us bow our shamed heads and in sack cloth and ashes declare that when in awful war we raise our weapons against the enemies of mankind, so, too, and in that same hour here at home we raise our hands to Heaven and pledge our sacred honor to make our own America a real land of the free:

2　To stop lynching and mob violence.

3　To stop disfranchisement for race and sex.

4　To abolish Jim Crow cars.

5　To resist the attempt to establish an American ghetto.

6　To stop race discrimination in Trade Unions, in Civil Service, in places of public accommodation, and in the Public School.

7　To secure Justice for all men in the courts.

8　To insist that individual desert and ability shall be the test of real American manhood and not adventitious differences of race or color or descent.

9　Awake! Put on they strength, America—put on thy beautiful robes. Become not a bye word and jest among the nations by the hypocrisy of your word and contradiction of your deed's. Russia has abolished the ghetto—shall we restore it? India is overthrowing caste—shall we upbuild it? China is establishing democracy—shall we strengthen our Southern oligarchy?

10   In five wars and now the sixth we black men have fought for your freedom and honor. Wherever the American flag floats today, black hands have helped to plant it. American Religion, American Industry, American Literature, American Music and American Art are as much the gift of the American Negro as of the American white man. This is as much our country as yours, and as much the world's as ours. We Americans, black and white, are the servants of all mankind and ministering to a greater, fairer heaven. Let us be true to our mission. No land that loves to lynch "niggers" can lead the hosts of Almighty God.

The Autobiography of W. E. B. Du Bois

1   There was a day when the world rightly called Americans honest even if crude; earning their living by hard work; telling the truth no matter whom it hurt; and going to war only in what they believed a just cause after nothing else seemed possible. Today we are lying, stealing, and killing. We call all this by finer names: Advertising, Free Enterprise, and National Defense. But names in the end deceive no one; today we use science to help us deceive our fellows; we take wealth that we never earned and we are devoting all our energies to kill, maim and drive insane, men, women, and children who dare refuse to do what we want done. No nation threatens us. We threaten the world.

2   Our President says that Foster Dulles was the wisest man he knew. If Dulles was wise, God help our fools—the fools who rule us and are today running wild in order to shoot a football into the sky where Sputnik rolls in peace around the earth. And they know why we fail, these military masters of men: we haven't taught our children mathematics and physics. No, it is because we have not taught our children to read and write or to behave like human beings and not like hoodlums. Every child on my street is whooping it up with toy guns and big boys with real pistols. When Elvis Presley goes through the motions of copulation on the public stage it takes the city police force to hold back teenage children from hysteria. The highest ambition of an American boy today is to be a millionaire. The highest ambition of an American girl is to be a movie star. Of the ethical actions which lie back of these ideals, little is said or learned. What are we doing about it? Half the Christian churches of New York are trying to ruin the free public schools in

order to install religious dogma in them; and the other half are too interested in Venezuelan oil to prevent the best center in Brooklyn from fighting youthful delinquency, or prevent a bishop from kicking William Howard Melish into the street and closing his church. Which of the hundreds of churches sitting half empty protests about this? They hire Billy Graham to replace the circus in Madison Square Garden.

3   Howard Melish is one of the few Christian clergymen for whom I have the highest respect. Honest and conscientious, believing sincerely in much of the Christian dogma, which I reject, but working honestly and without hypocrisy, for the guidance of the young, for the uplift of the poor and ignorant, and for the betterment of his city and his country, he has been driven from his work and his career ruined by a vindictive bishop of his church, with no effective protest from most of the Christian ministry and membership or of the people of the United States. The Melish case is perhaps at once the most typical and frightening illustration of present American religion and my reaction. Here is a young man of ideal character, of impeccable morals; a hard worker, especially among the poor and unfortunate, with fine family relations. His father had helped build one of the most popular Episcopal churches in the better part of Brooklyn. He himself had married a well-educated woman, and had three sons in school. The community about it was changing from well-to-do people of English and Dutch descent, to white-collar and laboring folk of Italian, Negro and Puerto Rican extraction. Trinity church, under the Melishes, adapted itself to changing needs, and invited neighborhood membership. It was not a large church, but it was doing the best work among the young and foreign-born of any institution in Brooklyn.

4   The young rector took one step for which the bishop, most of his fellow clergymen and the well-to-do community, with its business interests, pilloried him. He joined and became an official of the National Council of American-Soviet Friendship. He was accused immediately of favoring communism, and to appease criticism he gave up his official position in this organization, but refused to resign his membership. Allegedly for this reason the bishop, most of the clergy and the well-to-do community proceeded to force him out of the church. The real reason behind their fight was anger because a rich, white, "respectable" church was being surrendered to workers and Negroes. It became a renewed battle between Episcopal authority and democratic rule. That his parish wanted to retain Melish as rector was unquestionable. Through the use of technicalities in the canon law and in accord with the decision of Catholic judges who believed in Episcopal power, Howard Melish lost his church, had his

life work ruined, the church itself closed, and its local influence ended. There was vigorous protest against this by a few devoted colleagues, many of them Jews and liberals. But the great mass of the Episcopal church membership was silent and did nothing.

5   All this must not be mentioned even if you know it and see it. America must never be criticized even by honest and sincere men. America must always be praised and extravagantly praised, or you lose your job or are ostracized or land in jail. Criticism is treason, and treason or the hint of treason testified to by hired liars may be punished by shameful death. I saw Ethel Rosenberg lying beautiful in her coffin beside her mate. I tried to stammer futile words above her grave. But not over graves should we shout this failure of justice, but from the housetops of the world.

6   Honest men may and must criticize America. Describe how she has ruined her democracy, sold out her jury system, and led her seats of justice astray. The only question that may arise is whether this criticism is based on truth, not whether it has been openly expressed.

7   What is truth? What can it be when the President of the United States, guiding the nation, stands up in public and says: "*The world also thinks of us as a land which has never enslaved anyone.*" Everyone who heard this knew it was not true. Yet here stands the successor of George Washington who bought, owned, and sold slaves; the successor of Abraham Lincoln who freed four million slaves after they had helped him win victory over the slaveholding South. And so far as I have seen, not a single periodical, not even a Negro weekly, has dared challenge or even criticize that falsehood.

8   Perhaps the most extraordinary characteristic of current America is the attempt to reduce life to buying and selling. Life is not love unless love is sex and bought and sold. Life is not knowledge save knowledge of technique, of science for destruction. Life is not beauty except beauty for sale. Life is not art unless its price is high and it is sold for profit. All life is production for profit, and for what is profit but for buying and selling again?

9   Even today the contradictions of American civilization are tremendous. Freedom of political discussion is difficult: elections are not free and fair. Democracy is for us to a large extent unworkable. In business there is a tremendous amount of cheating and stealing; gambling in card games, on television and on the stock exchange is widely practiced. It is common custom for distinguished persons to sign books, articles, and speeches that they did not write; for men of brains to compose and sell opinions which they do not believe. Ghost writing is a profession. The greatest power in the land is not thought or ethics,

but wealth, and the persons who exercise the power of wealth are not necessarily its owners, but those who direct its use, and the truth about this direction is so far as possible kept a secret. We do not know who owns our vast property and resources, so that most of our argument concerning wealth and its use must be based on guesswork. Those responsible for the misuse of wealth escape responsibility, and even the owners of capital often do not know for what it is being used and how. The criterion of industry and trade is the profit that it accrues, not the good which it does either its owners or the public. Present profit is valued higher than future need. We waste materials. We refuse to make repairs. We cheat and deceive in manufacturing goods. We have succumbed to an increased use of lying and misrepresentation. In the last ten years at least a thousand books have been published to prove that the fight to preserve Negro slavery in America was a great and noble cause, led by worthy men of eminence.

10   I know the United States. It is my country and the land of my fathers. It is still a land of magnificent possibilities. It is still the home of noble souls and generous people. But it is selling its birthright. It is betraying its mighty destiny I was born on its soil and educated in its schools. I have served my country to the best of my ability. I have never knowingly broken its laws or unjustly attacked its reputation. At the same time I have pointed out its injustices and crimes and blamed it, rightly as I believe, for its mistakes. It has given me education and some of its honors, for which I am thankful.

11   Today the United States is the leading nation in the world, which apparently believes that war is the only way to settle present disputes and difficulties. For this reason it is spending fantastic sums of money, and wasting wealth and energy on the preparation for war, which is nothing less than criminal. Yet the United States dare not stop spending money for war. If she did her whole economy, which is today based on preparation for war, might collapse. Therefore, we prepare for a Third World War; we spread our soldiers and arms over the earth and we bribe every nation we can to become our allies. We are taxing our citizens into poverty, crime and unemployment, and systematically distorting the truth about socialism. We have used the horror of germ warfare. Some of our leaders are ready to use it again.

12   The use of history for distortion and not for education has led to another of our greatest present evils; and that is to make fear of socialism and communism so great that we have withdrawn our efforts toward the education of children, the war on disease, and the raising of the standards of living. We encourage the increase of debt to

finance present enjoyment; and above all we use newsgathering and opinion, radio and television, magazines and books, to make most Americans believe that the threat of war, especially on the part of the Soviet Union against the United States, justifies heavy taxation and tremendous expenditure for war preparation.

13   This propaganda began when our tremendous profits from the First World War encouraged American business to believe that the United States was about to replace Great Britain as ruler of most of mankind. The rise and spread of socialism contradicted this ambition, and made the projected American century quail in fright before the century of communism. We determined therefore to overthrow communism by brute force. Gradually we discovered the impossibility of this, unless we risked suicide. We saw communism increasing education, science and productivity. We now face the possibility of co-existence with the communist world, and competition between the methods of capitalism and the methods of socialism. It is at this crisis that I had the opportunity to live seven months in a world of socialism, which is striving toward communism as an ideal.

14   This is what I call decadence. It could not have happened 50 years ago. In the day of our fiercest controversy we have not dared thus publicly to silence opinion. I have lived through disagreement, vilification, and war and war again. But in all that time, I have never seen the right of human beings to think so challenged and denied as today.

15   The day after I was born, Andrew Johnson was impeached. He deserved punishment as a traitor to the poor Southern whites and poorer freedmen. Yet during his life, no one denied him the right to defend himself. A quarter of a century ago, I tried to state and carry into realization unpopular ideas against a powerful opposition—in the white South, in the reactionary North, and even among my own people. I found my thought being misconstrued and I planned an organ of propaganda, *The Crisis*, where I would be free to say what I believed. This was no easy sailing. My magazine reached but a fraction of the nation. It was bitterly attacked and once the government suppressed it. But in the end I maintained a platform of radical thinking on the Negro question which influenced many minds. War and depression ended my independence of thought and forced me to return to teaching, but with the certainty that I had at least started a new line of belief and action. Then they stopped my teaching.

16   As a result of my work and that of others, the Supreme Court began to restore democracy in the South and finally outlawed discrimination in public services based on color. This caused rebellion in the South

which the nation is afraid to meet. The Negro stands bewildered and attempt is made by appointments to unimportant offices and trips abroad to bribe him into silence. His art and literature cease to function. Only the children like those at Little Rock stand and fight.

17   The Yale sophomore who replaced a periodical of brains by a book of pictures concealed in advertisements, proposed that America rule the world. This failed because we could not rule ourselves. But Texas to the rescue, as Johnson proposes that America take over outer space. Somewhere beyond the Moon there must be sentient creatures rolling in inextinguishable laughter at the antics of our Earth.

18   We tax ourselves into poverty and crime so as to make the rich richer and the poor poorer and more evil. We know the cause of this: it is to permit our rich business interests to stop socialism and to prevent the ideals of communism from ever triumphing on earth. The aim is impossible. Socialism progresses and will progress. All we can do is to silence and jail its promoters and make world war on communism. I believe in socialism. I seek a world where the ideals of communism will triumph— to each according to his need, from each according to his ability. For this I will work as long as I live. And I still live.

19   I just live. I plan my work, but plan less for shorter periods. I live from year to year and day to day. I expect snatches of pain and discomfort to come and go. And then reaching back to my archives, I whisper to the great Majority: To the Almighty Dead, into whose pale approaching faces, I stand and stare; you whose thoughts, deeds and dreams have made men wise with all wisdom and stupid with utter evil. In every name of God, bend out and down, you who are the infinite majority of all mankind and with your thoughts, deeds, dreams and memories, overwhelm, outvote, and coerce this remnant of human life which lingers on, imagining themselves wisest of all who have lived just because they still survive. Whither with wide revelation will they go with their stinking pride and empty boasting, whose ever recurring lies only you the Dead have known all too well? Teach living man to jeer at this last civilization which seeks to build heaven on Want and Ill of most men and vainly builds on color and hair rather than on decency of hand and heart. Let your memories teach these wilful fools all which you have forgotten and ruined and done to death.

20   You are not and yet you are: your thoughts, your deeds, above all your dreams still live. So too, your deeds and what you forgot—these lived as your bodies died. With these we also live and die, realize and kill. Our dreams seek Heaven, our deeds plumb Hell. Hell lies about us in our Age: blithely we push into its stench and flame. Suffer us not.

Eternal Dead to stew in this Evil—the Evil of South Africa, the Evil of Mississippi; the Evil of Evils which is what we hope to hold in Asia and Africa, in the southern Americas and islands of the Seven Seas. Reveal, Ancient of Days, the Present in the Past and prophesy the End in the Beginning. For this is a beautiful world; this is a wonderful America, which the founding fathers dreamed until their sons drowned it in the blood of slavery and devoured it in greed. Our children must rebuild it. Let then the Dreams of the Dead rebuke the Blind who think that what is will be forever and teach them that what was worth living for must live again and that which merited death must stay dead. Teach us, Forever Dead, there is no Dream but Deed, there is no Deed but Memory.

Mary McLeod Bethune

(1875–1955)

Born July 10, 1875, near Mayesville, South Carolina, the 15th of 17 children, Mary Mcleod Bethune became one of the most important educators and civil rights leaders of the twentieth century. In 1900, she established two schools in Palatka, Florida. Four years later, she moved on to Daytona, Florida, where she established Daytona Educational and Industrial Institute, which initially consisted of five African American girls in a rented house. The school expanded and merged with Cookman Institute; the whole enterprise became, in 1929, Bethune-Cookman College. Bethune was a founder of the National Council of Negro Women and served as president of the organization from 1935 to 1949. She was also a member of the "Black Cabinet," a group of African Americans who had considerable access to the White House during the presidency of Franklin Delano Roosevelt. "Certain Unalienable Rights" was published in Rayford Logan's What the Negro Wants *(1944).*

Certain Unalienable Rights

1   It is a quiet night in December, 1773. A British merchant ship rides easily at anchor in Boston Harbor. Suddenly, some row boats move out from the shore. Dark stealthy figures in the boats appear to be Indians in buckskin jackets and with feathers in their hair; but as they reach the ship, clamber abroad, climb down into the hold and carry out boxes of the cargo, the muffled voices speak English words. Their voices grow

more excited and determined as they open the boxes and dump the King's tea into the ocean. The Boston Tea Party is in full swing. Resentment has reached flood tide. "Taxation without representation is tyranny!" The spark of the American Revolution has caught flame and the principle of the "consent of the governed" has been established by a gang disguised as Indians who take the law into their own hands. In this action a small and independent people struck out against restrictions and tyranny and oppression and gave initial expression to the ideal of a nation "that all men are created equal, that they are endowed by their Creator with certain unalienable Rights."

2   It is a Sunday night in Harlem in the year of our Lord 1943. Along the quiet streets dimmed out against the possibility of Axis air attack, colored Americans move to and fro or sit and talk and laugh. Suddenly electric rumor travels from mouth to ear: "A black soldier has been shot by a white policeman and has died in the arms of his mother." No one stops to ask how or why or if it be true. Crowds begin to gather. There is a rumbling of anger and resentment impelled by all the anger and all the resentment of all colored Americans in all the black ghettos in all the cities in America—the resentment against the mistreatment of Negroes in uniform, against restriction and oppression and discrimination breaks loose. Crowds of young people in blind fury strike out against the only symbols of this oppression which are near at hand. Rocks hurtle, windows crash, stores are broken open. Merchants' goods are tumbled into the streets, destroyed or stolen. Police are openly challenged and attacked. There are killings and bodily injury. For hours a veritable reign of terror runs through the streets. All efforts at restraint are of no avail. Finally the blind rage blows itself out.

3   Some are saying that a band of hoodlums have challenged law and order to burn and pillage and rob. Others look about them to remember riots in Detroit and Los Angeles and Beaumont. They will look further and recall cities laid in ruins by a global war in which the forces of tyranny and oppression and race supremacy attempt to subdue and restrain all the freedom of the world. They are thinking deeply to realize that there is a ferment aloose among the oppressed little people everywhere, a "groping of the long inert masses." They will see depressed and repressed masses all over the world swelling to the breaking point against the walls of ghettos, against economic, social and political restrictions; they will find them breaking open the King's boxes and throwing the tea into the ocean and storming the Bastilles stirred by the clarion call of the Four Freedoms. They are

striking back against all that the Axis stands for. They are rising to achieve the ideals "that all men are created equal, that they are endowed by their Creator with certain unalienable Rights, that among these are Life, Liberty and the pursuit of Happiness." With the crash of the guns and the whir of the planes in their ears, led by the fighting voices of a Churchill and a Franklin Roosevelt, a Chiang Kai-shek and a Stalin, they are realizing that "Governments are instituted among Men" to achieve these aims and that these governments derive "their just power from the consent of the governed." They are a part of a peoples' war. The little people want "out." Just as the Colonists at the Boston Tea Party wanted "out" from under tyranny and oppression and taxation without representation, the Chinese want "out," the Indians want "out," and colored Americans want "out."

4   Throughout America today many people are alarmed and bewildered by the manifestation of this world ferment among the Negro masses. We say we are living in a period of "racial tension." They seem surprised that the Negro should be a part to this world movement. Really, all true Americans should not be surprised by this logical climax of American education. For several generations colored Americans have been brought up on the Boston Tea Party and the Declaration of Independence; on the principle of equality of opportunity, the possession of inalienable rights, the integrity and sanctity of the human personality. Along with other good Americans the Negro has been prepared to take his part in the fight against an enemy that threatens all these basic American principles. He is fighting now on land and sea and in the air to beat back these forces of oppression and tyranny and discrimination. Why, then, should we be surprised when at home as well as abroad he fights back against these same forces?

5   One who would really understand this racial tension which has broken out into actual conflict in riots as in Harlem, Detroit, and Los Angeles, must look to the roots and not be confused by the branches and the leaves. The tension rises out of the growing internal pressure of Negro masses to break through the wall of restriction which restrains them from full American citizenship. This mounting power is met by the unwillingness of white America to allow any appreciable breach in this wall.

6   The hard core of internal pressure among the Negro masses in the United States today is undoubtedly their resentment over the mistreatment of colored men in the armed forces. The Negro faces restrictions in entering certain branches of the service, resistance to being

assigned posts according to his ability; and above all there is the failure of the Army and his government to protect him in the uniform of his country from actual assault by civilians.

7   Letters from the men in Army camps have streamed into the homes of their parents and friends everywhere, telling of this mistreatment by officers, military police and civilians, of their difficulties in getting accommodations on trains and buses, of numerous incidents of long, tiresome journeys without meals and other concrete evidences of the failure of their government to protect and provide for its men, even when they are preparing to fight in defense of the principles of that government.

8   They need no agitation by newspaper accounts or the stimulation of so-called leaders. These things are the intimate experiences of the masses themselves. They know them and feel them intensely and resent them bitterly.

9   You must add to these deep-seated feelings a whole series of repercussions of the frustrated efforts of Negroes to find a place in war production: the absolute denial of employment in many cases, or employment far below the level of their skills, numerous restrictions in their efforts to get training, resistance of labor unions to the improving and utilization of their skills on the job. Pile on to these their inability to get adequate housing even for those employed in war work, and often, where houses are available, restrictions to segregated units in temporary war housing. At the same time they see around them unlimited opportunities offered to other groups to serve their country in the armed forces, to be employed at well-paying jobs, to get good housing financed by private concerns and FHA funds.

10   Even those observers who have some understanding of the Negro's desire to break through all these restrictions will charge it to superficial causes, such as the agitation of the Negro press and leaders; or they counsel the Negro to "go slow." It is as though they admit that the patient is sick with fever and diagnosis reveals that he needs twelve grains of quinine, but they decide that because he is a Negro they had better give him only six. They admit that he is hungry and needs to be fed, but because he is a Negro they suggest that a half meal will suffice. This approach, of course, is a historical hang-over. It is a product of the half-hearted and timorous manner in which we have traditionally faced the Negro problem in America.

11   In order to maintain slavery, it was necessary to isolate black men from every possible manifestation of our culture. It was necessary to teach that they were inferior beings who could not profit from that

culture. After the slave was freed, every effort has persisted to maintain "white supremacy" and wall the Negro in from every opportunity to challenge this concocted "supremacy." Many Americans said the Negro could not learn and they "proved" it by restricting his educational opportunities. When he surmounted these obstacles and achieved a measure of training, they said he did not know how to use it and proved it by restricting his employment opportunities. When it was necessary to employ him, they saw to it that he was confined to laborious and poorly-paid jobs. After they had made every effort to guarantee that his economic, social and cultural levels were low, they attributed his status to his race. Therefore, as he moved North and West after Reconstruction and during the Industrial Revolution, they saw to it that he was confined to living in veritable ghettos with convenants that were as hard and resistant as the walls of the ghettos of Warsaw.

12   They met every effort on his part to break through these barriers with stern resistance that would brook no challenge to our concept of white supremacy. Although they guaranteed him full citizenship under the Constitution and its Amendments, they saw to it that he was largely disfranchised and had little part in our hard won ideal of "the consent of the governed." In the midst of this anachronism, they increasingly educated his children in the American way of life—in its ideals of equality of all men before the law, and opportunities for the fullest possible development of the individual.

13   As this concept took hold among the Negro masses, it has evidenced itself through the years in a slow, growing, relentless pressure against every restriction which denied them their full citizenship. This pressure, intensified by those of other races who really believed in democracy, began to make a break through the walls here and there. It was given wide-spread impetus by the objectives of the New Deal with its emphasis on the rise of the forgotten man. With the coming of the Second World War, all the Negro's desires were given voice and support by the world leaders who fought back against Hitler and all he symbolizes. His efforts to break through have responded to Gandhi and Chiang Kai-shek, to Churchill and Franklin Roosevelt.

14   The radios and the press of the world have drummed into his ears the Four Freedoms, which would lead him to think that the world accepts as legitimate his claims as well as those of oppressed peoples all over the world. His drive for status has now swept past even most of his leaders, and has become imbedded in mass-consciousness which is pushing out of the way all the false prophets, be they white or black—or, be they ar home or abroad.

15   The Negro wants to break out into the free realm of democratic citizenship. We can have only one of two responses. Either we must let him out wholly and completely in keeping with our ideals, or we must mimic Hitler and shove him back.

16   What, then, does the Negro want? His answer is very simple. He wants only what all other Americans want. He wants opportunity to make real what the Declaration of Independence and the Constitution and Bill of Rights say; what the Four Freedoms establish. While he knows these ideals are open to no man completely he wants only his equal chance to attain them. The Negro today wants specifically:

1. *Government leadership in building favorable public opinion.* Led by the President himself, the federal government should initiate a sound program carried out through appropriate federal agencies designed to indicate the importance of race in the war and post-war period. The cost of discrimination and segregation to a nation at war and the implications of American racial attitudes for our relationships with the other United Nations and their people should be delineated. Racial myths and superstitions should be exploded. The cooperation of the newspapers, the radio and the screen should be sought to replace caricature and slander with realistic interpretations of sound racial relationships.

2. *The victory of democracy over dictatorship.* Under democracy the Negro has the opportunity to work for an improvement in his status through the intelligent use of his vote, the creation of a more favorable public opinion, and the development of his native abilities. The ideals of democracy and Christianity work for equality. These ideals the dictatorships disavow. Experience has taught only too well the implications for him and all Americans of a Nazi victory.

3. *Democracy in the armed forces.* He wants a chance to serve his country in all branches of the armed forces to his full capacity. He sees clearly the fallacy of fostering discrimination and segregation in the very forces that are fighting against discrimination and segregation all over the world. He believes that the government should fully protect the persons and the rights of all who wear the uniform of its armed forces.

4. *The protection of his civil rights and an end to lynching.* He wants full protection of the rights guaranteed all Americans by the Constitution: equality before the law, the right to jury

trial and service, the eradication of lynching. Demanding these rights for himself, he will not be misled into any anti-foreign, Red-baiting, or anti-Semitic crusade to deny these rights to others. Appalled by the conditions prevailing in Washington, he joins in demanding the ballot for the District of Columbia and the protection of his rights now denied him within the shadow of the Capitol.

5. *The free ballot.* He wants the abolition of the poll tax and of the "white primary"; he wants universal adult suffrage. He means to use it to vote out all the advocates of racism and vote in those whose records show that they actually practise democracy.

6. *Equal access to employment opportunities.* He wants the chance to work and advance in any job for which he has the training and capacity. To this end he wants equal access to training opportunities. In all public programs, federal, state and local, he wants policy-making and administrative posts as well as rank and file jobs without racial discrimination. He wants a fair share of jobs under Civil Service.

7. *Extension of federal programs in public housing, health, social security, education and relief under federal control.* Low income and local prejudice often deprive him of these basic social services. Private enterprise or local government units cannot or will not provide them. For efficiency and equity in administration of these programs, the Negro looks to the federal government until such time as he has gained the full and free use of the ballot in all states.

8. *Elimination of racial barriers in labor unions.* He demands the right of admission on equal terms to the unions having jurisdiction over the crafts or industries in which he is employed. He urges that job control on public works be denied to any union practising discrimination.

9. *Realistic interracial co-operation.* He realizes the complete interdependence of underprivileged white people and Negroes, North and South—laborers and sharecroppers alike. He knows that they stay in the gutter together or rise to security together; that the hope of democracy lies in their cooperative effort to make their government responsive to their needs; that national unity demands their sharing together more fully in the benefits of freedom—not "one as the hand and separate as the fingers," but one as the clasped hands of friendly cooperation.

17   Here, then, is a program for racial advancement and national unity. It adds up to the sum of the rights, privileges and responsibilities of full American citizenship. This is all that the Negro asks. He will not willingly accept less. As long as America offers less, she will be that much less a democracy. The whole way is the American way.

18   What can the Negro do himself to help get what he wants?

> 1. In the first place, he should accept his responsibility for a full part of the job of seeing to it that whites and Negroes alike understand the current intensity of the Negro's fight for status as a part of a world people's movement. As individuals and as members of organizations, we must continue to use every channel open to affect public opinion, to get over to all Americans the real nature of this struggle. Those of us who accept some measure of responsibility for leadership, must realize that in such people's movements, the real leadership comes up out of the people themselves. All others who would give direction to such a movement must identify themselves with it, become a part of it, and interpret it to others. We must make plain to America that we have reached a critical stage in the assimilation of colored people.
>
> We have large and growing numbers of young and older Negroes who have achieved by discipline and training a measure of culture which qualifies them for advanced status in our American life. To deny this opportunity creates on the one hand frustration with its attendant disintegration, and, on the other, deprives American civilization of the potential fruits of some thirteen millions of its sons and daughters.
>
> Through our personal and group contacts with other racial groups, we must increasingly win their understanding and support. Only in this way can the swelling force among minority racial groups be channeled into creative progress rather than exploded into riots and conflicts, or dissipated in hoodlumism. While we seek on the one side to "educate" white America, we must continue relentlessly to make plain to ourselves and our associates the increased responsibility that goes with increased rights and privileges. Our fight for Fair Employment Practices legislation must go hand and hand with "Hold Your Job" campaigns; our fight for anti-poll tax legislation must be supported equally by efforts of Negroes themselves to exercise fully and intelligently the right of franchise where they have it.

2. We must challenge, skillfully but resolutely, every sign of restriction or limitation on our full American citizenship. When I say challenge, I mean we must seek every opportunity to place the burden of responsibility upon him who denies it, if we simply accept and acquiesce in the face of discrimination, we accept the responsibility ourselves and allow those responsible to salve their conscience by believing that they have our acceptance and concurrence. We should, therefore, protest openly everything in the newspapers, on the radio, in the movies that smacks of discrimination or slander. We must take the seat that our ticket calls for and place upon the proprietor the responsibility of denying it to us.

We must challenge everywhere the principle and practice of enforced racial segregation. We must make it clear that where groups and individuals are striving for social and economic status, group isolation one from the other allows the rise of misunderstanding and suspicion, providing rich soil for the seeds of antagonism and conflict. Recently in the city of Detroit, there was no rioting in the neighborhoods where whites and Negroes lived as neighbors, and there was no conflict in the plants where they worked side by side on the assembly-lines. Whenever one has the price or can fill the requirements for any privilege which is open to the entire public, that privilege must not be restricted on account of race.

Our appeal must be made to the attributes of which the Anglo-Saxon is so proud—his respect for law and justice, his love of fair-play and true sportsmanship.

3. We must understand that the great masses of our people are farmers and workers, and that their hopes for improvement in a large measure lie in association with organizations whose purpose is to improve their condition. This means membership in and support of labor and farmer unions. Within these organizations it means continuous efforts with our allies of all racial groups to remove all barriers which operate in the end to divide workers and defeat all of their purpose. The voice of organized labor has become one of the most powerful in the land and unless we have a part in that voice our people will not be heard.

4. We must take a full part in the political life of our community, state and nation. We must learn increasingly about political organization and techniques. We must prepare for and fight for places on the local, state, and national committees of our

political parties. This is a representative government and the only way that our representatives can reflect our desires is for us to register and vote. In a large measure the whole of our national life is directed by the legislation and other activities of our governmental units. The only way to affect their action and to guarantee their democratic nature is to have a full hand in electing individuals who represent us. The national election of 1944 represents one of the most crucial in the life of this nation and of the world. The Congressional representatives that are elected to office will have a large hand in the type of peace treaty to be adopted and the entire nature of our post-war domestic economy. All of our organizations and individuals who supply leadership must fully acquaint our people with the requirements of registering and voting, see to it that they are cognizant of the issues involved and get out to register and vote.

Negro women and their organizations have a tremendous responsibility and opportunity to offer leadership and support to this struggle of the racial group to attain improved cultural status in America. We have always done a full part of this job. Now with large numbers of our men in the armed forces and with considerable numbers of new people who have migrated into our communities to take their part in war production, we have a bigger job and a greater opportunity than ever. Our women know too well the disintegrating effect upon our family life of our low economic status. Discrimination and restriction have too often meant to us broken homes and the delinquency of our children. We have seen our dreams frustrated and our hopes broken. We have risen, however, out of our despair to help our men climb up the next rung of the ladder. We see now more than a glimmer of light on the horizon of a new hope. We feel behind us the surge of all women of China and India and of Africa who see the same light and look to us to march with them. We will reach out our hands to all women who struggle forward—white, black, brown, yellow—all. If we have the courage and tenacity of our forebears, who stood firmly like a rock against the lashings of slavery and the disruption of Reconstruction, we shall find a way to do for our day what they did for theirs. Above all we Negro women of all levels and classes must realize that this forward movement is a march of the masses and that all of us must go forward with it or be pushed aside by it. We will do our part. In order for us to have peace and justice and democracy for all, may I urge that we follow the example of the great humanitarian—Jesus Christ—in exemplifying in our lives both by word and action the fatherhood of God and the brotherhood of man?

Martin Luther King, Jr.

(1929–1968)

Born on January 15, 1929, in Atlanta, Georgia, the most famous civil rights leader of the 20th century was originally named Michael King, after his father, who was a prominent minister. The elder King changed his name after returning from a trip to Europe, where he was inspired by the legacy of Martin Luther. The younger King attended Morehouse College, graduating in 1948. He attended Crozer Seminary and then earned a PhD in theology from Boston University in 1955. He became nationally known while leading the Montgomery bus boycott in 1955 and 1956. In 1964, King was awarded the Nobel Peace Prize; he was the youngest person ever to win the award. He was assassinated in Memphis on April 4, 1968, while in town to support a strike by sanitation workers. In the aftermath of his death, there were riots in more than 100 American cities. King's birthday became a national holiday on November 2, 1983. His books include Stride toward Freedom: The Montgomery Story *(1958)*, Strength to Love *(1963)*, Where Do We Go from Here: Chaos or Community? *(1967), and the posthumously published* The Trumpet of Conscience *(1968). The following readings include King's speech at the Holt Street Baptist Church; his famous "I Have a Dream" speech from the 1963 March on Washington; and selections from* Where Do We Go from Here?.

Speech at Holt Street Baptist Church

[*5 December 1955*]
Montgomery, Ala.

1 My friends, we are certainly very happy to see each of you out this evening. We are here this evening for serious business. [*Audience:*] (*Yes*) We are here in a general sense because first and foremost we are American citizens (*That's right*) and we are determined to apply our

citizenship to the fullness of its meaning. (*Yeah, That's right*) We are here also because of our love for democracy (*Yes*), because of our deep-seated belief that democracy transformed from thin paper to thick action (*Yes*) is the greatest form of government on earth. (*That's right*)

2 But we are here in a specific sense, because of the bus situation in Montgomery. (*Yes*) We are here because we are determined to get the situation corrected. This situation is not at all new. The problem has existed over endless years. (*That's right*) For many years now Negroes in Montgomery and so many other areas have been inflicted with the paralysis of crippling fears (*Yes*) on buses in our community. (*That's right*) On so many occasions, Negroes have been intimidated and humiliated and impressed—oppressed—because of the sheer fact that they were Negroes. (*That's right*) I don't have time this evening to go into the history of these numerous cases. Many of them now are lost in the thick fog of oblivion (*Yes*), but at least one stands before us now with glaring dimensions. (*Yes*)

3 Just the other day, just last Thursday to be exact, one of the finest citizens in Montgomery (*Amen*)—not one of the finest Negro citizens (*That's right*), but one of the finest citizens in Montgomery—was taken from a bus (*Yes*) and carried to jail and arrested (*Yes*) because she refused to get up to give her seat to a white person. (*Yes. That's right*) Now the press would have us believe that she refused to leave a reserved section for Negroes (*Yes*), but I want you to know this evening that there is no reserved section. (*All right*) The law has never been clarified at that point. (*Hell no*) Now I think I speak with, with legal authority— not that I have any legal authority, but I think I speak with legal authority behind me (*All right*)—that the law, the ordinance, the city ordinance has never been totally clarified.* (*That's right*)

4 Mrs. Rosa Parks is a fine person. (*Well, well said*) And, since it had to happen, I'm happy that it happened to a person like Mrs. Parks, for nobody can doubt the boundless outreach of her integrity. (*Sure enough*) Nobody can doubt the height of her character (*Yes*), nobody can doubt the depth of her Christian commitment and devotion to the teachings of Jesus. (*All right*) And I'm happy since it had to happen, it happened to a person that nobody can call a disturbing factor in the community. (*All right*) Mrs. Parks is a fine Christian person,

---

* By custom bus drivers could request that black passengers move to the rear, one row at a time, when the forward white section was filled and additional white passengers had to be accommodated.

unassuming, and yet there is integrity and character there. And just because she refused to get up, she was arrested.

5   And you know, my friends, there comes a time when people get tired of being trampled over by the iron feet of oppression. [*thundering applause*] There comes a time, my friends, when people get tired of being plunged across the abyss of humiliation, where they experience the bleakness of nagging despair. (*Keep talking*) There comes a time when people get tired of being pushed out of the glittering sunlight of life's July and left standing amid the piercing chill of an alpine November. (*That's right*) [*applause*] There comes a time. (*Yes sir, Teach*) [*applause continues*]

6   We are here, we are here this evening because we're tired now. (*Yes*) [*applause*] And I want to say that we are not here advocating violence. (*No*) We have never done that. (*Repeat that, Repeat that*) [*applause*] I want it to be known throughout Montgomery and throughout this nation (*Well*) that we are Christian people. (*Yes*) [*applause*] We believe in the Christian religion. We believe in the teachings of Jesus. (*Well*) The only weapon that we have in our hands this evening is the weapon of protest. (*Yes*) [*applause*] That's all.

7   And certainly, certainly, this is the glory of America, with all of its faults. (*Yeah*) This is the glory of our democracy. If we were incarcerated behind the iron curtains of a Communistic nation we couldn't do this. If we were dropped in the dungeon of a totalitarian regime we couldn't do this. (*All right*) But the great glory of American democracy is the right to protest for right. (*That's right*) [*applause*] My friends, don't let anybody make us feel that we are to be compared in our actions with the Ku Klux Klan or with the White Citizens Council. [*applause*] There will be no crosses burned at any bus stops in Montgomery. (*Well, That's right*) There will be no white persons pulled out of their homes and taken out on some distant road and lynched for not cooperating. [*applause*] There will be nobody amid, among us who will stand up and defy the Constitution of this nation. [*applause*] We only assemble here because of our desire to see right exist. [*applause*] My friends, I want it to be known that we're going to work with grim and bold determination to gain justice on the buses in this city. [*applause*]

8   And we are not wrong, we are not wrong in what we are doing. (*Well*) If we are wrong, the Supreme Court of this nation is wrong. (*Yes sir*) [*applause*] If we are wrong, the Constitution of the United States is wrong. (*Yes*) [*applause*] If we are wrong, God Almighty is wrong. (*That's right*) [*applause*] If we are wrong, Jesus of Nazareth

was merely a utopian dreamer that never came down to earth. (*Yes*) [*applause*] If we are wrong, justice is a lie (*Yes*). Love has no meaning. [*applause*] And we are determined here in Montgomery to work and fight until justice runs down like water (*Yes*) [*applause*], and righteousness like a mighty stream.* (*Keep talking*) [*applause*]

9   I want to say that in all of our actions we must stick together. (*That's right*) [*applause*] Unity is the great need of the hour (*Well, That's right*), and if we are united we can get many of the things that we not only desire but which we justly deserve. (*Yeah*) And don't let anybody frighten you. (*Yeah*) We are not afraid of what we are doing (*Oh no*), because we are doing it within the law. (*All right*) There is never a time in our American democracy that we must ever think we're wrong when we protest. (*Yes sir*) We reserve that right. When labor all over this nation came to see that it would be trampled over by capitalistic power, it was nothing wrong with labor getting together and organizing and protesting for its rights. (*That's right*)

10   We, the disinherited of this land, we who have been oppressed so long, are tired of going through the long night of captivity. And now we are reaching out for the daybreak of freedom and justice and equality. [*applause*] May I say to you my friends, as I come to a close, and just giving some idea of why we are assembled here, that we must keep—and I want to stress this, in all of our doings, in all of our deliberations here this evening and all of the week and while—whatever we do, we must keep God in the forefront. (*Yeah*) Let us be Christian in all of our actions. (*That's right*) But I want to tell you this evening that it is not enough for us to talk about love, love is one of the pivotal points of the Christian face, faith. There is another side called justice. And justice is really love in calculation. (*All right*) Justice is love correcting that which revolts against love. (*Well*)

11   The Almighty God himself is not the only, not the, not the God just standing out saying through Hosea, "I love you, Israel." He's also the God that stands up before the nations and said: "Be still and know that I'm God (*Yeah*), that if you don't obey me I will break the backbone of your power (*Yeah*) and slap you out of the orbits of your international and national relationships."** (*That's right*) Standing beside love is always justice, and we are only using the tools of justice. Not only are we using the tools of persuasion, but we've come to see that

---

*Amos 5:24.
**King refers to Hosea 11:1 ("When Israel was a child, I loved him"). He may also refer to Psalm 46:10 ("Be still, and know that I am God; I will be exalted among the nations, I will be exalted in the earth!").

we've got to use the tools of coercion. Not only is this thing a process of education, but it is also a process of legislation. [*applause*]

12   As we stand and sit here this evening and as we prepare ourselves for what lies ahead, let us go out with a grim and bold determination that we are going to stick together. [*applause*] We are going to work together. [*applause*] Right here in Montgomery, when the history books are written in the future (*Yes*), somebody will have to say, "There lived a race of people (*Well*), a *black* people (*Yes sir*), 'fleecy locks and black complexion' (*Yes*), a people who had the moral courage to stand up for their rights.* [*applause*] And thereby they injected a new meaning into the veins of history and of civilization." And we're gonna do that. God grant that we will do it before it is too late. (*Oh yeah*) As we proceed with our program let us think of these things. (*Yes*) [*applause*]

I Have a Dream

1   I am happy to join with you today in what will go down in history as the greatest demonstration for freedom in the history of our nation.

2   Fivescore years ago, a great American, in whose symbolic shadow we stand today, signed the Emancipation Proclamation. This momentous decree came as a great beacon light of hope to millions of Negro slaves who had been seared in the flames of withering injustice. It came as a joyous daybreak to end the long night of their captivity.

3   But one hundred years later, the Negro still is not free; one hundred years later, the life of the Negro is still sadly crippled by the manacles of segregation and the chains of discrimination; one hundred years later, the Negro lives on a lonely island of poverty in the midst of a vast ocean of material prosperity; one hundred years later, the Negro is still languished in the corners of American society and finds himself in exile in his own land.

4   So we've come here today to dramatize a shameful condition. In a sense we've come to our nation's capital to cash a check. When the architects of our republic wrote the magnificent words of the Constitution and the Declaration of Independence, they were signing a promissory note to which every American was to fall heir. This note

---

*The phrase "fleecy locks and black complexion" is from a poem, "The Negro's Complaint" (1788), by British poet William Cowper. In later speeches King included longer quotations from this poem.

was the promise that all men, yes, black men as well as white men, would be guaranteed the unalienable rights of life, liberty, and the pursuit of happiness.

5   It is obvious today that America has defaulted on this promissory note in so far as her citizens of color are concerned. Instead of honoring this sacred obligation, America has given the Negro people a bad check; a check which has come back marked "insufficient funds." We refuse to believe that there are insufficient funds in the great vaults of opportunity of this nation. And so we've come to cash this check, a check that will give us upon demand the riches of freedom and the security of justice.

6   We have also come to this hallowed spot to remind America of the fierce urgency of now. This is no time to engage in the luxury of cooling off or to take the tranquilizing drug of gradualism. Now is the time to make real the promises of democracy; now is the time to rise from the dark and desolate valley of segregation to the sunlit path of racial justice; now is the time to lift our nation from the quicksands of racial injustice to the solid rock of brotherhood; now is the time to make justice a reality for all God's children. It would be fatal for the nation to overlook the urgency of the moment. This sweltering summer of the Negro's legitimate discontent will not pass until there is an invigorating autumn of freedom and equality.

7   Nineteen sixty-three is not an end, but a beginning. And those who hope that the Negro needed to blow off steam and will now be content, will have a rude awakening if the nation returns to business as usual.

8   There will be neither rest nor tranquility in America until the Negro is granted his citizenship rights. The whirlwinds of revolt will continue to shake the foundations of our nation until the bright day of justice emerges.

9   But there is something that I must say to my people who stand on the warm threshold which leads into the palace of justice. In the process of gaining our rightful place we must not be guilty of wrongful deeds.

10   Let us not seek to satisfy our thirst for freedom by drinking from the cup of bitterness and hatred. We must forever conduct our struggle on the high plane of dignity and discipline. We must not allow our creative protest to degenerate into physical violence. Again and again we must rise to the majestic heights of meeting physical force with soul force.

11   The marvelous new militancy which has engulfed the Negro community must not lead us to a distrust of all white people, for many of our white brothers, as evidenced by their presence here today, have come to realize that their destiny is tied up with our destiny and they have come to realize that their freedom is inextricably bound to our freedom. This offense we share mounted to storm the battlements of injustice must be carried forth by a biracial army. We cannot walk alone.

12   And as we walk, we must make the pledge that we shall always march ahead. We cannot turn back. There are those who are asking the devotees of civil rights, "When will you be satisfied?" We can never be satisfied as long as the Negro is the victim of the unspeakable horrors of police brutality.

13   We can never be satisfied as long as our bodies, heavy with fatigue of travel, cannot gain lodging in the motels of the highways and the hotels of the cities. We cannot be satisfied as long as the Negro's basic mobility is from a smaller ghetto to a larger one.

14   We can never be satisfied as long as our children are stripped of their selfhood and robbed of their dignity by signs stating "for whites only." We cannot be satisfied as long as a Negro in Mississippi cannot vote and a Negro in New York believes he has nothing for which to vote. No, we are not satisfied, and we will not be satisfied until justice rolls down like waters and righteousness like a mighty stream.

15   I am not unmindful that some of you have come here out of excessive trials and tribulation. Some of you have come fresh from narrow jail cells. Some of you have come from areas where your quest for freedom left you battered by the storms of persecution and staggered by the winds of police brutality. You have been the veterans of creative suffering. Continue to work with the faith that unearned suffering is redemptive.

16   Go back to Mississippi; go back to Alabama; go back to South Carolina; go back to Georgia; go back to Louisiana; go back to the slums and ghettos of the northern cities, knowing that somehow this situation can, and will be changed. Let us not wallow in the valley of despair.

17   So I say to you, my friends, that even though we must face the difficulties of today and tomorrow, I still have a dream. It is a dream deeply rooted in the American dream that one day this nation will rise up and live out the true meaning of its creed—we hold these truths to be self-evident, that all men are created equal.

18   I have a dream that one day on the red hills of Georgia, sons of former slaves and sons of former slave-owners will be able to sit down together at the table of brotherhood.

19   I have a dream that one day, even the state of Mississippi, a state sweltering with the heat of injustice, sweltering with the heat of oppression, will be transformed into an oasis of freedom and justice.

20   I have a dream my four little children will one day live in a nation where they will not be judged by the color of their skin but by content of their character. I have a dream today!

21   I have a dream that one day, down in Alabama, with its vicious racists, with its governor having his lips dripping with the words of interposition and nullification, that one day, right there in Alabama, little black boys and black girls will be able to join hands with little white boys and white girls as sisters and brothers. I have a dream today!

22   I have a dream that one day every valley shall be exalted, every hill and mountain shall be made low, the rough places shall be made plain, and the crooked places shall be made straight and the glory of the Lord will be revealed and all flesh shall see it together.

23   This is our hope. This is the faith that I go back to the South with.

24   With this faith we will be able to hew out of the mountain of despair a stone of hope. With this faith we will be able to transform the jangling discords of our nation into a beautiful symphony of brotherhood.

25   With this faith we will be able to work together, to pray together, to struggle together, to go to jail together, to stand up for freedom together, knowing that we will be free one day. This will be the day when all of God's children will be able to sing with new meaning— "my country 'tis of thee; sweet land of liberty; of thee I sing; land where my fathers died, land of the pilgrim's pride; from every mountain side, let freedom ring"—and if America is to be a great nation, this must become true.

26   So let freedom ring from the prodigious hilltops of New Hampshire.

27   Let freedom ring from the mighty mountains of New York.

28   Let freedom ring from the heightening Alleghenies of Pennsylvania.

29   Let freedom ring from the snow-capped Rockies of Colorado.

30   Let freedom ring from the curvaceous slopes of California.

31   But not only that.

32   Let freedom ring from Stone Mountain of Georgia.

33   Let freedom ring from Lookout Mountain of Tennessee.

34   Let freedom ring from every hill and molehill of Mississippi, from every mountainside, let freedom ring.

35   And when we allow freedom to ring, when we let it ring from every village and hamlet, from every state and city, we will be able to speed

up that day when all of God's children—black men and white men, Jews and Gentiles, Catholics and Protestants—will be able to join hands and to sing in the words of the old Negro spiritual, "Free at last, free at last thank God Almighty, we are free at last."*

Where Do We Go from Here?

1   To define much of white America as self-deluded on the commitment to equality and to apprehend the broad base on which it rests are not to enthrone pessimism. The racism of today is real, but the democratic spirit that has always faced it is equally real. The value in pulling racism out of its obscurity and stripping it of its rationalizations lies in the confidence that it can be changed. To live with the pretense that racism is a doctrine of a very few is to disarm us in fighting it frontally as scientifically unsound, morally repugnant and socially destructive. The prescription for the cure rests with the accurate diagnosis of the disease. A people who began a national life inspired by a vision of a society of brotherhood can redeem itself. But redemption can come only through a humble acknowledgment of guilt and an honest knowledge of self.

2   Jesus once told a parable of a young man who left home and wandered into a far country, where he sought life in adventure after adventure. But he found only frustration and bewilderment. The farther he moved from his father's house, the closer he came to the house of despair. After the boy had wasted all, a famine developed in the land, and he ended up seeking food in a pig's trough. But the story does not end here. In a state of disillusionment, frustration and homesickness, the boy "came to himself" and said, "I will arise and go to my father, and will say unto him, Father, I have sinned against heaven, and before thee." The prodigal son was not himself when he left his father's house or when he dreamed that pleasure was the end of life. Only when he made up his mind to go home and be a son again did he come to himself. The boy returned home to find a loving father waiting with outstretched arms and a heart filled with joy.

Negro History Bulletin 21 (May 1968): 16–17.

3   This is an analogy to what white America confronts today. Like all human analogies, it is imperfect, but it does suggest some parallels worth considering. America has strayed to the far country of racism. The home that all too many Americans left was solidly structured idealistically. Its pillars were soundly grounded in the insights of our Judeo-Christian heritage: all men are made in the image of God; all men are brothers; all men are created equal; every man is heir to a legacy of dignity and worth: every man has rights that are neither conferred by nor derived from the state, they are God-given. What a marvelous foundation for any home! What a glorious place to inhabit! But America strayed away; and this excursion has brought only confusion and bewilderment. It has left hearts aching with guilt and minds distorted with irrationality. It has driven wisdom from the throne. This long and callous sojourn in the far country of racism has brought a moral and spiritual famine to the nation.

4   *But it is not too late to return home.* If America would come to herself and return to her true home, "one nation, indivisible, with liberty and justice for all," she would give the democratic creed a new authentic ring, enkindle the imagination of mankind and fire the souls of men. If she fails, she will be victimized with the ultimate social psychosis that can lead only to national suicide.

5   In 1944 Gunnar Myrdal, the Swedish economist, wrote in *An American Dilemma*:

> . . . the Negro problem is not only America's greatest failure but also America's incomparably great opportunity for the future. If America should follow its own deepest convictions, its well-being at home would be increased directly. At the same time America's prestige and power abroad would rise immensely. The century-old dream of American patriots, that America should give to the entire world its own freedoms and its own faith, would come true. America can demonstrate that justice, equality and cooperation are possible between white and colored people. . . . *America is free to choose whether the Negro shall remain her liability or become her opportunity.*

6   This is white America's most urgent challenge today. If America is to respond creatively to the challenge, many individuals, groups and agencies must rise above the hypocrisies of the past and begin to take an immediate and determined part in changing the face of their nation. If the country has not yet emerged with a massive program to end

the blight surrounding the life of the Negro, one is forced to believe that the answers have not been forthcoming because there is as yet no genuine and widespread conviction that such fundamental changes are needed, and needed now.

7   As a first step on the journey home, the journey to full equality, we will have to engage in a radical reordering of national priorities. As the *Carnegie Quarterly* declares: "A great deal of money is spent in this country every day, for education and for housing, freeways, war, national parks, liquor, cosmetics, advertising and a lot of other things. It is a question of the allocation of money, which means the establishing of priorities."

8   Are we more concerned with the size, power and wealth of our society or with creating a more just society? The failure to pursue justice is not only a moral default. Without it social tensions will grow and the turbulence in the streets will persist despite disapproval or repressive action. Even more, a withered sense of justice in an expanding society leads to corruption of the lives of all Americans. All too many of those who live in affluent America ignore those who exist in poor America; in doing so, the affluent Americans will eventually have to face themselves with the question that Eichmann chose to ignore: How responsible am I for the well-being of my fellows? To ignore evil is to become an accomplice to it.

9   Today the exploration of space is engaging not only our enthusiasm but our patriotism. Developing it as a global race we have intensified its inherent drama and brought its adventure into every living room, nursery, shop and office. No such fervor or exhilaration attends the war on poverty. There is impatience with its problems, indifference toward its progress and hostility toward its errors. Without denying the value of scientific endeavor, there is a striking absurdity in committing billions to reach the moon where no people live, while only a fraction of that amount is appropriated to service the densely populated slums. If these strange values persist, in a few years we can be assured that when we set a man on the moon, with an adequate telescope he will be able to see the slums on earth with their intensified congestion, decay and turbulence. On what scale of values is this a program of progress?

10   In the wasteland of war, the expenditure of resources knows no restraints; here our abundance is fully recognized and enthusiastically squandered. The recently revealed mis-estimate of the war budget amounts to $10 billion for a single year. The error alone is more than five times the amount committed to antipoverty programs. If we

reversed investments and gave the armed forces the antipoverty budget, the generals could be forgiven if they walked off the battlefield in disgust. The Washington *Post* has calculated that we spend $332,000 for each enemy we kill. It challenges the imagination to contemplate what lives we could transform if we were to cease killing. The security we profess to seek in foreign adventures we will lose in our decaying cities. The bombs in Vietnam explode at home; they destroy the hopes and possibilities for a decent America.

11   A considerable part of the Negro's efforts of the past decades has been devoted, particularly in the South, to attaining a sense of dignity. For us, enduring the sacrifices of beatings, jailings and even death was acceptable merely to have access to public accommodations. To sit at a lunch counter or occupy the front seat of a bus had no effect on our material standard of living, but in removing a caste stigma it revolutionized our psychology and elevated the spiritual content of our being. Instinctively we struck out for dignity first because personal degradation as an inferior human being was even more keenly felt than material privation.

12   But dignity is also corroded by poverty no matter how poetically we invest the humble with simple graces and charm. No worker can maintain his morale or sustain his spirit if in the market place his capacities are declared to be worthless to society. The Negro is no longer ashamed that he is black—he should never have permitted himself to accept the absurd concept that white is more virtuous than black, but he was crushed by the propaganda that superiority had a pale countenance. That day is fast coming to an end. However, in his search for human dignity he is handicapped by the stigma of poverty in a society whose measure of value revolves about money. If the society changes its concepts by placing the responsibility on its system, not on the individual, and guarantees secure employment or a minimum income, dignity will come within reach of all. For Negroes, the goal on which they have placed the highest priority, which the emancipation from slavery was intended to assure, will finally be attained.

13   Meanwhile, any discussion of the problems of inequality is meaningless unless a time dimension is given to programs for their solution. The Great Society is only a phrase so long as no date is set for the achievement of its promises. It is disquieting to note that President Johnson in his message to Congress on the Demonstration Cities program stated, "If we can begin now the planning from which action

will flow, the hopes of the twentieth century will become the realities of the twenty-first." On this timetable many Negroes not yet born and virtually all now alive will not experience equality. The virtue of patience will become a vice if it accepts so leisurely an approach to social change.

* * *

14 A final challenge that we face as a result of our great dilemma is to be ever mindful of enlarging the whole society, and giving it a new sense of values as we seek to solve our particular problem. As we work to get rid of the economic strangulation that we face as a result of poverty, we must not overlook the fact that millions of Puerto Ricans, Mexican Americans, Indians and Appalachian whites are also poverty-stricken. Any serious war against poverty must of necessity include them. As we work to end the educational stagnation that we face as a result of inadequate segregated schools, we must not be unmindful of the fact, as Dr. James Conant has said, the whole public school system is using nineteenth-century educational methods in conditions of twentieth-century urbanization, and that quality education must be enlarged for all children. By and large, the civil rights movement has followed this course, and in so doing has contributed infinitely more to the nation than the eradication of racial injustice. In winning rights for ourselves we have produced substantial benefits for the whole nation.

15 In the days ahead we must not consider it unpatriotic to raise certain basic questions about our national character. We must begin to ask, "Why are there forty million poor people in a nation overflowing with such unbelievable affluence?" Why has our nation placed itself in the position of being God's military agent on earth, and intervened recklessly in Vietnam and the Dominican Republic? Why have we substituted the arrogant undertaking of policing the whole world for the high task of putting our own house in order?

16 All these questions remind us that there is a need for a radical restructuring of the architecture of American society. For its very survival's sake, America must re-examine old presuppositions and release itself from many things that for centuries have been held sacred. For the evils of racism, poverty and militarism to die, a new set of values must be born. Our economy must become more person centered than property- and profit-centered. Our government must depend more on its moral power than on its military power.

17   Let us, therefore, not think of our movement as one that seeks to integrate the Negro into all the existing values of American society. Let us be those creative dissenters who will call our beloved nation to a higher destiny, to a new plateau of compassion, to a more noble expression of humaneness.

18   We are superbly equipped to do this. We have been seared in the flames of suffering. We have known the agony of being the underdog. We have learned from our have not status that it profits a nation little to gain the whole world of means and lose the end, its own soul. We must have a passion for peace born out of wretchedness and the misery of war. Giving our ultimate allegiance to the empire of justice, we must be that colony of dissenters seeking to imbue our nation with the ideals of a higher and nobler order. So in dealing with our particular dilemma, we will challenge the nation to deal with its larger dilemma.

19   This is the challenge. If we will dare to meet it honestly, historians in future years will have to say there lived a great people—a black people—who bore their burdens of oppression in the heat of many days and who, through tenacity and creative commitment, injected new meaning into the veins of American life.

Cornel West
(1953–)

Born June 2, 1953, in Tulsa, Oklahoma, Cornel West is one of the preeminent scholars and intellectuals among contemporary African Americans. He earned a bachelor's degree from Harvard University and a PhD from Princeton University. He taught at Union Theological Seminary and Yale Divinity School, and directed Princeton's Department of Afro-American Studies before accepting a post at Harvard in 1993, where in 1998 he was named the first Alphonse J. Fletcher University Professor. In 2002, he returned to the faculty of Princeton. His books include Prophesy Deliverance!: An Afro-American Revolutionary Christianity *(1982),* Keeping Faith: Philosophy and Race in America *(1993),* Race Matters *(1993), and* The Cornel West Reader *(1999). "Beyond Multiculturalism & Eurocentrism" is taken from* Prophetic Thought in Postmodern Times *(1993). "A Twilight Civilization" is included in* The Future of the Race *(1996, co-authored with Henry Louis Gates, Jr.).*

Beyond Multiculturalism & Eurocentrism

1 I think it is very important as we reflect on prophetic thought in post-modern times, in these very, very deep and difficult crises of our day, to always view ourselves as part of a tradition. A long and grand tradition trying to forge a sense of dignity and decency, keeping alive quests for excellence and elegance. That is very much what I am. I stand very much on the shoulders of the deep love of my family. My mother and father and brothers and sisters.

2 My grandmother, who is here in Tulsa and who has been struggling and doing so very well and she is unable to be here today. We love her deeply because she gives us such inspiration. She is unable to be here because she is not well enough and yet she is still well enough to give us a sense of possibility. I talked to her until 3:00 a.m. last night. Already it was worth coming to Tulsa, just for that dialogue. Not that the dialogue with you won't be as rich, but if it is I will have a double blessing.

3 Let me begin, then by talking about prophetic thought in post-modern times and what it means to go beyond multiculturalism and eurocentrism. But I want to begin first by defining what I mean by the term "prophetic thought." There are four basic components, four fundamental features, four constitutive elements.

DISCERNMENT

4 The first element of prophetic thought has to do with discernment. Prophetic thought must have the capacity to provide a broad and deep analytical grasp of the present in light of the past. Discernment. We can call it an analytical moment. It is a moment in which one must accent a nuanced historical sense. What I mean by nuanced historical sense is an ability to keep track, to remain attuned to the ambiguous legacies and hybrid cultures in history.

5 This is very important as we shall see when we talk about multiculturalism and eurocentrism, because it means from the very beginning we must call into question any notions of pure traditions or pristine heritages, or any civilization or culture having a monopoly on virtue or insight. Ambiguous legacies, hybrid cultures. By hybrid, of course,

we mean cross-cultural fertilization. Every culture that we know is a result of the weaving of antecedent cultures. Elements of antecedent cultures create something new based on that which came before.

6　This is so true of the United States, of course. There is no jazz without European instruments. But this is true all the way back to the beginning of the human adventure in Mesopotamia, Egypt and Pakistan, and Northern China off the Yellow River. So when we talk about Europe, we are not talking about anything monolithic or homogeneous. When we talk about multiculturalism we are talking about a particular critique of something which is already multicultural.

7　Which means that the very terms themselves, multiculturalism and eurocentrism, are for me not analytical categories, they are categories to be analyzed with a nuanced historical sense, and also a subtle social analysis. By subtle social analysis, I mean powerful descriptions and persuasive explanations of wealth and status and prestige. We have to keep track at any social moment of who is bearing most of the social cost. This is what it means to look at the world from the vantage point of those below.

8　I believe, in fact, that the condition of truth is to allow the suffering to speak. It doesn't mean that those who suffer have a monopoly on truth, but it means that the condition of truth to emerge must be in tune with those who are undergoing social misery—socially induced forms of suffering.

CONNECTION

9　This brings me to the second moment or constitutive element. It's about human connection. By this I mean a value of empathy. Empathy is something that is, unfortunately, waning in our time. Empathy is the capacity to get in contact with the anxieties and frustrations of others. To attempt to put yourself in their shoes. An attempt to get inside their skin.

10　There is a wonderful essay that William James wrote in 1903 upon the occasion of the U.S. invasion, occupation and annexation of the Philippines. It is called, "On a Certain Blindness in Human Beings." In this essay, William James raises the question of why it is that so many of his fellow citizens are unable to empathetically identify with Filipinos as human beings, but rather cast them as pictures and portraits—often stereotypical pictures and portraits.

11　The moment of human connection means never losing sight of the humanity of others. Always attempting to remain in contact with the humanity of others. It's a profoundly moral moment, this second component of the prophetic prospective.

TRACKING HYPOCRISY

12   The third moment is one of what we could call loosely, keeping track of human hypocrisy, in a self-critical, not a self-righteous mode. By keeping track of human hypocrisy, I mean accenting boldly, and defiantly, the gap between principles and practice, between promise and performance, between rhetoric and reality.

13   It has to do with courage because one must take a risk in pointing out human hypocrisy, and one must point out human hypocrisy while remaining open to having others point out that of your own. This is why it is self-critical. This is why a conception of the prophetic in our time cannot be one that claims we have unmediated access to God. But, rather, we are fallen vessels through which more critique is brought to bear on ourselves. We are often complicit with the very thing we are criticizing. It is a form of intellectual humility. But it still takes a stand.

HOPE

14   The last moment, the fourth moment, is one of human hope. And hope, for me, is one of the most difficult things to talk about in the latter part of the twentieth century. What a ghastly century we have lived in. So many millions of people whose lives have been taken or their life's chances crushed.

15   And there are so many hope peddlers who are manipulative, charlatan-like, blinding, obscuring. And yet, we must talk about hope. To talk about human hope is to engage in an audacious attempt to galvanize and energize, to inspire and to invigorate world-weary people. Because that is what we are. We are world-weary; we are tired. For some of us there are misanthropic skeletons hanging in our closet. And by misanthropic I mean the notion that we have given up on the capacity of human beings to do *anything* right. The capacity of human communities to solve any problem.

16   We must face that skeleton as a challenge, not a conclusion. But be honest about it. Weary, and keep alive the notion that history is incomplete, that the world is unfinished, that the future is open-ended and that what we think and what we do can make a difference.

17   If you give up on that notion then there is no hope and all you have is sophisticated analysis. Ironic reflection. Even narcissistic forms of

intellectual engagement. If you don't think what you think and what you do can make a difference, then the possibility of human hope wanes.

MULTICULTURALISM AND EUROCENTRISM

18   Given these four components, then, how are we to think about multi-culturalism and eurocentrism? I am sure that most of you know that there has been a lot of talk about multiculturalism these days. It is a buzzword. It is often undefined. It tends to function in a rather promiscuous manner, to lie down with any perspective, any orientation. So we need to handle it. It is a rather elusive and amorphous term.

19   The same is true with eurocentrism. What do we mean by euro-centrism? Which particular European nation do you have in mind? Which classes of europeans do you have in mind? Certainly, Sicilian peasants don't have the same status as Oxbridge elites. What Europe do you have in mind?

20   We begin with the first moment of this lecture. There are three historical coordinates that will help us "situate and contextualize" this debate that is going on, as Brother "John [Bolin who introduced this lecture series] puts it.

THE VALUE OF THE AGE OF EUROPE

21   The first historical coordinate is the fact that we have yet to fully come to terms with the recognition that we live 48 years after the end of the Age of Europe. Between 1492 and 1945, powerful nations between the Ural mountains and the Atlantic Ocean began to shape the world in their own image. Break throughs in oceanic transportation, break throughs in agricultural production, break throughs in the consolidation of nation status, break-throughs in urbanization, led toward a take-off.

22   1492, the problem of degrading other people and the expulsion of Jews and Muslims and wars in Spain. 1492, Christopher Columbus shows up in what to him is a New World. It is not new to indigenous peoples; they have been there for thousands of years, two hundred nations, as those of you who are here tonight in Tulsa know quite intimately.

23   But the New World concept was part of an expansionism, keeping in mind our ambiguous legacies. We don't want to romanticize and we don't want to trivialize. There were structures of domination already here before the Europeans got here. The plight of indigenous women,

for example. It doesn't mean that the wiping out of indigenous peoples by disease and conquest somehow gets European conquistadors off the hook. But it means that there was always, already, oppression. In new forms it was brought.

24   1492, publication of the first grammar book in Indo-European languages by Antonio de Nebrija in Spanish. Language, of course, being the benchmark in the foundation of a culture. This is what is so interesting about multiculturalism these days. The fact that the dialogue takes place in English already says something. For me, English is an imperial language. My wife is Ethiopian and she dreams in Amharic. I dream in English. That says something about us culturally. We still love each other, but it says something about us culturally. Namely, that I am part of a profoundly hybrid culture. I happen to speak the very language of the elite who tell me that I am not part of the human family, as David Walker said in his Appeal of September 1829. And she speaks Amharic, a different elite, in a different empire, an Ethiopian empire. Different hybridity. Different notions about what it means to be multicultural in this regard.

25   1492, a crucial year. Between 1492 and 1945, we see unprecedented levels of productivity. We see what, in my view, is the grand achievement of the Age of Europe. Because it was in some way marvelous, and it was in some other ways quite ugly. What was marvelous about it was the attempt to institutionalize critiques of illegitimate forms of authority. Let me say that slowly: The attempt to hammer out not just critical gestures but critiques that could be sustained of arbitrary forms of power. That's what the Reformation was about in its critique of the Catholic Church.

26   Think what you will about Martin Luther. He was bringing critique to bear on what he perceived to be arbitrary forms of power. That is what the Enlightenment was about, fighting against national churches that had too much unaccountable power leading to too many lives crushed. That's what liberalism was about against absolute monarchy. That is what women's movements are about against male authority. That's what anti-racist movements are about against white supremacist authority.

27   They are building on traditions of critique and resistance. And, during the age of Europe, given levels of productivity, there were grand experiments. Each and every one of them flawed, but grand experiments to try to live in large communities while institutionalizing critiques of illegitimate forms of authority. This was the makings of the democratic ideal, to which accountability to ordinary

people became not just an abstract possibility, but realizable. As I say, it was deeply flawed.

28   The greatest experiment as we know, began in 1776. But they were institutionalizing these critiques. It didn't apply to white men who had no property. It didn't apply to women. It didn't apply to slaves, people of African descent in the United States who were 21 percent of the population at that time. But that is not solely the point. It is in part the point. But it is not fully the point. The courageous attempt to build a democratic experiment in which the uniqueness of each and every one of us, the sanctity of each and every one of us who has been made equal in the eyes of God becomes at least possible.

29   That democratic idea is one of the grand contributions of the Age of Europe even given the imperial expansion, the colonial subjugation of Africa and Asia, the perrucious and vicious crimes against working people and people of color and so forth. So ambiguous legacy means, in talking about multiculturalism, we have got to keep two ideas in our minds at the same time. The achievements as well as the downfalls. The grand contributions and the vicious crimes.

THE END OF THE AGE OF EUROPE AND THE RISE OF THE UNITED STATES

30   1945. The Age of Europe is over. Europe is a devastated and divided continent. Mushroom clouds over Nagasaki and Hiroshima. Indescribable concentration camps in Germany. Again, Europe's inability to come to terms with the degradation of others. Now upon the hills of a divided continent emerges the first new nation. The U.S.A. Henry James called it a "hotel civilization." A hotel is a fusion between the market and the home. The home, a symbol of warmth and security, hearth. The market, dynamic, mobile, the quest for comfort and convenience. Both home and market. Deeply privatistic phenomenon. By privatistic, I mean being distant from, even distrustful of, the public interest and the common good.

31   In the first new nation, American civilization with tremendous difficulty was trying to define its national identity. What ought to be the common interest. What ought to be the common good. It is quite striking in fact that this first new nation doesn't even raise the question of what it means to be a citizen until after the Civil War, when they have to decide what is the status of the freed men and women, the exenslaved persons. The first new nation, a heterogenous population.

People come from all around the world. In quest for what? Opportunity. In quest for what? A decent life. The quest for what? More comfort and convenience.

32   In 1945, we thought it would be—not "we," but Henry Luce did at least—the American Century. It only lasted 28 years. For the first time in human history, Americans created a modern social structure that looks like a diamond rather than a pyramid. Mass middle class, owing to the GI Bill, Federal Housing Administration programs, Workers' Compensation, Unemployment Compensation. The Great Society that played such a fundamental role in moving persons from working class to middle class in the United States. And yet, the distinctive feature of American civilization in its negative mode, would be the institutionalizing of a discourse of whiteness and blackness.

33   The issue of race. Race is not a moral mistake of individuals, solely. It is a feature of institutions and structures that insures that one group of people have less access to resources, both material and intangible. By material, I mean money, housing, food, health care. By intangible, I mean things like self-confidence. I mean things like self-respect and self-regard and self-esteem. The discourse of whiteness and blackness would result in the incessant bombardment of people of color. Attacks on black beauty. Attacks on black intelligence. You can still get tenure in some universities for arguing that black people are not as intelligent as others. Where did that come from?

34   We are not concerned about eye color, not concerned about the shape of ears. But we are still concerned about pigmentation. It has a history. Of attacks on black intelligence. Attacks on black possibility. What is fascinating about this discourse, that in many ways is distinctive to the USA, though South Africa shares it as well, is that those who came to the United States didn't realize they were white until they got here. They were told they were white. They had to learn they were white. An Irish peasant coming from British imperial abuse in Ireland during the potato famine in the 1840s, arrives in the States. You ask him or her what they are. They say "I am Irish." No, you're white. "What do you mean I am white?" And they point me out. Oh, I see what you mean. This is a strange land.

35   Jews from Ukraine and Poland and Russia undergoing ugly pogroms, assaults and attacks, arrive in Ellis Island. They are told they have to choose, either white or black. They say neither, but they are perceived as white. They say I will not go with the goyim, the goyim have treated me like whites treat black people here. But, I am certainly not black either.

36   This is the 1880s. This is a time in which that peculiar American institution in which a black woman, a man, a child was swinging from a tree every two and a half days for thirty years. An institution unique to the United States called lynching, that "strange fruit that Southern trees bear" which Billy Holiday sang so powerfully about. It's happening every other day. And many Jews would say, no baby, I'm sure not identifying with these folk.

37   Arbitrary use of power. Unaccountable. Segregated laws, Jim and Jane Crow unaccountable. But yet, this new nation, after 1945, would emerge to the center of the historical stage. We now come to the third historical coordinate, the first was the end of the Age of Europe, the second was the emergence of the United States as a world power, and the third is the decolonization of the Third World.

THE DECOLONIZATION OF THE THIRD WORLD

38 By decolonization, I mean the quest of colonized people around the world, between 1945 and 1974, to break the back of European maritime empires. 1947, India. Exemplary anti-colonial struggle. Young preacher, 26 years old, Dexter Avenue Baptist Church, Montgomery, Alabama. He and couragous others look to India for anti-colonial strategy. Nonviolent struggle. Applies the same techniques and strategies to try to break the back of an apartheid-like rule of law in the United States.

39   The civil rights movement was part of a larger international attempt to bring critiques to bear on the empire building that had taken place during the heyday of the Age of Europe namely the nineteenth century. '47 India, '49 China, '57 Ghana, '59 Cuba, '60 Guinea. We go on and on and on. '74 Angola. South Africa as yet to come. There is no way, of course, of looking past some of the colossal failures of the post-colonial regimes in some of those places, or the greed and corruption of the post-colonial elites, like Moi in Kenya, or Mengistu in Ethiopia, or Mobutu. The list is long.

40   But the decolonization points out the degree to which we are living in a fundamentally different world. In 1945, the UN had 45 nations; there are now 172 and there will be more soon given the disintegration of the Soviet Empire. It is a different world.

41   This is a way of situating broadly what the debate between multiculturalism and eurocentrism is about. But it forces us to call into question anyone who would criticize eurocentrism, as if, as I said before, it is monolithic. Because there are struggles going on in Europe between

a whole host of different peoples with different cultures and different nations. And one has to begin with a nuanced historical sense in laying bare a genealogy or a history of the very term Europe itself.

42   Before the debate begins, when was Europe used for the first time as a noun? Christmas, 800, Charles the Great. Pope Leo III puts the crown upon his head. There's only Lombards and the Franks. Two out of eight clans. No Alamans. No Bavarians. An attempt to impose a unity from above. Arab caliphs threatening, Empress Irene in Greek Christendom. Unstable. Historians tell us that without Mohammed, Charlemagne would have been inconceivable. That is what Henri Pirenne says in his magisterial reading of this moment. And yet, at the same time, the attempt to conceive of Europe as some kind of homogenous entity collapses. 843. Partition. At Verdun. Territorial principalities. Their particularisms. Their multiplicities expand and surface. Europe as an entity is not taken seriously.

43   Second attempt, 1458. Pope Pius II, five years after the Turkish invasion of Constantinople. Responding to the Turkish menace, Europe is attempting to forge some collective identity. Reformation. Churches under national government, particularism again. Multiplicity again.

44   Last attempt made, 1804. Napoleon puts crown on his own head. And he calls himself not Emperor of Europe, but Emperor of France.

45   Francis II, withdrew himself as Emperor, and said I am simply part of Austria now. After May, 1804, the collapse of Napoleon and we see the emergence of nationalism. A new tribalism in the human adventure. A nationalism that would strain the moral imagination. Populations around the world remain to this day in this central tribal division of humankind.

46   That is what is going on in Yugoslavia, that is what is going on in Russia. That is what is going on in Ethiopia between the Tigrans and the Amhara, and the Oromo. Nationalism. And, this nationalism would dictate the rules of power during the heyday of the Age of Europe. So strong that people would be willing die for it. That is pretty deep. That is pretty deep, that we all have to impose or endow some sense of meaning to our lives and one test is what we are willing to die for. And citizens around the world are willing to die for their nation-state. That's how deep the thread of nationalism is. That particular form of tribalism. And by calling it tribalism, I am not using that in a degrading sense. Because all of us are born under circumstances not of our own choosing, in particular families, clans, tribes and what-have-you. We all need protection. Tribes protect. Nation-states protect.

47   We all need identity. Tribes provide identity. But, of course, prophetic critique, and of course, in my view the Christian version of the prophetic critique, is that when any form of tribalism becomes a form of idolatry, then a critique and resistance must be brought to bear. When any form of tribalism becomes a justification for hiding and concealing social misery, critique and resistance must be brought to bear.

ECONOMIC & SOCIAL DECLINE

48   Let's come closer in our first moment of discernment. In our present moment here, and I will be saying more about this in the last lecture, but I want to touch on this now. From 1973 to 1989 was a period of national decline. For the first time since the '30s. Levels of productivity nearly freeze. A 0.4 percent increase in 1973–4.

49   There are reasons that we need not go into as to fragility of the debt structure linked to Third World nations. It has much to do, of course, with the rise of OPEC and the Third World monopoly of one of the crucial resources of the modern world, oil. We saw that in January [1991, during the Gulf War]. I think most of us are convinced that if the major resource of Kuwait was artichokes we would not have responded so quickly.

50   Which doesn't take away from the rhetoric of the liberation of Kuwait. Kuwaitis were, in fact, living under vicious and repressive regime under Sadaam Hussein. But there are a whole lot of regimes where people are living that we don't respond to. The rise of OPEC in '74 made a fundamental difference. The slowdown of the U.S. economy. No longer expanding. The unprecedented economic boom no longer in place. And since 1974, the real wages—by real wages I mean inflation-adjusted wages of non-supervisory workers in America—have declined. Which means social slippage, which means downward mobility that produces fear.

51   Material uncertainty becomes real. As you can imagine, it serves as a raw ingredient for scapegoating. And from '73 to '89, we have seen much scapegoating. The major scapegoats have been women and black people, especially at the behest of certain wings of the Republican Party. We don't want to tar the Republican Party as a whole, but yes indeed, in '68 Nixon was talking about busing as a racially coded term. Harry Dent, the same architect of the strategy that led to the walkout of Strom Thurmond in 1948, due to the civil rights plank in the party, and the

formation of the Dixiecrats. The same Harry Dent who served as the principal architect in '48 and lingered in '68.

52 Kevin Phillips wrote a book in '69 called *The New Republican Majority* which is an appeal to race to convince white working class ethnic workers that black people were receiving too much and were unjustified in what they were receiving and that whites were getting a raw deal and ought to come to the Republican Party.

53 Thomas and Mary Edsall tell the story in their recent *Chain Reaction. The impact of rights and race and taxes on American politics.* '76 the Democrats ride on the coattails of Watergate, but they have very little substance. In '80, Ronald Reagan consolidates it all and begins his campaign in Philadelphia, Mississippi and says state rights forever. Racially coded language. Political realignment. The Republican Party becomes essentially a lily-white party. Which is not to say that all Republicans are racist. It is a lily-white party.

54 Another feature is inadequate education for workers so that the products that they produce cannot compete. Japan, Taiwan and South Korea surge. Even Brazil. Stubborn incapacity to generate resources for the public square. No New Taxes, read my lips. Inability to generate resources means public squalor alongside private opulence.

THE RAVAGES OF THE CULTURE OF CONSUMPTION

55 Added to these problems is the undeniable cultural decay, which is in fact quite unprecedented in American history. This is what frightens me more than anything else. By unprecedented cultural decay I mean the social breakdown of the nurturing system for children. The inability to transmit meaning, value, purpose, dignity, decency to children.

56 I am not just talking about the one out of five children who live in poverty. I am not just talking about the one out of two black and two out of five brown children who live in poverty. I am talking about the state of their souls. The deracinated state of their souls. By deracinated I mean rootless. The denuded state of their souls. By denuded, I mean culturally naked. Not to have what is requisite in order to make it through life. Missing what's needed to navigate through the terrors and traumas of death and disease and despair and dread and disappointment. And thereby falling prey to a culture of consumption. A culture that promotes addiction to stimulation. A culture obsessed with bodily stimulation. A culture obsessed with consuming as the only way of preserving some vitality of a self.

57   You are feeling down, go to the mall. Feeling down, turn on the
TV. The TV with its spectator passivity. You are receiving as a spectator, with no sense of agency, no sense of making a difference. You
are observing the collapse of an empire and feeling unable to do anything about it, restricted to just listening to Dan Rather talk about
it. A market culture that promotes a market morality.

58   A market morality has much to do with the unprecedented violence of our social fabric. The sense of being haunted every minute of
our lives in our homes and on the street. Because a market morality
puts money-making, buying and selling, or hedonistic self-indulgence
at the center of one's behavior. Human life has little value. I want
it, I want it now. Quick fix, I've got the gun, give it to me. It affects
us all. I know some people try to run and move out to the suburbs and
the technoburbs and so forth, but it effects us all. Market morality.

59   We should keep in mind that one of the great theorists of market society, namely Adam Smith, wrote a book in 1776, *The Wealth
of Nations*. It is a powerful book in many ways. He talked about ways
in which you generate wealth, but he also wrote a book in 1759 called
The Theory of Moral Sentiments. And in that book Adam Smith
argues that a market culture cannot sustain a market economy.

60   You need market forces as necessary conditions for the preservation of liberties in the economy. But when the market begins to
hold sway in every sphere of a person's life, market conceptions of
the self, market conceptions of time, you put a premium on distraction over attention, stimulation over concentration, then disintegrate sets in. Also in this book, Adam Smith talks about the values
of virtue and propriety, and especially the value of sympathy that
he shared with his fellow Scot, David Hume. And when these non-
market values lose influence or when their influence wanes, then you
have got a situation of Hobbes' war of all against all, of cultural
anarchy and social chaos.

61   Emile Durkheim put it another way, put it well when he said that
a market culture evolves around a notion of contract, but every con-
tractual relation presupposes precontractual commitments. So, a contract means nothing if there is no notion of truth telling and promise
keeping. It has no status. It collapses. Now all we have is manipulative relations. I don't know how many of you have been reading
Michael Levine's book, *The Money Culture*. I don't want to make an
advertisement for it, but the book looks at what happens when a market culture begins to take over the center of a person's life. It tells stories about a Wall Street speculator who is upset because he only made

550 million dollars in a year. He has got to make 555, and he is willing to take a risk and break the law to do it.

62 You say, what is going on? It cannot be solely a question of pointing fingers at individuals. We are talking about larger cultural tendencies that affect each and every one of us. It takes the form of self-destructive nihilism in poor communities, in very poor communities. The lived experience of meaninglessness and hopelessness and lovelessness. Of self-paralyzing pessimism among stable working-class and lower working-class people in which they feel as if their life, their standard of living is declining, they are convinced that the quality of life is declining. And yet, they are looking for quick solutions. I think in part that is what David Duke is all about. It is not just that the people who support him are racist, though, of course, many are. It's that they are looking for a quick solution to a downward slide they experience in their lives. He speaks to it in his own xenophobically coded language. The racist coded language. He is gaining ground.

63 There is a self-indulgent hedonism and self-serving cynicism for those at the top. To simply let it collapse and pull back. Public school, nothing to do with it. Public transportation, nothing to do with it. Public health, nothing to do with it. Privatize them because I have access to resources that allow me to privatize in such a way that I can have quality. The rest, do what you will, make it on your own.

64 In such a context, is it a surprise then, that we see tribal frenzy and xenophobic strife? Multiculturalism and eurocentrism; two notions that go hand in hand. Our attempts on the one hand to respond to the tribal frenzy and xenophobic strife, and yet in their vulgar versions they contribute to it. These are highly unfortunate times which prepackage a debate resulting in even more polarization because it obscures and obfuscates what is fundamentally at stake in our moment. Intellectually, as I noted before, this means preserving the nuanced historical sense. But how do you preserve a historical sense in a market culture that effaces the past? A past that comes back to us through televisual means solely in the form of icons.

65 You go into any school today, who are the great figures? Martin Luther King, Jr. That is fine. Can you tell me something about context that produced him. There is no King without a movement, there is movement without King. King is part of a tradition. But all we have is icons. George Washington. Icon. He was part of an armed revolutionary movement. He picked up guns and threw out the British imperialists. And he tried to institutionalize his conception of democracy. Grand but flawed, as I said before.

66   How do we preserve a sense of history in such a moment? What a challenge. But this is what is intellectually at stake. It makes no sense. Students read Toni Morrison and simply look in her text and see themselves rather than the challenge of a great artist who is dealing with collective memory and community breakdown in *Beloved*, for example. Challenge. If you look in a text and see yourself, that is market education, done in the name of education. But education must not be about a cathartic quest for identity. It must foster credible sensibilities for an active critical citizenry.

67   How do we preserve critical sensibility in a market culture? In our churches, in our synagogues, in our mosques, they are often simply marketing identity. It must be a rather thin identity, this market. It won't last long. Fashion, fad. Someone benefitting, usually the elites who do the marketing and benefiting. How deep does one's identity cut? Most importantly, what is the moral content of one's identity? What are the political consequences of one's identity? These are the kinds of questions that one must ask in talking about multiculturalism and eurocentrism.

68   If one is talking about critiques of racism, critiques of patriarchy, critiques of homophobia, then simply call it that. Eurocentrism is not identical with racism. So, you deny the John Brown's of the world. You deny the anti-racist movement in the heart of Europe. Eurocentrism is not the same as male supremacists. Why? Because every culture we know has been patriarchal in such an ugly way and that you deny the anti-patriarchal movements within the heart of Europe. And the same is so with homophobia. Demystify the categories in order to stay tuned to the complexity of the realities. That is what I am calling for. That is the role of prophetic thinkers and prophetic activists who are willing to build on discernment, human connection. Who are willing to hold up human hypocrisy, including their own and also willing to hold up the possibility of human hope.

69   What I shall attempt to do tomorrow [in the second lecture] is to look at a distinctive American tradition that makes democracy its object of focus, its object of investigation, namely, American pragmatism. And pragmatism has nothing to do with practicalism or opportunism, which is the usual meaning of that term which you see in your newspapers. So and so was pragmatic. No principles, just did what had to be done. No, no. That is not what we will be talking about. American pragmatism is a distinct philosophical tradition that begins with Charles Sanders Peirce, through William James,

through John Dewey, and Sidney Hook and W. E. B. Du Bois, all the way up to the present. And, it makes democracy a basic focus.

70 Its fundamental focus and question is, what are the prospects of democracy? How do you promote individuality and allow it to flower and flourish? I will be linking this tradition with the deep sense of the tragic, which I think the pragmatic tradition lacks. I will try to show ways in which Christian resources can be brought to bear to keep track of the sense of the tragic without curtailing agency. Without curtailing possibilities for action and then I will end [in the third lecture] with what the future of prophetic thought looks like. And I will try to answer some of those questions about whether indeed we can even talk about preserving a historical sense and subtle analysis in a culture that is so saturated by market sensibilities. Thank you so very much.

A Twilight Civilization

1 In our time—at the end of the twentieth century—the crisis of race in America is still raging. The problem of black invisibility and namelessness, however, remains marginal to the dominant accounts of our past and present and is relatively absent from our pictures of the future. In this age of globalization, with its impressive scientific and technological innovations in information, communication, and applied biology, a focus on the lingering effects of racism seems outdated and antiquated. The global cultural bazaar of entertainment and enjoyment, the global shopping mall of advertising and marketing, the global workplace of blue-collar and white-collar employment, and the global financial network of computerized transactions and megacorporate mergers appear to render any talk about race irrelevant.

2 Yet with the collapse of the Soviet Empire, the end of the Cold War, and the rise of Japan, corrupt and top-heavy nation-states are being eclipsed by imperial corporations as public life deteriorates due to class polarization, racial balkanization, and especially a predatory market culture. With the vast erosion of civic networks that nurture and care for citizens—such as families, neighborhoods, and schools—and with what might be called the gangsterization

of everyday life, characterized by the escalating fear of violent attack, vicious assault, or cruel insult, we are witnessing a pervasive cultural decay in American civilization. Even public discourse has degenerated into petty name-calling and finger-pointing—with little room for mutual respect and empathetic exchange. Increasing suicides and homicides, alcoholism and drug addiction, distrust and disloyalty, coldheartedness and mean-spiritedness, isolation and loneliness, cheap sexual thrills and cowardly patriarchal violence are still other symptoms of this decay. Yet race—in the coded language of welfare reform, immigration policy, criminal punishment, affirmative action, and suburban privatization—remains a central signifier in the political debate.

3   As in late nineteenth-century Russia and early twentieth-century Central Europe, the ruling political right hides and conceals the privilege and wealth of the few (the 1 percent who own 48 percent of the net financial wealth, the top 10 percent who own 86 percent, the top 20 percent who have 94 percent!) and pits the downwardly mobile middlers against the downtrodden poor. This age-old strategy of scapegoating the most vulnerable, frightening the most insecure, and supporting the most comfortable constitutes a kind of iron law signaling the decline of modern civilizations, as in Tolstoy's Russia and Kafka's Central Europe: chaotic and inchoate rebellion from below, withdrawal and retreat from public life from above, and a desperate search for authoritarian law and order, at any cost, from the middle. In America, this suggests not so much a European style of fascism but rather a homespun brand of authoritarian democracy—the systemic stigmatizing, regulating, and policing of the degraded "others"—women, gays, lesbians, Latinos, Jews, Asians, Indians, and especially black people. As Sinclair Lewis warned over a half-century ago, fascism, American-style, can happen here.

4   Welfare reform means, on the ground, poor people (disproportionately black) with no means of support. Criminal punishment means hundreds of thousands of black men in crowded prisons—many in there forever. And suburban privatization means black urban poor citizens locked into decrepit public schools, dilapidated housing, inadequate health care, and unavailable child care. Furthermore, the lowest priorities on the global corporate agenda of the political right—the low quantity of jobs with a living wage and the low quality of life for children—have the greatest consequences for the survival of any civilization. Instead, we have generational layers of unemployed and underemployed people (often uncounted in our

national statistics) and increasing numbers of hedonistic and nihilistic young people (of all classes, races, genders, and regions) with little interest in public life and with little sense of moral purpose.

5   This is the classic portrait of a twilight civilization whose dangerous rumblings—now intermittent in much of America but rampant in most of black urban America—will more than likely explode in the twenty-first century if we stay on the present conservative course. In such a bleak scenario—given the dominant tendencies of our day—Du Bois's heralded Talented Tenth will by and large procure a stronger foothold in the well-paid professional managerial sectors of the global economy and more and more will become intoxicated with the felicities of a parvenu bourgeois existence. The heroic few will attempt to tell unpleasant truths about our plight and bear prophetic witness to our predicament as well as try to organize and mobilize (and be organized and mobilized by) the economically devastated, culturally degraded, and politically marginalized black working poor and very poor. Since a multiracial alliance of progressive middlers, liberal slices of the corporate elite, and subversive energy from below is the only vehicle by which some form of radical democratic accountability can redistribute resources and wealth and restructure the economy and government so that all benefit, the significant secondary efforts of the black Talented Tenth alone in the twenty-first century will be woefully inadequate and thoroughly frustrating. Yet even progressive social change—though desirable and necessary—may not turn back the deeper and deadly processes of cultural decay in late twentieth-century America.

6   As this Talented Tenth comes to be viewed more and more with disdain and disgust by the black working poor and very poor, not only class envy but class hatred in black America will escalate—in the midst of a more isolated and insulated black America. This will deepen the identity crisis of the black Talented Tenth—a crisis of survivor's guilt and cultural rootlessness. As the glass ceilings (limited promotions) and golden cuffs (big position and good pay with little or no power) remain in place for most, though not all, blacks in corporate America, we will see anguish and hedonism intensify among much of the Talented Tenth. The conservative wing of black elites will climb on the band-wagon of the political right—some for sincere reasons, most for opportunistic ones—as the black working poor and very poor try to cope with the realities of death, disease, and destruction. The progressive wing of the black elite will split into a vociferous (primarily male-led) black nationalist camp that opts for self-help

at the lower and middle levels of the entrepreneurial sectors of the global economy and a visionary (disproportionately woman-led) radical democratic camp that works assiduously to keep alive a hope— maybe the last hope—for a twilight civilization that once saw itself as the "last best hope of earth."

7   After ninety-five years of the most courageous and unflagging devotion to black freedom witnessed in the twentieth century, W. E. B. Du Bois not only left America for Africa but concluded,

> I just cannot take any more of this country's treatment. We leave for Ghana October 5th and I set no date for return. . . . Chin up, and fight on, but realize that American Negroes can't win.

8   In the end, Du Bois's Enlightenment worldview, Victorian strategies, and American optimism failed him. He left America in militant despair—the very despair he had avoided earlier—and mistakenly hoped for the rise of a strong postcolonial and united Africa. Echoing Tolstoy's claim that "it's intolerable to live in Russia. . . . I've decided to emigrate to England forever" (though he never followed through) and Kafka's dream to leave Prague and live in Palestine (though he died before he could do so), Du Bois concluded that black strivings in a twilight civilization were unbearable for him yet still imperative for others—even if he could not envision black freedom in America as realizable.

9   For those of us who stand on his broad shoulders, let us begin where he ended—with his militant despair; let us look candidly at the tragicomic and absurd character of black life in America in the spirit of John Coltrane and Toni Morrison; let us continue to strive with genuine compassion, personal integrity, and human decency to fight for radical democracy in the face of the frightening abyss—or terrifying inferno—of the twenty-first century, clinging to "a hope not hopeless but unhopeful."

Writing Assignments

1. David Walker is clear in his warning toward the close of "Our Wretchedness in Consequence of the Preachers of the Religion of Jesus Christ." But how does he develop his indictment of American society? What is his specific formulation of an ideal, and how does

he make the case that America has departed from or failed to live up to that ideal? Explain how you agree or disagree with Walker.

2. Analyze how Walker's text compares and contrasts with those of Frederick Douglass. Consider such matters as the message, the selection and arrangement of details, the forcefulness or tone of the arguments, the degree of specificity, and vocabulary. Do you consider either style to be more effective?

3. "In all things purely social we can be as separate as the fingers, yet one as the hand in all things essential to human progress." What is your reaction to this remark from Booker T. Washington's "Speech at the Atlanta Exposition," which was a central statement of his social, economic, and political philosophy? Explain in detail whether you feel Washington's approach represented a reasonable strategy in 1895 or is a viable one for today?

4. Make a list of what you consider the key points to be in the chapter from Washington's *The Future of the American Negro*. Discuss how these ideas compare and contrast with the specific assertions of Ida B. Wells-Barnett and W. E. B. Du Bois in *A Red Record* and "The Niagara Movement," respectively.

5. Choose two writers/speakers from among Du Bois, Mary McLeod Bethune, Martin Luther King, Jr., and Cornel West. Explain the similarities and differences of style and message you detect in the works of the figures you select. Which viewpoints are most compelling or convincing to you? Which viewpoints are least compelling or convincing?

DISCOURSES OF BLACK NATIONALISM

In *The Souls of Black Folk* (1903), W. E. B. Du Bois published his classic statement about the divided psyche or "double consciousness" of African Americans. He wrote that, "one ever feels his twoness,—an American, a Negro; two souls, two thoughts, two unreconciled strivings; two warring ideals in one dark body, whose dogged strength alone keeps it from being torn asunder." Although these words are among the most memorable issued by Du Bois, he had for years expressed the same sentiment in phrasing almost as remarkable. In his 1897 essay "The Conservation of Races," included in this chapter, he addressed the same issue of the bifurcated self:

> Here, then, is the dilemma, and it is a puzzling one, I admit. No Negro who has given earnest thought to the situation of his people in America has failed to ask himself at some time: What, after all, am I? Am I an American or am I a Negro? Can I be both? Or is it my duty to cease to be a Negro as soon as possible and be an American? If I strive as a Negro, am I not perpetuating the very cleft that threatens and separates Black and White America? Is not my only possible practical aim the subduction of all that is Negro in me to the American? Does my black blood place upon me any more obligation to assert my nationality than German, or Irish or Italian blood would?

Generally speaking, when African Americans emphasize their culturally distinctive aspects and advocate social and political action based on ethnic separatism (more Negro than American), they are operating under the concept of *Black nationalism*. Simplicity of definition ends at this point, however. Closer inspection reveals Black nationalism to be a cluster of related beliefs or theories by Blacks concerning the Black liberation struggle.

In its strongest or classic form, Black nationalism represents a desire for an independent territory to be maintained and defended by Blacks. Often the proposed land is in Africa, but other sites in the Americas, including within the United States, have been mentioned. Another variety opposes the creation of a separate nation-state but argues for community control of institutions in African American neighborhoods. A third form, usually combined in some way with the two previous notions, involves the belief that African American political aspirations should be consciously connected to the activities of all Black Africans and other Blacks of African descent. This is commonly referred to as *Pan-Africanism*. Yet other manifestations of Black nationalism are mainly cultural or religious; they may involve observances like Kwanzaa, ethnic dress and naming, or a sense of Black messianism, sometimes called Ethiopianism because of the embrace of the sentiment conveyed in Psalms 68:31—"Princes shall come out of Egypt, Ethiopia shall soon stretch out her hands unto God." African Americans often view themselves as having a divine destiny apart from the rest of American society.

But even the distinctions listed above fail to exhaust the dimensions of Black nationalist thought. Regarding the question of settling in Africa, for example, some have advanced this cause for purely commercial reasons, even envisioning themselves as rulers over native Africans. On the other hand, others have clearly articulated a desire to work hand-in-hand with native Africans for social uplift.

Overall, there are myriad and complex issues surrounding Black nationalism. The concept is traceable to the colonial period and has evolved alongside the integrationist or pluralist impulses often expressed in jeremiads. It has flourished, and most likely will continue to flower, during periods when African Americans are mostly pessimistic about the prospects for social justice. It has also been frequently entwined, in all but its most extreme separatist versions, with rhetoric that espouses an ultimately common destiny for Blacks and other Americans. The problem articulated by Du Bois more than a century ago remains a relevant description of the mindset of millions of African Americans, including a fair sampling of literary artists, who are undoubtedly attracted to at least some aspect of Black nationalism.

Indeed, no one reflected the ambivalence concerning Black nationalism more intensely than Du Bois himself (thus his inclusion both here and in the chapter on jeremiads). He was at times the prototypical African American Jeremiah, clearly buying into the ideal of the American promise and viewing African American destiny in the context of that promise. At other times, he seemed more preoccupied, as evident in "The Conservation of Races," with Black cultural ideals, "race organizations," and Pan-Africanism. But Du Bois was far from a classic Black nationalist. He opposed the idea of a separate nation-state and even attacked Marcus Garvey for propagating the idea.

David Walker perhaps experienced as much double consciousness as Du Bois. Elements of both the African American jeremiad and Black nationalist thought are present in his *Appeal* (1829). That is why Walker is also represented both in the previous chapter and this one. In part of the *Appeal*, Walker writes as a Pan-Africanist. His intended audience is partly described as "the coloured citizens of the world," and he argues that freedom for Africans in the United States is integrally related to the "entire emancipation of your enslaved brethren all over the world." He cites the Haitian revolution of 1804 as an example of action that should be undertaken by oppressed Blacks. He also describes whites as "natural enemies," which, if so, seemingly rules out forever the prospect of peaceful co-existence. If the oppression of African Americans results from natural causes as opposed, say, to social declension, then the only alternatives for freedom are conquest or separation. In the end, however, Walker does not argue for a separate nation-state.

Maria Stewart, a friend and colleague of Walker's, shares several of his ideas and much of his rhetoric. She, in fact, pays tribute to him as a freedom fighter with the cryptic line in "Address at the African Masonic Hall," her 1833 speech, "There was one, although he sleeps, his memory lives." Her tone, like Walker's, is militant at times. She supports separate educational institutions for people of African descent and also trades in Black messianism as indicated by her statement, "Ethiopia shall again stretch forth her hands unto God." However, this religious nationalism, a commonplace stance among Blacks, is firmly linked by Stewart to demands for social equality in the United States. She was a staunch opponent of colonization and envisioned that liberated Africans could eventually benefit from American society.

Although Du Bois and, before him, Walker and Stewart deplored the notion of territorial Black separatism, there were various proposals and efforts over many decades to establish Black settlements beyond the authority of the United States government. Samuel Delany's is a prominent example, although Delany, in fact, made several different proposals concerning colonization.

Of the orators and writers represented in this chapter, Garvey is the least ambiguous. Despite the fact that Blacks had been present in the Americas for more than 300 years, Garvey dismisses any thoughts about hybridity or the idea that a new people had been created. He levels Africanity, insisting on race purity. He argues in "Africa for the Africans" (1923), that, with respect to the nature of Blacks in Africa and in the diaspora, there is "absolutely no difference." Garvey is thus the classic Black separatist in his quest to establish for the Negro "a government of his own." In addition, like Walker and Stewart, he promotes Ethiopianism, emphasizing once more the "stretching of the hand."

The most direct link between Garvey and the most revered proponent of Black nationalism in the latter half of the 20th century, Malcolm X, is Elijah Muhammad, the first prominent leader of the Nation of Islam. In Malcolm's speech, "The Black Revolution" (1963), we see his reference to Muhammad as the "godsent shepherd" and how he credits his major lines of reasoning to Muhammad. The overall tenor is that of classic Black nationalism: "In short, we don't want to be segregated by the white man, we don't want to be integrated with the white man, we want to be separated from the white man." Malcolm does prophesize, with the stridency of a jeremiad, the possible doom of America, but he doesn't believe such fate would result from America's inability to fulfill an ideal promise. He had no faith in that promise.

After Malcolm's split with the Nation of Islam in 1964, he reconceptualized Black nationalism, disconnecting it from any one particular religious interpretation, allowing for political activity other than territorial separatism, and incorporating an international perspective. His influential speech "The Ballot or the Bullet" (1964) epitomizes his reorientation. In it, he is more flexible in his philosophy and approach, and makes new demands on the American political system.

Malcolm's influence has been felt profoundly by many literary figures. One of the most important essayists and poets to emerge after Malcolm's death is Haki Madhubuti, whose "Standing As an African Man" (1994), is a probing meditation on the relevance of Black nationalism in the contemporary world. Madhubuti's central questions, "where do I belong and what is the price I have to pay for being where and who I am?," are essentially the same as those posed by Du Bois.

Further Reading

Cruse, Harold. *The Crisis of the Negro Intellectual: A Historical Analysis of the Failure of Black Leadership.* New York: Morrow, 1967.

Essien-Udom, E. U. *Black Nationalism: A Search for an Identity in America.* Chicago: University of Chicago Press, 1962.

Moses, Wilson, ed. *Classical Black Nationalism: From the American Revolution to Marcus Garvey.* New York: New York UP, 1996.

Stuckey, Sterling. *Slave Culture: Nationalist Theory and the Foundations of Black America.* New York: Oxford UP, 1987.

David Walker

(1785–1830)

For biographical information about David Walker, see page 936. The following excerpts from the Appeal *employ a different argument strategy from the excerpt included in Chapter Nine.*

Appeal, &c.

PREAMBLE.

1   *My dearly beloved Brethren and Fellow Citizens.*

2   Having travelled over a considerable portion of these United States, and having, in the course of my travels, taken the most accurate observations of things as they exist—the result of my observations has warranted the full and unshaken conviction, that we, (coloured people of these United States,) are the most degraded, wretched, and abject set of beings that ever lived since the world began, and I pray God that none like us ever may live again until time shall be no more. They tell us of the Israelites in Egypt, the Helots in Sparta, and of the Roman Slaves, which last were made up from almost every nation under heaven, whose sufferings under those ancient and heathen nations, were, in comparison with ours, under this enlightened and Christian nation, no more than a cypher—or,

in other words, those nations of antiquity, had but little more among them than the name and form of slavery; while wretchedness and endless miseries were reserved, apparently in a phial, to be poured out upon our fathers, ourselves and our children, by *Christian* Americans!

3   These positions I shall endeavour, by the help of the Lord, to demonstrate in the course of this APPEAL, to the satisfaction of the most incredulous mind—and may God Almighty, who is the Father of our Lord Jesus Christ, open your hearts to understand and believe the truth.

4   The *causes*, my brethren, which produce our wretchedness and miseries, are so very numerous and aggravating, that I believe the pen only of a Josephus or a Plutarch, can well enumerate and explain them. Upon subjects, then, of such incomprehensible magnitude, so impenetrable, and so notorious, I shall be obliged to omit a large class of, and content myself with giving you an exposition of a few of those, which do indeed rage to such an alarming pitch, that they cannot but be a perpetual source of terror and dismay to every reflecting mind.

5   I am fully aware, in making this appeal to my much afflicted and suffering brethren, that I shall not only be assailed by those whose greatest earthly desires are, to keep us in abject ignorance and wretchedness, and who are of the firm conviction that Heaven has designed us and our children to be slaves and *beasts of burden* to them and their children. I say, I do not only expect to be held up to the public as an ignorant, impudent and restless disturber of the public peace, by such avaricious creatures, as well as a mover of insubordination—and perhaps put in prison or to death, for giving a superficial exposition of our miseries, and exposing tyrants. But I am persuaded, that many of my brethren, particularly those who are ignorantly in league with slaveholders or tyrants, who acquire their daily bread by the blood and sweat of their more ignorant brethren—and not a few of those too, who are too ignorant to see an inch beyond their noses, will rise up and call me cursed—Yea, the jealous ones among us will perhaps use more abject subtlety, by affirming that this work is not worth perusing, that we are well situated, and there is no use in trying to better our condition, for we cannot. I will ask one question here.—Can our condition be any worse?—Can it be more mean and abject? If there are any changes, will they not be for the better, though they may appear for the worst at first? Can they get us any lower? Where can they get us? They are afraid to treat us worse, for they know well, the day they do it they are gone. But against all accusations which may or can be preferred

against me, I appeal to Heaven for my motive in writing—who knows that my object is, if possible, to awaken in the breasts of my afflicted, degraded and slumbering brethren, a spirit of inquiry and investigation respecting our miseries and wretchedness in this REPUBLICAN LAND OF LIBERTY !!!!!!

6   The sources from which our miseries are derived, and on which I shall comment, I shall not combine in one, but shall put them under distinct heads and expose them in their turn; in doing which, keeping truth on my side, and not departing from the strictest rules of morality, I shall endeavour to penetrate, search out, and lay them open for your inspection. If you cannot or will not profit by them, I shall have done *my* duty to you, my country and my God.

7   And as the inhuman system of *slavery*, is the *source* from which most of our miseries proceed, I shall begin with that *curse to nations*, which has spread terror and devastation through so many nations of antiquity, and which is raging to such a pitch at the present day in Spain and in Portugal. It had one tug in England, in France, and in the United States of America; yet the inhabitants thereof, do not learn wisdom, and erase it entirely from their dwellings and from all with whom they have to do. The fact is, the labour of slaves comes too cheap to the avaricious usurpers, and is (as they think) of such great utility to the country where it exists, that those who are actuated by sordid avarice only, overlook the evils, which will as sure as the Lord lives, follow after the good. In fact, they are so happy to keep in ignorance and degradation, and to receive the homage and the labour of the slaves, they forget that God rules in the armies of heaven and among the inhabitants of the earth, having his ears continually open to the cries, tears and groans of his oppressed people; and being a just and holy Being will at one day appear fully in behalf of the oppressed, and arrest the progress of the avaricious oppressors; for although the destruction of the oppressors God may not effect by the oppressed, yet the Lord our God will bring other destructions upon them—for not unfrequently will he cause them to rise up one against another, to be split and divided, and to oppress each other, and sometimes to open hostilities with sword in hand.

8   Some may ask, what is the matter with this united and happy people?—Some say it is the cause of political usurpers, tyrants, oppressors, &c. But has not the Lord an oppressed and suffering people among them? Does the Lord condescend to hear their cries and see their tears in consequence of oppression? Will he let the oppressors rest comfortably and happy always? Will he not cause the very children of the

oppressors to rise up against them, and ofttimes put them to death? "God works in many ways his wonders to perform."

9   I will not here speak of the destructions which the Lord brought upon Egypt, in consequence of the oppression and consequent groans of the oppressed—of the hundreds and thousands of Egyptians whom God hurled into the Red Sea for afflicting his people in their land—of the Lord's suffering people in Sparta or Lacedemon, the land of the truly famous Lycurgus—nor have I time to comment upon the cause which produced the fierceness with which Sylla usurped the title, and absolutely acted as dictator of the Roman people—the conspiracy of Cataline—the conspiracy against, and murder of Caesar in the Senate house—the spirit with which Marc Antony made himself master of the commonwealth—his associating Octavius and Lipidus with himself in power—their dividing the provinces of Rome among themselves—their attack and defeat, on the plains of Phillippi, of the last defenders of their liberty, (Brutus and Cassius)—the tyranny of Tiberius, and from him to the final overthrow of Constantinople by the Turkish Sultan, Mahomed II. A.D. 1453.

10   I say, I shall not take up time to speak of the *causes* which produced so much wretchedness and massacre among those heathen nations, for I am aware that you know too well, that God is just, as well as merciful!—I shall call your attention a few moments to that *Christian* nation, the Spaniards—while I shall leave almost unnoticed, that avaricious and cruel people, the Portuguese, among whom all true hearted Christians and lovers of Jesus Christ, must evidently see the judgments of God displayed. To show the judgments of God upon the Spaniards, I shall occupy but a little time, leaving a plenty of room for the candid and unprejudiced to reflect.

11   All persons who are acquainted with history, and particularly the Bible, who are not blinded by the God of this world, and are not actuated solely by avarice—who are able to lay aside prejudice long enough to view candidly and impartially, things as they were, are, and probably will be—who are willing to admit that God made man to serve Him *alone*, and that man should have no other Lord or Lords but Himself—that God Almighty is the *sole proprietor* or *master* of the WHOLE human family, and will not on any consideration admit of a colleague, being unwilling to divide his glory with another—and who can dispense with prejudice long enough to admit that we are *men*, notwithstanding our *improminent noses* and *woolly heads*, and believe that we feel for our fathers, mothers, wives and children, as well as the whites do for theirs.—I say, all

who are permitted to see and believe these things, can easily recognize the judgments of God among the Spaniards. Though others may lay the cause of the fierceness with which they cut each other's throats, to some other circumstances, yet they who believe that God is a God of justice, will believe that SLAVERY *is the principal cause.*

12   While the Spaniards are running about upon the field of battle cutting each other's throats, has not the Lord an afflicted and suffering people in the midst of them, whose cries and groans in consequence of oppression are continually pouring into the ears of the God of justice? Would they not cease to cut each other's throats, if they could? But how can they? The very support which they draw from government to aid them in perpetrating such enormities, does it not arise in a great degree from the wretched victims of oppression among them? And yet they are calling for PEACE!—PEACE!! Will any peace be given unto them? Their destruction may indeed be procrastinated awhile, but can it continue long, while they are oppressing the Lord's people? Has He not the hearts of all men in His hand? Will he suffer one part of his creatures to go on oppressing another like brutes always, with impunity? And yet, those avaricious wretches are calling for PEACE!!!! I declare, it does appear to me, as though some nations think God is asleep, or that he made the Africans for nothing else but to dig their mines and work their farms, or they cannot believe history, sacred or profane.

13   I ask every man who has a heart, and is blessed with the privilege of believing—Is not God a God of justice to *all* his creatures? Do you say he is? Then if he gives peace and tranquillity to tyrants, and permits them to keep our fathers, our mothers, ourselves and our children in eternal ignorance and wretchedness, to support them and their families, would he be to us a God of *justice?* I ask, O ye *Christians!!!* who hold us and our children in the most abject ignorance and degradation, that ever a people were afflicted with since the world began—I say, if God gives you peace and tranquillity, and suffers you thus to go on afflicting us, and our children, who have never given you the least provocation—would he be to us *a God of justice?* If you will allow that we are MEN, who feel for each other, does not the blood of our fathers and of us their children, cry aloud to the Lord of Sabaoth against you, for the cruelties and murders with which you have, and do continue to afflict us. But it is time for me to close my remarks on the suburbs, just to enter more fully into the interior of this system of cruelty and oppression.

ARTICLE *I.*

Our Wretchedness in Consequence of Slavery.

14   My beloved brethren:—The Indians of North and of South America—the Greeks—the Irish, subjected under the king of Great Britain—the Jews, that ancient people of the Lord—the inhabitants of the islands of the sea—in fine, all the inhabitants of the earth, (except however, the sons of Africa) are called *men*, and of course are, and ought to be free. But we, (coloured people) and our children are *brutes!!* and of course are, and *ought to be* SLAVES to the American people and their children forever!! to dig their mines and work their farms; and thus go on enriching them, from one generation to another with our *blood* and our *tears!!!!*

15   I promised in a preceding page to demonstrate to the satisfaction of the most incredulous, that we, (coloured people of these United States of America) are the *most wretched*, *degraded* and *abject* set of beings that *ever lived* since the world began, and that the white Americans having reduced us to the wretched state of *slavery*, treat us in that condition *more cruel* (they being an enlightened and Christian people,) than any heathen nation did any people whom it had reduced to our condition. These affirmations are so well confirmed in the minds of all unprejudiced men, who have taken the trouble to read histories, that they need no elucidation from me. But to put them beyond all doubt, I refer you in the first place to the children of Jacob, or of Israel in Egypt, under Pharaoh and his people. Some of my brethren do not know who Pharaoh and the Egyptians were—I know it to be a fact, that some of them take the Egyptians to have been a gang of *devils*, not knowing any better, and that they (Egyptians) having got possession of the Lord's people, treated them *nearly* as cruel as *Christian Americans* do us, at the present day. For the information of such, I would only mention that the Egyptians, were Africans or coloured people, such as we are—some of them yellow and others dark—a mixture of Ethiopians and the natives of Egypt—about the same as you see the coloured people of the United States at the present day.—I say, I call your attention then, to the children of Jacob, while I point out particularly to you his son Joseph, among the rest, in Egypt.

16   "And Pharaoh, said unto Joseph, thou shalt be over my house, and according unto thy word shall all my people be ruled: only in the throne will I be greater than thou."*

*See Genesis, chap. xli.

17   "And Pharaoh said unto Joseph, see, I have set thee over all the land of Egypt."*

18   "And Pharaoh said unto Joseph, I am Pharaoh, and without thee shall no man lift up his hand or foot in all the land of Egypt."**

19   Now I appeal to heaven and to earth, and particularly to the American people themselves, who cease not to declare that our condition is not *hard*, and that we are comparatively satisfied to rest in wretchedness and misery, under them and their children. Not, indeed, to show me a coloured President, a Governor, a Legislator, a Senator, a Mayor, or an Attorney at the Bar.—But to show me a man of colour, who holds the low office of a Constable, or one who sits in a Juror Box, even on a case of one of his wretched brethren, throughout this great Republic!!—But let us pass Joseph the son of Israel a little farther in review, as he existed with that heathen nation.

21   "And Pharaoh called Joseph's name Zaphnathpaaneah; and he gave him to wife Asenath the daughter of Potipherah priest of On. And Joseph went out over all the land of Egypt."***

22   Compare the above, with the American institutions. Do they not institute laws to prohibit us from marrying among the whites? I would wish, candidly, however, before the Lord, to be understood, that I would not give a *pinch of snuff* to be married to any white person I ever saw in all the days of my life. And I do say it, that the black man, or man of colour, who will leave his own colour (provided he can get one, who is good for any thing) and marry a white woman, to be a double slave to her, just because she is *white*, ought to be treated by her as he surely will be, viz: as a NIGER[*sic*]!!!! It is not, indeed, what I care about intermarriages with the whites, which induced me to pass this subject in review; for the Lord knows, that there is a day coming when they will be glad enough to get into the company of the blacks, notwithstanding, we are, in this generation, levelled by them, almost on a level with the brute creation: and some of us they treat even worse than they do the brutes that perish. I only made this extract to show how much lower we are held, and how much more cruel we are treated by the Americans, than were the children of Jacob, by the Egyptians.—We will notice the sufferings of Israel some further, under *heathen Pharaoh*, compared with ours under the *enlightened Christians of America.*

*xli. 44.
**xli. 44.
*** xli. 45.

23   "And Pharaoh spake unto Joseph, saying, thy father and thy brethren are come unto thee:"

24   "The land of Egypt is before thee: in the best of the land make thy father and brethren to dwell; in the land of Goshen let them dwell: and if thou knowest any men of activity among them, then make them rulers over my cattle."*

25   I ask those people who treat us so *well*, Oh! I ask them, where is the most barren spot of land which they have given unto us? Israel had the most fertile land in all Egypt. Need I mention the very notorious fact, that I have known a poor man of colour, who laboured night and day, to acquire a little money, and having acquired it, he vested it in a small piece of land, and got him a house erected thereon, and having paid for the whole, he moved his family into it, where he was suffered to remain but nine months, when he was cheated out of his property by a white man, and driven out of door! And is not this the case generally? Can a man of colour buy a piece of land and keep it peaceably? Will not some white man try to get it from him, even if it is in a *mud hole?* I need not comment any farther on a subject, which all, both black and white, will readily admit. But I must, really, observe that in this very city, when a man of colour dies, if he owned any real estate it most generally falls into the hands of some white person. The wife and children of the deceased may weep and lament if they please, but the estate will be kept snug enough by its white possessor.

26   But to prove farther that the condition of the Israelites was better under the Egyptians than ours is under the whites, I call upon the professing Christians, I call upon the philanthropist, I call upon the very tyrant himself, to show me a page of history, either sacred or profane, on which a verse can be found, which maintains, that the Egyptians heaped the *insupportable insult* upon the children of Israel, by telling them that they were not of the *human family*. Can the whites deny this charge? Have they not, after having reduced us to the deplorable condition of slaves under their feet, held us up as descending originally from the tribes of *Monkeys* or *Orang-Outangs?* O! my God! I appeal to every man of feeling—is not this insupportable? Is it not heaping the most gross insult upon our miseries, because they have got us under their feet and we cannot help ourselves? Oh! pity us we pray thee, Lord Jesus, Master.—

*Genesis, chap. xlvii, 5, 6.

Has Mr. Jefferson declared to the world, that we are inferior to the whites, both in the endowments of our bodies and of minds? It is indeed surprising, that a man of such great learning, combined with such excellent natural parts, should speak so of a set of men in chains. I do not know what to compare it to, unless, like putting one wild deer in an iron cage, where it will be secured, and hold another by the side of the same, then let it go, and expect the one in the cage to run as fast as the one at liberty. So far, my brethren, were the Egyptians from heaping these insults upon their slaves, that Pharaoh's daughter took Moses, a son of Israel for her own, as will appear by the following.

27   "And Pharaoh's daughter said unto her, [Moses' mother] take this child away, and nurse it for me, and I will pay thee thy wages. And the woman took the child [Moses] and nursed it.

28   "And the child grew, and she brought him unto Pharaoh's daughter and he became her son. And she called his name Moses: and she said because I drew him out of the water."*

29   In all probability, Moses would have become Prince Regent to the throne, and no doubt, in process of time but he would have been seated on the throne of Egypt. But he had rather suffer shame, with the people of God, than to enjoy pleasures with that wicked people for a season. O! that the coloured people were long since of Moses' excellent disposition, instead of courting favour with, and telling news and lies to our *natural enemies*, against each other— aiding them to keep their hellish chains of slavery upon us. Would we not long before this time, have been respectable men, instead of such wretched victims of oppression as we are? Would they be able to drag our mothers, our fathers, our wives, our children and ourselves, around the world in chains and handcuffs as they do, to dig up gold and silver for them and theirs? This question, my brethren, I leave for you to digest; and may God Almighty force it home to your hearts. Remember that unless you are united, keeping your tongues within your teeth, you will be afraid to trust your secrets to each other, and thus perpetuate our miseries under the *Christians!!!!!* Addition.—Remember, also to lay humble at the feet of our Lord and Master Jesus Christ, with prayers and fastings. Let our enemies go on with their butcheries, and at once fill up their cup. Never make an attempt to gain our freedom or *natural right*,

*See Exodus, chap. ii. 9, 10.

from under our cruel oppressors and murderers, until you see your
way clear*—when that hour arrives and you move, be not afraid or
dismayed; for be you assured that Jesus Christ the King of heaven
and of earth who is the God of justice and of armies, will surely
go before you. And those enemies who have for hundreds of years
stolen our *rights*, and kept us ignorant of Him and His divine worship, he will remove. Millions of whom, are this day, so ignorant
and avaricious, that they cannot conceive how God can have an
attribute of justice, and show mercy to us because it pleased Him
to make us black—which colour, Mr. Jefferson calls unfortunate!!!!!! As though we are not as thankful to our God, for having made us as it pleased himself, as they (the whites,) are for
having made them white. They think because they hold us in their
infernal chains of slavery, that we wish to be white or of their
color—but they are dreadfully deceived—we wish to be just as it
pleased our Creator to have made us, and no avaricious and unmerciful wretches, have any business to make slaves of, or hold us in
slavery. How would they like for us to make slaves of, and hold
them in cruel slavery, and murder them as they do us?—But is Mr.
Jefferson's assertions true? viz. "that it is unfortunate for us that
our Creator has been pleased to make us *black*." We will not take
his say so, for the fact. The world will have an opportunity to see
whether it is unfortunate for us, that our Creator *has made us*
darker than the *whites*.

30   Fear not the number and education of our *enemies*, against whom
we shall have to contend for our lawful right; guaranteed to us by our
Maker; for why should we be afraid, when God is, and will continue,
(if we continue humble) to be on our side?

31   The man who would not fight under our Lord and Master Jesus
Christ, in the glorious and heavenly cause of freedom and of God—
to be, delivered from the most wretched, abject and servile slavery,
that ever a people was afflicted with since the foundation of the world,
to the present day—ought to be kept with all of his children or family, in slavery, or in chains, to be butchered by his *cruel enemies*.

---

*It is not to be understood here, that I mean for us to wait until God shall take us by the hair of
our heads and drag us out of abject wretchedness and slavery, nor do I mean to convey the idea
for us to wait until our enemies shall make preparations, and call us to seize those preparations,
take it away from them, and put every thing before us to death, in order to gain our freedom
which God has given us. For you must remember that we are men as well as they. God has been
pleased to give us two eyes, two hands, two feet, and some sense in our heads as well as they.
They have no more right to hold us in slavery than we have to hold them, we have just as much
right, in the sight of God, to hold them and their children in slavery and wretchedness, as they
have to hold us, and no more.

32   I saw a paragraph, a few years since, in a South Carolina paper, which, speaking of the barbarity of the Turks, it said: "The Turks are the most barbarous people in the world—they treat the Greeks more like *brutes* than human beings." And in the same paper was an advertisement, which said: "Eight well built Virginia and Maryland *Negro fellows* and four *wenches* will positively be *sold* this day, *to the highest bidder!*" And what astonished me still more was, to see in this same *humane* paper!! the cuts of three men, with clubs and budgets on their backs, and an advertisement offering a considerable sum of money for their apprehension and delivery. I declare, it is really so amusing to hear the Southerners and Westerners of this country talk about *barbarity*, that it is positively, enough to make a man *smile*.

33   The sufferings of the Helots among the Spartans, were somewhat severe, it is true, but to say that theirs, were as severe as ours among the Americans, I do most strenuously deny—for instance, can any man show me an article on a page of ancient history which specifies, that, the Spartans chained, and handcuffed the Helots, and dragged them from their wives and children, children from their parents, mothers from their suckling babes, wives from their husbands, driving them from one end of the country to the other? Notice the Spartans were heathens, who lived long before our Divine Master made his appearance in the flesh.

34   Can Christian Americans deny these barbarous cruelties? Have you not, Americans, having subjected us under you, added to these miseries, by insulting us in telling us to our face, because we are helpless, that we are not of the human family? I ask you, O! Americans, I ask you, in the name of the Lord, can you deny these charges? Some perhaps may deny, by saying, that they never thought or said that we were not men. But do not actions speak louder than *words?*—have they not made provisions for the Greeks, and Irish? Nations who have never done the least thing for them, while *we*, who have enriched their country with our blood and tears—have dug up gold and silver for them and their children, from generation to generation, and are in more miseries than any other people under heaven, are not seen, but by comparatively, a handful of the American people? There are indeed, more ways to kill a dog, besides choking it to death with butter. Further—The Spartans or Lacedemonians, had some frivolous pretext, for enslaving the Helots, for they (Helots) while being free inhabitants of Sparta, stirred up an intestine commotion, and were, by the Spartans subdued, and made prisoners of

war. Consequently they and their children were condemned to perpetual slavery.*

35   I have been for years troubling the pages of historians, to find out what our fathers have done to the *white Christians of America*, to merit such condign punishment as they have inflicted on them, and do continue to inflict on us their children. But I must aver, that my researches have hitherto been to no effect. I have therefore, come to the immoveable conclusion, that they (Americans) have, and do continue to punish us for nothing else, but for enriching them and their country. For I cannot conceive of any thing else. Nor will I ever believe otherwise, until the Lord shall convince me.

36   The world knows, that slavery as it existed among the Romans, (which was the primary cause of their destruction) was, comparatively speaking, no more than a *cypher*, when compared with ours under the Americans. Indeed I should not have noticed the Roman slaves, had not the very learned and penetrating Mr. Jefferson said, "when a master was murdered, all his slaves in the same house, or within hearing, were condemned to death."**—Here let me ask Mr. Jefferson, (but he is gone to answer at the bar of God, for the deeds done in his body while living,) I therefore ask the whole American people, had I not rather die, or be put to death, than to be a slave to any tyrant, who takes not only my own, but my wife and children's lives by the inches? Yea, would I meet death with avidity far! far!! in preference to such *servile submission* to the murderous hands of tyrants. Mr. Jefferson's very severe remarks on us have been so extensively argued upon by men whose attainments in literature, I shall never be able to reach, that I would not have meddled with it, were it not to solicit each of my brethren, who has the spirit of a man, to buy a copy of Mr. Jefferson's *Notes on Virginia*, and put it in the hand of his son. For let no one of us suppose that the refutations which have been written by our white friends are enough—they are *whites*—we are *blacks*.

37   We, and the world wish to see the charges of Mr. Jefferson refuted by the blacks *themselves*, according to their chance; for we must remember that what the whites have written respecting this subject, is other men's labours, and did not emanate from the blacks. I know well, that there are some talents and learning among the coloured people of this

---

*See Dr. Goldsmith's *History of Greece*–page 9. See also, Plutarch's *Lives*. The Helots subdued by Agis, king of *Sparta*.
** See his *Notes on Virginia*, page 210.

country, which we have not a chance to develop, in consequence of oppression; but our oppression ought not to hinder us from acquiring all we can. For we will have a chance to develop them by and by. God will not suffer us, always to be oppressed. Our sufferings will come to an *end*, in spite of all the Americans this side of *eternity*. Then we will want all the learning and talents among ourselves, and perhaps more, to govern ourselves.—"Every dog must have its day," the American's is coming to an end.

38   But let us review Mr. Jefferson's remarks respecting us some further. Comparing our miserable fathers, with the learned philosophers of Greece, he says:

> Yet notwithstanding these and other discouraging circumstances among the Romans, their slaves were often their rarest artists. They excelled too, in science, insomuch as to be usually employed as tutors to their master's children; Epictetus, Terence and Phaedrus, were slaves,—but they were of the race of whites. It is not their *condition* then, but *nature*, which has produced the distinction.*

See this, my brethren!! Do you believe that this assertion is swallowed by millions of the whites? Do you know that Mr. Jefferson was one of as great characters as ever lived among the whites? See his writings for the world, and public labours for the United States of America. Do you believe that the assertions of such a man, will pass away into oblivion unobserved by this people and the world? If you do you are much mistaken—See how the American people treat us— have we souls in our bodies? Are we men who have any spirits at all? I know that there are many *swell-bellied* fellows among us, whose greatest object is to fill their stomachs. Such I do not mean—I am after those who know and feel, that we are MEN, as well as other people, to them, I say, that unless we try to refute Mr. Jefferson's arguments respecting us, we will only establish them.

39   But the slaves among the Romans. Every body who has read history, knows, that as soon as a slave among the Romans obtained his freedom, he could rise to the greatest eminence in the State, and there was no law instituted to hinder a slave from buying his freedom. Have not the Americans instituted laws to hinder us from obtaining our freedom? Do any deny this charge? Read the laws of Virginia, North

*See his *Notes on Virginia*, page 211.

Carolina, &c. Further: have not the Americans instituted laws to prohibit a man of colour from obtaining and holding any office whatever,
under the government of the United States of America? Now, Mr.
Jefferson tells us, that our condition is not so hard, as the slaves were
under the Romans!!!!!!

40   It is time for me to bring this article to a close. But before I close
it, I must observe to my brethren that at the close of the first Revolution in this country, with Great Britain, there were but thirteen
States in the Union, now there are twenty-four, most of which are
slaveholding States, and the whites are dragging us around in chains
and in handcuffs, to their new States and Territories to work their
mines and farms, to enrich them and their children—and millions
of them believing firmly that we being a little darker than they, were
made by our Creator to be an inheritance to them and their children
for ever—the same as a parcel of *brutes*.

41   Are we MEN!!—I ask you, O my brethren! are we MEN? Did our
Creator make us to be slaves to dust and ashes like ourselves? Are
they not dying worms as well as we? Have they not to make their
appearance before the tribunal of Heaven, to answer for the deeds
done in the body, as well as we? Have we any other Master but Jesus
Christ alone? Is he not their Master as well as ours?—What right then,
have we to obey and call any other Master, but Himself? How we
could be so *submissive* to a gang of men, whom we cannot tell whether
they are *as good* as ourselves or not, I never could conceive. However,
this is shut up with the Lord, and we cannot precisely tell—but I
declare, we judge men by their works.

42   The whites have always been an unjust, jealous, unmerciful, avaricious and bloodthirsty set of beings, always seeking after power and
authority.—We view them all over the confederacy of Greece, where
they were first known to be any thing, (in consequence of education) we see them there, cutting each other's throats—trying to subject each other to wretchedness and misery—to effect which, they
used all kinds of deceitful, unfair, and unmerciful means. We view
them next in Rome, where the spirit of tyranny and deceit raged still
higher. We view them in Gaul, Spain, and in Britain.—In fine, we view
them all over Europe, together with what were scattered about in Asia
and Africa, as heathens, and we see them acting more like devils than
accountable men. But some may ask, did not the blacks of Africa, and
the mulattoes of Asia, go on in the same way as did the whites of
Europe. I answer, no—they never were half so avaricious, deceitful
and unmerciful as the whites, according to their knowledge.

43   But we will leave the whites or Europeans as heathens, and take a view of them as Christians, in which capacity we see them as cruel, if not more so than ever. In fact, take them as a body, they are ten times more cruel, avaricious and unmerciful than ever they were; for while they were heathens, they were bad enough it is true, but it is positively a fact that they were not quite so audacious as to go and take vessel loads of men, women and children, and in cold blood, and through devilishness, throw them into the sea, and murder them in all kind of ways. While they were heathens, they were too ignorant for such barbarity. But being Christians, enlightened and sensible, they are completely prepared for such hellish cruelties.

44   Now suppose God were to give them more sense, what would they do? If it were possible, would they not *dethrone* Jehovah and seat themselves upon his throne? I therefore, in the name and fear of the Lord God of Heaven and of earth, divested of prejudice either on the side of my colour or that of the whites, advance my suspicion of them, whether they are *as good by nature* as we are or not. Their actions, since they were known as a people, have been the reverse, I do indeed suspect them, but this, as I before observed, is shut up with the Lord, we cannot exactly tell, it will be proved in succeeding generations.—The whites have had the essence of the gospel as it was preached by my master and his apostles—the Ethiopians have not, who are to have it in its meridian splendor—the Lord will give it to them to their satisfaction. I hope and pray my God, that they will make good use of it, that it may be well with them.*

ARTICLE II.

Our Wretchedness in Consequence of Ignorance.

45   Ignorance, my brethren, is a mist, low down into the very dark and almost impenetrable abyss in which, our fathers for many centuries have been plunged. The Christians, and enlightened of Europe, and

*It is my solemn belief, that if ever the world becomes Christianized, (which must certainly take place before long) it will be through the means, under God of the *Blacks*, who are now held in wretchedness, and degradation, by the white *Christians* of the world, who before they learn to do justice to us before our Maker–and be reconciled to us, and reconcile us to them, and by that means have clear consciences before God and man.–Send out Missionaries to convert the Heathens, many of whom after they cease to worship gods, which neither see nor hear, become ten times more the children of Hell, then ever they were, why what is the reason? Why the reason is obvious, they must learn to do justice at home, before they go into distant lands, to display their charity, Christianity, and benevolence; when they learn to do justice, God will accept their offering, (no man may think that I am against Missionaries for I am not, my object is to see justice done at home, before we go to convert the heathens.)

some of Asia, seeing the ignorance and consequent degradation of our fathers, instead of trying to enlighten them, by teaching them that religion and light with which God had blessed them, they have plunged them into wretchedness ten thousand times more intolerable, than if they had left them entirely to the Lord, and to add to their miseries, deep down into which they have plunged them tell them, that they are an *inferior* and *distinct race* of beings, which they will be glad enough to recall and swallow by and by. Fortune and misfortune, two inseparable companions, lay rolled up in the wheel of events, which have from the creation of the world, and will continue to take place among men until God shall dash worlds together.

46   When we take a retrospective view of the arts and sciences—the wise legislators—the Pyramids, and other magnificent buildings— the turning of the channel of the river Nile, by the sons of Africa or of Ham, among whom learning originated, and was carried thence into Greece, where it was improved upon and refined. Thence among the Romans, and all over the then enlightened parts of the world, and it has been enlightening the dark and benighted minds of men from then, down to this day. I say, when I view retrospectively, the renown of that once mighty people, the children of our great progenitor I am indeed cheered. Yea further, when I view that mighty son of Africa, HANNIBAL, one of the greatest generals of antiquity, who defeated and cut off so many thousands of the white Romans or murderers, and who carried his victorious arms, to the very gate of Rome, and I give it as my candid opinion, that had Carthage been well united and had given him good support, he would have carried that cruel and barbarous city by storm. But they were disunited, as the coloured people are now, in the United States of America, the reason our natural enemies are enabled to keep their feet on our throats.

47   Beloved brethren—here let me tell you, and believe it, that the Lord our God, as true as he sits on his throne in heaven, and as true as our Saviour died to redeem the world, will give you a Hannibal, and when the Lord shall have raised him up, and given him to you for your possession, O my suffering brethren! remember the divisions and consequent sufferings of *Carthage* and of *Hayti*. Read the history particularly of Hayti, and see how they were butchered by the whites, and do you take warning. The person whom God shall give you, give him your support and let him go his length, and behold in him the salvation of your God. God will indeed, deliver you through him from your deplorable and wretched condition under the

Christians of America. I charge you this day before my God to lay no obstacle in his way, but let him go.

48   The whites want slaves, and want us for their slaves, but some of them will curse the day they ever saw us. As true as the sun ever shone in its meridian splendor, my colour will root some of them out of the very face of the earth. They shall have enough of making slaves of, and butchering, and murdering us in the manner which they have. No doubt some may say that I write with a bad spirit, and that I being a black, wish these things to occur. Whether I write with a bad or a good spirit, I say if these things do not occur in their proper time, it is because of the world in which we live does not exist, and we are deceived with regard to its existence.—It is immaterial however to me, who believe, or who refuse—though I should like to see the whites repent peradventure God may have mercy on them, some however, have gone so far that their cup must be filled.

49   But what need have I to refer to antiquity, when Hayti, the glory of the blacks and terror of tyrants, is enough to convince the most avaricious and stupid of wretches—which is at this time, and I am sorry to say it, plagued with that scourge of nations, the Catholic religion; but I hope and pray God that she may yet rid herself of it, and adopt in its stead the Protestant faith; also, I hope that she may keep peace within her borders and be united, keeping a strict look out for tyrants, for if they get the least chance to injure her, they will avail themselves of it, as true as the Lord lives in heaven. But one thing which gives me joy is, that they are men who would be cut off to a man, before they would yield to the combined forces of the whole world—in fact, if the whole world was combined against them, it could not do any thing with them, unless the Lord delivers them up.

50   Ignorance and treachery one against the other—a grovelling servile and abject submission to the lash of tyrants, we see plainly, my brethren, are not the natural elements of the blacks, as the Americans try to make us believe; but these are misfortunes which God has suffered our fathers to be enveloped in for many ages, no doubt in consequence of their disobedience to their maker, and which do, indeed, reign at this time among us, almost to the destruction of all other principles: for I must truly say, that ignorance, the mother of treachery and deceit, gnaws into our very vitals. Ignorance, as it now exists among us, produces a state of things, Oh my Lord! too horrible to present to the world. Any man who is curious to see the full force of ignorance developed among the coloured people of the United States of America, has only to go into the southern and western states of this

confederacy, where, if he is not a tyrant, but has the feelings of a human being, who can feel for a fellow creature, he may see enough to make his very heart bleed! He may see there, a son take his mother, who bore almost the pains of death to give him birth, and by the command of a tyrant, strip her as naked as she came into the world, and apply the cowhide to her, until she falls a victim to death in the road! He may see a husband take his dear wife, not unfrequently in a pregnant state, and perhaps far advanced, and beat her for an unmerciful wretch, until his infant falls a lifeless lump at her feet!

51   Can the Americans escape God Almighty? If they do, can he be to us a God of Justice? God is just, and I know it—for he has convinced me to my satisfaction—I cannot doubt him. My observer may see fathers beating their sons, mothers their daughters, and children their parents, all to pacify the passions of unrelenting tyrants. He may also, see them telling news and lies, making mischief one upon another. These are some of the productions of ignorance, which he will see practised among my dear brethren, who are held in unjust slavery and wretchedness, by avaricious and unmerciful tyrants, to whom, and their hellish deeds, I would suffer my life to be taken before I would submit. And when my curious observer comes to take notice of those who are said to be free, (which assertion I deny) and who are making some frivolous pretentions to common sense, he will see that branch of ignorance among the slaves assuming a more cunning and deceitful course of procedure.—He may see some of my brethren in league with tyrants, selling their own brethren into *hell upon earth*, not dissimilar to the exhibitions in Africa, but in a more secret, servile and abject manner. Oh Heaven! I am full!!! I can hardly move my pen!!! and as I expect some will try to put me to death, to strike terror into others, and to obliterate from their minds the notion of freedom, so as to keep my brethren the more secure in wretchedness, where they will be permitted to stay but a short time (whether tyrants believe it or not)—I shall give the world a development of facts, which are already witnessed in the courts of heaven. My observer may see some of those ignorant and treacherous creatures (coloured people) sneaking about in the large cities, endeavouring to find out all strange coloured people, where they work and where they reside, asking them questions, and trying to ascertain whether they are runaways or not, telling them, at the same time, that they always have been, are, and always will be, friends to their brethren; and, perhaps, that they themselves are absconders, and a thousand such treacherous lies to get the better information of the more

ignorant!!! There have been and are at this day in Boston, New York, Philadelphia, and Baltimore, coloured men, who are in league with tyrants, and who receive a great portion of their daily bread, of the moneys which they acquire from the blood and tears of their more miserable brethren, whom they scandalously delivered into the hands of our *natural enemies!!!!!!*

52 To show the force of degraded ignorance and deceit among us some farther, I will give here an extract from a paragraph, which may be found in the *Columbian Centinel* of this city, for September 9, 1829, on the first page of which, the curious may find an article, headed

"Affray and Murder."

Portsmouth, (Ohio) Aug. 22, 1829

A most shocking outrage was committed in Kentucky, about eight miles from this place, on 14th inst. A negro driver, by the name of Gordon, who had purchased in Maryland about sixty negroes, was taking them, assisted by an associate named Allen, and the wagoner who conveyed the baggage, to the Mississippi. The men were handcuffed and chained together, in the usual manner for driving those poor wretches, while the women and children were suffered to proceed without incumbrance. It appears that, by means of a file the negroes, unobserved, had succeeded in separating the iron which bound their hands, in such a way as to be able to throw them off at any moment. About 8 o'clock in the morning, while proceeding on the state road leading from Greenup to Vanceburg, two of them dropped their shackles and commenced a fight, when the wagoner (Petit) rushed in with his whip to compel them to desist. At this moment, every negro was found to be perfectly at liberty; and one of them seizing a club, gave Petit a violent blow on the head, and laid him dead at his feet; and Allen, who came to his assistance, met a similar fate, from the contents of a pistol fired by another of the gang. Gordon was then attacked, seized and held by one of the negroes, whilst another fired twice at him with a pistol, the ball of which each time grazed his head, but not proving effectual, he was beaten with clubs, and left for dead. They then commenced pillaging the wagon, and with an axe split open the trunk of Gordon, and rifled it of the money, about $2,400. Sixteen of the negroes then took to the woods; Gordon, in the mean time, not being materially injured, was enabled, by the assistance of one of the women, to mount his horse and flee; pursued, however, by one of the gang on another horse, with a drawn pistol; fortunately he escaped with his life barely, arriving at a plantation, as the negro came in sight; who then turned about and retreated.

The neighborhood was immediately rallied, and a hot pursuit given—which, we understand, has resulted in the capture of the whole gang and the recovery of the greatest part of the money. Seven of the negro men and one woman, it is said were engaged in the murders, and will be brought to trial at the next court in Greenupsburg.

53   Here, my brethren, I want you to notice particularly in the above article, the *ignorant* and *deceitful actions* of this coloured woman. I beg you to view it candidly, as for ETERNITY!!!! Here a *notorious wretch*, with two other confederates had SIXTY of them in a gang, driving them like *brutes*—the men all in chains and handcuffs, and by the help of God they got their chains and handcuffs thrown off, and caught two of the wretches and put them to death, and beat the other until they thought he was dead, and left him for dead; however, he deceived them, and rising from the ground, this *servile woman* helped him upon his horse, and he made his escape.

54   Brethren, what do you think of this? Was it the natural *fine feelings* of this woman, to save such a wretch alive? I know that the blacks, take them half enlightened and ignorant, are more humane and merciful than the most enlightened and refined European that can be found in all the earth. Let no one say that I assert this because I am prejudiced on the side of my colour, and against the whites or Europeans. For what I write, I do it candidly, for my God and the good of both parties: Natural observations have taught me these things; there is a solemn awe in the hearts of the blacks, as it respects *murdering* men:* whereas the whites, (though they are great cowards) where they have the advantage, or think that there are any prospects of getting it, they murder all before them, in order to subject men to wretchedness and degradation under them. This is the natural result of pride and avarice. But I declare, the actions of this black woman are really insupportable. For my own part, I cannot think it was any thing but servile deceit, combined with the most gross ignorance: for we must remember that *humanity, kindness* and the *fear of the Lord*, does not consist in protecting *devils*.

*Which is the reason the whites take the advantage of us.

55   Here is a set of wretches, who had SIXTY of them in a gang, driving them around the country like *brutes*, to dig up gold and silver for them, (which they will get enough of yet.) Should the lives of such creatures be spared? Are God and Mammon in league? What has the Lord to do with a gang of desperate wretches, who go *sneaking about the country like robbers*—light upon his people wherever they can get a chance, binding them with chains and handcuffs, beat and murder them as they would rattlesnakes? Are they not the Lord's enemies? Ought they not to be destroyed? Any person who will save such wretches from destruction, is fighting against the Lord, and will receive his just recompense. The black men acted like *blockheads*. Why did they not make sure of the wretch? He would have made sure of them, if he could. It is just the way with black men—eight white men can frighten fifty of them; whereas, if you can only get courage into the blacks, I do declare it, that one good black man can put to death six white men; and I give it as a fact, let twelve black men get well armed for battle, and they will kill and put to flight fifty whites.—The reason is, the blacks, once you get them started, they glory in death. The whites have had us under them for more than three centuries, murdering, and treating us like brutes; and, as Mr. Jefferson wisely said, they have never *found us out*—they do not know, indeed, that there is an unconquerable disposition in the breasts of the blacks, which, when it is fully awakened and put in motion, will be subdued, only with the destruction of the animal existence. Get the blacks started, and if you do not have a gang of tigers and lions to deal with, I am a deceiver of the blacks and of the whites.

56   How sixty of them could let that wretch escape unkilled, I cannot conceive—they will have to suffer as much for the two whom, they secured, as if they had put one hundred to death: if you commence, make sure work—do not trifle, for they will not trifle with you— they want us for their slaves, and think nothing of murdering us in order to subject us to that wretched condition—therefore, if there is an *attempt* made by us, kill or be killed. Now, I ask you, had you not rather be killed than to be a slave to a tyrant, who takes the life of your mother, wife, and dear little children? Look upon your mother, wife and children, and answer God Almighty! and believe this, that it is no more harm for you to kill a man, who is trying to kill you, than it is for you to take a drink of water when thirsty; in fact, the man who will stand still and let another murder him, is worse than an infidel, and, if he has common sense, ought not to be pitied.

57   The actions of this deceitful and ignorant coloured woman in saving the life of a desperate wretch, whose avaricious and cruel object was to drive her, and her companions in miseries, through the country like cattle, to make his fortune on their carcasses, are but too much like that of thousands of our brethren in these states: if any thing is whispered by one, which has any allusion to the melioration of their dreadful condition, they run and tell tyrants, that they may be, enabled to keep them the longer in wretchedness and miseries. Oh! coloured people of these United States, I ask you, in the name of that God who made us, have we, in consequence of oppression, nearly lost the spirit of man, and, in no very trifling degree, adopted that of brutes? Do you answer, no?—I ask you, then, what set of men can you point me to, in all the world, who are so abjectly employed by their oppressors, as we are by our *natural enemies*?

58   How can, Oh! how can those enemies but say that we and our children are not of the HUMAN FAMILY, but were made by our Creator to be an inheritance to them and theirs for ever? How can the slaveholders but say that they can bribe the best coloured person, in the country, to sell his brethren for a trifling sum of money, and take that atrocity to confirm them in their avaricious opinion, that we were made to be slaves to them and their children? How could Mr. Jefferson but say,*

I advance it therefore as a suspicion only, that the blacks, whether originally a distinct race, or made distinct by time and circumstances, are *inferior* to the whites in the endowments both of body and mind?

59   "It," says he, "is not against experience to suppose, that different species of the same genus, or varieties of the same species, may possess different qualifications." [Here, my brethren, listen to him.]

Will not a lover of natural history, then, one who views the gradations in all the races of *animals* with the eye of philosophy, excuse an effort to keep those in the department of MAN as *distinct* as nature has formed them?

I hope you will try to find out the meaning of this verse—its widest sense and all its bearings: whether you do or not, remember the whites

*See his *Notes on Virginia*, page 213.

do. This very verse, brethren, having emanated from Mr. Jefferson, a much greater philosopher the world never afforded, has in truth injured us more, and has been as great a barrier to our emancipation as any thing that has ever been advanced against us. I hope you will not let it pass unnoticed. He goes on further, and says:

> This *unfortunate* difference of colour, and *perhaps of faculty*, is a powerful obstacle to the emancipation of these people. Many of their advocates, while they wish to vindicate the liberty of human nature are anxious also to preserve its *dignity* and *beauty*. Some of these, embarrassed by the question, 'What further is to be done with them?' join themselves in opposition with those who are actuated by sordid avarice only.

60 Now I ask you candidly, my suffering brethren in time, who are candidates for the eternal worlds, how could Mr. Jefferson but have given the world these remarks respecting us, when we are so submissive to them, and so much servile deceit prevail among ourselves— when we so *meanly* submit to their murderous lashes, to which neither the Indians nor any other people under Heaven would submit? No, they would die to a man, before they would suffer such things from men who are no better than themselves, and *perhaps not so good.* Yes, how can our friends but be embarrassed, as Mr. Jefferson says, by the question, "What further is to be done with these people?" For while they are working for our emancipation, we are, by our treachery, wickedness and deceit, working against ourselves and our children— helping ours, and the enemies of God, to keep us and our dear little children in their infernal chains of slavery!!! Indeed, our friends cannot but relapse and join themselves "with those who are actuated by *sordid avarice* only!!!"

61 For my own part, I am glad Mr. Jefferson has advanced his positions for your sake; for you will either have to contradict or confirm him by your own actions, and not by what our friends have said or done for us; for those things are other men's labours, and do not satisfy the Americans, who are waiting for us to prove to them ourselves, that we are MEN, before they will be willing to admit the fact; for I pledge you my sacred word of honour, that Mr. Jefferson's remarks respecting us, have sunk deep into the hearts of millions of the whites, and never will be removed this side of eternity.—For how can they, when we are confirming him every day, by our *groveling submissions* and *treachery?* I aver, that when I look

over these United States of America, and the world, and see the
ignorant deceptions and consequent wretchedness of my brethren,
I am brought ofttimes solemnly to a stand, and in the midst of my
reflections I exclaim to my God "Lord didst thou make us to be
slaves to our brethren, the whites?" But when I reflect that God
is just, and that millions of my wretched brethren would meet death
with glory—yea, more, would plunge into the very mouths of can-
nons and be torn into particles as minute as the atoms which compose the elements of the earth, in preference to a mean submission
to the lash of tyrants, I am with streaming eyes, compelled to shrink
back into nothingness before my Maker, and exclaim again, thy will
be done, O Lord God Almighty.

62   Men of colour, who are also of sense, for you particularly is my
APPEAL designed. Our more ignorant brethren are not able to penetrate its value. I call upon you therefore to cast your eyes upon the
wretchedness of your brethren, and to do your utmost to enlighten
them—*go to work and enlighten your brethren!*—Let the Lord see
you doing what you can to rescue them and yourselves from degradation. Do any of you say that you and your family are free and happy
and what have you to do with the wretched slaves and other people? So can I say, for I enjoy as much freedom as any of you, if I am
not quite as well off as the best of you. Look into our freedom and
happiness, and see of what kind they are composed!! They are of
the very lowest kind—they are the very *dregs!*—they are the most
servile and abject kind, that ever a people was in possession of! If any
of you wish to know how FREE you are, let one of you start and go
through the southern and western States of this country, and unless
you travel as a slave to a white man (a servant is a slave to the man
whom he serves) or have your free papers, (which if you are not careful they will get from you) if they do not take you up and put you
in jail, and if you cannot give good evidence of your freedom, sell you
into eternal slavery, I am not a living man: or any man of colour,
immaterial who he is, or where he came from, if he is not *the fourth
from the negro race!!* (as we are called) the white Christians of America will serve him the same they will sink him into wretchedness and
degradation for ever while he lives. And yet some of you have the
hardihood to say that you are free and happy! May God have mercy
on your freedom and happiness!!

63   I met a coloured man in the street a short time since, with a
string of boots on his shoulders; we fell into conversation, and in

course of which, I said to him, what a miserable set of people we are! He asked, why?—Said I, we are so subjected under the whites, that we cannot obtain the comforts of life, but by cleaning their boots and shoes, old clothes, waiting on them, shaving them &c. Said he, (with the boots on his shoulders) "I am completely happy!!! I never want to live any better or happier than when I can get a plenty of boots and shoes to clean!!!" Oh! how can those who are actuated by avarice only, but think, that our Creator made us to be an inheritance to them for ever, when they see that our greatest glory is centered in such mean and low objects? Understand me, brethren, I do not mean to speak against the occupations by which we acquire enough and sometimes scarcely that, to render ourselves and families comfortable through life. I am subjected to the same inconvenience, as you all.—My objections are, to our *glorying* and being *happy* in such low employments; for if we are men, we ought to be thankful to the Lord for the past, and for the future. Be looking forward with thankful hearts to higher attainments than *wielding the razor* and *cleaning boots and shoes.* The man whose aspirations are not *above,* and even *below* these, is indeed, ignorant and wretched enough.

64   I advance it therefore to you, not as a *problematical,* but as an unshaken and for ever immoveable *fact,* that your full glory and happiness, as well as all other coloured people under Heaven, shall never be fully consummated, but with the *entire emancipation of your enslaved brethren all over the world.* You may therefore, go to work and do what you can to rescue, or join in with tyrants to oppress them and yourselves, until the Lord shall come upon you all like a thief in the night. For I believe it is the will of the Lord that our greatest happiness shall consist in working for the salvation of our whole body. When this is accomplished a burst of glory will shine upon you, which will indeed astonish you and the world. Do any of you say this never will be done? I assure you that God will accomplish it—if nothing else will answer, he will hurl tyrants and devils into *atoms* and make way for his people. But O my brethren! I say unto you again, you must go to work and prepare the way of the Lord.

65   There is a great work for you to do, as trifling as some of you may think of it. You have to prove to the Americans and the world, that we are MEN, and not *brutes,* as we have been represented, and by millions treated. Remember, to let the aim of your labours among your brethren, and particularly the youths, be the dissemination of

education and religion.* It is lamentable, that many of our children go to school, from four until they are eight or ten, and sometimes fifteen years of age, and leave school knowing but a little more about the grammar of their language than a horse does about handling a musket—and not a few of them are really so ignorant, that they are unable to answer a person correctly, general questions in geography, and to hear them read, would only be to disgust a man who has a taste for reading; which, to do well, as trifling as it may appear to some, (to the ignorant in particular) is a great part of learning.

66   Some few of them, may make out to scribble tolerably well, over a half sheet of paper, which I believe has hitherto been a powerful obstacle in our way, to keep us from acquiring knowledge. An ignorant father, who knows no more than what nature has taught him, together with what little he acquires by the senses of hearing and seeing, finding his son able to write a neat hand, sets it down for granted that he has as good learning as any body; the young, ignorant gump, hearing his father or mother, who perhaps may be ten times more ignorant, in point of literature, than himself, extolling his learning, struts about, in the full assurance, that his attainments in literature are sufficient to take him through the world, when, in fact, he has scarcely any learning at all!!!!

67   I promiscuously fell in conversation once, with an elderly coloured man on the topics of education, and of the great prevalency of ignorance among us: Said he, "I know that our people are very ignorant but my son has a good education. I spent a great deal of money on his education: he can write as well as any white man, and I assure you that no one can fool him," &c. Said I, what else can your son do, besides writing a good hand? Can he post a set of books in a mercantile manner? Can he write a neat piece of composition in prose or in verse? To these interrogations he answered in the negative. Said I, did your son learn, while he was at school, the width and depth of English Grammar? To which he also replied in the negative, telling me his son did not learn those things. Your son, said I, then has hardly any learning at all—he is almost as ignorant, and more so, than many of those who never went to school one day in all their lives. My friend

*Never mind what the ignorant ones among us may say, many of whom when you speak to them for their good, and try to enlighten their minds, laugh at you, and perhaps tell you plump to your face, that they want no instruction from you or any other Niger, and all such aggravating language. Now if you are a man of understanding and sound sense, I conjure you in the name of the Lord, and of all that is good, to impute their actions to ignorance, and wink at their follies, and do your very best to get around them some way or other, for remember they are your brethren; and I declare to you that it is for your interests to teach and enlighten them.

got a little put out, and so walking off, said that his son could write as well as any white man. Most of the coloured people, when they speak of the education of one among us who can write a neat hand, and who perhaps knows nothing but to scribble and puff pretty fair on a small scrap of paper, immaterial whether his words are grammatical, or spelt correctly, or not; if it only looks beautiful, they say he has as good an education as any white man—he can write as well as any white man, &c. The poor, ignorant creature, hearing, this, he is ashamed, forever after, to let any person see him humbling himself to another for knowledge but going about trying to deceive those who are more ignorant than himself, he at last falls an ignorant victim to death in wretchedness.

68   I pray that the Lord may undeceive my ignorant brethren, and permit them to throw away pretensions, and seek after the substance of learning. I would crawl on my hands and knees through mud and mire, to the feet of a learned man, where I would sit and humbly supplicate him to instil into me, that which neither devils nor tyrants could remove, only with my life—for coloured people to acquire learning in this country, make tyrants quake and tremble on their sandy foundation. Why, what is the matter? Why, they know that their infernal deeds of cruelty will be made known to the world. Do you suppose one man of good sense and learning would submit himself, his father, mother, wife and children, to be slaves to a wretched man like himself, who, instead of compensating him for his labours, chains, handcuffs and beats him and family almost to death, leaving life enough in them, however, to work for, and call him master? No! no! he would cut his devilish throat from ear to ear, and well do slaveholders know it. The bare name of educating the coloured people, scares our cruel oppressors almost to death. But if they do not have enough to be frightened for yet, it will be, because they can always keep us ignorant, and because God approbates their cruelties, with which they have been for centuries murdering us. The whites shall have enough of the blacks, yet, as true as God sits on his throne in Heaven.

69   Some of our brethren are so very full of learning, that you cannot mention any thing to them which they do not know better than yourself!!—nothing is strange to them!!—they knew every thing years ago!—if any thing should be mentioned in company where they are, immaterial how important it is respecting us or the world, if they had not divulged it; they make light of it, and affect to have known it long before it was mentioned and try to make all in the

room, or wherever you may be, believe that your conversation is nothing!!—not worth hearing! All this is the result of ignorance and illbreeding; for a man of good-breeding, sense and penetration, if he had heard a subject told twenty times over, and should happen to be in company where one should commence telling it again, he would wait with patience on its narrator, and see if he would tell it as it was told in his presence before—paying the most strict attention to what is said, to see if any more light will be thrown on the subject: for all men are not gifted alike in telling, or even hearing the most simple narration. These ignorant, vicious, and wretched men, contribute almost as much injury to our body as tyrants themselves, by doing so much for the promotion of ignorance amongst us; for they, making such pretensions to knowledge, such of our youth as are seeking after knowledge, and can get access to them, take them as criterions to go by, who will lead them into a channel, where, unless the Lord blesses them with the privilege of seeing their folly, they will be irretrievably lost forever, while in time!!!

70   I must close this article by relating the very heart-rending fact, that I have examined schoolboys and young men of colour in different parts of the country, in the most simple parts of Murray's English Grammar, and not more than one in thirty was able to give a correct answer to my interrogations. If anyone contradicts me, let him step out of his door into the streets of Boston, New York, Philadelphia, or Baltimore, (no use to mention any other, for the Christians are too charitable further south or west!)—I say, let him who disputes me, step out of his door into the streets of either of those four cities, and promiscuously collect one hundred schoolboys, or young men of colour, *who have been to school*, and who are considered by the coloured people to have received an excellent education, because, perhaps, some of them can write a good hand, but who, notwithstanding their neat writing, may be almost as ignorant, in comparison, as a horse.—And, I say it, he will hardly find (in this enlightened day, and in the midst of this *charitable* people) five in one hundred, who, are able to correct the false grammar of their language.—The cause of this almost universal ignorance among us, I appeal to our schoolmasters to declare.

71   Here is a fact, which I this very minute take from the mouth of a young coloured man, who has been to school in this state (Massachusetts) nearly nine years, and who knows grammar this day, *nearly* as well as he did the day he first entered the schoolhouse, under a white master. This young man says: "My master would never allow

me to study grammar." I asked him, why? "The school committee," said he "forbid the coloured children learning grammar—they would not allow any but the white children to study grammar." It is a notorious fact, that the major part of the white Americans, have, ever since we have been among them, tried to keep us ignorant, and make us believe that God made us and our children to be slaves to them and theirs. *Oh! my God, have mercy on Christian Americans!!!*

Maria Stewart

(1803–1879)

On September 21, 1832, Maria Stewart mounted the podium in to deliver a lecture to the New England Anti-Slavery Society. It was the first public speech by an African American woman before a mixed audience of men and women. Born in Hartford, Connecticut, Stewart was an associate of David Walker in Boston during the 1820s. Her brief speaking career (1832–1834) is largely captured in abolitionist William Lloyd Garrison's newpaper, The Liberator. After Stewart's husband, who was a successful businessman, died in 1829, she was swindled by white businessmen and left bankrupt. She subsequently taught school for 30 years in Boston, New York, Baltimore, and Washington. Stewart is author of Religion and the Pure Principles of Morality, the Sure Foundation on Which We Must Build *(1831);* Productions of Mrs. Maria W. Stewart *(1835), from which the following reading was taken; and* Meditations from the Pen of Mrs. Maria W. Stewart *(1879). The address that follows was delivered in Boston on February 27, 1833.*

Address at the African Masonic Hall*

1 African rights and liberty is a subject that ought to fire the breast of every free man of color in these United States, and excite in his bosom a lively, deep, decided and heart-felt interest. When I cast my eyes on the long list of illustrious names that are enrolled on the bright annals of fame among the whites, I turn my eyes within, and

---

*Maria Stewart, Address at the African Masonic Hall, Boston, February 27, 1833, in
*Productions of Mrs. Maria W. Stewart, Presented to the First African Baptist Church and
Society, of the City of Boston* (Boston: Friends of Freedom and Virtue, 1835).

ask my thoughts, "Where are the names of *our* illustrious ones?" It must certainly have been for the want of energy on the part of the free people of color, that they have been long willing to bear the yoke of oppression. It must have been the want of ambition and force that has given the whites occasion to say, that our natural abilities are not as good, and our capacities by nature inferior to theirs. They boldly assert, that, did we possess a natural independence of soul, and feel a love for liberty within our breasts, some one of our sable race, long before this, would have testified it, notwithstanding the disadvantages under which we labor. We have made ourselves appear altogether unqualified to speak in our own defence, and are therefore looked upon as objects of pity and commiseration. We have been imposed upon, insulted and derided on every side; and now, if we complain, it is considered as the height of impertinence. We have suffered ourselves to be considered as dastards, cowards, mean, faint-hearted wretches; and on this account, (not because of our complexion,) many despise us, and would gladly spurn us from their presence.

2   These things have fired my soul with a holy indignation, and compelled me thus to come forward, and endeavor to turn their attention to knowledge and improvement; for knowledge is power. I would ask, is it blindness of mind, or stupidity of soul, or the want of education, that has caused our men who are 60 or 70 years of age, never to let their voices be heard, nor their hands be raised in behalf of their color? Or has it been for the fear of offending the whites? If it has, O ye fearful ones, throw off your fearfulness, and come forth in the name of the Lord, and in the strength of the God of Justice, and make yourselves useful and active members in society; for they admire a noble and patriotic spirit in others; and should they not admire it in us? If you are men, convince them that you possess the spirit of men; and as your day, so shall your strength be. Have the sons of Africa no souls? feel they no ambitious desires? shall the chains of ignorance forever confine them? shall the insipid appellation of "clever negroes," or "good creatures," any longer content them? Where can we find among ourselves the man of science, or a philosopher, or an able statesman, or a counsellor at law? Show me our fearless and brave, our noble and gallant ones. Where are our lecturers on natural history, and our critics in useful knowledge? There may be a few such men among us, but they are rare. It is true, our fathers bled and died in the revolutionary war, and others fought bravely under the command of Jackson, in defence of liberty. But where is the man that has distinguished himself in these

modern days by acting wholly in the defence of African rights and liberty? There was one, although he sleeps, his memory lives.

3   I am sensible that there are many highly intelligent gentlemen of color in these United States, in the force of whose arguments, doubtless, I should discover my inferiority; but if they are blest with wit and talent, friends and fortune, why have they not made themselves men of eminence, by striving to take all the reproach that is cast upon the people of color, and in endeavoring to alleviate the woes of their brethren in bondage? Talk, without effort, is nothing; you are abundantly capable, gentlemen, of making yourselves men of distinction; and this gross neglect, on your part, causes my blood to boil within me. Here is the grand cause which hinders the rise and progress of the people of color. It is their want of laudable ambition and requisite courage.

4   Individuals have been distinguished according to their genius and talents, ever since the first formation of man, and will continue to be while the world stands. The different grades rise to honor and respectability as their merits may deserve. History informs us that we sprung from one of the most learned nations of the whole earth; from the seat, if not the parent of science; yes, poor, despised Africa was once the resort of sages and legislators of other nations, was esteemed the school for learning, and the most illustrious men in Greece flocked thither for instruction. But it was our gross sins and abominations that provoked the Almighty to frown thus heavily upon us, and give our glory unto others. Sin and prodigality have caused the downfall of nations, kings and emperors; and were it not that God in wrath remembers mercy, we might indeed despair; but a promise is left us; "Ethiopia shall again stretch forth her hands unto God."

5   But it is of no use for us to boast that we sprung from this learned and enlightened nation, for this day a thick mist of moral gloom hangs over millions of our race. Our condition as a people has been low for hundreds of years, and it will continue to be so, unless, by true piety and virtue, we strive to regain that which we have lost. White Americans, by their prudence, economy and exertions, have sprung up and become one of the most flourishing nations in the world, distinguished for their knowledge of the arts and sciences, for their polite literature. While our minds are vacant, and starving for want of knowledge, theirs are filled to overflowing. Most of our color have been taught to stand in fear of the white man, from their earliest infancy, to work as soon as they could walk, and call "master," before they scarce could lisp the name of *mother*. Continual fear and laborious servitude have in some degree lessened in us that natural force and energy which belong to man; or

else, in defiance of opposition, our men, before this, would have nobly and boldly contended for their rights. But give the man of color an equal opportunity with the white from the cradle to manhood, and from manhood to the grave, and you would discover the dignified statesman, the man of science, and the philosopher. But there is no such opportunity for the sons of Africa, and I fear that our powerful ones are fully determined that there never shall be. Forbid, ye Powers on high, that it should any longer be said that our men possess no force. O ye sons of Africa, when will your voices be heard in our legislative halls, in defiance of your enemies, contending for equal rights and liberty? How can you, when you reflect from what you have fallen, refrain from crying mightily unto God, to turn away from us the fierceness of his anger, and remember our transgressions against us no more forever. But a God of infinite purity will not regard the prayers of those who hold religion in one hand, and prejudice, sin and pollution in the other; he will not regard the prayers of self-righteousness and hypocrisy. Is it possible, I exclaim; that for the want of knowledge, we have labored for hundreds of years to support others, and been content to receive what they chose to give us in return? Cast your eyes about, look as far as you can see; all, all is owned by the lordly white, except here and there a lowly dwelling which the man of color, midst deprivations, fraud and opposition, has been scarce able to procure. Like king Solomon, who put neither nail nor hammer to the temple, yet received the praise; so also have the white Americans gained themselves a name, like the names of the great men that are in the earth, while in reality we have been their principal foundation and support. We have pursued the shadow, they have obtained the substance; we have performed the labor, they have received the profits; we have planted the vines, they have eaten the fruits of them.

6   I would implore our men, and especially our rising youth, to flee from the gambling board and the dance-hall; for we are poor, and have no money to throw away. I do not consider dancing as criminal in itself, but it is astonishing to me that our young men are so blind to their own interest and the future welfare of their children, as to spend their hard earnings for this frivolous amusement; for it has been carried on among us to such an unbecoming extent, that it has became absolutely disgusting. "Faithful are the wounds of a friend, but the kisses of an enemy are deceitful." Had those men among us, who have had an opportunity, turned their attention as assiduously to mental and moral improvement as they have to gambling and dancing, I might have remained quietly at home, and they stood contending in my place. These polite accomplishments will never enrol your names on the bright annals of

fame, who admire the belle void of intellectual knowledge, or applaud the dandy that talks largely on politics, without striving to assist his fellow in the revolution, when the nerves and muscles of every other man forced him into the field of action. You have a right to rejoice, and to let your hearts cheer you in the days of your youth; yet remember that for all these things, God will bring you into judgment. Then, O ye sons of Africa, turn your mind from these perishable objects, and contend for the cause of God and the rights of man. Form yourselves into temperance societies. There are temperate men among you; then why will you any longer neglect to strive, by your example, to suppress vice in all its abhorrent forms? You have been told repeatedly of the glorious results arising from temperance, and can you bear to see the whites arising in honor and respectability, without endeavoring to grasp after that honor and respectability also?

7   But I forbear. Let our money, instead of being thrown away as heretofore, be appropriated for schools and seminaries of learning for our children and youth. We ought to follow the example of the whites in this respect. Nothing would raise our respectability, add to our peace and happiness, and reflect so much honor upon us, as to be ourselves the promoters of temperance, and the supporters, as far as we are able, of useful and scientific knowledge. The rays of light and knowledge have been hid from our view; we have been taught to consider ourselves as scarce superior to the brute creation; and have performed the most laborious part of American drudgery. Had we as a people received one half the early advantages the whites have received, I would defy the government of these United States to deprive us any longer of our rights.

8   I am informed that the agent of the Colonization Society has recently formed an association of young men, for the purpose of influencing those of us to go to Liberia who may feel disposed. The colonizationists are blind to their own interest, for should the nations of the earth make war with America, they would find their forces much weakened by our absence; or should we remain here, can our "brave soldiers," and "fellow-citizens," as they were termed in time of calamity, condescend to defend the rights of the whites, and be again deprived of their own, or sent to Liberia in return? Or, if the colonizationists are real friends to Africa, let them expend the money which they collect, in erecting a college to educate her injured sons in this land of gospel light and liberty; for it would be most thankfully received on our part, and convince us of the truth of their professions, and save time, expense and anxiety. Let them place before us noble objects, worthy of pursuit, and see if we prove ourselves to be those unambitious

negroes they term us. But ah! methinks their hearts are so frozen towards us, they had rather their money should be sunk in the ocean than to administer it to our relief; and I fear, if they dared, like Pharaoh, king of Egypt, they would order every male child among us to be drowned. But the most high God is still as able to subdue the lofty pride of these white Americans, as He was the heart of that ancient rebel. They say, though we are looked upon as *things*, yet we sprang from a scientific people. Had our men the requisite force and energy, they would soon convince them by their efforts both in public and private, that they were men, or things in the shape of men. Well may the colonizationists laugh us to scorn for our negligence; well may they cry, "Shame to the sons of Africa." As the burden of the Israelites was too great for Moses to bear, so also is our burden too great for our noble advocate to bear. You must feel interested, my brethren, in what he undertakes, and hold up his hands by your good works, or in spite of himself, his soul will become discouraged, and his heart will die within him; for he has, as it were, the strong bulls of Bashan to contend with.

9   It is of no use for us to wait any longer for a generation of well educated men to arise. We have slumbered and slept too long already; the day is far spent; the night of death approaches; and you have sound sense and good judgment sufficient to begin with, if you feel disposed to make a right use of it. Let every man of color throughout the United States, who possesses the spirit and principles of a man, sign a petition to Congress, to abolish slavery in the District of Columbia, and grant you the rights and privileges of common free citizens; for if you had had faith as a grain of mustard seed, long before this the mountains of prejudice might have been removed. We are all sensible that the Anti-Slavery Society has taken hold of the arm of our whole population, in order to raise them out of the mire. Now all we have to do is, by a spirit of virtuous ambition to strive to raise ourselves; and I am happy to have it in my power thus publicly to say, that the colored inhabitants of this city, in some respects, are beginning to improve. Had the free people of color in these United States nobly and boldly contended for their rights, and showed a natural genius and talent, although not so brilliant as some; had they held up, encouraged and patronized each other, nothing could have hindered us from being a thriving and flourishing people. There has been a fault among us. The reason why our distinguished men have not made themselves more influential is, because they fear that the strong current of opposition through which they must pass, would cause their downfall and prove their overthrow. And what gives rise to this

opposition? Envy. And what has it amounted to? Nothing. And who are the cause of it? Our whited sepulchres, who want to be great, and don't know how; who love to be called of men "Rabbi, Rabbi," who put on false sanctity, and humble themselves to their brethren, for the sake of acquiring the highest place in the synagogue, and the uppermost seats at the feast. You, dearly beloved, who are the genuine followers of our Lord Jesus Christ, the salt of the earth and the light of the world, are not so culpable. As I told you, in the very first of my writing, I tell you again, I am but as a drop in the bucket—as one particle of the small dust of the earth. God will surely raise up those among us who will plead the cause of virtue, and the pure principles of morality, more eloquently than I am able to do.

10   It appears to me that America has become like the great city of Babylon, for she has boasted in her heart,—"I sit a queen, and am no widow, and shall see no sorrow"? She is indeed a seller of slaves and the souls of men; she has made the Africans drunk with the wine of her fornication; she has put them completely beneath her feet, and she means to keep them there; her right hand supports the reins of government, and her left hand the wheel of power, and she is determined not to let go her grasp. But many powerful sons and daughters of Africa will shortly arise, who will put down vice and immorality among us, and declare by Him that sitteth upon the throne, that they will have their rights; and if refused, I am afraid they will spread horror and devastation around. I believe that the oppression of injured Africa has come up before the Majesty of Heaven; and when our cries shall have reached the ears of the Most High, it will be a tremendous day for the people of this land; for strong is the arm of the Lord God Almighty.

11   Life has almost lost its charms for me; death has lost its sting and the grave its terrors; and at times I have a strong desire to depart and dwell with Christ, which is far better. Let me entreat my white brethren to awake and save our sons from dissipation, and our daughters from ruin. Lend the hand of assistance to feeble merit; plead the cause of virtue among our sable race; so shall our curses upon you be turned into blessings; and though you should endeavor to drive us from these shores, still we will cling to you the more firmly; nor will we attempt to rise above you: we will presume to be called your equals only.

12   The unfriendly whites first drove the native American from his much loved home. Then they stole our fathers from their peaceful and quiet dwellings, and brought them hither, and made bond-men and bond-women of them and their little ones; they have obliged our brethren to labor, kept them in utter ignorance, nourished them in

vice, and raised them in degradation; and now that we have enriched their soil, and filled their coffers, they say that we are not capable of becoming like white men, and that we never can rise to respectability in this country. They would drive us to a strange land. But before I go, the bayonet shall pierce me through. African rights and liberty is a subject that ought to fire the breast of every free man of color in these United States, and excite in his bosom a lively, deep, decided and heart-felt interest.

Martin Robison Delany

(1812–1885)

Born May 6, 1812, in Charles Town, Virginia, to a free woman (and thus legally free), Martin Robison Delany migrated to Pennsylvania as a youth. Possessing intellectual energy that was a match for anyone's in the nineteenth century, he was a steadfast critic of slavery and a proponent of Black self-reliance. At times, he favored emigration to Africa as a solution to the plight of African Americans. Delany, serving as a major, was the highest-ranking African American in the Union army during the Civil War and was the first Black to be given a field command. Prior to that experience, he studied medicine at Harvard University, co-edited the North Star *with Frederick Douglass from 1847 to 1849, lived for awhile in Canada, and wrote voluminously. In 1852, he published* The Condition, Elevation, Emigration, and Destiny of the Colored People of the United States, *the first book-length study of the situation of Blacks in America. The* Anglo-American *ran his novel,* Blake, or the Huts of America, *in 1859 and 1861–1862.*

A Glance at Ourselves— Conclusion.

> With broken hopes—sad devastation;
> A race *resigned* to DEGRADATION!

1 We have said much to our young men and women, about their vocation and calling: we have dwelt much upon the menial position of our people in this country. Upon this point we cannot say too much,

because there is a seeming satisfaction and seeking after such positions manifested on their part, unknown to any other people. There appears to be, a want of a sense of propriety or *self-respect*, altogether inexplicable; because young men and women among us, many of whom have good trades and homes, adequate to their support, voluntarily leave them, and seek positions, such as servants, waiting maids, coachmen, nurses, cooks in gentlemens' kitchen, on such like occupations, when they can gain a livelihood at something more respectable, or elevating in character. And the worse part of the whole matter is, that they have become so accustomed to it, it has become so "fashionable," that it seems to have become second nature, and they really become offended, when it is spoken against.

2   Among the German, Irish, and other European peasantry who come to this country, it matters not what they were employed at before and after they come; just so soon as they can better their condition by keeping shops, cultivating the soil, the young men and women going to night-schools, qualifying themselves for usefulness, and learning trades—they do so. Their first and last care, object and aim is, to better their condition by raising themselves above the condition that necessity places them in. We do not say too much, when we say, as an evidence of the deep degradation of our race. In the United States, that there are those among us, the wives and daughters, some of the *first ladies*, (and who dare say they are not the "first," because they belong to the "first class" and associate where any body among us can?) whose husbands are industrious, able and willing to support them, who voluntarily leave home, and become chamber-maids, and stewardesses, upon vessels and steamboats, in all probability, to enable them to obtain some more fine or costly article of dress or furniture.

3   We have nothing to say against those whom *necessity* compels to do these things, those who can do no better; we have only to do with those who can, and will not, or do not do better. The whites are always in the advance, and we either standing still or retrograding; as that which does not go forward, must either stand in one place or go back. The father in all probability is a farmer, mechanic, or man of some independent business; and the wife, sons and daughters, are chamber-maids, on vessels, nurses and waiting-maids, or coachmen and cooks in families. This is retrogradation. The wife, sons, and daughters should be elevated above this condition as a necessary consequence.

4   If we did not love our race superior to others, we would not concern ourself about their degradation; for the greatest desire of our heart is, to see them stand on a level with the most elevated of

mankind. No people are ever elevated above the condition of their *females;* hence, the condition of the *mother* determines the condition of the child. To know the position of a people. It is only necessary to know the *condition* of their *females;* and despite themselves, they cannot rise above their level. Then what is our condition? Our *best ladies* being washer-women, chamber-maids, children's traveling nurses, and common house servants, and menials, we are all a degraded, miserable people, inferior to any other people as a whole, on the face of the globe.

5   These great truths, however unpleasant, must be brought before the minds of our people in its true and proper light, as we have been too delicate about them, and too long concealed them for fear of giving offence. It would have been infinitely better for our race, if these facts had been presented before us half a century ago—we would have been now proportionably benefitted by it.

6   As an evidence of the degradation to which we have been reduced, we dare premise, that this chapter will give offence to many, very many, and why? Because they may say, "He dared to say that the occupation of a *servant* is a degradation." It is not necessarily degrading; it would not be, to one or a few people of a kind; but a *whole race of servants* are a degradation to that people.

7   Efforts made by men of qualifications for the tolling and degraded millions among the whites, neither gives offence to that class, nor is it taken unkindly by them; but received with manifestations of gratitude; to know that they are thought to be, equally worthy of, and entitled to stand on a level with the elevated classes; and they have only got to be informed of the way to raise themselves, to make the effort and do so as far as they can. But how different with us. Speak of our position in society, and it at once gives insult. Though we are servants; among ourselves we claim to be *ladies* and *gentlemen,* equal in standing, and as the popular expression goes, "Just as good as any body"—and so believing, we make no efforts to raise above the common level of menials; because the *best* being in that capacity, all are content with the position. We cannot at the same time, be domestic and lady; servant and gentleman. We must be the one or the other. Sad, sad indeed, is the thought, that hangs drooping in our mind, when contemplating the picture drawn before us. Young men and women, "we write these things unto you, because ye are strong," because the writer, a few years ago, gave unpardonable offence to many of the young people of Philadelphia and other places, because he dared to tell them, that he thought too much of them, to be

content with seeing them the servants of other people. Surely, she that could be the mistress, would not be the maid; neither would he that could be the master, be content with being the servant; then why be offended, when we point out to you, the way that leads from the menial to the mistress or the master. All this we seem to reject with fixed determination, repelling with anger, every effort on the part of our intelligent men and women to elevate us, with true Israelitish degradation, in reply to any suggestion or proposition that may be offered, "Who made thee a ruler and judge?"

8   The writer is no "Public Man," in the sense in which this is understood among our people, but simply an humble individual, endeavoring to seek a livelihood by a profession obtained entirely by his own efforts, without relatives and friends able to assist him; except such friends as he gained by the merit of his course and conduct, which he here gratefully acknowledges; and whatever he has accomplished, other young men may, by making corresponding efforts, also accomplish.

9   We have advised an emigration to Central and South America, and even to Mexico and the West Indies, to those who prefer either of the last named places, all of which are free countries, Brazil being the only real slave-holding State in South America—there being nominal slavery in Dutch Guiana, Peru, Buenos Ayres, Paraguay, and Uraguay, in all of which places colored people have equally in social, civil, political, and religious privileges; Brazil making it punishable with death to import slaves into the empire.

10   Our oppressors, when urging us to go to Africa, tell us that we are better adapted to the climate than they—that the physical condition of the constitution of colored people better endures the heat of warm climates than that of the whites; this we are willing to *admit*, without argument, without adducing the physiological reason why, that colored people can and do stand warm climates better than whites; and find an answer fully to the point in the fact, that they also stand *all other* climates, cold, temperate, and modified, that white people can stand; therefore, according to our oppressors' own showing, we are a *superior race*, being endowed with properties fitting us for *all parts* of the earth; while they are only adapted to *certain* parts. Of course, this proves our right and duty to live wherever we may *choose*; while the white race may only live where they *can*. We are content with the fact, and have ever claimed it. Upon this rock, they and we shall ever agree.

11   Of the West India Islands, Santa Cruz, belonging to Denmark; Porto Rico, and Cuba with its little adjuncts, belonging to Spain, are

the only slave-holding Islands among them—three-fifths of the whole population of Cuba being colored people, who cannot and will not much longer endure the burden and the yoke. They only want intelligent leaders of their own color, when they are ready at any moment to charge to the conflict—to liberty or death. The remembrance of the noble mulatto, PLACIDO, the gentleman, scholar, poet, and intended Chief Engineer of the Army of Liberty and Freedom in Cuba; and the equally noble black, CHARLES BLAIR, who was to have been Commander-in-Chief, who were shamefully put to death in 1844, by that living monster, Captain General O'Donnell, is still fresh and indelible to the mind of every bondman of Cuba.

12   In our own country, the United States, there are *three million five hundred thousand slaves;* and we, the nominally free colored people, are *six hundred thousand* in number; estimating one-sixth to be men, we have *one hundred thousand* able bodied freemen, which will make a powerful auxiliary in any country in which we may become adopted—an ally not to be despised by any power on earth. We love our country, dearly love her, but she don't love us—she despises us, and bids us begone, driving us from her embraces; but we shall not go where she desires us; but when we do go, whatever love we have for her, we shall love the country none the less that receives us as her adopted children.

13   For the want of business habits and training, our energies have become paralyzed; our young men never think of business, any more than if they were so many bondmen, without the right to pursue any calling they may think most advisable. With our people in this country, dress and good appearances have been made the only test of gentlemen and lady-ship, and that vocation which offers the best opportunity to dress and appear well, has generally been preferred, however mental and degrading, by our young people, without even, in the majority of cases, an effort to do better; indeed, in many instances, refusing situations equally lucrative, and superior in position; but which would not allow us much display of dress and personal appearance. This, if we ever expect to rise, must be discarded from among us, and a high and respectable position assumed.

14   One of our great temporal curses is our consummate poverty. We are the poorest people, as a class, in the world of civilized mankind—abjectly, miserably poor, no one scarcely being able to assist the other. To this, of course, there are noble exceptions; but that which is common to, and the very process by which white men exist, and succeed in life, is unknown to colored men in general. In any and every

considerable community may be found, some one of our white fellow-citizens, who is worth more than all the colored people in that community put together. We consequently have little or no efficiency. We must have means to be practically efficient in all the undertakings of life; and to obtain them, it is necessary that we should be engaged in lucrative pursuits, trades, and general business transactions. In order to be thus engaged, it is necessary that we should occupy positions that afford the facilities for such pursuits. To compete now with the mighty odds of wealth, social and religious preferences, and political influences of this country, at this advanced stage of its national existence, we never may expect. A new country, and new beginning, is the only true, rational, politic remedy for our disadvantageous position: and that country we have already pointed out, with triple golden advantages, all things considered, to that of any country to which it has been the province of man to embark.

15   Every other than we, have at various periods of necessity, been a migratory people; and all when oppressed, shown a greater abhorrence of oppression. If not a greater love of liberty, than we. We cling to our oppressors as the objects of our love. It is true that our enslaved brethren are here, and we have been led to believe that it is necessary for us to remain, on that account. Is it true, that all should remain in degradation, because a part are degraded? We believe no such thing. We believe it to be the duty of the Free, to elevate themselves in the most speedy and effective manner possible; as the redemption of the bondman depends entirely upon the elevation of the freeman; therefore, to elevate the free colored people of America, anywhere upon this continent; forebodes the speedy redemption of the slaves. We shall hope to hear no more of so fallacious a doctrine—the necessity of the free remaining in degradation, for the sake of the oppressed. Let us apply, first, the lever to ourselves; and the force that elevates us to the position of manhood's considerations and honors, will cleft the manacle of every slave in the land.

16   When such great worth and talents—for want of a better sphere—of men like Rev. Jonathan Robinson, Robert Douglass, Frederick A. Hinton, and a hundred others that might be named, were permitted to expire in a barber-shop; and such living men as may be found in Boston, New York, Philadelphia, Baltimore, Richmond, Washington City, Charleston, (S.C.) New Orleans, Cincinnati, Louisville, St. Louis, Pittsburg, Buffalo, Rochester, Albany, Utica, Cleveland, Detroit, Milwaukie, Chicago, Columbus, Zanesville, Wheeling, and a hundred other places, confining themselves to Barber-shops and waiterships in

Hotels; certainly the necessity of such a course as we have pointed out, must be cordially acknowledged; appreciated by every brother and sister of oppression; and not rejected as heretofore, as though they preferred inferiority to equality. These minds must become "unfettered," and have "space to rise." This cannot be in their present positions. A continuance in any position, becomes what is termed "Second Nature:" it begets an *adaptation*, and *reconciliation of mind* to such condition. It changes the whole physiological condition of the system, and adapts man and woman to a higher or lower sphere in the pursuits of life. The offsprings of slaves and peasantry, have the general characteristics of their parents; and nothing but a different course of training and education, will change the character.

17   The slave may become a lover of his master, and learn to forgive him for continual deeds of maltreatment and abuse; just us the Spaniel would couch and fondle at the feet that kick him; because he has been taught to reverence them, and consequently, becomes adapted in body and mind to his condition. Even the shrubbery-loving Canary, and lofty-soaring Eagle, may be tamed to the cage, and learn to love it from habit of confinement. It has been so with us in our position among our oppressors; we have been so prone to such positions, that we have learned to love them. When reflecting upon this all important, and to us, all absorbing subject; we feel in the agony and anxiety of the moment, as though we could cry out in the language of a Prophet of old: "Oh that my head were waters, and mine eyes a fountain of tears, that I might weep day and night for the" degradation "of my people! Oh that I had in the wilderness a lodging place of way-faring men; that I might leave my people, and go from them!"

18   The Irishman and German in the United States, are very different persons to what they were when in Ireland and Germany, the countries of their nativity. There their spirits were depressed and downcast; but the instant they set their foot upon unrestricted soil; free to act and untrammeled to move; their physical condition undergoes a change, which in time becomes physiological, which is transmitted to the offspring, who when born under such circumstances, is a decidedly different being to what it would have been, had it been born under different circumstances.

19   A child born under oppression, has all the elements of servility in its constitution; who when born under favorable circumstances, has to the contrary, all the elements of freedom and independence of feeling. Our children then, may not be expected, to maintain that position and

manly bearing; born under the unfavorable circumstances with which we are surrounded in this country; that we so much desire. To use the language of the talented Mr. Whipper, "they cannot be raised in this country, without being stoop shouldered." Heaven's pathway stands unobstructed, which will lead us into a Paradise of bliss. Let us go on and possess the land, and the God of Israel will be our God.

20   The lessons of every school book, the pages of every history, and columns of every newspaper, are so replete with stimuli to nerve us on to manly aspirations, that those of our young people, who will now refuse to enter upon this great theatre of Polynesian adventure, and take their position on the stage of Central and South America, where a brilliant engagement, of certain and most triumphant success, in the drama of human equality awaits them; then, with the blood of *slaves*, write upon the lintel of every door in sterling Capitals, to be gazed and hissed at by every passer by—

> Doomed by the Creator
> To servility and degradation;
> The SERVANT of the *white man*.
> And despised of every nation!

A Project for an Expedition of Adventure, to the Eastern Coast of Africa

1   Every people should be the originators of their own designs, the projector of their own schemes, and creators of the events that lead to their destiny—the consummation of their desires.

2   Situated as we are, in the United States, many, and almost insurmountable obstacles present themselves. We are four-and-a-half millions in numbers, free and bond; six hundred thousand free, and three-and-a-half millions bond.

3   We have native hearts and virtues, just as other nations; which in their pristine purity are noble, potent, and worthy of example. We are a nation within a nation;—as the Poles in Russia, the Hungarians in Austria, the Welsh, Irish, and Scotch in the British dominions.

4   But we have been, by our oppressors, despoiled of our purity, and corrupted in our native characteristics, so that we have inherited their vices, and but few of their virtues, leaving us in character, really a *broken people.*

5   Being distinguished by complexion, we are still singled out— although having merged in the habits and customs of our oppressors—as a distinct nation of people; as the Poles, Hungarians, Irish, and others, who still retain their native peculiarities, of language, habits, and various other traits. The claims of no people, according to established policy and usage, are respected by any nation, until they are presented in a national capacity.

6   To accomplish so great and desirable an end, there should be held, a great representative gathering of the colored people of the United States; not what is termed a National Convention, represented en masse, such as have been, for the last few years, held at various times and places; but a true representation of the intelligence and wisdom of the colored freemen; because it will be futile and an utter failure, to attempt such a project without the highest grade of intelligence.

7   No great project was ever devised without the consultation of the most mature intelligence, and discreet discernment and precaution.

8   To effect this, and prevent intrusion and improper representation, there should be a CONFIDENTIAL COUNCIL held; and circulars issued, only to such persons as shall be *known* to the projectors to be equal to the desired object.

9   The authority from whence the call should originate, to be in this wise:—The originator of the scheme, to impart the contemplated Confidential Council, to a limited number of known, worthy gentlemen, who agreeing with the project, endorse at once the scheme, when becoming joint proprietors in interest, issue a *Confidential Circular,* leaving blanks for *date, time,* and *place of holding* the Council; sending them to trusty, worthy, and suitable colored freemen, in all parts of the United States, and the Canadas, inviting them to attend; who when met in Council, have the right to project any scheme they may think proper for the general good of the whole people—provided, that the project is laid before them after its maturity.

10   By this Council to be appointed, a Board of Commissioners, to consist of three, five, or such reasonable number as may be decided

upon, one of whom shall be chosen as Principal or Conductor of the Board, whose duty and business shall be, to go on an expedition to the EASTERN COAST OF AFRICA, to make researches for a suitable location on that section of the coast, for the settlement of colored adventurers from the United States, and elsewhere. Their mission should be to all such places as might meet the approbation of the people; as South America, Mexico, the West Indies, &c.

11   The Commissioners all to be men of decided qualifications, to embody among them, the qualifications of physician, botanist, chemist, geologist, geographer, and surveyor,—having a sufficient knowledge of these sciences, for practical purposes.

12   Their business shall be, to make a topographical, geographical, geological, and botanical examination, into such part or parts as they may select, with all other useful information that may be obtained; to be recorded in a journal kept for that purpose.

13   The Council shall appoint a permanent Board of Directors, to manage and supervise the doings of the Commissioners, and to whom they shall be amenable for their doings, who shall hold their offices until successors shall be appointed.

14   A National Confidential Council, to be held once in three years; and sooner, if necessity or emergency should demand it; the Board of Directors giving at least three months' notice, by circulars and newspapers. And should they fail to perform their duty, twenty-five of the representatives from any six States, of the former Council, may issue a call, authentically bearing their names, as sufficient authority for such a call. But when the Council is held for the reception of the report of the Commissioners, a general mass convention should then take place, by popular representation.

MANNER OF RAISING FUNDS

15   The National Council shall appoint one or two Special Commissioners, to England and France, to solicit, in the name of the Representatives of a Broken Nation, of four-and-a-half millions, the necessary outfit and support, for any period not exceeding three years, of such an expedition. Certainly, what England and France would do, for a little nation—mere nominal nation, of five thousand civilized Liberians, they would be willing and ready to do, for five millions; if they be but authentically represented, in a national capacity. What was due to Greece, enveloped by Turkey, should be due to us, enveloped by the United States; and we believe would be respected,

if properly presented. To England and France, we should look for sustenance, and the people of those two nations—as they would have every thing to gain from such an adventure and eventual settlement on the EASTERN COAST OF AFRICA—the opening of an immense trade being the consequence. The whole Continent is rich in minerals, and the most precious metals, as but a superficial notice of the topographical and geological reports from that country, plainly show to any mind versed in the least, in the science of the earth.

16   The Eastern Coast of Africa has long been neglected, and never but little known, even to the ancients; but has ever been our choice part of the Continent. Bounded by the Red Sea, Arabian Sea, and Indian Ocean, it presents the greatest facilities for an immense trade, with China, Japan, Siam, Hindoostan, in short, all the East Indies— of any other country in the world. With a settlement of enlightened freemen, who with the immense facilities, must soon grow into a powerful nation. In the Province of Berbera, south of the Strait of Babelmandel, or the great pass, from the Arabian to the Red Sea, the whole commerce of the East must touch this point.

17   Also, a great rail road could be constructed from here, running with the Mountains of the Moon, clearing them entirely, except making one mountain pass, at the western extremity of the Mountains of the Moon, and the southeastern terminus of the Kong Mountains; entering the Province of Dahomey, and terminating on the Atlantic Ocean West; which would make the GREAT THOROUGHFARE for all the trade with the East Indies and Eastern Coast of Africa, and the Continent of America. All the world would pass through Africa upon this rail road, which would yield a revenue infinitely greater than any other investment in the world.

18   The means for prosecuting such a project—as stupendous as it may appear—will be fully realised in the prosecution of the work. Every mile of the road, will thrice pay for itself. In the development of the rich treasures that now lie hidden in the bowels of the earth. There is no doubt, that in some one section of twenty-five miles, the developments of gold would more than pay the expenses of any one thousand miles of the work. This calculation may, to those who have never given this subject a thought, appear extravagant, and visionary; but to one who has had his attention in this direction for years, it is clear enough. But a few years will witness a development of gold, precious metals, and minerals in Eastern Africa, the Moon and Kong Mountains, ten-fold greater than all the rich productions of California.

19   There is one great physiological fact in regard to the colored race—which, while it may not apply to all colored persons, is true of those having black skins—that they can bear *more different* climates than the white race. They bear *all* the temperates and extremes, while the other can only bear the temperates and *one* of the extremes. The black race is endowed with natural properties, that adapt and fit them for temperate, cold, and hot climates; while the white race is only endowed with properties that adapt them to temperate and cold climates; being unable to stand the warmer climates; In them, the white race cannot work, but become perfectly indolent, requiring somebody to work for them—and these, are always people of the black race.

20   The black race may be found, inhabiting in healthful improvement, every part of the globe where the white race reside; while there are parts of the globe where the black race reside, that the white race cannot live in health.

21   What part of mankind is the "denizen of every soil, and the lord of terrestrial creation," if it be not the black race? The Creator has indisputably adapted us for the "denizens of *every soil*," all that is left for us to do, is to *make* ourselves the "*lords*" of terrestrial creation." The land is ours—there it lies with inexhaustible resources; let us go and possess it. In Eastern Africa must rise up a nation, to whom all the world must pay commercial tribute.

W. E. B. Du Bois

(1868–1963)

For biographical information about Du Bois, see page 56. The following paper, delivered at the inaugural meeting of the American Negro Academy, demonstrates Du Bois's enthusiasm for separate institutions for African Americans.

The Conservation of Races*

1   The American Negro has always felt an intense personal interest in discussions as to the origins and destinies of races: primarily because back of most discussions of race with which he is familiar, have lurked certain assumptions as to his natural abilities, as

*W. E. B. Du Bois, *The Conservation of Races*, American Negro Academy Occasional Papers, no. 2 (Washington, D.C., 1897).

to his political, intellectual and moral status, which he felt were wrong. He has, consequently, been led to deprecate and minimize race distinctions, to believe intensely that out of one blood God created all nations, and to speak of human brotherhood as though it were the possibility of an already dawning to-morrow.

2 Nevertheless, in our calmer moments we must acknowledge that human beings are divided into races; that in this country the two most extreme types of the world's races have met, and the resulting problem as to the future relations of these types is not only of intense and living interest to us, but forms an epoch in the history of mankind.

3 It is necessary, therefore, in planning our movements, in guiding our future development, that at times we rise above the pressing, but smaller questions of separate schools and cars, wage-discrimination and lynch law, to survey the whole question of race in human philosophy and to lay, on a basis of broad knowledge and careful insight, those large lines of policy and higher ideals which may form our guiding lines and boundaries in the practical difficulties of every day. For it is certain that all human striving must recognize the hard limits of natural law, and that any striving, no matter how intense and earnest, which is against the constitution of the world, is vain. The question, then, which we must seriously consider is this: What is the real meaning of Race; what has, in the past, been the law of race development, and what lessons has the past history of race development to teach the rising Negro people?

4 When we thus come to inquire into the essential difference of races we find it hard to come at once to any definite conclusion. Many criteria of race differences have in the past been proposed, as color, hair, cranial measurements and language. And manifestly, in each of these respects, human beings differ widely. They vary in color, for instance, from the marble-like pallor of the Scandinavian to the rich, dark brown of the Zulu, passing by the creamy Slav, the yellow Chinese, the light brown Sicilian and the brown Egyptian. Men vary, too, in the texture of hair from the obstinately straight hair of the Chinese to the obstinately tufted and frizzled hair of the Bushman. In measurement of heads, again, men vary: from the broad-headed Tartar to the medium-headed European and the narrow-headed Hottentot; or, again in language, from the highly-inflected Roman tongue to the monosyllabic Chinese. All these physical characteristics are patent enough, and if they agreed with each other it would be very easy to classify mankind. Unfortunately for scientists, however, these criteria of race are most exasperatingly intermingled. Color does not agree

with texture of hair, for many of the dark races have straight hair; nor does color agree with the breadth of the head, for the yellow Tartar has a broader head than the German; nor, again, has the science of language as yet succeeded in clearing up the relative authority of these various and contradictory criteria. The final word of science, so far, is that we have at least two, perhaps three, great families of human beings—the whites and Negroes, possibly the yellow race. That other races have arisen from the intermingling of the blood of these two. This broad division of the world's races which men like Huxley and Raetzel have introduced as more nearly true than the old five-race scheme of Blumenbach, is nothing more than an acknowledgment that, so far as purely physical characteristics are concerned, the differences between men do not explain all the differences of their history. It declares, as Darwin himself said, that great as is the physical unlikeness of the various races of men their likenesses are greater, and upon this rests the whole scientific doctrine of Human Brotherhood.

5   Although the wonderful developments of human history teach that the grosser physical differences of color, hair and bone go but a short way toward explaining the different roles which groups of men have played in Human Progress, yet there are differences—subtle, delicate and elusive, though they may be—which have silently but definitely separated men into groups. While these subtle forces have generally followed the natural cleavage of common blood, descent and physical peculiarities, they have at other times swept across and ignored these. At all times, however, they have divided human beings into races, which, while they perhaps transcend scientific definition, nevertheless, are clearly defined to the eye of the Historian and Sociologist.

6   If this be true, then the history of the world is the history, not of individuals, but of groups, not of nations, but of races, and he who ignores or seeks to override the race idea in human history ignores and overrides the central thought of all history. What, then, is a race? It is a vast family of human beings, generally of common blood and language, always of common history, traditions and impulses, who are both voluntarily and involuntarily striving together for the accomplishment of certain more or less vividly conceived ideals of life.

7   Turning to real history, there can be no doubt, first, as to the widespread, nay, universal, prevalence of the race idea, the race spirit, the race ideal, and as to its efficiency as the vastest and most ingenious invention for human progress. We, who have been reared and trained under the individualistic philosophy of the Declaration of Independence and the laisser-faire philosophy of Adam Smith, are loath to see and

loath to acknowledge this patent fact of human history. We see the Pharaohs, Caesars, Toussaints and Napoleons of history and forget the vast races of which they were but epitomized expressions. We are apt to think in our American impatience, that while it may have been true in the past that closed race groups made history, that here in conglomerate America *nous avons changer tout cela*—we have changed all that, and have no need of this ancient instrument of progress. This assumption of which the Negro people are especially fond, can not be established by a careful consideration of history.

8   We find upon the world's stage today eight distinctly differentiated races, in the sense in which History tells us the word must be used. They are, the Slavs of eastern Europe, the Teutons of middle Europe, the English of Great Britain and America, the Romance nations of Southern and Western Europe, the Negroes of Africa and America, the Semitic people of Western Asia and Northern Africa, the Hindoos of Central Asia and the Mongolians of Eastern Asia. There are, of course, other minor race groups, as the American Indians, the Esquimaux and the South Sea Islanders; these larger races, too, are far from homogeneous; the Slav includes the Czech, the Magyar, the Pole and the Russian; the Teuton includes the German, the Scandinavian and the Dutch; the English include the Scotch, the Irish and the conglomerate American. Under Romance nations the widely-differing Frenchman, Italian, Sicilian and Spaniard are comprehended. The term Negro is, perhaps, the most indefinite of all, combining the Mulattoes and Zamboes of America and the Egyptians, Bantus and Bushmen of Africa. Among the Hindoos are traces of widely differing nations, while the great Chinese, Tartar, Corean and Japanese families fall under the one designation—Mongolian.

9   The question now is: What is the real distinction between these nations? Is it the physical differences of blood, color and cranial measurements? Certainly we must all acknowledge that physical differences play a great part; and that, with wide exceptions and qualifications, these eight great races of to-day follow the cleavage of physical race distinctions; the English and Teuton represent the white variety of mankind; the Mongolian, the yellow; the Negroes, the black. Between these are many crosses and mixtures, where Mongolian and Teuton have blended into the Slav, and other mixtures have produced the Romance nations and the Semites. But while race differences have followed mainly physical race lines, yet no mere physical distinctions would really define or explain the deeper differences—the cohesiveness and continuity of these groups. The deeper differences are spiritual,

psychical, differences—undoubtedly based on the physical, but infinitely transcending them. The forces that bind together the Teuton nations are, then, first, their race identity and common blood; secondly, and more important, a common history, common laws and religion, similar habits of thought and a conscious striving together for certain ideals of life. The whole process which has brought about these race differentiations has been a growth, and the great characteristic of this growth has been the differentiation of spiritual and mental differences between great races of mankind and the integration of physical differences.

10   The age of nomadic tribes of closely related individuals represents the maximum of physical differences. They were practically vast families, and there were as many groups as families. As the families came together to form cities the physical differences lessened, purity of blood was replaced by the requirement of domicile, and all who lived within the city bounds became gradually to be regarded as members of the group; *i.e.*, there was a slight and slow breaking down of physical barriers. This, however, was accompanied by an increase of the spiritual and social differences between cities. This city became husbandmen, this, merchants, another warriors, and so on. The *ideals of life* for which the different cities struggled were different. When at last cities began to coalesce into nations there was another breaking down of barriers which separated groups of men. The larger and broader differences of color, hair and physical proportions were not by any means ignored, but myriads of minor differences disappeared, and the sociological and historical races of men began to approximate the present division of races as indicated by physical researches. At the same time the spiritual and physical differences of race groups which constituted the nations became deep and decisive. The English nation stood for constitutional liberty and commercial freedom; the German nation for science and philosophy; the Romance nations stood for literature and art, and the other race groups are striving, each in its own way, to develope for civilization its particular message, its particular ideal, which shall help to guide the world nearer and nearer that perfection of human life for which we all long, that

   "one far off Divine event."

11   This has been the function of race differences up to the present time. What shall be its function in the future? Manifestly some of the great races of today—particularly the Negro race—have not as yet given to

civilization the full spiritual message which they are capable of giving. I will not say that the Negro race has as yet given no message to the world, for it is still a mooted question among scientists as to just how far Egyptian civilization was Negro in its origin; if it was not wholly Negro, it was certainly very closely allied. Be that as it may, however the fact still remains that the full, complete Negro message of the whole Negro race has not as yet been given to the world: that the message and ideal of the yellow race have not been completed, and that the striving of the mighty Slavs has but begun. The question is, then: How shall this message be delivered; how shall these various ideals be realized? The answer is plain: By the development of these race groups, not as individuals, but as races. For the development of Japanese genius, Japanese literature and art, Japanese spirit, only Japanese, bound and welded together, Japanese inspired by one vast ideal, can work out in its fullness the wonderful message which Japan has for the nations of the earth. For the development of Negro genius, of Negro literature and art, of Negro spirit, only Negroes bound and welded together, Negroes inspired by one vast ideal, can work out in its fullness the great message we have for humanity. We cannot reverse history; we are subject to the same natural laws as other races, and if the Negro is ever to be a factor in the world's history—if among the gaily-colored banners that deck the broad ramparts of civilization is to hang one uncompromising black, then it must be placed there by black hands, fashioned by black heads and hallowed by the travail of 200,000,000 black hearts beating in one glad song of jubilee.

12   For this reason, the advance guard of the Negro people—the 8,000,000 people of Negro blood in the United States of America—must soon come to realize that if they are to take their just place in the van of Pan-Negroism, then their destiny is *not* absorption by the white Americans. That if in America it is to be proven for the first time in the modern world that not only Negroes are capable of evolving individual men like Toussaint, the Saviour, but are a nation stored with wonderful possibilities of culture, then their destiny is not a servile imitation of Anglo-Saxon culture, but a stalwart originality which shall unswervingly follow Negro ideals.

13   It may, however, be objected here that the situation of our race in America renders this attitude impossible; that our sole hope of salvation lies in our being able to lose our race identity in the commingled blood of the nation; and that any other course would merely increase the friction of races which we call race prejudice, and against which we have so long and so earnestly fought.

14   Here, then, is the dilemma, and it is a puzzling one, I admit. No Negro who has given earnest thought to the situation of his people in America has failed, at some time in life, to find himself at these cross-roads; has failed to ask himself at some time: What, after all, am I? Am I an American or am I a Negro? Can I be both? Or is it my duty to cease to be a Negro as soon as possible and be an American? If I strive as a Negro, am I not perpetuating the very cleft that threatens and separates Black and White America? Is not my only possible practical aim the subduction of all that is Negro in me to the American? Does my black blood place upon me any more obligation to assert my nationality than German, or Irish or Italian blood would?

15   It is such incessant self-questioning and the hesitation that arises from it, that is making the present period a time of vacillation and contradiction for the American Negro; combined race action is stifled, race responsibility is shirked, race enterprises languish, and the best blood, the best talent, the best energy of the Negro people cannot be marshalled to do the bidding of the race. They stand back to make room for every rascal and demagogue who chooses to cloak his self-ish deviltry under the veil of race pride.

16   Is this right? Is it rational? Is it good policy? Have we in America a distinct mission as a race—a distinct sphere of action and an opportunity for race development, or is self-obliteration the highest end to which Negro blood dare aspire?

17   If we carefully consider what race prejudice really is, we find it, historically, to be nothing but the friction between different groups of people; it is the difference in aim, in feeling, in ideals of two different races; if, now, this difference exists touching territory, laws, language, or even religion, it is manifest that these people cannot live in the same territory without fatal collision; but if, on the other hand, there is substantial agreement in laws, language and religion; if there is a satisfactory adjustment of economic life, then there is no reason why, in the same country and on the same street, two or three great national ideals might not thrive and develop, that men of different races might not strive together for their race ideals as well, perhaps even better, than in isolation. Here, it seems to me, is the reading of the riddle that puzzles so many of us. We are Americans, not only by birth and by citizenship, but by our political ideals, our language, our religion. Farther than that, our Americanism does not go. At that point, we are Negroes, members of a vast historic race that from the very dawn of creation has slept, but half awakening in the dark forests of its African fatherland. We are the first fruits of this new

nation, the harbinger of that black to-morrow which is yet destined to soften the whiteness of the Teutonic to-day. We are that people whose subtle sense of song has given America its only American music, its only American fairy tales, its only touch of pathos and humor amid its mad money-getting plutocracy. As such, it is our duty to conserve our physical powers, our intellectual endowments, our spiritual ideals; as a race we must strive by race organization, by race solidarity, by race unity to the realization of that broader humanity which freely recognizes differences in men, but sternly deprecates inequality in their opportunities of development.

18   For the accomplishment of these ends we need race organizations: Negro colleges, Negro newspapers, Negro business organizations, a Negro school of literature and art, and an intellectual clearing house, for all these products of the Negro mind, which we may call a Negro Academy. Not only is all this necessary for positive advance, it is absolutely imperative for negative defense. Let us not deceive ourselves at our situation in this country. Weighted with a heritage of moral iniquity from our past history, hard pressed in the economic world by foreign immigrants and native prejudice, hated here, despised there and pitied everywhere; our one haven of refuge is ourselves, and but one means of advance, our own belief in our great destiny, our own implicit trust in our ability and worth. There is no power under God's high heaven that can stop the advance of eight thousand thousand honest, earnest, inspired and united people. But—and here is the rub—they *must* be honest, fearlessly criticising their own faults, zealously correcting them; they must be *earnest*. No people that laughs at itself, and ridicules itself, and wishes to God it was anything but itself ever wrote its name in history; it *must* be inspired with the Divine faith of our black mothers, that out of the blood and dust of battle will march a victorious host, a mighty nation, a peculiar people, to speak to the nations of earth a Divine truth that shall make them free. And such a people must be united; not merely united for the organized theft of political spoils, not united to disgrace religion with whoremongers and ward-heelers; not united merely to protest and pass resolutions, but united to stop the ravages of consumption among the Negro people, united to keep black boys from loafing, gambling and crime; united to guard the purity of black women and to reduce that vast army of black prostitutes that is today marching to hell; and united in serious organizations, to determine by careful conference and thoughtful interchange of opinion the broad lines of policy and action for the American Negro.

19   This, is the reason for being which the American Negro Academy has. It aims at once to be the epitome and expression of the intellect of the black-blooded people of America, the exponent of the race ideals of one of the world's great races. As such, the Academy must, if successful, be

      (*a*). Representative in character.
      (*b*). Impartial in conduct.
      (*c*). Firm in leadership.

20   It must be representative in character; not in that it represents all interests or all factions, but in that it seeks to comprise something of the *best* thought, the most unselfish striving and the highest ideals. There are scattered in forgotten nooks and corners throughout the land, Negroes of some considerable training, of high minds, and high motives, who are unknown to their fellows, who exert far too little influence. These the Negro Academy should strive to bring into touch with each other and to give them a common mouthpiece.

21   The Academy should be impartial in conduct; while it aims to exalt the people it should aim to do so by truth—not by lies, by honesty—not by flattery. It should continually impress the fact upon the Negro people that they must not expect to have things done for them—they MUST DO FOR THEMSELVES; that they have on their hands a vast work of self-reformation to do, and that a little less complaint and whining, and a little more dogged work and manly striving would do us more credit and benefit than a thousand Force or Civil Rights bills.

22   Finally, the American Negro Academy must point out a practical path of advance to the Negro people; there lie before every Negro today hundreds of questions of policy and right which must be settled and which each one settles now, not in accordance with any rule, but by impulse or individual preference; for instance: What should be the attitude of Negroes toward the educational qualification for voters? What should be our attitude toward separate schools? How should we meet discriminations on railways and in hotels? Such questions need not so much specific answers for each part as a general expression of policy, and nobody should be better fitted to announce such a policy than a representative honest Negro Academy.

23   All this, however, must come in time after careful organization and long conference. The immediate work before us should be practical and have direct bearing upon the situation of the Negro. The historical work of collecting the laws of the United States and of

the various States of the Union with regard to the Negro is a work of such magnitude and importance that no body but one like this could think of undertaking it. If we could accomplish that one task we would justify our existence.

24   In the field of Sociology an appalling work lies before us. First, we must unflinchingly and bravely face the truth, not with apologies, but with solemn earnestness. The Negro Academy ought to sound a note of warning that would echo in every black cabin in the land: *Unless we conquer our present vices they will conquer us*; we are diseased, we are developing criminal tendencies, and an alarmingly large percentage of our men and women are sexually impure. The Negro Academy should stand and proclaim this over the housetops, crying with Garrison: *I will not equivocate, I will not retreat a single inch, and I will be heard.* The Academy should seek to gather about it the talented, unselfish men, the pure and nobleminded women, to fight an army of devils that disgraces our manhood and our womanhood. There does not stand today upon God's earth a race more capable in muscle, in intellect, in morals, than the American Negro, if he will bend his energies in the right direction; if he will

> *Burst his birth's invidious bar*
> *And grasp the skirts of happy chance,*
> *And breast the blows of circumstance,*
> *And grapple with his evil star.*

25   In science and morals, I have indicated two fields of work for the Academy. Finally, in practical policy, I wish to suggest the following *Academy Creed*:

1. We believe that the Negro people, as a race, have a contribution to make to civilization and humanity, which no other race can make.

2. We believe it the duty of the Americans of Negro descent, as a body, to maintain their race identity until this mission of the Negro people is accomplished, and the ideal of human brotherhood has become a practical possibility.

3. We believe that, unless modern civilization is a failure, it is entirely feasible and practicable for two races in such essential political, economic and religious harmony as the white and colored people of America, to develop side by side in

peace and mutual happiness, the peculiar contribution which each has to make to the culture of their common country.

4. As a means to this end we advocate, not such social equality between these races as would disregard human likes and dislikes, but such a social equilibrium as would, throughout all the complicated relations of life, give due and just consideration to culture, ability, and moral worth, whether they be found under white or black skins.

5. We believe that the first and greatest step toward the settlement of the present friction between the races—commonly called the Negro Problem—lies in the correction of the immorality, crime and laziness among the Negroes themselves, which still remains as a heritage from slavery. We believe that only earnest and long continued efforts on our own part can cure these social ills.

6. We believe that the second great step toward a better adjustment of the relations between the races, should be a more impartial selection of ability in the economic and intellectual world, and a greater respect for personal liberty and worth, regardless of race. We believe that only earnest efforts on the part of the white people of this country will bring much needed reform in these matters.

7. On the basis of the foregoing declaration, and firmly believing in our high destiny, we, as American Negroes, are resolved to strive in every honorable way for the realization of the best and highest aims, for the development of strong manhood and pure womanhood, and for the rearing of a race ideal in America and Africa, to the glory of God and the uplifting of the Negro people.

Marcus Garvey
(1887–1940)

Marcus Mosiah Garvey, leader of the Universal Negro Improvement Association (UNIA), the largest Black political organization in American history, was born August 17, 1887, in St. Ann's Bay, Jamaica. As a youth he was trained to be a printer, then sought work in Kingston and abroad, in Central America and Europe. In England, he worked

for Duse Mohammed Ali on the Pan-African journal Africa Times.
*Partly inspired by Booker T. Washington's model of institution build-
ing and self-reliance, Garvey journeyed to the United States in 1916 to
explore possibilities for social activism. He founded the UNIA in
Harlem in 1917 and operated several business ventures including the
publication* Negro World *and, most famously, the Black Star
Steamship Line. The shipping company failed in 1921; Garvey was
indicted the following year for mail fraud involving stock sales. He
spent almost three years in federal prison and was deported in 1927.
Although his ideas frequently were the target of criticism by the likes of
W. E. B. Du Bois, that is, when Du Bois was stressing integration,
Garvey's message of self-determination was embraced by millions of
African Americans in his time—and by legions since. Many of Garvey's
speeches and essays, including the following readings, are collected in*
The Philosophy and Opinions of Marcus Garvey; or, Africa for the
Africans, *a work originally compiled in two volumes by his wife, Amy
Jacques Garvey, and published in 1923 and 1925.*

Africa for the Africans

1   For five years the Universal Negro Improvement Association has been
advocating the cause of Africa for the Africans—that is, that the
Negro peoples of the world should concentrate upon the object of
building up for themselves a great nation in Africa.

2   When we started our propaganda toward this end several of the
so-called intellectual Negroes who have been bamboozling the race
for over half a century said that we were crazy, that the Negro peoples of the western world were not interested in Africa and could not
live in Africa. One editor and leader went so far as to say at his so-called
Pan-African Congress that American Negroes could not live in Africa,
because the climate was too hot. All kinds of arguments have been
adduced by these Negro intellectuals against the colonization of Africa
by the black race. Some said that the black man would ultimately work
out his existence alongside of the white man in countries founded and
established by the latter. Therefore, it was not necessary for Negroes
to seek an independent nationality of their own. The old time stories
of "African fever," "African bad climate," "African mosquitos,"
"African savages," have been repeated by these "brainless intellectuals" of ours as a scare against our people in America and the West Indies
taking a kindly interest in the new program of building a racial empire

of our own in our Motherland. Now that years have rolled by and the Universal Negro Improvement Association has made the circuit of the world with its propaganda, we find eminent statesmen and leaders of the white race coming out boldly advocating the cause of colonizing Africa with the Negroes of the western world. A year ago Senator Mac-Cullum of the Mississippi Legislature introduced a resolution in the House for the purpose of petitioning the Congress of the United States of America and the President to use their good influence in securing from the Allies sufficient territory in Africa in liquidation of the war debt, which territory should be used for the establishing of an independent nation for American Negroes. About the same time Senator France of Maryland gave expression to a similar desire in the Senate of the United States. During a speech on the "Soldiers' Bonus." He said: "We owe a big debt to Africa and one which we have too long ignored. I need not enlarge upon our peculiar interest in the obligation to the people of Africa. Thousands of Americans have for years been contributing to the missionary work which has been carried out by the noble men and women who have been sent out in that field by the churches of America."

GERMANY TO THE FRONT

3   This reveals a real change on the part of prominent statesmen in their attitude on the African question. Then comes another suggestion from Germany, for which Dr. Heinrich Schnee, a former Governor of German East Africa, is author. This German statesman suggests in an interview given out in Berlin, and published in New York, that America takes over the mandatories of Great Britain and France in Africa for the colonization of American Negroes. Speaking on the matter, he says "As regards the attempt to colonize Africa with the surplus American colored population, this would in a long way settle the vexed problem, and under the plan such as Senator France has outlined, might enable France and Great Britain to discharge their duties to the United States, and simultaneously ease the burden of German reparations which is paralyzing economic life."

4   With expressions as above quoted from prominent world statesmen, and from the demands made by such men as Senators France and McCullum, it is clear that the question of African nationality is not a far-fetched one, but is as reasonable and feasible as was the idea of an American nationality.

A "PROGRAM" AT LAST

5 I trust that the Negro peoples of the world are now convinced that the work of the Universal Negro Improvement Association is not a visionary one, but very practical, and that it is not so far fetched, but can be realized in a short while if the entire race will only co-operate and work toward the desired end. Now that the work of our organization has started to bear fruit we find that some of these "doubting Thomases" of three and four years ago are endeavoring to mix themselvves up with the popular idea of rehabilitating Africa in the interest of the Negro They are now advancing spurious "programs" and in a short while will endeavor to force themselves upon the public as advocates and leaders of the African idea.

6 It is felt that those who have followed the career of the Universal Negro Improvement Association will not allow themselves to be deceived by these Negro opportunists who have always sought to live off the ideas of other people.

THE DREAM OF A NEGRO EMPIRE

7 It is only a question of a few more years when Africa will be completely colonized by Negroes, as Europe is by the white race. What we want is an independent African nationality, and if America is to help the Negro peoples of the world establish such a nationality, then we welcome the assistance.

8 It is hoped that when the time comes for American and West Indian Negroes to settle in Africa, they will realize their responsibility and their duty. It will not be to go to Africa for the purpose of exercising an over-lordship over the natives, but it shall be the purpose of the Universal Negro Improvement Association to have established in Africa that brotherly co-operation which will make the interests of the African native and the American and West Indian Negro one and the same, that is to say, we shall enter into a common partnership to build up Africa in the interests of our race.

ONENESS OF INTERESTS

9 Everybody knows that there is absolutely no difference between the native African and the American and West Indian Negroes, in that we are descendants from one common family stock. It is only a matter of accident that we have been divided and kept apart for over three

hundred years, but it is felt that when the time has come for us to get back together, we shall do so in the spirit of brotherly love, and any Negro who expects that he will be assisted here, there or anywhere by the Universal Negro Improvement Association to exercise a haughty superiority over the fellows of his own race, makes a tremenduous mistake. Such men had better remain where they are and not attempt to become in any way interested in the higher development of Africa.

10   The Negro has had enough of the vaunted practice of race superiority as inflicted upon him by others, therefore he is not prepared to tolerate a similar assumption on the part of his own people. In America and the West Indies, we have Negroes who believe themselves so much above their fellows as to cause them to think that any readjustment in the affairs of the race should be placed in their hands for them to exercise a kind of an autocratic and despotic control as others have done to us for centuries. Again I say, it would be advisable for such Negroes to take their hands and minds off the now popular idea of colonizing Africa in the interest of the Negro race, because their being identified with this new program will not in any way help us because of the existing feeling among Negroes everywhere not to tolerate the infliction of race or class superiority upon them, as is the desire of the self-appointed and self-created race leadership that we have been having for the last fifty years.

THE BASIS OF AN AFRICAN ARISTOCRACY.

11   The masses of Negroes in America, the West Indies, South and Central America are in sympathetic accord with the aspirations of the native Africans. We desire to help them build up Africa as a Negro Empire, where every black man, whether he was born in Africa or in the Western world, will have the opportunity to develop on his own lines under the protection of the most favorable democratic institutions.

12   It will be useless, as before stated, for bombastic Negroes to leave America and the West Indies to go to Africa, thinking that they will have privileged positions to inflict upon the race that bastard aristocracy that they have tried to maintain in this Western world at the expense of the masses. Africa shall develop an aristocracy of its own, but it shall be based upon service and loyalty to race. Let all Negroes work toward that end. I feel that it is only a question of a few more years before our program will be accepted not only by the few statesmen of America who are now interested in it, but by the strong statesmen of the world, as the only solution to the great race problem. There

is no other way to avoid the threatening war of the races that is bound to engulf all mankind, which has been prophesied by the world's greatest thinkers; there is no better method than by apportioning every race to its own habitat.

13   The time has really come for the Asiatics to govern themselves in Asia, as the Europeans are in Europe and the Western world, so also is it wise for the Africans to govern themselves at home and thereby bring peace and satisfaction to the entire human family.

The Future As I See It

1   It comes to the individual, the race, the nation, once in a life time to decide upon the course to be pursued as a career. The hour has now struck for the individual Negro as well as the entire race to decide the course that will be pursued in the interest of our own liberty.

2   We who make up the Universal Negro Improvement Association have decided that we shall go forward, upward and onward toward the great goal of human liberty. We have determined among ourselves that all barriers placed in the way of our progress must be removed, must be cleared away for we desire to see the light of a brighter day.

THE NEGRO IS READY

3   The Universal Negro Improvement Association for five years has been proclaiming to the world the readiness of the Negro to carve out a pathway for himself in the course of life. Men of other races and nations have become alarmed at this attitude of the Negro in his desire to do things for himself and by himself. This alarm has become so universal that organizations have been brought into being here, there and everywhere for the purpose of deterring and obstructing this forward move of our race. Propaganda has been waged here, there and everywhere for the purpose of misinterpreting the intention of this organization; some have said that this organization seeks to create discord and discontent among the races; some say we are organized for the purpose of hating other people. Every sensible, sane and honest-minded person knows that the Universal Negro Improvement Association has no such intention. We are organized for the absolute purpose of bettering our condition, industrially, commercially, socially, religiously and politically. We are

organized not to hate other men, but to lift ourselves, and to demand respect of all humanity. We have a program that we believe to be righteous; we believe it to be just, and we have made up our minds to lay down ourselves on the altar of sacrifice for the realization of this great hope of ours, based upon the foundation of righteousness. We declare to the world that Africa must be free, that the entire Negro race must be emancipated from industrial bondage, peonage and serfdom; we make no compromise, we make no apology in this our declaration. We do not desire to create offense on the part of other races, but we are determined that we shall be heard, that we shall be given the rights to which we are entitled.

THE PROPAGANDA OF OUR ENEMIES

4 For the purpose of creating doubts about the work of the Universal Negro Improvement Association, many attempts have been made to cast shadow and gloom over our work. They have even written the most uncharitable things about our organization; they have spoken so unkindly of our effort, but what do we care? They spoke unkindly and uncharitably about all the reform movements that have helped in the betterment of humanity. They maligned the great movement of the Christian religion; they maligned the great liberation movements of America, of France, of England, of Russia; can we expect, then, to escape being maligned in this, our desire for the liberation of Africa and the freedom of four hundred million Negroes of the world?

5 We have unscrupulous men and organizations working in opposition to us. Some trying to capitalize the new spirit that has come to the Negro to make profit out of it to their own selfish benefit; some are trying to set back the Negro from seeing the hope of his own liberty, and thereby poisoning our people's mind against the motives of our organization; but every sensible far-seeing Negro in this enlightened age knows what propaganda means. It is the medium of discrediting that which you are opposed to, so that the propaganda of our enemies will be of little avail as soon as we are rendered able to carry to our peoples scattered throughout the world the true message of our great organization.

"CROCODILES" AS FRIENDS

6 Men of the Negro race, let me say to you that a greater future is in store for us; we have no cause to lose hope, to become faint-hearted. We must realize that upon ourselves depend our destiny, our future;

we must carve out that future, that destiny, and we who make up the Universal Negro Improvement Association have pledged ourselves that nothing in the world shall stand in our way, nothing in the world shall discourage us, but opposition shall make us work harder, shall bring us closer together so that as one man the millions of us will march on toward that goal that we have set for ourselves. The new Negro shall not be deceived. The new Negro refuses to take advice from anyone who has not felt with him, and suffered with him. We have suffered for three hundred years, therefore we feel that the time has come when only those who have suffered with us can interpret our feelings and our spirit. It takes the slave to interpret the feelings of the slave; it takes the unfortunate man to interpret the spirit of his unfortunate brother; and so it takes the suffering Negro to interpret the spirit of his comrade. It is strange that so many people are interested in the Negro now, willing to advise him how to act, and what organizations he should join, yet nobody was interested in the Negro to the extent of not making him a slave for two hundred and fifty years, reducing him to industrial peonage and serfdom after he was freed; it is strange that the same people can be so interested in the Negro now, as to tell him what organization he should follow and what leader he should support.

7   Whilst we are bordering on a future of brighter things, we are also at our danger period, when we must either accept the right philosophy, or go down by following deceptive propaganda which has hemmed us in for many centuries.

DECEIVING THE PEOPLE

8   There is many a leader of our race who tells us that everything is well, and that all things will work out themselves and that a better day is coming. Yes, all of us know that a better day is coming; we all know that one day we will go home to Paradise, but whilst we are hoping by our Christian virtues to have an entry into Paradise we also realize that we are living on earth, and that the things that are practised in Paradise are not practiced here. You have to treat this world as the world treats you; we are living in a temporal, material age, an age of activity, an age of racial, national selfishness. What else can you expect but to give back to the world what the world gives to you, and we are calling upon the four hundred million Negroes of the world to take a decided stand, a determined stand, that we shall occupy a firm position; that position shall be an emancipated race and a free

nation of our own. We are determined that we shall have a free country; we are determined that we shall have a flag; we are determined that we shall have a government second to none in the world.

AN EYE FOR AN EYE

9 Men may spurn the idea, they may scoff at it; the metropolitan press of this country may deride us; yes, white men may laugh at the idea of Negroes talking about government; but let me tell you there is going to be a government, and let me say to you also that whatsoever you give, in like measure it shall be returned to you. The world is sinful, and therefore man believes in the doctrine of an eye for an eye, a tooth for a tooth. Everybody believes that revenge is God's, but at the same time we are men, and revenge sometimes springs up, even in the most Christian heart.

10   Why should man write down a history that will react against him? Why should man perpetrate deeds of wickedness upon his brother which will return to him in like measure? Yes, the Germans maltreated the French in the Franco-Prussian war of 1870, but the French got even with the Germans in 1918. It is history, and history will repeat itself. Beat the Negro, brutalize the Negro, kill the Negro, burn the Negro, imprison the Negro, scoff at the Negro, deride the Negro, it may come back to you one of these fine days, because the supreme destiny of man is in the hands of God. God is no respecter of persons, whether that person be white, yellow or black. Today the one race is up, tomorrow it has fallen; today the Negro seems to be the footstool of the other races and nations of the world; tomorrow the Negro may occupy the highest rung of the great human ladder.

11   But, when we come to consider the history of man, was not the Negro a power, was he not great once? Yes, honest students of history can recall the day when Egypt, Ethiopia and Timbuctoo towered in their civilizations, towered above Europe, towered above Asia. When Europe was inhabited by a race of cannibals, a race of savages, naked men, heathens and pagans, Africa was peopled with a race of cultured black men, who were masters in art, science and literature; men who were cultured and refined; men who, it was said, were like the gods. Even the great poets of old sang in beautiful sonnets of the delight it afforded the gods to be in companionship with the Ethiopians. Why, then, should we lose hope! Black men, you were once great; you shall be great again. Lose not courage, lose not faith, go forward. The thing to do is to get organized; keep separated and

you will be exploited, you will be robbed, you will be killed. Get organized, and you will compel the world to respect you. If the world fails to give you consideration, because you are black men, because you are Negroes, four hundred millions of you shall, through organization, shake the pillars of the universe and bring down creation, even as Samson brought down the temple upon his head and upon the heads of the Philistines.

AN INSPIRING VISION

12 So Negroes, I say, through the Universal Negro Improvement Association, that there is much to live for. I have a vision of the future, and I see before me a picture of a redeemed Africa, with her dotted cities, with her beautiful civilization, with her millions of happy children, going to and fro. Why should I lose hope, why should I give up and take a back place in this age of progress! Remember that you are men, that God created you Lords of this creation. Lift up yourselves, men, take yourselves out of the mire and hitch your hopes to the stars; yes, rise as high as the very stars themselves. Let no man pull you down, let no man destroy your ambition, because man is but your companion, your equal; man is your brother; he is not your lord; he is not your sovereign master.

13   We of the Universal Negro Improvement Association feel happy; we are cheerful. Let them connive to destroy us; let them organize to destroy us; we shall fight the more. Ask me personally the cause of my success, and I say opposition; oppose me, and I fight the more, and if you want to find out the sterling worth of the Negro, oppose him, and under the leadership of the Universal Negro Improvement Association he shall fight his way to victory, and in the days to come, and I believe not far distant, Africa shall reflect a splendid demonstration of the worth of the Negro, of the determination of the Negro, to set himself free and to establish a government of his own.

First Speech After Release From Tombs Prison Delivered At Liberty Hall, New York City, September, 13, 1923.

1   "Ladies and Gentlemen:

2   "It is needless for me to say that the pleasure of meeting you in Liberty Hall, the shrine of Negro inspiration, after an enforced absence of three months, is beyond my ability to express.

3   "The news of the trial of the celebrated case of fraud, and my so-called conviction, have made the circuit of the world, and black humanity everywhere, even to the remotest parts of our homeland, Africa, have formed their opinion of Western twentieth century civilization and justice, as controlled and administered by the white man.

4   "My absence from you did not leave me despondent, nor desolate, for in the daily silence of the passing hours in my cell I thought of you, the warriors of true liberty, who were working for the consummation of our ideal—a free and redeemed Africa, and my meditations led me into greater flights of hope that shall strengthen me for the nobler work of self-sacrifice for the cause that we represent.

5   "The amusing part of my trial is that I was indicted along with others for conspiracy to use the United States mails to defraud in the promotion of the Black Star Line Steamship Company, yet my conviction was void of conspiracy, in that I alone was convicted, and, if I understand my conviction clearly, I was convicted for selling stock in the Black Star Line after I knew it to be insolvent. The difference between us and the trial court is that they wanted a conviction, caring not how it came about, and they had it to suit themselves, to the extent that all the others, who had more to do with the actual selling of stock than I, went free, because they were not wanted, while I received the fullest penalty that the law could impose—five years in the penitentiary, the maximum fine of one thousand dollars as provided by law, and the entire cost of the case, a condition not generally imposed but, maybe, once in twentyfive years.

6   "Our point of view is that we cannot defraud ourselves in the sense of promoting the Black Star Line, for the idea of a line of steamships operated by Negroes for the promotion of their industrial, commercial, fraternal and material well-being can never be insolvent or bankrupt; for, as long as the race lasts, and as long as humanity indulges in the pursuit of progress and achievements, the new Negro will be found doing his part to hold a place in the affairs of the world. It is true that we have been defrauded, but it was done, not by those of us who love our work and our race, but by disloyal and dishonest ones, whom we thought had the same feelings as we do, and by crooked white men, who were not even ashamed of hiding their crookedness. One white man said in court that he sold us a ship when he knew it was not worth the money paid for it. Another took $25,000. and an additional $11,000. to buy the Phyllis Wheatley to go to Africa, which never materialized, and which money was never returned, the reason of which supplied the legal cause for my indictmemnt. And yet it is said in the law of those who tried me that there was fraud and I should pay the penalty.

7   "The Black Star Line, as we all know, was but a small attempt, or experiment, of the race to fit and prepare ourselves for the bigger effort in the direction of racial self-reliance and self-determination. To say that we have failed, because a few black and white unscrupulous persons deceived and robbed us, is to admit that the colonization scheme of America failed because a few Pilgrim Fathers died at Plymouth, and that the fight of the Allies to save the world for a new civilization failed, because the Crown Prince met with early success at Verdun. The Black Star Line was only part of an honest effort on the part of real Negroes to re-establish themselves as a worthy people among the other races and nations of the earth, and but a small contribution in the plan of a free and redeemed African nation for the Negro peoples of the world. The idea of a Black Steamship Line, therefore, can only fail when the Negro race has completely passed away, and that means eternity.

8   "I was convicted, not because any one was defrauded in the temporary failure of the Black Star Line brought about by others, but because I represented, even as I do now, a movement for the real emancipation of my race. I was convicted because I talked about Africa and about its redemption for Negroes. I was convicted because an atmosphere of hostility was created around me. I was convicted because wicked enemies, malicious and jealous members of my own race, misrepresented me to those in authority for the purpose of discrediting and destroying me.

9   "I would not blame the few white persons who contributed to my conviction, neither would I blame the Government and the illiberal of the white race who had prejudices against me. They knew no better than the information they received from treacherous, malicious and jealous Negroes who, for the sake of position and privilege, will sell their own mothers.

10   "I feel, however, that these white persons and the Government have now the opportunity of learning the truth, not only about my case and my conviction, but about the differences in the Negro race, that set one against the other.

APPEALING THE CASE.

11   "I have no fear of the ultimate outcome of my case. I shall take it to the highest courts in the land, and from there to the bar of international public opinion, and even though I go to jail because of prejudice, I will have left behind for our generations a record of injustice that will be our guide in the future rise of Ethiopia's glory. Nevertheless, I believe that the higher courts of this country will not mingle prejudice with justice and condemn a man simply because he is black and attempts to do good for his race and his fellow men.

12   "Whatsoever happens, the world may know that the jail or penitentiary has no terrors for me. Guilty men are afraid of jail, but I am as much at home in jail for the cause of human rights as I am in my drawing room, the only difference being that I have not my good wife's company even as I know how glad she would have been to share my lot, but hers must be a life of sacrifice also, painful though it be. When my life is fully given for the cause, and she is left behind, I trust that you will give her the consideration that is due a faithful and devoted wife, who gave up her husband for the cause of human service. During my trial cowards tried to blemish her character, but it is an accepted truth that character is not blemished from without; it is from within, and the noblest souls that ever peopled this world were those maligned and outraged by the vile and wicked.

13   "Service to my race is an undying passion with me, so the greater the persecution, the greater my determination to serve.

14   "As leader of the Universal Negro Improvement Association, of which the Black Star Line was an auxiliary, I must state that the millions of our members in this country and abroad look to America as a national friend, and, citizens and residents as we are, we are

jealous of her fair name among the other nations of the world and zealous in the effort to be to her loyal and true.

15   "The Universal Negro Improvement Association seeks to do for Africa similarly what the Pilgrims and, later George Washington sought to do for America. We Negroes want a government of our own in Africa, so that we can be nationally, if not industrially and commercially, removed from competition in race, a condition that will make both races better friends, with malice toward none, but respect and appreciation for each.

16   "Our greatest trouble, however, is with our own people. There are some in the race who are not in sympathy with an independent Negro nation. To them 'they have lost nothing in Africa.' They believe in the amalgamation of races for the production of new racial and national types; hence their doctrine of social equality and the creating of a new American race Feeling as they do, divides us into two separate and distinct schools of thought, and, apparently, we are now at war with each other, and they have gained the first victory in having me (through their misrepresentation) indicted and convicted for the purpose of rendering me *hors de combat*.

17   "We who believe in race purity are going to fight the issue out for the salvation of both races, and this can only be satisfactorily done when we have established for the Negro a nation of his own. We believe that the white race should protect itself against racial contamination, and the Negro should do the same. Nature intended us morally (and may I not say socially?) apart, otherwise there never would have been this difference. Our sins will not make the world better; hence, to us of the Universal Negro Improvement Association the time has come to rebuild our ancient and proud race.

18   "My personal suffering for the program of the Universal Negro Improvement Association is but a drop in the bucket of sacrifice. To correct the evils surrounding our racial existence is to undertake a task as pretentious and difficult as dividing the sea or uprooting the Rock of Gibraltar; but, with the grace of God, all things are possible, for in truth there is prophecy that 'Ethiopia shall stretch forth her hand, and Princes shall come out of Egypt.'

19   "We are expecting the co-operation and support of liberal White America in the promulgation of the ideal of race purity, and the founding of a nation for Negroes in Africa, so that those who, after proper industrial and other adjustments, desire to return to their original native homeland can do so in peace and security.

20   "Now that the world is readjusting itself and political changes and distributions are being made of the earth's surface, there is absolutely no reason why certain parts of Africa should not be set aside absolutely for the Negro race as our claim and heritage. If this is not done, then we may as well look forward to eternal confusion among the races.

SUPERSTATE FOR NEGROES.

21   "Negro men will never always feel satisfied with being ruled, governed and dictated to by other races. As in my case, I would never feel absolutely satisfied with being tried and judged by a white judge, district attorney and jury, for it is impossible for them to correctly interpret the real feelings of my race and appreciate my effort in their behalf; hence, the prejudice from which I suffer. A white man before a black district attorney, judge and jury would feel the same way, and thus we have the great problem that can only be solved by giving the Negro a government of his own. The Black Star Line was an effort in this direction and bore a relationship to the Universal Negro Improvement Association as the Shipping Board does to the Government. My effort was not correctly understood, and that is why some people have become prejudiced toward me. Yet in the final presentation of truth the fair-minded is bound to come to the conclusion that the program of the Universal Negro Improvement Association is reasonable and proper for the solution of the vexed question of races.

Malcolm X

(1925–1965)

Named Malcolm Little upon his birth in Omaha, Nebraska, on May 19, 1925, Malcolm X, also known by his Arabic name of El-Hajj Malik El-Shabazz, is among the most important orators, intellectuals, and autobiographers to emerge on the world scene in the latter half of the twentieth century. His father, Earl Little, a minister influenced by Marcus Garvey, was killed under mysterious circumstances, some suggest by white supremacists. His mother, Louise Little, could not thrive under the strain of raising her children amid poverty and racism; she eventually spent 25 years in a mental institution. Malcolm X (the X represents the unknown surnames of his African ancestors) spent time in Lansing, Michigan, before moving to Roxbury, Massachusetts, to live with his sister Ella. He became attracted to hustling, and, shuffling between Roxbury and Harlem, he engaged in several illegal enterprises. In 1946, he was sent to prison in Massachusetts for a series of house burglaries. Embarking upon an ambitious program of self-improvement while incarcerated, he read voraciously and honed his speaking skills, at one point leading a prison debate team to victory over a team from the Massachusetts Institute of Technology. Having embraced Islam during his stay in prison, Malcolm X, upon his release, worked for Elijah Muhammad's organization, eventually becoming the Nation of Islam's national spokesperson. After making what Elijah Muhammad considered to be intemperate remarks following the assassination of President Kennedy, Malcolm X was relieved by Muhammad of most of his responsibilities. During this period, Malcolm X announced his departure from the Nation of Islam, a split that may have been inevitable given his intellectual curiosity and his concerns about the moral conduct of Nation of Islam leadership. In the spring of 1964, he formed the Organization of Afro-American Unity, his attempt to lead a secular political movement that would be driven by principles of Black Nationalism. Malcolm X was assassinated on February 21, 1965, as he prepared to deliver a speech at the Audobon Ballroom in New York City. Members of the Nation of Islam were convicted of the murder. The speeches of Malcolm X, who was undoubtedly the greatest inspiration for Black Power activists and artists in the 1960s and 1970s, have been collected in such volumes as Malcolm X Speaks *(1965),* By Any Means Necessary *(1970), and* The End of White World Supremacy *(1971). The* Autobiography of Malcolm X, *which he composed with the assistance of Alex Haley, was released posthumously in 1965. The version of "The Black Revolution" included in this chapter was delivered at the Abyssinian Baptist Church in Harlem. The enclosed version of "The Ballot or the Bullet" was delivered at Cory Methodist Church in Cleveland.*

The Black Revolution

1   Malcolm X: Dr. Powell, distinguished guests, brothers and sisters, friends, and even our enemies. As a follower and minister of The Honorable Elijah Muhammad, who is the Messenger of Allah to the American so-called Negro, I am very happy to accept Dr. Powell's invitation to be here this evening at the Abyssinian Baptist Church and to express or at least to try to represent The Honorable Elijah Muhammad's views on this most timely topic, the black revolution.

2   First, however, there are some questions we have to put to you. Since the black masses here in America are now in open revolt against the American system of segregation, will these same black masses turn toward integration or will they turn toward complete separation? Will these awakened black masses demand integration into the white society that enslaved them or will they demand complete separation from that cruel white society that has enslaved them? Will the exploited and oppressed black masses seek integration with their white exploiters and white oppressors or will these awakened black masses truly revolt and separate themselves completely from this wicked race that has enslaved us?

3   These are just some quick questions that I think will provoke some thoughts in your minds and my mind. How can the so-called Negroes who call themselves enlightened leaders expect the poor black sheep to integrate into a society of bloodthirsty white wolves, white wolves who have already been sucking on our blood for over four hundred years here in America? Or will these black sheep also revolt against the "false shepherd," the handpicked Uncle Tom Negro leader, and seek complete separation so that we can escape from the den of the wolves rather than be integrated with wolves in this wolves' den? And since we are in church and most of us here profess to believe in God, there is another question: When the "good shepherd" comes will he integrate his long-lost sheep with white wolves? According to the Bible when God comes he won't even let his sheep integrate with goats. And if his sheep can't be safely integrated with goats they certainly aren't safe integrated with wolves. The Honorable Elijah Muhammad teaches us that no people on earth fit the Bible's symbolic picture about the Lost Sheep more so than America's twenty million so-called Negroes and there has never in history been a more vicious and blood-thirsty wolf than the American white man. He teaches us that for four hundred years America has been nothing but a wolves' den for twenty million so-called Negroes, twenty million second-class citizens, and this black revolution that is developing against the white wolf today is developing because The Honorable Elijah Muhammad, a godsent shepherd, has opened the eyes of our people. And the black masses can now see that we have all been here in this white doghouse long, too long. The black masses don't want segregation nor do we want integration. What we want is complete separation. In short, we don't want to be segregated by the white man, we don't want to be integrated with the white man, we want to be separated from the white man. And now our religious leader and teacher, The Honorable

Elijah Muhammad, teaches us that this is the only intelligent and lasting solution to the present race problem. In order to fully understand why the Muslim followers of The Honorable Elijah Muhammad actually reject hypocritical promises of integration it must first be understood by everyone that we are a religious group, and as a religious group we can in no way be equated or compared to the non-religious civil rights groups. We are Muslims because we believe in Allah. We are Muslims because we practice the religion of Islam. The Honorable Elijah Muhammad teaches us that there is but one God, the creator and sustainer of the entire universe, the all-wise, all-powerful Supreme Being. The great God whose proper name is Allah. The Honorable Elijah Muhammad also teaches us that Islam is an Arabic word that means "complete submission to the will of Allah or obedience to the God of truth, God of peace, the God of righteousness, the God whose proper name is Allah." And he teaches us that the word Muslim is used to describe one who submits to God, one who obeys God. In other words a Muslim is one who strives to live a life of righteousness. You may ask what does the religion of Islam have to do with the American so-called Negro's changing attitude toward himself, toward the white man, toward segregation, toward integration, and toward separation, and what part will this religion of Islam play in the current black revolution that is sweeping the American continent today? The Honorable Elijah Muhammad teaches us that Islam is the religion of naked truth, naked truth, undressed truth, truth that is not dressed up, and he says that truth is the only thing that will truly set our people free. Truth will open our eyes and enable us to see the white wolf as he really is. Truth will stand us on our own feet. Truth will make us walk for ourselves instead of leaning on others who mean our people no good. Truth not only shows us who our real enemy is, truth also gives us the strength and the know-how to separate ourselves from that enemy. Only a blind man will walk into the open embrace of his enemy, and only a blind people, a people who are blind to the truth about their enemies, will seek to embrace or integrate with that enemy. Why, Jesus himself prophesied. You shall know the truth and it shall make you free. Beloved brothers and sisters, Jesus never said that Abraham Lincoln would make us free. He never said that the Congress would make us free. He never said that the Senate or Supreme Court or John Kennedy would make us free. Jesus two thousand years ago looked down the wheel of time and saw your and my plight here today and he knew the tricky high court, Supreme Court, desegregation decisions would only lull you into a deeper sleep, and the tricky promises of the hypocritical politicians on civil rights legislation would only be designed to advance you and me from ancient slavery to modern slavery. But Jesus did prophesy that when Elijah comes in the spirit and power of truth he said that Elijah would teach you the truth. Elijah would guide you with truth and Elijah would protect you with truth and make you free indeed. And brothers and sisters, that Elijah, the one whom Jesus has said was to come, has come and is in America today in the person of The Honorable Elijah Muhammad.

4   This Elijah, the one whom they said was to come and who has come, teaches those of us who are Muslims that our white slave masters have always known the truth and they have always known that truth alone would set us free. Therefore this same American white man kept the truth hidden from our people. He kept us in the darkness of ignorance. He made us spiritually blind by depriving us of the light of truth. During the four hundred years that we have spent confined to the darkness of ignorance here in this land of bondage, our American enslavers have given us an overdose of their own white-controlled Christian religion, but have kept all other religions hidden from us, especially the religion of Islam. And for this reason, Almighty God Allah, the God of our forefathers, has raised The Honorable Elijah Muhammad from the midst of our downtrodden people here in America. And this same God has missioned The Honorable Elijah Muhammad to spread the naked truth to America's twenty million so-called Negroes, and the truth alone will make you and me free.

5   The Honorable Elijah Muhammad teaches us that there is but one God whose proper name is Allah, and one religion, the religion of Islam, and that this one God will not rest until he has used his religion to establish one world—a universal, one-world brotherhood. But in order to set up his righteous world God must first bring down this wicked white world. The black revolution against the injustices of the white world is all part of God's divine plan. God must destroy the world of slavery and evil in order to establish a world based upon freedom, justice, and equality. The followers of The Honorable Elijah Muhammad religiously believe that we are living at the end of this wicked world, the world of colonialism, the world of slavery, the end of the Western world, the white world or the Christian world, or the end of the wicked white man's Western world of Christianity.

6   The Honorable Elijah Muhammad teaches us that the symbolic stories in all religious scriptures paint a prophetic picture of today. He says that the Egyptian House of Bondage was only a prophetic picture of

America. Mighty Babylon was only a prophetic picture of America. The wicked cities of Sodom and Gomorrah painted only a prophetic picture of America. No one here in this church tonight can deny that America is the mightiest government on earth today, the mightiest, the richest, and the wickedest. And no one in this church tonight dare deny that America's wealth and power stemmed from 310 years of slave labor contributed from the American so-called Negro.

7   The Honorable Elijah Muhammad teaches us that these same so-called American Negroes are God's long-lost people who are symbolically described in the Bible as the Lost Sheep or the Lost Tribe of Israel. We who are Muslims believe in God, we believe in his scriptures, we believe in prophecy. Nowhere in the scriptures did God ever integrate his enslaved people with their slave masters. God always separates his oppressed people from their oppressor and then destroys the oppressor. God has never deviated from his divine pattern in the past and The Honorable Elijah Muhammad says that God will not deviate from that divine pattern today. Just as God destroyed the enslavers in the past, God is going to destroy this wicked white enslaver of our people here in America.

8   God wants us to separate ourselves from this wicked white race here in America because this American House of Bondage is number one on God's list for divine destruction today. I repeat: This American House of Bondage is number one on God's list for divine destruction today. He warns us to remember Noah never taught integration, Noah taught separation; Moses never taught integration, Moses taught separation. The innocent must always be given a chance to separate themselves from the guilty before the guilty are executed. No one is more innocent than the poor, blind, American so-called Negro who has been led astray by blind Negro leaders, and no one on earth is more guilty than the blue-eyed white man who has used his control and influence over the Negro leader to lead the rest of our people astray.

9   Beloved brothers and sisters here, a beautiful here at the Abyssinian Baptist Church in Harlem, because of America's evil deeds against the so-called Negroes, like Egypt and Babylon before her, America herself now stands before the bar of justice. America herself is now facing her day of judgment, and she can't escape because God Himself is the judge. If America can't atone for the crimes she has committed against the twenty million so-called Negroes, if she can't undo the evils that she has brutally and mercilessly heaped upon our people these past four hundred years, The Honorable Elijah Muhammad says that America has signed her own doom. And you, our people,

would be foolish to accept her deceitful offers of integration at this late date into her doomed society.

10   Can America escape? Can America atone? And if so how can she atone for these crimes? In my conclusion I must point out that The Honorable Elijah Muhammad says a desegregated theater, a desegregated lunch counter won't solve our problem. Better jobs won't solve our problems. An integrated cup of coffee isn't sufficient pay for four hundred years of slave labor. He also says that a better job, a better job in the white man's factory, or a better job in the white man's business, or a better job in the white man's industry or economy is, at best, only a temporary solution. He says that the only lasting and permanent solution is complete separation on some land that we can call our own. Therefore, The Honorable Elijah Muhammad says that this problem can be solved and solved forever just by sending our people back to our own homeland or back to our own people, but that this government should provide the transportation plus everything else we need to get started again in our own country. This government should give us everything we need in the form of machinery, material, and finance—enough to last for twenty to twenty-five years until we can become an independent people and an independent nation in our own land. He says that if the American government is afraid to send us back to our own country and to our own people, then America should set aside some separated territory right here in the Western hemisphere where the two races can live apart from each other, since we certainly don't get along peacefully while we are together.

11   The Honorable Elijah Muhammad says that the size of the territory can be judged according to our population. If a seventh of the population of this country is black, then give us a seventh of the territory, a seventh part of the country. And that is not asking too much because we already worked for the man for four hundred years.

12   He says it must not be in the desert, but where there is plenty of rain and much mineral wealth. We want fertile, productive land on which we can farm and provide our own people with food, clothing, and shelter. He says that this government should supply us on that territory with the machinery and other tools needed to dig into the earth. Give us everything we need for twenty to twenty-five years until we can produce and supply our own needs.

13   And in my conclusion I repeat: We want no part of integration with this wicked race that enslaved us. We want complete separation from this wicked race of devils. But he also says we should not be expected

to leave America empty-handed. After four hundred years of slave labor, we have some back pay coming. A bill that is owed to us and must be collected. If the government of America truly repents of its sins against our people and atones by giving us our true share of the land and the wealth, then America can save herself. But if America waits for God to step in and force her to make a just settlement, God will take this entire continent away from the white man. And the Bible says that God can then give the kingdom to whomsoever he pleases. I thank you.

The Ballot or the Bullet

1   Mr. Moderator, Brother Lomax, brothers and sisters, friends and enemies: I just can't believe everyone in here is a friend and I don't want to leave anybody out. The question tonight, as I understand it, is "The Negro Revolt, and Where Do We Go From Here?" or "What Next?" In my little humble way of understanding it, it points toward either the ballot or the bullet.

2   Before we try and explain what is meant by the ballot or the bullet, I would like to clarify something concerning myself. I'm still a Muslim, my religion is still Islam. That's my personal belief. Just as Adam Clayton Powell is a Christian minister who heads the Abyssinian Baptist Church in New York, but at the same time takes part in the political struggles to try and bring about rights to the black people in this country; and Dr. Martin Luther King is a Christian minister down in Atlanta, Georgia, who heads another organization fighting for the civil rights of black people in this country; and Rev. Galamison, I guess you've heard of him, is another Christian minister in New York who has been deeply involved in the school boycotts to eliminate segregated education; well, I myself am a minister, not a Christian minister, but a Muslim minister; and I believe in action on all fronts by whatever means necessary.

3   Although I'm still a Muslim, I'm not here tonight to discuss my religion. I'm not here to try and change your religion. I'm not here to argue or discuss anything that we differ about, because it's time for us to submerge our differences and realize that it is best for us to first see that we have the same problem, a common problem—a problem that will make you catch hell whether you're a Baptist, or a

Methodist, or a Muslim, or a nationalist. Whether you're educated or illiterate, whether you live on the boulevard or in the alley, you're going to catch hell just like I am. We're all in the same boat and we all are going to catch the same hell from the same man. He just happens to be a white man. All of us have suffered here, in this country, political oppression at the hands of the white man, economic exploitation at the hands of the white man, and social degradation at the hands of the white man.

4   Now in speaking like this, it doesn't mean that we're anti-white, but it does mean we're anti-exploitation, we're anti-degradation, we're anti-oppression. And if the white man doesn't want us to be anti-him, let him stop oppressing and exploiting and degrading us. Whether we are Christians or Muslims or nationalists or agnostics or atheists, we must first learn to forget our differences. If we have differences, let us differ in the closet; when we come out in front, let us not have anything to argue about until we get finished arguing with the man. If the late President Kennedy could get together with Khrushchev and exchange some wheat, we certainly have more in common with each other than Kennedy and Khrushchev had with each other.

5   If we don't do something real soon, I think you'll have to agree that we're going to be forced either to use the ballot or the bullet. It's one or the other in 1964. It isn't that time is running out—time has run out! 1964 threatens to be the most explosive year America has ever witnessed. The most explosive year. Why? It's also a political year. It's the year when all of the white politicians will be back in the so-called Negro community jiving you and me for some votes. The year when all of the white political crooks will be right back in your and my community with their false promises, building up our hopes for a letdown, with their trickery and their treachery, with their false promises which they don't intend to keep. As they nourish these dissatisfactions, it can only lead to one thing, an explosion; and now we have the type of black man on the scene in America today—I'm sorry, Brother Lomax—who just doesn't intend to turn the other cheek any longer.

6   Don't let anybody tell you anything about the odds are against you. If they draft you, they send you to Korea and make you face 800 million Chinese. If you can be brave over there, you can be brave right here. These odds aren't as great as those odds. And if you fight here, you will at least know what you're fighting for.

7   I'm not a politician, not even a student of politics; in fact, I'm not a student of much of anything. I'm not a Democrat, I'm not a Republican, and I don't even consider myself an American. If you and I were

Americans, there'd be no problem. Those Hunkies that just got off the boat, they're already Americans; Polacks are already Americans; the Italian refugees are already Americans. Everything that came out of Europe, every blue-eyed thing, is already an American. And as long as you and I have been over here, we aren't Americans yet.

8   Well, I am one who doesn't believe in deluding myself. I'm not going to sit at your table and watch you eat, with nothing on my plate, and call myself a diner. Sitting at the table doesn't make you a diner, unless you eat some of what's on that plate. Being here in America doesn't make you an American. Being born here in America doesn't make you an American. Why, if birth made you American, you wouldn't need any legislation, you wouldn't need any amendments to the Constitution, you wouldn't be faced with civil-rights filibustering in Washington, D. C., right now. They don't have to pass civil-rights legislation to make a Polack an American.

9   No, I'm not an American. I'm one of the 22 million black people who are the victims of Americanism. One of the 22 million black people who are the victims of democracy, nothing but disguised hypocrisy. So, I'm not standing here speaking to you as an American, or a patriot, or a flag-saluter, or a flag-waver—no, not I. I'm speaking as a victim of this American system. And I see America through the eyes of the victim. I don't see any American dream: I see an American nightmare.

10   These 22 million victims are waking up. Their eyes are coming open. They're beginning to see what they used to only look at. They're becoming politically mature. They are realizing that there are new political trends from coast to coast. As they see these new political trends, it's possible for them to see that every time there's an election the races are so close that they have to have a recount. They had to recount in Massachusetts to see who was going to be governor, it was so close. It was the same way in Rhode Island, in Minnesota, and in many other parts of the country. And the same with Kennedy and Nixon when they ran for president. It was so close they had to count all over again. Well, what does this mean? It means that when white people are evenly divided, and black people have a bloc of votes of their own, it is left up to them to determine who's going to sit in the White House and who's going to be in the dog house.

11   It was the black man's vote that put the present administration in Washington, D.C. Your vote, your dumb vote, your ignorant vote, your wasted vote put in an administration in Washington, D.C., that

has seen fit to pass every kind of legislation imaginable, saving you until last, then filibustering on top of that. And your and my leaders have the audacity to run around clapping their hands and talk about how much progress we're making. And what a good president we have. If he wasn't good in Texas, he sure can't be good in Washington, D.C. Because Texas is a lynch state. It is in the same breath as Mississippi no different; only they lynch you in Texas with a Texas accent and lynch you in Mississippi with a Mississippi accent. And these Negro leaders have the audacity to go and have some coffee in the White House with a Texan, a Southern cracker—that's all he is—and then come out and tell you and me that he's going to be better for us because, since he's from the South, he knows how to deal with the Southerners. What kind of logic is that? Let Eastland be president, he's from the South too. He should be better able to deal with them than Johnson.

12   In this present administration they have in the House of Representatives 257 Democrats to only 177 Republicans. They control two-thirds of the House vote. Why can't they pass something that will help you and me? In the Senate, there are 67 senators who are of the Democratic Party. Only 33 of them are Republicans. Why, the Democrats have got the government sewed up, and you're the one who sewed it up for them. And what have they given you for it? Four years in office, and just now getting around to some civil-rights legislation. Just now, after everything else is gone, out of the way, they're going to sit down now and play with you all summer long—the same old giant con game that they call filibuster. All those are in cahoots together. Don't you ever think they're not in cahoots together, for the man that is heading the civil-rights filibuster is a man from Georgia named Richard Russell. When Johnson became president, the first man he asked for when he got back to Washington, D.C., was "Dicky"—that's how tight they are. That's his boy, that's his pal, that's his buddy. But they're playing that old con game. One of them makes believe he's for you, and he's got it fixed where the other one is so tight against you, he never has to keep his promise.

13   So it's time in 1964 to wake up. And when you see them coming up with that kind of conspiracy, let them know your eyes are open. And let them know you got something else that's wide open too. It's got to be the ballot or the bullet. The ballot or the bullet. If you're afraid to use an expression like that, you should get on out of the country, you should get back in the cotton patch, you should get back in the alley. They get all the Negro vote, and after

they get it, the Negro gets nothing in return. All they did when they got to Washington was give a few big Negroes big jobs. Those big Negroes didn't need big jobs, they already had jobs. That's camouflage, that's trickery, that's treachery, window-dressing. I'm not trying to knock out the Democrats for the Republicans, we'll get to them in a minute. But it is true—you put the Democrats first and the Democrats put you last.

14   Look at it the way it is. What alibis do they use, since they control Congress and the Senate? What alibi do they use when you and I ask, "Well, when are you going to keep your promise?" They blame the Dixiecrats. What is a Dixiecrat? A Democrat, A Dixiecrat is nothing but a Democrat in disguise. The titular head of the Democrats is also the head of the Dixiecrats, because the Dixiecrats are a part of the Democratic Party. The Democrats have never kicked the Dixiecrats out of the party. The Dixiecrats bolted themselves once, but the Democrats didn't put them out. Imagine, these lowdown Southern segregationists put the Northern Democrats down. But the Northern Democrats have never put the Dixiecrats down. No, look at that thing the way it is. They have got a con game going on, a political con game, and you and I are in the middle. It's time for you and me to wake up and start looking at it like it is, and trying to understand it like it is; and then we can deal with it like it is.

15   The Dixiecrats in Washington, D.C., control the key committees that run the government. The only reason the Dixiecrats control these committees is because they have seniority. The only reason they have seniority is because they come from states where Negroes can't vote. This is not even a government that's based on democracy. It is not a government that is made up of representatives of the people. Half of the people in the South can't even vote. Eastland is not even supposed to be in Washington. Half of the senators and congressmen who occupy these key positions in Washington, D.C., are there illegally, are there unconstitutionally.

16   I was in Washington, D.C., a week ago Thursday, when they were debating whether or not they should let the bill come onto the floor. And in the back of the room where the Senate meets, there's a huge map of the United States, and on that map it shows the location of Negroes throughout the country. And it shows that the Southern section of the country, the states that are most heavily concentrated with Negroes, are the ones that have senators and congressmen standing up filibustering and doing all other kinds of trickery to keep the Negro from being able to vote. This is pitiful. But it's not pitiful for us any

longer; it's actually pitiful for the white man, because soon now, as the Negro awakens a little more and sees the vise that he's in, sees the bag that he's in, sees the real game that he's in, then the Negro's going to develop a new tactic.

17 These senators and congressmen actually violate the constitutional amendments that guarantee the people of that particular state or county the right to vote. And the Constitution itself has within it the machinery to expel any representative from a state where the voting rights of the people are violated. You don't even need new legislation. Any person in Congress right now, who is there from a state or a district where the voting rights of the people are violated, that particular person should be expelled from Congress. And when you expel him, you've removed one of the obstacles in the path of any real meaningful legislation in this country. In fact, when you expel them, you don't need new legislation, because they will be replaced by black representatives from counties and districts where the black man is in the majority, not in the minority.

18 If the black man in these Southern states had his full voting rights, the key Dixiecrats in Washington, D.C., which means the key Democrats in Washington, D.C., would lose their seats. The Democratic Party itself would lose its power. It would cease to be powerful as a party. When you see the amount of power that would be lost by the Democratic Party if it were to lose the Dixiecrat wing, or branch, or element, you can see where it's against the interests of the Democrats to give voting rights to Negroes in states where the Democrats have been in complete power and authority ever since the Civil War. You just can't belong to that party without analyzing it.

19 I say again, I'm not anti-Democrat, I'm not anti-Republican, I'm not anti-anything. I'm just questioning their sincerity, and some of the strategy that they've been using on our people by promising them promises that they don't intend to keep. When you keep the Democrats in power, you're keeping the Dixiecrats in power. I doubt that my good Brother Lomax will deny that. A vote for a Democrat is a vote for a Dixiecrat. That's why, in 1964, it's time now for you and me to become more politically mature and realize what the ballot is for; what we're supposed to get when we cast a ballot; and that if we don't cast a ballot, it's going to end up in a situation where we're going to have to cast a bullet. It's either a ballot or a bullet.

20 In the North, they do it a different way. They have a system that's known as gerrymandering, whatever that means. It means when Negroes become too heavily concentrated in a certain area,

and begin to gain too much political power, the white man comes along and changes the district lines. You may say, "Why do you keep saying white man?" Because it's the white man who does it. I haven't ever seen any Negro changing any lines. They don't let him get near the line. It's the white man who does this. And usually, it's the white man who grins at you the most, and pats you on the back, and is supposed to be your friend. He may be friendly, but he's not your friend.

21   So, what I'm trying to impress upon you, in essence, is this: You and I in America are faced not with a segregationist conspiracy, we're faced with a government conspiracy. Everyone who's filibustering is a senator—that's the government. Everyone who's finagling in Washington, D.C., is a congressman—that's the government. You don't have anybody putting blocks in your path but people who are a part of the government. The same government that you go abroad to fight for and die for is the government that is in a conspiracy to deprive you of your voting rights, deprive you of your economic opportunities, deprive you of decent housing, deprive you of decent education. You don't need to go to the employer alone, it is the government itself, the government of America, that is responsible for the oppression and exploitation and degradation of black people in this country. And you should drop it in their lap. This government has failed the Negro. This so-called democracy has failed the Negro. And all these white liberals have definitely failed the Negro.

22   So, where do we go from here? First, we need some friends. We need some new allies. The entire civil-rights struggle needs a new interpretation, a broader interpretation. We need to look at this civil-rights thing from another angle—from the inside as well as from the outside. To those of us whose philosophy is black nationalism, the only way you can get involved in the civil-rights struggle is give it a new interpretation. That old interpretation excluded us. It kept us out. So, we're giving a new interpretation to the civil-rights struggle, an interpretation that will enable us to come into it, take part in it. And these handkerchief-heads who have been dillydallying and pussyfooting and compromising—we don't intend to let them pussyfoot and dillydally and compromise any longer.

23   How can you thank a man for giving you what's already yours? How then can you thank him for giving you only part of what's already yours? You haven't even made progress, if what's being given to you, you should have had already. That's not progress. And I love my Brother Lomax, the way he pointed out we're right back where

we were in 1954. We're not even as far up as we were in 1954. We're behind where we were in 1954. There's more segregation now than there was in 1954. There's more racial animosity, more racial hatred, more racial violence today in 1964, than there was in 1954. Where is the progress?

24   And now you're facing a situation where the young Negro's coming up. They don't want to hear that "turn-the-other-cheek" stuff, no. In Jacksonville, those were teenagers, they were throwing Molotov cocktails. Negroes have never done that before. But it shows you there's a new deal coming in. There's new thinking coming in. There's new strategy coming in. It'll be Molotov cocktails this month, hand grenades next month, and something else next month. It'll be ballots, or it'll be bullets. It'll be liberty, or it will be death. The only difference about this kind of death—it'll be reciprocal. You know what is meant by "reciprocal"? That's one of Brother Lomax's words, I stole it from him. I don't usually deal with those big words because I don't usually deal with big people. I deal with small people. I find you can get a whole lot of small people and whip hell out of a whole lot of big people. They haven't got anything to lose, and they've got everything to gain. And they'll let you know in a minute: "It takes two to tango; when I go, you go."

25   The black nationalists, those whose philosophy is black nationalism, in bringing about this new interpretation of the entire meaning of civil rights, look upon it as meaning, as Brother Lomax has pointed out, equality of opportunity. Well, we're justified in seeking civil rights, if it means equality of opportunity, because all we're doing there is trying to collect for our investment. Our mothers and fathers invested sweat and blood. Three hundred and ten years we worked in this country without a dime in return—I mean without a *dime* in return. You let the white man walk around here talking about how rich this country is, but you never stop to think how it got rich so quick. It got rich because you made it rich.

26   You take the people who are in this audience right now. They're poor, we're all poor as individuals. Our weekly salary individually amounts to hardly anything. But if you take the salary of everyone in here collectively it'll fill up a whole lot of baskets. It's a lot of wealth. If you can collect the wages of just these people right here for a year, you'll be rich—richer than rich. When you look at it like that, think how rich Uncle Sam had to become, not with this handful, but millions of black people. Your and my mother and father, who didn't work an eight-hour shift, but worked from "can't see" in the

morning until "can't see" at night, and worked for nothing, making the white man rich, making Uncle Sam rich.

27   This is our investment. This is our contribution—our blood. Not only did we give of our free labor, we gave of our blood. Every time he had a call to arms, we were the first ones in uniform. We died on every battlefield the white man had. We have made a greater sacrifice than anybody who's standing up in America today. We have made a greater contribution and have collected less. Civil rights, for those of us whose philosophy is black nationalism, means: "Give it to us now. Don't wait for next year. Give it to us yesterday, and that's not fast enough."

28   I might stop right here to point out one thing. Whenever you're going after something that belongs to you, anyone who's depriving you of the right to have it is a criminal. Understand that. Whenever you are going after something that is yours, you are within your legal rights to lay claim to it. And anyone who puts forth any effort to deprive you of that which is yours, is breaking the law, is a criminal. And this was pointed out by the Supreme Court decision. It outlawed segregation. Which means segregation is against the law. Which means a segregationist is breaking the law. A segregationist is a criminal. You can't label him as anything other than that. And when you demonstrate against segregation, the law is on your side. The Supreme Court is on your side.

29   Now, who is it that opposes you in carrying out the law? The police department itself. With police dogs and clubs. Whenever you demonstrate against segregation, whether it is segregated education, segregated housing, or anything else, the law is on your side, and anyone who stands in the way is not the law any longer. They are breaking the law, they are not representatives of the law. Any time you demonstrate against segregation and a man has the audacity to put a police dog on you, kill that dog, kill him, I'm telling you, kill that dog. I say it, if they put me in jail tomorrow, kill—that—dog. Then you'll put a stop to it. Now, if these white people in here don't want to see that kind of action, get down and tell the mayor to tell the police department to pull the dogs in. That's all you have to do. If you don't do it, someone else will.

30   If you don't take this kind of stand, your little children will grow up and look at you and think "shame." If you don't take an uncompromising stand—I don't mean go out and get violent; but at the same time you should never be nonviolent unless you run into some nonviolence. I'm nonviolent with those who are nonviolent with me. But

when you drop that violence on me, then you've made me go insane, and I'm not responsible for what I do. And that's the way every Negro should get. Any time you know you're within the law, within your legal rights, within your moral rights, in accord with justice, then die for what you believe in. But don't die alone. Let your dying be reciprocal. This is what is meant by equality. What's good for the goose is good for the gander.

31   When we begin to get in this area, we need new friends, we need new allies. We need to expand the civil-rights struggle to a higher level—to the level of human rights. Whenever you are in a civil-rights struggle, whether you know it or not, you are confining yourself to the jurisdiction of Uncle Sam. No one from the outside world can speak out in your behalf as long as your struggle is a civil-rights struggle. Civil rights comes within the domestic affairs of this country. All of our African brothers and our Asian brothers and our Latin-American brothers cannot open their mouths and interfere in the domestic affairs of the United States. And as long as it's civil rights, this comes under the jurisdiction of Uncle Sam.

32   But the United Nations has what's known as the charter of human rights, it has a committee that deals in human rights. You may wonder why all of the atrocities that have been committed in Africa and in Hungary and in Asia and in Latin America are brought before the UN, and the Negro problem is never brought before the UN. This is part of the conspiracy. This old, tricky, blue-eyed liberal who is supposed to be your and my friend, supposed to be in our corner, supposed to be subsidizing our struggle, and supposed to be acting in the capacity of an adviser, never tells you anything about human rights. They keep you wrapped up in civil rights. And you spend so much time barking up the civil-rights tree, you don't even know there's a human-rights tree on the same floor.

33   When you expand the civil-rights struggle to the level of human rights, you can then take the case of the black man in this country before the nations in the UN. You can take it before the General Assembly. You can take Uncle Sam before a world court. But the only level you can do it on is the level of human rights. Civil rights keeps you under his restrictions, under his jurisdiction. Civil rights keeps you in his pocket. Civil rights means you're asking Uncle Sam to treat you right. Human rights are something you were born with. Human rights are your God-given rights. Human rights are the rights that are recognized by all nations of this earth. And any time any one violates your human rights, you can take them to the world court. Uncle

Sam's hands are dripping with blood, dripping with the blood of the black man in this country. He's the earth's number-one hypocrite. He has the audacity—yes, he has—imagine him posing as the leader of the free world. The free world!—and you over here singing "We Shall Overcome." Expand the civil-rights struggle to the level of human rights, take it into the United Nations, where our African brothers can throw their weight on our side, where our Asian brothers can throw their weight on our side, where our Latin-American brothers can throw their weight on our side, and where 800 million Chinamen are sitting there waiting to throw their weight on our side.

34   Let the world know how bloody his hands are. Let the world know the hypocrisy that's practiced over here. Let it be the ballot or the bullet. Let him know that it must be the ballot or the bullet.

35   When you take your case to Washington, D.C., you're taking it to the criminal who's responsible; it's like running from the wolf to the fox. They're all in cahoots together. They all work political chicanery and make you look like a chump before the eyes of the world. Here you are walking around in America, getting ready to be drafted and sent abroad, like a tin soldier, and when you get over there, people ask you what are you fighting for, and you have to stick your tongue in your cheek. No, take Uncle Sam to court, take him before the world.

36   By ballot I only mean freedom. Don't you know—I disagree with Lomax on this issue—that the ballot is more important than the dollar? Can I prove it? Yes. Look in the UN. There are poor nations in the UN; yet those poor nations can get together with their voting power and keep the rich nations from making a move. They have one nation—one vote, everyone has an equal vote. And when those brothers from Asia, and Africa and the darker parts of this earth get together, their voting power is sufficient to hold Sam in check. Or Russia in check. Or some other section of the earth in check. So, the ballot is most important.

37   Right now, in this country, if you and I, 22 million African-Americans—that's what we are—Africans who are in America. You're nothing but Africans. Nothing but Africans. In fact, you'd get farther calling yourself African instead of Negro. Africans don't catch hell. You're the only one catching hell. They don't have to pass civil-rights bills for Africans. An African can go anywhere he wants right now. All you've got to do is tie your head up. That's right go anywhere you want. Just stop being a Negro. Change your name to Hoogaga-gooba. That'll show you how silly the white man is. You're dealing

with a silly man. A friend of mine who's very dark put a turban on his head and went into a restaurant in Atlanta before they called themselves desegregated. He went into a white restaurant, he sat down, they served him, and he said, "What would happen if a Negro came in here?" And there he's sitting, black as night, but because he had his head wrapped up the waitress looked back at him and says, "Why, there wouldn't no nigger dare come in here."

38   So, you're dealing with a man whose bias and prejudice are making him lose his mind, his intelligence, every day. He's frightened. He looks around and sees what's taking place on this earth, and he sees that the pendulum of time is swinging in your direction. The dark people are waking up. They're losing their fear of the white man. No place where he's fighting right now is he winning. Everywhere he's fighting, he's fighting someone your and my complexion. And they're beating him. He can't win any more. He's won his last battle. He failed to win the Korean War. He couldn't win it. He had to sign a truce. That's a loss. Any time Uncle Sam, with all his machinery for warfare, is held to a draw by some rice-eaters, he's lost the battle. He had to sign a truce. America's not supposed to sign a truce. She's supposed to be bad. But she's not bad any more. She's bad as long as she can use her hydrogen bomb, but she can't use hers for fear Russia might use hers. Russia can't use hers, for fear that Sam might use his. So, both of them are weaponless. They can't use the weapon because each's weapon nullifies the other's. So the only place where action can take place is on the ground. And the white man can't win another war fighting on the ground. Those days are over. The black man knows it, the brown man knows it, the red man knows it, and the yellow man knows it. So they engage him in guerrilla warfare. That's not his style. You've got to have heart to be a guerrilla warrior, and he hasn't got any heart. I'm telling you now.

39   I just want to give you a little briefing on guerrilla warfare because, before you know it, before you know it—It takes heart to be a guerrilla warrior because you're on your own. In conventional warfare you have tanks and a whole lot of other people with you to back you up, planes over your head and all that kind of stuff. But a guerrilla is on his own. All you have is a rifle, some sneakers and a bowl of rice, and that's all you need—and a lot of heart. The Japanese on some of those islands in the Pacific, when the American soldiers landed, one Japanese sometimes could hold the whole army off. He'd just wait until the sun went down, and when the sun went down they were all equal. He would take his little blade and slip from bush to bush,

and from American to American. The white soldiers couldn't cope with that. Whenever you see a white soldier that fought in the Pacific, he has the shakes, he has a nervous condition, because they scared him to death.

40   The same thing happened to the French up in French Indochina. People who just a few years previously were rice farmers got together and ran the heavily-mechanized French army out of Indochina. You don't need it—modern warfare today won't work. This is the day of the guerrilla. They did the same thing in Algeria. Algerians, who were nothing but Bedouins, took a rifle and sneaked off to the hills, and de Gaulle and all of his highfalutin' war machinery couldn't defeat those guerrillas. Nowhere on this earth does the white man win in a guerrilla warfare. It's not his speed. Just as guerrilla warfare is prevailing in Asia and in parts of Africa and in parts of Latin America, you've got to be mighty naive, or you've got to play the black man cheap, if you don't think some day he's going to wake up and find that it's got to be the ballot or the bullet.

41   I would like to say, in closing, a few things concerning the Muslim Mosque, Inc., which we established recently in New York City. It's true we're Muslims and our religion is Islam, but we don't mix our religion with our politics and our economics and our social and civil activities—not any more. We keep our religion in our mosque. After our religious services are over, then as Muslims we become involved in political action, economic action and social and civic action. We become involved with anybody, anywhere, any time and in any manner that's designed to eliminate the evils, the political, economic and social evils that are afflicting the people of our community.

42   The political philosophy of black nationalism means that the black man should control the politics and the politicians in his own community; no more. The black man in the black community has to be re-educated into the science of politics so he will know what politics is supposed to bring him in return. Don't be throwing out any ballots. A ballot is like a bullet. You don't throw your ballots until you see a target, and if that target is not within your reach, keep your ballot in your pocket. The political philosophy of black nationalism is being taught in the Christian church. It's being taught in the NAACP. It's being taught in CORE meetings. It's being taught in SNCC [Student Nonviolent Coordinating Committee] meetings. It's being taught in Muslim meetings. It's being taught where nothing but atheists and agnostics come together. It's being taught everywhere. Black people are fed up with the dillydallying, pussyfooting, compromising

approach that we've been using toward getting our freedom. We want freedom *now*, but we're not going to get it saying "We Shall Overcome." We've got to fight until we overcome.

43   The economic philosophy of black nationalism is pure and simple. It only means that we should control the economy of our community. Why should white people be running all the stores in our community? Why should white people be running the banks of our community? Why should the economy of our community be in the hands of the white Why? If a black man can't move his store into a white community, you tell me why a white man should move his store into a black community. The philosophy of black nationalism involves a re-education program in the black community in regards to economics. Our people have to be made to see that any time you take your dollar out of your community and spend it in a community where you don't live, the community where you live will get poorer and poorer, and the community where you spend your money will get richer and richer. Then you wonder why where you live is always a ghetto or a slum area. And where you and I are concerned, not only do we lose it when we spend it out of the community, but the white man has got all our stores in the community tied up; so that though we spend it in the community, at sundown the man who runs the store takes it over across town somewhere. He's got us in a vise.

44   So the economic philosophy of black nationalism means in every church, in every civic organization, in every fraternal order, it's time now for our people to become conscious of the importance of controlling the economy of our community. If we own the stores, if we operate the businesses, if we try and establish some industry in our own community, then we're developing to the position where we are creating employment for our own kind. Once you gain control of the economy of your own community, then you don't have to picket and boycott and beg some cracker downtown for a job in his business.

45   The social philosophy of black nationalism only means that we have to get together and remove the evils, the vices, alcoholism, drug addiction, and other evils that are destroying the moral fiber of our community. We ourselves have to lift the level of our community, the standard of our community to a higher level, make our own society beautiful so that we will be satisfied in our own social circles and won't be running around here trying to knock our way into a social circle where we're not wanted.

46   So I say, in spreading a gospel such as black nationalism, it is not designed to make the black man re-evaluate the white man—

you know him already—but to make the black man re-evaluate himself. Don't change the white man's mind—you can't change his mind, and that whole thing about appealing to the moral conscience of America—America's conscience is bankrupt. She lost all conscience long time ago. Uncle Sam has no conscience. They don't know what morals are. They don't try and eliminate an evil because it's evil, or because it's illegal, or because it's immoral; they eliminate it only when it threatens their existence. So you're wasting your time appealing to the moral conscience of a bankrupt man like Uncle Sam. If he had a conscience, he'd straighten this thing out with no more pressure being put upon him. So it is not necessary to change the white man's mind. We have to change our own mind. You can't change his mind about us. We've got to change our own minds about each other. We have to see each other with new eyes. We have to see each other as brothers and sisters. We have to come together with warmth so we can develop unity and harmony that's necessary to get this problem solved ourselves. How can we do this? How can we avoid jealousy? How can we avoid the suspicion and the divisions that exist in the community? I'll tell you how.

47   I have watched how Billy Graham comes into a city, spreading what he calls the gospel of Christ, which is only white nationalism. That's what he is. Billy Graham is a white nationalist; I'm a black nationalist. But since it's the natural tendency for leaders to be jealous and look upon a powerful figure like Graham with suspicion and envy, how is it possible for him to come into a city and get all the cooperation of the church leaders? Don't think because they're church leaders that they don't have weaknesses that make them envious and jealous—no, everybody's got it. It's not an accident that when they want to choose a cardinal [as Pope] over there in Rome, they get in a closet so you can't hear them cussing and fighting and carrying on.

48   Billy Graham comes in preaching the gospel of Christ, he evangelizes the gospel, he stirs everybody up, but he never tries to start a church. If he came in trying to start a church, all the churches would be against him. So, he just comes in talking about Christ and tells everybody who gets Christ to go to any church where Christ is; and in this way the church cooperates with him. So we're going to take a page from his book.

49   Our gospel is black nationalism. We're not trying to threaten the existence of any organization, but we're spreading the gospel of black nationalism. Anywhere there's a church that is also preaching and practicing the gospel of black nationalism, join that church. If the

NAACP is preaching and practicing the gospel of black nationalism, join the NAACP. If CORE is spreading and practicing the gospel of black nationalism, join CORE. Join any organization that has a gospel that's for the uplift of the black man. And when you get into it and see them pussyfooting or compromising, pull out of it because that's not black nationalism. We'll find another one.

50 And in this manner, the organizations will increase in number and in quantity and in quality, and by August, it is then our intention to have a black nationalist convention which will consist of delegates from all over the country who are interested in the political, economic and social philosophy of black nationalism. After these delegates convene, we will hold a seminar, we will hold discussions, we will listen to everyone. We want to hear new ideas and new solutions and new answers. And at that time, if we see fit then to form a black nationalist party, we'll form a black nationalist party. If it's necessary to form a black nationalist army, we'll form a black nationalist army. It'll be the ballot or the bullet. It'll be liberty or it'll be death.

51 It's time for you and me to stop sitting in this country, letting some cracker senators, Northern crackers and Southern crackers, sit there in Washington, D.C., and come to a conclusion in their mind that you and I are supposed to have civil rights. There's no white man going to tell me anything about *my* rights. Brothers and sisters, always remember, if it doesn't take senators and congressmen and presidential proclamations to give freedom to the white man, it is not necessary for legislation or proclamation or Supreme Court decisions to give freedom to the black man. You let that white man know, if this is a country of freedom, let it be a country of freedom; and if it's not a country of freedom, change it.

52 We will work with anybody, anywhere, at any time, who is genuinely interested in tackling the problem head-on, nonviolently as long as the enemy is nonviolent, but violent when the enemy gets violent. We'll work with you on the voter-registration drive, we'll work with you on rent strikes, we'll work with you on school boycotts—I don't believe in any kind of integration; I'm not even worried about it because I know you're not going to get it anyway; you're not going to get it because you're afraid to die; you've got to be ready to die if you try and force yourself on the white man, because he'll get just as violent as those crackers in Mississippi, right here in Cleveland. But we will still work with you on the school boycotts because we're against a segregated school system. A segregated school system produces children who, when they graduate, graduate with crippled

minds. But this does not mean that a school is segregated because it's all black. A segregated school means a school that is controlled by people who have no real interest in it whatsoever.

53   Let me explain what I mean. A segregated district or community is a community in which people live, but outsiders control the politics and the economy of that community. They never refer to the white section as a segregated community. It's the all-Negro section that's a segregated community. Why? The white man controls his own school, his own bank, his own economy, his own politics, his own everything, his own community—but he also controls yours. When you're under someone else's control, you're segregated. They'll always give you the lowest or the worst that there is to offer, but it doesn't mean you're segregated just because you have your own. You've got to *control* your own. Just like the white man has control of his, you need to control yours.

54   You know the best way to get rid of segregation? The white man is more afraid of separation than he is of integration. Segregation means that he puts you away from him, but not far enough for you to be out of his jurisdiction; separation means you're gone. And the white man will integrate faster than he'll let you separate. So we will work with you against the segregated school system because it's criminal, because it is absolutely destructive, in every way imaginable, to the minds of the children who have to be exposed to that type of crippling education.

55   Last but not least, I must say this concerning the great controversy over rifles and shotguns. The only thing that I've ever said is that in areas where the government has proven itself either unwilling or unable to defend the lives and the property of Negroes, it's time for Negroes to defend themselves. Article number two of the constitutional amendments provides you and me the right to own a rifle or a shotgun. It is constitutionally legal to own a shotgun or a rifle. This doesn't mean you're going to get a rifle and form battalions and go out looking for white folks, although you'd be within your rights—I mean, you'd be justified; but that would be illegal and we don't do anything illegal. If the white man doesn't want the black man buying rifles and shotguns, then let the government do its job. That's all. And don't let the white man come to you and ask you what you think about what Malcolm says—why, you old Uncle Tom. He would never ask you if he thought you were going to say, "Amen!" No, he is making a Tom out of you.

56   So, this doesn't mean forming rifle clubs and going out looking for people, but it is time, in 1964, if you are a man, to let that man know.

If he's not going to do his job in running the government and providing you and me with the protection that our taxes are supposed to be for, since he spends all those billions for his defense budget, he certainly can't begrudge you and me spending $12 or $15 for a single-shot, or double-action. I hope you understand. Don't go out shooting people, but any time, brothers and sisters, and especially the men in this audience—some of you wearing Congressional Medals of Honor, with shoulders this wide, chests this big, muscles that big— any time you and I sit around and read where they bomb a church and murder in cold blood, not some grownups, but four little girls while they were praying to the same god the white man taught them to pray to, and you and I see the government go down and can't find who did it.

57   Why, this man—he can find Eichmann hiding down in Argentina somewhere. Let two or three American soldiers, who are minding somebody else's business way over in South Vietnam, get killed, and he'll send battleships, sticking his nose in their business. He wanted to send troops down to Cuba and make them have what he calls free elections—this old cracker who doesn't have free elections in his own country. No, if you never see me another time in your life, if I die in the morning, I'll die saying one thing: the ballot or the bullet, the ballot or the bullet.

58   If a Negro in 1964 has to sit around and wait for some cracker senator to filibuster when it comes to the rights of black people, why, you and I should hang our heads in shame. You talk about a march on Washington in 1963, you haven't seen anything. There's some more going down in '64. And this time they're not going like they went last year. They're not going singing "We Shall Overcome." They're not going with white friends. They're not going with placards already painted for them. They're not going with round-trip tickets. They're going with oneway tickets.

59   And if they don't want that non-nonviolent army going down there, tell them to bring the filibuster to a halt. The black nationalists aren't going to wait. Lyndon B. Johnson is the head of the Democratic Party. If he's for civil rights, let him go into the Senate next week and declare himself. Let him go in there right now and declare himself. Let him go in there and denounce the Southern branch of his party. Let him go in there right now and take a moral stand—right now, not later. Tell him, don't wait until election time. If he waits too long, brothers and sisters, he will be responsible for letting a condition develop in this country which will create a climate that

will bring seeds up out of the ground with vegetation on the end of them looking like something these people never dreamed of. In 1964, it's the ballot or the bullet. Thank you.

Haki R. Madhubuti

(1942–)

Haki R. Madhubuti was born on February 23, 1942, in Little Rock, Arkansas, with the name Donald Luther Lee. He grew up in Detroit, Michigan. Although his mother, Maxine Lee, lived a tragic and brief life, she cultivated in her son a love of literature. Generally acknowledged as one of the leading poets of the Black Arts Movement, his most well-known poetry volumes include Think Black *(1966),* Black Pride *(1968),* Don't Cry, Scream *(1969),* We Walk the Way of the New World *(1970), and* GroundWork: New and Selected Poems *(1996). His other books, some of which contain poetry along with nonfiction, include* From Plan to Planet *(1973),* Enemies: The Clash of Races *(1978),* Earthquakes and Sunrise Missions: Poetry and Essays of Black Revival 1973–1983 *(1984),* Black Men: Obsolete, Single, Dangerous? *(1990), and* Claiming Earth: Race, Rage, Redemption *(1994), from which the following reading is taken. Madhubuti, who holds an MFA from the University of Iowa, is a Distinguished Professor of English at Chicago State University.*

Standing as an African Man

BLACK MEN IN A SEA OF WHITENESS

Where do I belong and what is the price I have to pay for being where and who I am?

1 Study the faces of children that look like you. Walk your streets, count the smiles and bright eyes, and make a mental note of their ages. At what age do our children cease to smile naturally, smile full-teeth, uninhibited, expecting full life? At what age will memory of lost friends, and lost relatives, deaden their eyes? Where does childhood stop in much of our community? At seven, eight? How many killings, rapes, beatings, verbal and mental abuse, hustles, get over programs, drug infestations, drive-by shootings/drive-by leaders must they

witness before their eyes dry up for good and their only thought is: "Will I make it to the age of twenty-five?" When the life in the eyes of our children do not gleam brightly with future and hope, we cease being nurturers and become repairers of broken spirits and stolen souls. This is the state we are now in and too often it is too late.

Where do I belong and what is the price I have to pay for being where and who I am?

2 If you don't know, you can't do.

3 Who do we buy our food from? Who do we rent our apartments from? Who do we buy our clothes, furniture, cars, and life bettering needs from? Whose land do we walk, sleep, live, play, work, get high, chase women, lie, steal, produce children and die on? Why is it that 800,000 Black men and 50,000 Black women populated the nation's prisons? Is race a factor in a land where white people control most things of value? Is race a factor in a country where young Black boys and men are dying quicker than their birth rate? When do we declare war on our own destruction? Why is it that the Blacker one is the worse it is? Who taught Black people that killing Black people is all right and sometimes honorable?

This is Our Charge!

4 Study the landscape. Read the music in your hearts. Remember the beauty of mothers, sisters, and the women in our lives that talked good about us. Remember when we talked good about us. Remember when we talked good about them. Understand the importance of ideas.

This is Our Mission!

5 Pick up a book. Challenge the you in you. Rise above the limited expectations of people who do not like you and never will like you. Rise above the self-hatred that slowly eats your heart, mind, and spirit away. Find like-minded brothers. Study together. Talk together. Find each others hearts. Ask the right questions. Why are we poor? Why are our children not educated? Why are our children dying at such an unbelievable rate? Why are we landless? What does land ownership have to do with race? What does wealth have to do with race? Why do we hate being called African and Black? What does Africa mean to me, us? Why is Africa in a state of confusion and civil war?

Why is there no work in our communities? What is the difference between a producer and a consumer? What do we produce that is sold and used world-wide? Whose knowledge is most valuable for the development of Black (African) people? Would I kill myself and others that look like me if I loved myself and those that look like me? Where does self-love come from? Who taught me, us, self-hatred? Is self-hatred an idea? Is self-love an idea? Whose ideas do we tap-dance to? Whose ideas do we impress each other with? Are African (Black) ideas crucial to our discourse and development? Can a Black person be multi-cultural if he/she does not have his/her culture first? When do we declare war on ignorance, intellectual betrayal, self-destruction, pimpism, weakening pleasures, European worldviews, beggar mentalities, and white world supremacy? Is race an idea? When will we use the race idea to benefit us?

Where do I belong and what is the price I have to pay for being where and who I am?

6   We belong among the people worldwide that look like us. We belong to a world where we produce rather than consume. We belong to a world where the measurement of Black beauty and worth is internal and cultural.

7   We belong where our education is not anti-us.

8   We belong among African men who are brothers and brothers who are Africans. How will we recognize them?

You will recognize your brothers
by the way they act and move throughout the world.
there will be a strange force about them,
there will be unspoken answers in them.
this will be obvious not only to you but to many.
the confidence they have in themselves and in
their people will be evident in their quiet saneness.
the way they relate to women will be
clean, complementary, responsible, with honesty and as partners.
the way they relate to children will be
strong and soft full of positive direction and as example.
the way they relate to men
will be that of questioning our position in this world,
will be one of planning for movement and change,
will be one of working for their people,
will be one of gaining and maintaining trust within the culture.

these men at first will seem strange and unusual but
this will not be the case for long.
they will train others and the discipline they display
will become a way of life for many.
they know that this is difficult
but this is the life that they have chosen
for themselves, for us, for life:
they will be the examples.
they will be the answers,
they will be the first line builders,
they will be the creators,
they will be the first to give up the weakening pleasures,
they will be the first to share a black value system,
they will be the workers,
they will be the scholars,
they will be the providers,
they will be the historians,
they will be the doctors, lawyers, farmers, priests
and all that is needed for development and growth.
you will recognize these brothers
and
they will not betray you.

Writing Assignments

1. Last but not least among the complaints that David Walker makes in "Our Wretchedness in Consequence of Ignorance" is that Black schoolboys are often denied instruction in grammar. Discuss how Walker's charge relates to all of the other points he makes, to his position as an author, and to your role as a student.

2. Maria Stewart compares the United States to Babylon relative to the status of people of African descent. Explain in detail whether the Babylon metaphor is appropriate today as a description of the nation.

3. Samuel Delany writes, "To know the condition of a people, it is only necessary to know the condition of their women; and despite themselves, they cannot rise above their level." Explore whether Delany's observation coincides with your own view of history or of the present situation of African Americans?

4. In your estimation, is Du Bois's notion of "double consciousness" as relevant today as it was a century ago? Discuss the ways in which it still rings true or has lost power as a method of analysis.

5. As you consider the works of Delany, Du Bois, Marcus Garvey, Malcolm X, and Haki Madhubuti, which proposals do you find most captivating or most worthy of being implemented today? What are the weaknesses, if any, in the various ideas of these authors?

CHAPTER ELEVEN

STATEMENTS OF FEMINISM

The history of American feminism often has been characterized as the domain of white, middle-class, heterosexual, educated women. However, African American women were a visible presence in the second wave American women's movement, and a look at the early years of American history reveals the enormous role that African American women played in the initial struggle for gender equality. Long before the 1960s and 1970s, women were active in the fight for equal rights (although the participants may not have self-identified as "feminists"), and African American women were a major force in what we now call the first wave feminist movement. Acts of resistance against structures of patriarchy are a central tenet in African American feminism; however, equally strong is the fight for racial and class equality, as Black womanhood is not circumscribed solely by issues of gender. Thus, it is not surprising that early African American feminists were also abolitionists.

During the antislavery movements of the nineteenth century, activists such as Sojourner Truth, Frances E. W. Harper, and Ida B. Wells were dedicated to social reform, and their agendas addressed not only slavery and racism, but also sexism. Sojourner Truth, whose most famous speeches are included in this volume, linked these oppressive systems when she argued: "There is a great stir about colored men getting their rights, but not a word about the colored women; and if colored men get their rights, and not colored women get theirs, you see the colored men will be masters over the women, and it will be just as bad as it was before. . . . I have done a great deal of work; as much as a man, but did not get so much pay." Here, Truth speaks to the economic disadvantage of women and the role that African American men, although victimized by racism, can play in the oppression of women. It is important to note that there is a current debate regarding the veracity of the published accounts of Truth's most famous oration, "Ar'n't I a Woman?" This oral text was first reported in the *Anti-Slavery Bugle* in 1851 and subsequently recorded in a more dialectic and less straightforward manner by Frances Gage (the president of the women's rights convention in Akron, Ohio) in the 1878 edition of Truth's *Narrative of Sojourner Truth*. While the former account is now believed to be more reliable, Gage's version, responsible for having created the famous refrain "ar'n't I a woman?," is the more popular. This controversy raises serious concerns regarding issues of voice, agency, and stereotypical constructs of Black female identity. Nonetheless, the power of Truth's message is timeless and continues to have currency for present-day feminists.

Indeed, more than a century later, bell hooks would label these interlocking forms of oppression "white supremacist capitalist patriarchy" to capture the ways in which gender discrimination functions simultaneously with class and racial subjugation. Furthermore, as hooks explains, the term indicates how all people, regardless of gender and race, can be complicit with these institutionalized forces of oppression. It is noteworthy that Sojourner Truth, an illiterate woman born in the eighteenth century, sounds a similar chord to hooks, one of the leading intellectuals of our time, for it suggests that Black feminist theory is not merely an academic exercise, but is rooted in the historical exigencies of African American women's lives.

The interdependence of gender, race, and class also emerges in Alice Walker's theory of "Womanism," which demarcates the unique life experiences of African American women, historically and presently. Recognizing that there is no monolithic Black female experience, Walker presents a rather open-ended definition of womanism in *In Search of Our Mothers' Gardens* (1983), which by her own account parallels feminism, arguing that "womanist is to feminist, as purple to lavender." Walker explains that this term is rooted in the language and culture of Black America, defining it as follows: "From the black folk expressions of mothers to female children, 'You acting womanish,' i.e. like a woman." She further defines the concept as describing a woman who is "committed to survival and wholeness of entire people, male and female." Like hooks, Walker is intent on establishing a more comprehensive paradigm for gender, racial, class, and sexual parity. Many women of color have opted for this term over "feminism" because of the latter's implicit association with white feminism. In fact, there often has been an uneasy alliance of African American women with the larger white

American feminist movement because of its marginalization of women of color and working-class women from its agendas. Indeed, the treatment of African American women in the movement is illustrated perhaps most profoundly by the initial reaction to Truth's oration at the women's rights convention: the white women in the crowd wanted to prevent Truth from speaking. Efforts like those to silence Truth, which have continued in various forms throughout the twentieth century, suggest to some the necessity of creating a parallel but separate movement.

The idea of difference is a primary concern in one of Audre Lorde's famous speeches, "The Master's Tools Will Never Dismantle the Master's House" (1979). While echoing some of the same concerns posed by other writers in this chapter, Lorde's impassioned plea calls for a new paradigm of interracial women's coalitions—one predicated not on a patriarchal standard that rejects or elides the very material differences of race, class, sexuality, and age, but rather on a recognition that these differences represent a strength of the women's movement. Lorde writes, "The failure of academic feminists to recognize difference as a crucial strength is a failure to reach beyond the first patriarchal lesson." Likewise, Jordan's essays, "A New Politics of Sexuality" and "Report from the Bahamas," undermine romanticized notions of community, claiming, "the usual race and class concepts of connection, or gender assumptions of unity, do not apply very well. I doubt they ever did."

Beyond the marginalization of African American women in white feminist associations, Black women were at times characterized by Black men as race traitors for speaking on behalf of gender parity. In fact, some race leaders opined that feminism was a divisive issue that enervated the "more important" matter of racial equality. bell hooks takes up this concern in her 1996 essay, reprinted in this chapter, "Feminism: It's a Black Thing," when she argues: "As long as individual black males (and some females) feel that their freedom cannot be attained without the establishment of patriarchal power and privilege, they will see black female struggles for self-determination, our engagement with feminist movement, as threatening. Convinced that the struggle to 'save' the black race is really first and foremost about saving the lives of black males, they will not only continually insist that their 'sufferings' are greater than those of black females, they will believe that the proud assertion of sexist politics registers a meaningful opposition to racism."

While this position still has cultural currency, two notable exceptions to this narrow focus of racial politics were Frederick Douglass and W. E. B. Du Bois, both of whom recognized the simultaneous plight of gender

and race inequality in America. In fact, Douglass, an outspoken abolitionist, acknowledged that the social movement to abolish slavery actually provided a structure for the rights of women. His newspaper, *The
North Star*, provided favorable coverage of the Seneca Falls Convention
of 1848, considered by many historians to be the beginning of the
American women's movement. Douglass attended this watershed gathering. As an advocate for women's rights, he championed the female
suffragist movement, as did Du Bois, who is clearly one of the most respected leaders of the twentieth century. In fact, Du Bois conflated the
civil rights of white women with African Americans, claiming that
"[E]very argument for Negro suffrage is an argument for women's suffrage; every argument for woman suffrage is an argument for Negro
suffrage; both are great moments in democracy."

Despite the progressiveness of these towering male intellectuals,
there has been resistance to Black feminism, at times manifest as a vocal
backlash against the representation of men in African American
women's literature. Alice Walker's *The Color Purple* (1982), excerpted
in this chapter, and Steven Spielberg's filmic adaptation of the novel en-
gendered perhaps the staunchest criticism. Despite this oftentimes public debate, many moments of mutual cooperation and dialogue sprang
forth from these important literary and theoretical treatises. The final
words of June Jordan's "Where Is the Love" (1978) indicate that being
a feminist does not constitute an oppositional stance; rather, it is about
love of humankind, "everywhere, that I work and live, now, as a feminist trusting that I will learn to love myself well enough to love you
(whoever you are), well enough so that you will love me well enough so
that we will know exactly where is the love: that it is here, between us,
and growing stronger and growing stronger."

African American women's fight for gender equality was comple-
mented by the literary outpouring of female authors in the latter half of
the twentieth century. African American feminist thought is realized in
activism and academic work, written and oral texts, fictional prose and
critical essays. Indeed, the range of Black feminist work is monumental,
but perhaps the most well-known venue has been in the African
American women's literary movement. Certainly, the literary expression
of African American women writers since the 1970s was not the starting
point for the history of an African American female literary tradition.
Black women have been writing in America for centuries. A woman,
Lucy Terry, in 1746, wrote the earliest known piece of African
American literature, "Bars Fight," (published in 1855), and Phillis
Wheatley was the first African American to publish a book (1773).

Nevertheless, it is important to recognize the impact of the Black women's literary renaissance of the late twentieth century (what Henry Louis Gates, Jr. has called the "explosion of black women's writing"). What is particularly significant about these writers is their insistence on paying tribute to their literary foremothers. While intertextuality in the African American tradition is indisputable, as this anthology evidences, there is an especially notable homage that Black women writers pay to their female ancestors. The selections in this chapter bespeak this impulse to remember.

Sojourner Truth is remembered and honored by Alice Walker and June Jordan in pieces collected in this chapter. Jordan's poem "A Song of Sojourner Truth" (1980) chronicles the indomitable spirit of Truth, and Walker's essay "A Name Is Sometimes an Ancestor Saying Hi, I'm with You" (1988) identifies the trace of this foremother in her own name. Walker's sense of a collective African American female identity is also evident in her relationship to the late Zora Neale Hurston, another literary forebear that Walker has claimed as a foremother. Walker's essay "Looking for Zora," collected in "The Middle Passage, Mourning, and Survival" chapter of this anthology, solidifies her relationship to Hurston and provides a paradigm for reclaiming the lives and work of African American writers who have fallen into obscurity, a preoccupation of many contemporary female authors. Indeed, Jordan's "Where Is the Love?" acknowledges a little-known Harlem Renaissance writer, Georgia Douglas Johnson. Jordan writes: "From the terrible graves of a traditional conspiracy against my sisters in art, I must exhume the works of women writers and poets such as Georgia Douglas Johnson (who?)." Recognizing that African American women writers' work bears the imprint of their literary forebears, Jordan asks the reader to consider why female authors are often disremembered.

Johnson's poems "My Little Dreams" (1918) and "The Heart of a Woman" (1918) are good companion pieces to Gwendolyn Brooks's *Maud Martha* (1953). The quiet despair in Johnson's poems is palpable and captures the unfulfilled life of the title character in Brooks's novel. Like the woman in Johnson's "Heart of a Woman," whose heart is portrayed as a caged bird (an image from Paul Laurence Dunbar's "Sympathy," and one which Maya Angelou also draws on in her famous autobiography, *I Know Why the Caged Bird Sings*), Maud Martha lives an interior life that is constrained by racism, classism, and sexism, as well as color prejudice from within her own community. The narrative, with its terse chapters and sparsely written prose, enacts the silencing and repressed anger of the protagonist. However, as the excerpts in this chapter attest, Maud Martha's role as mother enables her voice and galvanizes her strength.

This chapter concludes with the vibrant voice of Joan Morgan. Like many Black feminists, Morgan acknowledges the contributions of her feminist foremothers from Sojourner Truth to June Jordan to Alice Walker to bell hooks, yet addresses what she sees as the unique concerns of the "post-feminist" generation. Morgan's contemporary viewpoint notwithstanding, her brand of feminism is in line with that of other writers in this chapter, as it fights against cultural restraints while simultaneously registering the vitality and beauty of African American women's lives.

Further Reading

Christian, Barbara. *Black Feminist Criticism: Perspectives on Black Women Writers.* New York: Pergamon Press, 1985.

Collins, Patricia Hill. *Black Feminist Thought: Knowledge, Consciousness, and the Politics of Empowerment.* New York: Routledge, 2000.

Davis, Angela Y. *Women, Race and Class.* New York: Random House, 1983.

Gates, Henry Louis, Jr. *Reading Black, Reading Feminist: A Critical Anthology.* New York: Meridian, 1990.

Giddings, Paula. *When and Where I Enter: The Impact of Black Women on Sex and Race in America.* New York: Bantam Books, 1984.

hooks, bell. *Feminist Theory: From Margin to Center.* Boston: South End Press, 1984.

Hull, Gloria T., Patricia Bell Scott, and Barbara Smith. *But Some of Us Are Brave: Black Women's Studies.* Old Westbury, NY: Feminist Press, 1982.

Lewis, David Levering. *W. E. B. Du Bois: Biography of a Race, 1868–1919.* New York: Henry Holt and Company, 1993.

Lorde, Audre. *Sister Outsider: Essays and Speeches.* Trumansburg, NY: Crossing Press, 1984.

McDowell, Deborah E. *"The Changing Same": Black Women's Literature, Criticism, and Theory.* Bloomington: Indiana UP, 1995.

Pryse, Marjorie, and Hortense J. Spillers, eds. *Conjuring: Black Women, Fiction, and Literary Tradition.* Bloomington, Indiana UP, 1985.

Walker, Alice. *In Search of Our Mothers' Gardens: Feminist Prose.* San Diego: Harcourt Brace Jovanovich, 1983.

Sojourner Truth
(1797–1883)

Born Isabella Van Wagener in Ulster County, New York, Sojourner Truth was enslaved first by a wealthy Dutch master and then was sold a number of times during the first 30 years of her life. During this time, she bore at least five children and took one of them with her when she fled her final captor. New York abolished slavery in 1827, the year after Truth escaped, and soon thereafter she successfully sued to retrieve her son Peter from enslavement in Alabama. After a profound religious conversion, she assumed the name Sojourner Truth to exemplify her newfound identity as an itinerant preacher, abolitionist, and feminist. In 1850, Truth published The Narrative of Sojourner Truth: A Bondswoman of Olden Time, *recorded by Olive Gilbert. The narrative went through seven editions, with major revisions in its later editions. These revisions included the addition of* Book of Life, *which set forth personal correspondence from Truth's friends, as well as newspaper accounts of her activities. However, it is Truth's passionate 1850s human rights speeches for which she is most well known, and two of these (one has two versions) are reprinted below.*

Speech Delivered to The Woman's Rights Convention, Akron, Ohio (1851)
[Campbell Version]

1   Well, children, where there is so much racket there must be something out o' kilter. I think that 'twixt the Negroes of the South and the women of the North all a-talking about rights, the white men will be in a fix pretty soon.

2   But what's all this here talking about? That man over there says that women need to be helped into carriages, and lifted over ditches, and to have the best place everywhere. Nobody ever helps me into carriages, or over mud puddles or gives me any best place *(and raising herself to her full height and her voice to a pitch like rolling thunder, she asked),* and aren't I a woman? Look at me!

Look at my arm! *(And she bared her right arm to the shoulder, showing her tremendous muscular power.)* I have plowed, and planted, and gathered into barns, and no man could head me—and aren't I a woman? I could work as much and eat as much as a man (when I could get it), and bear the lash as well—and aren't I a woman? I have borne thirteen children and seen them almost all sold off into slavery, and when I cried out with a mother's grief, none but Jesus heard—and aren't I a woman? Then they talk about this thing in the head—what's this they call it? *("Intellect," whispered someone near.)* That's it honey. What's that got to do with woman's rights or Negroes' rights? If my cup won't hold but a pint and yours holds a quart, wouldn't you be mean not to let me have my little half-measure full? *(And she pointed her significant finger and sent a keen glance at the minister who had made the argument. The cheering was long and loud.)*

3   Then that little man in black there, he says women can't have as much rights as man, 'cause Christ wasn't a woman. Where did your Christ come from? *(Rolling thunder could not have stilled that crowd as did those deep, wonderful tones, as she stood there with outstretched arms and eye of fire. Raising her voice still louder, she repeated,)* Where did your Christ come from? From God and a woman. Man had nothing to do with him. *(Oh! what a rebuke she gave the little man.)*

4   *(Turning again to another objector, she took up the defense of mother Eve. I cannot follower [sic] her through it all. It was pointed, and witty, and solemn, eliciting at almost every sentence deafening applause; and she ended [sic] by asserting that)* If the first woman God ever made was strong enough to turn the world upside down, all alone, these together *(and she glanced her eye over us)*, ought to be able to turn it back and get it right side up again; and now they are asking to do it, the men better let them. *(Long-continued cheering.)*

5   'Bliged to you for hearing on me, and now old Sojourner hasn't got anything more to say.

[Gage Version]

1   "Well, chilern, whar dar is so much racket dar must be something out o' kilter. I tink dat 'twixt de niggers of de Souf and de women at

de Norf all a talkin' 'bout rights, de white men will be in a fix pretty soon. But what's all dis here talkin' 'bout? Dat man ober dar say dat women needs to be helped into carriages, and lifted ober ditches, and to have de best place every whar. Nobody eber help me into carriages, or ober mud puddles, or gives me any best place [and raising herself to her full hight [*sic*] and her voice to a pitch like rolling thunder, she asked], and ar'n't I a woman? Look at me! Look at my arm! [And she bared her right arm to the shoulder, showing her tremendous muscular power.] I have plowed, and planted, and gathered into barns, and no man could head me—and ar'n't I a woman? I could work as much and eat as much as a man (when I could get it), and bear de lash as well—and ar'n't I a woman? I have borne thirteen chilern and seen 'em mos' all sold off into slavery, and when I cried out with a mother's grief, none but Jesus heard—and ar'n't I a woman? Den dey talks 'bout dis ting in de head—what dis dey call it?" "Intellect," whispered some one near. "Dat's it honey. What's dat got to do with women's rights or niggers' rights? If my cup won't hold but a pint and yourn holds a quart, would n't ye be mean not to let me have my little half-measure full?" And she pointed her significant finger and sent a keen glance at the minister who had made the argument. The cheering was long and loud.

2   "Den dat little man in black dar, he say women can't have as much rights as man, cause Christ want a woman. What did your Christ come from?" Rolling thunder could not have stilled that crowd as did those deep, wonderful tones, as she stood there with outstretched arms and eye of fire. Raising her voice still louder, she repeated, "What did your Christ come from? From God and a woman. Man had nothing to do with him." Oh! what a rebuke she gave the little man.

3   Turning again to another objector, she took up the defense of mother Eve. I cannot follow her through it all. It was pointed, and witty, and solemn, eliciting at almost every sentence deafening applause; and she ended by asserting that "if de fust woman God ever made was strong enough to turn the world upside down, all 'lone, dese togedder [and she glanced her eye over us] ought to be able to turn it back and get it right side up again, and now dey is asking to do it, de men better let em." Long, continued cheering. " 'Bleeged to you for hearin' on me, and now ole Sojourner ha'n't got nothing more to say."

Speech Delivered to the First Annual Meeting of the American Equal Rights Association (May 9, 1867)

1   My friends, I am rejoiced that you are glad, but I don't know how you will feel when I get through. I come from another field—the country of the slave. They have got their liberty—so much good luck to have slavery partially destroyed; not entirely. I want it root and branch destroyed. Then we will all be free indeed. I feel that if I have to answer for the deeds done in my body just as much as a man, I have a right to have just as much as a man. There is a great stir about colored men getting their rights, but not a word about the colored women; and if colored men get their rights, and not colored women get theirs, you see the colored men will be masters over the women, and it will be just as bad as it was before. So I am for keeping the thing going while things are stirring; because if we wait till it is still, it will take a great while to get it going again. White women are a great deal smarter, and know more than colored women, while colored women do not know scarcely anything. They go out washing, which is about as high as a colored woman gets, and their men go about idle, strutting up and down; and when the women come home, they ask for their money and take it all, and then scold because there is no food. I want you to consider on that, chil'n. I call you chil'n; you are somebody's chil'n, and I am old enough to be mother of all that is here.

2   I want women to have their rights. In the courts women have no right, no voice; nobody speaks for them. I wish woman to have her voice there among the pettifoggers. If it is not a fit place for women, it is unfit for men to be there.

3   I am above eighty years old; it is about time for me to be going. I have been forty years a slave and forty years free, and would be here forty years more to have equal rights for all. I suppose I am kept here because something remains for me to do; I suppose I am yet to help break the chain.

4   I have done a great deal of work; as much as a man, but did not get so much pay. I used to work in the field and bind grain, keeping up with the cradler; but men doing no more, got twice as much pay. So with the German women. They work in the field and do as much work, but do not get the pay. We do as much, we eat as much, we want as much.

5   I suppose I am about the only colored woman that goes about to speak for the rights of the colored woman. I want to keep the thing stirring, now that the ice is cracked. What we want is a little money. You men know that you get as much again as women when you write, or for what you do. When we get our rights, we shall not have to come to you for money, for then we shall have money enough in our own pockets; and may be you will ask us for money. But help us now until we get it. It is a good consolation to know that when we have got this battle once fought we shall not be coming to you any more.

6   You have been having our right so long, that you think, like a slave-holder, that you own us. I know that it is hard for one who has held the reins for so long to give up; it cuts like a knife. It will feel all the better when it closes up again. I have been in Washington about three years, seeing about these colored people. Now colored men have a right to vote. There ought to be equal rights more then ever, since colored people have got their freedom.

7   I am going to talk several times while I am here; so now I will do a little singing. I have not heard any singing since I came here.

8   *(Accordingly, suiting the action to the word, Sojourner sang,)* We are going home. There, children, *(said she,)* in heaven we shall rest from all our labors; first do all we have to do here. There I am determined to go, not to stop short of that beautiful place, and I do not mean to stop till I get there, and meet you there, too.

Anna Julia Cooper

(1858–1964)

Born enslaved in Raleigh, North Carolina, Anna Julia Cooper was educated at St. Augustine Normal School, where she eventually became a member of the faculty. In 1881, Cooper attended Oberlin College, where she earned a bachelor's degree in 1884 and later a master's degree in mathematics. After receiving her M.A., she moved to Washington, D.C., to teach at M Street School, also known as Washington Colored High School, where she became principal in 1902. In

*1925, Cooper graduated with a Ph.D. from the University of Paris,
making her one of the first African Americans to receive a doctorate.
The following essay is from Cooper's collection of essays and speeches,
A Voice from the South by a Black Woman of the South (1892), a
landmark feminist text, which connects gender equality to racial justice. Cooper, recognizing the direct relationship between higher education and racial progress, was a particularly staunch advocate for the
education of African American women.*

Womanhood: A Vital Element in the Regeneration and Progress of a Race (1886)

1 The two sources from which, perhaps, modern civilization has derived
its noble and ennobling ideal of woman are Christianity and the Feudal System.

2 In Oriental countries woman has been uniformly devoted to a life
of ignorance, infamy, and complete stagnation. The Chinese shoe of
to-day does not more entirely dwarf, cramp, and destroy her physical powers, than have the customs, laws, and social instincts, which
from remotest ages have governed our Sister of the East, enervated
and blighted her mental and moral life.

3 Mahomet makes no account of woman whatever in his polity.
The Koran, which, unlike our Bible, was a product and not a
growth, tried to address itself to the needs of Arabian civilization
as Mahomet with his circumscribed powers saw them. The Arab was
a nomad. Home to him meant his present camping place. That deity
who, according to our western ideals, makes and sanctifies the
home, was to him a transient bauble to be toyed with so long as it
gave pleasure and then to be thrown aside for a new one. As a personality, an individual soul, capable of eternal growth and unlimited development, and destined to mould and shape the civilization
of the future to an incalculable extent, Mahomet did not know

woman. There was no hereafter, no paradise for her. The heaven of the Mussulman is peopled and made gladsome not by the departed wife, or sister, or mother, but by *houri*—a figment of Mahomet's brain, partaking of the ethereal qualities of angels, yet imbued with all the vices and inanity of Oriental women. The harem here, and—"dust to dust" hereafter, this was the hope, the inspiration, the *summum bonum* of the Eastern woman's life! With what result on the life of the nation, the "Unspeakable Turk," the "sick man" of modern Europe can to-day exemplify.

4   Says a certain writer: "The private life of the Turk is vilest of the vile, unprogressive, unambitious, and inconceivably low." And yet Turkey is not without her great men. She has produced most brilliant minds; men skilled in all the intricacies of diplomacy and statesmanship; men whose intellects could grapple with the deep problems of empire and manipulate the subtle agencies which check-mate kings. But these minds were not the normal outgrowth of a healthy trunk. They seemed rather ephemeral excrescencies which shoot far out with all the vigor and promise, apparently, of strong branches; but soon alas fall into decay and ugliness because there is no soundness in the root, no life-giving sap, permeating, strengthening and perpetuating the whole. There is a worm at the core! The home-life is impure! and when we look for fruit, like apples of Sodom, it crumbles within our grasp into dust and ashes.

5   It is pleasing to turn from this effete and immobile civilization to a society still fresh and vigorous, whose seed is in itself, and whose very name is synonymous with all that is progressive, elevating and inspiring, viz., the European bud and the American flower of modern civilization.

6   And here let me say parenthetically that our satisfaction in American institutions rests not on the fruition we now enjoy, but springs rather from the possibilities and promise that are inherent in the system, though as yet, perhaps, far in the future.

7   "Happiness," says Madame de Staël, "consists not in perfections attained, but in a sense of progress, the result of our own endeavor under conspiring circumstances *toward* a goal which continually advances and broadens and deepens till it is swallowed up in the Infinite." Such conditions in embryo are all that we claim for the land of the West. We have not yet reached our ideal in

American civilization. The pessimists even declare that we are not marching in that direction. But there can be no doubt that here in America is the arena in which the next triumph of civilization is to be won; and here too we find promise abundant and possibilities infinite.

8   Now let us see on what basis this hope for our country primarily and fundamentally rests. Can any one doubt that it is chiefly on the homelife and on the influence of good women in those homes? Says Macaulay: "You may judge a nation's rank in the scale of civilization from the way they treat their women." And Emerson, "I have thought that a sufficient measure of civilization is the influence of good women." Now this high regard for woman, this germ of a prolific idea which in our own day is bearing such rich and varied fruit, was ingrafted into European civilization, we have said, from two sources, the Christian Church and the Feudal System. For although the Feudal System can in no sense be said to have originated the idea, yet there can be no doubt that the habits of life and modes of thought to which Feudalism gave rise, materially fostered and developed it; for they gave us chivalry, than which no institution has more sensibly magnified and elevated woman's position in society.

9   Tacitus dwells on the tender regard for woman entertained by these rugged barbarians before they left their northern homes to overrun Europe. Old Norse legends too, and primitive poems, all breathe the same spirit of love of home and veneration for the pure and noble influence there presiding—the wife, the sister, the mother.

10   And when later on we see the settled life of the Middle Ages "oozing out," as M. Guizot expresses it, from the plundering and pillaging life of barbarism and crystallizing into the Feudal System, the tiger of the field is brought once more within the charmed circle of the goddesses of his castle, and his imagination weaves around them a halo whose reflection possibly has not yet altogether vanished.

11   It is true the spirit of Christianity had not yet put the seal of catholicity on this sentiment. Chivalry, according to Bascom, was but the toning down and softening of a rough and lawless period. It gave a roseate glow to a bitter winter's day. Those who looked out from castle windows revelled in its "amethyst tints." But God's poor, the weak, the unlovely, the commonplace were still freezing and starving none the less in unpitied, unrelieved loneliness.

12 Respect for woman, the much lauded chivalry of the Middle Ages, meant what I fear it still means to some men in our own day—respect for the elect few among whom they expect to consort.

13 The idea of the radical amelioration of womankind, reverence for woman as woman regardless of rank, wealth, or culture, was to come from that rich and bounteous fountain from which flow all our liberal and universal ideas—the Gospel of Jesus Christ.

14 And yet the Christian Church at the time of which we have been speaking would seem to have been doing even less to protect and elevate woman than the little done by secular society. The Church as an organization committed a double offense against woman in the Middle Ages. Making of marriage a sacrament and at the same time insisting on the celibacy of the clergy and other religious orders, she gave an inferior if not an impure character to the marriage relation, especially fitted to reflect discredit on woman. Would this were all or the worst! but the Church by the licentiousness of its chosen servants invaded the household and established too often as vicious connections those relations which it forbade to assume openly and in good faith. "Thus," to use the words of our authority, "the religious corps became as numerous, as searching, and as unclean as the frogs of Egypt, which penetrated into all quarters, into the ovens and kneading troughs, leaving their filthy trail wherever they went." Says Chaucer with characteristic satire, speaking of the Friars:

> *Women may now go safely up and doun,*
> *In every bush, and under every tree,*
> *Ther is non other incubus but he,*
> *And he ne will don hem no dishonour.*

Henry, Bishop of Liege, could unblushingly boast the birth of twenty-two children in fourteen years.

15 It may help us under some of the perplexities which beset our way in "the one Catholic and Apostolic Church" to-day, to recall some of the corruptions and incongruities against which the Bride of Christ has had to struggle in her past history and in spite of which she has kept, through many vicissitudes, the faith once delivered to the saints. Individuals, organizations, whole sections of the Church militant may outrage the Christ whom they profess, may ruthlessly trample under foot both the spirit and the letter of his precepts, yet not till we hear the voices

audibly saying "Come let us depart hence," shall we cease to believe and cling to the promise, "*I am with you to the end of the world.*"

> *Yet saints their watch are keeping,*
> *The cry goes up "How long!"*
> *And soon the night of weeping*
> *Shall be the morn of song.*

However much then the facts of any particular period of history may seem to deny it, I for one do not doubt that the source of the vitalizing principle of woman's development and amelioration is the Christian Church, so far as that church is coincident with Christianity.

16   Christ gave ideals not formulae. The Gospel is a germ requiring millennia for its growth and ripening. It needs and at the same time helps to form around itself a soil enriched in civilization, and perfected in culture and insight without which the embryo can neither be unfolded or comprehended. With all the strides our civilization has made from the first to the nineteenth century, we can boast not an idea, not a principle of action, not a progressive social force but was already mutely foreshadowed, or directly enjoined in that simple tale of a meek and lowly life. The quiet face of the Nazarene is ever seen a little way ahead, never too far to come down to and touch the life of the lowest in days the darkest, yet ever leading onward, still onward, the tottering childish feet of our strangely boastful civilization.

17   By laying down for woman the same code of morality, the same standard of purity, as for man; by refusing to countenance the shameless and equally guilty monsters who were gloating over her fall,—graciously stooping in all the majesty of his own spotlessness to wipe away the filth and grime of her guilty past and bid her go in peace and sin no more; and again in the moments of his own careworn and footsore dejection, turning trustfully and lovingly, away from the heartless snubbing and sneers, away from the cruel malignity of mobs and prelates in the dusty marts of Jerusalem to the ready sympathy, loving appreciation and unfaltering friendship of that quiet home at Bethany; and even at the last, by his dying bequest to the disciple whom he loved, signifying the protection and tender regard to be extended to that sorrowing mother and ever afterward to the sex she represented;—throughout his life and in his death he has given to men a rule and guide for the estimation of woman as an equal, as a helper, as a friend, and as a sacred charge to be sheltered and cared for with a brother's love and sympathy, lessons which nineteen centuries' gigantic strides in knowledge, arts, and sciences, in

social and ethical principles have not been able to probe to their depth or to exhaust in practice.

18   It seems not too much to say then of the vitalizing, regenerating, and progressive influence of womanhood on the civilization of to-day, that, while it was foreshadowed among Germanic nations in the far away dawn of their history as a narrow, sickly and stunted growth, it yet owes its catholicity and power, the deepening of its roots and broadening of its branches to Christianity.

19   The union of these two forces, the Barbaric and the Christian, was not long delayed after the Fall of the Empire. The Church, which fell with Rome, finding herself in danger of being swallowed up by barbarism, with characteristic vigor and fertility of resources, addressed herself immediately to the task of conquering her conquerors. The means chosen does credit to her power of penetration and adaptability, as well as to her profound, unerring, all-compassing diplomacy; and makes us even now wonder if aught human can successfully and ultimately withstand her far-seeing designs and brilliant policy, or gainsay her well-earned claim to the word *Catholic*.

20   She saw the barbarian, little more developed than a wild beast. She forbore to antagonize and mystify his warlike nature by a full blaze of the heartsearching and humanizing tenets of her great Head. She said little of the rule "If thy brother smite thee on one cheek, turn to him the other also"; but thought it sufficient for the needs of those times, to establish the so-called "Truce of God" under which men were bound to abstain from butchering one another for three days of each week and on Church festivals. In other words, she respected their individuality: non-resistance pure and simple being for them an utter impossibility, she contented herself with less radical measures calculated to lead up finally to the full measure of the benevolence of Christ.

21   Next she took advantage of the barbarian's sensuous love of gaudy display and put all her magnificent garments on. She could not capture him by physical force, she would dazzle him by gorgeous spectacles. It is said that Romanism gained more in pomp and ritual during this trying period of the Dark Ages than throughout all her former history.

22   The result was she carried her point. Once more Rome laid her ambitious hand on the temporal power, and allied with Charlemagne, aspired to rule the world through a civilization dominated by Christianity and permeated by the traditions and instincts of those sturdy barbarians.

23   Here was the confluence of the two streams we have been tracing, which, united now, stretch before us as a broad majestic river. In regard to woman it was the meeting of two noble and ennobling forces, two kindred ideas the resultant of which, we doubt not, is destined to be a potent force in the betterment of the world.

24   Now after our appeal to history comparing nations destitute of this force and so destitute also of the principle of progress, with other nations among whom the influence of woman is prominent coupled with a brisk, progressive, satisfying civilization,—if in addition we find this strong presumptive evidence corroborated by reason and experience, we may conclude that these two equally varying concomitants are linked as cause and effect; in other words, that the position of woman in society determines the vital elements of its regeneration and progress.

25   Now that this is so on *a priori* grounds all must admit. And this not because woman is better or stronger or wiser than man, but from the nature of the case, because it is she who must first form the man by directing the earliest impulses of his character.

26   Byron and Wordsworth were both geniuses and would have stamped themselves on the thought of their age under any circumstances; and yet we find the one a savor of life unto life, the other of death into death. "Byron, like a rocket, shot his way upward with scorn and repulsion, flamed out in wild, explosive, brilliant excesses and disappeared in darkness made all the more palpable."

27   Wordsworth lent of his gifts to reinforce that "power in the Universe which makes for righteousness" by taking the harp handed him from Heaven and using it to swell the strains of angelic choirs. Two locomotives equally mighty stand facing opposite tracks; the one to rush headlong to destruction with all its precious freight, the other to toil grandly and gloriously up the steep embattlements to Heaven and to God. Who—who can say what a world of consequences hung on the first placing and starting of these enormous forces!

28   Woman, Mother,—your responsibility is one that might make angels tremble and fear to take hold! To trifle with it, to ignore or misuse it, is to treat lightly the most sacred and solemn trust ever confided by God to human kind. The training of children is a task on which an infinity of weal or woe depends. Who does not covet it? Yet who does not stand awestruck before its momentous issues! It is a matter of small moment, it seems to me, whether that lovely girl in whose accomplishments you take such pride and delight, can

enter the gay and crowded salon with the ease and elegance of this or that French or English gentlewoman, compared with the decision as to whether her individuality is going to reinforce the good or the evil elements of the world. The lace and the diamonds, the dance and the theater, gain a new significance when scanned in their bearings on such issues. Their influence on the individual personality, and through her on the society and civilization which she vitalizes and inspires—all this and more must be weighed in the balance before the jury can return a just and intelligent verdict as to the innocence or banefulness of these apparently simple amusements.

29   Now the fact of woman's influence on society being granted, what are its practical bearings on the work which brought together this conference of colored clergy and laymen in Washington? "We come not here to talk." Life is too busy, too pregnant with meaning and far reaching consequences to allow you to come this far for mere intellectual entertainment.

30   The vital agency of womanhood in the regeneration and progress of a race, as a general question, is conceded almost before it is fairly stated. I confess one of the difficulties for me in the subject assigned lay in its obviousness. The plea is taken away by the opposite attorney's granting the whole question.

31   "Woman's influence on social progress"—who in Christendom doubts or questions it? One may as well be called on to prove that the sun is the source of light and heat and energy to this many-sided little world.

32   Nor, on the other hand, could it have been intended that I should apply the position when taken and proven, to the needs and responsibilities of the women of our race in the South. For is it not written, "Cursed is he that cometh after the king?" and has not the King already preceded me in "The Black Woman of the South"?

33   They have had both Moses and the Prophets in Dr. Crummell and if they hear not him, neither would they be persuaded though one came up from the South.

34   I would beg, however, with the Doctor's permission, to add my plea for the *Colored Girls* of the South:—that large, bright, promising fatally beautiful class that stand shivering like a delicate plantlet before the fury of tempestuous elements, so full of promise and possibilities, yet so sure of destruction; often without a father to whom they dare apply the loving term, often without a stronger brother to espouse their cause and defend their honor with his life's

blood; in the midst of pitfalls and snares, waylaid by the lower classes of white men, with no shelter, no protection nearer than the great blue vault above, which half conceals and half reveals the one Care-Taker they know so little of. Oh, save them, help them, shield, train, develop, teach, inspire them! Snatch them, in God's name, as brands from the burning! There is material in them well worth your while, the hope in germ of a staunch, helpful, regenerating womanhood on which, primarily, rests the foundation stones of our future as a race.

35   It is absurd to quote statistics showing the Negro's bank account and rent rolls, to point to the hundreds of newspapers edited by colored men and lists of lawyers, doctors, professors, D.D.'s, LL.D.'s, etc., etc., etc., while the source from which the life-blood of the race is to flow is subject to taint and corruption in the enemy's camp.

36   True progress is never made by spasms. Real progress is growth. It must begin in the seed. Then, "first the blade, then the ear, after that the full corn in the ear." There is something to encourage and inspire us in the advancement of individuals since their emancipation from slavery. It at least proves that there is nothing irretrievably wrong in the shape of the black man's skull, and that under given circumstances his development, downward or upward, will be similar to that of other average human beings.

37   But there is no time to be wasted in mere felicitation. That the Negro has his niche in the infinite purposes of the Eternal, no one who has studied the history of the last fifty years in America will deny. That much depends on his own right comprehension of his responsibility and rising to the demands of the hour, it will be good for him to see; and how best to use his present so that the structure of the future shall be stronger and higher and brighter and nobler and holier than that of the past, is a question to be decided each day by every one of us.

38   The race is just twenty-one years removed from the conception and experience of a chattel, just at the age of ruddy manhood. It is well enough to pause a moment for retrospection, introspection, and prospection. We look back, not to become inflated with conceit because of the depths from which we have arisen, but that we may learn wisdom from experience. We look within that we may gather together once more our forces, and, by improved and more practical methods, address ourselves to the tasks before us. We look forward with hope and trust that the same God whose guiding hand led our fathers through and out of the gall and bitterness of oppression, will

still lead and direct their children, to the honor of His name, and for their ultimate salvation.

39   But this survey of the failures or achievements of the past, the difficulties and embarrassments of the present, and the mingled hopes and fears for the future, must not degenerate into mere dreaming nor consume the time which belongs to the practical and effective handling of the crucial questions of the hour; and there can be no issue more vital and momentous than this of the womanhood of the race.

40   Here is the vulnerable point, not in the heel, but at the heart of the young Achilles; and here must the defenses be strengthened and the watch redoubled.

41   We are the heirs of a past which was not our fathers' moulding. "Every man the arbiter of his own destiny" was not true for the American Negro of the past: and it is no fault of his that he finds himself to-day the inheritor of a manhood and womanhood impoverished and debased by two centuries and more of compression and degradation.

42   But weaknesses and malformations, which to-day are attributable to a vicious schoolmaster and a pernicious system, will a century hence be rightly regarded as proofs of innate corruptness and radical incurability.

43   Now the fundamental agency under God in the regeneration, the retraining of the race, as well as the ground work and starting point of its progress upward, must be the *black woman*.

44   With all the wrongs and neglects of her past, with all the weakness, the debasement, the moral thralldom of her present, the black woman of to-day stands mute and wondering at the Herculean task devolving upon her. But the cycles wait for her. No other hand can move the lever. She must be loosed from her hands and set to work.

45   Our meager and superficial results from past efforts prove their futility; and every attempt to elevate the Negro, whether undertaken by himself or through the philanthropy of others, cannot but prove abortive unless so directed as to utilize the indispensable agency of an elevated and trained womanhood.

46   A race cannot be purified from without. Preachers and teachers are helps, and stimulants and conditions as necessary as the gracious rain and sunshine are to plant growth. But what are rain and dew and sunshine and cloud if there be no life in the plant germ? We must go to the root and see that that is sound and healthy and vigorous; and not deceive ourselves with waxen flowers and painted leaves of mock chlorophyll.

47   We too often mistake individuals' honor for race development and so are ready to substitute pretty accomplishments for sound sense and earnest purpose.

48   A stream cannot rise higher than its source. The atmosphere of homes is no rarer and purer and sweeter than are the mothers in those homes. A race is but a total of families. The nation is the aggregate of its homes. As the whole is sum of all its parts, so the character of the parts will determine the characteristics of the whole. These are all axioms and so evident that it seems gratuitous to remark it; and yet, unless I am greatly mistaken, most of the unsatisfaction from our past results arises from just such a radical and palpable error, as much almost on our own part as on that of our benevolent white friends.

49   The Negro is constitutionally hopeful and proverbially irrepressible; and naturally stands in danger of being dazzled by the shimmer and tinsel of superficials. We often mistake foliage for fruit and overestimate or wrongly estimate brilliant results.

50   The late Martin R. Delany, who was an unadulterated black man, used to say when honors of state fell upon him, that when he entered the council of kings the black race entered with him; meaning, I suppose, that there was no discounting his race identity and attributing his achievements to some admixture of Saxon blood. But our present record of eminent men, when placed beside the actual status of the race in America to-day, proves that no man can represent the race. Whatever the attainments of the individual may be, unless his home has moved on *pari passu*, he can never be regarded as identical with or representative of the whole.

51   Not by pointing to sun-bathed mountain tops do we prove that Phoebus warms the valleys. We must point to homes, average homes, homes of the rank and file of horny handed toiling men and women of the South (where the masses are) lighted and cheered by the good, the beautiful, and the true,—then and not till then will the whole plateau be lifted into the sunlight.

52   Only the BLACK WOMAN can say "when and where I enter, in the quiet, undisputed dignity of my womanhood, without violence and without suing or special patronage, then and there the whole *Negro race enters with me.*" Is it not evident then that as individual workers for this race we must address ourselves with no half-hearted zeal to this feature of our mission. The need is felt and must be recognized by all. There is a call for workers, for missionaries, for men and women with the double consecration of a fundamental love of

humanity and a desire for its melioration through the Gospel; but superadded to this we demanded an intelligent and sympathetic comprehension of the interests and special needs of the Negro.

53   I see not why there should not be an organized effort for the protection and elevation of our girls such as the White Cross League in England. English women are strengthened and protected by more than twelve centuries of Christian influences, freedom and civilization; English girls are dispirited and crushed down by no such all-leveling prejudice as that supercilious caste spirit in America which cynically assumes "A Negro woman cannot be a lady." English womanhood is beset by no such snares and traps as betray the unprotected, untrained colored girl of the South, whose only crime and dire destruction often is her unconscious and marvelous beauty. Surely then if English indignation is aroused and English manhood thrilled under the leadership of a Bishop of the English church to build up bulwarks around their wronged sisters, Negro sentiment cannot remain callous and Negro efforts nerveless in view of the imminent peril of the mothers of the next generation. *"I am my Sister's keeper!"* should be the hearty response of every man and woman of the race, and this conviction should purify and exalt the narrow, selfish and petty personal aims of life into a noble and sacred purpose.

54   We need men who can let their interest and gallantry extend outside the circle of their aesthetic appreciation; men who can be a father, a brother, a friend to every weak, struggling unshielded girl. We need women who are so sure of their own social footing that they need not fear leaning to lend a hand to a fallen or falling sister. We need men and women who do not exhaust their genius splitting hairs on aristocratic distinctions and thanking God they are not as others; but earnest, unselfish souls, who can go into the highways and byways, lifting up and leading, advising and encouraging with the truly catholic benevolence of the Gospel of Christ.

55   As Church workers we must confess our path of duty is less obvious; or rather our ability to adapt our machinery to our conception of the peculiar exigencies of this work as taught by experience and our own consciousness of the needs of the Negro, is as yet not demonstrable. Flexibility and aggressiveness are not such strong characteristics of the Church to-day as in the Dark Ages.

56   As a Mission field for the Church the Southern Negro is in some aspects most promising; in others, perplexing. Aliens neither in language and customs, nor in associations and sympathies, naturally

of deeply rooted religious instincts and taking most readily and kindly to the worship and teachings of the Church, surely the task of proselytizing the American Negro is infinitely less formidable than that which confronted the Church in the Barbarians of Europe. Besides, this people already look to the Church as the hope of their race. Thinking colored men almost uniformly admit that the Protestant Episcopal Church with its quiet, chaste dignity and decorous solemnity, its instructive and elevating ritual, its bright chanting and joyous hymning, is eminently fitted to correct the peculiar faults of worship—the rank exuberance and often ludicrous demonstrativeness of their people. Yet, strange to say, the Church, claiming to be missionary and Catholic, urging that schism is sin and denominationalism inexcusable, has made in all these years almost no inroads upon this semi-civilized regionalism.

57   Harvests from this over ripe field of home missions have been gathered in by Methodists, Baptists, and not least by Congregationalists, who were unknown to the Freedmen before their emancipation.

58   Our clergy numbers less than two dozen priests of Negro blood and we have hardly more than one self-supporting colored congregation in the entire Southland. While the organization known as the A. M. E. Church has 14,063 ministers, itinerant and local, 4,069 self-supporting churches, 4,275 Sunday-schools, with property valued at $7,772,284, raising yearly for church purposes $1,427,000.

59   Stranger and more significant than all, the leading men of this race (I do not mean demagogues and politicians, but men of intellect, heart, and race devotion, men to whom the elevation of their people means more than personal ambition and sordid gain—and the men of that stamp have not all died yet) the Christian workers for the race, of younger and more cultured growth, are noticeably drifting into sectarian churches, many of them declaring all the time that they acknowledge the historic claims of the Church, believe her apostolicity, and would experience greater personal comfort, spiritual and intellectual, in her revered communion. It is a fact which any one may verify for himself, that representative colored men, professing that in their heart of hearts they are Episcopalians, are actually working in Methodist and Baptist pulpits; while the ranks of the Episcopal clergy are left to be filled largely by men who certainly suggest the propriety of a *"perpetual* Diaconate" if they cannot be said to have created the necessity for it.

60   Now where is the trouble? Something must be wrong. What is it?

61   A certain Southern Bishop of our Church reviewing the situation, whether in Godly anxiety or in "Gothic antipathy" I know not, deprecates the fact that the colored people do not seem *drawn* to the Episcopal Church, and comes to the sage conclusion that the Church is not adapted to the rude untutored minds of the Freedmen, and that they may be left to go to the Methodists and Baptists whither their racial proclivities undeniably tend. How the good Bishop can agree that all-foreseeing Wisdom, and Catholic Love would have framed his Church as typified in his seamless garment and unbroken body, and yet not leave it broad enough and deep enough and loving enough to seek and save and hold seven millions of God's poor, I cannot see.

62   But the doctors while discussing their scientifically conclusive diagnosis of the disease, will perhaps not think it presumptuous in the patient if he dares to suggest where at least the pain is. If this be allowed, a *Black woman of the South* would beg to point out two possible oversights in this southern work which may indicate in part both a cause and a remedy for some failure. The first is *not calculating for the Black man's personality*; not having respect, if I may so express it, to his manhood or deferring at all to his conceptions of the needs of his people. When colored persons have been employed it was too often as machines or as manikins. There has been no disposition, generally, to get the black man's ideal or to let his individuality work by its own gravity, as it were. A conference of earnest Christian men have met at regular intervals for some years past to discuss the best methods of promoting the welfare and development of colored people in this country. Yet, strange as it may seem, they have never invited a colored man or even intimated that one would be welcome to take part in their deliberations. Their remedial contrivances are purely theoretical or empirical, therefore, and the whole machinery devoid of soul.

63   The second important oversight in my judgment is closely allied to this and probably grows out of it, and that is not developing Negro womanhood as an essential fundamental for the elevation of the race, and utilizing this agency in extending the work of the Church.

64   Of the first I have possibly already presumed to say too much since it does not strictly come within the province of my subject.

However, Macaulay somewhere criticises the Church of England as not knowing how to use fanatics, and declares that had Ignatius Loyola been in the Anglican instead of the Roman communion, the Jesuits would have been schismatics instead of Catholics; and if the religious awakenings of the Wesleys had been in Rome, she would have shaven their heads, tied ropes around their waists, and sent them out under her own banner and blessing. Whether this be true or not, there is certainly a vast amount of force potential for Negro evangelization rendered latent, or worse, antagonistic by the halting, uncertain, I had almost said, *trimming* policy of the Church in the South. This may sound both presumptuous and ungrateful. It is mortifying, I know, to benevolent wisdom, after having spent itself in the execution of well conned theories for the ideal development of a particular work, to hear perhaps the weakest and humblest element of that work asking "what does thou?"

65   Yet so it will be in life. The "thus far and no further" pattern cannot be fitted to any growth in God's kingdom. The universal law of development is "onward and upward." It is God-given and inviolable. From the unfolding of the germ in the acorn to reach the sturdy oak, to the growth of a human soul into the full knowledge and likeness of its Creator, the breadth and scope of the movement in each and all are too grand, too mysterious, too like God himself, to be encompassed and locked down in human molds.

66   After all the Southern slave owners were right: either the very alphabet of intellectual growth must be forbidden and the Negro dealt with absolutely as a chattel having neither rights nor sensibilities; or else the clamps and irons of mental and moral, as well as civil compression must be riven asunder and the truly enfranchised soul led to the entrance of that boundless vista through which it is to toil upwards to its beckoning God as the buried seed germ to meet the sun.

67   A perpetual colored diaconate, carefully and kindly superintended by the white clergy; congregations of shiny faced peasants with their clean white aprons and sunbonnets catechised at regular intervals and taught to recite the creed, the Lord's prayer and the ten commandments—duty towards God and duty towards neighbor, surely such well tended sheep ought to be grateful to their shepherds and content in that station of life to which it pleased God to call them. True, like the old professor lecturing to his solitary student, we make no provisions here for irregularities. "Questions

must be kept till after class," or dispensed with altogether. That some do ask questions and insist on answers, in class too, must be both impertinent and annoying. Let not our spiritual pastors and masters however be grieved at such self-assertion as merely signifies we have a destiny to fulfill and as men and women we must *be about our Father's business.*

68   It is a mistake to suppose that the Negro is prejudiced against a white ministry. Naturally there is not a more kindly and implicit follower of a white man's guidance than the average colored peasant. What would to others be an ordinary act of friendly or pastoral interest he would be more inclined to regard gratefully as a condescension. And he never forgets such kindness. Could the Negro be brought near to his white priest or bishop, he is not suspicious. He is not only willing but often longs to unburden his soul to this intelligent guide. There are no reservations when he is convinced that you are his friend. It is a saddening satire on American history and manners that it takes something to convince him.

69   That our people are not "drawn" to a church whose chief dignitaries they see only in the chancel, and whom they reverence as they would a painting or an angel, whose life never comes down to and touches theirs with the inspiration of an objective reality, may be "perplexing" truly (American caste and American Christianity both being facts) but it need not be surprising. There must be something of human nature in it, the same as that which brought about that "the Word was made flesh and dwelt among us" that He might "draw" us towards God.

70   Men are not "drawn" by abstractions. Only sympathy and love can draw, and until our Church in America realizes this and provides a clergy that can come in touch with our life and have a fellow feeling for our woes, without being imbedded and frozen up in their "Gothic antipathies," the good bishops are likely to continue "perplexed" by the sparsity of colored Episcopalians.

71   A colored priest of my acquaintance recently related to me, with tears in his eyes, how his reverend Father in God, the Bishop who had ordained him, had met him on the cars on his way to the diocesan convention and warned him, not unkindly, not to take a seat in the body of the convention with the white clergy. To avoid disturbance of their godly placidity he would of course please sit back and somewhat apart. I do not imagine that that clergyman had very much heart for the Christly (!) deliberations of that convention.

72   To return, however, it is not on this broader view of Church work, which I mentioned as a primary cause of its halting progress with the colored people, that I am to speak. My proper theme is the second oversight of which in my judgment our Christian propagandists have been guilty: or, the necessity of church training, protecting and uplifting our colored womanhood as indispensable to the evangelization of the race.

73   Apelles did not disdain even that criticism of his lofty art which came from an uncouth cobbler; and may I not hope that the writer's oneness with her subject both in feeling and in being may palliate undue obtrusiveness of opinions here. That the race cannot be effectually lifted up till its women are truly elevated we take as proven. It is not for us to dwell on the needs, the neglects, and the ways of succor, pertaining to the black woman of the South. The ground has been ably discussed and an admirable and practical plan proposed by the oldest Negro priest in America, advising and urging that special organizations such as Church Sisterhoods and industrial schools be advised to meet her pressing needs in the Southland. That some such movements are vital to the life of this people and the extension of the Church among them, is not hard to see. Yet the pamphlet fell still-born from the press. So far as I am informed the Church has made no motion towards carrying out Dr. Crummell's suggestion.

74   The denomination which comes next [to] our own in opposing the proverbial emotionalism of Negro worship in the South, and which in consequence like ours receives the cold shoulder from the old heads, resting as we do under the charge of not "having religion" and not believing in conversion—the Congregationalists—have quietly gone to work on the young, have established industrial and training schools, and now almost every community in the South is yearly enriched by a fresh infusion of vigorous young hearts, cultivated heads, and helpful hands that have been trained at Fisk, at Hampton, in Atlanta University, and in Tuskegee, Alabama.

75   These young people are missionaries actual or virtual both here and in Africa. They have learned to love the methods and doctrines of the Church which trained and educated them; and so Congregationalism surely and steadily progresses.

76   Need I compare these well known facts with results shown by the Church in the same field and during the same or even a longer time.

77   The institution of the Church in the South to which she mainly
looks for the training of her colored clergy and for the help of the
"Black Woman" and "Colored Girl" of the South, has graduated
since the year 1868, when the school was founded, *five young
women*, and while yearly numerous young men have been kept and
trained for the ministry by the charities of the Church, the number of indigent females who have here been supported, sheltered
and trained, is phenomenally small. Indeed, to my mind, the attitude of the Church toward this feature of her work is as if the
solution of the problem of Negro missions depended solely on sending a quota of deacons and priests into the field, girls being a sort
of *tertium quid* whose development may be promoted if they can
pay their way and fall in with the plans mapped out for the training of the other sex. Now I would ask in all earnestness, does not
this force potential deserve by education and stimulus to be made
dynamic? Is it not a solemn duty incumbent on all colored churchmen to make it so? Will not the aid of the Church be given to prepare our girls in head, heart, and hand for the duties and
responsibilities that await the intelligent wife, the Christian mother,
the earnest, virtuous, helpful woman, at once both the lever and the
fulcrum for uplifting the race.

78   As Negroes and churchmen we cannot be indifferent to these questions. They touch us most vitally on both sides. We believe in the Holy
Catholic Church. We believe that however gigantic and apparently
remote the consummation, the Church will go on conquering and to
conquer till the kingdoms of this world, not excepting the black man
and the black woman of the South, shall have become the kingdoms
of the Lord and of his Christ.

79   That past work in this direction has been unsatisfactory we must
admit. That without a change of policy results in the future will be as
meagre, we greatly fear. Our life as a race is at stake. The dearest interests of our hearts are in the scale. We must either break away from dear
old landmarks and plunge out in any line and every line that enables
us to meet the pressing need of our people, or we must ask the Church
to allow and help us, untrammelled by the prejudices and theories of
individuals, to work aggressively under her direction as we alone can,
with God's help, for the salvation of our people.

80   The time is ripe for action. Self-seeking and ambition must be
laid on the altar. The battle is one of sacrifice and hardship, but

our duty is plain. We have been recipients of missionary bounty in some sort for twenty-one years. Not even the senseless vegetable is content to be a mere reservoir. Receiving without giving is an anomaly in nature. Nature's cells are all little workshops for manufacturing sunbeams, the product to be *given out* to earth's inhabitants in warmth, energy, thought, action. Inanimate creation always pays back an equivalent.

81   Now, *How much owest thou my Lord?* Will his account be overdrawn if he call for singleness of purpose and self-sacrificing labor for your brethren? Having passed through your drill school, will you refuse a general's commission even if it entail responsibility, risk and anxiety, with possibly some adverse criticism? Is it too much to ask you to step forward and direct the work for your race along those lines which you know to be of first and vital importance?

82   Will you allow these words of Ralph Waldo Emerson? "In ordinary," says he,

we have a snappish criticism which watches and contradicts the opposite party. We want the will which advances and dictates [acts]. Nature has made up her mind that what cannot defend itself, shall not be defended. Complaining never so loud and with never so much reason, is of no use. What cannot stand must fall; *and the measure of our sincerity and therefore of the respect of men is the amount of health and wealth we will hazard in the defense of our right.*

Victoria Earle Matthews
(1861–1907)

Orator, writer, journalist, and social activist Victoria Earle Matthews was born in Fort Valley, Georgia, on May 27, 1861, to an enslaved woman, Caroline Smith, who escaped her captivity by fleeing to New York. Smith returned to Georgia eight years later to win custody of her daughter. After marrying William Matthews and having a son, Matthews began working as a journalist and was quite successful, becoming a correspondent for the Boston Advocate *and the* New York Globe. *Her articles and her public lectures were driven by timely social issues, including anti-lynching crusades, social welfare reform, and women's rights. In keeping with her human rights campaign,*

Matthews founded societies dedicated to the protection of African American girls and women, including the White Rose Industrial Association, initiated in 1897. In addition to her work for social reform, Matthews also wrote children's short stories and a novella, Aunt Lindy, *in 1893.*

The Awakening of The Afro-American Woman (1897)

1   The awakening to life of any of the forces of nature is the most mysterious as it is the sublimest of spectacles. Through all nature there runs a thread of life. We watch with equal interest and awe the transformation of the rosebud into the flower and the babe into manhood. The philosopher has well said that the element of life runs through all nature and links the destinies of earth with the destinies of the stars. This is a beautiful and ennobling thought; while it binds to earth it yet lifts us to heaven. It gives us strength in adversity, when the storms beat and the thunders peal forth their diapason and confusion reigns supreme everywhere; it tempers our joys with soberness when prosperity hedges us about as the dews of the morning hedge about with gladness the modest violet shyly concealed by the wayside. Life is the most mysterious as it is the most revealed force in nature. Death does not compare with it in these qualities, for there can be no death without life. It is from this point of view that we must regard the tremendous awakening of the Afro-American womanhood, during the past three decades from the double night of ages of slavery in which it was locked in intellectual and moral eclipse. It has been the awakening of a race from the nightmare of 250 years of self-effacement and debasement. It is not within the power of any one who has stood outside of Afro-American life to adequately estimate the extent of the effacement and debasement, and, therefore, of the gracious awakening which has quickened into life the slumbering forces and filled with hope and gladness the souls of millions of the womanhood of our land. To the God of love and tenderness and pity and justice we ascribe the fullness of our thanks and prayers for the transformation from the death of slavery to the life

of freedom. All the more are we grateful to the moral and Christian forces of the world, the Christian statesmen and soldiers and scholars who were the divine instruments who made it possible for this womanhood to stand in this august presence to-day, this vast army laboring for the upbuilding of the Master's kingdom among men; for it is true as Longfellow said:

> *Were half the power that fills the world with terror,*
> *Were half the wealth bestowed on camps and courts,*
> *Given to redeem the human mind from error,*
> *There were no need of arsenals and forts.*

The auction block of brutality has been changed into the forum of reason, the slave mart has been replaced by the schoolroom and the church.

2   As I stand here to-day clothed in the garments of Christian womanhood, the horrible days of slavery, out of which I came, seem as a dream that is told, some horror incredible. Indeed, could they have been, and are not? They were; they are not; this is the sum and substance, the shame and the glory of the tale that I would tell, of the message that I would bring.

3   In the vast economy of nature, cycles of time are of small moment, years are as hours, and seconds bear but small relation to the problem, yet they are as the drops of rain that fall to earth and lodge in the fastnesses of the mountain from which our rivers are formed that feed the vast expanse of ocean. So in the history of a race lifting itself out of its original condition of helplessness, time is as necessary an element as is opportunity, in the assisting forces of humankind.

4   When we remember that the God who created all things is no respector [*sic*] of persons, that the black child is beloved of Him as the white child, we can more easily fix the responsibility that rests upon the Christian womanhood of the country to join with us in elevating the head, the heart and the soul of Afro-American womanhood. As the great Frederick Douglass once said, in order to measure the heights to which we have risen we must first measure the depths to which we were dragged. It is from this point of observation that we must regard the awakening of the Afro-American womanhood of the land. And what is this awakening? What is its distinguishing characteristics? It would seem superfluous to ask or to answer questions so obvious, but the lamentable truth is, that the womanhood of the United States, of the world, knows almost

absolutely nothing of the hope and aspirations, of the joys and the sorrows, of the wrongs, and of the needs of the black women of this country, who came up out of the effacement and debasement of American slavery into the dazzling sunlight of freedom. My friends, call to mind the sensations of the prisoner of Chillon, as he walked out of the dungeon where the flower of his life had been spent, into the open air, and you will be able to appreciate in some sense our feelings in 1865,

> *When the war drums throbbed no longer*
> *And the battle flags were furled.*

5   What a past was ours! There was no attribute of womanhood which had not been sullied—aye, which had not been despoiled in the crucible of slavery. Virtue, modesty, the joys of maternity, even hope of mortality, all those were the heritage of this womanhood when the voice of Lincoln and the sword of Grant, as the expression of the Christian opinion of the land, bade them stand forth, without let or hindrance, as arbiters of their own persons and wills. They had no past to which they could appeal for anything. It had destroyed, more than in the men, all that a woman holds sacred, all that ennobles womanhood. She had but the future.

6   From such small beginnings she was compelled to construct a home. She who had been an outcast, the caprice of brutal power and passion, who had been educated to believe that morality was an echo, and womanly modesty a name; she who had seen father and brother and child torn from her and hurried away into ever-lasting separation—this creature was born to life in an hour and expected to create a home.

> *Home, sweet home;*
> *Be it ever so humble,*
> *There's no place like home.*

7   My friends, more, home is the noblest, the most sacred spot in a Christian nation. It is the foundation upon which nationality rests, the pride of the citizen and the glory of the Republic. This woman was expected to build a home for 4,500,000 people, of whom she was the decisive unit. No Spartan mother ever had a larger task imposed upon her shoulders; no Spartan mother ever acquitted herself more

heroically than this Afro-American woman has done. She has done it almost without any assistance from her white sister; who, in too large a sense, has left her to work out her own destiny in fear and trembling. The color of the skin has been an almost insurmountable barrier between them, despite the beautiful lines of the gentle Cowper, that—

Skin may differ,
But affection
Dwells in black and white the same.

8   I am not unmindful, however, of the Northern women who went into the South after the war as the missionary goes into the dark places of the world, and helped the Afro-American women to lay the foundation of her home broad and deep in the Christian virtues. For years they did this in the schoolroom and their labors naturally had their reflex in the home life of their pupils.

9   Broadly speaking, my main statement holds, however, that these women, starting empty handed, were left to make Christian homes where a Christian citizenship should be nurtured. The marvel is not that they have succeeded, not that they are succeeding, but that they did not fail, *utterly fail.* I believe the God who brought them out of the Valley of the Shadow, who snatched them from the hand of the white rapist, the base slave master whose unacknowledged children are to be found in every hamlet of the Republic, guided these women, and guides them in the supreme work of building their Christian homes. The horrors of the past were forgotten in the joyous labor that presented itself. Even the ineffaceable wrongs of the past, while not forgotten, were forgiven in the spirit of the Master, who even forgave those who took His life.

10   If there had been no other awakening than this, if this woman who had stood upon the auction block possessed of no rights that a white man was bound to respect, and none which he did respect, if there had been no other awakening of the Afro-American woman than this, that she made a home for her race, an abiding place for husband, and son, and daughter, it would be glory enough to embalm her memory in song and story. As it is, it will be her sufficient monument through all time that out of nothing she created something, and that something the dearest, the sweetest, the strongest institution in Christian government.

11   But she has done more than this. The creation of a home is the central feature of her awakening, but around this are many other

features which show her strong title to the countenance and respect of the sisterhood of the world. She has meekly taken her place by her husband, in the humble occupations of life as a bread winner, and by her labors and sacrifices has helped to rear and educate 50,000 young women, who are active instructors in the Christian churches of the land. In the building up of the Master's kingdom she has been and she is an active and a positive influence; indeed, in this field she has proven, as her white sister has proven, the truth of Napoleon Bonaparte's sententious but axiomatic truth, that "The hand that rocks the cradle rules the world." It is not too much to say that the 7,000,000 Afro-American church memberships would fall to pieces as a rope of sand if the active sympathy and support of the Afro-American women were withdrawn. It is demonstrable that these women are the arch of the Afro-American temple. But these women who came out of slavery have done more than this. They have not only made Christian homes for their families, and educated 50,000 Sunday-school workers, but they have given to the State 25,000 educated school teachers, who are to-day the hope and inspiration of the whole race. The black women who came out of slavery in the past thirty years, have accomplished these tremendous results as farm-laborers and house servants, and they deserve the admiration of mankind for the glorious work that they have accomplished. In the past few years the educated daughters of these ex-slave women have aroused themselves to the necessity of systematic organization for their own protection, and for strengthening their race where they find it is weak, and to this end they have in the several States 243 regularly organized and officered clubs in the Afro-American Women's National Association; there are besides hundreds of social clubs and temperance organizations working in their own way for a strong Christian womanhood. Indeed, the impulse of aspiration after the strong and the good in our civilization is manifest on all hands in our womanhood. It is all so grounded in Christian morality that we may safely conclude that it is built upon a rock and cannot be shaken by the fury of the storms.

12   The awakening of the Afro-American woman is one of the most promising facts in our national life. That she deserves the active sympathy and co-operation of all the female forces of the Republic, I think I have sufficiently shown. We need them. We have always needed them. We need them in the work of religion, of education, of temperance, of morality, of industrialism; and above all we need their assistance in combatting the public opinion and laws that degrade our womanhood because it is black and not white; for of a truth, and as

a universal law, an injury to one woman is an injury to all women. As long as the affections are controlled by legislation in defiance of Christian law, making infamous the union of black and white, we shall have unions without the sanction of the law, and children without legal parentage, to the degradation of black womanhood and the disgrace of white manhood. As one woman, as an Afro-American woman, I stand in this great Christian presence to-day and plead that the marriage and divorce laws be made uniform throughout the Republic, and that they shall not control, but legalize, the union of mutual affections. Until this shall have been done, Afro-American womanhood will have known no full and absolute awakening. As the laws now stand, they are the greatest demoralizing forces with which our womanhood has to contend. They serve as the protection of the white man, but they leave us defenceless, indeed. I ask the Christian womanhood of this great organized Army of Christ, to lend us their active co-operation in coercing the law-makers of the land in throwing around our womanhood the equal protection of the State to which it is entitled. A slave regulation should not be allowed to prevail in a free government. A barbarous injustice should not receive the sanction of a Christian nation. The stronger forces of society should scorn to crush to the earth one of the weakest forces.

13   Next to these degrading marriage and divorce laws which prevail in two [*sic*] many States of the Republic, the full awakening of the Afro-American woman to her rightful position in society, are the separate car regulations which prevail in most of the States of the South. They were conceived in injustice; they are executed with extraordinary cowardice. Their entire operation tends to degrade Afro-American womanhood. None who are familiar with their operation will dispute this statement of facts. From this exalted forum, and in the name of the large army of Afro-American women, I appeal to the Christian sentiment which dominates this organization, to assist us in righting the wrongs growing out of these regulations, to the end that our womanhood may be sustained in its dignity and protected in its weakness, and the heavenly Father, who hath declared, "righteousness exalteth a nation, but sin is a reproach to any people," will give His benediction to the laws made just.

14   I am moved here further to invoke your patience and sympathy in the efforts of our awakening womanhood to care for the aged and infirm, for the orphan and outcast; for the reformation of the penal institutions of the Southern States, for the separation of male and female convicts, and above all for the establishment of juvenile

reformatories [in] those States for both races, to the end that the shame of it may be removed that children of tender age should be herded with hardened criminals from whose life all of moral sensibility has vanished forever.

15   I feel moved to speak here in this wise for a whole race of women whose rise or fall, whose happiness or sorrow, whose degradation or exaltation are the concern of Christian men and women everywhere. I feel moved to say in conclusion that in all Christian and temperance work, in all that lifts humanity from its fallen condition to a more perfect resemblance of Him in whose image it was made, in all that goes to make our common humanity stronger and better and more beautiful; the Afro-American women of the Republic will "do their duty as God shall give them light to do it."

Georgia Douglas Johnson

(1877–1966)

Poet Georgia Douglas Johnson was born in Atlanta, Georgia, on September 10, 1877, but lived the majority of her life in Washington, D.C. Johnson, who graduated from Atlanta University in 1896 (and received an honorary doctoral degree from the university in 1965), married a Washington attorney and raised two sons. Despite the geographic distance, she became active in the Harlem Renaissance, hosting what became knows as the "S Street Salon," attended by such notable figures as Langston Hughes, Jean Toomer, Alain Locke, and Jessie Redmon Fauset. Publishing four volumes of poetry, The Heart of a Woman *(1918),* Bronze: A Book of Verse *(1922),* An Autumn Love Cycle *(1928), and* Share My World *(1962), Johnson also wrote plays and newspaper columns. She is considered one of the most important female voices of the Harlem Renaissance.*

The Heart of a Woman

The heart of a woman goes forth with the dawn,
As a lone bird, soft winging, so restlessly on,
In the wake of those echoes the heart calls home.
Afar o'er life's turrets and vales does it roam

5 The heart of a woman falls back with the night,
And enters some alien cage in its plight,
And tries to forget it has dreamed of the stars
While it breaks, breaks, breaks on the sheltering bars.

My Little Dreams

I'm folding up my little dreams
  Within my heart tonight,
And praying I may soon forget
  The torture of their sight.

5 For time's deft fingers scroll my brow
  With fell relentless art—
I'm folding up my little dreams
  Tonight, within my heart.

Free

1 The funeral was over. The wife and the mistress sat facing each
other in the old fashioned parlor of their common home, waiting
for the will to be read. A September drizzle had set in and lent to
the somber air of the house an added gloom. Stray bits of faded
leaves and flowers from the many lovely floral wreathes were here
and there upon the green plush carpet that covered the rectangular surface of the quiet room. Nashville had not seen such a long
procession of carriages as had curled through her narrow streets
at this noon hour in many a year. Dr. Ryan had been very popular. These two strangely linked women had just returned from the
cemetery where all that remained of the tie that bound them, the
late Paul Ryan—had been laid to rest. What would happen now
that his portly, beaming, and genial personality had left them—
poles apart together?

2   As Martha Ryan, hidden in the thick crepe of her black veil sat
in church, her mind was darting here and there, picking at the tangled threads of her life. What would she do now? Always he had made

decisions for her, now he lay there so still and cold in front of the altar as the preacher's voice threw sweet flattering words across his upturned face. Even when she had tried once to put her foot down on his bringing this young woman Rose Delaney to live right in the house with them, twenty-five years ago . . . twenty-five long years! Had called her his new nurse, her lips curled in derision. For her, this baby-eyed woman, he had decided against her, his own wife. But the whole town knew the truth . . . you can't throw dust in people's eyes . . . nurse . . . nurse forsooth! And what could she do about it? Nothing, she was old and the girl was young!

3   Out of one corner of her eye she could see Rose's head bowed beside her. She was weeping, and well she might, for now, her protector was gone, and she herself was boss. At last, boss in her own house, and out she'd go! Her friends had taunted her long enough, she'd show them how she'd handle the situation. Martha tightened her lips in determination. Tears, tears, let her cry, cry her eyes out. He'd stood between them and taken her part! Protected her against his own wife. Men were queer. Yet he had been good to her. She'd had nothing, nothing of which to complain but this, this one thing. Strange how numb and far-away like she had felt at the funeral, not like it was her own dead she was burying, but maybe the feeling would come later and then. . . . So now, here she was back home at last, waiting, waiting to hear his last commands!

4   The clock on the mantle struck two. Martha shivered. Lawyer Green had promised to follow them from the funeral. He should be here now. Said he just had to stop by his office and get the will. The will! What did it say? Would it leave her anything? Yes, she guessed it would. Something anyhow, so's she could go away—somewhere! Martha sighed, free, free from her at last!

5   Rose Delaney sitting across from Mrs. Ryan, her black hat a little awry, had noted the sign and seen the shiver. She was keenly aware of her deep agitation. Something called to her from this woman's silence . . . she had always administered to her, served her . . . she needed her even now. Interestingly, she arose, casting a solicitious glance toward the brooding woman as she announced timidly that she was going to make a cup of hot tea. "You're chilly," she added, "it was awfully damp under foot at the cemetery."

6   A faint sound came from Mrs. Ryan's throat, whether of approval or not Rose couldn't make out, but she passed on out to the little kitchen where the soft tinkle of china was soon heard.

7   To make a cup of tea was an easy pleasure for Rose. She liked to serve, but somehow, today her hands seemed strangely awkward and she stumbled as she moved about the little kitchen. She was saying "Goodbye, Goodbye," to every little pot and pan that hung so shiny on the wall. She had loved to make them shine, for the woman with sad, sad questioning eyes liked them so. She had done her best. The day was over and now she must go—go away from this refuge that she had learned to love, this home, hers no longer.

8   As she placed the little silver tray before the tense woman with the steaming odor of the fragrant tea stealing upward she thought she detected a faint softening of her face, a small relaxation of the set jaw. She wasn't sure.

9   Sitting there with her hat still slantwise on her bowed head, Rose looked like a lonely traveler who sits in the station without a time table waiting for the next train with no fixed destination—just going!

10   A ring at the front door. Rose jumped. "It must be Lawyer Green," she murmured. She started for the door, then stopped suddenly and looked toward Mrs. Ryan; she was conscious of the new situation, its tenseness—was she expected to go—There was no movement, no sign from the still woman bent over her tea. Rose walked toward the door. As she moved away, Mrs. Ryan gradually raised her head and fixed her gaze upon Rose's retreating form. She had not been unmindful of Rose's hesitation about the door—aha! She had realized at once the change that had come about—she wasn't sure of herself anymore, not that she had been forward before, in fact, she had always deferred to her, served her well, had been kind and considerate, nursing her, but as her eyes followed the form moving bent and slow, another thought— another thought awoke like a thunder-clap in her mind! A new thought, so strangely new that she felt stunned . . . this woman who moved so slowly before her was not a young woman—she was old! old!!! Rose too was old. The years had passed and even Rose had lost her youth.

11   Mrs. Ryan was sitting in a kind of daze when Rose led Lawyer Green into the room. She paid no heed to his apologetic words, just sat gazing into space. Her mind had rushed back over the years to that day so long ago when Rose had first come into her home—a lovely young brown-eyed girl. Breaking away from her thoughts she fastened her eyes upon Rose as upon a stranger. This woman was new to her, new in her oldness. There was something sweet and comforting in the thought.

12   The tall solemn faced lawyer dropped awkwardly into a chair. He had a difficult duty to perform.

13   "I ask you two ladies to hear the will at once because—because
. . ." He cleared his throat in embarrassment, then finished, "I
thought it best for you both to have an understanding."

14   Placing his horn-rimmed glasses firmly on his nose, he looked at
both women apprehensively and began reading: "I, Paul Ryan, being
of sound mind—." He read on and on. There were several small
bequests to former patients and to the hospital, and then—"The
house and all my remaining property I bequeath and devise to my
wife Martha Ryan, and my adopted daughter, Rose Delaney, equally
share and share alike—"

15   The eyes of the two women met, hung together for a moment, and
then Rose's glance fell.

16   The lawyer finished and again cleared his throat. "I'm sorry."

17   "I'm sorry," Rose whispered faintly. "I'll go away of course, Mrs.
Ryan."

18   'Either of you can sell your share of the house to the other," the
lawyer added. "You'd be willing to sell wouldn't you, Miss Delaney?"

19   "Oh certainly yes—anything Mrs. Ryan suggests will be all right
with me. I'll cause no trouble at all. Now if you will excuse me I'll
get a few things together and be leaving." She looked bewilderedly
about her and stumbled from the room.

20   Lawyer Green looked at the set face of the widowed woman,
arose and tried to offer some further advice. "Everything will be all
right, I'm sure, Mrs. Ryan. Just consult me when you've come to
a decision. The will is a little peculiar, but—ah—ah—the situation is a bit unusual."

21   She continued to hold the door ajar, her eyes following the lawyer's
retreating form as it grew dimmer and dimmer and then vanished
down the street.

22   How quiet it was, both outside and in. Not a sound. Death-like
in the street. She closed the door—still, how still outside. Her foot-
fall was hushed in the red velvet carpet. Her world had come to an
end—All things had come to an end.

23   Descending the stairs slowly came a bowed figure. She seemed
to be feeling her way blindly, one hand slipping along the balustrade,
the other holding a brown valise.

24   Martha stood near the door—waiting. She wondered why she
waited. She didn't know. . . . Was it to say "Good-bye"? Did you
stop to say "Good-bye" when you were asking, even demanding that
some one should leave your house?

25 Rose knew that she was waiting for her to go—had waited for twenty-five years, waited for this moment for nearly a life-time!

26 Nearer and nearer crept the drooping form—she came alongside, set down the valise and slowly lifted her swimming eyes to Martha's face. Haltingly, how haltingly, she formed the words—her throat tightening like cords about them, they seemed squeezed from it.

27 "Well, well, I'll . . . be . . . going. . . . " Martha's lips pressed more firmly together, her eyes following Rose's every move as she bent down to pick up the valise. A kind of stupor seemed to hold her speechless, she just watched and watched. Why didn't she say, "It's time you were going!" But no, she just stood still and watched wordless. Motionless.

28 How still the house was. Still and empty. It would be more still and empty . . . there would be no one to do little things for her . . . nurse her . . . comfort her . . . decide for her . . . no one to lean upon. . . . With a start she awoke to the moment. . . . Rose was going, her hand was turning the knob. . . . Martha watched with growing panic. . . . Rose paused a moment on the threshold, she looked back! and then Mrs. Ryan flung open her arms and cried brokenly, "Rose!"

Gwendolyn Brooks

(1917–2000)

Born June 7, 1917, in Topeka, Kansas, Gwndolyn Brooks was the eldest child of David and Keziah Brooks. Just weeks after Brooks's birth, the family relocated to Chicago, where Brooks was educated in first a predominantly white school, then a predominantly Black school, and finally the integrated Englewood High School, from which she graduated. In 1936, she graduated from Wilson Junior College. Brooks's first book of poetry, A Street in Bronzeville *(1945), was widely acclaimed and led to a two-year Guggenheim Fellowship. In 1949, Brooks published her second volume of poetry,* Annie Allen, *for which she won a Pulitzer Prize in 1950, making her the first African American to win the award. In 1953, Brooks published her one and only novel,* Maud Martha, *a poetic, sparse account of a young woman's maturation from childhood to adulthood, which is excerpted below. Other volumes of poems include* Bronzeville Boys and Girls *(1956), a collection for children;* The Bean Eaters *(1961);* In the Mecca *(1968); and* Riot *(1969), a response to the 1968 riots following the assassination of Martin Luther King, Jr. In her role as 1968 poet laureate of Illinois and also in her 1972 autobiography,* Report from Part One, *Brooks expressed eagerness for her poetry to reach a large Black audience.*

Maud Martha

IF YOU'RE LIGHT AND HAVE LONG HAIR

1 Came the invitation that Paul recognized as an honor of the first water, and as sufficient indication that he was, at last, a social somebody. The invitation was from the Foxy Cats Club, the club of clubs. He was to be present, in formal dress, at the Annual Foxy Cats Dawn Ball. No chances were taken: "Top hat, white tie and tails" hastily followed the "Formal dress," and that elucidation was in bold type.

2 Twenty men were in the Foxy Cats Club. All were good-looking. All wore clothes that were rich and suave. All "handled money," for their number consisted of well-located barbers, policemen, "government men" and men with a lucky touch at the tracks. Certainly the Foxy Cats Club was not a representative of that growing group of South Side organizations devoted to moral and civic improvements, or to literary or other cultural pursuits. If that had been so, Paul would have chucked his bid (which was black and silver, decorated with winking cat faces) down the toilet with a yawn. "That kind of stuff" was hardly understood by Paul, and was always dismissed with an airy "dicty," "hincty" or "high-falutin'." But no. The Foxy Cats devoted themselves solely to the business of being "hep," and each year they spent hundreds of dollars on their wonderful Dawn Ball, which did not begin at dawn, but was scheduled to end at dawn. "Ball," they called the frolic, but it served also the purposes of party, feast and fashion show. Maud Martha, watching him study his invitation, watching him lift his chin, could see that he considered himself one of the blessed.

3 *Who—what kind soul had recommended him!*

4 "He'll have to take me," thought Maud Martha. "For the envelope is addressed 'Mr. and Mrs.,' and I opened it. I guess he'd like to leave me home. At the Ball, there will be only beautiful girls, or real stylish ones. There won't be more than a handful like me. My type is not a Foxy Cat favorite. But he can't avoid taking me—since he hasn't yet thought of words or ways strong enough, and at the same time soft enough—for he's kind: he doesn't like to injure—to carry across to me the news that he is not to be held permanently by my type, and that he can go on with this marriage only if I put no ropes or questions around him. Also, he'll want to humor me, now that I'm pregnant."

5   She would need a good dress. That, she knew, could be a problem, on his grocery clerk's pay. He would have his own expenses. He would have to rent his topper and tails, and he would have to buy a fine tie, and really excellent shoes. She knew he was thinking that on the strength of his appearance and sophisticated behavior at this Ball might depend his future admission (for why not dream?) to *membership*, actually, in the Foxy Cats Club!

6   "I'll settle," decided Maud Martha, "on a plain white princess-style thing and some blue and black satin ribbon. I'll go to my mother's. I'll work miracles at the sewing machine.

7   "On that night, I'll wave my hair. I'll smell faintly of lily of the valley."

8   The main room of the Club 99, where the Ball was held, was hung with green and yellow and red balloons, and the thick pillars, painted to give an effect of marble, and stretching from floor to ceiling, were draped with green and red and yellow crepe paper. Huge ferns, rubber plants and bowls of flowers were at every corner. The floor itself was a decoration, golden, glazed. There was no overhead light; only wall lamps, and the bulbs in these were romantically dim. At the back of the room, standing on a furry white rug, was the long banquet table, dressed in damask, accented by groups of thin silver candlesticks bearing white candles, and laden with lovely food: cold chicken, lobster, candied ham fruit combinations, potato salad in a great gold dish, corn sticks, a cheese fluff in spiked tomato cups, fruit cake, angel cake, sunshine cake. The drinks were at a smaller table nearby, behind which stood a genial mixologist, quick with maraschino cherries, and with lemon, ice and liquor. Wines were there, and whiskey, and rum, and egg-nog made with pure cream.

9   Paul and Maud Martha arrived rather late, on purpose. Rid of their wraps, they approached the glittering floor. Bunny Bates's orchestra was playing Ellington's "Solitude."

10   Paul, royal in rented finery, was flushed with excitement. Maud Martha looked at him. Not very tall. Not very handsomely made. But there was that extraordinary quality of maleness. Hiding in the body that was not *too* yellow, waiting to spring out at her, surround her (she liked to think)—that maleness. The Ball stirred her. The Beauties, in their gorgeous gowns, bustling, supercilious; the young men, who at other times most unpleasantly blew their noses, and darted surreptitiously into alleys to relieve themselves, and sweated and swore at their jobs, and scratched their more intimate parts,

now smiling, smooth, overgallant; the drowsy lights; the smells of food and flowers, the smell of Murray's pomade, the body perfumes, natural and superimposed; the sensuous heaviness of the wine-colored draperies at the many windows; the music, now steamy and slow, now as clear and fragile as glass, now raging, passionate, now moaning and thickly gray. The Ball made toys of her emotions, stirred her variously. But she was anxious to have it end, she was anxious to be at home again, with the door closed behind herself and her husband. Then, he might be warm. There might be more than the absent courtesy he had been giving her of late. Then, he might be the tree she had a great need to lean against, in this "emergency." There was no telling what dear thing he might say to her, what little gem let fall.

11   But, to tell the truth, his behavior now was not very promising of gems to come. After their second dance he escorted her to a bench by the wall, left her. Trying to look nonchalant, she sat. She sat, trying not to show the inferiority she did not feel. When the music struck up again, he began to dance with someone red-haired and curved, and white as a white. Who was she? He had approached her easily, he had taken her confidently, he held her and conversed with her as though he had known her well for a long, long time. The girl smiled up at him. Her gold-spangled bosom was pressed—was pressed against that maleness—

12   A man asked Maud Martha to dance. He was dark, too. His mustache was small.

13   "Is this your first Foxy Cats?" he asked.

14   "What?" Paul's cheek was on that of Gold-Spangles.

15   "First Cats?"

16   "Oh. Yes." Paul and Gold-Spangles were weaving through the noisy twisting couples, were trying, apparently, to get to the reception hall.

17   "Do you know that girl? What's her name?" Maud Martha asked her partner, pointing to Gold-Spangles. Her partner looked, nodded. He pressed her closer.

18   "That's Maella. That's Maella."

19   "Pretty, isn't she?" She wanted him to keep talking about Maella. He nodded again.

20   "Yep. She has 'em howling along the stroll, all right, all right."

21   Another man, dancing past with an artificial redhead, threw a whispered word at Maud Martha's partner, who caught it eagerly, winked. "Solid, ol' man," he said. "Solid, Jack." He pressed Maud Martha closer. "You're a babe," he said. "You're a real babe." He reeked excitingly of tobacco, liquor, pinesoap, toilet water, and Sen Sen.

22   Maud Martha thought of her parents' back yard. Fresh. Clean. Smokeless. In her childhood, a snowball bush had shone there, big above the dandelions. The snowballs had been big, healthy. Once, she and her sister and brother had waited in the back yard for their parents to finish readying themselves for a trip to Milwaukee. The snowballs had been so beautiful, so fat and startlingly white in the sunlight, that she had suddenly loved home a thousand times more than ever before, and had not wanted to go to Milwaukee. But as the children grew, the bush sickened. Each year the snowballs were smaller and more dispirited. Finally a summer came when there were no blossoms at all. Maud Martha wondered what had become of the bush. For it was not there now. Yet she, at least, had never seen it go.

23   "Not," thought Maud Martha, "that they love each other. It oughta be that simple. Then I could lick it. It oughta be that easy. But it's my color that makes him mad. I try to shut my eyes to that, but it's no good. What I am inside, what is really me, he likes okay. But he keeps looking at my color, which is like a wall. He has to jump over it in order to meet and touch what I've got for him. He has to jump away up high in order to see it. He gets awful tired of all that jumping."

24   Paul came back from the reception hall. Maella was clinging to his arm. A final cry of the saxophone finished that particular slice of the blues. Maud Martha's partner bowed, escorted her to a chair by a rubber plant, bowed again, left.

25   "I could," considered Maud Martha, "go over there and scratch her upsweep down. I could spit on her back. I could scream. 'Listen,' I could scream, 'I'm making a baby for this man and I mean to do it in peace.' "

26   But if the root was sour what business did she have up there hacking at a leaf?

A BIRTH

27   After dinner, they washed dishes together. Then they undressed, and Paul got in bed, and was asleep almost instantly. She went down the long public hall to the bathroom, in her blue chenille robe. On her way back down the squeezing dark of the hall she felt—something softly separate in her. Back in the bedroom, she put on her gown, then stepped to the dresser to smear her face with cold cream. But when she turned around to get in the bed she couldn't move. Her legs cramped painfully, and she had a tremendous desire to eliminate which somehow she felt she would never be able to gratify.

28   "Paul!" she cried. As though in his dreams he had been waiting to hear that call, and that call only, he was up with a bound.

29   "I can't move."

30   He rubbed his eyes.

31   "Maudie, are you kidding?"

32   "I'm not kidding, Paul. I can't move."

33   He lifted her up and laid her on the bed, his eyes stricken.

34   "Look here, Maudie. Do you think you're going to have that baby tonight?"

35   "No—no. These are just what they call 'false pains.' I'm not going to have the baby tonight. Can you get—my gown off?"

36   "Sure. Sure."

37   But really he was afraid to touch her. She lay nude on the bed for a few moments, perfectly still. Then all of a sudden motion came to her. Whereas before she had not been able to move her legs, now she could not keep them still.

38   "Oh, my God," she prayed aloud. "Just let my legs get *still five minutes.*" God did not answer the prayer.

39   Paul was pacing up and down the room in fright.

40   "Look here. I don't think those are false pains. I think you're going to have that baby tonight."

41   "Don't say that, Paul," she muttered between clenched teeth. "I'm not going to have the baby tonight."

42   "I'm going to call your mother."

43   "Don't do that, Paul. She can't stand to see things like this. Once she got a chance to see a still-born baby, but she fainted before they even unwrapped it. She can't stand to see things like this. False pains, that's all. Oh, GOD, why don't you let me keep my legs still!"

44   She began to whimper in a manner that made Paul want to vomit. His thoughts traveled to the girl he had met at the Dawn Ball several months before. Cool. Sweet. Well-groomed. Fair.

45   "You're going to have that baby *now.* I'm going down to call up your mother and a doctor."

46   "DON'T YOU GO OUT OF HERE AND LEAVE ME ALONE! Damn. DAMN!"

47   "All right. All right. I won't leave you alone. I'll get the woman next door to come in. But somebody's got to get a doctor here."

48   "Don't you sneak out! Don't you *sneak* out!" She was pushing down with her stomach now. Paul, standing at the foot of the bed with his hands in his pockets, saw the creeping insistence of what he thought was the head of the child.

49   "Oh, my Lord!" he cried. "It's coming! It's coming!"

50   He walked about the room several times. He went to the dresser and began to brush his hair. She looked at him in speechless contempt. He went out of the door, and ran down the three flights of stairs two or three steps at a time. The telephone was on the first floor. No sooner had he picked up the receiver than he heard Maud Martha give what he was sure could *only* be called a "bloodcurdling scream." He bolted up the stairs, saw her wriggling on the bed, said softly, "Be right back," and bolted down again. First he called his mother's doctor, and begged him to come right over. Then he called the Browns.

51   "Get her to the hospital!" shouted Belva Brown. "You'll have to get her to the hospital right away!"

52   "I can't. She's having the baby now. She isn't going to let anybody touch her. I tell you, she's having the baby."

53   "Don't be a fool. Of course she can get to the hospital. Why, she mustn't have it there in the house! I'm coming over there. I'll take her myself. Be sure there's plenty of gas in that car."

54   He tried to reach his mother. She was out—had not returned from a revival meeting.

55   When Paul ran back up the stairs, he found young Mrs. Cray, who lived in the front apartment of their floor, attending his shrieking wife.

56   "I heard 'er yellin', and thought I'd better come in, seein' as how you all is so confused. Got a doctor comin'?"

57   Paul sighed heavily. "I just called one. Thanks for coming in. This—this came on all of a sudden, and I don't think I know what to do."

58   "Well, the thing to do is get a doctor right off. She's goin' to have the baby soon. Call *my* doctor." She gave him a number. "Whichever one gets here first can work on her. Ain't no time to waste."

59   Paul ran back down the stairs and called the number. "What's the doctor's address?" he yelled up. Mrs. Cray yelled it down. He went out to get the doctor personally. He was glad of an excuse to escape. He was sick of hearing Maudie scream. He had had no idea that she could scream that kind of screaming. It was awful. How lucky he was that he had been born a man. How lucky he was that he had been born a man!

60   Belva arrived in twenty minutes. She was grateful to find another woman present. She had come to force Maud Martha to start for the hospital, but a swift glance told her that the girl would not leave her bed for many days. As she said to her husband and Helen later on, "The baby was all ready to spill out."

61   When her mother came in the door Maud Martha tightened her lips, temporarily forgetful of her strange pain. (But it wasn't pain. It was something else.) "Listen. If you're going to make a fuss, go on out. I'm having enough trouble without you making a fuss over everything."

62   Mrs. Cray giggled encouragingly. Belva said bravely, "I'm not going to make a fuss. You'll see. Why, there's nothing to make a fuss *about*. You're just going to have a baby, like millions of other women. Why should I make a fuss?"

63   Maud Martha tried to smile but could not quite make it. The sensations were getting grindingly sharp. She screamed longer and louder, explaining breathlessly in between times, "I just can't help it. Excuse me."

64   "Why, go on and scream," urged Belva. "You're supposed to scream. That's your privilege. I'm sure *I* don't mind." Her ears were splitting, and over and over as she stood there looking down at her agonized daughter, she said to herself, "Why doesn't the doctor come? Why doesn't the doctor come? I know I'm going to faint." She and Mrs. Cray stood, one on each side of the bed, purposelessly holding a sheet over Maud Martha, under which they peeped as seldom as they felt was safe. Maud Martha kept asking, "Has the head come?" Presently she felt as though her whole body were having a bowel movement. The head came. Then, with a little difficulty, the wide shoulders. Then easily, with soft and slippery smoothness, out slipped the rest of the body and the baby was born. The first thing it did was sneeze.

65   Maud Martha laughed as though she could never bear to stop. "Listen to him sneeze. My little baby. Don't let him drown, Mrs. Cray." Mrs. Cray looked at Maud Martha, because she did not want to look at the baby. "How you know it's a him?" Maud Martha laughed again.

66   Belva also refused to look at the baby. "See, Maudie," she said, "see how brave I was? The baby is born, and I didn't get nervous or faint or anything. Didn't I tell you?"

67   "Now isn't that nice," thought Maud Martha. "Here I've had the baby, and she thinks I should praise her for having stood up there and looked on." Was it, she suddenly wondered, as hard to watch suffering as it was to bear it?

68   Five minutes after the birth, Paul got back with Mrs. Cray's doctor, a large silent man, who came in swiftly, threw the sheet aside without saying a word, cut the cord. Paul looked at the new human being. It appeared gray and greasy. Life was hard, he thought. What had he done to deserve a stillborn child? But there it was, lying dead.

69   "It's dead, isn't it?" he asked dully.

70   "Oh, get out of here!" cried Mrs. Cray, pushing him into the kitchen and shutting the door.

71   "Girl," said the doctor. Then grudgingly, "Fine girl."

72   "Did you hear what the doctor said, Maudie?" chattered Belva. "You've got a daughter, the doctor says." The doctor looked at her quickly.

73   "Say, you'd better go out and take a walk around the block. You don't look so well."

74   Gratefully, Belva obeyed. When she got back, Mrs. Cray and the doctor had oiled and dressed the baby—dressed her in an outfit found in Maud Martha's top dresser drawer. Belva looked at the newcomer in amazement.

75   "Well, she's a little beauty, isn't she!" she cried. She had not expected a handsome child.

76   Maud Martha's thoughts did not dwell long on the fact of the baby. There would be all her life long for that. She preferred to think, now, about how well she felt. Had she ever in her life felt so well? She felt well enough to get up. She folded her arms triumphantly across her chest, as another young woman, her neighbor to the rear, came in.

77   "Hello, Mrs. Barksdale!" she hailed. "Did you hear the news? I just had a baby, and I feel strong enough to go out and shovel coal! Having a baby is *nothing*, Mrs. Barksdale. Nothing at all."

78   "Aw, yeah?" Mrs. Barksdale smacked her gum admiringly. "Well, from what I heard back there a while ago, didn't seem like it was nothing. Girl, I didn't know anybody *could* scream that loud." Maud Martha tittered. Oh, she felt fine. She wondered why Mrs. Barksdale hadn't come in while the screaming was going on; she had missed it all.

79   People. Weren't they sweet. She had never said more than "Hello, Mrs. Barksdale" and "Hello, Mrs. Cray" to these women before. But as soon as something happened to her, in they trooped. People were sweet.

80   The doctor brought the baby and laid it in the bed beside Maud Martha. Shortly before she had heard it in the kitchen—a bright delight had flooded through her upon first hearing that part of Maud Martha Brown Phillips expressing itself with a voice of its own. But now the baby was quiet and returned its mother's stare with one that seemed equally curious and mystified but perfectly cool and undisturbed.

June Jordan

(1936–2002)

Born July 9, 1936, in Harlem, New York, Jordan was the only child of Granville and Mildred Jordan, Jamaican immigrants. After graduating from high school, Jordan attended Barnard College and the University of Chicago. Nicknamed "the universal poet," Jordan, who had also published under her married name, June Meyers, is best known for her poetry, which powerfully addresses human rights issues from the Americas to Palestine to South Africa. A complex thinker and writer, Jordan addressed intraracial class stratification, language as a site of power, and struggles common to Black women in the Diaspora. Her first poetry collection, Who Look at Me *(1968), was followed by numerous volumes, including* New Days: Poems of Exile and Return *(1974),* Things That I Do in the Dark: Selected Poetry *(1977), which was edited by Toni Morrison, and* Living Room: New Poems, 1980–1984 *(1985). She also wrote essay collections, a novel entitled* His Own Where *(1970), children's books, plays, and a libretto. "A Song of Sojourner Truth," from her 1980 collection,* Passion: New Poems, 1977–1980, *"Where Is the Love?," from her first volume of essays,* Civil Wars *(1981), and "A New Politics of Sexuality" and "Report from the Bahamas," both included in* Some of Us Did Not Die: New and Selected Essays of June Jordan *(2002), are included in this chapter. Jordan was a professor of African American Studies at the University of California, Berkeley, where she directed the Poetry for the People Program.*

A Song of Sojourner Truth

Dedicated to Bernice Reagon

The trolley cars was rollin and the passengers all white
when Sojourner just decided it was time to take a seat
The trolley cars was rollin and the passengers all white
When Sojourner decided it was time to take a seat
5 It was time she felt to rest a while and ease up
on her feet
So Sojourner put her hand out
tried to flag the trolley down
So Sojourner put her hand out
10 for the trolley crossin town
And the driver did not see her

the conductor would not stop
But Sojourner yelled, "It's me!"
And put her body on the track
15 "It's me!" she yelled, "And yes,
I walked here but I ain walkin back!"
The trolley car conductor and the driver was afraid
to roll right over her and leave her lying dead
So they opened up the car and Sojourner took a seat
20 So Sojourner sat to rest a while and eased up on her feet

REFRAIN:

Sojourner had to be just crazy
tellin all that kinda truth
I say she musta been plain crazy
plus they say she was uncouth
25 talkin loud to any crowd
talkin bad insteada sad
She just had to be plain crazy
talkin all that kinda truth

If she had somewhere to go she said
30 *I'll ride*
If she had somewhere to go she said
I'll ride
jim crow or no
she said *I'll go*
35 just like the lady
that she was in all the knowing darkness
of her pride
she said *I'll ride*
she said *I'll talk*
40 she said *A Righteous Mouth*
ain nothin you should hide
she said she'd ride
just like the lady
that she was in all the knowing darkness
45 of her pride
she said *I'll ride*

They said she's Black and ugly and they said she's
really rough
They said if you treat her like a dog

50   well that'll be plenty good enough
     And Sojourner said
     I'll ride
     And Sojourner said
     I'll go
55   I'm a woman and this hell has made me tough
     (Thank God!)
     This hell has made me tough
     I'm a strong Black woman
     and Thank God!

     REFRAIN:

60   Sojourner had to be just crazy
     tellin all that kinda truth
     I say she musta been plain crazy
     plus they say she was uncouth
     talkin loud to any crowd
65   talkin bad insteada sad
     She just had to be plain crazy
     talkin all that kinda truth

Where Is the Love?

1   The 1978 National Black Writers Conference at Howard University culminated with an extremely intense public seminar entitled *Feminism and the Black Woman Writer*. This was an historic, unprecedented event tantamount to conceding that, under such a heading, there might be something to discuss! Acklyn Lynch, Sonia Sanchez, Barbara Smith, and myself were the panelists chosen to present papers to the standing room only audience. I had been asked, also, to moderate the proceedings and therefore gave the opening statement, *Where Is the Love?*, which was later published in *Essence* magazine.

2   From phone calls and other kinds of gossip, I knew that the very scheduling of this seminar had managed to divide people into camps prepared for war. Folks were so jumpy, in fact, that when I walked into the theater I ran into several Black feminists and then several Black men who, I suppose, just to be safe, had decided not to speak

to anyone outside the immediate circle of supportive friends they had brought with them.

3   The session was going to be hot. Evidently, feminism was being translated into lesbianism, into something interchangeable with lesbianism, and the taboo on feminism, within the Black intellectual community, had long been exceeded in its orthodox severity only by the taboo on the subject of the lesbian. I say within the intellectual Black community, because, minus such terms as *feminist* and *lesbian*, the phenomena of self-directed Black women or the phenomena of Black women loving other women have hardly been uncommon, let alone unbelievable, events to Black people not privy to theoretical strife about correct and incorrect Black experience.

4   This blurring of issues seemed to me incendiary and obnoxious. Once again, the Black woman writer would be lost to view as issues of her sex life claimed public attention at the expense of intellectual and aesthetic focus upon her work. Compared to the intellectual and literary criticism accorded to James Baldwin and Richard Wright, for example, there is damned little attention paid to their bedroom activities. In any case, I do not believe that feminism is a matter, first or last, of sexuality.

5   The seminar was going to be a fight. It was not easy to prepare for this one. From my childhood in Brooklyn I knew that your peers would respect you if you could hurt somebody. Much less obvious was how to elicit respect as somebody who felt and who meant love.

6   I wanted to see if it was possible to say things that people believe they don't want to hear, without having to kick ass and without looking the fool for holding out your hand. Was there some way to say, to insist on, each, perhaps disagreeable, individual orientation and nonetheless leave the union of Black men and Black women, as a people, intact? I felt that there had to be: If the individual cannot exist then who will be the people?

7   I expected that we, Black panelists and audience, together, would work out a way to deal, even if we didn't want to deal. And that's what happened, at Howard. We did. Nobody walked out. Nobody stopped talking. The session ended because we ran out of time.

8   As I think about anyone or anything—whether history or literature or my father or political organizations or a poem or a film—as I seek to evaluate the potentiality, the life-supportive commitment/possibilities of anyone or any thing, the decisive question is, always, *where is the love?* The energies that flow from hatred, from

negative and hateful habits and attitudes and dogma do not promise something good, something I would choose to cherish, to honor with my own life. It is always the love, whether we look to the spirit of Fannie Lou Hamer, or to the spirit of Agostinho Neto, it is always the love that will carry action into positive new places, that will carry your own nights and days beyond demoralization and away from suicide.

9   I am a feminist, and what that means to me is much the same as the meaning of the fact that I am Black: it means that I must undertake to love myself and to respect myself as though my very life depends upon self-love and self-respect. It means that I must everlastingly seek to cleanse myself of the hatred and the contempt that surrounds and permeates my identity, as a woman, and as a Black human being, in this particular world of ours. It means that the achievement of self-love and self-respect will require inordinate, hourly vigilance, and that I am entering my soul into a struggle that will most certainly transform the experience of all the peoples of the earth, as no other movement can, in fact, hope to claim: because the movement into self-love, self-respect, and self-determination is the movement now galvanizing the true, the unarguable majority of human beings everywhere. This movement explicitly demands the testing of the viability of a moral idea: that the health, the legitimacy of any status quo, any governing force, must be measured according to the experiences of those who are, comparatively, powerless. Virtue is not to be discovered in the conduct of the strong vis-à-vis the powerful, but rather it is to be found in our behavior and policies affecting those who are different, those who are weaker, or smaller than we. How do the strong, the powerful, treat children? How do we treat the aged among us? How do the strong and the powerful treat so-called minority members of the body politic? How do the powerful regard women? How do they treat us?

10   Easily you can see that, according to this criterion, the overwhelming reality of power and government and tradition is evil, is diseased, is illegitimate, and deserves nothing from us—no loyalty, no accommodation, no patience, no understanding—except a clear-minded resolve to utterly change this total situation and, thereby, to change our own destiny.

11   As a Black woman, as a Black feminist, I exist, simultaneously, as part of the powerless and as part of the majority peoples of the world in two ways: I am powerless as compared to any man because women, per se, are kept powerless by men/by the powerful; I am powerless as compared to anyone white because Black and Third World

peoples are kept powerless by whites/by the powerful. I am the majority because women constitute the majority gender. I am the majority because Black and Third World peoples constitute the majority of life on this planet.

12   And it is here, in this extreme, inviolable coincidence of my status as a Black feminist, my status as someone twice stigmatized, my status as a Black woman who is twice kin to the despised majority of all the human life that there is, it is here, in that extremity, that I stand in a struggle against suicide. And it is here, in this extremity, that I ask, of myself, and of any one who would call me *sister, Where is the love?*

13   The love devolving from my quest for self-love and self-respect and self-determination must be, as I see it, something you can verify in the ways that I present myself to others, and in the ways that I approach people different from myself. How do I reach out to the people I would like to call my sisters and my brothers and my children and my lovers and my friends? If I am a Black feminist serious in the undertaking of self-love, then it seems to me that the legitimate, the morally defensible character of that self-love should be such that I gain and gain and gain in the socio-psychic strength needed so that I may, without fear, be able and willing to love and respect women, for example, who are not like me: women who are not feminists, women who are not professionals, women who are not as old or as young as I am, women who have neither job nor income, women who are not Black.

14   And it seems to me that the socio-psychic strength that should follow from a morally defensible Black feminism will mean that I become able and willing, without fear, to love and respect all men who are willing and able, without fear, to love and respect me. In short, if the acquirement of my self-determination is part of a worldwide, an inevitable, and a righteous movement, then I should become willing and able to embrace more and more of the whole world, without fear, and also without self-sacrifice.

15   This means that, as a Black feminist, I cannot be expected to respect what somebody else calls self-love if that concept of self-love requires my suicide to any degree. And this will hold true whether that somebody else is male, female, Black, or white. My Black feminism means that you cannot expect me to respect what somebody else identifies as the Good of The People, if that so-called Good (often translated into *manhood* or *family* or *nationalism*) requires the deferral or the diminution of my self-fulfillment. We *are* the people. And, as Black women, we are most of the people, any people, you care to

talk about. And, therefore, nothing that is Good for The People is good unless it is good for me, as I determine myself.

16   When I speak of Black feminism, then, I am speaking from an exacerbated consciousness of the truth that we, Black women, huddle together, miserably, on the very lowest levels of the economic pyramid. We, Black women, subsist among the most tenuous and least likely economic conditions for survival.

17   When I speak of Black feminism, then, I am not speaking of sexuality. I am not speaking of heterosexuality or lesbianism or homosexuality or bisexuality; whatever sexuality anyone elects for his or her pursuit is not my business, nor the business of the state. And, furthermore, I cannot be persuaded that one kind of sexuality, as against another, will necessarily provide for the greater happiness of the two people involved. I am not talking about sexuality. I am talking about love, about a steady-state deep caring and respect for every other human being, a love that can only derive from a secure and positive self-love.

18   As a Black woman/feminist, I must look about me, with trembling, and with shocked anger, at the endless waste, the endless suffocation of my sisters: the bitter sufferings of hundreds of thousands of women who are the sole parents, the mothers of hundreds of thousands of children, the desolation and the futility of women trapped by demeaning, lowest-paying occupations, the unemployed, the bullied, the beaten, the battesed, the ridiculed, the slandered, the trivialized, the raped, and the sterilized, the lost millions and multimillions of beautiful, creative, and momentous lives turned to ashes on the pyre of gender identity. I must look about me and, as a Black feminist, I must ask myself: *Where is the love?* How is my own lifework serving to end these tyrannies, these corrosions of sacred possibility?

19   As a Black feminist poet and writer I must look behind me with trembling, and with shocked anger, at the fate of Black women writers until now. From the terrible graves of a traditional conspiracy against my sisters in art, I must exhume the works of women writers and poets such as Georgia Douglas Johnson (who?).

20   In the early flush of the Harlem Renaissance, Georgia Johnson accomplished an astonishing, illustrious life experience. Married to Henry Lincoln Johnson, U.S. Recorder of Deeds in Washington, D.C., the poet, in her own right, became no less than Commissioner of Conciliation for the U.S. Department of Labor (*who was that again? Who?*). And she, this poet, furthermore enjoyed the intense, promotional attention of Dean Kelley Miller, here at Howard, and W. E. B. DuBois, and William Stanley Braithwaite, and Alain Locke. And she

published three volumes of her own poetry and I found her work in Countee Cullen's anthology, *Caroling Dusk*, where, Countee Cullen reports, she, Georgia Douglas Johnson, thrived as a kind of Gwendolyn Brooks, holding regular Saturday night get-togethers with the young Black writers of the day.

21   And what did this poet of such acclaim, achievement, connection, and generosity, what did this poet have to say in her poetry, and who among us has ever heard of Georgia Douglas Johnson? And is there anybody in this room who can tell me the name of two or three other women poets from the Harlem Renaissance? And why did she die, and why does the work of all women die with no river carrying forward the record of such grace? How is it the case that whether we have written novels or poetry or whether we have raised our children or cleaned and cooked and washed and ironed, it is all dismissed as "women's work"; it is all, finally, despised as nothing important, and there is no trace, no echo of our days upon the earth?

22   Why is it not surprising that a Black woman as remarkably capable and gifted and proven as Georgia Douglas Johnson should be the poet of these pathetic, beggarly lines:

> *I'm folding up my little dreams*
> *within my heart tonight*
> *And praying I may soon forget*
> *the torture of their sight*
> *   "My Little Dreams"*

How long, how long will we let the dreams of women serve merely to torture and not to ignite, to enflame, and to ennoble the promise of the years of every lifetime? And here is Georgia Douglas Johnson's poem "The Heart of a Woman":

> *The heart of a woman goes forth with the dawn,*
> *As a lovebird, softwinging, so restlessly on,*
> *Afar o'er life's turrets and vales does it roam*
> *In the wake of those echoes the heart calls home.*
>
> *The heart of a woman falls back with the night*
> *And enters some alien cage in its plight,*
> *And tries to forget it has dreamed of the stars,*
> *While it breaks, breaks, breaks on the sheltering bars.*

23   And it is against such sorrow, and it is against such suicide, and it is against such deliberated strangulation of the possible lives of women, of my sisters, and of powerless peoples—men and children— everywhere, that I work and live, now, as a feminist trusting that I will learn to love myself well enough to love you (whoever you are), well enough so that you will love me well enough so that we will know exactly where is the love: that it is here, between us, and growing stronger and growing stronger.

A New Politics of Sexuality*

1   As a young worried mother, I remember turning to Dr. Benjamin Spock's *Common Sense Book of Baby and Child Care* just about as often as I'd pick up the telephone. He was God. I was ignorant but striving to be good: a good Mother. And so it was there, in that best-seller pocketbook of do's and don't's, that I came upon this doozie of a guideline: Do not wear miniskirts or other provocative clothing because that will upset your child, especially if your child happens to be a boy. If you give your offspring "cause" to think of you as a sexual being, he will, at the least, become disturbed; you will derail the equilibrium of his notions about your possible identity and meaning in the world.

2   It had never occurred to me that anyone, especially my son, might look upon me as an asexual being. I had never supposed that "asexual" was some kind of positive designation I should, so to speak, lust after. I was pretty surprised by Dr. Spock. However, I was also, by habit, a creature of obedience. For a couple of weeks I actually experimented with lusterless colors and dowdy tops and bottoms, self-consciously hoping thereby to prove myself as a lusterless and dowdy and, therefore, excellent female parent.

3   Years would have to pass before I could recognize the familiar, by then, absurdity of a man setting himself up as the expert on a subject

*This essay was adapted from the author's keynote address to the Bisexual, Gay, and Lesbian Student Association at Stanford University on April 29, 1991. It was published in *The Progressive*, July 1991.

that presupposed women as the primary objects for his patriarchal dis-course—on motherhood, no less! Years passed before I came to perceive the perversity of dominant power assumed by men, and the perver-sity of self-determining power ceded to men by women.

4 A lot of years went by before I understood the dynamics of what anyone could summarize as the Politics of Sexuality.

5 I believe the Politics of Sexuality is the most ancient and prob-ably the most profound arena for human conflict. Increasingly, it seems clear to me that deeper and more pervasive than any other oppression, than any other bitterly contested human domain, is the oppression of sexuality, the exploitation of the human domain of sexuality for power.

6 When I say sexuality, I mean gender: I mean male subjugation of human beings because they are female. When I say sexuality, I mean heterosexual institutionalization of rights and privileges denied to homosexual men and women. When I say sexuality I mean gay or lesbian contempt for bisexual modes of human relationship.

7 The Politics of Sexuality therefore subsumes all of the different ways in which some of us seek to dictate to others of us what we should do, what we should desire, what we should dream about, and how we should behave ourselves, generally. From China to Iran, from Nigeria to Czechoslovakia, from Chile to California, the politics of sexuality—enforced by traditions of state-sanctioned violence plus religion and the law—reduces to male domination of women, het-erosexist tyranny, and, among those of us who are in any case deemed despicable or deviant by the powerful, we find intolerance for those who choose a different, a more complicated—for example, an inter-racial or bisexual—mode of rebellion and freedom.

8 We must move out from the shadows of our collective subjuga-tion—as people of color/as women/as gay/as lesbian/as bisexual human beings.

9 I can voice my ideas without hesitation or fear because I am speak-ing, finally, about myself. I am Black and I am female and I am a mother and I am bisexual and I am a nationalist and I am an anti-nationalist. And I mean to be fully and freely all that I am!

10 Conversely, I do not accept that any white or Black or Chinese man—I do not accept that, for instance, Dr. Spock—should presume to tell me, or any other woman, how to mother a child. He has no right. He is not a mother. My child is not his child. And, likewise, I do not accept that anyone—any woman or any man who is not inextricably

part of the subject he or she dares to address—should attempt to tell any of us, the objects of her or his presumptuous discourse, what we should do or what we should not do.

11 Recently, I have come upon gratuitous and appalling pseudoliberal pronouncements on sexuality. Too often, these utterances fall out of the mouths of men and women who first disclaim any sentiment remotely related to homophobia, but who then proceed to issue outrageous opinions like the following:

- That it is blasphemous to compare the oppression of gay, lesbian, or bisexual people to the oppression, say, of black people, or of the Palestinians.
- That the bottom line about gay or lesbian or bisexual identity is that you can conceal it whenever necessary and, so, therefore, why don't you do just that? Why don't you keep your deviant sexuality in the closet and let the rest of us—we who suffer oppression for reasons of our ineradicable and always visible components of our personhood such as race or gender—get on with our more necessary, our more beleaguered struggle to survive?

12 Well, number one: I believe I have worked as hard as I could, and then harder than that, on behalf of equality and justice—for African-Americans, for the Palestinian people, and for people of color everywhere.

13 And no, I do not believe it is blasphemous to compare oppressions of sexuality to oppressions of race and ethnicity: Freedom is indivisible or it is nothing at all besides sloganeering and temporary, short-sighted, and short-lived advancement for a few. Freedom is indivisible, and either we are working for freedom or you are working for the sake of your self-interests and I am working for mine.

14 If you can finally go to the bathroom wherever you find one, if you can finally order a cup of coffee and drink it wherever coffee is available, but you cannot follow your heart—you cannot respect the response of your own honest body in the world—then how much of what kind of freedom does any one of us possess?

15 Or, conversely, if your heart and your honest body can be controlled by the state, or controlled by community taboo, are you not then, and in that case, no more than a slave ruled by outside force?

16 *What tyranny could exceed a tyranny that dictates to the human heart, and that attempts to dictate the public career of an honest human body?*

17   Freedom is indivisible; the Politics of Sexuality is not some optional "special-interest" concern for serious, progressive folk.

18   And, on another level, let me assure you: if every single gay or lesbian or bisexual man or woman active on the Left of American politics decided to stay home, there would be *no* Left left.

19   One of the things I want to propose is that we act on that reality: that we insistently demand reciprocal respect and concern from those who cheerfully depend upon our brains and our energies for their, and our, effective impact on the political landscape.

20   Last spring, at Berkeley, some students asked me to speak at a rally against racism. And I did. There were four or five hundred people massed on Sproul Plaza, standing together against that evil. And, on the next day, on that same plaza, there was a rally for bisexual and gay and lesbian rights, and students asked me to speak at that rally. And I did. There were fewer than seventy-five people stranded, pitiful, on that public space. And I said then what I say today: That was disgraceful! There should have been just one rally. One rally: freedom is indivisible.

21   As for the second, nefarious pronouncement on sexuality that now enjoys mass-media currency; the idiot notion of keeping yourself in the closet—that is very much the same thing as the suggestion that black folks and Asian-Americans and Mexican-Americans should assimilate and become as "white" as possible—in our walk/talk/music/food/values—or else. Or else? Or else we should, deservedly, perish.

22   Sure enough, we have plenty of exposure to white everything so why would we opt to remain our African/Asian/Mexican selves? The answer is that suicide is absolute, and if you think you will survive by hiding who you really are, you are sadly misled: there is no such thing as partial or intermittent suicide. You can only survive if you—who you really are—do survive.

23   Likewise, we who are not men and we who are not heterosexist—we, sure enough, have plenty of exposure to male-dominated/heterosexist this and that.

24   But a struggle to survive cannot lead to suicide: suicide is the opposite of survival. And so we must not conceal/assimilate/integrate into the would-be dominant culture and political system that despises us. Our survival requires that we alter our environment so that we can live and so that we can hold each other's hands and so that we can kiss each other on the streets, and in the daylight of our existence,

without terror and without violent and sometimes fatal reactions from the busybodies of America.

25　Finally, I need to speak on bisexuality. I do believe that the analogy is interracial or multiracial identity. I do believe that the analogy for bisexuality is a multicultural, multi-ethnic, multiracial world view. Bisexuality follows from such a perspective and leads to it, as well.

26　Just as there are many men and women in the United States whose parents have given them more than one racial, more than one ethnic identity and cultural heritage to honor; and just as these men and women must deny no given part of themselves except at the risk of self-deception and the insanities that must issue from that; and just as these men and women embody the principle of equality among races and ethnic communities; and just as these men and women falter and anguish and choose and then falter again and then anguish and then choose yet again how they will honor the irreducible complexity of their God-given human being—even so, there are many men and women, especially young men and women, who seek to embrace the complexity of their total, always-changing social and political circumstance.

27　They seek to embrace our increasing global complexity on the basis of the heart and on the basis of an honest human body. Not according to ideology. Not according to group pressure. Not according to anybody's concept of "correct."

28　This is a New Politics of Sexuality. And even as I despair of identity politics—because identity is given and principles of justice/equality/freedom cut across given gender and given racial definitions of being, and because I will call you my brother, I will call you my sister, on the basis of what you *do* for justice, what you *do* for equality, what you *do* for freedom and *not* on the basis of who you are, even so I look with admiration and respect upon the new, bisexual politics of sexuality.

29　This emerging movement politicizes the so-called middle ground: Bisexuality invalidates either/or formulation, either/or analysis. Bisexuality means I am free and I am as likely to want and to love a woman as I am likely to want and to love a man, and what about that? Isn't that what freedom implies?

30　If you are free, you are not predictable and you are not controllable. To my mind, that is the keenly positive, politicizing significance of bisexual affirmation:

31   To insist upon complexity, to insist upon the validity of all of the components of social/sexual complexity, to insist upon the equal validity of all of the components of social/sexual complexity.

32   This seems to me a unifying, 1990s mandate for revolutionary Americans planning to make it into the twenty-first century on the basis of the heart, on the basis of an honest human body, consecrated to every struggle for justice, every struggle for equality, every struggle for freedom.

Report from the Bahamas

1   I am staying in a hotel that calls itself The Sheraton British Colonial. One of the photographs advertising the place displays a middle-aged Black man in a waiter's tuxedo, smiling. What intrigues me most about the picture is just this: while the Black man bears a tray full of "colorful" drinks above his left shoulder, both of his feet, shoes and trouser-legs, up to ten inches above his ankles, stand in the also "colorful" Caribbean salt water. He is so delighted to serve you he will wade into the water to bring you Banana Daquiris while you float! More precisely, he will wade into the water, fully clothed, oblivious to the ruin of his shoes, his trousers, his health, and he will do it with a smile.

2   I am in the Bahamas. On the phone in my room, a spinning complement of plastic pages offers handy index clues such as CAR RENTAL and CASINOS. A message from the Ministry of Tourism appears among these travellers tips. Opening with a paragraph of "WELCOME," the message then proceeds to "A PAGE OF HISTORY," which reads as follows:

> New World History begins on the same day that modern Bahamian history begins—October 12, 1492. That's when Columbus stepped ashore—British influence came first with the Eleutherian Adventurers of 1647—After the Revolutions, American Loyalists fled from the newly independent states and settled in the Bahamas. Confederate blockade-runners used the island as a haven during the War between the States, and after the War, a number of Southerners moved to the Bahamas. . . .

3   There it is again. Something proclaims itself a legitimate history and all it does is track white Mr. Columbus to the British Eleutherians

through the Confederate Southerners as they barge into New World surf, land on New World turf, and nobody saying one word about the Bahamian people, the Black peoples, to whom the only thing new in their island world was this weird succession of crude intruders and its colonial consequences.

4   This is my consciousness of race as I unpack my bathing suit in the Sheraton British Colonial. Neither this hotel nor the British nor the long ago Italians nor the white Delta airline pilots belong here, of course. And every time I look at the photograph of that fool standing in the water with his shoes on I'm about to have a West Indian fit, even though I know he's no fool; he's a middle-aged Blackman who needs a job and this is his job—pretending himself a servile ancillary to the pleasures of the rich. (Compared to his options in life, I am a rich woman. Compared to most of the Black Americans arriving for this Easter weekend on a three nights four days' deal of bargain rates, the middle-aged waiter is a poor Black man.)

5   We will jostle along with the other (white) visitors and join them in the tee shirt shops or, laughing together, learn ruthless rules of negotiation as we, Black Americans as well as white, argue down the price of handwoven goods at the nearby straw market while the merchants, frequently toothless Black women seated on the concrete in their only presentable dress, humble themselves to our careless games:

6   "Yes? You like it? Eight dollar."

7   "Five."

8   "I give it to you. Seven."

9   And so it continues, this weird succession of crude intruders that, now, includes me and my brothers and sisters from the North.

10   This is my consciousness of class as I try to decide how much money I can spend on Bahamian gifts for my family back in Brooklyn. No matter that these other Black women incessantly weave words and flowers into the straw hats and bags piled beside them on the burning dusty street. No matter that these other Black women must work their sense of beauty into these things that we will take away as cheaply as we dare, or they will do without food.

11   We are not white, after all. The budget is limited. And we are harmlessly killing time between the poolside rum punch and "The Native Show on the Patio" that will play tonight outside the hotel restaurant.

12   This is my consciousness of race and class and gender identity as I notice the fixed relations between these other Black women and myself. They sell and I buy or I don't. They risk not eating. I risk going broke on my first vacation afternoon.

13   We are not particularly women anymore; we are parties to a transaction designed to set us against each other.

14   "Olive" is the name of the Black woman who cleans my hotel room.
On my way to the beach I am wondering what "Olive" would say if I
told her why I chose The Sheraton British Colonial; if I told her I wanted
to swim. I wanted to sleep. I did not want to be harassed by the mid-
dleaged waiter, or his nephew. I did not want to be raped by anybody
(white or Black) at all and I calculated that my safety as a Black woman
alone would best be assured by a multinational hotel corporation. In
my experience, the big guys take customer complaints more seriously
than the little ones. I would suppose that's one reason why they're big;
they don't like to lose money anymore than I like to be bothered when
I'm trying to read a goddamned book underneath a palm tree I paid
$264 to get next to. A Black woman seeking refuge in a multinational
corporation may seem like a contradiction to some, but there you are.
In this case it's a coincidence of entirely different self-interests: Sher-
aton/cash = June Jordan's short run safety.

15   Anyway, I'm pretty sure "Olive" would look at me as though I
came from someplace as far away as Brooklyn. Then she'd probably allow herself one indignant query before righteously removing her
vacuum cleaner from my room; "and why in the first place you come
down you without your husband?"

16   I cannot imagine how I would begin to answer her.

17   My "rights" and my "freedom" and my "desire" and a slew of
other New World values; what would they sound like to this Black
woman described on the card atop my hotel bureau as "Olive the
Maid?" "Olive" is older than I am and I may smoke a cigarette while
she changes the sheets on my bed. Whose rights? Whose freedom?
Whose desire?

18   And why should she give a shit about mine unless I do something, for real, about hers?

19   It happens that the book that I finished reading under a palm
tree earlier today was the novel, *The Bread Givers*, by Anzia Yezierska. Definitely autobiographical, Yezierska lays out the difficulties
of being both female and "a person" inside a traditional Jewish family at the start of the 20th century. That any Jewish woman became
anything more than the abused servant of her father or her husband
is really an improbable piece of news. Yet Yezierska managed such
an unlikely outcome for her own life. In *The Bread Givers*, the heroine also manages an important, although partial, escape from traditional Jewish female destiny. And in the unpardonable, despotic

father, the Talmudic scholar of that Jewish family, did I not see my own and hate him twice, again? When the heroine, the young Jewish child, wanders the streets with a filthy pail she borrows to sell herring in order to raise the ghetto rent and when she cries, "Nothing was before me but the hunger in our house, and no bread for the next meal if I didn't sell the herring. No longer like a fire engine, but like a houseful of hungry mouths my heart cried, 'herring—herring! Two cents apiece!'" who would doubt the ease, the sisterhood of conversation possible between that white girl and the Black women selling straw bags on the streets of paradise because they do not want to die? And is it not obvious that the wife of that Talmudic scholar and "Olive," who cleans my room here at the hotel, have more in common than I can claim with either one of them?

20   This is my consciousness of race and class and gender identity as I collect wet towels, sunglasses, wristwatch, and head towards a shower.

21   I am thinking about the boy who loaned this novel to me. He's white and he's Jewish and he's pursuing an independent study project with me, at the State University where I teach whether or not I feel like it, where I teach without stint because, like the waiter, I am no fool. It's my job and either I work or I do without everything you need money to buy. The boy loaned me the novel because he thought I'd be interested to know how a Jewish-American writer used English so that the syntax, and therefore the cultural habits of mind expressed by the Yiddish language, could survive translation. He did this because he wanted to create another connection between us on the basis of language, between his knowledge/his love of Yiddish and my knowledge/my love of Black English.

22   He has been right about the forceful survival of the Yiddish. And I had become excited by this further evidence of the written voice of spoken language protected from the monodrone of "standard" English, and so we had grown closer on this account. But then our talk shifted to student affairs more generally, and I had learned that this student does not care one way or the other about currently jeopardized Federal Student Loan Programs because, as he explained it to me, they do not affect him. He does not need financial help outside his family. My own son, however, is Black. And I am the only family help available to him and that means, if Reagan succeeds in eliminating Federal programs to aid minority students, he will have to forget about furthering his studies, or he or I or both of us will have to hit the numbers pretty big. For these reasons of difference, the student and I had moved away from each other, even while we continued to talk.

23   My consciousness turned to race, again, and class.

24   Sitting in the same chair as the boy, several weeks ago, a graduate student came to discuss her grade. I praised the excellence of her
final paper; indeed it had seemed to me an extraordinary pulling
together of recent left brain/right brain research with the themes of
transcendental poetry.

25   She told me that, for her part, she'd completed her reading of
my political essays. "You are so lucky!" she exclaimed.

26   "What do you mean by that?"

27   "You have a cause. You have a purpose to your life."

28   I looked carefully at this white woman; what was she really saying to me?

29   "What do you mean?" I repeated.

30   "Poverty. Police violence. Discrimination in general."

31   (Jesus Christ, I thought: Is that her idea of lucky?)

32   "And how about you?" I asked.

33   "Me?"

34   "Yeah, you. Don't you have a cause?"

35   "Me? I'm just a middle aged woman: a housewife and a mother.
I'm a nobody."

36   For a while, I made no response.

37   First of all, speaking of race and class and gender in one breath,
what she said meant that those lucky preoccupations of mine, from
police violence to nuclear wipe-out, were not shared. They were mine
and not hers. But here she sat, friendly as an old stuffed animal,
beaming good will or more "luck" in my direction.

38   In the second place, what this white woman said to me meant that
she did not believe she was "a person" precisely because she had
fulfilled the traditional female functions revered by the father of that
Jewish immigrant, Anzia Yezierska. And the woman in front of me
was not a Jew. That was not the connection. The link was strictly
female. Nevertheless, how should that woman and I, another female
connect, beyond this bizarre exchange?

39   If she believed me lucky to have regular hurdles of discrimination then why shouldn't I insist that she's lucky to be a middle class
white Wasp female who lives in such well-sanctioned and normative
comfort that she even has the luxury to deny the power of the privileges that paralyze her life?

40   If she deserts me and "my cause" where we differ, if, for example, she abandons me to "my" problems of race, then why should I
support her in "her" problems of housewifely oblivion?

41   Recollection of this peculiar moment brings me to the shower in the bathroom cleaned by "Olive." She reminds me of the usual Women's Studies curriculum because it has nothing to do with her or her job: you won't find "Olive" listed anywhere on the reading list. You will likewise seldom hear of Anzia Yezierska. But yes, you will find, from Florence Nightingale to Adrienne Rich, a white procession of independently well-to-do women writers. (Gertrude Stein/Virginia Woolf/Hilda Doolittle are standard names among the "essential" women writers.)

42   In other words, most of the women of the world—Black and First World and white who work because we must—most of the women of the world persist far from the heart of the usual Women's Studies syllabus.

43   Similarly, the typical Black History course will slide by the majority experience it pretends to represent. For example, Mary McLeod Bethune will scarcely receive as much attention as Nat Turner, even though Black women who bravely and efficiently provided for the education of Black people hugely outnumber those few Black men who led successful or doomed rebellions against slavery. In fact, Mary McLeod Bethune may not receive even honorable mention because Black History too often apes those ridiculous white history courses which produce such dangerous gibberish as The Sheraton British Colonial "history" of the Bahamas. Both Black and white history courses exclude from their central consideration those people who neither killed nor conquered anyone as the means to new identity, those people who took care of every one of the people who wanted to become "a person," those people who still take care of the life at issue: the ones who wash and who feed and who teach and who diligently decorate straw hats and bags with all of their historically unrequired gentle love: the women.

> Oh the old rugged cross
> on a hill far away
> Well I cherish the old rugged cross

44   It's Good Friday in the Bahamas. Seventy-eight degrees in the shade. Except for Sheraton territory, everything's closed.

45   It so happens that for truly secular reasons I've been fasting for three days. My hunger has now reached nearly violent proportions. In the hotel sandwich shop, the Black woman handling the counter complains about the tourists; why isn't the shop closed and why don't the tourists stop eating for once in their lives. I'm famished and I order

chicken salad and cottage cheese and lettuce and tomato and a hard boiled egg and a hot cross bun and apple juice.

46   She eyes me with disgust.

47   To be sure, the timing of my stomach offends her serious religious practices. Neither one of us apologizes to the other. She seasons the chicken salad to the peppery max while I listen to the loud radio gospel she plays to console herself. It's a country Black version of "The Old Rugged Cross."

48   As I heave much chicken into my mouth tears start. It's not the pepper. I am, after all, a West Indian daughter. It's the Good Friday music that dominates the humid atmosphere.

   Well I cherish the old rugged cross

49   And I am back, faster than a 747, in Brooklyn, in the home of my parents where we are wondering, as we do every year, if the sky will darken until Christ has been buried in the tomb. The sky should darken if God is in His heavens. And then, around 3 p.m., at the conclusion of our mournful church service at the neighborhood St. Phillips, and even while we dumbly stare at the black cloth covering the gold altar and the slender unlit candles, the sun should return through the high gothic windows and vindicate our waiting faith that the Lord will rise again, on Easter.

50   How I used to bow my head at the very name of Jesus: ecstatic to abase myself in deference to His majesty.

51   My mouth is full of salad. I can't seem to eat quickly enough. I can't think how I should lessen the offense of my appetite. The other Black woman on the premises, the one who disapprovingly prepared this very tasty break from my fast, makes no remark. She is no fool. This is a job that she needs. I suppose she notices that at least I included a hot cross bun among my edibles. That's something in my favor. I decide that's enough.

52   I am suddenly eager to walk off the food. Up a fairly steep hill I walk without hurrying. Through the pastel desolation of the little town, the road brings me to a confectionary pink and white plantation house. At the gates, an unnecessarily large statue of Christopher Columbus faces me down, or tries to. His hand is fisted to one hip. I look back at him, laugh without deference, and turn left.

53   It's time to pack it up. Catch my plane. I scan the hotel room for things not to forget. There's that white report card on the bureau.

54   "Dear Guests:" it says, under the name "Olive." "I am your maid for the day. Please rate me: Excellent. Good. Average. Poor. Thank you."

55   I tuck this memento from the Sheraton British Colonial into my notebook. How would "Olive" rate *me*? What would it mean for us to seem "good" to each other? What would that rating require?

56   But I am hastening to leave. Neither turtle soup nor kidney pie nor any conch shell delight shall delay my departure. I have rested, here, in the Bahamas, and I'm ready to return to my usual job, my usual work. But the skin on my body has changed and so has my mind. On the Delta flight home I realize I am burning up, indeed.

57   So far as I can see, the usual race and class concepts of connection, or gender assumptions of unity, do not apply very well. I doubt that they ever did. Otherwise why would Black folks forever bemoan our lack of solidarity when the deal turns real. And if unity on the basis of sexual oppression is something natural, then why do we women, the majority people on the planet, still have a problem?

58   The plane's ready for takeoff. I fasten my seatbelt and let the tumult inside my head run free. Yes: race and class and gender remain as real as the weather. But what they must mean about the contact between two individuals is less obvious and, like the weather, not predictable.

59   And when these factors of race and class and gender absolutely collapse is whenever you try to use them as automatic concepts of connection. They may serve well as indicators of commonly felt conflict, but as elements of connection they seem about as reliable as precipitation probability for the day after the night before the day.

60   It occurs to me that much organizational grief could be avoided if people understood that partnership in misery does not necessarily provide for partnership for change: *When we get the monsters off our backs all of us may want to run in very different directions.*

61   And not only that: even though both "Olive" and "I" live inside a conflict neither one of us created, and even though both of us therefore hurt inside that conflict, I may be one of the monsters she needs to eliminate from her universe and, in a sense, she may be one of the monsters in mine.

62   I am reaching for the words to describe the difference between a common identity that has been imposed and the individual identity any one of us will choose, once she gains that chance.

63   That difference is the one that keeps us stupid in the face of new, specific information about somebody else with whom we are supposed to have a connection because a third party, hostile to both of us, has

worked it so that the two of us, like it or not, share a common enemy. *What happens beyond the idea of that enemy and beyond the consequences of that enemy?*

64   I am saying that the ultimate connection cannot be the enemy. The ultimate connection must be the need that we find between us. It is not only who you are, in other words, but what we can do for each other that will determine the connection.

65   I am flying back to my job. I have been teaching contemporary women's poetry this semester. One quandary I have set myself to explore with my students is the one of taking responsibility without power. We had been wrestling ideas to the floor for several sessions when a young Black woman, a South African, asked me for help, after class.

66   Sokutu told me she was "in a trance" and that she'd been unable to eat for two weeks.

67   "What's going on?" I asked her, even as my eyes startled at her trembling and emaciated appearance.

68   "My husband. He drinks all the time. He beats me up. I go to the hospital. I can't eat. I don't know what/anything."

69   In my office, she described her situation. I did not dare to let her sense my fear and horror. She was dragging about, hour by hour, in dread. Her husband, a young Black South African, was drinking himself into more and more deadly violence against her.

70   Sokutu told me how she could keep nothing down. She weighed 90 lbs. at the outside, as she spoke to me. She'd already been hospitalized as a result of her husband's battering rage.

71   I knew both of them because I had organized a campus group to aid the liberation struggles of Southern Africa.

72   Nausea rose in my throat. What about this presumable connection: this husband and this wife fled from that homeland of hatred against them, and now what? He was destroying himself. If not stopped, he would certainly murder his wife.

73   She needed a doctor, right away. It was a medical emergency. She needed protection. It was a security crisis. She needed refuge for battered wives and personal therapy and legal counsel. She needed a friend.

74   I got on the phone and called every number in the campus directory that I could imagine might prove helpful. Nothing worked. There were no institutional resources designed to meet her enormous, multifaceted, and ordinary woman's need.

75   I called various students. I asked the Chairperson of the English Department for advice. I asked everyone for help.

76 Finally, another one of my students, Cathy, a young Irish woman active in campus IRA activities, responded. She asked for further details. I gave them to her.

77 "Her husband," Cathy told me, "is an alcoholic. You have to understand about alcoholics. It's not the same as anything else. And it's a disease you can't treat any old way."

78 I listened, fearfully. Did this mean there was nothing we could do?

79 "That's not what I'm saying," she said. "But you have to keep the alcoholic part of the thing central in everybody's mind, otherwise her husband will kill her. Or he'll kill himself."

80 She spoke calmly. I felt there was nothing to do but to assume she knew what she was talking about.

81 "Will you come with me?" I asked her, after a silence. "Will you come with me and help us figure out what to do next?"

82 Cathy said she would but that she felt shy: Sokutu comes from South Africa. What would she think about Cathy?

83 "I don't know," I said. "But let's go."

84 We left to find a dormitory room for the young batterred wife.

85 It was late, now, and dark outside.

86 On Cathy's VW that I followed behind with my own car, was the sticker that reads BOBBY SANDS FREE AT LAST. My eyes blurred as I read and reread the words. This was another connection: Bobby Sands and Martin Luther King Jr. and who would believe it? I would not have believed it; I grew up terrorized by Irish kids who introduced me to the word "nigga."

87 And here I was following an Irish woman to the room of a Black South African. We were going to that room to try to save a life together.

88 When we reached the little room, we found ourselves awkward and large. Sokutu attempted to treat us with utmost courtesy, as though we were honored guests. She seemed surprised by Cathy, but mostly Sokutu was flushed with relief and joy because we were there, with her.

89 I did not know how we should ever terminate her heartfelt courtesies and address, directly, the reason for our visit: her starvation and her extreme physical danger.

90 Finally, Cathy sat on the floor and reached out her hands to Sokutu.

91 "I'm here," she said quietly, "Because June has told me what has happened to you. And I know what it is. Your husband is an alcoholic. He has a disease. I know what it is. My father was an alcoholic. He killed himself. He almost killed my mother. I want to be your friend."

92   "Oh," was the only small sound that escaped from Sokutu's mouth. And then she embraced the other student. And then everything changed and I watched all of this happen so I know that this happened: this connection.

93   And after we called the police and exchanged phone numbers and plans were made for the night and for the next morning, the young South African woman walked down the dormitory hallway, saying goodbye and saying thank you to us.

94   I walked behind them, the young Irish woman and the young South African, and I saw them walking as sisters walk, hugging each other, and whispering and sure of each other and I felt how it was not who they were but what they both know and what they were both preparing to do about what they know that was going to make them both free at last.

95   And I look out the windows of the plane and I see clouds that will not kill me and I know that someday soon other clouds may erupt to kill us all.

96   And I tell the stewardess No thanks to the cocktails she offers me. But I look about the cabin at the hundred strangers drinking as they fly and I think even here and even now I must make the connection real between me and these strangers everywhere before those other clouds unify this ragged bunch of us, too late.

Alice Walker

(1944–)

For biographical information, see page 78. The Color Purple, excerpted below, is written in the epistolary form and traces Celie's growth from an abused teenager to a strong-willed, independent woman. As the following passage reveals, Celie's spiritual development is predicated on recognizing and dismissing the insidious forms of patriarchal power.

The Color Purple

1 Dear Nettie,

2 I don't write to God no more, I write to you.

3 What happen to God? ast Shug.

4 Who that? I say.

5   She look at me serious.

6   Big a devil as you is, I say, you not worried bout no God, surely.

7   She say, Wait a minute. Hold on just a minute here. Just because I don't harass it like some peoples us know don't mean I ain't got religion.

8   What God do for me? I ast.

9   She say, Celie! Like she shock. He gave you life, good health, and a good woman that love you to death.

10   Yeah, I say, and he give me a lynched daddy, a crazy mama, a low-down dog of a step pa and a sister I probably won't ever see again. Anyhow, I say, the God I been praying and writing to is a man. And act just like all the other mens I know. Trifling, forgitful and lowdown.

11   She say, Miss Celie, You better hush. God might hear you.

12   Let 'im hear me, I say. If he ever listened to poor colored women the world would be a different place, I can tell you.

13   She talk and she talk, trying to budge me way from blasphemy. But I blaspheme much as I want to.

14   All my life I never care what people thought bout nothing I did, I say. But deep in my heart I care about God. What he going to think. And come to find out, he don't think. Just sit up there glorying in being deaf, I reckon. But it ain't easy, trying to do without God. Even if you know he ain't there, trying to do without him is a strain.

15   I is a sinner, say Shug. Cause I was born. I don't deny it. But once you find out what's out there waiting for us, what else can you be?

16   Sinners have more good times, I say.

17   You know why? she ast.

18   Cause you ain't all the time worrying bout God, I say.

19   Naw, that ain't it, she say. Us worry bout God a lot. But once us feel loved by God, us do the best us can to please him with what us like.

20   You telling me God love you, and you ain't never done nothing for him? I mean, not go to church, sing in the choir, feed the preacher and all like that?

21   But if God love me, Celie, I don't have to do all that. Unless I want to. There's a lot of other things I can do that I speck God likes.

22   Like what? I ast.

23   Oh, she say. I can lay back and just admire stuff. Be happy. Have a good time.

24   Well, this sound like blasphemy sure nuff.

25   She say, Celie, tell the truth, have you ever found God in church? I never did. I just found a bunch of folks hoping for him to show. Any God

I ever felt in church I brought in with me. And I think all the other folks did too. They come to church to *share* God, not find God.

26   Some folks didn't have him to share, I said. They the ones didn't speak to me while I was there struggling with my big belly and Mr. _____ children.

27   Right, she say.

28   Then she say: Tell me what your God look like, Celie.

29   Aw naw, I say. I'm too shame. Nobody ever ast me this before, so I'm sort of took by surprise. Besides, when I think about it, it don't seem quite right. But it all I got. I decide to stick up for him, just to see what Shug say.

30   Okay, I say. He big and old and tall and graybearded and white. He wear white robes and go barefooted.

31   Blue eyes? she ast.

32   Sort of bluish-gray. Cool. Big though. White lashes, I say.

33   She laugh.

34   Why you laugh? I ast. I don't think it so funny. What you expect him to look like, Mr. _____?

35   That wouldn't be no improvement, she say. Then she tell me this old white man is the same God she used to see when she prayed. If you wait to find God in church, Celie, she say, that's who is bound to show up, cause that's where he live.

36   How come? I ast.

37   Cause that's the one that's in the white folks' white bible.

38   Shug! I say. God wrote the bible, white folks had nothing to do with it.

39   How come he look just like them, then? she say. Only bigger? And a heap more hair. How come the bible just like everything else they make, all about them doing one thing and another, and all the colored folks doing is gitting cursed?

40   I never thought bout that.

41   Nettie say somewhere in the bible it say Jesus' hair was like lamb's wool, I say.

42   Well, say Shug, if he came to any of these churches we talking bout he'd have to have it conked before anybody paid him any attention. The last thing niggers want to think about they God is that his hair kinky.

43   That's the truth, I say.

44   Ain't no way to read the bible and not think God white, she say. Then she sigh. When I found out I thought God was white, and a man, I lost interest. You mad cause he don't seem to listen to your prayers. Humph! Do the mayor listen to anything colored say? Ask Sofia, she say.

45   But I don't have to ast Sofia. I know white people never listen to colored, period. If they do, they only listen long enough to be able to tell you what to do.

46   Here's the thing, say Shug. The thing I believe. God is inside you and inside everybody else. You come into the world with God. But only them that search for it inside find it. And sometimes it just manifest itself even if you not looking, or don't know what you looking for. Trouble do it for most folks, I think. Sorrow, lord. Feeling like shit.

47   It? I ast.

48   Yeah, It. God ain't a he or a she, but a It.

49   But what do it look like? I ast.

50   Don't look like nothing, she say. It ain't a picture show. It ain't something you can look at apart from anything else, including yourself. I believe God is everything, say Shug. Everything that is or ever was or ever will be. And when you can feel that, and be happy to feel that, you've found It.

51   Shug a beautiful something, let me tell you. She frown a little, look out cross the yard, lean back in her chair, look like a big rose.

52   She say, My first step from the old white man was trees. Then air. Then birds. Then other people. But one day when I was sitting quiet and feeling like a motherless child, which I was, it come to me: that feeling of being part of everything, not separate at all. I knew that if I cut a tree, my arm would bleed. And I laughed and I cried and I run all around the house. I knew just what it was. In fact, when it happen, you can't miss it. It sort of like you know what, she say, grinning and rubbing high up on my thigh.

53   *Shug!* I say.

54   Oh, she say. God love all them feelings. That's some of the best stuff God did. And when you know God loves 'em you enjoys 'em a lot more. You can just relax, go with everything that's going, and praise God by liking what you like.

55   God don't think it dirty? I ast.

56   Naw, she say. God made it. Listen, God love everything you love—and a mess of stuff you don't. But more than anything else, God love admiration.

57   You saying God vain? I ast.

58   Naw, she say. Not vain, just wanting to share a good thing. I think it pisses God off if you walk by the color purple in a field somewhere and don't notice it.

59   What it do when it pissed off? I ast.

60   Oh, it make something else. People think pleasing God is all God
      care about. But any fool living in the world can see it always trying
      to please us back.

61   Yeah? I say.

62   Yeah, she say. It always making little surprises and springing them
      on us when us least expect.

63   You mean it want to be loved, just like the bible say.

64   Yes, Celie, she say. Everything want to be loved. Us sing and dance,
      make faces and give flower bouquets, trying to be loved. You ever notice
      that trees do everything to git attention we do except walk?

65   Well, us talk and talk bout God, but I'm still adrift. Trying to chase
      that old white man out of my head. I been so busy thinking bout
      him I never truly notice nothing God make. Not a blade of corn (how
      it do that?) not the color purple (where it come from?). Not the lit-
      tle wildflowers. Nothing.

66   Now that my eyes opening, I feels like a fool. Next to any little
      scrub of a bush in my yard, Mr. _____'s evil sort of shrink. But not
      altogether. Still, it is like Shug say. You have to git man off your eye-
      ball, before you can see anything a'tall.

67   Man corrupt everything, say Shug. He on your box of grits, in your
      head, and all over the radio. He try to make you think he everywhere.
      Soon as you think he everywhere, you think he God. But he ain't.
      Whenever you trying to pray, and man plop himself on the other
      end of it, tell him to git lost, say Shug. Conjure up flowers, wind,
      water, a big rock.

68   But this hard work, let me tell you. He been there so long, he don't
      want to budge. He threaten lightening, floods and earthquakes. Us fight.
      I hardly pray at all. Every time I conjure up a rock, I throw it.

69   Amen

                                    * * *

70 Dear Nettie,

71   When I told Shug I'm writing to you instead of to God, she laugh.
      Nettie don't know these people, she say. Considering who I been writ-
      ing to, this strike me funny.

72   It was Sofia you saw working as the mayor's maid. The woman
      you saw carrying the white woman's packages that day in town. Sofia
      Mr. _____'s son Harpo's wife. Polices lock her up for sassing the
      mayor's wife and hitting the mayor back. First she was in prison

working in the laundry and dying fast. Then us got her move to the mayor's house. She had to sleep in a little room up under the house, but it was better than prison. Flies, maybe, but no rats.

73   Anyhow, they kept her eleven and a half years, give her six months off for good behavior so she could come home early to her family. Her bigger children married and gone, and her littlest children mad at her, don't know who she is. Think she act funny, look old and dote on that little white gal she raise.

74   Yesterday us all had dinner at Odessa's house. Odessa Sofia's sister. She raise the kids. Her and her husband Jack. Harpo's woman Squeak, and Harpo himself.

75   Sofia sit down at the big table like there's no room for her. Children reach cross her like she not there. Harpo and Squeak act like a old married couple. Children call Odessa mama. Call Squeak little mama. Call Sofia "Miss." The only one seem to pay her any tention at all is Harpo and Squeak's little girl, Suzie Q. She sit cross from Sofia and squinch up her eyes at her.

76   As soon as dinner over, Shug push back her chair and light a cigarette. Now is come the time to tell yall, she say.

77   Tell us what? Harpo ast.

78   Us leaving, she say.

79   Yeah? say Harpo, looking round for the coffee. And then looking over at Grady.

80   Us leaving, Shug say again. Mr. _____ look struck, like he always look when Shug say she going anywhere. He reach down and rub his stomach, look off side her head like nothing been said.

81   Grady say, Such good peoples, that's the truth. The salt of the earth. But—time to move on.

82   Squeak not saying nothing. She got her chin glued to her plate. I'm not saying nothing either. I'm waiting for the feathers to fly.

83   Celie is coming with us, say Shug.

84   Mr._____'s head swivel back straight. Say what? he ast.

85   Celie is coming to Memphis with me.

86   Over my dead body, Mr._____say.

87   You satisfied that what you want, Shug say, cool as clabber.

88   Mr._____start up from his seat, look at Shug, plop back down again. He look over at me. I thought you was finally happy, he say. What wrong now?

89   You a lowdown dog is what's wrong, I say. It's time to leave you and enter into the Creation. And your dead body just the welcome mat I need.

90 Say what? he ast. Shock.

91 All round the table folkses mouths be dropping open.

92 You took my sister Nettie away from me, I say. And she was the only person love me in the world.

93 Mr._____start to sputter. ButButButButBut. Sound like some kind of motor.

94 But Nettie and my children coming home soon, I say. And when she do, all us together gon whup your ass.

95 Nettie and your children! say Mr._____.You talking crazy.

96 I got children, I say. Being brought up in Africa. Good schools, lots of fresh air and exercise. Turning out a heap better than the fools you didn't even try to raise.

97 Hold on, say Harpo.

98 Oh, hold on hell, I say. If you hadn't tried to rule over Sofia the white folks never would have caught her.

99 Sofia so surprise to hear me speak up she ain't chewed for ten minutes.

100 That's a lie, say Harpo.

101 A little truth in it, say Sofia.

102 Everybody look at her like they surprise she there. It like a voice speaking from the grave.

103 You was all rotten children, I say. You made my life a hell on earth. And your daddy here ain't dead horse's shit.

104 Mr._____reach over to slap me. I jab my case knife in his hand.

105 You bitch, he say. What will people say, you running off to Memphis like you don't have a house to look after?

106 Shug say, Albert. Try to think like you got some sense. Why any woman give a shit what people think is a mystery to me.

107 Well, say Grady, trying to bring light. A woman can't git a man if peoples talk.

108 Shug look at me and us giggle. Then us laugh sure nuff. Then Squeak start to laugh. Then Sofia. All us laugh and laugh.

109 Shug say, Ain't they something? Us say um *hum*, and slap the table, wipe the water from our eyes.

110 Harpo look at Squeak. Shut up Squeak, he say. It bad luck for women to laugh at men.

111 She say, Okay. She sit up straight, suck in her breath, try to press her face together.

112 He look at Sofia. She look at him and laugh in his face. I already had my bad luck, she say. I had enough to keep me laughing the rest of my life.

113   Harpo look at her like he did the night she knock Mary Agnes
down. A little spark fly cross the table.

114   I got six children by this crazy woman, he mutter.

115   Five, she say.

116   He so outdone he can't even say, Say what?

117   He look over at the youngest child. She sullen, mean, mischeevous
and too stubborn to live in this world. But he love her best of all.
Her name Henrietta.

118   Henrietta, he say.

119   She say, Yesssss . . . like they say it on the radio.

120   Everything she say confuse him. Nothing, he say. Then he say,
Go git me a cool glass of water.

121   She don't move.

122   Please, he say.

123   She go git the water, put it by his plate, give him a peck on the
cheek. Say, Poor Daddy. Sit back down.

124   You not gitting a penny of my money, Mr._____say to me. Not
one thin dime.

125   Did I ever ast you for money? I say. I never ast you for nothing.
Not even for your sorry hand in marriage.

126   Shug break in right there. Wait, she say. Hold it. Somebody
else going with us too. No use in Celie being the only one taking the
weight.

127   Everybody sort of cut they eyes at Sofia. She the one they can't
quite find a place for. She the stranger.

128   It ain't me, she say, and her look say, Fuck you for entertaining
the thought. She reach for a biscuit and sort of root her behind deeper
into her seat. One look at this big stout graying, wildeyed woman and
you know not even to ast. Nothing.

129   But just to clear this up neat and quick, she say, I'm home. Period.

130   Her sister Odessa come and put her arms round her. Jack move
up close.

131   Course you is, Jack say.

132   Mama crying? ast one of Sofia children.

133   Miss Sofia too, another one say.

134   But Sofia cry quick, like she do most things.

135   Who going? she ast.

136   Nobody say nothing. It so quiet you can hear the embers dying
back in the stove. Sound like they falling in on each other.

137   Finally, Squeak look at everybody from under her bangs. Me, she
say. I'm going North.

138   You going What? say Harpo. He so surprise. He begin to sputter, sputter, just like his daddy. Sound like I don't know what.

139   I want to sing, say Squeak.

140   Sing! say Harpo.

141   Yeah, say Squeak. Sing. I ain't sung in public since Jolentha was born. Her name Jolentha. They call her Suzie Q.

142   You ain't had to sing in public since Jolentha was born. Everything you need I done provided for.

143   I need to sing, say Squeak.

144   Listen Squeak, say Harpo. You can't go to Memphis. That's all there is to it.

145   Mary Agnes, say Squeak.

146   Squeak, Mary, Agnes, what difference do it make?

147   It make a lot, say Squeak. When I was Mary Agnes I could sing in public.

148   Just then a little knock come on the door.

149   Odessa and Jack look at each other. Come in, say Jack.

150   A skinny little white woman stick most of herself through the door.

151   Oh, you all are eating dinner, she say. Excuse me.

152   That's all right, say Odessa. Us just finishing up. But there's plenty left. Why don't you sit down and join us. Or I could fix you something to eat on the porch.

153   Oh lord, say Shug.

154   It Eleanor Jane, the white girl Sofia used to work for.

155   She look round till she spot Sofia, then she seem to let her breath out. No thank you, Odessa, she say. I ain't hungry. I just come to see Sofia.

156   Sofia, she say. Can I see you on the porch for a minute.

157   All right, Miss Eleanor, she say. Sofia push back from the table and they go out on the porch. A few minutes later us hear Miss Eleanor sniffling. Then she really boo-hoo.

158   What the matter with her? Mr. _____ ast.

159   Henrietta say, Prob-limbszzzz . . . like somebody on the radio.

160   Odessa shrug. She always underfoot, she say.

161   A lot of drinking in that family, say Jack. Plus, they can't keep that boy of theirs in college. He get drunk, aggravate his sister, chase women, hunt niggers, and that ain't all.

162   That enough, say Shug. Poor Sofia.

163   Pretty soon Sofia come back in and sit down.

164   What the matter? ast Odessa.

165   A lot of mess back at the house, say Sofia.

166   You got to go back up there? Odessa ast.

167   Yeah, say Sofia. In a few minutes. But I'll try to be back before the children go to bed.

168   Henrietta ast to be excuse, say she got a stomach ache.

169   Squeak and Harpo's little girl come over, look up at Sofia, say, You gotta go Misofia?

170   Sofia say, Yeah, pull her up on her lap. Sofia on parole, she say. Got to act nice.

171   Suzie Q lay her head on Sofia chest. Poor Sofia, she say, just like she heard Shug. Poor Sofia.

172   Mary Agnes, darling, say Harpo, look how Suzie Q take to Sofia.

173   Yeah, say Squeak, children know good when they see it. She and Sofia smile at one nother.

174   Go on sing, say Sofia, I'll look after this one till you come back.

175   You will? say Squeak.

176   Yeah, say Sofia.

177   And look after Harpo, too, say Squeak. Please ma'am.

178   Amen

* * *

179 Dear Nettie,

180   Well, you know wherever there's a man, there's trouble. And it seem like, going to Memphis, Grady was all over the car. No matter which way us change up, he want to sit next to Squeak.

181   While me and Shug sleeping and he driving, he tell Squeak all about life in North Memphis, Tennessee. I can't half sleep for him raving bout clubs and clothes and forty-nine brands of beer. Talking so much bout stuff to drink make me have to pee. Then us have to find a road going off into the bushes to relieve ourselves.

182   Mr. _____ try to act like he don't care I'm going.

183   You'll be back, he say. Nothing up North for nobody like you. Shug got talent, he say. She can sing. She got spunk, he say. She can talk to anybody. Shug got looks, he say. She can stand up and be notice. But what you got? You ugly. You skinny. You shape funny. You too scared to open your mouth to people. All you fit to do in Memphis is be Shug's maid. Take out her slop-jar and maybe cook her food. You not that good a cook either. And this house ain't been clean good since my first wife died. And nobody crazy or backward enough to want to marry you, neither. What you gon do? Hire yourself out to farm? He laugh. Maybe somebody let you work on they railroad.

184   Any more letters come? I ast.

185   He say, What?

186   You heard me, I say. Any more letters from Nettie come?

187   If they did, he say. I wouldn't give 'em to you. You two of a kind, he say. A man try to be nice to you, you fly in his face.

188   I curse you, I say.

189   What that mean? he say.

190   I say, Until you do right by me, everything you touch will crumble.

191   He laugh. Who you think you is? he say. You can't curse nobody. Look at you. You black, you pore, you ugly, you a woman. Goddam, he say, you nothing at all.

192   Until you do right by me, I say, everything you even dream about will fail. I give it to him straight, just like it come to me. And it seem to come to me from the trees.

193   Whoever heard of such a thing, say Mr. _____. I probably didn't whup your ass enough.

194   Every lick you hit me you will suffer twice, I say. Then I say, You better stop talking because all I'm telling you ain't coming just from me. Look like when I open my mouth the air rush in and shape words.

195   Shit, he say. I should have lock you up. Just let you out to work.

196   The jail you plan for me is the one in which you will rot, I say.

197   Shug come over to where us talking. She take one look at my face and say Celie! Then she turn to Mr. _____. Stop Albert, she say. Don't say no more. You just going to make it harder on yourself.

198   I'll fix her wagon! say Mr. _____, and spring toward me.

199   A dust devil flew up on the porch between us, fill my mouth with dirt. The dirt say, Anything you do to me, already done to you.

200   Then I feel Shug shake me. Celie, she say. And I come to myself.

201   I'm pore, I'm black, I may be ugly and can't cook, a voice say to everything listening. But I'm here.

202   Amen, say Shug. Amen, amen.

A Name Is Sometimes An Ancestor Saying Hi, I'm With You

1   There are always people in history (or herstory) who help us, and whose "job" it is, in fact, to do this. One way of looking at history (whether oral or written) is as a method that records characteristics and vibrations of our helpers, whose spirits we may feel but of whose objective reality as people who once lived we may not know. Now these people—our "spirit helpers," as indigenous peoples time after time in all cultures have referred to them—always create opportunities that make a meeting with and recognition of them unavoidable.

2   Sojourner Truth is one such figure for me. Even laying aside such obvious resemblances as the fact that we are both as concerned about the rights of women as the rights of men, and that we share a certain "mystical" bent, Sojourner ("Walker"—in the sense of traveler, journeyer, wanderer) Truth (which "Alice" means in Old Greek) is also my name. How happy I was when I realized this. It is one of those "synchronicities" (some might say conceits) of such reassuring proportions that even when I've been tempted to rename myself "Treeflower" or "Weed" I have resisted.

3   I get a power from this name that Sojourner Truth and I share. And when I walk into a room of strangers who are hostile to the words of women, I do so with her/our cloak of authority—as black women and beloved expressions of the Universe (i.e., children of God)—warm about me.

4   She smiles within my smile. That irrepressible great heart rises in my chest. Every experience that roused her passion against injustice in her lifetime shines from my eyes.

5   This feeling of being loved and supported by the Universe in general and by certain recognizable spirits in particular is bliss. No other state is remotely like it. And perhaps that is what Jesus tried so hard to teach: that the transformation required of us is not simply to be "like" Christ, but to *be* Christ.

6   The spirit of our helpers incarnates in us, making us more ourselves by extending us far beyond. And to that spirit there is no "beginning" as we know it (although we might finally "know" a historical figure who at one time expressed it) and no end. Always a

hello, from the concerned spiritual ancestor you may not even have known you had—but this could strike at any time. Never a good-bye.

1986

---

bell hooks

(1952–)

Born Gloria Watkins in Hopkinsville, Kentucky, on September 25, 1952, bell hooks assumed her pseudonym as a tribute to her maternal great-grandmother. hooks received her BA in 1973 from Stanford University, an MA in 1976 from the University of Wisconsin, and a PhD in 1983 from the University of California, Santa Cruz. After her first two books, Ain't I a Woman: Black Women and Feminism *(1981) and* Feminist Theory: From Margin to Center *(1984), hooks was recognized as a leading feminist intellectual of our time. She is a prolific writer, publishing numerous volumes of essays on the intersection of feminism with the politics of race, class, sexuality, and nationhood. hooks's essays bridge the chasm between theoretical discourse and everyday speech, making her work accessible and far-reaching. hooks's other volumes include* Talking Back: Thinking Feminist, Thinking Black *(1989),* Yearning: Race, Gender and Cultural Politics *(1990),* Black Looks: Race and Representation *(1992),* Outlaw Culture: Resisting Representations *(1994),* Teaching to Transgress: Education as the Practice of Freedom *(1994),* Art on My Mind *(1995), and a discussion with Cornel West,* Breaking Bread: Insurgent Black Intellectual Life *(1991). hooks, whose most recent work,* All About Love: New Visions *(2000),* Salvation: Black People and Love *(2001), and* Communion: The Female Search for Love *(2002) is a professor at the City College of New York.*

Feminism: It's a Black Thing

1 More black men than ever before acknowledge that sexism is a problem in black life. Yet rarely is that acknowledgment linked with progressive political struggle to end sexism, to critique and challenge patriarchy. While these black men can acknowledge that sexism is an issue, they tend to see it as a "natural" response, one that need not be altered. In more recent years some black males link sexist thinking and

action to their sense of victimization by racist exploitation and oppression. Extreme expressions of sexism, misogyny, made visible by overt exploitation of women by men, become in their minds a dysfunctional response to racism rather than a perspective that exists both apart from and in conjunction with racism.

2   Such thinking enables black males to assume no direct accountability for a politics of sexism that in reality does not have its origin in racist aggression. To see sexism as an outcome of racist victimization is to construct a worldview wherein black males can easily deflect attention away from the power and privileges accorded them by maleness within white supremacist capitalist patriarchy, however relative, even as they simultaneously undermine the seriousness of sexist exploitation by insisting that the problem is ultimately, and always, only racism. This overlapping of the two systems of domination, in ways that deflect attention away from black male accountability for sexist exploitation of black females, was evoked in a recent interview with black male journalist Nathan McCall, highlighting the publication of his autobiographical work *Makes Me Wanna Holler*. McCall comments: "If you hate what's black it doesn't matter if it's a man or a woman. And if it's a woman it's even more convenient because women are subjugated. It's understood that the only folks in this world who are at the mercy of black men are black women." While there are culprits in racist aggression against black males, there are no culprits who subjugate black women in McCall's rhetoric. Female subjugation is presented as "natural," already in place, not something black men create, only something they exploit. McCall shares his understanding of black male sexist aggression towards black females: "A common response to oppression, or abuse, is to become an abuser. Black men don't have the traditional avenues that other men in this society have for expressing what we consider manhood." These assumptions, presented as fact, are dangerous. They belie the reality that white men, and individual men from diverse groups who have access to all the traditional avenues of power and privilege, willingly perpetuate sexism and sexist exploitation and oppression. Concurrently, as long as access to patriarchal power and privilege in all avenues of life is presented as the balm that will heal the wounds inflicted on black men by racist victimization then maintaining sexism will be seen as essential not only to black male freedom but to the well-being of all black people.

3   When black men like Nathan McCall acknowledge a structure of sexist exploitation and/or oppression in black life that promotes the

systematic abuse of black females, without in any way offering a critique or challenge to that structure, they reinscribe the assumption that sexist brutality cannot change or be eradicated. This tacit acceptance of a system they acknowledge to be wrong is a form of complicity. That complicity for seeing sexism in black life yet viewing it unproblematically is often shared by white individuals, even some liberal and progressive white feminists, who ignore and in some cases condone black male sexism when it is articulated as a response to racist aggression.

4   Linking sexism and racism in ways that condone one as a response to the other in contemporary society pits black males and females against one another. As long as individual black males (and some females) feel that their freedom cannot be attained without the establishment of patriarchal power and privilege, they will see black female struggles for self-determination, our engagement with feminist movement, as threatening. Convinced that the struggle to "save" the black race is really first and foremost about saving the lives of black males, they will not only continually insist that their "sufferings" are greater than those of black females, they will believe that the proud assertion of sexist politics registers a meaningful opposition to racism. Mainstream white culture has shown that it is far more willing to listen and respond to the dilemmas of black men when those dilemmas are articulated not as the harsh aftermath of white supremacist aggression and assault that affects all black folks but instead when these issues are mediated by a discourse of tragic, "failed," emasculated manhood. Within contemporary white supremacist capitalist patriarchy, the discourse of an unrealized wounded black manhood, which is constantly in jeopardy or under assault, that responds to victimization with brutal threatening aggression, is played out in public rhetoric that defines black males as an "endangered" species. Black males who are usually astute in their critique of racist stereotypes of black masculinity have not raised objections to the use of dehumanizing language that links black males to a public rhetoric that is usually evoked to talk about the extinction of wild animals. Instead some black males opportunistically exploited the racist/sexist rhetoric implied in the phrase "endangered species" to call attention to the serious impact of racism on black male lives. However, by not questioning this rhetoric they implicitly endorse the notion that there exists a black "bestial" masculinity, so central to racist/sexist iconography, that must be properly controlled, because it represents a danger to itself and others. Embedded in much of this rhetoric is the assumption that young black males

would not represent a "danger" to white society if they could all be in training to be mature patriarchs. Conservative whites, and even some liberals, seem to be able to respond to the real dilemmas that affect black males only if the rhetoric that explains these problems shifts from white accountability to a focus on gender, wherein the creation of a context for "healthy" black masculinity to flourish is perceived to be the remedy and not confronting and changing white supremacy. As a consequence both black males and white society invest in a rhetoric of self-recovery for black males that explicitly perpetuates and maintains sexism and patriarchy.

5   Much of the recent emphasis on the need for special schools for black boys invests in a rhetoric of patriarchal thinking that uncritically embraces sexist-defined notions of manhood as the cure for all that ails black males. No one talks about the need for black girls to have positive black male role models that would offer them the kind of affirmation and care that could enhance their self-esteem. No one insists that young black males need positive black female role models whom they respect and treat with regard. All the rhetoric that privileges the self-esteem of black male children over that of girls maintains and perpetuates the assumption that sexist-defined sex roles are healthy, are the key to creating a non-dysfunctional black family. A major focus in schools for all black males is a militaristic emphasis on discipline. This seems especially significant since it was Daniel Patrick Moynihan who first suggested in his racist formulations of a theory of black matriarchy a sexist paradigm that would explain black male dysfunction by suggesting that they were castrated and emasculated by strong black females who prevented them from realizing manhood. His suggestion was that black males should enter the military, a world without women, wherein they could self-actualize. It is tragically ironic that black folks who once clearly saw the racism in this attempt to blame the problems black men face living in a white supremacist society on black females are now employing a similar mode of analysis. The notion that schools for all black boys which teach a patriarchal pedagogy, one that emphasizes both coercive discipline and obedience to authority, are a corrective to dysfunctional behavior is one that completely erases the extent to which patriarchal thinking promotes dysfunction. A recent article in *Black Issues* in *Higher Education* positively highlighted Detroit's African-centered academies for boys. The author states: "Discipline is one of the cornerstones of the academies' overall program. Teachers don't cut youngsters any slack. Students dress in uniforms which are

inspected regularly, and must speak clearly and assertively in full sentences, and address adults in a proper manner." While it is positive for young black males and females to learn discipline and self-responsibility, those attitudes, values, and habits of being can be taught with pedagogical strategies that are liberatory, that do not rely on coercive control and punishment to reinforce positive behavior. It is obvious that militaristic models of education effectively teach young males behavior that may lead them to be more positively disciplined, etc. However, there is an extremely negative dimension to this coercive hierarchical model of education that no one talks about. If these young males are being taught to be disciplined within a learning community where they are also learning patriarchal thinking, how will they respond to females who do not conform to their expectations. As adult men will they attempt to subordinate black females using a discipline and punish model. Significantly, all the schools for young black males described in this article are called by the name of important black male figures—Paul Robeson, Malcolm X, or Marcus Garvey. Supporters of these schools, and others like them around the nation, rarely question the teaching of patriarchal perspectives. Even the critics are more concerned with whether there should be "African-centered" schools than with the issue of gender. In white supremacist capitalist patriarchy it is often just assumed that black gender relations will necessarily be retrograde, inferior to those of whites, be they conservative or progressive. Despite the cultural impact of feminist movement, most white and black critics in contemporary mass media do not extend the same critical awareness to gender issues when black folks are the center of attention. Individuals who support separate schools for black boys that emphasize a militaristic patriarchal pedagogy or for that matter any of the folks who push patriarchy using the guise of building strong black families do not have to confront an interrogating public, demanding hard evidence that patriarchy is healing to the psyches of black males who are assaulted by racism. There is no evidence that suggests patriarchal black males who are successful in the arena of work, who are not in prisons, who are not committing crimes on the street, are more humane in their relationships with black females or less powerful males than unsuccessful black males whom society deems dysfunctional and/or criminal. There is plenty of evidence to substantiate the reality that black men who have obtained class power, status, and privilege, like their white counterparts, often dominate females in assaultive coercive ways to maintain sexist power. Concurrently, many of the negative ways black males interact with one another, using coercive violence or assaultive verbal harassment, are behavior patterns reinforced by sexist constructions of masculine identity. Yet the extent to which embracing feminist thinking and practice could transform black male identity is never presented as an option by that public claiming to be concerned about the quality of life for black males in white supremacist capitalist patriarchy.

6   So far only small numbers of black males willingly engage feminist critique, seeing it from a standpoint that enables them to divest of learned engagement with patriarchal thinking that is fundamentally undermining and disenabling. Many black males accept and perpetuate sexist/racist notions about black manhood not only because they can receive more sympathetic attention from the dominant culture by focusing on a wounded masculinity but because by endorsing sexist thinking they also strengthen their alliances with white males. Throughout the history of black male presence in the United States, masculine physical prowess has been one of the few arenas where they are perceived as heterosexuals. Negative representations of lesbians and gay men abound in black life, precisely because they create a context of fear and condemnation that closes off the possibility that black heterosexuals will study and learn from the critical thinking and writing of black homosexuals. Much of the compelling critique and challenge to black male engagement with sexist thinking, with patriarchy, exists primarily in the work of gay black men. If straight black men never seek this literature and/or repudiate it, they deprive themselves of life-affirming and life-sustaining discussions of black masculinity. Homophobic thinking and action is a barrier that often prevents black males and females from choosing to learn about feminist thinking.

7   At the peak of contemporary feminist movement black males were one-upping white males by representing themselves as that group of males who had not capitulated to feminist demands that they rethink sexism. That repudiation of feminist thinking was highlighted when black males responded to the feminist fiction writing of black females like Alice Walker by once again flaunting their sexism and accusing her and other black women of being traitors to the race. To support the race, to not be seen as traitors, black women were and are still being told to express racial allegiance by passively accepting sexism and sexist domination. Recent anti-feminist backlash has led to the positive highlighting of black male sexism and phallocentrism. In public spheres of homo-social bonding black males inspire

alternately fear and envy in white males by flaunting the "it's a dick thing" masculinity. Willingness to flaunt sexist behavior, coercive masculine domination of females, is one of the ways black males receive respect and admiration as well as rewards from white male peers. Often mainstream white culture condemns black male sexism if it impinges on its freedom even as it rewards it if the targets of that rage remain black females, less powerful black males, and advocates of feminist movement. The production and dissemination of rap music that perpetuates sexist and/or misogynist thinking, that condones the assertion of male domination over females by any means necessary, is a site of cultural production where black males are alternately punished and rewarded for this conduct. The punishment usually takes the form of public critique and censorship. Ultimately, the positive response to sexist and/or misogynist rap music (fame, wealth) reinforces the reality that these attitudes and values will be rewarded in this society. If black males find that they can make much more money flaunting lyrics that are sexist and misogynist, it is mainstream consumer culture that creates the demand for this product. If white supremacist capitalist patriarchy rewards black males for sexist behavior whether in the entertainment, sports, or political arena (i.e., the Thomas hearings) there are few incentives for black males to divest of sexist thinking.

8   Ultimately, sexist aggression by black males towards black females creates a cultural climate in black life where gender wars and conflicts claim the attention and energy that could be constructively used to create strategies for radical intervention that would challenge and undermine the existing racist and sexist systems of domination. As long as the vast majority of black males are brainwashed into thinking that sexist thinking enhances their lives, white patriarchy need never fear being dismantled by progressive black male insurrection. Nationalist black leaders male and female, whether they be in conservative religious organizations or represent themselves as spokespersons of more radical movements for liberation, continue to suffer failures of insight that lead them to invest in the notion that patriarchy is the only possible system of social organization that can bring stability to black family life and to the race.

9   Unfortunately, as long as the misguided assumption that patriarchal power compensates black males for the trauma of living in a white supremacist society and experiencing the trauma of perpetual racist assault is accepted without question, then the reproduction of sexist thinking and action will remain the norm in black

life. Concurrently the negative consequences of sexist black male domination will remain a taboo subject. Those of us who break the silence will be continually cast as traitors. Until this silence is repeatedly broken, African Americans will never be able to constructively address issues of positive gender identity formation, domestic violence, rape, incest, or black male-on-male violence. We will not be able to challenge and critique sexism if the destructive impact of patriarchal thinking is always denied, covered up, masked as a response to racial victimization.

10   Individual, progressive black heterosexual males who engage a critique of domination that takes feminist thinking and practice seriously as a radical alternative to the push to institutionalize potentially exploitative and oppressive patriarchal regimes in black life must be more willing to act politically so that their counter hegemonic presence is visible. Working in collective solidarity with black women who are active in progressive movements for black self-determination that incorporate fully a feminist standpoint, these black men represent a vanguard group that could begin and sustain a cultural revolution that could vigilantly contest, challenge, and change sexism and misogyny in black life. All too often the anti-feminist perspective is the only voice that masses of black people have the opportunity to hear. It is this voice that most intimately addresses black folks across class. Progressive black women and men often end up speaking the most to mainstream white culture. While this speaking is necessary intervention, it must be coupled with an equally intense effort to address gender issues with strategies that articulate ways the struggle to end sexism can positively transform black life in diverse black communities. Black males who cling to sexist thinking and fantasies of patriarchal power need to know that a concrete engagement with feminist thinking would allow them to examine the ways their acceptance of patriarchal notions of masculine identity undermine their capacity to live fully and freely. No matter how clearly and passionately black women active in feminist thinking and progressive black liberation struggle critique patriarchal thinking and action, it ultimately deprives black males of the opportunity to construct self and identity in ways that are truly liberatory, that do not require the subordination and domination of anyone else, and ultimately only the testimony of black males can bear witness to this truth. We need to hear more from black males who repudiate domination as the only possible means of social intercourse between themselves and black females. We need

to hear from those black males who are not sadomasochistically seduced by images of black females "at the mercy of black men." We need to hear from black males who have turned their gaze away from the colonizer's face and are able to look at gender and race with new eyes. Black men who can hear anew the prophetic words of Malcolm X urging us to change our minds: "We've got to change our own minds about each other. We have to see each other with new eyes. We have to see each other as brothers and sisters. We have to come together with warmth." Any black male or female who seriously contemplates this message of radical black self-determination would necessarily embrace the struggle to end sexism and sexist domination in black life. It is that struggle that offers us the hope of mutual intimacy, of a redemptive love that can extend beyond the limitations of utopian fantasies of family and nation, that can transcend narrowly constructed paradigms of identity formation and fixed sexual practice, a redemptive love that can indiscriminately offer every black male and female the hope that our suffering within white supremacist capitalist patriarchy will cease, that our wounds can be healed, that the struggle for black liberation can be realized in the politics of daily life.

Audre Lorde

(1934–1992)

Audrey Geraldine Lorde, the youngest of three girls, was born to Grenadian immigrants, Frederic Byron and Linda Belmar, in New York City on February 18, 1934. Bespeaking Lorde's spirit of self-determination, at the age of five she dropped the "y" in Audrey because she was disturbed by her printed name's unevenness. She attended Catholic schools, then earned a bachelor's degree from Hunter College in 1959 and a master's degree in Library Science from Columbia University in 1961. Lorde worked as a librarian and was a poet in residence at Tougaloo College in Jackson, Mississippi. In 1980, she became an English professor at Hunter College, and, in 1991, she was named poet laureate of New York. She is well known as a feminist poet; her works include The First Cities *(1968),* Cables to Rage *(1970),* From Land Where Other People Live *(1973), which was nominated for the National Book Award,* Coal *(1976), and* The Black Unicorn *(1978). In addition to her poetry, Lorde's prose broke a number of barriers:* The Cancer Journals, *published in 1980, marks the first published reflection of an African American woman's experiences with*

breast cancer, and her 1982 "biomythography," Zami: A New Spelling
of My Name, is a first-person account of the struggles that Lorde faced
as an African American lesbian in a homophobic society. Lorde boldly
affirmed her multiple identities in prose, essays, and poetry.

The Master's Tools Will Never Dismantle the Master's House*

1   I agreed to take part in a New York University Institute for the
Humanities conference a year ago, with the understanding that I
would be commenting upon papers dealing with the role of difference
within the lives of american women: difference of race, sexuality,
class, and age. The absence of these considerations weakens any feminist discussion of the personal and the political.

2   It is a particular academic arrogance to assume any discussion
of feminist theory without examining our many differences, and without a significant input from poor women, Black and Third World
women, and lesbians. And yet, I stand here as a Black lesbian feminist, having been invited to comment within the only panel at this
conference where the input of Black feminists and lesbians is represented. What this says about the vision of this conference is sad, in
a country where racism, sexism, and homophobia are inseparable. To
read this program is to assume that lesbian and Black women have
nothing to say about existentialism, the erotic, women's culture and
silence, developing feminist theory, or heterosexuality and power. And
what does it mean in personal and political terms when even the two
Black women who did present here were literally found at the last
hour? What does it mean when the tools of a racist patriarchy are
used to examine the fruits of that same patriarchy? It means that only
the most narrow perimeters of change are possible and allowable.

3   The absence of any consideration of lesbian consciousness or the
consciousness of Third World women leaves a serious gap within this
conference and within the papers presented here. For example, in a

*Comments at "The Personal and the Political Panel," Second Sex Conference, New York,
September 29, 1979.

paper on material relationships between women, I was conscious of an either/or model of nurturing which totally dismissed my knowledge as a Black lesbian. In this paper there was no examination of mutuality between women, no systems of shared support, no interdependence as exists between lesbians and women-identified women. Yet it is only in the patriarchal model of nurturance that women "who attempt to emancipate themselves pay perhaps too high a price for the results," as this paper states.

4   For women, the need and desire to nurture each other is not pathological but redemptive, and it is within that knowledge that our real power is rediscovered. It is this real connection which is so feared by a patriarchal world. Only within a patriarchal structure is maternity the only social power open to women.

5   Interdependency between women is the way to a freedom which allows the *I* to be, not in order to be used, but in order to be creative. This is a difference between the passive *be* and the active *being*.

6   Advocating the mere tolerance of difference between women is the grossest reformism. It is a total denial of the creative function of difference in our lives. Difference must be not merely tolerated, but seen as a fund of necessary polarities between which our creativity can spark like a dialectic. Only then does the necessity for interdependency become unthreatening. Only within that interdependency of different strengths, acknowledged and equal, can the power to seek new ways of being in the world generate, as well as the courage and sustenance to act where there are no charters.

7   Within the interdependence of mutual (nondominant) differences lies that security which enables us to descend into the chaos of knowledge and return with true visions of our future, along with the concomitant power to effect those changes which can bring that future into being. Difference is that raw and powerful connection from which our personal power is forged.

8   As women, we have been taught either to ignore our differences, or to view them as causes for separation and suspicion rather than as forces for change. Without community there is no liberation, only the most vulnerable and temporary armistice between an individual and her oppression. But community must not mean a shedding of our differences, nor the pathetic pretense that these differences do not exist.

9   Those of us who stand outside the circle of this society's definition of acceptable women; those of us who have been forged in the crucibles of difference—those of us who are poor, who are lesbians, who are Black, who are older—know that *survival is not an academic skill.*

It is learning how to stand alone, unpopular and sometimes reviled, and how to make common cause with those others identified as outside the structures in order to define and seek a world in which we can all flourish. It is learning how to take our differences and make them strengths. *For the master's tools will never dismantle the master's house.* They may allow us temporarily to beat him at his own game, but they will never enable us to bring about genuine change. And this fact is only threatening to those women who still define the master's house as their only source of support.

10   Poor women and women of Color know there is a difference between the daily manifestations of marital slavery and prostitution because it is our daughters who line 42nd Street. If white american feminist theory need not deal with the differences between us, and the resulting difference in our oppressions, then how do you deal with the fact that the women who clean your houses and tend your children while you attend conferences on feminist theory are, for the most part, poor women and women of Color? What is the theory behind racist feminism?

11   In a world of possibility for us all, our personal visions help lay the groundwork for political action. The failure of academic feminists to recognize difference as a crucial strength is a failure to reach beyond the first patriarchal lesson. In our world, divide and conquer must become define and empower.

12   Why weren't other women of Color found to participate in this conference? Why were two phone calls to me considered a consultation? Am I the only possible source of names of Black feminists? And although the Black panelist's paper ends on an important and powerful connection of love between women, what about interracial cooperation between feminists who don't love each other?

13   In academic feminist circles, the answer to these questions is often, "We did not know who to ask." But that is the same evasion of responsibility, the same cop-out, that keeps Black women's art out of women's exhibitions, Black women's work out of most feminist publications except for the occasional "Special Third World Women's Issue," and Black women's texts off your reading lists. But as Adrienne Rich pointed out in a recent talk, white feminists have educated themselves about such an enormous amount over the past ten years, how come you haven't also educated yourselves about Black women and the differences between us—white and Black—when it is key to our survival as a movement?

14   Women of today are still being called upon to stretch across the gap of male ignorance and to educate men as to our existence and our

needs. This is an old and primary tool of all oppressors to keep the oppressed occupied with the master's concerns. Now we hear that it is the task of women of Color to educate white women—in the face of tremendous resistance—as to our existence, our differences, our relative roles in our joint survival. This is a diversion of energies and a tragic repetition of racist patriarchal thought.

15   Simone de Beauvoir once said: "It is in the knowledge of the genuine conditions of our lives that we must draw our strength to live and our reasons for acting."

16   Racism and homophobia are real conditions of all our lives in this place and time. *I urge each one of us here to reach down into that deep place of knowledge inside herself and touch that terror and loathing of any difference that lives there. See whose face it wears.* Then the personal as the political can begin to illuminate all our choices.

Joan Morgan

(1965–)

Feminist, cultural critic, and award-winning journalist Joan Morgan was born May 25, 1965, in Jamaica, and raised in the South Bronx. After graduating from Wesleyan University, Morgan began her writing career at The Village Voice. *She has also written for* Vibe, Spin *and* Ms., *and is currently the executive editor of* Essence *magazine. The following excerpt, "the f-word" is from Morgan's* When Chickenheads Come Home to Roost . . . My Life as a Hip-Hop Feminist, *published in 1999. In ten personal, thought-provoking and candid pieces, Morgan's debut book offers an astute analysis of hip-hop culture, the complexities of contemporary Black women's lives—including marriage, motherhood and feminism—and the interconnectedness of money, sex, and power. Morgan, who is married and has one son, currently lives in Brooklyn, New York.*

the f-word

On our quests to create ourselves we brown girls play dress up. What is most fascinating about this ritual of imitation is what we choose to mimic—what we reach for in our mothers' closets. We move right on past the unglamorous garb of our mothers' day-to-day realities— the worn housedresses or beat-up slippers—and reach instead for the intimates. Slip our sassy little selves into their dressiest of dresses and sexiest of lingerie like being grown is like Christmas or Kwanzaa and can't come fast enough.

Then we practice the deadly art of attitude—rollin' eyes, necks, and hips in mesmerizing synchronization, takin' out imaginary violators with razor-sharp tongues. Perhaps to our ingenuous eyes transforming ourselves into invincible Miss Thangs is the black woman's only armature against the evils of the world.

Interestingly enough, we do not imitate our mothers at their weakest or most vulnerable. Shedding silent midnight tears, alone and afraid. That we don't do until much later, when we are fully grown, occasionally trippin' and oblivious to our behavior's origins.

It took years to realize that the same process was true of my feminism. For a very long time I was a black woman completely unaware that I faced the world in my mother's clothes . . .

1   I became a black feminist writer in the least feminist of ways. It happened one night in Harlem, up on Sugar Hill with a man the goddess had thrown in my path to grant me the sufferice I thought I needed to become a real woman. I was the young lover of a celebrated griot of black post-modernism, an icon of eighties black bohemia. He was a seductively brilliant brother with limited emotional skills, a penchant for younger women, and a Pygmalion obsession of legendary notoriety.

2   At twenty-four, I'd already been an assistant manager at a major retail store, an aspiring actress, and a very good teacher, but I still had no idea what I wanted to be when I grew up. So I stepped into my lover's life like I arrived in Harlem—willing and pliable—fresh outta lockdown in South Bronx soul prisons and armed with fly-girl attitude and wanna-be bohemian desire. In short, I was as ghetto a Galatea as you could get.

3   The night I became a black feminist writer was so like every other night that the details are rendered indiscernible. For poetry's sake I would like to say it started with one of those tender post-coital moments, brown limb entwined with brown limb, discussing the implications of wildin', race, and rape in the Central Park Jogger case. This is unlikely. My lover was not tender and we were not particularly compatible.

4   More likely than not, the conversation took place over the phone, with him in his space and me in mine, enjoying the magic of an unobstructed Sugar Hill view. To my right, Yankee Stadium and the rest of the Boogie-Down served as backdrop for the nocturnal adventures of

the Polo Grounds. On the left was Amsterdam, then Broadway, painted colorful and loud by the nonstop traffic of an ever-growing Dominican presence. But I was probably looking straight ahead, down the block, past my lover's building, past Harlem, Central Park, the Empire State Building, and somewhere past that—the rest of the world. And that's when I told him that *writing an article about the racial implications of the Central Park Jogger case without discussing gender was, like, bananas 'cause yes the coverage was racist, but that doesn't change the fact that the woman was raped and probably by some brown boys. I mean damn, wasn't anybody gonna say she wasn't a victim becuz she was white, she was a victim becuz she was a woman and what did he think, that if I was a black investment banker who happened to be in the park that night I wouldn't be raped 'cause homeboys woulda been like, "Now we can't hit it 'cuz she a sista"? And if it was a sista lying there where would we be 'cuz talking about niggas and sexism is like, mad taboo. So maybe, just maybe while we're busy being mad at the white folks we could also take a minute to acknowledge that sexism and violence against women occurs in our community too and our men are no better or worse than anybody else's.*

5   My lover's kindness lay in the generosity of his talent, his unfailing ability to pull out diamonds where others see only coal. He called his editor early that morning and told her about my midnight rave. When she asked if I could write, he doggedly ignored my lack of experience, cast aside the fact that I'd never expressed as much as passing desire, and said simply, "Yes. She can." Thirty-six hours later I turned in my first feature for a national weekly paper.

6   The piece got considerable play and I was rechristened Joan Morgan—Black Feminist Writer. It took a year of being published before I would call myself a writer. It took that long to figure out I had something valuable to say. My lover's work was done when I did, and we went our separate ways.

7   Coming out as a black feminist, however, was another matter entirely.

8   Feminism claimed me long before I claimed it. The foundation was laid by women who had little use for the word. Among them the three country women—mother, daughter, and sister—who brought me into this world sans hospital, electricity, or running water. (My father was off doing whatever it is island men do while their women give birth to girl children.) Shortly after, my mother left Jamaica to see for herself that the streets of the Bronx were not paved with gold. They were paved with things more frightening than she

could have imagined. So she armed her children with the King's English, good character, and explicit instructions to kick the ass of any knucklehead stupid enough to come for us. In the meantime, she cleaned white folks' homes, put herself and two kids through college, and proceeded to travel the world.

9   There were others. The mothers of friends. The grande dame Genevieve survived burying a husband, three children, and a daughter-in-law and taught us a woman commands a great deal of power when she remains, above all else, a lady. Sassy Aunt Claire* kicked a drug addiction square in the ass to resume her perpetual love affair with life. Lois's fierce spirit was the harness that held her child back from the grave, until cancer caused her to slip and fall into her own. And of course, Marvelous Melba aka Grand Diva Emeritus who loved magic and flowers and sensual things and was always down to share a few secrets over a good cappuccino. I did not know that feminism is what you called it when black warrior women moved mountains and walked on water. Growing up in their company, I considered these things ordinary.

10   The spirits of these women were nowhere to be found in the feminism I discovered in college. Feminists on our New England campus came in two flavas—both variations of vanilla. The most visible were the braless, butch-cut, anti-babes, who seemed to think the solution to sexism was reviling all things male (except, oddly enough, their clothing and mannerisms) and sleeping with each other. They used made up words like "womyn," "femynists," and threw mad shade if you asked them directions to the "Ladies' Room." The others—straight and more femme—were all for the liberation of women as long as it did not infringe on their sense of entitlement. They felt their men should *share* the power to oppress. They were the spiritual descendants of the early suffragettes and absolutely not to be trusted.

11   This is not to say that our differences were so great that the wave of feminist activism on campus left me totally unaffected. I stuck my toes in the water. I was adamantly pro-choice, attended speakouts against rape and domestic violence, and made sure to vote for candidates who paid lip-service to equal pay for equal work, protecting planned parenthood, legalized abortion, and quality child care. But feminism definitely felt like white women's shit.

12   White girls don't call their men "brothers" and that made their struggle enviably simpler than mine. Racism and the will to survive

*Not her real name.

it creates a sense of intra-racial loyalty that makes it impossible for black women to turn our backs on black men—even in their ugliest and most sexist of moments. I needed a feminism that would allow us to continue loving ourselves *and* the brothers who hurt us without letting race loyalty buy us early tombstones.

13   Being the bastion of liberal education it was, the university's curriculum did expose me to feminists of color. (Unfortunately this happened far more frequently in African-American Studies courses than it did in Women's Studies). Dedicated professors—male and female—exhumed the voices of Sojourner Truth, Ida B. Wells, Frances Harper, and Mary Church Terrell and let me know that black women had been making it their bidness to speak out against sexism and racism for over 250 years. (That it took almost twelve years of formal education to find out our contribution to African-American history was more than Harriet Tubman or Coretta Scott King made me seriously question if only white folks were guilty of revisionist history.) Discovering the works of Alice Walker, Angela Davis, Audre Lorde, Paula Giddings, and bell hooks—black women who claimed the f-word boldly—not only enabled me to understand the complex and often complicit relationship between both isms; it empowered me with language to express the unique oppression that comes with being colored and a woman.

14   I was eternally grateful, but I was not a feminist.

15   When I thought about feminism—women who were living and breathing it daily—I thought of white women or black female intellectuals. Academics. Historians. Authors. Women who had little to do with my everyday life. The sistas in my immediate proximity grew up in the 'hood, summered in the Hamptons, swapped spit on brightly lit Harlem corners, and gave up more than a li'l booty in Ivy League dorms. They were ghetto princesses with a predilection for ex–drug dealers. They got their caesars cut at the barbershop and perms at the Dominican's uptown. They were mack divas who rolled wit posses fifteen bitches deep and lived for Kappa beach parties, the Garage, the Roxy, and all things hip-hop. Black feminists were some dope sistas, respected elders most def, but they were not my contemporaries. They were not crew. And for most of my twenties, crew was what mattered.

16   But I was also a twenty-four-year-old who'd begun writing highly volatile articles on black male sexism and the conspiracy of protective silence that surrounds it. If I wasn't going to call myself a feminist, I'd

better come up with something. Folks like to know what to call you when they're cussing you out.

17 Thanks to Marc Christian* I found this out with a quickness.

18 Marc Christian was a sorcerer with a loft on the borderline of black Harlem and El Barrio. A photographer by trade, he was haunted by visions of unearthed black beauty, so he made a business outta making black folks beautiful. He called it "reminding them who they are." In his unspectacular loft, with its dingy white walls and worn wood floors, Marc Christian worked magic on the regular. Boxers with badly bludgeoned faces were given the regality of Zulu warriors; nude brown girls with Hottentot asses made love to his lenses like they grew up finding themselves in *Vogue*; ciphers of old drunk men recovered bits of spirits long ago sent swimming in Wild Irish Rose bottles. All he asked in return was for a little bit of their souls. He usually got it. Marc Christian was highly skilled in the art of seduction and a very pretty nigga. So when he called talkin' 'bout, "Yeah, baby, I read the article, your stunning debut. Now come bring your fine ass over here so I can talk to you 'bout this heavy shit you gettin' into," I dropped everything and jumped in a cab. Like most folks, I was defenseless against his juju.

19 Truth be told I couldn't wait to step into Marc Christian's loft with some semblance of a creative identity. I remembered the many times I sat awestruck and envious while he and my lover parleyed with various members of New York's Niggerati. I was hardly a member of that illustrious set, but for once "the work" was mine. I wanted to kick it with Marc up on his roof where the world was spread out like a humongous smorgasbord that extended as far as spirit, will, and appetite would take you. Of course, getting him to stop working would probably require some *brujeria* of my own but I was determined to have his undivided attention. As soon as I walked in the front door I knew this would not be the case. Marc Christian had company. Three men. Strangers who were expecting me.

20 Foolishly, I'd forgotten Marc Christian occasionally satiated his hunger for drama by mixing highly incendiary elements. At his prompting, each one of the men had read the article and was prepared to do battle. I had no choice but to go for mine.

21 "So you're the sista who wrote the article?" asked the first, in a tone less curious than caustic. He was young. A Latino homeboy with ghetto allegiances and bohemian aspirations. He and his compadre—a Queens

*Not his real name.

cutie with Trini roots—were Marc Christian's newest apprentices. As fellow creative spirits they gave me my props for "getting the work out there." They were upset, however, that my article didn't emphasize the impact of the rape on their lives.

22 It was a valid point. The city's current climate was undeniably ill. The rape became a self-righteous hook that racists conveniently hung their prejudices on. Brothers all over were forced to watch powerless as the media reduced them to savages and white women gripped their pocketbooks even harder in fear. Faced with these brothers' pain, it was easy to see why a critical article written by a black woman for a predominantly white paper felt not only traitorous but hurtful. Despite my convictions my Black Male Empathy Reflex was kickin' like a motherfucka.

23 Just as I began to question my ability to deal with such obviously divided loyalties Stranger #3 took center stage. He was in his early forties, some kinda horn player and bedecked in sixties attire, down to his ill-fitting high-waters. "Alla this was bullshit!" he declared ceremoniously and advised the young ones to step aside so he could "set the record straight."

24 Pausing only to hear the leftover conga beats that still played in his head, Money black-power-pimp strolled across the floor and kicked it faux Last Poets.

> *My siss-tah, don't you seee?*
> *You are be-ing yoused.*
> *Thisss is how the cracker da-feets*
> *the BLACK man every-time.*
> *He captures the minds*
> *of our women*
> *and uses them*
> *to speak out a-gainst us.*
> *Don't you seeee.*
> *My siss-tah*
> *You are a tool of the white man . . .*

25 It's been said Marc Christian could sometimes read minds so I offered him a piece of my own. *Alright, you've had your fun. Now why don't you reel your boy back in before he plays himself. You know damn well those wanna-be revolutionary theatrics are wasted on folks who were only around for five years of the sixties . . .* His only reply was the hint of a grin.

26   Unchecked, the asshole who considered himself the heavy artillery continued.

> *My siss-tah my siss-tah my siss-tah*
> *Do ya even like men?*
> *'cuz ya could be one a dem*
> *funny girls*
> *(UH-HUH, UH-HUH)*
> *then in that case you'd need something else to save ya*
> *(ha-ha)*

27   He said this of course, this little bit of a man (with feet and hands smaller than nobody's business), as if I'd consider being mistaken for a lesbian an insult instead of an inaccuracy. For a second I couldn't tell what pissed me off more, the assumption that any woman who is willing to call a black man out on his shit *must* be eating pussy or his depiction of me as a brainwashed Sappho, waving the American flag in one hand and a castrated black male penis in the other. As it turns out, there wasn't time to decide; he finished his malediction by throwing down the gauntlet.

> *Ya know Marc Christian?*
> *Ya know what we got here?*
> *my brotha*
> *We got us one dem*
> *FEM-in-ists.*
> *Are you a feminist*
> *my siss-tah? . . .*

28   And there it was, the f-word all up in my face daring me to blanket myself in the yarns I'd spun to justify my rejection. *Go on, girl. Deny me and tell this fool about cha lover and the butch-cut white girls and see if he gives a fuck.* Searching for a viable, less volatile alternative I did a quick mental check of the popular epithets. Strong Black Woman. Womanist. Warrior Woman. Nubian Queen. Bitch. Gangsta Bitch. Bitches With Problems. Hos With Attitude. None of them offered even the hint of protection.

29   Finally, I realized that in the face of sexism it didn't matter what I called myself. Semantics would not save me from the jerks I was bound to run into if I continued to do this for a living nor would it save women from the violence of teenage boys who suffered from their

own misconceptions of power and manhood. If I truly believed that the empowerment of the black community had to include its women, or that sexism stood stubbornly in the way of black men and women loving each other or sistas loving themselves, if I acknowledged this both in print and in person then in any sexist's eyes I was a feminist. Once I recognized these manifestations of black-on-black love as the dual heart-beats of black feminism, I was purged of doubt. I accepted his challenge with confidence.

30   *Since my sexual preference could not be of any relevance to you, whatcha really wanna know is how I feel about brothas. It's simple. I love black men like I love no other. And I'm not talking sex or aesthetics, I'm talking about loving y' all enough to be down for the drama— stomping anything that threatens your existence. Now only a fool loves that hard without asking the same in return. So yeah, I demand that black men fight sexism with the same passion they battle racism. I want you to annihilate anything that endangers sistas' welfare—including violence against women—because my survival walks hand in hand with yours. So, my brotha, if loving y'all fiercely and wanting it back makes me a feminist then I'm a feminist. So be it.*

31   As our cab made its way through the Harlem night, I'd asked Marc Christian if luring unsuspecting friends into the dens of wolves was a regular practice. He replied with a severity I'd never seen from him. "The article was damn good, but you are better. Your work comes from your heart and the truth is some powerful shit. That's black magic. When people find out you got that they gonna keep trying to tear you apart. You already know you got skills. Tonight was about getting your *cojónes.*"

32   The moment catapulted me across time and the bridge, back to my family's small South Bronx apartment. I'd run upstairs one day to tell my mother about a bigger, older girl who kept threatening to kick my ass becuz our family dressed in clean clothes, spoke decent English, and dared not to be on welfare. My attempts to ignore her only infuriated her more and that day she pushed the issue by shoving me. I told my mother in the hopes she would go downstairs and hit her (and if need be her mother) or tell her to leave me alone. Instead, she said, "If she hits you again, fight her—pick up something if you have to—but if I hear you stood there and let her beat your ass I'm gonna come downstairs and beat yours." And she went back

to whatever she was doing. Minutes later, my nemesis hit me again, and I beat the child bloody.

33   "So how did I do, Marc?" I asked in a voice that belonged more to the ten-year-old girl telling her mom the details of her battle than the young woman sitting next to him. "You mean the *cojónes?*" he said and let out a sorcerer's laugh that charmed even the gypsy cab driver who'd been impatiently waiting for my departure. "Baby, you gonna be just fine. You got a bigger dick than most niggas I know." And with that I said good night and tucked my friend's departing words safely away in my treasure chest of talismans.

Writing Assignments

1. How are Sojourner Truth's concerns regarding race, gender, and class in "Ar'n't I a Woman" revisited by later feminists' works in the chapter? What are the similarities and dissimilarities among the different authors' perspectives? Do you think that in today's society there are other concerns for Black feminists?

2. Both Gwendolyn Brooks' *Maud Martha* and Alice Walker's *The Color Purple* make use of distinct narrative styles. Analyze both content and form of each text and consider what the narrative structure reveals about of the protagonist's inner life.

3. Examine June Jordan's and Alice Walker's reflections on Sojourner Truth's and Georgia Douglas Johnson's works. How are these latter authors participating in what Walker refers to as "herstory"?

4. Although initially perceiving feminism as the domain of white women and Black female intellectuals, Joan Morgan learns to adopt the "f-word." Why does she label her feminism hip-hop feminism? What is your response to the argument that popular hip-hop and rap have misogynic tendencies? Discuss Morgan's hip-hop feminism in terms of Walker's womanism, paying particlar attention to how each woman defines the contours of feminism for Black women.

CHAPTER TWELVE

THE BLACK AESTHETIC

For our purposes, the term *aesthetic* implies consideration of what is valuable and beautiful in literature. As such, virtually all African American literary activity reflects to some degree what may be called a *Black aesthetic*. In the tradition, there has always been artistic production and reception based upon some sense of African American pride, taste, and exquisiteness. This work has departed in some measure—sometimes very slightly and at other times dramatically—from what may be called a Eurocentric orientation. Innumerable African American writers also have argued for emancipation and equality. In the process of doing so, some have promoted distinctly Black verbal expression. In previous chapters, we have seen these impulses manifested in such forms as spirituals, folktales, blues, and Black vernacular speech. We have seen writers ranging from Zora Neale Hurston to Etheridge Knight incorporate these patterns of representation in their works. In this chapter, however, we focus on a period when the idea of a Black aesthetic was formalized in theoretical terms and became a codified prescription that was dominant. It became, in short, *the* Black Aesthetic. This period spanned roughly 10 years from the mid-1960s to the mid-1970s an expanse of time also cited as the dates of the closely related Black Arts Movement. With an exception or two, we have placed writing from the 1960s and the 1970s literally in the middle of the chapter. In addition, we have included earlier writing that prefigured and perhaps set the tone for later articulations of Black pride and Black power during the Black Aesthetic/Black Arts phase. We have also featured a sampling of relatively recent work that draws inspiration, in some cases quite directly, from the Black

Aesthetic/Black Arts undertaking, thus demonstrating the continuing influence of that brand of cultural politics.

What, then, was *the* Black Aesthetic? In an essay titled "The Black Arts Movement" (1968), poet and critic Larry Neal wrote, "Black art is the aesthetic and spiritual sister of the Black Power concept. . . . It proposes a separate symbolism, mythology, critique, and iconology." In other words, the emphasis was cultural Black nationalism that aligned with the militant Black nationalist politics of the post-Civil Rights era. Of course, not all expressions of cultural nationalism led the creators to engage in nationalist political organizing, nor was all nationalist organizing militant to the same extent. But there was a widespread feeling that the purpose of Black art was, as Maulana Karenga put it in his essay "Black Art" (1968), to "expose the enemy, praise the people and support the revolution." Therefore, there was rejection of the traditional notion, regarded as Eurocentric, that art should exist apart from political considerations, an idea also known as "art for art's sake." Instead, writers and critics denounced the white power structure as well as integrationist African American leaders and the "Black bourgeoisie." Emphasis was placed on the struggles and manners of the African American masses.

Although the blues and jazz experiments of Langston Hughes, the musings about Africa by Countee Cullen, and the militance of Claude McKay all preceded the 1960s, the Black aestheticians combined radical political postures and artistic forms in new ways, often stressing the rhythms of Black speech and music. However revolutionary of spirit, a poet probably would not have received an enthusiastic welcome at street festivals in 1969 reading a large selection of Shakespearean sonnets, one of McKay's preferred forms. Stylistically, the Black Aesthetic also involved semantic inversion. For example, "endarkened" could come to mean possession of knowledge as opposed to "enlightened." The object of such a move was to counteract the color bias inherent in the English language, where "white" is invariably associated with the positive and "black" with the negative, a fact famously recognized by Malcolm X while voraciously reading the dictionary during his stint in prison. Similarly, to have a "black heart" is in traditional English semantics to be evil. But immoral people are certainly not the intended primary audience for Amiri Baraka's "Poem for Black Hearts" (1969).

Strictly speaking, the Black Aesthetic in its theoretical heyday was subsumed under the Black Arts Movement. The latter entity consisted of aesthetic theory and artistry *plus* an infrastructure of cultural centers, academic programs, and publishing outlets. When people speak of the Black Arts Movement as something that ended around 1975, they are actually referring to the fact that a political and cultural network had become so eroded by that time that the term *movement* would be an overblown description of the activity that remained. Yet many of the participants in the Black Aesthetic/Black Arts Movement are still working in line with the goals of that movement, and they have enlisted new recruits, so there is no definitive note of finality. As for antecedents, we can turn, as has been hinted, to the Harlem Renaissance.

Considered by many to have been a phenomenon more or less of the 1920s, the Harlem Renaissance was a cultural flowering that represents one of the high peaks of Black literary expression. Figures associated with the era include W. E. B. Du Bois, Langston Hughes, Countee Cullen, Claude McKay, Nella Larsen, Zora Neale Hurston, Jessie Faucet, Wallace Thurman, Helene Johnson, James Weldon Johnson, and Arna Bontemps. A principal text edited by Alain Locke in 1925, *The New Negro: Voices of the Harlem Renaissance*, attempted to capture the spirit of the times. In his introduction to the book, a publication that included all of the writers mentioned above, Locke spoke of a "New Negro," a person or artist committed to self-determination and higher levels of artistic achievement. True expression for him involved portraying the Negro in a variety of guises. Seeing in past American cultural production, Black and otherwise, a collection of "aunties," "mammies," and "uncles," as well as types like Sambo and Uncle Tom, Locke wished to see Blacks depicted with self-respect and without sentimentality. In addition, as his political mission was decidedly integrationist, Locke wanted African American writing held to so-called universal standards. He saw literature as a tool in political struggle because it was illustrative of African American humanity and potential. In this regard, his approach was similar to that of James Weldon Johnson, who three years earlier had edited another key text of the Harlem Renaissance, *The Book of American Negro Poetry*. As Johnson wrote in the introduction, "No people that has produced great literature and art has ever been looked upon by the world as distinctly inferior." Whether that is true is certainly questionable, at the least. Perhaps how one is "acted upon" is more important than how one is "looked upon."

At any rate, neither Locke nor Johnson represented fully the aesthetics of the writers of the Harlem Renaissance, who themselves reflected various degrees of a Black aesthetic. Some were more oriented toward so-called high culture and its traditional expressive forms. Others were more interested in the Black vernacular. Some traded in both. Writers like Hughes, Cullen, McKay, and Helene Johnson, though dissimilar in some respects, all reflected sensibilities that anticipated the dominant strand of African American writing of the 1960s. For example, there is Hughes's straightforward affirmation of Black beauty in "My People" (1923), and Cullen's grappling with the issue of his African roots in "Heritage" (1925). Cullen is no pan-Africanist; he is questioning—not claiming—the importance of Africa. But his question is taken up exuberantly in the 1960s. McKay's call for self-defense in "If We Must Die" (1919), and Helene Johnson's racial pride as exhibited in pieces like "Poem" (1927) and "Sonnet to a Negro in Harlem" (1927) fit, albeit not always most smoothly, into a Black aesthetic mold.

Margaret Walker, a poet who bridges the gap between the Harlem Renaissance and the 1960s, is an important precursor to the Black Arts Movement. Although she was quite adept at manipulating traditional verse forms, she also employed a freer lyricism and in virtually all of her work celebrated common Black folk. This is evident in "For My People" (1937, 1942).

Considered together, the writing of Quincy Troupe, Amiri Baraka, John A. Williams, Haki Madhubuti, Nikki Giovanni, Larry Neal, Sarah Webster Fabio, Toni Cade Bambara, Sonia Sanchez, and Gil Scott-Heron indicate the range of Black aesthetics during the 1960s and 1970s. To be sure, not all of these writers agreed with all the ideas of *the* Black Aesthetic, but collectively they evince the love of Blackness, stylistic departures, and militant politics for which critics were calling. (Of course, some of the critics were themselves calling for these artistic elements.)

Several fairly recent anthologies further the tradition. For instance, Derrick Gilbert's *Catch the Fire!!!: A Cross-Generational Anthology of Contemporary African-American Poetry* (1998) contributes to, as he phrases it," a continuum of centuries of tradition." He avoids sometimes fashionable talk about a New Black Renaissance and stresses, rather, the continuity between the old and the new. Fittingly, the first line of Gilbert's "The Revolution Will Be on the Big Screen" (2000) is "My man Gil Scott-Heron once said:." Tony Medina, Samiya Bashir, and Quraysh Lansana's *Role Call: A Generational Anthology of Social & Political Black Literature and Art* (2000) also aims to build explicitly upon the Black Arts Movement. Their book champions a "new Black Power—one that is spiritually grounded, forged in multiple alliances, and based on the credo that each of our experiences matter." It is no coincidence that *Role Call* was published by Third World Press, which was founded in 1967 by Haki Madhubuti and still functions as an example of Black Aesthetic/Black Arts ideas put into practice.

Further Reading

Gilbert, Derek I. M., ed. *Catch the Fire!!!: A Cross-Generational Anthology of Contemporary African-American Poetry*. New York: Riverhead, 1998.

Jones, LeRoi and Larry Neal, eds. *Black Fire: An Anthology of African American Writing*. New York: Morrow, 1968.

Karenga, Maulana. (1968) "Black Art: Mute Matter Given Form and Function." In *Black Poets and Prophets*, W. King and E. Anthony (eds.). New York: Mentor, 1972, 174–180.

Locke, Alain, ed. (1925) *The New Negro: Voices of the Harlem Renaisance*. New York: Atheneum, 1992.

Medina, Tony, Samiya A. Bashir, and Quarishi Ali Lansana, eds. *Role Call: A Generational Anthology of Social and Political Black Art & Literature*. Chicago: Third World Press, 2002.

Neal, Larry, "The Black Arts Movement." *The Drama Review* (1968), Vol. 12, No. 4.

Redmond, Eugene B. *Drumvoices: The Mission of Afro-American Poetry: A Critical History*. Garden City, N.Y.: Anchor Press, 1976.

Langston Hughes

(1902–1967)

For biographical information about Langston Hughes, see page 458. "My People" was originally published as "Poem" in the August 1923 issue of the Crisis.

My People

The night is beautiful.
So the faces of my people.

The stars are beautiful.
So the eyes of my people.

5 Beautiful, also, is the sun.
Beautiful, also, are the souls of my people.

Countee Cullen

(1903–1946)

For biographical information about Countee Cullen, see page 63.
"Heritage" and "From the Dark Tower" are two of his most recognized
poems.

Heritage

(For Harold Jackman)

What is Africa to me:
Copper sun or scarlet sea,
Jungle star or jungle track,
Strong bronzed men, or regal black
5 Women from whose loins I sprang
When the birds of Eden sang?
One three centuries removed
From the scenes his fathers loved,
Spicy grove, cinnamon tree,
10 *What is Africa to me?*

So I lie, who all day long
Want no sound except the song
Sung by wild barbaric birds
Goading massive jungle herds,
15 Juggernauts of flesh that pass
Trampling tall defiant grass
Where young forest lovers lie,
Plighting troth beneath the sky.
So I lie, who always hear,
20 Though I cram against my ear
Both my thumbs, and keep them there,
Great drums throbbing through the air.
So I lie, whose fount of pride,
Dear distress, and joy allied,
25 Is my somber flesh and skin,
With the dark blood dammed within
Like great pulsing tides of wine

That, I fear, must burst the fine
Channels of the chafing net
30 Where they surge and foam and fret.
Africa? A book one thumbs
Listlessly, till slumber comes.
Unremembered are her bats
Circling through the night, her cats
35 Crouching in the river reeds,
Stalking gentle flesh that feeds
By the river brink; no more
Does the bugle-throated roar
Cry that monarch claws have leapt
40 From the scabbards where they slept.
Silver snakes that once a year
Doff the lovely coats you wear,
Seek no covert in your fear
Lest a mortal eye should see;
45 What's your nakedness to me?
Here no leprous flowers rear
Fierce corollas in the air;
Here no bodies sleek and wet,
Dripping mingled rain and sweat,
50 Tread the savage measures of
Jungle boys and girls in love.
What is last year's snow to me,
Last year's anything? The tree
Budding yearly must forget
55 How its past arose or set—
Bough and blossom, flower, fruit,
Even what shy bird with mute
Wonder at her travail there,
Meekly labored in its hair.
60 *One three centuries removed*
From the scenes his father loved,
Spicy grove, cinnamon tree,
What is Africa to me?

So I lie, who find no peace
65 Night or day, no slight release
From the unremittant beat
Made by cruel padded feet

Walking through my body's street.
Up and down they go, and back,
70 Treading out a jungle track.
So I lie, who never quite
Safely sleep from rain at night—
I can never rest at all
When the rain begins to fall;
75 Like a soul gone mad with pain
I must match its weird refrain;
Ever must I twist and squirm,
Writhing like a baited worm,
While its primal measures drip
80 Through my body, crying, "Strip!
Doff this new exuberance.
Come and dance the Lover's Dance!"
In an old remembered way
Rain works on me night and day.

85 Quaint, outlandish heathen gods
Black men fashion out of rods,
Clay, and brittle bits of stone,
In a likeness like their own,
My conversion came high-priced;
90 I belong to Jesus Christ,
Preacher of humility;
Heathen gods are naught to me.

Father, Son, and Holy Ghost,
So I make an idle boast;
95 Jesus of the twice-turned cheek,
Lamb of God, although I speak
With my mouth thus, in my heart,
Do I play a double part.
Ever at Thy glowing altar
100 Must my heart grow sick and falter,
Wishing He I served were black,
Thinking then it would not lack
Precedent of pain to guide it,
Let who would or might deride it;
105 Surely then this flesh would know
Yours had borne a kindred woe.

Lord, I fashion dark gods, too,
Daring even to give You
Dark despairing features where,
110 Crowned with dark rebellious hair,
Patience wavers just so much as
Mortal grief compels, while touches
Quick and hot, of anger, rise
To smitten cheek and weary eyes.
115 Lord, forgive me if my need
Sometimes shapes a human creed.

All day long and all night through,
One thing only must I do:
Quench my pride and cool my blood,
120 *Lest I perish in the flood.*
Lest a hidden ember set
Timber that I thought was wet
Burning like the dryest flax,
Melting like the merest wax,
125 *Lest the grave restore its dead.*
Not yet has my heart or head
In the least way realized
They and I are civilized.

From the Dark Tower

(To Charles S. Johnson)

We shall not always plant while others reap
The golden increment of bursting fruit,
Not always countenance, abject and mute.
That lesser men should hold their brothers cheap;
5 Not everlastingly while others sleep
Shall we beguile their limbs with mellow flute,
Not always bend to some more subtle brute;
We were not made eternally to weep.

The night whose sable breast relieves the stark,
10 White stars is no less lovely being dark,
And there are buds that cannot bloom at all
In light, but crumple, piteous, and fall;
So in the dark we hide the heart that bleeds,
And wait, and tend our agonizing seeds.

Claude McKay

(1889–1948)

Festus Claudius McKay was born on September 15, 1889, in rural Jamaica. He first gained attention as a poet with the publication, in 1912, of two volumes, Songs of Jamaica *and* Constab Ballads. *He left Jamaica for the United States to enroll at Booker T. Washington's Tuskegee Institute. However, he stayed only for a couple of months before enrolling at Kansas State University. After two years, he left school to move to Harlem, where he pursued a writing career full time. He gained national attention when "If We Must Die" appeared in the July 1919 issue of the* Liberator *magazine. The poem, published after a series of race riots in cities across the country, was embraced widely as a call to resist injustice. Winston Churchill, though he did not credit McKay, later used the poem to rally British troops during World War II. McKay became one of the major voices of the Harlem Renaissance, producing work that evinced both race and class consciousness. His books include the poetry volumes* Spring in New Hampshire *(1920) and* Harlem Shadows *(1922); the novels* Home to Harlem *(1928),* Banjo *(1929), and* Banana Bottom *(1933); the short story collection* Gingertown *(1932); the autobiography* A Long Way from Home *(1937); and the nonfiction book* Harlem: Negro Metropolis *(1940). The following pieces are from* Selected Poems of Claude McKay *(1953).*

If We Must Die

If we must die, let it not be like hogs
Hunted and penned in an inglorious spot,
While round us bark the mad and hungry dogs,
Making their mock at our accursed lot.
5 If we must die. O let us nobly die,

So that our precious blood may not be shed
In vain; then even the monsters we defy
Shall be constrained to honor us though dead!
O kinsmen! we must meet the common foe!
10 Though far outnumbered let us show us brave,
And for their thousand blows deal one deathblow!
What though before us lies the open grave?
Like men we'll face the murderous, cowardly pack,
Pressed to the wall, dying, but fighting back!

Enslaved

Oh when I think of my long-suffering race,
For weary centuries despised, oppressed,
Enslaved and lynched, denied a human place
In the great life line of the Christian West;
5 And in the Black Land disinherited,
Robbed in the ancient country of its birth,
My heart grows sick with hate, becomes as lead,
For this my race that has no home on earth.
Then from the dark depths of my soul I cry
10 To the avenging angel to consume
The white man's world of wonders utterly;
Let it be swallowed up in earth's vast womb,
Or upward roll as sacrificial smoke
To liberate my people from its yoke!

Outcast

For the dim regions whence my fathers came
My spirit, bondaged by the body, longs.
Words felt, but never heard, my lips would frame;
My soul would sing forgotten jungle songs.
5 I would go back to darkness and to peace,
But the great western world holds me in fee,
And I may never hope for full release

While to its alien gods I bend my knee.
Something in me is lost, forever lost,
10 Some vital thing has gone out of my heart.
And I must walk the way of life a ghost
Among the sons of earth, a thing apart;
For I was born, far from my native clime,
Under the white man's menace, out of time.

Helene Johnson

(1906–1995)

Helen Johnson (Helene was a pen name) was born on July 7, 1906, in Boston. After attending Boston University, she moved to New York City in 1926. A friend and neighbor of Zora Neale Hurston, Johnson was the youngest of the poets associated with the Harlem Renaissance. Johnson did not publish much in her later years, but during the 1920s and 1930s her work appeared in many magazines and anthologies.

Poem

Little brown boy,
Slim, dark, big-eyed,
Crooning love songs to your banjo
Down at the Lafayette
5 Gee, boy, I love the way you hold your head,
High sort of and a bit to one side,
Like a prince, a jazz prince. And I love
Your eyes flashing, and your hands,
And your patent-leathered feet,
10 And your shoulders jerking the jig-wa.
And I love your teeth flashing,
And the way your hair shines in the spotlight
Like it was the real stuff.
Gee, brown boy. I loves you all over.

15 I'm glad I'm a jig. I'm glad I can
Understand your dancin' and your
Singin', and feel all the happiness
And joy and don't-care in you.
Gee, boy, when you sing, I can close my ears
20 And hear tomtoms just as plain.
Listen to me, will you, what do I know
About tomtoms? But I like the word, sort of,
Don't you? It belongs to us.
Gee, boy, I love the way you hold your head,
25 And the way you sing and dance,
And everything.
Say, I think you're wonderful. You're
All right with me,
You are.

1927

Sonnet to a Negro in Harlem

You are disdainful and magnificent—
Your perfect body and your pompous gait,
Your dark eyes flashing solemnly with hate,
Small wonder that you are incompetent
5 To imitate those whom you so despise—
Your shoulders towering high above the throng,
Your head thrown back in rich, barbaric song,
Palm trees and mangoes stretched before your eyes.
Let others toil and sweat for labor's sake
10 And wring from grasping hands their meed of gold.
Why urge ahead your supercilious feet?
Scorn will efface each footprint that you make.
I love your laughter arrogant and bold.
You are too splendid for this city street.

1927

Margaret Walker

(1915–1998)

*For biographical information about Margaret Walker, see page 260.
"For My People," written when she was still in her twenties, is her
most celebrated poem.*

For My People

For my people everywhere singing their slave songs repeatedly:
    their dirges and their ditties and their blues and jubilees,
    praying their prayers nightly to an unknown god, bending
    their knees humbly to an unseen power;

5 For my people lending their strength to the years, to the gone years
    and the now years and the maybe years, washing ironing
    cooking scrubbing sewing mending hoeing plowing digging
    planting pruning patching dragging along never gaining
    never reaping never knowing and never understanding;

10 For my playmates in the clay and dust and sand of Alabama
    backyards playing baptizing and preaching and doctor and
    jail and soldier and school and mama and cooking and
    playhouse and concert and store and hair and Miss Choomby
    and company;

15 For the cramped bewildered years we went to school to learn to
    know the reasons why and the answers to and the people who
    and the places where and the days when, in memory of the
    bitter hours when we discovered we were black and poor and
    small and different and nobody cared and nobody wondered
20   and nobody understood;

For the boys and girls who grew in spite of these things to be man
    and woman, to laugh and dance and sing and play and drink
    their wine and religion and success, to marry their playmates
    and bear children and then die of consumption
25   and anemia and lynching.

For my people thronging 47th Street in Chicago and Lenox Avenue
    in New York and Rampart Street in New Orleans, lost

disinherited dispossessed and happy people filling the
cabarets and taverns and other people's pockets needing
30   bread and shoes and milk and land and money and
something—something all our own;

For my people walking blindly spreading joy, losing time being
lazy, sleeping when hungry, shouting when burdened,
drinking when hopeless, tied and shackled and tangled
35   among ourselves by the unseen creatures who tower over us
omnisciently and laugh;

For my people blundering and groping and floundering in the dark
of churches and schools and clubs and societies, associations
and councils and committees and conventions, distressed and
40   disturbed and deceived and devoured by money-hungry
glory-craving leeches, preyed on by facile force of state and
fad and novelty, by false prophet and holy believer;

For my people standing staring trying to fashion a better way from
confusion, from hypocrisy and misunderstanding, trying to
45   fashion a world that will hold all the people, all the faces, all
the adams and eves and their countless generations;

Let a new earth rise. Let another world be born. Let a bloody
peace be written in the sky. Let a second generation full of
courage issue forth: let a people loving freedom come to
50   growth. Let a beauty full of healing and a strength of final
clenching be the pulsing in our spirits and our blood. Let the
martial songs be written, let the dirges disappear. Let a race
of men now rise and take control.

Gwendolyn Brooks
(1917–2000)

For biographical information about Gwendolyn Brooks, see page 1182.

The Mother

Abortions will not let you forget.
You remember the children you got that you did not get,

The damp small pulps with a little or with no hair,
The singers and workers that never handled the air.
5 You will never neglect or beat
Them, or silence or buy with a sweet.
You will never wind up the sucking-thumb
Or scuttle off ghosts that come.
You will never leave them, controlling your luscious sigh,
10 Return for a snack of them, with gobbling mother-eye.

I have heard in the voices of the wind the voices of my dim killed
    children.
I have contracted. I have eased
My dim dears at the breasts they could never suck.
I have said, Sweets, if I sinned, if I seized
15 Your luck
And your lives from your unfinished reach,
If I stole your births and your names,
Your straight baby tears and your games,
Your stilted or lovely loves, your tumults, your marriages, aches,
    and your deaths,
20 If I poisoned the beginnings of your breaths,
Believe that even in my deliberateness I was not deliberate.
Though why should I whine,
Whine that the crime was other than mine?—
Since anyhow you are dead.
25 Or rather, or instead,
You were never made.
But that too, I am afraid,
Is faulty: oh, what shall I say, how is the truth to be said?
You were born, you had body, you died.
30 It is just that you never giggled or planned or cried.

Believe me, I loved you all.
Believe me, I knew you, though faintly, and I loved, I loved you
All.

Malcolm X

For Dudley Randall

Original.
Ragged-round.
Rich-robust.

He had the hawk-man's eyes.
5   We gasped. We saw the maleness.
The maleness raking out and making guttural the air
and pushing us to walls.

And in a soft and fundamental hour
a sorcery devout and vertical
10 beguiled the world.

He opened us—
who was a key,

who was a man.

Quincy Troupe
(1939–)

For biographical information about Quincy Troupe, see page 469. The following selection is taken from his 1996 volume Avalanche.

Old Black Ladies Standing on Bus Stop Corners # 2

for my grandmother, Leona Smith

blue black & bow bent under, beautiful
blue black & bow bent under, beautiful
blue black & bow bent under, beautiful

& it never did matter
5 whether the weather
was flame-tongue-licked
or as cold as a welldigger's asshole
in late december when santa claus
was working his cold money bullshit
10 that made financiers grin ear to ear
all the way to secret bank vaults
overflowing with marble eyes
of dirt-poor children

blue black & bow bent under, beautiful
15 *blue black & bow bent under, beautiful*
blue black & bow bent under, beautiful

never did matter
whether the days were storm raked
unzipped by lightning streaking clouds
20 dropping tornadoes that skipped crazy
to their own exploding beat
shooting hailstone death—
that popped like old bones—
crashing into the skulled
25 sunken eyes of tired old ladies
tired old black ladies
standing on bus stop corners
pain wrapped as shawls around their necks

blue black & bow bent under, beautiful

30 & "mama" it didn't matter
that your pained scarred feet overworked
numb legs grew down out of old worn dresses
seemingly fragile, gaunt & skeletal frail
as two old mop sticks—scarecrow legs—
35 didn't matter because you stood there anyway
defying nature's chameleon weather—
cold as a welldigger's asshole, then oven-hot—
defying all reason, you stood
there, testifying over 300 years
40 stretching back, of madness & treason

blue black & bow bent under, beautiful

no, it didn't matter
because the beauty of your heroic life
grown lovely in twisted swamps
45 grown lovely in a loveless land
grown pure & full from wombs
of concrete blood & bones.
of concrete blood & bones & death
of death & sweat chained to breath
50 didn't matter dark proud flower
who stood tall scrubbed by cold
& rain & hear & age carrying
the foreign name given your grandfather—
who swayed body high
55 twisting & turning in the breeze
like billie's "strange fruit"—

because you stood there anyway
unforgettably silent in your standing
beautiful work-scarred black lady
60 numb legs & bow bent under beautiful
stood there on pain-scarred feet overworked
numb legs
& bow bent under beautiful
under the memory of your grandfather swaying high
65 up there in a burning southern breeze

now sweet music love sings soft tender beauty
                         deep in your washed aging windows—
& you give me strength
                         during the mad, bizarre days—

70 & we have learned to love your life
& will vindicate the pain & silence of your life
the memory of your grandfather with the foreign name
& who sways high up there in history over your legs
                         blue black & bow bent under beautiful
75 the weight of over 300 years carried
of blood & bones & death in mud
of breath & sweat chained to death
                         numb legs & bow bent under beautiful
under the memory of your grandfather
80 swaying high up there in the burning breeze

didn't matter whether the weather was flame-tongue-licked
or as cold as a welldigger's asshole in late december
because you stood there anyway
in full bloom of your strength & rare beauty
85 & made us strong

blue black & bow bent under, beautiful
blue black & bow bent under, beautiful
blue black & bow bent under, beautiful

Amiri Baraka

(1934–)

For biographical information about Amiri Baraka, see page 221. The
three poems that follow epitomize his artistic position in the latter part
of the 1960s.

A Poem Some People Will Have to Understand

Dull unwashed windows of eyes
and buildings of industry. What
industry do I practice? A slick
colored boy, 12 miles from his
5 home. I practice no industry.
I am no longer a credit
to my race. I read a little,
scratch against silence slow spring
afternoons.
10   I had thought, before, some years ago
that I'd come to the end of my life.
    Watercolor ego. Without the preciseness
a violent man could propose.
    But the wheel, and the wheels,
15 wont let us alone. All the fantasy
    and justice, and dry charcoal winters

All the pitifully intelligent citizens
    I've forced myself to love.

    We have awaited the coming of a natural
20   phenomenon. Mystics and romantics, knowledgeable workers
    of the land.
    But none has come.
     (*Repeat*)
25   but none has come.
Will the machinegunners please step forward?

Black Art

Poems are bullshit unless they are
teeth or trees or lemons piled
on a step. Or black ladies dying
of men leaving nickel hearts
5 beating them down. Fuck poems
and they are useful, wd they shoot
come at you, love what you are,
breathe like wrestlers, or shudder
strangely after pissing. We want live
10 words of the hip world live flesh &
coursing blood. Hearts Brains
Souls splintering fire. We want poems
like fists beating niggers out of Jocks
or dagger poems in the slimy bellies
15 of the owner-jews. Black poems to
smear on girdlemamma mulatto bitches
whose brains are red jelly stuck
between 'lizabeth taylor's toes. Stinking
Whores! We want "poems that kill."
20 Assassin poems, Poems that shoot
guns. Poems that wrestle cops into alleys
and take their weapons leaving them dead
with tongues pulled out and sent to Ireland. Knockoff
poems for dope selling wops or slick halfwhite
25 politicians Airplane poems, rrrrrrrrrrrrrrrr

rrrrrrrrrrrrrr . . . tuhtuhtuhtuhtuhtuhtuhtuhtuh
. . . rrrrrrrrrrrrrrrr . . . Setting fire and death to
whities ass. Look at the Liberal
Spokesman for the jews clutch his throat
30 & puke himself into eternity . . . rrrrrrr
There's a negroleader pinned to
a bar stool in Sardi's eyeballs melting
in hot flame Another negroleader
on the steps of the white house one
35 kneeling between the sheriff's thighs
negotiating cooly for his people.
Agggh . . . stumbles across the room . . .
Put it on him, poem. Strip him naked
to the world! Another bad poem cracking
40 steel knuckles in a jewlady's mouth
Poem scream poison gas on beasts in green berets
Clean out the world for virtue and love,
Let there be no love poems written
until love can exist freely and
45 cleanly. Let Black People understand
that they are the lovers and the sons
of lovers and warriors and sons
of warriors Are poems & poets &
all the loveliness here in the world

50 We want a black poem. And a
Black World.
Let the world be a Black Poem
And Let All Black People Speak This Poem
Silently
55 or LOUD

A Poem for Black Hearts

For Malcolm's eyes, when they broke
the face of some dumb white man, For
Malcolm's hands raised to bless us
all black and strong in his image
5 of ourselves, For Malcolm's words
fire darts, the victor's tireless

thrusts, words hung above the world
change as it may, he said it, and
for this he was killed, for saying,
10 and feeling, and being///change, all
collected hot in his heart, For Malcolm's
heart, raising us above our filthy cities,
for his stride, and his beat, and his address
to the grey monsters of the world, For Malcolm's
15 pleas for your dignity, black men, for your life,
black man, for the filling of your minds
with righteousness, For all of him dead and
gone and vanished from us, and all of him which
clings to our speech black god of our time.
20 For all of him, and all of yourself, look up,
black man, quit stuttering and shuffling, look up,
black man, quit whining and stooping, for all of him,
For Great Malcolm a prince of the earth, let nothing in us rest
until we avenge ourselves for his death, stupid animals
25 that killed him, let us never breathe a pure breath if
we fail, and white men call us faggots till the end of
the earth.

John A. Williams

(1925–)

Fiction writer, journalist, and poet John Alfred Williams was born on December 5, 1925, near Jackson, Mississippi, though he grew up in Syracuse, New York. After serving in the navy during World War II, he returned to Syracuse and earned a degree from Syracuse University. He is best known for his novels, including The Angry Ones *(1960),* Night Song *(1961),* Sissie *(1963),* The Man Who Cried I Am *(1967),* Sons of Darkness, Sons of Light *(1969),* Captain Blackman *(1972),* The Junior Bachelor Society *(1976),* !Click Song *(1982),* The Berhama Account *(1985), and* Clifford's Blues *(1999). The following excerpt is from* The Man Who Cried I Am, *Williams's most celebrated work and one of the most accomplished novels of the 1960s. The central character, writer Maxwell Reddick, suffers from rectal cancer and is reminiscing about his life, career, and American society. This selection depicts a conversation between Reddick and Harry Ames, who is based on Richard Wright, about the Black writer's mission.*

The Man Who Cried I Am

1   One press day afternoon, in the fall, Max lay on his couch reading. Beside him rested a clipboard; sometimes while reading, a passage triggered ideas. The desk light was on and there was paper in the typewriter. His hemorrhoids had been bothering him; it was best to take it easy. But, whenever he glanced at the empty clipboard, the desk, and the typewriter with its surly white paper waiting to be filled, he felt uneasy and guilty about lying down.

2   He forced himself to read. A little later he felt chills and then was suddenly nervous. He shifted his position. Then he got up and turned off the desk light and returned to the couch. Once more he rose and went to the desk and ripped the paper out of the typewriter. But now his hands were shaking. He was overwhelmed by the idea that he was not a writer, but a pretender, like so many others he had met in Harlem or down on 8th Street. No real writer would be lying on his can when there was work to be done. He had stumbled into a dead-end street, that was all. A writer had to stand the silences that came with being alone, and he hated being lonely and yet it comforted him. You could think when you were alone, and writers needed to think.

3   He picked up the clipboard and tossed it across the room where it clattered against a wall and fell to the floor. Dilemma. How in the hell did it happen? What had started it? He could get out; he wasn't going to spend the rest of his life like Harry—never knowing what the next phone call or mail delivery would or wouldn't bring; never knowing what life would hold for you at forty-nine or fifty-nine. No. He was going to apply himself; he was going to scheme and jive, dance in the sandbox, Tom, kiss behinds, and wind up managing editor of the *Democrat*. He had a little prestige now. No one else at the office had written a novel and they weren't planning to, either!

4   His chills and shakes persisted. He thought he would feel better outside. He pulled on a sweater and walked rapidly to the corner and then across the street into the park. There he sat in the sun, but even as he did, his mind floated up words to describe what he was seeing and feeling. A young sharpie in draped coat and pegged pants strolled by, arms held stiffly behind his back. A barge, bellydeep in water, steamed slowly up the Hudson, froth leaping from its bows. Max looked at the Palisades and descriptions came for that sheer mass of stone rising from the west bank of the river. And words came for the color of the sun, for the sounds of the children playing near him, for the arching spiral

of a battered football and the taut freckled face that watched its flight. The words kept coming, even when he closed his eyes, words and ways of using them that he knew no newspaper could ever use.

5   He was twenty-four and he knew he hadn't lived much. He hadn't been anywhere, really, not even to Niagara Falls, the Canadian side. Going to college had only taught him that he would never be able to read all the things he wanted to or should. And if he hadn't read so much or traveled so much, how in hell could he feel so much?

6   Why me? He asked himself bitterly. He looked at the bouncing back of the sharpie. Why couldn't I have been like him? Anybody who walked like that and dressed like that, well, he seemed to be able to live life as he found it. Why can't *I* wear zoot suits, dance the Lindy better, until my nuts fall, laugh like hell instead of just smiling? Why can't *I* be loud and loose and drunker than I ever let myself get? Why am I the way I am? Mutant, freak, caprice, fluke. Maxwell Reddick.

7   He thought about his childhood, his parents, and dismissed them. No, it went beyond that, beyond them. He remembered a childhood photo. He still had it, somewhere. It was a photo which, when his parents had passed it around, drew the comment: "Three? He looks so old and wise." Was there something in that silly photo that could give him answers? So old, so wise, God, about *what?* He would study it once more when he returned to his apartment. What in the world had made him look so old and wise at only three? His family had never starved. His parents had been good to him and perhaps even loved him, coming late in their lives as he had. He didn't know, had never assumed that they had not loved or at least liked him. That had to count for something, although the old man was hell on wheels right up until they laid him out, four years to the exact day and hour after his mother had died. What did that mean? That look he had at three . . . Which spermatozoid, which ovum, preserved for generations in the secret places of bodies, had sensed the presence of each other, finally, and, fiercely subcopulating, created him? Had they come out of the past at all, the future? But why, *why?*

8   The next time he saw Harry, Max asked, "Do you ever question the way you are, why you're a writer?"

9   "Every day."

10   Max waited for him to go on. It was a Saturday afternoon and the uptown bar had not yet filled with dapper Negroes starting the second leg of the weekend; Friday night was the first; Saturday into Sunday was the second, which was brought to an end only by habit of going to church Sunday morning or sleeping into Sunday afternoon.

11   Harry laughed. "Well, you're colored and you wonder how come you're a writer because there is no tradition of colored writers. Are we related to some ancient Yoruba folklorist, to Phillis Wheatley? I think about that. Then, somehow, it doesn't matter about the tradition; what matters is now. You wrote a book, Max, and published it. As I see it, that makes you, like me, a very special person among all the people who've ever lived. That's cause for some pride, I think; that's cause to produce more books. That also makes you dangerous because they don't burn people anymore, they burn books, and they don't always have bonfires. I love it like this; let there be a little danger to life, otherwise life is a lie.

12   "I'm the way I am, the kind of writer I am, and you may be too, because I'm a black man; therefore, we're in rebellion; we've got to be. We have no other function as valid as that one." Harry grinned. "I've been in rebellion, and a writer, I guess, ever since I discovered that even colored folks wanted to keep me away from books so I could never learn just how bad it all was. Maybe, too, to keep me from laughing at them. For taking it. My folks had a deathly fear of books."

13   Harry took a deep drink of his beer and gazed moodily around the bar, then he said, "There's something wrong with this ritual these people have here. Oh, hell, I like kicking it around all weekend, too, but that doesn't mean I can't see what's going on. A writer worth his salt is not going to write about how damned lovely it is; it isn't, that's why so many people tell themselves it is. But they don't want to hear what you've got to say if it isn't the same thing they can see or believe, and that's going to make you a target. Talk about sitting ducks! You against them, and all you've got is a beat-up typewriter and some cheap rag bond. And your head.

14   "If your first book is any indication, you're a rebel, too, just as you should be. Don't be guilty if you make it and Negroes themselves start shooting you down; your subject will always be America or Americans. You didn't make the bed; you just have to lie in it. Even so, when my name is mentioned, I want people to jerk up and look for trouble; I want trouble to be my middle name when I write about America. I wouldn't like it if a single person slept well. We—you, me, Warren and the others—have that function. I'll tell you why.

15   "In our society which is white—we are intruders they say—there has got to be something inherently horrible about having the sicknesses and weaknesses of that society described by a person who is a victim of them; for if he, the victim, is capable of describing what they have believed nonexistent, then they, the members of the majority, must choose

between living the truth, which can be pretty grim, and the lie, which isn't much better. But at least they will then have the choice.

16   "It must be pretty awful for a white man to learn that one of the things wrong with this society is that it is not based on dollars directly or alone, but dollars denied men who are black so dollars can go into the pockets of men who are white: It must make white men ponder a kind of weakness that will make them deny work to black men so that work can be done by men who are white. How it must anger them to know finally that we know they deny women who are white to black men, while they have taken black women at will for generations.

17   "And don't they know or want to know that the absence of black voices in the state legislatures and in Congress, unheard since the Reconstruction, wounds them to the death? How painful would it be for them to admit that millions of acres of black men's lands were ripped from them by night riders and county clerks, and are still being held by the descendants of the thieves? Very painful. They'd have to give back those lands, those dollars, that work.

18   "Ah yeah, there's quite enough to be in rebellion about," Harry said, morosely. "I quit the Party because I became damned sick and tired of white men telling me when I should suffer, where and how and what for. And, Max, I was suffering all the time! And I got tired of writing what I knew was wrong for me, our people, our time, our country. I got tired of seeing young Negroes, *young*, man! beat when they drifted into the Party looking for hope and found nothing but another version of white man's hell. Karl Marx was not thinking about niggers when he engineered *The Communist Manifesto*; if he was, why didn't he *say* so? None of the 'great documents' of the West ever acknowledged a racial problem tied to an economic problem, tied to a social problem, tied to a religious problem, tied to a whole nation's survival. And that's why, man, none of them, unamended, are worth the paper they were written on." Harry jabbed himself in the chest. "Somewhere you know this and you're thinking twice about starting to work. Your job is to tell those people to stop lying, not only to us, but to themselves. You've written and in the process, somewhere in that African body of yours, something said, 'I am—a writer, a man, something, but here for today. Here for right now.' "

19   Harry waved to the waiter for more beer.

20   "That could make a man start thinking he's pretty important stuff, couldn't it, Harry?"

21   "Damn, Max. Don't you understand? If you don't have the perspective of yourself, can you expect other people to have it?"

22   But during the next weeks no amount of talking seemed to help. Max had a thousand abortive starts on the new novel, but none of them went past page three or four. In despair, he turned to his essays, but finally came to distrust them; he could not begin one with a question and answer it logically. "Does American democracy work?" Logically the essay could be completed by adding two letters: "No."

23   When he wrote, Max wanted to soar, to sing golden arias. But Zutkin's editor friends wanted emotion: anger, unreasonable black fury; screeching, humiliation, pain, subjects which evaded the essay; articles, yes; the essay, no. Do not sing, Max, the editors seemed to be saying. Instead, tell us, in your own words, in ten thousand words or less, just how much we've hurt you! We will pay handsomely for that revelation.

24   Until the Moses Boatwright case, few of the Harlem doings had touched Max. There were murders, yes, and reefer raids, the burglaries. There were the big bands at the Savoy and the Apollo; the Garvey diehards, the Ras Tafarian street fights, the dances. After Moses Boatwright Max didn't want to sing at all, ever. Or, he knew it would take him a long time to learn how to sing again and even if he did, he would never sing the way he imagined he could. Maybe he would sing a rumbling, threatening basso like Harry Ames.

Haki Madhubuti

(1942–)

For biographical information about Haki Madhubuti, see page 1136.

Back Again, Home

(confessions of an ex-executive)

Pains of insecurity surround me;
   shined shoes,
   conservative suits,
   button down shirts with silk ties.
5   bi-weekly payroll.

Ostracized, but not knowing why;
   executive haircut,

clean shaved,
    "yes" instead of "yeah" and "no" instead of "naw",
10   hours, nine to five. (after five he's alone)

"Doing an excellent job, keep it up;"
    promotion made—semi-monthly payroll,
    very quiet—never talks,
    budget balanced—saved the company money,
15   quality work—production tops.
    He looks sick. (but there is a smile in his eyes)

He resigned, we wonder why;
    let his hair grow—a mustache too,
    out of a job—broke and hungry,
20   friends are coming back—bring food,
    not quiet now—trying to speak,
    what did he say?

"Back Again,

      BLACK AGAIN

25   Home."

We Walk the Way of the New World

1.

we run the dangercourse.
the way of the stocking caps & murray's grease.
(if u is modern u used duke greaseless hair pomade)
jo jo was modern/ an international nigger
5   born: jan. 1, 1863 in new york, mississippi.
his momma was mo militant than he was/is
jo jo bes no instant negro
his development took all of 106 years
& he was the first to be stamped "made in USA"
10 where he arrived bow-legged a curve ahead of the 20th
    century's new weapon: television.

which invented, "how to win and influence people"
& gave jo jo his how/ ever look: however u want me.

we discovered that with the right brand of cigarettes
15 that one, with his best girl,
cd skip thru grassy fields in living color
& in slow-motion: Caution: niggers, cigarette smoking
           will kill u & yr/health.
& that the breakfast of champions is: blackeyed peas & rice.
20 & that God is dead & Jesus is black and last seen on 63rd
           street in a gold & black dashiki, sitting in a
           pink hog speaking swahili with a pig-latin
           accent.
& that integration and coalition are synonymous,
25 & that the only thing that really mattered was: who could get the
highest on the least or how to expand & break one's mind.

in the coming world
new prizes are
to be given

30 we *ran* the dangercourse,
now, it's a silent walk/ a careful eye
jo jo is there
to his mother he is unknown
(she accepted with a newlook: what wd u do if someone loved u?)
35 jo jo is back
& he will catch all the new jo jo's as they wander in & out
and with a fan-like whisper say: you ain't no
           tourist
           and Harlem ain't for
40   sight-seeing, brother.

2.

Start with the itch and there will be no scratch. Study yourself.
Watch yr/every movement as u skip thru-out the southside of
    chicago.
be hip to yr/actions.

45 our dreams are realities
traveling the nature-way.
we meet them

at the apex of their utmost
meanings/means;
50 we walk in cleanliness
down state st/or Fifth Ave.
& wicked apartment buildings shake
as their windows announce our presence
as we jump into the interior
55 & cut the day's evil away.
We walk in cleanliness
the newness of it all
becomes us
our women listen to us
60 and learn.
We teach our children thru
our actions.

We'll become owners of the   New World
the New World.
65 will run it as unowners
for
we will live in it too
& will want to be remembered
as   realpeople.

Nikki Giovanni

(1943–)

Born in Knoxville, Tennessee, on June 7, 1943, Yolande Cornelia Giovanni Jr. grew up in the Cincinnati area. She is one of the poets closely identified with the Black Arts Movement; for a time, she was the best-selling African American author in the United States. A graduate of Fisk University, where she was active in the Student Nonviolent Coordinating Committee (SNCC), she is Professor of English and Gloria D. Smith Professor of Black Studies at Virginia Tech, where she has taught since 1987. Her works include the poetry collections Black Feeling, Black Talk *(1968),* Black Judgment *(1968),* My House *(1972),* The Women and the Men *(1975),* Selected Poems of Nikki Giovanni *(1996),* Love Poems *(1997),* Blues for All the Changes *(1999), and* Quilting the Black-Eyed Pea *(2002). Additional works include the nonfiction books* Gemini: An Extended Autobiographical Statement on My First Twenty-Five Years of Being a Black Poet *(1971) and* Racism 101 *(1994), as well as the recordings* Truth Is on Its Way *(1971) and* The Way I Feel *(1974).*

Black Power
(For All the Beautiful Black Panthers East)

But the whole thing is a miracle—See?

We were just standing there
talking—not touching or smoking
Pot
5 When this cop told
Tyrone
Move along buddy—take your whores
outa here

And this tremendous growl
10 From out of nowhere
Pounced on him

Nobody to this very day
Can explain
How it happened

15 And none of the zoos or circuses
Within fifty miles
Had reported
A panther
Missing

Poem for Black Boys
(With Special Love to James)

Where are your heroes, my little Black ones
You are the Indian you so disdainfully shoot
Not the big bad sheriff on his faggoty white horse

You should play run-away-slave
5 or Mau Mau
These are more in line with your history

Ask your mothers for a Rap Brown gun
Santa just may comply if you wish hard enough
Ask for CULLURD instead of Monopoly
10 DO NOT SIT IN DO NOT FOLLOW KING
GO DIRECTLY TO STREETS
This is a game you can win

As you sit there with your all understanding eyes
You know the truth of what I'm saying
15 Play Back-to-Black
Grow a natural and practice vandalism
These are useful games (some say a skill is even learned)

There is a new game I must tell you of
It's called Catch the Leader Lying
20 (and knowing your sense of the absurd
you will enjoy this)

Also a company called Revolution has just issued
a special kit for little boys
called Burn Baby
25 I'm told it has full instructions on how to siphon gas
and fill a bottle

Then our old friend. Hide and Seek becomes valid
Because we have much to seek and ourselves to hide
from a lecherous dog

30 And this poem I give is worth much more
than any nickel bag
or ten cent toy
And you will understand all too soon
That you, my children of battle, are your heroes
35 You must invent your own games and teach us old ones
how to play

The Great Pax Whitie

In the beginning was the word
And the word was
Death

And the word was nigger
5 And the word was death to all niggers
And the word was death to all life
And the word was death to all
    peace be still

The genesis was life
10 The genesis was death
In the genesis of death
Was the genesis of war
    be still peace be still

In the name of peace
15 They waged the wars
    ain't they got no shame

In the name of peace
Lot's wife is now a product of the Morton company
    nah, they ain't got no shame

20 Noah packing his wife and kiddies up for a holiday
row row row your boat
But why'd you leave the unicorns, noah
Huh? why'd you leave them
While our Black Madonna stood there
25 Eighteen feet high holding Him in her arms
Listening to the rumblings of peace
    be still be still

CAN I GET A WITNESS? WITNESS? WITNESS?
He wanted to know
30 And peter only asked who is that dude?
Who is that Black dude?
Looks like a troublemaker to me
And the foundations of the mighty mighty
Ro Man Cat holic church were laid

35   hallelujah jesus
      nah, they ain't got no shame

Cause they killed the Carthaginians
in the great appian way
And they killed the Moors
40 "to civilize a nation"

And they just killed the earth
And blew out the sun
In the name of a god
Whose genesis was white
45 And war wooed god
And america was born
Where war became peace
And genocide patriotism
And honor is a happy slave
50 cause all god's chillun need rhythm
And glory hallelujah why can't peace
         be still

The great emancipator was a bigot
         ain't they got no shame
55 And making the world safe for democracy
Were twenty million slaves
         nah, they ain't got no shame
And they barbecued six million
To raise the price of beef
60 And crossed the 38th parallel
To control the price of rice
         ain't we never gonna see the light

And champagne was shipped out of the East
While kosher pork was introduced
65 To Africa
         Only the torch can show the way

In the beginning was the deed
And the deed was death

And the honkies are getting confused
70   peace be still

So the great white prince
Was shot like a nigger in texas
And our Black shining prince was murdered
like that thug in his cathedral
75 While our nigger in memphis
was shot like their prince in dallas
And my lord
         ain't we never gonna see the light

The rumblings of this peace must be stilled
80   be stilled be still

ahh Black people
ain't we got no pride?

Larry Neal
(1937–1981)

*Lawrence Paul Neal was born on September 5, 1937, in Atlanta,
Georgia. He grew up in Philadelphia and attended nearby Lincoln
University and the University of Pennsylvania. Neal moved to New
York City in 1964 and became active in literary circles. He collaborat-
ed with Amiri Baraka on several projects, including* Black Fire: An
Anthology of Afro-American Writing *(1968), of which he was co-edi-
tor. In addition to critical essays, Neal published two volumes of poetry,* Black Boogaloo: Notes on Black Liberation *(1969) and* Hoodoo
Hollerin' Bebop Ghosts *(1971); and two plays,* The Glorious Monster
in the Bell of the Horn *(1976) and* In an Upstate Motel *(1981). While
attending a theater workshop at Colgate University on January 6,
1981, Neal died of a heart attack at the age of 43.*

Black Writing

Is love for our people, to tell the plain-truth, and though it hurts we
grow more beautiful in each others eyes; and the lies we have been
told melt in the fires of black love-understanding. Art should make
us stronger. bring more into the knowledge of our hidden strength,
the magic power lurking in Smokey Robinson's voice. Coltrane in there
informing our lives also. The best artistic acts, of this epoch, move
toward shattering bull-shit illusions. Hear them singing, it is not only
about lonely-love, the sex things, but portends the destruction of America. James Brown when he is best James Brown, and that is not working for some slick politician portends the death of America, and the rise
of the new consciousness. Listen to black life. Know its history. Its pain.
The sound it makes as it wakes up. The essential spiritual nature of this
our culture has helped us to survive. Do you dig it? If So What Do
We Do About it? Ah say move wid it.

One Spark Can Light a Prairie Fire

Rap Brown strolls out of his cell,
     lean
panther of these days wearing
         basketball sneaks
5   and blowing the hard line.
his lines are hard; but mixed loosely with the memory
         of soft summer louisannas,
         alabama sundays
         lurk there too
10   in the hard cadence
         of his words

blowing the hard line, Rap changes shape
         before the larger shapes
         in the crowd facing him.

15 some eyes speak jive
some move weak, proving
that they are shucking;
a few believe, gaining
strength from the fire
20 he lays on their asses.

now he leans into his words, into the audience
            to jab the air
         with the sharper edge of his voice.

Brown becomes elastic, continues to change
25   the voice is the same
         but the body becomes
         an old nigger slave
         with red chains in his eyes

the crowd blinks.
30   the panther speaks of cherry pie
         and violence, shouts go up
         and the shapes become tired warriors
         in subversive apartment buildings

the shapes grow larger and congeal
35   in black around Brown.

soon Brown is indistinguishable from the other shapes
almost faceless now.

they have swallowed Brown,
the death-love gives way
40   to the hard impulse within them.

Brown breaks into a hip boogoloo, only there is a hand grenade in
his hands instead of a microphone.

The crowd blinks. Brown has turned into an M-1 carbine
a shell splatters upside Johnson's head,
45   a large nigger-sharp switchblade descends
and chops J. Edgar Hoover's head off also.

the black shapes are turned on with power.
the black shapes boogaloo with hand grenades,
this is our Apollo.

50   the flames get hotter
like magic, the jails
are emptied and filled again
the flames get hotter,
the cities like dry prairies
55   burn.
when the ashes cleared, we touched.

Sarah Webster Fabio

(1928–1979)

*Born on January 20, 1928, in Nashville, Tennessee, Sarah Webster
Fabio lent great talent and energy to the Black Arts Movement. She
attended Spelman College briefly and then Fisk University, where she
worked with Arna Bontemps. Family obligations—a husband and five
children—limited her literary, cultural, and political activity during
her early years. However, she had made her way to the West Coast by
the 1960s, and while working at Merritt College in Oakland she
became a part of the political and cultural fervor in the Bay Area. She
published the poetry volumes* Saga of a Black Man *(1968),* A Mirror, A
Soul *(1969), and* Rainbow Signs *(1973), as well as* No Crystal Stair: A

Socio-Drama of the History of Black Women in the U.S.A. *(1967).*
Sarah Webster Fabio, perhaps just hitting her stride as an artist, died
of cancer at the age of 51.

Black Man's Feast

His desires, growing
from timid heights
on homecomings, birthdays,
holiday celebrations,
5 looming tall on his
taste buds and leaden;
then, in the exuberance
of his black mood, he'd
call for greens, pot likker,
10 cole slaw, cracklin' bread,
and chitterlings; hog head
and maw, pig feet and ears
and black-eyed peas—
these gourmet dishes of his
15 impoverished past.

Confronted with this repast,
he'd conjure up the memory
of his ugly-money days when
it maddened him to spend his
20 torn-muscle treasures for
the trivial idiocies of
a second-hand civilization.
Dressed to kill in hard-pressed,
outmoded garments, he'd survey
25 his store of pinched-penny
purchases and mourn the passing
of his thin, rainy-day dimes
dribbled away on pews and prayers,
grave plots, and poll tax
30 irrelevancies.

He'd remember when he,
African bushman, (or his

father or father's father)
had stalked big game, absorbing
35 the animal strength of his prize
in the ritual of eating viscera:
later, it was he,
American slave, (or his
mother, or mother's mother)
40 whose reward for soulless toil
was special rations of
these same intestines,
burnt-out bacon ends, bone-
and-gristle inedibles
45 to turn with will and magic
into succulent sustenance.

Now, basking in the warmth
of his gladder money days,
he swallows hungrily
50 his easy-purchased pleasure food—
yet still feasts on the gall
of his gastronomical past.

Evil Is No Black Thing

1.

Ahab's gaily clad fisherfriends,
questing under the blue skies after
the albino prize find the green sea
cold and dark at its deep center,
5 but calm—unperturbed by the fates
of men and whales.

Rowing shoreward, with wet and empty
hands, their sun-rich smiles fuzz
with bafflement as the frothing
10 surf buckles underneath and their
sea-scarred craft is dashed to pieces
near the shore: glancing backward,
the spiralling waves are white-capped.

2.

Evil is no black thing: black
15 the rain clouds attending a storm
but the fury of it neither begins
nor ends there. Weeping tear-clear
rain, trying to contain the hoarse
blue-throated thunder and the fierce
20 quick-silver tongue of lightning, bands
of clouds wring their hands.

Once I saw dark clouds in Texas
stand by idly while a Northeaster
screamed its icy puffs, ringtailing
25 rainddrops, rolling them into baseballs
of hail, then descending upon the
tin-roofed houses, unrelentingly
battering them down.

3.

And the night is blackest where
30 gay throated cuckoos sing among the
dense firs of the Black Forest, where
terrible flurries of snow are blinding
bright: somewhere, concealed here deeply,
lies a high-walled town, whitewashed.

35 Seen at sunset, only the gaping ditch
and overhanging, crooked tree are painted
pitch to match the night: but I've seen
a dying beam of light reach through
the barred windows of a shower chamber,
40 illuminating its blood-scratched walls.

4.

Evil is no black thing: black
may be the undertaker's hearse
and so many of the civil trappings
of death, but not its essence:
45 the riderless horse, the armbands

and veils of mourning, the grave shine
darkly; but these are the rituals
of the living.

One day I found its meaning as I
50 rushed breathless through a wind-parched
field, stumbling unaware: suddenly there
it was, laying at my feet, hidden
beneath towering golden rods,
a criss-crossed pile of
55 sun-bleached bones.

Tripping with Black Writing

1 The move toward liberation from slave to serf to self, for Black folk, has meant a long, arduous trip. The history of this development, which we might call "The Black Experience," has been chronicled in the annals of Black Literature. Always the movement has had to be bilateral—that is, both external and internal; language has played an important part in communicating the experience from within and without. And while Blacks have had to define and validate Black reality, they, concurrently, have had to protest and protect themselves from exploitation and dehumanization. They had to not only devise ways of speaking in tongues so that "the man" could not always understand everything, but also had to speak out of both sides of their mouths—hurrahing Black; badmouthing White.

2 Original hoodoo, badmouthing the man, forerunners of the "Stomp Me, O Lord" slave accounts and protests Black-perspective accounts of what was really going down with the wind, start with Lucy Terry, digging the scene of an Indian Massacre, 1746:

> And had not her petticoats stopt her
> The awful creatures had not cotched her
> And tommyhawked her on the head
> And left her on the ground for dead.

3   Or Jupiter Hammon on *An Evening Thought, Salvation by Christ, with Penitential Cries*, turning hearts and souls away from an unbearable reality to spiritualism:

> *Lord turn our dark benighted Souls;*
> *Give us a true Motion,*
> *And let the Hearts of all the World,*
> *Make Christ their Salvation.*

4   Early turnings; trying to turn these bedeviled mothers around, shame them in their human trafficking; these wrenchings of conscience from those short on conscience but long on bread and black gold—earliest forms of Black power. Image-making from early days from pure spirit and communication with nature. Nation-building from the ground. Loss of king-of-the-jungle images, lion-and-panther form. Beaten to the ground; gagged and shackled, but singing free:

> *Keep a-inching along*
> *like a poor inch worm*
> *JESUS IS COMING BY AND BY.*

5   Or George Moses Horton transcending that hell-bound scene in *On Liberty and Slavery*, rapping on "the man," calling on the ancestors' spirit world:

> *Say unto foul oppression, Cease:*
> *Ye tyrants rage no more,*
> *And let the joyful trump of peace,*
> *Now bid the vassal soar.*
> *Soar on the pinions of that dove*
> *Which long has cooed for thee,*
> *And breathed her notes from Afric's grove.*
> *The Sound of liberty. . . .*

6   And with *The Life of Olanudah Equiano or Gustavus Vassa, The African, Written by Himself*, the beginning of the Black gift to American Mainstream Literature, a new genre—the slave narrative. "For-real" world literature. Gustavus Vassa running it down how he was run across the world, making giant steps, building civilization. Born in Benin, slaved in Virginia and Pennsylvania, farmed-out on a

Caribbean plantation, working out as an abolitionist in England—
as a self-made man. Bootstrap pulling; defying laws of gravity and
gravitation. Gaming for self, and bootstrap-yanking for brother boots.

7 Getting that soul together in times of dehumanization and desecra-
tion of the souls of Black men. *Life and Times*, Frederick Douglass,
a put-down as early as 1845; altogether in 1881. Whipping it to the
original outhouse ruler of the "Harry Sam" vintage, Abe Lincoln; running down such a heavy game that runaway slave turns presidential adviser and Consul General to Haiti. Shades of Papa Doc!
Wearing two faces. Seer. Invoking spirits, calling for an exorcism of
the spirit and body of racism manifested by *Dred Scott* decision and
the act of nullifying the Fourteenth Amendment in 1883. Instances
of bad Supreme Court decisions which made him cry out:

> But when a deed is done for slavery, caste, and oppression; and
> a blow is struck at human progress, whether so intended or
> not, the heart of humanity sickens in sorrow and writhes in
> pain. It makes us feel as if some one were stamping upon the
> graves of our mothers, or desecrating our sacred temples. Only
> base men and oppressors can rejoice in a triumph of injus-
> tice over the weak and defenseless, for weakness ought itself
> to protect from assaults of pride, prejudice, and power . . . .
>
> No man can put a chain about the ankle of his fellow-man,
> without at last finding the other end of it about his own neck.
>
> The lesson of all the ages upon this point is, that a wrong
> done to one man is a wrong done to all men. It may not be
> felt at the moment, and the evil may be long delayed, but so
> sure as there is a moral government of the universe, so sure
> will the harvest of evil come.

8 Stomp us, O Lord! Getting into the power of speaking in tongues.
W.E.B. DuBois. *The Souls of Black Folk*. Those of the double con-
sciousness, born with veils over their eyes . . . From *Darkwater*, "A
Litany at Atlanta, Done at Atlanta, in the Day of Death, 1906":

> . . . Wherefore do we pray? Is not the God of the fathers dead?
> Have not seers seen in Heaven's halls Thine hearsed and life-
> less form stark amidst the black and rolling smoke of sin,
> where all along bow bitter forms of endless dead? . . . Thou
> art still the God of our black fathers, and in Thy soul's soul

sit some soft darkenings of the evening, some shadowings of the velvet night.

9   Stomp us, O Lord! James Weldon Johnson raising *God's Trombones*, giving a new folk "Creation," rhapsodizing about Africa's prodigal son's return home. Setting the beat of marching feet on the road to victory in "Lift Every Voice and Sing":

> . . . *Stony the road we trod,*
> *Bitter the chastening rod,*
> *Felt in the days when hope unborn had died;*
> *Yet with a steady beat,*
> *Have not our weary feet*
> *Come to the place for which our fathers sighed?*

10   Speaking in tongues. Uncle Julius, in "The Goophered Grapevine," describes one of Sycorax's daughters, Aun' Peggy, who has goophered, cunju'd, bewitched the scuppernon' vineyard:

> She sa'ntered 'roun' mongs' de vimes, en tuk a leaf fum dis one, en a grape-hull fum dat one, en a grape-seed fum annuder one; en den a little twig fum here, en a little pinch er dirt fum dere,—en put it all in a big black bottle, wid a snake's toof en a speckle'hen's gall en some ha'rs fum a black cat's tail, en den fill' de bottle wid scuppernon' wine.

11   Speaking in tongues and running his games. Charles Chesnutt. And Paul Laurence Dunbar running it down how "We wear the Mask/That grins and lies." An African orientation . . .

12   Alain Locke—that necessary critic for *The New Negro;* a special critic for a special time. Harlem Renaissance. Fathering Negritude. Giving the possibility of showing forth a triumph of spirit and mind. A decolonized mind shining through colonial language. Locke sees Caliban's early move:

> . . . Then eventually came the time when the hectic rhetoric and dogged moralism had to fall back in sheer exhaustion on the original basis of cultural supply. Through Dunbar,—part of whose poetry, nevertheless, reflects the last stand of this rhetorical advance, Negro poetry came penitently back to the

folk-tradition, and humbled itself to dialect for fresh spiritual food and raiment.

13   William Stanley Braithwaite, who gave America the possibility of an American poetry, speaks of Dunbar as closing one age in Black poetry and beginning another. Check out the Sesqui-Centennial Edition of *Braithwaite's Anthology of Magazine Verse for 1926, Yearbook of American Poetry*. Black poetry—a main tributary of mainstream American poetry. A Black man willing to bring an indigenous, nonderivative poetry into being. He got lost in the shuffle after 1929. But he'd done his thing. Sterlling Brown, one of the most capable writers using Black form chronicling the literary movement in *Negro Caravan*. Sterling Brown in his *Negro Poetry and Drama* said this:

"Dialect, or the speech of the people, is capable of expressing whatever the people are. And the folk Negro is a great deal more than a buffoon or a plaintive minstrel. Poets more intent upon learning the ways of the folk, their speech, and their character, that is to say better poets, could have smashed the mold. But first they would have had to believe in what they were doing. And this was difficult in a period of conciliation and middle class striving for recognition and respectability."

14   Early there was a self-consciousness and a mold which a deriding white America put on Black folk speech. This meant that many feigned representing folk speech, according to Brown, by:

"A few pat phrases, a few stock situations and characteristics, some misspelling: these were the chief things necessary. The wit and beauty possible to folk speech, the folk-shrewdness, the humanity, the stoicism of these people they seldom say."

15   The Harlem Renaissance period closed the credibility gap between the Black man, his articulation of his experience, and his selfhood. Zora Neal [*sic*] Hurston, anthropologist, throwing light on language. Open the way for today's freedom-wigged freaks. Stone-cold, bad-blood revolutionaries. Escapees from prisons of Anglo rhetoric. Frontiersmen in the lumbering netherlands of Black language. Medicine men schooled in witchcraft, black magic, the voodoo of words. Immortalized, subterranean, out-of-this-world travelers. Dutchmen. LeRois. LeRoi Joneses. Quick-change sleight-of-hand magicians.

Dons. Don Lees. Changing. "Change your enemy change your change change change your enemy change change . . . change your mind nigger." Killens. Killens' chilluns. On their jobs. Taking care of business. "Deniggerizing the world." Voodoo cowboys. Loop Garoo Kids. Riding loose—cool ones—into the whirlwind of change; who, as they gallop into town, have a "posse of spells phone in sick." Ishmaels. Ishmael Reeds. Yeah. Yellow Back Radio Done Show Good Broke-Down. Up against the wall, Prospero.

16 Calibans all. Exploding Prospero's premises with extraordinary, forreal, supernatural departures. Trips. More benevolent despotism, spelled Tyranny. Any way you look at it. And his gift of language—his "prison in which Caliban's achievements will be realized and restricted"—is a boomerang. New-breed Blacks, those desperadoes who "Take the Money and Run," leave "the man" behind bound and bankrupt; marooned on a barren island of derivative Anglo-Saxon, European-like culture. Walled in by the "law and order" of his own restrictive rhetoric. And those newly free? They are on their jobs making jujus, working their mojos, peeping Chuck's hold cards.

17 Understanding the real meaning of his excessive articulation of so much nonsense. Seers and sages. Reporters such as Eldridge Cleaver sending back messages about the "technologically gifted moon men": "I heard what he said; he said 'oink.' " LeRoi Jones-created criminals intent on robbing the family of its jewels in *Home on the Range*. Mystified, momentarily, with the father's talk, "Crillilly bagfest. Gobble Gobble. Gobble." But understand their task is to give these robots the gift of soul, of language of the real world. Once more, Mr. Tooful: "I was born in Kansas City in 1920. My father was the vice-president of a fertilizer company. Before that we were phantoms. . . ." Which explains all that shit. Packaged under the brand name of "Standard English," mainstream American literature. Or Sister Carolyn Rodgers taking a look at the spineless, flat imitation in "Portrait of a White Nigger!" who "talks like/a biscuit that will/not rise . . . got a jelly mind/and shimmy thighs"; whose purpose in life is reduced to an endless search trying "to find the MAGIC that/will/PRESTO"/Black/off/ . . ."

18 No mere children of nature these. They are indeed, Sycorax-the-Sorceress' offspring. With magic potions to tame the beasts of nature. With so many thumping, twangling instruments giving the beat. Informing William Melvin Kelley and his likes that he moves to the rhythms of *A Different Drummer*. Dere's Us'ns and dere's *Dem*, Magic

knowledge. Source of power found rooted in the residue of a well-spring of aged and ageless African native culture—soul. Spooky Stuff. Sins of the father's revisited! Great balls of fire!!! Brother, brush off your Br'er Rabbit's foot. Shine up your John-The-Conqueror root. Whip up your own brand gris-gris. It's Voodoo time again.

19 LeRoi Jones, dramatizing the dilemma. Don Lee, chronicling the changes. Ishmael Reed, S-p-e-l-l-i-n-g it out. Nikki Giovanni, recording "Records": "a negro needs to kill/something/trying to record/that this country must be/destroyed/if we are to live/must be destroyed if we are to live/must be destroyed if we are to live." Jimmy Garret, bucking the whitewashed system. White power—the same which done got his mama—challenged to a duel. By a deathly game of dozens, in the one-act *And We Own the Night*. Cracker-walled prisons of rhetoric crumbled before the double-whammied eyes of crumb-snatching blues logic, Semple-fied by Langston Hughes, passed on as sacrament to Stanley Crouch and Dante. Stone walls of martial law and bad conditions failing to imprison the spirit of Blacks. Etheridge Knight, breaking through in *Cell Song*, answering the call to "take/your words and scrape/the sky, shake rain/on the desert, sprinkle/salt on the tail/of a girl . . ." And Sonia Sanchez preparing for *Homecoming*: "Leaving behind me/all those hide and/seek faces . . . I have learned it/ain't like they say/in the newspapers." Soul talk for soul folk. *Boss Soul*, by Sarah Fabio: ". . . gut bucket, gospel spiritual, jazz/touching cords of Feeling any live person/has to tune into or turn on to that/special deepdown/inside you thing."

20 New Day. Dawn. Light of Broken Night. Night breaks. Night trippers. Check out the Bad, Bold scene of the Mojo workers. Dig the star-crossed bones uncovered by Ishmael Reed in *15 Nigromancers From Now*. If you dare. Any day or night—or seance in between—get on down to what's really there. Clean-picked bones. The skulls of ones who talked too much. Get to that. Another necessary trip: *Amistad*, with Charles Harris and John Williams piloting.

21   Black writers, finding themselves up a tree with "the man's" rhetoric and aesthetic, which hangs them up, lynching their black visions, cut it loose. All the way—swinging free. Flying home. Wings flapping, raucously, in the breeze. So many unnatural demands from the establishment, the tradition, beamed into a subject people from a hostile, alien culture, shined off as irrelevant, self-defeating. Needing to respond as integral beings not having to compromise integrity. Bringing black

perspective, black aesthetic, black rhetoric, black language to add authenticity to the felt reality. Knowing America has no rhetoric matching its racist reality; no reality matching its "universal" and "democratic" idealistic state of existence. Knowing the simple-minded, fascist, pseudo-Europeanized mandate of "universality" to be a funky issue in any aesthetic consideration. A hustle to make walleyed, white-eyed America the all-seeing Cyclops of our age.

22   Giving the finger to blind justice. Peeping the loosened blindfold. Peeping her peeping; favoring the apples of her eye—rotten though they may be. Playing the game of dozens with her. Combating her status-quo games. Knowing the truth about this society. One that devaluates the lives of a people for the duration of its existence. One that dehumanizes them for fun and profit. A mere matter of pragmatism and utilitarianism. Knowing that society to be guilty of: emasculating manhood; deflowering womanhood; exploiting spirit and soul; blinding vision; binding motion; dulling sensitivity; gagging speech.

23   Black Writing—repressed, suppressed, ignored, denounced. Black Writers having rained upon them not respect, riches, rewards, but disrespect, discouragement, nonrecognition, deculturation, assimilation, isolation, starvation, expatriation, derangement, criminal indictment. LeRoi Jones's case but a recent and flagrant example of a system's way of dealing with creative liberated black minds. The same brutal white backlash that cut the cord of David Walker's life after his writing of his "Appeal" in the early nineteenth century still tears at the flesh of articulate Blacks of the recent past and the present—men such as Malcolm X, Martin Luther King, Eldridge Cleaver, Bobby Seale.

24   No turning back, though. This is the day of Biggers and ghosts of Biggers. Black writers—most of them poets plus—have always been barometers, even when America kept bell jars on them. Have always been/still are/will be. Always traveling with ears to the ground; attuned to the drumbeats of the age. Check out the Harlem Renaissance poets, such as Langston Hughes, Claude McKay, Sterling Brown. Check out the post depression poets of the thirties, including Richard Wright. Check out Margaret Walker's words to her people in the early forties. Check out the poets in *Beyond the Blues*, a time when Black poetry was so far underground it had to travel to England for publication. Check out Black poets publishing with Broadside Press, Third World Press, Success Press. Check out Black periodicals—*Journal of Black Poetry*, *Black Dialogue*, *Negro Digest*, *Liberator*.

25   Take the A-Train to Black liberation. Black writing of the seventies will be the Sweet Chariots of our time: swinging low/swing-
ing high/swinging free. Communicant, Continuum, Change,
Consummation.

Toni Cade Bambara

(1939–1995)

*Toni Cade Bambara was born in New York City on March 25, 1939.
She took the name Bambara when she discovered through some old
family papers that her grandmother had used it. Bambara taught at
several schools, including the City College of New York, Spelman, Rutgers, and Duke. She edited the important anthology* The Black Woman
(1970), as well as Tales and Stories for Black Folks *(1971). Her fiction
includes the short story collections* Gorilla, My Love *(1972) and* The
Sea Birds Are Still Alive *(1977), and the novel* The Salt Eaters *(1980).
Bambara had a number of writing and film projects underway, and
was involved in several activist efforts, when she succumbed to cancer
on December 9, 1995.*

The Lesson

1   Back in the days when everyone was old and stupid or young and
foolish and me and Sugar were the only ones just right, this lady
moved on our block with nappy hair and proper speech and no
makeup. And quite naturally we laughed at her, laughed the way
we did at the junk man who went about his business like he was some
big-time president and his sorry-ass horse his secretary. And we kinda
hated her too, hated the way we did the winos who cluttered up our
parks and pissed on our handball walls and stank up our hallways
and stairs so you couldn't halfway play hide-and-seek without a goddamn gas mask. Miss Moore was her name. The only woman on the
block with no first name. And she was black as hell, cept for her
feet, which were fish-white and spooky. And she was always planning
these boring-ass things for us to do, us being my cousin, mostly, who
lived on the block cause we all moved North the same time and to the
same apartment then spread out gradual to breathe. And our parents would yank our heads into some kinda shape and crisp up our

clothes so we'd be presentable for travel with Miss Moore, who always looked like she was going to church, though she never did. Which is just one of the things the grownups talked about when they talked behind her back like a dog. But when she came calling with some sachet she'd sewed up or some gingerbread she'd made or some book, why then they'd all be too embarrassed to turn her down and we'd get handed over all spruced up. She'd been to college and said it was only right that she should take responsibility for the young ones' education, and she not even related by marriage or blood. So they'd go for it. Specially Aunt Gretchen. She was the main gofer in the family. You got some ole dumb shit foolishness you want somebody to go for, you send for Aunt Gretchen. She been screwed into the go-along for so long, it's a blood-deep natural thing with her. Which is how she got saddled with me and Sugar and Junior in the first place while our mothers were in a la-de-da apartment up the block having a good ole time.

2   So this one day Miss Moore rounds us all up at the mailbox and it's purdee hot and she's knockin herself out about arithmetic. And school suppose to let up in summer I heard, but she don't never let up. And the starch in my pinafore scratching the shit outta me and I'm really hating this nappy-head bitch and her goddamn college degree. I'd much rather go to the pool or to the show where it's cool. So me and Sugar leaning on the mailbox being surly, which is a Miss Moore word. And Flyboy checking out what everybody brought for lunch. And Fat Butt already wasting his peanut-butter-and-jelly sandwich like the pig he is. And Junebug punchin on Q.T.'s arm for potato chips. And Rosie Giraffe shifting from one hip to the other waiting for somebody to step on her foot or ask her if she from Georgia so she can kick ass, preferably Mercedes'. And Miss Moore asking us do we know what money is, like we a bunch of retards. I mean real money, she say, like it's only poker chips or monopoly papers we lay on the grocer. So right away I'm tired of this and say so. And would much rather snatch Sugar and go to the Sunset and terrorize the West Indian kids and take their hair ribbons and their money too. And Miss Moore files that remark away for next week's lesson on brotherhood, I can tell. And finally I say we oughta get to the subway cause it's cooler and besides we might meet some cute boys. Sugar done swiped her mama's lipstick, so we ready.

3   So we heading down the street and she's boring us silly about what things cost and what our parents make and how much goes for rent and how money ain't divided up right in this country. And then she

gets to the part about we all poor and live in the slums, which I don't feature. And I'm ready to speak on that, but she steps out in the street and hails two cabs just like that. Then she hustles half the crew in with her and hands me a five-dollar bill and tells me to calculate 10 percent tip for the driver. And we're off. Me and Sugar and Junebug and Flyboy hangin out the window and hollering to everybody, putting lipstick on each other cause Flyboy a faggot anyway, and making farts with our sweaty armpits. But I'm mostly trying to figure how to spend this money. But they all fascinated with the meter ticking and Junebug starts laying bets as to how much it'll read when Flyboy can't hold his breath no more. Then Sugar lays bets as to how much it'll be when we get there. So I'm stuck. Don't nobody want to go for my plan, which is to jump out at the next light and run off to the first bar-b-que we can find. Then the driver tells us to get the hell out cause we there already. And the meter reads eighty-five cents. And I'm stalling to figure out the tip and Sugar say give him a dime. And I decide he don't need it bad as I do, so later for him. But then he tries to take off with Junebug foot still in the door so we talk about his mama something ferocious. Then we check out that we on Fifth Avenue and everybody dressed up in stockings. One lady in a fur coat, hot as it is. White folks crazy.

4   "This is the place," Miss Moore say, presenting it to us in the voice she uses at the museum. "Let's look in the windows before we go in."

5   "Can we steal?" Sugar asks very serious like she's getting the ground rules squared away before she plays. "I beg your pardon," say Miss Moore, and we fall out. So she leads us around the windows of the toy store and me and Sugar screamin, "This is mine, that's mine, I gotta have that, that was made for me, I was born for that," till Big Butt drowns us out.

6   "Hey, I'm goin to buy that there."

7   "That there? You don't even know what it is, stupid."

8   "I do so," he say punchin on Rosie Giraffe. "It's a microscope."

9   "Whatcha gonna do with a microscope, fool?"

10   "Look at things."

11   "Like what, Ronald?" ask Miss Moore. And Big Butt ain't got the first notion. So here go Miss Moore gabbing about the thousands of bacteria in a drop of water and the somethinorother in a speck of blood and the million and one living things in the air around us is invisible to the naked eye. And what she say that for? Junebug go to town on that "naked" and we rolling. Then Miss Moore ask what it cost. So we all jam into the window smudgin it up and the price

tag say $300. So then she ask how long'd take for Big Butt and Junebug to save up their allowances. "Too long," I said. "Yeh," adds Sugar, "outgrown it by that time." And Miss Moore say no, you never outgrow learning instruments. "Why, even medical students and interns and," blah, blah, blah. And we ready to choke Big Butt for bringing it up in the first damn place.

12   "This here costs four hundred eighty dollars," say Rosie Giraffe. So we pile up all over her to see what she pointin out. My eyes tell me it's a chunk of glass cracked with something heavy and different-color inks dripped into the splits, then the whole thing put into a oven or something. But for $480 it don't make sense.

13   "That's a paperweight made of semi-precious stones fused together under tremendous pressure," she explains slowly, with her hands doing the mining and all the factory work.

14   "So what's a paperweight?" asks Rosie Giraffe.

15   "To weigh paper with, dumbbell," say Flyboy, the wise man from the East.

16   "Not exactly," say Miss Moore, which is what she say when you warm or way off too. "It's to weigh paper down so it won't scatter and make your desk untidy." So right away me and Sugar curtsy to each other and then to Mercedes who is more the tidy type.

17   "We don't keep paper on top of the desk in my class," say Junebug, figuring Miss Moore crazy or lyin one.

18   "At home, then," she say. "Don't you have a calendar and a pencil case and a blotter and a letter-opener on your desk at home where you do your homework?" And she know damn well what our homes look like cause she nosys around in them every chance she gets.

19   "I don't even have a desk," say Junebug. "Do we?"

20   "No. And I don't get no homework neither," say Big Butt.

21   "And I don't even have a home," say Flyboy like he do at school to keep the white folks off his back and sorry for him. Send this poor kid to camp posters, is his specialty.

22   "I do," say Mercedes. "I have a box of stationery on my desk and a picture of my cat. My godmother bought the stationery and the desk. There's a big rose on each sheet and the envelopes smell like roses."

23   "Who wants to know about your smelly-ass stationery," say Rosie Giraffe fore I can get my two cents in.

24   "It's important to have a work area all your own so that . . ."

25   "Will you look at this sailboat, please," say Flyboy, cuttin her off and pointin to the thing like it was his. So once again we tumble all over each other to gaze at this magnificent thing in the toy store which

is just big enough to maybe sail two kittens across the pond if you strap them to the posts tight. We all start reciting the price tag like we in assembly. "Handcrafted sailboat of fiberglass at one thousand one hundred ninety-five dollars."

26 "Unbelievable," I hear myself say and am really stunned. I read it again for myself just in case the group recitation put me in a trance. Same thing. For some reason this pisses me off. We look at Miss Moore and she lookin at us, waiting for I dunno what.

27 Who'd pay all that when you can buy a sailboat set for a quarter at Pop's, a tube of glue for a dime, and a ball of string for eight cents? "It must have a motor and a whole lot else besides," I say. "My sailboat cost me about fifty cents."

28 "But will it take water?" say Mercedes with her smart ass.

29 "Took mine to Alley Pond Park once," say Flyboy. "String broke. Lost it. Pity."

30 "Sailed mine in Central Park and it keeled over and sank. Had to ask my father for another dollar."

31 "And you got the strap," laugh Big Butt. "The jerk didn't even have a string on it. My old man wailed on his behind."

32 Little Q.T. was staring hard at the sailboat and you could see he wanted it bad. But he too little and somebody'd just take it from him. So what the hell. "This boat for kids, Miss Moore?"

33 "Parents silly to buy something like that just to get all broke up," say Rosie Giraffe.

34 "That much money it should last forever," I figure.

35 "My father'd buy it for me if I wanted it."

36 "Your father, my ass," say Rosie Giraffe getting a chance to finally push Mercedes.

37 "Must be rich people shop here," say Q.T.

38 "You are a very bright boy," say Flyboy. "What was your first clue?" And he rap him on the head with the back of his knuckles, since Q.T. the only one he could get away with. Though Q.T. liable to come up behind you years later and get his licks in when you half expect it.

39 "What I want to know is," I say to Miss Moore though I never talk to her, I wouldn't give the bitch that satisfaction, "is how much a real boat costs? I figure a thousand'd get you a yacht any day."

40 "Why don't you check that out," she say, "and report back to the group?" Which really pains my ass. If you gonna mess up a perfectly good swim day least you could do is have some answers. "Let's go in," she say like she got something up her sleeve. Only she don't lead the

way. So me and Sugar turn the corner to where the entrance is, but when we get there I kinda hang back. Not that I'm scared, what's there to be afraid of, just a toy store. But I feel funny, shame. But what I got to be shamed about? Got as much right to go in as anybody. But somehow I can't seem to get hold of the door, so I step away for Sugar to lead. But she hangs back too. And I look at her and she looks at me and this is ridiculous. I mean, damn, I have never ever been shy about doing nothing or going nowhere. But then Mercedes steps up and then Rosie Giraffe and Big Butt crowd in behind and shove, and next thing we all stuffed into the doorway with only Mercedes squeezing past us, smoothing out her jumper and walking right down the aisle. Then the rest of us tumble in like a glued-together jigsaw done all wrong. And people lookin at us. And it's like the time me and Sugar crashed into the Catholic church on a dare. But once we got in there and everything so hushed and holy and the candles and the bowin and the handkerchiefs on all the drooping heads, I just couldn't go through with the plan. Which was for me to run up to the altar and do a tap dance while Sugar played the nose flute and messed around in the holy water. And Sugar kept givin me the elbow. Then later teased me so bad I tied her up in the shower and turned it on and locked her in. And she'd be there till this day if Aunt Gretchen hadn't finally figured I was lyin about the boarder takin a shower.

41　　Same thing in the store. We all walkin on tiptoe and hardly touchin the games and puzzles and things. And I watched Miss Moore who is steady watchin us like she waitin for a sign. Like Mama Drewery watches the sky and sniffs the air and takes note of just how much slant is in the bird formation. Then me and Sugar bump smack into each other, so busy gazing at the toys, specially the sailboat. But we don't laugh and go into our fat-lady bump-stomach routine. We just stare at that price tag. Then Sugar run a finger over the whole boat. And I'm jealous and want to hit her. Maybe not her, but I sure want to punch somebody in the mouth.

42　　"Watcha bring us here for, Miss Moore?"

43　　"You sound angry, Sylvia. Are you mad about something?" Givin me one of them grins like she tellin a grown-up joke that never turns out to be funny. And she's lookin very closely at me like maybe she plannin to do my portrait from memory. I'm mad, but I won't give her that satisfaction. So I slouch around the store being very bored and say, "Let's go."

44　　Me and Sugar at the back of the train watchin the tracks whizzin by large then small then gettin gobbled up in the dark. I'm thinkin about this tricky toy I saw in the store. A clown that somersaults on a bar then does chin-ups just cause you yank lightly at his leg. Cost $35. I could see me askin my mother for a $35 birthday clown. "You wanna who that costs what?" she'd say, cocking her head to the side to get a better view of the hole in my head. Thirty-five dollars could buy new bunk beds for Junior and Gretchen's boy. Thirty-five dollars and the whole household could go visit Granddaddy Nelson in the country. Thirty-five dollars would pay for the rent and the piano bill too. Who are these people that spend that much for performing clowns and $1,000 for toy sailboats? What kinda work they do and how they live and how come we ain't in on it? Where we are is who we are, Miss Moore always pointin out. But it don't necessarily have to be that way, she always adds then waits for somebody to say that poor people have to wake up and demand their share of the pie and don't none of us know what kind of pie she talkin about in the first damn place. But she ain't so smart cause I still got her four dollars from the taxi and she sure ain't gettin it. Messin up my day with this shit. Sugar nudges me in my pocket and winks.

45   Miss Moore lines us up in front of the mailbox where we started from, seem like years ago, and I got a headache for thinkin so hard. And we lean all over each other so we can hold up under the draggy-ass lecture she always finishes us off with at the end before we thank her for borin us to tears. But she just looks at us like she readin tea leaves. Finally she say, "Well, what did you think of F.A.O. Schwarz?"

46   Rosie Giraffe mumbles, "White folks crazy."

47   "I'd like to go there again when I get my birthday money," says Mercedes, and we shove her out the pack so she has to lean on the mailbox by herself.

48   "I'd like a shower. Tiring day," said Flyboy.

49   Then Sugar surprises me by sayin, "You know, Miss Moore, I don't think all of us here put together eat in a year what that sailboat costs." And Miss Moore lights up like somebody goosed her. "And?" she say, urging Sugar on. Only I'm standin on her foot so she don't continue.

50   "Imagine for a minute what kind of society it is in which some people can spend on a toy what it would cost to feed a family of six or seven. What do you think?"

51   "I think," say Sugar pushing me off her feet like she never done before, cause I whip her ass in a minute, "that this is not much of a democracy if you ask me. Equal chance to pursue happiness means an equal crack at the dough, don't it?" Miss Moore is besides herself and I am disgusted with Sugar's treachery. So I stand on her foot

one more time to see if she'll shove me. She shuts up, and Miss Moore looks at me, sorrowfully I'm thinkin. And somethin weird is goin on, I can feel it in my chest.

52   "Anybody else learn anything today?" lookin dead at me. I walk away and Sugar has to run to catch up and don't even seem to notice when I shrug her arm off my shoulder.

53   "Well, we got four dollars anyway," she said.

54   "Uh hunh."

55   "We could go to Hascombs and get half a chocolate layer and then go to the Sunset and still have plenty money for potato chips and ice-cream sodas."

56   "Uh hunh."

57   "Race you to Hascombs," she say.

58   We start down the block and she gets ahead which is O.K. by me cause I'm goin to the West End and then over to the Drive to think this day through. She can run if she want to and even run faster. But ain't nobody gonna beat me at nuthin.

Sonia Sanchez

(1934–)

For biographical information about Sonia Sanchez, see page 514.

Listenen to Big Black at S.F. State

no mo meetings
where u talk bout
whitey, the cracker
who done u wrong
5   (like some sad/bitch
who split in the middle of yo/comen)
just.   gitting.   stronNNNger.
                 maken warriors
outa boys.
10   blk/woooomen

                              outa girls.
                                    moven in &
        out of blkness
                  till it runs this
15   400/yr/old/road/show
        (called
              amurica.
                    now liven off its re/runs.)
                                          off the road.
20 no mo tellen the man he is
                                a dead/die/en/motha/
        fucka.
                just a sound of drums.
                          the sonnnnnNNg of chiefs
25 pouren outa our blk/sections.
                aree-um-doo-doo-doooooo-WORK
                aree-um-doo-doo-doooooo-LOVE
                arem-doooo-UNITY
                arem-doooo-LAND
30   arem-doooo-WAR
                arem-doooo-BUILDEN

        aree-um-doo-doo-dooooo. MalcolMmmm
        aree-um-doo-doo-dooooo. ElijahHHH
        aree-um-doo-doo-dooooo. Imamuuuu

35   just the sonnnng of chiefs.
                loud with blk/nation/hood
                              builden.

This Is Not a Small Voice

   This is not a small voice
   you hear   this is a large
   voice coming out of these cities.
   This is the voice of LaTanya.
5 Kadesha. Shaniqua. This
   is the voice of Antoine.
   Darryl. Shaquille.

Running over waters
navigating the hallways
10 of our schools spilling out
on the corners of our cities and
no epitaphs spill out of their river mouths.

This is not a small love
you hear   this is a large
15 love, a passion for kissing learning
on its face.
This is a love that crowns the feet with hands
that nourishes, conceives, feels the water sails
mends the children,
20 folds them inside our history where they
toast more than the flesh
where they suck the bones of the alphabet
and spit out closed vowels.
This is a love colored with iron and lace.
25 This is a love initialed Black Genius.

This is not a small voice
you hear.

From a Black Feminist Conference Reflections on Margaret Walker: Poet

1 chicago/october 1977/saturday afternoon/margaret walker walks her
red clay mississippi walk into a room of feminists, a strong gust of
a woman, raining warm honeysuckle kisses and smiles, and I fold
myself into her and hear a primordial black song sailing down the
guinea coast.

2 her face. ordained with lines. confesses poems. halleluyas. choruses. she
turns leans her crane like neck on the edge of the world. emphasizing

us. in this hotel/village/room. heavy with women. our names become known to us.

3 there is an echo about her. of black people rhyming of a woman celebrating herself and a people. words ripen on her mouth like pomegranates. this pecan/color/woman. short limbed with lightning. and i swallow her whole as she pulls herself up from youth, shaking off those early chicago years where she and wright and others turned a chicago desert into a well spring of words.

4 eyes. brillant/southern eyes torpedoing the room with sun eyes/dressed like a woman seeing thru riddles offering asylum from ghosts.

5 she stands over centuries as she talks. hands on waist. a feminine memory washed up from another shore. she opens her coat. a light colored blouse dances against dark breasts. her words carved from ancestral widows rain children and the room contracts with color.

6 her voice turns the afternoon brown. this black woman poet. removing false veils, baptizes us with syllables. woman words. entering and leaving at will:

Let a new earth rise. Let another world be born. Let a bloody peace be written in the sky. Let a second generation full of courage issue forth; let a people loving freedom come to growth. Let a beauty full of healing and a strength of final clenching be the pulsing in our spirits and our blood. Let the martial songs be written, let the dirges disappear. Let a race of men now rise and take control.*

7 walking back to my room i listen to the afternoon play it again and again scatter myself over evening walls and passageways wet with her footprints. in my room i collect papers. breasts. and listen to our mothers hummmmmming

*"For My People" by Margaret Walker

Remembering and Honoring Toni Cade Bambara

how to respond to the genius
of our sister Toni Cade Bambara? How to
give praise to this brilliant. Hard. Sweet
talking Toni. Who knew everything.
5 Read everything. Saw everything?

I guess if we remember Willie Kgositsile's lines:

> *if you sing of workers you have praised her*
> *if you sing of brotherhood and sisterhood you*
> *have praised her*
> *if you sing of liberation you have praised her*
> *if you sing of peace you have praised her*
> *you have praised her without knowing*
> *her name*
> *her name is Spear of the Nation . . .*

I would also add:

> *her name is clustered on the hills*
> *for she has sipped at the edge of rivers*
> *her words have the scent of the earth*
> *and the genius of the stars*
> *i have stored in my blood the*
> *memory of your voice Toni linking continents*
> *making us abandon Catholic minds.*
> *You spread yourself rainbowlike*
> *across seas*
> *Your voice greeting foreign trees*
> *Your voice stalking the evening stars.*

And a generation of people began to question their
silence. Their poverty. Their scarcity. Because you had
10 asked the most important question we can ask ourselves:

What are we pretending not to know today? The premise
as you said, my sister, being that colored people on the

planet earth really know everything there is to know. And
if one is not coming to grips with the knowledge, it must
15 mean that one is either scared or pretending to be stupid.

You open your novel with the simple but profound
question: Do we want to be well? And you said in an
interview with Sister Zala Chandler that the answer tends
to be "No! to be whole politically, psychically, spiritually,
20 culturally, intellectually, aesthetically, physically, and
economically whole—is of profound significance. It is
significant because there is a correlative to this. There is a
responsibility to self and to history that is developed once
you are whole, once you are well, once you acknowledge
25 your powers."

Amiri Baraka wrote that Jimmy Baldwin was God's black
revolutionary mouth. So were you Toni. You made us
laugh resistance laughter. You taught us how to improvise
change shapes sometimes change skins. We learned that if
30 we are to be, sometimes we must have been there already
and have people wondering about us:

> *You asking about them colored folk?*
> *They were just here. Ain't they still there*
> *in place in Harlem, in Washington in*
> *Chicago? i just seen em a second ago*
> *they wuz dancing at the Palladium,*
> *picking cotton, having a picnic in*
> *the park drinking walking they*
> *sanctified walk talking they*
> *fast talk brushing the nightmare*
> *of America off they foreheads.*
> *Look there they be. That's them laughing*
> *that loud laugh over there. No that*
> *ain't them. They gone again like the wind.*
> *Oh. You asking for them people from*
> *forever ago time sifting time through*
> *hands, announcing they are here intend*
> *to be here. Listen. Listen You can hear*
> *them breathing breaths not even invented*
> *yet. laughing their resistance, hee hee hee.*
> *You got to find me to get me.*

Get on board children.
This Bambara liberation train
of the spirit, soul. This Bambara
train doing what Audre Lorde said:
forever moving history beyond nightmare
into structures for the future. . .

Get on board this liberation train called Bambara. Cmon
lil children. And Toni had many children. She taught us
how to organize. Be. Their names are Aishah, Mungu,
35 Karma, Kevin, D Knowledge, Ras, Nora, Louis, Tony,
Morani, Gar.

This is how i lay down my Praise:

What seas came from her eyes!
What oceans connected us from her
Southern and Eastern bones!
What waterfall of Bambara words transformed
Our lives, our hands into miracle songs!

This is how i lay down my love:

We are not Robert Oppenheimer quoting
Indian literature: I have become death.
We are. Must be. Must quote,
i have become life
and oppose all killings, murderings,
rapings, invasions, executions,
imperialist actions.
i have become life
and i burn silver, red,
black with life for our children
for the universe for the sake
of being human.

What we know today is that this
earth cannot support murderers,
imperialists, rapists, racists, sexists,
homophobes. This earth cannot
support those who would invent
just for the sake of inventing
and become death.

We must all say i have
become life, look at me
i have become life
i move like the dawn with a tint of
blue in my hair
i say, i say
i have become life and
i walk a path that clears
away the debris of
pornographers.
i have become life, light,
life, light, life,
light and i move
with my eyes
My hands holding up life
for the world.
i have become life . . .

Gil Scott-Heron

(1949–)

Born in Chicago on April 1, 1949, Gil Scott-Heron was among the most
popular voices to emerge in the 1970s. A musician as well as writer, he
began publishing and performing while still a student at Lincoln Uni-
versity. His novel The Vulture *appeared in 1970; that same year he col-*
laborated with Brian Jackson on the album Small Talk at 125ᵗʰ *and*
Lenox (also the title of his accompanying first volume of poetry). Subse-
quent recordings include Pieces of a Man *(1970),* Winter in America
(1974), The Best of Gil Scott-Heron *(1984), and* Evolution & Flash-
*back: The Very Best of Gil Scott-Heron *(1999). Much of his poetry is*
collected in Now and Then: The Poems of Gil Scott-Heron *(2001). The*
following poem is taken from So Far, So Good *(1990).*

The Revolution Will Not Be Televised

You will not be able to stay home, brother.
You will not be able to plug in, turn on and cop out.
You will not be able to lose yourself on scag and
skip out for beer during commercials because
5 The revolution will not be televised.

The revolution will not be televised.
The revolution will not be brought to you by Xerox in four parts
    without commercial interruption.
The revolution will not show you pictures of Nixon blowing a bugle
    and leading a charge by John Mitchell, General Abramson and
    Spiro Agnew to eat hog maws confiscated from a Harlem
    sanctuary.
The revolution will not be televised.

10 The revolution will not be brought to you by
The Schaeffer Award Theatre and will not star
Natalie Wood and Steve McQueen or Bullwinkle and Julia.
The revolution will not give your mouth sex appeal.
The revolution will not get rid of the nubs.
15 The revolution will not make you look five pounds thinner.
The revolution will not be televised, brother.

There will be no pictures of you and Willie Mae
pushing that shopping cart down the block on the dead run
or trying to slide that color t.v. in a stolen ambulance.
20 NBC will not be able to predict the winner at 8:32 on reports from
    twenty-nine districts.
The revolution will not be televised.

There will be no pictures of pigs shooting down brothers
on the instant replay.
There will be no pictures of pigs shooting down brothers
25 on the instant replay.
The will be no slow motion or still lifes of Roy Wilkins strolling
    through Watts in a red, black and green liberation jumpsuit that
    he has been saving for just the proper occasion.

Green Acres, Beverly Hillbillies and Hooterville Junction
will no longer be so damned relevant
and women will not care if Dick finally got down with Jane
30 on Search for Tomorrow
because black people will be in the streets looking for
A Brighter Day.
The revolution will not be televised.

There will be no highlights on the Eleven O'Clock News
35 and no pictures of hairy armed women liberationists
and Jackie Onassis blowing her nose.

The theme song will not be written by Jim Webb or Francis Scott Key
nor sung by Glen Campbell, Tom Jones, Johnny Cash.
Englebert Humperdink or Rare Earth.
40   The revolution will not be televised.
The revolution will not be right back after a
message about a white tornado, white lightning
or white people.
You will not have to worry about a dove in your bedroom,
the tiger in your tank or the giant in your toilet bowl.
45   The revolution will not go better with coke.
The revolution will not fight germs that may cause bad breath.
The revolution *will* put you in the driver's seat.
The revolution will not be televised
               will not be televised
                  not be televised
                     be televised
The revolution will be no re-run, brothers.
50   The revolution will be LIVE.

Derrick I. M. Gilbert (a.k.a. D-Knowledge)

(1970–)

*A native of Long Beach, California, Derrick Gilbert did graduate work
in sociology at UCLA and has published essays in several academic
journals. He has, however, made a greater mark as a poet. Gilbert has
performed with such artists as Me'Shell Ndege'Ocello; Arrested Development; and Earth, Wind and Fire. He recorded the CD* All That And
a Bag of Words *(1995), edited* Catch the Fire!!!: A Cross-Generational
Anthology of Contemporary African-American Poetry *(1998), and
published the poetry collection* HennaMan *(2000).*

The Revolution Will Be on the Big Screen

My man Gil Scott-Heron once said:
"You will not be able to stay home, brother
You will not be able to plug in, turn on, and cop out

You will not be able to lose yourself on scag and
5   skip out for beer during commercial because
The Revolution will not be televised"

Gil Scott may have a point
The Revolution will not be televised
But it will be a major motion picture
10   The Revolution will not be televised
But the Revolution will be on the big screen.

The Revolution will be a billion-dollar production
Written by John Grisham and directed by Steven Spielberg
The Revolution will star Kevin Costner and Julia Roberts
15   And they will teach people of color
How to revolt . . . how to rebel . . . how to kill . . . and how to scream
The Revolution will be on the big screen.

The Revolution will have one Latino extra (Edward James Olmos)
Playin' a thief
20   One Asian extra (Jackie Chan)
Playin' an eighth-degree cook
And one Native American extra
Played by a moccasin-wearing Bruce Willis
Runnin' down Florence and Normandie
25   Yellin' "yeepeekayyay!"
The Revolution will be on the big screen.

The Revolution will have two Black supporting actors
One: Morgan Freeman
'Cause Daisy's been resurrected
30   And she needs a ride back down South
Two: Denzel Washington
Who will be killed in the first three minutes
By Kevin Costner
For looking at Julia Roberts
35   For more than four seconds
While Kevin Costner will have a picture of Whitney Houston
Burnin' in his wallet
The Revolution will be on the big screen.

The Revolution will be coming soon to a theater near you
40   And will get two thumbs-up from Siskel and Ebert
And will make more many than *Jurassic Park* and *E.T.*

The Revolution will cost $8.50 to see or $5.50 if you got a student ID
The Revolution will go good with popcorn, bonbons, and licorice
The Revolution will be on the big screen.

45 The Revolution will have a multiplatinum sound track
With subversive songs sung by
Marilyn Manson, Madonna, and the Spice Girls
The Revolution will be advertised on billboards, buses, Web sites,
   T-shirts
And with Hitler's lost testicle reincarnated as a Chihuahua
50 Leading the coup for Toco Bell
"Viya la revolución, suckers"
The Revolution will be on the big screen.

The Revolution will be distributed internationally
The Revolution will be seen in Cuba, Croatia, and Haiti
55 The Revolution will be on the big screen.

The Revolution will have a sequel
The Revolution will have a part III
The Revolution will be too large for TV
Too large for the little screen
60 ("It's going to be huge, man")
The Revolution will not be televised
Will not be televised/Not be televised
But
The Revolution will be on the big screen.

Reparation

Once upon a time
Called always
I asked a partner of mine
If he was registered to vote
5 He said:
Now, G
Why the hell should I vote
Votin' don't really change nothin'
Votin' don't really do nothin' for the
10 Afrocentric/revolutionary/hypo-melanated

BLACKMAN/True God
You know what I'm sayin'

Another partner of mine
Occupyin' the same mind
15 Space
Replied
In an extended tone:
Well, homie
You know I'm real busy these days
20 And/well
I just haven't had time
To register
Let alone
Vote
25 BAM
Was his next decibel
As he threw down a bone
And yelled
"Domino"

30 Then this righteous sistah
I really respect
Awkwardly said:
Well . . .
You know I'm registered to vote
35 But damn, brotherman
I haven't really stayed up on the issues
So
I think I'll pass this time
But
40 Next go around
I'll represent
Well/well
Seems like many of our peeps.
Don't wanna vote
45 Don't know how to vote
And don't know what to vote for
Don't know that young boys and girls
Were gaged with Mississippi urine-drenched ballots
Until their ears and noses bled yellow
50 So that we could vote

Don't know that grandmothers saturated billy clubs
With blistered and bruised blood
So that we could vote
Don't know that grandfathers had ancestral fingers
55 Chip/chip CHOPPED off
With crick/crack CRACKERED up
Butcher knifes
But still X'd their names
With crimson blood from severed veins
60 So that we could vote

Don't know
That if we don't vote
We'll find ourselves livin' in a world
Where Jim Crow is resurrected and elected president
65 And where Willie Lynch is scientifically reincarnated from a
Time-capsuled decomposed
Putrid test tube
And immediately appointed vice president

Don't know
70 That if we don't get politically
Active/aware
Beware
We'll find ourselves living in a world where
To be young, gifted, and Black
75 Is a code phrase
For a COINTELPRO-plan to have ghetto youth
Young, gifted, and addicted to smack
Don't know that if we don't act up
An initiative will pass that makes
80 Listenin' to rap/havin' braids or locks
And wearin' baggy clothes
All be federal offenses
Punishable by life on
Crack

85 Don't know that if we don't vote
Historically Black colleges will be eradicated
Affirmative action programs will be annihilated
That the only Blacks at White universities
Will be required to play with the athletic boosters' balls

90 And that the only place Blacks will receive
    Scholarships
    Will be at U. Penn/Penn State
    Or the penitentiary in any state
    'Cause it's one/two/three strikes your out
95 In the U.S.A.
    And
    BAM
    Will be the sound we'll ubiquitously hear
    As our brain cells are eternally slammed
100 "Domino"

    And I don't care how cool we are
    If we don't vote
    We won't be able to escape the perspiration
    Caused by the bureaucratic heat
105 If we don't grab hold of the ballot
    We'll experience infinite millimeter bullets
    Shattering our cranial domes
    And as we piece back our dismembered collective consciousness
    We'll have disunity seizures
110 Frantically runnin' down the street
    Shakin' and breakin'
    Realizin'
    The Ku Klux Klan has obtained nonprofit status
    David Duke is president
115 Every March 3 is Rodney King Day
    Or better yet
    National Beat a Nigger Day
    And on Thomas Jefferson's birthday it is
    Legal for any white male to rape any Black female
120 As long as he hallucinates through history yellin' Sally
    Then we'll all collect accumulated (dis)interest on
    Never received reparations
    'Cause every Black person will be given 40 acres of
    Teenage mutant mule shh

125 And
    Don't go sayin' that votin' don't change nothin'
    'Cause
    If we don't vote

We'll soon find ourselves pickin'
130 Spoiled cotton candy with swollen fingers
In jagged cracks through decaying concrete soil
With genocidal pus oozing off split fingertips
'Cause if we don't register
Learn wassup
135 And check in at the ballot box
We'll soon find ourselves
Propositioned into
Chattel slavery
Talkin' 'bout
140 Massa
We sho iz wishin' youd set us free
Someday
Someday
Someday

Why I Would Never Buy a Jeep Cherokee

This country
America
The so-called beautiful
Ignores the religious freedom of
5 The native people
Steals water and other natural resources from
The native people
Dumps toxic waste onto the lands of
The native people
10 Pumps gin and whiskey juice into the homes of
The native people
And
Fails to live up to over 400 treaties signed with
The native people
15 But then
This country
America

The so-called beautiful
Proclaims to honor
20 The native people
By naming sports teams
After them
Teams like
The Atlanta Braves
25 The Cleveland Indians
The Chicago Black Hawks
The Washington Redskins
The Kansas City Chiefs
The Florida State Seminoles
30 And
The University of Illinois Fighting Illini
But
That's not honoring
That's objectifying
35 That's caricaturizing
That's humiliating
That's stereotyping
That's degrading
That's exploiting
40 And
That's the same as
Having teams like
The San Francisco Sambos
The Jackson State Jungle Bunnies
45 The Seattle Spearchuckers
The New Orleans Niggers
The Detroit Darkies
The Cincinnati Coons
The San Diego Spics
50 The Green Bay Greasers
The Baltimore Beaners
The Washington Wetbacks
The Chicago Chinks
The Golden State Gooks
55 The Kansas City Kikes
The St. Louis Semites
The New Jersey Jews
The New York Hymies

The Houston Honkies
60 The Oklahoma Ofays
The UCLA Crackers
The Phoenix Rednecks
The Pittsburgh Peckerwoods
The Wichita White Trash
65 And
The Brigham Young Blue-eyed Devils
But
That's not honoring
That's objectifying
70 That's caricaturizing
That's humiliating
That's stereotyping
That's degrading
That's exploiting
75 And
That's why I would never buy a Jeep Cherokee
Never buy a Jeep Cherokee
Jeep Cherokee never buy
Never buy
80 Never . . .
Buy
Never . . .
Bye

Tony Medina

(1966–)

Tony Medina was born January 10, 1966, in the South Bronx, raised
in the Throgs Neck Housing Projects, and currently lives in Harlem.
He is the author or editor of 12 books for adults and children, the
most recent of which is the poetry collection Committed to Breathing
(2003). Named by Writer's Digest *as one of 10 poets to watch in the*
new millennium, Medina's poetry, fiction, and essays appear in over
20 anthologies and two CD compilations. His children's books,
DeShawn Days *(2001) and* Love to Langston *(2002)—both illustrated*
by R. Gregory Christie—have garnered several awards, including the

Parent's Guide Children's Media Award, the Paterson Prize for Books
for Young People, and the Rhode Island Children's Book Award.
Among his three anthologies, In Defense of Mumia (1996, with S. E.
Anderson) won The American Booksellers Association's Firecracker
Alternative Book Award and Bum Rush the Page: A Def Poetry Jam
(2001, with Louis Reyes Rivera) was named a Best Book of 2002 by
The Washington Post's Book World. Medina, who has taught English
and creative writing at several colleges and universities, has recently
earned his MA and PhD in Poetry and American and African American Literature from Binghamton University. The following selections
are from Committed to Breathing.

Doorway Dirge

bullets open
into flames
peal back
flesh in search
5 of blood and
          bone
41 points of light
leak out onto
hands clutching keys
10 the latch not yet
          undone
what slumps
in the vestibule
a grin full of teeth
15 pressing down hard
onto a tongue
surprised twisted
jew, sparks
ricocheting off wood
20 and metal
the last breath of air
gasps in the silence
of a mind too shooked
to scream

The Movie I Would Make

A black man is killed in the vestibule of his apartment building,
trying to get home from work. He was shot 451 times with a sub-
machine gun, a bazooka, and a tank by 4 white cops who claimed
they thought the pizza box he was carrying looked like a gun.

5 They said it wasn't a murder; it was a tragedy, it was a mistake.

As the black forewoman reads the Not Guilty verdict to a
euphoric white courtroom, the black bailiff, visibly shaken,
takes out his gun and blows each smiling officer's brains out,
places his weapon on the defendant's table, and says, *Now we have*
10 *justice . . . you can arrest me now.*

The only black woman juror with a child is surprised to learn that
her son was killed by a cop who mistook his skin color for a gun.

New York is engulfed in flames as protesters take to the street,
destroying property on the Upper East Side.

15 Negro Politician turns to the camera and says,
I'm the one paid to be the moderator.

Closing credits roll as a reggae-like song begins to blare:

Amadou Diallo
        One more reason to kill
20 *Eleanor Bumpers*
        One more reason to kill
Michael Stewart
        One more reason to kill
Phillip Pannel
25   *One more reason to kill*
Anthony Baez
        One more reason to kill . . .
And the list goes on and on and on . . .

Cut to:

30 Juan Gonzalez in interview on WBAI Radio, New York.

"You have a book signing at a store called
A Clean Well-Lighted Place."

"Yes . . . we're all trying to stay out
of the dim light these days."

This Week's *Ebony/Jet*
Showcase's Top Ten Hip
Hop Video Singles

1. Every Bitch Ain't No Hoe
2. Bitch Ass Punks in Basic Training
   (*From the Motion Picture Sound Track*)
3. Savor the Flava Off My Crusty Ass Drawers—No Shit, Yo!
4. What Evuh it Take II Get Yo Mack On
5. LaQuisha's Hustle
6. Ode to Iceberg Slim
   (*Also Available On CD ROM*)
7. Man, Fuck George Washington! Big Daddy Cotton Candy
   Need to Be on a Dollar Bill. Yo! Word Da Muh! Word Da Muh!
8. HIV is E–Z to Get if You Just All About
   Gettin Paid -N- Gettin Laid
9. Multi-Various Ways to Kill Some Cops
10. ILL Literate Reprieve
    (*From the Board of Education Mass Choir
    Featuring Spoken Word Voice-overs
    from Maya Angelou & Nikki Giovanni*)

Taxes

It was a savage inquest in which nothing was resolved other than I
still had to pay my taxes. I tried to hold out until the final lottery numbers were selected but somehow that got delayed-by-sports, the weather
and three or four commercials. By this time I was on welfare mort-
gaging off my ribcage in exchange for government surplus cheese. The
eviction proceedings were swift and final. We set up shop at a nearby
park, hiding what was left of our valuables in a pup tent made of Glad
Ziploc plastic bags. To keep up with world events we stayed indoors

mornings, reading bits and pieces of newspapers, which lined the inside of the tent, keeping the heat in. We did this till high noon when the sun began melting our shelters, magnifying down through the newspaper, boring a hole through the business section. Some of our neighbors, who slept late, turned into toast. Their charcoal broiled tears giving them a weird gentle glean of butter spread appearance. We thought they died in the fire, but were relieved to hear their yelling when, alarmed, they jumped up screaming from the pigeons frantically pecking through the smoke trails rising up off what almost became their charred remains. They ran towards the sprinklers like giant baked potatoes. This always seemed to amuse the kids lining up in the yard for school. Some kids were scolded by their teachers for talking in line. It wasn't that they were deliberately mischievous. They just articulated their disposition to breakfast treats as birds flew by with worms in their mouths. How we envied those birds whose eating habits were not enslaved by check out counters and money. Some of us would wake up early to pretend that were sleeping in order to try and wrest a few worms from their mouths. But we abandoned that dreadfully desperate attempt when we caught ourselves feeding the schoolyard kids' hysteria as if we were cartoon characters. And it wasn't such a bad idea, some of us thought, to be cartoons, finding ourselves caught up in animated tragic comedies where you could die and come back to life, where in one scene you could be blown to smithereens by a huge bomb with a long fuse, and in another get up, piece yourself back together, dust yourself off and drive off in an ACME truck, trying to run your assailant off the side of some off. And at least with cartoons we wouldn't have to go to the store or order out or spend our days rummaging through garbage cans for food. We would simply have to draw a couple of chicken thighs and some biscuits and mashed potatoes. But life isn't that simple.

Kenneth Carroll

(1959–)

Born in Washington, D.C., in 1959, Kenneth Carroll has written poems, plays, and numerous articles. He is a founding member of the SRock Writers Collective, and he is a past president of the African American Writers Guild. His poetry book is So What!: For the White Dude Who Said This Ain't Poetry *(1997).*

On Watching the Republican Convention
(and the password is . . .)

       when the republicans want to say,
"all them bastard colored folk need to be
shipped back to africa or locked up"
            they say.
5 *"family values"*
       when the republicans want to say,
"all these coons need to be put back
on plantations where they belong"
            they say,
10 *"returning america to its glorious past"*
hmpf,
              and they say
niggas talk funny.

So What!

(for the white dude who said this ain't poetry)

a faucet dripping arrogance in sycophantic half steps
a literary tarzan trying to save the natives from they own ignorance
short on knowledge, long on knowing he instructs without reference.

ain't poetry?

5 "no dialectics needed sambo, your thing just is not poetry."
said the gold coast representative
never been in the mines
never sweated riches but 'bwana knows best'

a minute man wit a culture thirty seconds old
10 ain't poetry? mmmm . . .
maybe if i threw soup cans in it

or something obscure dark & cryptic
alluded to hackneyed over-hyped dead writers
& avoided references to the dark continent of
15   my origin this work could be saved

ain't poetry?
minute rice analysis
cracker instant oats
pour in europe and stir: a cold water recipe
20   . . . meanwhile my village dances to simmering rhythms
spiced by intellectual development measured in tens
of thousands of years

homer, his lips stuck to the chilly nipple
of his mother's frozen breast,
25   could only dream civilizations
as dark men & women built pyramids
& shaped words to fit eternity
poets retired & came back as ancestor spirits
while greece contemplated a working alphabet & gods
30   but this shit ain't poetry cause johnny come lately say so
   . . . and he should know

ain't poetry?
our systems were a mystery
alexander burned all that he & aristotle couldn't understand
35   the ensuing blaze warmed the ice-capade continent
as the pillaging plagiarizers worked their un-magic in the fire's light

ain't poetry?
the sails on your scholar-ship are bloody
you scribble death upon the pages on the world
40   persecuting your brightest stars, preferring
whoring scribes who search for insignificance
to entertain the inane
   . . . so dis ain't poetry . . . so you dis'n me?

ain't poetry, huh?   ain't india either sucka!
45   what is round, rotating and will never
fit into a box marked trite poetic conventions:
the world and it's inhabitants—
you are trying to fold the world in half
to place it neatly into your square mind

50 ain't poetry?
ain't dat a bitch!
a new-jack dis
half empty memory-banks
culture validated by gun powder
55 your qualifications are shaky
like a bamboo bridge stretched across
the white supremacist waters of your existence
you are still preaching the missionary position
as the natives re-read the karma sutra

60 a day late, a dollar short
always missing the bus
you are peeing in the snow
while we design a papyrus for the living
a patronizing peeping tom
65 seeing in but unable to decipher
without an oxford interpreter

we are a black fire
burning across the pages of your random house guide
to modern american poetry
70 where you cannot find references to shine or even signifying monkeys
we have left your meter in shambles
as we laugh at you tripping over lemons piled on the steps

the drumming you hear coming from the hills ain't poetry either
(but of course it is!)
75 it is the maroons planning your demise
it is ritual music and david walker's appeal
it is brown hips dancing verses
it is what it feels like to be kissed by full lips

it is natural
80 like sun ra returning in a charlie parker space ship
from galaxies wit no names
while europe sails the wrong way
in search of a short cut to imperialism

damn columbus, you are lost and desperate
85 and denying the only music you really hear
you riffin with a trumpet that plays one note
while the planet be's and bops

like coltrane star-hopping through
the theloniosphere as a white boy
90 from downbeat points to the heavens & screams,
"that ain't music, that ain't music!"

we are like miles,
a black whirlwind
wit a red trumpet,
95 blowing blue stanzas
saying, so what!
yeah goddamn it
SO WHAT!

Writing Assignments

1. Choose two poets from the group of Langston Hughes, Countee
Cullen, Helene Johnson, Claude McKay, Margaret Walker, and Gwendolyn Brooks. Compare and contrast the degree, forcefulness, or
complexity with which the poets you choose affirm African American identity. Also compare and contrast the poets' style. Cullen, Johnson, and McKay all write sonnets, for example, but they do not all
use the same form of the sonnet in the poetry that appears in this
chapter. To develop your paper, you probably will want to read additional poetry by the poets you select.

2. Choose a poet from the group of Quincy Troupe, Amiri Baraka, Haki
Madhubuti, Nikki Giovanni, Larry Neal, Sarah Webster Fabio, and
Sonia Sanchez. Also select a poet from the group mentioned in the
assignment above. In terms of message and style, compare and contrast the work of the two poets, and indicate which poet you favor.

3. How does the fiction of John A. Williams and Toni Cade Bambara
complement the Black Arts poetry of the 1960s and 1970s? In which
ways is their writing similar to that of the poets? In which ways,
beyond the obvious difference of genre, is their writing different from
that of the poets? What is your response to the message and technique of the fiction writers?

4. Read additional poems by Derrick Gilbert, Tony Medina, or Kenneth
Carroll. How does the poet's work in terms of content and form compare and contrast with selected poetry (you do the selecting) of the
Black Arts era? Comment on whether the more recent work compares
favorably with the poetry of the past.

Select Chronology of African American Literature

1760 "An Evening Thought: Salvation, by Christ, with Penitential Cries," by Jupiter Hammon. First poem published and first publication overall by an African American.

1773 *Poems on Various Subjects, Religious and Moral*, by Phillis Wheatley, published in London. First book published by an African American.

1789 *The Interesting Narrative of the Life of Olaudah Equiano, or Gustavus Vassa, the African.* First major slave narrative.

1829 *David Walker's Appeal, in Four Articles; Together with a Preamble, to the Coloured Citizens of the World, but in Particular, and Very Expressly, to those of the United States of America.*

1831 *Religion and the Pure Principles of Morality, the Sure Foundation on Which We Must Build*, by Maria Stewart.

1832 Maria Stewart becomes first women born in the United States to deliver a political lecture in public to a mixed-gender audience.

1838 Frederick Douglass escapes from enslavement in Maryland.

1845 *Narrative of the Life of Frederick Douglass, an American Slave, Written by Himself.*

1851 Sojourner Truth delivers the speech—famous for the refrain "ar'n't I a womn?"—at the Second Woman's Rights Convention in Akron, Ohio.

1853 *Clotel; or, The President's Daughter*, by William Wells Brown, published in London. First African American novel.

1859 *Our Nig*, by Harriet E. Wilson. First novel by an African American woman and first African American novel published in the United States.

The Anglo-African Magazine is founded by Thomas Hamilton. Regarded as the first African American literary journal. Published until 1865.

1861 *Incidents in the Life of a Slave Girl: Written by Herself*, by
      Harriet Jacobs. Most comprehensive slave narrative by an African
      American woman.

1861–
1865 American Civil War.

1895 Booker T. Washington delivers "The Atlanta Exposition Address"
      at the Cotton States and International Exposition. Also known
      as "The Atlanta Compromise," it expresses a policy of accom-
      modation regarding segregation.

1896 *Plessy v. Ferguson* decision by the United States Supreme Court,
      which offered a doctrine of "separate but equal," allowed states
      to impose public segregation.

1903 *The Souls of Black Folk*, by W. E. B. Du Bois.

1910 *Crisis* magazine is established by W. E. B. Du Bois. Functioned
      as a periodical for the NAACP and as a literary magazine. Still
      published by the NAACP.

1913 Beginning of The Great Migration. Millions of African Americans
      began to move from the rural South to the North, West, and to
      Southern cities.

1922 *The Book of American Negro Poetry*, edited by James Weldon
      Johnson. Arguably the beginning of the peak years of the cultur-
      al movement known as the Harlem Renaissance.

1923 *Cane*, by Jean Toomer.

      Opportunity magazine, journal of the National Urban League,
      is founded. Key outlet for emerging writers during the 1920s.
      Published until 1949.

1925 *Color*, by Countee Cullen.

      The New Negro, edited by Alain Locke.

1926 *The Weary Blues*, by Langston Hughes.

1927 *Caroling Dusk*, edited by Countee Cullen.

1929 Stock market crash ushered in the Great Depression. Signaled the
      end of the peak years of the Harlem Renaissance and a slowing
      of the pace of African American migration.

1937 *Their Eyes Were Watching God*, by Zora Neale Hurston.

1940 *Native Son*, by Richard Wright.

The Big Sea, by Langston Hughes.

1949 Founding of the College Language Association, which evolved from the Association of Teachers of English in Negro Colleges. Published *CLA-Bulletin* from 1941 to 1957 and the *CLA Journal* beginning in 1957.

Gwendolyn Brooks publishes *Annie Allen*, her second book of poetry.

1950 Gwendolyn Brooks becomes the first African American to win a Pulitzer Prize; honor bestowed for *Annie Allen*.

Founding of the Harlem Writers Guild by John Oliver Killens, Rosa Guy, John Henrik Clarke, and others.

1952 *Invisible Man*, by Ralph Ellison.

1953 Ellison becomes first African American to win the National Book Award.

1954 *Brown v. the Board of Education of Topeka, Kansas*, a decision by the United States Supreme Court that struck against the practice of "separate but equal." Ruling spurred the modern Civil Rights Movement.

1959 *A Raisin in the Sun*, by Lorraine Hansberry. First Broadway play by an African American woman. Winner of the New York Drama Critics Circle Award; Hansberry is the first African American to receive the award.

"The American Negro Writer and His Roots" conference sponsored in New York City by the American Society of African Culture.

1961 *Negro Digest*, which had been published as a general-interest magazine from 1942 to 1951 by John H. Johnson, resumes publication under the editorship of Hoyt Fuller and becomes a crucial literary outlet. The name was changed to *Black World* in 1970; the last issue was published in 1976.

1962 Umbra Workshop founded on the Lower East Side in New York City by Ishmael Reed, Calvin Hernton, Askia M. Touré, and others.

1963   More than 200,000 people assemble in Washington, D. C., to participate in the March on Washington for Jobs and Freedom organized by A. Philip Randolph and Bayard Rustin. From the steps of the Lincoln Memorial, Martin Luther King, Jr. delivers his climactic, 17-minute "I Have a Dream" speech.

1964   Free Southern Theatre founded in Jackson, Mississippi, by Doris Derby, Gilbert Moses, and John O'Neal. In 1969, became BLKARTSOUTH.

1965   Assassination of Malcolm X. Release of *The Autobiography of Malcom X*.

Black Arts Repertory Theatre/School (BARTS) founded in Harlem by Amiri Baraka and others.

Broadside Press founded in Detroit by Dudley Randall.

Watts Writers Workshop established in Los Angeles by Budd Schulberg.

1966   *Journal of Black Poetry* established in San Francisco by Joe Goncalves. Published until 1973.

"The Image of the Negro in American Literature" conference at Fisk University.

1967   Third World Press founded in Chicago by Haki Madhubuti (then known as Don L. Lee), Carolyn Rogers, and Johari Amini.

Negro American Literature Forum founded at Indiana State University by John F. Bayliss. Became known as *Black American Literature Forum* (BALF) in 1976 and as *African American Review* (AAR) in 1992.

"The Black Writer and Human Rights" conference at Fisk University.

Organization of Black American Culture (OBAC) founded in Chicago by Hoyt Fuller and others.

1968   Assassination of Martin Luther King, Jr.

Black Fire: An Anthology of Afro-American Writing, edited by Amiri Baraka (then LeRoi Jones) and Larry Neal.

"The Black Writer's Vision for America" conference at Fisk University.

1970 *The Black Woman*, edited by Toni Cade Bambara.

1973 The Phillis Wheatley Poetry Festival at Jackson State College; celebrates the 200th anniversary of the publication of Wheatley's *Poems on Various Subjects*.

1974 "The Image of Black Folk in American Literature" conference at Howard University.

1976 Literary journal *Callaloo* founded at Southern University in Baton Rouge, Louisiana. Developed under the editorship of Charles H. Rowell.

1982 *The Color Purple*, by Alice Walker.

1983 Alice Walker wins the Pulitzer Prize and National Book Award for *The Color Purple*.

1986 First National Black Writers Conference held at Medgar Evers College of the City University of New York. Subsequent conferences in 1988, 1991, 1996, 2000, and 2003.

1987 Rita Dove wins the Pulitzer Prize for *Thomas and Beulah* (1986).

      August Wilson wins the Pulitzer Prize for *Fences* (1986).

      Beloved, by Toni Morrison.

1988 Toni Morrison wins the Pulitzer for *Beloved* (1987).

1989 "Looking Back with Pleasure: A Celebration" conference held in Salt Lake City, Utah.

1990 August Wilson becomes the first African American two-time winner of the Pulitzer Prize for Drama when he is honored for *The Piano Lesson*.

1991 Gwendolyn Brooks Writers Conference begins annual run at Chicago State University.

1993 Maya Angelou reads her poem, "On the Pulse of Morning," at Bill Clinton's inauguration. First African American poet to perform at a presidential inauguration.

      Rita Dove named Poet Laureate of the United States.

      Toni Morrison becomes the first African American to win the Nobel Prize for Literature.

1994 "Furious Flower" poetry conference at James Madison University.

2000 "Looking Back with Pleasure II: A Celebration" conference held in Salt Lake City, Utah.

2002 Conference commemorating the 100th anniversary of the birth of Langston Hughes convened at the University of Kansas.

2003 Conference commemorating the 100th anniversary of the publication of *The Souls of Black Folk* convened at Northwestern University.

Credits

Sterling A. Brown, All lines from "Ma Rainey" from *The Collected Poems of Sterling A. Brown*, edited by Michael S. Harper, copyright 1932 by Harcourt Brace & Co., renewed 1960 by Sterling A. Brown. Reprinted by permission of HarperCollins Publishers, Inc.

——, All lines from "New St. Louis Blues" from *The Collected Poems of Sterling A. Brown*, edited by Michael S. Harper, copyright 1932 by Harcourt Brace & Co., renewed 1960 by Sterling A. Brown. Originally appeared in Southern Road. Reprinted by permission of HarperCollins Publishers, Inc.

Kenneth Carroll, "On Watching the Republican Convention" and "So What!" from *So What!*, copyright © 1997 by Kenneth Carroll, reprinted by permission of the author.

Xam Wilson Cartiér, "Be-Bop, Re-Bop & All Those Obligatos," "Double or Nothing and All That Jazz" and "A Matter of Taste" from *Be-Bop, Re-Bop* by Xam Wilson Cartiér, copyright © 1987 by Xam Wilson Cartiér. Used by permission of Ballantine Books, a division of Random House, Inc.

Charles W. Chesnutt, "Goophered Grapevine" (originally appeared in the *Atlantic Monthly* in 1887) and "PO' Sandy" from *The Conjure Woman* by Charles W. Chesnutt, 1899.

Wanda Coleman, "Fast Eddie," "Flight of the California Condor (2)" and "Dominoes," copyright © 1998 by Wanda Coleman. Reprinted from *Bathwater Wine* by Black Sparrow Press (imprint of David R. Godine, Publisher, Inc.) with the permission from the author.

——, "Low English," "South Central Los Angeles Deathtrip 1982" and "Sears Life" copyright © 2001 by Wanda Coleman. Reprinted from *Mercurochrome* by Published by Black Sparrow Press (imprint of David R. Godine, Publisher, Inc), with the permission from the author.

Anna Julia Cooper, Material from *A Voice from the South by a Black Woman of the South* by Anna Julia Cooper. The Aldine Printing House, Xenia, OH (1892).

Jayne Cortez, "Into This Time" and "Solo Finger Solo" from *Jazz Fan Looks Back*, copyright © 2002 by Jayne Cortez, reprinted by permission of Hanging Loose Press.

Countee Cullen, Reprinted by Permission of GRM Associates, Inc., Agents for the Estate of Ida M. Cullen. "A Brown Girl Dead" and "Heritage" from the book *Color* by Countee Cullen, copyright © 1925 by Harper & Brothers; copyright renewed 1953 by Ida M. Cullen.

——, Reprinted by permission of GRM Associates, Inc., Agents for the Estate of Ida M. Cullen. "From the Dark Tower" from the book *Copper Sun* by Countee Cullen; copyright © 1927 by Harper & Brothers; copyright renewed 1955 by Ida M. Cullen.

Daryl Cumber Dance, "The Signifying Monkey" and "Stagolee" from *My People: 400 Years of African American Folklore*, edited by Daryl Cumber Dance. Copyright © 2001 by Daryl Cumber Dance. Used by permission of W. W. Norton & Company, Inc.

Julie Dash, "The Sorcerer as told by Miz Emma Julia" from *Daughters of the Dust* by Julie Dash, copyright © 1997 by Geechee Girl Productions, Inc. Used by permission of Dutton Signet, a division of Penguin Group (USA) Inc.

Martin R. Delaney, "A Glance at Ourselves-Conclusion" and "A Project for an Expedition of Adventure to the Eastern Coast of Africa" from *The Condition, Elevation, Emigration and Destiny of the Colored People of the United States, Politically Considered* by Martin R. Delaney (1852)

Frederick Douglass, "The Blood of the Slave on the Skirts of the Northern People" by Frederick Douglass, which appeared in *The North Star*, November 17, 1848.

———, Footnotes to "Emancipation, Racism, and the Work Before Us" by Frederick Douglass as published in *The Frederick Douglas Papers: Series One, Volume 3, 1855-63* edited by John W. Blassingame, copyright © 1985 by Yale University. Published and reprinted by permission of Yale University Press.

Rita Dove, "The Zulus" from *Fifth Sunday*, Callaloo Series, copyright © 1985 by Rita Dove. Reprinted by permission of the author.

———, "Maple Valley Branch Library, 1967" from *On the Bus with Rosa Parks* by Rita Dove. Copyright © 1999 by Rita Dove. Used by permission of W. W. Norton & Company, Inc.

———, "My Mother Enters the Work Force" from *On the Bus with Rosa Parks*, W. W. Norton, copyright © 1999 by Rita Dove. Reprinted by permission of the author.

W. E. B. Du Bois, "XI of the Passing of the First-born" from *The Souls of Black Folk* by W. E. B. Du Bois, Published by A. C. McClurg & Company, 1903.

———, "The Niagara Movement Address at founding of Niagara Movement, pamphlet, 1906" by W. E. B. Du Bois

———, "Awake America" by W. E. B. Du Bois from the *Crisis 14* Magazine (Sept 1917)

———, Pages 415-423 from *The Autobiography of W. E. B. Du Bois* by W. E. B. Du Bois, reprinted by permission of International Publishers.

———, "The Conservation of Races," American Negro Academy Occasional Papers, no. 2, Washington, D.C. (1897)

Henry Dumas, "Ark of Bones" from *Ark of Bones and Other Stories* edited by Eugene Redmond and Hale Chatfield, copyright © 1970 by Carbondale, Southern Illinois University Press, reprinted by permission of Eugene Redmond.

Paul Laurence Dunbar, "A Death Song" and "An Ante-Bellum Sermon" from *The Collected Poetry of Paul Laurence Dunbar* by Paul Laurence Dunbar. Published by Dodd, Mead and Company (1913).

———, "The Hamiltons," "A Farewell Dinner," "The Thief," "From a Clear Sky," "The Justice of Men," "Outcasts," "In New York," "An Evening Out," "His Heart's Desire," "A Visitor from Home," "Broken Hopes," "All the World's a Stage," "The Oakleys," "Frankenstein," "Dear, Damned, Delightful Town," "Shaggs's Theory" and "A Yellow Journal" from *The Sport of the Gods* by Paul Laurence Dunbar, (1901).

Ralph Ellison, Excerpt from *Invisible Man* by Ralph Ellison, copyright 1947, 1948, 1952 by Ralph Ellison. Copyright renewed 1975, 1976, 1980 by Ralph Ellison. Used by permission of Random House, Inc.

Olaudah Equiano, Chapter 11 from *The Interesting Narrative of the Life of Olaudah Equiano (1789)*.

Mari Evans, "Liberation Blues," and "Lee Morgan" from *A Dark and Splendid Mass* by Mari Evans, copyright © 1992 by Mari Evans, published by Harlem River Press, used by permission of the author.

Sarah Webster Fabio, "Black Man's Feast," "Evil is No Black Thing" and "Tripping With Black Writing," copyright © 1971 by Sarah Webster Fabio. Reprinted by permission of Cheryl Fabio-Bradford. All rights reserved.

Arthur Flowers, Excerpt from Chapter 2 in *Another Good Loving Blues* by Arthur Flowers, copyright © 1993 by Arthur Flowers. Reprinted by permission of Ellen Levine Literary Agency / Trident Media Group.

Ernest Gaines, "Grant Bello aka Cherry" from *A Gathering of Old Men* by Ernest Gaines, copyright © 1983 by Ernest Gaines. Used by permission of Alfred A. Knopf, a division of Random House, Inc.

——, "Speech Delivered to the First Annual Meeting of the American Equal Rights Association" from *History of Woman Suffrage, Vol. 2 (1861-1876)*. Rochester, NY: Charles Mann, 1881.

Alice Walker, "Burial" and "View from Rosehill Cemetery" from *Revolutionary Petunias & Other Poems*, copyright © 1971 by Alice Walker, reprinted by permission of Harcourt, Inc.

——, "Looking for Zora" from *In Search of Our Mothers' Gardens: Womanist Prose*, copyright © 1975 by Alice Walker, reprinted by permission of Harcourt, Inc.

——, Letters from *The Color Purple*, copyright © 1982 by Alice Walker, reprinted by permission of Harcourt, Inc.

——, "A Name Is Sometimes an Ancestor Saying Hi, I'm With You" from *Living by the Word: Selected Writings 1973-1987*, copyright © 1986 by Alice Walker, reprinted by permission of Harcourt, Inc.

David Walker, Preamble and Articles I, II and III from *David Walker's Appeal*, Published by David Walker in 1829.

Margaret Walker, "Southern Song" and "For My People" from *For My People*, copyright 1942 by Margaret Walker, Published by Yale University Press, reprinted by permission of The University of Georgia Press.

Booker T. Washington, "Speech at the Atlanta Exposition" also known as "The Atlanta Compromise Speech" was delivered on September 18, 1895 by Booker T. Washington and published in *Up from Slavery* in 1901.

——, Chapter IV from *The Future of the American Negro* by Booker T. Washington (1899)

Ida B. Wells-Barnett, Chapter X, "The Remedy" from *A Red Record: Tabulated Statistics and Alleged Causes of Lynchings in the United States* by Ida B. Wells-Barnett (1892).

——, Introduction by Ida B. Wells-Barnett from *Mob Rule in New Orleans* Chicago, IL (1900).

Cornel West, Jr., "A Twilight Civilization" from *The Future of the Race* by Henry Louis Gates, Jr. and Cornel West, copyright © 1996 by Henry Louis Gates, Jr., and Cornel West. Used by permission of Alfred A. Knopf, a division of Random House, Inc.

Cornel West, "Beyond Multiculturalism and Eurocentrism" from *Prophetic Thought in Postmodern Times*, copyright © 1993 by Cornel West, reprinted by permission of the author.

Phillis Wheatley, "Letter to Samson Occum" (1765).

——, "On Being Brought from Africa to America" by Phillis Wheatley, Boston, MA, published by A. Bell, for Cox and Berry (1773).

Colson Whitehead, Pages 112-117 from *John Henry Days* by Colson Whitehead, copyright © 2001 Colson Whitehead. Used by permission of Doubleday, a division of Random House, Inc.

John Edgar Wideman, From pages 111-120 in *Brothers and Keepers* by John Edgar Wideman, copyright © 1984 by John Edgar Wideman. Reprinted by permission of Henry Holt and Company, LLC.

John A. Williams, Excerpt from *The Man Who Cried I Am*, copyright © 1967, 1985 by John A. Williams, reprinted by permission of the author.

August Wilson, "Scene Four, Act One" from *Joe Turner's Come and Gone* by August Wilson, copyright 1988 by August Wilson. Used by permission of Dutton Signet, a division of Penguin Group (USA) Inc.

Richard Wright, "Big Boy Leaves Home" from *Uncle Tom's Children* by Richard Wright. Copyright 1936, 1937, 1938 by Richard Wright. Copyright © renewed 1964, 1964, 1966 by Ellen Wright. Reprinted by permission of HarperCollins Publishers.

Index

Additional Titles of Interest

Note to Instructors: Any of these Penguin-Putnam, Inc. titles can be packaged with this book for a special discount up to 60% off the retail price. Contact your local Allyn & Bacon/Longman publisher's representative for details on how to create a Penguin-Putnam, Inc. Value Package.

Frederick Douglass, *Narrative of the Life of Frederick Douglass*

W. E. B. Du Bois, *The Souls of Black Folk*

Lorraine Hansberry, *A Raisin in the Sun*

Harriet Jacobs, *Incidents in the Life of a Slave Girl*

Martin Luther King, Jr., *Why We Can't Wait*

Nella Larsen, *Passing*

James McBride, *The Color of Water*

Toni Morrison, *Beloved*

Toni Morrison, *Sula*

Toni Morrison, *The Bluest Eye*

Gloria Naylor, *The Women of Brewster Place*

Patricia Raybon, *My First White Friend*

Sojourner Truth, *The Narrative of Sojourner Truth*

August Wilson, *Fences*

August Wilson, *Joe Turner's Come and Gone*